WEST'S LAW SCHOOL ADVISORY BOARD

THE INTERACTIVE CASEBOOK SERIES™

FEDERAL COURTS

A Contemporary Approach

FIFTH EDITION

By

Donald L. Doernberg
PROFESSOR OF LAW
PACE UNIVERSITY SCHOOL OF LAW

Evan Tsen Lee
PROFESSOR OF LAW
UNIVERSITY OF CALIFORNIA,
HASTINGS COLLEGE OF THE LAW

WEST®

Mat #41313691

610 Opperman Drive
St. Paul, MN 55123
1-800-313-9378

Printed in the United States of America

ISBN: 978–0–314–28368–9

The First Edition was dedicated:

To my Fathers

D.L.D.

To Lilly, Clarence, Christine, and A.D.

C.K.W.

The Second Edition was dedicated:

To Cyndy

D.L.D.

To Gloria

C.K.W.

The Third Edition was dedicated:

To Chris Felts

D.L.D.

To the memories of Harriet Tubman, W.E.B. DuBois, and John Brown

C.K.W.

To my Father

D.H.Z.

The Fourth Edition was dedicated:

To Don Zeigler

D.L.D.

To Brenda, Marvin, Terry and Oliver

C.K.W.

To Brannon Heath

D.H.Z.

The Fifth Edition is dedicated:

To the thousands of students with whom I have been privileged to work over the past thirty-four years, and to all those yet to come

D.L.D.

To "my judge"

The Hon. William H. Orrick, Jr.

A man of the law

A man of the people

E.T.L.

Preface

The fifth edition opens two new chapters, as it were, in the development of this book. First, there is a significant changing of the guard in the editing crew. Keith Wingate has taken his well-deserved retirement from the academy, and Don Zeigler's life was tragically cut short. With Evan Lee now on board, we are more open than ever to new ideas about structure, coverage, technology, and methodological perspectives. We will always strive to be the best pedagogical vehicle in the field, and we invite comments, criticisms, and suggestions to help us achieve that goal.

Second, we have converted the text to make it interactive. Students purchasing a new book will also receive a one-year license to the electronic version. (Students purchasing a used book will be able to purchase a license separately.) The electronic version offers the greater flexibility, largely because of hyperlinks that go to other materials in the text or to on-line materials that students may want to consult, such as Black's Law Dictionary (the Black's definition of terms of art in opinions will pop up when the user places the mouse cursor on the differently colored text), cited cases, secondary sources and some specially prepared materials that will help to amplify the text, *e.g.* the complaints in *American Well Works v. Layne & Bowler* and *E. Edelmann Co. v. Triple-A Specialty Co.* in Chapter 3.

The interactive format even provides the paper version with some distinct advantages. The new format allows authors to insert some notes and questions within the text of opinions. This has allowed us to call students' attention to passages in the opinions that students might otherwise read too quickly, and we hope that these intra-case materials will influence students to read the remainder of the case differently. This should help students understand the cases on a deeper level when they prepare for class, which in turn will allow more in-depth class discussion.

Format aside, we have also changed some chapters to make them more teachable. Chapter 1 now draws attention to two key dichotomies: one between constitutional and prudential standing and the other between challenges to legislation and state action on the one hand and judicial review of federal agency action on the other. The chapter is now actually shorter, despite the addition of two prudential standing cases(*Powers v. Ohio* and *Coates v. Cincinnati*) and the substitution of *Zivotovsky v. Clinton* for *United States v. Nixon* in the political question materials. The saving in length comes primarily in the restructuring and condensation of the extensive textual material on standing, which we think had become overwhelming in their complexity and depth, perhaps useful to a full-length seminar dealing only with justiciability, but less than optimal for a survey course.

Chapter 2 now includes *Boumediene v. Bush*, because its relevance to a course in Federal Courts is greater with respect to jurisdiction-stripping than with respect to habeas corpus, which is where the case previously resided within the book.

Chapter 3 also saw a major change. *Gunn v. Minton*, which the Court decided just before this volume went to press, confirms the burial of *Merrell Dow Pharmaceuticals, Inc. v. Thompson* that *Grable* presaged. Accordingly, *Merrell Dow* now appears only in an introductory note, with *Grable* and *Gunn* as main cases. Whether the *Grable-Gunn* approach will work any better than *Merrell Dow* remains to be seen.

Chapter 4 sees the addition of *Stern v. Marshall*, which may signal some rethinking by the Court on how Article I courts ought to function. The chapter structure otherwise remains the same.

Outside of tightening up the voluminous legislative history in *Monell v. Dept. of Social Services*, the biggest change to Chapter 6 is the deletion of the lengthy "Note on Protected and Unprotected Interests." It was our judgment that the many restrictions placed on procedural due process claims in the 1970s and 1980s was more appropriate for a Constitutional Law course. The subject requires more space than we could give it. On the other hand, we have of course added a substantial discussion of *Pearson v. Callahan* as it effectively overrules *Saucier v. Katz*.

Chapter 7 now includes *Pennhurst State School & Hospital v. Halderman*. That case had been in the first three editions, but appeared only as textual note material in the fourth. We think that was a mistake. *Pennhurst* deals so centrally with the underlying themes of the Eleventh Amendment and state sovereign immunity, and the clash in theories between Justice Powell's majority opinion and Justice Stevens's dissent is so clear that we think it makes a fine case with which to end the chapter.

In the same vein, Chapter 11 (Habeas Corpus) is also more manageable. On reflection, it seemed to us that over time the chapter had gravitated from its initial focus on habeas as elaborating federal courts doctrine to materials more appropriate to a course in post-conviction remedies. The grinding detail of the Court's treatment of the Antiterrorism and Effective Death Penalty Act did not so much elaborate the institutional role of the federal courts as it did the ins and outs of post-conviction practice and the Court's retrenchment with respect to interpreting some constitutional rights—a subject better covered in the Constitutional Law course. Accordingly, the Chapter now covers only five main cases—*Williams (Michael) v. Taylor*, *Teague v. Lane*, *Williams (Terry) v. Taylor*, *Cullen v. Pinholster* and *Coleman v. Thompson*. Discussion of the war on terror has moved to Chapter 2, Congressional Control of Federal Jurisdiction, and includes only *Boumediene* as a main case.

The hardest decision with Chapter 11 was to delete the materials on habeas corpus in the executive detention context. Our judgment was that a meaningful treatment of this newly rejuvenated area was more appropriate for Constitutional Law because, unlike habeas corpus to review state custody, it presented only separation-of-powers issues, not judicial federalism issues as well. Equally important is the reality that no Constitutional Law course will cover habeas to review the legality of state custody, and few students will ever take a course on post-conviction remedies.

Chapters 5, 8, 9 and 10 remain the essentially the same as in the fourth edition. Other changes in the areas that these chapters cover have been incremental rather than dramatic. The (shortened) note materials cover those changes.

We continue to use editing conventions to limit length and remove matter that does not contribute to understanding. Within the cases, we omit without ellipsis citations that are not of pedagogical importance and some of the Court's footnotes. The remaining footnotes in cases retain their original numbers. Where the Court is clearly quoting itself, we omit the citation unless it is peculiarly important to understanding the substantive point. Similarly, when the Court quotes a clearly identified source (for example an IRS policy in *Allen v. Wright)*, we have omitted the citation unless it is necessary for understanding. Authors' footnotes within cases are lettered rather than numbered; other authors' footnotes are consecutively numbered within each chapter. Within the material we have written, we have avoided endless repetition of citations; if we have recently cited a case, we then refer to it by its commonly-used short name. When citing state-court cases, we have included both the official reporter citation and citations to the West regional and individual-state reporters. The current version of the Bluebook may frown on it, but we think it is a service to the reader.

Donald L. Doernberg

Evan Tsen Lee

March, 2013

Acknowledgments

From Professor Doernberg:

I would be more than remiss—indeed, an ingrate—not to acknowledge the contribution that Don Zeigler made to my life, personal and professional, in the forty-four years during which I was privileged to know him. To attempt to recite even the highlights of our relationship would be to damn with faint praise. I am a better human being because of him.

For many years I was also fortunate enough to work with Keith Wingate on the first four editions of this book. Countless students have benefited from his contributions, and I count myself among them. I received the news of his coming retirement with some dismay. First of all, he's younger than I. Much more important, however, is what future students will be missing. I have learned from him, both in the subject matter of this volume but also about things like professional judgment, calmness in the face of adversity, and generosity of spirit.

I am grateful also to my colleagues, both at here and at other schools, for their patience in listening to my maunderings about Federal Courts over the years and for making helpful suggestions. I include, without intending to slight anyone, Patti Alleva, Jack Beermann, Jay Carlisle, Erwin Chemerinsky, Dan Meltzer, Michael Mushlin, Ed Purcell, Bob Pushaw, Marty Redish, Tom Rowe and Michelle Simon.

Much of my work would not have been possible without the help of fine research assistants, who worked hard with me and cared enough to tell me bluntly when I was headed off in a wrong direction or had overlooked something that they could see from the perspective of current students. Much of the additional material that the new format of the book makes possible is a direct result of their insight from that perspective. I hope and expect that this will make the book a better teaching and learning tool. I want specifically to thank Lauren Bachtel, Ann Marie Bermont, Michael DiCato, Gillian Kirsch, Katherine Leisch, Tanya Manderson, and Monika A. Urbanowicz for their much appreciated hard work.

From Professor Lee:

Writing acknowledgements for this revision is easy. My wife Susan and my children, M.G. and Michael, make everything in my life possible. Beyond that, I have to thank Keith Wingate for informally involving me in this volume many years ago and Don Doernberg for his patience with a casebook neophyte. Then there are my colleagues across the country from whom I have learned so much—Vik Amar, Ash Bhagwat, Erwin Chemerinsky, Rick Marcus, Henry Monaghan, Jim Pfander, Ed Purcell, Suzanna Sherry, Larry Yackle—to name just a few. Finally, although Felix Frankfurter may be the father of the academic field of Federal Jurisdiction, for me, everything in American public law begins and ends with John Marshall.

Preface to the First Edition

Federal Courts is one of the most difficult courses in the law school curriculum. The concepts are highly abstract; the doctrine is remarkably complex; the courts are open to the well-founded suspicion that their application of the doctrine is often inconsistent. Consequently, the subject presents an unusual challenge for casebook authors: to create a text that stimulates productive thought about the complexities without inundating the student with masses of impenetrable material or uncollated detail.

Federal Courts is first and foremost, a course about power. Though many of the issues concern private disputes and individual rights, two fundamental power relationships underlie them: the states versus the federal government—federalism—and the federal judiciary versus Congress—separation of powers. Moreover, many of those power struggles are played out in the context of disputes between the individual and government, a third type of power relationship. Indeed, the way federalism and separation-of-powers battles are resolved often has a major impact on the power balance between individual and government. The federal courts' primary role is to regulate these conflicts. That is what makes the federal courts special—not just another hierarchical court system.

The importance of the themes of federalism and separation of powers in the study of federal courts requires more attention to American history than in many other courses. The law of contracts, for example, was not directly affected by the Civil War; the law of federal courts was and still is. Political events stimulated many important developments in the law of federal courts. Understanding those causal relationships helps to explain federal courts doctrine.

We have elected, in choosing materials for this book, to focus on those two themes. Apparently disparate topics have in common the underlying themes of federalism and separation of powers, and it is easier to understand the forces that move the Supreme Court in a particular area if one has focused on them in other areas. Most of the chapters involve both themes, and the notes and questions following the main cases attempt to stimulate thought in those terms. Accordingly, we have elected to omit topics that do not illustrate these themes as well, such as the original jurisdiction of the Supreme Court and appellate review within the federal system.

We think there are three things a well-constructed casebook should do. First, it should present the basic themes in the subject matter in an integrated manner that demonstrates their development and interrelationships. Second, it should help students develop their analytical skills by challenging them to deal with case materials that are not too predigested and to grasp not merely the holdings of the cases but also their broader implications. Third, it should be a workable teaching and study tool that does not present the instructor with a volume of material that cannot reasonably be covered or that is often covered in some other course, as diversity is. We hope we have charted a middle course between casebooks that contain little interpretive guidance and those that are such exhaustive scholarly exercises that they would serve as excellent research tools but are unsuited to pedagogy. The notes and questions that follow each case are designed to assist the student to understand both the individual case and its doctrinal implications. To be sure, many of the questions have no clear answers. We intend them to elicit debate on the hard issues and to explore the arguments on both sides of controversial decisions, but we have tried to avoid questions that require knowledge that students cannot reasonably have.

The chapter sequence reflects the two themes. Chapter 1, Justiciability, is a good starting point both because it is a collection of threshold doctrines and because it introduces federalism and separation of powers. Justiciability is difficult to cover as a single unit of a multi-unit course. The doctrine, particularly with respect to standing, is so convoluted that it would make a fine two-credit seminar in its own right. We have elected to cover each of the justifiability sub-doctrines with a single case supplemented by extensive notes and text commentary, resisting considerable temptation to add cases to flesh out parts of the doctrine at the expense of greatly increased length. Running throughout Chapter 1 is the primary question of whether Congress or the Supreme Court is the guardian of federalism and separation of powers.

Broadly speaking, Chapters 2, 3, and 4 concern subject matter jurisdiction, another collection of threshold doctrines. Chapter 2 discusses congressional control of federal jurisdiction. With the exception of the original jurisdiction of the Supreme Court, the federal courts derive no jurisdiction directly from the Constitution. Article III, § 2, functions primarily to enable Congress to confer jurisdiction if it wishes. That is why, almost invariably, one must find a statutory implementation of the general Article III authorization in order successfully to invoke federal jurisdiction. Chapter 2 focuses on how much latitude Congress has in conferring or withholding jurisdiction from the Supreme Court and the lower federal courts.

Chapter 3 turns to federal question jurisdiction. Most first-year Civil Procedure courses introduce the subject, but it deserves more study. A delayed return often helps cement concepts that may seem hopelessly amorphous when encountered in the first year. The doctrine is difficult, particularly with respect to declaratory judgment cases, but it illustrates the interaction between Congress and the courts and between the federal and state judicial systems.

Chapter 4, Legislative Courts, introduces a peculiar separation-of-powers problem. Most of the separation-of-powers issues raised in this volume concern whether the federal judiciary is trenching upon the powers of the other branches of the federal government, particularly Congress. In the area of legislative courts, the question is reversed, and the issue becomes whether Congress, by creating non-Article III courts, is infringing the power of the judiciary. It is an odd and interesting role reversal, casting Congress, not the courts' as the potential constitutional miscreant.

Chapter 5, Federal Common Law, further develops a subject often introduced in Civil Procedure. In our experience, few first-year students really grasp the mechanics of *Erie's* vertical choice-of-law process; fewer still understand the methods of creating federal common law when it is needed. Moreover, we suspect it is highly unusual, if not entirely unheard of, for first-year courses to focus on the separation-of-powers implications of these issues. Yet, increasingly in recent years, voices in the academy and on the bench have suggested that the *Erie* doctrine in its broadest sense properly contemplates both of the themes that animate this volume.

Chapter 6 is a place-setter; it explores the functions and limits of the Civil Rights Act of 1871, 42 U.S.C.A. § 1983. Litigation under that statute need not be in the federal courts, but most of it is. Congress intended the statute to interpose federal power between states and individuals, even though it did not make jurisdiction over § 1983 actions exclusively federal. But most of the problems that Chapters 7 and 8 discuss are played out in § 1983 litigation, so it is well to begin with a sound idea of what that section contemplates.

Chapter 7 examines the states' constitutional insulation from suits in federal court and demonstrates the importance of history in the study of federal courts. The Eleventh Amendment's roots extend back well before the Constitution, into the colonial experience with abusive central control of local affairs. The Amendment is a graphic reminder both that the battle between federal and state power is not merely historical, but continues today and that the power of the federal courts is a key part of that struggle. Moreover, it is the federal courts, primarily the Supreme Court, that determine the scope of the Amendment and thus their own power vis-à-vis the states.

Chapter 8 amplifies the federalism power struggle and begins a series of three chapters that focus on that struggle in a particular context. In these chapters we see the federal courts acting (or refusing to act) with respect to state courts particularly. Here the federalism clash is manifest in the collision of two judicial systems. Chapter 8 covers statutory and judge-made doctrines of restraint that define whether the federal courts can take a dispute away from the state courts. The Anti-Injunction Act, 28 U.S.C.A. § 2283, the doctrine of exhaustion of administrative remedies, and the abstention doctrines the Supreme Court has created all have obvious federalism implications. But they also raise important separation-of-powers questions of whether the Court is being faithful to congressional jurisdictional commands. Finally, these doctrines raise significant questions about the state courts' willingness and ability to vindicate federal rights.

Chapters 9 and 10 continue the study of federal court and state court interaction, but in a different context. Here the focus is not on the federal courts preventing state court consideration, but rather upon federal courts reviewing state adjudications. Chapter 9 discusses Supreme Court review of state court decisions. The idea of taking a case "all the way to the Supreme Court" has great colloquial currency, but not all cases can be heard there. In addition, there are a variety of doctrines that the Court invokes (apart from its discretionary certiorari policy) to weed out cases that, for one reason or another, it thinks it cannot or ought not hear. It may seem surprising that the Court lacks subject matter jurisdiction over a case with a federal constitutional issue, but that is sometimes true. Chapter 9 explores why. This Chapter also presents the only circumstance in which a federal court, as a formal matter, sits in review of a state court. The federalism implications early-on provoked a constitutional crisis in *Martin v. Hunter's Lessee,* a case well known to all students of constitutional law. The crisis has abated; the issue survives.

Finally, Chapter 10, Federal Habeas Corpus Challenges to State Custody, presents cases in which federal courts, though not as a formal matter sitting in review of state court proceedings, are in fact doing exactly that. Here, the federalism clash is intensified. In Chapter 9, the Supreme Court reviews state court judgments. In the realm of federal habeas corpus, however, the inferior federal courts may review the judgment of the highest court of a state. Moreover, the cases are far more numerous, so federal habeas corpus acts as a constant irritant to the states. Congress has provided the basic statutory framework, but the Supreme Court has played a major role in determining the degree of irritation. Consequently, federal habeas corpus is a good place to end, because we come full circle with respect to the underlying themes of this book. Even as the Supreme Court monitors federal habeas corpus on behalf of federalism, it collides with congressional authorizations of the use of the writ, thus raising separation-of-powers problems. Federal habeas corpus provides a good stage from which to present the continuing importance of these themes and an institutional question of overriding importance: As between Congress and the Court, who should be the guardian of federalism and who should be the guardian of separation of powers?

Donald L. Doernberg

C. Keith Wingate

January, 1994

Table of Contents

CHAPTER 6: *The Federal Forum, the Fourteenth Amendment, and Section 1983* ... 563

CHAPTER 7: *The Eleventh Amendment* ... 643

Table of Cases

The principal cases are in **bold** type. Cases cited or discussed in the text are in roman type. References are to pages. Cases cited in principal cases and within other quoted materials are not included.

Table of Secondary Authorities

Materials from which excerpts appear are in **bold** type. Materials cited or discussed in the text are roman in type. References are to pages. Materials cited in principal cases and within other quoted materials are not included.

Chadbourn, James H. & A. Leo Levin, *Original Jurisdiction of Federal Questions,* 90 U.PA.L.REV. 639 (1942), 291

Chemerinsky, Erwin, *Ending the Parity Debate,* 71 B.U.L.REV. 593 (1991), 18

CHEMERINSKY, ERWIN, FEDERAL JURISDICTION (5th ed. 2007), 60, 152, 798, 821, 835, 870, 900, 1080, 1083

Cohen, William, *The Broken Compass: The Requirement that a Case Arise "Directly" under Federal Law,* 115 U.PA.L.REV. 890 (1967), 373

III THE CORRESPONDENCE AND PUBLIC PAPERS OF JOHN JAY 1763-1826 (Henry P. Johnston ed. 1971), 25

Currie, David P., Ex parte Young *After Seminole Tribe,* 72 N.Y.U.L.REV. 547 (1997), 754

DePalma, Anthony, *Warming Report Warns of Increased Flooding,* N.Y. TIMES (July 11, 2007), 118

DOERNBERG, DONALD L., IDENTITY CRISIS: FEDERAL COURTS IN A PSYCHOLOGICAL WILDERNESS (2001), 278

Doernberg, Donald L., *Juridical Chameleons in the "New Erie" Canal,* 1990 UTAH L.REV. 759, 526

Doernberg, Donald L., *There's No Reason for It; It's Just Our Policy: Why the Well-Pleaded Complaint Rule Sabotages the Purposes of Federal Question Jurisdiction,* 38 HASTINGS L.J. 597 (1987), 303

Doernberg, Donald L. & Michael B. Mushlin, *The Trojan Horse: How the Declaratory Judgment Act Created a Cause of Action and Expanded Federal Jurisdiction While the Supreme Court Wasn't Looking,* 36 U.C.L.A.L.REV. 529 (1989), 373

Eisenberg, Theodore, *Congressional Authority to Restrict Lower Federal Court Jurisdiction,* 83 YALE L.J. 498 (1974), 216

Ely, John Hart, *The Irrepressible Myth of* Erie, 87 HARV.L.REV. 693 (1974), 428

Eskridge, William N. Jr. & Philip P. Frickey, *Quasi-Constitutional Law: Clear Statement Rules As Constitutional Lawmaking,* 45 VAND.L.REV. 593 (1992), 701

Fallon, Richard H. Jr. & Daniel J. Meltzer, *New Law, Non-retroactivity and Constitutional Remedies,* 104 HARV.L.REV. 1731 (1991), 1121

Fallon, Richard H. Jr., *Of Legislative Courts, Administrative Agencies, and Article III,* 101 HARV.L.REV. 915 (1988), 402

Farina, Cynthia R., *Statutory Interpretation and the Balance of Power in the Administrative State,* 89 COLUM.L. REV. 452 (1989), 13

THE FEDERALIST NO. 47 (James Madison) (Jacob E. Cooke ed. 1961), 9

THE FEDERALIST NO. 48 (James Madison) (Jacob E. Cooke ed. 1961), 13

THE FEDERALIST NO. 81 (James Madison) (Jacob E. Cooke ed. 1961), 259, 260, 646, 743, 744, 781

Feld, Alan L., *Separation of Political Powers: Boundaries or Balance?,* 21 GA.L. REV. 171 (1986), 13

Merrill, Thomas W., *The Judicial Prerogative,* 12 PACE L.REV. 327 (1992), 526

Merrill, Thomas, *The Common Law Powers of Federal Courts,* 52 U.CHI.L.REV. 1 (1985), 438

Neuborne, Burt, *Parity Revisited: The Uses of a Judicial Forum of Excellence,* 44 DEPAUL L.REV. 797 (1995), 19

Neuborne, Burt, *The Myth of Parity*, 90 HARV.L.REV. 1105 (1977), 14, 18, 834

Nichol, Gene R. Jr., *Ripeness and the Constitution,* 54 U.CHI.L.REV. 153 (1987), 152

Nichol, Gene, *Causation As a Standing Requirement: The Unprincipled Use of Judicial Restraint,* 69 KY.L.J. 185 (1981), 60

Nichol, Gene, *Rethinking Standing,* 72 CALIF.L.REV. 68 (1984), 60

Note, *Moore v. Sims: A Further Expansion of the* Younger *Abstention Doctrine,* 1 PACE L.REV. 149 (1980), 869

NOWAK, JOHN E. & RONALD D. ROTUNDA, CONSTITUTIONAL LAW (8th ed. 2010), 981

Peller, Gary, *In Defense of Federal Habeas Corpus Relitigation,* 16 HARV.C.R.-C.L. L. REV. 579 (1982), 1086

Pildes, Richard H., *Democracy, Anti-Democracy and the Canon,* 17 CONST. COMMENT. 295 (2000), 662

Purcell, Edward A. Jr., *The Particularly Dubious Case of* Hans v. Louisiana: *An Essay on Law, History, and "Federal Courts,"* 81 N.CAR.L.REV. 1927 (2003), 656

Ratner, Leonard, *Congressional Power over the Appellate Jurisdiction of the Supreme Court*, 109 U.PA.L.REV. 157 (1960), 196

Ratner, Leonard, *Executive Privilege, Self Incrimination, and the Separation of Powers Illusion,* 22 U.C.L.A.L.REV. 92 (1974), 8

Redish, Martin H., *Abstention, Separation of Powers, and the Limits of the Judicial Function,* 94 YALE L.J. 71 (1984), 561, 796, 830

Redish, Martin H., *Federal Common Law, Political Legitimacy, and the Interpretive Process: An "Institutionalist" Perspective,* 83 NW.U.L. REV. 761 (1989), 526, 561

REDISH, MARTIN H., FEDERAL JURISDICTION: TENSIONS IN THE ALLOCATION OF JUDICIAL POWER (2d ed. 1990), 213, 330, 493

RITZ, WILFRED, REWRITING THE HISTORY OF THE JUDICIARY ACT OF 1789 (1990), 439

Rowe, Thomas D. Jr., Rooker-Feldman: *Worth Only the Powder to Blow It Up?,* 74 NOTRE DAME L.REV. 1081 (1999), 1081

Rowe, Thomas D. Jr. & Edward L. Baskauskas, *"Inextricably Intertwined" Explicable at Last?* Rooker-Feldman *Analysis After the Supreme Court's* ExxonMobil *Decision,* 2006 FED. CTS. L. REV. 1 (2006), 1053

SCALIA, JOHN, BUREAU OF JUSTICE STATISTICS SPECIAL REPORT: PRISONER PETITIONS FILED IN U.S. DISTRICT COURTS, 2000, WITH TRENDS 1980-2000 (2002), 1090

SHAKESPEARE, WILLIAM, HAMLET, 1013

Shapiro, David L., *Jurisdiction and Discretion,* 60 N.Y.U.L.REV. 543, (1985), 291

Prologue

Federalism: A Foreword[a]

Henry J. Friendly[*]
86 Yale L.J. 1019 (1977).

It should never be forgotten that this slogan, "Our Federalism," born in the early struggling days of our Union of States, occupies a highly important place in our Nation's history and its future.[1]

It was fitting that in his last term Mr. Justice Black should have bequeathed to the American people the phrase "Our Federalism" and the discussion accompanying it—the most eloquent statement on the subject since Chief Justice Chase's reference to "an indestructible Union, composed of indestructible States." It was fitting also that he should have emphasized Our Federalism's historic origins. The United States under the Constitution was born federalist; it did not truly choose federalism or have federalism thrust upon it. As Chief Justice Chase had said, "Both the States and the United States existed before the Constitution." The genius of the Framers lay in devising a unique form of federalism—one in which a national government was authorized to act directly on the people within the powers confided to it rather than solely on the states, and was endowed with an amplitude of powers which might or might not be used as the future would

a Reprinted by permission of The Yale Law Journal Company from The Yale Law Journal, vol. 86, pp. 1019–34.

* Senior Judge, United States Court of Appeals for the Second Circuit; Presiding Judge Special Court under Rail Reorganization Act of 1973.

1 Younger v. Harris, 401 U.S. 37, 44–45 (1971) (Black, J.). The Justice regarded the phrase as embodying "the belief that the National Government will fare best if the States and their institutions are left free to perform their separate functions in their separate ways." He elaborated:

> The concept does not mean blind deference to "States' Rights" any more than it means centralization of control over every important issue in our National Government and its courts. The Framers rejected both these courses. What the concept does represent is a system in which there is sensitivity to the legitimate interests of both State and National Governments, and in which the National Government, anxious though it may be to vindicate and protect federal rights and federal interests, always endeavors to do so in ways that will not unduly interfere with the legitimate activities of the States.

dictate. As Mr. Justice Holmes was later to say, the Framers "called into life a being the development of which could not have been foreseen completely by the most gifted of its begetters."

Despite the Marshall Court's resounding affirmation of the breadth of the powers conferred on the national government, the use made of these powers through the first century of our history under the Constitution was restrained. Congress moved speedily to exercise its powers with respect to patents and copyrights. The national government conducted foreign affairs, raised and supported an exceedingly modest army and, over considerable protest, provided and maintained an even more modest navy, waged some foreign wars, borrowed and coined money, levied taxes (primarily import tariffs), created the first and second Banks of the United States, spent money both to purchase the Louisiana Territory and, again over much objection, to make internal improvements, and then, under the impulse of Jacksonian democracy, it withdrew from the banking field. Beyond this the national government did relatively little, and some of what it did, notably the Fugitive Slave Acts, would not be proudly regarded today. Few people remember that until 1867 we had bankruptcy acts for only seven years, 1800 to 1803 and 1841 to 1843.

The judiciary made relatively little attempt to rush in where the legislative and executive branches were unwilling to tread. Chief Justice Marshall himself authored *Barron v. Mayor of Baltimore,* which held that the guarantees of the Bill of Rights applied only to the federal government, not to the states; he thought the question to be "of great importance, but not of much difficulty." After what Professor Gunther calls "gropings," the Supreme Court arrived at the celebrated formulation of *Cooley v. Board of Wardens* that when Congress had not acted to utilize the commerce power, the states were precluded from nondiscriminatory action only when "subjects of this power are in their nature national, or admit only of one uniform system, or plan of regulation." Judged by today's standards, Congress did little indeed.

The watershed was the war between the states, the adoption of the three Reconstruction amendments, especially the Fourteenth, and enactment of the various civil rights acts with jurisdiction in the federal courts to enforce them. Although these amendments were doubtless intended primarily to safeguard the rights of the newly emancipated Negroes, Mr. Justice Miller's prophecy that this would be practically their sole effect turned out to be an exceedingly poor one. In time the due process and equal protection clauses of the Fourteenth Amendment would vest the federal judiciary, particularly the Supreme Court, with a roving authority to invalidate state statutes and, for almost all practical purposes, to reverse the decision in *Barron v. Mayor of Baltimore*. Along with these enactments Congress adopted the National Bank Act of 1864 and the Bankruptcy Act of 1867. As important as these substantive changes was the Act of March 3, 1875, which for the first time (except for the abortive Judiciary Act of 1801) vested the federal courts with general federal question jurisdiction, although subject to a jurisdictional amount.

Still another score of years elapsed, however, before enactment of the two statutes that were the real beginnings of federal regulation of interstate business—the Interstate Commerce Act of 1887, adopted in response to the Supreme Court's holding that state regulation of interstate railroad rates was not permissible under the Cooley doctrine, and the Sherman Antitrust Act of 1890. These were followed, again after the lapse of some years, by a burst of legislation in the first Wilson administration—the Clayton Act of 1914, the Federal Trade Commission Act of the same year, the Shipping Act of 1916, and, perhaps most important though least litigated, the Federal Reserve Act of 1913. The early 1920s saw four other important pieces of legislation extending federal regulatory power: the Transportation Act, 1920, which transformed the Interstate Commerce Act by placing "the railroad systems of the country more completely than ever under the fostering guardianship and control of the Commission," the Federal Water Power Act, the Packers and Stockyard Act, 1921, and the Radio Act of 1927—the forerunner of the Federal Communications Act.

Contemplating what then seemed a rather amazing array of new statutes extending national power, this writer was prompted to say in 1928:

> The steady expansion of the jurisdiction of the federal courts, especially since Reconstruction days, has been but a reflex of the general growth of federal political power. That growth will not abate, since it is responsive to deep social and economic causes.

Although this must rate as an excellent prediction, little did the author know what the next few years would bring.

If the war between the states was a watershed, the New Deal was a tidal wave. Two remarkable statutes, the Securities Act of 1933 and the Securities Exchange Act of 1934, elevated the national government from a negligible to a predominant role with respect to the issuance of and dealings in securities and the operation of the stock exchanges. An equally dramatic change in the field of labor regulation was wrought by the National Labor Relations Act of 1935 and the Fair Labor Standards Act of 1938. The Securities Exchange Act, unlike the Securities Act, provides for exclusive federal jurisdiction. Although the National Labor Relations Act does not, a good deal of preemption is furnished by the judicially fashioned rule that "[w]hen it is clear or may fairly be assumed that the activities which a State purports to regulate are protected by Section 7 of the National Labor Relations Act, or constitute an unfair labor practice under Section 8, due regard for the federal enactment requires that state jurisdiction must yield." Even when litigation under this statute can proceed in the state courts, the latter must follow not only the text of the statute but also "federal common law"—a concept representing an advance in federal power that far outweighed the abandonment in the *Erie* case of "the spurious uniformity of *Swift v. Tyson.*"

These major assertions of federal power were accompanied by a host of others—the Tennessee Valley Authority Act of 1933, the Banking Acts of 1933 and 1935, the Public Utility Holding Company Acts of 1935, the expansion of the Interstate Commerce Act to include motor carriers and water carriers, the Civil Aeronautics Act, the Federal Power Act, the Commodity Exchange Act, the Robinson–Patman Act, the 1938 amendments to the Federal Trade Commission Act and to the Securities Exchange Act, the Natural Gas Act, the Federal Food, Drug, and Cosmetic Act, the Trust Indenture Act of 1939, and the Investment Company and Investment Advisers Acts. Perhaps an even more important alteration in the national-state balance was worked by a statute that could hardly have then been thought of as creating such a change—the Social Security Act of 1935, or more accurately the portions of that Act which established assistance programs to be administered by the states in accordance with federal standards, with the national government supplying varying percentages of funds. In this and similar enactments Congress has found a new and powerful tool to bring the states into line with national thinking under penalty of losing the largesse from the federal fisc.

After some slowing of the congressional mill during the 1940s and 1950s, the legislative expansion of national power resumed in the next two decades. Of prime importance was the effort, after the lapse of nearly a century, to utilize Section 5 of the Fourteenth Amendment, which empowers the Congress "to enforce, by appropriate legislation, the provisions of this article." Here the basic enactments are the Civil Rights Acts of 1957, the Voting Rights Act of 1965, the Civil Rights Act of 1964, Title VIII of the Civil Rights Act of 1968, and the Age Discrimination in Employment Act of 1967. Along with this has come a whole rash of statutes utilizing the commerce power for the promotion of safety[73] and the protection of borrowers and consumers.[74] Still more important is a series of

73 The single most important is the Occupational Safety and Health Act of 1970. Others are the National Traffic and Motor Vehicle Safety Act of 1966, the Highway Safety Act of 1966, the Natural Gas Pipeline Safety Act of 1963, the Federal Coal Mine Health and Safety Act of 1969, the Ports and Waterways Safety Act of 1972, the Federal Railroad Safety Act of 1970, the Consumer Product Safety Act, the Motor Vehicle and Schoolbus Safety Amendments of 1974, the Transportation Safety Act of 1974, the Highway Safety Act of 1976, and the Consumer Product Safety Commission Improvements Act of 1976.

74 These include: the Consumer Credit Protection Act, the Interstate Land Sales Full Disclosure Act, the Fair Credit Reporting Act, the Fair Credit Billing Act, the Real Estate Settlement Procedures Act of 1974, the Magnuson–Moss Warranty–Federal Trade Commission Improvement Act, the Equal Credit Opportunity Act, the Home Mortgage Disclosure Act of 1973, and the Consumer Leasing Act of 1976. * * *

laws placing the weight of the national government behind efforts to protect the environment.[75] Considerably more troubling to me, from the standpoint of policy and even from that of constitutionality, has been what seems a knee-jerk tendency of Congress to seek to remedy any serious abuse by invoking the commerce power as a basis for the expansion of the federal criminal law into areas of scant federal concern.

The judiciary has made its own contribution to the growth of national power. I have already referred to one that seems to me wholly salutary—the development of federal common law. More controversial has been the selective incorporation doctrine whereby the due process clause of the Fourteenth Amendment has been held to make applicable to the states all the provisions of the first eight amendments except the Second, Third, and Seventh, the indictment clause of the Fifth, and the excessive bail protection of the Eighth.[78] This constitutional revolution, effectively overruling *Twining v. New Jersey* and *Adamson v. California,* became an even greater force for federalizing state criminal procedure as a result of the expansion of federal habeas corpus for state prisoners wrought initially by *Brown v. Allen* and expanded by *Fay v. Noia*. In the wake of Supreme Court decisions, notably *Monroe v. Pape*, there has been an unparalleled resort to the long-dormant civil rights acts of the Reconstruction period—not simply to prevent discrimination against blacks but to redress many other sorts of constitutional deprivations, particularly in state prisons. In carrying out this mission, federal courts have felt authorized to take on an enormous degree of supervision of the operations of state prisons and mental institutions and to impose affirmative obligations on the states. One federal court, in an effort to obtain minority representation, has ordered the complete remodeling of a city government. The risks of confrontation are serious.

Other potent weapons for increased national power recently forged by the Supreme Court are the expansion of the hearing component of due process evidenced by *Sniadach v. Family Finance Corp.* and *Goldberg v. Kelly* and their numer-

---

75 The basic statute is the National Environmental Policy Act of 1969. Other important statutes are the Water Quality Improvement Act of 1970, the Clean Air Amendments of 1970, the Federal Water Pollution Control Act Amendments of 1972, the Federal Environmental Pesticide Control Act of 1972, the Noise Control Act of 1972, and the Deepwater Port Act of 1974.

78 The principal decisions accomplishing this include: *Mapp v. Ohio* (4th Amendment exclusionary rule); *Robinson v. California* (8th Amendment prohibition of cruel and unusual punishment); *Gideon v. Wainwright* (6th Amendment right to counsel); *Ker v. California* (4th Amendment exclusionary rule); *Malloy v. Hogan* (5th Amendment right to remain silent); *Pointer v. Texas* (6th Amendment right to confront witnesses); *Klopher v. North Carolina* (6th Amendment right to a speedy trial); *Washington v. Texas* (6th Amendment right to compulsory process); *Duncan v. Louisiana* (6th Amendment right to jury trial); *Benton v. Maryland* (5th Amendment prohibition of double jeopardy); *In re Winship* (proof beyond reasonable doubt). The Court has never had to say whether the Eighth Amendment's prohibition against excessive bail applies to the states, although the lower courts have held that it does, and the Court itself has hinted as much. * * *

ous progeny, the revival of substantive due process thought by some to be implicit in *Roe v. Wade,* and the holding that the Civil Rights Act of 1871 was an "expressly authorized" exception to the statute prohibiting federal court injunctions against proceedings in state courts. In addition, the Court has diluted the "reasonable ground—good faith" defense for state officials (in the particular case, members of school boards) from liability for damages under the civil rights laws by a qualification that this defense would not apply if the officer "knew or reasonably should have known that the action he took within his sphere of official responsibility" would violate a plaintiff's constitutional rights.

As if this were not enough, many believe—with much reason—that further expansion of national power is required. A former chairman of the Securities Exchange Commission, having closely and critically examined what he terms "the Delaware syndrome," has called for a federal law imposing minimum standards of fiduciary responsibility and fairness on all corporations engaged in commerce with more than $1 million of assets and 300 shareholders. The proliferation of state statutes designed to aid management in retaining control of interstate enterprises that are locally based or even that simply have property within the state has led the framers of the proposed ALI Federal Securities Code to provide for preemption in the area of tender offers and takeovers. The Code proposes other preemption; some believe it should propose more to avoid the costs and delays of largely duplicative requirements in a field effectively regulated by the national government. Companies that have complied with federal environmental standards naturally object to being obliged to start all over again with the states. The adoption of many new federal statutes for the protection of consumers and borrowers may raise again the question of preemption not only in those areas but in the entire field of unfair competition and antitrust law with respect to interstate or foreign transactions. And surely we will see a federal law dealing with major aircraft accidents where there are plaintiffs from many states and defendants who can be sued in a variety of courts, state and federal, with consequences enticing to choice-of-law buffs but considerably less appealing to litigants.

Yet the movement has not been all in one direction. The cases stemming from the decision with which we began, *Younger v. Harris,* afford one illustration. The Court has advanced from its position in *Younger* that a federal court may not enjoin a pending state criminal proceeding brought in good faith even when the federal court plaintiff is suing under the Civil Rights Act, and from its simultaneous holding applying the same rule to declaratory judgments. The Court has recently held that a federal court may enjoin neither state criminal proceedings begun after the federal complaint was filed but before proceedings of substance had taken place in the federal court, nor state civil proceedings "in aid of and closely related to criminal statutes, nor state contempt proceedings." * * *

The rising tide of imposition of procedural due process on the states was checked at the 1975 Term by three decisions requiring higher thresholds for showing a legally protected interest in liberty or property. Despite the dismissal of certiorari in a case that was expected to settle the question, there may still be hope that the Court will retreat from its unexplained and, in the writer' view, ill-advised intimations that state prisoners seeking relief under the Civil Rights Act need not exhaust administrative remedies which the state has provided; if it does not, Congress may be persuaded to act. Federal habeas corpus was substantially restricted when the Court held it unavailable for Fourth Amendment claims of state prisoners to whom the state had provided an opportunity for full and fair litigation in its own courts. Any reader familiar with views I expressed some years ago will not be surprised to learn that I applaud this result, although I would have preferred to have seen it reached by a thoroughgoing judicial reconsideration of the whole subject of collateral attack on criminal convictions or, failing that, by legislation * * *.

Furthermore the Eleventh Amendment still lives, to the extent of barring federal court actions by private persons seeking funds in the state treasury even when the funds have come there through alleged violation of federal regulations concerning a federal welfare program; per contra, however, when Congress has authorized damage awards in legislation enacted pursuant to Section 5 of the Fourteenth Amendment * * *. [Consider] Professor Gunther's provocative questions:

> What are the values, historical and contemporary, of federalism? Can it still be said that federalism increases liberty, encourages diversity, promotes creative experimentation and responsive self-government? Or is it a legalistic obstruction, a harmful brake on governmental responses to pressing social issues, a shield for selfish vested interests? Is federalism a theme that constitutional law must grapple with simply because it is *there,* in the Constitution? Is the prime challenge it poses that of minimizing the obstacles that the complexities of federalism put in the way of meeting modern needs? Or does federalism embody more appealing values that deserve some of the imaginative enthusiasm with which modern constitutional law embraces the promotion of such values as equality and freedom of speech?

Clearly Mr. Justice Black, who played no small part in strengthening the role of the national government at the expense of the states, would have answered the second and the final question with a resounding "Yes." So, for what it is worth, would I. Although some state governments may be ignorant or venal, many are far-seeing and courageous; and not all wisdom reposes in Washington. There is still truth in Mr. Justice Brandeis' renowned observation:

> It is one of the happy incidents of the federal system that a single courageous State may, if its citizens choose, serve as a laboratory; and try novel social and economic experiments without risk to the rest of the country.

No-fault insurance is a sufficient example; we may end up with a uniform federal system or minimum federal standards, but we should never have had anything save for experimentation by the states. We must stand in awe and admiration of the design of the Framers and of the success of the Supreme Court in fleshing it out—preventing one state from getting in the way of others and endowing the central government with power to act on a national basis when Congress finds this to be warranted, but leaving to the states the final decision on the bulk of day-to-day matters that can best be decided by those who are closest to them. While I expect we shall be forced to pursue the centripetal path of the last century, we should not rush along it too fast or too far; the question whether action by the national government is needed should always be asked. To paraphrase T.R. Powell, how fast is too fast and far too far are matters on which the writer of a foreword need not express an opinion.

Preliminary Thoughts on Separation of Powers and the Judiciary

One hesitates to play on a double bill opposite Henry Friendly, even in a prologue; it seems both presumptuous and a sure way to be on the short end of an invidious comparison. Yet, for balance it is necessary to introduce the second great theme that animates these materials. We are all poorer for Judge Friendly's not having written on separation of powers as he did on federalism. But even his silence teaches; the Supreme Court's role in elaborating this theme with respect to the functioning of the federal courts has generally been far less noticeable than its corresponding role with respect to federalism.

"Separation of powers" is a ringing phrase in American constitutional history. It brings to mind the talismanic incantation[1] of "checks and balances" and visions of bicameralism,[2] presidential veto,[3] impeachment,[4] the Senate's power to approve

---

1 Yet, as Professor Ratner warns, "[N]o matter how solemnly reiterated, the phrase provides no talismanic precept." Leonard Ratner, *Executive Privilege, Self Incrimination, and the Separation of Powers Illusion*, 22 U.C.L.A. L. REV. 92, 93 (1974).

2 U.S. CONST. art. I, § 1.

3 U.S. CONST. art. I, § 7, cl. 2.

4 U.S. CONST. art. I, § 2, cl. 5; U.S. CONST. art. I, § 3, cl. 6, 7; U.S. CONST. art. II, § 4.

treaties,[5] its "advise and consent" power generally,[6] the House of Representatives' special role as the originator of all revenue bills,[7] and judicial review.[8] Those who drafted the Constitution were much concerned with separation of powers, and James Madison devoted a substantial portion of the Federalist essays to it.

> One of the principal objections inculcated by the more respectable adversaries to the constitution, is its supposed violation of the political maxim, that the legislative, executive and judiciary departments ought to be separate and distinct. In the structure of the federal government, no regard, it is said, seems to have been paid to this essential precaution in favor of liberty. The several departments of power are distributed and blended in such a manner, as at once to destroy all symmetry and beauty of form; and to expose some of the essential parts of the edifice to the danger of being crushed by the disproportionate weight of other parts.
>
> No political truth is certainly of greater intrinsic value or is stamped with the authority of more enlightened patrons of liberty than that on which the objection is founded. The accumulation of all powers legislative, executive and judiciary in the same hands, whether of one, a few or many, and whether hereditary, self-appointed, or elective, may justly be pronounced the very definition of tyranny. Were the federal constitution therefore really chargeable with this accumulation of power or with a mixture of powers having a dangerous tendency to such an accumulation, no further arguments would be necessary to inspire a universal reprobation of the system.
>
> * * *
>
> [I]n saying "there can be no liberty where the legislative and executive powers are united in the same person, or body of magistrates," or "if the power of judging be not separated from the legislative and executive powers," [Montesquieu] did not mean that these departments ought to have no *partial agency* in, or no *controul* over the acts of each other. His meaning, as his own words import, and still more conclusively as illustrated by the example in his eye, can amount to no more than this, that where the *whole* power of one department is exercised by the same hands which possess the *whole* power of another department, the fundamental principles of a free constitution, are subverted. * * *[9]

Thus did Madison endeavor to show that the checks and balances system, though it blended powers, was nonetheless consistent with and essential to separation of powers.

---

5 U.S. Const. art. II, § 2, cl. 2.

6 *Id*.

7 U.S. Const. art. I, § 7, cl. 1.

8 Marbury v. Madison, 5 U.S. (1 Cranch) 137 (1803).

9 The Federalist No. 47, at 323–26 (James Madison) (Jacob E. Cooke ed. 1961).

Constitutional law courses abound with the great decisions on separation of powers: *Marbury v. Madison*,[10] *Youngstown Sheet and Tube Co. v. Sawyer*,[11] *United States v. Nixon*,[12] *Bowsher v. Synar*,[13] *United States v. United States District Court*,[14] and *Immigration and Naturalization Service v. Chadha*,[15] to name but a few. Most of the best known decisions on separation of powers concern what the legislative and executive branches may or may not do. On occasion, however, the Supreme Court discusses separation-of-powers restraints on what the judiciary may do. One scholar notes:

> The Supreme Court, after a fragile start, has evolved into the authoritative interpreter of the U.S. Constitution, short of amendment. Judicial review of national and state action converts the tribunal into a continuous constitutional convention, which mediates between forces of continuity and change in a "living" Constitution. * * * The primary mission of the Supreme Court throughout American history has been to enforce the supremacy and uniformity of national law and of federally-created rights of individuals in the states. Enforcing separation of powers is secondary. * * * Notwithstanding its role as ultimate interpreter, the branch of the national government limited most by Supreme Court interpretation of separation of powers is the judiciary itself.[16]

Concerns about separation of powers underlie much of the Court's jurisprudence in the area of justiciability. The Article III doctrines of standing, ripeness, mootness, political questions, advisory opinions, and the overarching concept of "case or controversy" all implicate separation of powers. The Court has often declared that the case-or-controversy requirement of Article III is a specific manifestation of separation of powers because it requires the courts to limit themselves to concrete disputes, avoiding broader policy questions and more general disagreements about what the law ought to be, questions the Court reminds us are more properly left to the political branches.[17]

Separation of powers also plays a more subtle part in how the federal courts operate. The power to declare legislation unconstitutional clearly brings the judiciary into potential conflict with at least the legislature and possibly with the

---

10 5 U.S. (1 Cranch) 137 (1803) (establishing judicial review of federal legislation).

11 343 U.S. 579 (1952) (confirming judicial review of executive acts—here the government's seizure of steel mills to terminate a labor dispute during the Korean War).

12 418 U.S. 683 (1974) (confirming judicial authority to review claims of executive privilege in dispute between the President and the special prosecutor investigating the Watergate break-in).

13 478 U.S. 714 (1986) (overturning congressional assignment of executive functions to Comptroller General, a legislative department official).

14 407 U.S. 297 (1972) (overturning executive's claim of authority to order searches in domestic national security cases without judicial supervision).

15 462 U.S. 919 (1983) (disapproving legislative veto of executive branch actions unless the congressional veto goes through the normal legislative process).

16 J. Woodford Howard, Jr., *Supreme Court Enforcement of Separation of Powers: A Balance Sheet, in* SEPARATION OF POWERS IN THE AMERICAN POLITICAL SYSTEM 81, 88 (Barbara B. Knight ed. 1989).

17 *See, e.g.*, Allen v. Wright, 468 U.S. 737 (1984), discussed in Chapter 1.

executive. Beyond that, every time a court interprets a statute, it gives meaning to the act of a coordinate branch. When we speak of the role of the courts in legislative interpretation, we are concerned with separation of powers. Should the courts, for example, search for "legislative intent," or should they confine themselves to the unadorned words of statutes no matter how clear the underlying intent of the legislature may be?[18] If the courts ignore legislative intent in favor of plain meaning, does the practice exalt separation of powers or, to the extent that a clear legislative purpose is frustrated, offend it? An example may help demonstrate the difficulty of the problem.

Suppose Congress enacts a statute creating new substantive rights for individuals, but not explicitly creating a private cause of action for enforcement of those rights. Should the courts do so? If not, congressional purpose to create effective rights may be ignored. If so, the courts may be cast into the role of "supplemental legislators," effectively amending legislation to include what the political branches omitted.[19]

The preceding example leads to the more general question of whether, in this age of statutes and administrative regulation, courts ought ever to formulate rules of law. The venerable clash of *Swift v. Tyson*[20] on one hand and *Erie Railroad v. Tompkins*[21] on the other represents a substantial federalism problem, but there are separation-of-powers undertones as well. Is it appropriate for courts to make law?

Two factors complicate that inquiry. First, the demarcation between interpretation and creation is by no means clear. Second, on occasion the legislature may invite or command the judiciary to construct rules of law.[22] In such cases, is separation of powers more offended if the courts accept or refuse the assignment?

Most of the topics covered in this volume involve separation-of-powers problems. The interplay between justiciability and separation of powers has already been noted. Congressional power to define the jurisdiction of the federal courts

18 Justice Scalia, at least, has suggested the latter.

> [Examination of legislative history] is appropriate * * * if one assumes that the task of a court of law is to plumb the intent of the particular Congress that enacted a particular provision. That methodology is not mine nor, I think, the one that courts have traditionally followed. It is our task, as I see it, not to enter the minds of the Members of Congress—who need have nothing in mind in order for their votes to be both lawful and effective—but rather to give fair and reasonable meaning to the text of the United States Code, adopted by various Congresses at various times.

Pennsylvania v. Union Gas Co., 491 U.S. 1, 29–30 (1989) (Scalia, J., concurring and dissenting).

19 Justices Stevens and Powell debated this problem vigorously in Cannon v. University of Chicago, 441 U.S. 677 (1979). *See generally* Chapter 5, Section C, Part 3.

20 41 U.S. (16 Pet.) 1 (1842).

21 304 U.S. 64 (1938).

22 *See, e.g.*, Textile Workers Union v. Lincoln Mills, 353 U.S. 448 (1957). *See generally* Chapter 5, Section C, Part 2.

within the limits of Article III represents an enormous influence by the legislature on the judiciary.[23] At the same time, the Supreme Court's efforts to construe jurisdictional statutes also affect the distribution of power among all three branches. Congress has often created "legislative" or "Article I" courts, the judges of which do not enjoy the protections available under Article III.[24] Does the existence of such courts violate separation of powers? To the extent that Congress assigns to them questions that are contemplated by Article III, § 2, is that a separate violation?

In addition to construing jurisdictional statutes, the Court occasionally recognizes that jurisdiction exists but elects not to exercise it. The abstention doctrines[25] demonstrate this phenomenon. One might not initially characterize abstention doctrines as interbranch conflicts, but they may be. When Congress grants jurisdiction, should the Court consider the grant an invitation, or is it more like an offer that cannot be refused? Although the Court has, for the most part, developed abstention doctrines narrowly, it could theoretically create a new doctrine, deciding to abstain from exercising all diversity jurisdiction, for example.[26] If it did, would the new doctrine pose a separation-of-powers problem because of the obvious frustration of congressional intent to retain diversity jurisdiction? With respect to the more limited abstention doctrines, is the difference one in kind or merely in degree?

Complicating this entire inquiry is the fact that the Constitution never discusses separation of powers in so many words. To some extent, the document's organization exemplifies separation of powers, but the separation is far from total. In part, the elaborate system of checks and balances, by making the three branches to some extent interdependent, represents a rejection of rigid separation. James Madison thought that important. "[U]nless these departments be so far connected and blended as to give to each a constitutional control over the others, the degree of separation which the maxim requires, as essential to a free government,

---

23 *See generally* Chapter 2.

24 *See generally* Chapter 4.

25 *See generally* Chapter 8.

26 The Court has developed a more limited sort of abstention with respect to diversity.

> [T]here are two important areas, domestic relations cases and probate matters, where, by a judge-made exception to the [diversity] statute, the federal courts will not act though diversity is present. These two exceptions were first developed at a time when the diversity statute granted jurisdiction of "suits of a civil nature in law or in equity," and it was thought that the domestic relations and probate cases, being matters that would have been heard in the ecclesiastical courts, did not fit this description. The 1948 Judicial Code substituted the term "civil action" for the phrase used in the older statutes, but the exceptions have persisted. Today the exceptions may more rationally be defended on the ground that these are areas of the law in which the states have an especially strong interest and a well-developed competence for dealing with them.

CHARLES A. WRIGHT & MARY KAY KANE, LAW OF FEDERAL COURTS § 25, at 160-161 (7th ed. 2011) (footnote omitted).

can never in practice be duly maintained."[27] The tension between the "separate spheres" view of separation of powers and what Professor Jack Beermann has called the "overlapping" model[28] has generated much scholarly attention.[29] The Constitution's imprecision makes these problems even more difficult and subtle than they might otherwise be. Moreover, whether the federal courts act or refrain from acting because of separation of powers, they necessarily affect the relationship of the federal government to the states. As you go through this volume, keep in mind the underlying eddies and currents of interbranch relationships and their effects not merely on how each branch functions within itself, but upon federalism as well.

Some Observations on Parity

Some cases cannot proceed in the federal courts because there is no subject matter jurisdiction. Others *must* proceed in those courts because Congress has made federal jurisdiction exclusive, as in patent and copyright cases. For the third group, however—cases for which both federal and state courts have subject matter jurisdiction—what difference does the choice of forum make? We are all familiar with cases (many encountered in the course in Civil Procedure) in which the parties do battle over the choice of forum. Often those battles turn on geography: the plaintiff wants to litigate her claim in Guam, while the defendant prefers Miami. One can readily understand issues of convenience and witness-availability that often underlie such disputes. The choice between federal and state court, however, is frequently not predominantly geographic. Recall that in *World-Wide Volkswagen Corp. v. Woodson*, 444 U.S. 286 (1980), the plaintiffs deliberately joined a non-diverse party in an attempt to keep the case in the state courts, and the defendants fought that assertion of personal jurisdiction (successfully) precisely so that they could remove the case to federal court. Why? The plaintiffs' counsel believed that state court juries were consistently more favorable to plaintiffs than were federal court juries (a belief apparently shared by the defense). Counsel attempted to keep the case in the state courts to enhance the chances of a favorable result.

World-Wide Volkswagen exemplifies the on-going debate about what is called "parity": the question of whether there are qualitative differences in adjudication between state and federal courts. *Erie Railroad Co. v. Tompkins* was one attempt by the Supreme Court to deal with a demonstrated lack of parity, one stemming from

27 The Federalist No. 48, at 332 (James Madison) (Jacob E. Cooke ed. 1961).

28 Jack M. Beermann, *"Bad" Judicial Activism and Liberal Federal–Courts Doctrine: A Comment on Professor Doernberg and Professor Redish*, 40 Case W.Res.L.Rev. 1053, 1062 n. 37 (1989–90).

29 *See, e.g.*, Alan L. Feld, *Separation of Political Powers: Boundaries or Balance?*, 21 Ga.L.Rev. 171 (1986); Cynthia R. Farina, *Statutory Interpretation and the Balance of Power in the Administrative State*, 89 Colum.L.Rev. 452 (1989).

choice-of-law differences between state and federal courts. Before Erie, suing in state court usually meant that state law would apply to key issues in a case, and suing in federal court meant that federal common law would apply, choice of forum was often equivalent to choice of result.[30] Although Erie sought to eliminate one particular kind of forum/result linkage, many remain. Battles between litigants over personal jurisdiction often deal less with convenience than with the parties' recognition that forum choice-of-law rules can determine the outcome of disputes touching more than one state. It is still true, to some extent, that choosing among available state forums may directly and predictably determine the outcome in some cases.

The choice between federal and state courts often involves considerations far less tangible than choice of law. Many academics, practitioners, and litigants believe that the federal courts are qualitatively better.[31] One observes the manifestations of these beliefs primarily in two phenomena. Plaintiffs vote with their feet, by electing to file in one forum or the other. Defendants vote with motion (or removal) papers, seeking dismissal, removal, transfer, or abstention. The parity debate outside of academia plays itself out in those terms, with the underlying motivations rarely being discussed. Others have approached the subject more directly. As Professor Neuborne indicates in the following excerpt, the debate is quite important, not least because the Supreme Court quite explicitly bases some of its jurisdictional and other decisional rules on the assumption that there is no qualitative difference between the two court systems, or at least none of which the courts ought to take notice.

The Myth of Parity[b]

Burt Neuborne
90 HARV.L.REV. 1105 (1977).

In *Stone v. Powell*, Justice Powell responded to the assertion that federal habeas corpus review of state exclusionary rule determinations was essential to the vigorous enforcement of the fourth amendment by rejecting any notion that federal judges are institutionally more receptive to federal constitutional norms than are their state counterparts. Rather, Justice Powell appeared to assume that state and federal courts are functionally interchangeable forums likely to provide equivalent protection for federal constitutional rights. If it existed, this assumed

30 Perhaps the most famous example is Black & White Taxicab & Transfer Company v. Brown & Yellow Taxicab & Transfer Company, 276 U.S. 518 (1928), where the plaintiff changed the state of its incorporation so that it could bring a diversity action to enforce a contract that was lawful under federal common law but that the state courts would have declared invalid.

31 Some or many judges in both systems may agree, but they are far less likely to make their feelings known for obvious institutional reasons.

b

parity between state and federal courts, which characterizes much of the current Court's approach to problems of federal jurisdiction, would render the process of allocating judicial business between state and federal forums an outcome-neutral exercise unrelated to the merits.

Unfortunately, I fear that the parity which Justice Powell celebrated in Stone exists only in his understandable wish that it were so. I suggest that the assumption of parity is, at best, a dangerous myth, fostering forum allocation decisions which channel constitutional adjudication under the illusion that state courts will vindicate federally secured constitutional rights as forcefully as would the lower federal courts. At worst, it provides a pretext for funneling federal constitutional decisionmaking into state courts precisely because they are less likely to be receptive to vigorous enforcement of federal constitutional doctrine. As a result, I view forum allocation decisions like Stone not as outcome-neutral allocations of judicial business but as indirect decisions on the merits, which weaken disfavored federal constitutional rights by remitting their enforcement to less receptive state forums.

The attempt by lawyers to utilize an ostensibly outcome-neutral federalism analysis to influence indirectly the merits of constitutional litigation is hardly new. During the past century, litigators have consistently advanced ostensibly outcome-neutral federalism arguments, assertedly unrelated to the merits, to channel constitutional adjudication into forums calculated to advance the substantive interests of their clients. Although the political persuasion and economic status of the constitutional litigants have varied with the changing nature of the rights invoked, one factor has remained constant: interests and groups seeking expansive definition and vigorous application of federal constitutional rights have sought a federal judicial forum while their opponents, attempting to narrow federal rights and weaken their implementation, have emphasized the facially neutral federalism concerns which argue in favor of state judicial enforcement of federal constitutional rights.

* * *

One of the current Court's most vigorous proponents for channelling constitutional challenges against state officials into the state courts has been Justice Rehnquist.[89] Professor David Shapiro, recently assessing Justice Rehnquist's performance on the Court, has suggested that his opinions have been guided by three basic principles:

(1) Conflicts between an individual and the government should, whenever possible, be resolved against the individual;

---

89 *See, e.g.*, Paul v. Davis, 424 U.S. 693 (1976); Rizzo v. Goode, 423 U.S. 362 (1976); Doran v. Salem Inn, Inc., 422 U.S. 922 (1975); Huffman v. Pursue, Ltd., 420 U.S. 592 (1975).

(2) Conflicts between state and federal authority, * * * should, whenever possible, be resolved in favor of the states; and

(3) Questions of the exercise of federal jurisdiction, * * * should, whenever possible, be resolved against such exercise.[90]

As Professor Shapiro noted, these principles "often overlap and reinforce each other." I suggest that not only do they "often overlap"; they are, in fact, integrally related by the perception that state judicial forums are less likely to operate as strong countermajoritarian power centers than are federal district courts. Were one to reformulate Professor Shapiro's first proposition more charitably, it might read:

In a democracy, actions bearing the imprimatur of democratic decisionmaking should be overturned by courts only when absolutely necessary; all doubts should be resolved in favor of upholding a collective societal judgment.

If the views of Justice Rehnquist and those of a current majority of his brethren reflect not merely a preference for government at the expense of the individual, but rather a principled theory of deference to majoritarian decisionmaking,[92] the Court's increasing preference for state court adjudication and its distrust of federal jurisdiction are explicable as the logical forum allocation corollaries to its major substantive premise. As subsidiary propositions they rest, I suggest, on an understanding that the only judicial forums in our system capable of enforcing countermajoritarian checks in a sustained, effective manner are the federal courts and that, to the extent that constitutional cases can be shifted from federal to state trial courts, the capacity of individuals to mount successful challenges to collective decisions will be substantially diminished. It is the recognition of that fact and its troubling ramifications for the viability of constitutional rights—and not an uncritical assumption of parity—which should be the critical factor in current federal-state forum allocation decisions.

Professor Neuborne addresses the issue of parity head-on, but even defining the terms of debate is not easy. Professor Susan Herman notes that

Parties to the parity debate have framed the issue in a variety of ways: whether federal and state court judges are "equally talented and equally sympathetic" to federal constitutional claims; whether state court judges show "widespread disregard" for federal constitutional claims; or whether the federal and state courts can be considered "functionally interchangeable."[32]

90 David Shapiro, *Mr. Justice Rehnquist: A Preliminary View*, 90 HARV.L.REV. 293, 294 (1976).

92 Justice Rehnquist has articulated such a view in William H. Rehnquist, *The Notion of a Living Constitution*, 54 TEX.L.REV. 693 (1976). *But see* National League of Cities v. Usery, 426 U.S. 833 (1976).

32 Susan N. Herman, *Why Parity Matters*, 71 B.U.L.REV. 651, 651-52 (1991) (footnotes omitted).

Professor Michael Wells observes that parity is an ambiguous term that can be interpreted in two ways:

> The assertion of parity between state and federal courts may refer to a claim that a litigant will receive a constitutionally adequate hearing on a federal claim in state court. In contrast with this "weak" sense of parity, the "strong" sense of the term signifies the fungible nature of state and federal courts and the absence of a systematic difference in outcomes whether cases are allotted to state or federal courts.[33]

He finds that "most participants in the parity debate believe in the weak sense of parity," but that there is a consensus that "strong" parity does not exist.[34]

In the 1950s and 1960s, Supreme Court decisions mandating desegregation met considerable resistance from some state courts. Many state judges, particularly (though not exclusively) in the South, were hostile to plaintiffs who sought to take advantage of the Court's (and other federal courts') decisions. Simultaneously, the Warren Court expanded federal constitutional rights in criminal cases through the process of incorporation, applying Bill of Rights provisions to the states through the Due Process Clause of the Fourteenth Amendment, both on direct review and collateral attack on state criminal convictions through federal habeas corpus. The Court was obviously concerned that individuals asserting constitutional rights against state governments did not receive fair adjudication on the state level, and it therefore saw federal courts as necessary to enforce federal constitutional rights against state encroachment.[35] This concern assumed, though it did not articulate, a lack of parity between state and federal courts.

In the late 1960s and early 1970s, appointments of conservative Justices resulted in a resurgence of deference to state power. While the Warren Court saw federal courts as essential to enforcing expanded federal constitutional rights, the more conservative Burger Court restricted the availability of federal remedies. The Court had an increasing tendency to channel constitutional challenges to state action into the state courts, basing its forum allocation choices on concerns about federalism, judicial economy, and the federal courts' caseload. Apart from the Court's explicit bows to parity, as Professor Neuborne mentioned, one sees its judicial philosophy in the expansion of door-closing doctrines, such as *Younger* abstention and *Pullman* abstention, and the Court's creation of new barriers to federal adjudication, such as *Colorado River* abstention.[36]

---

33 Michael Wells, *Behind the Parity Debate: The Decline of the Legal Process Tradition in the Law of Federal Courts*, 71 B.U.L.Rev. 609, 610 (1991).

34 *Id.* at 610-11.

35 *See, e.g., Brown v. Allen*, 344 U.S. 443, 511 (1953) (Frankfurter, J., concurring) (noting that "even the highest state courts" had failed to uphold federal constitutional rights).

36 Chapter 8 discusses the abstention doctrines.

The modern parity debate ensued when the Court began to express its view that state courts were as competent as federal courts to adjudicate federal constitutional challenges and restricted federal court power based on an assumption of parity.[37] As Professor Neuborne noted, "The Supreme Court * * * presently seems bent on resolving forum allocation decisions by assuming that no factors exist which render federal district courts more effective than state trial or appellate courts for the enforcement of federal constitutional rights."[38] Professor Erwin Chemerinsky suggested that the Court "profess[ed] parity to justify diverting cases to state courts, which, the Court believed, would rule quite differently from their federal counterparts."[39] Professor Herman posited the Court's willingness to tolerate some disparity at the expense of federal constitutional rights, "because this cost offsets what the Court perceives as the enormous countervailing cost of not adequately respecting the values of federalism."[40]

Professor Neuborne, an experienced constitutional litigator, generated academic debate when he urged that the importance of having constitutional claims heard by a "more sympathetic and competent forum" be considered along with the traditional factors of judicial economy and caseload when allocating business between state and federal courts. He argued that federal courts, rather than state courts, were the appropriate forum to adjudicate federal constitutional rights and identified three institutional characteristics of the federal judiciary responsible for federal superiority in adjudicating federal claims: 1) the greater prestige and higher pay of federal judgeships, which help to attract superior talent, 2) the long-standing federal tradition of upholding federal constitutional rights, and 3) the fact that federal judges enjoy lifetime tenure and are thus shielded from public pressures when enforcing counter-majoritarian rights (unlike state trial judges who must undergo periodic elections, thereby making them vulnerable to majoritarian pressure when deciding constitutional cases). These factors permitted Professor Neuborne to argue that institutional differences, not "bad faith," account for state judges being less likely than federal judges to resolve arguable issues in favor of protecting federal constitutional rights.[41]

Much has changed since the debate over parity emerged. Openly ideological appointments to the federal judiciary have altered the federal courts and, per-

---

37 *See, e.g,, Stone v. Powell*, 428 U.S. 465, 494 n.35 (1976) (noting that the Court was "unwilling to assume that there now exists a general lack of appropriate sensitivity to constitutional rights in the trial and appellate courts of the several States"); *Huffman v. Pursue, Ltd.*, 420 U.S. 592, 611 (1975) (refusing to "base a rule on the assumption that state judges will not be faithful to constitutional responsibilities).

38 Burt Neuborne, *The Myth of Parity*, 90 HARV.L.REV. 1105, 1118 (1977).

39 Erwin Chemerinsky, *Ending the Parity Debate*, 71 B.U.L.REV. 593, 598 (1991).

40 Susan N. Herman, *Why Parity Matters*, 71 B.U.L.REV. 651, 655 (1991).

41 Professor Redish thinks the point beyond debate. "So many obvious, undisputed institutional differences between state and federal courts exist that one must truly close one's eyes to avoid seeing them." Martin H. Redish, *Judicial Parity, Litigant Choice, and Democratic Theory: A Comment on Federal Jurisdiction and Constitutional Rights*, 36 U.C.L.A.L.REV. 329, 332 (1988).

haps equally important, perceptions of the federal courts. Some state courts have emerged as champions of state constitutional jurisprudence, protecting individual rights at the state level as the Supreme Court has withdrawn federal constitutional protection. Eighteen years after *The Myth of Parity*, Professor Neuborne observed that ever since its publication, academicians have disputed "the existence of qualitative differences between state and federal courts and it has been impossible to resolve the dispute empirically, principally because no agreement exists about what we mean as better."[42]

Ending the Parity Debate[c]

Erwin Chemerinsky
71 B.U.L.Rev. 593 (1991).

* * *

In the 1990s, parity seems a relic of an earlier time and a previous set of issues. First, there now is great uncertainty about how to compare the quality of federal and state courts. In the 1950s and 1960s, the desirability of courts enforcing desegregation orders and complying with Bill of Rights provisions was largely accepted in academic circles. But the standard for evaluating courts is now unsettled. More protection of individual liberties is hardly accepted as an unquestioned good: there is a deep division among scholars and on the bench as to the appropriate role for the judiciary. Even the desirability of rights as a concept has come under attack. Furthermore, if federal courts are more likely than state courts to protect individual liberties aggressively, there is no agreement that this is desirable. It is impossible to discuss parity without having some agreed upon baseline for comparison. Unfortunately, no baseline appears to exist.

Second, the domination of federal courts by judges appointed by Republican presidents undermines any basis for confidence in the federal bench as a source of systematic protection of individual liberties. More than half of the current federal judges were appointed by President Ronald Reagan. From 1968 until at least 1992, for twenty of twenty-four years, Republicans will have occupied the White House and selected federal judges. If the assumption of federal courts superiority stemmed, in part, from years of Democratic appointees, then this sustained period of Republican domination diminishes any basis for greater trust in federal courts.

42 Burt Neuborne, *Parity Revisited: The Uses of a Judicial Forum of Excellence*, 44 DePaul L.Rev. 797, 798 (1995).

c Volume 71:4, Boston University Law Review (1991) 598-600. Reprinted with permission of Dean Erwin Chemerinsky.

Third, the differences between federal and state courts do not necessarily translate into decisions that are more protective of individual liberties. Most commentators appear to believe that the general quality of the federal bench is greater than the average quality of state judges. But there is no reason to believe that "better" judges will produce decisions that systematically favor individual rights. Jurists such as Justice Antonin Scalia and Ninth Circuit Judge Alex Kozinski are respected for their brilliance, but they hardly instill confidence that federal courts will protect individual rights more often than their state counterparts.

Nor does the greater independence of federal courts necessarily mean that state judges are more likely to compromise constitutional rights. Although all federal judges have life tenure, state court judges generally have some degree of insulation by virtue of features such as long terms, a tradition of non-partisanship and strong support for incumbent judges, and non-contested retention elections. A survey of twenty years of election data from 1964 to 1984 found that in 1,864 judicial elections, only twenty-two judges (1.2%) were defeated. Electoral accountability only undermines state judicial independence if state court judges fear that voters will use their decisions as the basis for casting their votes. But how many cases are of sufficient visibility to influence voters? Realistically, it is unlikely that many cases are decided differently because of fear of voter rejection at the next election. In fact, it appears that few voters are able to distinguish between judges in retention elections.

Fourth and finally, the analytical problems in demonstrating parity or the lack thereof seem insurmountable. * * * [P]arity is an empirical question—which court system will perform better at a particular task—for which no empirical answer is likely to exist. Additionally, the usefulness of any empirical answer is questionable. At best, data could provide an aggregate comparison of all state courts with all federal courts. State courts differ greatly from one another, however, and federal courts lack homogeneity as well. The parity question demands an overall comparison of the federal courts with the state courts. This comparison appears largely useless given the likelihood that on some issues, in some places, at some times, the federal courts will seem preferable for vindicating rights, while at other times and places the state courts will appear to be better. Absent marked overall differences between the systems, there is no reason to engage in a comparison.

All of the above suggests that the parity debate is futile and dangerous. If the defense of federal court jurisdiction in constitutional rights cases rests on the assumption of federal court superiority, then there is little reason to preserve such jurisdiction if parity is assumed. This is not to suggest that Congress is likely to eliminate section 1331 or that the Court will gut it in the foreseeable future. Rather, emphasizing the parity issue poses a risk for those who believe in the availability of federal courts for constitutional cases. The more the question is phrased in terms of parity, the more it seems that federal court jurisdiction should be based exclusively on this judgment. A meaningful approach to federal jurisdiction must transcend the focus on parity.

Perhaps so, but it is difficult to ignore the elephant in the room, and one might even posit that the appropriately zealous advocate cannot ethically ignore the real-world concerns upon which the parity debate focuses. As Professor Herman observed, "parity will continue to be an issue * * * because the issue arises every time a litigant chooses whether to raise a constitutional claim in federal or state court."[55] Professor Chemerinsky may be correct on a theoretical level that it would be better that the debate end, but there seems to be little doubt that it will continue without resolution.

43 Susan N. Herman, *Why Parity Matters*, 71 B.U.L.Rev. 651, 662 (1991).

Chapter 1

Justiciability

A. Introduction

"Justiciability" is a word unique to federal courts law. It roughly signifies that litigation is in a form appropriate for adjudication in federal court. "Justiciability" subsumes several doctrines that, like subject matter jurisdiction, are threshold matters.

At the federal level, justiciability concerns in large part, though not exclusively, limitations on jurisdiction that flow from Article III's so-called Case-or-Controversy Clause. Whether litigation constitutes a case or controversy depends on whether the parties are those appropriate to seek judicial intervention (standing), whether the dispute is sufficiently well-developed (ripeness) and not too far along (mootness) to justify resort to the courts, and whether there is a true practical dispute between the parties as opposed to a question of merely academic interest (advisory opinions). Only the political question doctrine does not easily fit the case-or-controversy mold.

FYI

As you may know already, lawyers and judges use the term "doctrine" as a synonym for "rule" or "set of rules."

At its core, "standing" doctrine is about whether the plaintiff is the appropriate person to present the dispute to the courts. The Supreme Court has stated, for example, that people who merely have ideological differences with legislation may not challenge it in federal court. But the standing doctrine has become by far the most complicated of the justiciability doctrines and now also touches on the remedial discretion of district courts, the appropriateness of certain subject matter for federal court adjudication, and free-floating separation-of-powers concerns.

Make the Connection

Be sure to locate these themes in *Allen v. Wright.*

Ripeness involves whether a dispute has progressed far enough to make judicial review appropriate. For example, a married couple's challenge to an abortion-restricting statute is not ripe for adjudication unless the woman is pregnant, even if the woman should avoid pregnancy for medical reasons and even if the couple alleges the detrimental effect of having to choose between refraining from normal sexual relations or endangering the woman's health through a possible pregnancy.[1] The courts consider such a controversy too hypothetical and speculative to permit judicial review.

A dispute can also be "too ripe." A case is "moot" if the dispute between the parties is stale; the controversy is no longer "live." But there are exceptions. First, a defendant may in bad faith seek to manipulate the doctrine, discontinuing a challenged practice when an action is filed but reinstituting it after the litigation is dismissed. A federal court will not allow such manipulation. Second, some problems are of such limited duration that judicial resolution cannot be obtained quickly enough. For example, if a pregnant woman wants to take an experimental drug during her pregnancy because she and her physician believe it promotes fetal health, and the government opposes its use, nine months may well elapse before the courts can resolve the controversy. If the woman and her physician seek to sue on behalf of the class of all women in that circumstance, should the court dismiss the case for mootness after she gives birth? If it does, no one is likely ever to be able to challenge the policy.

Finally, under the political question doctrine, courts occasionally refuse to adjudicate disputes because the Constitution commits them to other branches of government or because the Court determines that the other branches are better suited to resolve them. Historically, such cases have included questions of whether a particular state government complies with the requirements of the Guaranty Clause,[2] whether questions of legislative apportionment are justiciable,[3] whether the United States may fund and participate in an undeclared war,[4] and whether the Senate has constitutionally conducted an impeachment trial.[5]

---

1 *See* Roe v. Wade, 410 U.S. 113, 127 (1973).

2 U.S. CONST. art. IV, § 4. *See* Luther v. Borden, 48 U.S. (7 How.) 1 (1849).

3 *See, e.g.,* Baker v. Carr, 369 U.S. 186 (1962); Colegrove v. Green, 328 U.S. 549 (1946). *Baker,* discussed more fully at page 179, is particularly interesting because while it reaffirmed *Colegrove's* holding that apportionment questions are nonjusticiable under the Guaranty Clause, it held that they are justiciable as equal protection matters.

4 *See* Crockett v. Reagan, 720 F.2d 1355 (D.C.Cir.1983) (constitutionality of United States' assistance to El Salvador); DaCosta v. Laird, 471 F.2d 1146 (2d Cir.1973) (constitutionality of aerial operations in Cambodia); Head v. Nixon, 342 F.Supp. 521 (E.D.La.), *aff'd,* 468 F.2d 951 (5th Cir.1972) (constitutionality of Vietnam war generally).

5 Nixon v. United States, 506 U.S. 224 (1993).

B. Advisory Opinions

The prohibition on federal courts issuing "advisory opinions" could well be considered another "justiciability" doctrine. The first specific mentions of advisory opinions appear in a famous letter from then-Secretary of State Thomas Jefferson to the Supreme Court and the Court's subsequent reply to President Washington, on whose behalf Jefferson had written.[6] Washington and Jefferson clearly entertained doubts about the propriety of the Court acting in such a manner.

> **Take Note**
>
> This correspondence is part of the "canon" of federal court jurisprudence. Ignorance of this is considered a sign that one lacks sophistication in federal practice.

Gentlemen:

The war which has taken place among the powers of Europe produces frequent transactions within our ports and limits, on which questions arise of considerable difficulty, and of greater importance to the peace of the United States. These questions depend for their solution on the construction of our treaties, on the laws of nature and nations, and on the laws of the land, and are often presented under circumstances *which do not give a cognisance of them to the tribunals of the country.* Yet their decision is so little analogous to the ordinary functions of the executive, as to occasion much embarrassment and difficulty to them. The President therefore would be much relieved if he found himself free to refer questions of this description to the opinions of the judges of the Supreme Court of the United States, whose knowledge of the subject would secure as against errors dangerous to the peace of the United States, and their authority to insure the respect of all parties. He has therefore asked the attendance of such of the judges as could be collected in time for the occasion, to know, in the first place, their opinion, whether the public may, with propriety, be availed of their *advice on these questions*? And if they may, to present, for their advice, the abstract questions which have already occurred, or may soon occur, from which they will themselves strike out such as any circumstance might, in their opinion, forbid them to pronounce on. I have the honour to be with sentiments of the most perfect respect, gentlemen, Your most obedient and humble servant * * * .

Chief Justice Jay's response to President Washington confirmed Washington's and Jefferson's suspicions about the Court's limited role.

Sir:

We have considered the previous question stated in a letter written by your direction to us by the Secretary of State on the 18th of last month, [regarding]

---

6 III THE CORRESPONDENCE AND PUBLIC PAPERS OF JOHN JAY 1763-1826 486-87 (Henry P. Johnston ed. 1971).

> the lines of separation drawn by the Constitution between the three departments of the government. These being in certain respects checks upon each other, and our being judges of a court in the last resort, are considerations which afford strong arguments against the propriety of our extra-judicially deciding the questions alluded to, especially as the power given by the Constitution to the President, of calling on the heads of departments for opinions, seems to have been *purposely* as well as expressly united to the *executive* departments.
>
> We exceedingly regret every event that may cause embarrassment to your administration, but we derive consolation from the reflection that your judgment will discern what is right, and that your usual prudence, decision, and firmness will surmount every obstacle to the preservation of the rights, peace, and dignity of the United States.
>
> We have the honour to be, with perfect respect, sir, your most obedient and humble servants.

The Court thus refused, as a matter of separation of powers, to permit itself to be drawn by request into the decision of questions that apparently could not assume ordinary judicial form.[7]

One might disapprove of advisory opinions either as a matter of constitutional imperative or in the view that they are bad policy. The Supreme Court has repeatedly linked advisory opinions with the Case-or-Controversy Clause, leaving little doubt that the prohibition is constitutionally based.[8] Moreover, the Court has made clear that the Case-or-Controversy Clause helps to implement the more general principle of separation of powers by keeping the courts from addressing problems in the absence of a specific, limited conflict, much as the legislative and executive branches do. *See Flast v. Cohen,* 392 U.S. 83 (1968). The federal courts thus avoid general, prescriptive pronouncements thought to be more appropriate for the other branches, simultaneously avoiding entanglement in the workings of the other branches and preserving their own independence and legitimacy.

The Jefferson-Jay correspondence involved "pure advice seeking" by the executive from the judiciary. Congress, from time to time, endeavors to authorize particular forms of cases in traditional judicial form, but the Court has not always been willing to permit adjudication in such circumstances. In 1792, a congressional scheme called for the federal courts to make preliminary findings

7 Some have suggested that that is a small set of questions indeed. *See, e.g.,* ALEXIS DE TOCQUEVILLE, DEMOCRACY IN AMERICA 207 (Henry Steele Commager ed. 1965) ("Scarcely any question arises in the United States which does not become, sooner or later, a subject of judicial debate.").

8 *See, e.g.,* City of Los Angeles v. Lyons, 461 U.S. 95, 129 n. 20 (1983) ("[A] court must have the power to fashion some appropriate remedy. This concern, an aspect of the more general case or controversy requirement, reflects the view that the adjudication of rights which a court is powerless to enforce is tantamount to an advisory opinion.") *See also* New York State Club Association, Inc. v. City of New York, 487 U.S. 1, 8 n. 2 (1988); Flast v. Cohen, 392 U.S. 83, 96 n. 14 (1968).

and recommendations to the Secretary of War about disability benefits to be paid to Revolutionary War veterans. The Secretary was authorized to disregard the courts' findings. Although the Supreme Court itself did not expressly hold the statute unconstitutional, five of the Court's six Justices, serving as Circuit Court judges, found that the scheme violated separation of powers because it subjected individual judicial actions to review and revision by executive officials. *Hayburn's Case,* 2 U.S. (2 Dall.) 408 (1792). The decisions in *Hayburn's Case* and in more recent cases have been taken to signify that a case is not justiciable unless the judiciary's decision will have final, not merely preliminary, effect. Moreover, when a case is justiciable, the finality principle means that Congress cannot reverse the final decision by the judicial branch by mandating a new judicial proceeding with a different result. *See Plaut v. Spendthrift Farm, Inc.*, 514 U.S. 211 (1995), at page 254. The Judiciary has the power not only to consider cases, but also to decide them dispositively. The next logical step was for Congress to attempt to create and authorize a case in traditional judicial form in which the judicial decision *would* be final. Such an attempt resulted in the following case.

Muskrat v. United States

Supreme Court of the United States, 1911.
219 U.S. 346.

MR. JUSTICE DAY delivered the opinion of the Court:

These cases arise under an act of Congress undertaking to confer jurisdiction upon the court of claims, and upon this Court, on appeal, to determine the validity of certain acts of Congress hereinafter referred to.

Case No. 330 was brought by David Muskrat and J. Henry Dick, in their own behalf, and in behalf of others in a like situation, to determine the constitutional validity of the act of Congress of April 26, 1906 and to have the same declared invalid in so far as the same undertook to increase the number of persons entitled to share in the final distribution of lands and funds of the Cherokees beyond those enrolled on September 1, 1902, in accordance with the act of Congress passed July 1, 1902. The acts subsequent to that of July 1, 1902, have the effect to increase the number of persons entitled to participate in the division of the Cherokee lands and funds, by permitting the enrolment of children who were minors, living on March 4, 1906, whose parents had theretofore been enrolled as members of the Cherokee tribe, or had applications pending for that purpose.

Case No. 331 was brought by Brown and Gritts on their own behalf and on behalf of other Cherokee citizens having a like interest in the property allotted under the act of July 1, 1902. Under this act, Brown and Gritts received allotments. The subsequent act of March 11, 1904 empowered the Secretary of the

Interior to grant rights of way for pipe lines over lands allotted to Indians under certain regulations. Another act purported to extend to a period of twenty-five years the time within which full-blooded Indians of the Cherokee, Choctaw, Chickasaw, Creek, and Seminole tribes were forbidden to alienate, sell, dispose of, or encumber certain of their lands.

The object of the petition of Brown and Gritts was to have the subsequent legislation of 1904 and 1906 declared to be unconstitutional and void, and to have the lands allotted to them under the original act of July 1, 1902, adjudged to be theirs free from restraints upon the rights to sell and convey the same. From this statement it is apparent that the purpose of the proceedings instituted in the court of claims, and now appealed to this Court, is to restrain the enforcement of such legislation subsequent to the act of July 1, 1902, upon the ground that the same is unconstitutional and void. The court of claims sustained the validity of the acts and dismissed the petitions.

These proceedings were begun under the supposed authority of an act of Congress passed March 1, 1907 (a part of the Indian appropriation bill). As that legislation is important in this connection, so much of the act as authorized the beginning of these suits is here inserted in full:

> That William Brown and Levi B. Gritts, on their own behalf and on behalf of all other Cherokee citizens, having like interests in the property allotted under the act of July first, nineteen hundred and two, entitled, "An Act to Provide for the Allotment of Lands of the Cherokee Nation, for the Disposition of Town Sites Therein, and for Other Purposes," and David Muskrat and J. Henry Dick, on their own behalf, and on behalf of all Cherokee citizens enrolled as such for allotment as of September first, nineteen hundred and two, be, and they are hereby, authorized and empowered to institute their suits in the court of claims to determine the validity of any acts of Congress passed since the said act of July first, nineteen hundred and two, in so far as said acts, or any of them, attempt to increase or extend the restrictions upon alienation, encumbrance, or the right to lease the allotments of lands of Cherokee citizens, or to increase the number of persons entitled to share in the final distribution of lands and funds of the Cherokees beyond those enrolled for allotment as of September first, nineteen hundred and two, and provided for in the said act of July first, nineteen hundred and two.
>
> And jurisdiction is hereby conferred upon the court of claims, with the right of appeal, by either party, to the Supreme Court of the United States, to hear, determine, and adjudicate each of said suits.
>
> The suits brought hereunder shall be brought on or before September first, nineteen hundred and seven, against the United States as a party defendant, and, for the speedy disposition of the questions involved, preference shall be given to the same by said courts, and by the Attorney General, who is hereby charged with the defense of said suits.

> Upon the rendition of final judgment by the court of claims or the Supreme Court of the United States, denying the validity of any portion of the said acts authorized to be brought into question, in either or both of said cases, the court of claims shall determine the amount to be paid the attorneys employed by the above-named parties in the prosecution thereof for services and expenses, and shall render judgment therefor, which shall be paid out of the funds in the United States Treasury belonging to the beneficiaries, under the said act of July first, nineteen hundred and two.

This act is the authority for the maintenance of these two suits.

The first question in these cases, as in others, involves the jurisdiction of the Court to entertain the proceeding, and that depends upon whether the jurisdiction conferred is within the power of Congress, having in view the limitations of the judicial power, as established by the Constitution of the United States.

* * *

The subject underwent a complete examination [when] * * * an act of Congress was held invalid which undertook to confer jurisdiction upon the court of claims, and thence by appeal to this Court, the judgment, however, not to be paid until an appropriation had been estimated therefor by the Secretary of the Treasury; and * * * the result was that neither court could enforce its judgment by any process, and whether it was to be paid or not depended on the future action of the Secretary of the Treasury and of Congress. "The Supreme Court," says the Chief Justice,

> does not owe its existence or its powers to the legislative department of the government. It is created by the Constitution, and represents one of the three great divisions of power in the government of the United States, to each of which the Constitution has assigned its appropriate duties and powers, and made each independent of the other in performing its appropriate functions. The power conferred on this Court is exclusively judicial, and it cannot be required or authorized to exercise any other.

* * *

It therefore becomes necessary to inquire what is meant by the judicial power thus conferred by the Constitution upon this Court, and, with the aid of appropriate legislation, upon the inferior courts of the United States. "Judicial power," says Mr. Justice Miller, in his work on the Constitution, "is the power of a court to decide and pronounce a judgment and carry it into effect between persons and parties who bring a case before it for decision."

As we have already seen, by the express terms of the Constitution, the exercise of the judicial power is limited to "cases" and "controversies." Beyond this it does not extend, and unless it is asserted in a case or controversy within the meaning of the Constitution, the power to exercise it is nowhere conferred.

What, then, does the Constitution mean in conferring this judicial power with the right to determine "cases" and "controversies." A "case" was defined by Mr. Chief Justice Marshall as early as the leading case of Marbury v. Madison to be a suit instituted according to the regular course of judicial procedure. And what more, if anything, is meant in the use of the term "controversy?" That question was dealt with by Mr. Justice Field, at the circuit. Of these terms that learned justice said:

> The judicial article of the Constitution mentions cases and controversies. The term "controversies," if distinguishable at all from "cases," is so in that it is less comprehensive than the latter, and includes only suits of a civil nature. By cases and controversies are intended the claims of litigants brought before the courts for determination by such regular proceedings as are established by law or custom for the protection or enforcement of rights, or the prevention, redress, or punishment of wrongs. Whenever the claim of a party under the Constitution, laws, or treaties of the United States takes such a form that the judicial power is capable of acting upon it, then it has become a case. The term implies the existence of present or possible adverse parties, whose contentions are submitted to the court for adjudication.

The power being thus limited to require an application of the judicial power to cases and controversies, Is the act which undertook to authorize the present suits to determine the constitutional validity of certain legislation within the constitutional authority of the court? This inquiry in the case before us includes the broader question, When may this Court, in the exercise of the judicial power, pass upon the constitutional validity of an act of Congress? That question has been settled from the early history of the Court, the leading case on the subject being Marbury v. Madison.

In that case Chief Justice Marshall, who spoke for the Court, was careful to point out that the right to declare an act of Congress unconstitutional could only be exercised when a proper case between opposing parties was submitted for judicial determination; that there was no general veto power in the Court upon the legislation of Congress; and that the authority to declare an act unconstitutional sprang from the requirement that the Court, in administering the law and pronouncing judgment between the parties to a case, and choosing between the requirements of the fundamental law established by the people and embodied in the Constitution and an act of the agents of the people, acting under authority of the Constitution, should enforce the Constitution as the supreme law of the land. The Chief Justice demonstrated, in a manner which has been regarded as settling the question, that with the choice thus given between a constitutional requirement and a conflicting statutory enactment, the plain duty of the Court was to follow and enforce the Constitution as the supreme law established by the people. And the Court recognized, in *Marbury v. Madison* and subsequent cases, that the exercise of this great power could only be invoked in cases which came regularly before the courts for determination * * * .

Again, in the case of *Cohens v. Virginia*, Chief Justice Marshall, amplifying and reasserting the doctrine of *Marbury v. Madison*, recognized the limitations upon the right of this Court to declare an act of Congress unconstitutional, and granting that there might be instances of its violation which could not be brought within the jurisdiction of the courts, and referring to a grant by a state of a patent of nobility as a case of that class, and conceding that the Court would have no power to annul such a grant, said:

> This may be very true; but by no means justifies the inference drawn from it. The article does not extend the judicial power to every violation of the Constitution which may possibly take place, but to "a case in law or equity" in which a right under such law is asserted in a court of justice. If the question cannot be brought into a court, then there is no case in law or equity, and no jurisdiction is given by the words of the article. But if, in any controversy depending in a court, the cause should depend on the validity of such a law, that would be a case arising under the Constitution, to which the judicial power of the United States would extend.

* * *

Applying the principles thus long settled by the decisions of this Court to the act of Congress undertaking to confer jurisdiction in this case, we find that William Brown and Levi B. Gritts * * * are authorized and empowered to institute suits in the court of claims to determine the validity of acts of Congress passed since the act of July 1, 1902 * * * .

> **FYI**
>
> The United States Court of Federal Claims is the tribunal for parties suing the federal government for money damages. The judges on the Court of Federal Claims serve 15-year terms. Appeal from a judgment of that court goes to the United States Court of Appeals for the District of Columbia Circuit.

The jurisdiction was given for that purpose first to the Court of Claims, and then upon appeal to this Court. That is, the object and purpose of the suit is wholly comprised in the determination of the constitutional validity of certain acts of Congress; and furthermore, in the last paragraph of the section, should a judgment be rendered in the Court of Claims or this Court, denying the constitutional validity of such acts, then the amount of compensation to be paid to attorneys employed for the purpose of testing the constitutionality of the law is to be paid out of funds in the Treasury of the United States belonging to the beneficiaries, the act having previously provided that the United States should be made a party, and the Attorney General be charged with the defense of the suits.

It is therefore evident that there is neither more nor less in this procedure than an attempt to provide for a judicial determination, final in this Court, of the constitutional validity of an act of Congress. Is such a determination within the judicial power conferred by the Constitution, as the same has been interpreted and defined in the authoritative decisions to which we have referred? We think it is not. That judicial power, as we have seen, is the right to determine actual controversies arising between adverse litigants, duly instituted in courts of proper jurisdiction. The right to declare a law unconstitutional arises because an act of Congress relied upon by one or the other of such parties in determining their rights is in conflict with the fundamental law. The exercise of this, the most important and delicate duty of this Court, is not given to it as a body with revisory power over the action of Congress, but because the rights of the litigants in justiciable controversies require the court to choose between the fundamental law and a law purporting to be enacted within constitutional authority, but in fact beyond the power delegated to the legislative branch of the government. This attempt to obtain a judicial declaration of the validity of the act of Congress is not presented in a "case" or "controversy," to which, under the Constitution of the United States, the judicial power alone extends. It is true the United States is made a defendant to this action, but it has no interest adverse to the claimants. The object is not to assert a property right as against the government, or to demand compensation for alleged wrongs because of action upon its part. The whole purpose of the law is to determine the constitutional validity of this class of legislation, in a suit not arising between parties concerning a property right necessarily involved in the decision in question, but in a proceeding against the government in its sovereign capacity, and concerning which the only judgment required is to settle the doubtful character of the legislation in question. Such judgment will not conclude private parties, when actual litigation brings to the court the question of the constitutionality of such legislation. In a legal sense the judgment could not be executed, and amounts in fact to no more than an expression of opinion upon the validity of the acts in question. Confining the jurisdiction of this Court within the limitations conferred by the Constitution, which the Court has hitherto been careful to observe, and whose boundaries it has refused to transcend, we think the Congress, in the act of March 1, 1907, exceeded the limitations of legislative authority, so far as it required of this Court action not judicial in its nature within the meaning of the Constitution.

Nor can it make any difference that the petitioners had brought suits in the supreme court of the District of Columbia to enjoin the Secretary of the Interior from carrying into effect the legislation subsequent to the act of July 1, 1902, which suits were pending when the jurisdictional act here involved was passed. The latter act must depend upon its own terms and be judged by the authority which it undertakes to confer. If such actions as are here attempted, to determine the validity of legislation, are sustained, the result will be that this Court, instead of keeping within the limits of judicial power, and deciding cases or controversies arising between opposing parties, as the Constitution intended it should, will be required to give opinions in the nature of advice concerning legislative action,—a function never conferred upon it by the Constitution, and against the exercise of which this Court has steadily set its face from the beginning.

The questions involved in this proceeding as to the validity of the legislation may arise in suits between individuals, and when they do and are properly brought before this Court for consideration they, of course, must be determined in the exercise of its judicial functions. For the reasons we have stated, we are constrained to hold that these actions present no justiciable controversy within the authority of the Court, acting within the limitations of the Constitution under which it was created. As Congress, in passing this act, as a part of the plan involved, evidently intended to provide a review of the judgment of the court of claims in this Court, as the constitutionality of important legislation is concerned, we think the act cannot be held to intend to confer jurisdiction on that court separately considered.

The judgments will be reversed and the cases remanded to the Court of Claims, with directions to dismiss the petitions for want of jurisdiction.

Notes and Questions

1. Would this matter be justiciable in a suit with the proper parties?

2. Does Congress's goal here differ in any substantial way from what a declaratory judgment seeks to accomplish? If the federal Declaratory Judgment Act (not enacted until 1934) had been in effect in 1911, could the Court have entertained an action to determine the constitutionality of the post-1902 legislation? Or does *Muskrat* suggest that the Declaratory Judgment Act is unconstitutional?

3. Early opinion held that declaratory judgments presented insurmountable constitutional problems because they "looked" advisory.[9] In one of the first cases involving a declaratory judgment, the Michigan Supreme Court reacted harshly not just to the friendly nature of the suit (in which the defendant admitted all of the allegations of the plaintiff's complaint), but to the declaratory judgment device itself, declaring

9 There was also concern that such disputes were not ripe. Note 3 at page 153 discusses this aspect of declaratory judgments.

the Michigan Declaratory Judgment Act unconstitutional. *See Anway v. Grand Rapids Railway*, 211 Mich. 592, 179 N.W. 350 (1920). A trio of United States Supreme Court cases in the late 1920's also viewed declaratory judgments as inherently violating federal constitutional limitations. The Court reversed itself five years later, repudiating what it referred to as the "denunciatory dicta" of the earlier cases, and eventually ruled that the Declaratory Judgment Act of 1934 was constitutional. *See Aetna Life Ins. Co. v. Haworth*, 300 U.S. 227 (1937).

4. It would be a mistake to conclude that any congressional attempt to authorize judicial review of particular matters is necessarily void as seeking an advisory opinion. In *South Carolina v. Katzenbach*, 383 U.S. 301 (1966), the state challenged several provisions of the Voting Rights Act of 1964, particularly one that automatically suspended state voting regulations enacted after November 1, 1964, until approval by the United States Attorney General or a declaratory judgment by the United States District Court for the District of Columbia that the new regulations did not violate the Fifteenth Amendment. Section 5 of the Act authorized such declaratory judgments actions. Georgia, appearing ***amicus curiae***, argued that the provision sought to authorize advisory opinions and therefore violated Article III. The Court disagreed.

> Nor has Congress authorized the District Court to issue advisory opinions, in violation of the principles of Article III * * * . The Act automatically suspends the operation of voting regulations enacted after November 1, 1964, and furnishes mechanisms for enforcing the suspension. A State or political subdivision wishing to make use of a recent amendment to its voting laws therefore has a concrete and immediate "controversy" with the Federal Government.

It's Latin to Me!

Amicus curiae is Latin for "friend of the court." Governments, trade associations, and academics often file such briefs to help the court deal with cutting-edge issues of law.

Does the Court's approach in South Carolina v. Katzenbach suggest alternative strategies for Congress in a situation like that in *Muskrat*?

5. In *Camreta v. Greene*, 131 S.Ct. 2020 (2011), the Court heard an appeal in a case involving officials' immunities from private suit, in this instance on a claim that the officials' actions had violated the Fourth Amendment. The United States Court of Appeals for the Ninth Circuit ruled against the officials on the Fourth Amendment issue, but found that they were entitled to qualified immunity and affirmed the District Court's grant of summary judgment. The case is unusual because the plaintiff did not seek Supreme Court review, despite the unfavorable immunity ruling below, but the victorious officials did ask the Court to review the Ninth Circuit's ruling on

the Fourth Amendment issue. The *Camreta* Court granted the petition for certiorari but did not review the Fourth Amendment issue, finding that the case had become moot. However, the Court did grant relief to the officials. "In line with our normal practice when mootness frustrates a party's right to appeal, we vacate the part of the Ninth Circuit's opinion that decided the Fourth Amendment issue." As that sentence implies, the Court recognized the officials' right to appeal, which the Court had noted at the beginning of the same paragraph: "We conclude that this Court generally may review a lower court's constitutional ruling at the behest of a government official granted immunity."

One is apt to read that sentence too quickly, overlooking its remarkable implications. Suppose the case had not been moot when it reached the Supreme Court. Presumably the Court would have considered the Fourth Amendment issue on its merits. Suppose further that the Court differed from the Ninth Circuit on the Fourth Amendment issue and reversed the lower court's ruling. What would be the effect of the Supreme Court's decision on the case? What judgment would the Court issue? The Ninth Circuit affirmed the grant of summary judgment to the defendants. Would the Supreme Court's ruling overturn that result?

How extensively will the Court interpret its power to review in such cases? Can you think of other circumstances in which the Court might allow the victorious party below—a party who has gotten all of the relief that it requested—to seek review of an unfavorable ruling on one or more issues? Does the Court have jurisdiction to review in such circumstances? The statute controlling the Court's power to review in *Camreta*, 28 U.S.C. § 2254, reads as follows:

Cases in the courts of appeals may be reviewed by the Supreme Court by the following methods:

(1) By writ of certiorari granted upon the petition of any party to any civil or criminal case, before or after rendition of judgment or decree;

(2) By certification at any time by a court of appeals of any question of law in any civil or criminal case as to which instructions are desired, and upon such certification the Supreme Court may give binding instructions or require the entire record to be sent up for decision of the entire matter in controversy.

Note subsection (1)'s specification that *any* party may seek review, a point on which the *Camreta* Court relied. Compare § 1254 with 28 U.S.C. § 1257, the statute governing review of state court decisions. Does the Court have as much latitude to review state court decisions as it has declared it has with respect to federal decisions? In this connection, consider the effect of the adequate-and-independent-state-ground rule, discussed in Chapter 9 of the text.

Justice Kennedy dissented, arguing that it was improper for the Court to review the Ninth Circuit's ruling on the Fourth Amendment issue because the Court's judgment would do nothing to change the judgment of the Ninth Circuit that affirmed the grant of summary judgment. "[O]ur power is to correct wrong judgments, not to revise opinions," he wrote.

C. Standing

The law of standing in federal court runs along two distinct analytical tracks, and the failure to appreciate that duality can lead to serious mistakes. The first "track" applies to lawsuits challenging the legality of legislation, the conduct of federal officials, and state action. The first principal case, *Allen v. Wright,* illustrates the rules that apply in this category. The second "track" applies to requests for judicial review of federal agency action. *Massachusetts v. EPA* illustrates the rules that apply there.

1. Standing to Challenge Legislation, Federal Officials' Conduct, and State Action

Allen v. Wright

Supreme Court of the United States, 1984.
468 U.S. 737.

JUSTICE O'CONNOR delivered the opinion of the Court.

Parents of black public school children allege in this nationwide class action that the Internal Revenue Service (IRS) has not adopted sufficient standards and procedures to fulfill its obligation to deny tax-exempt status to racially discriminatory private schools. They assert that the IRS thereby harms them directly and interferes with the ability of their children to receive an education in desegregated public schools. The issue before us is whether plaintiffs have standing to bring this suit. We hold that they do not.

I

The Internal Revenue Service denies tax-exempt status * * * and hence eligibility to receive charitable contributions deductible from income taxes to racially discriminatory private schools. The IRS policy requires that a school applying for tax-exempt status show that it "admits the students of any race to all the rights, privileges, programs, and activities generally accorded or made available to students at that school and that the school does not discriminate on the basis of race in administration of its educational policies, admissions policies, scholarship and loan programs, and athletic and other school-administered programs." To carry out this policy, the IRS has established guidelines and procedures for determining whether a particular school is in fact racially nondiscriminatory. Failure to comply with the guidelines "will ordinarily result in the proposed revocation of" tax-exempt status.

* * *

The IRS rules require a school applying for tax-exempt status to give a breakdown along racial lines of its student body and its faculty and administrative staff, as well as of scholarships and loans awarded. They also require the applicant school to state the year of its organization, and to list "incorporators, founders, board members, and donors of land or buildings," and state whether any of the organizations among these have an objective of maintaining segregated public or private school education. The rules further provide that, once given an exemption, a school must keep specified records to document the extent of compliance with the IRS guidelines. Finally, the rules announce that any information concerning discrimination at a tax-exempt school is officially welcomed.

Make the Connection

One might wonder why this case is not on the "administrative review" track of standing law, since the plaintiffs are complaining about the way the Internal Revenue Service administers certain regulations. The reason is that the plaintiffs did not first petition the IRS. Thus, this lawsuit is not an appeal from an adverse agency ruling. This is something you would normally learn in Administrative Law.

In 1976 respondents challenged these guidelines and procedures in a suit filed in Federal District Court against the Secretary of the Treasury and the Commissioner of Internal Revenue. The plaintiffs named in the complaint are parents of black children who, at the time the complaint was filed, were attending public schools in seven States in school districts undergoing desegregation. They brought this nationwide class action "on behalf of themselves and their children, and * * * on behalf of all other parents of black children attending public school systems undergoing, or which may in the future undergo, desegregation pursuant to court order [or] HEW regulations and guidelines, under state law, or voluntarily." They estimated that the class they seek to represent includes several million persons.

Respondents allege in their complaint that many racially segregated private schools were created or expanded in their communities at the time the public schools were undergoing desegregation. According to the complaint, many such private schools, including 17 schools or school systems identified by name in the complaint (perhaps some 30 schools in all), receive tax exemptions either directly or through the tax-exempt status of "umbrella" organizations that operate or support the schools. Respondents allege that, despite the IRS policy of denying tax-exempt status to racially discriminatory private schools and despite the IRS guidelines and procedures for implementing that policy, some of the tax-exempt racially segregated private schools created or expanded in desegregating districts in fact have racially discriminatory policies. Respondents allege that the IRS grant of tax exemptions to such racially discriminatory schools is unlawful.

Respondents allege that the challenged Government conduct harms them in two ways. The challenged conduct

> (a) constitutes tangible federal financial aid and other support for racially segregated educational institutions, and
>
> (b) fosters and encourages the organization, operation and expansion of institutions providing racially segregated educational opportunities for white children avoiding attendance in desegregating public school districts and thereby interferes with the efforts of federal courts, HEW and local school authorities to desegregate public school districts which have been operating racially dual school systems.

Thus, respondents do not allege that their children have been the victims of discriminatory exclusion from the schools whose tax exemptions they challenge as unlawful. Indeed, they have not alleged at any stage of this litigation that their children have ever applied or would ever apply to any private school. Rather, respondents claim a direct injury from the mere fact of the challenged Government conduct and, as indicated by the restriction of the plaintiff class to parents of children in desegregating school districts, injury to their children's opportunity to receive a desegregated education. The latter injury is traceable to the IRS grant of tax exemptions to racially discriminatory schools, respondents allege, chiefly because contributions to such schools are deductible from income taxes and the "deductions facilitate the raising of funds to organize new schools and expand existing schools in order to accommodate white students avoiding attendance in desegregating public school districts."

Respondents request only prospective relief. They ask for a declaratory judgment that the challenged IRS tax-exemption practices are unlawful. They also ask for an injunction requiring the IRS to deny tax exemptions to a considerably broader class of private schools than the class of racially discriminatory private schools. Under the requested injunction, the IRS would have to deny tax-exempt status to all private schools which have insubstantial or nonexistent minority enrollments, which are located in or serve desegregating public school districts, and which either—

(1) were established or expanded at or about the time the public school districts in which they are located or which they serve were desegregating;

(2) have been determined in adversary judicial or administrative proceedings to be racially segregated; or

(3) cannot demonstrate that they do not provide racially segregated educational opportunities for white children avoiding attendance in desegregating public school systems.

Finally, respondents ask for an order directing the IRS to replace its 1975 guidelines with standards consistent with the requested injunction.

* * * The District Court * * * granted the defendants' motion to dismiss the complaint, concluding that respondents lack standing, that the judicial task proposed by respondents is inappropriately intrusive for a federal court, and that awarding the requested relief would be contrary to the will of Congress expressed in the 1979 ban on strengthening IRS guidelines.

The United States Court of Appeals for the District of Columbia reversed, concluding that respondents have standing to maintain this lawsuit. The court acknowledged that Simon v. Eastern Kentucky Welfare Rights Org. "suggests that litigation concerning tax liability is a matter between taxpayer and IRS, with the door barely ajar for third party challenges." The court concluded, however, that the *Simon* case is inapposite because respondents claim no injury dependent on taxpayers' actions: "[t]hey claim indifference as to the course private schools would take." Instead, the court observed, "[t]he sole injury [respondents] claim is the denigration they suffer as black parents and schoolchildren when their government graces with tax-exempt status educational institutions in their communities that treat members of their race as persons of lesser worth." The court held this denigration injury enough to give respondents standing * * * . The court accordingly remanded the case to the District Court for further proceedings, enjoining the defendants meanwhile from granting tax-exempt status to any racially discriminatory school.

* * * We granted certiorari, and now reverse.

II

A

Article III of the Constitution confines the federal courts to adjudicating actual "cases" and "controversies." As the Court [has] explained, the "case or controversy" requirement defines with respect to the Judicial Branch the idea of separation of powers on which the Federal Government is founded. The several doctrines that have grown up to elaborate that requirement are "founded in concern about the proper—and properly limited—role of the courts in a democratic society."

> All of the doctrines that cluster about Article III—not only standing but mootness, ripeness, political question, and the like—relate in part, and in different though overlapping ways, to an idea, which is more than an intuition but less than a rigorous and explicit theory, about the constitutional and prudential limits to the powers of an unelected, unrepresentative judiciary in our kind of government.

Vander Jagt v. O'Neill, 699 F.2d 1166, 1178-79 (1983) (Bork, J., concurring). The case-or-controversy doctrines state fundamental limits on federal judicial power in our system of government.

The Art. III doctrine that requires a litigant to have "standing" to invoke the power of a federal court is perhaps the most important of these doctrines. "In essence the question of standing is whether the litigant is entitled to have the court decide the merits of the dispute or of particular issues." Standing doctrine embraces several judicially self-imposed limits on the exercise of federal jurisdiction, such as the general prohibition on a litigant's raising another person's legal rights, the rule barring adjudication of generalized grievances more appropriately addressed in the representative branches, and the requirement that a plaintiff's complaint fall within the zone of interests protected by the law invoked. The requirement of standing, however, has a core component derived directly from the Constitution. A plaintiff must allege personal injury fairly traceable to the defendant's allegedly unlawful conduct and likely to be redressed by the requested relief.

Like the prudential component, the constitutional component of standing doctrine incorporates concepts concededly not susceptible of precise definition. The injury alleged must be, for example, " 'distinct and palpable,' " and not "abstract" or "conjectural" or "hypothetical." The injury must be "fairly" traceable to the challenged action, and relief from the injury must be "likely" to follow from a favorable decision. These terms cannot be defined so as to make application of the constitutional standing requirement a mechanical exercise.

* * * [T]he law of Art. III standing is built on a single basic idea—the idea of separation of powers. It is this fact which makes possible the gradual clarification of the law through judicial application. * * *

* * * Typically, * * * the standing inquiry requires careful judicial examination of a complaint's allegations to ascertain whether the particular plaintiff is entitled to an adjudication of the particular claims asserted. Is the injury too abstract, or otherwise not appropriate, to be considered judicially cognizable? Is the line of

causation between the illegal conduct and injury too attenuated? Is the prospect of obtaining relief from the injury as a result of a favorable ruling too speculative? These questions and any others relevant to the standing inquiry must be answered by reference to the Art. III notion that federal courts may exercise power only "in the last resort, and as a necessity," and only when adjudication is "consistent with a system of separated powers and [the dispute is one] traditionally thought to be capable of resolution through the judicial process."

B

Respondents allege two injuries in their complaint to support their standing to bring this lawsuit. First, they say that they are harmed directly by the mere fact of Government financial aid to discriminatory private schools. Second, they say that the federal tax exemptions to racially discriminatory private schools in their communities impair their ability to have their public schools desegregated.

In the Court of Appeals, respondents apparently relied on the first injury. Thus, the court below asserted that "[t]he sole injury [respondents] claim is the denigration they suffer" as a result of the tax exemptions. In this Court, respondents have not focused on this claim of injury. Here they stress the effect of the tax exemptions on their "equal educational opportunities," renewing reliance on the second injury described in their complaint.

Because respondents have not clearly disclaimed reliance on either of the injuries described in their complaint, we address both allegations of injury. We conclude that neither suffices to support respondents' standing. The first fails under clear precedents of this Court because it does not constitute judicially cognizable injury. The second fails because the alleged injury is not fairly traceable to the assertedly unlawful conduct of the IRS.[19]

1

Respondents' first claim of injury can be interpreted in two ways. It might be a claim simply to have the Government avoid the violation of law alleged in respondents' complaint. Alternatively, it might be a claim of stigmatic injury, or

19 The "fairly traceable" and "redressability" components of the constitutional standing inquiry were initially articulated by this Court as "two facets of a single causation requirement." C. WRIGHT, LAW OF FEDERAL COURTS § 13, at 68 n.43 (4th ed. 1983). To the extent there is a difference, it is that the former examines the causal connection between the assertedly unlawful conduct and the alleged injury, whereas the latter examines the causal connection between the alleged injury and the judicial relief requested. Cases such as this, in which the relief requested goes well beyond the violation of law alleged, illustrate why it is important to keep the inquiries separate if the "redressability" component is to focus on the requested relief. Even if the relief respondents request might have a substantial effect on the desegregation of public schools, whatever deficiencies exist in the opportunities for desegregated education for respondents' children might not be traceable to IRS violations of law—grants of tax exemptions to racially discriminatory schools in respondents' communities.

denigration, suffered by all members of a racial group when the Government discriminates on the basis of race. Under neither interpretation is this claim of injury judicially cognizable.

This Court has repeatedly held that an asserted right to have the Government act in accordance with law is not sufficient, standing alone, to confer jurisdiction on a federal court. [T]he Court rejected a claim of citizen standing to challenge Armed Forces Reserve commissions held by Members of Congress as violating the Incompatibility Clause of Art. I, § 6, cl. 2, of the Constitution. As citizens, the Court held, plaintiffs alleged nothing but "the abstract injury in nonobservance of the Constitution * * * ." More recently, we rejected a claim of standing to challenge a Government conveyance of property to a religious institution. Insofar as the plaintiffs relied simply on " 'their shared individuated right' " to a Government that made no law respecting an establishment of religion, we held that plaintiffs had not alleged a judicially cognizable injury. "[A]ssertion of a right to a particular kind of Government conduct, which the Government has violated by acting differently, cannot alone satisfy the requirements of Art. III without draining those requirements of meaning." Respondents here have no standing to complain simply that their Government is violating the law.

Neither do they have standing to litigate their claims based on the stigmatizing injury often caused by racial discrimination. There can be no doubt that this sort of noneconomic injury is one of the most serious consequences of discriminatory government action and is sufficient in some circumstances to support standing. Our cases make clear, however, that such injury accords a basis for standing only to "those persons who are personally denied equal treatment" by the challenged discriminatory conduct.

[T]he Court [has] held that the plaintiff had no standing to challenge a club's racially discriminatory membership policies because he had never applied for membership. [T]he Court [has also] held that the plaintiffs had no standing to challenge racial discrimination in the administration of their city's criminal justice system because they had not alleged that they had been or would likely be subject to the challenged practices. * * * In each of those cases, the plaintiffs alleged official racial discrimination comparable to that alleged by respondents here. Yet standing was denied in each case because the plaintiffs were not personally subject to the challenged discrimination. Insofar as their first claim of injury is concerned, respondents are in exactly the same position: * * * they do not allege a stigmatic injury suffered as a direct result of having personally been denied equal treatment.

The consequences of recognizing respondents' standing on the basis of their first claim of injury illustrate why our cases plainly hold that such injury is not judicially cognizable. If the abstract stigmatic injury were cognizable, standing would extend nationwide to all members of the particular racial groups against which the Government was alleged to be discriminating by its grant of a tax exemption to a racially discriminatory school, regardless of the location of that school. All such persons could claim the same sort of abstract stigmatic injury respondents assert in their first claim of injury. A black person in Hawaii could challenge the grant of a tax exemption to a racially discriminatory school in Maine. Recognition of standing in such circumstances would transform the federal courts into "no more than a vehicle for the vindication of the value interests of concerned bystanders." Constitutional limits on the role of the federal courts preclude such a transformation.

2

It is in their complaint's second claim of injury that respondents allege harm to a concrete, personal interest that can support standing in some circumstances. The injury they identify—their children's diminished ability to receive an education in a racially integrated school—is, beyond any doubt, not only judicially cognizable but, * * * one of the most serious injuries recognized in our legal system. Despite the constitutional importance of curing the injury alleged by respondents, however, the federal judiciary may not redress it unless standing requirements are met. In this case, respondents' second claim of injury cannot support standing because the injury alleged is not fairly traceable to the Government conduct respondents challenge as unlawful.[22]

The illegal conduct challenged by respondents is the IRS' grant of tax exemptions to some racially discriminatory schools. The line of causation between that conduct and desegregation of respondents' schools is attenuated at best. From the perspective of the IRS, the injury to respondents is highly indirect and "results from the independent action of some third party not before the court." As the Court pointed out in *Warth v. Seldin,* "the indirectness of the injury * * * may make it substantially more difficult to meet the minimum requirement of Article III * * * ."

22 Respondents' stigmatic injury, though not sufficient for standing in the abstract form in which their complaint asserts it, is judicially cognizable to the extent that respondents are personally subject to discriminatory treatment. The stigmatic injury thus requires identification of some concrete interest with respect to which respondents are personally subject to discriminatory treatment. That interest must independently satisfy the causation requirement of standing doctrine. * * *

In this litigation, respondents identify only one interest that they allege is being discriminatorily impaired—their interest in desegregated public-school education. Respondents' asserted stigmatic injury, therefore, is sufficient to support their standing in this litigation only if their school-desegregation injury independently meets the causation requirement of standing doctrine.

The diminished ability of respondents' children to receive a desegregated education would be fairly traceable to unlawful IRS grants of tax exemptions only if there were enough racially discriminatory private schools receiving tax exemptions in respondents' communities for withdrawal of those exemptions to make an appreciable difference in public-school integration. Respondents have made no such allegation. It is, first, uncertain how many racially discriminatory private schools are in fact receiving tax exemptions. Moreover, it is entirely speculative, as respondents themselves conceded in the Court of Appeals, whether withdrawal of a tax exemption from any particular school would lead the school to change its policies. It is just as speculative whether any given parent of a child attending such a private school would decide to transfer the child to public school as a result of any changes in educational or financial policy made by the private school once it was threatened with loss of tax-exempt status. It is also pure speculation whether, in a particular community, a large enough number of the numerous relevant school officials and parents would reach decisions that collectively would have a significant impact on the racial composition of the public schools.

The links in the chain of causation between the challenged Government conduct and the asserted injury are far too weak for the chain as a whole to sustain respondents' standing. [T]he Court [has] held that standing to challenge a Government grant of a tax exemption to hospitals could not be founded on the asserted connection between the grant of tax-exempt status and the hospitals' policy concerning the provision of medical services to indigents. The causal connection depended on the decisions hospitals would make in response to withdrawal of tax-exempt status, and those decisions were sufficiently uncertain to break the chain of causation between the plaintiffs' injury and the challenged Government action. The chain of causation is even weaker in this case. It involves numerous third parties (officials of racially discriminatory schools receiving tax exemptions and the parents of children attending such schools) who may not even exist in respondents' communities and whose independent decisions may not collectively have a significant effect on the ability of public-school students to receive a desegregated education.

The idea of separation of powers that underlies standing doctrine explains why our cases preclude the conclusion that respondents' alleged injury "fairly can be traced to the challenged action" of the IRS. That conclusion would pave the way generally for suits challenging, not specifically identifiable Government violations of law, but the particular programs agencies establish to carry out their legal obligations. Such suits, even when premised on allegations of several instances of violations of law, are rarely if ever appropriate for federal-court adjudication.

> Carried to its logical end, [respondents'] approach would have the federal courts as virtually continuing monitors of the wisdom and soundness of Ex-

ecutive action; such a role is appropriate for the Congress acting through its committees and the "power of the purse"; it is not the role of the judiciary, absent actual present or immediately threatened injury resulting from unlawful governmental action.

The same concern for the proper role of the federal courts is reflected in cases like *O'Shea v. Littleton*, *Rizzo v. Goode*, and *City of Los Angeles v. Lyons*. In all three cases plaintiffs sought injunctive relief directed at certain systemwide law enforcement practices. The Court held in each case that, absent an allegation of a specific threat of being subject to the challenged practices, plaintiffs had no standing to ask for an injunction. Animating this Court's holdings was the principle that "[a] federal court * * * is not the proper forum to press" general complaints about the way in which government goes about its business.

* * * Most relevant to this case is the principle [that]:

> When a plaintiff seeks to enjoin the activity of a government agency, even within a unitary court system, his case must contend with "the well-established rule that the Government has traditionally been granted the widest latitude in the 'dispatch of its own internal affairs.' "

When transported into the Art. III context, that principle, grounded as it is in the idea of separation of powers, counsels against recognizing standing in a case brought, not to enforce specific legal obligations whose violation works a direct harm, but to seek a restructuring of the apparatus established by the Executive Branch to fulfill its legal duties. The Constitution, after all, assigns to the Executive Branch, and not to the Judicial Branch, the duty to "take Care that the Laws be faithfully executed." U.S. CONST., Art. II, § 3. We could not recognize respondents' standing in this case without running afoul of that structural principle.[26]

* * *

III

"The necessity that the plaintiff who seeks to invoke judicial power stand to profit in some personal interest remains an Art. III requirement." Respondents have not met this fundamental requirement. The judgment of the Court of Appeals is accordingly reversed, and the injunction issued by that court is vacated.

It is so ordered.

---

26 We disagree with Justice Stevens' suggestions that separation of powers principles merely underlie standing requirements, have no role to play in giving meaning to those requirements, and should be considered only under a distinct justiciability analysis. Moreover, our analysis of this case does not rest on the more general proposition that no consequence of the allocation of administrative enforcement resources is judicially cognizable. Rather, we rely on separation of powers principles to interpret the "fairly traceable" component of the standing requirement.

JUSTICE BRENNAN, dissenting.

Once again, the Court "uses 'standing to slam the courthouse door against plaintiffs who are entitled to full consideration of their claims on the merits.' " And once again, the Court does so by "wax[ing] eloquent" on considerations that provide little justification for the decision at hand. This time, however, the Court focuses on "the idea of separation of powers," as if the mere incantation of that phrase provides an obvious solution to the difficult questions presented by these cases.

One could hardly dispute the proposition that Article III of the Constitution, by limiting the judicial power to "cases" or "controversies," embodies the notion that each branch of our National Government must confine its actions to those that are consistent with our scheme of separated powers. But simply stating that unremarkable truism provides little, if any, illumination of the standing inquiry that must be undertaken by a federal court faced with a particular action filed by particular plaintiffs. "The question whether a particular person is a proper party to maintain the action does not, by its own force, raise separation of powers problems related to improper judicial interference in areas committed to other branches of the Federal Government."

The Court's attempt to obscure the standing question must be seen, therefore, as no more than a cover for its failure to recognize the nature of the specific claims raised by the respondents in these cases. By relying on generalities concerning our tripartite system of government, the Court is able to conclude that the respondents lack standing to maintain this action without acknowledging the precise nature of the injuries they have alleged. In so doing, the Court displays a startling insensitivity to the historical role played by the federal courts in eradicating race discrimination from our nation's schools—a role that has played a prominent part in this Court's decisions. Because I cannot join in such misguided decisionmaking, I dissent.

* * *

II

Persons seeking judicial relief from an Article III court must have standing to maintain their cause of action. At a minimum, the standing requirement is not met unless the plaintiff has "such a personal stake in the outcome of the controversy as to assure that concrete adverseness which sharpens the presentation of issues upon which the court so largely depends." Under the Court's cases, this "personal stake" requirement is satisfied if the person seeking redress has suffered, or is threatened with, some "distinct and palpable injury," and if there is some causal connection between the asserted injury and the conduct being challenged.

A

In these cases, the respondents have alleged at least one type of injury that satisfies the constitutional requirement of "distinct and palpable injury."[3] In particular, they claim that the IRS' grant of tax-exempt status to racially discriminatory private schools directly injures their children's opportunity and ability to receive a desegregated education. As the complaint specifically alleges, the IRS action being challenged

> fosters and encourages the organization, operation and expansion of institutions providing racially segregated educational opportunities for white children avoiding attendance in desegregating public school districts and thereby interferes with the efforts of federal courts, HEW and local school authorities to desegregate public school districts which have been operating racially dual school systems.

The Court acknowledges that this alleged injury is sufficient to satisfy constitutional standards. It does so only grudgingly, however, without emphasizing the significance of the harm alleged. Nonetheless, we have consistently recognized throughout the last 30 years that the deprivation of a child's right to receive an education in a desegregated school is a harm of special significance; surely, it satisfies any constitutional requirement of injury in fact. Just last Term, for example, we acknowledged that "[a]n unbroken line of cases following Brown v. Board of Education establishes beyond doubt this Court's view that racial discrimination in education violates a most fundamental national public policy, *as well as the rights of individuals.*" ([E]mphasis added). "The right of a student not to be segregated on racial grounds in schools * * * is indeed so fundamental and pervasive that it is embraced in the concept of due process of law."

3 Because I conclude that the second injury alleged by the respondents is sufficient to satisfy constitutional requirements, I do not need to reach what the Court labels the "stigmatic injury." I note, however, that the Court has mischaracterized this claim of injury by misreading the complaint filed by the respondents. In particular, the respondents have not simply alleged that, as blacks, they have suffered the denigration injury "suffered by all members of a racial group when the Government discriminates on the basis of race." Rather, the complaint, fairly read, limits the claim of stigmatic injury from illegal governmental action to black children attending public schools in districts that are currently desegregating yet contain discriminatory private schools benefitting [*sic*] from illegal tax exemptions. Thus, the Court's "parade of horribles" concerning black plaintiffs from Hawaii challenging tax exemptions granted to schools in Maine is completely irrelevant for purposes of Article III standing in this action. Indeed, even if relevant, that criticism would go to the scope of the class certified or the relief granted in the lawsuit, issues that were not reached by the District Court or the Court of Appeals and are not now before this Court.

In the analogous context of housing discrimination, the Court has similarly recognized that the denial of an opportunity to live in an integrated community is injury sufficient to satisfy the constitutional requirements of standing. In particular, we have recognized that injury is properly alleged when plaintiffs claim a deprivation "of the social and professional benefits of living in an integrated society." Noting "the importance of the 'benefits [obtained] from interracial associations,' " as well as the oft-stated principle "that noneconomic injuries may suffice to provide standing," we have consistently concluded that such an injury is "sufficient to satisfy the constitutional standing requirement of actual or threatened harm."

* * *

B

Fully explicating the injury alleged helps to explain why it is fairly traceable to the governmental conduct challenged by the respondents. As the respondents specifically allege in their complaint:

> Defendants have fostered and encouraged the development, operation and expansion of many of these racially segregated private schools by recognizing them as "charitable" organizations described in Section 501(c)(3) of the Internal Revenue Code, and exempt from federal income taxation under Section 501(a) of the Code. Once the schools are classified as tax-exempt * * *, contributions made to them are deductible from gross income on individual and corporate income tax returns * * * . Moreover, [the] organizations * * * are also exempt from federal social security taxes * * * and from federal unemployment taxes * * * . The resulting exemptions and deductions provide tangible financial aid and other benefits which support the operation of racially segregated private schools. In particular, the resulting deductions facilitate the raising of funds to organize new schools and expand existing schools in order to accommodate white students avoiding attendance in desegregating public school districts. Additionally, the existence of a federal tax exemption amounts to a federal stamp of approval which facilitates fund raising on behalf of racially segregated private schools. Finally, by supporting the development, operation and expansion of institutions providing racially segregated educational opportunities for white children avoiding attendance in desegregating public schools, defendants are thereby interfering with the efforts of courts, HEW and local school authorities to desegregate public school districts which have been operating racially dual school systems.

Viewed in light of the injuries they claim, the respondents have alleged a direct causal relationship between the government action they challenge and the injury they suffer: their inability to receive an education in a racially integrated school is directly and adversely affected by the tax-exempt status granted by the IRS to racially discriminatory schools in their respective school districts. Common sense alone would recognize that the elimination of tax-exempt status for racially discriminatory private schools would serve to lessen the impact that those institutions have in defeating efforts to desegregate the public schools.

The Court admits that "[t]he diminished ability of respondents' children to receive a desegregated education would be fairly traceable to unlawful IRS grants of tax exemptions * * * if there were enough racially discriminatory private schools receiving tax exemptions in respondents' communities for withdrawal of those exemptions to make an appreciable difference in public-school integration," but concludes that "[r]espondents have made no such allegation." With all due respect, the Court has either misread the complaint or is improperly requiring the respondents to prove their case on the merits in order to defeat a motion to dismiss. For example, the respondents specifically refer by name to at least 32 private schools that discriminate on the basis of race and yet continue to benefit illegally from tax-exempt status. Eighteen of those schools—including at least 14 elementary schools, two junior high schools, and one high school—are located in the city of Memphis, Tennessee, which has been the subject of several court orders to desegregate. Similarly, the respondents cite two private schools in Orangeburg, South Carolina that continue to benefit from federal tax exemptions even though they practice race discrimination in school districts that are desegregating pursuant to judicial and administrative orders. At least with respect to these school districts, as well as the others specifically mentioned in the complaint, there can be little doubt that the respondents have identified communities containing "enough racially discriminatory private schools receiving tax exemptions * * * to make an appreciable difference in public-school integration."

Moreover, the Court has previously recognized the existence, and constitutional significance, of such direct relationships between unlawfully segregated school districts and government support for racially discriminatory private schools in those districts. In *Norwood v. Harrison*, for example, we considered a Mississippi program that provided textbooks to students attending both public and private schools, without regard to whether any participating school had racially discriminatory policies. In declaring that program constitutionally invalid, we noted that "a state may not induce, encourage or promote private persons to accomplish what it is constitutionally forbidden to accomplish." We then spoke directly to the causal relationship between the financial aid provided by the state textbook program and the constitutional rights asserted by the students and their parents:

> The District Court laid great stress on the absence of a showing by appellants that "any child enrolled in private school, if deprived of free textbooks, would withdraw from private school and subsequently enroll in the public schools." * * * *We do not agree with the District Court in its analysis of the legal consequences of this uncertainty, for the Constitution does not permit the State to aid discrimination even when there is no precise causal relationship between state*

> *financial aid to a private school and the continued well-being of that school. A State may not grant the type of tangible financial aid here involved if that aid has a significant tendency to facilitate, reinforce, and support private discrimination.*

([E]mphasis added). Thus, Norwood explicitly stands for the proposition that governmental aid to racially discriminatory schools is a direct impediment to school desegregation.

* * *

[T]he Court is forced to place primary reliance on our decision in Simon v. Eastern Kentucky Welfare Rights Org. In that case, the Court denied standing to plaintiffs who challenged an IRS revenue ruling that granted charitable status to hospitals even though they failed to operate to the extent of their financial ability when refusing medical services for indigent patients. The Court found that the injury alleged was not one "that fairly can be traced to the challenged action of the defendant." In particular, it was "purely speculative" whether the denial of access to hospital services alleged by the plaintiffs fairly could be traced to the government's grant of tax-exempt status to the relevant hospitals, primarily because hospitals were likely making their service decisions without regard to the tax implications.

Even accepting the correctness of the causation analysis included in that decision, however, it is plainly distinguishable from the case at hand. The respondents in this case do not challenge the denial of any service by a tax-exempt institution; admittedly, they do not seek access to racially discriminatory private schools. Rather, the injury they allege, and the injury that clearly satisfies constitutional requirements, is the deprivation of their children's opportunity and ability to receive an education in a racially integrated school district. This injury, as the Court admits, and as we have previously held, is of a kind that is directly traceable to the governmental action being challenged. The relationship between the harm alleged and the governmental action cannot simply be deemed "purely speculative" * * * .

III

More than one commentator has noted that the causation component of the Court's standing inquiry is no more than a poor disguise for the Court's view of the merits of the underlying claims. The Court today does nothing to avoid that criticism. What is most disturbing about today's decision, therefore, is not the standing analysis applied, but the indifference evidenced by the Court to the detrimental effects that racially segregated schools, supported by tax-exempt status from the federal government, have on the respondents' attempt to obtain an education in a racially integrated school system. I cannot join such indifference, and would give the respondents a chance to prove their case on the merits.

JUSTICE STEVENS, with whom JUSTICE BLACKMUN joins, dissenting.

Three propositions are clear to me: (1) respondents have adequately alleged "injury in fact"; (2) their injury is fairly traceable to the conduct that they claim to be unlawful; and (3) the "separation of powers" principle does not create a jurisdictional obstacle to the consideration of the merits of their claim.

* * *

II

In final analysis, the wrong the respondents allege that the Government has committed is to subsidize the exodus of white children from schools that would otherwise be racially integrated. The critical question in this case, therefore, is whether respondents have alleged that the Government has created that kind of subsidy.

* * *

An organization that qualifies for preferential treatment under § 501(c)(3) of the Internal Revenue Code, because it is "operated exclusively for * * * charitable * * * purposes," 26 U.S.C. § 501(c)(3), is exempt from paying federal income taxes, and under § 170 of the Code, persons who contribute to such organizations may deduct the amount of their contributions when calculating their taxable income. Only last Term we explained the effect of this preferential treatment:

> Both tax exemptions and tax-deductibility are a form of subsidy that is administered through the tax system. A tax exemption has much the same effect as a cash grant to the organization of the amount of tax it would have to pay on its income. Deductible contributions are similar to cash grants of the amount of a portion of the individual's contributions.

The purpose of this scheme, like the purpose of any subsidy, is to promote the activity subsidized; the statutes "seek to achieve the same basic goal of encouraging the development of certain organizations through the grant of tax benefits." If the granting of preferential tax treatment would "encourage" private segregated school to conduct their "charitable" activities, it must follow that the withdrawal of the treatment would "discourage" them, and hence promote the process of desegregation.[2]

---

2 Respondents' complaint is premised on precisely this theory. The complaint * * * describes a number of private schools which receive preferential tax treatment and which allegedly discriminate on the basis of race, providing white children with "a racially segregated alternative to attendance" in the public schools which respondents' children attend. The complaint then states:

> There are thousands of other racially segregated private schools which operate or serve desegregating public school districts and which function under the umbrella of organizations which have received, applied for, or will apply for, federal tax exemptions. Moreover, many additional

* * *

We have held that when a subsidy makes a given activity more or less expensive, injury can be fairly traced to the subsidy for purposes of standing analysis because of the resulting increase or decrease in the ability to engage in the activity.

* * *

This causation analysis is nothing more than a restatement of elementary economics: when something becomes more expensive, less of it will be purchased. Sections 170 and 501(c)(3) are premised on that recognition. If racially discriminatory private schools lose the "cash grants" that flow from the operation of the statutes, the education they provide will become more expensive and hence less of their services will be purchased. Conversely, maintenance of these tax benefits makes an education in segregated private schools relatively more attractive, by decreasing its cost. Accordingly, without tax exempt status, private schools will either not be competitive in terms of cost, or have to change their admissions policies, hence reducing their competitiveness for parents seeking "a racially segregated alternative" to public schools, which is what respondents have alleged many white parents in desegregating school districts seek.[5] In either event the process of desegregation will be advanced in the same way that it was advanced in *Gilmore* and *Norwood*—the withdrawal of the subsidy for segregated schools means the incentive structure facing white parents who seek such schools for their children will be altered. Thus, the laws of economics, not to mention the laws of Congress embodied in §§ 170 and 501(c)(3), compel the conclu-

> public school districts will in the future begin desegregating pursuant to court order or [government] regulations and guidelines, under state law or voluntarily. Additional racially segregated private schools may be organized or expanded, many of which will be operated by organizations which have received, applied for, or will apply for federal tax exemptions. As in the case of those representative organizations and private schools described in paragraphs 39-48, supra, such organizations and schools provide, or will provide, white children with a racially segregated alternative to desegregating public schools. *By recognizing these organizations as exempt from federal taxation, defendants facilitate their development, operation and expansion and the provision of racially segregated educational opportunities for white children avoiding attendance in desegregating public school systems. Defendants thereby also interfere with the efforts of federal courts, [the Federal Government] and local school authorities to eliminate racially dual school systems.*

([E]mphasis supplied). Thus, like Justice Brennan, I do not understand why the Court states that the complaint contains no allegation that the tax benefits received by private segregated schools "make an appreciable difference to public school integration," unless the Court requires "intricacies of pleading that would have gladdened the heart of Baron Parke." Chayes, *The Role of the Judge in Public Law Litigation*, 89 HARV.L.REV. 1281, 1305 (1976).

5 It is this "racially segregated alternative" to public schools—the availability of schools that "receive tax exemptions on the basis of adopting and certifying—but not implementing—a policy of nondiscrimination," which respondents allege white parents have found attractive, and which would either lose their cost advantage or their character as a segregated alternative if denied tax exempt status because of their discriminatory admissions policies.

sion that the injury respondents have alleged—the increased segregation of their children's schools because of the ready availability of private schools that admit whites only—will be redressed if these schools' operations are inhibited through the denial of preferential tax treatment.

III

Considerations of tax policy, economics, and pure logic all confirm the conclusion that respondents' injury in fact is fairly traceable to the Government's allegedly wrongful conduct. The Court therefore is forced to introduce the concept of "separation of powers" into its analysis. The Court writes that the separation of powers "explains why our cases preclude the conclusion" that respondents' injury is fairly traceable to the conduct they challenge.

* * *

In short, I would deal with the question of the legal limitations on the IRS' enforcement discretion on its merits, rather than by making the untenable assumption that the granting of preferential tax treatment to segregated schools does not make those schools more attractive to white students and hence does not inhibit the process of desegregation. I respectfully dissent.

Notes and Questions

1. Above all, *Allen* stands for the basic proposition that, when challenging legislation, federal official action (as here), or state action, the plaintiff must properly plead three things: injury-in-fact, causation, and redressability. The plaintiff must personally be among the injured; the injury must be "fairly traceable" (caused by) the defendant's alleged wrongful conduct, and the plaintiff's prayed-for remedy must be likely to redress the injury effectively. The Supreme Court has consistently held that these prerequisites for standing are required by Article III of the Constitution.

2. Both the constitutional and prudential components of the standing inquiry have developed over time, and each deserves individualized attention.

a) *Constitutional Components—Injury in Fact.* Note that Article III does not use the words "injury," "causation," or "redressability." Nor does it use the word "standing." Indeed, the "Case or Controversy" Clause isn't a "clause" at all; the word "cases" is used to denote some types of jurisdiction, and the word "controversies" denotes the rest. The standing doctrine and its requirements of injury-in-fact, causation, and redressability are inferences drawn from Article III and from the structure of the Constitution, specifically, the principle of separation of powers that runs through it. No Supreme

Court Justice has ever questioned these inferences. That Article III mandates this three-prong requirement for standing is now black-letter law. Given that the injury-in-fact requirement is part of Article III, by what process does the Court determine whether an alleged injury is constitutionally sufficient? What criteria does, or should, it use? In the general case, how does it give meaning to its view of injury in fact?

A major source of confusion in standing law is the difference between "injury-in-fact" and the violation of legal rights. There were many cases in the early 20th century in which businesses challenged new regulations that would have eliminated their ***de facto*** market monopolies under previous regulations. The courts rejected these challenges on the ground that, although the plaintiff undoubtedly suffered harm (loss of profits), it failed to show the violation of a legal right to a monopoly. Today, the law of standing requires just the opposite. To have standing, the plaintiff must show a real-world harm ("injury-in-fact"). Whether it can show a violation of legal rights is a matter for the "merits" of the case.

It's Latin to Me!

1. Actual; existing in fact; having effect even though not formally or legally recognized <a de facto contract> 2. Illegitimate but in effect <a de facto government>.

Is it possible to access the constitutional sufficiency of an injury without consideration of the nature of the legal rights which have allegedly been violated? Is a plaintiff's loss of sleep too abstract an injury to support the standing requirements of Article III? Or does it depend on the nature of the substantive claim he is asserting? If one of the plaintiffs in *Allen* alleged that he was unable to sleep because racially discriminatory schools obtained tax-exempt status under the challenged guidelines, would such a claimed injury be too abstract to support standing? Suppose a plaintiff in a nuisance case alleged that the barking of a neighbor's dog interfered with his ability to sleep. Would such an injury be too abstract to support standing? Is the first plaintiff's loss of sleep different from that of the second plaintiff? An excellent article argues that the Court's entire standing jurisprudence is really a mischaracterized examination of the merits of the cases. " '[I]njury in fact' is a meaningless concept when applied to a plaintiff who is telling the truth about the injury she feels she has suffered, for injury can only be assessed against some normative structure. In the legal system, injury is assessed against the normative structure provided by particular rights." William A. Fletcher, *The Structure of Standing*, 98 YALE L.J. 221, 248-49 (1988). Judge Fletcher argues that when the Court asks if someone has been injured in fact, it is really asking whether the hurt that the plaintiff perceives is one that society is prepared to remedy through the legal system. He views that inquiry as indistinguishable from whether the plaintiff can state, in federal terms, "a claim upon which relief may be granted." FED.R.CIV.P. 12(b)(6). Many scholars agree with Judge Fletcher's thesis.

Courts analyze standing for *each individual remedy* that the plaintiff has requested. One who sues for money damages almost always has standing to pursue that remedy because such a suit almost invariably alleges that the defendant caused his or her injury, and the law presumes that money damages will redress that injury. But if the plaintiff goes on to ask for an injunction or declaratory relief, standing problems may appear. For example, in *City of Los Angeles v. Lyons,* 461 U.S. 95 (1981), the plaintiff complained that he had been choked into unconsciousness by police who stopped him for a minor traffic violation. Los Angeles police policy permitted officers to use either of two chokeholds in circumstances that did not justify deadly force; sixteen people had died as a result of police chokeholds. The Court found Lyons lacked standing because he could not demonstrate that he was a) likely to be arrested again and b) likely to be choked even if he was arrested. Justice Marshall, joined by three colleagues, dissented:

> By fragmenting the standing inquiry and imposing a separate standing hurdle with respect to each form of relief sought, the decision today departs significantly from this Court's traditional conception of the standing requirement and of the remedial powers of the federal courts. We have never required more than that a plaintiff have standing to litigate a claim. Whether he will be entitled to obtain particular forms of relief should he prevail has never been understood to be an issue of standing. * * *
>
> Our cases uniformly state that the touchstone of the Article III standing requirement is the plaintiff's personal stake in the underlying dispute, not in the particular types of relief sought. Once a plaintiff establishes a personal stake in the dispute, he has done all that is necessary * * * .

See also Rizzo v. Goode, 423 U.S. 362 (1976); *O'Shea v. Littleton,* 414 U.S. 488 (1974). Should the Court continue to evaluate standing according to the type of relief sought? If it does, what are the implications for plaintiffs' ability to seek systemic relief?

Camreta v. Greene, 131 S.Ct. 2020 (2011), saw the Court accept for review an appeal from state officials of a Ninth Circuit ruling that their conduct had violated the Fourth Amendment, although the Circuit found they were entitled to qualified immunity and affirmed the summary judgment in their favor. The majority stated its rationale for allowing review:

> If the official regularly engages in that conduct as part of his job (as Camreta does), he suffers injury caused by the adverse constitutional ruling. So long as it continues in effect, he must either change the way he performs his duties or risk a meritorious damages action. Only by overturning the ruling on appeal can the official gain clearance to engage in the conduct in the future. He thus can demonstrate, as we demand, injury, causation, and redressability.[4]

Is the Court's position consistent with *City of Los Angeles v. Lyons*, the chokehold case?

4 Contrary to the dissent's view, the injury to the official thus occurs independent of any future suit brought by a third party. Indeed, no such suit is likely to arise because the prospect of damages liability will force the official to change his conduct.

In *Raines v. Byrd,* 521 U.S. 811 (1997), the Court declined to reach the issue of the constitutionality of the Line Item Veto Act, 2 U.S.C.A. Secs. 681, *et seq.* The Justices found that members of Congress who had voted against the Act lacked standing, despite Congress's attempt to create it by statute. The Court ruled that no member who had voted against the Act had any personal stake likely to be redressed by invalidation of the Act. Chief Justice Rehnquist also noted that the harm to any member of Congress was equally shared by all members.

In *Bond v. United States*, 131 S.Ct. 2355 (2011), Bond sought to challenge the statute underlying her conviction on the ground that "Congress exceeded its powers under the Constitution, thus intruding upon the sovereignty and authority of the States * * * ," in violation of the Tenth Amendment. The government took the position that she lacked standing to do so, arguing that she was asserting the state's constitutional interest rather than her own. The district and circuit courts upheld the government's position. The government then changed its mind, conceding that she had standing. Granting review, the Supreme Court appointed an amicus curiae to defend the judgment of the circuit court. A unanimous Court ruled that the defendant did have standing.

Justice Kennedy's opinion for the Court criticized an earlier decision (upon which *amicus* relied) for imprecision in vocabulary. *Tennessee Electric Power Co. v. TVA* (1939) had said that "the problem with the power companies' suit was a lack of 'standing' or a 'cause of action.' It treated those concepts as interchangeable." The *Bond* Court criticized *Tennessee Power* for that reason, although Justice Kennedy did observe that "the distinct concepts can be difficult to keep separate." That may reflect Judge Fletcher's suggestion, *see supra* at 54, that standing often acts as a stand-in (so to speak) for the question of whether the plaintiff can state a claim upon which relief may be granted. Yet the Court continues to insist that the inquiries are different. "Still, the question whether a plaintiff states a claim for relief 'goes to the merits' in the typical case, not the justiciability of a dispute, and conflation of the two concepts can cause confusion."

Perhaps so, but some of the Court's other decisions appear to support the conflation. In *Rakas v. Illinois*, 439 U.S. 128 (1978), the Court pronounced the vocabulary of standing inappropriate in Fourth Amendment cases.

> [H]aving rejected petitioners' target theory and reaffirmed the principle that the "rights assured by the Fourth Amendment are personal rights, [which] * * * may be enforced by exclusion of evidence only at the instance of one whose own protection was infringed by the search and seizure," the question necessarily arises whether it serves any useful analytical purpose to consider this principle a matter of standing, distinct from the merits of a defendant's Fourth Amendment claim. We can think of no decided cases of this Court that would have come out differently had we concluded, as we do now, that the type of standing require-

> ment discussed in *Jones* and reaffirmed today is more properly subsumed under substantive Fourth Amendment doctrine. Rigorous application of the principle that the rights secured by this Amendment are personal, in place of a notion of "standing," will produce no additional situations in which evidence must be excluded. The inquiry under either approach is the same. But we think the better analysis forthrightly focuses on the extent of a particular defendant's rights under the Fourth Amendment, rather than on any theoretically separate, but invariably intertwined concept of standing.

Id. at 138-39 (footnote and citation omitted). And the Court has adhered to that approach, discussing Fourth Amendment cases in terms of whether the individual had a "reasonable expectation of privacy" rather than in terms of standing and criticizing a state supreme court for continuing the older form of analysis. *Minnesota v. Carter*, 525 U.S. 83, 87-88 (1998).

Bond is of interest also because the Court clearly rejected the suggestion of two distinguished scholars that the federal courts should regard standing and separation-of-powers issues as nonjusticiable. Justice Kennedy pointed out that federalism deals with two concerns:

> The Framers concluded that allocation of powers between the National Government and the States enhances freedom, first by protecting the integrity of the governments themselves, and second by protecting the people, from whom all governmental powers are derived.
>
> Federalism has more than one dynamic. It is true that the federal structure serves to grant and delimit the prerogatives and responsibilities of the States and the National Government vis-a-vis one another. The allocation of powers in our federal system preserves the integrity, dignity, and residual sovereignty of the States. The federal balance is, in part, an end in itself, to ensure that States function as political entities in their own right.
>
> But that is not its exclusive sphere of operation. Federalism is more than an exercise in setting the boundary between different institutions of government for their own integrity. "State sovereignty is not just an end in itself: 'Rather, federalism secures to citizens the liberties that derive from the diffusion of sovereign power.' "
>
> Some of these liberties are of a political character. The federal structure allows local policies "more sensitive to the diverse needs of a heterogeneous society," permits "innovation and experimentation," enables greater citizen "involvement in democratic processes," and makes government "more responsive by putting the States in competition for a mobile citizenry." Federalism secures the freedom of the individual.

"Actual or imminent" injury. The Court has made it clear that the claimant's injury-in-fact must be "actual or imminent." The most recent pronouncement on what constitutes "imminent" came in *Clapper v. Amnesty International USA*, 133 S.Ct.

1138 (2013) , where a 5-4 majority held that the plaintiffs (human rights and media organizations) lacked standing to mount a constitutional challenge to 50 U.S.C. § 1881a, which Congress added to the Foreign Intelligence Surveillance Act of 1978 to eliminate some previously existing obstacles to wiretapping non-Americans outside the United States. Citing language first used in *Whitmore v. Arkansas*, 495 U.S. 149, 158 (1990), Justice Alito's opinion for the Court held that the plaintiffs had failed to demonstrate that surveillance of either the plaintiffs or foreign persons with whom the plaintiffs were in contact was "certainly impending." The Court explicitly rejected the Second Circuit's standard of "objectively reasonable likelihood."

The Court also rejected the plaintiffs' alternative theory of standing, which was that they had already suffered injury because the prospect of surveillance had forced them to take "costly and burdensome" protective measures. "[R]espondents cannot manufacture standing merely by inflicting harm on themselves based on their fears of hypothetical future harm that is not certainly impending," the majority stated.

Although nothing in the majority opinion limits its "certainly impending" standard of imminence to national security cases, there is some reason to doubt its universal applicability. In addition to characterizing the plaintiffs' possible injury as dependent on a parlay of events, many of which were in the control of persons not before the Court, Justice Alito took pains to detail the procedural safeguards that Congress built into § 1881a. Given the Foreign Intelligence Surveillance Court's well-documented record of virtually never refusing the Government's requests, the majority's review of safeguards may have had the additional purpose of suggesting that § 1881a treads a careful path around constitutional values.

Nor did the majority attempt to refute Justice Breyer's point in dissent that numerous previous cases had found imminence of injury on facts that appeared less certain than in the case *sub judice*. For example, in *Pennell v. City of San Jose*, 485 U.S. 1, 8 (1988), the Court found standing where there was a "'*realistic danger of sustaining a direct injury* as a result of the statute's operation'" (emphasis in original). The "certainly impending" language in previous cases, stated Justice Breyer, signified what was "sufficient" to demonstrate imminence rather than what was "necessary" to demonstrate it.

b) *Constitutional Components—Traceability & Redressability.* Traceability and redressability are linked causation requirements that look in different directions. "Traceability" refers to whether the plaintiff's injury arises from the defendant's action. It is, in other words, backward-looking. "Redressability," on the other hand, is forward-looking, asking whether the relief requested is likely to improve the situation for the plaintiff.

If the plaintiff is an intended beneficiary of a criminal statute enacted to protect a class of people, does non-enforcement of the statute give rise to a cognizable injury sufficient to create standing, or must the plaintiff demonstrate that but for the non-enforcement of the statute she would not have suffered injury, and that if the statute is enforced the injury will cease? How close a causal connection should the plaintiff have to demonstrate? In *Linda R.S. v. Richard D.*, 410 U.S. 614 (1973), a Texas statutory scheme allowed prosecution of parents who did not pay child support for legitimate children, but did not permit prosecution of defaulting parents of illegitimate children. The plaintiff argued that the scheme violated the Equal Protection Clause. The Court's denial of standing rested upon its perception that granting relief would have made it no more probable (or insufficiently probable) that support payments to the individual plaintiff would commence. On the Court's rationale, would the defaulting parent of a legitimate child have had standing to challenge the statutory scheme, at least if threatened with prosecution? Manifestly, such an individual would benefit directly from a judicial victory; no prosecution could ensue. If the Court had allowed standing in that case, what anomalies would that have created?

For a plaintiff seeking equitable relief, should standing doctrine require the plaintiff to demonstrate that the relief requested will "cure" the plaintiff's problem? If so, to what degree of certainty must the plaintiff prove redressability? *See Simon v. Eastern Kentucky Welfare Rights Organization*, 426 U.S. 26 (1976). In *Simon*, the Court found no standing to challenge IRS's continuing allowance of charitable-organization status to hospitals that allegedly did not offer service to those unable to pay. The Court reasoned that there was not a sufficient showing that removal of the hospitals' tax exempt status would cause them to change the behavior of which the plaintiffs complained.

Why should traceability and redressability be viewed as components of Article III standing? Might these requirements stem from the Court's oft-repeated insistence that a plaintiff have a "personal stake in the outcome of the controversy," first articulated in *Baker v. Carr*, 369 U.S. 186 (1962)? How much certainty of redress should be required before a federal court can act? "Substantial likelihood"? Commentators have assailed the Court's jurisprudence in this area as too malleable.

Food for Thought

Does it make any difference whether a case is dismissed for lack of standing, for failure of the plaintiff to state a claim upon which relief may be granted, or for failure of proof? Dismissal for lack of standing would have no preclusive effect; dismissal for failure of proof certainly would.

Allan Bakke, a white male, was denied admission to the University of California at Davis Medical School and challenged the school's practice of setting aside sixteen spots for minority students out of an entering class of 100. The state argued that Bakke lacked standing based on the redressability requirement. Even if the affirmative action program were declared unconstitutional, Bakke still might not be admitted to the medical school. In other words, if the Court characterized Bakke's injury as a denial of admission, there was no assurance that a favorable court decision would redress the injury. But the Court chose

> a different characterization of the harm. The Court stated that Bakke's injury was an inability to compete for all 100 spots and, therefore, a judicial decision declaring the set-aside of sixteen spots unconstitutional would remedy the injury and give him a chance to compete for all the slots.

ERWIN CHEMERINSKY, FEDERAL JURISDICTION, § 2.3, at 80-81 (6th. ed. 2012) (footnotes omitted). *See also* Gene Nichol, *Causation As a Standing Requirement: The Unprincipled Use of Judicial Restraint,* 69 KY.L.J. 185 (1981); Gene Nichol, *Rethinking Standing,* 72 CALIF.L.REV. 68, 79 (1984).

The Court took a narrow view of redressability in *Steel Company v. Citizens for a Better Environment*, 523 U.S. 83 (1998). Plaintiff CBE sued under the Emergency Planning and Community Right-to-Know Act of 1986 (EPCRA), alleging that the defendant had failed timely to file reports required by the Act with respect to the presence of toxic or other hazardous chemicals at its site. After the plaintiff had notified defendant and relevant federal and state officials of the non-filing, defendant filed all of the overdue reports. Plaintiff nonetheless exercised its statutory right to sue. Defendant moved to dismiss for lack of subject matter jurisdiction and for failure to state a claim upon which relief could be granted, arguing that by the time the action was filed, there was no violation and that EPCRA does not authorize an action for past violations. All nine Justices concurred in the judgment directing dismissal of the action, but reached that conclusion via different routes. The Court's majority declined to reach the question of whether deprivation of information is an injury-in-fact that satisfies Article III, holding instead that the complaint could not satisfy the redressability requirement that the majority identified as one of the "irreducible constitutional minim[a] of standing * * * ."

The complaint asks for (1) a declaratory judgment that petitioner violated EPCRA; (2) authorization to inspect periodically petitioner's facility and records (with costs borne by petitioner); (3) an order requiring petitioner to provide respondent copies of all compliance reports submitted to the EPA; (4) an order requiring petitioner to pay civil penalties of $25,000 per day for each violation of §§ 11022 and 11023; (5) an award of all respondent's "costs, in connection with the investigation and prosecution of this matter, including reasonable attorney and expert witness fees, as authorized by Section 326(f) of [EPCRA]"; and (6) any such further relief as the court deems appropriate. None of the specific items of relief sought, and none that we can envision as "appropriate" under the general request, would serve to reimburse respondent for losses caused by the late reporting, or to eliminate any effects of that late reporting upon respondent.

Since it was undisputed that the defendant had failed timely to file the reports, thus violating the Act, the request for declaratory relief did not support standing. Civil penalties, the only damages authorized by the Act, were payable to the United States, not to the plaintiff. Thus, the request for civil penalties did not meet the redressability requirement. Moreover, the majority noted that "[t]he litigation must give the plaintiff some other benefit besides reimbursement of costs that are a byproduct of the litigation itself." Consequently, the request for investigation and prosecution costs did not establish standing. The majority recognized that deterrence of future injury could be remedial for Article III purposes, but demurred at recognizing it in this case. "If respondent had alleged a continuing violation or the imminence of a future violation, the injunctive relief requested would remedy that alleged harm. But there is no allegation here—and on the facts of the case, there seems no basis for it." The Court also rejected the notion that voluntary cessation of illegal activity gives rise to a presumption that the activity will be resumed, distinguishing this situation from a case where the defendant argues mootness after voluntary cessation. If the defendant here had characterized the ground for dismissal as mootness because it had filed the required forms, do you think the majority would have had to come out the other way? Was the result determined simply by defendant's artfulness in selecting the basis for objecting to the action, combined with plaintiff's inartfulness in failing to allege the likelihood of continuing violations?

3. When should a court determine standing? In *Gladstone, Realtors v. Village of Bellwood*, 441 U.S. 91, 115 n. 31 (1979), the Court said: "Although standing generally is a matter dealt with at the earliest stages of litigation, usually on the pleadings, it sometimes remains to be seen whether the factual allegations of the complaint necessary for standing will be supported adequately by the evidence adduced at trial." When the court determines standing at the pleading stage, the plaintiff merely need make "plausible allegations" that satisfy the standing requirements. When standing is determined at the summary judgment stage, the plaintiff will have to produce some evidence demonstrating that the requirements have been met. At least with respect to requirements mandated by Article III, standing is, for some purposes at least, akin to subject matter jurisdiction. Thus, if the parties fail to raise an Article III standing problem, the court is required to raise it ***sua sponte***.

4. In *Sprint Communications Co., L.P. v. APPC Services Inc.*, 554 U.S. 269 (2008), the Court addressed a question that one would think had been settled long before: "[W]hether an assignee of a legal claim for money owed has standing to pursue that claim in federal court, even when the assignee has promised to remit the proceeds of the litigation to the assignor." In other words, do debt collectors have standing to sue in federal court on behalf of their clients? "Because history and precedent make clear that such an assignee has long been permitted to bring suit," wrote Justice Breyer for the majority, "we conclude that the assignee does have standing."

It's Latin to Me!

"Without prompting or suggestion; on its own motion"

Chief Justice Roberts, writing for himself and three other dissenters, complained that the majority's real rationale was to elevate expediency over separation-of-powers principles.

5. *Sprint Communications* permitted an assignee standing to sue even though any recovery would go to the assignor. Under a longstanding federal statute, the False Claims Act, a private individual may sue someone who has profited off false representations to the federal government. The incentive for whistleblower ("relator") is a share of the recovery. In *Vermont Agency of Natural Resources v. U.S. ex rel. Stevens*, 529 U.S. 765 (2000), the relator brought an action under the False Claims Act against his former employer, a state agency, for submitting false claims to the Environmental Protection Agency. Writing for the majority, Justice Scalia stated

> We believe, however, that adequate basis for the relator's suit for his bounty is to be found in the doctrine that the assignee of a claim has standing to assert the injury in fact suffered by the assignor. The FCA can reasonably be regarded as effecting a partial assignment of the Government's damages claim. Although we have never expressly recognized "representational standing" on the part of assignees, we have routinely entertained their suits, and also suits by subrogees, who have been described as "equitable assign[ees]." We conclude, therefore, that the United States' injury in fact suffices to confer standing on respondent Stevens.

In an omitted footnote, Justice Scalia noted that "we are asserting that a *qui tam* relator is, in effect, suing as a *partial* assignee of the United States." If the assignee of a claim can assert the assignor's injury-in-fact, then the standing problem here disappears, does it not?

6. There is enough in these opinions to keep standing watchers guessing for a long time, because both the majority and dissenting opinion portend large changes in the way in which the Court has viewed the problem of standing. Consider first the majority opinion in *Sprint Communications*. The law has long recognized subrogation; it arises commonly when an insurance company pays its insured for the insured's loss and then sues on the claim that the insured had against the party who caused the loss. In effect, the insurance company purchases the insured's claim. Of course, in the traditional rubric of standing, the insurance company has suffered no direct injury-in-fact, so there is nothing to redress.

Hollingsworth v. Perry

Supreme Court of the United States, 2013.
133 S.Ct. 2652.

CHIEF JUSTICE ROBERTS delivered the opinion of the Court.

The public is currently engaged in an active political debate over whether same-sex couples should be allowed to marry. That question has also given rise to litigation. In this case, petitioners, who oppose same-sex marriage, ask us to decide whether the Equal Protection Clause "prohibits the State of California from defining marriage as the union of a man and a woman." Respondents, same-sex couples who wish to marry, view the issue in somewhat different terms: For them, it is whether California—having previously recognized the right of same-sex couples to marry—may reverse that decision through a referendum.

Federal courts have authority under the Constitution to answer such questions only if necessary to do so in the course of deciding an actual "case" or "controversy." As used in the Constitution, those words do not include every sort of dispute, but only those "historically viewed as capable of resolution through the judicial process." This is an essential limit on our power: It ensures that we act *as judges,* and do not engage in policymaking properly left to elected representatives.

For there to be such a case or controversy, it is not enough that the party invoking the power of the court have a keen interest in the issue. That party must also have "standing," which requires, among other things, that it have suffered a concrete and particularized injury. Because we find that petitioners do not have standing, we have no authority to decide this case on the merits, and neither did the Ninth Circuit.

I

In 2008, the California Supreme Court held that limiting the official designation of marriage to opposite-sex couples violated the equal protection clause of the California Constitution. Later that year, California voters passed the ballot initiative at the center of this dispute, known as Proposition 8. That proposition amended the California Constitution to provide that "[o]nly marriage between a man and a woman is valid or recognized in California." Shortly thereafter, the California

Practice Pointer

Do you perceive that same-sex marriage advocates took this non-decision as a political victory, as its immediate effect was to allow such marriages to go forward in California? If it was perceived as a victory for same-sex marriage, did the Court gain anything in terms of judicial statesmanship by refusing to decide the merits?

Supreme Court rejected a procedural challenge to the amendment, and held that the Proposition was properly enacted under California law.

According to the California Supreme Court, Proposition 8 created a "narrow and limited exception" to the state constitutional rights otherwise guaranteed to same-sex couples. Under California law, same-sex couples have a right to enter into relationships recognized by the State as "domestic partnerships," which carry "the same rights, protections, and benefits, and shall be subject to the same responsibilities, obligations, and duties under law * * * as are granted to and imposed upon spouses." In *In re Marriage Cases*, the California Supreme Court concluded that the California Constitution further guarantees same-sex couples "all of the constitutionally based incidents of marriage," including the right to have that marriage "officially recognized" as such by the State. Proposition 8, the court explained in Strauss [v. Horton, involving a procedural challenge to the initiative], left those rights largely undisturbed, reserving only "the official designation of the term 'marriage' for the union of opposite-sex couples as a matter of state constitutional law."

Respondents, two same-sex couples who wish to marry, filed suit in federal court, challenging Proposition 8 under the Due Process and Equal Protection Clauses of the Fourteenth Amendment to the Federal Constitution. The complaint named as defendants California's Governor, attorney general, and various other state and local officials responsible for enforcing California's marriage laws. Those officials refused to defend the law, although they have continued to enforce it throughout this litigation. The District Court allowed petitioners—the official proponents of the initiative—to intervene to defend it. After a 12–day bench trial, the District Court declared Proposition 8 unconstitutional, permanently enjoining the California officials named as defendants from enforcing the law, and "directing the official defendants that all persons under their control or supervision" shall not enforce it.

Those officials elected not to appeal the District Court order. When petitioners did, the Ninth Circuit asked them to address "why this appeal should not be dismissed for lack of Article III standing." After briefing and argument, the Ninth Circuit certified a question to the California Supreme Court:

> Whether under Article II, Section 8 of the California Constitution, or otherwise under California law, the official proponents of an initiative measure possess either a particularized interest in the initiative's validity or the authority to assert the State's interest in the initiative's validity, which would enable them to defend the constitutionality of the initiative upon its adoption or appeal a judgment invalidating the initiative, when the public officials charged with that duty refuse to do so.

The California Supreme Court agreed to decide the certified question, and answered in the affirmative. Without addressing whether the proponents have a particularized interest of their own in an initiative's validity, the court concluded that "[i]n a postelection challenge to a voter-approved initiative measure, the official proponents of the initiative are authorized under California law to appear and assert the state's interest in the initiative's validity and to appeal a judgment invalidating the measure when the public officials who ordinarily defend the measure or appeal such a judgment decline to do so."

> **FYI**
>
> The vast majority of states have enacted "certification" statutes authorizing state supreme courts to decide uncertain questions of state law referred to them by federal courts. Most such statutes permit federal district courts to certify questions, but California's only permits federal appellate courts to certify. The state court does not decide the entire case, only the discrete question that was certified. For more on certification, see Chapter 8. If Congress enacted a statute permitting state courts to certify federal questions to federal courts, would it violate Article III?

Relying on that answer, the Ninth Circuit concluded that petitioners had standing under federal law to defend the constitutionality of Proposition 8. California, it reasoned, " 'has standing to defend the constitutionality of its [laws],' " and States have the "prerogative, as independent sovereigns, to decide for themselves who may assert their interests." "All a federal court need determine is that the state has suffered a harm sufficient to confer standing and that the party seeking to invoke the jurisdiction of the court is authorized by the state to represent its interest in remedying that harm."

On the merits, the Ninth Circuit affirmed the District Court. * * *

We granted certiorari to review that determination, and directed that the parties also brief and argue "Whether petitioners have standing under Article III, § 2, of the Constitution in this case."

> **Practice Pointer**
>
> Note that the California Supreme Court lacked the power to deciding the entire standing question. It could decide only that the State of California delegated litigating authority to the initiative's authors. The ultimate question of standing in federal court is a federal question.

II

Article III of the Constitution confines the judicial power of federal courts to deciding actual "Cases" or "Controversies." One essential aspect of this requirement is that any person invoking the power of a federal court must demonstrate standing to do so. This requires the litigant to prove that he has suffered a concrete and particularized injury that is fairly traceable to the challenged conduct, and is likely to be redressed by a favorable judicial decision. In other words, for a federal court to have authority under the Constitution to settle a dispute, the party before it must seek a remedy for a personal and tangible harm. "The presence of a disagreement, however sharp and acrimonious it may be, is insufficient by itself to meet Art. III's requirements."

The doctrine of standing, we recently explained, "serves to prevent the judicial process from being used to usurp the powers of the political branches." *Clapper v. Amnesty Int'l USA* (2013). In light of this "overriding and time-honored concern about keeping the Judiciary's power within its proper constitutional sphere, we must put aside the natural urge to proceed directly to the merits of [an] important dispute and to 'settle' it for the sake of convenience and efficiency." ([F]ootnote omitted).

Most standing cases consider whether a plaintiff has satisfied the requirement when filing suit, but Article III demands that an "actual controversy" persist throughout all stages of litigation. That means that standing "must be met by persons seeking appellate review, just as it must be met by persons appearing in courts of first instance." *Arizonans for Official English v. Arizona* (1997). We therefore must decide whether petitioners had standing to appeal the District Court's order.

Respondents initiated this case in the District Court against the California officials responsible for enforcing Proposition 8. The parties do not contest that respondents had Article III standing to do so. Each couple expressed a desire to marry and obtain "official sanction" from the State, which was unavailable to them given the declaration in Proposition 8 that "marriage" in California is solely between a man and a woman.

> **Practice Pointer**
>
> Do not be thrown by the fact that this case concerns the standing of people trying to defend the litigation. Anyone who makes any claim in federal court must have standing to raise that claim.

After the District Court declared Proposition 8 unconstitutional and enjoined the state officials named as defendants from enforcing it, however, the inquiry under Article III changed. Respondents no longer had any injury to redress—they had won—and the state officials chose not to appeal.

The only individuals who sought to appeal that order were petitioners, who had intervened in the District Court. But the District Court had not ordered them to do or refrain from doing anything. To have standing, a litigant must seek relief for an injury that affects him in a "personal and individual way." He must possess a "direct stake in the outcome" of the case. Here, however, petitioners had no "direct stake" in the outcome of their appeal. Their only interest in having the District Court order reversed was to vindicate the constitutional validity of a generally applicable California law.

We have repeatedly held that such a "generalized grievance," no matter how sincere, is insufficient to confer standing. A litigant "raising only a generally available grievance about government—claiming only harm to his and every citizen's interest in proper application of the Constitution and laws, and seeking relief that no more directly and tangibly benefits him than it does the public at large—does not state an Article III case or controversy."

Petitioners argue that the California Constitution and its election laws give them a " 'unique,' 'special,' and 'distinct' role in the initiative process—one 'involving both authority and responsibilities that differ from other supporters of the measure.' " True enough—but only when it comes to the process of enacting the law. Upon submitting the proposed initiative to the attorney general, petitioners became the official "proponents" of Proposition 8. As such, they were responsible for collecting the signatures required to qualify the measure for the ballot. After those signatures were collected, the proponents alone had the right to file the measure with election officials to put it on the ballot. Petitioners also possessed control over the arguments in favor of the initiative that would appear in California's ballot pamphlets.

Pet. had role in initiative process

But once Proposition 8 was approved by the voters, the measure became "a duly enacted constitutional amendment or statute." Petitioners have no role—special or otherwise—in the enforcement of Proposition 8. They therefore have no "personal stake" in defending its enforcement that is distinguishable from the general interest of every citizen of California.

Article III standing "is not to be placed in the hands of 'concerned bystanders,' who will use it simply as a 'vehicle for the vindication of value interests.' " No matter how deeply committed petitioners may be to upholding Proposition 8 or how "zealous [their] advocacy," that is not a "particularized" interest sufficient to create a case or controversy under Article III.

III

A

Without a judicially cognizable interest of their own, petitioners attempt to invoke that of someone else. They assert that even if they have no cognizable interest in appealing the District Court's judgment, the State of California does, and they may assert that interest on the State's behalf. It is, however, a "fundamental restriction on our authority" that "[i]n the ordinary course, a litigant must assert his or her own legal rights and interests, and cannot rest a claim to relief on the legal rights or interests of third parties." There are "certain, limited exceptions" to that rule. But even when we have allowed litigants to assert the interests of others, the litigants themselves still "must have suffered an injury in fact, thus giving [them] a sufficiently concrete interest in the outcome of the issue in dispute."

In *Diamond v. Charles*, for example, we refused to allow Diamond, a pediatrician engaged in private practice in Illinois, to defend the constitutionality of the State's abortion law. In that case, a group of physicians filed a constitutional challenge to the Illinois statute in federal court. The State initially defended the law, and Diamond, a professed "conscientious object[or] to abortions," intervened to defend it alongside the State.

After the Seventh Circuit affirmed a permanent injunction against enforcing several provisions of the law, the State chose not to pursue an appeal to this Court. But when Diamond did, the state attorney general filed a " 'letter of interest,' " explaining that the State's interest in the proceeding was " 'essentially coterminous with the position on the issues set forth by [Diamond].' " That was not enough, we held, to allow the appeal to proceed. As the Court explained, "[e]ven if there were circumstances in which a private party would have standing to defend the constitutionality of a challenged statute, this [was] not one of them," because Diamond was not able to assert an injury in fact of his own. And without "any judicially cognizable interest," Diamond could not "maintain the litigation abandoned by the State."

For the reasons we have explained, petitioners have likewise not suffered an injury in fact, and therefore would ordinarily have no standing to assert the State's interests.

B

Petitioners contend that this case is different, because the California Supreme Court has determined that they are "authorized under California law to appear and assert the state's interest" in the validity of Proposition 8. The court below agreed: "All a federal court need determine is that the state has suffered a harm sufficient to confer standing and that the party seeking to invoke the jurisdiction of the court is authorized by the state to represent its interest in remedying that harm." As petitioners put it, they "need no more show a personal injury, separate from the State's indisputable interest in the validity of its law, than would California's Attorney General or did the legislative leaders held to have standing in *Karcher v. May* (1987)."

In *Karcher*, we held that two New Jersey state legislators—Speaker of the General Assembly Alan Karcher and President of the Senate Carmen Orechio—

could intervene in a suit against the State to defend the constitutionality of a New Jersey law, after the New Jersey attorney general had declined to do so. "Since the New Jersey Legislature had authority under state law to represent the State's interests in both the District Court and the Court of Appeals," we held that the Speaker and the President, in their official capacities, could vindicate that interest in federal court on the legislature's behalf.

Far from supporting petitioners' standing, however, *Karcher* is compelling precedent against it. The legislators in that case intervened in their official capacities as Speaker and President of the legislature. No one doubts that a State has a cognizable interest "in the continued enforceability" of its laws that is harmed by a judicial decision declaring a state law unconstitutional. To vindicate that interest or any other, a State must be able to designate agents to represent it in federal court. That agent is typically the State's attorney general. But state law may provide for other officials to speak for the State in federal court, as New Jersey law did for the State's presiding legislative officers in *Karcher*.

What is significant about *Karcher* is what happened after the Court of Appeals decision in that case. Karcher and Orechio lost their positions as Speaker and President, but nevertheless sought to appeal to this Court. We held that they could not do so. We explained that while they were able to participate in the lawsuit in their official capacities as presiding officers of the incumbent legislature, "since they no longer hold those offices, they lack authority to pursue this appeal."

The point of *Karcher* is not that a State could authorize private parties to represent its interests; Karcher and Orechio were permitted to proceed only because they were state officers, acting in an official capacity. As soon as they lost that capacity, they lost standing. Petitioners here hold no office and have always participated in this litigation solely as private parties.

* * *

C

Both petitioners and respondents seek support from dicta in *Arizonans for Official English v. Arizona*. The plaintiff in *Arizonans for Official English* filed a constitutional challenge to an Arizona ballot initiative declaring English " 'the official language of the State of Arizona.' " After the District Court declared the initiative unconstitutional, Arizona's Governor announced that she would not pursue an appeal. Instead, the principal sponsor of the ballot initiative—the Arizonans for Official English Committee—sought to defend the measure in the Ninth Circuit. Analogizing the sponsors to the Arizona Legislature, the Ninth Circuit held that the Committee was "qualified to defend [the initiative] on appeal," and affirmed the District Court.

Before finding the case mooted by other events, this Court expressed "grave doubts" about the Ninth Circuit's standing analysis. We reiterated that "[s]tanding to defend on appeal in the place of an original defendant * * * demands that the litigant possess 'a direct stake in the outcome.' " We recognized that a legislator authorized by state law to represent the State's interest may satisfy standing requirements, as in *Karcher*, but noted that the Arizona committee and its members were "not elected representatives, and we [we]re aware of no Arizona law appointing initiative sponsors as agents of the people of Arizona to defend, in lieu of public officials, the constitutionality of initiatives made law of the State."

Petitioners argue that, by virtue of the California Supreme Court's decision, they are authorized to act " 'as agents of the people' of California." But that Court never described petitioners as "agents of the people," or of anyone else. Nor did the Ninth Circuit. The Ninth Circuit asked—and the California Supreme Court answered—only whether petitioners had "the authority to assert the State's interest in the initiative's validity." All that the California Supreme Court decision stands for is that, so far as California is concerned, petitioners may argue in defense of Proposition 8. This "does not mean that the proponents become de facto public officials"; the authority they enjoy is "simply the authority to participate as parties in a court action and to assert legal arguments in defense of the state's interest in the validity of the initiative measure." That interest is by definition a generalized one, and it is precisely because proponents assert such an interest that they lack standing under our precedents.

> **Food for Thought**
>
> In what sense is the initiative authors' interest "generalized" if they have been given "authority to * * * assert legal arguments in defense of the state's interest in the validity of the initiative measure"? Does it make any difference that, under California law, taxpayers have broad standing to challenge the validity of laws?

And petitioners are plainly not agents of the State—"formal" or otherwise. As an initial matter, petitioners' newfound claim of agency is inconsistent with their representations to the District Court. When the proponents sought to intervene in this case, they did not purport to be agents of California. They argued instead that "no other party in this case w[ould] adequately represent their interests as official proponents." It was their "unique legal status" as official proponents—not an agency relationship with the people of California—that petitioners claimed "endow[ed] them with a significantly protectable interest" in ensuring that the District Court not "undo[ ] all that they ha[d] done in obtaining * * * enactment" of Proposition 8.

More to the point, the most basic features of an agency relationship are missing here. Agency requires more than mere authorization to assert a particular interest. "An essential element of agency is the principal's right to control the agent's actions." 1 Restatement (Third) of Agency § 1.01, Comment f (2005). Yet petitioners answer to no one; they decide for themselves, with no review, what arguments to make and how to make them. Unlike California's attorney general, they are not elected at regular intervals—or elected at all. No provision provides for their removal. As one *amicus* explains, "the proponents apparently have an unelected appointment for an unspecified period of time as defenders of the initiative, however and to whatever extent they choose to defend it."

Pet. ≠ state agents

"If the relationship between two persons is one of agency * * * , the agent owes a fiduciary obligation to the principal." But petitioners owe nothing of the sort to the people of California. Unlike California's elected officials, they have taken no oath of office. As the California Supreme Court explained, petitioners are bound simply by "the same ethical constraints that apply to all other parties in a legal proceeding." They are free to pursue a purely ideological commitment to the law's constitutionality without the need to take cognizance of resource constraints, changes in public opinion, or potential ramifications for other state priorities.

Finally, the California Supreme Court stated that "[t]he question of who should bear responsibility for any attorney fee award * * * is entirely distinct from the question" before it. But it is hornbook law that "a principal has a duty to indemnify the agent against expenses and other losses incurred by the agent in defending against actions brought by third parties if the agent acted with actual authority in taking the action challenged by the third party's suit." If the issue of fees is entirely distinct from the authority question, then authority cannot be based on agency.

Neither the California Supreme Court nor the Ninth Circuit ever described the proponents as agents of the State, and they plainly do not qualify as such.

IV

The dissent eloquently recounts the California Supreme Court's reasons for deciding that state law authorizes petitioners to defend Proposition 8. We do not "disrespect[ ]" or "disparage[ ]" those reasons. Nor do we question California's sovereign right to maintain an initiative process, or the right of initiative proponents to defend their initiatives in California courts, where Article III does not apply. But as the dissent acknowledges, standing in federal court is a question of federal law, not state law. And no matter its reasons, the fact that a State thinks a private party should have standing to seek relief for a generalized grievance cannot override our settled law to the contrary.

The Article III requirement that a party invoking the jurisdiction of a federal court seek relief for a personal, particularized injury serves vital interests going to the role of the Judiciary in our system of separated powers. "Refusing to entertain generalized grievances ensures that * * * courts exercise power that is judicial in nature," and ensures that the Federal Judiciary respects "the proper—and properly limited—role of the courts in a democratic society[.]" States cannot alter that role simply by issuing to private parties who otherwise lack standing a ticket to the federal courthouse.

* * *

We have never before upheld the standing of a private party to defend the constitutionality of a state statute when state officials have chosen not to. We decline to do so for the first time here.

Because petitioners have not satisfied their burden to demonstrate standing to appeal the judgment of the District Court, the Ninth Circuit was without jurisdiction to consider the appeal. The judgment of the Ninth Circuit is vacated, and the case is remanded with instructions to dismiss the appeal for lack of jurisdiction.

It is so ordered.

> **Practice Pointer**
>
> In theory, dismissal of the appeal left only the District Court's injunction against the enforcement of Proposition 8, but in practice the precise effect of the District Court's order became the subject of intense controversy in the California courts—an important reminder that, in litigation, it is possible to win the big battle and still lose the war.

Justice Kennedy, with whom Justice Thomas, Justice Alito and Justice Sotomayor join, dissenting.

The Court's opinion is correct to state, and the Supreme Court of California was careful to acknowledge, that a proponent's standing to defend an initiative in federal court is a question of federal law. Proper resolution of the justiciability question requires, in this case, a threshold determination of state law. The state-law question is how California defines and elaborates the status and authority of an initiative's proponents who seek to intervene in court to defend the initiative after its adoption by the electorate. Those state-law issues have been addressed in a meticulous and unanimous opinion by the Supreme Court of California.

Under California law, a proponent has the authority to appear in court and assert the State's interest in defending an enacted initiative when the public officials charged with that duty refuse to do so. The State deems such an appearance essential to the integrity of its initiative process. Yet the Court today concludes that this state-defined status and this state-conferred right fall short of meeting federal requirements because the proponents cannot point to a formal delegation of authority that tracks the requirements of the Restatement of Agency. But the State Supreme Court's definition of proponents' powers is binding on this Court. And that definition is fully sufficient to establish the standing and adversity that are requisites for justiciability under Article III of the United States Constitution.

In my view Article III does not require California, when deciding who may appear in court to defend an initiative on its behalf, to comply with the Restatement of Agency or with this Court's view of how a State should make its laws or structure its government. The Court's reasoning does not take into account the fundamental principles or the practical dynamics of the initiative system in California, which uses this mechanism to control and to bypass public officials—the same officials who would not defend the initiative, an injury the Court now leaves unremedied. The Court's decision also has implications for the 26 other States that use an initiative or popular referendum system and which, like California, may choose to have initiative proponents stand in for the State when public officials decline to defend an initiative in litigation. In my submission, the Article III requirement for a justiciable case or controversy does not prevent proponents from having their day in court.

These are the premises for this respectful dissent.

I

As the Court explains, the State of California sustained a concrete injury, sufficient to satisfy the requirements of Article III, when a United States District Court nullified a portion of its State Constitution. To determine whether justiciability continues in appellate proceedings after the State Executive acquiesced in the District Court's adverse judgment, it is necessary to ascertain what persons, if any, have "authority under state law to represent the State's interests" in federal court.

As the Court notes, the California Elections Code does not on its face prescribe in express terms the duties or rights of proponents once the initiative becomes law. If that were the end of the matter, the Court's analysis would have somewhat more force. But it is not the end of the matter. It is for California, not this Court, to determine whether and to what extent the Elections Code provisions are instructive and relevant in determining the authority of proponents to assert the State's interest in postenactment judicial proceedings. And it is likewise not for this Court to say that a State must determine the substance and meaning of its laws by statute, or by judicial decision, or by a combination of the two. That, too, is for the State to decide.

This Court, in determining the substance of state law, is "bound by a state court's construction of a state statute." And the Supreme Court of California, in response to the certified question submitted to it in this case, has determined that State Elections Code provisions directed to initiative proponents do inform and instruct state law respecting the rights and status of proponents in postelection judicial proceedings. Here, in reliance on these statutes and the California Constitution, the State Supreme Court has held that proponents do have authority "under California law to appear and assert the state's interest in the initiative's validity and appeal a judgment invalidating the measure when the public officials who ordinarily defend the measure or appeal such a judgment decline to do so."

The reasons the Supreme Court of California gave for its holding have special relevance in the context of determining whether proponents have the authority to seek a federal-court remedy for the State's concrete, substantial, and continuing injury. As a class, official proponents are a small, identifiable group. Because many of their decisions must be unanimous, they are necessarily few in number. Their identities are public. Their commitment is substantial. They know and understand the purpose and operation of the proposed law, an important requisite in defending initiatives on complex matters such as taxation and insurance. Having gone to great lengths to convince voters to enact an initiative, they have a stake in the outcome and the necessary commitment to provide zealous advocacy.

Thus, in California, proponents play a "unique role * * * in the initiative process." They "have a unique relationship to the voter-approved measure that makes them especially likely to be reliable and vigorous advocates for the measure and to be so viewed by those whose votes secured the initiative's enactment into law." * * * Proponents' authority under state law is not a contrivance. It is not a fictional construct. It is the product of the California Constitution and the California Elections Code. There is no basis for this Court to set aside the California Supreme Court's determination of state law.

* * *

II

A

The Court concludes that proponents lack sufficient ties to the state government. It notes that they "are not elected," "answer to no one," and lack " 'a fiduciary obligation' " to the State. But what the Court deems deficiencies in the proponents' connection to the State government, the State Supreme Court saw as essential qualifications to defend the initiative system. The very object of the initiative system is to establish a lawmaking process that does not depend upon state officials. In California, the popular initiative is necessary to implement "the theory that all power of government ultimately resides in the people." The right to adopt initiatives has been described by the California courts as "one of the most precious rights of [the State's] democratic process." That historic role for the initiative system "grew out of dissatisfaction with the then governing public officials and a widespread belief that the people had lost control of the political process." The initiative's "primary purpose," then, "was to afford the people the ability to propose and to adopt constitutional amendments or statutory provisions that their elected public officials had refused or declined to adopt."

The California Supreme Court has determined that this purpose is undermined if the very officials the initiative process seeks to circumvent are the only parties who can defend an enacted initiative when it is challenged in a legal proceeding. Giving the Governor and attorney general this *de facto* veto will erode one of the cornerstones of the State's governmental structure. And in light of the frequency with which initiatives' opponents resort to litigation, the impact of that veto could be substantial. As a consequence, California finds it necessary to vest the responsibility and right to defend a voter-approved initiative in the initiative's proponents when the State Executive declines to do so.

> **Food for Thought**
>
> Why does Justice Kennedy think that it is the responsibility of the federal judiciary to protect the operation of state initiative systems? If California wanted to stop its governor and attorney general from subverting the initiative system, surely it could provide for the impeachment of such executive officers when they fail to defend initiatives in court, could it not?

Yet today the Court demands that the State follow the Restatement of Agency. There are reasons, however, why California might conclude that a conventional agency relationship is inconsistent with the history, design, and purpose of the initiative process. The State may not wish to associate itself with proponents or their views outside of the "extremely narrow and limited" context of this litigation, or to bear the cost of proponents' legal fees. The State may also wish to avoid the odd conflict of having a formal agent of the State (the initiative's proponent) arguing in favor of a law's validity while state officials (*e.g.*, the attorney general) contend in the same proceeding that it should be found invalid.

Furthermore, it is not clear who the principal in an agency relationship would be. It would make little sense if it were the Governor or attorney general, for that would frustrate the initiative system's purpose of circumventing elected officials who fail or refuse to effect the public will. If there is to be a principal, then, it must be the people of California, as the ultimate sovereign in the State. But the Restatement may offer no workable example of an agent representing a principal composed of nearly 40 million residents of a State.

And if the Court's concern is that the proponents are unaccountable, that fear is neither well founded nor sufficient to overcome the contrary judgment of the State Supreme Court. It must be remembered that both elected officials and initiative proponents receive their authority to speak for the State of California directly from the people. The Court apparently believes that elected officials are acceptable "agents" of the State, but they are no more subject to ongoing supervision of their principal— *i.e.,* the people of the State—than are initiative proponents. At most, a Governor or attorney general can be recalled or voted out of office in a subsequent election, but proponents, too, can have their authority terminated or their initiative overridden by a subsequent ballot measure. Finally, proponents and their attorneys, like all other litigants and counsel who appear before a federal court, are subject to duties of candor, decorum, and respect for the tribunal and co-parties alike, all of which guard against the possibility that initiative proponents will somehow fall short of the appropriate standards for federal litigation.

B

Contrary to the Court's suggestion, this Court's precedents do not indicate that a formal agency relationship is necessary. In *Karcher v. May* (1987), the Speaker of the New Jersey Assembly (Karcher) and President of the New Jersey Senate (Orechio) intervened in support of a school moment-of-silence law that the State's Governor and attorney general declined to defend in court. In considering the question of standing, the Court looked to New Jersey law to determine whether Karcher and Orechio "had authority under state law to represent the State's interest in both the District Court and Court of Appeals." The Court concluded that they did. Because the "New Jersey Supreme Court ha[d] granted applications of the Speaker of the General Assembly and the President of the Senate to intervene as parties-respondent on behalf of the legislature in defense of a legislative enactment," the *Karcher* Court held that standing had been proper in the District Court and Court of Appeals. By the time the case arrived in this Court, Karcher and Orechio had lost their presiding legislative offices, without which they lacked the authority to represent the State under New Jersey law. This, the Court held, deprived them of standing. Here, by contrast, proponents' authority under California law is not contingent on officeholder status, so their standing is unaffected by the fact that they "hold no office" in California's Government

Arizonans for Official English v. Arizona (1997), is consistent with the premises of this dissent, not with the rationale of the Court's opinion. There, the Court noted its serious doubts as to the aspiring defenders' standing because there was "no Arizona law appointing initiative sponsors as agents of the people of Arizona to defend, in lieu of public officials, the constitutionality of initiatives made law of the State." The Court did use the word "agents"; but, read in context, it is evident that the Court's intention was not to demand a formal agency relationship in compliance with the Restatement. Rather, the Court used the term as shorthand for a party whom "state law authorizes" to "represent the State's interests" in court.

Both the Court of Appeals and the Supreme Court of California were mindful of these precedents and sought to comply with them. The state court, noting the importance of *Arizonans*, expressed its understanding that "the high court's doubts as to the official initiative proponents' standing in that case were based, at least in substantial part, on the fact that the court was not aware of any 'Arizona law appointing initiative sponsors as agents of the people of Arizona to defend * * * the constitutionality of initiatives made law of the State.' " Based on this passage, it concluded that "nothing in [*Arizonans for Official English*] indicates that if a state's law does authorize the official proponents of an initiative to assert the state's interest in the validity of a challenged state initiative when the public officials who ordinarily assert that interest have declined to do so, the proponents would not have standing to assert the state's interest in the initiative's validity in a federal lawsuit."

The Court of Appeals, too, was mindful of this requirement. Although that panel divided on the proper resolution of the merits of this case, it was unanimous in concluding that proponents satisfy the requirements of Article III. Its central premise, ignored by the Court today, was that the "State's highest court [had] held that California law provides precisely what the *Arizonans* Court found lacking in Arizona law: it confers on the official proponents of an initiative the authority to assert the State's interests in defending the constitutionality of that initiative, where state officials who would ordinarily assume that responsibility choose not to do so." ([M]ajority opinion). The Court of Appeals and the State Supreme Court did not ignore *Arizonans for Official English*; they were faithful to it. * * *

III

There is much irony in the Court's approach to justiciability in this case. A prime purpose of justiciability is to ensure vigorous advocacy, yet the Court insists upon litigation conducted by state officials whose preference is to lose the case. The doctrine is meant to ensure that courts are responsible and constrained in their power, but the Court's opinion today means that a single district court can make a decision with far-reaching effects that cannot be reviewed. And rather than honor the principle that justiciability exists to allow disputes of public policy to be resolved by the political process rather than the courts, here the Court refuses to allow a State's authorized representatives to defend the outcome of a democratic election.

The Court's opinion disrespects and disparages both the political process in California and the well-stated opinion of the California Supreme Court in this case. The California Supreme Court, not this Court, expresses concern for vigorous representation; the California Supreme Court, not this Court, recognizes the necessity to avoid conflicts of interest; the California Supreme Court, not this Court, comprehends the real interest at stake in this litigation and identifies the most proper party to defend that interest. The California Supreme Court's opinion reflects a better understanding of the dynamics and principles of Article III than does this Court's opinion.

Of course, the Court must be cautious before entering a realm of controversy where the legal community and society at large are still formulating ideas and approaches to a most difficult subject. But it is shortsighted to misconstrue principles of justiciability to avoid that subject. As the California Supreme Court recognized, "the question before us involves a fundamental procedural issue that may arise with respect to *any* initiative measure, without regard to its subject matter." If a federal court must rule on a constitutional point that either confirms or rejects the will of the people expressed in an initiative, that is when it is most necessary, not least necessary, to insist on rules that ensure the most committed and vigorous adversary arguments to inform the rulings of the courts.

* * *

In the end, what the Court fails to grasp or accept is the basic premise of the initiative process. And it is this. The essence of democracy is that the right to make law rests in the people and flows to the government, not the other way around. Freedom resides first in the people without need of a grant from government. The California initiative process embodies these principles and has done so for over a century. "Through the structure of its government, and the character of those who exercise government authority, a State defines itself as sovereign." In California and the 26 other States that permit initiatives and popular referendums, the people have exercised their own inherent sovereign right to govern themselves. The Court today frustrates that choice by nullifying, for failure to comply with the Restatement of Agency, a State Supreme Court decision holding that state law authorizes an enacted initiative's proponents to defend the law if and when the State's usual legal advocates decline to do so. The Court's opinion fails to abide by precedent and misapplies basic principles of justiciability. Those errors necessitate this respectful dissent.

Food for Thought

Does the last sentence of the previous paragraph beg the question? Are the majority and dissent in this case not disagreeing about whether "a federal court must rule on a constitutional point"? The majority holds that the Court should not, and may not, rule on the merits of the constitutional question with the litigation in this posture, while the dissent believes that the Court should reach the merits.

Notes and Questions

1. Majority and dissent in Perry argue for judicial restraint in deference to democratic process. Can they both be right? The majority presumably wishes to leave states free to define marriage as they see fit, unfettered by an equal protection ruling. The dissent argues that failure to recognize standing in this case allows California's governor and attorney general to sabotage the state's initiative system, which verges on plebiscite democracy. Is "democracy" too indeterminate a concept to decide Perry or even to decide the justiciability of most challenges to the constitutionality of government action? After all, there may be multiple plausible views about what constitutes the "most democratic" course.

2. Preliminary to deciding whether petitioners (Prop. 8's authors) had standing to appeal, the Ninth Circuit asked the California Supreme Court whether the petitioners either had a "particularized interest in the statute's validity" or "authority to assert the State's interest in the initiative's validity." (Chapter 8 covers certification of state-law questions to state supreme courts more generally.) Because the California Supreme Court found that state law did clothe the petitioners with authority to represent the state's interest, the Ninth Circuit had no occasion to decide whether petitioners had a particularized interest in Prop. 8's validity.

The majority, to the contrary, does examine petitioners' interest and finds that petitioners' interest is undifferentiated from that of any other members of the public. Perhaps it is true that, if the governor and attorney general decline to challenge the judgment on appeal, no one else has standing to prosecute the appeal. Yet that is exactly what the "generalized grievance" doctrine holds—that no one has standing to sue for injuries common to all—and Chief Justice Roberts's opinion explicitly cites that doctrine in support of finding no standing.

In your opinion, did they? On the one hand, how is their interest different from anyone else in California who wishes the state to define marriage as only between persons of the opposite sex? On the other hand, as the dissent states, can one deny that the initiative's authors are "necessarily few in number" and that their "commitment is substantial" in terms of time and money, gathering signatures and paying the official fees?

Suppose that instead of the California Supreme Court's ruling on these petitioners' authority to represent the state's interest, California's constitution provided,

> With respect to any provision of the California Constitution or statutes that shall become law through the initiative and referendum process, in the event that the Attorney General shall decline to defend the constitutionality of such provision under the United States Constitution or the California Constitution, the proponents of the initiative shall represent the State of California in place of the Attorney General.

On the majority's reasoning, would the *Hollingsworth* petitioners then be able to proceed, or would the Article III problem remain? Bear in mind that the California Attorney General's authority to represent the state comes ultimately from the same state constitution.

3. A key component of the majority's reasoning is that the agency relationship between the state and the initiative's authors is insufficient to support an assignment of the state's interest. Is the majority assuming that Article III contains a body of agency law within it? If so, should the law of agency at the time of the framing and ratification control, rather than the modern third edition of the Restatement of Agency? Or does the majority instead operate on the assumption that it is free to fashion interstitial common law here, much in the way that federal courts look to state law for a statute of limitations when a federal statutory cause of action is silent on the limitations provision? On interstitial federal common law more generally, see Chapter 5, Section C.

The dissenters regret that the Court "demands that the State follow the Restatement of Agency." Do they ever offer an alternative description of the relationship they find so critical—*i.e.*, the one between the state and the initiative's authors? Justice Kennedy could have likened the initiative's authors to private attorneys general, who step into the state's shoes for limited litigation purposes. Can you think of a reason why the dissenters bypassed that analogy?

4. It remains to be seen whether any state can comply sufficiently with the Restatement of Agency to effectively confer standing on initiative authors to defend the legality of their work product in federal court. Normally lack of standing in federal court is not fatal to one's hopes for judicial vindication, as Article III does not apply in state court. The plaintiff can simply walk across the street, as it were. Where the standing of initiative proponents to defend their work is involved, however, the state courts will not generally be an option. Those challenging the federal constitutionality of state initiatives may bring their suits in federal court, and there is no device to remove such a case to state court. Initiative authors could take the litigating initiative in state court, suing for a declaration of validity, but those looking for a declaration of invalidity could remove to federal court. Thus, one might conclude that the finding of no standing in *Perry* is more serious than in most cases challenging the constitutionality of state action.

United States v. Windsor

Supreme Court of the United States, 2013.
133 S.Ct. 2675.

JUSTICE KENNEDY delivered the opinion of the Court.

Two women then resident in New York were married in a lawful ceremony in Ontario, Canada, in 2007. Edith Windsor and Thea Spyer returned to their home in New York City. When Spyer died in 2009, she left her entire estate to Windsor. Windsor sought to claim the estate tax exemption for surviving spouses. She was barred from doing so, however, by a federal law, the Defense of Marriage Act, which excludes a same-sex partner from the definition of "spouse" as that term is used in federal statutes. Windsor paid the taxes but filed suit to challenge the constitutionality of this provision. The United States District Court and the Court of Appeals ruled that this portion of the statute is unconstitutional and ordered the United States to pay Windsor a refund. This Court granted certiorari and now affirms the judgment in Windsor's favor.

I

In 1996, as some States were beginning to consider the concept of same-sex marriage and before any State had acted to permit it, Congress enacted the Defense of Marriage Act (DOMA). DOMA contains two operative sections: Section 2, which has not been challenged here, allows States to refuse to recognize same-sex marriages performed under the laws of other States.

Section 3 is at issue here. It amends the Dictionary Act in Title 1, § 7, of the United States Code to provide a federal definition of "marriage" and "spouse." Section 3 of DOMA provides as follows:

> In determining the meaning of any Act of Congress, or of any ruling, regulation, or interpretation of the various administrative bureaus and agencies of the United States, the word "marriage" means only a legal union between one man and one woman as husband and wife, and the word "spouse" refers only to a person of the opposite sex who is a husband or a wife.

§3 @ issue

The definitional provision does not by its terms forbid States from enacting laws permitting same-sex marriages or civil unions or providing state benefits to residents in that status. The enactment's comprehensive definition of marriage for purposes of all federal statutes and other regulations or directives covered by its terms, however, does control over 1,000 federal laws in which marital or spousal status is addressed as a matter of federal law.

Edith Windsor and Thea Spyer met in New York City in 1963 and began a long-term relationship. Windsor and Spyer registered as domestic partners when New York City gave that right to same-sex couples in 1993. Concerned about Spyer's health, the couple made the 2007 trip to Canada for their marriage, but they continued to reside in New York City. The State of New York deems their Ontario marriage to be a valid one.

Spyer died in February 2009, and left her entire estate to Windsor. Because DOMA denies federal recognition to same-sex spouses, Windsor did not qualify for the marital exemption from the federal estate tax, which excludes from taxation "any interest in property which passes or has passed from the decedent to his surviving spouse." Windsor paid $363,053 in estate taxes and sought a refund. The Internal Revenue Service denied the refund, concluding that, under DOMA, Windsor was not a "surviving spouse." Windsor commenced this refund suit in the United States District Court for the Southern District of New York. She contended that DOMA violates the guarantee of equal protection, as applied to the Federal Government through the Fifth Amendment.

> **Practice Pointer**
>
> If one pays a disputed amount of federal income tax under protest, one may sue in United States District Court for a refund. If one refuses to pay the amount, he or she is relegated to United States Tax Court, which is not an Article III tribunal.

While the tax refund suit was pending, the Attorney General of the United States notified the Speaker of the House of Representatives, pursuant to 28 U.S.C. § 530D, that the Department of Justice would no longer defend the constitutionality of DOMA's § 3. Noting that "the Department has previously defended DOMA against * * * challenges involving legally married same-sex couples," the Attorney General informed Congress that "the President has concluded that given a number of factors, including a documented history of discrimination, classifications based on sexual orientation should be subject to a heightened standard of scrutiny." The Department of Justice has submitted many § 530D letters over the years refusing to defend laws it deems unconstitutional, when, for instance, a federal court has rejected the Government's defense of a statute and has issued a judgment against it. This case is unusual, however, because the § 530D letter was not preceded by an adverse judgment. The letter instead reflected the Executive's own conclusion, relying on a definition still being debated and considered in the courts, that heightened equal protection scrutiny should apply to laws that classify on the basis of sexual orientation.

Although "the President * * * instructed the Department not to defend the statute in *Windsor*," he also decided "that Section 3 will continue to be enforced by the Executive Branch" and that the United States had an "interest in providing

Congress a full and fair opportunity to participate in the litigation of those cases." The stated rationale for this dual-track procedure (determination of unconstitutionality coupled with ongoing enforcement) was to "recogniz[e] the judiciary as the final arbiter of the constitutional claims raised."

Food for Thought

Justice Kennedy seems to praise the President for leaving the merits to the judiciary on the ground that the courts should be the "final arbiter" of the constitutional question. But there is another possibility: the President could be trying to deflect political responsibility for a divisible social issue onto the judiciary.

In response to the notice from the Attorney General, the Bipartisan Legal Advisory Group (BLAG) of the House of Representatives voted to intervene in the litigation to defend the constitutionality of § 3 of DOMA. The Department of Justice did not oppose limited intervention by BLAG. The District Court denied BLAG's motion to enter the suit as of right, on the rationale that the United States already was represented by the Department of Justice. The District Court, however, did grant intervention by BLAG as an interested party.

On the merits of the tax refund suit, the District Court ruled against the United States. It held that § 3 of DOMA is unconstitutional and ordered the Treasury to refund the tax with interest. Both the Justice Department and BLAG filed notices of appeal, and the Solicitor General filed a petition for certiorari before judgment. Before this Court acted on the petition, the Court of Appeals for the Second Circuit affirmed the District Court's judgment. It applied heightened scrutiny to classifications based on sexual orientation, as both the Department and Windsor had urged. The United States has not complied with the judgment. Windsor has not received her refund, and the Executive Branch continues to enforce § 3 of DOMA.

In granting certiorari on the question of the constitutionality of § 3 of DOMA, the Court requested argument on two additional questions: whether the United States' agreement with Windsor's legal position precludes further review and whether BLAG has standing to appeal the case. All parties agree that the Court has jurisdiction to decide this case; and, with the case in that framework, the Court appointed Professor Vicki Jackson as *amicus curiae* to argue the position that the Court lacks jurisdiction to hear the dispute. She has ably discharged her duties.

FYI

It is not uncommon for the Court to appoint a prominent lawyer to argue an important position not represented by any of the parties.

* * *

II

It is appropriate to begin by addressing whether either the Government or BLAG, or both of them, were entitled to appeal to the Court of Appeals and later to seek certiorari and appear as parties here.

There is no dispute that when this case was in the District Court it presented a concrete disagreement between opposing parties, a dispute suitable for judicial resolution. "[A] taxpayer has standing to challenge the collection of a specific tax assessment as unconstitutional; being forced to pay such a tax causes a real and immediate economic injury to the individual taxpayer." ([E]mphasis deleted). Windsor suffered a redressable injury when she was required to pay estate taxes from which, in her view, she was exempt but for the alleged invalidity of § 3 of DOMA.

The decision of the Executive not to defend the constitutionality of § 3 in court while continuing to deny refunds and to assess deficiencies does introduce a complication. Even though the Executive's current position was announced before the District Court entered its judgment, the Government's agreement with Windsor's position would not have deprived the District Court of jurisdiction to entertain and resolve the refund suit; for her injury (failure to obtain a refund allegedly required by law) was concrete, persisting, and unredressed. The Government's position—agreeing with Windsor's legal contention but refusing to give it effect—meant that there was a justiciable controversy between the parties, despite what the claimant would find to be an inconsistency in that stance. Windsor, the Government, BLAG, and the *amicus* appear to agree upon that point. The disagreement is over the standing of the parties, or aspiring parties, to take an appeal in the Court of Appeals and to appear as parties in further proceedings in this Court.

The *amicus'* position is that, given the Government's concession that § 3 is unconstitutional, once the District Court ordered the refund the case should have ended; and the *amicus* argues the Court of Appeals should have dismissed the appeal. The *amicus* submits that once the President agreed with Windsor's legal position and the District Court issued its judgment, the parties were no longer adverse. From this standpoint the United States was a prevailing party below, just as Windsor was. Accordingly, the *amicus* reasons, it is inappropriate for this Court to grant certiorari and proceed to rule on the merits; for the United States seeks no redress from the judgment entered against it.

This position, however, elides the distinction between two principles: the jurisdictional requirements of Article III and the prudential limits on its exercise. The latter are "essentially matters of judicial self-governance." The Court has kept these two strands separate: "Article III standing, which enforces the Constitution's case-or-controversy requirement, and prudential standing, which embodies 'judicially self-imposed limits on the exercise of federal jurisdiction.' "

Food for Thought

The Court's statement that the constitutional and prudential strands have been kept separate involves some wishful thinking. For example, the Court has sometimes said that the "prohibition against generalized grievances" is rooted in Article III; other times it has said that it is prudential. In *Federal Election Commission v. Akins*, the Court explicitly acknowledged the conflict and refused to resolve it.

The requirements of Article III standing are familiar:

> First, the plaintiff must have suffered an "injury in fact"—an invasion of a legally protected interest which is (a) concrete and particularized, and (b) "actual or imminent, not 'conjectural or hypothetical.' " Second, there must be a causal connection between the injury and the conduct complained of—the injury has to be "fairly * * * trace[able] to the challenged action of the defendant, and not * * * th[e] result [of] the independent action of some third party not before the court." Third, it must be "likely," as opposed to merely "speculative," that the injury will be "redressed by a favorable decision." ([F]ootnote and citations omitted).

Rules of prudential standing, by contrast, are more flexible "rule[s] * * * of federal appellate practice," designed to protect the courts from "decid[ing] abstract questions of wide public significance even [when] other governmental institutions may be more competent to address the questions and even though judicial intervention may be unnecessary to protect individual rights."

In this case the United States retains a stake sufficient to support Article III jurisdiction on appeal and in proceedings before this Court. The judgment in question orders the United States to pay Windsor the refund she seeks. An order directing the Treasury to pay money is "a real and immediate economic injury," indeed as real and immediate as an order directing an individual to pay a tax. That the Executive may welcome this order to pay the refund if it is accompanied by the constitutional ruling it wants does not eliminate the injury to the national Treasury if payment is made, or to the taxpayer if it is not. The judgment orders the United States to pay money that it would not disburse but for the court's order. The Government of the United States has a valid legal argument that it is injured even if the Executive disagrees with § 3 of DOMA, which results in Windsor's liability for the

Food for Thought

But hasn't the government inflicted the injury on itself by simply refusing to pay the refund?

tax. Windsor's ongoing claim for funds that the United States refuses to pay thus establishes a controversy sufficient for Article III jurisdiction. It would be a different case if the Executive had taken the further step of paying Windsor the refund to which she was entitled under the District Court's ruling.

This Court confronted a comparable case in *INS v. Chadha* (1983). A statute by its terms allowed one House of Congress to order the Immigration and Naturalization Service (INS) to deport the respondent Chadha. There, as here, the Executive determined that the statute was unconstitutional, and "the INS presented the Executive's views on the constitutionality of the House action to the Court of Appeals." The INS, however, continued to abide by the statute, and "the INS brief to the Court of Appeals did not alter the agency's decision to comply with the House action ordering deportation of Chadha." This Court held "that the INS was sufficiently aggrieved by the Court of Appeals decision prohibiting it from taking action it would otherwise take," regardless of whether the agency welcomed the judgment. The necessity of a "case or controversy" to satisfy Article III was defined as a requirement that the Court's " 'decision will have real meaning: if we rule for Chadha, he will not be deported; if we uphold [the statute], the INS will execute its order and deport him.' " This conclusion was not dictum. It was a necessary predicate to the Court's holding that "prior to Congress' intervention, there was adequate Art. III adverseness." The holdings of cases are instructive, and the words of *Chadha* make clear its holding that the refusal of the Executive to provide the relief sought suffices to preserve a justiciable dispute as required by Article III. In short, even where "the Government largely agree[s] with the opposing party on the merits of the controversy," there is sufficient adverseness and an "adequate basis for jurisdiction in the fact that the Government intended to enforce the challenged law against that party."

It is true that "[a] party who receives all that he has sought generally is not aggrieved by the judgment affording the relief and cannot appeal from it." But this rule "does not have its source in the jurisdictional limitations of Art. III. In an appropriate case, appeal may be permitted * * * at the behest of the party who has prevailed on the merits, so long as that party retains a stake in the appeal satisfying the requirements of Art. III."

While these principles suffice to show that this case presents a justiciable controversy under Article III, the prudential problems inherent in the Executive's unusual position require some further discussion. The Executive's agreement with Windsor's legal argument raises the risk that instead of a " 'real, earnest and vital controversy,' " the Court faces a "friendly, non-adversary, proceeding * * * [in which] 'a party beaten in the legislature [seeks to] transfer to the courts an inquiry as to the constitutionality of the legislative act.' " Even when Article III permits the exercise of federal jurisdiction, prudential considerations demand that the

Court insist upon "that concrete adverseness which sharpens the presentation of issues upon which the court so largely depends for illumination of difficult constitutional questions."

There are, of course, reasons to hear a case and issue a ruling even when one party is reluctant to prevail in its position. Unlike Article III requirements—which must be satisfied by the parties before judicial consideration is appropriate—the relevant prudential factors that counsel against hearing this case are subject to "countervailing considerations [that] may outweigh the concerns underlying the usual reluctance to exert judicial power." One consideration is the extent to which adversarial presentation of the issues is assured by the participation of *amici curiae* prepared to defend with vigor the constitutionality of the legislative act. With respect to this prudential aspect of standing as well, the *Chadha* Court encountered a similar situation. It noted that "there may be prudential, as opposed to Art. III, concerns about sanctioning the adjudication of [this case] in the absence of any participant supporting the validity of [the statute]. The Court of Appeals properly dispelled any such concerns by inviting and accepting briefs from both Houses of Congress." *Chadha* was not an anomaly in this respect. The Court adopts the practice of entertaining arguments made by an *amicus* when the Solicitor General confesses error with respect to a judgment below, even if the confession is in effect an admission that an Act of Congress is unconstitutional.

In the case now before the Court the attorneys for BLAG present a substantial argument for the constitutionality of § 3 of DOMA. BLAG's sharp adversarial presentation of the issues satisfies the prudential concerns that otherwise might counsel against hearing an appeal from a decision with which the principal parties agree. Were this Court to hold that prudential rules require it to dismiss the case, and, in consequence, that the Court of Appeals erred in failing to dismiss it as well, extensive litigation would ensue. The district courts in 94 districts throughout the Nation would be without precedential guidance not only in tax refund suits but also in cases involving the whole of DOMA's sweep involving over 1,000 federal statutes and a myriad of federal regulations. For instance, the opinion of the Court of Appeals for the First Circuit, addressing the validity of DOMA in a case involving regulations of the Department of Health and Human Services, likely would be vacated with instructions to dismiss, its ruling and guidance also then erased. Rights and privileges of hundreds of thousands of persons would be adversely affected, pending a case in which all prudential concerns about justiciability are absent. That numerical prediction may not be certain, but it is certain that the cost in judicial resources and expense of litigation for all persons adversely affected would be immense. True, the very extent of DOMA's mandate means that at some point a case likely would arise without the prudential concerns raised here; but the costs, uncertainties, and alleged harm and injuries likely would continue for a time measured in years before the issue is resolved. In these unusual and urgent circumstances, the very term "prudential" counsels that it is a proper exercise of the Court's responsibility to take jurisdiction. For these reasons, the prudential and Article III requirements are met here; and, as a consequence, the Court need not decide whether BLAG would have standing to challenge the District Court's ruling and its affirmance in the Court of Appeals on BLAG's own authority.

> **Food for Thought**
>
> Note that the considerations in the preceding paragraph substantially overlap the Court's criteria for the grant of certiorari.

The Court's conclusion that this petition may be heard on the merits does not imply that no difficulties would ensue if this were a common practice in ordinary cases. The Executive's failure to defend the constitutionality of an Act of Congress based on a constitutional theory not yet established in judicial decisions has created a procedural dilemma. On the one hand, as noted, the Government's agreement with Windsor raises questions about the propriety of entertaining a suit in which it seeks affirmance of an order invalidating a federal law and ordering the United States to pay money. On the other hand, if the Executive's agreement with a plaintiff that a law is unconstitutional is enough to preclude judicial review, then the Supreme Court's primary role in determining the constitutionality of a law that has inflicted real injury on a plaintiff who has brought a justiciable legal claim would become only secondary to the President's. This would undermine the clear dictate of the separation-of-powers principle that "when an Act of Congress is alleged to conflict with the Constitution, '[i]t is emphatically the province and duty of the judicial department to say what the law is.' " Similarly, with respect to the legislative power, when Congress has passed a statute and a President has signed it, it poses grave challenges to the separation of powers for the Executive at a particular moment to be able to nullify Congress' enactment solely on its own initiative and without any determination from the Court.

The Court's jurisdictional holding, it must be underscored, does not mean the arguments for dismissing this dispute on prudential grounds lack substance. Yet the difficulty the Executive faces should be acknowledged. When the Executive makes a principled determination that a statute is unconstitutional, it faces a difficult choice. Still, there is no suggestion here that it is appropriate for the Executive as a matter of course to challenge statutes in the judicial forum rather than making the case to Congress for their amendment or repeal. The integrity of the political process would be at risk if difficult constitutional issues were simply referred to the Court as a routine exercise. But this case is not routine. And the capable defense of the law by BLAG ensures that these prudential issues do not cloud the merits question, which is one of immediate importance to the Federal Government and to hundreds of thousands of persons. These circumstances support the Court's decision to proceed to the merits.

* * *

The class to which DOMA directs its restrictions and restraints are those persons who are joined in same-sex marriages made lawful by the State. DOMA singles out a class of persons deemed by a State entitled to recognition and protection to enhance their own liberty. It imposes a disability on the class by refusing to acknowledge a status the State finds to be dignified and proper. DOMA instructs all federal officials, and indeed all persons with whom same-sex couples interact, including their own children, that their marriage is less worthy than the marriages of others. The federal statute is invalid, for no legitimate purpose overcomes the purpose and effect to disparage and to injure those whom the State, by its marriage laws, sought to protect in personhood and dignity. By seeking to displace this protection and treating those persons as living in marriages less respected than others, the federal statute is in violation of the Fifth Amendment. This opinion and its holding are confined to those lawful marriages.

The judgment of the Court of Appeals for the Second Circuit is affirmed.

It is so ordered.

JUSTICE SCALIA, with whom JUSTICE THOMAS joins, and with whom THE CHIEF JUSTICE joins as to Part I, dissenting.

This case is about power in several respects. It is about the power of our people to govern themselves, and the power of this Court to pronounce the law. Today's opinion aggrandizes the latter, with the predictable consequence of diminishing the former. We have no power to decide this case. And even if we did, we have no power under the Constitution to invalidate this democratically adopted legislation. The Court's errors on both points spring forth from the same diseased root: an exalted conception of the role of this institution in America.

I

A

The Court is eager—*hungry*—to tell everyone its view of the legal question at the heart of this case. Standing in the way is an obstacle, a technicality of little interest to anyone but the people of We the People, who created it as a barrier against judges' intrusion into their lives. They gave judges, in Article III, only the "judicial Power," a power to decide not abstract questions but real, concrete "Cases" and "Controversies." Yet the plaintiff and the Government agree entirely on what should happen in this lawsuit. They agree that the court below got it right; and they agreed in the court below that the court below that one got it right as well. What, then, are we *doing* here?

The answer lies at the heart of the jurisdictional portion of today's opinion, where a single sentence lays bare the majority's vision of our role. The Court says that we have the power to decide this case because if we did not, then our "primary role in determining the constitutionality of a law" (at least one that "has inflicted real injury on a plaintiff") would "become only secondary to the President's." But wait, the reader wonders—Windsor won below, and so *cured* her injury, and the President was glad to see it. True, says the majority, but judicial review must march on regardless, lest we "undermine the clear dictate of the separation-of-powers principle that when an Act of Congress is alleged to conflict with the Constitution, it is emphatically the province and duty of the judicial department to say what the law is." ([I]nternal quotation marks and brackets omitted).

That is jaw-dropping. It is an assertion of judicial supremacy over the people's Representatives in Congress and the Executive. It envisions a Supreme Court standing (or rather enthroned) at the apex of government, empowered to decide all constitutional questions, always and everywhere "primary" in its role.

This image of the Court would have been unrecognizable to those who wrote and ratified our national charter. They knew well the dangers of "primary" power, and so created branches of government that would be "perfectly coordinate by the terms of their common commission," none of which branches could "pretend to an exclusive or superior right of settling the boundaries between their respective powers." THE FEDERALIST, NO. 49 (J. Madison). The people did this to protect themselves. They did it to guard their right to self-rule against the black-robed supremacy that today's majority finds so attractive. So it was that Madison could confidently state, with no fear of contradiction, that there was nothing of "greater intrinsic value" or "stamped with the authority of more enlightened patrons of liberty" than a government of separate and coordinate powers.

For this reason we are quite forbidden to say what the law is whenever (as today's opinion asserts) " 'an Act of Congress is alleged to conflict with the Constitution.' " We can do so only when that allegation will determine the outcome of a lawsuit, and is contradicted by the other party. The "judicial Power" is not, as the majority believes, the power " 'to say what the law is,' " giving the Supreme Court the "primary role in determining the constitutionality of laws." The majority must have in mind one of the foreign constitutions that pronounces such primacy for its constitutional court and allows that primacy to be exercised in contexts other than a lawsuit. The judicial power as Americans have understood it (and their English ancestors before them) is the power to adjudicate, with conclusive effect, disputed government claims (civil or criminal) against private persons, and disputed claims by private persons against the government or other private persons. Sometimes (though not always) the parties before the court disagree not with regard to the facts of their case (or not *only* with regard to the facts) but with regard to the applicable law—in which event (and *only* in which event) it becomes the " 'province and duty of the judicial department to say what the law is.' "

In other words, declaring the compatibility of state or federal laws with the Constitution is not only not the "primary role" of this Court, it is not a separate, free-standing role *at all.* We perform that role incidentally—by accident, as it were—when that is necessary to resolve the dispute before us. Then, and only then, does it become " 'the province and duty of the judicial department to say what the law is.' " That is why, in 1793, we politely declined the Washington Administration's request to "say what the law is" on a particular treaty matter that was not the subject of a concrete legal controversy. And that is why, as our opinions have said, some questions of law will *never* be presented to this Court, because there will never be anyone with standing to bring a lawsuit. As Justice Brandeis put it, we cannot "pass upon the constitutionality of legislation in a friendly, non-adversary, proceeding"; absent a " 'real, earnest and vital controversy between individuals,' " we have neither any work to do nor any power to do it. Our authority begins and ends with the need to adjudge the rights of an injured party who stands before us seeking redress.

Food for Thought

Isn't it possible that the role of the United States Supreme Court has changed since the Founding -- that it had to change to accommodate the massive growth of federal law, the federal government, and the Nation? And isn't it possible that the text of Article III is sufficiently broad to accommodate that change?

That is completely absent here. Windsor's injury was cured by the judgment in her favor. And while, in ordinary circumstances, the United States is injured by a directive to pay a tax refund, this suit is far from ordinary. Whatever injury the United States has suffered will surely not be redressed by the action that it, as a litigant, asks us to take. The final sentence of the Solicitor General's brief on the merits reads: "For the foregoing reasons, the judgment of the court of appeals *should be affirmed.*" ([E]mphasis added). That will not cure the Government's injury, but carve it into stone. One could spend many fruitless afternoons ransacking our library for any other petitioner's brief seeking an affirmance of the judgment against it. What the petitioner United States asks us to do in the case before us is exactly what the respondent Windsor asks us to do: not to provide relief from the judgment below but to say that that judgment was correct. And the same was true in the Court of Appeals: Neither party sought to undo the judgment for Windsor, and so that court should have dismissed the appeal (just as we should dismiss) for lack of jurisdiction. Since both parties agreed with the judgment of the District Court for the Southern District of New York, the suit should have ended there. The further proceedings have been a contrivance, having no object in mind except to elevate a District Court judgment that has no precedential effect in other courts, to one that has precedential effect throughout the Second Circuit, and then (in this Court) precedential effect throughout the United States.

We have never before agreed to speak—to "say what the law is"—where there is no controversy before us. In the more than two centuries that this Court has existed as an institution, we have never suggested that we have the power to decide a question when every party agrees with both its nominal opponent *and the court below* on that question's answer. The United States reluctantly conceded that at oral argument.

The closest we have ever come to what the Court blesses today was our opinion in *INS v. Chadha* (1983). But in that case, two parties to the litigation disagreed with the position of the United States and with the court below: the House and Senate, which had intervened in the case. Because *Chadha* concerned the validity of a mode of congressional action—the one-house legislative veto—the House and Senate were threatened with destruction of what they claimed to be one of their institutional powers. The Executive choosing not to defend that power,[2] we permitted the House and Senate to intervene. Nothing like that is present here.

To be sure, the Court in *Chadha* said that statutory aggrieved-party status was "not altered by the fact that the Executive may agree with the holding that the statute in question is unconstitutional." But in a footnote to that statement, the Court acknowledged Article III's separate requirement of a "justiciable case or controversy," and stated that *this* requirement was satisfied "because of the presence of the two Houses of Congress as adverse parties." Later in its opinion, the *Chadha* Court remarked that the United States' announced intention to enforce the statute also sufficed to permit judicial review, even absent congressional participation. That remark is true, as a description of the judicial review conducted in the Court of Appeals, where the Houses of Congress had not intervened. (The case originated in the Court of Appeals.) There, absent a judgment setting aside the INS order, Chadha faced deportation. This passage of our opinion seems to be addressing that initial standing in the Court of Appeals, as indicated by its quotation from the lower court's opinion. But if it was addressing standing to pursue the appeal, the remark was both the purest dictum (as congressional intervention at that point made the required adverseness "beyond doubt,") and quite incorrect. When a private party has a judicial decree safely in hand to prevent his injury,

2 There the Justice Department's refusal to defend the legislation was in accord with its longstanding (and entirely reasonable) practice of declining to defend legislation that in its view infringes upon Presidential powers. There is no justification for the Justice Department's abandoning the law in the present case. The majority opinion makes a point of scolding the President for his "failure to defend the constitutionality of an Act of Congress based on a constitutional theory not yet established in judicial decisions." But the rebuke is tongue-in-cheek, for the majority gladly gives the President what he wants. Contrary to all precedent, it decides this case (and even decides it the way the President wishes) *despite* his abandonment of the defense and the consequent absence of a case or controversy.

additional judicial action requires that a party injured by the decree *seek to undo it*. In *Chadha*, the intervening House and Senate fulfilled that requirement. Here no one does.

The majority's discussion of the requirements of Article III bears no resemblance to our jurisprudence. It accuses the *amicus* (appointed to argue against our jurisdiction) of "elid[ing] the distinction between * * * the jurisdictional requirements of Article III and the prudential limits on its exercise." It then proceeds to call the requirement of adverseness a "prudential" aspect of standing. *Of standing*. That is incomprehensible. A plaintiff (or appellant) can have all the standing in the world—satisfying all three standing requirements of *Lujan* that the majority so carefully quotes—and yet no Article III controversy may be before the court. Article III requires not just a plaintiff (or appellant) who has standing to complain but *an opposing party* who denies the validity of the complaint. It is not the *amicus* that has done the eliding of distinctions, but the majority, calling the quite separate Article III requirement of adverseness between the parties an element (which it then pronounces a "prudential" element) of standing. The question here is not whether, as the majority puts it, "the United States retains a stake sufficient to support Article III jurisdiction," the question is whether there is any controversy (which requires *contradiction*) between the United States and Ms. Windsor. There is not.

I find it wryly amusing that the majority seeks to dismiss the requirement of party-adverseness as nothing more than a "prudential" aspect of the sole Article III requirement of standing. (Relegating a jurisdictional requirement to "prudential" status is a wondrous device, enabling courts to ignore the requirement whenever they believe it "prudent"—which is to say, a good idea.) Half a century ago, a Court similarly bent upon announcing its view regarding the constitutionality of a federal statute achieved that goal by effecting a remarkably similar *but completely opposite* distortion of the principles limiting our jurisdiction. The Court's notorious opinion in *Flast v. Cohen* (1968), held that *standing* was merely an element (which it pronounced to be a "prudential" element) of the sole Article III requirement of *adverseness*. We have been living with the chaos created by that power-grabbing decision ever since, as we will have to live with the chaos created by this one.

The authorities the majority cites fall miles short of supporting the counterintuitive notion that an Article III "controversy" can exist without disagreement between the parties. In *Deposit Guaranty Nat. Bank v. Roper* (1980), the District Court had entered judgment in the individual plaintiff's favor based on the defendant bank's offer to pay the full amount claimed. The plaintiff, however, sought to appeal the District Court's denial of class certification under Federal Rule of Civil Procedure 23. There was a continuing dispute between the parties concerning the issue raised on appeal. The same is true of the other case cited by the majority, *Camreta v. Greene* (2011). There the District Court found that the defendant state officers had violated the Fourth Amendment, but rendered judgment in their favor because they were entitled to official immunity, application of the Fourth Amendment to their conduct not having been clear at the time of violation. The officers sought to appeal the holding of Fourth Amendment violation, which would circumscribe their future conduct; the plaintiff continued to insist that a Fourth Amendment violation had occurred. The "prudential" discretion to which both those cases refer was the discretion to *deny* an appeal even when a live controversy exists—not the discretion to *grant* one when it does not. The majority can cite no case in which this Court entertained an appeal in which both parties urged us to affirm the judgment below. And that is because the existence of a controversy is not a "prudential" requirement that we have invented, but an essential element of an Article III case or controversy. The majority's notion that a case between friendly parties can be entertained so long as "adversarial presentation of the issues is assured by the participation of *amici curiae* prepared to defend with vigor" the other side of the issue, effects a breathtaking revolution in our Article III jurisprudence.

It may be argued that if what we say is true some Presidential determinations that statutes are unconstitutional will not be subject to our review. That is as it should be, when both the President and the plaintiff agree that the statute is unconstitutional. Where the Executive is enforcing an unconstitutional law, suit will of course lie; but if, in that suit, the Executive admits the unconstitutionality of the law, the litigation should end in an order or a consent decree enjoining enforcement. This suit saw the light of day only because the President enforced the Act (and thus gave Windsor standing to sue) even though he believed it unconstitutional. He could have equally chosen (more appropriately, some would say) neither to enforce nor to defend the statute he believed to be unconstitutional—in which event Windsor would not have been injured, the District Court could not have refereed this friendly scrimmage, and the Executive's determination of unconstitutionality would have escaped this Court's desire to blurt out its view of the law. The matter would have been left, as so many matters ought to be left, to a tug of war between the President and the Congress, which has innumerable means (up to and including impeachment) of compelling the President to enforce the laws it has written. Or the President could have evaded presentation of the constitutional issue to this Court simply by declining to appeal the District Court and Court of Appeals dispositions he agreed with. Be sure of this much: If a President wants to insulate his judgment of unconstitutionality from our review, he can. What the views urged in this dissent produce is not insulation from judicial review but insulation from Executive contrivance.

The majority brandishes the famous sentence from *Marbury v. Madison* (1803) that "[i]t is emphatically the province and duty of the judicial department to say what the law is." ([I]nternal quotation marks omitted). But that sentence neither says nor implies that it is *always* the province and duty of the Court to say what the law is—much less that its responsibility in that regard is a "primary" one. The very next sentence of Chief Justice Marshall's opinion makes the crucial qualification that today's majority ignores: "*Those who apply the rule to particular cases,* must of necessity expound and interpret that rule." ([E]mphasis added). Only when a "particular case" is before us—that is, a controversy that it is our business to resolve under Article III—do we have the province and duty to pronounce the law. For the views of our early Court more precisely addressing the question before us here, the majority ought instead to have consulted the opinion of Chief Justice Taney in *Lord v. Veazie* (1850):

> The objection in the case before us is * * * that the plaintiff and defendant have the same interest, and that interest adverse and in conflict with the interest of third persons, whose rights would be seriously affected if the question of law was decided in the manner that both of the parties to this suit desire it to be.
>
> A judgment entered under such circumstances, and for such purposes, is a mere form. The whole proceeding was in contempt of the court, and highly reprehensible * * * . A judgment in form, thus procured, in the eye of the law is no judgment of the court. It is a nullity, and no writ of error will lie upon it. This writ is, therefore, dismissed.

There is, in the words of *Marbury,* no "necessity [to] expound and interpret" the law in this case; just a desire to place this Court at the center of the Nation's life.

B

A few words in response to the theory of jurisdiction set forth in Justice Alito's dissent: Though less far reaching in its consequences than the majority's conversion of constitutionally required adverseness into a discretionary element of standing, the theory of that dissent similarly elevates the Court to the "primary" determiner of constitutional questions involving the separation of powers, and, to boot, increases the power of the most dangerous branch: the "legislative department," which by its nature "draw[s] all power into its impetuous vortex." The Federalist, No. 48, at 309 (J. Madison). Heretofore in our national history, the President's failure to "take Care that the Laws be faithfully executed," U.S. Const., Art. II, § 3, could only be brought before a judicial tribunal by someone whose concrete interests were harmed by that alleged failure. Justice Alito would create a system in which Congress can hale the Executive before the courts not only to vindicate its own institutional powers to act, but to correct a perceived inadequacy in the execution of its laws. This would lay to rest Tocqueville's praise of our judicial system as one which "intimately bind[s] the case made for the law with the case made for one man," one in which legislation is "no longer exposed to the daily aggression of the parties," and in which "[t]he political question that [the judge] must resolve is linked to the interest" of private litigants. That would be replaced by a system in which Congress and the Executive can pop immediately into court, in their institutional capacity, whenever the President refuses to implement a statute he believes to be unconstitutional, and whenever he implements a law in a manner that is not to Congress's liking.

* * *

II

For the reasons above, I think that this Court has, and the Court of Appeals had, no power to decide this suit. We should vacate the decision below and remand to the Court of Appeals for the Second Circuit, with instructions to dismiss the appeal. Given that the majority has volunteered its view of the merits, however, I proceed to discuss that as well.

* * *

Some will rejoice in today's decision, and some will despair at it; that is the nature of a controversy that matters so much to so many. But the Court has cheated both sides, robbing the winners of an honest victory, and the losers of the peace that comes from a fair defeat. We owed both of them better. I dissent.

JUSTICE ALITO, with whom JUSTICE THOMAS joins as to Parts II and III, dissenting.

* * *

I

I turn first to the question of standing. In my view, the United States clearly is not a proper petitioner in this case. The United States does not ask us to overturn the judgment of the court below or to alter that judgment in any way. Quite to the contrary, the United States argues emphatically in favor of the correctness of that judgment. We have never before reviewed a decision at the sole behest of a party that took such a position, and to do so would be to render an advisory opinion, in violation of Article III's dictates. For the reasons given in Justice Scalia's dissent, I do not find the Court's arguments to the contrary to be persuasive.

Whether the Bipartisan Legal Advisory Group of the House of Representatives (BLAG) has standing to petition is a much more difficult question. It is also a significantly closer question than whether the intervenors in Hollingsworth

v. Perry—which the Court also decides today—have standing to appeal. It is remarkable that the Court has simultaneously decided that the United States, which "receive[d] all that [it] ha[d] sought" below, is a proper petitioner in this case but that the intervenors in *Hollingsworth*, who represent the party that lost in the lower court, are not. In my view, both the *Hollingsworth* intervenors and BLAG have standing.[1]

A party invoking the Court's authority has a sufficient stake to permit it to appeal when it has " 'suffered an injury in fact' that is caused by 'the conduct complained of' and that 'will be redressed by a favorable decision.' " Camreta v. Greene (2011). In the present case, the House of Representatives, which has authorized BLAG to represent its interests in this matter, suffered just such an injury.

In INS v. Chadha (1983), the Court held that the two Houses of Congress were "proper parties" to file a petition in defense of the constitutionality of the one-house veto statute (internal quotation marks omitted). Accordingly, the Court granted and decided petitions by both the Senate and the House, in addition to the Executive's petition. That the two Houses had standing to petition is not surprising: The Court of Appeals' decision in *Chadha*, by holding the one-house veto to be unconstitutional, had limited Congress' power to legislate. In discussing Article III standing, the Court suggested that Congress suffered a similar injury whenever federal legislation it had passed was struck down, noting that it had "long held that Congress is the proper party to defend the validity of a statute when an agency of government, as a defendant charged with enforcing the statute, agrees with plaintiffs that the statute is inapplicable or unconstitutional."

The United States attempts to distinguish *Chadha* on the ground that it "involved an unusual statute that vested the House and the Senate themselves each with special procedural rights—namely, the right effectively to veto Executive action." But that is a distinction without a difference: just as the Court of Appeals decision that the *Chadha* Court affirmed impaired Congress' power by striking down the one-house veto, so the Second Circuit's decision here impairs Congress' legislative power by striking down an Act of Congress. The United States has not explained why the fact that the impairment at issue in *Chadha* was "special" or "procedural" has any relevance to whether Congress suffered an injury. Indeed, because legislating is Congress' central function, any impairment of that function is a more grievous injury than the impairment of a procedural add-on.

* * *

I appreciate the argument that the Constitution confers on the President alone the authority to defend federal law in litigation, but in my view, as I have

1 Our precedents make clear that, in order to support our jurisdiction, BLAG must demonstrate that it had Article III standing in its own right, quite apart from its status as an intervenor.

explained, that argument is contrary to the Court's holding in *Chadha,* and it is certainly contrary to the *Chadha* Court's endorsement of the principle that "Congress is the proper party to defend the validity of a statute" when the Executive refuses to do so on constitutional grounds.[3] Accordingly, in the narrow category of cases in which a court strikes down an Act of Congress and the Executive declines to defend the Act, Congress both has standing to defend the undefended statute and is a proper party to do so.

Notes and Questions

1. There were six votes to find standing in *Windsor*, on two distinct theories. The majority found that the United States suffered injury-in-fact and qualified for prudential standing on the strength of BLAG's adversary presentation. Justice Alito denied that the United States had standing, but he concluded that Congress had standing under the unusual circumstances. Only Justice Scalia, Justice Thomas and Chief Justice Roberts found no standing on anyone's part.

2. One point of disagreement between the majority and Justice Scalia was where adverseness fits into the standing equation. The majority characterized it as a prudential matter—a "flexible rule of federal appellate practice"—while Justice Scalia insisted that adverseness is at the core of Article III. The majority tried to win this argument by way of the negative implication canon, *expressio unius est exclusio alterius* (that which is not expressed is excluded). In Lujan v. Defenders of Wildlife (1992) the Court (speaking through Justice Scalia) listed three requirements of Article III standing: injury-in-fact, causation, and redressability. Because adverseness of the parties' positions did not appear in that list, the *Windsor* majority inferred that adverseness was not a requirement of Article III. Justice Scalia's response was that adverseness may not be a requirement for standing, but it is a prerequisite for a "case or controversy."

3. All the justices agreed on one point—the unusual posture of the case because of t. he combination of two facts: the administration conceded the invalidity of the statute but continued to. refuse to pay Windsor her refund. If the administration had conceded invalidity and paid the refund, there would be no case or controversy, as even the majority acknowledged. If the administration had refused to pay the refund and argued that the statute was valid, the government would clearly have had standing to appeal, and BLAG's participation would not have been necessary. But the administration quite plainly attempted to preserve judicial review by not paying the refund, even though it agreed with Windsor's claim.

---

3 Buckley v. Valeo (1976), is not to the contrary. The Court's statements there concerned enforcement, not defense.

Did the majority and dissent view the propriety of the administration's actions through different lenses? Justice Scalia stated:

> This suit saw the light of day only because the President enforced the Act (and thus gave Windsor standing to sue) even though he believed it unconstitutional. He could have equally chosen (more appropriately, some would say) neither to enforce nor to defend the statute he believed to be unconstitutional, *see* Presidential Authority to Decline to Execute Unconstitutional Statutes, 18 Op. Off. Legal Counsel[a] 199 (Nov. 2, 1994)—in which event Windsor would not have been injured, the District Court could not have refereed this friendly scrimmage, and the Executive's determination of unconstitutionality would have escaped this Court's desire to blurt out its view of the law.

Justice Kennedy's majority opinion seemed more sympathetic, if guarded:

> [T]he difficulty the Executive faces should be acknowledged. When the Executive makes a principled determination that a statute is unconstitutional, it faces a difficult choice. Still, there is no suggestion here that it is appropriate for the Executive as a matter of course to challenge statutes in the judicial forum rather than making the case to Congress for their amendment or repeal. The integrity of the political process would be at risk if difficult constitutional issues were simply referred to the Court as a routine exercise. But this case is not routine.

4. *Windsor* gets to the very roots of the justification for judicial review. In asserting that it would be unacceptable to leave the President as the sole arbiter of DOMA's constitutionality, Justice Kennedy's opinion for the Court invokes that most famous of sentences from *Marbury v. Madison:* "It is emphatically the province and duty of the judicial department to say what the law is." Justice Scalia accused the majority of not understanding the true meaning of this declaration:

> [T]hat sentence neither says nor implies that it is *always* the province and the duty of the Court to say what the law is—much less that its responsibility in that regard is a "primary" one. The very next sentence of Chief Justice Marshall's opinion makes the crucial qualification that today's majority ignores: "*Those who apply the rule to particular cases,* must of necessity expound and interpret that rule." Only when a "particular case" is before us—that is, a controversy that it is our business to resolve under Article III—do we have the province and duty to pronounce the law.

Justice Scalia's view of *Marbury* and judicial review is commonly associated with Justices Brandeis and Frankfurter, and widely held even today among the elites of the federal bench and bar. This view holds that pronouncements of law are a necessary evil—in the course of deciding concrete cases, courts cannot avoid resolving some legal questions along the way. Courts, including those of last resort, exist to resolve properly presented conflicts between truly adverse parties. Any declaration of law is incidental to the settlement of the dispute between the parties at bar. As Justice

---

a Justice Scalia once served in the Office of Legal Counsel.

Scalia stated in his dissent, "We perform that role incidentally—by accident, as it were—when that is necessary to resolve the dispute before us."

Justice Kennedy's opinion for the Court was less explicit about the theory of judicial review on which it relied. But there were clues. "[I]f the Executive's agreement with a plaintiff that a law is unconstitutional is enough to preclude judicial review," warned the Court, "then the Supreme Court's primary role in determining the constitutionality of a law that has inflicted real injury on a plaintiff who has brought a justiciable legal claim would become only secondary to the President's." Justice Scalia was unconcerned by this scenario: "That is as it should be."[1] Yet Justices Scalia and Thomas and Chief Justice Roberts were alone on the Court in thinking that this would be a tenable state of affairs. Even Justice Alito, in his separate dissent, concluded, "[I]n the narrow category of cases in which a court strikes down an Act of Congress and the Executive declines to defend Congress both has standing to defend the undefended statute and is a proper party to do so." Thus, six justices were ultimately unwilling to allow the President to nullify a statute in this manner.

A relatively narrow view could be attributed to these six justices—*i.e.*, that the Court must be available to referee constitutional disagreements between the President and Congress. Neither of these branches can be trusted to have the last word on such disagreements because of the potential for self-dealing. Justice Scalia might respond that the Court is not immune to self-dealing.

A somewhat different view might be attributed to a subset of these justices—perhaps the three who would have found standing in both *Windsor* and *Perry* (Kennedy, Alito, and Sotomayor). That view would be that no executive, whether federal or state, should be able to nullify legislation by simple non-enforcement. In *Perry,* it was California's governor and attorney general who might be said to have nullified Proposition 8; in *Windsor,* it was the President who would have nullified DOMA had he ordered a refund to Windsor. Even then, however, Justices Kennedy and Sotomayor would not have found standing if the government had paid Windsor ("It would be a different case if the Executive had taken the further step of paying Windsor"). Presumably Justice Alito would have allowed BLAG to sue even if Windsor were out of the case, as he found that BLAG had suffered injury-in-fact.

The broadest possible theory of judicial review that could be used to justify standing in *Windsor* would be the notion that courts must generally have the final word on

---

21 [1] Consider, however, the ramifications of the President's authority to which Justice Scalia adverted. If Congress passes a statute (and in this case, the President signed the statute into law) and the President refuses to execute it, does Congress have any remedy? Would it matter if Congress had passed the statute over the President's veto? Do you think the President's refusal to execute a law conflicts with the duties imposed by Article II, § 1, cl. 7 ("preserve, protect and defend the Constitution of the United States")? If it does, then is refusal to execute a law an impeachable offense? If it does not, then does each president have a *de facto* power to impose an unchallengeable veto on any statute throughout that president's administration?

the constitutionality of governmental action, and that they should have that say earlier than later. The underlying principle here is one of institutional settlement; the main purpose of courts of last resort, at least, is to provide guidance to primary actors and lower courts. The efficiency of private ordering depends on clear and stable default rules. People need to know where they stand in relation to government so they can figure out the best way to go about their lives. Lower courts need to know the law so they can enforce it consistently, thereby reinforcing stable settlement values. If the courts are shut out of too many constitutional questions, various local, state, and federal government agencies will have the last word, leaving too much room for inconsistency and uncertainty. It is a challenge to square such a theory of judicial review with traditional notions of Article III, and it is not a safe bet that any of the current Justices subscribe to it. But the modern popular interpretation of *Marbury's* most famous sentence seems to be moving away from the notion that courts only make law by accident and toward the notion that the Supreme Court must generally be the arbiter of constitutional questions, traditional limitations notwithstanding.

---

2. Standing to Seek Judicial Review of Adverse Federal Agency Action

Massachusetts v. Environmental Protection Agency

Supreme Court of the United States, 2007.
549 U.S. 497.

JUSTICE STEVENS delivered the opinion of the Court.

A well-documented rise in global temperatures has coincided with a significant increase in the concentration of carbon dioxide in the atmosphere. Respected scientists believe the two trends are related. For when carbon dioxide is released into the atmosphere, it acts like the ceiling of a greenhouse, trapping solar energy and retarding the escape of reflected heat. It is therefore a species—the most important species—of a "greenhouse gas."

Calling global warming "the most pressing environmental challenge of our time," a group of States, local governments, and private organizations, alleged in a petition for certiorari that the Environmental Protection Agency (EPA) has abdicated its responsibility under the Clean Air Act to regulate the emissions of four greenhouse gases, including carbon dioxide. Specifically, petitioners asked us to answer two questions concerning the meaning of § 202(a)(1) of the Act: whether EPA has the statutory authority to regulate greenhouse gas emissions from new motor vehicles; and if so, whether its stated reasons for refusing to do so are consistent with the statute.

In response, EPA, supported by 10 intervening States and six trade associations, correctly argued that we may not address those two questions unless at least one petitioner has standing to invoke our jurisdiction under Article III of the Constitution. Notwithstanding the serious character of that jurisdictional argument and the absence of any conflicting decisions construing § 202(a)(1), the unusual importance of the underlying issue persuaded us to grant the writ.

I

Section 202(a)(1) * * * provides:

> The [EPA] Administrator shall by regulation prescribe (and from time to time revise) in accordance with the provisions of this section, standards applicable to the emission of any air pollutant from any class or classes of new motor vehicles or new motor vehicle engines, which in his judgment cause, or contribute to, air pollution which may reasonably be anticipated to endanger public health or welfare * * * ."

statute @ issue

The Act defines "air pollutant" to include "any air pollution agent or combination of such agents, including any physical, chemical, biological, radioactive * * * substance or matter which is emitted into or otherwise enters the ambient air." "Welfare" is also defined broadly: among other things, it includes "effects on * * * weather * * * and climate."

When Congress enacted these provisions, the study of climate change was in its infancy. In 1959, shortly after the U.S. Weather Bureau began monitoring atmospheric carbon dioxide levels, an observatory in Mauna Loa, Hawaii, recorded a mean level of 316 parts per million. This was well above the highest carbon dioxide concentration—no more than 300 parts per million—revealed in the 420,000-year-old ice-core record. By the time Congress drafted § 202(a)(1) in 1970, carbon dioxide levels had reached 325 parts per million.[10]

* * *

Meanwhile, the scientific understanding of climate change progressed. In 1990, the Intergovernmental Panel on Climate Change (IPCC), a multinational scientific body organized under the auspices of the United Nations, published its first comprehensive report on the topic. Drawing on expert opinions from across the globe, the IPCC concluded that "emissions resulting from human activities are

10 A more dramatic rise was yet to come: In 2006, carbon dioxide levels reached 382 parts per million, a level thought to exceed the concentration of carbon dioxide in the atmosphere at any point over the past 20-million years.

substantially increasing the atmospheric concentrations of * * * greenhouse gases [which] will enhance the greenhouse effect, resulting on average in an additional warming of the Earth's surface."

Responding to the IPCC report, the United Nations convened the "Earth Summit" in 1992 in Rio de Janeiro. The first President Bush attended and signed the United Nations Framework Convention on Climate Change (UNFCCC), a nonbinding agreement among 154 nations to reduce atmospheric concentrations of carbon dioxide and other greenhouse gases for the purpose of "prevent[ing] dangerous anthropogenic [*i.e.*, human-induced] interference with the [Earth's] climate system." The Senate unanimously ratified the treaty.

Some five years later—after the IPCC issued a second comprehensive report in 1995 concluding that "[t]he balance of evidence suggests there is a discernible human influence on global climate"—the UNFCCC signatories met in Kyoto, Japan, and adopted a protocol that assigned mandatory targets for industrialized nations to reduce greenhouse gas emissions. Because those targets did not apply to developing and heavily polluting nations such as China and India, the Senate unanimously passed a resolution expressing its sense that the United States should not enter into the Kyoto Protocol. President Clinton did not submit the protocol to the Senate for ratification.

II

On October 20, 1999, a group of 19 private organizations filed a rulemaking petition asking EPA to regulate "greenhouse gas emissions from new motor vehicles under § 202 of the Clean Air Act." Petitioners maintained that 1998 was the "warmest year on record"; that carbon dioxide, methane, nitrous oxide, and hydrofluorocarbons are "heat trapping greenhouse gases"; that greenhouse gas emissions have significantly accelerated climate change; and that the IPCC's 1995 report warned that "carbon dioxide remains the most important contributor to [man-made] forcing of climate change." The petition further alleged that climate change will have serious adverse effects on human health and the environment. As to EPA's statutory authority, the petition observed that the agency itself had already confirmed that it had the power to regulate carbon dioxide. In 1998, Jonathan Z. Cannon, then EPA's General Counsel, prepared a legal opinion concluding that "CO_2 emissions are within the scope of EPA's authority to regulate," even as he recognized that EPA had so far declined to exercise that authority. Cannon's successor, Gary S. Guzy, reiterated that opinion before a congressional committee just two weeks before the rulemaking petition was filed.

Fifteen months after the petition's submission, EPA requested public comment on "all the issues raised in [the] petition," adding a "particular" request for comments on "any scientific, technical, legal, economic or other aspect of these issues that may be relevant to EPA's consideration of this petition." EPA received more than 50,000 comments over the next five months.

Before the close of the comment period, the White House sought "assistance in identifying the areas in the science of climate change where there are the greatest certainties and uncertainties" from the National Research Council, asking for a response "as soon as possible." The result was a 2001 report titled Climate Change: An Analysis of Some Key Questions (NRC Report), which, drawing heavily on the 1995 IPCC report, concluded that "[g]reenhouse gases are accumulating in Earth's atmosphere as a result of human activities, causing surface air temperatures and subsurface ocean temperatures to rise. Temperatures are, in fact, rising."

On September 8, 2003, EPA entered an order denying the rulemaking petition.

* * *

III

Petitioners, now joined by intervenor States and local governments, sought review of EPA's order in the United States Court of Appeals for the District of Columbia Circuit. Although each of the three judges on the panel wrote a separate opinion, two judges agreed "that the EPA Administrator properly exercised his discretion under § 202(a)(1) in denying the petition for rule making." The court therefore denied the petition for review.

* * *

IV

Article III of the Constitution limits federal-court jurisdiction to "Cases" and "Controversies." Those two words confine "the business of federal courts to questions presented in an adversary context and in a form historically viewed as capable of resolution through the judicial process." It is therefore familiar learning that no justiciable "controversy" exists when parties seek adjudication of a political question, when they ask for an advisory opinion, or when the question sought to be adjudicated has been mooted by subsequent developments,. This case suffers from none of these defects.

The parties' dispute turns on the proper construction of a congressional statute, a question eminently suitable to resolution in federal court. Congress has moreover authorized this type of challenge to EPA action. That authorization is of critical importance to the standing inquiry: "Congress has the power to define injuries and articulate chains of causation that will give rise to a case or controversy where none existed before." *Lujan v. Defenders of Wildlife*, 504 U.S. 555, 580

[1992] (Kennedy, J., concurring in part and concurring in judgment). "In exercising this power, however, Congress must at the very least identify the injury it seeks to vindicate and relate the injury to the class of persons entitled to bring suit." We will not, therefore, "entertain citizen suits to vindicate the public's non-concrete interest in the proper administration of the laws."

> **Food for Thought**
>
> Note that this could not happen in a case where the plaintiff was challenging the legality of state action or a congressional act. The Supreme Court permits Congress to lessen the redressability and imminence requirements for standing, but only with respect to requests for judicial review of federal agency action.

EPA maintains that because greenhouse gas emissions inflict widespread harm, the doctrine of standing presents an insuperable jurisdictional obstacle. We do not agree. At bottom, "the gist of the question of standing" is whether petitioners have "such a personal stake in the outcome of the controversy as to assure that concrete adverseness which sharpens the presentation of issues upon which the court so largely depends for illumination." As Justice Kennedy explained in his *Lujan* concurrence:

> While it does not matter how many persons have been injured by the challenged action, the party bringing suit must show that the action injures him in a concrete and personal way. This requirement is not just an empty formality. It preserves the vitality of the adversarial process by assuring both that the parties before the court have an actual, as opposed to professed, stake in the outcome, and that the legal questions presented * * * will be resolved, not in the rarified [*sic*] atmosphere of a debating society, but in a concrete factual context conducive to a realistic appreciation of the consequences of judicial action.

To ensure the proper adversarial presentation, *Lujan* holds that a litigant must demonstrate that it has suffered a concrete and particularized injury that is either actual or imminent, that the injury is fairly traceable to the defendant, and that it is likely that a favorable decision will redress that injury. However, a litigant to whom Congress has "accorded a procedural right to protect his concrete interests,"—-here, the right to challenge agency action unlawfully withheld—"can assert that right without meeting all the normal standards for redressability and immediacy." When a litigant is vested with a procedural right, that litigant has standing if there is some possibility that the requested relief will prompt the injury-causing party to reconsider the decision that allegedly harmed the litigant.

const. standing

Only one of the petitioners needs to have standing to permit us to consider the petition for review. We stress here, as did Judge Tatel below, the special position and interest of Massachusetts. It is of considerable relevance that the party seeking review here is a sovereign State and not, as it was in *Lujan*, a private individual.

Well before the creation of the modern administrative state, we recognized that States are not normal litigants for the purposes of invoking federal jurisdiction. As Justice Holmes explained in *Georgia v. Tennessee Copper Co.* (1907), a case in which Georgia sought to protect its citizens from air pollution originating outside its borders:

> **FYI**
>
> A quotation by one of the more historically revered Supreme Court justices, such as Chief Justice John Marshall, or Justices Oliver Wendell Holmes or Louis D. Brandeis, tends to carry more weight than quotations by other justices.

> The case has been argued largely as if it were one between two private parties; but it is not. The very elements that would be relied upon in a suit between fellow-citizens as a ground for equitable relief are wanting here. The State owns very little of the territory alleged to be affected, and the damage to it capable of estimate in money, possibly, at least, is small. This is a suit by a State for an injury to it in its capacity of *quasi*-sovereign. In that capacity the State has an interest independent of and behind the titles of its citizens, in all the earth and air within its domain. It has the last word as to whether its mountains shall be stripped of their forests and its inhabitants shall breathe pure air.

Just as Georgia's "independent interest * * * in all the earth and air within its domain" supported federal jurisdiction a century ago, so too does Massachusetts' well-founded desire to preserve its sovereign territory today. That Massachusetts does in fact own a great deal of the "territory alleged to be affected" only reinforces the conclusion that its stake in the outcome of this case is sufficiently concrete to warrant the exercise of federal judicial power.

When a State enters the Union, it surrenders certain sovereign prerogatives. Massachusetts cannot invade Rhode Island to force reductions in greenhouse gas emissions, it cannot negotiate an emissions treaty with China or India, and in some circumstances the exercise of its police powers to reduce in-state motor-vehicle emissions might well be pre-empted.

These sovereign prerogatives are now lodged in the Federal Government, and Congress has ordered EPA to protect Massachusetts (among others) by prescribing standards applicable to the "emission of any air pollutant from any class or classes of new motor vehicle engines, which in [the Administrator's] judgment cause, or contribute to, air pollution which may reasonably be anticipated to endanger public health or welfare." Congress has moreover recognized a concomitant procedural right to challenge the rejection of its rulemaking petition as arbitrary and capricious. Given that procedural right and Massachusetts' stake in protecting its quasi-sovereign interests, the Commonwealth is entitled to special solicitude in our standing analysis.[17]

With that in mind, it is clear that petitioners' submissions as they pertain to Massachusetts have satisfied the most demanding standards of the adversarial process. EPA's steadfast refusal to regulate greenhouse gas emissions presents a risk of harm to Massachusetts that is both "actual" and "imminent." There is, moreover, a "substantial likelihood that the judicial relief requested" will prompt EPA to take steps to reduce that risk.

The Injury

The harms associated with climate change are serious and well recognized. Indeed, the NRC Report itself—which EPA regards as an "objective and independent assessment of the relevant science,"—identifies a number of environmental changes that have already inflicted significant harms, including "the global retreat of mountain glaciers, reduction in snow-cover extent, the earlier spring melting of rivers and lakes, [and] the accelerated rate of rise of sea levels during the 20th century relative to the past few thousand years * * * ."

Petitioners allege that this only hints at the environmental damage yet to come. According to the climate scientist Michael MacCracken, "qualified scientific experts involved in climate change research" have reached a "strong consensus" that global warming threatens (among other things) a precipitate rise in sea levels by the end of the century, "severe and irreversible changes to natural ecosystems," a "significant reduction in water storage in winter snowpack in mountainous regions with direct and important economic consequences," and an increase in

17 The Chief Justice accuses the Court of misreading *Tennessee Copper* and "devis[ing] a new doctrine of state standing." But no less an authority than HART & WECHSLER'S THE FEDERAL COURTS AND THE FEDERAL SYSTEM understands *Tennessee Copper* as a standing decision. Indeed, it devotes an entire section to chronicling the long development of cases permitting States "to litigate as *parens patriae* to protect quasi-sovereign interests—*i.e.*, public or governmental interests that concern the state as a whole."

Drawing on *Massachusetts v. Mellon* (1923) and *Alfred L. Snapp & Son, Inc. v. Puerto Rico ex rel. Barez*, 458 U.S. 592 (1982), the Chief Justice claims that we "overloo[k] the fact that our cases cast significant doubt on a State's standing to assert a quasi-sovereign interest * * * against the Federal Government." Not so. *Mellon* itself disavowed any such broad reading when it noted that the Court had been "called upon to adjudicate, not rights of person or property, not rights of dominion over physical domain, [and] *not quasi sovereign rights actually invaded or threatened*." ([E]mphasis added). In any event, we held in *Georgia v. Pennsylvania R. Co.* (1945) that there is a critical difference between allowing a State "to protect her citizens from the operation of federal statutes" (which is what *Mellon* prohibits) and allowing a State to assert its rights under federal law (which it has standing to do). Massachusetts does not here dispute that the Clean Air Act *applies* to its citizens; it rather seeks to assert its rights under the Act.

the spread of disease. He also observes that rising ocean temperatures may contribute to the ferocity of hurricanes.[18]

That these climate-change risks are "widely shared" does not minimize Massachusetts' interest in the outcome of this litigation. According to petitioners' unchallenged affidavits, global sea levels rose somewhere between 10 and 20 centimeters over the 20th century as a result of global warming. These rising seas have already begun to swallow Massachusetts' coastal land. Because the Commonwealth "owns a substantial portion of the state's coastal property," it has alleged a particularized injury in its capacity as a landowner. The severity of that injury will only increase over the course of the next century: If sea levels continue to rise as predicted, one Massachusetts official believes that a significant fraction of coastal property will be "either permanently lost through inundation or temporarily lost through periodic storm surge and flooding events." Remediation costs alone, petitioners allege, could run well into the hundreds of millions of dollars.[21]

Causation

EPA does not dispute the existence of a causal connection between man-made greenhouse gas emissions and global warming. At a minimum, therefore, EPA's refusal to regulate such emissions "contributes" to Massachusetts' injuries.

EPA nevertheless maintains that its decision not to regulate greenhouse gas emissions from new motor vehicles contributes so insignificantly to petitioners' injuries that the agency cannot be haled into federal court to answer for them. For the same reason, EPA does not believe that any realistic possibility exists that the relief petitioners seek would mitigate global climate change and remedy their injuries. That is especially so because predicted increases in greenhouse gas emissions from developing nations, particularly China and India, are likely to offset any marginal domestic decrease.

18 In this regard, MacCracken's 2004 affidavit—drafted more than a year in advance of Hurricane Katrina—was eerily prescient. Immediately after discussing the "particular concern" that climate change might cause an "increase in the wind speed and peak rate of precipitation of major tropical cyclones (i.e., hurricanes and typhoons)," MacCracken noted that "[s]oil compaction, sea level rise and recurrent storms are destroying approximately 20-30 square miles of Louisiana wetlands each year. These wetlands serve as a 'shock absorber' for storm surges that could inundate New Orleans, significantly enhancing the risk to a major urban population."

21 In dissent, the Chief Justice dismisses petitioners' submissions as "conclusory," presumably because they do not quantify Massachusetts' land loss with the exactitude he would prefer. He therefore asserts that the Commonwealth's injury is "conjectur[al]." Yet the likelihood that Massachusetts' coastline will recede has nothing to do with whether petitioners have determined the precise metes and bounds of their soon-to-be-flooded land. Petitioners maintain that the seas are rising and will continue to rise, and have alleged that such a rise will lead to the loss of Massachusetts' sovereign territory. No one, save perhaps the dissenters, disputes those allegations. Our cases require nothing more.

But EPA overstates its case. Its argument rests on the erroneous assumption that a small incremental step, because it is incremental, can never be attacked in a federal judicial forum. Yet accepting that premise would doom most challenges to regulatory action. Agencies, like legislatures, do not generally resolve massive problems in one fell regulatory swoop. They instead whittle away at them over time, refining their preferred approach as circumstances change and as they develop a more-nuanced understanding of how best to proceed. That a first step might be tentative does not by itself support the notion that federal courts lack jurisdiction to determine whether that step conforms to law.

And reducing domestic automobile emissions is hardly a tentative step. Even leaving aside the other greenhouse gases, the United States transportation sector emits an enormous quantity of carbon dioxide into the atmosphere—according to the MacCracken affidavit, more than 1.7 billion metric tons in 1999 alone. That accounts for more than 6% of worldwide carbon dioxide emissions. To put this in perspective: Considering just emissions from the transportation sector, which represent less than one-third of this country's total carbon dioxide emissions, the United States would still rank as the third-largest emitter of carbon dioxide in the world, outpaced only by the European Union and China. Judged by any standard, U.S. motor-vehicle emissions make a meaningful contribution to greenhouse gas concentrations and hence, according to petitioners, to global warming.

The Remedy

While it may be true that regulating motor-vehicle emissions will not by itself *reverse* global warming, it by no means follows that we lack jurisdiction to decide whether EPA has a duty to take steps to *slow* or *reduce* it. Because of the enormity of the potential consequences associated with man-made climate change, the fact that the effectiveness of a remedy might be delayed during the (relatively short) time it takes for a new motor-vehicle fleet to replace an older one is essentially irrelevant. Nor is it dispositive that developing countries such as China and India are poised to increase greenhouse gas emissions substantially over the next century: A reduction in domestic emissions would slow the pace of global emissions increases, no matter what happens elsewhere.

We moreover attach considerable significance to EPA's "agree[ment] with the President that 'we must address the issue of global climate change,' " and to EPA's ardent support for various voluntary emission-reduction programs. As Judge Tatel observed in dissent below, "EPA would presumably not bother with such efforts if it thought emissions reductions would have no discernable impact on future global warming."

In sum—at least according to petitioners' uncontested affidavits—the rise in sea levels associated with global warming has already harmed and will continue to harm Massachusetts. The risk of catastrophic harm, though remote, is nevertheless real. That risk would be reduced to some extent if petitioners received the relief they seek. We therefore hold that petitioners have standing to challenge the EPA's denial of their rulemaking petition.[24]

* * *

[The Court's discussion of the merits is omitted.]

VIII

The judgment of the Court of Appeals is reversed, and the case is remanded for further proceedings consistent with this opinion.

It is so ordered.

CHIEF JUSTICE ROBERTS, with whom JUSTICE SCALIA, JUSTICE THOMAS, and JUSTICE ALITO join, dissenting.

Global warming may be a "crisis," even "the most pressing environmental problem of our time." Indeed, it may ultimately affect nearly everyone on the planet in some potentially adverse way, and it may be that governments have done too little to address it. It is not a problem, however, that has escaped the attention of policymakers in the Executive and Legislative Branches of our Government, who continue to consider regulatory, legislative, and treaty-based means of addressing global climate change.

Apparently dissatisfied with the pace of progress on this issue in the elected branches, petitioners have come to the courts claiming broad-ranging injury, and

---

24 In his dissent, the Chief Justice expresses disagreement with the Court's holding in United States v. Students Challenging Regulatory Agency Procedures (SCRAP) (1973). He does not, however, disavow this portion of Justice Stewart's opinion for the Court:

> Unlike the specific and geographically limited federal action of which the petitioner complained in *Sierra Club* (1972), the challenged agency action in this case is applicable to substantially all of the Nation's railroads, and thus allegedly has an adverse environmental impact on all the natural resources of the country. Rather than a limited group of persons who used a picturesque valley in California, all persons who utilize the scenic resources of the country, and indeed all who breathe its air, could claim harm similar to that alleged by the environmental groups here. But we have already made it clear that standing is not to be denied simply because many people suffer the same injury. Indeed some of the cases on which we relied in *Sierra Club* demonstrated the patent fact that persons across the Nation could be adversely affected by major governmental actions. *To deny standing to persons who are in fact injured simply because many others are also injured, would mean that the most injurious and widespread Government actions could be questioned by nobody.* We cannot accept that conclusion." ([C]itations omitted and emphasis added).

It is moreover quite wrong to analogize the legal claim advanced by Massachusetts and the other public and private entities who challenge EPA's parsimonious construction of the Clean Air Act to a mere "lawyer's game."

attempting to tie that injury to the Government's alleged failure to comply with a rather narrow statutory provision. I would reject these challenges as nonjusticiable. Such a conclusion involves no judgment on whether global warming exists, what causes it, or the extent of the problem. Nor does it render petitioners without recourse. This Court's standing jurisprudence simply recognizes that redress of grievances of the sort at issue here "is the function of Congress and the Chief Executive," not the federal courts. I would vacate the judgment below and remand for dismissal of the petitions for review.

I

* * *

Our modern framework for addressing standing is familiar: "A plaintiff must allege personal injury fairly traceable to the defendant's allegedly unlawful conduct and likely to be redressed by the requested relief." Applying that standard here, petitioners bear the burden of alleging an injury that is fairly traceable to the Environmental Protection Agency's failure to promulgate new motor vehicle greenhouse gas emission standards, and that is likely to be redressed by the prospective issuance of such standards.

Before determining whether petitioners can meet this familiar test, however, the Court changes the rules. It asserts that "States are not normal litigants for the purposes of invoking federal jurisdiction," and that given "Massachusetts' stake in protecting its quasi-sovereign interests, the Commonwealth is entitled to *special solicitude* in our standing analysis." ([E]mphasis added).

Relaxing Article III standing requirements because asserted injuries are pressed by a State, however, has no basis in our jurisprudence, and support for any such "special solicitude" is conspicuously absent from the Court's opinion. The general judicial review provision cited by the Court affords States no special rights or status. The Court states that "Congress has ordered EPA to protect Massachusetts (among others)" through the statutory provision at issue and that "Congress has * * * recognized a concomitant procedural right to challenge the rejection of its rulemaking petition as arbitrary and capricious." The reader might think from this unfortunate phrasing that Congress said something about the rights of States in this particular provision of the statute. Congress knows how to do that when it wants to, but it has done nothing of the sort here. Under the law on which petitioners rely, Congress treated public and private litigants exactly the same.

Nor does the case law cited by the Court provide any support for the notion that Article III somehow implicitly treats public and private litigants differently. The Court has to go back a full century in an attempt to justify its novel standing rule, but even there it comes up short. The Court's analysis hinges on Georgia v. Tennessee Copper Co. (1907)—a case that did indeed draw a distinction between a State and private litigants, but solely with respect to available remedies. The case had nothing to do with Article III standing.

In *Tennessee Copper,* the State of Georgia sought to enjoin copper companies in neighboring Tennessee from discharging pollutants that were inflicting "a wholesale destruction of forests, orchards and crops" in bordering Georgia counties. Although the State owned very little of the territory allegedly affected, the Court reasoned that Georgia—in its capacity as a "*quasi*-sovereign"—"has an interest independent of and behind the titles of its citizens, in all the earth and air within its domain." The Court explained that while "[t]he very elements that would be relied upon in a suit between fellow-citizens as a ground for equitable relief [were] wanting," a State "is not lightly to be required to give up *quasi*-sovereign rights for pay." Thus while a complaining private litigant would have to make do with a *legal* remedy—one "for pay"—the State was entitled to *equitable* relief.

In contrast to the present case, there was no question in *Tennessee Copper* about Article III injury. There was certainly no suggestion that the State could show standing where the private parties could not; there was no dispute, after all, that the private landowners had "an action at law." *Tennessee Copper* has since stood for nothing more than a State's right, in an original jurisdiction action, to sue in a representative capacity as ***parens patriae***. Nothing about a State's ability to sue in that capacity dilutes the bedrock requirement of showing injury, causation, and redressability to satisfy Article III.

> **It's Latin to Me!**
>
> "*Parens patriae*" means "parent of the nation." In this case, it means a state suing on behalf of its citizens.

A claim of *parens patriae* standing is distinct from an allegation of direct injury. Far from being a substitute for Article III injury, *parens patriae* actions raise an additional hurdle for a state litigant: the articulation of a "quasi-sovereign interest" "*apart* from the interests of particular private parties." ([E]mphasis added). Just as an association suing on behalf of its members must show not only that it represents the members but that at least one satisfies Article III requirements, so too a State asserting quasi-sovereign interests as *parens patriae* must still show that its citizens satisfy Article III. Focusing on Massachusetts's interests as quasi-sovereign makes the required showing here harder, not easier. The Court, in effect, takes what has always been regarded as a *necessary* condition for *parens patriae* standing—a quasi-sovereign interest—and converts it into a *sufficient* showing for purposes of Article III.

What is more, the Court's reasoning falters on its own terms. The Court asserts that Massachusetts is entitled to "special solicitude" due to its "quasi-sovereign interests," but then applies our Article III standing test to the asserted injury of the State's loss of coastal property. In the context of *parens patriae* standing, however, we have characterized state ownership of land as a "nonsovereign interes[t]" because a State "is likely to have the same interests as other similarly situated proprietors."

On top of everything else, the Court overlooks the fact that our cases cast significant doubt on a State's standing to assert a quasi-sovereign interest—as opposed to a direct injury—against the Federal Government. As a general rule, we have held that while a State might assert a quasi-sovereign right as *parens patriae* "for the protection of its citizens, it is no part of its duty or power to enforce their rights in respect of their relations with the Federal Government. In that field it is the United States, and not the State, which represents them."

All of this presumably explains why petitioners never cited *Tennessee Copper* in their briefs before this Court or the D.C. Circuit. It presumably explains why not one of the legion of *amici* supporting petitioners ever cited the case. And it presumably explains why not one of the three judges writing below ever cited the case either. Given that one purpose of the standing requirement is " 'to assure that concrete adverseness which sharpens the presentation of issues upon which the court so largely depends for illumination,' " it is ironic that the Court today adopts a new theory of Article III standing for States without the benefit of briefing or argument on the point.[1]

II

It is not at all clear how the Court's "special solicitude" for Massachusetts plays out in the standing analysis, except as an implicit concession that petitioners cannot establish standing on traditional terms. But the status of Massachusetts as a State cannot compensate for petitioners' failure to demonstrate injury in fact, causation, and redressability.

When the Court actually applies the three-part test, it focuses, as did the dissent below, on the State's asserted loss of coastal land as the injury in fact. If petitioners rely on loss of land as the Article III injury, however, they must ground the rest of the standing analysis in that specific injury. That alleged injury must be "concrete and particularized," and "distinct and palpable." Central to this

1 The Court seems to think we do not recognize that *Tennessee Copper* is a case about *parens patriae* standing, but we have no doubt about that. The point is that nothing in our cases (or HART & WECHSLER) suggests that the prudential requirements for *parens patriae* standing, can somehow substitute for, or alter the content of, the "irreducible constitutional minimum" requirements of injury in fact, causation, and redressability under Article III. * * *

concept of "particularized" injury is the requirement that a plaintiff be affected in a "personal and individual way," and seek relief that "directly and tangibly benefits him" in a manner distinct from its impact on "the public at large." Without "particularized injury, there can be no confidence of 'a real need to exercise the power of judicial review' or that relief can be framed 'no broader than required by the precise facts to which the court's ruling would be applied.' "

The very concept of global warming seems inconsistent with this particularization requirement. Global warming is a phenomenon "harmful to humanity at large," and the redress petitioners seek is focused no more on them than on the public generally—it is literally to change the atmosphere around the world.

If petitioners' particularized injury is loss of coastal land, it is also that injury that must be "actual or imminent, not conjectural or hypothetical," "real and immediate," and "certainly impending."

As to "actual" injury, the Court observes that "global sea levels rose somewhere between 10 and 20 centimeters over the 20th century as a result of global warming" and that "[t]hese rising seas have already begun to swallow Massachusetts' coastal land." But none of petitioners' declarations supports that connection. One declaration states that "a rise in sea level due to climate change is occurring on the coast of Massachusetts, in the metropolitan Boston area," but there is no elaboration. And the declarant goes on to identify a "significan[t]" *non*-global-warming cause of Boston's rising sea level: land subsidence. Thus, aside from a single conclusory statement, there is nothing in petitioners' 43 standing declarations and accompanying exhibits to support an inference of actual loss of Massachusetts coastal land from 20th century global sea level increases. It is pure conjecture.

The Court's attempts to identify "imminent" or "certainly impending" loss of Massachusetts coastal land fares no better. One of petitioners' declarants predicts global warming will cause sea level to rise by 20 to 70 centimeters *by the year 2100*. Another uses a computer modeling program to map the Commonwealth's coastal land and its current elevation, and calculates that the high-end estimate of sea level rise would result in the loss of significant state-owned coastal land. But the computer modeling program has a conceded average error of about 30 centimeters and a maximum observed error of 70 centimeters. As an initial matter, if it is possible that the model underrepresents the elevation of coastal land to an extent equal to or in excess of the projected sea level rise, it is difficult to put much stock in the predicted loss of land. But even placing that problem to the side, accepting a century-long time horizon and a series of compounded estimates renders requirements of imminence and immediacy utterly toothless. "Allegations of possible future injury do not satisfy the requirements of Art. III. A threatened injury must be *certainly impending* to constitute injury in fact."

III

Petitioners' reliance on Massachusetts's loss of coastal land as their injury in fact for standing purposes creates insurmountable problems for them with respect to causation and redressability. To establish standing, petitioners must show a causal connection between that specific injury and the lack of new motor vehicle greenhouse gas emission standards, and that the promulgation of such standards would likely redress that injury. As is often the case, the questions of causation and redressability overlap. And importantly, when a party is challenging the Government's allegedly unlawful regulation, or lack of regulation, of a third party, satisfying the causation and redressability requirements becomes "substantially more difficult."

Petitioners view the relationship between their injuries and EPA's failure to promulgate new motor vehicle greenhouse gas emission standards as simple and direct: Domestic motor vehicles emit carbon dioxide and other greenhouse gases. Worldwide emissions of greenhouse gases contribute to global warming and therefore also to petitioners' alleged injuries. Without the new vehicle standards, greenhouse gas emissions-and therefore global warming and its attendant harms-have been higher than they otherwise would have been; once EPA changes course, the trend will be reversed.

The Court ignores the complexities of global warming, and does so by now disregarding the "particularized" injury it relied on in step one, and using the dire nature of global warming itself as a bootstrap for finding causation and redressability. First, it is important to recognize the extent of the emissions at issue here. Because local greenhouse gas emissions disperse throughout the atmosphere and remain there for anywhere from 50 to 200 years, it is global emissions data that are relevant. According to one of petitioners' declarations, domestic motor vehicles contribute about 6 percent of global carbon dioxide emissions and 4 percent of global greenhouse gas emissions. The amount of global emissions at issue here is smaller still; § 202(a)(1) of the Clean Air Act covers only *new* motor vehicles and *new* motor vehicle engines, so petitioners' desired emission standards might reduce only a fraction of 4 percent of global emissions.

* * *

Petitioners are never able to trace their alleged injuries back through this complex web to the fractional amount of global emissions that might have been limited with EPA standards. In light of the bit-part domestic new motor vehicle greenhouse gas emissions have played in what petitioners describe as a 150-year global phenomenon, and the myriad additional factors bearing on petitioners' alleged injury—the loss of Massachusetts coastal land—the connection is far too speculative to establish causation.

IV

Redressability is even more problematic. To the tenuous link between petitioners' alleged injury and the indeterminate fractional domestic emissions at issue here, add the fact that petitioners cannot meaningfully predict what will come of the 80 percent of global greenhouse gas emissions that originate outside the United States. As the Court acknowledges, "developing countries such as China and India are poised to increase greenhouse gas emissions substantially over the next century," so the domestic emissions at issue here may become an increasingly marginal portion of global emissions, and any decreases produced by petitioners' desired standards are likely to be overwhelmed many times over by emissions increases elsewhere in the world.

Petitioners offer declarations attempting to address this uncertainty, contending that "[i]f the U.S. takes steps to reduce motor vehicle emissions, other countries are very likely to take similar actions regarding their own motor vehicles using technology developed in response to the U.S. program." In other words, do not worry that other countries will contribute far more to global warming than will U.S. automobile emissions; someone is bound to invent something, and places like the People's Republic of China or India will surely require use of the new technology, regardless of cost. The Court previously has explained that when the existence of an element of standing "depends on the unfettered choices made by independent actors not before the courts and whose exercise of broad and legitimate discretion the courts cannot presume either to control or to predict," a party must present facts supporting an assertion that the actor will proceed in such a manner. The declarations' conclusory (not to say fanciful) statements do not even come close.

No matter, the Court reasons, because *any* decrease in domestic emissions will "slow the pace of global emissions increases, no matter what happens elsewhere." Every little bit helps, so Massachusetts can sue over any little bit.

The Court's sleight-of-hand is in failing to link up the different elements of the three-part standing test. What must be *likely* to be redressed is the particular injury in fact. The injury the Court looks to is the asserted loss of land. The Court contends that regulating domestic motor vehicle emissions will reduce carbon dioxide in the atmosphere, *and therefore* redress Massachusetts's injury. But even if regulation *does* reduce emissions—to some indeterminate degree, given events elsewhere in the world—the Court never explains why that makes it *likely* that the injury in fact—the loss of land—will be redressed. Schoolchildren know that a kingdom might be lost "all for the want of a horseshoe nail," but "likely" redressability is a different matter. The realities make it pure conjecture to suppose that EPA regulation of new automobile emissions will *likely* prevent the loss of Massachusetts coastal land.

V

Petitioners' difficulty in demonstrating causation and redressability is not surprising given the evident mismatch between the source of their alleged injury—catastrophic global warming—and the narrow subject matter of the Clean Air Act provision at issue in this suit. The mismatch suggests that petitioners' true goal for this litigation may be more symbolic than anything else. The constitutional role of the courts, however, is to decide concrete cases—not to serve as a convenient forum for policy debates.

When dealing with legal doctrine phrased in terms of what is "fairly" traceable or "likely" to be redressed, it is perhaps not surprising that the matter is subject to some debate. But in considering how loosely or rigorously to define those adverbs, it is vital to keep in mind the purpose of the inquiry. The limitation of the judicial power to cases and controversies "is crucial in maintaining the tripartite allocation of power set forth in the Constitution." In my view, the Court today—addressing Article III's "core component of standing"—fails to take this limitation seriously.

To be fair, it is not the first time the Court has done so. Today's decision recalls the previous high-water mark of diluted standing requirements, United States v. Students Challenging Regulatory Agency Procedures (SCRAP) (1973). *SCRAP* involved "[p]robably the most attenuated injury conferring Art. III standing" and "surely went to the very outer limit of the law"—until today. In *SCRAP*, the Court based an environmental group's standing to challenge a railroad freight rate surcharge on the group's allegation that increases in railroad rates would cause an increase in the use of nonrecyclable goods, resulting in the increased need for natural resources to produce such goods. According to the group, some of these resources might be taken from the Washington area, resulting in increased refuse that might find its way into area parks, harming the group's members.

Over time, *SCRAP* became emblematic not of the looseness of Article III standing requirements, but of how utterly manipulable they are if not taken seriously as a matter of judicial self-restraint. *SCRAP* made standing seem a lawyer's game, rather than a fundamental limitation ensuring that courts function as courts and not intrude on the politically accountable branches. Today's decision is *SCRAP* for a new generation.[2]

2 The difficulty with *SCRAP*, and the reason it has not been followed, is not the portion cited by the Court. Rather, it is the *attenuated* nature of the injury there, and here, that is so troubling. Even in *SCRAP*, the Court noted that what was required was "something more than an ingenious academic exercise in the conceivable," and we have since understood the allegation there to have been "that the string of occurrences alleged would happen *immediately*." That is hardly the case here.

The Court says it is "quite wrong" to compare petitioners' challenging "EPA's parsimonious construction of the Clean Air Act to a mere 'lawyer's game.' " Of course it is not the legal challenge that is merely "an ingenious academic exercise in the conceivable," but the assertions made in support of standing.

Perhaps the Court recognizes as much. How else to explain its need to devise a new doctrine of state standing to support its result? The good news is that the Court's "special solicitude" for Massachusetts limits the future applicability of the diluted standing requirements applied in this case. The bad news is that the Court's self-professed relaxation of those Article III requirements has caused us to transgress "the proper—and properly limited—role of the courts in a democratic society."

> **FYI**
>
> Many consider SCRAP an outlier. One probably ought not cite it as the only authority for the existence of standing in a case.

I respectfully dissent.

Notes and Questions

1. The majority, quoting Lujan v. Defenders of Wildlife (1992) (*see* page 120), asserts that if Congress creates a procedural right, then Congress also has the power to relax the ordinary requirements of redressability and immediacy of the harm threatened. If those requirements are functions of Article III standing, how is it possible for Congress to create exceptions to them? For a discussion of this conundrum, *see* Evan T. Lee & Josephine K. Ellis, *The Standing Doctrine's Dirty Little Secret*, 107 Nw. U. L. Rev. 169 (2012).

2. What is the constitutional basis for declaring states to be "special" litigants for purposes of standing? Does the *Tennessee Copper* case that Justice Stevens cites stand for that proposition, or does it merely recognize that states *qua* states have certain substantive rights, violation of which may give rise to injuries-in-fact of a type that individuals cannot suffer?

3. a) What precisely is the injury-in-fact that Massachusetts claims? If it is the loss of coastal land, is the Chief Justice correct in his dissent that it is neither impending nor redressable? *See* Anthony DePalma, *Warming Report Warns of Increased Flooding*, N.Y. Times (July 11, 2007) ("One-hundred-year floods could come as often as once every 10 years by the end of this century, Long Island lobsters could disappear and New York apples could be just a memory if nothing is done to reduce greenhouse gas emissions, according to a new report on the impact of global warming by the Union of Concerned Scientists.") If it is harm to the climate, is he correct that it is not individualized?

b) If Massachusetts' injury is the loss of coastal land, which, as Justice Stevens notes, gives rise to "a particularized injury in its capacity as a landowner," then is it proper simultaneously to treat Massachusetts as a state? In other words, is the majority trying to have it both ways, characterizing Massachusetts as a state entitled to special rules for purposes of satisfying the imminence and redressability inquiries but as an individual for purposes of the injury-in-fact inquiry?

4. Near the beginning of the dissent, the Chief Justice argues that the Court's standing jurisprudence merely remits Massachusetts to the political process for addressing this difficulty. Massachusetts, of course, may have the view that the political process has already spoken and that it is simply trying to get the courts to enforce the very statute that Congress passed. Is the Chief Justice saying that the law is unconstitutional, or is he instead saying that a law may confer specific rights without those rights being judicially enforceable? If it is the latter, does that raise separation-of-powers problems?

At bottom, is the Chief Justice's real concern with standing, or is it that he thinks that Massachusetts either cannot or should not prevail on the merits? Note his comments on page 115 on the speculative nature of Massachusetts's injury. Is the dissent subtly equating the only-partial-effectiveness of relief with the causation inquiry?

---

3. *Note On Further Problems With The Court's Standing Jurisprudence*

a. Constitutional Standing

(1) Generalized Grievances

Massachusetts v. EPA is only the latest case to consider widely-shared harms as injuries-in-fact. What the Court now refers to as a separate "prohibition against generalized grievances" was actually the start of the Article III standing doctrine, tracing back to *Fairchild v. Hughes,* 258 U.S. 126 (1922). Over the years, the line of cases that followed *Fairchild* culminated in the "injury-in-fact," "causation" and "redressability" requirements. For the historical progression, placed in social and political context, *see* EVAN TSEN LEE, JUDICIAL RESTRAINT IN AMERICA: HOW THE AGELESS WISDOM OF FEDERAL COURTS WAS INVENTED (2011). *Ex parte Levitt,* 302 U.S. 633 (1937), is a representative example of the early cases. In 1937, a brave attorney challenged Hugo Black's appointment to the Supreme Court on the ground that Black had been a member of the Senate when it passed a bill increasing the retirement pay of associate justices. The plaintiff argued that the appointment violated the Ineligibility Clause (art. I, § 6, cl. 2): "No Senator or Representative shall, during the Time for which he was elected, be appointed to any civil Office under the Authority of the United States, * * * the Emoluments whereof shall have been encreased during such time * * * ." The Court, in a *per curiam* opinion, found the plaintiff lacked standing and never reached the merits. Suppose that Levitt was correct on the merits. What remedy would he or anyone else have?

The Vietnam War sparked many judicial challenges to various governmental practices. *United States v. Richardson*, 418 U.S. 166 (1974), refused to find standing for a taxpayer challenging the CIA's accounting methods as inconsistent with the Accounts Clause, U.S. CONST. art. I, § 9, cl. 7. In *Schlesinger v. Reservists Committee to Stop the War*, 418 U.S. 208 (1974), present and former members of military reserve units challenged the constitutionality of members of Congress also holding reserve commissions in violation of the Incompatibility Clause, U.S. CONST. art. I, § 6, cl. 2. There, too, the Court refused to find standing and made it clear that what it called "generalized grievances" were insufficient to satisfy the Case-or-Controversy Clause. In *Schlesinger*, as in *Richardson*, the Court asserted that the plaintiffs' remedy was political, not judicial.

What are the advantages and disadvantages of remitting citizens to the political process to raise issues about the constitutionality of governmental conduct? What are the disadvantages of permitting cases like *Levitt*, *Richardson* and *Schlesinger* to be resolved by the judiciary?

Although the Court has said contradictory things about whether the prohibition against generalized grievances is constitutionally mandated or prudential, the fact that current Article III standing doctrine devolved from the early generalized grievance cases strongly suggests that it is constitutional. Of course, if it is only prudential, Congress may freely make exceptions to it. Even if "generalized grievances" is a constitutional component, Congress may be able effectively to create standing. Congress can create new substantive property or liberty rights and thereby create the possibility of new "injuries in fact." For example, the patent laws define a substantive right—the right not to have others copy and sell one's invention—and thereby create a new type of injury-in-fact. The common law of torts, property, or contracts would not have recognized the inventor's loss of business because someone copied his invention as a cognizable legal injury. When Congress does so, it can authorize private rights of action by those injured in the enjoyment of the newly-created rights. Must the injury be individualized? *Lujan v. Defenders of Wildlife*, *supra*, seems to say so. Part of the Endangered Species Act, 16 U.S.C.A. § 1531 *et seq.* (1982), requires each federal agency to insure that its actions not threaten any protected species. Another provision permits a civil suit by "any person" to enjoin violations. When a dispute arose over whether the Act applies to federal involvement outside the United States, Defenders of Wildlife and several of its individual members sued to establish that it does. The plaintiffs alleged that defendants' actions threatened species in Egypt and Sri Lanka, but did not allege that the individual plaintiffs had concrete plans to visit those areas again. The Court refused to find standing, but in the course of doing so, stated:

> Vindicating the *public* interest (including the public interest in government observance of the Constitution and laws) is the function of Congress and the Chief Executive. The question presented here is whether the public interest in

> proper administration of the laws * * * can be converted into an individual right by a statute that denominates it as such, and that permits all citizens * * * to sue. If the concrete injury requirement has the separation-of-powers significance we have always said, the answer must be obvious: To permit Congress to convert the undifferentiated public interest in executive officers' compliance with the law into an "individual right" vindicable in the courts is to permit Congress to transfer from the President to the courts the Chief Executive's most important constitutional duty, to "take Care that the Laws be faithfully executed * * * ."

Does this passage suggest that Congress may create standing, but to do so it must find a way to convert what would otherwise be a mere "generalized grievance" into a violation that can visit a specific and distinctive harm on an individual? Does this possibility operate the same way with respect to constitutional and statutory rights?

In *Federal Election Commission v. Akins*, 524 U.S. 11 (1998), the Court again considered Congress's ability to create standing. The Federal Election Campaign Act (FECA) mandates limits on the amounts that individuals, corporations, political committees and political parties can directly contribute to candidates for federal office. Part of FECA imposes both recordkeeping and disclosure requirements on political committees, which the Act defines as "any committee, club, association or other group of persons which receives" or makes certain defined contributions or expenditures.[10] The *Akins* plaintiffs challenged the FEC's refusal to treat the American Israel Public Affairs Committee (AIPAC) as a political committee. They asserted that AIPAC was violating certain provisions of FECA and demanded that FEC order AIPAC to make the disclosures required of a political committee under FECA. There was a lively dispute between the plaintiffs and AIPAC about the nature of some of the latter's revenue (contributions) and disbursements (expenditures). FEC sought and received summary judgment in the district court, which upheld FEC's interpretation of FECA's requirements. A panel of the District of Columbia Circuit affirmed on the substantive point after finding that the plaintiffs had standing. The *en banc* Circuit vacated the panel decision, agreeing on the standing point but finding that the plaintiff's interpretation of FECA was correct. Accordingly, it reversed the district court's grant of summary judgment and remanded.

When the case reached the Supreme Court, a six-Member majority agreed with the District of Columbia Circuit that there was standing, but vacated the Circuit decision and remanded so that the FEC could reconsider whether, under proposed new FEC rules concerning who qualified as a member of organizations like AIPAC, AIPAC was a political committee within the meaning of FECA.

10 The definition is somewhat more complex because it goes into what constitutes contributions to such committees and qualifying expenditures by them, but the precise contours are not important here.

With respect to standing, the majority rejected FEC arguments that the plaintiffs satisfied neither the constitutional nor the prudential requirements of the Court's doctrine. Regarding the prudential standing challenge, the Court found that Congress explicitly authorized people like the *Akins* plaintiffs—a group of voters—to challenge FEC dismissal of an administrative complaint demanding that the FEC proceed against an entity under FECA, thus bringing voters within the "zone of interests" that the statute protected.

The FEC's constitutional standing argument fared no better. FEC argued that the plaintiffs had suffered no injury-in-fact, and that their case was analogous to *United States v. Richardson*, *supra* at 120, because they expressed only a generalized grievance. The *Akins* majority noted that *Richardson* refused to find standing because the Court found "no 'logical nexus' between the [plaintiffs'] asserted status of taxpayer and the claimed failure of the Congress to require the Executive to supply a more detailed report of the [CIA's] expenditures." By contrast, the court noted that the *Akins* plaintiffs wanted the information they said FECA required to "help them (and others to whom they would communicate it) to evaluate candidates for public office, especially candidates who received assistance from AIPAC, and to evaluate the role that AIPAC's financial assistance might play in a specific election." Thus, having the FECA information might directly affect the plaintiffs' exercise of their franchise, validating congressional creation of voter standing. The Court also noted that *Richardson* was a taxpayer-standing, not a voter-standing, case.

Ultimately, the Court characterized the generalized-grievance attack as the FEC's strongest argument, but rejected it (explicitly without placing the generalized-grievance doctrine squarely in either the constitutional or prudential standing requirements), finding that the plaintiffs' interest in obtaining the information was neither abstract nor undifferentiated from the entitlement of the populace generally. "[T]he informational injury here, directly related to voting, the most basic of political rights, is sufficiently concrete and specific such that the fact that it is widely shared does not deprive Congress of constitutional power to authorize its vindication in the federal courts."

(2) *Taxpayer Standing*

Although "taxpayer standing" analysis falls within the larger category of "generalized grievances," the courts often speak of it as if it were a separate rule. When government embarks upon a course of conduct alleged to be unconstitutional and the conduct requires expenditure of public funds, should a federal taxpayer have standing to challenge the perceived misuse of tax revenues? For many years, the Court's answer has been a uniform "no." *See Frothingham v. Mellon*, 262 U.S. 447 (1923), in which the Court, although noting that municipal taxpayer standing had been upheld, refused to find standing for a taxpayer challenging the constitutionality of a federal expenditure.

> [T]he relation of a taxpayer of the United States to the federal government is very different. His interest in the moneys of the treasury—partly realized from taxation and partly from other sources—is shared with millions of others, is comparatively minute and indeterminable, and the effect upon future taxation, of any payment out of the funds, so remote, fluctuating and uncertain, that no basis is afforded for an appeal to the preventive powers of a court of equity * * * . If one taxpayer may champion and litigate such a cause, then every other taxpayer may do the same, not only in respect of the statute here under review, but also in respect of every other public appropriation act and statute whose administration requires the outlay of public money, and whose validity may be questioned. The bare suggestion of such a result, with its attendant inconveniences, goes far to sustain the conclusion which we have reached, that a suit of this character cannot be maintained.

Would or should the answer be different if the challenged expenditure were a substantial part of the federal budget, or if the individual taxpayer pays enough in taxes to make an identifiable contribution? What if the tax is not general, but is a specialized "use" tax?

In the only exception to denial of taxpayer standing, a sharply divided Court ruled in *Flast v. Cohen*, 392 U.S. 83 (1968), that a taxpayer had standing to challenge action that specifically violated the taxing power itself. The plaintiffs presented an Establishment Clause challenge to federal expenditures of funds to support education in religious schools. A five-to-four majority found standing for the plaintiffs as taxpayers. The Court's analysis—heavily criticized even by sympathetic academics over the years—purported to apply to a wide variety of claims by taxpayers. Chief Justice Warren's opinion asserted that taxpayer standing was permissible whenever "there is a logical nexus between the status asserted and the claim sought to be adjudicated." In *Flast*, this requirement was satisfied because there was a logical nexus between being a federal taxpayer on the one hand and the challenged Congressional action on the other hand, which had been made under the Taxing and Spending Clause. The *Flast* Court's locution, however, was couched in terms that would govern taxpayer suits generally.

The Court has never overruled *Flast*, but in recent years it appears to have narrowed *Flast* to its facts. In *Valley Forge Christian College v. Americans United for Separation of Church and State*, 454 U.S. 464 (1982), the federal government granted surplus property to a religious college. The plaintiff challenged the grant under the Establishment Clause, citing *Flast*. This time, the Court found no standing because the grant had been made under Congress's power to dispose of property, not the taxing and spending power. In *Hein v. Freedom from Religion Foundation, Inc.*, 551 U.S. 587 (2007), the White House allocated funds to its Office of Faith-Based and Community Initiatives and corresponding centers. The Court found that the plaintiff had no standing to challenge the allocation under *Flast*. Although it was true that Congress gave the executive branch the money under its taxing and spending powers, it was a general allocation of funds, with no specification that the money was to be used for a program to benefit religious programs, as in Flast.

Most recently, in *Arizona Christian School Tuition Organization v. Winn*, 131 S.Ct. 1436 (2011), Arizona law provided tax credits for contributions to school tuition organizations, or STOs. STOs use these contributions to provide scholarships to students attending private schools, many of which are religious. Plaintiff challenged the tax credit provision as a violation of Establishment Clause. Writing for the majority, Justice Kennedy distinguished *Flast* on the ground that *Winn* involved tax credits rather than direct governmental expenditures:

> The distinction between governmental expenditures and tax credits refutes respondents' assertion of standing. When Arizona taxpayers choose to contribute to STOs, they spend their own money, not money the State has collected from respondents or from other taxpayers. Arizona's [challenged tax credit] does not "extrac[t] and spen[d]" a conscientious dissenter's funds in service of an establishment, " 'force a citizen to contribute three pence only of his property' " to a sectarian organization. On the contrary, respondents and other Arizona taxpayers remain free to pay their own tax bills, without contributing to an STO. Respondents are likewise able to contribute to an STO of their choice, either religious or secular. And respondents also have the option of contributing to other charitable organizations, in which case respondents may become eligible for a tax deduction or a different tax credit. The STO tax credit is not tantamount to a religious tax or to a tithe and does not visit the injury identified in *Flast*. It follows that respondents have neither alleged an injury for standing purposes under general rules nor met the *Flast* exception. Finding standing under these circumstances would be more than the extension of *Flast* "to the limits of its logic."

Winn was a 5-4 decision, with Justices Scalia and Thomas separately calling for an outright overruling of *Flast*. Justice Kagan, joined by Justices Ginsburg, Breyer, and Sotomayor, accused the majority of having effectively eviscerated *Flast*. For now, a taxpayer still has standing to challenge a direct governmental expenditure specifically designated for religious organizations, but it is doubtful whether taxpayer standing exists in any other context.

One could be forgiven for thinking that the real dispute in the religion-standing cases, from *Flast* to *Valley Forge* to *Winn*, has far less to do with standing as a concept of justiciability than with the Justices' deep disagreements about what the Establishment Clause really means. The *Winn* majority seizes particularly on Madison's Memorial and Remonstrance as a way of focusing on establishment as a dollars-and-cents issue only. The dissent implicitly accedes to the majority's characterization when Justice Kagan argues on economic grounds, making her point that there is no functional difference between a government payout and a tax credit. (Note, however, that she subsequently suggests that "it's not about the money.")

(3) *Citizen Standing*

"Citizen standing" also falls within the larger category of "generalized grievances," but there are isolated situations where Congress can create something akin to citizen standing. The most obvious example is the Freedom of Information Act (FOIA). It is well established that one has standing to sue for enforcement of a non-exempt document request, even if he or she has no connection with the subject matter of the requested documents. Another question is, may state law allow citizen-standing actions in the state courts that would not qualify as Article III cases or controversies? If so, may the Supreme Court review the ensuing state court decisions without running afoul of Article III? The Court has suggested an affirmative answer to both questions, with some significant qualifications.

In *ASARCO Inc. v. Kadish*, 490 U.S. 605 (1989), taxpayers sought a declaration that a state law concerning mineral leases on state lands was invalid. They prevailed in the state court, after which the defendant class of mineral lessees sought Supreme Court review. The Court held that Article III standing existed, although it recognized that had the action been commenced in the federal courts, long-established law would have required its dismissal because the taxpayer plaintiffs would have been unable to demonstrate injury-in-fact and thus would have lacked standing under *Frothingham v. Mellon*, *supra*. Nonetheless, the Court found that the defendant class, having suffered an adverse judgment in the state courts that would have invalidated their mineral leases, did have standing.

Although the Court stated clearly that the plaintiffs would have lacked standing in an original federal action, it did not address the question, not presented by the case in its posture on review, of whether there would have been Supreme Court jurisdiction to review if the state courts had ruled adversely to the plaintiffs. To be sure, the plaintiffs would have lacked standing to commence their action in the federal district court, but after an adverse state court ruling, would they have been in position to claim that the state court's erroneous judgment then caused them injury and, in effect, conferred standing?

The latest case to present the state-versus-federal standing problem is *DaimlerChrysler Corp. v. Cuno*, 547 U.S. 332 (2006). Taxpayers in Ohio, including some in Toledo, sued DaimlerChrysler and municipal and state tax officials objecting to local (a municipal tax exemption) and state tax benefits (in the form of a property tax credit) offered to the company in exchange for its agreement to expand its Jeep plant in Toledo. The plaintiffs argued that the benefits would have the effect of increasing their own tax burdens and violated the Commerce Clause. They commenced the action in the Ohio state courts, but DaimlerChrysler removed the case to the federal courts. Plaintiffs moved to remand, expressing doubts that they could satisfy the federal requirements for standing. The district court denied the remand, finding that the plaintiffs had standing under the municipal taxpayer rule that Massachusetts v. Mellon (1923), a companion case to Frothingham had recognized. That court denied relief under the Commerce Clause. The Sixth Circuit agreed with the district court as to the municipal tax exemption but disagreed as to the state franchise tax credit. Both sides sought certiorari.

In what one certainly must view as creative lawyering, the plaintiffs argued that since jurisdiction over the municipal tax exemption claim was secure, the federal courts could hear the *state*-taxpayers claims under their supplemental jurisdiction. The Court declined this invitation as well, noting that it had read *United Mine Workers v. Gibbs* (1966) narrowly, and relying for that assertion in part on *Owen Equipment & Erection Co. v. Kroger* (1978) and *Finley v. United States* (1989).[11] In the course of the discussion of *Gibbs*, the Court limited *Gibbs*'s one-constitutional-case approach to Article III considerations other than standing.[12] The Chief Justice noted the gate-opening effects that the plaintiffs' suggested "ancillary-standing" reading of *Gibbs* would have and turned away from the parade of horribles that the Court envisioned.[13]

So saying, the Court reversed the Sixth Circuit's grant of relief and remanded the case with directions that the plaintiffs' challenge to the state franchise tax credit be dismissed, leaving in place the judgment of the lower courts upholding the municipal property tax exemption. It is at this point that interesting questions begin to arise. Why, for example, did the Court not remand with directions that the district court remand the case to the state court from which it came, pursuant to 28 U.S.C. § 1447(c)?[14] It is true, of course, that the statute refers to remand

11 The latter reliance was perhaps a bit odd, given that the Court recognized in *Exxon Mobil Corp. v. Allapattah Services, Inc.* (2005) that the supplemental jurisdiction statute, 28 U.S.C. § 1367, had overruled *Finley*, a fact that Chief Justice Roberts noted in the sentence following his *Finley* citation.

12 What we have never done is apply the rationale of *Gibbs* to permit a federal court to exercise supplemental jurisdiction over a claim that does not by itself satisfy those elements of the Article III inquiry, such as constitutional standing, that "serv[e] to identify those disputes which are appropriately resolved through the judicial process * * * ." We see no reason to read the language of *Gibbs* so broadly, particularly since our standing cases confirm that a plaintiff must demonstrate standing for each claim he seeks to press. * * * We have insisted, for instance, that "a plaintiff must demonstrate standing separately for each form of relief sought."

13 Yet if *Gibbs*' "common nucleus" formulation announced a new definition of "case" or "controversy" for all Article III purposes, a federal court would be free to entertain moot or unripe claims, or claims presenting a political question, if they "derived from" the same "operative fact[s]" as another federal claim suffering from non of these defects. Plaintiffs' reading of *Gibbs*, therefore, would amount to a significant revision of our precedent interpreting Article III. With federal courts thus deciding issues they would not otherwise be authorized to decide, the " 'tripartite allocation of power' " that Article III is designed to maintain would quickly erode; our emphasis on the standing requirement's role in maintaining this separation would be rendered hollow rhetoric. As we have explained, "[t]he actual-injury requirement would hardly serve the purpose * * * of preventing courts from undertaking tasks assigned to the political branches[,] if once a plaintiff demonstrated harm from one particular inadequacy in government administration, the court were authorized to remedy *all* inadequacies in that administration."

14 In pertinent part, the statute reads: "If at any time before final judgment it appears that the district court lacks subject matter jurisdiction, the case shall be remanded."

"before final judgment," but that term has varying meanings, depending on the context. For purposes of the preclusion doctrines, for example, a judgment is final even while it is on appeal and may serve as the predicate for either claim or issue preclusion. In this sense, the Supreme Court's action in the case certainly did not come before final judgment. On the other hand, in the law of federal habeas corpus, a judgment is not final for purposes of beginning the statute of limitations period until "the date on which the judgment became final by the conclusion of direct review or the expiration of the time for seeking such review."[15] Using that standard, perhaps the Court should have directed the district court to remand. As a practical matter, it may make little difference, since the plaintiffs retain the option of refiling in the state court under the Ohio law discussed in the next paragraph.

The Court has said that the Article III standing requirements are jurisdictional, preventing the federal courts from considering the plaintiffs' claims on the merits. Those requirements do not, of course, apply to the state courts. If plaintiffs refile their state court claim[16] that the state tax credit is unlawful, what should happen? Although the case as originally filed was removable (because the Supreme Court had not spoken definitively on the issue), the Court's decision in DaimlerChrysler now makes clear that the case is not removable because there is no jurisdiction.[17]

Assume the plaintiffs do litigate their challenge to the state tax credit in the state courts. Under ASARCO, Inc. v. Kadish, if the plaintiffs win the defendants presumably would have standing to seek review of the Ohio Supreme Court's decision in the United States Supreme Court. Thus, under DaimlerChrysler, defendants lack Article III standing to invoke the removal jurisdiction of the federal courts but have standing under *ASARCO* to invoke the Supreme Court's appellate jurisdiction. Can these cases be harmonized, or are the results simply inconsistent?

Suppose instead that the defendants were to prevail in the Ohio Supreme Court. Do the plaintiffs then acquire Article III standing under ASARCO, which found that an adverse state judgment can itself create injury-in-fact that permits Supreme Court review? If nothing else, would such a situation require the Supreme Court to decide the merits of the plaintiffs' constitutional claims with respect to the state-tax-credit claim? If that is not the case, has DaimlerChrysler (in

15 28 U.S.C. § 2244(d)(1)(A) (2000).

16 Ohio law allows refiling in this situation either until the end of the normal limitation period or within one year from the Supreme Court's decision, whichever is later. *See* OHIO REV. CODE ANN. § 2305.19(a) (2005).

17 Indeed, counsel now seeking to remove the case would run a considerable risk of Rule 11 sanctions, since there is no longer a good-faith argument that there is federal jurisdiction.

combination with ASARCO) bequeathed a situation in which the decision of the Ohio Supreme Court may or may not create Article III standing, depending which way it goes? Some might think that anomalous. Either plaintiffs or defendants might seek review of the same Fourteenth Amendment issues: whether the state tax credit violates the Due Process or Equal Protection Clauses. Does resolution of the Article III standing issue depend on who asks the question?[18]

b. Prudential Standing

In recent years, the Court has begun to refer to a "prudential standing" doctrine. This is misleading; there are actually several distinct prudentially-based standing rules that have little to do with one another.

One is the prohibition against asserting the rights of other persons. The rule is variously referred to as "the rule against third-party standing," or sometimes as the "rule prohibiting ***jus tertii*** standing."

The content of the rule is that a party may only assert his or her own legal rights. In other words, even if one suffers "injury-in-fact," he or she generally must also show that the rights violated by the defendant belong to the plaintiff. But there are multiple exceptions to this rule.

It's Latin to Me!

A third person's right.

Food for Thought

Professor Lee finds the phrase "third-party standing" misleading. In his view, the claimant is trying to assert the legal right of a third party, not the "standing" of the third party. The claimant must have his or her own standing based on his or her own injury. On the other hand, Professor Doernberg thinks "third-party standing" aptly describes what happens when the claimant asserts the rights of a third party.

18 The Court has created this sort of anomaly before. In Franchise Tax Board v. Construction Laborer' Vacation Trust, text at 359, the question to which both parties wanted an answer in the form of a declaratory judgment was, "Does ERISA pre-empt?" The Court made clear that there was federal question jurisdiction if the Trust commenced an action asking the question but not if the Franchise Tax Board commenced an action asking the same question.

(1) The Rule Against Asserting the Rights of Third Parties.

Powers v. Ohio

Supreme Court of the United States, 1991.
499 U.S. 400.

JUSTICE KENNEDY delivered the opinion of the Court.

Jury service is an exercise of responsible citizenship by all members of the community, including those who otherwise might not have the opportunity to contribute to our civic life. Congress recognized this over a century ago in the Civil Rights Act of 1875, which made it a criminal offense to exclude persons from jury service on account of their race. *See* 18 U.S.C. § 243. In a trilogy of cases decided soon after enactment of this prohibition, our Court confirmed the validity of the statute, as well as the broader constitutional imperative of race neutrality in jury selection. * * * In the many times we have confronted the issue since those cases, we have not questioned the premise that racial discrimination in the qualification or selection of jurors offends the dignity of persons and the integrity of the courts. Despite the clarity of these commands to eliminate the taint of racial discrimination in the administration of justice, allegations of bias in the jury selection process persist. In this case, petitioner alleges race discrimination in the prosecution's use of peremptory challenges. Invoking the Equal Protection Clause and federal statutory law, and relying upon well-established principles of standing, we hold that a criminal defendant may object to race-based exclusions of jurors effected through peremptory challenges whether or not the defendant and the excluded juror share the same races.

I

Petitioner Larry Joe Powers, a white man, was indicted in Franklin County, Ohio, on two counts of aggravated murder and one count of attempted aggravated murder. Each count also included a separate allegation that petitioner had a firearm while committing the offense. Powers pleaded not guilty and invoked his right to a jury trial.

In the jury selection process, Powers objected when the prosecutor exercised his first peremptory challenge to remove a black venireperson. Powers requested the trial court to compel the prosecutor to explain, on the record, his reasons for excluding a black person. The trial court denied the request and excused the juror. The State proceeded to use nine more peremptory challenges, six of which removed black venirepersons from the jury. Each time the prosecution challenged a black prospective juror, Powers renewed his objections, citing our decision in Batson v. Kentucky (1986).

His objections were overruled. The record does not indicate that race was somehow implicated in the crime or the trial; nor does it reveal whether any black persons sat on petitioner's petit jury or if any of the nine jurors petitioner excused by peremptory challenges were black persons.

> **FYI**
>
> *Batson* held that prosecutors may not exercise peremptory challenges to prospective jurors based on race.

The empaneled jury convicted Powers on counts of murder, aggravated murder, and attempted aggravated murder, each with the firearm specifications, and the trial court sentenced him to a term of imprisonment of 53 years to life. Powers appealed his conviction to the Ohio Court of Appeals, contending that the prosecutor's discriminatory use of peremptories violated the Sixth Amendment's guarantee of a fair cross section in his petit jury, the Fourteenth Amendment's Equal Protection Clause, and Article I, §§ 10 and 16, of the Ohio Constitution. Powers contended that his own race was irrelevant to the right to object to the prosecution's peremptory challenges. The Court of Appeals affirmed the conviction, and the Supreme Court of Ohio dismissed Powers' appeal on the ground that it presented no substantial constitutional question.

Petitioner sought review before us, renewing his Sixth Amendment fair cross section and Fourteenth Amendment equal protection claims. While the petition for certiorari was pending, we decided *Holland v. Illinois*, 493 U.S. 474 (1990). In *Holland* it was alleged the prosecution had used its peremptory challenges to exclude from the jury members of a race other than the defendant's. We held the Sixth Amendment did not restrict the exclusion of a racial group at the peremptory challenge stage. Five members of the Court there said a defendant might be able to make the objection on equal protection grounds. After our decision in *Holland*, we granted Powers' petition for certiorari limited to the question whether, based on the Equal Protection Clause, a white defendant may object to the prosecution's peremptory challenges of black venirepersons. We now reverse and remand.

II

For over a century, this Court has been unyielding in its position that a defendant is denied equal protection of the laws when tried before a jury from which members of his or her race have been excluded by the State's purposeful conduct. "The Equal Protection Clause guarantees the defendant that the State will not exclude members of his race from the jury venire on account of race * * * . Although a defendant has no right to a "petit jury composed in whole or in part of persons of [the defendant's] own race," * * * he or she does have the right to be tried by a jury whose members are selected by nondiscriminatory criteria.

[In Batson,] we considered a situation similar to the one before us today, but with one exception: Batson, the defendant who complained that black persons were being excluded from his petit jury, was himself black. During the voir dire examination of the venire for Batson's trial, the prosecutor used his peremptory challenges to strike all four black persons on the venire, resulting in a petit jury composed only of white persons. * * * [W]e held that a defendant can raise an equal protection challenge to the use of peremptories at his own trial by showing that the prosecutor used them for the purpose of excluding members of the defendant's race. * * *

The State contends that our holding in the case now before us must be limited to the circumstances prevailing in *Batson* and that in equal protection analysis the race of the objecting defendant constitutes a relevant precondition for a *Batson* challenge. Because Powers is white, the State argues, he cannot object to the exclusion of black prospective jurors. This limitation on a defendant's right to object conforms neither with our accepted rules of standing to raise a constitutional claim nor with the substantive guarantees of the Equal Protection Clause and the policies underlying federal statutory law.

In Batson, we spoke of the harm caused when a defendant is tried by a tribunal from which members of his own race have been excluded. But we did not limit our discussion in *Batson* to that one aspect of the harm caused by the violation. Batson "was designed 'to serve multiple ends,' " only one of which was to protect individual defendants from discrimination in the selection of jurors. * * * Batson recognized that a prosecutor's discriminatory use of peremptory challenges harms the excluded jurors and the community at large.

The opportunity for ordinary citizens to participate in the administration of justice has long been recognized as one of the principal justifications for retaining the jury system. * * * In Balzac v. Porto Rico (1922), Chief Justice Taft wrote for the Court:

> The jury system postulates a conscious duty of participation in the machinery of justice * * * . One of its greatest benefits is in the security it gives the people that they, as jurors actual or possible, being part of the judicial system of the country can prevent its arbitrary use or abuse.

And, over 150 years ago, Alexis de Tocqueville remarked:

> [T]he institution of the jury raises the people itself, or at least a class of citizens, to the bench of judicial authority [and] invests the people, or that class of citizens, with the direction of society.

* * *

> * * * The jury * * * invests each citizen with a kind of magistracy; it makes them all feel the duties which they are bound to discharge towards society; and the part which they take in the Government. By obliging men to turn their attention to affairs which are not exclusively their own, it rubs off that individual egotism which is the rust of society.
>
> * * *
>
> I do not know whether the jury is useful to those who are in litigation; but I am certain it is highly beneficial to those who decide the litigation; and I look upon it as one of the most efficacious means for the education of the people which society can employ." * * *

Jury service preserves the democratic element of the law, as it guards the rights of the parties and ensures continued acceptance of the laws by all of the people. * * * It "affords ordinary citizens a valuable opportunity to participate in a process of government, an experience fostering, one hopes, a respect for law." * * * Indeed, with the exception of voting, for most citizens the honor and privilege of jury duty is their most significant opportunity to participate in the democratic process.

* * *

We hold that the Equal Protection Clause prohibits a prosecutor from using the State's peremptory challenges to exclude otherwise qualified and unbiased persons from the petit jury solely by reason of their race, a practice that forecloses a significant opportunity to participate in civic life. An individual juror does not have a right to sit on any particular petit jury, but he or she does possess the right not to be excluded from one on account of race.

III

We must consider whether a criminal defendant has standing to raise the equal protection rights of a juror excluded from service in violation of these principles. In the ordinary course, a litigant must assert his or her own legal rights and interests, and cannot rest a claim to relief on the legal rights or interests of third parties. *Department of Labor v. Triplett*, 494 U.S. 715, 720 (1990); *Singleton v. Wulff*, 428 U.S. 106 (1976). This fundamental restriction on our authority admits of certain, limited exceptions. We have recognized the right of litigants to bring actions on behalf of third parties, provided three important criteria are satisfied: The litigant must have suffered an "injury in fact," thus giving him or her a "sufficiently concrete interest" in the outcome of the issue in dispute, * * * the litigant must have a close relation to the third party, * * * and there must exist some hindrance to the third party's ability to protect his or her own interests.

* * * These criteria have been satisfied in cases where we have permitted criminal defendants to challenge their convictions by raising the rights of third parties. *See, e.g., Eisenstadt v. Baird*, 405 U.S. 438 (1972); *Griswold v. Connecticut*, 381 U.S. 479 (1965); *see also McGowan v. Maryland*, 366 U.S. 420 (1961). By similar reasoning, we have permitted litigants to raise third-party rights in order to prevent possible future prosecution. *See, e.g., Doe v. Bolton*, 410 U.S. 179 (1973).

The discriminatory use of peremptory challenges by the prosecution causes a criminal defendant cognizable injury, and the defendant has a concrete interest in challenging the practice. * * * This is not because the individual jurors dismissed by the prosecution may have been predisposed to favor the defendant; if that were true, the jurors might have been excused for cause. Rather, it is because racial discrimination in the selection of jurors "casts doubt on the integrity of the judicial process," * * * and places the fairness of a criminal proceeding in doubt.

The jury acts as a vital check against the wrongful exercise of power by the State and its prosecutors. * * * The intrusion of racial discrimination into the jury selection process damages both the fact and the perception of this guarantee. "Jury selection is the primary means by which a court may enforce a defendant's right to be tried by a jury free from ethnic, racial, or political prejudice, * * * or predisposition about the defendant's culpability * * *. Active discrimination by a prosecutor during this process condones violations of the United States Constitution within the very institution entrusted with its enforcement, and so invites cynicism respecting the jury's neutrality and its obligation to adhere to the law. The cynicism may be aggravated if race is implicated in the trial, either in a direct way as with an alleged racial motivation of the defendant or a victim, or in some more subtle manner as by casting doubt upon the credibility or dignity of a witness, or even upon the standing or due regard of an attorney who appears in the cause.

Unlike the instances where a defendant seeks to object to the introduction of evidence obtained illegally from a third party, * * * here petitioner alleges that the primary constitutional violation occurred during the trial itself. A prosecutor's wrongful exclusion of a juror by a race-based peremptory challenge is a constitutional violation committed in open court at the outset of the proceedings. The overt wrong, often apparent to the entire jury panel, casts doubt over the obligation of the parties, the jury, and indeed the court to adhere to the law throughout the trial of the cause. The voir dire phase of the trial represents the "jurors' first introduction to the substantive factual and legal issues in a case." * * * The influence of the voir dire process may persist through the whole course of the trial proceedings. * * * If the defendant has no right to object to the prosecutor's improper exclusion of jurors, and if the trial court has no duty to make a prompt inquiry when the defendant shows, by adequate grounds, a likelihood of impropriety in the exercise of a challenge, there arise legitimate doubts that the jury has been chosen by proper means. The composition of the trier of fact itself is called in question, and the irregularity may pervade all the proceedings that follow.

The purpose of the jury system is to impress upon the criminal defendant and the community as a whole that a verdict of conviction or acquittal is given in accordance with the law by persons who are fair. The verdict will not be accepted or understood in these terms if the jury is chosen by unlawful means at the outset. Upon these considerations, we find that a criminal defendant suffers a real injury when the prosecutor excludes jurors at his or her own trial on account of race.

We noted in Singleton that in certain circumstances "the relationship between the litigant and the third party may be such that the former is fully, or very nearly, as effective a proponent of the right as the latter." * * * Here, the relation between petitioner and the excluded jurors is as close as, if not closer than, those we have recognized to convey third-party standing in our prior cases. *See, e.g.*, Griswold v. Connecticut, *supra* (Planned Parenthood official and a licensed physician can raise the constitutional rights of contraceptive users with whom they had professional relationships); Craig v. Boren (1976) (licensed beer vendor has standing to raise the equal protection claim of a male customer challenging a statutory scheme prohibiting the sale of beer to males under the age of 21 and to females under the age of 18); Department of Labor v. Triplett, 494 U.S. 715 (1990) (attorney may challenge an attorney's fees restriction by asserting the due process rights of the client). Voir dire permits a party to establish a relation, if not a bond of trust, with the jurors. This relation continues throughout the entire trial and may in some cases extend to the sentencing as well.

Both the excluded juror and the criminal defendant have a common interest in eliminating racial discrimination from the courtroom. A venireperson excluded from jury service because of race suffers a profound personal humiliation heightened by its public character. The rejected juror may lose confidence in the court and its verdicts, as may the defendant if his or her objections cannot be heard. This congruence of interests makes it necessary and appropriate for the defendant to raise the rights of the juror. And, there can be no doubt that petitioner will be a motivated, effective advocate for the excluded venirepersons' rights. Petitioner has much at stake in proving that his jury was improperly constituted due to an equal protection violation, for we have recognized that discrimination in the jury selection process may lead to the reversal of a conviction. * * *

The final inquiry in our third-party standing analysis involves the likelihood and ability of the third parties, the excluded venirepersons, to assert their own rights. * * * We have held that individual jurors subjected to racial exclusion have the legal right to bring suit on their own behalf. * * * As a practical matter, however, these challenges are rare. * * * Indeed, it took nearly a century after the

Fourteenth Amendment and the Civil Rights Act of 1875 came into being for the first such case to reach this Court. * * *

The barriers to a suit by an excluded juror are daunting. Potential jurors are not parties to the jury selection process and have no opportunity to be heard at the time of their exclusion. Nor can excluded jurors easily obtain declaratory or injunctive relief when discrimination occurs through an individual prosecutor's exercise of peremptory challenges. Unlike a challenge to systematic practices of the jury clerk and commissioners such as we considered in *Carter*, it would be difficult for an individual juror to show a likelihood that discrimination against him at the voir dire stage will recur. *See* Los Angeles v. Lyons, 461 U.S. 95 (1983). And, there exist considerable practical barriers to suit by the excluded juror because of the small financial stake involved and the economic burdens of litigation. * * * The reality is that a juror dismissed because of race probably will leave the courtroom possessing little incentive to set in motion the arduous process needed to vindicate his own rights. * * *

We conclude that a defendant in a criminal case can raise the third-party equal protection claims of jurors excluded by the prosecution because of their race.

* * *

It remains for the trial courts to develop rules, without unnecessary disruption of the jury selection process, to permit legitimate and well-founded objections to the use of peremptory challenges as a mask for race prejudice. In this case, the State concedes that, if we find the petitioner has standing to object to the prosecution's use of the peremptory challenges, the case should be remanded. We find that petitioner does have standing. The judgment is reversed, and the case is remanded for further proceedings not inconsistent with our opinion.

It is so ordered.

JUSTICE SCALIA, with whom THE CHIEF JUSTICE joins, dissenting.

[In the first two sections, Justice Scalia disagreed with the majority's Equal Protection analysis.]

* * *

III

In any event, the Court's third-party standing analysis is not correct. The Court fails to establish what we have described as the very first element of third-party standing: the requirement of "injury in fact." * * * The Court's attempt at constructing an injury in fact to petitioner goes as follows: When the prosecution takes race into account in exercising its peremptory challenges, it "casts doubt on the integrity of the judicial process," and "invites cynicism respecting the jury's neutrality and its obligation to adhere to the law," * * * as a result of which "[t]he verdict will not be accepted or understood as fair" * * * . The Court must, of course, speak in terms of the perception of fairness rather than its reality, since only last Term we held categorically that the exclusion of members of a particular race from a jury does not produce an unfair jury, and suggested that in some circumstances it may increase fairness. * * * But in any event, how do these alleged perceptions of unfairness, these "castings of doubt" and "invitations to cynicism," establish that the defendant has been injured in fact? They plainly do not. Every criminal defendant objecting to the introduction of some piece of evidence or to some trial procedure on the ground that it violates the rights of a third party can claim a similar "perception of unfairness," but we deny standing. "Injury in perception" would seem to be the very antithesis of "injury in fact." As the very words suggest, the latter sort of injury must be "distinct and palpable," *Warth v. Seldin* (1975), "particular [and] concrete," *United States v. Richardson*, 418 U.S. 166, 177 (1974), "specific [and] objective," *Laird v. Tatum*, 408 U.S. 1, 14 (1972). Today's opinion makes a mockery of that requirement. It does not even pretend that the peremptory challenges here have caused this defendant tangible injury and concrete harm-but rather (with careful selection of both adjectives and nouns) only a " cognizable injury," producing a "concrete interest in challenging the practice." * * * I have no doubt he now has a cognizable injury; the Court has made it true by saying so. And I have no doubt he has a concrete interest in challenging the practice at issue here; he would have a concrete interest in challenging a mispronunciation of one of the jurors' names, if that would overturn his conviction. But none of this has anything to do with injury in fact.

* * *

I respectfully dissent.

Notes and Questions

1. Despite the fact that *Powers* occurs in a criminal context, it is only one in a line of cases concerning when a party has standing to assert the legal rights of a non-party. The general rule is that one must assert his or her own legal rights and not those belonging to others. The exception is when (1) the party challenging the government action has a "close relationship" with the rightholder; and (2) when there are obstacles to the rightholder asserting his or her own rights. Even when the exception applies, the party challenging the government action must be able to demonstrate his or her own "injury-in-fact." Do you agree that the criminal defendant in *Powers* suffered his

own injury-in-fact when the peremptories were exercised in a racially discriminatory manner?

Powers may be exceptional because of the Court's special solicitude for the public perception of integrity in criminal proceedings. It may also be significant that *Powers* involves allegations of race discrimination. Another well-known case involving the assertion of the legal rights of third parties is *Barrows v. Jackson,* 346 U.S. 249 (1953), in which neighbors sued a landowner who had sold her house to an African-American family in violation of a racially restrictive covenant. The covenant plainly violated the buyers' Equal Protection rights, but could the *seller* assert the *buyers'* rights against the damages lawsuit? The Court held that under these "unique" circumstances she could.

Both *Powers* and *Barrows* involved race discrimination, but the Court has made exceptions to the general rule in less compelling circumstances. In *Craig v. Boren,* 429 U.S. 190 (1976), an Oklahoma statute prohibited the purchase of alcohol by males under the age of 21 and by females under the age of 18. A vendor challenged the constitutionality of the law in federal court. The vendor clearly demonstrated his own injury, loss of sales, but the legal right he asserted did not belong to him. It was an Equal Protection right belonging to males between 18 and 21 who wanted to buy alcohol. The Court found that the vendor had standing to assert their rights. Were there really serious obstacles to the males asserting their rights in court? Was there really a close relationship between the vendors and the males who wanted to purchase alcohol?

2. What authorizes the Court to recognize "prudential" restrictions on the standing doctrine? The Court has made it clear that an absence of Article III standing creates a jurisdictional defect; does an absence of prudential standing call for the same treatment? Must a court raise a matter of prudential standing ***sua sponte***, or are such defects less structural and therefore only for the parties to raise? Case law provides no clear answer.

3. Another exception to the general prohibition against asserting the rights of others is referred to as the "First Amendment overbreadth doctrine." Because of what the Warren Court viewed as the importance of having clear rules about what speech could be punished, so as not to bring about undue self-censorship, the Court permitted some litigants to challenge laws as violating the First Amendment—even if their own conduct was not constitutionally protected. In other words, they were permitted to assert the legal rights of hypothetical persons whose constitutionally protected speech would fall within the prohibition of the challenged law. Here is an example.

Coates v. Cincinnati

Supreme Court of the United States, 1971.
402 U.S. 611.

MR. JUSTICE STEWART delivered the opinion of the Court.

A Cincinnati, Ohio, ordinance makes it a criminal offense for "three or more persons to assemble * * * on any of the sidewalks * * * and there conduct themselves in a manner annoying to persons passing by * * * ." The issue before us is whether this ordinance is unconstitutional on its face.

The appellants were convicted of violating the ordinance, and the convictions were ultimately affirmed by a closely divided vote in the Supreme Court of Ohio, upholding the constitutional validity of the ordinance. * * * The record brought before the reviewing courts tells us no more than that the appellant Coates was a student involved in a demonstration and the other appellants were pickets involved in a labor dispute. For throughout this litigation it has been the appellants' position that the ordinance on its face violates the First and Fourteenth Amendments of the Constitution. * * *

In rejecting this claim and affirming the convictions the Ohio Supreme Court did not give the ordinance any construction at variance with the apparent plain import of its language. The court simply stated:

> The ordinance prohibits, ***inter alia***, "conduct * * * annoying to persons passing by." The word "annoying" is a widely used and well understood word; it is not necessary to guess its meaning. "Annoying" is the present participle of the transitive verb "annoy" which means to trouble, to vex, to impede, to incommode, to provoke, to harass or to irritate.

> Non constat jus civile a posteriori
>
> **It's Latin to Me!**
>
> *Inter alia* means "among other things."

> We conclude, as did the Supreme Court of the United States in *Cameron v. Johnson*, 390 U.S. 611 [1968] in which the issue of the vagueness of a statute was presented, that the ordinance "clearly and precisely delineates its reach in words of common understanding. It is a 'precise and narrowly drawn regulatory statute (ordinance) evincing a legislative judgment that certain specific conduct be * * * proscribed.' " * * *

Beyond this, the only construction put upon the ordinance by the state court was its unexplained conclusion that "the standard of conduct which it specifies is not dependent upon each complainant's sensitivity." But the court did not indicate upon whose sensitivity a violation does depend--the sensitivity of the judge or jury, the sensitivity of the arresting officer, or the sensitivity of a hypothetical reasonable man.[3]

We are thus relegated, at best, to the words of the ordinance itself. If three or more people meet together on a sidewalk or street corner, they must conduct themselves so as not to annoy any police officer or other person who should happen to pass by. In our opinion this ordinance is unconstitutionally vague because it subjects the exercise of the right of assembly to an unascertainable standard, and unconstitutionally broad because it authorizes the punishment of constitutionally protected conduct.

Conduct that annoys some people does not annoy others. Thus, the ordinance is vague, not in the sense that it requires a person to conform his conduct to an imprecise but comprehensible normative standard, but rather in the sense that no standard of conduct is specified at all. As a result, "men of common intelligence must necessarily guess at its meaning." * * *

It is said that the ordinance is broad enough to encompass many types of conduct clearly within the city's constitutional power to prohibit. And so, indeed, it is. The city is free to prevent people from blocking sidewalks, obstructing traffic, littering streets, committing assaults, or engaging in countless other forms of antisocial conduct. It can do so through the enactment and enforcement of ordinances directed with reasonable specificity toward the conduct to be prohibited. * * * It cannot constitutionally do so through the enactment and enforcement of an ordinance whose violation may entirely depend upon whether or not a policeman is annoyed.

But the vice of the ordinance lies not alone in its violation of the due process standard of vagueness. The ordinance also violates the constitutional right of free assembly and association. Our decisions establish that mere public intolerance or animosity cannot be the basis for abridgment of these constitutional freedoms. * * * The First and Fourteenth Amendments do not permit a State to make criminal the exercise of the right of assembly simply because its exercise may

3 Cf. Chaplinsky v. New Hampshire, 315 U.S. 568, where this Court upheld a statute that punished "offensive, derisive or annoying" words. The state courts had construed the statute as applying only to such words "as have a direct tendency to cause acts of violence by the persons to whom, individually, the remark is addressed." The state court also said:

> The word "offensive" is not to be defined in terms of what a particular addressee thinks. * * * The test is what men of common intelligence would understand would be words likely to cause an average addressee to fight. * * * The English language has a number of words and expressions which by general consent are "fighting words" when said without a disarming smile. * * * Such words, as ordinary men know, are likely to cause a fight. So are threatening, profane or obscene revilings. Derisive and annoying words can be taken as coming within the purview of the statute as heretofore interpreted only when they have this characteristic of plainly tending to excite the addressee to a breach of the peace." This Court was 'unable to say that the limited scope of the statute as thus construed contravenes the constitutional right of free expression.

be 'annoying' to some people. If this were not the rule, the right of the people to gather in public places for social or political purposes would be continually subject to summary suspension through the good-faith enforcement of a prohibition against annoying conduct. And such a prohibition, in addition, contains an obvious invitation to discriminatory enforcement against those whose association together is 'annoying' because their ideas, their lifestyle, or their physical appearance is resented by the majority of their fellow citizens.[6]

The ordinance before us makes a crime out of what under the Constitution cannot be a crime. It is aimed directly at activity protected by the Constitution. We need not lament that we do not have before us the details of the conduct found to be annoying. It is the ordinance on its face that sets the standard of conduct and warns against transgression. The details of the offense could no more serve to validate this ordinance than could the details of an offense charged under an ordinance suspending unconditionally the right of assembly and free speech.

The judgment is reversed.

MR. JUSTICE WHITE, with whom THE CHIEF JUSTICE and MR. JUSTICE BLACKMUN join, dissenting.

* * *

Even accepting the overbreadth doctrine with respect to statutes clearly reaching speech, the Cincinnati ordinance does not purport to bar or regulate speech as such. It prohibits persons from assembling and "conduct[ing]'" themselves in a manner annoying to other persons. Even if the assembled defendants in this case were demonstrating and picketing, we have long recognized that picketing is not solely a communicative endeavor and has aspects which the State is entitled to regulate even though there is incidental impact on speech. In *Cox v. Louisiana* (1965), the Court held valid on its face a statute forbidding picketing and parading near a courthouse. This was deemed a valid regulation of conduct rather than pure speech. The conduct reached by the statute was "subject to regulation even though [it was] intertwined with expression and association." * * * The Court then went on to consider the statute as applied to the facts of record.

In the case before us, I would deal with the Cincinnati ordinance as we would with the ordinary criminal statute. The ordinance clearly reaches certain conduct but may be illegally vague with respect to other conduct. The statute is not infirm on its face and since we have no information from this record as to what conduct was charged against these defendants, we are in no position to judge the statute

6 The alleged discriminatory enforcement of this ordinance figured prominently in the background of the serious civil disturbances that took place in Cincinnati in June 1967.

as applied. That the ordinance may confer wide discretion in a wide range of circumstances is irrelevant when we may be dealing with conduct at its core.

I would therefore affirm the judgment of the Ohio Supreme Court.

Notes and Questions

1. There are two distinct but overlapping rationales in *Coates*. The first is that the ordinance was unconstitutionally vague, which has nothing to do with standing. The second is that the ordinance violates the First Amendment because, so far as the Court could tell, it authorized the punishment of protected speech as well as unprotected action.

In *Coates*, it was not at all clear whether the petitioner's conduct was protected by the First Amendment. This did not stop the Court from determining that the ordinance, unlimited by the Ohio courts, could authorize punishment of all kinds of protected speech. Thus, without saying so, the Court permitted Coates standing to assert the First Amendment rights of hypothetical persons whose speech would be punishable under the ordinance. This is the First-Amendment-overbreadth doctrine.

The Burger, Rehnquist, and Roberts Courts have been more reluctant to invoke the doctrine than was the Warren Court. In *Broadrick v. Oklahoma,* 413 U.S. 601 (1973), the Court held that the overbreadth rule does not apply unless the law is *substantially* overbroad. In theory, at least, this inquiry requires a court to imagine all possible applications of a law and then determine whether a substantial number of those applications would violate the First Amendment. If not, then the person challenging the statute will win only if his or her own conduct is constitutionally protected.

2. The First Amendment overbreadth doctrine can be viewed as a sliver of a much larger issue: when may a litigant mount a "facial" challenge to a law versus merely an "as-applied" challenge? A facial challenge, if successful, renders the law unenforceable in any future case. An as-applied challenge, if successful, makes the law unenforceable only in cases that are factually similar to the case at bar. In recent years, the Supreme Court has permitted fewer and fewer facial challenges.

The metaphysics of facial versus as-applied challenges are daunting, and the Court has not been discursive on the subject. There are at least four ways to characterize the difference. One would be as a matter of substantive constitutional law, as in the First Amendment overbreadth cases. Arguably, *Coates* finds that the First Amendment itself compels facial invalidation of the law.

A second view would be that the First Amendment itself may not compel facial invalidation, but instead that the Court has employed facial invalidation as a prophylactic approach to protecting First Amendment rights. This second view might be characterized as "constitutional common law," analogous to *Miranda v. Arizona*'s relationship to the Sixth Amendment.

A third view would be that whether a law may be challenged facially or whether it must be considered on a case-by-case basis is a form of "severability" analysis. Usually, severability refers to whether the remainder of a statute can survive the invalidation of one section. Here, severability would refer to whether constitutional applications of the law can survive the existence of its unconstitutional applications. The severability view is not mutually exclusive to the first two views.

Fourth, the facial versus as-applied distinction can be seen as a matter of standing. When one is permitted to make a facial challenge, he or she arguably has been given standing to sue on behalf of hypothetical persons whose hypothetical protected activity would be condemned by the law in question. When one is relegated to an as-applied challenge, one only has standing to assert his or her own legal entitlements. If the claimant's conduct itself is not protected, the case is at an end. Whether the law might be unconstitutionally applied to the rights of others will be left for another day. In recent years, the Supreme Court has strongly favored the as-applied approach on the ground that it reflects judicial restraint, and that it leads to better decisions because of the dangers inherent in hypothesizing.

---

(2) *The "Zone of Interests" Requirement.*

In cases where the plaintiff seeks judicial review of adverse federal administrative agency action, he or she must satisfy all the Article III requirements for standing (unless Congress has relaxed them in a permissible manner). In addition, however, the plaintiff seeking judicial review of agency action must satisfy an additional requirement: the interest that the plaintiff seeks to vindicate must be arguably within the zone of interests that the statute upon which she relies protects or regulates. *Association of Data Processing Service Organizations v. Camp*, 397 U.S. 150 (1970), originally articulated that test. The Comptroller of the Currency had ruled that national banks could provide data processing services to other banks and to bank customers "as an incident to their banking services." Petitioners, a data processors' association and a data processing firm, challenged the ruling, alleging that it was inconsistent with a federal statute that allowed banks to engage in incidental activities only when such activities were "necessary to carry on the business of banking." Additionally, the petitioners argued that the Comptroller's ruling violated another federal statute that restricted banks to performing "bank services" for banks. The Supreme Court asserted that it was easy to identify those whose interests were directly affected by the statutes and concluded that competitors of the banks providing data processing services were within the statutorily protected zone of interests. The Court introduced the zone-of-interests test as a rejection of the previously-used protected-legal-interest test. "The 'legal interest' test goes to the merits. The question of standing is different."[19]

In 1987, the Court elaborated further.

> The "zone of interest" test is a guide for deciding whether, in view of Congress' evident intent to make agency action presumptively reviewable, a particular plaintiff should be heard to complain of a particular agency decision. In cases where the plaintiff is not itself the subject of the contested regulatory action, the test denies a right of review if the plaintiff's interests are so marginally related to or inconsistent with the purposes implicit in the statute that it cannot reasonably be assumed that Congress intended to permit the suit. The test is not meant to be especially demanding; in particular, there need be no indication of congressional purpose to benefit the would-be plaintiff.

Clarke v. Securities Industry Association, 479 U.S. 388, 399-400 (1987). Does the quotation distinguish the zone-of-interests test from the legally-protected-interest test that *Data Processing* purported to reject, or is Justice Brennan correct that the new test is merely the old traveling *incognito*?

National Credit Union Administration v. First National Bank & Trust Co., 522 U.S. 479 (1998), is a more recent example of the Court's application of the zone-of-interests test. Respondents, five banks and the American Bankers Association, challenged the National Credit Union Administration's (NCUA) interpretation of a federal statute it administered. The statute limited membership of federal credit unions to "groups having a common bond of occupation or association, or to groups within a well-defined neighborhood, community, or rural district." Before 1982, NCUA had interpreted the common bond provision to require that all members of the credit union be united by occupation, but it changed its interpretation in 1982 to apply only to each employer group within multi-group credit unions. Thus, as long as each employer group was united by a common bond, federal credit unions could be composed of entirely unrelated groups and still meet the requirements of the statute. When the NCUA allowed a particular credit union to add several unrelated employer groups, respondents sued. The Supreme Court again declared that in applying the zone-of-interests test there is no need to determine whether Congress intended the statutory provision to benefit those in the plaintiff's position. Rather, a court must first ascertain the interests the statute arguably protects and then ask if the plaintiff's interests are among them.

19 At least for Justice Brennan, the change in vocabulary was not sufficient.

> I had thought we discarded the notion of any additional requirement when we discussed standing solely in terms of its constitutional content in Flast v. Cohen. By requiring a second, nonconstitutional step, the Court comes very close to perpetuating the discredited requirement that conditioned standing on a showing by the plaintiff that the challenged governmental action invaded one of his legally protected interests.

The Court found that one of the protected interests was an interest in limiting the markets that federal credits can serve by limiting their membership and restricting the availability of their services to members only. As competitors, respondents also had an interest in limiting the markets the credit unions could serve, and the NCUA's interpretation of the statute affected that interest by allowing the credit unions to increase their base of customers. Consequently, respondents were arguably within the statute's zone of protected interests and had standing.

Four Justices joined in a vigorous dissent, arguing that the majority's application of the zone-of-interests test was inconsistent with precedent and all but eliminated the requirement. The majority's view of the relevant protected interest amounted to an examination of the interest in *enforcing* the statute. The common-bond requirement limited the customers a credit union can serve, and because respondents were competitors, they also had an interest in the same limitation. Thus, according to the majority, respondents had an interest in enforcing the statute. Instead, the dissent argued that the critical inquiry should be whether the injury of which the plaintiff complains is within the zone of interests the statute seeks to protect. The dissenters concluded that neither the statutory language, its operation, nor the circumstances surrounding its enactment demonstrated congressional intent to restrict competition. Thus, the injury plaintiffs asserted was not within the statute's zone of protected interests. The dissent argued that Congress required a common bond among members of federal credit unions to ensure that, as lenders, credit unions would be more knowledgeable about their borrowers and that the borrowers would be more reluctant to default.

Does *National Credit Union Administration* say that Congress may protect an interest (for purposes of standing) without having intended to do so? The majority opinion quoted *Clarke*'s assertion that "there need be no indication of congressional purpose to benefit the would-be plaintiff." Was it suggesting that Congress may not actually have intended to benefit the plaintiff but might have if it had thought about it, thus making this test a watered-down version of congressional intent? Alternatively, did it mean that reasonable people could conclude that a legislature intended the benefit claimed by the plaintiff, even if the particular legislature that passed the statute did not? In short, just what did the juxtaposition of these themes in the majority opinion mean? The only limitation the majority seemed to express on a plaintiff's coming within the zone-of-interests test was " 'if the plaintiff's interests * * * are [only] marginally related to or inconsistent with the purposes implicit in the statute.' "

The dissent, on the other hand, seemed to read the test as one of congressional intent. Is the dissent correct that the majority made the zone-of-interest test simply a mutated form of the constitutionally-required injury-in-fact? If injury-in-fact is all that the majority is talking about, what of its exclusion from standing of plaintiffs whose interests are only "marginally related to or inconsistent with the purposes implicit in the statute"? To the extent that the majority's test is not simply injury-in-fact, does it become a form of sophisticated causation requirement, with the Court asserting that it is unwilling to find that challenged agency action proximately caused plaintiffs' the injury-in-fact?

Suppose the Federal Communications Commission, acting pursuant to a congressional grant of authority, denies television broadcast stations permission to offer electronically-based services (such as shopping, banking, or other informational services) other than entertainment, simply because the FCC thinks it too difficult to regulate such a broad spectrum of operations. Such a decision would permit (perhaps implicitly encourage) development of cable services. If the FCC were then to overcome its concerns and reverse its ruling, would cable companies have standing to object?

Should the zone-of-interests test apply in litigation seeking relief under constitutional provisions? Is it possible in a principled way to speak of the zone of interests addressed by a constitutional provision?

Suppose a state passes a law requiring a locally-regulated industry to purchase a certain percentage of its raw materials from in-state sources, a change from the commercial practice formerly followed by the industry. It is clear that former suppliers in other states might challenge the law under the Commerce Clause. May the states in which the former suppliers are located file their own judicial challenges on the ground that the new statute has deprived them of tax revenues that they otherwise would have gotten from raw material sales? Is such a state within the zone of interests protected by the Commerce Clause? In *Wyoming v. Oklahoma* the majority found standing but did not mention the zone-of-interests test. Justice Scalia, joined by Chief Justice Rehnquist and Justice Thomas, dissented on the ground that Wyoming's interests were at best only marginally related to those protected by the Commerce Clause, since Wyoming was not itself seeking to engage in interstate commerce.

In at least one area, the Court has used zone-of-interest analysis as part of its inquiry in constitutional cases, though it has assiduously avoided labeling it as such. In a line of cases restricting defendants' standing to challenge searches and seizures on Fourth Amendment grounds, the Court articulated its findings in terms of the defendants' "reasonable expectation of privacy." *See, e.g., Rawlings v. Kentucky,* 448 U.S. 98 (1980); *United States v. Payner,* 447 U.S. 727 (1980); *Rakas v. Illinois,* 439 U.S. 128 (1978). In each of those cases, the Court held that defendants convicted on the basis of evidence seized in violation of the Fourth Amendment had no standing because they had no reasonable expectation of privacy in the area searched. Clearly each search caused a defendant injury in fact; the seized evidence was crucial to conviction. Was the Court saying, in effect, that the defendants were outside the zone of interests of the Fourth Amendment? Explicit application of the zone-of-interest test, a prudential rather than constitutional requirement, would allow Congress prospectively to overrule the Court's standing analysis. In the Fourth Amendment cases, the Court eliminated that possibility by declaring, in *Rakas:*

> the question necessarily arises whether it serves any useful analytical purpose to consider this principle as a matter of standing, distinct from the merits of a defendant's Fourth Amendment claim * * * . [T]he type of standing requirement * * * reaffirmed today is more properly subsumed under substantive Fourth Amendment doctrine * * * . The inquiry under either approach is the same. But we think the better analysis forthrightly focuses on the extent of a particular defendant's rights under the Fourth Amendment, rather than on any theoretically separate, but invariably intertwined concept of standing.

Does the Court's recognition of the interrelationship of standing and the merits support the argument that all standing inquiries ought instead to be treated as questions about the merits?

(3) *Organizational Standing*

May an organization ever bring suit on behalf of one or more of its members? May it do so even if the participation of individual members upon whose behalf the suit is brought is essential to the action? The Supreme Court faced these issues in *United Food and Commercial Workers Union Local 751* v. *Brown Group, Inc.*, 517 U.S. 544 (1996). A federal statute, the Worker Adjustment and Retraining Notification Act (the WARN Act), requires certain employers to provide workers or their union at least 60 days' notice before a mass layoff or plant closing. The Act authorizes employees to bring suit to obtain back pay for each day of the violation and specifically authorizes the union to bring suit on their behalf in the alternative. In a previous case the Court had set forth a three part test for situations where an organization would have standing to bring suit on behalf of a member: 1) the members would otherwise have standing to sue on their own behalf; 2) the interests the group seeks to protect are germane to its purpose; and 3) neither the claim asserted nor the remedy sought requires the participation of individual group members in the action. The participation of the individual union members was required so that their right to damages and the amount thereof could be determined based upon particularized proof. Thus, the Court had to determine whether Congress could constitutionally authorize the union to bring suit upon the employees' behalf, despite the fact that their individual presence was required.

The Court held that Congress had that power, characterizing the requirement that the presence of individual group members not be required as prudential. In its view the first and second requirements assured vigorous advocacy on the part of the organization in pursing a claim for which its member had Article III standing, and there was no constitutional necessity for anything else.

In an organizational standing case, is it essential that the organization itself have suffered some injury? A footnote in *United Food and Commercial Workers Union* asserted that the Court's holding made it unnecessary for it to address the issue. If the organization need not suffer any injury, how is the constitutional requirement of injury-in-fact met? Can Congress authorize any third-party to bring suit on behalf of an injured plaintiff?

D. Ripeness

Abbott Laboratories v. Gardner

Supreme Court of the United States, 1967.
387 U.S. 136.

MR. JUSTICE HARLAN delivered the opinion of the Court.

In 1962 Congress amended the Federal Food, Drug, and Cosmetic Act to require manufacturers of prescription drugs to print the "established name" of the drug "prominently and in type at least half as large as that used thereon for any proprietary name or designation for such drug," on labels and other printed material. The "established name" is one designated by the Secretary of Health, Education, and Welfare; the "proprietary name" is usually a trade name under which a particular drug is marketed. The underlying purpose of the 1962 amendment was to bring to the attention of doctors and patients the fact that many of the drugs sold under familiar trade names are actually identical to drugs sold under their "established" or less familiar trade names at significantly lower prices. The Commissioner of Food and Drugs, exercising authority delegated to him by the Secretary, published proposed regulations designed to implement the statute. After inviting and considering comments submitted by interested parties the Commissioner promulgated the following regulation for the "efficient enforcement" of the Act: "If the label or labeling of a prescription drug bears a proprietary name or designation for the drug or any ingredient thereof, the established name, if such there be, corresponding to such proprietary name or designation, shall accompany each appearance of such proprietary name or designation." A similar rule was made applicable to advertisements for prescription drugs.

The present action was brought by a group of 37 individual drug manufacturers and by the Pharmaceutical Manufacturers Association, of which all the petitioner companies are members, and which includes manufacturers of more than 90% of the Nation's supply of prescription drugs. They challenged the regulations on the ground that the Commissioner exceeded his authority under the statute by promulgating an order requiring labels, advertisements, and other printed matter relating to prescription drugs to designate the established name of the particular drug involved every time its trade name is used anywhere in such material.

The District Court, on cross motions for summary judgment, granted the declaratory and injunctive relief sought, finding that the statute did not sweep so broadly as to permit the Commissioner's "every time" interpretation. The Court of Appeals for the Third Circuit reversed without reaching the merits of the case. It held first that under the statutory scheme provided by the Federal Food, Drug, and Cosmetic Act pre-enforcement review of these regulations was unauthorized and therefore beyond the jurisdiction of the District Court. Second, the Court of Appeals held that no "actual case or controversy" existed and, for that reason, that no relief under the Administrative Procedure Act or under the Declaratory Judgment Act was in any event available. Because of the general importance of the question, and the apparent conflict with the decision of the Court of Appeals for the Second Circuit, we granted certiorari.

I

[The Court concluded that there is no indication that Congress intended to preclude pre-enforcement review of this agency action under the Administrative Procedure Act, "which embodies the basic presumption of judicial review to one 'suffering legal wrong because of the agency action, or adversely affected or aggrieved by agency action within the meaning of a relevant statute,' 5 U.S.C. § 702, so long as no statute precludes such relief or the action is not one committed by law to agency discretion."]

II

A further inquiry must, however, be made. The injunctive and declaratory judgment remedies are discretionary, and courts traditionally have been reluctant to apply them to administrative determinations unless these arise in the context of a controversy "ripe" for judicial resolution. Without undertaking to survey the intricacies of the ripeness doctrine it is fair to say that its basic rationale is to prevent the courts, through avoidance of premature adjudication, from entangling themselves in abstract disagreements over administrative policies, and also to protect the agencies from judicial interference until an administrative decision has been formalized and its effects felt in a concrete way by the challenging parties. The problem is best seen in a twofold aspect, requiring us to evaluate both the fitness of the issues for judicial decision and the hardship to the parties of withholding court consideration.

As to the former factor, we believe the issues presented are appropriate for judicial resolution at this time. First, all parties agree that the issue tendered is a purely legal one: whether the statute was properly construed by the Commissioner to require the established name of the drug to be used every time the proprietary name is employed. Both sides moved for summary judgment in the District Court, and no claim is made here that further administrative proceedings are contemplated. It is suggested that the justification for this rule might vary with different circumstances, and that the expertise of the Commissioner is relevant to passing upon the validity of the regulation. This of course is true, but the suggestion overlooks the fact that both sides have approached this case as one purely of congressional intent, and that the Government made no effort to justify the regulation in factual terms.

Second, the regulations in issue we find to be "final agency action" within the meaning of § 10 of the Administrative Procedure Act as construed in judicial decisions. An "agency action" includes any "rule," defined by the Act as "an agency statement of general or particular applicability and future effect designed to implement, interpret, or prescribe law or policy." The cases dealing with judicial review of administrative actions have interpreted the "finality" element in a pragmatic way.

* * *

We find decision in the present case following ***a fortiori*** from * * * precedents. The regulation challenged here, promulgated in a formal manner after announcement in the Federal Register and consideration of comments by interested parties is quite clearly definitive. There is no hint that this regulation is informal or only the ruling of a subordinate official or tentative. It was made effective upon publication, and the Assistant General Counsel for Food and Drugs stated in the District Court that compliance was expected.

> **It's Latin to Me!**
>
> "*A fortiori*" means "all the more." For example, if recklessly killing someone is a crime, then intentionally killing someone is *a fortiori* a crime.

The Government argues, however, that the present case can be distinguished from cases like *Frozen Food Express* on the ground that in those instances the agency involved could implement its policy directly, while here the Attorney General must authorize criminal and seizure actions for violations of the statute. In the context of this case, we do not find this argument persuasive. These regulations are not meant to advise the Attorney General, but purport to be directly authorized by the statute. Thus, if within the Commissioner's authority, they have the status of law and violations of them carry heavy criminal and civil sanctions.

Also, there is no representation that the Attorney General and the Commissioner disagree in this area; the Justice Department is defending this very suit. It would be adherence to a mere technicality to give any credence to this contention. Moreover, the agency does have direct authority to enforce this regulation in the context of passing upon applications for clearance of new drugs, or certification of certain antibiotics.

This is also a case in which the impact of the regulations upon the petitioners is sufficiently direct and immediate as to render the issue appropriate for judicial review at this stage. These regulations purport to give an authoritative interpretation of a statutory provision that has a direct effect on the day-to-day business of all prescription drug companies; its promulgation puts petitioners in a dilemma that it was the very purpose of the Declaratory Judgment Act to ameliorate. As the District Court found on the basis of uncontested allegations, "Either they must comply with the every time requirement and incur the costs of changing over their promotional material and labeling or they must follow their present course and risk prosecution." The regulations are clear-cut, and were made effective immediately upon publication; as noted earlier the agency's counsel represented to the District Court that immediate compliance with their terms was expected. If petitioners wish to comply they must change all their labels, advertisements, and promotional materials; they must destroy stocks of printed matter; and they must invest heavily in new printing type and new supplies. The alternative to compliance—continued use of material which they believe in good faith meets the statutory requirements, but which clearly does not meet the regulation of the Commissioner—may be even more costly. That course would risk serious criminal and civil penalties for the unlawful distribution of "misbranded" drugs.

It is relevant at this juncture to recognize that petitioners deal in a sensitive industry, in which public confidence in their drug products is especially important. To require them to challenge these regulations only as a defense to an action brought by the Government might harm them severely and unnecessarily. Where the legal issue presented is fit for judicial resolution, and where a regulation requires an immediate and significant change in the plaintiffs' conduct of their affairs with serious penalties attached to noncompliance, access to the courts under the Administrative Procedure Act and the Declaratory Judgment Act must be permitted, absent a statutory bar or some other unusual circumstance, neither of which appears here.

The Government does not dispute the very real dilemma in which petitioners are placed by the regulation, but contends that "mere financial expense" is not a justification for pre-enforcement judicial review. It is of course true that cases in this Court dealing with the standing of particular parties to bring an action have held that a possible financial loss is not by itself a sufficient interest to sustain a judicial challenge to governmental action. But there is no question in the present case that petitioners have sufficient standing as plaintiffs: the regulation is directed at them in particular; it requires them to make significant changes in their everyday business practices; if they fail to observe the Commissioner's rule they are quite clearly exposed to the imposition of strong sanctions. * * *

The Government further contends that the threat of criminal sanctions for noncompliance with a judicially untested regulation is unrealistic; the Solicitor General has represented that if court enforcement becomes necessary, "the Department of Justice will proceed only civilly for an injunction * * * or by condemnation." We cannot accept this argument as a sufficient answer to petitioners' petition. This action at its inception was properly brought and this subsequent representation of the Department of Justice should not suffice to defeat it.

Finally, the Government urges that to permit resort to the courts in this type of case may delay or impede effective enforcement of the Act. We fully recognize the important public interest served by assuring prompt and unimpeded administration of the Pure Food, Drug, and Cosmetic Act, but we do not find the Government's argument convincing. First, in this particular case, a pre-enforcement challenge by nearly all prescription drug manufacturers is calculated to speed enforcement. If the Government prevails, a large part of the industry is bound by the decree; if the Government loses, it can more quickly revise its regulation.

* * *

Reversed and remanded.

Notes and Questions

1. The Commissioner of the Food and Drug Administration issued a regulation that provided that he could immediately suspend certification service to any company that refused to permit authorized FDA employees unrestricted access to any company facilities involved in manufacturing color additives. Cosmetics containing additives that have not been certified cannot be sold in interstate commerce. Companies could challenge suspension of certification services through an administrative procedure and were entitled to judicial review of adverse determinations. Although it was unclear whether the Commissioner would actually order inspections and, if so, under what circumstances, several cosmetics companies sued, alleging that the Commissioner had exceeded his authority when he issued the regulation. Among other things, the companies were concerned that safeguards the Commissioner might devise would not adequately protect their trade secrets. Was the dispute ripe for adjudication? *See Toilet Goods Association v. Gardner,* 387 U.S. 158 (1967) (case unripe because it was not clear

whether inspection would actually be ordered, and there was no real harm in making the companies wait until inspection occurred).

2. There are potential difficulties distinguishing ripeness from standing. One might ask three questions: 1) whether the type of injury alleged by the plaintiff is justiciable, 2) whether the plaintiff personally has suffered or will suffer the injury, and 3) whether the plaintiff is sufficiently close to suffering the injury to make judicial intervention appropriate. Consider the following:

> In measuring whether the litigant has asserted an injury that is real and concrete rather than speculative and hypothetical, the ripeness inquiry merges almost completely with standing analysis. The standing requirement, the cornerstone of the Burger Court's article III jurisprudence, demands that a litigant show that he personally "has suffered some threatened or actual injury" as the result of the conduct of the defendant. This requirement of particularized actual injury repeatedly has been treated by the Court not only as constitutionally mandated, but as the very core of the standing determination.
>
> What then is the distinction between the standing doctrine's demand for "threatened or actual injury" and the ripeness cases' focus on "direct and immediate" harm? Analytically, the two concepts could be segregated, despite the similar phraseology of their standards. The standing doctrine might be used to analyze the nature and magnitude of *present* injuries. Only if such harms could be considered concrete, objective, and judicially cognizable would the standing barrier be overcome. The ripeness requirement, on the other hand, would focus on the substantiality of threatened or actually pending *future* injuries. Applying injury analysis on a forward-looking time frame, the ripeness demand would measure the present effects and hardships imposed by the threat of future government action. In theory, therefore, each doctrine could serve distinct but related functions.
>
> It is clear, however, that no such line of demarcation can be located in the cases. The "natural" overlap between standing and ripeness analysis occurs in the measurement of the cognizability of contingent or threatened harms. In such cases, the Burger Court appears to have used the two lines of inquiry interchangeably.

Gene R. Nichol, Jr., *Ripeness and the Constitution,* 54 U.CHI.L.REV. 153, 172-73 (1987) (footnotes omitted). Dean Nichol is not alone in his view. *See, e.g.,* ERWIN CHEMERINSKY, FEDERAL JURISDICTION § 2.4.1, at 117-18 (5th ed. 2007).

Dean Nichol's reservations about the limitations of the present/future dichotomy seem well-founded in at least some cases. For example, in *City of Los Angeles v. Lyons,* 461 U.S. 95 (1983), the plaintiff challenged a city police practice of using chokeholds when deadly force was not justified. Although the plaintiff had been choked, the Court found him without *standing* to seek injunctive relief against the practice because he could not show with any certainty that he would ever be choked again. The Court clearly viewed Lyons as a standing case, but under Dean Nichol's hypothesis it appears that it should be a ripeness case.

On the other hand, in *Renne v. Geary,* 501 U.S. 312 (1991), the Court considered challenges to a California constitutional provision that prohibited party endorsements of candidates for judicial, school, county or city offices. The Court found the challenges non-justiciable, noting in part:

> [W]e have no reason to believe that § 6(b) had any impact on the conduct of those involved. The committee made these endorsements "despite objections from some that such endorsements are prohibited" by the provision at issue. Nothing in the record suggests that any action was taken to enforce § 6(b) as a result of those endorsements. We know of no adverse consequences suffered by the Republican Committee or its members due to the apparent violation of § 6(b).

Although the Court sounds like it is discussing injury-in-fact, it concluded that no "ripe controversy" existed. Under Dean Nichol's model, the Court would have focused on the "nature and magnitude of *present* injuries" and therefore would have discussed standing.

Does the standing inquiry turn upon the certainty that the plaintiff will suffer injury or be a member of the affected class, while ripeness asks when an injury clearly threatening the plaintiff is likely to occur? Does this formulation do any better at describing the results reached by the Court? At bottom, does it make any difference whether a case is dismissed as unripe or for plaintiff's lack of standing?

3. Cases seeking declaratory relief can obviously present ripeness problems. The Court disparaged early declaratory judgment statutes as attempts to permit adjudication of cases that presented no Article III case or controversy. *See, e.g., Willing v. Chicago Auditorium Association,* 277 U.S. 274 (1928); *Liberty Warehouse v. Grannis,* 273 U.S. 70 (1927). But the Court's hostility seemed to erode five years later in *Nashville, Chattanooga & St. Louis Railway v. Wallace,* 288 U.S. 249 (1933), and in 1937, the Court had no trouble affirming the federal Declaratory Judgment Act's constitutionality. *Aetna Life Ins. Co. v. Haworth,* 300 U.S. 227 (1937). It is important to remember, however, that while one of the purposes of declaratory judgment statutes is to accelerate the commencement of litigation, the Supreme Court's approval does not mean that all ripeness problems have disappeared. One still must analyze each case under the Court's ripeness standards.

The Court continues to struggle with the distinction between standing and ripeness and with declaratory judgment actions. *Medimmune, Inc. v. Genentech, Inc.*, 549 U.S. 118 (2007), involved a dispute between a patentee (Genentech) and a patent licensee (Medimmune). The license covered an existing patent and a pending application for a second patent, and it required royalty payments to continue until the relevant patent expired or was authoritatively declared not to bar any particular product. Medimmune had been manufacturing Synagis for some years and did not pay royalties on it, apparently because neither party thought the existing patent covered the product. When the Patent Office issued the second patent, the patentee advised the licensee to begin paying royalties on Synagis. The licensee wanted to challenge the patent as invalid and unenforceable and further wanted to establish that Synagis did not infringe the second patent. The licensee faced the classic dilemma of an alleged patent infringer: pay royalties, discontinue the challenged activity or persist in its conduct, with the risk, as Justice Scalia noted, of incurring treble damages, liability for attorney's fees and an injunction preventing further manufacture and sale of the product, which accounted for more than 80% of Medimmune's revenues in recent years. Medimmune paid the demanded royalties "under protest and with reservation of all of [its] rights." It commenced an action seeking declaratory relief. The Court had to decide:

> whether Article III"s limitation of federal courts' jurisdiction to "Cases" and "Controversies," reflected in the "actual controversy" requirement of the Declaratory Judgment Act * * * requires a patent licensee to terminate or be in breach of its license agreement before it can seek a declaratory judgment that the underlying patent is invalid, unenforceable, or not infringed.
>
> Finding that the matter satisfied the case-or-controversy requirement, the Court reversed the lower courts' dismissal of the declaratory judgment claim and remanded.

Justice Scalia's opinion for an eight-Member majority observed that "Aetna [Life Ins. Co. v. Haworth (1937)] and the cases following it do not draw the brightest of lines between those declaratory-judgment actions that satisfy the case-or-controversy requirement and those that do not." The potential justiciability difficulty arose because the licensee's under-protest royalty payments prevented hostile action by the patentee, so the issue was whether the threat to the licensee was sufficient. The Court noted the difficulty in characterizing the problem:

> The justiciability problem that arises, when the party seeking declaratory relief is himself preventing the complained-of injury from occurring, can be described in terms of standing (whether plaintiff is threatened with "imminent" injury in fact " 'fairly * * * trace[able] to the challenged action of the defendant,' " or in terms of ripeness (whether there is sufficient "hardship to the parties [in] withholding court consideration" until there is enforcement action. As respondents acknowledge, standing and ripeness boil down to the same question in this case.

That may be so, given the Court's convoluted standing jurisprudence. Consider, however, whether the Justices might find the characterization of the problem simpler if they confined the standing inquiry to the question of identity (whether the party suing is the proper plaintiff) and remitted questions of timing (*imminent* injury in fact) to the ripeness inquiry.

The Court noted that where threatened government action is concerned, the Court has not required plaintiffs to risk liability or prosecution before suing, and Justice Scalia found no reason to use a different approach when the threatened action comes from a private source. Citing established precedents (including Ex parte Young

(1908) (*infra* at 663) and *Steffel v. Thompson* (1974) (*infra* at 837)), the Court noted that "[i]n each of these cases, the plaintiff had eliminated the imminent threat of harm by simply not doing what he claimed the right to do. * * * . That did not preclude subject-matter jurisdiction because the threat-eliminating behavior was effectively coerced."

4. Justice Harlan mentions several factors that affect whether issues are fit for judicial determination. Does the Court suggest that the more fact-specific a dispute, the less appropriate is early judicial intervention? Why might that be a desirable rule?

In San Jose, California, a city rent control ordinance provided that hearing officers could consider hardship to tenants when evaluating a landlord's application for a rent increase. A landlords' association and individual landlords challenged the ordinance, arguing that it violated the Due Process and Equal Protection Clauses and, separately, that it was a constitutionally impermissible taking. The Court ruled on the merits of the first two challenges, but declined to adjudicate the takings challenge.

> We think it would be premature to consider this contention on the present record. As things stand, there simply is no evidence that the "tenant hardship clause" has in fact ever been relied upon by a Hearing Officer to reduce a rent below the figure it would have been set at on the basis of the other factors set forth in the Ordinance. In addition, there is nothing in the Ordinance requiring that a Hearing Officer in fact reduce a proposed rent increase on grounds of tenant hardship. Section 5703.29 does make it mandatory that hardship be considered—it states that "the Hearing Officer *shall* consider the economic hardship imposed on the present tenant"—but it then goes on to state that if "the proposed increase constitutes an unreasonably severe financial or economic hardship * * * he *may* order that the excess of the increase" be disallowed. ([E]mphasis added). Given the "essentially ad hoc, factual inquir[y]" involved in the takings analysis, we have found it particularly important in takings cases to adhere to our admonition that "the constitutionality of statutes ought not be decided except in an actual factual setting that makes such a decision necessary." [F]or example, we found that a challenge to the Surface Mining Control and Reclamation Act of 1977 was "premature" and "not ripe for judicial resolution," because the property owners had not identified any property that had allegedly been taken by the Act, nor had they sought administrative relief from the Act's restrictions on surface mining. Similarly, in this case we find that the mere fact that a Hearing Officer is enjoined to consider hardship * * * does not present a sufficiently concrete factual setting for the adjudication of the takings claim appellants raise here.

Pennell v. City of San Jose, 485 U.S. 1, 9-10 (1988).

Contrast *Yee v. City of Escondido*, 503 U.S. 519 (1992), with *Pennell*. Owners of mobile home parks challenged a local rent control ordinance as a constitutionally impermissible taking, arguing it effectively gave mobile home owners a transferable right of perpetual occupation of the park owner's land and simultaneously regulated the rents a park owner could charge. Said the Court:

> As a preliminary matter, we must address respondent's assertion that a regulatory taking claim is unripe because petitioners have not sought rent increases. While respondent is correct that a claim that the ordinance effects a regulatory taking as applied to petitioners' property would be unripe for this reason * * * petitioners mount a facial challenge to the ordinance. They allege in this Court that the ordinance does not " 'substantially advance' " a " 'legitimate state interest' " no matter how it is applied. * * * As this allegation does not depend on the extent to which petitioners are deprived of the economic use of their particular pieces of property or the extent to which these particular petitioners are compensated, petitioners' facial challenge is ripe.

Are *Pennell* and *Yee* reconcilable? Are they consistent with *Abbott Laboratories*?

How much development of the fact pattern underlying a dispute of law should the Court demand? In *Poe v. Ullman*, 367 U.S. 497 (1961), physicians and their patients challenged Connecticut statutes that prohibited use of contraceptives or giving medical advice as to their use.

> In proceedings seeking declarations of law [the state] court has ruled that these statutes would be applicable in the case of married couples and even under claim that conception would constitute a serious threat to the health or life of the female spouse.
>
> Appellants' complaints * * * do not * * * allege that appellee Ullman threatens to prosecute [them]. The allegations are merely that, in the course of his public duty, he intends to prosecute any offenses against Connecticut law, and that he claims that use of and advice concerning contraceptives would constitute offenses.

The majority ruled that despite Ullman's statements of intention to prosecute violations, the controversy was not ripe. The Court relied in part upon the fact that the statutes had been on the books for nearly a century without enforcement.[20] Justice Harlan, later to author *Gardner*, dissented.

> I do not think these appeals may be dismissed for want of "ripeness" as that concept has been understood in its "varied applications." There is no lack of "ripeness" in the sense that is exemplified by [many prior] cases. In all of those cases the lack of ripeness inhered in the fact that the need for some further procedure, some further contingency of application or interpretation, whether judicial, administrative or executive, or some further clarification of the intentions of the claimant, served to make remote the issue which was sought to be presented to the Court. Certainly the appellants have stated in their pleadings fully and unequivocally what it is that they intend to do; no clarifying or resolving contingency stands in their way before they may embark on that conduct. Thus there is no circumstance besides that of detection or prosecution to make remote the particular controversy. And it is clear beyond cavil that the mere fact that a con-

20 Griswold v. Connecticut, 381 U.S. 479 (1965), held those statutes unconstitutional, vacating the convictions of several persons prosecuted under the century-old statute.

troversy such as this is rendered still more unavoidable by an actual prosecution, is not alone sufficient to make the case too remote, not ideally enough "ripe" for adjudication, at the prior stage of anticipatory relief.

Moreover, it follows from what has already been said that there is no such want of ripeness as was presented in * * * [cases] where the records presented for adjudication a controversy so artificially truncated as to make the cases not susceptible to intelligent decision. I cannot see what further elaboration is required to enable us to decide the appellants' claims, and indeed neither the plurality opinion nor the concurring opinion—notwithstanding the latter's characterization of this record as "skimpy"—suggests what mere grist is needed before the judicial mill could turn.

For a more modern setting, consider *Steffel v. Thompson,* 415 U.S. 452 (1974), *infra* at 837, where plaintiff challenged the constitutionality of a statute that would have prohibited him from distributing leaflets at a local shopping center. He had twice been warned to stop distributing leaflets or face arrest, and his companion, who continued to distribute, was arrested. The Court ruled on the merits. Would the plaintiffs in *Poe* have been better off if only they had been able to get Ullman to threaten them specifically? What if they could have arranged for someone else to be prosecuted?

5. The second component of the ripeness inquiry revolves around the hardship to the parties of withholding judicial resolution. Justice Harlan makes clear that this factor is critical, yet the Court has not been particularly rigorous or consistent in applying it. Consider the following cases.

a) The Hatch Act prohibits federal employees from participating in political campaigns. The penalty for engaging in the prohibited activity is dismissal from federal employment. If federal employees who wish to campaign sue to have the Hatch Act declared unconstitutional, is the matter ripe? *United Public Workers v. Mitchell,* 330 U.S. 75 (1947), held that it was not.

b) Although the Hatch Act still exists, members of a federal employees union allege that they desire to participate in a wide variety of political activities, including running for local office, being a delegate to a party convention, and campaigning for various candidates, but have refrained because of the statute. Democratic and Republican political organizations allege that they cannot get people to run for certain local offices or even to be members of Democratic or Republican committees because of the Act. Is an action brought by those groups under the Declaratory Judgment Act ripe? *United States Civil Service Commission v. National Association of Letter Carriers,* 413 U.S. 548 (1973), held that it was, but did not overrule *Mitchell.*

c) A state statute forbids discharge of sewage from boats, though officials have stated that they will not seek to enforce the statute until on-shore pumping facilities are available. A group of ship owners wishes to challenge the statute's constitutionality. They have already begun modifying their vessels to comply with the law when it is finally implemented. Is an action to declare the statute unconstitutional ripe? *Lake Carriers' Association v. MacMullan*, 406 U.S. 498 (1972), says it is.

d) Can one harmonize *Mitchell*, never overruled, with the latter two cases? In 1974, the Court said, "Where the inevitability of the operation of a statute against certain individuals is patent, it is irrelevant to the existence of a justiciable controversy that there will be a time delay before the disputed provisions will come into effect." *Regional Rail Act Reorganization Cases*, 419 U.S. 102, 143 (1974). Does that language suggest that the Court would view *Mitchell* differently today? In any event, how much harm must a plaintiff allege from the withholding of judicial relief in order to make a case ripe?

6. Is ripeness a constitutional or prudential concern? To be sure, at some point a plaintiff's request for pre-enforcement review of a proposed statute or regulation will raise substantial case-or-controversy problems. Should those be dealt with under the rubric of ripeness or standing? If a prospective plaintiff seeking pre-enforcement review has suffered an injury in fact for standing purposes, is there any legitimate constitutional or prudential policy reason to superimpose a ripeness requirement also?

E. Mootness

Defunis v. Odegaard

Supreme Court of the United States, 1974.
416 U.S. 312.

PER CURIAM.

> **It's Latin to Me!**
>
> "*Per curiam*" means "by the court." For various reasons, the court will sometimes use this designation rather than attributing authorship to a single justice. The press colloquially refers to a *per curiam* decision as an "unsigned" opinion.

In 1971 the petitioner Marco DeFunis, Jr., applied for admission as a first-year student at the University of Washington Law School, a state-operated institution. The size of the incoming first-year class was to be limited to 150 persons, and the Law School received some 1,600 applications for these 150 places. DeFunis was eventually notified that he had been denied admission. He thereupon commenced this suit in a Washington trial court, contending that the procedures and criteria employed by the Law School Admissions Committee invidiously discriminated against him on account of his race in violation of the Equal Protection Clause of the Fourteenth Amendment to the United States Constitution.

DeFunis brought the suit on behalf of himself alone, and not as the representative of any class, against the various respondents, who are officers, faculty members, and members of the Board of Regents of the University of Washington. He asked the trial court to issue a mandatory injunction commanding the respondents to admit him as a member of the first-year class entering in September 1971, on the ground that the Law School admissions policy had resulted in the unconstitutional denial of his application for admission. The trial court agreed with his claim and granted the requested relief. DeFunis was, accordingly, admitted to the Law School and began his legal studies there in the fall of 1971. On appeal, the Washington Supreme Court reversed the judgment of the trial court and held that the Law School admissions policy did not violate the Constitution. By this time DeFunis was in his second year at the Law School.

He then petitioned this Court for a writ of certiorari, and Mr. Justice Douglas, as Circuit Justice, stayed the judgment of the Washington Supreme Court pending the "final disposition of the case by this Court." By virtue of this stay, DeFunis has remained in law school, and was in the first term of his third and final year when this Court first considered his certiorari petition in the fall of 1973. Because of our concern that DeFunis' third-year standing in the Law School might have rendered this case moot, we requested the parties to brief the question of mootness before we acted on the petition. In response, both sides contended that the case was not moot. The respondents indicated that, if the decision of the Washington Supreme Court were permitted to stand, the petitioner could complete the term for which he was then enrolled but would have to apply to the faculty for permission to continue in the school before he could register for another term.[2]

We granted the petition for certiorari on November 19, 1973. The case was in due course orally argued on February 26, 1974.

In response to questions raised from the bench during the oral argument, counsel for the petitioner has informed the Court that DeFunis has now registered "for his final quarter in law school." Counsel for the respondents have made clear that the Law School will not in any way seek to abrogate this registration. In light of DeFunis' recent registration for the last quarter of his final law school year, and the Law School's assurance that his registration is fully effective, the insistent question again arises whether this case is not moot, and to that question we now turn.

2 By contrast, in their response to the petition for certiorari, the respondents had stated that DeFunis "will complete his third year (of law school) and be awarded his J.D. degree at the end of the 1973-74 academic year regardless of the outcome of this appeal."

The starting point for analysis is the familiar proposition that "federal courts are without power to decide questions that cannot affect the rights of litigants in the case before them." The inability of the federal judiciary "to review moot cases derives from the requirement of Art. III of the Constitution under which the exercise of judicial power depends upon the existence of a case or controversy." Although as a matter of Washington state law it appears that this case would be saved from mootness by "the great public interest in the continuing issues raised by this appeal," the fact remains that under Art. III "[e]ven in cases arising in the state courts, the question of mootness is a federal one which a federal court must resolve before it assumes jurisdiction."

The respondents have represented that, without regard to the ultimate resolution of the issues in this case, DeFunis will remain a student in the Law School for the duration of any term in which he has already enrolled. Since he has now registered for his final term, it is evident that he will be given an opportunity to complete all academic and other requirements for graduation, and, if he does so, will receive his diploma regardless of any decision this Court might reach on the merits of this case. In short, all parties agree that DeFunis is now entitled to complete his legal studies at the University of Washington and to receive his degree from that institution. A determination by this Court of the legal issues tendered by the parties is no longer necessary to compel that result, and could not serve to prevent it. DeFunis did not cast his suit as a class action, and the only remedy he requested was an injunction commanding his admission to the Law School. He was not only accorded that remedy, but he now has also been irrevocably admitted to the final term of the final year of the Law School course. The controversy between the parties has thus clearly ceased to be "definite and concrete" and no longer "touch[es] the legal relations of parties having adverse legal interests."

It matters not that these circumstances partially stem from a policy decision on the part of the respondent Law School authorities. The respondents, through their counsel, the Attorney General of the State, have professionally represented that in no event will the status of DeFunis now be affected by any view this Court might express on the merits of this controversy. And it has been the settled practice of the Court, in contexts no less significant, fully to accept representations such as these as parameters for decision.

There is a line of decisions in this Court standing for the proposition that the "voluntary cessation of allegedly illegal conduct does not deprive the tribunal of power to hear and determine the case, *i.e.*, does not make the case moot." These decisions and the doctrine they reflect would be quite relevant if the question of mootness here had arisen by reason of a unilateral change in the admissions procedures of the Law School. For it was the admissions procedures that were the target of this litigation, and a voluntary cessation of the admissions practices complained of could make this case moot only if it could be said with assurance "that 'there is no reasonable expectation that the wrong will be repeated.' " Otherwise, "[t]he defendant is free to return to his old ways," and this fact would be enough to prevent mootness because of the "public interest in having the legality of the practices settled." But mootness in the present case depends not at all upon a "voluntary cessation" of the admissions practices that were the subject of this litigation. It depends, instead, upon the simple fact that DeFunis is now in the final quarter of the final year of his course of study, and the settled and unchallenged policy of the Law School to permit him to complete the term for which he is now enrolled.

It might also be suggested that this case presents a question that is "capable of repetition, yet evading review," and is thus amenable to federal adjudication even though it might otherwise be considered moot. But DeFunis will never again be required to run the gantlet of the Law School's admission process, and so the question is certainly not "capable of repetition" so far as he is concerned. Moreover, just because this particular case did not reach the Court until the eve of the petitioner's graduation from Law School, it hardly follows that the issue he raises will in the future evade review. If the admissions procedures of the Law School remain unchanged, there is no reason to suppose that a subsequent case attacking those procedures will not come with relative speed to this Court, now that the Supreme Court of Washington has spoken. This case, therefore, in no way presents the exceptional situation in which the *Southern Pacific Terminal* doctrine might permit a departure from "[t]he usual rule in federal cases * * * that an actual controversy must exist at stages of appellate or certiorari review, and not simply at the date the action is initiated."

Because the petitioner will complete his law school studies at the end of the term for which he has now registered regardless of any decision this Court might reach on the merits of this litigation, we conclude that the Court cannot, consistently with the limitations of Art. III of the Constitution, consider the substantive constitutional issues tendered by the parties.[5] Accordingly, the judgment of the Supreme Court of Washington is

Food for Thought

In Southern Pacific Terminal v. Interstate Commerce Comm'n, which gave birth to the "capable of repetition, yet evading review" rule in 1911, there was no mention that the issue had to be capable of repetition with respect to the claimant then at bar. It could be capable of repetition with respect to anyone. The *DeFunis* Court does not mention that it changed the rule to restrict it to the individual in the case before the court. Is this change a good one?

5 It is suggested in dissent that "[a]ny number of unexpected events—illness, economic necessity, even academic failure—might prevent his graduation at the end of the term." "But such speculative contingencies afford no basis for our passing on the substantive issues [the petitioner] would have us decide," in the absence of "evidence that this is a prospect of 'immediacy and reality.' "

vacated, and the cause is remanded for such proceedings as by that court may be deemed appropriate.

It is so ordered.

MR. JUSTICE BRENNAN, with whom MR. JUSTICE DOUGLAS, MR. JUSTICE WHITE, and MR. JUSTICE MARSHALL concur, dissenting.

I respectfully dissent. Many weeks of the school term remain, and petitioner may not receive his degree despite respondents' assurances that petitioner will be allowed to complete this term's schooling regardless of our decision. Any number of unexpected events—illness, economic necessity, even academic failure—might prevent his graduation at the end of the term. Were that misfortune to befall, and were petitioner required to register for yet another term, the prospect that he would again face the hurdle of the admissions policy is real, not fanciful; for respondents warn that "Mr. DeFunis would have to take some appropriate action to request continued admission for the remainder of his law school education, and *some discretionary action by the University on such request would have to be taken.*" ([E]mphasis supplied). Thus, respondents' assurances have not dissipated the possibility that petitioner might once again have to run the gantlet of the University's allegedly unlawful admissions policy. The Court therefore proceeds on an erroneous premise in resting its mootness holding on a supposed inability to render any judgment that may affect one way or the other petitioner's completion of his law studies. For surely if we were to reverse the Washington Supreme Court, we could insure that, if for some reason petitioner did not graduate this spring, he would be entitled to re-enrollment at a later time on the same basis as others who have not faced the hurdle of the University's allegedly unlawful admissions policy.

In these circumstances, and because the University's position implies no concession that its admissions policy is unlawful, this controversy falls squarely within the Court's long line of decisions holding that the "[m]ere voluntary cessation of allegedly illegal conduct does not moot a case." Since respondents' voluntary representation to this Court is only that they will permit petitioner to complete this term's studies, respondents have not borne the "heavy burden," of demonstrating that there was not even a "mere possibility" that petitioner would once again be subject to the challenged admissions policy. On the contrary, respondents have positioned themselves so as to be "free to return to [their] old ways."

* * *

[I]n endeavoring to dispose of this case as moot, the Court clearly disserves the public interest. The constitutional issues which are avoided today concern vast numbers of people, organizations, and colleges and universities, as evidenced by the filing of twenty-six *amicus curiae* briefs. Few constitutional questions in recent history have stirred as much debate, and they will not disappear. They must inevitably return to the federal courts and ultimately again to this Court. Because avoidance of repetitious litigation serves the public interest, that inevitability counsels against mootness determinations, as here, not compelled by the record. Although the Court should, of course, avoid unnecessary decisions of constitutional questions, we should not transform principles of avoidance of constitutional decisions into devices for sidestepping resolution of difficult cases.

* * *

Notes and Questions

1. a) Is the majority accurate that "all parties agree that DeFunis is now entitled to receive his degree"? Does not Justice Brennan's dissent argue persuasively that the parties only agreed that DeFunis could finish the current term? It is far from unheard-of for circumstances to arise that cause a student unexpectedly to have to take a leave of absence or otherwise to interrupt his legal education. Should that possibility, which the majority calls a "speculative contingency," be sufficient to avoid a finding of mootness? If not, should the Court consider the effect on scarce judicial resources if DeFunis were forced to reapply and, presumably, to relitigate constitutional claims that have already been through three levels of courts?

b) Perhaps the majority is correct that the case is moot, but for a different reason. Even if DeFunis did not finish his degree program without interruption, upon seeking re-entry he would be competing for a seat with potential transfer and visiting students, not with the incoming first-year class. Is the school's affirmative action policy relevant at all? Even if it is, does its application in the new context present issues sufficiently similar to the original issues to warrant hearing the case?

2. Four primary categories of cases present special mootness problems. Whether they are actually moot cases that the courts hear or are not moot at all, it is important to understand each category. Consider the following.

a) A defendant is convicted, the conviction secured in part through the use of evidence the defendant claims was obtained in violation of his Fourth and Fourteenth Amendment rights. The state courts refuse bail pending appeal. After pursuing his appeals through the state court system, the defendant successfully petitions for a writ of certiorari. One month before oral argument, the defendant is released. Is the case moot? *See Sibron v. New York*, 392 U.S. 40 (1968).

In contrast with *Sibron*, consider the following. An inmate serving a sentence is released on parole. Subsequently, his parole is revoked in a proceeding that the inmate claims is constitutionally tainted. He seeks federal habeas corpus relief from his reincarceration. Does his release from custody upon the expiration of his complete sentence moot the habeas proceeding? *See Spencer v. Kemna*, 523 U.S. 1 (1998) (yes, because presumption that collateral consequences flow from criminal convictions does not extend to parole revocations).

An individual discharged from employment sues claiming discrimination. The company reinstates the individual in circumstances that make it clear that the reinstatement is not simply a ruse to dispose of the pending litigation. Is the case moot? *See Firefighters Local 1784 v. Stotts*, 467 U.S. 561 (1984) (not moot).

Sibron, Kemna, and Stotts address mootness in the context of what has been called "collateral consequences." Clearly the complaining parties are primarily interested in the sentence of imprisonment and the loss of employment. But are there other matters at stake than merely whether Sibron or Kemna is in jail or the fire fighter is on the job? If so, are they sufficient to avoid mootness?

b) *Roe v. Wade*, 410 U.S. 113 (1973), deals with one of the most important social issues of the past few decades. Yet should the Court have decided it at all? By the time the case reached the Supreme Court, the plaintiff was no longer pregnant. The majority observed, "the normal 266-day human gestation period is so short that the pregnancy will come to term before the usual appellate process is complete. If that termination makes a case moot, pregnancy litigation seldom will survive much beyond the trial stage, and appellate review will effectively be denied." Without disputing the Court's factual conclusion, one may nonetheless ask whether the Court could have done anything to affect the plaintiff's legal situation. If not, was the case moot?

Suppose a newly-arrived domiciliary of a state seeks to register to vote only to be told that there is a one-year residency requirement. He brings a federal action challenging the requirement on First and Fourteenth Amendment grounds, and secures a preliminary injunction requiring the state to permit him to vote in the upcoming election. If the next election will not occur until after he has been a state resident for one year, does his case become moot as soon as he casts his ballot? Suppose instead that he obtains a final judgment from the federal district court declaring the state statute unconstitutional. If, pending the state's appeal, the election occurs or the plaintiff completes his year of residence, does the case then become moot? If not, why not? If so, should the appellate court remand with directions to dismiss the case as moot? *See Dunn v. Blumstein*, 405 U.S. 330 (1972) (reaching merits because claim is "capable of repetition yet evading review"). *But cf. Golden v. Zwickler*, 394 U.S. 103 (1969) (too unlikely that situation would recur).

Is the "capable of repetition, yet evading review" case truly not moot, or is it a circumstance in which the ordinary strictures of the mootness doctrine have been loosened? If the latter, then must it not be the case that the mootness doctrine is at least partially prudential and not dictated by Article III? Chief Justice Rehnquist asked whether the case-or-controversy view of the mootness doctrine is accurate.

> The Court implies in its opinion, and the dissent [by Justice Scalia] expressly states, that the mootness doctrine is based upon Art. III of the Constitution. There is no doubt that our recent cases have taken that position * * * . But it seems very doubtful that the earliest case I have found discussing mootness, was premised on constitutional constraints; Justice Gray's opinion in that case nowhere mentions Art. III.
>
> If it were indeed Art. III which—by reason of its requirement of a case or controversy for the exercise of federal judicial power—underlies the mootness doctrine, the "capable of repetition yet evading review" exception relied upon by the Court in this case would be incomprehensible. If our mootness doctrine were forced upon us by the case or controversy requirement of Art. III itself, we would have no more power to decide lawsuits which are "moot" but which also raise questions which are capable of repetition but evading review than we would to decide cases which are "moot" but raise no such questions.
>
> * * *
>
> The logical conclusion to be drawn from [earlier "capable of repetition"] cases, and from the historical development of the principle of mootness, is that while an unwillingness to decide moot cases may be connected to the case or controversy requirement of Art. III, it is an attenuated connection that may be overridden where there are strong reasons to override it.

Honig v. Doe, 484 U.S. 305, 330-31 (1988) (Rehnquist, Ch. J., concurring). Chief Justice Rehnquist further suggested that the Court ought to be especially reluctant to dismiss a case as moot where the supervening events occurred after the decision to review.

> To me the unique and valuable ability of this Court to decide a case—we are, at present, the only Art. III court which can decide a federal question in such a way as to bind all other courts—is sufficient reason either to abandon the doctrine of mootness altogether in cases which this Court has decided to review, or at least to relax the doctrine of mootness in such a manner as the dissent accuses the majority of doing here. I would leave the mootness doctrine as established by our cases in full force and effect when applied to the earlier stages of a lawsuit, but I believe that once this Court has undertaken a consideration of a case, an exception to that principle is just as much warranted as where a case is "capable of repetition, yet evading review."

Justice Scalia dissented sharply, arguing that mootness is an inescapable component of Article III. "There is no more reason to intuit that mootness is merely a prudential doctrine than to intuit that initial standing is. Both doctrines have equivalently deep roots in the common-law understanding, and hence the constitutional understanding, of what makes a matter appropriate for judicial disposition." At the same time, he seemed to approve, with limitations, the capable-of-repetition exception.

Jurisdiction on the basis that a dispute is "capable of repetition, yet evading review" is limited to the "exceptional situatio[n]" * * * where the following two circumstances simultaneously occur " '(1) the challenged action [is] in its duration too short to be fully litigated prior to its cessation or expiration, and (2) there [is] a reasonable expectation that the same complaining party would be subjected to the same action again.' "

Was Chief Justice Rehnquist's advocacy of mootness as a prudential doctrine weakened by his admission that it may have at least an attenuated connection with Article III? What, exactly, does he mean by that phrase? If Article III compels the mootness doctrine, how can even the strongest policy reason override it? For an article arguing that justiciability generally and mootness particularly ought to be regarded as non-constitutional doctrines, see Evan T. Lee, *Deconstitutionalizing Justiciability: The Example of Mootness*, 105 HARV.L.REV. 603 (1992). For a more nuanced argument, see Matthew I. Hall, *The Partially Prudential Doctrine of Mootness*, 77 GEO. WASH. L. REV. 562 (2008).

c) If a plaintiff seeks to enjoin a policy or practice and the defendant announces that it has discontinued the conduct, does that moot the case? The Court has generally held that it does not, on the theory that the defendant remains free to resume the challenged practice. The leading case is *United States v. W.T. Grant Co.*, 345 U.S. 629 (1953), in which the federal government's challenge to corporate interlocking directorships on antitrust grounds was met by the corporations' announcement that they had abandoned and would not resume the practice. The Court refused to dismiss on mootness grounds. The Justices did say that "[t]he case may nevertheless be moot if the defendant can demonstrate that there is no reasonable expectation the wrong will be repeated. The burden is a heavy one."

Suppose that instead of merely announcing the cessation of a practice, a governmental entity repeals the statute or ordinance that aggrieved the plaintiff. Should that sort of formalized voluntary cessation moot the action? Nothing, obviously, then prevents reenactment of the challenged provision. *See generally Kremens v. Bartley*, 431 U.S. 119 (1977). *But see City of Mesquite v. Aladdin's Castle, Inc.*, 455 U.S. 283 (1982).

Alteration of a challenged statute presents an even more difficult mootness question. How much of a change is sufficient to moot the original question? The Court split on this issue in *Northeastern Florida Chapter of the Associated General Contractors of America v. City of Jacksonville*, 508 U.S. 656 (1993), where the petitioner originally challenged a municipal set-aside ordinance that required 10% of city contract expenditures to go to minority businesses. The petitioner challenged the ordinance on equal protection grounds, winning preliminary relief in the district court but suffering reversal in the Eleventh Circuit for lack of standing. Three weeks after the Supreme Court granted certiorari, Jacksonville replaced the ordinance with one that (a) applied only to women and blacks, rather than all minorities, (b) established participation "goals" of 5 to 16%, and (c) provided five alternative methods for reaching the goals. Jacksonville moved to dismiss the case as moot; the Court refused, arguing that the new ordinance worked no essential change in petitioner's complaint. Justices O'Connor and Blackmun dissented, arguing that

> precedents establish that, where a challenged statute is replaced with more narrowly drawn legislation pending our review, and the plaintiff seeks only prospective relief, we generally should decline to decide the case. The controversy with respect to the old statute is moot, because a declaration of its invalidity or an injunction against the law's future enforcement would not benefit the plaintiff. Where we cannot be sure how the statutory changes will affect the plaintiff's claims, dismissal avoids the possibility that our decision will prove advisory.

See also Diffenderfer v. Central Baptist Church of Miami, Inc., 404 U.S. 412 (1972) (*per curiam*); *Fusari v. Steinberg*, 419 U.S. 379 (1975).

The Court's hesitation about letting defendants too easily escape with insincere and temporary changes of behavior is understandable. But consider a circumstance in which a plaintiff fears that the defendant is about to undertake an unlawful activity. Is such a case ripe? Ordinarily, the plaintiff bears a heavy burden to show that the complained-of activity is imminent. Why should that burden be shifted to the defendant in circumstances of voluntary cessation?

Why doesn't *DeFunis* survive the mootness challenge as a "voluntary cessation" case? The University had no intention of abandoning its policy and candidly conceded that if anything interrupted DeFunis's march to his diploma, the policy might again apply to him. Does that meet the "heavy burden" upon which the Court insisted in *W.T. Grant*?

d) Does mooting the claim of a class representative require dismissal of the action? That pattern can arise in many contexts. In *Sosna v. Iowa*, 419 U.S. 393 (1975), the class representative challenged Iowa's one-year residency prerequisite for divorce actions. The plaintiff lost on the merits in the district court. Before the Supreme Court could review the case, Ms. Sosna satisfied the residency requirement. The Court refused to find the case moot, although the majority noted that "[i]f appellant had sued only on her own behalf, both the fact that she now satisfies the one-year residency requirement and the fact that she has obtained a divorce elsewhere would make this case moot and require dismissal." In addition, the Court declined to categorize the case as one "capable of repetition, yet evading review," recognizing the extreme unlikelihood that the plaintiff would again face the durational residency requirement. "The controversy may exist, however, between a named defendant and a member of the class represented by the named plaintiff, even though the claim of the named plaintiff has become moot." The majority was similarly untroubled by the named plaintiff's unrepresentativeness of the class when the case was reviewed. "In the present suit, where it is unlikely that segments of the class appellant represents would have interests conflicting with those she has sought to advance, and where the interests of that class have been competently urged at each level of the proceeding, we believe that the test of Rule 23(a) is met."

Justice White dissented vigorously, arguing that Sosna lacked standing to represent the class, since she no longer had any personal stake in the outcome. He chided the majority with language from the Court's then-recent decision in *O'Shea v. Littleton*, 414 U.S. 488 (1974):

> [I]f none of the named plaintiffs purporting to represent a class establishes the requisite of a case or controversy with the defendants, none may seek relief on behalf of himself or any other member of the class." * * * In reality, there is no longer a named plaintiff in the case, no member of the class before the Court. The unresolved issue, the attorney, and a class of unnamed litigants remain. None of the anonymous members of the class is present to direct counsel and ensure that class interests are being properly served. For all practical purposes, this case has become one-sided and has lost the adversary quality necessary to satisfy the constitutional "case or controversy" requirement. A real issue unquestionably remains, but the necessary adverse party to press it has disappeared.
>
> The Court thus dilutes the jurisdictional command of Art. III to a mere prudential guideline.

Whether one agrees with the rationale or not, the Court has been quite consistent in allowing certified class actions to proceed despite the disappearance of the claims of the named parties. But what if the class has not been certified when the representative's claims become moot? In *United States Parole Commission v. Geraghty*, 445 U.S. 388 (1980), a prisoner challenged the Parole Commission's guidelines. The district court refused to certify the plaintiff class, and before Geraghty's appeal from the denial of certification could be decided, he was released from custody. Does that not moot the case? The Court ruled that it did not. Yet, despite the Court's confident assertion that the plaintiff retained sufficient personal stake in the controversy to satisfy Article III, what, exactly, was the plaintiff's personal stake, and how did it differ from that of anyone else with an interest in prison problems and parole guidelines? *See also Deposit Guaranty National Bank v. Roper*, 445 U.S. 326 (1980), decided the same day as *Geraghty*.

Is the Court's approach to class actions and the mootness doctrine sound? If the Court were to reverse its position, what would be the practical effects?

3. In *Friends of the Earth, Inc. v. Laidlaw Environmental Services (TOC), Inc.*, 528 U.S. 167 (2000), the Court seemed to create some distance between the standing and mootness doctrines. In a case involving the citizen-suit provisions of the Clean Water Act, the Court stated:

> [T]he Court of Appeals confused mootness with standing. The confusion is understandable, given this Court's repeated statements that the doctrine of mootness

can be described as "the doctrine of standing set in a time frame: The requisite personal interest that must exist at the commencement of the litigation (standing) must continue throughout its existence (mootness)."

Careful reflection on the long-recognized exceptions to mootness, however, reveals that the description of mootness as "standing set in a time frame" is not comprehensive. As just noted, a defendant claiming that its voluntary compliance moots a case bears the formidable burden of showing that it is absolutely clear the allegedly wrongful behavior could not reasonably be expected to recur. By contrast, in a lawsuit brought to force compliance, it is the plaintiff's burden to establish standing by demonstrating that, if unchecked by the litigation, the defendant's allegedly wrongful behavior will likely occur or continue, and that the "threatened injury [is] certainly impending." Thus, in *Lyons*, as already noted, we held that a plaintiff lacked initial standing to seek an injunction against the enforcement of a police chokehold policy because he could not credibly allege that he faced a realistic threat arising from the policy. Elsewhere in the opinion, however, we noted that a citywide moratorium on police chokeholds—an action that surely diminished the already slim likelihood that any particular individual would be choked by police—would not have mooted an otherwise valid claim for injunctive relief, because the moratorium by its terms was not permanent. The plain lesson of these cases is that there are circumstances in which the prospect that a defendant will engage in (or resume) harmful conduct may be too speculative to support standing, but not too speculative to overcome mootness.

Furthermore, if mootness were simply "standing set in a time frame," the exception to mootness that arises when the defendant's allegedly unlawful activity is "capable of repetition, yet evading review" could not exist. * * * Standing admits of no similar exception; if a plaintiff lacks standing at the time the action commences, the fact that the dispute is capable of repetition yet evading review will not entitle the complainant to a federal judicial forum.

We acknowledged the distinction between mootness and standing most recently in *Steel Co.*:

> The United States * * * argues that the injunctive relief does constitute remediation because "there is a presumption of [future] injury when the defendant has voluntarily ceased its illegal activity in response to litigation," even if that occurs before a complaint is filed * * *. This makes a sword out of a shield. The "presumption" the Government refers to has been applied to refute the assertion of mootness by a defendant who, when sued in a complaint that alleges present or threatened injury, ceases the complained-of activity * * * . It is an immense and unacceptable stretch to call the presumption into service as a substitute for the allegation of present or threatened injury upon which initial standing must be based.

Standing doctrine functions to ensure, among other things, that the scarce resources of the federal courts are devoted to those disputes in which the parties have a concrete stake. In contrast, by the time mootness is an issue, the case has been brought and litigated, often (as here) for years. To abandon the case at an advanced stage may prove more wasteful than frugal. This argument from sunk costs does not license courts to retain jurisdiction over cases in which one or both of the parties plainly lacks a continuing interest, as when the parties have settled or a plaintiff pursuing a nonsurviving claim has died. But the argument surely highlights an important difference between the two doctrines.

4. *Tory v. Cochran*, 544 U.S. 734 (2005), held that a case resulting in an injunction restraining Mr. Tory from picketing and making any oral or written public statements about the well-known attorney Johnnie Cochran was not mooted by Mr. Cochran's death. California law did not automatically render the injunction invalid upon Mr. Cochran's death; apparently, a court order was necessary to determine its continued force. Moreover, the widow had an interest in enforcing the injunction. The Court also concluded, however, that the injunction as written amounted to an overly broad prior restraint on speech because the basic reason for the injunction, which was to keep Tory from trying to coerce Mr. Cochran to pay " 'amounts of money to which Tory was not entitled' as a 'tribute' or a 'premium' for desisting * * * ," had lost much of its force. The Court remanded to the state courts to consider whether a more narrowly tailored injunction was appropriate.

F. Political Questions

Zivotofsky ex rel. Zivotofsky v. Clinton

Supreme Court of the United States, 2012.
132 S.Ct. 1421.

CHIEF JUSTICE ROBERTS delivered the opinion of the Court.

Congress enacted a statute providing that Americans born in Jerusalem may elect to have "Israel" listed as the place of birth on their passports. The State Department declined to follow that law, citing its longstanding policy of not taking a position on the political status of Jerusalem. When sued by an American who invoked the statute, the Secretary of State argued that the courts lacked authority to decide the case because it presented a political question. The Court of Appeals so held.

We disagree. The courts are fully capable of determining whether this statute may be given effect, or instead must be struck down in light of authority conferred on the Executive by the Constitution.

I

A

In 2002, Congress enacted the Foreign Relations Authorization Act, Fiscal Year 2003. Section 214 of the Act is entitled "United States Policy with Respect to Jerusalem as the Capital of Israel." The first two subsections express Congress's "commitment" to relocating the United States Embassy in Israel to Jerusalem. The third bars funding for the publication of official Government documents that do not list Jerusalem as the capital of Israel. The fourth and final provision, § 214(d), is the only one at stake in this case. Entitled "Record of Place of Birth as Israel for Passport Purposes," it provides that "[f]or purposes of the registration of birth, certification of nationality, or issuance of a passport of a United States citizen born in the city of Jerusalem, the Secretary shall, upon the request of the citizen or the citizen's legal guardian, record the place of birth as Israel."

The State Department's Foreign Affairs Manual states that "[w]here the birthplace of the applicant is located in territory disputed by another country, the city or area of birth may be written in the passport." The manual specifically directs that passport officials should enter "JERUSALEM" and should "not write Israel or Jordan" when recording the birthplace of a person born in Jerusalem on a passport.

Section 214(d) sought to override this instruction by allowing citizens born in Jerusalem to have "Israel" recorded on their passports if they wish. In signing the Foreign Relations Authorization Act into law, President George W. Bush stated his belief that § 214 "impermissibly interferes with the President's constitutional authority to conduct the Nation's foreign affairs and to supervise the unitary executive branch." He added that if the section is "construed as mandatory," then it would "interfere with the President's constitutional authority to formulate the position of the United States, speak for the Nation in international affairs, and determine the terms on which recognition is given to foreign states." He concluded by emphasizing that "U.S. policy regarding Jerusalem has not changed." The President made no specific reference to the passport mandate in § 214(d).

B

Petitioner Menachem Binyamin Zivotofsky was born in Jerusalem on October 17, 2002, shortly after § 214(d) was enacted. Zivotofsky's parents were American citizens and he accordingly was as well, by virtue of congressional enactment. Zivotofsky's mother filed an application for a consular report of birth abroad and a United States passport. She requested that his place of birth be listed as "Jerusalem, Israel" on both documents. U.S. officials informed Zivotofsky's mother that State Department policy prohibits recording "Israel" as Zivotofsky's place of birth.

Pursuant to that policy, Zivotofsky was issued a passport and consular report of birth abroad listing only "Jerusalem."

Zivotofsky's parents filed a complaint on his behalf against the Secretary of State. Zivotofsky sought a declaratory judgment and a permanent injunction ordering the Secretary to identify his place of birth as "Jerusalem, Israel" in the official documents. The District Court granted the Secretary's motion to dismiss the complaint on the grounds that Zivotofsky lacked standing and that his complaint presented a nonjusticiable political question.

The Court of Appeals for the D.C. Circuit reversed, concluding that Zivotofsky did have standing. It then observed that while Zivotofsky had originally asked that "Jerusalem, Israel" be recorded on his passport, "[b]oth sides agree that the question now is whether § 214(d) entitles [him] to have just 'Israel' listed as his place of birth." The D.C. Circuit determined that additional factual development might be helpful in deciding whether this question was justiciable, as the parties disagreed about the foreign policy implications of listing "Israel" alone as a birthplace on the passport. It therefore remanded the case to the District Court.

The District Court again found that the case was not justiciable. It explained that "[r]esolving [Zivotofsky's] claim on the merits would necessarily require the Court to decide the political status of Jerusalem." Concluding that the claim therefore presented a political question, the District Court dismissed the case for lack of subject matter jurisdiction.

The D.C. Circuit affirmed. It reasoned that the Constitution gives the Executive the exclusive power to recognize foreign sovereigns, and that the exercise of this power cannot be reviewed by the courts. Therefore, "deciding whether the Secretary of State must mark a passport * * * as Zivotofsky requests would necessarily draw [the court] into an area of decisionmaking the Constitution leaves to the Executive alone." The D.C. Circuit held that the political question doctrine prohibits such an intrusion by the courts, and rejected any suggestion that Congress's decision to take "a position on the status of Jerusalem" could change the analysis.

Judge Edwards concurred in the judgment, but wrote separately to express his view that the political question doctrine has no application to this case. He explained that the issue before the court was whether § 214(d) "impermissibly intrude[s] on the President's exclusive power to recognize foreign sovereigns." That question, he observed, involves "commonplace issues of statutory and constitutional interpretation" plainly within the constitutional authority of the Judiciary to decide. Reaching the merits, Judge Edwards determined that designating Israel as a place of birth on a passport is a policy "in furtherance of the recognition power." Because in his view the Constitution gives that power exclusively to the President, Judge Edwards found § 214(d) unconstitutional. For this reason, he concluded that Zivotofsky had no viable cause of action, and concurred in affirming the dismissal of the complaint.

sep. of powers

Zivotofsky petitioned for certiorari, and we granted review.

II

The lower courts concluded that Zivotofsky's claim presents a political question and therefore cannot be adjudicated. We disagree.

In general, the Judiciary has a responsibility to decide cases properly before it, even those it "would gladly avoid." *Cohens v. Virginia*, 6 Wheat. 264, 404, 5 L.Ed. 257 (1821). Our precedents have identified a narrow exception to that rule, known as the "political question" doctrine. We have explained that a controversy "involves a political question * * * where there is 'a textually demonstrable constitutional commitment of the issue to a coordinate political department; or a lack of judicially discoverable and manageable standards for resolving it.' " In such a case, we have held that a court lacks the authority to decide the dispute before it.

The lower courts ruled that this case involves a political question because deciding Zivotofsky's claim would force the Judicial Branch to interfere with the President's exercise of constitutional power committed to him alone. The District Court understood Zivotofsky to ask the courts to "decide the political status of Jerusalem." This misunderstands the issue presented. Zivotofsky does not ask the courts to determine whether Jerusalem is the capital of Israel. He instead seeks to determine whether he may vindicate his statutory right, under § 214(d), to choose to have Israel recorded on his passport as his place of birth.

For its part, the D.C. Circuit treated the two questions as one and the same. That court concluded that "[o]nly the Executive—not Congress and not the courts—has the power to define U.S. policy regarding Israel's sovereignty over Jerusalem," and also to "decide how best to implement that policy." Because the Department's passport rule was adopted to implement the President's "exclusive and unreviewable constitutional power to keep the United States out of the debate over the status of Jerusalem," the validity of that rule was itself a "nonjusticiable political question" that "the Constitution leaves to the Executive alone." Indeed, the D.C. Circuit's opinion does not even mention § 214(d) until the fifth of its six paragraphs of analysis, and then only to dismiss it as irrelevant: "That Congress took a position on the status of Jerusalem and gave Zivotofsky a statutory cause of action * * * is of no moment to whether the judiciary has [the] authority to resolve this dispute * * * ."

The existence of a statutory right, however, is certainly relevant to the Judiciary's power to decide Zivotofsky's claim. The federal courts are not being asked to supplant a foreign policy decision of the political branches with the courts' own unmoored determination of what United States policy toward Jerusalem should be. Instead, Zivotofsky requests that the courts enforce a specific statutory right. To resolve his claim, the Judiciary must decide if Zivotofsky's interpretation of the statute is correct, and whether the statute is constitutional. This is a familiar judicial exercise.

Moreover, because the parties do not dispute the interpretation of § 214(d), the only real question for the courts is whether the statute is constitutional. At least since *Marbury v. Madison*, we have recognized that when an Act of Congress is alleged to conflict with the Constitution, "[i]t is emphatically the province and duty of the judicial department to say what the law is. That duty will sometimes involve the "[r]esolution of litigation challenging the constitutional authority of one of the three branches," but courts cannot avoid their responsibility merely "because the issues have political implications."

In this case, determining the constitutionality of § 214(d) involves deciding whether the statute impermissibly intrudes upon Presidential powers under the Constitution. If so, the law must be invalidated and Zivotofsky's case should be dismissed for failure to state a claim. If, on the other hand, the statute does not trench on the President's powers, then the Secretary must be ordered to issue Zivotofsky a passport that complies with § 214(d). Either way, the political question doctrine is not implicated. "No policy underlying the political question doctrine suggests that Congress or the Executive * * * can decide the constitutionality of a statute; that is a decision for the courts."

The Secretary contends that "there is 'a textually demonstrable constitutional commitment' " to the President of the sole power to recognize foreign sovereigns and, as a corollary, to determine whether an American born in Jerusalem may choose to have Israel listed as his place of birth on his passport. Perhaps. But there is, of course, no exclusive commitment to the Executive of the power to determine the constitutionality of a statute. The Judicial Branch appropriately exercises that authority, including in a case such as this, where the question is whether Congress or the Executive is "aggrandizing its power at the expense of another branch."

Our precedents have also found the political question doctrine implicated when there is " 'a lack of judicially discoverable and manageable standards for resolving' " the question before the court. Framing the issue as the lower courts did, in terms of whether the Judiciary may decide the political status of Jerusalem, certainly raises those concerns. They dissipate, however, when the issue is recognized to be the more focused one of the constitutionality of § 214(d). Indeed, both sides offer detailed legal arguments regarding whether § 214(d) is constitutional in light of powers committed to the Executive, and whether Congress's own powers with respect to passports must be weighed in analyzing this question.

For example, the Secretary reprises on the merits her argument on the political question issue, claiming that the Constitution gives the Executive the exclusive power to formulate recognition policy. She roots her claim in the Constitution's declaration that the President shall "receive Ambassadors and other public Ministers." U.S. CONST., Art. II, § 3. According to the Secretary, "[c]enturies-long Executive Branch practice, congressional acquiescence, and decisions by this Court" confirm that the "receive Ambassadors" clause confers upon the Executive the exclusive power of recognition.

The Secretary observes that "President Washington and his cabinet unanimously decided that the President could receive the ambassador from the new government of France without first consulting Congress." She notes, too, that early attempts by the Legislature to affect recognition policy were regularly "rejected in Congress as inappropriate incursions into the Executive Branch's constitutional authority." And she cites precedents from this Court stating that "[p]olitical recognition is exclusively a function of the Executive."

The Secretary further contends that § 214(d) constitutes an impermissible exercise of the recognition power because "the decision as to how to describe the place of birth * * * operates as an official statement of whether the United States recognizes a state's sovereignty over a territorial area." The Secretary will not "list[ ] as a place of birth a country whose sovereignty over the relevant territory the United States does not recognize." Therefore, she claims, "listing 'Israel' as the place of birth would constitute an official decision by the United States to begin to treat Jerusalem as a city located within Israel."

For his part, Zivotofsky argues that, far from being an exercise of the recognition power, § 214(d) is instead a "legitimate and permissible" exercise of Congress's "authority to legislate on the form and content of a passport." He points the Court to Professor Louis Henkin's observation that " 'in the competition for power in foreign relations,' Congress has 'an impressive array of powers expressly enumerated in the Constitution.' " Zivotofsky suggests that Congress's authority to enact § 214(d) derives specifically from its powers over naturalization, U.S. CONST., Art. I, § 8, cl. 4, and foreign commerce, *id.*, § 8, cl. 3. According to Zivotofsky, Congress has used these powers to pass laws regulating the content and issuance of passports since 1856.

Zivotofsky contends that § 214(d) fits squarely within this tradition. He notes that the State Department's designated representative stated in her deposition for this litigation that the "place of birth" entry is included only as "an element of identification." Moreover, Zivotofsky argues, the "place of birth" entry cannot be taken as a means for recognizing foreign sovereigns, because the State Department authorizes recording unrecognized territories—such as the Gaza Strip and the West Bank—as places of birth.

Further, Zivotofsky claims that even if § 214(d) does implicate the recognition power, that is not a power the Constitution commits exclusively to the Executive. Zivotofsky argues that the Secretary is overreading the authority granted to the President in the "receive Ambassadors" clause. He observes that in the Federalist Papers, Alexander Hamilton described the power conferred by this clause as "more a matter of dignity than of authority," and called it "a circumstance, which will be without consequence in the administration of the government." Zivotofsky also points to other clauses in the Constitution, such as Congress's power to declare war, that suggest some congressional role in recognition. He cites, for example, an 1836 message from President Jackson to Congress, acknowledging that it is unclear who holds the authority to recognize because it is a power "no where expressly delegated" in the Constitution, and one that is "necessarily involved in some of the great powers given to Congress."

Zivotofsky argues that language from this Court's precedents suggesting the recognition power belongs exclusively to the President is inapplicable to his claim, because that language appeared in cases where the Court was asked to alter recognition policy developed by the Executive in the absence of congressional opposition. Finally, Zivotofsky contends that even if the "receive Ambassadors" clause confers some exclusive recognition power on the President, simply allowing a choice as to the "place of birth" entry on a passport does not significantly intrude on that power.

Recitation of these arguments—which sound in familiar principles of constitutional interpretation—is enough to establish that this case does not "turn on standards that defy judicial application." Resolution of Zivotofsky's claim demands careful examination of the textual, structural, and historical evidence put forward by the parties regarding the nature of the statute and of the passport and recognition powers. This is what courts do. The political question doctrine poses no bar to judicial review of this case.

* * *

The judgment of the Court of Appeals for the D.C. Circuit is vacated, and the case is remanded for further proceedings consistent with this opinion.

It is so ordered.

JUSTICE SOTOMAYOR, with whom JUSTICE BREYER joins as to Part I, concurring in part and concurring in the judgment.

As this case illustrates, the proper application of *Baker's* six factors has generated substantial confusion in the lower courts. I concur in the Court's conclusion that this case does not present a political question. I write separately, however, because I understand the inquiry required by the political question doctrine to be more demanding than that suggested by the Court.

[In *Baker v. Carr*, 369 U.S. 186 (1962), the Court set forth six factors for determining whether litigation presents a nonjusticiable political question:

> [A] textually demonstrable constitutional commitment of the issue to a coordinate political department; or a lack of judicially discoverable and manageable standards for resolving it; or the impossibility of deciding without an initial policy determination of a kind clearly for nonjudicial discretion; or the impossibility of a court's undertaking independent resolution without expressing lack of the respect due coordinate branches of government; or an unusual need for unquestioning adherence to a political decision already made, or the potentiality of embarrassment from multifarious pronouncements by various departments on one question.

The majority in *Zivotofsky* applies only the first two factors of the *Baker* test.]

I

The political question doctrine speaks to an amalgam of circumstances in which courts properly examine whether a particular suit is justiciable—that is, whether the dispute is appropriate for resolution by courts. The doctrine is "essentially a function of the separation of powers," *Baker v. Carr* (1962), which recognizes the limits that Article III imposes upon courts and accords appropriate respect to the other branches' exercise of their own constitutional powers.

* * *

In my view, the *Baker* factors reflect three distinct justifications for withholding judgment on the merits of a dispute. When a case would require a court to decide an issue whose resolution is textually committed to a coordinate political department, as envisioned by *Baker's* first factor,

Food for Thought

The next section may be *Zivotofsky's* most important contribution to political question jurisprudence. Justice Sotomayor's incisive categorization of *Baker's* six factors provides a good roadmap for applying the doctrine.

abstention is warranted because the court lacks authority to resolve that issue. In such cases, the Constitution itself requires that another branch resolve the question presented.

The second and third *Baker* factors reflect circumstances in which a dispute calls for decisionmaking beyond courts' competence. " 'The judicial Power' created by Article III, § 1, of the Constitution is not whatever judges choose to do," but rather the power "to act in the manner traditional for English and American courts." That traditional role involves the application of some manageable and cognizable standard within the competence of the Judiciary to ascertain and employ to the facts of a concrete case. When a court is given no standard by which to adjudicate a dispute, or cannot resolve a dispute in the absence of a yet-unmade policy determination charged to a political branch, resolution of the suit is beyond the judicial role envisioned by Article III. This is not to say, of course, that courts are incapable of interpreting or applying somewhat ambiguous standards using familiar tools of statutory or constitutional interpretation. But where an issue leaves courts truly rudderless, there can be "no doubt of [the] validity" of a court's decision to abstain from judgment.

The final three *Baker* factors address circumstances in which prudence may counsel against a court's resolution of an issue presented. Courts should be particularly cautious before forgoing adjudication of a dispute on the basis that judicial intervention risks "embarrassment from multifarious pronouncements by various departments on one question," would express a "lack of the respect due coordinate branches of government," or because there exists an "unusual need for unquestioning adherence to a political decision already made." We have repeatedly rejected the view that these thresholds are met whenever a court is called upon to resolve the constitutionality or propriety of the act of another branch of Government. A court may not refuse to adjudicate a dispute merely because a decision "may have significant political overtones" or affect "the conduct of this Nation's foreign relations." Nor may courts decline to resolve a controversy within their traditional competence and proper jurisdiction simply because the question is difficult, the consequences weighty, or the potential real for conflict with the policy preferences of the political branches. The exercise of such authority is among the "gravest and most delicate dut[ies] that this Court is called on to perform."

Rare occasions implicating *Baker*'s final factors, however, may present an "'unusual case'" unfit for judicial disposition. Because of the respect due to a coequal and independent department, for instance, courts properly resist calls to question the good faith with which another branch attests to the authenticity of its internal acts. Likewise, we have long acknowledged that courts are particularly ill suited to intervening in exigent disputes necessitating unusual need for "attributing finality to the action of the political departments," or creating acute "risk [of] embarrassment of our government abroad, or grave disturbance at home," Finally, it may be appropriate for courts to stay their hand in cases implicating delicate questions concerning the distribution of political authority between coordinate branches until a dispute is ripe, intractable, and incapable of resolution by the political process.

When such unusual cases arise, abstention accommodates considerations inherent in the separation of powers and the limitations envisioned by Article III, which conferred authority to federal courts against a common-law backdrop that recognized the propriety of abstention in exceptional cases. The political questions envisioned by *Baker's* final categories find common ground, therefore, with many longstanding doctrines under which considerations of justiciability or comity lead courts to abstain from deciding questions whose initial resolution is better suited to another time.

To be sure, it will be the rare case in which *Baker's* final factors alone render a case nonjusticiable. But our long historical tradition recognizes that such exceptional cases arise, and due regard for the separation of powers and the judicial role envisioned by Article III confirms that abstention may be an appropriate response.

* * *

Notes and Questions

1. Is the political question doctrine constitutional or prudential? If it is constitutional, from what part of the Constitution does it spring? If it is prudential, what should the courts do when a matter arguably involving the doctrine is nonetheless explicitly within their Article III jurisdiction and an appropriate statutory jurisdictional grant?

2. *Baker v. Carr*, 369 U.S. 186 (1962), is still considered the authoritative modern statement of the political question doctrine. There, the Court considered whether questions of legislative apportionment were justiciable. It found that they are, but carefully distinguished the Guaranty Clause, Art. IV, § 4, from the Equal Protection Clause as possible bases for decision. As to the former, the Court reaffirmed its position in *Colegrove v. Green*, 328 U.S. 549 (1946), that issues arising under the Guaranty Clause are nonjusticiable. The *Baker* Court, on the other hand, ruled on the basis of equal protection.

Consider the degree to which Justice Sotomayor's concurrence in *Zivotofsky* clarifies the application of the six-factor *Baker* test. It certainly does seem that the first "factor" is not a factor at all; if the Constitution commits a matter exclusively to another branch, then how can any mere policy consideration make it appropriate for adjudication? The rest of the factors appear to exhibit concern for the quality of judicial craftsmanship and the desire not to interfere unduly with the conduct of international affairs.

3. If the political question doctrine is a servant of separation of powers within the federal government, why are Guaranty Clause cases necessarily nonjusticiable political questions? Why is not any Guaranty Clause case involving state government, as *Luther v. Borden*, 48 U.S. (7 How.) 1 (1849), did, justiciable? *Luther* involved disputes between supporters of conflicting governments in the state of Rhode Island. After 1783, Rhode Island did not adopt a new state constitution, but continued to operate the form of government established by charter in the seventeenth century. In 1841, some of the people of Rhode Island purported to hold a constitutional convention and to adopt a state constitution, under which elections were held and a new government declared. The "charter government" did not yield to those proceedings, but convened its own constitutional convention, which resulted in certification of a new government. In *Luther*, the plaintiff called upon the Supreme Court to adjudicate a trespass claim that depended upon a determination of which of the two "governments" of Rhode Island should be recognized as the lawful government. The plaintiff relied upon the Guaranty Clause, U.S. CONST. art. IV, § 4: "The United States shall guarantee to every State in this Union, a Republican Form of Government, and shall protect each of them against Invasion; and on Application of the Legislature, or of the Executive (when the Legislature cannot be convened), against domestic Violence." The Supreme Court found the dispute a nonjusticiable political question, declining to place any federal *imprimatur* on either of the two state governments. It observed that the courts of the state had determined the legitimacy of one of the governments as a matter of state law in which the federal courts could not intervene. Additionally, the Court concluded that the Guaranty Clause gave Congress the power to decide what government was the established one in a state. Congress had to decide what government was established before it could decide whether it was "republican" or not. By admitting the senators and representatives from a state, Congress recognized the authority by which they were designated to represent the state and, hence, the state government's republican character.

Does the text of the Guaranty Clause indicate that disputes concerning it are not subject to judicial review?

4. Suppose Congress passed a statute specially conferring on the federal courts subject matter jurisdiction with respect to a class of cases (involving the legislature) that the Court had determined were political questions. Which way would the separation of powers argument then cut? Alternatively, to the extent that the doctrine is a function of separation of powers, should the burden be on Congress affirmatively to exclude from federal jurisdiction classes of cases that it does not want the federal courts to adjudicate because they are "political"?

5. What does it mean for an issue to be committed to a coordinate branch? Consider the following cases.

a) The House of Representatives refuses to seat one of its members who has been re-elected, excluding him on the ground that in a previous term he had filed false travel vouchers seeking reimbursement to which he was not entitled and had otherwise misused government funds. Article I, § 5 declares that each house of Congress is the judge of the qualifications of its own members and that it may "determine the Rules of its Proceedings, punish its Members for disorderly Behaviour, and, with the Concurrence of two thirds, expel a Member." On the other hand, Article I, § 2, cl. 2 lists the qualifications for membership in the House and limits them to age, citizenship, and residence. The excluded member and his constituents sue to compel the House to seat him on the grounds that he meets all of the qualification requirements. Should the case be dismissed as non-justiciable? *See Powell v. McCormack*, 395 U.S. 486 (1969) (justiciable).

b) The House of Representatives impeached a federal judge convicted of making false statements to a jury. The Senate referred the matter to a committee of ten senators pursuant to one of its standing rules. The committee filed a full report to the Senate recommending conviction. The entire Senate considered the report, and the Senate allowed the judge to make a personal appeal to the full body. The Senate then voted to remove him from office. When he filed suit in federal court to challenge the Senate's process, did it present a political question? Does Article I's text stating that the Senate shall have the "sole" power to try all impeachments constitute an exclusive commitment of the matter to another branch? Does the word "try" provide sufficiently clear judicial standards for determining whether the Senate gave the judge proper process? *See Nixon v. United States*, 506 U.S. 224 (1993) (answering the first question affirmatively and the second negatively).

c) Certain Tribes sue several counties of a state for damages representing the fair rental value of land allegedly conveyed from the Tribes to the state in violation of a treaty providing that "no sale of lands made by any Indians, or any nation or tribe of Indians within the United States, shall be valid to any person * * * unless * * * held under the authority of the United States." The state's purchase of the land (nearly 200 years before the lawsuit) was not supervised by the federal government. Article I, § 3 explicitly gives Congress responsibility for Indian affairs. Was the case justiciable? *See County of Oneida v. Oneida Indian Nation*, 470 U.S. 226 (1985) (not a political question).

d) Federal statutes require the Secretary of Commerce to certify nations violating whale harvesting quotas set by the International Whaling Commission, an organization established by a fifteen-nation treaty to which the United States is a party. The statutes require economic sanctions against such nations. The United States and Japan enter into a bilateral agreement concerning whale harvests that the Secretary of Commerce thinks do not undermine the treaty. Plaintiffs sue to compel the Secretary to certify Japan as being in violation of the treaty. Was the case justiciable? *See Japan Whaling Association v. American Cetacean Society*, 478 U.S. 221 (1986) (not a political question).

e) When the United States announced in late 1978 that it would recognize the People's Republic of China on January 1, 1979, President Carter also gave notice to the Republic of China that he would abrogate the Mutual Defense Treaty of 1954 between that nation and the United States, pursuant to an article of that Treaty that permitted cancellation on one year's notice. Members and one former member of Congress challenged the President's power to cancel a treaty without senatorial or congressional consultation and approval. Was the case justiciable? *See Goldwater v. Carter*, 444 U.S. 996 (1979) (plurality found a political question).

f) In 1924, Congress proposed a child labor amendment to the Constitution. In 1937, the Kansas Senate divided evenly on whether to ratify the amendment, and the state's lieutenant governor then cast his vote for ratification. After the Kansas House had also ratified the amendment, some members of both houses sued the Kansas Secretary of State, seeking to compel him to erase an endorsement of the Senate resolution approving the amendment. The Secretary of State of Kansas argued that the federal courts should not hear cases concerning state legislatures' ratification procedures. The plaintiffs argued that the proposed amendment had lost its vitality by lapse of time and that the Kansas legislature therefore could not ratify it. Was the case justiciable? *See Coleman v. Miller*, 307 U.S. 433 (1939) (finding a political question).

6. In *Bush v. Gore*, 531 U.S. 98 (2000), the United States Supreme Court essentially resolved the disputed presidential election of that year. The election depended upon which candidate received Florida's electoral votes, and the Florida popular vote was extremely close. In a suit filed by then Vice-President Al Gore, one of the candidates, the Florida Supreme Court had ordered manual recounts in all Florida counties where "undervotes," ballots that the vote scanning machines had reported as not indicating a preference for president, had not been subject to manual tabulation. After Governor George W. Bush of Texas, the other major candidate sought review, the Supreme Court reversed the Florida Supreme Court's order and remanded the case for further proceedings in a five-to-four decision. In a *per curiam* opinion the Court concluded that the Florida court's manual recount order did not meet the minimum standards required by the Equal Protection Clause. There were no uniform guidelines as to how the voters' intent was to be discerned when ballots had not been marked properly, and different counties had followed, and presumably would follow, different standards in tabulating the votes.

Justice Breyer dissented, in an opinion joined in part by Justices Stevens, Ginsburg, and Souter. He contended that the state court could have resolved the equal protection problem by imposing a uniform standard upon remand. Therefore, he did not think the Supreme Court had to act to vindicate a fundamental constitutional right. Justice Breyer went on to discuss why the majority action was not only legally wrong, but unfortunate. He noted that in characterizing political disputes that the federal courts should refrain from deciding, the Court should consider the strangeness of the issue, its intractability to judicial judgment, its momentousness, and the vulnerability of the courts as important factors, and he found that there are all present in the case. Breyer asserted that by acting in such a politicized dispute in such a divided manner, the majority risked undermining public confidence in the Court as an institution. Do you agree? If so, does that mean the Court should in no circumstances have decided the equal protection issue or that it would have been all right to decide it if it appeared that all Justices agreed?

Chapter 2

Congressional Control of Federal Jurisdiction

A. Introduction

Members of Congress have often introduced bills that would have prohibited the Supreme Court, the lower federal courts, or both from exercising jurisdiction over cases dealing with controversial issues. Over the last two decades, these have included abortion, busing, and school prayer. The members who introduce these bills generally disagree with Supreme Court interpretations of some provision of the Constitution. By restricting the jurisdiction of the federal courts, they hope to minimize the effect of the Court's decisions. They believe that state courts or non-Article III tribunals will hand down more palatable decisions. The constitutionality of jurisdiction-stripping proposals is a serious question that goes to the heart of separation of powers. In addition, important federalism issues arise such legislation would limit the federal courts' ability to enforce federal rights (often against the states themselves), transferring that role to the state courts.

The Constitution clearly gives Congress some power over the appellate jurisdiction of the Supreme Court. Article III, § 2, allows the Court appellate jurisdiction "with such exceptions, and under such regulations as the Congress shall make." The first Congress exercised that power by limiting the circumstances in which the Supreme Court could review state court interpretations of federal law. The first Judiciary Act[1] authorized Supreme Court review of such determinations only if the state court rejected the contention of the party relying upon federal law. Thus, from the beginning of our history, Congress has determined which state court cases are eligible for Supreme Court review. But how broad is that power? Could Congress completely eliminate appellate review by the Supreme Court? Could it prohibit the Court from exercising appellate jurisdiction over a category of constitutional cases because of disagreement with the Court's decisions, as many jurisdiction-limiting bills have attempted to do?

Similar questions regarding the jurisdiction of the lower federal courts also arise. One of the great controversies at the Constitutional Convention was the existence of federal courts other than the Supreme Court. Many delegates

1 Act of Sept. 29, 1789, § 25, 1 Stat. 73, 85. This section of the statute is reproduced in *Murdock v. City of Memphis* in Chapter 9 at pages 910-11.

thought lower federal courts were essential to the new national government's survival. Others, however, argued that a large federal judiciary would permit too much federal encroachment on state courts and state power. The solution was a compromise. Article III, § 1, does not mandate the existence of the lower federal courts, but rather provides for "such inferior courts as the Congress may from time to time ordain and establish." Consequently, many scholars contend that because Congress has the power to create or eliminate inferior federal courts, it has plenary power over their jurisdiction and has exercised it since the Judiciary Act of 1789. For example, the Act provided trial court jurisdiction in diversity cases only when the amount in controversy exceeded $500 and did not grant any jurisdiction over civil cases that arose under federal law. Indeed, with minor exceptions, Congress did not grant the lower federal courts jurisdiction over federal question cases until 1875.[2] Some argue that this history demonstrates that although proposals to strip the lower federal courts of jurisdiction over specific categories of cases may be unwise, they are not unconstitutional.

Others have questioned this conclusion by pointing to other language in the text of Article III or to other constitutional provisions. Article III does say that "[t]he judicial Power * * * *shall* be vested * * * ," (emphasis added) not that it may be vested. Additionally, some have argued that any jurisdiction-stripping statute would violate another constitutional provision by excluding classes of litigants or cases entitled to constitutional protection. As with congressional control of the appellate jurisdiction of the Supreme Court, the issue continues to be the subject of heated debate.

Questions also arise as to whether Congress can totally preclude federal court review of specific issues by both cutting off the appellate jurisdiction of the Supreme Court and stripping the lower federal courts of jurisdiction as well. Even if one accepts congressional power to engage in either course of conduct, would it be unconstitutional for Congress to do both? Some scholars contend that the federal judicial power has to be available in either its appellate or original form over all federal question cases. As with the other issues discussed above, there is still debate among scholars on this matter. However, the so-called "War on Terror" has made the debate more than academic. Congress has severely limited the rights of aliens either suspected of being or determined to be enemy combatants to assert federal constitutional challenges to their confinement. It has further limited the federal forums that can hear those challenges that are allowed. Thus, the federal courts themselves may soon have to answer the questions which thus far have primarily been discussed by scholars.

---

2 Congress did briefly grant general federal question jurisdiction in the famous Midnight Judges Act that spawned Marbury v. Madison, 5 U.S. (1 Cranch) 137 (1803), but the incoming Jeffersonian Congress repealed the grant a year later. Act of Feb. 13, 1801, ch. 4, § 11, 2 Stat. 89, 92, *repealed by* Act of Mar. 8, 1802, ch. 8, § 1, 2 Stat. 132. There were also, from time to time, specialized grants of federal question jurisdiction, discussed in Chapter 3 at page 278 n.4.

B. Congressional Control Of The Appellate Jurisdiction of the Supreme Court

Ex Parte McCardle

Supreme Court of the United States, 1869.
74 U.S. (7 Wall.) 506.

[Following the Civil War, newspaperman William H. McCardle wrote several editorials that contained bitter attacks on Reconstruction and the military leaders responsible for implementing it. Military authorities arrested and held him pursuant to the Military Reconstruction Act of 1867, which was the legislative foundation of Congress' reconstruction program. The Act established military jurisdiction in 10 Southern states and authorized military commissions to try civilians accused of violating its provisions. McCardle was charged with libel, impeding Reconstruction, inciting to insurrection and disorder, and disturbing the peace. He petitioned a federal circuit court for a writ of habeas corpus, alleging that he was being held in military custody in violation of his constitutional rights. The court held that his imprisonment was lawful, but ordered his release on bond pending appeal to the Supreme Court.

McCardle appealed pursuant to the Habeas Corpus Act of 1867. Prior to that statute, the Supreme Court had exercised appellate jurisdiction over cases in which persons held under federal authority sought habeas relief, pursuant to section 14 of the Judiciary Act of 1789. The Habeas Corpus Act of 1867 authorized the federal courts for the first time to issue writs of habeas corpus whenever persons held in *state* custody challenged it on federal grounds. In addition, the Act provided an alternate basis for federal habeas relief for those held in federal custody and an alternate authorization of Supreme Court review.

When McCardle's appeal reached the Court, the government moved to dismiss on the ground that the Court lacked jurisdiction. The Court unanimously found jurisdiction based upon the Habeas Corpus Act of 1867. *Ex Parte McCardle*, 73 U.S. (6 Wall.) 318, 18 L.Ed. 816 (1868). The Court then heard argument on the merits. Before the Court announced a decision, Congress passed the Repealer Act (over President Johnson's veto), which provided that so much of the Habeas Corpus Act of 1867 "as authorizes an appeal from the judgment of the circuit court to the Supreme Court of the United States, or the exercise of any such jurisdiction by said Supreme Court on appeals which have been made or may hereafter be taken, be, and the same is, hereby repealed." Congress evidently wanted to prevent the Court from hearing McCardle's appeal and ruling on the constitutionality of the Military Reconstruction Act and Reconstruction itself. The government again moved to dismiss for lack of jurisdiction.]

THE CHIEF JUSTICE delivered the opinion of the court.

The first question necessarily is that of jurisdiction; for, if the act of March, 1868, takes away the jurisdiction defined by the act of February, 1867, it is useless, if not improper, to enter into any discussion of other questions.

It is quite true, as was argued by the counsel for the petitioner, that the appellate jurisdiction of this court is not derived from acts of Congress. It is, strictly speaking, conferred by the Constitution. But it is conferred "with such exceptions and under such regulations as Congress shall make."

It is unnecessary to consider whether, if Congress had made no exceptions and no regulations, this court might not have exercised general appellate jurisdiction under rules prescribed by itself. For among the earliest acts of the first Congress, at its first session, was the act of September 24th, 1789, to establish the judicial courts of the United States. That act provided for the organization of this court, and prescribed regulations for the exercise of its jurisdiction.

The source of that jurisdiction, and the limitations of it by the Constitution and by statute, have been on several occasions subjects of consideration here. In the case of *Durousseau v. The United States* particularly, the whole matter was carefully examined, and the court held, that while "the appellate powers of this court are not given by the judicial act, but are given by the Constitution," they are, nevertheless, "limited and regulated by that act, and by such other acts as have been passed on the subject." The court said, further, that the judicial act was an exercise of the power given by the Constitution to Congress "of making exceptions to the appellate jurisdiction of the Supreme Court." "They have described affirmatively," said the court, "its jurisdiction, and this affirmative description has been understood to imply a negation of the exercise of such appellate power as is not comprehended within it."

Food for Thought

The last paragraph is an important rhetorical device. If "it is unnecessary to consider," why is the Court talking about it? Clearly the purpose of the Court is to implant in the reader's mind the notion that the Court's appellate jurisdiction is constitutionally endowed and therefore that congressional limits should be few and far between.

The principle that the affirmation of appellate jurisdiction implies the negation of all such jurisdiction not affirmed having been thus established, it was an almost necessary consequence that acts of Congress, providing for the exercise of jurisdiction, should come to be spoken of as acts granting jurisdiction, and not as acts making exceptions to the constitutional grant of it.

The exception to appellate jurisdiction in the case before us, however, is not an inference from the affirmation of other appellate jurisdiction. It is made in terms. The provision of the act of 1867, affirming the appellate jurisdiction of this court in cases of habeas corpus is expressly repealed. It is hardly possible to imagine a plainer instance of positive exception.

We are not at liberty to inquire into the motives of the legislature. We can only examine into its power under the Constitution; and the power to make exceptions to the appellate jurisdiction of this court is given by express words.

What, then, is the effect of the repealing act upon the case before us? We cannot doubt as to this. Without jurisdiction the court cannot proceed at all in any cause. Jurisdiction is power to declare the law, and when it ceases to exist, the only function remaining to the court is that of announcing the fact and dismissing the cause. And this is not less clear upon authority than upon principle.

Several cases were cited by the counsel for the petitioner in support of the position that jurisdiction of this case is not affected by the repealing act. But none of them, in our judgment, afford any support to it. They are all cases of the exercise of judicial power by the legislature, or of legislative interference with courts in the exercising of continuing jurisdiction.

On the other hand, the general rule, supported by the best elementary writers, is, that "when an act of the legislature is repealed, it must be considered, except as to transactions past and closed, as if it never existed."

* * *

It is quite clear, therefore, that this court cannot proceed to pronounce judgment in this case, for it has no longer jurisdiction of the appeal; and judicial duty is not less fitly performed by declining ungranted jurisdiction than in exercising firmly that which the Constitution and the laws confer.

Counsel seem to have supposed, if effect be given to the repealing act in question, that the whole appellate power of the court, in cases of habeas corpus, is denied. But this is an error. The act of 1868 does not except from that jurisdiction any cases but appeals from Circuit Courts under the act of 1867. It does not affect the jurisdiction which was previously exercised.

The appeal of the petitioner in this case must be dismissed for want of jurisdiction.

Notes and Questions

1. Should the Court have found the Repealer Act ineffective because it had already heard arguments on the merits? Would it matter if the Court had not only heard arguments on the merits, but had discussed the case in conference? If the Court had already reached a decision but had simply not published its opinion, should that alter the result?

2. Could the Court have decided McCardle's appeal on the merits without ignoring the Repealer Act? If so, should it have?

3. Did the Repealer Act make an "exception" to the appellate jurisdiction of the Supreme Court? Or did it simply "take back" what Congress had given?

Ex Parte Yerger

Supreme Court of the United States, 1869.
75 U.S. (8 Wall.) 85.

[Military authorities acting pursuant to the Military Reconstruction Act of 1867 arrested Yerger, also a newspaper editor, and charged him with murder. The Act provided for trial by military commission without a jury. Yerger was not and had never been connected with the United States' armed forces. He filed a petition for a writ of habeas corpus in the Circuit Court of the United States for the Southern District of Mississippi. That court found his imprisonment lawful and dismissed the habeas petition. Yerger appealed to the Supreme Court pursuant to section 14 of the Judiciary Act of 1789. "On the suggestion of the Attorney-General," the Court directed argument on the issue of jurisdiction.]

THE CHIEF JUSTICE delivered the opinion of the court.

* * *

The general question of jurisdiction in this case resolves itself necessarily into two other questions:

1. Has the court jurisdiction, in a case like the present, to inquire into the cause of detention, alleged to be unlawful, and to give relief, if the detention be found to be in fact unlawful, by the writ of habeas corpus, under the Judiciary Act of 1789?

2. If, under that act, the court possessed this jurisdiction, has it been taken away by the second section of the act of March, 27, 1868, repealing so much

of the act of February 5, 1867, as authorizes appeals from Circuit Courts to the Supreme Court?

Neither of these questions is new here. The first has, on several occasions, received very full consideration, and very deliberate judgment.

A cause, so important as that which now invokes the action of this court, seems however to justify a reconsideration of the grounds upon which its jurisdiction has been heretofore maintained.

The great writ of habeas corpus has been for centuries esteemed the best and only sufficient defence of personal freedom.

In England, after a long struggle, it was firmly guaranteed by the famous Habeas Corpus Act of May 27, 1679, "for the better securing of the liberty of the subject," which, as Blackstone says, "is frequently considered as another Magna Charta."

It was brought to America by the colonists, and claimed as among the immemorial rights descended to them from their ancestors.

Naturally, therefore, when the confederated colonies became United States, and the formation of a common government engaged their deliberations in convention, this great writ found prominent sanction in the Constitution. That sanction is in these words: "The privilege of the writ of habeas corpus shall not be suspended unless when in cases of rebellion or invasion the public safety may require it."

The terms of this provision necessarily imply judicial action. In England, all the higher courts where open to applicants for the writ, and it is hardly supposable that, under the new government, founded on more liberal ideas and principles, any court would be, intentionally, closed to them.

We find, accordingly, that the first Congress under the Constitution, after defining, by various sections of the act of September 24, 1789, the jurisdiction of the District Courts, the Circuit Courts, and the Supreme Court in other cases, proceeded, in the 14th section, to enact, "that all the beforementioned courts of the United States shall have power to issue writs of ***scire facias,*** habeas corpus, and all other writs, not specially provided by statute, which may be necessary for the exercise of their respective jurisdictions, and agreeable to the principles and usages of law." In

Non constat
jus civile
a posteriori

It's Latin to Me!

This ancient English writ directed the sheriff to make the record known to a specified party.

the same section, it was further provided "that either of the Justices of the Supreme Court, as well as Judges of the District Courts, shall have power to grant writs of habeas corpus for the purpose of an inquiry into the cause of commitment; provided that writs of habeas corpus shall in no case extend to prisoners in jail, unless they are in custody, under, or by color of the authority of the United States, or are committed for trial before some court of the same, or are necessary to be brought into court to testify."

* * *

The judicial power of the United States extends to all cases in law and equity arising under the Constitution, the laws of the United States, and treaties made under their authority, and to large classes of cases determined by the character of the parties, or the nature of the controversy.

That part of this judicial power vested in this court is defined by the Constitution in these words:

> In all cases affecting ambassadors, other public ministers, and consuls, and those in which a State shall be a party, the Supreme Court shall have original jurisdiction. In all the other cases before mentioned, the Supreme Court shall have appellate jurisdiction, both as to law and fact, with such exceptions, and under such regulations as the Congress shall make.

If the question were new one, it would, perhaps, deserve inquiry whether Congress might not, under the power to make exceptions from this appellate jurisdiction, extend the original jurisdiction to other cases than those expressly enumerated in the Constitution; and especially, in view of the constitutional guaranty of the writ of habeas corpus, to cases arising upon petition for that writ.

But, in the case of *Marbury v. Madison*, it was determined, upon full consideration, that the power to issue writs of mandamus, given to this court by the 13th section of the Judiciary Act, is, under the Constitution, an appellate jurisdiction, to be exercised only in the revision of judicial decisions. And this judgment has ever since been accepted as fixing the construction of this part of the Constitution.

It was pronounced in 1803. In 1807 the same construction was given to the provision of the 14th section relating to the writ of habeas corpus.

* * *

The doctrine of the Constitution and of the cases thus far may be summed up in these propositions:

(1) The original jurisdiction of this court cannot be extended by Congress to any other cases than those expressly defined by the Constitution.

(2) The appellate jurisdiction of this court, conferred by the Constitution, extends to all other cases within the judicial power of the United States.

(3) This appellate jurisdiction is subject to such exceptions, and must be exercised under such regulations as Congress, in the exercise of its discretion, has made or may see fit to make.

(4) Congress not only has not excepted writs of habeas corpus and mandamus from this appellate jurisdiction, but has expressly provided for the exercise of this jurisdiction by means of these writs.

* * *

The great and leading intent of the Constitution and the law must be kept constantly in view upon the examination of every question of construction.

That intent, in respect to the writ of habeas corpus, is manifest. It is that every citizen may be protected by judicial action from unlawful imprisonment. To this end the act of 1789 provided that every court of the United States should have power to issue the writ. The jurisdiction thus given in law to the Circuit and District Courts is original; that given by the Constitution and the law to this court is appellate. Given in general terms, it must necessarily extend to all cases to which the judicial power of the United States extends, other than those expressly excepted from it.

* * *

We are obligated to hold, therefore, that in all cases where a Circuit Court of the United States has, in the exercise of its original jurisdiction, caused a prisoner to be brought before it, and has, after inquiring into the cause of detention, remanded him to the custody from which he was taken, this court, in the exercise of its appellate jurisdiction, may, by the writ of habeas corpus, aided by the writ of certiorari, revise the decision of the Circuit Court, and if it be found unwarranted by law, relieve the prisoner from the unlawful restraint to which he has been remanded.

This conclusion brings us to the inquiry whether the 2d section of the act of March 27th, 1868, takes away or affects the appellate jurisdiction of this court under the Constitution and the acts of Congress prior to 1867.

In *McCardle's* case * * * we expressed the opinion that it does not, and we have now re-examined the grounds of that opinion.

The circumstances under which the act of 1868 was passed were peculiar.

On the 5th of February, 1867, Congress passed the act to which reference has already been made, extending the original jurisdiction by habeas corpus of the District and Circuit Courts, and of the several judges of these courts, to all cases of restraint of liberty in violation of the Constitution, treaties, or laws of the United States. This act authorized appeals to this court from judgments of the Circuit Court, but did not repeal any previous act conferring jurisdiction by habeas corpus, unless by implication.

* * *

The effect of the act was to oust the court of its jurisdiction of the particular case then before it on appeal, and it is not to be doubted that such was the effect intended. Nor will it be questioned that legislation of this character is unusual and hardly to be justified except upon some imperious public exigency.

It was, doubtless, within the constitutional discretion of Congress to determine whether such an exigency existed; but it is not to be presumed that an act, passed under such circumstances, was intended to have any further effect than that plainly apparent from its terms.

It is quite clear that the words of the act reach, not only all appeals pending, but all future appeals to this court under the act of 1867; but they appear to be limited to appeals taken under that act.

The words of the repealing section are, "that so much of the act approved February 5th, 1867, as authorizes an appeal from the judgment of the Circuit Court to the Supreme Court of the United States, or the exercise of any such jurisdiction by said Supreme Court on appeals which have been, or may be hereafter taken, be, and the same is hereby repealed."

These words are not of doubtful interpretation. They repeal only so much of the act of 1867 as authorized appeals, or the exercise of appellate jurisdiction by this court. They affected only appeals and appellate jurisdiction authorized by that act. They do not purport to touch the appellate jurisdiction conferred by the Constitution, or to except from it any cases not excepted by the act of 1789. They reach no act except the act of 1867.

* * *

We could come to no other conclusion without holding that the whole appellate jurisdiction of this court, in cases of habeas corpus, conferred by the Constitution, recognized by law, and exercised from the foundation of the government hitherto, has been taken away, without the expression of such intent, and by mere implication, through the operation of the acts of 1867 and 1868.

* * *

The argument having been confined, by direction of the court, to the question of jurisdiction, this opinion is limited to that question. The jurisdiction of the court to issue the writ prayed for is affirmed.

Notes and Questions

1. Despite finding jurisdiction, the Court never did decide Yerger's constitutional claims on the merits. Following the jurisdictional decision, the military dismissed the charges, again avoiding Supreme Court review of the constitutionality of Reconstruction.

2. Do *McCardle* and *Yerger* establish congressional power completely to eliminate the appellate jurisdiction of the Supreme Court? Do they at least establish congressional power to eliminate Supreme Court review in a specific category of constitutional cases?

3. In *Felker v. Turpin*, 518 U.S. 651 (1996), the issue of congressional power to control the appellate jurisdiction of the Supreme Court again arose in the context of statutory restrictions on the review of habeas petitions. The Antiterrorism and Effective Death Penalty Act of 1996 places severe restrictions on a state prisoner's second or successive federal habeas application. The prospective applicant must move the court of appeals for leave to file such an application in the district court. A three-judge appellate panel plays a "gatekeeping" role by determining whether the prisoner has made a showing sufficient to meet the statutory requirements. Title 28 U.S.C. § 106(b)(3)(E) of the Act provides that "[t]he grant or denial of an authorization by a court of appeals to file a second or successive application shall not be appealable and shall not be the subject of a petition for rehearing or for a writ of certiorari." When the Eleventh Circuit denied Felker's motion for leave to file a second habeas petition, he sought certiorari from the Supreme Court, arguing that the statute unconstitutionally restricts the Court's jurisdiction. The Court granted certiorari but unanimously rejected his claim. After an extended discussion of *Yerger*, the Court "for reasons similar to those stated in" that case concluded that the Act had not repealed its power to entertain original habeas petitions pursuant to 28 U.S.C. § 2241, pointing out that the provision does not mention that jurisdiction. Consequently, the Court held that there was no substantial argument that the Act deprives it of appellate jurisdiction in violation of Article III. The Court then denied Felker's petition for an original writ of habeas corpus.

Congressional Power Over the Appellate Jurisdiction of the Supreme Court

Leonard Ratner

109 U.PA.L.REV. 157, 160-161 (1960)[a]

* * *

The Constitution gives the Supreme Court appellate jurisdiction "with such Exceptions, and under such Regulations as the Congress shall make" over all cases within the judicial power of the United States originating in state or lower federal courts. From time to time since 1796 the Supreme Court has used language in its opinions suggesting that by virtue of the exceptions and regulations clause its appellate jurisdiction is subject to unlimited congressional control, and this language has generally been regarded as establishing that Congress has such power.

Constitutional authority to create and abolish inferior federal courts gives Congress plenary control over their jurisdiction. If Congress also has plenary control over the appellate jurisdiction of the Supreme Court, then Congress may constitutionally do any of the following:

(1) Deprive the Supreme Court of all appellate jurisdiction and abolish the lower federal courts, thereby confining the judiciary of the United States to a single court exercising original jurisdiction over cases affecting ambassadors, public ministers, and consuls, or in which a state is a party.

(2) Deprive the Supreme Court of appellate jurisdiction and other federal courts of all jurisdiction over cases involving the validity, under the Constitution, of state statutes or the conduct of state officials, thereby leaving to the highest court of each state the final determination of such questions.

(3) Deprive the Supreme Court of appellate jurisdiction over any case arising under the Constitution, laws, or treaties of the United States, thereby allowing the federal courts of appeals and the highest state courts to become, in their respective jurisdictions, the final interpreters of federal law.

If such legislation is permissible, Congress can by statute profoundly alter the structure of American government. It can all but destroy the coordinate judicial branch and thus upset the delicately poised constitutional system of checks and balances. It can distort the nature of the federal union by permitting each state to decide for itself the scope of its authority under the Constitution. It can reduce the supreme law of the land as defined in article VI to a hodgepodge of inconsistent decisions by making fifty state courts and eleven federal courts of appeals the final judges of the meaning and application of the Constitution, laws, and treaties of the United States.

* * *

Does the exceptions and regulations clause confer power of such magnitude upon Congress? The answer requires an analysis of the function of the Supreme Court as a part of the governmental structure created by the Constitution.

* * *

One of the most significant aspects of the federal union is disclosed by the declaration in article VI of the Constitution that "this Constitution, and the Laws of the United States which shall be made in Pursuance thereof; and all Treaties made, or which shall be made, under the Authority of the United States, shall be the supreme Law of the Land; and the Judges in every State shall be bound thereby, any Thing in the Constitution or Laws of any State to the Contrary notwithstanding." This constitutional mandate requires (a) that there shall be one supreme federal law throughout the land and (b) that in the event of conflict between that law and the law or authority of any state, the federal law shall prevail.

supremacy clause

The supremacy clause standing alone, however, is no more than an exhortation. A tribunal with nationwide authority is needed to interpret and apply the supreme law. Such a tribunal is created by article III, which vests the judicial power of the United States in one Supreme Court and such inferior courts as Congress may establish and extends that power to every case involving the supreme law of the land. The only court created by the article is designated as supreme in contrast to the inferior courts which Congress in its discretion may establish. That court alone is expressly given appellate jurisdiction over cases involving the supreme law of the land whether those cases are initiated in state or federal courts. It is thus the constitutional instrument for implementing the supremacy clause. As such, its essential appellate functions under the Constitution are: (1) to provide a tribunal for the ultimate resolution of inconsistent or conflicting interpretations of federal law by state and federal courts, and (2) to provide a tribunal for maintaining the supremacy of federal law when it conflicts with state law or is challenged by state authority.

The process of carrying out these functions is necessarily a flexible one. A Supreme Court decision is not required in every case that involves a state challenge to federal law or an interpretation of federal law in conflict with other cases. A measure of inconsistency in the interpretation and application of federal law is inevitable, and immediate correction is not always imperative. But some avenue must remain open to permit ultimate resolution by the Supreme Court of persistent conflicts between state and federal law or in the interpretation of federal law by lower courts. For this purpose discretionary review through certiorari can be as effective as mandatory review by writ of error or appeal. Although these essential functions would not ordinarily be disrupted by a procedural limitation restricting the availability of Supreme Court review in some but not all cases involving a particular subject, legislation denying the Court jurisdiction to review any case involving that subject would effectively obstruct those functions in the proscribed area.

Congressional Power to Curtail Federal Court Jurisdiction: An Opinionated Guide to the Ongoing Debate

Gerald Gunther

36 STAN.L.REV. 895, 901-08 (1984)[b]

* * *

On its face, the exceptions clause of article III, section 2, seems to grant a quite unconfined power to Congress to withhold from the Court a large number of classes of cases potentially within its appellate jurisdiction. Moreover, those who would find substantial constitutional restraints on congressional power over Supreme Court appellate jurisdiction within article III itself face formidable obstacles in the historical congressional practice and in numerous statements by the Supreme Court. Nevertheless, there have been extensive academic efforts to articulate substantial internal limits on congressional authority.

* * *

Far and away the most widely voiced modern argument for internal limitations is that the "exceptions" power of Congress cannot be exercised in a way that would interfere with the "essential" or "core" functions of the Supreme Court. The origin of the argument is traceable to a remark in the deservedly famous Socratic dialogue written by the late Henry Hart in 1953. Hart suggested (with somewhat ambiguous import) that the "exceptions" power cannot be used in a manner that "will destroy the essential role of the Supreme Court in the constitutional plan." The most insistent modern advocate of this type of limit is Leonard Ratner. In Ratner's view, the "essential constitutional functions of the Court" are "to maintain the supremacy and uniformity of federal law." A plenary congressional "exceptions" power, he insists, is "not consistent with the constitutional plan."

Although much of the modern academic literature goes on at considerable length to explain why Ratner's thesis is unpersuasive, he does not stand alone in advocating this "essential functions" limit. Recently, his position has been adopted in substance by a powerful ally outside of academia—William French Smith, the Reagan Administration's Attorney General. In May 1982, Attorney General Smith sent a lengthy letter to Senator Strom Thurmond, the Chairman of the Senate Judiciary Committee, in response to inquiries about the constitutionality of the portion of the Helms bill that would withdraw the Court's appellate jurisdiction over cases relating to "voluntary" prayers. The Attorney General, while recognizing that "the question of the limits of Congress' authority under the Exceptions Clause is an extraordinarily difficult one," argued that Congress may not constitutionally "make 'exceptions' to Supreme Court jurisdiction which would intrude upon the core functions of the Supreme Court as an independent and equal branch in our system of separation of powers." Rather, "Congress can limit the Supreme Court's appellate jurisdiction only up to the point where it impairs the Court's core functions in the constitutional scheme."

What are the pros and cons of the widely debated "essential" or "core" functions position? Proponents of the thesis cannot readily (and do not) rely on the constitutional language: there is simply no "essential functions" limit on the face of the exceptions clause. They claim to find helpful language in some Supreme Court opinions, but they discount the far more numerous statements from the Court suggesting a very broad congressional authority by arguing that the Court has really never had to face a situation in which Congress sought to bar all access to the Court in an "essential" area. Proponents rely above all on historical expectations and structural considerations allegedly demonstrating that appellate review must be available to assure that the Court will be able to provide the "essential" uniformity and supremacy of important (especially constitutional) issues of federal law. Critics of the thesis question the legitimacy of importing the "essential functions" limit into the Constitution, emphasize the vague, slippery, open-ended nature of the limit, and challenge its various underpinnings at length.

The most concrete source of the arguments lies in statements made by the Supreme Court itself. The advocates of an "essential functions" limit can indeed point to various dicta endorsing the desirability of Court review to ensure the supremacy and uniformity of federal law. An early, extensive, and eloquent example is in Joseph Story's opinion for the Court in *Martin v. Hunter's Lessee*, which sustained the constitutionality of section 25 of the 1789 Judiciary Act against an attack from the highest court of Virginia. But, as I have argued elsewhere, Justice Story's statements are more plausibly read as exhortations regarding desirable policy than as expressions of constitutional commands, particularly in view of his own later decisions and his contemporaneous legislative lobbying activities advocating congressional extension of the Judiciary Act. In any event, as critics such as William Van Alstyne have pointed out, the Court's sporadic paeans of praise to uniformity and supremacy seem far outweighed by its considerably more frequent expressions of deference to congressional delineations of appellate jurisdiction.

* * *

But the main support invoked by those who assert a broad "essential functions" limit on the "exceptions" power does not rest on such slender reeds. Instead the arguments rely most heavily on general expectations, historical and contemporary, about the Supreme Court's role—on the "constitutional plan" and its evolution. The main question raised by this kind of argument is whether it confuses the familiar with the necessary, the desirable with the constitutionally mandated. In recent decades, the Court certainly has enjoyed very broad statutory jurisdiction to review constitutional rulings by state and lower federal courts. The central and expanding role of the Court in our modern polity helps explain the recurrent outrage expressed in the media and in academia in response to proposed congressional assertions of power over jurisdiction. But is there sufficient basis, in history and in principle, for insistence upon substantial internal, article III restraints on congressional power?

The strongest basis for such restraints lies in expectations reflected in the debates at the Constitutional Convention. The major point of controversy during the evolution of article III was whether the Constitution should mandate the establishment of lower federal courts. Nationalists insisted that lower federal courts were necessary to assure adequate enforcement of federal law; localists countered that state judges, compelled to apply federal law under the supremacy clause, were adequate for the initial interpretation and enforcement of federal requirements, and that ultimate review by the Supreme Court would assure sufficient supremacy and uniformity. In one of the Convention's great compromises, article III emerged: the article mandated the creation of the Supreme Court, but left to the discretion of Congress the establishment of any "inferior" courts.

Advocates of the "essential functions" limit on congressional power can draw some legitimate comfort from these debates, for an expectation of Supreme Court review of state court judgments was indeed widespread. But is that expectation tantamount to a constitutional limitation on congressional authority over appellate jurisdiction? After all, the same Convention did insert the exceptions clause, the textual nub of the controversy. Even more damaging to the case for an unreachable, "essential" Court role of assuring supremacy and uniformity is congressional practice, beginning in the earliest period, when there was a considerable overlap among delegates to the Constitutional Convention and members of the First Congress. The Judiciary Act of 1789 did not grant to the Court all of the potential article III appellate jurisdiction, even in constitutional cases, necessary to assure that the Supreme Court would be the ultimate provider of both supremacy and uniformity. Rather, section 25 of the Act, dealing with review of state court decisions, was essentially a supremacy-assuring device; it was not primarily concerned with uniformity. Supreme Court review was available only when a state court denied a federal claim; when the state court sustained a federal claim, even when its reading of federal law differed from that of federal tribunals, review was unavailable. Such was the scheme of the jurisdictional statutes for more than a century, until 1914. Proponents of the "essential functions" thesis have difficulty explaining the long life of the section 25 scheme. They counter that section 25 did, after all, assure supremacy. But their thesis is that assurance of uniformity as well as supremacy is the "essential function" of the Court, and uniformity was conspicuously lacking from the congressionally devised and judicially implemented jurisdictional scheme until Congress chose to modify it early in this century.

The advocates of a narrow reading of the "exceptions" power then fall back to a broader ground: the alleged implications of the role of an independent judiciary in a system of separation of powers. A large part of Attorney General Smith's narrow reading of the "exceptions" power, for example, is based on just such premises. "Essential to the principle of separation of powers," he argues, "was the proposition that no one Branch of Government should have the power to eliminate the fundamental constitutional role of either of the other Branches." But of course the constitutional scheme is one of checks and balances as well as separation. Article III does provide for an independent judiciary, but independence does not mean total insulation of the judicial branch any more than it does for the other branches. No one denies, for example, that the political branches govern the selection of personnel for the Bench, a selection process that often has a profound impact on the course of decisions. And article III does not specify the size of the Supreme Court, leaving open the technique of "packing" the Court that Franklin D. Roosevelt advocated—a technique widely recognized as constitutionally authorized albeit criticizable in the strongest terms as a matter of policy. Ultimately, arguments stemming from the lack of power of one branch to interfere with the "fundamental constitutional role" of another tend to be question-begging. Even the proponents of the "essential" or "core" functions limitation recognize that Congress may legitimately react to constitutional rulings through the constitutional amendment route; they simply insist that that is the only legitimate route. But the question remains whether the "fundamental constitutional role" of the Court leaves any significant role for Congress under its "exceptions" power. In a sense, then, much of the debate turns on whether arguments about sensible and desirable judicial structures can be converted into constitutionally mandated ones. Much of the "essential functions" theory of Professor Ratner and Attorney General Smith strikes me as failing to heed the warning I voiced earlier about confusing wisdom and constitutionality, confusing what Congress ought not to do with what it cannot do.

Notes and Questions

1. As Professor Gunther points out, Professor Henry Hart originated the "essential functions" theory in an article written more than sixty ago and still frequently cited in debates on this topic. *See* Henry L. Hart, *The Power of Congress to Limit the Jurisdiction of Federal Courts: An Exercise in Dialectic,* 66 HARV.L.REV. 1362 (1953).

2. Is there any language in Article III that supports the "essential functions" theory? If not, does the Exceptions Clause connote that while it may be desirable for the Court to perform the core functions set forth by the theory, it is not constitutionally mandated? If the Exceptions Clause embraces the essential functions theory, does Congress have a substantial role in determining the Supreme Court's appellate jurisdiction?

3. Do *McCardle* and *Yerger* support or contradict the "essential functions" theory?

4. Is Professor Gunther correct that the Judiciary Act of 1789 was inconsistent with the "essential functions" theory?

5. Is recognition of broad congressional power over the appellate jurisdiction of the Supreme Court a greater threat to the Court's independence than the checks on it that are universally recognized, such as selection of justices by the political branches or congressional power to determine the number of justices and thereby "pack" the Court?

6. Eliminating Supreme Court review over a particular category of constitutional cases would not eliminate the "undesirable" decisions that may motivate efforts to restrict the Court's appellate jurisdiction. State court judges have an obligation under the Supremacy Clause to follow Supreme Court precedents notwithstanding congressional opposition to them. The Court has often (particularly in recent years) asserted that state and federal courts are equally willing and able to apply federal constitutional principles. *See, e.g., Huffman v. Pursue, Ltd.,* 420 U.S. 592, 604 (1975); *Steffel v. Thompson,* 415 U.S. 452, 461 (1974) (both supporting federal abstention on the ground that intervention "reflect['s] negatively upon the state courts' ability to enforce constitutional principles."). *See generally* Chapter 8, Section D. If that assertion is

correct, what would Congress accomplish by eliminating Supreme Court review? If it is not, are there implications for the legitimacy of the jurisdiction-stripping legislation?

United States v. Klein

Supreme Court of the United States, 1872.
80 U.S. (13 Wall.) 128.

[In 1863, United States Treasury agents seized 664 bales of cotton belonging to V.F. Wilson, sold it, and paid the proceeds, $125,300, into the Treasury. Wilson had aided the Confederacy by signing, as surety, two official bonds of Confederate Army officers. After his death, the estate's administrators sued in the Court of Claims to recover the proceeds pursuant to the Abandoned and Captured Property Act, which conditioned recovery upon a showing that the property owner had never given any aid or comfort to the rebellion. *United States v. Padelford,* 76 U.S. (9 Wall.) 531, 19 L.Ed. 788 (1869), had held that even though Padelford had participated in the rebellion, his presidential pardon made him as innocent under the law as if he had never participated. Based on *Padelford,* the Court of Claims concluded that Wilson was relieved of any charge of disloyalty; he, too, had received a presidential pardon. Consequently, the court held that Klein, the surviving administrator, was entitled to the proceeds of the cotton sale. The government appealed to the Supreme Court.

While the appeal was pending, Congress attached the following *proviso* to an appropriations bill that was enacted:

> Provided, That no pardon or amnesty granted by the President, whether general or special, by proclamation or otherwise, nor any acceptance of such pardon or amnesty, nor oath taken, or other act performed in pursuance or as a condition thereof, shall be admissible in evidence on the part of any claimant in the Court of Claims as evidence in support of any claim against the United States, or to establish the standing of any claimant in said court, or his right to bring or maintain suit therein; nor shall any such pardon, amnesty, acceptance, oath, or other act as aforesaid, heretofore offered or put in evidence on behalf of any claimant in said court, be used or considered by said court, or by the appellate court on appeal from said court, in deciding upon the claim of said claimant, or any appeal therefrom, as any part of the proof to sustain the claim of the claimant, or to entitle him to maintain his action in said Court of Claims, or on appeal therefrom; but the proof of loyalty required by the Abandoned and Captured Property Act, and by the sections of several acts quoted, shall be made by proof of the matters required, irrespective of the effect of any executive proclamation, pardon, amnesty, or other act of condonation or oblivion. And in all cases where judgment shall have

> been heretofore rendered in the Court of Claims in favor of any claimant, on any other proof of loyalty than such as is above required and provided, and which is hereby declared to have been and to be the true intent and meaning of said respective acts, the Supreme Court shall, on appeal, have no further jurisdiction of the cause, and shall dismiss the same for want of jurisdiction.
>
> And provided further, That whenever any pardon shall have heretofore been granted by the President of the United States to any person bringing suit in the Court of Claims for the proceeds of abandoned or captured property under the said act, approved 12th March, 1863, and the acts amendatory of the same, and such pardon shall recite in substance that such person took part in the late rebellion against the government of the United States, or was guilty of any act of rebellion against, or disloyalty to, the United States; and such pardon shall have been accepted in writing by the person to whom the same issued without an express disclaimer of, and protestation against, such fact of guilt contained in such acceptance, such pardon and acceptance shall be taken and deemed in such suit in the said Court of Claims, and on appeal therefrom, conclusive evidence that such person did take part in, and give aid and comfort to, the late rebellion, and did not maintain true allegiance or consistently adhere to the United States; and on proof of such pardon and acceptance, which proof may be heard summarily on motion or otherwise, the jurisdiction of the court in the case shall cease, and the court shall forthwith dismiss the suit of such claimant.

The government then asked the Supreme Court to remand the case with the mandate that it be dismissed for want of jurisdiction.]

THE CHIEF JUSTICE delivered the opinion of the Court.

The general question in this case is whether or not the *proviso* relating to suits for the proceeds of abandoned and captured property in the Court of Claims, contained in the appropriation act of July 12th, 1870, debars the defendant in error from recovering, as administrator of V.F. Wilson, deceased, the proceeds of certain cotton belonging to the decedent, which came into the possession of the agents of the Treasury Department as captured or abandoned property, and the proceeds of which were paid by them according to law into the Treasury of the United States.

The answer to this question requires a consideration of the rights of property, as affected by the late civil war, in the hands of citizens engaged in hostilities against the United States.

It may be said in general terms that property in the insurgent States may be distributed into four classes:

1st. That which belonged to the hostile organizations or was employed in actual hostilities on land.

2d. That which at sea became lawful subject of capture and prize.

3d. That which became the subject of confiscation.

4th. A peculiar description, known only in the recent war, called captured and abandoned property.

The first of these descriptions of property, like property of other like kind in ordinary international wars, became, wherever taken, ipso facto, the property of the United States.

The second of these descriptions comprehends ships and vessels with their cargoes belonging to the insurgents or employed in aid of them; but property in these was not changed by capture alone but by regular judicial proceeding and sentence.

Accordingly it was provided in the Abandoned and Captured Property Act of March 12th, 1863, that the property to be collected under it "shall not include any kind or description used or intended to be used for carrying on war against the United States, such as arms, ordnance, ships, steamboats and their furniture, forage, military supplies, or munitions of war."

Almost all the property of the people in the insurgent States was included in the third description, for after sixty days from the date of the President's proclamation of July 25th, 1862, all the estates and property of those who did not cease to aid, countenance, and abet the rebellion became liable to seizure and confiscation, and it was made the duty of the President to cause the same to be seized and applied, either specifically or in the proceeds thereof, to the support of the army. But it is to be observed that tribunals and proceedings were provided, by which alone such property could be condemned, and without which it remained unaffected in the possession of the proprietors.

It is thus seen that, except to property used in actual hostilities, as mentioned in the first section of the act of March 12th, 1863, no titles were divested in the insurgent States unless in pursuance of a judgment rendered after due legal proceedings. The government recognized to the fullest extent the humane maxims of the modern law of nations, which exempt private property of non-combatant enemies from capture as booty of war. Even the law of confiscation was sparingly applied. The cases were few indeed in which the property of any not engaged in actual hostilities was subjected to seizure and sale.

The spirit which animated the government received special illustration from the act under which the present case arose. We have called the property taken into the custody of public officers under that act a peculiar species, and it was so. There is, so far as we are aware, no similar legislation mentioned in history.

The act directs the officers of the Treasury Department to take into their possession and make sale of all property abandoned by its owners or captured by the national forces, and to pay the proceeds into the national treasury.

That it was not the intention of Congress that the title to these proceeds should be divested absolutely out of the original owners of the property seems clear upon a comparison of different parts of the act.

We have already seen that those articles which became by the simple fact of capture the property of the captor, as ordnance, munitions of war, and the like, or in which third parties acquired rights which might be made absolute by decree, as ships and other vessels captured as prize, were expressly excepted from the operation of the act; and it is reasonable to infer that it was the purpose of Congress that the proceeds of the property for which the special provision of the act was made should go into the treasury without change of ownership. Certainly such was the intention in respect to the property of loyal men. That the same intention prevailed in regard to the property of owners who, though then hostile, might subsequently become loyal, appears probable from the circumstance that no provision is anywhere made for confiscation of it; while there is no trace in the statute book of intention to divest ownership of private property not excepted from the effect of this act, otherwise than by proceedings for confiscation.

In the case of *Padelford*, we held that the right to the possession of private property was not changed until actual seizure by proper military authority, and that actual seizure by such authority did not divest the title under the provisions of the Abandoned and Captured Property Act. The reasons assigned seem fully to warrant the conclusion. The government constituted itself the trustee for those who were by that act declared entitled to the proceeds of captured and abandoned property, and for those whom it should thereafter recognize as entitled. By the act itself it was provided that any person claiming to have been the owner of such property might prefer his claim to the proceeds thereof, and, on proof that he had never given aid or comfort to the rebellion, receive the amount after deducting expenses.

This language makes the right to the remedy dependent upon proof of loyalty, but implies that there may be proof of ownership without proof of loyalty. The property of the original owner is, in no case, absolutely divested. There is, as we have already observed, no confiscation, but the proceeds of the property have passed into the possession of the government, and restoration of the property is pledged to none except to those who have continually adhered to the government. Whether restoration will be made to others, or confiscation will be enforced, is left to be determined by considerations of public policy subsequently to be developed.

* * *

We conclude, therefore, that the title to the proceeds of the property which came to the possession of the government by capture or abandonment, with the exceptions already noticed, was in no case divested out of the original owner. It was for the government itself to determine whether these proceeds should be restored to the owner or not. The promise of the restoration of all rights of property decides that question affirmatively as to all persons who availed themselves of the proffered pardon. It was competent for the President to annex to his offer of pardon any conditions or qualifications he should see fit; but after those conditions and qualifications had been satisfied, the pardon and its connected promises took full effect. The restoration of the proceeds became the absolute right of the persons pardoned, on application within two years from the close of the war. It was, in fact, promised for an equivalent. "Pardon and restoration of political rights" were "in return" for the oath and its fulfilment. To refuse it would be a breach of faith not less "cruel and astounding" than to abandon the freed people whom the Executive had promised to maintain in their freedom.

What, then, was the effect of the provision of the act of 1870 upon the right of the owner of the cotton in this case? He had done certain acts which this court has adjudged to be acts in aid of the rebellion; but he abandoned the cotton to the agent of the Treasury Department, by whom it has been sold and the proceeds paid into the Treasury of the United States; and he took, and has not violated, the amnesty oath under the President's proclamation. Upon this case the Court of Claims pronounced him entitled to a judgment for the net proceeds in the treasury. This decree was rendered on the 26th of May, 1869; the appeal to this court made on the 3d of June, and was filed here on the 11th of December, 1869.

The judgment of the court in the case of *Padelford*, which, in its essential features, was the same with this case, was rendered on the 30th of April, 1870. It affirmed the judgment of the Court of Claims in his favor.

Soon afterwards the provision in question was introduced as a *proviso* to the clause in the general appropriation bill, appropriating a sum of money for the payment of judgments of the Court of Claims, and became a part of the act, with perhaps little consideration in either House of Congress.

This *proviso* declares in substance that no pardon, acceptance, oath, or other act performed in pursuance, or as a condition of pardon, shall be admissible in evidence in support of any claim against the United States in the Court of Claims, or to establish the right of any claimant to bring suit in that court; nor, if already put in evidence, shall be used or considered on behalf of the claimant, by said court, or by the appellate court on appeal. Proof of loyalty is required to be made according to the provisions of certain statutes, irrespective of the effect of any executive proclamation, pardon, or amnesty, or act of oblivion; and when judgment has been already rendered on other proof of loyalty, the Supreme Court, on appeal, shall have no further jurisdiction of the cause, and shall dismiss the same for want of jurisdiction. It is further provided that whenever any pardon, granted to any suitor in the Court of Claims, for the proceeds of captured and abandoned property, shall recite in substance that the person pardoned took part in the late rebellion, or was guilty of any act of rebellion or disloyalty, and shall have been accepted in writing without express disclaimer and protestation against the fact so recited, such pardon or acceptance shall be taken as conclusive evidence in the Court of Claims, and on appeal, that the claimant did give aid to the rebellion; and on proof of such pardon, or acceptance, which proof may be made summarily on motion or otherwise, the jurisdiction of the court shall cease, and the suit shall be forthwith dismissed.

The substance of this enactment is that an acceptance of a pardon, without disclaimer, shall be conclusive evidence of the acts pardoned, but shall be null and void as evidence of the rights conferred by it, both in the Court of Claims and in this court on appeal.

* * *

FYI

The presidents following the end of the Civil War gave out a controversially large number of pardons to Southerners. The Court that decided *Klein* was sympathetic to this conciliatory policy.

The Court of Claims is * * * constituted one of those inferior courts which Congress authorizes, and has jurisdiction of contracts between the government and the citizen, from which appeal regularly lies to this court.

Undoubtedly the legislature has complete control over the organization and existence of that court and may confer or withhold the right of appeal from its decisions. And if this act did nothing more, it would be our duty to give it effect. If it simply denied the right of appeal in a particular class of cases, there could be no doubt that it must be regarded as an exercise of the power of Congress to make "such exceptions from the appellate jurisdiction" as should seem to it expedient.

But the language of the *proviso* shows plainly that it does not intend to withhold appellate jurisdiction except as a means to an end. Its great and controlling purpose is to deny to pardons granted by the President the effect which this court had adjudged them to have. The *proviso* declares that pardons shall not be considered by this court on appeal. We had already decided that it was our duty to consider them and give them effect, in cases like the present, as equivalent to proof of loyalty. It provides that whenever it shall appear that any judgment of the Court of Claims shall have been founded on such pardons, without other proof of loyalty, the Supreme Court shall have no further jurisdiction of the case and shall dismiss the same for want of jurisdiction. The *proviso* further declares that every pardon granted to any suitor in the Court of Claims and reciting that the person pardoned has been guilty of any act of rebellion or disloyalty, shall, if accepted in writing without disclaimer of the fact recited, be taken as conclusive evidence in that court and on appeal, of the act recited; and on proof of pardon or acceptance, summarily made on motion or otherwise, the jurisdiction of the court shall cease and the suit shall be forthwith dismissed.

It is evident from this statement that the denial of jurisdiction to this court, as well as to the Court of Claims, is founded solely on the application of a rule of decision, in causes pending, prescribed by Congress. The court has jurisdiction of the cause to a given point; but when it ascertains that a certain state of things exists, its jurisdiction is to cease and it is required to dismiss the cause for want of jurisdiction.

It seems to us that this is not an exercise of the acknowledged power of Congress to make exceptions and prescribe regulations to the appellate power.

The court is required to ascertain the existence of certain facts and thereupon to declare that its jurisdiction on appeal has ceased, by dismissing the bill. What is this but to prescribe a rule for the decision of a cause in a particular way? In the case before us, the Court of Claims has rendered judgment for the claimant and an appeal has been taken to this court. We are directed to dismiss the appeal, if we find that the judgment must be affirmed, because of a pardon granted to the intestate of the claimants. Can we do so without allowing one party to the controversy to decide it in its own favor? Can we do so without allowing that the legislature may prescribe rules of decision to the Judicial Department of the government in cases pending before it?

We think not; and thus thinking, we do not at all question what was decided in the case of *Pennsylvania v. Wheeling Bridge Company*. In that case, after a decree in this court that the bridge, in the then state of the law, was a nuisance and must be abated as such, Congress passed an act legalizing the structure and making it a postroad; and the court, on a motion for process to enforce the decree, held that the bridge had ceased to be a nuisance by the exercise of the constitutional powers of Congress, and denied the motion. No arbitrary rule of decision was prescribed in that case, but the court was left to apply its ordinary rules to the new circumstances created by the act. In the case before us no new circumstances have been created by legislation. But the court is forbidden to give the effect to evidence which, in its own judgment, such evidence should have, and is directed to give it an effect precisely contrary.

We must think that Congress has inadvertently passed the limit which separates the legislative from the judicial power.

It is of vital importance that these powers be kept distinct. The Constitution provides that the judicial power of the United States shall be vested in one Supreme Court and such inferior courts as the Congress shall from time to time ordain and establish. The same instrument, in the last clause of the same article, provides that in all cases other than those of original jurisdiction, "the Supreme Court shall have appellate jurisdiction both as to law and fact, with such exceptions and under such regulations as the Congress shall make."

Congress has already provided that the Supreme Court shall have jurisdiction of the judgments of the Court of Claims on appeal. Can it prescribe a rule in conformity with which the court must deny to itself the jurisdiction thus conferred, because and only because its decision, in accordance with settled law, must be adverse to the government and favorable to the suitor? This question seems to us to answer itself.

The rule prescribed is also liable to just exception as impairing the effect of a pardon, and thus infringing the constitutional power of the Executive.

It is the intention of the Constitution that each of the great co-ordinate departments of the government—the Legislative, the Executive, and the Judicial—shall be, in its sphere, independent of the others. To the executive alone is intrusted the power of pardon; and it is granted without limit. Pardon includes amnesty. It blots out the offence pardoned and removes all its penal consequences. It may be granted on conditions. In these particular pardons, that no doubt might exist as to their character, restoration of property was expressly pledged, and the pardon was granted on condition that the person who availed himself of it should take and keep a prescribed oath.

Now it is clear that the legislature cannot change the effect of such a pardon any more than the executive can change a law. Yet this is attempted by the provision under consideration. The court is required to receive special pardons as evidence of guilt and to treat them as null and void. It is required to disregard pardons granted by proclamation on condition, though the condition has been fulfilled, and to deny them their legal effect. This certainly impairs the executive authority and directs the court to be instrumental to that end.

We think it unnecessary to enlarge. The simplest statement is the best.

We repeat that it is impossible to believe that this provision was not inserted in the appropriation bill through inadvertence; and that we shall not best fulfill the deliberate will of the legislature by Denying the motion to dismiss and Affirming the judgment of the Court of Claims; which is accordingly done.

MR. JUSTICE MILLER (with whom concurred MR. JUSTICE BRADLEY), dissenting.

I cannot agree to the opinion of the court just delivered in an important matter; and I regret this the more because I do agree to the proposition that the *proviso* to the act of July 12th, 1870, is unconstitutional, so far as it attempts to prescribe to the judiciary the effect to be given to an act of pardon or amnesty by the President. This power of pardon is confided to the President by the Constitution, and whatever may be its extent or its limits, the legislative branch of the government cannot impair its force or effect in a judicial proceeding in a constitutional court. But I have not been able to bring my mind to concur in the proposition that, under the act concerning captured and abandoned property, there remains in the former owner, who had given aid and comfort to the rebellion, any interest whatever in the property or its proceeds when it had been sold and paid into the treasury or had been converted to the use of the public under that act. I must construe this act, as all others should be construed, by seeking the intention of its framers, and the intention to restore the proceeds of such property to the loyal citizen, and to transfer it absolutely to the government in the case of those who had given active support to the rebellion, is to me too apparent to be disregarded. In the one case the government is converted into a trustee for the former owner; in the other it appropriates it to its own use as the property of a public enemy captured in war. Can it be inferred from anything found in the statute that Congress intended that this property should ever be restored to the disloyal? I am unable to discern any such intent. But if it did, why was not some provision made by which the title of the government could at some time be made perfect, or that of the owner established? Some judicial proceeding for confiscation would seem to be necessary if there remains in the disloyal owner any right or interest whatever. But there is no such provision, and unless the act intended to forfeit absolutely the right of the disloyal owner, the proceeds remain in a condition where the owner cannot maintain a suit for its recovery, and the United States can obtain no perfect title to it.

This statute has recently received the attentive consideration of the court in two reported cases.

In the case of the *United States v. Anderson*, in reference to the relation of the government to the money paid into the treasury under this act, and the difference between the property of the loyal and disloyal owner, the court uses language hardly consistent with the opinion just read. It says that Congress, in a spirit of liberality, constituted the government a trustee for so much of this property as belonged to the faithful Southern people, and while it directed that all of it should be sold and its proceeds paid into the treasury, gave to this class of persons an opportunity to establish their right to the proceeds. Again, it is said, that "the measure, in itself of great beneficence, was practically important only in its application to the loyal Southern people, and sympathy for their situation doubtless prompted Congress to pass it." These views had the unanimous concurrence of the court. If I understand the present opinion, however, it maintains that the government, in taking possession of this property and selling it, became the trustee of all the former owners, whether loyal or disloyal, and holds it for the latter until pardoned by the President, or until Congress orders it to be restored to him.

The other case which I refer to is that of United States v. Padelford. In that case the opinion makes a labored and successful effort to show that Padelford, the owner of the property, had secured the benefit of the amnesty proclamation before the property was seized under the same statute we are now considering. And it bases the right of Padelford to recover its proceeds in the treasury on the fact that before the capture his status as a loyal citizen had been restored, and with it all his rights of property, although he had previously given aid and comfort to the rebellion. In this view I concurred with all my brethren. And I hold now that as long as the possession or title of property remains in the party, the pardon or the amnesty remits all right in the government to forfeit or confiscate it. But where the property has already been seized and sold, and the proceeds paid into the treasury, and it is clear that the statute contemplates no further proceeding as necessary to divest the right of the former owner, the pardon does not and cannot restore that which has thus completely passed away. And if such was not the view of the court when Padelford's case was under consideration I am at a loss to discover a reason for the extended argument in that case, in the opinion of the court, to show that he had availed himself of the amnesty before the seizure of the property. If the views now advanced are sound, it was wholly immaterial whether Padelford was pardoned before or after the seizure.

Notes and Questions

1. Is *Klein* consistent with *McCardle*?

2. Did Congress have the power to disqualify classes of former property owners from receiving compensation? If so, why is the use of that power in *Klein* unconstitutional? How does it differ from other situations where Congress has amended statutes to achieve certain results?

Does *Klein* indicate that Congress cannot make such changes applicable to pending cases? Generally appellate courts apply the law as it exists at the time of their decisions, even if it was not the law at the time the suit was filed. *See* MARTIN REDISH, FEDERAL JURISDICTION: TENSIONS IN THE ALLOCATION OF JUDICIAL POWER 49 (2d ed. 1990). Does *Klein* establish an exception to this rule for cases where the federal government is a party? If so, why? If not, is *Klein* based upon some other exception to the general rule, or is the general rule mentioned above irrelevant to the decision? If the latter, what makes it irrelevant?

3. Can one characterize the statute in *Klein* as not making an exception to the Court's appellate jurisdiction? If so, what does it do? Does that raise constitutional concerns?

4. Does the discussion of separation of powers refer to possible congressional intrusion on the power of the judiciary, the pardon power of the President, or both? Should the answer affect the Court's analysis of the constitutionality of the statute?

5. Some scholars have distinguished between "internal" limitations on congressional power to make exceptions—those found within Article III itself—and "external" limitations—those found in other constitutional provisions. Is the limitation recognized by the Court in *Klein* internal or external? What difference does it make?

6. Does *Klein* answer the question of congressional power to restrict the Supreme Court's appellate jurisdiction over a category of cases because Congress disagrees with the Court's decisions?

C. Congressional Control of the Jurisdiction of the Lower Federal Courts

Sheldon v. Sill

Supreme Court of the United States, 1850.
49 U.S. (8 How.) 441.

MR. JUSTICE GRIER delivered the opinion of the court.

The only question which it will be necessary to notice in this case is, whether the Circuit Court had jurisdiction.

Sill, the complainant below, a citizen of New York, filed his bill in the Circuit Court of the United States for Michigan, against Sheldon, claiming to recover the amount of a bond and mortgage, which had been assigned to him by Hastings, the President of the Bank of Michigan.

Sheldon, in his answer, among other things, pleaded that "the bond and mortgage in controversy, having been originally given by a citizen of Michigan to another citizen of the same state, and the complainant being assignee of them, the Circuit Court had no jurisdiction."

The eleventh section of the Judiciary Act, which defines the jurisdiction of the Circuit Courts, restrains them from taking "cognizance of any suit to recover the contents of any promissory note or other chose in action, in favor of an assignee, unless a suit might have been prosecuted in such court to recover the contents, if no assignment had been made, except in cases of foreign bills of exchange."

The third article of the Constitution declares that "the judicial power of the United States shall be vested in one Supreme Court, and such inferior courts as the Congress may, from time to time, ordain and establish." The second section of the same article enumerates the cases and controversies of which the judicial power shall have cognizance, and, among others, it specifies "controversies between citizens of different states."

It has been alleged, that this restriction of the Judiciary Act, with regard to assignees of choses in action, is in conflict with this provision of the Constitution, and therefore void.

It must be admitted, that if the Constitution had ordained and established the inferior courts, and distributed to them their respective powers, they could not be restricted or divested by Congress. But as it has made no such distribution, one of two consequences must result,—either that each inferior court created by Congress must exercise all the judicial powers not given to the Supreme Court, or that Congress, having the power to establish the courts, must define their respective jurisdictions. The first of these inferences has never been asserted, and could not be defended with any show of reason, and if not, the latter would seem to follow as a necessary consequence. And it would seem to follow, also, that, having a right to prescribe, Congress may withhold from any court of its creation jurisdiction of any of the enumerated controversies. Courts created by statute can have no jurisdiction but such as the statute confers. No one of them can assert a just claim to jurisdiction exclusively conferred on another, or withheld from all.

The Constitution has defined the limits of the judicial power of the United States, but has not prescribed how much of it shall be exercised by the Circuit Court; consequently, the statute which does prescribe the limits of their jurisdiction, cannot be in conflict with the Constitution, unless it confers powers not enumerated therein.

Such has been the doctrine held by this court since its first establishment. To enumerate all the cases in which it has been either directly advanced or tacitly assumed would be tedious and unnecessary.

In the case of *Turner v. Bank of North America*, it was contended, as in this case, that, as it was a controversy between citizens of different states, the Constitution gave the plaintiff a right to sue in the Circuit Court, notwithstanding he was an assignee within the restriction of the eleventh section of the Judiciary Act. But the court said,— "The political truth is, that the disposal of the judicial power (except in a few specified instances) belongs to Congress; and Congress is not bound to enlarge the jurisdiction of the Federal courts to every subject, in every form which the Constitution might warrant." This decision was made in 1799; since that time, the same doctrine has been frequently asserted by this court.

The only remaining inquiry is, whether the complainant in this case is the assignee of a "chose in action," within the meaning of the statute.

* * *

The complainant in this case is the purchaser and assignee of a sum of money, a debt, a chose in action, not of a tract of land. He seeks to recover by this action a debt assigned to him. He is therefore the "assignee of a chose in action," within the letter and spirit of the act of Congress under consideration, and cannot support this action in the Circuit Court of the United States, where his assignor could not.

The judgment of the Circuit Court must therefore be reversed, for want of jurisdiction.

Notes and Questions

1. Why did Congress limit the lower federal courts' jurisdiction in assignment cases? Does *Sheldon* mean that Congress has the power to remove original jurisdiction over a category of constitutional cases because it is unhappy with federal decisions? Do the due process arguments made against congressional power to limit the appellate jurisdiction of the Supreme Court apply with the same force in this context?

2. Could Congress simply have never created any lower federal courts? In *Martin v. Hunter's Lessee*, 14 U.S. (1 Wheat.) 304, 331 (1816), Justice Story, in dicta, expressed the view that Congress had a duty to vest the whole judicial power of the United States either in original or appellate form in some federal court. He based this conclusion on the language of Article III, § 1: "the judicial power of the United States *shall* be

vested."[3] [Emphasis added.] He reasoned that state courts might lack jurisdiction to adjudicate some cases within the federal judicial power but not within the original jurisdiction of the Supreme Court.[4] Thus, without inferior federal courts, the whole Article III judicial power could not be vested, from which Justice Story inferred that the Constitution required Congress to create some inferior federal courts. Is Justice Story's view consistent with language or holding of *Sill,* the leading decision on this topic? Is it consistent with the rest of the language of Article III, § 1? Even if Justice Story is correct that the entire federal judicial power must be vested, does that necessarily require the creation of lower federal courts?

3. One scholar has concluded that even though Congress need not have initially created the lower federal courts, it cannot abolish them now without violating the Constitution. Theodore Eisenberg, *Congressional Authority to Restrict Lower Federal Court Jurisdiction,* 83 YALE L.J. 498 (1974). This theory relies upon the circumstances of Supreme Court review that the Framers expected. They probably believed that appellate review by the Supreme Court would provide litigants with Article III cases the federal hearing to which they were entitled, not anticipating that the Supreme Court would only be able to review a very small percentage of the cases in which litigants seek that review. Indeed, for the first 100 years of our history, there was no discretionary device for the Court to use to control its docket, as certiorari functions today. The existence today of discretionary review and the Court's inability to handle the volume of cases qualifying for federal adjudication means that to meet the Framers' original expectation that cases within the federal judicial power would be heard by a federal court, Article III must now be interpreted to prohibit the abolition of the inferior federal courts. This theory also recognizes, however, that the lower federal courts need not have jurisdiction over all cases within the judicial power if granting such jurisdiction would undermine the federal judicial system, because the Framers would not have demanded such a self-defeating exercise. Thus, in his view, current restrictions on federal jurisdiction, such as the amount-in-controversy limitation, are consistent with Article III.

Is Professor Eisenberg's interpretation of Article III compelled by, or at least consistent with, the constitutional text? If not, is the justification he offers for departing from the text persuasive?

---

3 Justice Story placed such heavy reliance upon the word "shall" after comparing the beginning language of the first three articles of the Constitution. He argued that no one, upon reading that the legislative power shall be vested in Congress or the executive power in the President, understood that language to mean that any further act of the legislature was required to make the vesting of power effective in those branches and urged that there was no reason to construe the parallel language of Article III differently.

4 Although Justice Story did not elaborate, his theory may have been that the jurisdiction of the state courts depended upon state constitutional and legislative grants, which might not include certain classes of federal cases. Thus, in his view, a federal case might be excluded from both state and federal courts. He apparently did not consider the possibility that the Constitution might compel states to entertain federal actions. *See Testa v. Katt,* 330 U.S. 386 (1947).

4. In *Lauf v. E.G. Shinner & Co., Inc.*, 303 U.S. 323 (1938), the Court confronted a provision of the Norris-LaGuardia Act, 29 U.S.C. §§ 101 *et seq.*, that prohibited federal courts from exercising jurisdiction to issue injunctions in labor disputes in the absence of specific findings. Congress had passed the statute in response to the widely-held view that federal courts had been hostile to the labor movement in the early decades of this century. The district court in *Lauf* enjoined the defendant union on the theory that the case was not a labor dispute within the meaning of the statute, and the court of appeals affirmed. The Supreme Court disagreed and noted:

> There can be no question of the power of Congress thus to define and limit the jurisdiction of the inferior courts of the United States. The District Court made none of the required findings save as to irreparable injury and lack of remedy at law. It follows that in issuing the injunction it exceeded its jurisdiction.

Is there a conceptual difference between congressional power to limit the remedies federal courts can provide in certain classes of cases and its power to exclude those cases from the courts' jurisdiction entirely? Is there any practical difference when the remedy denied is the only effective one?

Is congressional power over the remedies broader in statutory or constitutional cases? Does *Lauf* establish congressional power to prohibit federal courts from ordering busing in school desegregation cases? Does it mean that Congress has the power to oust the lower federal courts of jurisdiction over a category of constitutional cases, like school desegregation cases, altogether?

5. Assuming that Congress can prohibit the Supreme Court from exercising appellate jurisdiction in categories of constitutional cases and also has the power to prohibit the exercise of original jurisdiction over such cases in the lower federal courts, can it do both?

6. Can Congress eliminate state jurisdiction as well as federal jurisdiction over such categories of cases? In *Battaglia v. General Motors Corp.*, 169 F.2d 254 (2d Cir.1948), the Second Circuit considered a constitutional challenge to a federal statute that prohibited the exercise of jurisdiction by any court, state or federal. The court indicated that although Congress had the power to restrict the jurisdiction of the lower federal courts, "it must not so exercise that power as to deprive any person of life, liberty, or property without due process of law or to take private property without just compensation." Having said that, the court avoided declaring the statute

unconstitutional by finding that the plaintiffs had no established property right that could serve as the predicate for a due process analysis.[5]

7. For its part, in order to avoid the "serious constitutional question" that would otherwise arise, the Supreme Court has gone to great lengths in a series of cases to construe federal statutes not to eliminate judicial review completely. *See, e.g., Webster v. Doe,* 486 U.S. 592 (1988); *Johnson v. Robison,* 415 U.S. 361 (1974).

In *Oestereich v. Selective Service System Local Board No. 11,* 393 U.S. 233 (1968), however, the majority interpreted a statute to allow judicial review without relying on the need to avoid the constitutional issue. Oestereich was a divinity student and thus entitled to exemption from service under § 6(g) of the Military Selective Service Act of 1967. He had received the exemption, but when he returned his registration certificate to express his opposition to the involvement of the United States in the War in Vietnam, his Local Board responded by declaring him delinquent for failure to have the certificate in his possession and for failure to provide the Board with notice of his local status. It then reclassified him I-A: ready for induction. Oestereich filed an administrative appeal but lost and was ordered to report for induction. He sued, alleging that he was illegally deprived of his exemption and that his induction order was therefore void.

Generally, the courts had held that the Selective Service Act did not permit pre-induction judicial review of draft classifications. Registrants could challenge classifications in the courts in only two ways: by raising improper classification as a defense to criminal prosecution for refusing to be inducted or, if the registrant accepted induction, by seeking discharge from the military through a writ of habeas corpus. Then, in *Wolff v. Selective Service Local Board No. 16,* 372 F.2d 817 (2d Cir.1967), the court permitted pre-induction review of the punitive reclassification of two young men who had demonstrated against the war. Congress disliked the decision and amended the Selective Service Act. Thus, when Oestereich filed his complaint, the pertinent language of § 10(b)(3) provided:

> No judicial review shall be made of the classification or processing of any registrant by local boards, appeal boards, or the President, except as a defense to a criminal prosecution instituted under section 12 of this title, after the registrant has responded either affirmatively or negatively to an order to report for induction * * * .

Legislative history confirmed that Congress meant to restrict judicial review to the two situations generally recognized before *Wolff.* Nonetheless, the Supreme Court held that pre-induction judicial review was available to Oestereich.

5 The court's analysis is similar to the analysis the Supreme Court would later use in Paul v. Davis, 424 U.S. 693 (1976), to find that a state official's labeling an individual a convicted criminal without an adjudication was not actionable under the Due Process Clause of the Fourteenth Amendment because the individual had no constitutionally cognizable liberty or property interest in his reputation. *See generally* Chapter 6, Section B, Part 4.

The Court concluded that Congress had never authorized the use of delinquency regulations to deprive a registrant of an exemption to which he was entitled. Once a person had qualified for an exemption, he could not be deprived of it because of conduct unrelated to the basis for the exemption. If Oestereich's allegations were true, his local board had acted completely outside its authority. The Court distinguished cases where the Board evaluated evidence and exercised its discretion in determining whether a registrant qualified for a claimed exemption. In regard to the language of § 10(b)(3), the Court asserted:

> To hold that a person deprived of his statutory exemption in such a blatantly lawless manner must either be inducted and raise his protest through habeas corpus or defy induction and defend his refusal in a criminal prosecution is to construe the Act with unnecessary harshness. As the Solicitor General suggests, such literalness does violence to the clear mandate of § 6(g) governing the exemption. Our construction leaves § 10(b)(3) unimpaired in the normal operations of the Act.

Justice Harlan concurred in a separate opinion. He read Oestereich's claim as one that the procedure by which he was reclassified was unlawful. Such a challenge was beyond the competence of the Board to hear and determine. Consequently, if Oestereich was not allowed pre-induction judicial review in this case, he would be deprived of his liberty without the prior opportunity to challenge the legality of the procedure by which he was inducted. Justice Harlan thought such a construction "would raise serious constitutional problems."

Thus, until 2008, most of the Supreme Court's confrontations with statutes purporting to preclude all judicial review had resulted in the Court, perhaps straining a bit, construing the statutes to permit judicial review after all.[6] That approach avoided the serious constitutional question to which Justice Harlan adverted. But then came the attacks of September 11, 2001, followed by the War on Terror, consisting in part of an attempt to strip the federal courts of jurisdiction to issue writs of habeas corpus to prisoners detained at Guantanamo.

---

6 In United States v. Mendoza-Lopez, 481 U.S. 828 (1987), however, a majority held that a statutory scheme that made prior deportation a conclusive predicate for felonious unlawful entry violated due process because Congress had permitted too limited judicial review of administrative deportation orders.

Boumediene v. Bush

Supreme Court of the United States, 2008.
553 U.S. 723.

JUSTICE KENNEDY delivered the opinion of the Court.

Petitioners are aliens designated as enemy combatants and detained at the United States Naval Station at Guantanamo Bay, Cuba. There are others detained there, also aliens, who are not parties to this suit.

Petitioners present a question not resolved by our earlier cases relating to the detention of aliens at Guantanamo: whether they have the constitutional privilege of habeas corpus, a privilege not to be withdrawn except in conformance with the Suspension Clause, art. I, § 9, cl. 2. We hold these petitioners do have the habeas corpus privilege. Congress has enacted a statute, the Detainee Treatment Act of 2005 (DTA), that provides certain procedures for review of the detainees' status. We hold that those procedures are not an adequate and effective substitute for habeas corpus. Therefore § 7 of the Military Commissions Act of 2006 (MCA), operates as an unconstitutional suspension of the writ. We do not address whether the President has authority to detain these petitioners nor do we hold that the writ must issue. These and other questions regarding the legality of the detention are to be resolved in the first instance by the District Court.

Make the Connection

Note how many of the cases in which the Court has confronted attempts at jurisdiction-stripping come in habeas corpus cases.

I

Under the Authorization for Use of Military Force (AUMF), the President is authorized "to use all necessary and appropriate force against those nations, organizations, or persons he determines planned, authorized, committed, or aided the terrorist attacks that occurred on September 11, 2001, or harbored such organizations or persons, in order to prevent any future acts of international terrorism against the United States by such nations, organizations or persons."

In *Hamdi v. Rumsfeld* (2004), five Members of the Court recognized that detention of individuals who fought against the United States in Afghanistan "for the duration of the particular conflict in which they were captured, is so fundamental and accepted an incident to war as to be an exercise of the 'necessary and appropriate force' Congress has authorized the President to use." After *Hamdi*, the Deputy Secretary of Defense established Combatant Status Review Tribunals (CSRTs) to determine whether individuals detained at Guantanamo were "enemy combatants," as the Department defines that term. A later memorandum established procedures to implement the CSRTs. The Government maintains these procedures were designed to comply with the due process requirements identified by the plurality in Hamdi.

Interpreting the AUMF, the Department of Defense ordered the detention of these petitioners, and they were transferred to Guantanamo. Some of these individuals were apprehended on the battlefield in Afghanistan, others in places as far away from there as Bosnia and Gambia. All are foreign nationals, but none is a citizen of a nation now at war with the United States. Each denies he is a member of the al Qaeda terrorist network that carried out the September 11 attacks or of the Taliban regime that provided sanctuary for al Qaeda. Each petitioner appeared before a separate CSRT; was determined to be an enemy combatant; and has sought a writ of habeas corpus in the United States District Court for the District of Columbia.

The first actions commenced in February 2002. The District Court ordered the cases dismissed for lack of jurisdiction because the naval station is outside the sovereign territory of the United States. Rasul v. Bush (2002). The Court of Appeals for the District of Columbia Circuit affirmed. We granted certiorari and reversed, holding that 28 U.S.C. § 2241 extended statutory habeas corpus jurisdiction to Guantanamo. The constitutional issue presented in the instant cases was not reached in *Rasul*.

After Rasul, petitioners' cases were consolidated and entertained in two separate proceedings. In the first set of cases, Judge Richard J. Leon granted the Government's motion to dismiss, holding that the detainees had no rights that could be vindicated in a habeas corpus action. In the second set of cases Judge Joyce Hens Green reached the opposite conclusion, holding the detainees had rights under the Due Process Clause of the Fifth Amendment.

While appeals were pending from the District Court decisions, Congress passed the DTA. Subsection (e) of § 1005 of the DTA amended 28 U.S.C. § 2241 to provide that "no court, justice, or judge shall have jurisdiction to hear or consider * * * an application for a writ of habeas corpus filed by or on behalf of an alien detained by the Department of Defense at Guantanamo Bay, Cuba." Section 1005 further provides that the Court of Appeals for the District of Columbia Circuit shall have "exclusive" jurisdiction to review decisions of the CSRTs.

In Hamdan v. Rumsfeld (2006), the Court held this provision did not apply to cases (like petitioners') pending when the DTA was enacted. Congress responded by passing the MCA, which again amended § 2241. The text of the statutory amendment is discussed below. (Four Members of the *Hamdan* majority noted that "[n]othing prevent[ed] the President from returning to Congress to seek the authority he believes necessary." The authority to which the concurring opinion referred was the authority to "create military commissions of the kind at issue" in the case. Nothing in that opinion can be construed as an invitation for Congress to suspend the writ.)

Petitioners' cases were consolidated on appeal, and the parties filed supplemental briefs in light of our decision in Hamdan. The Court of Appeals' ruling is the subject of our present review and today's decision.

The Court of Appeals concluded that MCA § 7 must be read to strip from it, and all federal courts, jurisdiction to consider petitioners' habeas corpus applications; that petitioners are not entitled to the privilege of the writ or the protections of the Suspension Clause; and, as a result, that it was unnecessary to consider whether Congress provided an adequate and effective substitute for habeas corpus in the DTA.

We granted certiorari.

II

As a threshold matter, we must decide whether MCA § 7 denies the federal courts jurisdiction to hear habeas corpus actions pending at the time of its enactment. We hold the statute does deny that jurisdiction, so that, if the statute is valid, petitioners' cases must be dismissed.

As amended by the terms of the MCA, 28 U.S.C.A. § 2241(e) (Supp. 2007) now provides:

> (1) No court, justice, or judge shall have jurisdiction to hear or consider an application for a writ of habeas corpus filed by or on behalf of an alien detained by the United States who has been determined by the United States to have been properly detained as an enemy combatant or is awaiting such determination.

* * *

Section 7(b) of the MCA provides the effective date for the amendment of § 2241(e). It states:

> The amendment made by [MCA § 7(a)] shall take effect on the date of the enactment of this Act, and shall apply to all cases, without exception, pending on or after the date of the enactment of this Act which relate to any aspect of the detention, transfer, treatment, trial, or conditions of detention of an alien detained by the United States since September 11, 2001.

There is little doubt that the effective date provision applies to habeas corpus actions. Those actions, by definition, are cases "which relate to * * * detention."

* * *

We acknowledge, moreover, the litigation history that prompted Congress to enact the MCA. In Hamdan the Court found it unnecessary to address the petitioner's Suspension Clause arguments but noted the relevance of the clear statement rule in deciding whether Congress intended to reach pending habeas corpus cases. (Congress should "not be presumed to have effected such denial [of habeas relief] absent an unmistakably clear statement to the contrary"). This interpretive rule facilitates a dialogue between Congress and the Court. If the Court invokes a clear statement rule to advise that certain statutory interpretations are favored in order to avoid constitutional difficulties, Congress can make an informed legislative choice either to amend the statute or to retain its existing text. If Congress amends, its intent must be respected even if a difficult constitutional question is presented. The usual presumption is that Members of Congress, in accord with their oath of office, considered the constitutional issue and determined the amended statute to be a lawful one; and the Judiciary, in light of that determination, proceeds to its own independent judgment on the constitutional question when required to do so in a proper case.

If this ongoing dialogue between and among the branches of Government is to be respected, we cannot ignore that the MCA was a direct response to Hamdan's holding that the DTA's jurisdiction-stripping provision had no application to pending cases. The Court of Appeals was correct to take note of the legislative history when construing the statute, and we agree with its conclusion that the MCA deprives the federal courts of jurisdiction to entertain the habeas corpus actions now before us.

III

In deciding the constitutional questions now presented we must determine whether petitioners are barred from seeking the writ or invoking the protections of the Suspension Clause either because of their status, *i.e.*, petitioners' designation by the Executive Branch as enemy combatants, or their physical location, *i.e.*, their presence at Guantanamo Bay. The Government contends that noncitizens designated as enemy combatants and detained in territory located outside our Nation's borders have no constitutional rights and no privilege of habeas corpus. Petitioners contend they do have cognizable constitutional rights and that Congress, in seeking to eliminate recourse to habeas corpus as a means to assert those rights, acted in violation of the Suspension Clause.

We begin with a brief account of the history and origins of the writ. Our account proceeds from two propositions. First, protection for the privilege of habeas corpus was one of the few safeguards of liberty specified in a Constitution that, at the outset, had no Bill of Rights. In the system conceived by the Framers the writ had a centrality that must inform proper interpretation of the Suspension Clause. Second, to the extent there were settled precedents or legal commentaries in 1789 regarding the extraterritorial scope of the writ or its application to enemy aliens, those authorities can be instructive for the present cases.

A

The Framers viewed freedom from unlawful restraint as a fundamental precept of liberty, and they understood the writ of habeas corpus as a vital instrument to secure that freedom. Experience taught, however, that the common-law writ all too often had been insufficient to guard against the abuse of monarchial power. That history counseled the necessity for specific language in the Constitution to secure the writ and ensure its place in our legal system.

* * *

This history was known to the Framers. It no doubt confirmed their view that pendular swings to and away from individual liberty were endemic to undivided, uncontrolled power. The Framers' inherent distrust of governmental power was the driving force behind the constitutional plan that allocated powers among three independent branches. This design serves not only to make Government accountable but also to secure individual liberty. Because the Constitution's separation-of-powers structure, like the substantive guarantees of the Fifth and Fourteenth Amendments, protects persons as well as citizens, foreign nationals who have the privilege of litigating in our courts can seek to enforce separation-of-powers principles.

That the Framers considered the writ a vital instrument for the protection of individual liberty is evident from the care taken to specify the limited grounds for its suspension: "The Privilege of the Writ of Habeas Corpus shall not be suspended, unless when in Cases of Rebellion or Invasion the public Safety may require it." [U.S. CONST.,] [a]rt. I, § 9, cl. 2. The word "privilege" was used, perhaps, to avoid mentioning some rights to the exclusion of others. (Indeed, the only mention of the term "right" in the Constitution, as ratified, is in its clause giving Congress the power to protect the rights of authors and inventors.

Surviving accounts of the ratification debates provide additional evidence that the Framers deemed the writ to be an essential mechanism in the separation-of-powers scheme. In a critical exchange with Patrick Henry at the Virginia ratifying convention[,] Edmund Randolph referred to the Suspension Clause as an "exception" to the "power given to Congress to regulate courts." A resolution passed by the New York ratifying convention made clear its understanding that the Clause not only protects against arbitrary suspensions of the writ but also guarantees an affirmative right to judicial inquiry into the causes of detention.

* * *

Post-1789 habeas developments in England, though not bearing upon the Framers' intent, do verify their foresight. Those later events would underscore the need for structural barriers against arbitrary suspensions of the writ. Just as the writ had been vulnerable to executive and parliamentary encroachment on both sides of the Atlantic before the American Revolution, despite the Habeas Corpus Act of 1679, the writ was suspended with frequency in England during times of political unrest after 1789. * * *

In our own system the Suspension Clause is designed to protect against these cyclical abuses. The Clause protects the rights of the detained by a means consistent with the essential design of the Constitution. It ensures that, except during periods of formal suspension, the Judiciary will have a time-tested device, the writ, to maintain the "delicate balance of governance" that is itself the surest safeguard of liberty. The Clause protects the rights of the detained by affirming the duty and authority of the Judiciary to call the jailer to account. The separation-of-powers doctrine, and the history that influenced its design, therefore must inform the reach and purpose of the Suspension Clause.

B

The broad historical narrative of the writ and its function is central to our analysis, but we seek guidance as well from founding-era authorities addressing the specific question before us: whether foreign nationals, apprehended and detained in distant countries during a time of serious threats to our Nation's security, may assert the privilege of the writ and seek its protection. The Court has been careful not to foreclose the possibility that the protections of the Suspension Clause have expanded along with post-1789 developments that define the present scope of the writ. But the analysis may begin with precedents as of 1789, for the Court has said that "at the absolute minimum" the Clause protects the writ as it existed when the Constitution was drafted and ratified.

To support their arguments, the parties in these cases have examined historical sources to construct a view of the common-law writ as it existed in 1789—as have *amici* whose expertise in legal history the Court has relied upon in the past. The Government argues the common-law writ ran only to those territories over which the Crown was sovereign. Petitioners argue that jurisdiction followed the King's officers. Diligent search by all parties reveals no certain conclusions. In none of the cases cited do we find that a common-law court would or would not have granted, or refused to hear for lack of jurisdiction, a petition for a writ of habeas corpus brought by a prisoner deemed an enemy combatant, under a standard like the one the Department of Defense has used in these cases, and when held in a territory, like Guantanamo, over which the Government has total military and civil control.

We know that at common law a petitioner's status as an alien was not a categorical bar to habeas corpus relief. *See, e.g.*, Sommersett's Case (1772) (ordering an African slave freed upon finding the custodian's return insufficient); see generally *Khera v. Secretary of State for the Home Dept.*, [1984] ("Habeas corpus protection is often expressed as limited to 'British subjects.' Is it really limited to British nationals? Suffice it to say that the case law has given an emphatic 'no' to the question.") We know as well that common-law courts entertained habeas petitions brought by enemy aliens detained in England—"entertained" at least in the sense that the courts held hearings to determine the threshold question of entitlement to the writ.

* * *

We find the evidence as to the geographic scope of the writ at common law informative, but, again, not dispositive.

* * *

Each side in the present matter argues that the very lack of a precedent on point supports its position. The Government points out there is no evidence that a court sitting in England granted habeas relief to an enemy alien detained abroad; petitioners respond there is no evidence that a court refused to do so for lack of jurisdiction.

Both arguments are premised, however, upon the assumption that the historical record is complete and that the common law, if properly understood, yields a definite answer to the questions before us. There are reasons to doubt both assumptions. Recent scholarship points to the inherent shortcomings in the historical record. And given the unique status of Guantanamo Bay and the particular dangers of terrorism in the modern age, the common-law courts simply may not have confronted cases with close parallels to this one. We decline, therefore, to infer too much, one way or the other, from the lack of historical evidence on point.

IV

Drawing from its position that at common law the writ ran only to territories over which the Crown was sovereign, the Government says the Suspension Clause affords petitioners no rights because the United States does not claim sovereignty over the place of detention.

Guantanamo Bay is not formally part of the United States. And under the terms of the lease between the United States and Cuba, Cuba retains "ultimate sovereignty" over the territory while the United States exercises "complete jurisdiction and control." Under the terms of the 1934 Treaty, however, Cuba effectively has no rights as a sovereign until the parties agree to modification of the 1903 Lease Agreement or the United States abandons the base.

The United States contends, nevertheless, that Guantanamo is not within its sovereign control. This was the Government's position well before the events of September 11, 2001. And in other contexts the Court has held that questions of sovereignty are for the political branches to decide. Even if this were a treaty interpretation case that did not involve a political question, the President's construction of the lease agreement would be entitled to great respect.

We therefore do not question the Government's position that Cuba, not the United States, maintains sovereignty, in the legal and technical sense of the term, over Guantanamo Bay. But this does not end the analysis. Our cases do not hold it is improper for us to inquire into the objective degree of control the Nation asserts over foreign territory. * * * Accordingly, for purposes of our analysis, we accept the Government's position that Cuba, and not the United States, retains *de jure* sovereignty over Guantanamo Bay. As we did in Rasul, however, we take notice of the obvious and uncontested fact that the United States, by virtue of its complete jurisdiction and control over the base, maintains *de facto* sovereignty over this territory.

Were we to hold that the present cases turn on the political question doctrine, we would be required first to accept the Government's premise that *de jure* sovereignty is the touchstone of habeas corpus jurisdiction. This premise, however, is unfounded. For the reasons indicated above, the history of common-law habeas corpus provides scant support for this proposition; and, for the reasons indicated below, that position would be inconsistent with our precedents and contrary to fundamental separation-of-powers principles.

A

[Here the Court analyzes and rejects the Government's argument that, at least as applied to noncitizens, the Constitution does not extend beyond where the United States' *de jure* sovereignty ends.]

* * *

B

The Government's formal sovereignty-based test raises troubling separation-of-powers concerns as well. The political history of Guantanamo illustrates the deficiencies of this approach. The United States has maintained complete and uninterrupted control of the bay for over 100 years. At the close of the Spanish-American War, Spain ceded control over the entire island of Cuba to the United States and specifically "relinquishe[d] all claim[s] of sovereignty * * * and title."

From the date the treaty with Spain was signed until the Cuban Republic was established on May 20, 1902, the United States governed the territory "in trust" for the benefit of the Cuban people. And although it recognized, by entering into the 1903 Lease Agreement, that Cuba retained "ultimate sovereignty" over Guantanamo, the United States continued to maintain the same plenary control it had enjoyed since 1898. Yet the Government's view is that the Constitution had no effect there, at least as to noncitizens, because the United States disclaimed sovereignty in the formal sense of the term. The necessary implication of the argument is that by surrendering formal sovereignty over any unincorporated territory to a third party, while at the same time entering into a lease that grants total control over the territory back to the United States, it would be possible for the political branches to govern without legal constraint.

Our basic charter cannot be contracted away like this. The Constitution grants Congress and the President the power to acquire, dispose of, and govern territory, not the power to decide when and where its terms apply. Even when the United States acts outside its borders, its powers are not "absolute and unlimited" but are subject "to such restrictions as are expressed in the Constitution." Abstaining from questions involving formal sovereignty and territorial governance is one thing. To hold the political branches have the power to switch the Constitution on or off at will is quite another. The former position reflects this Court's recognition that certain matters requiring political judgments are best left to the political branches. The latter would permit a striking anomaly in our tripartite system of government, leading to a regime in which Congress and the President, not this Court, say "what the law is." Marbury v. Madison (1803).

These concerns have particular bearing upon the Suspension Clause question in the cases now before us, for the writ of habeas corpus is itself an indispensable mechanism for monitoring the separation of powers. The test for determining the scope of this provision must not be subject to manipulation by those whose power it is designed to restrain.

C

As we recognized in Rasul, the outlines of a framework for determining the reach of the Suspension Clause are suggested by the factors the Court relied upon in Johnson v. Eisentrager (1950). In addition to the practical concerns discussed above, the Eisentrager Court found relevant that each petitioner:

> (a) is an enemy alien; (b) has never been or resided in the United States; (c) was captured outside of our territory and there held in military custody as a prisoner of war; (d) was tried and convicted by a Military Commission sitting outside the United States; (e) for offenses against laws of war committed outside the United States; (f) and is at all times imprisoned outside the United States.

Based on this language from Eisentrager, and the reasoning in our other extraterritoriality opinions, we conclude that at least three factors are relevant in determining the reach of the Suspension Clause: (1) the citizenship and status of the detainee and the adequacy of the process through which that status determination was made; (2) the nature of the sites where apprehension and then detention took place; and (3) the practical obstacles inherent in resolving the prisoner's entitlement to the writ.

Applying this framework, we note at the onset that the status of these detainees is a matter of dispute. The petitioners, like those in Eisentrager, are not American citizens. But the petitioners in Eisentrager did not contest, it seems, the Court's assertion that they were "enemy alien[s]." In the instant cases, by contrast, the detainees deny they are enemy combatants. They have been afforded some process in CSRT proceedings to determine their status; but, unlike in Eisentrager, there has been no trial by military commission for violations of the laws of war. The difference is not trivial. The records from the Eisentrager trials suggest that, well before the petitioners brought their case to this Court, there had been a rigorous adversarial process to test the legality of their detention. The Eisentrager petitioners were charged by a bill of particulars that made detailed factual allegations against them. To rebut the accusations, they were entitled to representation by counsel, allowed to introduce evidence on their own behalf, and permitted to cross-examine the prosecution's witnesses.

In comparison the procedural protections afforded to the detainees in the CSRT hearings are far more limited, and, we conclude, fall well short of the procedures and adversarial mechanisms that would eliminate the need for habeas corpus review. Although the detainee is assigned a "Personal Representative" to assist him during CSRT proceedings, the Secretary of the Navy's memorandum makes clear that person is not the detainee's lawyer or even his "advocate." The Government's evidence is accorded a presumption of validity. The detainee is allowed to present "reasonably available" evidence, but his ability to rebut the Government's evidence against him is limited by the circumstances of his confinement and his lack of counsel at this stage. And although the detainee can seek review of his status determination in the Court of Appeals, that review process cannot cure all defects in the earlier proceedings.

As to the second factor relevant to this analysis, the detainees here are similarly situated to the Eisentrager petitioners in that the sites of their apprehension and detention are technically outside the sovereign territory of the United States. As noted earlier, this is a factor that weighs against finding they have rights under the Suspension Clause. But there are critical differences between Landsberg Prison, *circa* 1950, and the United States Naval Station at Guantanamo Bay in 2008. Unlike its present control over the naval station, the United States' control over the prison in Germany was neither absolute nor indefinite. Like all parts of occupied Germany, the prison was under the jurisdiction of the combined Allied Forces. The United States was therefore answerable to its Allies for all activities occurring there. The Allies had not planned a long-term occupation of Germany, nor did they intend to displace all German institutions even during the period of occupation. The Court's holding in Eisentrager was thus consistent with the Insular Cases, where it had held there was no need to extend full constitutional protections to territories the United States did not intend to govern indefinitely. Guantanamo Bay, on the other hand, is no transient possession. In every practical sense Guantanamo is not abroad; it is within the constant jurisdiction of the United States.

As to the third factor, we recognize, as the Court did in Eisentrager, that there are costs to holding the Suspension Clause applicable in a case of military detention abroad. Habeas corpus proceedings may require expenditure of funds by the Government and may divert the attention of military personnel from other pressing tasks. While we are sensitive to these concerns, we do not find them dispositive. Compliance with any judicial process requires some incremental expenditure of resources. Yet civilian courts and the Armed Forces have functioned along side each other at various points in our history. The Government presents no credible arguments that the military mission at Guantanamo would be compromised if habeas corpus courts had jurisdiction to hear the detainees' claims. And in light of the plenary control the United States asserts over the base, none are apparent to us.

The situation in Eisentrager was far different, given the historical context and nature of the military's mission in post-War Germany. When hostilities in the European Theater came to an end, the United States became responsible for an occupation zone encompassing over 57,000 square miles with a population of 18 million. In addition to supervising massive reconstruction and aid efforts the American forces stationed in Germany faced potential security threats from a defeated enemy. In retrospect the post-War occupation may seem uneventful. But at the time Eisentrager was decided, the Court was right to be concerned about judicial interference with the military's efforts to contain "enemy elements, guerilla fighters, and 'were-wolves.' "

Similar threats are not apparent here; nor does the Government argue that they are. The United States Naval Station at Guantanamo Bay consists of 45 square miles of land and water. The base has been used, at various points, to house migrants and refugees temporarily. At present, however, other than the detainees themselves, the only long-term residents are American military personnel, their families, and a small number of workers. The detainees have been deemed enemies of the United States. At present, dangerous as they may be if released, they are contained in a secure prison facility located on an isolated and heavily fortified military base.

There is no indication, furthermore, that adjudicating a habeas corpus petition would cause friction with the host government. No Cuban court has jurisdiction over American military personnel at Guantanamo or the enemy combatants detained there. While obligated to abide by the terms of the lease, the United States is, for all practical purposes, answerable to no other sovereign for its acts on the base. Were that not the case, or if the detention facility were located in an active theater of war, arguments that issuing the writ would be "impracticable or anomalous" would have more weight. Under the facts presented here, however, there are few practical barriers to the running of the writ. To the extent barriers arise, habeas corpus procedures likely can be modified to address them.

It is true that before today the Court has never held that noncitizens detained by our Government in territory over which another country maintains *de jure* sovereignty have any rights under our Constitution. But the cases before us lack any precise historical parallel. They involve individuals detained by executive order for the duration of a conflict that, if measured from September 11, 2001, to the present, is already among the longest wars in American history. The detainees, moreover, are held in a territory that, while technically not part of the United States, is under the complete and total control of our Government. Under these circumstances the lack of a precedent on point is no barrier to our holding.

We hold that Art. I, § 9, cl. 2, of the Constitution has full effect at Guantanamo Bay. If the privilege of habeas corpus is to be denied to the detainees now before us, Congress must act in accordance with the requirements of the Suspension Clause. This Court may not impose a *de facto* suspension by abstaining from these controversies. The MCA does not purport to be a formal suspension of the writ; and the Government, in its submissions to us, has not argued that it is. Petitioners, therefore, are entitled to the privilege of habeas corpus to challenge the legality of their detention.

V

In light of this holding the question becomes whether the statute stripping jurisdiction to issue the writ avoids the Suspension Clause mandate because Congress has provided adequate substitute procedures for habeas corpus. The Government submits there has been compliance with the Suspension Clause because the DTA review process in the Court of Appeals, provides an adequate substitute. Congress has granted that court jurisdiction to consider

> (i) whether the status determination of the [CSRT] * * * was consistent with the standards and procedures specified by the Secretary of Defense * * * and (ii) to the extent the Constitution and laws of the United States are applicable, whether the use of such standards and procedures to make the determination is consistent with the Constitution and laws of the United States.

The Court of Appeals, having decided that the writ does not run to the detainees in any event, found it unnecessary to consider whether an adequate substitute has been provided. In the ordinary course we would remand to the Court of Appeals to consider this question in the first instance. It is well settled, however, that the Court's practice of declining to address issues left unresolved in earlier proceedings is not an inflexible rule. Departure from the rule is appropriate in "exceptional" circumstances.

The gravity of the separation-of-powers issues raised by these cases and the fact that these detainees have been denied meaningful access to a judicial forum for a period of years render these cases exceptional. The parties before us have addressed the adequacy issue. While we would have found it informative to consider the reasoning of the Court of Appeals on this point, we must weigh that against the harms petitioners may endure from additional delay. And, given there are few precedents addressing what features an adequate substitute for habeas corpus must contain, in all likelihood a remand simply would delay ultimate resolution of the issue by this Court.

We do have the benefit of the Court of Appeals' construction of key provisions of the DTA. When we granted certiorari in these cases, we noted "it would be of material assistance to consult any decision" in the parallel DTA review proceedings pending in the Court of Appeals, specifically any rulings in the matter of *Bismullah v. Gates*. Although the Court of Appeals has yet to complete a DTA review proceeding, the three-judge panel in Bismullah has issued an interim order giving guidance as to what evidence can be made part of the record on review and what access the detainees can have to counsel and to classified information. In that matter the full court denied the Government's motion for rehearing *en banc*. The order denying rehearing was accompanied by five separate statements from members of the court, which offer differing views as to scope of the judicial review Congress intended these detainees to have.

Under the circumstances we believe the costs of further delay substantially outweigh any benefits of remanding to the Court of Appeals to consider the issue it did not address in these cases.

A

Our case law does not contain extensive discussion of standards defining suspension of the writ or of circumstances under which suspension has occurred. This simply confirms the care Congress has taken throughout our Nation's history to preserve the writ and its function. Indeed, most of the major legislative enactments pertaining to habeas corpus have acted not to contract the writ's protection but to expand it or to hasten resolution of prisoners' claims.

There are exceptions, of course. Title I of the Antiterrorism and Effective Death Penalty Act of 1996 (AEDPA), contains certain gatekeeping provisions that restrict a prisoner's ability to bring new and repetitive claims in "second or successive" habeas corpus actions. We upheld these provisions against a Suspension Clause challenge in *Felker v. Turpin (1996)*. The provisions at issue in *Felker,* however, did not constitute a substantial departure from common-law habeas procedures. The provisions, for the most part, codified the longstanding abuse-of-the-writ doctrine. AEDPA applies, moreover, to federal, postconviction review after criminal proceedings in state court have taken place. As of this point, cases discussing the implementation of that statute give little helpful instruction (save perhaps by contrast) for the instant cases, where no trial has been held.

The two leading cases addressing habeas substitutes, *Swain v. Pressley (1977)* and *United States v. Hayman (1952)*, likewise provide little guidance here. The statutes at issue were attempts to streamline habeas corpus relief, not to cut it back.

* * *

Unlike in *Hayman* and *Swain,* here we confront statutes, the DTA and the MCA, that were intended to circumscribe habeas review. * * * When Congress has intended to replace traditional habeas corpus with habeas-like substitutes, as was the case in *Hayman* and *Swain,* it has granted to the courts broad remedial powers to secure the historic office of the writ. * * *

In contrast the DTA's jurisdictional grant is quite limited. The Court of Appeals has jurisdiction not to inquire into the legality of the detention generally but only to assess whether the CSRT complied with the "standards and procedures specified by the Secretary of Defense" and whether those standards and procedures are lawful. If Congress had envisioned DTA review as coextensive with traditional habeas corpus, it would not have drafted the statute in this manner. Instead, it would have used language similar to what it used in the statutes at issue in *Hayman* and *Swain*. Unlike in *Hayman* and *Swain,* moreover, there has been no effort to preserve habeas corpus review as an avenue of last resort. No saving clause exists in either the MCA or the DTA. And MCA § 7 eliminates habeas review for these petitioners.

The differences between the DTA and the habeas statute that would govern in MCA § 7's absence, are likewise telling. In § 2241 (2000 ed.) Congress confirmed the authority of "any justice" or "circuit judge" to issue the writ. That statute accommodates the necessity for factfinding that will arise in some cases by allowing the appellate judge or Justice to transfer the case to a district court of competent jurisdiction, whose institutional capacity for factfinding is superior to his or her own. By granting the Court of Appeals "exclusive" jurisdiction over petitioners' cases, Congress has foreclosed that option. This choice indicates Congress intended the Court of Appeals to have a more limited role in enemy combatant status determinations than a district court has in habeas corpus proceedings. The DTA should be interpreted to accord some latitude to the Court of Appeals to fashion procedures necessary to make its review function a meaningful one, but, if congressional intent is to be respected, the procedures adopted cannot be as extensive or as protective of the rights of the detainees as they would be in a § 2241 proceeding. Otherwise there would have been no, or very little, purpose for enacting the DTA.

To the extent any doubt remains about Congress' intent, the legislative history confirms what the plain text strongly suggests: In passing the DTA Congress did not intend to create a process that differs from traditional habeas corpus process in name only. It intended to create a more limited procedure. See, *e.g.*, 151 Cong. Rec. S14263 (Dec. 21, 2005) (statement of Sen. Graham) (noting that the DTA "extinguish[es] these habeas and other actions in order to effect a transfer of jurisdiction over these cases to the DC Circuit Court" and agreeing that the bill "create[s] in their place a very limited judicial review of certain military administrative decisions"); *id.*, at S14268 (statement of Sen. Kyl) ("It is important to note that the limited judicial review authorized by paragraphs 2 and 3 of subsection (e) [of DTA § 1005] are not habeas-corpus review. It is a limited judicial review of its own nature").

It is against this background that we must interpret the DTA and assess its adequacy as a substitute for habeas corpus. The present cases thus test the limits of the Suspension Clause in ways that *Hayman* and *Swain* did not.

B

We do not endeavor to offer a comprehensive summary of the requisites for an adequate substitute for habeas corpus. We do consider it uncontroversial, however, that the privilege of habeas corpus entitles the prisoner to a meaningful opportunity to demonstrate that he is being held pursuant to "the erroneous application or interpretation" of relevant law. And the habeas court must have the power to order the conditional release of an individual unlawfully detained-though release need not be the exclusive remedy and is not the appropriate one in every case in which the writ is granted.

Indeed, common-law habeas corpus was, above all, an adaptable remedy. Its precise application and scope changed depending upon the circumstances. It appears the common-law habeas court's role was most extensive in cases of pretrial and noncriminal detention, where there had been little or no previous judicial review of the cause for detention. Notably, the black-letter rule that prisoners could not controvert facts in the jailer's return was not followed (or at least not with consistency) in such cases. Oakes, *Legal History in the High Court—Habeas Corpus*, 64 MICH. L. REV. 451, 457 (1966) ("[W]hen a prisoner applied for habeas corpus before indictment or trial, some courts examined the written depositions on which he had been arrested or committed, and others even heard oral testimony to determine whether the evidence was sufficient to justifying holding him for trial" (footnotes omitted)).

There is evidence from 19th-century American sources indicating that, even in States that accorded strong res judicata effect to prior adjudications, habeas courts in this country routinely allowed prisoners to introduce exculpatory evidence that was either unknown or previously unavailable to the prisoner. * * * The idea that the necessary scope of habeas review in part depends upon the rigor of any earlier proceedings accords with our test for procedural adequacy in the due process context. * * *

Accordingly, where relief is sought from a sentence that resulted from the judgment of a court of record, as [is] the case * * * in most federal habeas cases, considerable deference is owed to the court that ordered confinement. Likewise in those cases the prisoner should exhaust adequate alternative remedies before filing for the writ in federal court. Both aspects of federal habeas corpus review are justified because it can be assumed that, in the usual course, a court of record provides defendants with a fair, adversary proceeding. In cases involving state convictions this framework also respects federalism; and in federal cases it has added justification because the prisoner already has had a chance to seek review of his conviction in a federal forum through a direct appeal. The present cases fall outside these categories, however; for here the detention is by executive order.

Where a person is detained by executive order, rather than, say, after being tried and convicted in a court, the need for collateral review is most pressing. A criminal conviction in the usual course occurs after a judicial hearing before a tribunal disinterested in the outcome and committed to procedures designed to ensure its own independence. These dynamics are not inherent in executive detention orders or executive review procedures. In this context the need for habeas corpus is more urgent. The intended duration of the detention and the reasons for it bear upon the precise scope of the inquiry. Habeas corpus proceedings need not resemble a criminal trial, even when the detention is by executive order. But the writ must be effective. The habeas court must have sufficient authority to conduct a meaningful review of both the cause for detention and the Executive's power to detain.

To determine the necessary scope of habeas corpus review, therefore, we must assess the CSRT process, the mechanism through which petitioners' designation as enemy combatants became final. Whether one characterizes the CSRT process as direct review of the Executive's battlefield determination that the detainee is an enemy combatant-as the parties have and as we do-or as the first step in the collateral review of a battlefield determination makes no difference in a proper analysis of whether the procedures Congress put in place are an adequate substitute for habeas corpus. What matters is the sum total of procedural protections afforded to the detainee at all stages, direct and collateral.

Petitioners identify what they see as myriad deficiencies in the CSRTs. The most relevant for our purposes are the constraints upon the detainee's ability to rebut the factual basis for the Government's assertion that he is an enemy combatant. As already noted, at the CSRT stage the detainee has limited means to find or present evidence to challenge the Government's case against him. He does not have the assistance of counsel and may not be aware of the most critical allegations that the Government relied upon to order his detention. The detainee can confront witnesses that testify during the CSRT proceedings. But given that there are in effect no limits on the admission of hearsay evidence—the only requirement is that the tribunal deem the evidence "relevant and helpful,"—the detainee's opportunity to question witnesses is likely to be more theoretical than real.

The Government defends the CSRT process, arguing that it was designed to conform to the procedures suggested by the plurality in Hamdi. Setting aside the fact that the relevant language in Hamdi did not garner a majority of the Court, it does not control the matter at hand. None of the parties in Hamdi argued there had been a suspension of the writ. Nor could they. The § 2241 habeas corpus process remained in place. Accordingly, the plurality concentrated on whether the Executive had the authority to detain and, if so, what rights the detainee had under the Due Process Clause. True, there are places in the Hamdi plurality opinion where it is difficult to tell where its extrapolation of § 2241 ends and its analysis of the petitioner's Due Process rights begins. But the Court had no occasion to define the necessary scope of habeas review, for Suspension Clause purposes, in the context of enemy combatant detentions. The closest the plurality came to doing so was in discussing whether, in light of separation-of-powers concerns, § 2241 should be construed to forbid the District Court from inquiring beyond the affidavit Hamdi's custodian provided in answer to the detainee's habeas petition. The plurality answered this question with an emphatic "no."

Even if we were to assume that the CSRTs satisfy due process standards, it would not end our inquiry. Habeas corpus is a collateral process that exists, in Justice Holmes' words, to "cu[t] through all forms and g[o] to the very tissue of the structure. It comes in from the outside, not in subordination to the proceedings, and although every form may have been preserved opens the inquiry whether they have been more than an empty shell." Even when the procedures authorizing detention are structurally sound, the Suspension Clause remains applicable and the writ relevant. This is so, as Hayman and Swain make clear, even where the prisoner is detained after a criminal trial conducted in full accordance with the protections of the Bill of Rights. Were this not the case, there would have been no reason for the Court to inquire into the adequacy of substitute habeas procedures in Hayman and Swain. That the prisoners were detained pursuant to the most rigorous proceedings imaginable, a full criminal trial, would have been enough to render any habeas substitute acceptable *per se*.

Although we make no judgment as to whether the CSRTs, as currently constituted, satisfy due process standards, we agree with petitioners that, even when all the parties involved in this process act with diligence and in good faith, there is considerable risk of error in the tribunal's findings of fact. This is a risk inherent in any process that, in the words of the former Chief Judge of the Court of Appeals, is "closed and accusatorial." And given that the consequence of error may be detention of persons for the duration of hostilities that may last a generation or more, this is a risk too significant to ignore.

For the writ of habeas corpus, or its substitute, to function as an effective and proper remedy in this context, the court that conducts the habeas proceeding must have the means to correct errors that occurred during the CSRT proceedings. This includes some authority to assess the sufficiency of the Government's evidence against the detainee. It also must have the authority to admit and consider relevant exculpatory evidence that was not introduced during the earlier proceeding. Federal habeas petitioners long have had the means to supplement the record on review, even in the postconviction habeas setting. Here that opportunity is constitutionally required.

Consistent with the historic function and province of the writ, habeas corpus review may be more circumscribed if the underlying detention proceedings are more thorough than they were here. In two habeas cases involving enemy aliens tried for war crimes, for example, this Court limited its review to determining whether the Executive had legal authority to try the petitioners by military commission. Military courts are not courts of record. And the procedures used to try General Yamashita have been sharply criticized by Members of this Court. We need not revisit these cases, however. For on their own terms, the proceedings in [Application of] Yamashita (1946) and [Ex Parte] Quirin (1942), like those in Eisentrager, had an adversarial structure that is lacking here. *See* Yamashita (noting that General Yamashita was represented by six military lawyers and that "[t]hroughout the proceedings * * * defense counsel * * * demonstrated their professional skill and resourcefulness and their proper zeal for the defense with which they were charged"); Quirin (appointing counsel to represent the German saboteurs).

The extent of the showing required of the Government in these cases is a matter to be determined. We need not explore it further at this stage. We do hold that when the judicial power to issue habeas corpus properly is invoked the judicial officer must have adequate authority to make a determination in light of the relevant law and facts and to formulate and issue appropriate orders for relief, including, if necessary, an order directing the prisoner's release.

C

We now consider whether the DTA allows the Court of Appeals to conduct a proceeding meeting these standards. "[W]e are obligated to construe the statute to avoid [constitutional] problems" if it is " 'fairly possible' " to do so. There are limits to this principle, however. The canon of constitutional avoidance does not supplant traditional modes of statutory interpretation. *See* Clark v. Martinez (2005) ("The canon of constitutional avoidance comes into play only when, after the application of ordinary textual analysis, the statute is found to be susceptible of more than one construction; and the canon functions as *a means of choosing between them.*"). We cannot ignore the text and purpose of a statute in order to save it.

The DTA does not explicitly empower the Court of Appeals to order the applicant in a DTA review proceeding released should the court find that the standards and procedures used at his CSRT hearing were insufficient to justify detention. This is troubling. Yet, for present purposes, we can assume congressional silence permits a constitutionally required remedy. In that case it would be possible to hold that a remedy of release is impliedly provided for. The DTA might be read, furthermore, to allow the petitioners to assert most, if not all, of the legal claims they seek to advance, including their most basic claim: that the President has no authority under the AUMF to detain them indefinitely. (Whether the President has such authority turns on whether the AUMF authorizes—and the Constitution permits—the indefinite detention of "enemy combatants" as the Department of Defense defines that term. Thus a challenge to the President's authority to detain is, in essence, a challenge to the Department's definition of enemy combatant, a "standard" used by the CSRTs in petitioners' cases.) At oral argument, the Solicitor General urged us to adopt both these constructions, if doing so would allow MCA § 7 to remain intact.

The absence of a release remedy and specific language allowing AUMF challenges are not the only constitutional infirmities from which the statute potentially suffers, however. The more difficult question is whether the DTA permits the Court of Appeals to make requisite findings of fact. The DTA enables petitioners to request "review" of their CSRT determination in the Court of Appeals, but the "Scope of Review" provision confines the Court of Appeals' role to reviewing whether the CSRT followed the "standards and procedures" issued by the

Department of Defense and assessing whether those "standards and procedures" are lawful. Among these standards is "the requirement that the conclusion of the Tribunal be supported by a preponderance of the evidence * * * allowing a rebuttable presumption in favor of the Government's evidence."

Assuming the DTA can be construed to allow the Court of Appeals to review or correct the CSRT's factual determinations, as opposed to merely certifying that the tribunal applied the correct standard of proof, we see no way to construe the statute to allow what is also constitutionally required in this context: an opportunity for the detainee to present relevant exculpatory evidence that was not made part of the record in the earlier proceedings.

* * *

For present purposes * * * we can assume that * * * the DTA allows introduction and consideration of relevant exculpatory evidence that was "reasonably available" to the Government at the time of the CSRT but not made part of the record. Even so, the DTA review proceeding falls short of being a constitutionally adequate substitute, for the detainee still would have no opportunity to present evidence discovered after the CSRT proceedings concluded.

Under the DTA the Court of Appeals has the power to review CSRT determinations by assessing the legality of standards and procedures. This implies the power to inquire into what happened at the CSRT hearing and, perhaps, to remedy certain deficiencies in that proceeding. But should the Court of Appeals determine that the CSRT followed appropriate and lawful standards and procedures, it will have reached the limits of its jurisdiction. There is no language in the DTA that can be construed to allow the Court of Appeals to admit and consider newly discovered evidence that could not have been made part of the CSRT record because it was unavailable to either the Government or the detainee when the CSRT made its findings. This evidence, however, may be critical to the detainee's argument that he is not an enemy combatant and there is no cause to detain him.

This is not a remote hypothetical. One of the petitioners, Mohamed Nechla, requested at his CSRT hearing that the Government contact his employer. The petitioner claimed the employer would corroborate Nechla's contention he had no affiliation with al Qaeda. Although the CSRT determined this testimony would be relevant, it also found the witness was not reasonably available to testify at the time of the hearing. Petitioner's counsel, however, now represents the witness is available to be heard. If a detainee can present reasonably available evidence demonstrating there is no basis for his continued detention, he must have the opportunity to present this evidence to a habeas corpus court. Even under the Court of Appeals' generous construction of the DTA, however, the evidence identified by Nechla would be inadmissible in a DTA review proceeding. The role of an Article III court in the exercise of its habeas corpus function cannot be circumscribed in this manner.

By foreclosing consideration of evidence not presented or reasonably available to the detainee at the CSRT proceedings, the DTA disadvantages the detainee by limiting the scope of collateral review to a record that may not be accurate or complete. In other contexts, *e.g.*, in post-trial habeas cases where the prisoner already has had a full and fair opportunity to develop the factual predicate of his claims, similar limitations on the scope of habeas review may be appropriate. In this context, however, where the underlying detention proceedings lack the necessary adversarial character, the detainee cannot be held responsible for all deficiencies in the record.

The Government does not make the alternative argument that the DTA allows for the introduction of previously unavailable exculpatory evidence on appeal. It does point out, however, that if a detainee obtains such evidence, he can request that the Deputy Secretary of Defense convene a new CSRT. Whatever the merits of this procedure, it is an insufficient replacement for the factual review these detainees are entitled to receive through habeas corpus. The Deputy Secretary's determination whether to initiate new proceedings is wholly a discretionary one. And we see no way to construe the DTA to allow a detainee to challenge the Deputy Secretary's decision not to open a new CSRT pursuant to Instruction 5421.1. Congress directed the Secretary of Defense to devise procedures for considering new evidence, but the detainee has no mechanism for ensuring that those procedures are followed. DTA § 1005(e)(2)(C) makes clear that the Court of Appeals' jurisdiction is "limited to consideration of * * * whether the status determination of the Combatant Status Review Tribunal with regard to such alien was consistent with the standards and procedures specified by the Secretary of Defense * * * and * * * whether the use of such standards and procedures to make the determination is consistent with the Constitution and laws of the United States." DTA § 1005(e)(2)(A) further narrows the Court of Appeals' jurisdiction to reviewing "any final decision of a Combatant Status Review Tribunal that an alien is properly detained as an enemy combatant." The Deputy Secretary's determination whether to convene a new CSRT is not a "status determination of the Combatant Status Review Tribunal," much less a "final decision" of that body.

We do not imply DTA review would be a constitutionally sufficient replacement for habeas corpus but for these limitations on the detainee's ability to present exculpatory evidence. For even if it were possible, as a textual matter, to read into the statute each of the necessary procedures we have identified, we could not overlook the cumulative effect of our doing so. To hold that the detainees at Guantanamo may, under the DTA, challenge the President's legal authority to detain them, contest the CSRT's findings of fact, supplement the record on review with exculpatory evidence, and request an order of release would come close to reinstating the § 2241 habeas corpus process Congress sought to deny them. The language of the statute, read in light of Congress' reasons for enacting it, cannot bear this interpretation. Petitioners have met their burden of establishing that the DTA review process is, on its face, an inadequate substitute for habeas corpus.

Although we do not hold that an adequate substitute must duplicate § 2241 in all respects, it suffices that the Government has not established that the detainees' access to the statutory review provisions at issue is an adequate substitute for the writ of habeas corpus. MCA § 7 thus effects an unconstitutional suspension of the writ. In view of our holding we need not discuss the reach of the writ with respect to claims of unlawful conditions of treatment or confinement.

VI

A

In light of our conclusion that there is no jurisdictional bar to the District Court's entertaining petitioners' claims the question remains whether there are prudential barriers to habeas corpus review under these circumstances.

The Government argues petitioners must seek review of their CSRT determinations in the Court of Appeals before they can proceed with their habeas corpus actions in the District Court. As noted earlier, in other contexts and for prudential reasons this Court has required exhaustion of alternative remedies before a prisoner can seek federal habeas relief. Most of these cases were brought by prisoners in state custody and thus involved federalism concerns that are not relevant here. But we have extended this rule to require defendants in courts-martial to exhaust their military appeals before proceeding with a federal habeas corpus action.

The real risks, the real threats, of terrorist attacks are constant and not likely soon to abate. The ways to disrupt our life and laws are so many and unforeseen that the Court should not attempt even some general catalogue of crises that might occur. Certain principles are apparent, however. Practical considerations and exigent circumstances inform the definition and reach of the law's writs, including habeas corpus. The cases and our tradition reflect this precept.

In cases involving foreign citizens detained abroad by the Executive, it likely would be both an impractical and unprecedented extension of judicial power to assume that habeas corpus would be available at the moment the prisoner is taken into custody. If and when habeas corpus jurisdiction applies, as it does in these cases, then proper deference can be accorded to reasonable procedures for screening and initial detention under lawful and proper conditions of confinement and treatment for a reasonable period of time. Domestic exigencies, furthermore, might also impose such onerous burdens on the Government that here, too, the Judicial Branch would be required to devise sensible rules for staying habeas corpus proceedings until the Government can comply with its requirements in a responsible way. *Cf.* Ex parte Milligan ("If, in foreign invasion or civil war, the courts are actually closed, and it is impossible to administer criminal justice according to law, *then,* on the theatre of active military operations, where war really prevails, there is a necessity to furnish a substitute for the civil authority, thus overthrown, to preserve the safety of the army and society; and as no power is left but the military, it is allowed to govern by martial rule until the laws can have their free course"). Here, as is true with detainees apprehended abroad, a relevant consideration in determining the courts' role is whether there are suitable alternative processes in place to protect against the arbitrary exercise of governmental power.

The cases before us, however, do not involve detainees who have been held for a short period of time while awaiting their CSRT determinations. Were that the case, or were it probable that the Court of Appeals could complete a prompt review of their applications, the case for requiring temporary abstention or exhaustion of alternative remedies would be much stronger. These qualifications no longer pertain here. In some of these cases six years have elapsed without the judicial oversight that habeas corpus or an adequate substitute demands. And there has been no showing that the Executive faces such onerous burdens that it cannot respond to habeas corpus actions. To require these detainees to complete DTA review before proceeding with their habeas corpus actions would be to require additional months, if not years, of delay. The first DTA review applications were filed over a year ago, but no decisions on the merits have been issued. While some delay in fashioning new procedures is unavoidable, the costs of delay can no longer be borne by those who are held in custody. The detainees in these cases are entitled to a prompt habeas corpus hearing.

Our decision today holds only that the petitioners before us are entitled to seek the writ; that the DTA review procedures are an inadequate substitute for habeas corpus; and that the petitioners in these cases need not exhaust the review procedures in the Court of Appeals before proceeding with their habeas actions in the District Court. The only law we identify as unconstitutional is MCA § 7. Accordingly, both the DTA and the CSRT process remain intact. Our holding with regard to exhaustion should not be read to imply that a habeas court should intervene the moment an enemy combatant steps foot in a territory where the writ runs. The Executive is entitled to a reasonable period of time to determine a detainee's status before a court entertains that detainee's habeas corpus petition. The CSRT process is the mechanism Congress and the President set up to deal with these issues. Except in cases of undue delay, federal courts should refrain from entertaining an enemy combatant's habeas corpus petition at least until after the Department, acting via the CSRT, has had a chance to review his status.

B

Although we hold that the DTA is not an adequate and effective substitute for habeas corpus, it does not follow that a habeas corpus court may disregard the dangers the detention in these cases was intended to prevent. *Felker, Swain,* and *Hayman* stand for the proposition that the Suspension Clause does not resist innovation in the field of habeas corpus. Certain accommodations can be made to reduce the burden habeas corpus proceedings will place on the military without impermissibly diluting the protections of the writ.

In the DTA Congress sought to consolidate review of petitioners' claims in the Court of Appeals. Channeling future cases to one district court would no doubt reduce administrative burdens on the Government. This is a legitimate objective that might be advanced even without an amendment to § 2241. If, in a future case, a detainee files a habeas petition in another judicial district in which a proper respondent can be served, the Government can move for change of venue to the court that will hear these petitioners' cases, the United States District Court for the District of Columbia.

Another of Congress' reasons for vesting exclusive jurisdiction in the Court of Appeals, perhaps, was to avoid the widespread dissemination of classified information. The Government has raised similar concerns here and elsewhere. We make no attempt to anticipate all of the evidentiary and access-to-counsel issues that will arise during the course of the detainees' habeas corpus proceedings. We recognize, however, that the Government has a legitimate interest in protecting sources and methods of intelligence gathering; and we expect that the District Court will use its discretion to accommodate this interest to the greatest extent possible.

These and the other remaining questions are within the expertise and competence of the District Court to address in the first instance.

* * *

In considering both the procedural and substantive standards used to impose detention to prevent acts of terrorism, proper deference must be accorded to the political branches. Unlike the President and some designated Members of Congress, neither the Members of this Court nor most federal judges begin the day with briefings that may describe new and serious threats to our Nation and its people. The law must accord the Executive substantial authority to apprehend and detain those who pose a real danger to our security.

Officials charged with daily operational responsibility for our security may consider a judicial discourse on the history of the Habeas Corpus Act of 1679 and like matters to be far removed from the Nation's present, urgent concerns. Established legal doctrine, however, must be consulted for its teaching. Remote in time it may be; irrelevant to the present it is not. Security depends upon a sophisticated intelligence apparatus and the ability of our Armed Forces to act and to interdict. There are further considerations, however. Security subsists, too, in fidelity to freedom's first principles. Chief among these are freedom from arbitrary and unlawful restraint and the personal liberty that is secured by adherence to the separation of powers. It is from these principles that the judicial authority to consider petitions for habeas corpus relief derives.

Our opinion does not undermine the Executive's powers as Commander in Chief. On the contrary, the exercise of those powers is vindicated, not eroded, when confirmed by the Judicial Branch. Within the Constitution's separation-of-powers structure, few exercises of judicial power are as legitimate or as necessary as the responsibility to hear challenges to the authority of the Executive to imprison a person. Some of these petitioners have been in custody for six years with no definitive judicial determination as to the legality of their detention. Their access to the writ is a necessity to determine the lawfulness of their status, even if, in the end, they do not obtain the relief they seek.

Because our Nation's past military conflicts have been of limited duration, it has been possible to leave the outer boundaries of war powers undefined. If, as some fear, terrorism continues to pose dangerous threats to us for years to come, the Court might not have this luxury. This result is not inevitable, however. The political branches, consistent with their independent obligations to interpret and uphold the Constitution, can engage in a genuine debate about how best to preserve constitutional values while protecting the Nation from terrorism.

It bears repeating that our opinion does not address the content of the law that governs petitioners' detention. That is a matter yet to be determined. We hold that petitioners may invoke the fundamental procedural protections of habeas corpus. The laws and Constitution are designed to survive, and remain in force, in extraordinary times. Liberty and security can be reconciled; and in our system they are reconciled within the framework of the law. The Framers decided that habeas corpus, a right of first importance, must be a part of that framework, a part of that law.

The determination by the Court of Appeals that the Suspension Clause and its protections are inapplicable to petitioners was in error. The judgment of the Court of Appeals is reversed. The cases are remanded to the Court of Appeals with instructions that it remand the cases to the District Court for proceedings consistent with this opinion.

It is so ordered.

JUSTICE SOUTER, with whom JUSTICE GINSBURG and JUSTICE BREYER join, concurring.

I join the Court's opinion in its entirety and add this afterword only to emphasize two things one might overlook after reading the dissents.

Four years ago, this Court in Rasul v. Bush (2004) held that statutory habeas jurisdiction extended to claims of foreign nationals imprisoned by the United States at Guantanamo Bay, "to determine the legality of the Executive's potentially indefinite detention" of them. Subsequent legislation eliminated the statutory habeas jurisdiction over these claims, so that now there must be constitutionally based jurisdiction or none at all. Justice Scalia is thus correct that here, for the first time, this Court holds there is (he says "confers") constitutional habeas jurisdiction over aliens imprisoned by the military outside an area of *de jure* national sovereignty. But no one who reads the Court's opinion in Rasul could seriously doubt that the jurisdictional question must be answered the same way in purely constitutional cases, given the Court's reliance on the historical background of habeas generally in answering the statutory question. Indeed, the Court in Rasul directly answered the very historical question that Justice Scalia says is dispositive; it wrote that "[a]pplication of the habeas statute to persons detained at [Guantanamo] is consistent with the historical reach of the writ of habeas corpus." Justice Scalia dismisses the statement as dictum, but if dictum it was, it was dictum well considered, and it stated the view of five Members of this Court on the historical scope of the writ. Of course, it takes more than a quotation from Rasul, however much on point, to resolve the constitutional issue before us here, which the majority opinion has explored afresh in the detail it deserves. But whether one agrees or disagrees with today's decision, it is no bolt out of the blue.

A second fact insufficiently appreciated by the dissents is the length of the disputed imprisonments, some of the prisoners represented here today having been locked up for six years. Hence the hollow ring when the dissenters suggest that the Court is somehow precipitating the judiciary into reviewing claims that the military (subject to appeal to the Court of Appeals for the District of Columbia Circuit) could handle within some reasonable period of time. These suggestions of judicial haste are all the more out of place given the Court's realistic acknowledgment that in periods of exigency the tempo of any habeas review must reflect the immediate peril facing the country.

It is in fact the very lapse of four years from the time Rasul put everyone on notice that habeas process was available to Guantanamo prisoners, and the lapse of six years since some of these prisoners were captured and incarcerated, that stand at odds with the repeated suggestions of the dissenters that these cases should be seen as a judicial victory in a contest for power between the Court and the political branches. The several answers to the charge of triumphalism might start with a basic fact of Anglo-American constitutional history: that the power, first of the Crown and now of the Executive Branch of the United States, is necessarily limited by habeas corpus jurisdiction to enquire into the legality of executive detention. And one could explain that in this Court's exercise of responsibility to preserve habeas corpus something much more significant is involved than pulling and hauling between the judicial and political branches. Instead, though, it is enough to repeat that some of these petitioners have spent six years behind bars. After six years of sustained executive detentions in Guantanamo, subject to habeas jurisdiction but without any actual habeas scrutiny, today's decision is no judicial victory, but an act of perseverance in trying to make habeas review, and the obligation of the courts to provide it, mean something of value both to prisoners and to the Nation.

CHIEF JUSTICE ROBERTS, with whom JUSTICE SCALIA, JUSTICE THOMAS, and JUSTICE ALITO join, dissenting.

Today the Court strikes down as inadequate the most generous set of procedural protections ever afforded aliens detained by this country as enemy combatants. The political branches crafted these procedures amidst an ongoing military conflict, after much careful investigation and thorough debate. The Court rejects them today out of hand, without bothering to say what due process rights the detainees possess, without explaining how the statute fails to vindicate those rights, and before a single petitioner has even attempted to avail himself of the law's operation. And to what effect? The majority merely replaces a review system designed by the people's representatives with a set of shapeless procedures to be defined by federal courts at some future date. One cannot help but think, after surveying the modest practical results of the majority's ambitious opinion, that this decision is not really about the detainees at all, but about control of federal policy regarding enemy combatants.

The majority is adamant that the Guantanamo detainees are entitled to the protections of habeas corpus—its opinion begins by deciding that question. I regard the issue as a difficult one, primarily because of the unique and unusual jurisdictional status of Guantanamo Bay. I nonetheless agree with Justice Scalia's analysis of our precedents and the pertinent history of the writ, and accordingly join his dissent. The important point for me, however, is that the Court should have resolved these cases on other grounds. Habeas is most fundamentally a procedural right, a mechanism for contesting the legality of executive detention. The critical threshold question in these cases, prior to any inquiry about the writ's scope, is whether the system the political branches designed protects whatever rights the detainees may possess. If so, there is no need for any additional process, whether called "habeas" or something else.

Congress entrusted that threshold question in the first instance to the Court of Appeals for the District of Columbia Circuit, as the Constitution surely allows Congress to do. But before the D.C. Circuit has addressed the issue, the Court cashiers the statute, and without answering this critical threshold question itself. The Court does eventually get around to asking whether review under the DTA is, as the Court frames it, an "adequate substitute" for habeas, but even then its opinion fails to determine what rights the detainees possess and whether the DTA system satisfies them. The majority instead compares the undefined DTA process to an equally undefined habeas right-one that is to be given shape only in the future by district courts on a case-by-case basis. This whole approach is misguided.

It is also fruitless. How the detainees' claims will be decided now that the DTA is gone is anybody's guess. But the habeas process the Court mandates will most likely end up looking a lot like the DTA system it replaces, as the district court judges shaping it will have to reconcile review of the prisoners' detention with the undoubted need to protect the American people from the terrorist threat-precisely the challenge Congress undertook in drafting the DTA. All that today's opinion has done is shift responsibility for those sensitive foreign policy and national security decisions from the elected branches to the Federal Judiciary.

I believe the system the political branches constructed adequately protects any constitutional rights aliens captured abroad and detained as enemy combatants may enjoy. I therefore would dismiss these cases on that ground. With all respect for the contrary views of the majority, I must dissent. * * *

JUSTICE SCALIA, with whom THE CHIEF JUSTICE, JUSTICE THOMAS, and JUSTICE ALITO join, dissenting.

Today, for the first time in our Nation's history, the Court confers a constitutional right to habeas corpus on alien enemies detained abroad by our military forces in the course of an ongoing war. The Chief Justice's dissent, which I join, shows that the procedures prescribed by Congress in the Detainee Treatment Act provide the essential protections that habeas corpus guarantees; there has thus been no suspension of the writ, and no basis exists for judicial intervention beyond what the Act allows. My problem with today's opinion is more fundamental still: The writ of habeas corpus does not, and never has, run in favor of aliens abroad; the Suspension Clause thus has no application, and the Court's intervention in this military matter is entirely *ultra vires*.

I shall devote most of what will be a lengthy opinion to the legal errors contained in the opinion of the Court. Contrary to my usual practice, however, I think it appropriate to begin with a description of the disastrous consequences of what the Court has done today.

I

America is at war with radical Islamists. The enemy began by killing Americans and American allies abroad: 241 at the Marine barracks in Lebanon, 19 at the Khobar Towers in Dhahran, 224 at our embassies in Dar es Salaam and Nairobi, and 17 on the USS Cole in Yemen. On September 11, 2001, the enemy brought the battle to American soil, killing 2,749 at the Twin Towers in New York City, 184 at the Pentagon in Washington, D. C., and 40 in Pennsylvania. It has threatened further attacks against our homeland; one need only walk about buttressed and barricaded Washington, or board a plane anywhere in the country, to know that the threat is a serious one. Our Armed Forces are now in the field against the enemy, in Afghanistan and Iraq. Last week, 13 of our countrymen in arms were killed.

The game of bait-and-switch that today's opinion plays upon the Nation's Commander in Chief will make the war harder on us. It will almost certainly cause more Americans to be killed. That consequence would be tolerable if necessary to preserve a time-honored legal principle vital to our constitutional Republic. But it is this Court's blatant *abandonment* of such a principle that produces the decision today. The President relied on our settled precedent in *Johnson v. Eisentrager* (1950), when he established the prison at Guantanamo Bay for enemy aliens. Citing that case, the President's Office of Legal Counsel advised him "that the great weight of legal authority indicates that a federal district court could not properly exercise habeas jurisdiction over an alien detained at [Guantanamo Bay]." Had the law been otherwise, the military surely would not have transported prisoners there, but would have kept them in Afghanistan, transferred them to another of our foreign military bases, or turned them over to allies for detention. Those other facilities might well have been worse for the detainees themselves.

In the long term, then, the Court's decision today accomplishes little, except perhaps to reduce the well-being of enemy combatants that the Court ostensibly seeks to protect. In the short term, however, the decision is devastating. At least 30 of those prisoners hitherto released from Guantanamo Bay have returned to the battlefield. Some have been captured or killed. But others have succeeded in carrying on their atrocities against innocent civilians. In one case, a detainee released from Guantanamo Bay masterminded the kidnapping of two Chinese dam workers, one of whom was later shot to death when used as a human shield against Pakistani commandoes. Another former detainee promptly resumed his post as a senior Taliban commander and murdered a United Nations engineer and three Afghan soldiers. Still another murdered an Afghan judge. It was reported only last month that a released detainee carried out a suicide bombing against Iraqi soldiers in Mosul, Iraq.

These, mind you, were detainees whom *the military* had concluded were not enemy combatants. Their return to the kill illustrates the incredible difficulty of assessing who is and who is not an enemy combatant in a foreign theater of operations where the environment does not lend itself to rigorous evidence collection. Astoundingly, the Court today raises the bar, requiring military officials to appear before civilian courts and defend their decisions under procedural and evidentiary rules that go beyond what Congress has specified. As the Chief Justice's dissent makes clear, we have no idea what those procedural and evidentiary rules are, but they will be determined by civil courts and (in the Court's contemplation at least) will be more detainee-friendly than those now applied, since otherwise there would no reason to hold the congressionally prescribed procedures unconstitutional. If they impose a higher standard of proof (from foreign battlefields) than the current procedures require, the number of the enemy returned to combat will obviously increase.

But even when the military has evidence that it can bring forward, it is often foolhardy to release that evidence to the attorneys representing our enemies. And one escalation of procedures that the Court *is* clear about is affording the detainees increased access to witnesses (perhaps troops serving in Afghanistan?) and to classified information. During the 1995 prosecution of Omar Abdel Rahman, federal prosecutors gave the names of 200 unindicted co-conspirators to the "Blind Sheik's" defense lawyers; that information was in the hands of Osama Bin Laden within two weeks. In another case, trial testimony revealed to the enemy that the United States had been monitoring their cellular network, whereupon they promptly stopped using it, enabling more of them to evade capture and continue their atrocities.

And today it is not just the military that the Court elbows aside. A mere two Terms ago in Hamdan (2006), when the Court held (quite amazingly) that the Detainee Treatment Act of 2005 had not stripped habeas jurisdiction over Guantanamo petitioners' claims, four Members of today's five-Justice majority joined an opinion saying the following:

> Nothing prevents the President from returning to Congress to seek the authority [for trial by military commission] he believes necessary.
>
> Where, as here, no emergency prevents consultation with Congress, judicial insistence upon that consultation does not weaken our Nation's ability to deal with danger. To the contrary, that insistence strengthens the Nation's ability to determine-through democratic means-how best to do so. The Constitution places its faith in those democratic means."

Food for Thought

Consider how remarkable it is for a judge in *any* nation to comment that the judiciary might be able to "elbow aside" the military.

Turns out they were just kidding. For in response, Congress, at the President's request, quickly enacted the Military Commissions Act, emphatically reasserting that it did not want these prisoners filing habeas petitions. It is therefore clear that Congress and the Executive—*both* political branches—have determined that limiting the role of civilian courts in adjudicating whether prisoners captured abroad are properly detained is important to success in the war that some 190,000 of our men and women are now fighting. As the Solicitor General argued, "the Military Commissions Act and the Detainee Treatment Act * * * represent an effort by the political branches to strike an appropriate balance between the need to preserve liberty and the need to accommodate the weighty and sensitive governmental interests in ensuring that those who have in fact fought with the enemy during a war do not return to battle against the United States."

But it does not matter. The Court today decrees that no good reason to accept the judgment of the other two branches is "apparent." "The Government," it declares, "presents no credible arguments that the military mission at Guantanamo would be compromised if habeas corpus courts had jurisdiction to hear the detainees' claims." What competence does the Court have to second-guess the judgment of Congress and the President on such a point? None whatever. But the Court blunders in nonetheless. Henceforth, as today's opinion makes unnervingly clear, how to handle enemy prisoners in this war will ultimately lie with the branch that knows least about the national security concerns that the subject entails.

[Justice Scalia's detailed historical analysis is omitted.]

* * *

In sum, because I conclude that the text and history of the Suspension Clause provide no basis for our jurisdiction, I would affirm the Court of Appeals even if *Eisentrager* did not govern these cases.

* * *

Today the Court warps our Constitution in a way that goes beyond the narrow issue of the reach of the Suspension Clause, invoking judicially brainstormed separation-of-powers principles to establish a manipulable "functional" test for the extraterritorial reach of habeas corpus (and, no doubt, for the extraterritorial reach of other constitutional protections as well). It blatantly misdescribes important precedents, most conspicuously Justice Jackson's opinion for the Court in *Eisentrager*. It breaks a chain of precedent as old as the common law that prohibits judicial inquiry into detentions of aliens abroad absent statutory authorization. And, most tragically, it sets our military commanders the impossible task of proving to a civilian court, under whatever standards this Court devises in the future, that evidence supports the confinement of each and every enemy prisoner.

The Nation will live to regret what the Court has done today. I dissent.

Notes and Questions

1. How much of a precedent does *Boumediene* create with respect to Congress' power to strip the federal courts of subject matter jurisdiction generally? It is one of the few Supreme Court cases holding that an attempt to strip jurisdiction runs afoul of the Constitution, but it does so on the basis of the Suspension Clause. Is there any basis to argue that *Boumediene* also rests on general separation of powers principles? In other words, does *Boumediene* have any applicability outside the habeas context? Recall that *Yerger* and *Felker* were also habeas cases.

2. *Rasul v. Bush* (2004) held that § 2241, as then written, conferred federal jurisdiction over habeas petitions filed by aliens detained at Guantanamo Bay. Precedent established that § 2241 applied to aliens and that jurisdiction over a prisoner's custodian was sufficient to empower the federal courts to hear a petition, even though the prisoner was detained outside the United States. Prisoners detained by the U.S. military are held, ultimately, under the authority of the President and the Secretary of Defense, both of whom are subject to federal court jurisdiction. As Justice Scalia pointed out in dissent, *Rasul* thus raised the possibility that aliens detained by the United States anywhere in the world might file habeas petitions.

Boumediene recognizes that Congress intended the Military Commissions Act of 2006 to withdraw habeas jurisdiction over aliens detained as enemy combatants or who are awaiting such determination. *Boumediene* holds that the jurisdiction-stripping provision of the Act violates the Suspension Clause. If the constitutional right to habeas corpus extends to any case where a federal court has jurisdiction over a detainee's custodian, then the specter of a worldwide writ remains. In Section IV of the majority opinion, Justice Kennedy addresses the extraterritorial application of the Constitution. He concludes precedent shows "that questions of extraterritoriality turn on objective factors and practical concerns, not formalism." In Section IV C, he sets forth a three-factor test for determining the extraterritorial reach of the Suspension Clause. What are the three factors? Do you think this test increases or decreases the likelihood that federal courts will exercise worldwide habeas jurisdiction?

3. Much is said—and not said—in the majority opinion and in Chief Justice Roberts's dissent about whether the procedures set forth in the Detainee Treatment Act of 2005 (DTA) provide an adequate substitute for habeas corpus and about the procedures to be followed in habeas proceedings brought by Guantanamo detainees.

The majority holds that the procedures in the Act are not an adequate and effective substitute for habeas corpus, but declines "to offer a comprehensive summary of the requisites for an adequate substitute." In Section V-B of the majority opinion, Justice Kennedy sets forth some general characteristics of habeas proceedings, and discusses some of the procedural shortcomings of the DTA process, but the discussion is tentative and provides few specifics as to exactly what process is due the detainees. Chief Justice Roberts plainly is correct when he says:

> [The Court's] opinion fails to determine what rights the detainees possess and whether the DTA system satisfies them. The majority instead compares the undefined DTA process to an equally undefined habeas corpus right—one that is to be given shape only in the future by district courts on a case-by-case basis.

Why does the majority not provide more guidance? What practical problems might explain the majority's caution?

a. The DTA itself says very little about procedure. Instead, it delegates to the Secretary of Defense the duty to issue a report setting forth the procedures to be followed by Combatant Status Review Tribunals (CSRTs). The Act itself says only that those procedures "shall provide for periodic review of any new evidence that may become available relating to the enemy combatant status of a detainee," and that CSRTs shall assess the value of coerced statements. DTA, § 1005(a)(1)(A), (a)(3), (b)(1). The Act also gives the Court of Appeals for the District of Columbia Circuit "exclusive jurisdiction to determine the validity of any final decision of a [CSRT] that an alien is properly detained as an enemy combatant." DTA § 1005(e)(2)(A). The scope of review is limited to:

> (1) whether the status determination of the [CSRT] with regard to such alien was consistent with the standards and procedures specified by the Secretary of Defense for [CSRTs] (including the requirement that the conclusion of the Tribunal be supported by a preponderance of the evidence and allowing a rebuttable presumption in favor of the Government's evidence); and
>
> (2) to the extent the Constitution and law of the United States are applicable, whether the use of such standards and procedures to make the determination is consistent with the Constitution and laws of the United States.

DTA § 1005(e)(2)C). As is discussed below, an "Implementation Memorandum" sets forth CSRT procedures. The Chief Justice dwells at length on the procedural rights accorded under the Memorandum, while the majority barely mentions it, and then only to note the shortcomings of the procedures.

b. At the conclusion of Section V-B, the majority holds "that when the judicial power to issue habeas corpus properly is invoked the judicial officer must have adequate authority to make a determination in light of the relevant law and facts and to formulate and issue appropriate orders for relief, including, if necessary, an order directing the prisoner's release." It may be possible to give some content to this vague standard by identifying the deficiencies in CSRT procedures listed by the Court in Section V-B and in Section IV-C. What deficiencies does the Court identify? Of course, it does not necessarily follow that a subsequent habeas proceeding is constitutionally sufficient only if it affirmatively remedies every deficiency. Nonetheless, this exercise may help district judges specify procedural safeguards that will satisfy the Supreme Court.

c. The Court gives additional guidance by suggesting that the scope of habeas review "depends upon the rigor of any earlier proceedings." It contrasts the more usual habeas posture, where relief is sought from a conviction by a court of record, with *Boumediene*, where petitioners are detained by executive order, saying more process is due in the latter situation. But the Court again pulls its punch with the following Delphic statement: "Habeas corpus proceedings need not resemble a criminal trial, even when the detention is by executive order. But the writ must be effective." What procedural safeguards of a criminal trial might safely be subtracted without violating the Court's admonition that the writ "be effective?"

4. *Munaf v. Geren*, 553 U.S. 674 (2008), decided the same day as *Boumediene*, also speaks to the extraterritorial reach of habeas corpus. The Court explicitly notes that *Munaf* concerns only American citizens proceeding under the habeas statute, rather than (as in *Boumediene*) aliens proceeding under constitutional habeas corpus. Petitioners Mohammad Munaf and Shawqi Omar are American citizens who traveled to Iraq and allegedly committed crimes there. American forces arrested and detained them. American military tribunals found that both men posed a serious threat to the security of Iraq and designated them "security internees." Munaf was bound over to the Central Court of Iraq for criminal proceedings. He was found guilty, but an appellate court reversed his conviction, and he was awaiting a new trial when the Court decided his case. The petitioners asked the Court to enjoin the military from transferring them to Iraqi custody or allowing them to be tried by Iraqi courts. The Court unanimously held that 28 U.S.C. § 2241 extended to American citizens held overseas by American forces "operating subject to an American chain of command," even though those forces were acting as part of a multinational coalition. Section 2241 applies to persons held "in custody under or by color of the authority of the United States," and the Court held that petitioners were such persons. Reaching the merits, the Court denied relief. It likened petitioners to any American citizen accused of committing a crime in a foreign country. Precedent established that Iraq has a "sovereign right to prosecute Omar and Munaf for crimes committed on its soil." Justice Souter, joined by Justices Ginsburg and Breyer concurred, but noted that the Court reserved judgment on extreme cases where a detainee in U.S. custody would likely be tortured when transferred to a foreign government.

Although the Court denied relief, it held that the federal courts had jurisdiction to entertain the habeas petitions. In his opinion for the Court, Chief Justice Roberts notes that multinational forces are currently holding approximately 24,000 detainees in Iraq. Can all of these detainees now petition a federal district court for release?

Can the vast majority of these detainees be excluded from § 2241 because they are not American citizens? Recall that *Rasul*, along with a long line of other cases, clearly extends § 2241 to aliens. *Munaf* holds that § 2241 applies because the petitioners are in custody "under or by color of the authority of the United States." Are aliens held under the same authority somehow not in custody for § 2241 purposes? Justice Scalia, Chief Justice Roberts, and Justice Thomas dissented in *Rasul* on the ground that § 2241 should not apply to aliens detained by the U.S. military overseas, outside the sovereign borders of the United States. By agreeing that habeas lies in *Manuf*, have they changed their minds? By denying relief on the merits, the Court allows the military to transfer Manuf and Omar to Iraqi authorities for trial. What of cases, however, where Iraqi authorities do not want to press charges and the military is holding detainees for whatever reason the military chooses. Can detainees' petitions be as easily dismissed on the merits?

Plaut v. Spendthrift Farm, Inc.

Supreme Court of the United States, 1995.
514 U.S. 211.

JUSTICE SCALIA delivered the opinion of the Court.

The question presented in this case is whether § 27A(b) of the Securities Exchange Act of 1934, to the extent that it requires federal courts to reopen final judgments in private civil actions under § 10(b) of the Act, contravenes the Constitution's separation of powers or the Due Process Clause of the Fifth Amendment.

I

> **FYI**
> *Plaut* is not a case involving a congressional attempt to strip the federal courts of jurisdiction. It involves the closely related issue of which branch has the ultimate say about when federal court judgments are final.

In 1987, petitioners brought a civil action against respondents in the United States District Court for the Eastern District of Kentucky. The complaint alleged that in 1983 and 1984 respondents had committed fraud and deceit in the sale of stock in violation of § 10(b) of the Securities Exchange Act of 1934 and Rule 10b-5 of the Securities and Exchange Commission. The case was mired in pretrial proceedings in the District Court until June 20, 1991, when we decided *Lampf, Pleva, Lipkind, Prupis & Petigrow v. Gilbertson*, 501 U.S. 350 (1991). *Lampf* held that "[l]itigation instituted pursuant to § 10(b) and Rule 10b-5 must be commenced within one year after the discovery of the facts constituting the violation and within three years after such violation." We applied that holding to the plaintiff-respondents in *Lampf* itself, found their suit untimely, and reinstated a summary judgment previously entered in favor of the defendant-petitioners. On the same day we decided *James B. Beam Distilling Co. v. Georgia*, 501 U.S. 529 (1991), in which a majority of the Court held, albeit in different opinions, that a new rule of federal law that is applied to the parties in the case announcing the rule must be applied as well to all cases pending on direct review. The joint effect of *Lampf* and *Beam* was to mandate application of the 1-year/3-year limitations period to petitioners' suit. The District Court, finding that petitioners' claims were untimely under the *Lampf* rule, dismissed their action with prejudice on August 13, 1991. Petitioners filed no appeal; the judgment accordingly became final 30 days later.

On December 19, 1991, the President signed the Federal Deposit Insurance Corporation Improvement Act of 1991. Section 476 of the Act—a section that had nothing to do with FDIC improvements—became § 27A of the Securities Exchange Act of 1934. It provides:

> (a) Effect on pending causes of action "The limitation period for any private civil action implied under section 78j(b) of this title [§ 10(b) of the Securities Exchange Act of 1934] that was commenced on or before June 19, 1991, shall be the limitation period provided by the laws applicable in the jurisdiction, including principles of retroactivity, as such laws existed on June 19, 1991.
>
> (b) Effect on dismissed causes of action "Any private civil action implied under section 78j(b) of this title that was commenced on or before June 19, 1991—
>
> > (1) which was dismissed as time barred subsequent to June 19, 1991, and
> >
> > (2) which would have been timely filed under the limitation period provided by the laws applicable in the jurisdiction, including principles of retroactivity, as such laws existed on June 19, 1991, shall be reinstated on motion by the plaintiff not later than 60 days after December 19, 1991.

On February 11, 1992, petitioners returned to the District Court and filed a motion to reinstate the action previously dismissed with prejudice. The District Court found that the conditions set out in §§ 27A(b)(1) and (2) were met, so that petitioners' motion was required to be granted by the terms of the statute. It nonetheless denied the motion, agreeing with respondents that § 27A(b) is unconstitutional. The United States Court of Appeals for the Sixth Circuit affirmed. We granted certiorari.[1]

---

1 Last Term this Court affirmed, by an equally divided vote, a judgment of the United States Court of Appeals for the Fifth Circuit that held § 27A(b) constitutional. That ruling of course lacks precedential weight.

II

Respondents bravely contend that § 27A(b) does not require federal courts to reopen final judgments, arguing first that the reference to "the laws applicable in the jurisdiction * * * as such laws existed on June 19, 1991" (the day before *Lampf* was decided) may reasonably be construed to refer precisely to the limitations period provided in *Lampf* itself, in which case petitioners' action was time barred even under § 27A. It is true that "[a] judicial construction of a statute is an authoritative statement of what the statute meant before as well as after the decision of the case giving rise to that construction." But respondents' argument confuses the question of what the law *in fact* was on June 19, 1991, with the distinct question of what § 27A *means* by its *reference* to what the law was. We think it entirely clear that it does not mean the law enunciated in *Lampf*, for two independent reasons. First, *Lampf* provides a uniform, national statute of limitations (instead of using the applicable state limitations period, as lower federal courts had previously done.) If the statute referred to *that* law, its reference to the "laws applicable *in the jurisdiction*" (emphasis added) would be quite inexplicable. Second, if the statute refers to the law enunciated in *Lampf* it is utterly without effect, a result to be avoided if possible. It would say, in subsection (a), that the limitation period is what the Supreme Court has held to be the limitation period; and in subsection (b), that suits dismissed as untimely under *Lampf* which were timely under *Lampf* (a null set) shall be reinstated. To avoid a constitutional question by holding that Congress enacted and the President approved a blank sheet of paper would indeed constitute "disingenuous evasion."

As an alternative reason why § 27A(b) does not require the reopening of final judgments, respondents suggest that the subsection applies only to cases still pending in the federal courts when § 27A was enacted. This has only half the defect of the first argument, for it makes only half of § 27A purposeless—§ 27A(b). There is no need to "reinstate" actions that are still pending; § 27A(a) (the new statute of limitations) could and would be applied by the courts of appeals. On respondents' reading, the only consequence of § 27A(b) would be the negligible one of permitting the plaintiff in the pending appeal from a statute-of-limitations dismissal to return *immediately* to the district court, instead of waiting for the court of appeals' reversal. To enable § 27A(b) to achieve such an insignificant consequence, one must disregard the language of the provision, which refers generally to suits "dismissed as time barred." It is perhaps arguable that this does *not* include suits that are not yet *finally* dismissed, *i.e.*, suits still pending on appeal; but there is *no* basis for the contention that it includes *only* those. In short, there is no reasonable construction on which § 27A(b) does not require federal courts to reopen final judgments in suits dismissed with prejudice by virtue of *Lampf*.

III

Respondents submit that § 27A(b) violates both the separation of powers and the Due Process Clause of the Fifth Amendment. Because the latter submission, if correct, might dictate a similar result in a challenge to state legislation under the Fourteenth Amendment, the former is the narrower ground for adjudication of the constitutional questions in the case, and we therefore consider it first. We conclude that in § 27A(b) Congress has exceeded its authority by requiring the federal courts to exercise "the judicial Power of the United States," U.S. CONST., art. III, § 1, in a manner repugnant to the text, structure and traditions of Article III.

Our decisions to date have identified two types of legislation that require federal courts to exercise the judicial power in a manner that Article III forbids. The first appears in *United States v. Klein*, where we refused to give effect to a statute that was said "[t]o prescribe rules of decision to the Judicial Department of the government in cases pending before it." Whatever the precise scope of *Klein*, however, later decisions have made clear that its prohibition does not take hold when Congress "amend[s] applicable law." Section 27A(b) indisputably does set out substantive legal standards for the Judiciary to apply, and in that sense changes the law (even if solely retroactively).

The second type of unconstitutional restriction upon the exercise of judicial power identified by past cases is exemplified by *Hayburn's Case*, which stands for the principle that Congress cannot vest review of the decisions of Article III courts in officials of the Executive Branch. Yet under any application of § 27A(b) only courts are involved; no officials of other departments sit in direct review of their decisions. Section 27A(b) therefore offends neither of these previously established prohibitions.

Food for Thought

Though most scholars and judges continue to puzzle over *Klein's* exact meaning , the preceding passage demonstrates that Justice Scalia believes it stands for the proposition that Congress may dictate the results in pending cases but only if it amends the underlying rule of decision and does not attempt to cherry-pick the particular case it wants to influence.

We think, however, that § 27A(b) offends a postulate of Article III just as deeply rooted in our law as those we have mentioned. Article III establishes a "judicial department" with the "province and duty * * * to say what the law is" in particular cases and controversies. *Marbury v. Madison*. The record of history shows that the Framers crafted this charter of the judicial department with an expressed understanding that it gives the Federal Judiciary the power, not merely to rule on cases, but to *decide* them, subject to review only by superior courts in the Article III hierarchy—with an understanding, in short, that "a judgment conclusively resolves the case" because "a 'judicial Power' is one to render dispositive judgments." Easterbrook, *Presidential Review*, 40 CASE W. RES. L. REV. 905, 926 (1990). By retroactively commanding the federal courts to reopen final judgments, Congress has violated this fundamental principle.

A

The Framers of our Constitution lived among the ruins of a system of intermingled legislative and judicial powers, which had been prevalent in the colonies long before the Revolution, and which after the Revolution had produced factional strife and partisan oppression. In the 17th and 18th centuries colonial assemblies and legislatures functioned as courts of equity of last resort, hearing original actions or providing appellate review of judicial judgments. Often, however, they chose to correct the judicial process through special bills or other enacted legislation. It was common for such legislation not to prescribe a resolution of the dispute, but rather simply to set aside the judgment and order a new trial or appeal. Thus, as described in our discussion of *Hayburn's Case*, such legislation bears not on the problem of interbranch review but on the problem of finality of judicial judgments.

* * *

* * * [A] sense of a sharp necessity to separate the legislative from the judicial power, prompted by the crescendo of legislative interference with private judgments of the courts, triumphed among the Framers of the new Federal Constitution. The Convention made the critical decision to establish a judicial department independent of the Legislative Branch by providing that "the judicial Power of the United States shall be vested in one supreme Court, and in such inferior Courts as the Congress may from time to time ordain and establish." Before and during the debates on ratification, Madison, Jefferson, and Hamilton each wrote of the factional disorders and disarray that the system of legislative equity had produced in the years before the framing; and each thought that the separation of the legislative from the judicial power in the new Constitution would cure them. Madison's FEDERALIST No. 48, the famous description of the process by which "[t]he legislative department is every where extending the sphere of its activity, and drawing all power into its impetuous vortex," referred to the report of the Pennsylvania Council of Censors to show that in that State "cases belonging to the judiciary department [had been] frequently drawn within legislative cognizance and determination." Madison relied as well on Jefferson's Notes on the State of Virginia, which mentioned, as one example of the dangerous concentration of governmental powers into the hands of the legislature, that "the Legislature

* * * in many instances decided rights which should have been left to judiciary controversy." ([E]mphasis deleted).[4]

If the need for separation of legislative from judicial power was plain, the principal effect to be accomplished by that separation was even plainer. As Hamilton wrote in his exegesis of Article III, § 1, in FEDERALIST No. 81:

> It is not true * * * that the parliament of Great Britain, or the legislatures of the particular states, can rectify the exceptionable decisions of their respective courts, in any other sense than might be done by a future legislature of the United States. The theory neither of the British, nor the state constitutions, authorises the revisal of a judicial sentence, by a legislative act * * * . A legislature without exceeding its province cannot reverse a determination once made, in a particular case; though it may prescribe a new rule for future cases.

The essential balance created by this allocation of authority was a simple one. The Legislature would be possessed of power to "prescrib[e] the rules by which the duties and rights of every citizen are to be regulated," but the power of "[t]he interpretation of the laws" would be "the proper and peculiar province of the courts." The Judiciary would be, "from the nature of its functions, * * * the [department] least dangerous to the political rights of the constitution," not because its acts were subject to legislative correction, but because the binding effect of its acts was limited to particular cases and controversies. Thus, "though individual oppression may now and then proceed from the courts of justice, the general liberty of the people can never be endangered from that quarter: * * * so long as the judiciary remains truly distinct from both the legislative and executive."

Judicial decisions in the period immediately after ratification of the Constitution confirm the understanding that it forbade interference with the final judgments of courts. * * *

The state courts of the era showed a similar understanding of the separation of powers, in decisions that drew little distinction between the federal and state constitutions. * * *

By the middle of the 19th century, the constitutional equilibrium created by the separation of the legislative power to make general law from the judicial power to apply that law in particular cases was so well understood and accepted that it could survive even *Dred Scott v. Sandford*. * * * And the great constitutional scholar Thomas Cooley addressed precisely the question before us in his 1868

4 Read in the abstract these public pronouncements might be taken, as the Solicitor General does take them, to disapprove only the practice of having the legislature itself sit as a court of original or appellate jurisdiction. But against the backdrop of history, that reading is untenable. Many, perhaps a plurality, of the instances of legislative equity in the period before the framing simply involved duly enacted laws that nullified judgments so that new trials or judicial rulings on the merits could take place.

treatise: "If the legislature cannot thus indirectly control the action of the courts, by requiring of them a construction of the law according to its own views, it is very plain it cannot do so directly, by setting aside their judgments, compelling them to grant new trials, ordering the discharge of offenders, or directing what particular steps shall be taken in the progress of a judicial inquiry."

B

Section 27A(b) effects a clear violation of the separation-of-powers principle we have just discussed. It is, of course, retroactive legislation, that is, legislation that prescribes what the law was at an earlier time, when the act whose effect is controlled by the legislation occurred—in this case, the filing of the initial Rule 10b-5 action in the District Court. When retroactive legislation requires its own application in a case already finally adjudicated, it does no more and no less than "reverse a determination once made, in a particular case." THE FEDERALIST No. 81. Our decisions stemming from *Hayburn's Case*—although their precise holdings are not strictly applicable here—have uniformly provided fair warning that such an act exceeds the powers of Congress. * * * Today those clear statements must either be honored, or else proved false.

It is true, as petitioners contend, that Congress can always revise the judgments of Article III courts in one sense: When a new law makes clear that it is retroactive, an appellate court must apply that law in reviewing judgments still on appeal that were rendered before the law was enacted, and must alter the outcome accordingly. Since that is so, petitioners argue, federal courts must apply the "new" law created by § 27A(b) in finally adjudicated cases as well; for the line that separates lower court judgments that are pending on appeal (or may still be appealed), from lower-court judgments that are final, is determined by statute and so cannot possibly be a *constitutional* line. But a distinction between judgments from which all appeals have been forgone or completed, and judgments that remain on appeal (or subject to being appealed), is implicit in what Article III creates: not a batch of unconnected courts, but a judicial *department* composed of "inferior Courts" and "one supreme Court." Within that hierarchy, the decision of an inferior court is not (unless the time for appeal has expired) the final word of the department as a whole. It is the obligation of the last court in the hierarchy that rules on the case to give effect to Congress's latest enactment, even when that has the effect of overturning the judgment of an inferior court, since each court, at every level, must "decide according to existing laws." Having achieved finality, however, a judicial decision becomes the last word of the judicial department with regard to a particular case or controversy, and Congress may not declare by retroactive legislation that the law applicable *to that very case* was something other than what the courts said it was. Finality of a legal judgment is determined by statute, just as entitlement to a government benefit is a statutory creation; but that no more deprives the former of its constitutional significance for separation-of-powers analysis than it deprives the latter of its significance for due process purposes.

To be sure, § 27A(b) reopens (or directs the reopening of) final judgments in a whole class of cases rather than in a particular suit. We do not see how that makes any difference. The separation-of-powers violation here, if there is any, consists of depriving judicial judgments of the conclusive effect that they had when they were announced, not of acting in a manner—*viz.*, with particular rather than general effect—that is unusual (though, we must note, not impossible) for a legislature. To be sure, a general statute such as this one may reduce the perception that legislative interference with judicial judgments was prompted by individual favoritism; but it is legislative interference with judicial judgments nonetheless. Not favoritism, nor even corruption, but *power* is the object of the separation-of-powers prohibition. The prohibition is violated when an individual final judgment is legislatively rescinded for even the *very best* of reasons, such as the legislature's genuine conviction (supported by all the law professors in the land) that the judgment was wrong; and it is violated 40 times over when 40 final judgments are legislatively dissolved.

It is irrelevant as well that the final judgments reopened by § 27A(b) rested on the bar of a statute of limitations. The rules of finality, both statutory and judge-made, treat a dismissal on statute-of-limitations grounds the same way they treat a dismissal for failure to state a claim, for failure to prove substantive liability, or for failure to prosecute: as a judgment on the merits. Petitioners suggest, directly or by implication, two reasons why a merits judgment based on this particular ground may be uniquely subject to congressional nullification. First, there is the fact that the length and indeed even the very existence of a statute of limitations upon a federal cause of action is entirely subject to congressional control. But virtually *all* of the reasons why a final judgment on the merits is rendered on a federal claim are subject to congressional control. Congress can eliminate, for example, a particular element of a cause of action that plaintiffs have found it difficult to establish; or an evidentiary rule that has often excluded essential testimony; or a rule of offsetting wrong (such as contributory negligence) that has often prevented recovery. To distinguish statutes of limitations on the ground that they are mere creatures of Congress is to distinguish them not at all. The second supposedly distinguishing characteristic of a statute of limitations is that it can be extended, without violating the Due Process Clause, after the cause of the action arose and even after the statute itself has expired. But that also does not set statutes of limitations apart. To mention only one other broad category of judgment-producing legal rule: rules of pleading and proof can similarly be altered after the cause of action arises, and even, if the statute clearly so requires, after they have been applied in a case but before final judgment has been entered.

Petitioners' principle would therefore lead to the conclusion that final judgments rendered on the basis of a stringent (or, alternatively, liberal) rule of pleading or proof may be set aside for retrial under a new liberal (or, alternatively, stringent) rule of pleading or proof. This alone provides massive scope for undoing final judgments and would substantially subvert the doctrine of separation of powers.

The central theme of the dissent is a variant on these arguments. The dissent maintains that Lampf "announced" a new statute of limitations, in an act of "judicial * * * lawmaking" that "changed the law." That statement, even if relevant, would be wrong. The point decided in Lampf had never before been addressed by this Court, and was therefore an open question, no matter what the lower courts had held at the time. But the more important point is that Lampf as such is irrelevant to this case. The dissent itself perceives that "[w]e would have the same issue to decide had Congress enacted the Lampf rule," and that the Lampf rule's genesis in judicial lawmaking rather than, shall we say, legislative lawmaking, "should not affect the separation-of-powers analysis." Just so. The issue here is not the validity or even the source of the legal rule that produced the Article III judgments, but rather the immunity from legislative abrogation of those judgments themselves. The separation-of-powers question before us has nothing to do with Lampf, and the dissent's attack on Lampf has nothing to do with the question before us.

C

Apart from the statute we review today, we know of no instance in which Congress has attempted to set aside the final judgment of an Article III court by retroactive legislation. That prolonged reticence would be amazing if such interference were not understood to be constitutionally proscribed. The closest analogue that the Government has been able to put forward is the statute at issue in *United States v. Sioux Nation*, 448 U.S. 371 (1980). That law required the Court of Claims " '[n]otwithstanding any other provision of law * * * to review on the merits, without regard to the defense of res judicata or collateral estoppel,' " a Sioux claim for just compensation from the United States—even though the Court of Claims had previously heard and rejected that very claim. We considered and rejected separation-of-powers objections to the statute based upon Hayburn's Case and United States v. Klein. The basis for our rejection was a line of precedent that stood, we said, for the proposition that "Congress has the power to waive the res judicata effect of a prior judgment entered in the Government's favor on a claim against the United States." And our holding was as narrow as the precedent on which we had relied: "In sum, * * * Congress' mere waiver of the res judicata effect of a prior judicial decision rejecting the validity of a legal claim against the United States does not violate the doctrine of separation of powers."[5]

The Solicitor General suggests that even if Sioux Nation is read in accord with its holding, it nonetheless establishes that Congress may require Article III courts to reopen their final judgments, since "if res judicata were compelled by Article III to safeguard the structural independence of the courts, the doctrine would not be subject to waiver by any party litigant." But the proposition that legal defenses based upon doctrines central to the courts' structural independence can never be waived simply does not accord with our cases. Certainly one such doctrine consists of the "judicial Power" to disregard an unconstitutional statute; yet none would suggest that a litigant may never waive the defense that a statute is unconstitutional. What may follow from our holding that the judicial power unalterably includes the power to render final judgments, is not that waivers of res judicata are always impermissible, but rather that, as many federal Courts of Appeals have held, waivers of res judicata need not always be accepted—that trial courts may in appropriate cases raise the res judicata bar on their own motion. Waiver subject to the control of the courts themselves would obviously raise no issue of separation of powers, and would be precisely in accord with the language of the decision that the Solicitor General relies upon. We [have] held * * * that, although a litigant had consented to bring a state-law counterclaim before an Article I tribunal, we would nonetheless choose to consider his Article III challenge, because "where these Article III limitations are at issue, notions of consent and waiver cannot be *dispositive*."

Petitioners also rely on a miscellany of decisions upholding legislation that altered rights fixed by the final judgments of non-Article III courts, or administrative agencies, or that altered the prospective effect of injunctions entered by Article III courts. These cases distinguish themselves; nothing in our holding today calls them into question. Petitioners rely on general statements from some of these cases that legislative annulment of final judgments is not an exercise of judicial power. But even if it were our practice to decide cases by weight of prior dicta, we would find the many dicta that reject congressional power to revise the judgments of *Article III* courts to be the more instructive authority.

Finally, petitioners liken § 27A(b) to Federal Rule of Civil Procedure 60(b), which authorizes courts to relieve parties from a final judgment for grounds such as excusable neglect, newly discovered evidence, fraud, or "any other reason justifying relief * * * ." We see little resemblance. Rule 60(b), which authorizes discretionary judicial revision of judgments in the listed situations and in

5 The dissent quotes a passage from the opinion saying that Congress " 'only was providing a forum so that a new judicial review of the Black Hills claim could take place.' " That is quite consistent with the res judicata holding. Any party who waives the defense of res judicata provides a forum for a new judicial review.

other "extraordinary circumstances," does not impose any legislative mandate-to-reopen upon the courts, but merely reflects and confirms the courts' own inherent and discretionary power, "firmly established in English practice long before the foundation of our Republic," to set aside a judgment whose enforcement would work inequity. Thus, Rule 60(b), and the tradition that it embodies, would be relevant refutation of a claim that reopening a final judgment is always a denial of property without due process; but they are irrelevant to the claim that legislative instruction to reopen impinges upon the independent constitutional authority of the courts.

The dissent promises to provide "[a] few contemporary examples" of statutes retroactively requiring final judgments to be reopened, "to demonstrate that [such statutes] are ordinary products of the exercise of legislative power." That promise is not kept. The relevant retroactivity, of course, consists not of the requirement that there be set aside a judgment that has been rendered *prior to its being setting aside*—for example, a statute passed today which says that all default judgments rendered in the future may be reopened within 90 days after their entry. In that sense, *all* requirements to reopen are "retroactive," and the designation is superfluous. Nothing we say today precludes a law such as that. The finality that a court can pronounce is no more than what the law in existence at the time of judgment will permit it to pronounce. If the law then applicable says that the judgment may be reopened for certain reasons, that limitation is built into the judgment itself, and its finality is so conditioned. The present case, however, involves a judgment that Congress subjected to a reopening requirement which did not exist when the judgment was pronounced. The dissent provides not a single clear prior instance of such congressional action.

The dissent cites, first, Rule 60(b), which it describes as a "familiar remedial measure." As we have just discussed, Rule 60(b) does not provide a new remedy at all, but is simply the recitation of pre-existing judicial power. The same is true of another of the dissent's examples, 28 U.S.C. § 2255, which provides federal prisoners a statutory motion to vacate a federal sentence. This procedure " 'restates, clarifies and simplifies the procedure in the nature of the ancient writ of error *coram nobis*.' " It is meaningless to speak of these statutes as applying "retroactively," since they simply codified judicial practice that pre-existed. Next, the dissent cites the provision of the Soldiers' and Sailors' Civil Relief Act of 1940, which authorizes courts, upon application, to reopen judgments against members of the Armed Forces entered while they were on active duty. It could not be clearer, however, that this provision was not retroactive. It says: "If any judgment *shall be rendered* in any action or proceeding governed by this section against any person in military service during the period of such service * * * *such judgment* may * * * be opened * * * ." (Emphasis added).

The dissent also cites a provision of the Handicapped Children's Protection Act of 1986, which provided for the award of attorney's fees under the Education for All Handicapped Children Act of 1975. This changed the law regarding attorney's fees under the Education for All Handicapped Children Act, after our decision in *Smith v. Robinson* found such fees to be unavailable. The provision of the Statutes at Large adopting this amendment to the United States Code specified, in effect, that it would apply not only to proceedings brought after its enactment, but also to proceedings pending at the time of, or brought after, the decision in *Smith*. The amendment says nothing about reopening final judgments, and the retroactivity provision may well mean nothing more than that it applies not merely to new suits commenced after the date of its enactment, but also to *previously* filed (but not yet terminated) suits of the specified sort. This interpretation would be consistent with the only case the dissent cites, which involved a court-entered consent decree not yet fully executed. Alternatively, the statute can perhaps be understood to create a new cause of action for attorney's fees attributable to already concluded litigation. That would create no separation-of-powers problem, and would be consistent with this Court's view that "[a]ttorney's fee determinations * * * are 'collateral to the main cause of action' and 'uniquely separable from the cause of action to be proved at trial.' "

The dissent's perception that retroactive reopening provisions are to be found all about us is perhaps attributable to its inversion of the statutory presumption regarding retroactivity. Thus, it asserts that Rule 60(b) must be retroactive, since "[n]ot a single word in its text suggests that it does not apply to judgments entered prior to its effective date." This reverses the traditional rule, confirmed only last Term, that statutes do *not* apply retroactively *unless* Congress expressly states that they do. The dissent adds that "the traditional construction of remedial measures * * * support[s] construing [Rule 60(b)] to apply to past as well as future judgments." But [we have rejected] reliance on the vaguely remedial purpose of a statute to defeat the presumption against retroactivity * * * .

The dissent sets forth a number of hypothetical horribles flowing from our assertedly "rigid holding"—for example, the inability to set aside a civil judgment that has become final during a period when a natural disaster prevented the timely filing of a certiorari petition. That is horrible not because of our holding, but because the underlying statute *itself* enacts a "rigid" jurisdictional bar to entertaining untimely civil petitions. Congress could undoubtedly enact *prospective* legislation permitting, or indeed requiring, this Court to make equitable exceptions to an otherwise applicable rule of finality, just as district courts do pursuant to Rule 60(b). It is no indication whatever of the invalidity of the constitutional rule which we announce, that it produces unhappy consequences when a legislature lacks foresight, and acts belatedly to remedy a deficiency in the law. That is a routine result of constitutional rules.

* * *

Ultimately, the concurrence agrees with our judgment only "[b]ecause the law before us embodies risks of the very sort that our Constitution's 'separation of powers' prohibition seeks to avoid." But the doctrine of separation of powers is a *structural safeguard* rather than a remedy to be applied only when specific harm, or risk of specific harm, can be identified. In its major features (of which the conclusiveness of judicial judgments is assuredly one) it is a prophylactic device, establishing high walls and clear distinctions because low walls and vague distinctions will not be judicially defensible in the heat of interbranch conflict. * * * We think legislated invalidation of judicial judgments deserves the same categorical treatment accorded by Chadha to congressional invalidation of executive action. The delphic alternative suggested by the concurrence (the setting aside of judgments is all right so long as Congress does not "impermissibly tr[y] to *apply*, as well as *make*, the law,") simply prolongs doubt and multiplies confrontation. Separation of powers, a distinctively American political doctrine, profits from the advice authored by a distinctively American poet: Good fences make good neighbors.

* * *

We know of no previous instance in which Congress has enacted retroactive legislation requiring an Article III court to set aside a final judgment, and for good reason. The Constitution's separation of legislative and judicial powers denies it the authority to do so. Section 27A(b) is unconstitutional to the extent that it requires federal courts to reopen final judgments entered before its enactment. The judgment of the Court of Appeals is affirmed.

It is so ordered.

JUSTICE STEVENS, with whom JUSTICE GINSBURG joins, dissenting.

* * *

Throughout our history, Congress has passed laws that allow courts to reopen final judgments. Such laws characteristically apply to judgments entered before as well as after their enactment. When they apply retroactively, they may raise serious due process questions,[12] but the Court has never invalidated such a law

12 Because the Court finds a separation-of-powers violation, it does not reach respondents' alternative theory that § 27A(b) denied them due process under the Fifth Amendment, a theory the Court of Appeals did not identify as an alternative ground for its holding. In my judgment, the statute easily survives a due process challenge. Section 27A(b) is rationally related to a legitimate public purpose. Given the existence of statutes and rules, such as Rule 60(b), that allow courts to reopen apparently "final" judgments in various circumstances, respondents cannot assert an inviolable "vested right" in the District Court's post-*Lampf* dismissal of petitioners' claims. In addition, § 27A(b) did not upset any

on separation-of-powers grounds until today. Indeed, only last Term we recognized Congress' ample *power* to enact a law that "in effect 'restored' rights that [a party] reasonably and in good faith thought he possessed before the surprising announcement" of a Supreme Court decision. We conditioned our unambiguous restatement of the proposition that "Congress had the power to enact legislation that had the practical effect of restoring the status quo retroactively" only on Congress' clear expression of its intent to do so.

* * *

I

Respondents conducted a public offering of common stock in 1983. Petitioners, suing on behalf of themselves and other purchasers of the stock, filed a 10b-5 action in 1987 in the United States District Court for the Eastern District of Kentucky, alleging violations of substantive federal rules that had been in place since 1934. Respondents moved to dismiss the complaint as untimely because petitioners had filed it more than three years after the events in dispute. At that time, settled law in Kentucky and elsewhere in the United States directed federal courts to determine statutes of limitations applicable to 10b-5 actions by reference to state law. The relevant Kentucky statute provided a 3-year limitations period, which petitioners contended ran from the time the alleged fraud was or should have been discovered. A Magistrate agreed with petitioners and recommended denial of respondents' motion to dismiss, but by 1991 the District Court had not yet ruled on that issue. The factual question whether petitioners should have discovered respondents' alleged 10b-5 violations more than three years before they filed suit remained open for decision by an Article III judge on June 20, 1991.

On that day, this Court's decision in *Lampf* changed the law. The Court concluded that every 10b-5 action is time barred unless brought within three years of the alleged violation and one year of its discovery. Moreover, it applied that novel rule to pending cases. As Justice O'Connor pointed out in her dissent, the Court held the plaintiffs' suit "time barred under a limitations period that did not exist before," a holding that "depart[ed] drastically from our established practice and inflict[ed] an injustice on the [plaintiffs]." The inequitable consequences of *Lampf* reached beyond the parties to that case, injuring a large class of litigants that includes petitioners. Without resolving the factual issue that would have determined the timeliness of petitioners' complaint before *Lampf*, the District Court dismissed the instant action as untimely under the new limitations period dictated by this Court. Because *Lampf* had deprived them of any non-frivolous basis for

"settled expectations" of respondents. * * * Before 1991 no one could have relied either on the yet-to-be-announced rule in *Lampf* or on the Court's unpredictable decision to apply that rule retroactively. All of the reliance interests that ordinarily support a presumption against retroactivity militate in favor of allowing retroactive application of § 27A.

an appeal, petitioners acquiesced in the dismissal, which therefore became final on September 12, 1991.

Congress responded to *Lampf* by passing § 27A, which became effective on December 19, 1991. The statute changed the substantive limitations law, restoring the pre-*Lampf* limitations rule for two categories of 10b-5 actions that had been pending on June 19, 1991. Subsection (a) of § 27A applies to cases that were still pending on December 19, 1991. The courts of appeals have uniformly upheld the constitutionality of that subsection, and its validity is not challenged in this case. Subsection (b) applies to actions, like the instant case, that (1) were dismissed after June 19, 1991, and (2) would have been timely under the pre-*Lampf* regime. This subsection authorized the district courts to reinstate dismissed cases if the plaintiff so moved within 60 days after the effective date of § 27A. The amendment was not self-executing: Unless the plaintiff both filed a timely motion for reinstatement and then satisfied the court that the complaint had been timely filed under applicable pre-*Lampf* law, the dismissal would remain in effect.

In this case petitioners made the required showing, but the District Court refused to reinstate their case. Instead, it held § 27A(b) unconstitutional. The Court of Appeals for the Sixth Circuit, contrary to an earlier decision of the Fifth Circuit, affirmed.

* * *

III

The lack of precedent for the Court's holding is not, of course, a sufficient reason to reject it. Correct application of separation-of-powers principles, however, confirms that the Court has reached the wrong result. As our most recent major pronouncement on the separation of powers noted, "we have never held that the Constitution requires that the three branches of Government 'operate with absolute independence.' " Rather, our jurisprudence reflects "Madison's flexible approach to separation of powers." In accepting Madison's conception rather than any "hermetic division among the Branches," "we have upheld statutory provisions that to some degree commingle the functions of the Branches, but that pose no danger of either aggrandizement or encroachment." Today's holding does not comport with these ideals.

Section 27A shares several important characteristics with the remedial statutes discussed above. It does not decide the merits of any issue in any litigation but merely removes an impediment to judicial decision on the merits. The impediment it removes would have produced inequity because the statute's beneficiaries did not cause the impediment. It requires a party invoking its benefits to file a motion within a specified time and to convince a court that the statute entitles the party to relief. Most important, § 27A(b) specifies both a substantive rule to govern the reopening of a class of judgments—the pre-Lampf limitations rule—and a procedure for the courts to apply in determining whether a particular motion to reopen should be granted. These characteristics are quintessentially legislative. They reflect Congress' fealty to the separation of powers and its intention to avoid the sort of *ad hoc* excesses the Court rightly criticizes in colonial legislative practice. In my judgment, all of these elements distinguish § 27A from "judicial" action and confirm its constitutionality. A sensible analysis would at least consider them in the balance.

Instead, the Court myopically disposes of § 27A(b) by holding that Congress has no power to "requir[e] an Article III court to set aside a final judgment." That holding must mean one of two things. It could mean that Congress may not impose a mandatory duty on a court to set aside a judgment even if the court makes a particular finding, such as a finding of fraud or mistake, that Congress has not made. Such a rule, however, could not be correct. Although Rule 60(b), for example, merely authorizes federal courts to set aside judgments after making appropriate findings, Acts of Congress characteristically set standards that judges are obligated to enforce. Accordingly, Congress surely could add to Rule 60(b) certain instances in which courts *must* grant relief from final judgments if they make particular findings—for example, a finding that a member of the jury accepted a bribe from the prevailing party. The Court, therefore, must mean to hold that Congress may not *unconditionally* require an Article III court to set aside a final judgment. That rule is both unwise and beside the point of this case.

A simple hypothetical example will illustrate the practical failings of the Court's new rule. Suppose Congress, instead of endorsing the new limitations rule fashioned by the Court in Lampf, had decided to return to the pre-Lampf regime (or perhaps to enact a longer uniform statute). Subsection (a) of § 27 would simply have provided that the law in effect prior to June 19, 1991, would govern the timeliness of all 10b-5 actions. In that event, subsection (b) would still have been necessary to remedy the injustice caused by this Court's failure to exempt pending cases from its new rule. In my judgment, the statutory correction of the inequitable flaw in Lampf would be appropriate remedial legislation whether or not Congress had endorsed that decision's substantive limitations rule. The Court, unfortunately, appears equally consistent: Even though the class of dismissed 10b-5 plaintiffs in my hypothetical would have been subject to the same substantive rule as all other 10b-5 plaintiffs, the Court's reasoning would still reject subsection (b) as an impermissible exercise of "judicial" power.

The majority's rigid holding unnecessarily hinders the Government from addressing difficult issues that inevitably arise in a complex society. This Court, for example, lacks power to enlarge the time for filing petitions for certiorari in a civil case after 90 days from the entry of final judgment, no matter how strong the equities. If an Act of God, such as a flood or an earthquake, sufficiently disrupted communications in a particular area to preclude filing for several days, the majority's reasoning would appear to bar Congress from addressing the resulting inequity. If Congress passed remedial legislation that retroactively granted movants from the disaster area extra time to file petitions or motions for extensions of time to file, today's holding presumably would compel us to strike down the legislation as an attack on the finality of judgments. Such a ruling, like today's holding, would gravely undermine federal courts' traditional power "to set aside a judgment whose enforcement would work inequity."[16]

Even if the rule the Court announces today were sound, it would not control the case before us. In order to obtain the benefit of § 27A, petitioners had to file a timely motion and persuade the District Court they had timely filed their complaint under pre-*Lampf* law. In the judgment of the District Court, petitioners satisfied those conditions. Congress reasonably could have assumed, indeed must have expected, that some movants under § 27A(b) would fail to do so. The presence of an important condition that the District Court must find a movant to have satisfied before it may reopen a judgment distinguishes § 27A from the unconditional congressional directives the Court appears to forbid.

Moreover, unlike the colonial legislative commands on which the Court bases its holding, § 27A directed action not in "a civil case," but in a large category of civil cases.[17] The Court declares that a legislative direction to reopen a class of 40 cases is 40 times as bad as a direction to reopen a single final judgment because "power is the object of the separation-of-powers prohibition." This self-evident observation might be salient if § 27A(b) unconditionally commanded courts to reopen judgments even absent findings that the complaints were timely under pre-*Lampf* law. But Congress did not decide—and could not know how any court would decide—the timeliness issue in any particular case in the affected category. Congress, therefore, had no way to identify which particular plaintiffs would benefit from § 27A. It merely enacted a law that applied a substantive rule to a class of litigants, specified a procedure for invoking the rule, and left particular outcomes to individualized judicial determinations—a classic exercise of legislative power.

---

16 The Court also appears to bar retroactive application of changes in the criminal law. Its reasoning suggests that, for example, should Congress one day choose to abolish the federal death penalty, the new statute could not constitutionally save a death row inmate from execution if his conviction had become final before the statute was passed.

17 At the time Congress was considering the bill that became § 27A, a House Subcommittee reported that *Lampf* had resulted in the dismissal of 15 cases, involving thousands of plaintiffs in every State (of whom over 32,000 had been identified) and claims totaling over $692.25 million. In addition, motions to dismiss based on *Lampf* were then pending in 17 cases involving thousands of plaintiffs in every State and claims totaling over $4.578 billion.

"All we seek," affirmed a sponsor of § 27A, "is to give the victims [of securities fraud] a fair day in court." A statute, such as § 27A, that removes an unanticipated and unjust impediment to adjudication of a large class of claims on their merits poses no danger of "aggrandizement or encroachment."[19] This is particularly true for § 27A in light of Congress' historic primacy over statutes of limitations. The statute contains several checks against the danger of congressional overreaching. The Court in *Lampf* undertook a legislative function. Essentially, it supplied a statute of limitations for 10b-5 actions. The Court, however, failed to adopt the transition rules that ordinarily attend alterations shortening the time to sue. Congress, in § 27A, has supplied those rules. The statute reflects the ability of two coequal branches to cooperate in providing for the impartial application of legal rules to particular disputes. The Court's mistrust of such cooperation ill serves the separation of powers.[21]

IV

The Court has drawn the wrong lesson from the Framers' disapproval of colonial legislatures' appellate review of judicial decisions. The Framers rejected that practice, not out of a mechanistic solicitude for "final judgments," but because they believed the impartial application of rules of law, rather than the will of the majority, must govern the disposition of individual cases and controversies. Any legislative interference in the adjudication of the merits of a particular case carries the risk that political power will supplant evenhanded justice, whether the interference occurs before or after the entry of final judgment. Section 27A(b) neither commands the reinstatement of any particular case nor directs any result

---

19 Today's decision creates a new irony of judicial legislation. A challenge to the constitutionality of § 27A(a) could not turn on the sanctity of final judgments. Section 27A(a) benefits litigants who had filed appeals that *Lampf* rendered frivolous; petitioners and other law-abiding litigants whose claims *Lampf* rendered untimely had acquiesced in the dismissal of their actions. By striking down § 27A(b) on a ground that would leave § 27A(a) intact, the Court indulges litigants who protracted proceedings but shuts the courthouse door to litigants who proceeded with diligence and respect for the *Lampf* judgment.

21 Although I agree with Justice Breyer's general approach to the separation-of-powers issue, I believe he gives insufficient weight to two important features of § 27A. First, he fails to recognize that the statute restored a preexisting rule of law in order to remedy the manifest injustice produced by the Court's retroactive application of *Lampf*. The only " 'substantial deprivation' " Congress imposed on defendants was that properly filed lawsuits proceed to decisions on the merits. Second, he understates the class of defendants burdened by § 27A: He finds the statute underinclusive because it provided no remedy for potential plaintiffs who may have failed to file timely actions in reliance on pre-*Lampf* limitations law, but he denies the importance of § 27A(a), which provided a remedy for plaintiffs who appealed dismissals after *Lampf*. The coverage of § 27A is coextensive with the retroactive application of the general rule announced in *Lampf*. If Congress had enacted a statute providing that the *Lampf* rule should apply to all cases filed after the statute's effective date and that the pre-*Lampf* rule should apply to all cases filed before that date, Justice Breyer could not reasonably condemn the statute as special legislation. The only difference between such a statute and § 27A is that § 27A covered all cases pending on the date of *Lampf*—June 20, 1991—rather than on the effective date of the statute—December 19, 1991. In my opinion, § 27A has sufficient generality to avoid the characteristics of a bill of attainder.

on the merits. Congress recently granted a special benefit to a single litigant in a pending civil rights case, but the Court saw no need even to grant certiorari to review that disturbing legislative favor. In an ironic counterpoint, the Court today places a higher priority on protecting the Republic from the restoration to a large class of litigants of the opportunity to have Article III courts resolve the merits of their claims.

"We must remember that the machinery of government would not work if it were not allowed a little play in its joints." The three Branches must cooperate in order to govern. We should regard favorably, rather than with suspicious hostility, legislation that enables the judiciary to overcome impediments to the performance of its mission of administering justice impartially, even when, as here, this Court has created the impediment.[23] Rigid rules often make good law, but judgments in areas such as the review of potential conflicts among the three coequal Branches of the Federal Government partake of art as well as science. That is why we have so often reiterated the insight of Justice Jackson:

> The actual art of governing under our Constitution does not and cannot conform to judicial definitions of the power of any of its branches based on isolated clauses or even single Articles torn from context. While the Constitution diffuses power the better to secure liberty, it also contemplates that practice will integrate the dispersed powers into a workable government. It enjoins upon its branches separateness but interdependence, autonomy but reciprocity.

We have the authority to hold that Congress has usurped a judicial prerogative, but even if this case were doubtful I would heed Justice Iredell's admonition that "the Court will never resort to that authority, but in a clear and urgent case." An appropriate regard for the interdependence of Congress and the judiciary amply supports the conclusion that § 27A(b) reflects constructive legislative cooperation rather than a usurpation of judicial prerogatives.

Accordingly, I respectfully dissent.

---

23 Of course, neither the majority nor I would alter its analysis had Congress, rather than the Court, enacted the *Lampf* rule without any exemption for pending cases, then later tried to remedy such unfairness by enacting § 27A. Thus, the Court's attribution of § 27A to "the legislature's genuine conviction (supported by all the law professors in the land) that [*Lampf*] was wrong" is quite beside the point.

Notes and Questions

1. *Plaut* is different from the other cases discussed in this chapter because it clearly does not involve any attempt by Congress to limit the subject-matter jurisdiction of the federal courts as such. It does, however, concern limits on Congress's ability to control judicial authority. Congress attempted to mandate the results in several federal court actions, and the Supreme Court found the attempt unconstitutional on separation-of-powers grounds. Is the decision analogous to Klein? Why or why not? Does *Plaut* support the notion that the separation of powers restricts Congress's ability to limit the jurisdiction of the federal courts? If so, describe the restriction.

2. *Plaut* shows the impact of the "Case-or-Controversy Clause" (discussed in Chapter 1) in a new light. In Hayburn's Case, the Clause prevented the Supreme Court from giving advice to the other branches. Here, rather than circumscribing the judiciary, the Clause protects an area from incursion by the political branches. Read together, these cases demonstrate that the Case-or-Controversy Clause defines a boundary between mutually exclusive areas of federal power.

3. The boundary may, however, be movable. Congress certainly can define cases or controversies through its control over substantive law. When Congress creates new substantive rights that include private rights of action, for example, it expands the reach of the Case-or-Controversy Clause. It remains to decide when the boundary becomes fixed.

Justice Scalia's opinion seems to acknowledge that Congress can affect pending cases, changing the substantive law in a manner that controls pending cases, including those on appeal. Ex parte McCardle is an example of this power. Why is a congressional attempt to affect the result in a case like McCardle less of an intrusion on the judiciary's exclusive power over cases or controversies than the congressional attempt here? Are you satisfied with the Court's explanation?

Perhaps the Case-or-Controversy Clause really describes three areas: 1) an area outside of the Clause, closed to the courts because there is no case or controversy, as exemplified by Hayburn's Case and Muskrat v. United States, 2) an area within the Clause in which the political branches and the judiciary can both act (and in which the former can affect the latter's ability to act), exemplified by Ex parte McCardle, and 3) an area within the Clause from which the political branches are excluded, as exemplified by *Plaut*, though the judiciary may still act (for example, under Rule 60 or what Justice Scalia calls the judiciary's "inherent" power).

4. Part of the majority's job is to distinguish Sioux Nation, in which Congress allowed the plaintiff to bring an already adjudicated action a second time, notwithstanding res judicata. If Congress had parroted the Sioux Nation statute here, purporting to permit "review on the merits, without regard to any defense based upon either

res judicata or limitation of the time in which to commence an action," would the Court have come out the other way? If so, does *Plaut* merely represent a legislative drafting blunder? If not, what distinguishes *Plaut* from Sioux Nation?

5. The majority notes that "waivers of res judicata need not always be accepted." When will or should the courts decline to permit waiver of the defense? What standards do or should govern the decision? To the extent res judicata is a doctrine "central to the courts' structural independence," therefore permitting the courts to refuse to allow waiver, does that suggest that res judicata is part and parcel of defining a case or controversy within the meaning of Article III? If that is so, when is res judicata part of Article III and thereby not waivable? What can take it out of Article III so that it becomes waivable?

6. Justice Scalia and the majority decline to recognize Rule 60 as a legislative authorization to reopen final judgments, arguing that the Rule merely reflects the courts' inherent discretionary power over their own judgments. Does that argument read Rule 60 to be "utterly without effect, a result to be avoided if possible," as Justice Scalia said with respect to petitioners' reading of § 27A? Isn't Justice Scalia trying to have it both ways? If Rule 60 does nothing at all, then it seems to be subject to the vice he condemns (perhaps more so, given that the Court itself promulgates the Federal Rules of Civil Procedure). If Rule 60 does in some respect affect the judiciary's power with respect to final judgments, then it provides more support for petitioners than the Court acknowledges.

7. The majority seems to draw a sharp line between cases that are pending (including on appeal) and those in which no further action is possible. In effect, Justice Scalia takes the position that the judicial department has not spoken until a case is no longer subject to judicial action.

a) Given that Rule 60 permits (or, in Justice Scalia's terms, confirms the inherent power of) the judiciary to reopen judgments, when can one say with certainty that the judicial department has spoken? After all, the Rule itself contemplates judicial revision in some cases more than one year after the entry of judgment.

b) Is it so obvious that a judgment is not a judicial department decision until there are no further possibilities of judicial action? Certainly that is not universally true. In *Federated Department Stores v. Moitie*, 452 U.S. 394 (1981), the Court's opinion by then-Justice Rehnquist made clear that a judgment on appeal is entitled to full res judicata recognition, reaffirming *Reed v. Allen*, 286 U.S. 191 (1932):

> [A]n "erroneous conclusion" reached by the court in the first suit does not deprive the defendants in the second action "of their right to rely upon the plea of res judicata * * * . A judgment merely voidable because based upon an erroneous view of the law is not open to collateral attack, but can be corrected only by a direct review and not by bringing another action upon the same cause [of action]."

In the majority's view, an erroneous judgment is open to collateral *legislative* attack as long as it is on appeal or is appealable. Is that position reconcilable with the Court's twice-expressed disinclination to permit collateral *judicial* attack on such a judgment?

8. The dissent also has its problems. Are there any limits to Congress's ability to affect judgments that without legislative action would be regarded as final? The dissent attempts to distinguish statutes like that in *Plaut* from illegitimate legislative interference on the ground that the *Plaut* statute does not seek to determine the merits of the litigation, but simply to ensure that the judiciary reaches the merits. Are you persuaded?

9. The Prison Litigation Reform Act of 1995, codified as scattered sections of Titles 18, 28 and 42 U.S.C. is one of the newest statutes to raise separation-of-powers problems similar to those in *Plaut* and *Klein*.

a) On its face, the statute mandates vacating judgments that are "final" in the sense that the parties could have, and indeed may have, appealed (under 28 U.S.C. § 1291) the relief that the district court ordered. In response to the Act's passage, prison authorities in several states moved to terminate relief granted in previous litigation. Prisoners' representatives opposed the motions on the ground that the PLRA's authorization of such termination unconstitutionally intrudes upon Article III courts and their final judgments.

Consider first the potential *Plaut* problems. A court may properly modify an equitable decree when there has been a significant change in the factual or legal circumstances that make it inequitable to give the original order continued prospective application. Do you think 18 U.S.C. § 3626(b) violates the rule of *Plaut*? For *Plaut* purposes, should the courts distinguish between "final" judgments and "executory" judgments? *See Benjamin v. Jacobson*, 172 F.3d 144 (2d Cir. 1999) (*en banc*); *Taylor v. United States*, 181 F.3d 1017 (9th Cir. 1999) (*en banc*). Does it matter whether the underlying claims rest upon the Constitution rather than upon federal statutes?

b) Section 3626(e)(2) appears to direct a court to stay existing injunctive relief when the state has made a motion to terminate that relief pursuant to § 3626(b). Does the statute permit a court to exercise any discretion as to whether to enter the stay? *See Hadix v. Johnson*, 144 F.3d 925 (6th Cir. 1998). If it does not, does it then constitute a legislative incursion into the judicial process in violation of *Klein* or *Plaut*? *See French v. Duckworth*, 178 F.3d 437 (7th Cir. 1999).

c) With respect to *Klein*, do the provisions of § 3626(a) violate its rule? Has Congress permissibly prescribed a substantive standard that applies to pending cases, or has it endeavored to tell the federal courts how to weigh evidence and determine facts? *See Imprisoned Citizens Union v. Ridge*, 169 F.3d 178 (3d Cir. 1999). With respect to the

Act as a whole, do you think Congress wanted to influence the outcome this particular kind of dispute? Assuming that it did, is there anything improper about that?

How should one draw the line between permissible—even desirable—congressional involvement in formulation of substantive social policies and impermissible congressional involvement in the courts' function as adjudicators of particular disputes under the law? To what extent should *Plaut* and *Klein* limit Congress's undoubted entitlement to change substantive and jurisdictional law?

CHAPTER 3

Federal Question Jurisdiction

A. Introduction

The United States' legal system is federal; state and national governments exist side by side. The Constitution allocates power in some cases exclusively to the states or the federal government, but often to both concurrently. The scope of federal jurisdiction greatly affects the relationship between the federal and state governments. If federal jurisdiction is broad, cases that would otherwise be in the state courts can be brought in the federal courts, thus diminishing the role of the state courts. On the other hand, if federal jurisdiction is narrowly circumscribed, state power increases proportionally to the number of cases forced into the state courts.

Moreover, it is not just a question of numbers. The power to adjudicate a case often necessarily includes the power to adjudicate issues from the "other" level of government. Many cases present issues of federal and state law. The broader federal jurisdiction, the more hybrid cases and therefore the more state law issues the federal courts will adjudicate. This increases federal influence on state law. Conversely, if federal jurisdiction were narrower, state courts would adjudicate more hybrid cases and have a correspondingly greater influence on federal law.

Finally, the court hearing a case necessarily makes choice-of-law decisions about whether federal or state law applies to each issue. As a practical matter, of course, for many issues the choice is so obvious that one never consciously considers the question. For example, in a negligence action between citizens of the same state, that state rather than federal law governs the standard of care is so plain that no discussion of choice of law ensues. Nonetheless, the choices are being made, even if ***sub silentio***. Although this process is primarily important with respect to the existence and scope of federal common law, it is also significant for subject matter juris-

It's Latin to Me!

"Under silence; without notice being taken; without being expressly mentioned"

diction, since the jurisdictional decision will determine whether a federal or state court will make the choice-of-law decisions. Thus, a federal or state court to some extent determines for itself the questions to which it will apply the law of the "other" system.

Article III, § 2 of the Constitution establishes the scope of possible jurisdiction over cases involving questions of federal law.[1] Note, however, that the judicial power described in Article III, § 2, cl. 1 is not self-executing. Compare that clause with the next,[2] which, rather than describing the reach of the judicial power generally, vests jurisdiction in a named court. Under Article III, § 1, the inferior federal courts need not even have existed, and Art. III, § 2, cl. 1 has always been understood to describe the power that Congress may, if it wishes, vest in the federal courts.[3]

Except for a brief period in 1801-02, Congress did not confer general federal question jurisdiction on the lower federal courts until 1875.[4]

It is not clear whether Congress intended to grant the full scope of Article III jurisdiction to the federal trial courts, but note the similarity of language in the two provisions. The only contemporaneous comment was made by Senator Carpenter, who, after noting that prior enactments had not vested all constitutionally-allowed jurisdiction, said, "This bill gives precisely the power which the Constitution confers—nothing more, nothing less." Nonetheless, the Supreme Court has interpreted the constitutional provision more broadly than the statutory provision. As you begin to understand the differences between the constitutional and statutory standards

> **Go Online**
>
> Act of Mar. 3, 1875, ch. 137, § 1, 18 Stat. 470.

1 "The judicial Power shall extend to all Cases, in Law and Equity, arising under this Constitution, the Laws of the United States, and Treaties made, or which shall be made, under their Authority * * *."

2 "In all Cases affecting Ambassadors, other public Ministers and Consuls, and those in which a State shall be a Party, the Supreme Court shall have original Jurisdiction." U.S. CONST. art. III, § 2, cl. 2.

3 This is why it is necessary, in order to find subject matter jurisdiction in the inferior federal courts, to find a statute conferring the jurisdiction in addition to finding that the case falls within those described in Article III, § 2. A case merely within Article III does not by that fact alone gain entry to the district court. Were that not so, for example, Congress' attempt to limit diversity jurisdiction to cases exceeding $75,000 would be unavailing.

4 The common view is that Congress enacted only a few specialized grants of jurisdiction for the federal trial courts from time to time before 1875. From time to time, Congress permitted removal of cases of particular federal interest, especially those involving direct state challenges to federal powerIn the aftermath of the Civil War, some jurisdictional statutes shifted power away from the states to the federal government. Professor Doernberg contests that limited view. "[W]hen Congress was creating substantive federal law involving rights or obligations of individuals with respect to the federal government, it ordinarily did create inferior federal court jurisdiction for resolving disputes." DONALD L. DOERNBERG, IDENTITY CRISIS: FEDERAL COURTS IN A PSYCHOLOGICAL WILDERNESS 32-33 (2001). *See generally id.* at 30-37.

for federal question jurisdiction, consider whether the Court has drawn wise and workable distinctions. Initially, why might it be a good idea to interpret the constitutional provision more broadly?

As a final preliminary matter, one must keep in mind two distinct concepts regarding federal question jurisdiction. The first involves the placement of the federal issue—whether it comes up in the complaint, the answer, or elsewhere. The second concerns the substantiality of the federal issue. Regrettably, cases do not always fall neatly into one category or the other, and the Court has not always been clear either about which issue it is addressing or about precisely what the concept of substantiality, in this context, entails. Nonetheless, it is important to remember both issues and to be aware of the distinctions between them.

In this area, as in others, it is wise to be aware of the broader themes. Apart from whether a court should exercise jurisdiction in a particular case, consider the purpose of having any federal question jurisdiction. Why does the Constitution mention it? Why not leave preliminary adjudication of federal questions to the state courts, with review in the United States Supreme Court when necessary? After all, that system prevailed until 1875. What might have provoked Congress to make so broad a change?

B. Constitutional And Statutory "Arising Under"—Separate Strands Intertwined

Osborn v. Bank of the United States was the Court's first major case to focus on the scope of federal question jurisdiction, but it was not the Court's first consideration of subject matter jurisdiction more generally. Recall that in *Marbury v. Madison*, Chief Justice Marshall's opinion ultimately rested on an Article III jurisdictional question: whether Congress had the power to expand the Supreme Court's original jurisdiction, upon which Marbury relied in pursuit of his judgeship. The Court's clear answer was that Congress could not do so, and that provided the basis for Chief Justice Marshall's invocation of the power of judicial review. Contrast the Chief Justice's strict construction of the terms of Article III, § 2, cl. 2 with his far more expansive reading of the judicial power set out in § 2, cl. 1. "Arising under," which appears in the first clause, allowed him that latitude. Contrast that rather open language with the approach of the second clause, which enumerates the kinds of cases that the Court can hear originally and hammers home the exclusivity of that listing in the second sentence, which begins, "In all the other Cases before mentioned, the supreme Court shall have appellate jurisdiction * * * ."

Osborn arose at a time of considerable economic ferment. In the aftermath of the War of 1812, the economy boomed. Importation of foreign goods, largely suspended during the war, resumed with a vengeance. Exports surged but never kept pace with imports. One of the results was that more specie flowed out of the nation than into it.

American banking was in its formative stages, with no central banking policy and little to no regulation. Even the monetary system was underdeveloped. The country was on a bimetallic (gold/silver) standard, but because the legal ratio undervalued gold, silver coins, most not even minted in the United States, were the primary medium of circulation. Banks expanded with the economy, and many of them operated without being able to redeem their notes in specie. The banks were, in effect, inflated.

New England banks were more conservative and hewed more closely to traditional banking practices based on specie. The result was a monetary imbalance between New England and the rest of the country, and New England banks insisted on redeeming notes from less conservative banks at depreciated levels. The Second Bank of the United States was an attempted solution. It encouraged resumption of payments in specie, as of 1817, but when it decided to treat the notes of overextended banks as equivalent to specie, it sowed the seeds of a banking crisis.

In 1818-19, several large overseas debts, notably that relating to the Louisiana Purchase, came due, and those debts required repayment in specie. The Second Bank, to make those payments, had to pull back from its previous expansionist monetary policy.

> Beginning in the summer of 1818, the Bank precipitated the Panic of 1819 by a series of deflationary moves. The branches of the Bank were ordered to call on the state banks to redeem heave balances and notes held by the Bank. The requirement that each branch redeem the notes of every other branch was rescinded, thus ending the liability of the conservative eastern branches to redeem the notes of expansionist branches.

The result was a wave of bankruptcies, spurred by the rapid monetary contraction. It began the first recognizable American depression. Unemployment rose, bankruptcies increased even more, and the economy contracted drastically. The depression lasted until 1821. Hostility to the national bank was high, and states, especially those outside of the relatively conservative New England banking area, attempted to tax the bank to death. That response led to *M'Culloch v. Maryland* in 1819 and to *Osborn v. Bank of the United States*, which reached the Supreme Court in 1824. *M'Culloch*, you will recall from your course in Constitutional Law, dealt with federal supremacy under Article VI. Osborn turned to the more arcane question of federal judicial jurisdiction.

As you read the Chief Justice's majority opinion below, pay careful attention to his articulation of the ways to test whether a case arises under federal law. How many can you spot? By the same token, be sure to isolate Justice Johnson's arising-under test(s) so that you can compare and contrast them.

Justice Johnson's dissent is worth very careful attention, since you will discover as you go through the materials in this chapter how truly prescient he was about the future development of federal question jurisdiction. You will see also that he divides cases in which there might be an argument for inferior federal court jurisdiction into two categories. What are they, and how would he treat them differently for purposes of establishing jurisdiction?

Osborn v. Bank of The United States

Supreme Court of the United States, 1824.
22 U.S. (9 Wheat.) 738.

The bill filed in this cause, was exhibited in the Court below, at September term, 1819, in the name of the respondents, and signed by solicitors of the Court, praying an injunction to restrain Ralph Osborn, Auditor of the State of Ohio, from proceeding against the complainants, under an act of the Legislature of that State, passed February the 8th, 1819, entitled, "An act to levy and collect a tax from all banks, and individuals, and companies, and associations of individuals, that may transact banking business in this State, without being allowed to do so by the laws thereof." This act, after reciting that the Bank of the United States pursued its operations contrary to a law of the State, enacted, that if, after the 1st day of the following September, the said Bank, or any other, should continue to transact business in the State, it should be liable to an annual tax of 50,000 dollars on each office of discount and deposit. And that on the 15th day of September, the Auditor should charge such tax to the Bank, and should make out his warrant, under his seal of office, directed to any person, commanding him to collect the said tax, who should enter the banking house, and demand the same, and if payment should not be made, should levy the amount on the money or other goods of the Bank, the money to be retained, and the goods to be sold * * *. If no effects should be found in the banking room, the person having the warrant was authorized to go into every room, vault, &c. and to open every chest, &c. in search of what might satisfy his warrant.

[Pursuant to the statute, and despite the grant of an injunction by the circuit court forbidding such a seizure, an agent of Osborn's broke into the bank and seized approximately $100,000. The Bank returned to the federal courts seeking relief.]

MR. CHIEF JUSTICE MARSHALL delivered the opinion of the Court, and, after stating the case, proceeded as follows:

At the close of the argument, a point was suggested, of such vital importance, as to induce the Court to request that it might be particularly spoken to. That point is, the right of the Bank to sue in the Courts of the United States. It has been argued, and ought to be disposed of, before we proceed to the actual exercise of jurisdiction, by deciding on the rights of the parties.

The appellants contest the jurisdiction of the Court on two grounds:

1st. That the act of Congress has not given it.

2d. That, under the constitution, Congress cannot give it.

1. The first part of the objection depends entirely on the language of the act. The words are, that the Bank shall be "made able and capable in law," "to sue and be sued, plead and be impleaded, answer and be answered, defend and be defended, in all State Courts having competent jurisdiction, and in any Circuit Court of the United States."

Go Online

Consider the statutes to which the Court refers in these two paragraphs.

These words seem to the Court to admit of but one interpretation. They cannot be made plainer by explanation. They give, expressly, the right "to sue and be sued," "in every Circuit Court of the United States," and it would be difficult to substitute other terms which would be more direct and appropriate for the purpose. The argument of the appellants is founded on the opinion of this Court, in *The Bank of the United States v. Deveaux*. In that case it was decided, that the former Bank of the United States was not enabled, by the act which incorporated it, to sue in the federal Courts. The words of the 3d section of that act are, that the Bank may "sue and be sued," & c. "in Courts of record, or any other place whatsoever." The Court was of opinion, that these general words, which are usual in all acts of incorporation, gave only a general capacity to sue, not a particular privilege to sue in the Courts of the United States; and this opinion was strengthened by the circumstance that the 9th rule of the 7th section of the same act, subjects the directors, in case of excess in contracting debt, to be sued in their private capacity, "in any Court of record of the United States, or either of them." The express grant of jurisdiction to the federal Courts, in this case, was considered as having some influence on the construction of the general words of the 3d section, which does not mention those Courts. Whether this decision be right or wrong, it amounts only to a declaration, that a general capacity in the Bank to sue, without mentioning the Courts of the

Union, may not give a right to sue in those Courts. To infer from this, that words expressly conferring a right to sue in those Courts, do not give the right, is surely a conclusion which the premises do not warrant.

The act of incorporation, then, confers jurisdiction on the Circuit Courts of the United States, if Congress can confer it.

2. We will now consider the constitutionality of the clause in the act of incorporation, which authorizes the Bank to sue in the federal Courts.

In support of this clause, it is said, that the legislative, executive, and judicial powers, of every well constructed government, are co-extensive with each other; that is, they are potentially co-extensive. The executive department may constitutionally execute every law which the Legislature may constitutionally make, and the judicial department may receive from the Legislature the power of construing every such law. All governments which are not extremely defective in their organization, must possess, within themselves, the means of expounding, as well as enforcing, their own laws. If we examine the constitution of the United States, we find that its framers kept this great political principle in view. The 2d article vests the whole executive power in the President; and the 3d article declares, "that the judicial power shall extend to all cases in law and equity arising under this constitution, the laws of the United States, and treaties made, or which shall be made, under their authority."

This clause enables the judicial department to receive jurisdiction to the full extent of the constitution, laws, and treaties of the United States, when any question respecting them shall assume such a form that the judicial power is capable of acting on it. That power is capable of acting only when the subject is submitted to it by a party who asserts his rights in the form prescribed by law. It then becomes a case, and the constitution declares, that the judicial power shall extend to all cases arising under the constitution, laws, and treaties of the United States.

Make the Connection

To what concepts does the Chief Justice refer here? You probably studied them in your Constitutional Law course.

The suit of *The Bank of the United States v. Osborn* and others, is a case, and the question is, whether it arises under a law of the United States?

The appellants contend, that it does not, because several questions may arise in it, which depend on the general principles of the law, not on any act of Congress.

If this were sufficient to withdraw a case from the jurisdiction of the federal Courts, almost every case, although involving the construction of a law, would be withdrawn; and a clause in the constitution, relating to a subject of vital importance to the government, and expressed in the most comprehensive terms, would be construed to mean almost nothing. There is scarcely any case, every part of which depends on the constitution, laws, or treaties of the United States. The questions, whether the fact alleged as the foundation of the action, be real or fictitious; whether the conduct of the plaintiff has been such as to entitle him to maintain his action; whether his right is barred; whether he has received satisfaction, or has in any manner released his claims, are questions, some or all of which may occur in almost every case; and if their existence be sufficient to arrest the jurisdiction of the Court, words which seem intended to be as extensive as the constitution, laws, and treaties of the Union, which seem designed to give the Courts of the government the construction of all its acts, so far as they affect the rights of individuals, would be reduced to almost nothing.

In those cases in which original jurisdiction is given to the Supreme Court, the judicial power of the United States cannot be exercised in its appellate form. In every other case, the power is to be exercised in its original or appellate form, or both, as the wisdom of Congress may direct. With the exception of these cases, in which original jurisdiction is given to this Court, there is none to which the judicial power extends, from which the original jurisdiction of the inferior Courts is excluded by the constitution. Original jurisdiction, so far as the constitution gives a rule, is co-extensive with the judicial power. We find, in the constitution, no prohibition to its exercise, in every case in which the judicial power can be exercised. It would be a very bold construction to say, that this power could be applied in its appellate form only, to the most important class of cases to which it is applicable.

The constitution establishes the Supreme Court, and defines its jurisdiction. It enumerates cases in which its jurisdiction is original and exclusive; and then defines that which is appellate, but does not insinuate, that in any such case, the power cannot be exercised in its original form by Courts of original jurisdiction. It is not insinuated, that the judicial power, in cases depending on the character of the **cause**, cannot be exercised in the first instance, in the Courts of the Union, but must first be exercised in the tribunals of the State; tribunals over which the government of the Union has no adequate control, and which may be closed to any claim asserted under a law of the United States.

Food for Thought

Which of the definitions of "cause" do you think Chief Justice Marshall intends here? Why does it make a difference? Keep the possibilities in mind as you read the next several paragraphs.

We perceive, then, no ground on which the proposition can be maintained, that Congress is incapable of giving the Circuit Courts original jurisdiction, in any case to which the appellate jurisdiction extends.

We ask, then, if it can be sufficient to exclude this jurisdiction, that the case involves questions depending on general principles? A cause may depend on several questions of fact and law. Some of these may depend on the construction of a law of the United States; others on principles unconnected with that law. If it be a sufficient foundation for jurisdiction, that the title or right set up by the party, may be defeated by one construction of the constitution or law of the United States, and sustained by the opposite construction, provided the facts necessary to support the action be made out, then all the other questions must be decided as incidental to this, which gives that jurisdiction.

Those other questions cannot arrest the proceedings. Under this construction, the judicial power of the Union extends effectively and beneficially to that most important class of cases, which depend on the character of the cause. On the opposite construction, the judicial power never can be extended to a whole case, as expressed by the constitution, but to those parts of cases only which present the particular question involving the construction of the constitution or the law. We say it never can be extended to the whole case, because, if the circumstance that other points are involved in it, shall disable Congress from authorizing the Courts of the Union to take jurisdiction of the original cause, it equally disables Congress from authorizing those Courts to take jurisdiction of the whole cause, on an appeal, and thus will be restricted to a single question in that cause; and words obviously intended to secure to those who claim rights under the constitution, laws, or treaties of the United States, a trial in the federal Courts, will be restricted to the insecure remedy of an appeal upon an insulated point, after it has received that shape which may be given to it by another tribunal, into which he is forced against his will.

> **Make the Connection**
>
> Does this formulation sound familiar to you? Think back to Civil Procedure and the development of the *Erie* doctrine.

We think, then, that when a question to which the judicial power of the Union is extended by the constitution, forms an ingredient of the original cause, it is in the power of Congress to give the Circuit Courts jurisdiction of that cause, although other questions of fact or of law may be involved in it.

> **Make the Connection**
>
> Does this formulation sound familiar to you? In light of the discussion three paragraphs hence, what do you think the Court means by "the original cause"?

bank created by fed law

The case of the Bank is, we think, a very strong case of this description. The charter of incorporation not only creates it, but gives it every faculty which it possesses. The power to acquire rights of any description, to transact business of any description, to make contracts of any description, to sue on those contracts, is given and measured by its charter, and that charter is a law of the United States. This being can acquire no right, make no contract, bring no suit, which is not authorized by a law of the United States. It is not only itself the mere creature of a law, but all its actions and all its rights are dependent on the same law. Can a being, thus constituted, have a case which does not arise literally, as well as substantially, under the law?

Take the case of a contract, which is put as the strongest against the Bank.

When a Bank sues, the first question which presents itself, and which lies at the foundation of the cause, is, has this legal entity a right to sue? Has it a right to come, not into this Court particularly, but into any Court? This depends on a law of the United States. The next question is, has this being a right to make this particular contract? If this question be decided in the negative, the cause is determined against the plaintiff; and this question, too, depends entirely on a law of the United States. These are important questions, and they exist in every possible case. The right to sue, if decided once, is decided for ever; but the power of Congress was exercised antecedently to the first decision on that right, and if it was constitutional then, it cannot cease to be so, because the particular question is decided. It may be revived at the will of the party, and most probably would be renewed, were the tribunal to be changed. But the question respecting the right to make a particular contract, or to acquire a particular property, or to sue on account of a particular injury, belongs to every particular case, and may be renewed in every case. The question forms an original ingredient in every cause. Whether it be in fact relied on or not, in the defence, it is still a part of the cause, and may be relied on. The right of the plaintiff to sue, cannot depend on the defence which the defendant may choose to set up. His right to sue is anterior to that defence, and must depend on the state of things when the action is brought. The questions which the case involves, then, must determine its character, whether those questions be made in the cause or not.

The appellants say, that the case arises on the contract; but the validity of the contract depends on a law of the United States, and the plaintiff is compelled, in every case, to show its validity. The case arises emphatically under the law. The act of Congress is its foundation. The contract could never have been made, but under the authority of that act. The act itself is the first ingredient in the case, is its origin, is that from which every other part arises. That other questions may also arise, as the execution of the contract, or its performance, cannot change the case, or give it any other origin than the charter of incorporation. The action still originates in, and is sustained by, that charter.

The clause giving the Bank a right to sue in the Circuit Courts of the United States, stands on the same principle with the acts authorizing officers of the United States who sue in their own names, to sue in the Courts of the United States. The Postmaster General, for example, cannot sue under that part of the constitution which gives jurisdiction to the federal Courts, in consequence of the character of the party, nor is he authorized to sue by the Judiciary Act. He comes into the Courts of the Union under the authority of an act of Congress, the constitutionality of which can only be sustained by the admission that his suit is a case arising under a law of the United States. If it be said, that it is such a case, because a law of the United States authorizes the contract, and authorizes the suit, the same reasons exist with respect to a suit brought by the Bank. That, too, is such a case; because that suit, too, is itself authorized, and is brought on a contract authorized by a law of the United States. It depends absolutely on [t]hat law, and cannot exist a moment without its authority.

If it be said, that a suit brought by the Bank may depend in fact altogether on questions unconnected with any law of the United States, it is equally true, with respect to suits brought by the Postmaster General. The plea in bar may be payment, if the suit be brought on a bond, or nonassumpsit, if it be brought on an open account, and no other question may arise than what respects the complete discharge of the demand. Yet the constitutionality of the act authorizing the Postmaster General to sue in the Courts of the United States, has never been drawn into question. It is sustained singly by an act of Congress, standing on that construction of the constitution which asserts the right of the Legislature to give original jurisdiction to the Circuit Courts, in cases arising under a law of the United States.

The clause in the patent law, authorizing suits in the Circuit Courts, stands, we think, on the same principle. Such a suit is a case arising under a law of the United States. Yet the defendant may not, at the trial, question the validity of the patent, or make any point which requires the construction of an act of Congress. He may rest his defence exclusively on the fact, that he has not violated the right of the plaintiff. That this fact becomes the sole question made in the cause, cannot oust the jurisdiction of the Court, or establish the position, that the case does not arise under a law of the United States.

* * *

Upon the best consideration we have been able to bestow on this subject, we are of opinion, that the clause in the act of incorporation, enabling the Bank to sue in the Courts of the United States, is consistent with the constitution, and to be obeyed in all Courts.

* * *

Mr. Justice Johnson, dissenting.

The argument in this cause presents three questions: 1. Has Congress granted to the Bank of the United States, an unlimited right of suing in the Courts of the United States? 2. Could Congress constitutionally grant such a right? and 3. Has the power of the Court been legally and constitutionally exercised in this suit?

I have very little doubt that the public mind will be easily reconciled to the decision of the Court here rendered; for, whether necessary or unnecessary originally, a state of things has now grown up, in some of the States, which renders all the protection necessary, that the general government can give to this Bank. The policy of the decision is obvious, that is, if the Bank is to be sustained; and few will bestow upon its legal correctness, the reflection, that it is necessary to test it by the constitution and laws, under which it is rendered.

* * *

[In this section of the opinion, Justice Johnson took issue with the majority on Congress's intent. He argued that Marshall's view would ultimately make everything a federal question case. He thought, to the contrary, that Congress had intended not to create jurisdiction, but only to authorize the Bank to use its corporate name in bringing suit.]

* * *

I will dwell no longer on a point, which is in fact secondary and subordinate; for if Congress can vest this jurisdiction, and the people will it, the act may be amended, and the jurisdiction vested. I next proceed to consider, more distinctly, the constitutional question, on the right to vest the jurisdiction to the extent here contended for.

And here I must observe, that I altogether misunderstood the counsel, who argued the cause for the plaintiff in error, if any of them contended against the jurisdiction, on the ground that the cause involved questions depending on general principles. No one can question, that the Court which has jurisdiction of the principal question, must exercise jurisdiction over every question. Neither did I understand them as denying, that if Congress could confer on the Circuit Courts appellate, they could confer original jurisdiction. The argument went to deny the right to assume jurisdiction on a mere hypothesis. It was one of description, identity, definition; they contended, that until a question involving the construction or administration of the laws of the United States did actually arise, the ***casus fœderis*** was not presented

It's Latin to Me!

A case or event falling within the terms of a contract

on which the constitution authorized the government to take to itself the jurisdiction of the cause. That until such a question actually arose, until such a case was actually presented, ***non constat***, but the cause depended upon general principles, exclusively cognizable in the State Courts; that neither the letter nor the spirit of the constitution sanctioned the assumption of jurisdiction on the part of the United States at any previous stage.

It's Latin to Me!

It is not certain or agreed

And this doctrine has my hearty concurrence in its general application. A very simple case may be stated, to illustrate its bearing on the question of jurisdiction between the two governments. By virtue of treaties with Great Britain, aliens holding lands were exempted from alien disabilities, and made capable of holding, aliening, and transmitting their estates, in common with natives. But why should the claimants of such lands, to all eternity, be vested with the privilege of bringing an original suit in the Courts of the United States? It is true, a question might be made, upon the effect of the treaty, on the rights claimed by or through the alien; but until that question does arise, nay, until a decision against the right takes place, what end has the United States to subserve in claiming jurisdiction of the cause?

* * *

Efforts have been made to fix the precise sense of the constitution, when it vests jurisdiction in the general government, in "cases arising under the laws of the United States." To me, the question appears susceptible of a very simple solution; that all depends upon the identity of the case supposed; according to which idea, a case may be such in its very existence, or it may become such in its progress. An action may "live, move, and have its being," in a law of the United States; such is that given for the violation of a patent-right, and four or five different actions given by this act of incorporation; particularly that against the President and Directors for over-issuing; in all of which cases the plaintiff must count upon the law itself as the ground of his action. And of the other description, would have been an action of trespass, in this case, had remedy been sought for an actual levy of the tax imposed. Such was the case of the former Bank against *Deveaux*, and many others that have occurred in this Court, in which the suit, in its

Food for Thought

Justice Johnson had a high opinion of federal jurisdiction indeed. The quotation is from Paul's speech to the Corinthians in Areopagus, Acts 17:27-28, and "him" is a reference to God. He seems, therefore, to be analogizing federal law to the deity, thus taking the concept of federal supremacy to a new level.

form, was such as occur in ordinary cases, but in which the pleadings or evidence raised the question on the law or constitution of the United States. In this class of cases, the occurrence of a question makes the case, and transfers it, as provided for under the twenty-fifth section of the Judiciary Act, to the jurisdiction of the United States. And this appears to me to present the only sound and practical construction of the constitution on this subject; for no other cases does it regard as necessary to place under the control of the general government. It is only when the case exhibits one or the other of these characteristics, that it is acted upon by the constitution. Where no question is raised, there can be no contrariety of construction; and what else had the constitution to guard against? As to cases of the first description, ***ex necessitate rei***, the Courts of the United States must be susceptible of original jurisdiction; and as to all other cases, I should hold them, also, susceptible of original jurisdiction, if it were practicable, in the nature of things, to make out the definition of the case, so as to bring it under the constitution judicially, upon an original suit. But until the plaintiff can control the defendant in his pleadings, I see no practical mode of determining when the case does occur, otherwise than by permitting the cause to advance until the case for which the constitution provides shall actually arise. If it never occurs, there can be nothing to complain of; and such are the provisions of the twenty-fifth section. The cause might be transferred to the Circuit Court before an adjudication takes place; but I can perceive no earlier stage at which it can possibly be predicated of such a case, that it is one within the constitution; nor any possible necessity for transferring it then, or until the Court has acted upon it to the prejudice of the claims of the United States. It is not, therefore, because Congress may not vest an original jurisdiction, where they can constitutionally vest in the Circuit Courts *appellate* jurisdiction, that I object to this general grant of the right to sue; but, because that the peculiar nature of this jurisdiction is such, as to render it impossible to exercise it in a strictly original form, and because the principle of a possible occurrence of a question as a ground of jurisdiction, and placing the bounds of the constitution, and placing it on a ground which will admit of an *enormous accession,* if not an *unlimited assumption,* of jurisdiction.

Go Online

Justice Johnson's reference is to the statute allowing appeals to the Supreme Court from the courts of the states. Act of Sept. 24, 1789, ch. 20, § 25.

Food for Thought

Why did Justice Johnson think this statute was helpful to his argument about the jurisdiction of the inferior federal courts?

* * *

Notes and Questions

1. How many formulations of a standard did Chief Justice Marshall articulate in *Osborn*? Are they different formulations of the same approach, or are they alternative standards by which to adjudicate jurisdictional questions? If the latter, what problems does that pose for judges in the lower federal courts?

2. In *Osborn*, the Bank asserted that the Supremacy Clause forbade the Ohio tax, citing *M'Culloch v. Maryland*, 17 U.S. (4 Wheat.) 316 (1819). The case thus presented a clear and recently settled federal constitutional issue. Obviously, an authorization to the federal courts to hear cases in which the federal issue was so central would have been well within the bounds of Article III. But Marshall thought Congress had gone further by authorizing jurisdiction whenever the Bank of the United States was a party, even if the substantive issues involved were not federal. Thus, the jurisdictional statute, while constitutional as applied in *Osborn*, seemed to authorize a far broader scope of jurisdiction. Chief Justice Marshall therefore decided to evaluate the outer limits of the statute under constitutional standards.

a) Note that the Court hypothesized suits by or against the Bank that did not involve so central a federal issue, as in Marshall's contract example. What federal issue did Marshall think would arise in that kind of case? Why would such a suit present a more difficult case for federal jurisdiction?

b) Should Congress allow the federal courts to hear cases containing potential federal issues that neither party intends to raise? What policies might be served by allowing jurisdiction in such cases? What policies might be harmed?

3. At what point in a case should the court determine the existence of federal jurisdiction? What did the *Osborn* majority think? What did Justice Johnson think? What do you think, and why?

The Supreme Court and some commentators have suggested that federal jurisdiction must appear at the outset of the litigation—that is, when the complaint is filed. On the other hand, if a court should determine jurisdiction later, what stage is appropriate?

Go Online

See, e.g., James H. Chadbourn & A. Leo Levin, *Original Jurisdiction of Federal Questions*, 90 U.PA.L.REV. 639, 648 (1942); David L. Shapiro, *Jurisdiction and Discretion*, 60 N.Y.U.L.REV. 543, 567 (1985). How will it ever be possible, at the complaint stage, to know whether the defendant will contest a federal issue that the plaintiff identifies? *See* Ernest J. London, *"Federal Question" Jurisdiction—A Snare and a Delusion*, 57 MICH.L.REV. 835, 846-47 (1959).

4. Statutes similar to the one in Osborn continue to torment the Court. In *American National Red Cross v. Solicitor General*, 505 U.S. 247 (1992), the federal charter authorized the Red Cross "to

sue and be sued in courts of law and equity, State or Federal, within the jurisdiction of the United States." The issue, as in *Osborn*, was whether that language conferred subject matter jurisdiction on the federal courts for every action to which the Red Cross is a party. A five-to-four Court held that it did. The majority argued that cases from Deveaux (discussed in *Osborn*) onward "support the rule that a congressional charter's 'sue and be sued' provision may be read to confer federal court jurisdiction if, but only if, it specifically mentions the federal courts." Thus, the majority distinguished *Deveaux* but embraced *Osborn* and cases with similar statutes that followed it.

Justice Scalia, writing for the minority, argued strongly that the "capacity" language of the statute did not grant jurisdiction. He pointed out that the *Deveaux* Court had distinguished two statutory provisions. The first, quoted in *Osborn*, gave the bank capacity to be a litigant in courts of record. The second, not mentioned in *Osborn*, "provided that certain actions against the directors of the Bank 'may * * * be brought * * * in any court of record of the United States * * * .' " Justice Scalia argued that *Deveaux* turned upon the distinction between the language in the two statutory sections, not upon the happenstance of the mention of federal courts in an otherwise capacity-granting statute. He distinguished *Osborn* from *Deveaux* and *Red Cross*:

> By granting the Bank power to sue, not in all courts generally (as in Deveaux), but in *particular* federal courts, this suggested a grant of jurisdiction rather than merely of capacity to sue. And that suggestion was strongly confirmed by the fact that the Bank was empowered to sue in state courts "having competent jurisdiction," but in federal circuit courts *simpliciter*. If the statute had jurisdiction in mind as to the one, it must as to the other as well.

Justice Scalia also took issue with *Osborn's* reading of *Deveaux*:

> In distinguishing Deveaux, Osborn noted, *and apparently misunderstood* as the Court today does, that case's contrast between the "express grant of jurisdiction to the federal Courts" over suits against directors and the "general words" of the "sue and be sued" clause, "which [did] not mention those Courts." All it concluded from that, however, was that Deveaux established that "a general capacity in the Bank to sue, without mentioning the Courts of the Union, may not give a right to sue in those Courts." There does not logically follow from that the rule which the Court announces today: that *any* grant of a general capacity to sue with mention of federal courts will suffice to confer jurisdiction.

(Emphasis added). Justice Souter replied. "The dissent accuses us of repeating what it announces as Chief Justice Marshall's misunderstanding, in *Osborn*, of his own previous opinion in Deveaux. We are honored."

Is the majority's or the dissent's reasoning more persuasive? One's reaction, of course, may turn ultimately upon how persuasively *Osborn* made the case for broad interpretation of the statute. Does it make any difference that Congress has continued to enact similarly-worded statutes and apparently acquiesced in the Court's reading? The majority thought so.

[W]e do not face a clean slate. Beginning with Chief Justice Marshall's opinion [in Deveaux] in 1809, we have had several occasions to consider whether the "sue and be sued" provision of a particular federal corporate charter conferred original federal jurisdiction over cases to which that corporation was a party, and our readings of those provisions not only represented our best efforts at divining congressional intent retrospectively, but have also placed Congress on prospective notice of the language necessary and sufficient to confer jurisdiction * * * .

5. Note that *Osborn* contains the earliest clearly identifiable reference to what later became known as pendent and ancillary (now supplemental) jurisdiction, as Chief Justice Marshall espoused the principle that a court properly exercising jurisdiction may decide all questions presented, whether or not each has a federal component. The polar position is that federal courts should entertain only cases presenting federal questions exclusively. Is there a possible middle position?

6. Whether one agrees with it or not, the Court's interpretation of Article III, § 2's arising-under language is quite generous. Recall, however, that with the exception of the original jurisdiction of the Supreme Court, Article III, § 2's language is not self-executing; a statute must confer jurisdiction on the district and circuit courts. *See supra* at 278. We now move from consideration of Article III, § 2's language to Congress's statutory grants of jurisdiction to the lower courts. Keep in mind, though, that Article III lurks in the background, rendering unconstitutional any statute that exceeds the bounds *Osborn* sketched out.

Textile Workers Union v. Lincoln Mills

Supreme Court of the United States, 1957.
353 U.S. 448.

[The Court considered the relationship between Congress's powers under Article I of the Constitution and its power to provide federal question jurisdiction under Article III, particularly whether Congress may allow federal question jurisdiction in areas in which it *could* legislate under Article I, or whether, by contrast, it is restricted to areas in which it has legislated. The Labor Management Relations Act of 1947 (the Taft-Hartley Act) granted jurisdiction over actions concerning violations of labor-employer contracts. Congress had not, however, enacted substantive law concerning such contracts, which continued to be governed by state law. Clearly, however, Congress could have enacted such substantive law, exercising its power under the Commerce Clause.

The majority construed the jurisdictional grant to be a command to the federal courts to fashion a body of federal common law dealing with labor-management contractual relations. Then, finding that the contractual cause of action was based upon federal law, the majority had no trouble concluding that federal question jurisdiction existed. Justice Frankfurter dissented, arguing that Congress did not intend the federal courts to create federal common law in this area. That conclusion led him to explore the jurisdictional question at length.]

Food for Thought

Such a command raises other significant questions concerning the existence and scope of federal common law. *See* Chapter 5. For example, assuming that Congress did intend such a command, do not substantial separation-of-powers questions arise from delegation of comprehensive legislative authority? Is it appropriate for courts to act as legislatures merely because Congress has instructed them to do so?

The second ground of my dissent from the Court's action is more fundamental. Since I do not agree with the Court's conclusion that federal substantive law is to govern in actions under § 301, I am forced to consider * * * the constitutionality of a grant of jurisdiction to federal courts over contracts that came into being entirely by virtue of state substantive law, a jurisdiction not based on diversity of citizenship, yet one in which a federal court would, as in diversity cases, act in effect merely as another court of the State in which it sits. The scope of allowable federal judicial power that this grant must satisfy is constitutionally described as "Cases, in Law and Equity, arising under this Constitution, the Laws of the United States, and Treaties made, or which shall be made, under their Authority." While interpretive decisions are legion under general statutory grants of jurisdiction strikingly similar to this constitutional wording, it is generally recognized that the full constitutional power has not been exhausted by these statutes.

Almost without exception, decisions under the general statutory grants have tested jurisdiction in terms of the presence, as an integral part of plaintiff's cause of action, of an issue calling for interpretation or application of federal law. Although it has sometimes been suggested that the "cause of action" must derive from federal law, it has been found sufficient that some aspect of federal law is essential to plaintiff's success. The litigation-provoking problem has been the degree to which federal law must be in the forefront of the case and not collateral, peripheral or remote.

In a few exceptional cases, arising under special jurisdictional grants, the criteria by which the prominence of the federal question is measured against constitutional requirements have been found satisfied under circumstances suggesting a variant theory of the nature of these requirements. The first, and the leading case in the field, is *Osborn v. Bank of United States*. There, Chief Justice Marshall sustained federal jurisdiction in a situation—hypothetical in the case before him but presented by the companion case of *Bank of United States v. Planters' Bank*—involving suit by a federally incorporated bank upon a contract. Despite the assumption that the cause of action and the interpretation of the contract would be governed by state law, the case was found to "arise under the laws of the United States" because the propriety and scope of a federally granted authority to enter into contracts and to litigate might well be challenged. This reasoning was subsequently applied to sustain jurisdiction in actions against federally chartered railroad corporations.

> **FYI**
>
> The *Pacific Railroad Removal Cases*, 115 U.S. 1 (1885), reaffirmed *Osborn*'s ruling that any case involving a federally chartered corporation as a party arises under federal law. The Court went further than *Osborn*, however, because it applied the ruling to the arising-under language of the then-new federal question jurisdiction statute from which 28 U.S.C. § 1331 descended. *Osborn* and the *Pacific Railroad* cases are distinguishable, however. The United States created the Second National Bank to carry out federal monetary policy, as an instrument of the federal government. The railroads, on the other hand, although the federal government chartered them, were private enterprises. That difference may justify a broader view of jurisdiction in *Osborn* than in *Pacific Railroad*.

The traditional interpretation of this series of cases is that federal jurisdiction under the "arising" clause of the Constitution, though limited to cases involving potential federal questions, has such flexibility that Congress may confer it whenever there exists in the background some federal proposition that might be challenged, despite the remoteness of the likelihood of actual presentation of such a federal question.[4]

The views expressed in *Osborn* and the *Pacific Railroad Removal Cases* were severely restricted in construing general grants of jurisdiction. But the Court later sustained this jurisdictional section of the Bankruptcy Act of 1898:

> The United States district courts shall have jurisdiction of all controversies at law and in equity, as distinguished from proceedings in bankruptcy, between trustees as such and adverse claimants concerning the property acquired or claimed by the trustees, in the same manner and to the same extent only as though bankruptcy proceedings had not been instituted and such controversies had been between the bankrupts and such adverse claimants.

Under this provision the trustee could pursue in a federal court a private cause of action arising under and wholly governed by state law. To be sure, the cases did not discuss the basis of jurisdiction. It has been suggested that they merely

---

4 *Osborn* might possibly be limited on the ground that a federal instrumentality, the Bank of the United States, was involved, but such an explanation could not suffice to narrow the holding in the *Pacific Railroad Removal Cases*.

represent an extension of the approach of the *Osborn* case; the trustee's right to sue might be challenged on obviously federal grounds—absence of bankruptcy or irregularity of the trustee's appointment or of the bankruptcy proceedings. So viewed, this type of litigation implicates a potential federal question.

Apparently relying on the extent to which the bankruptcy cases involve only remotely a federal question, Mr. Justice Jackson concluded in *Tidewater Transfer Co.*, that Congress may confer jurisdiction on the District Courts as incidental to its powers under Article I. No attempt was made to reconcile this view with the restrictions of Article III; a majority of the Court recognized that Article III defined the bounds of valid jurisdictional legislation and rejected the notion that jurisdictional grants can go outside these limits.

With this background, many theories have been proposed to sustain the constitutional validity of § 301. Judge Wyzanski suggested, among other possibilities, that § 301 might be read as containing a direction that controversies affecting interstate commerce should be governed by federal law incorporating state law by reference, and that such controversies would then arise under a valid federal law as required by Article III. Whatever may be said of the assumption regarding the validity of federal jurisdiction under an affirmative declaration by Congress that state law should be applied as federal law by federal courts to contract disputes affecting commerce, we cannot argumentatively legislate for Congress when Congress has failed to legislate. To do so disrespects legislative responsibility and disregards judicial limitations.

FYI

Judge Charles Wyzanski of the federal district court in Massachusetts was an exceptionally distinguished judge to whom the Supreme Court often referred. He served from 1941 to 1986.

Another theory, relying on *Osborn* and the bankruptcy cases, has been proposed which would achieve results similar to those attainable under Mr. Justice Jackson's view, but which purports to respect the "arising" clause of Article III. Called "protective jurisdiction," the suggestion is that in any case for which Congress has the constitutional power to prescribe federal rules of decision and thus confer "true" federal question jurisdiction, it may, without so doing, enact a jurisdictional statute, which will provide a federal forum for the application of state statute and decisional law. Analysis of the "protective jurisdiction" theory might also be attempted in terms of the language of Article III—construing "laws" to include jurisdictional statutes where Congress could have legislated substantively in a field. This is but another way of saying that because Congress could have legislated substantively and thereby could give rise to litigation under a statute of the United States, it can provide a federal forum for state-created rights although it chose not to adopt state law as federal law or to originate federal rights.

Surely the truly technical restrictions of Article III are not met or respected by a beguiling phrase that the greater power here must necessarily include the lesser. In the compromise of federal and state interests leading to distribution of jealously guarded judicial power in a federal system, it is obvious that very different considerations apply to cases involving questions of federal law and those turning solely on state law. It may be that the ambiguity of the phrase "arising under the laws of the United States" leaves room for more than traditional theory could accommodate. But, under the theory of "protective jurisdiction," the "arising under" jurisdiction of the federal courts would be vastly extended. For example, every contract or tort arising out of a contract affecting commerce might be a potential cause of action in the federal courts, even though only state law was involved in the decision of the case. At least in Osborn and the bankruptcy cases, a substantive federal law was present somewhere in the background. But this theory rests on the supposition that Congress could enact substantive federal law to govern the particular case. It was not held in those cases, nor is it clear, that federal law could be held to govern the transactions of all persons who subsequently become bankrupt, or of all suits of a Bank of the United States.

"Protective jurisdiction," once the label is discarded, cannot be justified under any view of the allowable scope to be given to Article III. "Protective jurisdiction" is a misused label for the statute we are here considering. That rubric is properly descriptive of safeguarding some of the indisputable, staple business of the federal courts. It is a radiation of an existing jurisdiction. "Protective jurisdiction" cannot generate an independent source for adjudication outside of the Article III sanctions and what Congress has defined. The theory must have as its sole justification a belief in the inadequacy of state tribunals in determining state law. The Constitution reflects such a belief in the specific situation within which the Diversity Clause was confined. The intention to remedy such supposed defects was exhausted in this provision of Article III.[5] That this "protective" theory was not adopted by Chief Justice Marshall at a time when conditions might have presented more substantial justification strongly suggests its lack of constitutional merit. Moreover, Congress in its consideration of § 301 nowhere suggested dissatisfaction with the ability of state courts to administer state law properly. Its concern was to provide access to the federal courts for easier enforcement of state-created rights.

5 To be sure, the Court upheld the removal statute for suits or prosecutions commenced in a state court against federal revenue officers on account of any act committed under color of office. The Court, however, construed the action of Congress in defining the powers of revenue agents as giving them a substantive defense against prosecution under state law for commission of acts "warranted by the Federal authority they possess." That put federal law in the forefront as a defense. In any event, the fact that officers of the Federal Government were parties may be considered sufficient to afford access to the federal forum.

Another theory also relies on *Osborn* and the bankruptcy cases as an implicit recognition of the propriety of the exercise of some sort of "protective jurisdiction" by the federal courts. Professor Mishkin tends to view the assertion of such a jurisdiction, in the absence of any exercise of substantive powers, as irreconcilable with the "arising" clause since the case would then arise only under the jurisdictional statute itself, and he is reluctant to find a constitutional basis for the grant of power outside Article III. Professor Mishkin also notes that the only purpose of such a statute would be to insure impartiality to some litigant, an objection inconsistent with Article III's recognition of "protective jurisdiction" only in the specified situation of diverse citizenship. But where Congress has "an articulated and active federal policy regulating a field, the 'arising under' clause of Article III apparently permits the conferring of jurisdiction on the national courts of all cases in the area—including those substantively governed by state law." In such cases, the protection being offered is not to the suitor, as in diversity cases, but to the "congressional legislative program." Thus he supports § 301: "even though the rules governing collective bargaining agreements continue to be state-fashioned, nonetheless the mode of their application and enforcement may play a very substantial part in the labor-management relations of interstate industry and commerce—an area in which the national government has labored long and hard."

> **FYI**
>
> Professor Paul Mishkin, who taught at the University of Pennsylvania Law School for twenty-two years before moving on to Berkeley for the next three decades, was one of the country's leading scholars on the role of the federal courts.

Insofar as state law governs the case, Professor Mishkin's theory is quite similar to that advanced by Professors Hart and Wechsler and followed by the Court of Appeals for the First Circuit: The substantive power of Congress, although not exercised to govern the particular "case," gives "arising under" jurisdiction to the federal courts despite governing state law. The second "protective jurisdiction" theory has the dubious advantage of limiting incursions on state judicial power to situations in which the State's feelings may have been tempered by early substantive federal invasions.

Professor Mishkin's theory of "protective jurisdiction" may find more constitutional justification if there is not merely an "articulated and active" congressional policy regulating the labor field but also federal rights existing in the interstices of actions under § 301. Therefore, before resting on an interpretation of § 301 that would compel a declaration of unconstitutionality, we must * * * defer to the strong presumption—even as to such technical matters as federal jurisdiction—that Congress legislated in accordance with the Constitution.

* * *

* * * " 'But avoidance of a difficulty will not be pressed to the point of disingenuous evasion.' * * * 'Here the intention of the Congress is revealed too distinctly to permit us to ignore it because of mere misgivings as to power.' "

* * *

There is a point, however, at which the search may be ended with less misgiving regarding the propriety of judicial infusion of substantive provisions into § 301. The contribution of federal law might consist in postulating the right of a union, despite its amorphous status as an unincorporated association, to enter into binding collective-bargaining contracts with an employer. The federal courts might also give sanction to this right by refusing to comply with any state law that does not admit that collective bargaining may result in an enforceable contract. It is hard to see what serious federal-state conflicts could arise under this view. At most, a state court might dismiss the action, while a federal court would entertain it. Moreover, such a function of federal law is closely related to the removal of the procedural barriers to suit. Section 301 would be futile if the union's status as a contracting party were not recognized. The statement in § 301(b) that the acts of the agents of the union are to be regarded as binding upon the union may be used in support of this conclusion. This provision, not confined in its application to suits in the District Court under § 301(a), was primarily directed to responsibility of the union for its agents' actions in authorizing strikes or committing torts. It can be construed, however, as applicable to the formation of a contract. So applied, it would imply that a union must be regarded as contractually bound by the acts of its agents, which in turn presupposes that the union is capable of contract relations.

Of course, the possibility of a State's law being counter to such a limited federal proposition is hypothetical, and to base an assertion of federal law on such a possibility, one never considered by Congress, is an artifice. And were a State ever to adopt a contrary attitude, its reasons for so doing might be such that Congress would not be willing to disregard them. But these difficulties are inherent in any attempt to expand § 301 substantively to meet constitutional requirements.

Even if this limited federal "right" were read into § 301, a serious constitutional question would still be present. It does elevate the situation to one closely analogous to that presented in *Osborn*.[6] Section 301 would, under this view, imply

6 Enunciation of such a requirement could in fact bring federal law somewhat further to the forefront than was true of *Osborn*, the *Pacific Railroad Removal Cases*, or the bankruptcy cases in the few cases where an assertion could be made that state law did not sufficiently recognize collective agreements as contracts. But there appears to be no State that today possesses such a rule. Most and probably all cases arising under § 301—certainly the present ones—would never present such a problem.

that a union is to be viewed as a juristic entity for purposes of acquiring contract rights under a collective-bargaining agreement, and that it has the right to enter into such a contract and to sue upon it. This was all that was immediately and expressly involved in the *Osborn* case, although the historical setting was vastly different and the juristic entity in that case was completely the creature of federal law, one engaged in carrying out essential governmental functions. Most of these special considerations had disappeared, however, at the time and in the circumstances of the decision of the *Pacific Railroad Removal Cases*. There is force in the view that regards the latter as a "sport" and finds that the Court has so viewed it. * * * The question is whether we should now so consider it and refuse to apply its holding to the present situation.

> **What's That?**
>
> Justice Frankfurter uses "sport" in the sense of "an object of derision; laughingstock," in other words, something not to be taken seriously.

I believe that we should not extend the precedents of *Osborn* and the *Pacific Railroad Removal Cases* to this case even though there be some elements of analytical similarity. *Osborn*, the foundation for the *Removal Cases*, appears to have been based on premises that today * * * are subject to criticism. The basic premise was that every case in which a federal question might arise must be capable of being commenced in the federal courts, and when so commenced it might, because jurisdiction must be judged at the outset, be concluded there despite the fact that the federal question was never raised. Marshall's holding was undoubtedly influenced by his fear that the bank might suffer hostile treatment in the state courts that could not be remedied by an appeal on an isolated federal question. There is nothing in Article III that affirmatively supports the view that original jurisdiction over cases involving federal questions must extend to every case in which there is the potentiality of appellate jurisdiction. We also have become familiar with removal procedures that could be adapted to alleviate any remaining fears by providing for removal to a federal court whenever a federal question was raised. In view of these developments, we would not be justified in perpetuating a principle that permits assertion of original federal jurisdiction on the remote possibility of presentation of a federal question. Indeed, Congress, by largely withdrawing the jurisdiction that the *Pacific Railroad Removal Cases* recognized, and this Court, by refusing to perpetuate it under general grants of jurisdiction, have already done much to recognize the changed atmosphere.

Analysis of the bankruptcy power also reveals a superficial analogy to § 301. The trustee enforces a cause of action acquired under state law by the bankrupt. Federal law merely provides for the appointment of the trustee, vests the cause of action in him, and confers jurisdiction on the federal courts. Section 301 similarly takes the rights and liabilities which under state law are vested distributively in the individual members of a union and vests them in the union for purposes of actions in federal courts, wherein the unions are authorized to sue and be sued as an entity. While the authority of the trustee depends on the existence of a bankrupt and on the propriety of the proceedings leading to the trustee's appointment, both of which depend on federal law, there are similar federal propositions that may be essential to an action under § 301. Thus, the validity of the contract may in any case be challenged on the ground that the labor organization negotiating it was not the representative of the employees concerned, a question that has been held to be federal, or on the ground that subsequent change in the representative status of the union has affected the continued validity of the agreement. Perhaps also the qualifications imposed on a union's right to utilize the facilities of the National Labor Relations Board * * * might be read as restrictions on the right of the union to sue under § 301, again providing a federal basis for challenge to the union's authority. Consequently, were the bankruptcy cases to be viewed as dependent solely on the background existence of federal questions, there would be little analytical basis for distinguishing actions under § 301. But the bankruptcy decisions may be justified by the scope of the bankruptcy power, which may be deemed to sweep within its scope interests analytically outside the "federal question" category, but sufficiently related to the main purpose of bankruptcy to call for comprehensive treatment. Also, although a particular suit may be brought by a trustee in a district other than the one in which the principal proceedings are pending, if all the suits by the trustee, even though in many federal courts, are regarded as one litigation for the collection and apportionment of the bankrupt's property, a particular suit by the trustee, under state law, to recover a specific piece of property might be analogized to the ancillary or pendent jurisdiction cases in which, in the disposition of a cause of action, federal courts may pass on state grounds for recovery that are joined to federal grounds.

If there is in the phrase "arising under the laws of the United States" leeway for expansion of our concepts of jurisdiction, the history of Article III suggests that the area is not great and that it will require the presence of some substantial federal interest, one of greater weight and dignity than questionable doubt concerning the effectiveness of state procedure. The bankruptcy cases might possibly be viewed as such an expansion. But even so, not merely convenient judicial administration but the whole purpose of the congressional legislative program—conservation and equitable distribution of the bankrupt's estate in carrying out the constitutional power over bankruptcy—required the availability of federal jurisdiction to avoid expense and delay. Nothing pertaining to § 301 suggests vesting the federal courts with sweeping power under the Commerce Clause comparable to that vested in the federal courts under the bankruptcy power.

In the wise distribution of governmental powers, this Court cannot do what a President sometimes does in returning a bill to Congress. We cannot return this provision to Congress and respectfully request that body to face the responsibility placed upon it by the Constitution to define the jurisdiction of the lower courts with some particularity and not to leave these courts at large. Confronted as I am, I regretfully have no choice. For all the reasons elaborated in this dissent, even reading into § 301 the limited federal rights consistent with the purposes of that section, I am impelled to the view that it is unconstitutional in cases such as the present ones where it provides the sole basis for exercise of jurisdiction by the federal courts.

Notes and Questions

1. Can Congress grant federal jurisdiction in cases involving no existing federal substantive law but touching upon areas in which Congress could legislate? What interests would be served if that were allowed? What interests might be compromised?

2. A related issue surfaced in a slightly different way in *National Mutual Insurance Co. v. Tidewater Transfer Co.*, 337 U.S. 582 (1949). Congress conferred jurisdiction on the district courts for non-federal suits between citizens of the District of Columbia and citizens of a state. Well-established precedent held that the District of Columbia was not a state for purposes of Article III diversity jurisdiction, and the Court showed no disposition to overturn those cases. Nonetheless, a splintered Court upheld the grant. Justice Jackson, joined by two other Justices, took an expansive view of Congress's ability to create jurisdiction notwithstanding the apparent limits of Article III. Noting that Congress has plenary authority under Article I to govern the District of Columbia, he continued:

> However, it is contended that Congress may not combine this function, under Art. I, with those under Art. III, in district courts of the United States. One is that no jurisdiction other than that specified in Art. III can be imposed on courts that exercise the judicial power of the United States thereunder. The other is that Art. I powers over the District of Columbia must be exercised solely within that geographic area.
>
> * * * [A]lthough District of Columbia courts are Art. III courts, they can also exercise judicial power conferred by Congress pursuant to Art. I. The fact that District of Columbia courts, as local courts, can also be given administrative or legislative functions which other Art. III courts cannot exercise, does but emphasize the fact that, although the latter are limited to the exercise of judicial power, it may constitutionally be received from either Art. III or Art. I, and that congressional power over the District, flowing from Art. I, is plenary in every respect.

* * *

> We concluded that where Congress in the exercise of its powers under Art. I finds it necessary to provide those on whom its power is exerted with access to some kind of court or tribunal for determination of controversies that are within the traditional concept of the justiciable, it may open the regular federal courts to them regardless of lack of diversity of citizenship. The basis of the holdings we have discussed is that, when Congress deems that for such purposes it owes a forum to claimants and trustees, it may execute its power in this manner. The Congress, with equal justification, apparently considers that it also owes such a forum to the residents of the District of Columbia in execution of its power and duty under the same Article. We do not see how the one could be sustained and the other denied.

Does Justice Jackson's position suggest that the jurisdiction of Article III courts is actually limited not by that Article but by Article I? Under this theory, could Congress open the Article III courts to private disputes between parties regulated by statutes under the Commerce Clause, even if their dispute involved neither interpretation, application nor constitutionality of those statutes? If so, is the potential jurisdictional reach of Article III courts effectively illimitable? If not, how can such a case be distinguished from *Tidewater Transfer* ?

There's No Reason for It; It's Just Our Policy: Why the Well-Pleaded Complaint Rule Sabotages the Purposes of Federal Question Jurisdiction

Donald L. Doernberg
38 HASTINGS L.J. 597, 601-07 (1987)[a]

The constitutional language creating federal question jurisdiction has not changed since 1787. Congress first permitted the exercise of this jurisdiction in the famous "Midnight Judges Act" of 1801, which substantially tracked the constitutional language: "[T]he said circuit courts respectively shall have cognizance of * * * all cases in law or equity, arising under the constitution and laws of the United States, and treaties made, or which shall be made, under their authority." The Act did not, however, survive the Federalists' departure from power for long; it was repealed barely one year later by the Jeffersonian Congress.

It was not until 1875 that Congress again granted federal question jurisdiction to the inferior federal courts. The 1875 Act, still the foundation for such jurisdiction, provided:

> That the circuit courts of the United States shall have original cognizance, concurrent with the courts of the several States, of all suits of a civil nature at

> common law or in equity, where the matter in dispute exceeds, exclusive of costs, the sum or value of five hundred dollars, and arising under the Constitution or laws of the United States, or treaties made, or which shall be made, under their authority * * * .

This statute, too, substantially tracked the constitutional language, except that the 1875 statute specified that federal question jurisdiction shall be concurrent with the states and used "or" rather than "and" as a conjunction between "Constitution," "laws," and "treaties."

The 1875 Act also provided for removal jurisdiction in federal question cases for the first time:

> [A]ny suit of a civil nature, at law or in equity, now pending or hereafter brought in any State court where the matter in dispute exceeds, exclusive of costs, the sum or value of five hundred dollars, and arising under the Constitution or laws of the United States, or treaties made, or which shall be made, under their authority, * * * either party may remove said suit into the circuit court of the United States for the proper district.

The meaning of the provision is reasonably clear apart from what one may think of its grammar and syntax: arising-under cases were made removable at the instance of either party. One may wonder why a plaintiff might wish to remove a federal question case, since he might well have brought it in federal court initially. The only logical explanation is that plaintiffs were given removal power in the event that the answer or reply raised a federal question. No other explanation is plausible. The significance of this provision for the development of the *Mottley* rule should not be underestimated.

The 1875 statute contained one other paragraph destined to become central to the century-long debate about the meaning of "arising under." Section 5 provided:

> That if, in any suit commenced in a circuit court or removed from a State court to a circuit court of the United States, it shall appear to the satisfaction of said circuit court, at any time after such suit has been brought or removed thereto, that such suit does not really and substantially involve a dispute or controversy properly within the jurisdiction of said circuit court, * * * the said circuit court shall proceed no further therein, but shall dismiss the suit or remand it to the court from which it was removed as justice may require.

This language might suggest several meanings, and it has been the subject of some scholarly debate. It might suggest that a case arising under federal law within the meaning of the Constitution and the first section of the 1875 Act could nonetheless be considered too insubstantial to warrant the expenditure of federal judicial energy.[22] On the other hand, as Professor Forrester has contended, it might have been intended only to permit the court to review its subject matter jurisdiction ***sua sponte***, eliminating the need for a party to enter a plea in abatement. Finally, it may represent Congress' rejection, for statutory purposes, of Chief Justice Marshall's argument in *Osborn v. Bank of the United States* that an underlying federal issue, even if not disputed by the parties, was sufficient to confer jurisdiction under the constitutional provision. In any case, the 1875 Act used language that later became central to the morass surrounding the *Mottley* rule.

There is almost no legislative history concerning the intended scope of "arising under" in the 1875 Act, but what little exists is unambiguous. Senator Carpenter, recalling Justice Story's argument that Congress was constitutionally required to vest the full scope of federal judicial power in the inferior federal courts, declared, "This bill does [vest such power] * * * . This bill gives precisely the power which the Constitution confers—nothing more, nothing less."[26] The only contemporaneous commentator adopted Senator Carpenter's view, explaining Congress' action in light of the Civil War and the continuing reconstruction effort. Many later commentators have expressed a similar understanding.

> **Take Note!**
>
> Recall that the end of the Civil War opened the door to a vast shift of power from the states to the federal government, as Congress attempted to manage the confederacy states' re-entry to full participation in the nation's affairs. At the same time, federal legislation began to expand dramatically, largely under the Commerce Clause. Given that dual trend, it is not surprising that Congress would have sought to bring more cases with national implications into the federal courts.

Shortly after 1875, in cases construing the Act, the Court appeared to adopt this broad view. Its repeated citations of cases construing constitutional "arising under" jurisdiction suggests that the Court believed that Congress intended the constitutional language to define the scope of the statute. In 1893, referring to the statute as amended in 1887 and 1888, a unanimous Court declared:

> The intention of Congress is manifest, at least as to cases of which the courts of the several States have concurrent jurisdiction, and which involve a certain amount or value, to vest in the Circuit Courts of the United States full and effectual jurisdiction, as contemplated by the Constitution, over each of the classes of controversies above mentioned * * * .

22 * * * In Merrell Dow Pharmaceuticals v. Thompson, 478 U.S. 804 (1986), the Court seems also to have adopted this view of statutory arising-under jurisdiction. * * *

26 2 CONG.REC. 4986-87 (1874) (statement of Sen. Carpenter). Senator Carpenter (R.Wis.) was president *pro tempore* of the Senate and apparently the only legislator to comment on the 1875 Act on the Senate floor. The fact that Justice Story's interpretation of Congress' obligation was never widely adopted does nothing to undercut the scope or clarity of Senator Carpenter's remarks.

Notwithstanding this history, however, it is clear that the statutory provision has not generally been accorded the same breadth as the constitutional grant.

In 1887, Congress amended the 1875 Act in several respects. It made no change in the original jurisdiction of the trial courts except to increase the jurisdictional amount from $500 to $2000. The statutory language governing removal, however, was radically altered:

> [A]ny suit of a civil nature, at law or equity, arising under the Constitution or laws of the United States, or treaties made, or which shall be made, under their authority, of which the circuit courts of the United States are given original jurisdiction by the preceding section, which may now be pending, or which may hereafter be brought, in any State court, may be removed by the defendant or defendants therein to the circuit court of the United States for the proper district * * * .

This language reflects two significant changes. First, Congress deleted the language that had closely paraphrased the "arising under" clause of the Constitution and replaced it with a reference to the section of the statute conferring original jurisdiction, a section that had remained substantially unchanged from the 1875 version. Second, the plaintiff's power to remove was eliminated.

* * *

In 1888, Congress tried to clarify the poorly drafted language of the 1887 Act. But, the 1888 statute left the language conferring original jurisdiction unchanged, while amending the section dealing with removal jurisdiction to eliminate the run-on sentence. The amended section continued to restrict removal to defendants and to refer to the original jurisdiction language of the preceding section of the statute.

Beginning in 1911, Congress recodified the statutory provisions concerning original and removal jurisdiction on several occasions, making only minor changes in the language. Thus, for practical purposes, by 1888 Congress had settled on the final statutory contours of federal question jurisdiction, whether invoked originally or by removal.

Louisville and Nashville Railroad Company v. Mottley

Supreme Court of the United States, 1908.
211 U.S. 149.

The bill alleged that in September, 1871, plaintiffs, while passengers upon the defendant railroad, were injured by the defendant's negligence, and released their respective claims for damages in consideration of the agreement for transportation during their lives, expressed in the contract. It is alleged that the contract was performed by the defendant up to January 1, 1907, when the defendant declined to renew the passes. The bill then alleges that the refusal to comply with the contract was based solely upon that part of the act of Congress of June 29, 1906, 34 Stat. 584, which forbids the giving of free passes or free transportation. The bill further alleges: First, that the act of Congress referred to does not prohibit the giving of passes under the circumstances of this case; and, second, that if the law is to be construed as prohibiting such passes, it is in conflict with the Fifth Amendment of the Constitution, because it deprives the plaintiffs of their property without due process of law. The defendant demurred to the bill. The judge of the Circuit Court overruled the demurrer, entered a decree for the relief prayed for, and the defendant appealed directly to this court.

Go Online

Consider the relevant provision of the contract.

Go Online

Consider the relevant language of the statute.

MR. JUSTICE MOODY, after making the foregoing statement, delivered the opinion of the court.

Two questions of law were raised by the demurrer to the bill, were brought here by appeal, and have been argued before us. They are, first, whether that part of the act of Congress of June 29, 1906 (34 Stat. 584), which forbids the giving of free passes or the collection of any different compensation for transportation of passengers than that specified in the tariff filed, makes it unlawful to perform a contract for transportation of persons, who in good faith, before the passage of the act, had accepted such contract in satisfaction of a valid cause of action against the railroad; and, second, whether the statute, if it should be construed to render such a contract unlawful, is in violation of the Fifth Amendment of the Constitution of the United States. We do not deem it necessary, however, to consider either of these questions, because, in our opinion, the court below was without jurisdiction of the cause. Neither party has questioned that jurisdiction, but it is the duty of this court to see to it that the jurisdiction of the Circuit Court, which is defined and limited by statute, is not exceeded. This duty we have frequently performed of our own motion.

There was no diversity of citizenship and it is not and cannot be suggested that there was any ground of jurisdiction, except that the case was a "suit * * * arising under the Constitution and laws of the United States." It is the settled interpretation of these words, as used in this statute, conferring jurisdiction, that a suit arises under the Constitution and laws of the United States only when the plaintiff's statement of his own cause of action shows that it is based upon those laws or that Constitution. It is not enough that the plaintiff alleges some anticipated defense to his cause of action and asserts that the defense is invalidated by some provision of the Constitution of the United States. Although such allegations show that very likely, in the course of the litigation, a question under the Constitution would arise, they do not show that the suit, that is, the plaintiff's original cause of action, arises under the Constitution. In *Tennessee v. Union & Planters' Bank*, the plaintiff, the State of Tennessee, brought suit in the Circuit Court of the United States to recover from the defendant certain taxes alleged to be due under the laws of the State. The plaintiff alleged that the defendant claimed an immunity from the taxation by virtue of its charter, and that therefore the tax was void, because in violation of the provision of the Constitution of the United States, which forbids any State from passing a law impairing the obligation of contracts. The cause was held to be beyond the jurisdiction of the Circuit Court, the court saying, by Mr. Justice Gray, "a suggestion of one party, that the other will or may set up a claim under the Constitution or laws of the United States, does not make the suit one arising under that Constitution or those laws." Again, in *Boston & Montana Consolidated Copper & Silver Mining Company v. Montana Ore Purchasing Company*, the plaintiff brought suit in the Circuit Court of the United States for the conversion of copper ore and for an injunction against its continuance. The plaintiff then alleged, for the purpose of showing jurisdiction, in substance, that the defendant would set up in defense certain laws of the United States. The cause was held to be beyond the jurisdiction of the Circuit Court, the court saying, by Mr. Justice Peckham:

> It would be wholly unnecessary and improper in order to prove complainant's cause of action to go into any matters of defence which the defendants might possibly set up and then attempt to reply to such defence, and thus, if possible, to show that a Federal question might or probably would arise in the course of the trial of the case. To allege such defence and then make an answer to it before the defendant has the opportunity to itself plead or prove its own defence is inconsistent with any known rule of pleading so far as we are aware, and is improper.

The rule is a reasonable and just one that the complainant in the first instance shall be confined to a statement of its cause of action, leaving to the defendant to set up in his answer what his defence is and, if anything more than a denial of complainant's cause of action, imposing upon the defendant the burden of proving such defence.

Conforming itself to that rule the complainant would not, in the assertion or proof of its cause of action, bring up a single Federal question. The presentation of its cause of action would not show that it was one arising under the Constitution or laws of the United States.

The only way in which it might be claimed that a Federal question was presented would be in the complainant's statement of what the defence of defendants would be and complainant's answer to such defence. Under these circumstances the case is brought within the rule laid down in *Tennessee v. Union & Planters' Bank*. That case has been cited and approved many times since * * * .

The interpretation of the act which we have stated was first announced in *Metcalf v. Watertown*, and has since been repeated and applied [in seventeen other cases decided by the Supreme Court following *Metcalf*].

* * *

The application of this rule to the case at bar is decisive against the jurisdiction of the Circuit Court. * * *

Notes and Questions

1. The Mottleys were not to be denied their day in court, or even their day in federal court. They returned to the state courts and brought an action identical to the dismissed federal action. They succeeded in the Kentucky courts, but the railroad appealed to the United States Supreme Court, which finally ruled on the federal issues it had declined to adjudicate three years earlier. The Mottleys lost. *Louisville & Nashville Railroad v. Mottley*, 219 U.S. 467 (1911).

2. a) The rule from *Mottley*, commonly known as the well-pleaded complaint rule, substantially antedates *Mottley* itself. Nonetheless, *Mottley* is the case most often associated with the rule and cited for it.

b) In evaluating cases like *Mottley* to see if they qualify for statutory federal question jurisdiction, one should get into the habit of drafting the complaint. Only in that manner can one reliably determine the jurisdictional issue. What pleading standards should be used to determine whether a particular document satisfies the *Mottley* test?

A good test should distinguish between cases of artful pleading and those presenting substantial federal issues for adjudication.

3. What is achieved by limiting federal question jurisdiction in the manner mandated by *Mottley*? The only apparent issues between the parties were the applicability of the no-free-pass law to the Mottleys and its constitutionality. Does the Court's decision to refuse the case make sense?

4. Could Congress overrule *Mottley*? Should it? Is it significant that Congress has recodified federal question jurisdiction several times since *Mottley* without commenting on it?

5. How does the scope of statutory federal question jurisdiction as interpreted in *Mottley* differ from the scope of constitutional federal question jurisdiction as delineated in *Osborn*? What practical difference do the distinctions between Article III and statutory federal question jurisdiction make?

6. Some justify the *Mottley* rule by arguing that adjudication of federal issues in state courts can be followed by Supreme Court review, as in *Mottley* itself. Consider, however, whether that is realistic. As a practical matter, cases brought in the state courts have a slim chance of Supreme Court review. One result, then, of the *Mottley* rule is that the state courts may finally adjudicate important federal issues. Presumably the federal courts have greater expertise in federal law than the state courts and will make fewer errors dealing with it. If state courts make more errors, the Supreme Court may feel compelled to review cases it would otherwise not hear were they originally handled by the lower federal courts. Thus, lessening the case load of the district courts may be at the expense of the load of the Supreme Court, a body substantially less elastic in its work capacity than the District Court with its many hundreds of authorized judges.

7. The Court continues to insist on the Mottley rule even when one might suspect that the rule frustrates congressional intent. In *Holmes Group, Inc. v. Vornado Air Circulation Systems Inc.*, 535 U.S. 826 (2002), the plaintiff sought a declaratory judgment that it was not infringing the defendant's trade dress, and the defendant responded with a patent law counterclaim. The district court entered judgment for the plaintiff, but stayed all proceedings on the defendant's counterclaim. The defendant appealed to the Federal Circuit, which has exclusive jurisdiction over "an appeal from a final decision of a district court of the United States * * * if the jurisdiction of that court was based, in whole or in part,"[5] on 28 U.S.C. § 1338. The Federal Circuit rejected Holmes Group's challenge to its jurisdiction, vacated the decision of the district court because of intervening Court of Appeals' decisions, and remanded.

5 Pub. L. 106-113, 113 Stat. 1501 (1999) (current version at 28 U.S.C. § 1295 (2006) (eliminating the reference to § 1338)).

The Supreme Court held that because the well-pleaded-complaint rule applies to actions under § 1338 just as it does to actions under § 1331, the district court's jurisdiction could not rest on § 1338 because the *plaintiff* stated no patent claim. Justice Scalia's opinion reaffirmed that counterclaims cannot serve as the basis for arising-under jurisdiction. The defendant argued that Congress created the Federal Circuit and gave it exclusive jurisdiction in order to achieve uniformity in patent law. Justice Scalia rebuffed the suggestion that the exclusive appellate jurisdiction should come into play whenever a case contains a patent law counterclaim. "Our task here is not to determine what would further Congress's goal of ensuring patent-law uniformity, but to determine what the words of the statute must fairly be understood to mean. * * * It would be an unprecedented feat of interpretive **necromancy** to say that § 1338's 'arising under' language means one thing (the well-pleaded-complaint rule) in its own right, but something quite different (respondent's complaint-or-counterclaim rule) when referred to by § 1295(a)(1)." Justices Ginsburg and O'Connor argued that "when the claim stated in a compulsory counterclaim 'aris[es] under' federal patent law and is adjudicated on the merits by a federal district court, the Federal Circuit has exclusive appellate jurisdiction over that adjudication and other determinations made in the same case * * * ," although they concurred in the judgment because the district court had not actually adjudicated the patent counterclaim.

What's That?

The art of revealing the future by means of alleged communication with the dead.

8. Suppose that a plaintiff could plead federal law as an ingredient of a claim within the meaning of *Mottley* but elects not to do so and sues in the state courts. May the defendant remove the action on the ground that the plaintiff is avoiding federal law that properly should be part of the complaint? In *Metropolitan Life Ins. Co. v. Taylor*, 481 U.S. 58 (1987), the Court held that the Employee Retirement Income Security Act (ERISA) had so completely preempted state law that the plaintiff's attempt to plead a state claim was unavailing; ERISA had, in effect, federalized the state claim. *Metropolitan's theory followed Avco Corp. v. Machinists*, 390 U.S. 557 (1968), *affirming* 376 F.2d 337, 340 (6th Cir.1967), which had held, following Lincoln Mills, that the Labor Management Relations Act had entirely federalized the law of labor management relations, absorbing state law as federal common law whenever it did not conflict with federal policy, so that the parties' dispute, ostensibly arising from the collective bargaining contract, nonetheless arose under federal law within the meaning of § 1441 (and, by implication, of § 1331): "[s]tate law does not exist as an independent source of private rights to enforce collective bargaining contracts" governed by the Labor Management Relations Act.

On the other hand, in *Caterpillar, Inc. v. Williams*, 482 U.S. 386 (1987), the Supreme Court limited *Avco* by ruling that the Labor Management Relations Act preempted state law only with respect to contracts between employers and unions, not with respect to individual employment contracts between employers and employees. Although the employees could have proceeded under the collective bargaining agreement, they elected not to do so. The Court held that "[t]he [*Mottley*] rule makes the plaintiff the master of the claim; he or she may avoid federal jurisdiction by exclusive reliance on state law." Thus, Caterpillar seemed sharply to limit the reach of *Metropolitan* and *AVCO*.

> **FYI**
>
> *Sweeney v. Abramovitz*, 449 F.Supp. 213 (D. Conn.1978), went a step further, holding a complaint's elliptical indirect reference to a question of federal law essential to the plaintiff's claim did not prevent the defendant from removing to federal court.

Beneficial National Bank v. Anderson, 539 U.S. 1 (2003), returned to *Avco* preemption theory. Anderson sued Beneficial to recover damages, alleging that Beneficial charged interest in excess of that permitted by Alabama common law and an Alabama usury statute. However, the National Bank Act, 12 U.S.C. §§ 85, 86, in addition to specifying the maximum lawful rate of interest chargeable by national banks, includes a private right of action for debtors subjected to usurious interest charges. Plaintiff commenced his action in an Alabama state court, and defendant removed. The district court denied plaintiff's motion to remand, but the Eleventh Circuit reversed on the ground that the complaint did not allege a federal claim and that Congress had given no indication in the National Bank Act that it intended to permit removal of actions brought under § 86. A 6-to-3 majority of the Justices found that the National Bank Act so completely preempts the area that the plaintiff could not state a claim under Alabama law at all. Regarding removal, the majority effectively found that the Eleventh Circuit had improperly conceived the issue; the question was not whether Congress had indicated in § 86 that such actions were removable, but rather whether § 86 contained any indication that the ordinary removal rules of 28 U.S.C. § 1441 did not apply. With respect to the preemption issue, the Court stated that congressional intent to preempt state remedies was paramount: "Only if Congress intended § 86 to provide the exclusive cause of action for usury claims against national banks would the statute be comparable to the provisions that we construed in the *Avco* and *Metropolitan Life* cases." The majority wasted no time in finding that Congress did so intend, and therefore found that although the plaintiff may have thought that he was pleading two state claims, he was actually pleading a single federal claim.

Justice Scalia, joined by Justice Thomas, dissented. In his view, the long-established rule that the plaintiff is the master of the claim prevented the Court's majority from recharacterizing the plaintiff's state claims as a federal claim. Preemption, he argued, is simply one species of defense to a state claim. He therefore felt that the well-pleaded-complaint rule should have kept the case out of the federal court, on the authority of *Caterpillar's* statement that "a case may not be removed to federal court on the basis of the defense of pre-emption." Justice Scalia also mounted a frontal attack on *Avco's* legitimacy, arguing that *Avco* rested unjustifiably on dictum from *Lincoln* Mills that Justice Scalia thought the *Avco* Court had taken out of context. He saw *Metropolitan Life Ins. Co. v. Taylor* as an empty echo of Avco: "*Taylor*, in other words, rests upon a sort of statutory incorporation of *Avco*. *Avco* itself, on the other hand, continues to rest upon nothing."

Justice Scalia also questioned the entire notion of federalizing state claims. He distinguished the federal courts' occasional adoption of the content of a state rule as federal common law[6] from conversion of a state claim into a federal claim. In his view, complete federal preemption (which he did not dispute) compelled the conclusion that the state claims had met their demise, requiring dismissal of the action.

> [T]he mere fact that a state-law claim is invalid no more deprives it of its character as a state-law claim which does not raise a federal question, than does the fact that a federal claim is invalid deprives it of its character as a federal claim which [sic] does raise a federal question. The proper response to the presentation of a non-existent claim to a state court is dismissal, not the "federalize-and-remove" dance authorized by today's opinion.

CLICK FOR UPDATE
UPDATES FOUND ON PAGES 1191-1195

Is Justice Scalia's argument persuasive? If so, what drove the majority to expand *Avco* to cover this situation?

9. One of the authors has suggested abandoning the well-pleaded complaint rule and allowing any action presenting an outcome-determinative federal issue to be heard in the federal courts, either originally, by permitting the plaintiff to anticipate federal defenses or replies, or by removal at the instance of either party after a federal issue has been injected into the case by pleadings after the complaint. What new difficulties might adoption of that suggestion create? What old problems might it solve?

We now move back to the question of the scope of Article III arising-under jurisdiction. *Verlinden B.V. v. Central Bank of Nigeria* involves a different jurisdictional statute, § 1330 instead of § 1331, but the procedural history of the case required the Court to consider the scope of jurisdiction under both statutes and the question of whether § 1330 was consistent with Article III.

---

6 *United States v. Kimbell Foods, Inc.* (page 451 of the text) and *Semtek International Incorporated v. Lockheed Martin Corporation* (*infra* at 478) discuss and exemplify this phenomenon.

Verlinden B.V. v. Central Bank Of Nigeria

Supreme Court of the United States, 1983.
461 U.S. 480.

CHIEF JUSTICE BURGER delivered the opinion of the Court.

We granted certiorari to consider whether the Foreign Sovereign Immunities Act of 1976, by authorizing a foreign plaintiff to sue a foreign state in a United States District Court on a non-federal cause of action, violates Article III of the Constitution.

I

On April 21, 1975, the Federal Republic of Nigeria and petitioner Verlinden B.V., a Dutch corporation with its principal offices in Amsterdam, The Netherlands, entered into a contract providing for the purchase of 240,000 metric tons of cement by Nigeria. The parties agreed that the contract would be governed by the laws of the Netherlands and that disputes would be resolved by arbitration before the International Chamber of Commerce, Paris, France.

The contract provided that the Nigerian government was to establish an irrevocable, confirmed letter of credit for the total purchase price through Slavenburg's Bank in Amsterdam. According to petitioner's amended complaint, however, respondent Central Bank of Nigeria, an instrumentality of Nigeria, improperly established an unconfirmed letter of credit payable through Morgan Guaranty Trust Company in New York.

In August 1975, Verlinden subcontracted with a Liechtenstein corporation, Interbuco, to purchase the cement needed to fulfill the contract. Meanwhile, the ports of Nigeria had become clogged with hundreds of ships carrying cement, sent by numerous other cement suppliers with whom Nigeria also had entered contracts. In mid-September, Central Bank unilaterally directed its correspondent banks, including Morgan Guaranty, to adopt a series of amendments to all letters of credit issued in connection with the cement contracts. Central Bank also directly notified the suppliers that payment would be made only for those shipments approved by Central Bank two months before their arrival in Nigerian waters.

Verlinden then sued Central Bank in United States District Court for the Southern District of New York, alleging that Central Bank's actions constituted an anticipatory breach of the letter of credit. Verlinden alleged jurisdiction under § 2 of the Foreign Sovereign Immunities Act, 28 U.S.C. § 1330.[4] Respondent moved to dismiss for, among other reasons, lack of subject matter and personal jurisdiction.

The District Court first held that a federal court may exercise subject matter jurisdiction over a suit brought by a foreign corporation against a foreign sovereign. Although the legislative history of the Foreign Sovereign Immunities Act does not clearly reveal whether Congress intended the Act to extend to actions brought by foreign plaintiffs, Judge Weinfeld reasoned that the language of the Act is "broad and embracing. It confers jurisdiction over 'any nonjury civil action' against a foreign state." Moreover, in the District Court's view, allowing *all* actions against foreign sovereigns, including those initiated by foreign plaintiffs, to be brought in federal court was necessary to effectuate "the Congressional purpose of concentrating litigation against sovereign states in the federal courts in order to aid the development of a uniform body of federal law governing assertions of sovereign immunity." The District Court also held that Article III subject matter jurisdiction extends to suits by foreign corporations against foreign sovereigns, stating:

> [The Act] imposes a single, federal standard to be applied uniformly by both state and federal courts hearing claims brought against foreign states. In consequence, even though the plaintiff's claim is one grounded upon common law, the case is one that "arises under" a federal law because the complaint compels the application of the uniform federal standard governing assertions of sovereign immunity. In short, the Immunities Act injects an essential federal element into all suits brought against foreign states.

The District Court nevertheless dismissed the complaint, holding that a foreign instrumentality is entitled to sovereign immunity unless one of the exceptions specified in the Act applies. After carefully considering each of the exceptions upon which petitioner relied, the District Court concluded that none applied, and accordingly dismissed the action.[5]

---

4 Section 2, 28 U.S.C. § 1330, provides:

> (a) The district courts shall have original jurisdiction without regard to amount in controversy of any nonjury civil action against a foreign state as defined in section 1603(a) of this title as to any claim for relief in personam with respect to which the foreign state is not entitled to immunity either under sections 1605-1607 of this title or under any applicable international agreement.
>
> (b) Personal jurisdiction over a foreign state shall exist as to every claim for relief over which the district courts have jurisdiction under subsection (a) where service has been made under section 1608 of this title.

5 The District Court dismissed "for lack of personal jurisdiction." Under the Act, however, both statutory subject matter jurisdiction (otherwise known as "competence") and personal jurisdiction turn on application of the substantive provisions of the Act. Under § 1330(a), federal district courts are provided subject matter jurisdiction if a foreign state is "not entitled to immunity either under sections 1605-1607 * * * or under any applicable international agreement;" § 1330(b) provides personal jurisdiction wherever subject matter jurisdiction exists under subsection (a) and service of process has been made under § 1608 of the Act. Thus, if none of the exceptions to sovereign immunity set forth in the Act

The Court of Appeals for the Second Circuit affirmed, but on different grounds. The court agreed with the District Court that the Act was properly construed to permit actions brought by foreign plaintiffs. The court held, however, that the Act exceeded the scope of Article III of the Constitution. In the view of the Court of Appeals, neither the diversity clause nor the "arising under" clause of Article III is broad enough to support jurisdiction over actions by foreign plaintiffs against foreign sovereigns; accordingly it concluded that Congress was without power to grant federal courts jurisdiction in this case, and affirmed the District Court's dismissal of the action.

We granted certiorari, and we reverse and remand.

II

* * *

In 1976, Congress passed the Foreign Sovereign Immunities Act in order to free the Government from the case-by-case diplomatic pressures, to clarify the governing standards, and to "assur[e] litigants that * * * decisions are made on purely legal grounds and under procedures that insure due process." To accomplish these objectives, the Act contains a comprehensive set of legal standards governing claims of immunity in every civil action against a foreign state or its political subdivisions, agencies or instrumentalities.

For the most part, the Act codifies, as a matter of federal law, the restrictive theory of sovereign immunity. A foreign state is normally immune from the jurisdiction of federal and state courts, 28 U.S.C. § 1604, subject to a set of exceptions specified in §§ 1605 and 1607. Those exceptions include actions in which the foreign state has explicitly or impliedly waived its immunity, and actions based upon commercial activities of the foreign sovereign carried on in the United States or causing a direct effect in the United States. When one of these or the other specified exceptions applies, "the foreign state shall be liable in the same manner and to the same extent as a private individual under like circumstances."

Go Online

Sections 1606-07 are irrelevant here. Consider, however, § 1605. Of what does this statute remind you? What sort of statute does it sound like?

The Act expressly provides that its standards control in "the courts of the United States and of the States," and thus clearly contemplates that such suits may be brought in either federal or state courts. However, "[i]n view of the potential

applies, the District Court lacks both statutory subject matter jurisdiction and personal jurisdiction. The District Court's conclusion that none of the exceptions to the Act applied therefore signified an absence of both competence and personal jurisdiction.

sensitivity of actions against foreign states and the importance of developing a uniform body of law in this area," the Act guarantees foreign states the right to remove any civil action from a state court to a federal court. The Act also provides that any claim permitted under the Act may be brought from the outset in federal court. If one of the specified exceptions to sovereign immunity applies, a federal district court may exercise subject matter jurisdiction under § 1330(a); but if the claim does not fall within one of the exceptions, federal courts lack subject matter jurisdiction. In such a case, the foreign state is also ensured immunity from the jurisdiction of state courts by § 1604.

* * *

IV

We now turn to the core question presented by this case: whether Congress exceeded the scope of Article III of the Constitution by granting federal courts subject matter jurisdiction over certain civil actions by foreign plaintiffs against foreign sovereigns where the rule of decision may be provided by state law.

* * * Within Article III of the Constitution, we find two sources authorizing the grant of jurisdiction in the Foreign Sovereign Immunities Act: the diversity clause and the "arising under" clause. The diversity clause is not sufficiently broad to support a grant of jurisdiction over actions by foreign plaintiffs* * * . We conclude, however, that the "arising under" clause of Article III provides an appropriate basis for the statutory grant of subject matter jurisdiction to actions by foreign plaintiffs under the Act.

The controlling decision on the scope of Article III "arising under" jurisdiction is Chief Justice Marshall's opinion for the Court in *Osborn v. Bank of the United States*. In Osborn, the Court upheld the constitutionality of a statute that granted the Bank of the United States the right to sue in federal court on causes of action based upon state law. There, the Court concluded that the "judicial department may receive * * * the power of construing every * * * law" that "the Legislature may constitutionally make." The rule was laid down that

> it [is] a sufficient foundation for jurisdiction, that the title or right set up by the party, may be defeated by one construction of the constitution or law[s] of the United States, and sustained by the opposite construction.

Osborn thus reflects a broad conception of "arising under" jurisdiction, according to which Congress may confer on the federal courts jurisdiction over any case or controversy that might call for the application of federal law. The breadth of that conclusion has been questioned. It has been observed that, taken at its broadest, *Osborn* might be read as permitting "assertion of original federal jurisdiction on the remote possibility of presentation of a federal question." We need not now resolve that issue or decide the precise boundaries of Article III jurisdiction, however, since the present case does not involve a mere speculative possibility that a federal question may arise at some point in the proceeding. Rather, a suit against a foreign state under this Act necessarily raises questions of substantive federal law at the very outset, and hence clearly "arises under" federal law, as that term is used in Article III.

By reason of its authority over foreign commerce and foreign relations, Congress has the undisputed power to decide, as a matter of federal law, whether and under what circumstances foreign nations should be amenable to suit in the United States. Actions against foreign sovereigns in our courts raise sensitive issues concerning the foreign relations of the United States, and the primacy of federal concerns is evident.

To promote these federal interests, Congress exercised its Article I powers by enacting a statute comprehensively regulating the amenability of foreign nations to suit in the United States. The statute must be applied by the District Courts in every action against a foreign sovereign, since subject matter jurisdiction in any such action depends on the existence of one of the specified exceptions to foreign sovereign immunity, 28 U.S.C. § 1330(a). At the threshold of every action in a District Court against a foreign state, therefore, the court must satisfy itself that one of the exceptions applies—and in doing so it must apply the detailed federal law standards set forth in the Act. Accordingly, an action against a foreign sovereign arises under federal law, for purposes of Article III jurisdiction.

In reaching a contrary conclusion, the Court of Appeals relied heavily upon decisions construing 28 U.S.C. § 1331, the statute which grants district courts general federal question jurisdiction over any case that "arises under" the laws of the United States. The court placed particular emphasis on the so-called "well-pleaded complaint" rule, which provides, for purposes of statutory "arising under" jurisdiction, that the federal question must appear on the face of a well-pleaded complaint and may not enter in anticipation of a defense. In the view of the Court of Appeals, the question of foreign sovereign immunity in this case arose solely as a defense, and not on the face of Verlinden's well-pleaded complaint.

Although the language of § 1331 parallels that of the "arising under" clause of Article III, this Court never has held that statutory "arising under" jurisdiction is identical to Article III "arising under" jurisdiction. Quite the contrary is true. Section 1331, the general federal question statute, although broadly phrased,

> has been continuously construed and limited in the light of the history that produced it, the demands of reason and coherence, and the dictates of sound judicial policy which have emerged from the [statute's] function as a provi-

sion in the mosaic of federal judiciary legislation. *It is a statute, not a Constitution, we are expounding.*

([E]mphasis added).

> **FYI**
>
> The italicized language is from *Romero v. International Terminal Operating Co.*, 358 U.S. 354 (1959), and contrasts with Chief Justice Marshall's statement in *M'Culloch v. Maryland*: "We must never forget that it is *a constitution* we are expounding."

In an accompanying footnote, the Court further observed, "Of course the many limitations which have been placed on jurisdiction under § 1331 are not limitations on the constitutional power of Congress to confer jurisdiction on the federal courts." As these decisions make clear, Article III "arising under" jurisdiction is broader than federal question jurisdiction under § 1331, and the Court of Appeals' heavy reliance on decisions construing that statute was misplaced.

In rejecting "arising under" jurisdiction, the Court of Appeals also noted that § 2 of the Foreign Sovereign Immunities Act, 28 U.S.C. § 1330, is a jurisdictional provision.[22] Because of this, the court felt its conclusion compelled by prior cases in which this Court has rejected Congressional attempts to confer jurisdiction on federal courts simply by enacting jurisdictional statutes. * * *

From these cases, the Court of Appeals apparently concluded that a jurisdictional statute can never constitute the federal law under which the action arises, for Article III purposes. Yet the statutes at issue in these prior cases sought to do nothing more than grant jurisdiction over a particular class of cases. As the Court stated in The Propeller Genesee Chief, "The law * * * contains no regulations of commerce * * * . *It merely confers a new jurisdiction on the district courts; and this is its only object and purpose* * * * . It is evident * * * that Congress, in passing [the law], did not intend to exercise their power to regulate commerce * * * ." (Emphasis added).

In contrast, in enacting the Foreign Sovereign Immunities Act, Congress expressly exercised its power to regulate foreign commerce, along with other

22 Although a major function of the Act as a whole is to regulate jurisdiction of federal courts over cases involving foreign states, the Act's purpose is to set forth "comprehensive rules governing sovereign immunity." H.R.REP. NO. 94-1487, at 12. The Act also prescribes procedures for commencing lawsuits against foreign states in federal and state courts and specifies the circumstances under which attachment and execution may be obtained against the property of foreign states. In addition, the Act defines "Extent of Liability," setting out a general rule that the foreign sovereign is "liable in the same manner and to the same extent as a private individual," subject to certain specified exceptions, 28 U.S.C. § 1606. In view of our resolution of this case, we need not consider petitioner's claim that § 1606 itself renders every claim against a foreign sovereign a federal cause of action.

specified Article I powers. As the House Report clearly indicates, the primary purpose of the Act was to "se[t] forth comprehensive rules governing sovereign immunity"; the jurisdictional provisions of the Act are simply one part of this comprehensive scheme. The Act thus does not merely concern access to the federal courts. Rather, it governs the types of actions for which foreign sovereigns may be held liable in a court in the United States, federal or state. The Act codifies the standards governing foreign sovereign immunity as an aspect of substantive federal law, and applying those standards will generally require interpretation of numerous points of federal law. Finally, if a court determines that none of the exceptions to sovereign immunity applies, the plaintiff will be barred from raising his claim in any court in the United States—manifestly, "the title or right set up by the party, may be defeated by one construction of the * * * laws of the United States, and sustained by the opposite construction." *Osborn v. Bank of the United States*. That the inquiry into foreign sovereign immunity is labeled under the Act as a matter of jurisdiction does not affect the constitutionality of Congress' action in granting federal courts jurisdiction over cases calling for application of this comprehensive regulatory statute.

Congress, pursuant to its unquestioned Article I powers, has enacted a broad statutory framework governing assertions of foreign sovereign immunity. In so doing, Congress deliberately sought to channel cases against foreign sovereigns away from the state courts and into federal courts, thereby reducing the potential for a multiplicity of conflicting results among the courts of the 50 states. The resulting jurisdictional grant is within the bounds of Article III, since every action against a foreign sovereign necessarily involves application of a body of substantive federal law, and accordingly "arises under" federal law, within the meaning of Article III.

V

A conclusion that the grant of jurisdiction in the Foreign Sovereign Immunities Act is consistent with the Constitution does not end the case. An action must not only satisfy Article III but must also be supported by a statutory grant of subject matter jurisdiction. As we have made clear, deciding whether statutory subject matter jurisdiction exists under the Foreign Sovereign Immunities Act entails an application of the substantive terms of the Act to determine whether one of the specified exceptions to immunity applies.

In the present case, the District Court, after satisfying itself as to the constitutionality of the Act, held that the present action does not fall within any specified exception. The Court of Appeals, reaching a contrary conclusion as to jurisdiction under the Constitution, did not find it necessary to address this statutory question. Accordingly, on remand the Court of Appeals must consider whether jurisdiction exists under the Act itself. If the Court of Appeals agrees with the District Court on that issue, the case will be at an end. If, on the other hand, the Court of Appeals concludes that jurisdiction does exist under the statute, the action may then be remanded to the District Court for further proceedings.

It is so ordered.

Notes and Questions

1. What does *Verlinden* mean for the constitutional test(s) of federal question jurisdiction that *Osborn* articulated? Does it endorse *Osborn*? Which case involves a more expansive exercise of federal question jurisdiction?

2. What does *Verlinden* suggest about the well-pleaded complaint rule?

3. Since the federal question in *Verlinden* is the existence of sovereign immunity, and since sovereign immunity is tied to subject matter jurisdiction by 28 U.S.C.A. § 1330(a), did not the plaintiff satisfy Mottley because pursuant to FED.R.CIV.P. 8(a)(1) a complaint must plead subject matter jurisdiction? If that is so, then is the Court's discussion of the well-pleaded complaint rule merely *dictum*?

4. As a policy matter, is it desirable for cases like *Verlinden* to be in the federal courts at all? This country's only apparent connection with the case is through the correspondent bank, which is not even individually exposed to liability. In *Gully v. Meridian National Bank* (*infra* at 331), Justice Cardozo observed that a "case does not arise under a law renouncing a defense." The Foreign Sovereign Immunities Act, in these circumstances, does just that. Given that all of the parties are aliens, is not *Verlinden* the paradigmatic example of why the federal courts should not get involved in cases like this?

American Well Works Co. v. Layne & Bowler Co.

Supreme Court of the United States, 1916.
241 U.S. 257.

MR. JUSTICE HOLMES delivered the opinion of the court.

This is a suit begun in a state court, removed to the United States Court, and then, on motion to remand by the plaintiff, dismissed by the latter court, on the ground that the cause of action arose under the patent laws of the United States, that the state court had no jurisdiction, and that therefore the one to which it was removed had none. There is a proper certificate and the case comes here direct from the District Court.

> **FYI**
>
> Until 1986, removal jurisdiction was wholly derivative, so that the federal district court could not acquire subject matter jurisdiction if the state court had lacked it. This led to the anomalous result exemplified by the federal trial court here. The court, viewing the plaintiff's case as exclusively federal and therefore not within the jurisdiction of the state court, dismissed it after removal so that the plaintiff could refile the case in federal court. The addition of 28 U.S.C.A. § 1441(e) in 1986 (now redesignated § 1441(f)) eliminated this bizarre dance.

Of course the question depends upon the plaintiff's declaration. That may be summed up in a few words. The plaintiff alleges that it owns, manufactures and sells a certain pump, has or has applied for a patent for it, and that the pump is known as the best in the market. It then alleges that the defendants have falsely and maliciously libeled and slandered the plaintiff's title to the pump by stating that the pump and certain parts thereof are infringements upon the defendant's pump and certain parts thereof[,] and that without probable cause they have brought suits against some parties who are using the plaintiff's pump and that they are threatening suits against all who use it. The allegation of the defendants' libel or slander is repeated in slightly varying form but it all comes to statements to various people that the plaintiff was infringing the defendants' patent and that the defendant would sue both seller and buyer if the plaintiff's pump was used. Actual damage to the plaintiff in its business is alleged to the extent of $50,000 and punitive damages to the same amount are asked.

It is evident that the claim for damages is based upon conduct, or, more specifically, language, tending to persuade the public to withdraw its custom from the plaintiff and having that effect to its damage. Such conduct having such effect is equally actionable whether it produces the result by persuasion, by threats or by falsehood, and it is enough to allege and prove the conduct and effect, leaving the defendant to justify if he can. If the conduct complained of is persuasion, it may be justified by the fact that the defendant is a competitor, or by good faith and reasonable grounds. If it is a statement of fact, it may be justified, absolutely or with qualifications, by proof that the statement is true. But all such justifications are defences and raise issues that are no part of the plaintiff's case. In the present instance it is part of the plaintiff's case that it had a business to be damaged; whether built up by patents or without them does not matter. It is no part of it to prove anything concerning the defendants' patent or that the plaintiff did not infringe the same—still less to prove anything concerning any patent of its own. The material statement complained of is that the plaintiff infringes—which may be true notwithstanding the plaintiff's patent. That is merely a piece of evidence. Furthermore, the damage alleged presumably is rather the consequence of the threat to sue than of the statement that the plaintiff's pump infringed the defendants' rights.

Make the Connection

Recall from your Torts course that the common law originally presumed both falsity and damages from the mere publication of defamatory material, effectively making defamation a strict liability tort. With respect to defamation of private persons involving matters not of public concern, that is still true in many states, though the defendant may defend on the ground that the statement was true.

A suit for damages to business caused by a threat to sue under the patent law is not itself a suit under the patent law. And the same is true when the damage is caused by a statement of fact—that the defendant has a patent which is infringed. What makes the defendants' act a wrong is its manifest tendency to injure the plaintiff's business and the wrong is the same whatever the means by which it is accomplished. But whether it is a wrong or not depends upon the law of the State where the act is done, not upon the patent law, and therefore the suit arises under the law of the State. A suit arises under the law that creates the cause of action. The fact that the justification may involve the validity and infringement of a patent is no more material to the question under what law the suit is brought than it would be in an action of contract. If the State adopted for civil proceedings the saying of the old criminal law: the greater the truth the greater the libel, the validity of the patent would not come in question at all. In Massachusetts the truth would not be a defence if the statement was made from disinterested malevolence. The State is master of the whole matter, and if it saw fit to do away with actions of this type altogether, no one, we imagine, would suppose that they still could be maintained under the patent laws of the United States.

Judgment reversed.

Notes and Questions

1. Is the test *American Well Works* announced consistent with the approach to federal question jurisdiction Mottley exemplified? Was it appropriate for Justice Holmes to write the opinion without citing Mottley, either to follow, modify, or overrule it? The decision was only eight years old, and he was on the unanimous Court that announced it. Does Mottley shed any light on the proper disposition of *American Well Works*? Although today a plaintiff in a trade libel action must plead and prove the falsity of the defendant's statements, that was not the case when the Court decided *American Well Works*. Would today's pleading requirements for a trade libel action make a difference for Mottley purposes? If so, how?

2. Do you see any relationship between the Court's position here and Justice Johnson's dissent in Osborn?

3. Does *American Well Works* hold that federal question jurisdiction exists whenever federal law creates the cause of action?

In *Shoshone Mining Co. v. Rutter*, 177 U.S. 505 (1900), the Supreme Court refused jurisdiction in a case involving conflicting miners' claims to tracts of western land. Despite a federal cause of action in a comprehensive congressional scheme for resolving such disputes, the Court found no jurisdiction. Although Congress had authorized the cause of action for adverse claims, it had also provided that local law should govern most claims involving land. The Court pointed out that Congress had not even incorporated such law as a body of federal law; it had merely made its use permissible. The statute authorizing the adverse-claim action provided only that such claims could be brought in a "court of competent jurisdiction." The Court observed that in most cases, the controversy between the parties would be resolved on issues of fact or of local law, with no provision of federal law being disputed either as to its meaning or its application. The Justices expressed their concern about the federal courts being inundated with essentially local suits and found that although federal law created the underlying cause of action, Congress did not intend, merely by doing so, to expand federal jurisdiction. Does *American Well Works* overrule Shoshone?

3. Justice Holmes's test for federal question jurisdiction clearly has the advantage of simplicity. If this bright-line test were rigorously applied, new categories of cases would be included in and excluded from federal jurisdiction. For example, a dispute involving title to western lands originally granted under a federal land patent might arise under federal law, contrary to the result in Shoshone. On the other hand, disputes like that in American Well Works itself, where apparently the only contested issues revolve around the patents, would be consigned to the state courts. Are those boundaries desirable? If not, is the remedy to reinterpret the statute or to redraft it? If the latter, how?

Smith v. Kansas City Title & Trust Co.

Supreme Court of the United States, 1921.
255 U.S. 180.

MR. JUSTICE DAY delivered the opinion of the court.

A bill was filed in the United States District Court for the Western Division of the Western District of Missouri by a shareholder in the Kansas City Title & Trust Company to enjoin the Company, its officers, agents and employees from investing the funds of the Company in farm loan bonds issued by Federal Land Banks or Joint Stock Land Banks under authority of the Federal Farm Loan Act of July 17, 1916.

The relief was sought on the ground that these acts were beyond the constitutional power of Congress. The bill avers that the Board of Directors of the Company are about to invest its funds in the bonds to the amount of $10,000 in each of the classes described, and will do so unless enjoined by the court in this action. The bill avers the formation of twelve Federal Land Banks, and twenty-one Joint Stock Land Banks under the provisions of the act.

* * *

Section 27 of the act provides that Farm Loan Bonds issued under the provisions of the act by Federal Land Banks or Joint Stock Land Banks shall be a lawful investment for all fiduciary and trust funds, and may be accepted as security for all public deposits. The bill avers that the defendant Trust Company is authorized to buy, invest in and sell government, state and municipal and other bonds, but it cannot buy, invest in or sell any such bonds, papers, stocks or securities which are not authorized to be issued by a valid law or which are not investment securities, but that nevertheless it is about to invest in Farm Loan Bonds; that the Trust Company has been induced to direct its officers to make the investment by reason of its reliance upon the provisions of the Farm Loan Acts, especially §§ 21, 26 and 27, by which the Farm Loan Bonds are declared to be instrumentalities of the Government of the United States, and as such with the income derived therefrom, are declared to be exempt from federal, state, municipal and local taxation, and are further declared to be lawful investments for all fiduciary and trust funds. The bill further avers that the acts by which it is attempted to authorize the bonds are wholly illegal, void and unconstitutional and of no effect because unauthorized by the Constitution of the United States.

The bill prays that the acts of Congress authorizing the creation of the banks, especially §§ 21, 26 and 27 thereof, shall be adjudged and decreed to be unconstitutional, void and of no effect, and that the issuance of the Farm Loan Bonds, and the taxation exemption feature thereof, shall be adjudged and decreed to be invalid.

* * * The Kansas City Title & Trust Company filed a motion to dismiss in the nature of a general demurrer, and upon hearing the District Court entered a decree dismissing the bill. From this decree appeal was taken to this court.

No objection is made to the federal jurisdiction, either original or appellate, by the parties to this suit, but that question will be first examined. The Company is authorized to invest its funds in legal securities only. The attack upon the proposed investment in the bonds described is because of the alleged unconstitutionality of the acts of Congress undertaking to organize the banks and authorize the issue of the bonds. No other reason is set forth in the bill as a ground of objection to the proposed investment by the Board of Directors acting in the Company's behalf. As diversity of citizenship is lacking, the jurisdiction of the District Court depends upon whether the cause of action set forth arises under the Constitution or laws of the United States.

The general rule is that where it appears from the bill or statement of the plaintiff that the right to relief depends upon the construction or application of the Constitution or laws of the United States, and that such federal claim is not merely colorable, and rests upon a reasonable foundation, the District Court has jurisdiction under this provision.

At an early date, considering the grant of constitutional power to confer jurisdiction upon the federal courts, Chief Justice Marshall said: "A case in law or equity consists of the right of the one party, as well as of the other, and may truly be said to arise under the Constitution or a law of the United States, whenever its correct decision depends on the construction of either," and again, when "the title or right set up by the party may be defeated by one construction of the Constitution or law of the United States, and sustained by the opposite construction." *Osborn v. Bank of the United States*.

This characterization of a suit arising under the Constitution or laws of the United States has been followed in many decisions of this and other federal courts.

* * *

The jurisdiction of this court is to be determined upon the principles laid down in the cases referred to. In the instant case the averments of the bill show that the directors were proceeding to make the investments in view of the act authorizing the bonds about to be purchased, maintaining that the act authorizing them was constitutional and the bonds valid and desirable investments. The objecting shareholder avers in the bill that the securities were issued under an unconstitutional law, and hence of no validity. It is, therefore, apparent that the controversy concerns the constitutional validity of an act of Congress which is directly drawn in question. The decision depends upon the determination of this issue.

The general allegations as to the interest of the shareholder, and his right to have an injunction to prevent the purchase of the alleged unconstitutional securities by misapplication of the funds of the corporation, give jurisdiction * * * . We are, therefore, of the opinion that the District Court had jurisdiction under the averments of the bill, and that a direct appeal to this court upon constitutional grounds is authorized.

* * *

[The Court examined the constitutional grounds that Smith urged and concluded that his claims were without merit.]

It follows that the decree of the District Court is

Affirmed.

MR. JUSTICE HOLMES, dissenting.

No doubt it is desirable that the question raised in this case should be set at rest, but that can be done by the Courts of the United States only within the limits of the jurisdiction conferred upon them by the Constitution and the laws of the United States. As this suit was brought by a citizen of Missouri against a Missouri corporation the single ground upon which the jurisdiction of the District Court can be maintained is that the suit "arises under the Constitution or laws of the United States" within the meaning of § 24 of the Judicial Code. I am of opinion that this case does not arise in that way and therefore that the bill should have been dismissed.

It is evident that the cause of action arises not under any law of the United States but wholly under Missouri law. The defendant is a Missouri corporation and the right claimed is that of a stockholder to prevent the directors from doing an act, that is, making an investment, alleged to be contrary to their duty. But the scope of their duty depends upon the charter of their corporation and other laws of Missouri. If those laws had authorized the investment in terms the plaintiff would have had no case, and this seems to me to make manifest what I am unable to deem even debatable, that, as I have said, the cause of action arises wholly under Missouri law. If the Missouri law authorizes or forbids the investment according to the determination of this Court upon a point under the Constitution or acts of Congress, still that point is material only because the Missouri law saw fit to make it so. The whole foundation of the duty is Missouri law, which at its sole will incorporated the other law as it might incorporate a document. The other law or document depends for its relevance and effect not on its own force but upon the law that took it up, so I repeat once more the cause of action arises wholly from the law of the State.

But it seems to me that a suit cannot be said to arise under any other law than that which creates the cause of action. It may be enough that the law relied upon creates a part of the cause of action although not the whole, as held in Osborn v. Bank of the United States, which perhaps is all that is meant by the less guarded expressions in Cohens v. Virginia. I am content to assume this to be so, although the Osborn Case has been criticized and regretted. But the law must create at least a part of the cause of action by its own force, for it is the suit, not a question in the suit, that must arise under the law of the United States. The mere adoption by a state law of a United States law as a criterion or test, when the law of the United States has no force ***proprio vigore,*** does not cause a case under the state law to be also a case under the law of the United States, and so it has been decided by this Court again and again.

> Non constat / jus civile / a posteriori
>
> **It's Latin to Me!**
>
> "By its own strength"

I find nothing contrary to my views in Brushaber v. Union Pacific R.R. Co. It seems to me plain that the objection that I am considering was not before the mind of the Court or the subject of any of its observations, if open. I am confirmed in my view of that case by the fact that in the next volume of reports is a decision, reached not without discussion and with but a single dissent, that "a suit arises under the law that creates the cause of action." That was the *ratio decidendi* of American Well Works Co. v. Layne & Bowler Co. I know of no decisions to the contrary and see no reason for overruling it now.

> **FYI**
>
> Brushaber had found federal question jurisdiction in an action by a shareholder to enjoin a state-chartered corporation from complying with the income tax law on the ground that the law was inconsistent with the Sixteenth Amendment and other constitutional provisions. The district court dismissed the complaint as legally insufficient, and direct appeal lay to the Supreme Court. The Court ruled on the merits of the dispute with but a brief comment on jurisdiction, which the defendant had attacked as violating the Tax Injunction Act (forbidding federal courts to enjoin collection of state taxes, *see* 28 U.S.C. § 1341), *not* as failing to arise under federal law. Justice Holmes seems correct that the Brushaber Court was not even thinking about the jurisdictional issue presented shortly thereafter in American Well Works and that recurred in *Smith*.

Notes and Questions

1. Note the similarity between the test articulated in *Smith* and one test from Osborn v. Bank of the United States. Did the Court thus intend to signal that statutory federal question jurisdiction was co-extensive with the bounds described in Article III, § 2?

2. What did the complaint in *Smith* look like? Was Justice Holmes correct in asserting that the cause of action arose "not under any law of the United States, but *wholly* under Missouri law"? (Emphasis added).

3. In 1916, only five years before *Smith*, the Court had voted six to one[7] for Justice Holmes's law-that-creates-the-cause-of-action test. Chief Justice White and Justices Hughes, McReynolds, Pitney and Van Devanter joined Justice Holmes in refusing jurisdiction; Justice McKenna dissented. In 1921, a six-to-two Court found jurisdiction in *Smith* in a situation clearly inconsistent with Holmes's test. Justice McKenna, now in the majority, was joined by Chief Justice White and Justices Clarke, Day, Pitney and Van Devanter. Justice McReynolds was still with Justice Holmes, now in dissent. Justice Brandeis did not participate. Thus, Chief Justice White and Justices Van Devanter and Pitney, who had opposed jurisdiction in *American Well Works*, supported it in *Smith*. Why? Had three members of the Court changed their views on so fundamental a matter as subject matter jurisdiction within the space of five years? If so, why did none of them offer an explanation? Is it possible that they did not see their positions as inconsistent? Can you construct a view of *American Well Works* and *Smith* that permits simultaneous support of the results in each case? Note, however, that Justice Holmes's clear identification of his test as the *ratio decidendi of American Well Works* poses problems for an alternate view even if there is one.

4. Scholars have been hard pressed to reconcile *American Well Works* and *Smith*. Professor Hirschman noted that "[t]he almost simultaneous decisions in *Smith* and *American Well Works* set up a situation where two incompatible approaches to the problem enjoyed equal precedential status." Linda R. Hirschman, *Whose Law Is It Anyway? A Reconsideration of Federal Question Jurisdiction Over Cases of Mixed State and Federal Law*, 60 IND.L.J. 17, 31 (1984). She suggests that *American Well Works* is the more closely followed, *Smith* being aberrant. Professor Redish, however, compared *Smith* and *American Well Works* and suggested that "Prior to *Merrell Dow*, *Smith*'s expansion of the *American Well* principle had been widely followed in the federal courts * * * ." MARTIN H. REDISH, FEDERAL JURISDICTION: TENSIONS IN THE ALLOCATION OF JUDICAL POWER 103 (2d ed. 1990). Which rule seems better to fulfill the purposes of federal question jurisdiction?

---

7 Justice Lamar had died; his seat was vacant when the Court decided *American Well Works*. Justice Day did not participate in the decision.

5. Judge Friendly, partly because of clash between the theories of *Smith* and *American Well Works*, suggested that Holmes's test is "more useful for inclusion than for the exclusion for which it was intended." *T.B. Harms Co. v. Eliscu*, 339 F.2d 823, 827 (2d Cir.1964), *cert. denied* 381 U.S. 915 (1965). But, as Professor Redish points out:

> It is not even entirely accurate, however, to say that federal question jurisdiction exists whenever the cause of action is created by federal law, for on occasion federal question jurisdiction has been rejected even where the cause of action derived solely from federal law. *Shoshone Mining Co. v. Rutter* is an example.

MARTIN H. REDISH, FEDERAL JURISDICTION: TENSIONS IN THE ALLOCATION OF JUDICIAL POWER 103 (2d ed. 1990) (footnote omitted).

6. While it is a struggle to reconcile *American Well Works* and *Smith*, it is even more difficult to harmonize *Smith* with *Moore v. Chesapeake & Ohio Ry.*, 291 U.S. 205 (1934). Moore sought damages for injuries suffered during his employment by the railroad. He stated two counts, one under the Federal Employers Liability Act, the other under a parallel Kentucky provision, certain regulations of the Interstate Commerce Act, and the Federal Safety Appliance Act. Kentucky law incorporated federal law, stating that an employer's negligence could not be negated by the employee's contributory negligence or assumption of risk if the employer had violated any state or federal employee-safety statute.

The case is unusual because, although the plaintiff sued in federal court, he also argued that there was no federal question jurisdiction because the federal regulations and statute involved in his claim under Kentucky law required actions to be prosecuted in the employer's home state. Moore had sued in Indiana, his home; the defendant was a Virginia citizen. Moore thus invoked diversity jurisdiction and did not need federal question jurisdiction. The railroad sought dismissal for improper venue under the federal regulations. Moore countered that the action was not federal, and therefore was not governed by the ICC's special venue provisions. The Court agreed with Moore and held that the second cause of action arose under Kentucky law despite that law's wholesale adoption of federal safety standards.

Are *Smith* and *Moore* reconcilable? In light of the purposes of federal question jurisdiction, which case reaches a sounder result, or can they both be justified? Draft the complaint in *Moore*. What did the plaintiff have to allege to state his claim for relief? How would the federal issue arise?

Gully v. First National Bank

Supreme Court of the United States, 1936.
299 U.S. 109.

[During the Depression, First National Bank purchased the assets and assumed the liabilities of a predecessor national bank. One of the liabilities was a state tax obligation, assessed pursuant to a federal statute permitting such taxation, thus avoiding the constitutional problem addressed in *M'Culloch v. Maryland* (1819). The statute also prescribed that tax assessments be made either against the shareholders of such banks, to be collected from the banks themselves as agents, or against the banks directly based upon their income only. The Mississippi tax law echoed the federal statute.

Gully, the state tax collector, sued to collect the tax. The Bank removed to federal court, arguing that only by virtue of the federal enabling statute was Gully able to maintain the admittedly state-created claim for taxes. On the merits, the Bank argued that the tax violated the statute because it was assessed against the property, not the income, of the predecessor bank. The Fifth Circuit affirmed the district court judgment finding federal question jurisdiction and dismissing on the merits. The Supreme Court, speaking through Justice Cardozo, reversed, finding no jurisdiction.]

How and when a case arises "under the Constitution or laws of the United States" has been much considered in the books. Some tests are well established. To bring a case within the statute, a right or immunity created by the Constitution or laws of the United States must be an element, and an essential one, of the plaintiff's cause of action. The right or immunity must be such that it will be supported if the Constitution or laws of the United States are given one construction or effect, and defeated if they receive another. A genuine and present controversy, not merely a possible or conjectural one, must exist with reference thereto and the controversy must be disclosed upon the face of the complaint, unaided by the answer or by the petition for removal. Indeed, the complaint itself will not avail as a basis of jurisdiction in so far as it goes beyond a statement of the plaintiff's cause of action and anticipates or replies to a probable defense.

Make the Connection

Recall that Justice Johnson's dissent in *Osborn* made much the same argument, at pages 288-89, in connection with the scope of Article III's arising-under language.

Looking backward we can see that the early cases were less exacting than the recent ones in respect of some of these conditions. If a federal right was pleaded, the question was not always asked whether it was likely to be disputed. This is seen particularly in suits by or against a corporation deriving its charter from an act of Congress. Modern statutes have greatly diminished the importance of those decisions by narrowing their scope. Federal incorporation is now abolished as a ground of federal jurisdiction except where the United States holds more than one-half the stock. Partly under the influence of statutes disclosing a new legislative policy, partly under the influence of more liberal decisions, the probable course of the trial, the real substance of the controversy, has taken on a new significance. "A suit to enforce a right which takes its origin in the laws of the United States is not necessarily, or for that reason alone, one arising under those laws, for a suit does not so arise unless it really and substantially involves a dispute or controversy respecting the validity, construction or effect of such a law, upon the determination of which the result depends." Today, even more clearly than in the past, "the federal nature of the right to be established is decisive—not the source of the authority to establish it."

* * *

This Court has had occasion to point out how futile is the attempt to define a "cause of action" without reference to the context. To define broadly and in the abstract "a case arising under the Constitution or laws of the United States" has hazards of a kindred order. What is needed is something of that common-sense accommodation of judgment to kaleidoscopic situations which characterizes the law in its treatment of problems of causation. One could carry the search for causes backward, almost without end. Instead, there has been a selective process which picks the substantial causes out of the web and lays the other ones aside. As in problems of causation, so here in the search for the underlying law. If we follow the ascent far enough, countless claims of right can be discovered to have their source or their operative limits in the provisions of a federal statute or in the Constitution itself with its circumambient restrictions upon legislative power. To set bounds to the pursuit, the courts have formulated the distinction between controversies that are basic and those that are collateral, between disputes that are necessary and those that are merely possible. We shall be lost in a maze if we put that compass by.

Food for Thought

What makes an issue "substantial" for these purposes? *Smith* did not speak of substantiality, at least directly. Is Justice Cardozo adding something new to the test for federal question jurisdiction?

Notes and Questions

1. What restriction does *Gully* place on statutory federal question jurisdiction in addition to that imposed by Mottley? Should it be important that the federal enabling statute was the *sine qua non* of Gully's cause of action, even though that claim was state-created?

2. In Osborn, Chief Justice Marshall asserted that the potential existence of a federal question not raised by either party made the case a federal question case. Does Justice Cardozo reject that part of Osborn? What is the significance of his language about the remoteness of the federal issue?

3. Is there another way to reach the result in *Gully*? If the parties were to contest the federal issue, how would it come up?

Note on *Merrell Dow Pharmaceuticals, Inc. v. Thompson*

After Gully, fifty years elapsed before the Court again confronted the task of giving understandable meaning to statutory "arising under." (The Court twice addressed what it considered the special problem presented by cases seeking declaratory relief, *see infra* Chapter 3(C), but as you will see, those cases dealt with the particular problem of applying the established test rather than changing the test itself.) In *Merrell Dow Pharmaceuticals, Inc. v. Thompson*, 478 U.S. 804 (1986), the Justices attempted a refinement of the test that had evolved in Mottley, American Well Works, Smith and Gully.

The action concerned serious multiple *in utero* birth defects that Bendectin, a Merrell Dow drug, had allegedly caused the plaintiffs' babies. The plaintiffs alleged six counts, including common law negligence, breach of warranty, strict liability, liability, gross negligence and, in Count IV, negligence *per se* on the ground that Merrell Dow had misbranded Bendectin within the meaning of the Food, Drug and Cosmetic Act (FDCA) of 1938.

There was no question that Count IV contained a well-pleaded, outcome-determinative, contested issue of federal law, thus apparently satisfying the Mottley-Smith-Gully test. For Justice Stevens's five-to-four majority, that was not enough. Justice Stevens noted that FDCA created no private right of action, so that Merrell Dow's quest for federal jurisdiction lacked the benefit of American Well Works law-that-creates-the-cause-of-action test. He concluded that the 1938

Congress[8] would not have intended the plaintiffs' actions to come within 28 U.S.C. § 1331 because the federal issue was not sufficiently "substantial," though the content of that word remained mysterious. In part, he rested his conclusion on the absence of a federally created cause of action.

> The significance of the necessary assumption that there is no federal private cause of action * * * cannot be overstated. For the ultimate import of such a conclusion * * * is that it would flout congressional intent to provide a private federal remedy for the violation of the federal statute. We think it would similarly flout, or at least undermine, congressional intent to conclude that the federal courts might nonetheless exercise federal-question jurisdiction and provide remedies for violations of that federal statute solely because the violation of the federal statute is said to be a "rebuttable presumption" or a "proximate cause" under state law, rather than a federal action under federal law.

That led some lower courts in the years following Merrell Dow to conclude (erroneously) that the Court had returned to the *American Well Works* test. Yet, it was clear that the Court had not.

The opinion cited Smith with approval, though distinguishing it on the ground that Smith involved "the constitutionality of an important federal statute."[9] In the very next sentence, Justice Stevens quoted from Smith language that should have sounded a caution for the remainder of his analysis: "It is * * * apparent that the controversy concerns the constitutional validity of an act of Congress which is directly drawn in question. The decision depends upon the determination of this issue." The Smith Court thus had linked substantiality to outcome-determinativeness. In Merrell Dow, Justice Stevens decoupled the two concepts, which left substantiality without any clear meaning. Resting in part on the absence of a federally-created cause of action, Justice Stevens declared the federal issue in Count IV insufficiently substantial to support federal-question jurisdiction.

The Court gave no indication of what would be "sufficiently" substantial. (This calls to mind Justice Stewart's famous remark about the obscenity standard in *Jacobellis v. Ohio*, 378 U.S. 184, 197 (1964) (Stewart, J., concurring): "I shall not today attempt further to define the kinds of material I understand to be embraced within that shorthand description; and perhaps I could never succeed

8 One of the troubling things about the Court's analysis is why it was looking to the presumed intent of the 1938 Congress that passed FDCA to construe 28 U.S.C. § 1331, which the 1875 Congress had enacted and that subsequent Congresses had recodified without change. To the extent that one thinks congressional intent important in construing a statute, one ordinarily looks to the intent of the Congress that enacted the statute, not the inferred intent of a body that sat more than sixty years later and did not so much as mention the statute. The Court's reliance thus potentially raises the question with respect to future substantive statutes of which ones Congress silently intended to affect federal jurisdiction. In any event, how likely is it that the 1938 Congress, focusing on problems with the nation's food and drug supply, was also thinking about the scope of federal-question jurisdiction and the appropriate division of judicial business between the federal government and the states?

9 How the Court distinguishes between important federal statutes and unimportant federal statutes is left as an exercise for the reader.

in intelligibly doing so. But I know it when I see it, and the motion picture * * * in this case is not that.") If the majority meant that only constitutional questions qualified as substantial for § 1331 purposes, it could have said so. Similarly, if the Court meant simply to substitute the *American Well Works* test for *Mottley-Smith-Gully*, it could have said that, too, and the opinion would have been much shorter. Instead, the Court left "substantiality" as a marker of undefined content. Nineteen years later, the Court attempted a clarification.

Grable & Sons Metal Products, Inc. v. Darue Engineering & Manufacturing

Supreme Court of the United States, 2005.
545 U.S. 308.

JUSTICE SOUTER delivered the opinion of the Court.

* * *

The question is whether want of a federal cause of action to try claims of title to land obtained at a federal tax sale precludes removal to federal court of a state action with non-diverse parties raising a disputed issue of federal title law. We answer no, and hold that the national interest in providing a federal forum for federal tax litigation is sufficiently substantial to support the exercise of federal question jurisdiction over the disputed issue on removal, which would not distort any division of labor between the state and federal courts, provided or assumed by Congress.

I

> **Food for Thought**
>
> It is difficult enough to determine what Congress intends from the words it uses. How is the Court to determine what Congress "assumes"? Will it be possible for the Justices to distinguish their own assumptions from Congress's unstated ones?

In 1994, the Internal Revenue Service seized Michigan real property belonging to petitioner Grable & Sons Metal Products, Inc., to satisfy Grable's federal tax delinquency. Title 26 U.S.C. § 6335 required the IRS to give notice of the seizure, and there is no dispute that Grable received actual notice by certified mail before the IRS sold the property to respondent Darue Engineering & Manufacturing. Although Grable also received notice of the sale itself, it did not exercise its statutory right to redeem the property within 180 days of the sale, § 6337(b)(1), and after that period had passed, the Government gave Darue a quitclaim deed.

Five years later, Grable brought a quiet title action in state court, claiming that Darue's record title was invalid because the IRS had failed to notify Grable of its seizure of the property in the exact manner required by § 6335(a), which provides that written notice must be "given by the Secretary to the owner of the property [or] left at his usual place of abode or business." Grable said that the statute required personal service, not service by certified mail.

Darue removed the case to Federal District Court as presenting a federal question, because the claim of title depended on the interpretation of the notice statute in the federal tax law. The District Court declined to remand the case at Grable's behest after finding that the "claim does pose a significant question of federal law," and ruling that Grable's lack of a federal right of action to enforce its claim against Darue did not bar the exercise of federal jurisdiction. On the merits, the court granted summary judgment to Darue, holding that although § 6335 by its terms required personal service, substantial compliance with the statute was enough.

The Court of Appeals for the Sixth Circuit affirmed. On the jurisdictional question, the panel thought it sufficed that the title claim raised an issue of federal law that had to be resolved, and implicated a substantial federal interest (in construing federal tax law). The court went on to affirm the District Court's judgment on the merits. We granted certiorari on the jurisdictional question alone, to resolve a split within the Courts of Appeals on whether *Merrell Dow Pharmaceuticals Inc. v. Thompson* (1986) always requires a federal cause of action as a condition for exercising federal-question jurisdiction. We now affirm.

II

Darue was entitled to remove the quiet title action if Grable could have brought it in federal district court originally, 28 U.S.C. § 1441(a), as a civil action "arising under the Constitution, laws, or treaties of the United States," § 1331. This provision for federal-question jurisdiction is invoked by and large by plaintiffs pleading a cause of action created by federal law * * *. There is, however, another longstanding, if less frequently encountered, variety of federal "arising under" jurisdiction, this Court having recognized for nearly 100 years that in certain cases federal question jurisdiction will lie over state-law claims that implicate significant federal issues. *E.g.*, *Hopkins v. Walker* (1917). The doctrine captures the commonsense notion that a federal court ought to be able to hear claims recognized under state law that nonetheless turn on substantial questions of federal law, and thus justify resort to the experience, solicitude, and hope of uniformity that a federal forum offers on federal issues.

The classic example is *Smith v. Kansas City Title & Trust Co.* (1921), * * * , [which] held, in a somewhat generous statement of the scope of the doctrine, that a state-law claim could give rise to federal-question jurisdiction so long as it "appears from the [complaint] that the right to relief depends upon the construction or application of [federal law]."

The *Smith* statement has been subject to some trimming to fit earlier and later cases recognizing the vitality of the basic doctrine, but shying away from the expansive view that mere need to apply federal law in a state-law claim will suffice to open the "arising under" door. As early as 1912, this Court had confined federal-question jurisdiction over state-law claims to those that "really and substantially involv[e] a dispute or controversy respecting the validity, construction or effect of [federal] law." This limitation was the ancestor of Justice Cardozo's later explanation that a request to exercise federal-question jurisdiction over a state action calls for a "common-sense accommodation of judgment to [the] kaleidoscopic situations" that present a federal issue, in "a selective process which picks the substantial causes out of the web and lays the other ones aside." It has in fact become a constant refrain in such cases that federal jurisdiction demands not only a contested federal issue, but a substantial one, indicating a serious federal interest in claiming the advantages thought to be inherent in a federal forum.

But even when the state action discloses a contested and substantial federal question, the exercise of federal jurisdiction is subject to a possible veto. For the federal issue will ultimately qualify for a federal forum only if federal jurisdiction is consistent with congressional judgment about the sound division of labor between state and federal courts governing the application of § 1331. Thus, *Franchise Tax Bd.* explained that the appropriateness of a federal forum to hear an embedded issue could be evaluated only after considering the "welter of issues regarding the interrelation of federal and state authority and the proper management of the federal judicial system." Because arising-under jurisdiction to hear a state-law claim always raises the possibility of upsetting the state-federal line drawn (or at least assumed) by Congress, the presence of a disputed federal issue and the ostensible importance of a federal forum are never necessarily dispositive; there must always be an assessment of any disruptive portent in exercising federal jurisdiction.

These considerations have kept us from stating a "single, precise, all-embracing" test for jurisdiction over federal issues embedded in state-law claims between nondiverse parties. We have not kept them out simply because they appeared in state raiment, as Justice Holmes would have done, but neither have we treated "federal issue" as a password opening federal courts to any state action embracing a point of federal law. Instead, the question is, does a state-law claim necessarily raise a stated federal issue, actually disputed and substantial, which a federal forum may entertain without disturbing any congressionally approved balance of federal and state judicial responsibilities.

III

A

This case warrants federal jurisdiction. Grable's state complaint must specify "the facts establishing the superiority of [its] claim," and Grable has premised its superior title claim on a failure by the IRS to give it adequate notice, as defined by federal law. Whether Grable was given notice within the meaning of the federal statute is thus an essential element of its quiet title claim, and the meaning of the federal statute is actually in dispute; it appears to be the only legal or factual issue contested in the case. The meaning of the federal tax provision is an important issue of federal law that sensibly belongs in a federal court. The Government has a strong interest in the "prompt and certain collection of delinquent taxes," and the ability of the IRS to satisfy its claims from the property of delinquents requires clear terms of notice to allow buyers like Darue to satisfy themselves that the Service has touched the bases necessary for good title. The Government thus has a direct interest in the availability of a federal forum to vindicate its own administrative action, and buyers (as well as tax delinquents) may find it valuable to come before judges used to federal tax matters. Finally, because it will be the rare state title case that raises a contested matter of federal law, federal jurisdiction to resolve genuine disagreement over federal tax title provisions will portend only a microscopic effect on the federal-state division of labor. See n.3, *infra*.

This conclusion puts us in venerable company, quiet title actions having been the subject of some of the earliest exercises of federal-question jurisdiction over state-law claims. In *Hopkins*, the question was federal jurisdiction over a quiet title action based on the plaintiffs' allegation that federal mining law gave them the superior claim. Just as in this case, "the facts showing the plaintiffs' title and the existence and invalidity of the instrument or record sought to be eliminated as a cloud upon the title are essential parts of the plaintiffs' cause of action."[3] As in this case again, "it is plain that a controversy respecting the construction and effect of the [federal] laws is involved and is sufficiently real and substantial." This Court therefore upheld federal jurisdiction in *Hopkins*, as well as in * * * similar quiet title matters * * * . Consistent with those cases, the recognition of federal jurisdiction is in order here.

---

3 The quiet title cases also show the limiting effect of the requirement that the federal issue in a state-law claim must actually be in dispute to justify federal-question jurisdiction. In *Shulthis v. McDougal* (1912), this Court found that there was no federal question jurisdiction to hear a plaintiff's quiet title claim in part because the federal statutes on which title depended were not subject to "any controversy respecting their validity, construction, or effect." As the Court put it, the requirement of an actual dispute about federal law was "especially" important in "suit[s] involving rights to land acquired under a law of the United States," because otherwise "every suit to establish title to land in the central and western states would so arise [under federal law], as all titles in those States are traceable back to those laws."

B

Merrell Dow Pharmaceuticals Inc. v. Thompson (1986), on which Grable rests its position, is not to the contrary. *Merrell Dow* considered a state tort claim resting in part on the allegation that the defendant drug company had violated a federal misbranding prohibition, and was thus presumptively negligent under Ohio law. The Court assumed that federal law would have to be applied to resolve the claim, but after closely examining the strength of the federal interest at stake and the implications of opening the federal forum, held federal jurisdiction unavailable. Congress had not provided a private federal cause of action for violation of the federal branding requirement, and the Court found "it would * * * flout, or at least undermine, congressional intent to conclude that federal courts might nevertheless exercise federal-question jurisdiction and provide remedies for violations of that federal statute solely because the violation * * * is said to be a * * * 'proximate cause' under state law."

Because federal law provides for no quiet title action that could be brought against Darue, Grable argues that there can be no federal jurisdiction here, stressing some broad language in *Merrell Dow* (including the passage just quoted) that on its face supports Grable's position. But an opinion is to be read as a whole, and *Merrell Dow* cannot be read whole as overturning decades of precedent, as it would have done by effectively adopting the Holmes dissent in *Smith* and converting a federal cause of action from a sufficient condition for federal-question jurisdiction[5] into a necessary one.

In the first place, *Merrell Dow* disclaimed the adoption of any bright-line rule, as when the Court reiterated that "in exploring the outer reaches of § 1331, determinations about federal jurisdiction require sensitive judgments about congressional intent, judicial power, and the federal system." The opinion included a lengthy footnote explaining that questions of jurisdiction over state-law claims require "careful judgments," about the "nature of the federal interest at stake" (emphasis deleted). And as a final indication that it did not mean to make a federal right of action mandatory, it expressly approved the exercise of jurisdiction sustained in *Smith*, despite the want of any federal cause of action available to *Smith*'s shareholder plaintiff. *Merrell Dow* then, did not toss out, but specifically retained the contextual enquiry that had been *Smith's* hallmark for over 60 years. At the end of *Merrell Dow*, Justice Holmes was still dissenting.

Accordingly, *Merrell Dow* should be read in its entirety as treating the absence of a federal private right of action as evidence relevant to, but not dispositive of, the "sensitive judgments about congressional intent" that § 1331 requires. The

5 For an extremely rare exception to the sufficiency of a federal right of action, see *Shoshone Mining Co. v. Rutter* (1900).

absence of any federal cause of action affected Merrell Dow's result two ways. The Court saw the fact as worth some consideration in the assessment of substantiality. But its primary importance emerged when the Court treated the combination of no federal cause of action and no preemption of state remedies for misbranding as an important clue to Congress's conception of the scope of jurisdiction to be exercised under § 1331. The Court saw the missing cause of action not as a missing federal door key, always required, but as a missing welcome mat, required in the circumstances, when exercising federal jurisdiction over a state misbranding action would have attracted a horde of original filings and removal cases raising other state claims with embedded federal issues. For if the federal labeling standard without a federal cause of action could get a state claim into federal court, so could any other federal standard without a federal cause of action. And that would have meant a tremendous number of cases.

One only needed to consider the treatment of federal violations generally in garden variety state tort law. "The violation of federal statutes and regulations is commonly given negligence per se effect in state tort proceedings."[6] RESTATEMENT (THIRD) OF TORTS (proposed final draft) § 14, Comment *a*. A general rule of exercising federal jurisdiction over state claims resting on federal mislabeling and other statutory violations would thus have heralded a potentially enormous shift of traditionally state cases into federal courts. Expressing concern over the "increased volume of federal litigation," and noting the importance of adhering to "legislative intent," Merrell Dow thought it improbable that the Congress, having made no provision for a federal cause of action, would have meant to welcome any state-law tort case implicating federal law "solely because the violation of the federal statute is said to [create] a rebuttable presumption [of negligence] * * * under state law." ([I]nternal quotation marks omitted). In this situation, no welcome mat meant keep out. Merrell Dow's analysis thus fits within the framework of examining the importance of having a federal forum for the issue, and the consistency of such a forum with Congress's intended division of labor between state and federal courts.

As already indicated, however, a comparable analysis yields a different jurisdictional conclusion in this case. Although Congress also indicated ambivalence in this case by providing no private right of action to Grable, it is the rare state quiet title action that involves contested issues of federal law. Consequently, jurisdiction over actions like Grable's would not materially affect, or threaten to affect, the normal currents of litigation. Given the absence of threatening structural consequences and the clear interest the Government, its buyers, and its delinquents have in the availability of a federal forum, there is no good reason to shirk from

---

6 Other jurisdictions treat a violation of a federal statute as evidence of negligence or, like Ohio itself in Merrell Dow Pharmaceuticals Inc. v. Thompson (1986), as creating a rebuttable presumption of negligence. RESTATEMENT (THIRD) OF TORTS (proposed final draft) § 14, Comment *c*. Either approach could still implicate issues of federal law.

federal jurisdiction over the dispositive and contested federal issue at the heart of the state-law title claim.[7]

IV

The judgment of the Court of Appeals, upholding federal jurisdiction over Grable's quiet title action, is affirmed.

It is so ordered.

JUSTICE THOMAS, concurring.

The Court faithfully applies our precedents interpreting 28 U.S.C. § 1331 to authorize federal-court jurisdiction over some cases in which state law creates the cause of action but requires determination of an issue of federal law. In this case, no one has asked us to overrule those precedents and adopt the rule Justice Holmes set forth in *American Well Works Co. v. Layne & Bowler Co.* (1916) limiting § 1331 jurisdiction to cases in which federal law creates the cause of action pleaded on the face of the plaintiff's complaint. In an appropriate case, and perhaps with the benefit of better evidence as to the original meaning of § 1331's text, I would be willing to consider that course.

Jurisdictional rules should be clear. Whatever the virtues of the *Smith* standard, it is anything but clear.

Whatever the vices of the *American Well Works* rule, it is clear. Moreover, it accounts for the " 'vast majority' " of cases that come within § 1331 under our current case law—further indication that trying to sort out which cases fall within the smaller *Smith* category may not be worth the effort it entails. Accordingly, I would be willing in appropriate circumstances to reconsider our interpretation of § 1331.

Notes and Questions

1. *Grable* clears up some questions *Merrell Dow* left. Or does it? The Court acknowledges, albeit indirectly, that the majority opinion in *Merrell Dow* at the very least gave rise to some substantial misconceptions in the lower federal courts. For

7 At oral argument Grable's counsel espoused the position that after *Merrell Dow*, federal-question jurisdiction over state-law claims absent a federal right of action could be recognized only where a constitutional issue was at stake. There is, however, no reason in text or otherwise to draw such a rough line. As *Merrell Dow* itself suggested, constitutional questions may be the more likely ones to reach the level of substantiality that can justify federal jurisdiction. But a flat ban on statutory questions would mechanically exclude significant questions of federal law like the one this case presents.

example, one might have been tempted after Merrell Dow to conclude that a hybrid claim—that is, one with a state-created right of action that necessarily incorporated at least one substantive provision of federal law as an element—could never support federal question jurisdiction without there being a federal right of action. Justice Stevens certainly seemed to imply that when he said,

> We *simply* conclude that the congressional determination that there should be no federal remedy for the violation of this federal statute is *tantamount* to a congressional conclusion that the presence of a claimed violation of the statute as an element of a state cause of action is insufficiently "substantial" to confer federal-question jurisdiction.

(Footnote omitted; emphasis added.) And indeed, after Merrell Dow many federal courts held that federal courts could not hear hybrid claims under § 1331. It now appears that things are not quite as simple as Justice Stevens's statement suggested. The statute upon which Grable relied for relief, 26 U.S.C. § 6335, certainly creates neither a federal cause of action nor a substantive right, merely entitling tax delinquents to a particular mode of service of the notice of an IRS property seizure.

2. The Court states that a federal issue must be central to the lawsuit and "substantial" to support federal question jurisdiction and finds that the federal issue is substantial in *Grable*. Why? The Court supports its conclusion by adverting to the strong federal interest in the "prompt and certain collection of delinquent taxes." *Grable* is an action between two private parties over ownership of a piece of land. How, exactly, might decision of the case affect government tax collection?

3. By stressing the government's strong interest in collecting taxes, does Justice Souter imply that other federal interests are less important? Does he imply, for example, that the government has no particularly strong interest in controlling the labeling and distribution of drugs that may be harmful, as in Merrell Dow? Congress apparently thought there was some significant government interest when it passed the Food, Drug and Cosmetic Act in 1938. Does the Court suggest any principled basis for determining which federal statutes are important enough to support federal question jurisdiction in hybrid cases and which ones are not?

4. Does the Court also seem to assume that a federal court will be more likely than a state court to vindicate an IRS administrative action? A skeptic might observe, "So much for parity." *See supra* at 13-21, *infra at* 675 Note 4(b), 834 Note 8, 1084. In any event, do you agree?

5. a) Does Justice Souter's attempt to distinguish and cabin Merrell Dow persuade you? The Sixth Circuit's one-page opinion in Merrell Dow suggests an easier way. In *Grable*, the entire case must rise or fall according to the resolution of the federal issue. In Merrell Dow, by contrast, the Sixth Circuit pointed out that the plaintiffs had pleaded multiple counts, including one count of common law negligence, and so

could prevail on a negligence theory without demonstrating a violation of the Food, Drug and Cosmetic Act. Is that any better? Does the Sixth Circuit's reasoning suggest that the presence of the other counts somehow poisoned federal question jurisdiction that would otherwise have existed? If that were so, what would become of supplemental jurisdiction?

The problem may be that the Sixth Circuit evaluated the case as a whole, not count by count. Note its repeated reference to the plaintiffs' *causes* of action, as if considering them collectively. Federal question jurisdiction is claim-based, not case-based. See AMERICAN LAW INSTITUTE, FEDERAL JUDICIAL CODE REVISION PROJECT 5-7 (2004). If there is federal question jurisdiction with respect to one count, the federal court may also hear the remaining counts if either they have independent jurisdictional bases or if they qualify for supplemental jurisdiction under 28 U.S.C. § 1367. In any event, the character of the other counts does not undercut jurisdiction over the federal question count.

For whatever reason, Justice Stevens's majority opinion in Merrell Dow essentially ignored the Sixth Circuit's reasoning. It certainly did not adopt it. Justice Souter, too, implicitly eschews the Circuit's approach.

b) Instead, Justice Souter focuses on numbers. He asserts that finding federal question jurisdiction in *Grable* will result in few additional federal cases, while finding jurisdiction in Merrell Dow would have resulted in a flood of new federal filings. Whether his prediction about *Grable* is correct remains to be seen, but he clearly is right that more cases would have arisen under federal law if Merrell Dow had come out the other way.

6. Justice Souter's numbers analysis is pragmatic, but also problematic. One hopes that he is not suggesting that the most important federal issues come up the least often. If a federal issue is substantial (whatever that may mean after Merrell Dow and *Grable*), should the federal courts nonetheless decline to hear a hybrid claim concerning it if one can predict many similar cases arising? Does ubiquity connote lack of substantiality?

7. *Grable* brings forward in time, but does not clear up, a problem that Merrell Dow created. The fourth part of the Court's arising-under test is that "the federal issue will ultimately qualify for a federal forum only if federal jurisdiction is consistent with congressional judgment about the sound division of labor between state and federal courts governing the application of § 1331." To which Congress does Justice Souter refer, the Congress that passed the predecessor of § 1331 back in 1875, the most recent Congress to have reenacted that section, or the Congress that passed the tax statute under which Grable claimed its entitlement?

Since there was no Internal Revenue Service in 1875, one might hazard a guess that the Congress that passed the original § 1331 did not spend a lot of time thinking about whether it should include actions where the federal issue was one of proper service under the Internal Revenue Code of 1954. Do you think the Congress sitting in 1980, which recodified § 1331 (removing the previously existing jurisdictional amount, which had always tracked the jurisdictional floor of the diversity statute, § 1332), had a view on whether questions of the propriety of service under the relevant tax statute should suffice for federal question jurisdiction?

In 1954, Congress initially passed the section upon which Darue relied for federal question jurisdiction in removing the case. Congress has subsequently recodified the statute four times, in 1976, 1986, 1988 and 1998. Do you think any of those Congresses had a particular view of whether a dispute about whether there was proper notice under 26 U.S.C. § 6335(a) should come within the jurisdictional ambit of 28 U.S.C. § 1331? Assuming that those Congresses even had such a view, of what importance is it if it did not result in any legislative action with respect to § 1331?

This uncertainty suggests the Court is not really interested in congressional judgment. Yet, "there must always be an assessment of any disruptive portent in exercising federal jurisdiction." Who makes the assessment?

8. *Grable* suggests resolution of an issue that lingered after Merrell Dow—whether a state court had jurisdiction to hear a hybrid claim involving a federal statutory standard combined with a state cause of action when the federal statute did not create a private right of action. In Merrell Dow, Justice Stevens stated that the import of the lack of a private federal cause of action "is that it would flout congressional intent to provide a private federal remedy for violation of the federal statute." If, as on Justice Stevens's reading, Congress affirmatively did not want private enforcement of the statutory standard, would it flout congressional intent to allow a private remedy in the state courts? Commentators have argued that state courts should be able to hear hybrid claims unless Congress has explicitly preempted state enforcement of the federal statutory provision. *Grable* appears to adopt this standard. Justice Souter states that the Merrell Dow Court "treated the combination of no federal cause of action and no preemption of state remedies for misbranding as an important clue to Congress's conception of the scope of jurisdiction to be exercised under § 1331." Perhaps we read too much into this single sentence, but the implication seems to be that a hybrid claim may go forward in state court even if a federal court cannot hear it.

9. At two points in the opinion, Justice Souter refers to the necessity, when considering jurisdiction over a hybrid claim, of the federal issue being actually in dispute. The first appearance of the idea is in the last sentence of Part II; the second occurs in the third footnote of the opinion. Although he does not cite Gully v. First National Bank (*supra* at 331), he probably is echoing Justice Cardozo's admonition that "[a] genuine and present controversy, not merely a possible or conjectural one, must

exist with reference" to the federal issue. Do you think Justice Souter is suggesting that if the dispute in a hybrid-claim case exists only with respect to what the facts are and not with respect to what federal law is or how it applies to particular sets of facts, then there is no federal question jurisdiction?

Certainly that is not the case when federal law creates the cause of action. In an antitrust dispute, for example, the parties may agree entirely on what the Sherman Act requires and differ only on whether the defendant performed anti-competitive acts. Nonetheless, the federal courts clearly would have jurisdiction in such a case. Justice Souter, however, is quite explicit in footnote 3 when he adverts to "the requirement that the federal issue in a state-law claim must actually be in dispute to justify federal-question jurisdiction." Is he implying that the courts are to treat federally created claims and hybrid claims differently? What might be the policy justification for such a position?

10. After *Grable*, do we have a clearer idea of the criteria for deciding whether a case arises under federal law? Are the criteria any easier to apply than they were before Grable, or are we still looking at the shifting colors of Justice Cardozo's kaleidoscope?

The Court demonstrated the very next year that federal question jurisdiction remains in ferment. *Empire Healthchoice Assurance, Inc. v. McVeigh*, 547 U.S. 677 (2006), involved the federal government's health insurance plan for federal employees. The government contracted with private carriers to administer a variety of health plans funded by government and employee contributions into a special fund under the Federal Employees Health Benefits Act of 1959 (FEHBA). One section of that statute explicitly preempts state law on issues concerning "coverage or benefits" under the plans. It does not create a right of action, nor does it make reference to any subrogation or reimbursement rights of the carriers, although annual contracts between the government and the private insurance carriers oblige the carriers to attempt to recoup amounts paid for employees' medical care. The contracts further provide that employees enrolling in any of the plans agree either to reimburse the carrier for benefit payments if the employee recovers damages from a tort action with respect to the condition or to subrogate the carrier to their claims. A second section of FEHBA explicitly creates federal question jurisdiction for actions against the United States.

The dispute arose when a beneficiary's estate settled a tort action against alleged tortfeasors for more than $3,000,000. Although the carrier knew of the action, it did not participate in it. After the settlement, Empire Healthchoice filed a federal action seeking reimbursement from the estate of the $157,309 it had paid in benefits, and the case arrived in the Supreme Court on the issue of jurisdiction under § 1331.

The Court's analysis is complex because the jurisdictional question turned on whether Empire Healthchoice's reimbursement claim sounded in state law or federal common law, and it is difficult to understand the opinions without being familiar with the Court's recent federal-common-law jurisprudence, which appears in Chapter 5.[11]

If one views the reimbursement claim as a function of the contract between the employee and the carrier, then typical analysis would view it as a state law claim (with no federal component) and refuse jurisdiction. If one considers that the employee is a beneficiary of a contract created and controlled by federal law that requires federal law to govern all issues arising under the contract, then the matter may look more like a federal question case.

> **FYI**
>
> 5 U.S.C.A. § 8902(m)(1): "The terms of any contract under this chapter which relate to the nature, provision, or extent of coverage or benefits (including payments with respect to benefits) shall supersede and preempt any State or local law, or any regulation issued thereunder, which relates to health insurance or plans."

Five Justices took the former view, noting that Congress had preempted state law in a very limited way, referring only to coverage and benefits and not referring to jurisdiction at all. They contrasted that with Congress's explicit conferral of federal question jurisdiction for actions against the United States. The combination of the majority's refusal to find the federal courts should create federal common law to govern reimbursement claims and Congress's exclusion by implication of federal jurisdiction not involving claims against the United States caused those Justices to rule that the case did not arise under federal law for purposes of § 1331.

Justice Breyer wrote for the four dissenters, who included Justice Souter, the author of Grable. He described the reimbursement portions of the contract as "a few scattered islands in a sea of federal contractual provisions." Noting that reimbursed funds must go to the Treasury Department and back into the statutory fund, Justice Breyer argued that the case was pervasively federal and that federal common law should govern. Moreover, he saw the federal government as the real party in interest, another reason for federal common law to govern the dispute. That being the case, it was but a short step for him to find jurisdiction under § 1331. At the end of the day, however, he lacked the votes.

> **Food for Thought**
>
> It is quite possible that it should have been a longer step for Justice Breyer. He rather quickly equated his view that federal common law should govern the case with the conclusion that there was § 1331 jurisdiction. Yet, after *Merrell Dow*, that result is far from automatic. Recall that *Merrell Dow* insisted that, at least in the absence of a federally created right of action, the federal question in an otherwise state claim had to be "substantial," a criterion that Grable by no means repudiated. Justice Breyer did not acknowledge that part of the jurisdictional test.

---

11 Chapter 5 contains a more complete discussion of the federal common law battle in *Empire Healthchoice*, *infra* at 484-86.

It turned out that *Grable's* clarification needed clarification. Only seven years later, the Court returned to the subject.

Gunn v. Minton

Supreme Court of the United States, 2013.
133 S.Ct. 1059

CHIEF JUSTICE ROBERTS delivered the opinion of the Court.

Federal courts have exclusive jurisdiction over cases "arising under any Act of Congress relating to patents." 28 U.S.C. § 1338(a). The question presented is whether a state law claim alleging legal malpractice in the handling of a patent case must be brought in federal court.

I

In the early 1990s, respondent Vernon Minton developed a computer program and telecommunications network designed to facilitate securities trading. In March 1995, he leased the system—known as the Texas Computer Exchange Network, or TEXCEN—to R.M. Stark & Co., a securities brokerage. A little over a year later, he applied for a patent for an interactive securities trading system that was based substantially on TEXCEN. The U.S. Patent and Trademark Office issued the patent in January 2000.

Patent in hand, Minton filed a patent infringement suit in Federal District Court against the National Association of Securities Dealers, Inc. (NASD) and the NASDAQ Stock Market, Inc. He was represented by Jerry Gunn and the other petitioners. NASD and NASDAQ moved for summary judgment on the ground that Minton's patent was invalid under the "on sale" bar, 35 U.S.C. § 102(b). That provision specifies that an inventor is not entitled to a patent if "the invention was * * * on sale in [the United States], more than one year prior to the date of the application," and Minton had leased TEXCEN to Stark more than one year prior to filing his patent application. Rejecting Minton's argument that there were differences between TEXCEN and the patented system that precluded application of the on-sale bar, the District Court granted the summary judgment motion and declared Minton's patent invalid.

Minton then filed a motion for reconsideration in the District Court, arguing for the first time that the lease agreement with Stark was part of ongoing testing of TEXCEN and therefore fell within the "experimental use" exception to the on-sale bar. The District Court denied the motion.

Minton appealed to the U.S. Court of Appeals for the Federal Circuit. That court affirmed, concluding that the District Court had appropriately held Minton's experimental-use argument waived.

Minton, convinced that his attorneys' failure to raise the experimental-use argument earlier had cost him the lawsuit and led to invalidation of his patent, brought this malpractice action in Texas state court. His former lawyers defended on the ground that the lease to Stark was not, in fact, for an experimental use, and that therefore Minton's patent infringement claims would have failed even if the experimental-use argument had been timely raised. The trial court agreed, holding that Minton had put forward "less than a scintilla of proof" that the lease had been for an experimental purpose. It accordingly granted summary judgment to Gunn and the other lawyer defendants.

On appeal, Minton raised a new argument: Because his legal malpractice claim was based on an alleged error in a patent case, it "aris[es] under" federal patent law for purposes of 28 U.S.C. § 1338(a). And because, under § 1338(a), "[n]o State court shall have jurisdiction over any claim for relief arising under any Act of Congress relating to patents," the Texas court—where Minton had originally brought his malpractice claim—lacked subject matter jurisdiction to decide the case. Accordingly, Minton argued, the trial court's order should be vacated and the case dismissed, leaving Minton free to start over in the Federal District Court.

A divided panel of the Court of Appeals of Texas rejected Minton's argument. Applying the test we articulated in *Grable & Sons Metal Products, Inc. v. Darue Engineering & Mfg.*, 545 U.S. 308, 314 (2005), it held that the federal interests implicated by Minton's state law claim were not sufficiently substantial to trigger § 1338 "arising under" jurisdiction. It also held that finding exclusive federal jurisdiction over state legal malpractice actions would, contrary to *Grable*'s commands, disturb the balance of federal and state judicial responsibilities. Proceeding to the merits of Minton's malpractice claim, the Court of Appeals affirmed the trial court's determination that Minton had failed to establish experimental use and that arguments on that ground therefore would not have saved his infringement suit.

The Supreme Court of Texas reversed, relying heavily on a pair of cases from the U.S. Court of Appeals for the Federal Circuit. The Court concluded that Minton's claim involved "a substantial federal issue" within the meaning of *Grable* "because the success of Minton's malpractice claim is reliant upon the viability of the experimental use exception as a defense to the on-sale bar." Adjudication of Minton's claim in federal court was consistent with the appropriate balance between federal and state judicial responsibilities, it held, because "the federal government and patent litigants have an interest in the uniform application of patent law by courts well-versed in that subject matter."

Justice Guzman, joined by Justices Medina and Willett, dissented. The dissenting justices would have held that the federal issue was neither substantial nor disputed, and that maintaining the proper balance of responsibility between state and federal courts precluded relegating state legal malpractice claims to federal court.

We granted certiorari.

II

"Federal courts are courts of limited jurisdiction," possessing "only that power authorized by Constitution and statute." There is no dispute that the Constitution permits Congress to extend federal court jurisdiction to a case such as this one, *see Osborn v. Bank of United States*, 22 U.S. 738, 823–824 (1824); the question is whether Congress has done so.

As relevant here, Congress has authorized the federal district courts to exercise original jurisdiction in "all civil actions arising under the Constitution, laws, or treaties of the United States," 28 U.S.C. § 1331, and, more particularly, over "any civil action arising under any Act of Congress relating to patents," § 1338(a). Adhering to the demands of "[l]inguistic consistency," we have interpreted the phrase "arising under" in both sections identically, applying our § 1331 and § 1338(a) precedents interchangeably. For cases falling within the patent-specific arising under jurisdiction of § 1338(a), however, Congress has not only provided for federal jurisdiction but also eliminated state jurisdiction, decreeing that "[n]o State court shall have jurisdiction over any claim for relief arising under any Act of Congress relating to patents." § 1338(a). To determine whether jurisdiction was proper in the Texas courts, therefore, we must determine whether it would have been proper in a federal district court—whether, that is, the case "aris[es] under any Act of Congress relating to patents."

For statutory purposes, a case can "aris[e] under" federal law in two ways. Most directly, a case arises under federal law when federal law creates the cause of action asserted. *See American Well Works Co. v. Layne & Bowler Co.*, 241 U.S. 257, 260 (1916) ("A suit arises under the law that creates the cause of action"). As a rule of inclusion, this "creation" test admits of only extremely rare exceptions and accounts for the vast bulk of suits that arise under federal law. Minton's original patent infringement suit against NASD and NASDAQ, for example, arose under federal law in this manner because it was authorized by 35 U.S.C. §§ 271, 281.

But even where a claim finds its origins in state rather than federal law—as Minton's legal malpractice claim indisputably does—we have identified a "special and small category" of cases in which arising under jurisdiction still lies. In outlining the contours of this slim category, we do not paint on a blank canvas. Unfortunately, the canvas looks like one that Jackson Pollock got to first.

In an effort to bring some order to this unruly doctrine several Terms ago, we condensed our prior cases into the following inquiry: Does the "state-law claim necessarily raise a stated federal issue, actually disputed and substantial, which a federal forum may entertain without disturbing any congressionally approved balance of federal and state judicial responsibilities"? That is, federal jurisdiction over a state law claim will lie if a federal issue is: (1) necessarily raised, (2) actually disputed, (3) substantial, and (4) capable of resolution in federal court without disrupting the federal-state balance approved by Congress. Where all four of these requirements are met, we held, jurisdiction is proper because there is a "serious federal interest in claiming the advantages thought to be inherent in a federal forum," which can be vindicated without disrupting Congress's intended division of labor between state and federal courts.

III

Applying *Grable's* inquiry here, it is clear that Minton's legal malpractice claim does not arise under federal patent law. Indeed, for the reasons we discuss, we are comfortable concluding that state legal malpractice claims based on underlying patent matters will rarely, if ever, arise under federal patent law for purposes of § 1338(a). Although such cases may necessarily raise disputed questions of patent law, those cases are by their nature unlikely to have the sort of significance for the federal system necessary to establish jurisdiction.

A

To begin, we acknowledge that resolution of a federal patent question is "necessary" to Minton's case. Under Texas law, a plaintiff alleging legal malpractice must establish four elements: (1) that the defendant attorney owed the plaintiff a duty; (2) that the attorney breached that duty; (3) that the breach was the proximate cause of the plaintiff's injury; and (4) that damages occurred. In cases like this one, in which the attorney's alleged error came in failing to make a particular argument, the causation element requires a "case within a case" analysis of whether, had the argument been made, the outcome of the earlier litigation would have been different. To prevail on his legal malpractice claim, therefore, Minton must show that he would have prevailed in his federal patent infringement case if only petitioners had timely made an experimental-use argument on his behalf. That will necessarily require application of patent law to the facts of Minton's case.

B

The federal issue is also "actually disputed" here—indeed, on the merits, it is the central point of dispute. Minton argues that the experimental-use exception properly applied to his lease to Stark, saving his patent from the on-sale bar; petitioners argue that it did not. This is just the sort of " 'dispute * * * respecting the * * * effect of [federal] law' " that Grable envisioned.

C

Minton's argument founders on Grable's next requirement, however, for the federal issue in this case is not substantial in the relevant sense. In reaching the opposite conclusion, the Supreme Court of Texas focused on the importance of the issue to the plaintiff's case and to the parties before it. As our past cases show, however, it is not enough that the federal issue be significant to the particular parties in the immediate suit; that will *always* be true when the state claim "necessarily raise[s]" a disputed federal issue, as Grable separately requires. The substantiality inquiry under Grable looks instead to the importance of the issue to the federal system as a whole.

> **Take Note**
>
> Thus, it is clear that merely having an outcome determinative federal issue well-pleaded in the complaint is no longer sufficient, as it seemed to be in *Smith*. One now must satisfy some sort of separate substantiality measure with reference "to the federal system as a whole." As you read the remainder of the opinion, evaluate how good a job the Court does at explaining to the lower federal courts how they should carry out the inquiry.

In Grable itself, for example, the Internal Revenue Service had seized property from the plaintiff and sold it to satisfy the plaintiff's federal tax delinquency. Five years later, the plaintiff filed a state law quiet title action against the third party that had purchased the property, alleging that the IRS had failed to comply with certain federally imposed notice requirements, so that the seizure and sale were invalid. In holding that the case arose under federal law, we primarily focused not on the interests of the litigants themselves, but rather on the broader significance of the notice question for the Federal Government. We emphasized the Government's "strong interest" in being able to recover delinquent taxes through seizure and sale of property, which in turn "require[d] clear terms of notice to allow buyers * * * to satisfy themselves that the Service has touched the bases necessary for good title." The Government's "direct interest in the availability of a federal forum to vindicate its own administrative action" made the question "an important issue of federal law that sensibly belong[ed] in a federal court."

A second illustration of the sort of substantiality we require comes from *Smith v. Kansas City Title & Trust Co.*, 255 U.S. 180 (1921), which *Grable* described as "[t]he classic example" of a state claim arising under federal law. In *Smith*, the plaintiff argued that the defendant bank could not purchase certain bonds issued by the Federal Government because the Government had acted unconstitutionally in issuing them. We held that the case arose under federal law, because the "decision depends upon the determination" of "the constitutional validity of an act of Congress which is directly drawn in question." Again, the relevant point was not the importance of the question to the parties alone but rather the importance more generally of a determination that the Government "securities were issued under an unconstitutional law, and hence of no validity."

Here, the federal issue carries no such significance. Because of the backward-looking nature of a legal malpractice claim, the question is posed in a merely hypothetical sense: *If* Minton's lawyers had raised a timely experimental-use argument, would the result in the patent infringement proceeding have been different? No matter how the state courts resolve that hypothetical "case within a case," it will not change the real-world result of the prior federal patent litigation. Minton's patent will remain invalid.

Nor will allowing state courts to resolve these cases undermine "the development of a uniform body of [patent] law." Congress ensured such uniformity by vesting exclusive jurisdiction over actual patent cases in the federal district courts and exclusive appellate jurisdiction in the Federal Circuit. See 28 U.S.C. §§ 1338(a), 1295(a)(1). In resolving the nonhypothetical patent questions those cases present, the federal courts are of course not bound by state court case-within-a-case patent rulings. In any event, the state court case-within-a-case inquiry asks what would have happened in the prior federal proceeding if a particular argument had been made. In answering that question, state courts can be expected to hew closely to the pertinent federal precedents. It is those precedents, after all, that would have applied had the argument been made.

As for more novel questions of patent law that may arise for the first time in a state court "case within a case," they will at some point be decided by a federal court in the context of an actual patent case, with review in the Federal Circuit. If the question arises frequently, it will soon be resolved within the federal system, laying to rest any contrary state court precedent; if it does not arise frequently, it is unlikely to implicate substantial federal interests. The present case is "poles apart from *Grable*," in which a state court's resolution of the federal question "would be controlling in numerous other cases."

Minton also suggests that state courts' answers to hypothetical patent questions can sometimes have real-world effect on other patents through issue preclusion. Minton, for example, has filed what is known as a "continuation patent" application related to his original patent. See 35 U.S.C. § 120. He argues that, in evaluating this separate application, the patent examiner could be bound by the Texas trial court's interpretation of the scope of Minton's original patent. It is unclear whether this is true. The Patent and Trademark Office's Manual of Patent Examining Procedure provides that res judicata is a proper ground for rejecting a patent "only when the earlier decision was a decision of the Board of Appeals" or certain federal reviewing courts, giving no indication that state court decisions would have preclusive effect. In fact, Minton has not identified any case finding such preclusive effect based on a state court decision. But even assuming that a state court's case-within-a-case adjudication may be preclusive under some circumstances, the result would be limited to the parties and patents that had been before the state court. Such "fact-bound and situation-specific" effects are not sufficient to establish federal arising under jurisdiction.

Nor can we accept the suggestion that the federal courts' greater familiarity with patent law means that legal malpractice cases like this one belong in federal court. It is true that a similar interest was among those we considered in *Grable*. But the possibility that a state court will incorrectly resolve a state claim is not, by itself, enough to trigger the federal courts' exclusive patent jurisdiction, even if the potential error finds its root in a misunderstanding of patent law.

There is no doubt that resolution of a patent issue in the context of a state legal malpractice action can be vitally important to the particular parties in that case. But something more, demonstrating that the question is significant to the federal system as a whole, is needed. That is missing here.

D

It follows from the foregoing that *Grable*'s fourth requirement is also not met. That requirement is concerned with the appropriate "balance of federal and state judicial responsibilities." We have already explained the absence of a substantial federal issue within the meaning of *Grable*. The States, on the other hand, have "a special responsibility for maintaining standards among members of the licensed professions." Their "interest * * * in regulating lawyers is especially great since lawyers are essential to the primary governmental function of administering justice, and have historically been officers of the courts." We have no reason to suppose that Congress—in establishing exclusive federal jurisdiction over patent cases—meant to bar from state courts state legal malpractice claims simply because they require resolution of a hypothetical patent issue.

As we recognized a century ago, "[t]he Federal courts have exclusive jurisdiction of all cases arising under the patent laws, but not of all questions in which a patent may be the subject-matter of the controversy." In this case, although the state courts must answer a question of patent law to resolve Minton's legal malpractice claim, their answer will have no broader effects. It will not stand as binding precedent for any future patent claim; it will not even affect the validity of Minton's patent. Accordingly, there is no "serious federal interest in claiming the advantages thought to be inherent in a federal forum," Section 1338(a) does not deprive the state courts of subject matter jurisdiction.

The judgment of the Supreme Court of Texas is reversed, and the case is remanded for further proceedings not inconsistent with this opinion.

It is so ordered.

Notes and Questions

1. At least some things are clearer after *Gunn*. It seems finally to have interred the notion from Merrell Dow that the American Well Works test was making a comeback. Justice Souter's *Grable* opinion had discussed that reasonably explicitly, *see supra* at 339-40, but by the time the Court decided *Gunn*, the notion did not even draw a mention. To the extent that Merrell Dow seems yet to stand for anything, it is the Court's still free-floating idea of substantiality, now apparently entirely untethered from American Well Works.

2. Of how much help to future courts is the Chief Justice's methodical examination of the four-part Grable test? The first two parts merely echo Mottley and Gully, but the ghost of Merrell Dow looms over the third and fourth parts. With respect to the substantiality prong, has the Court adopted Merrell Dow's decoupling of the Smith analysis discussed *supra* at 333-35?

3. As for the fourth prong, what can one say? The Chief Justice speaks of "the federal-state balance approved by Congress" as if Congress, in passing almost any legislation, constantly thinks about the division of judicial labor between the federal judiciary and the states. How is one to know that Congress *was* thinking about an issue on which it is silent? Beyond that, even assuming that Congress actually thought about federal versus state jurisdictional reach when it passed the notice provision involved in Grable or the provisions of the patent statutes upon which Minton relied, how should a court discern *what* the silent Congress was thinking? Do you think future courts will actually be responding to what they think Congress thought about subject matter jurisdiction, or will they more likely be concerned (knowingly or not) with what *they* think Congress should have thought? What difference does it make anyway?

C. The Special Problem of Declaratory Judgment Cases

The federal Declaratory Judgment Act is a relative newcomer. The effort to have Congress and the federal courts recognize a legitimate role for declaratory judgments began in 1919 and did not bear fruit until 1934. In the interim, the Supreme Court, which originally had questioned whether federal courts could issue declaratory judgments consistently with the Case-or-Controversy Clause, came to the view that they could.

The end result of a successful request for declaratory relief is just what it sounds like: a declaration of the parties' rights and obligations. The judgment itself has no mandatory effect, although the second section of the Act allows the court to grant "further relief." Contrast a declaratory judgment action with what is often called a "coercive" action. The latter is a typical case seeking mandatory relief, and claimant's success in a coercive action requires the losing party to *do* something, whether it is to pay a money judgment, perform some specific action (a mandatory injunction) or refrain from continuing to perform some specific action (a prohibitory injunction).

Skelly Oil Co. v. Phillips Petroleum Co.

Supreme Court of the United States, 1950.
339 U.S. 667.

MR. JUSTICE FRANKFURTER delivered the opinion of the Court.

In 1945, Michigan-Wisconsin Pipe Line Company sought from the Federal Power Commission a certificate of public convenience and necessity, required by § 7(c) of the Natural Gas Act, for the construction and operation of a pipe line to carry natural gas from Texas to Michigan and Wisconsin. A prerequisite for such a certificate is adequate reserves of gas. To obtain these reserves Michigan-Wisconsin entered into an agreement with Phillips Petroleum Company on December 11, 1945, whereby the latter undertook to make available gas from the Hugoton Gas Field, sprawling over Kansas, Oklahoma and Texas, which it produced or purchased from others. Phillips had contracted with petitioners, Skelly Oil Company, Stanolind Oil and Gas Company, and Magnolia Petroleum Company, to purchase gas produced by them in the Hugoton Field for resale to Michigan-Wisconsin. Each contract provided that "in the event Michigan-Wisconsin Pipe Line Company shall fail to secure from the Federal Power Commission on or before [October 1, 1946] a certificate of public convenience and necessity for the construction and operation of its pipe line, Seller [a petitioner] shall have the right to terminate this contract by written notice to Buyer [Phillips] delivered to Buyer at any time after December 1, 1946, but before the issuance of such certificate." The legal significance of this provision is at the core of this litigation.

> **FYI**
>
> You may wonder about the significance of the October 1 date, given that, as the remainder of the sentence points out, Skelly could not actually exercise its cancellation right before December 1. The most likely explanation is that the contract went through several drafts before being signed, and the typist simply overlooked this iteration of the date rather than changing it to December 1. (Ah, the delights of global search and replace.)

The Federal Power Commission, in response to the application of Michigan-Wisconsin, on November 30, 1946, ordered that "A certificate of public convenience and necessity be and it is hereby issued to applicant [Michigan-Wisconsin], upon the terms and conditions of this order," listing among the conditions that there be no transportation or sale of natural gas by means of the sanctioned facilities until all necessary authorizations were obtained from the State of Wisconsin and the communities proposed to be served, that Michigan-Wisconsin should have the approval of the Securities and Exchange Commission for its plan of financing, that the applicant should file for the approval of the Commission a schedule of reasonable rates, and that the sanctioned facilities should not be used for the transportation of gas to Detroit and Ann Arbor except with due regard for the rights and duties of Panhandle Eastern Pipe Line Company, which had intervened before the Federal Power Commission, in its established service for resale in these areas, such rights and duties to be set forth in a supplemental order. It was also provided that Michigan-Wisconsin should have fifteen days from the issue of the supplemental order to notify the Commission whether the certificate "as herein issued is acceptable to it." Finally, the Commission's order provided that for purposes of computing the time within which applications for rehearing could be filed, "the date of issuance of this order shall be deemed to be the date of issuance of the opinions, or of the supplemental order referred to herein, whichever may be later."

News of the Commission's action was released on November 30, 1946, but the actual content of the order was not made public until December 2, 1946. Petitioners severally, on December 2, 1946, gave notice to Phillips of termination of their contracts on the ground that Michigan-Wisconsin had not received a certificate of public convenience and necessity. Thereupon Michigan-Wisconsin and Phillips brought suit against petitioners in the District Court for the Northern District of Oklahoma. Alleging that a certificate of public convenience and necessity, "within the meaning of said Natural Gas Act and said contracts" had been issued prior to petitioners' attempt at termination of the contracts, they invoked the Federal Declaratory Judgment Act for a declaration that the contracts were still "in effect and binding upon the parties thereto." Motions by petitioners to have

Michigan-Wisconsin dropped as a party plaintiff were sustained, but motions to dismiss the complaint for want of jurisdiction were denied. The case then went to the merits, and the District Court decreed that the contracts between Phillips and petitioners have not been "effectively terminated and that each of such contracts remain [*sic*] in full force and effect." The Court of Appeals for the Tenth Circuit affirmed, and we brought the case here, because it raises in sharp form the question whether a suit like this "arises under the Constitution, laws or treaties of the United States," 28 U.S.C. § 1331, so as to enable District Courts to give declaratory relief under the Declaratory Judgment Act.

"[T]he operation of the Declaratory Judgment Act is procedural only." *Aetna Life Ins. Co. v. Haworth* [1937]. Congress enlarged the range of remedies available in the federal courts but did not extend their jurisdiction. When concerned as we are with the power of the inferior federal courts to entertain litigation within the restricted area to which the Constitution and Acts of Congress confine them, "jurisdiction" means the kinds of issues which give right of entrance to federal courts. Jurisdiction in this sense was not altered by the Declaratory Judgment Act. Prior to that Act, a federal court would entertain a suit on a contract only if the plaintiff asked for an immediately enforceable remedy like money damages or an injunction, but such relief could only be given if the requisites of jurisdiction, in the sense of a federal right or diversity, provided foundation for resort to the federal courts. The Declaratory Judgment Act allowed relief to be given by way of recognizing the plaintiff's right even though no immediate enforcement of it was asked. But the requirements of jurisdiction—the limited subject matters which alone Congress had authorized the District Courts to adjudicate—were not impliedly repealed or modified.

If Phillips sought damages from petitioners or specific performance of their contracts, it could not bring suit in a United States District Court on the theory that it was asserting a federal right. And for the simple reason that such a suit would "arise" under the State law governing the contracts. Whatever federal claim Phillips may be able to urge would in any event be injected into the case only in anticipation of a defense to be asserted by petitioners. "Not every question of federal law emerging in a suit is proof that a federal law is the basis of the suit." *Gully v. First National Bank in Meridian* [1936]. Ever since *Metcalf v. City of Watertown* [1888], it has been settled doctrine that where a suit is brought in the federal courts "upon the sole ground that the determination of the suit depends upon some question of a federal nature, it must appear, at the outset, from the declaration or the bill of the party suing, that the suit is of that character." But "a suggestion of one party that the other will or may set up a claim under the Constitution or laws of the United States does not make the suit one arising under that Constitution or those laws." The plaintiff's claim itself must present a federal question "unaided by anything alleged in anticipation of avoidance of defenses which it is thought the defendant may interpose."

* * *

To be observant of these restrictions is not to indulge in formalism or sterile technicality. It would turn into the federal courts a vast current of litigation indubitably arising under State law, in the sense that the right to be vindicated was State-created, if a suit for a declaration of rights could be brought into the federal courts merely because an anticipated defense derived from federal law. Not only would this unduly swell the volume of litigation in the District Courts but it would also embarrass those courts—and this Court on potential review—in that matters of local law may often be involved, and the District Courts may either have to decide doubtful questions of State law or hold cases pending disposition of such State issues by State courts. To sanction suits for declaratory relief as within the jurisdiction of the District Courts merely because, as in this case, artful pleading anticipates a defense based on federal law would contravene the whole trend of jurisdictional legislation by Congress, disregard the effective functioning of the federal judicial system and distort the limited procedural purpose of the Declaratory Judgment Act. Since the matter in controversy as to which Phillips asked for a declaratory judgment is not one that "arises under the * * * laws * * * of the United States" and since as to Skelly and Stanolind jurisdiction cannot be sustained on the score of diversity of citizenship, the proceedings against them should have been dismissed.

* * *

Notes and Questions

1. What is the precise federal issue in *Skelly Oil*?

2. Declaratory judgment cases presented a new problem in federal question jurisdiction. After *Skelly Oil*, what steps should a court follow in deciding whether a declaratory judgment action arises under federal law?

3. Consider the structure of the complaint in *Skelly Oil*. Is it not likely that it satisfied the various tests for federal question jurisdiction under 28 U.S.C.A. § 1331? In that event, does the case represent another shift in the Court's approach to federal question jurisdiction? If so, should the Court have announced the shift more explicitly? If not, then why does Phillips's well-pleaded complaint that necessarily contains the federal issue not suffice to open the federal courthouse doors?

4. If Skelly Oil had been the plaintiff, seeking a declaration of invalidity of the contract, would it not have been necessary then for it to plead the untimeliness of the issuance of the Federal Power Commission certificate? Would that cause the result

to change? Phillips had a potential state claim for breach of contract in the event that Skelly refused to supply the natural gas. By pleading a declaratory judgment claim, Phillips sought to create federal question jurisdiction where there would have been none in an ordinary breach of contract action by Phillips. Can the same be said of Skelly Oil as a plaintiff?

5. In connection with the last note, consider *E. Edelmann & Co. v. Triple-A Specialty Co.*, 88 F.2d 852 (7th Cir.), cert. *denied*, 300 U.S. 680 (1937). An alleged patent infringer sued the patentee seeking a declaration of invalidity of the patent or of non-infringement of the patent by plaintiff's device, and an injunction to bar further wrongful allegations of infringement. The Seventh Circuit upheld jurisdiction. In *Franchise Tax Board v. Construction Laborers Vacation Trust*, 463 U.S. 1, 19 n.19 (1983), the Court cited Edelmann with approval, "on the theory that an infringement suit by the declaratory judgment defendant would raise a federal question over which the federal courts have exclusive jurisdiction."

Go Online

American Well and Edelman Complaints

Does *Edelmann* suggest an alternative strategy for the plaintiff in *American Well Works* were the case brought today? What would be the result under an *Edelmann* analysis? Is it consistent with *Skelly Oil?* As you read the next case, pay careful attention to whether the Court approves or disapproves the jurisdictional approaches of *American Well Works, Edelmann, and Skelly Oil.* As a preliminary matter, compare the complaints in *American Well Works and Edelmann.* How do they differ?

Franchise Tax Board Of California v. Construction Laborers Vacation Trust

Supreme Court of the United States, 1983.
463 U.S. 1.

JUSTICE BRENNAN delivered the opinion of the Court.

The principal question in dispute between the parties is whether the Employee Retirement Income Security Act of 1974 (ERISA), permits state tax authorities to collect unpaid state income taxes by levying on funds held in trust for the taxpayers under an ERISA-covered vacation benefit plan. The issue is an important one, which affects thousands of federally regulated trusts and all nonfederal tax collection systems, and it must eventually receive a definitive, uniform resolution. Nevertheless, for reasons involving perhaps more history than logic, we hold that the lower federal courts had no jurisdiction to decide the question in the case before us, and we vacate the judgment and remand the case with instructions to remand it to the state court from which it was removed.

I

None of the relevant facts is in dispute. Appellee Construction Laborers Vacation Trust for Southern California (CLVT) is a trust established by an agreement between four associations of employers active in the construction industry in southern California and the Southern California District Council of Laborers, an arm of the District Council and affiliated locals of the Laborers' International Union of North America. The purpose of the agreement and trust was to establish a mechanism for administering the provisions of a collective-bargaining agreement that grants construction workers a yearly paid vacation. The trust agreement expressly proscribes any assignment, pledge, or encumbrance of funds held in trust by CLVT. The Plan that CLVT administers is unquestionably an "employee welfare benefit plan" within the meaning of § 3 of ERISA, and CLVT and its individual trustees are thereby subject to extensive regulation * * * .

Appellant Franchise Tax Board is a California agency charged with enforcement of that State's personal income tax law. California law authorizes appellant to require any person in possession of "credits or other personal property or other things of value, belonging to a taxpayer" "to withhold * * * the amount of any tax, interest, or penalties due from the taxpayer * * * and to transmit the amount withheld to the Franchise Tax Board." Any person who, upon notice by the Franchise Tax Board, fails to comply with its request to withhold and to transmit funds becomes personally liable for the amounts identified in the notice.

In June 1980, the Franchise Tax Board filed a complaint in state court against CLVT and its trustees. Under the heading "First Cause of Action," appellant alleged that CLVT had failed to comply with three levies * * *,[4] concluding with

4 At several points in 1977 and 1978, appellant issued notices to CLVT requesting it to withhold and to transmit approximately $380 in unpaid taxes, interest, and penalties due from three individuals. CLVT did not dispute that the individuals in question were beneficiaries of its trust or that it was then holding vacation benefit funds for them. In each case, however, it acknowledged receipt of appellant's notice and informed appellant that it had requested an opinion letter from the Administrator for Pension and Welfare Benefit Programs of the United States Department of Labor as to whether it was permitted under ERISA to honor appellant's levy. CLVT also informed appellant that it would withhold the funds from the individual workers until it received an opinion from the Department of Labor, but that it would not transmit the funds to the Franchise Tax Board.

Appellant took no immediate action to enforce its levy, and in January 1980 CLVT finally received the opinion letter it had requested. The opinion letter concluded: "[I]t is the position of the Department of Labor that the process of any state judicial or administrative agency seeking to levy for unpaid taxes or unpaid unemployment insurance contributions upon benefits due a participant or beneficiary under the Plan is pre-empted under ERISA." Accordingly, on January 7, 1980, counsel for CLVT furnished appellant a copy of the opinion letter, informed appellant that CLVT lacked the power to honor appellant's levies, and stated their intention to recommend that CLVT should disburse the funds it had withheld to the employees in question.

the allegation that it had been "damaged in a sum * * * not to exceed $380.56 plus interest from June 1, 1980." Under the heading "Second Cause of Action," appellant incorporated its previous allegations and added:

> There was at the time of the levies alleged above and continues to be an actual controversy between the parties concerning their respective legal rights and duties. The Board [appellant] contends that defendants [CLVT] are obligated and required by law to pay over to the Board all amounts held * * * in favor of the Board's delinquent taxpayers. On the other hand, defendants contend that section 514 of ERISA preempts state law and that the trustees lack the power to honor the levies made upon them by the State of California.
>
> [D]efendants will continue to refuse to honor the Board's levies in this regard. Accordingly, a declaration by this court of the parties' respective rights is required to fully and finally resolve this controversy.

In a prayer for relief, appellant requested damages for defendants' failure to honor the levies and a declaration that defendants are "legally obligated to honor all future levies by the Board."

CLVT removed the case to the United States District Court for the Central District of California, and the court denied the Franchise Tax Board's motion for remand to the state court. On the merits, the District Court ruled that ERISA did not pre-empt the State's power to levy on funds held in trust by CLVT. CLVT appealed, and the Court of Appeals reversed. On petition for rehearing, the Franchise Tax Board renewed its argument that the District Court lacked jurisdiction over the complaint in this case. The petition for rehearing was denied, and an appeal was taken to this Court. We postponed consideration of our jurisdiction pending argument on the merits. We now hold that this case was not within the removal jurisdiction conferred by 28 U.S.C. § 1441, and therefore we do not reach the merits of the preemption question.

II

* * *

For this case—as for many cases where there is no diversity of citizenship between the parties—the propriety of removal turns on whether the case falls within the original "federal question" jurisdiction of the United States district courts * * * .

The most familiar definition of the statutory "arising under" limitation is Justice Holmes' statement, "A suit arises under the law that creates the cause of action." * * *

We have often held that a case "arose under" federal law where the vindication of a right under state law necessarily turned on some construction of federal law, and even the most ardent proponent of the Holmes test has admitted that it has been rejected as an exclusionary principle.

* * *

One powerful doctrine has emerged, however—the "well-pleaded complaint" rule—which as a practical matter severely limits the number of cases in which state law "creates the cause of action" that may be initiated in or removed to federal district court, thereby avoiding more-or-less automatically a number of potentially serious federal-state conflicts.

* * *

For better or worse, under the present statutory scheme as it has existed since 1887, a defendant may not remove a case to federal court unless the *plaintiff's* complaint establishes that the case "arises under" federal law.[9] "[A] right or immunity created by the Constitution or laws of the United States must be an element, and an essential one, of the plaintiff's cause of action."

* * *

The rule, however, may produce awkward results, especially in cases in which neither the obligation created by state law nor the defendant's factual failure to comply are in dispute, and both parties admit that the only question for decision is raised by a federal pre-emption defense. Nevertheless, it has been correctly understood to apply in such situations. As we said in *Gully*: "By unimpeachable authority, a suit brought upon a state statute does not arise under an act of Congress or the Constitution of the United States because prohibited thereby."[12]

---

9 The well-pleaded complaint rule applies to the original jurisdiction of the district courts as well as to their removal jurisdiction.

It is possible to conceive of a rational jurisdictional system in which the answer as well as the complaint would be consulted before a determination was made whether the case "arose under" federal law, or in which original and removal jurisdiction were not coextensive. Indeed, until the 1887 amendments to the 1875 Act, the well-pleaded complaint rule was not applied in full force to cases removed from state court; the defendant's petition for removal could furnish the necessary guarantee that the case necessarily presented a substantial question of federal law. Commentators have repeatedly proposed that some mechanism be established to permit removal of cases in which a federal defense may be dispositive. But those proposals have not been adopted.

12 Note, however, that a claim of federal pre-emption does not always arise as a defense to a coercive action. *See* n.20, *infra*. And, of course, the absence of original jurisdiction does not mean that there is no federal forum in which a pre-emption defense may be heard. If the state courts reject a claim of federal pre-emption, that decision may ultimately be reviewed on appeal by this Court.

III

Simply to state these principles is not to apply them to the case at hand. Appellant's complaint sets forth two "causes of action," one of which expressly refers to ERISA; if either comes within the original jurisdiction of the federal courts, removal was proper as to the whole case. Although appellant's complaint does not specifically assert any particular statutory entitlement for the relief it seeks, the language of the complaint suggests (and the parties do not dispute) that appellant's "first cause of action" states a claim under [state law], * * * and its "second cause of action" states a claim under California's Declaratory Judgment Act.

Go Online

Compare the federal Declaratory Judgment Act, 28 U.S.C. § 2201, with the California statute, CAL. CODE CIV. PROC. § 1060 as they read when the Court decided *Franchise Tax*. Is there a difference between them? Why might it matter?

As an initial proposition, then, the "law that creates the cause of action" is state law, and original federal jurisdiction is unavailable unless it appears that some substantial, disputed question of federal law is a necessary element of one of the well-pleaded state claims, or that one or the other claim is "really" one of federal law.

A

Take Note!

Justice Brennan appears to concede here that the California declaratory judgment statute creates a cause of action. That is important with respect to how the well-pleaded-complaint rule operates with respect to Count 2 of the complaint.]

Even though state law creates appellant's causes of action, its case might still "arise under" the laws of the United States if a well-pleaded complaint established that its right to relief under state law requires resolution of a substantial question of federal law in dispute between the parties. For appellant's first cause of action—to enforce its levy—a straightforward application of the well-pleaded complaint rule precludes original federal-court jurisdiction. California law establishes a set of conditions, without reference to federal law, under which a tax levy may be enforced; federal law becomes relevant only by way of a defense to an obligation created entirely by state law, and then only if appellant has made out a valid claim for relief under state law. The well-pleaded complaint rule was framed to deal with precisely such a situation. As we discuss above, since 1887 it has been settled law that a case may not be removed to federal court on the basis of a federal defense, including the defense of pre-emption, even if the defense is anticipated in the plaintiff's complaint, and even if both parties admit that the defense is the only question truly at issue in the case.

Appellant's declaratory judgment action poses a more difficult problem. Whereas the question of federal pre-emption is relevant to appellant's first cause of action only as a potential defense, it is a necessary element of the declaratory judgment claim. Under [state law], a party with an interest in property may bring an action for a declaration of another party's legal rights and duties with respect to that property upon showing that there is an "actual controversy relating to the legal rights and duties" of the parties. The only questions in dispute between the parties in this case concern the rights and duties of CLVT and its trustees under ERISA. Not only does appellant's request for a declaratory judgment under California law clearly encompass questions governed by ERISA, but appellant's complaint identifies no other questions as a subject of controversy between the parties. Such questions must be raised in a well-pleaded complaint for a declaratory judgment. Therefore, it is clear on the face of its well-pleaded complaint that appellant may not obtain the relief it seeks in its second cause of action ("[t]hat the court declare defendants legally obligated to honor all future levies by the Board upon [CLVT],") without a construction of ERISA and/or an adjudication of its pre-emptive effect and constitutionality—all questions of federal law.

Appellant argues that original federal-court jurisdiction over such a complaint is foreclosed by our decision in *Skelly Oil Co. v. Phillips Petroleum Co.* As we shall see, however, *Skelly Oil* is not directly controlling.

* * *

1. As an initial matter, we must decide whether the doctrine of *Skelly Oil* limits original federal-court jurisdiction under § 1331—and by extension removal jurisdiction under § 1441—when a question of federal law appears on the face of a well-pleaded complaint for a state-law declaratory judgment. Apparently, it is a question of first impression. As the passage quoted above makes clear, *Skelly Oil* relied significantly on the precise contours of the federal Declaratory Judgment Act as well as of § 1331. *Cf.* 339 U.S. at 674 (stressing the need to respect "the limited procedural purpose of the Declaratory Judgment Act"). The Court's emphasis that the Declaratory Judgment Act was intended to affect only the remedies available in a federal district court, not the court's jurisdiction, was critical to the Court's reasoning. Our interpretation of the federal Declaratory Judgment Act in *Skelly Oil* does not apply of its own force to *state* declaratory judgment statutes, many of which antedate the federal statute.[16]

16 California's Declaratory Judgment Act was enacted 13 years before the federal Act. California may well regard its statute as having a more substantive purpose than the federal Act as interpreted in *Skelly Oil*. According to the leading commentator on California procedure: "Declaratory relief is not a special proceeding. It is an action, classified as equitable by reason of the type of relief offered * * *."

Yet while *Skelly Oil* itself is limited to the federal Declaratory Judgment Act, fidelity to its spirit leads us to extend it to state declaratory judgment actions as well. If federal district courts could take jurisdiction, either originally or by removal, of state declaratory judgment claims raising questions of federal law, without regard to the doctrine of *Skelly Oil*, the federal Declaratory Judgment Act—with the limitations *Skelly Oil* read into it—would become a dead letter. For any case in which a state declaratory judgment action was available, litigants could get into federal court for a declaratory judgment despite our interpretation of § 2201, simply by pleading an adequate state claim for a declaration of federal law. Having interpreted the Declaratory Judgment Act of 1934 to include certain limitations on the jurisdiction of federal district courts to entertain declaratory judgment suits, we should be extremely hesitant to interpret the Judiciary Act of 1875 and its 1887 amendments in a way that renders the limitations in the later statute nugatory. Therefore, we hold that under the jurisdictional statutes as they now stand[17] federal courts do not have original jurisdiction, nor do they acquire jurisdiction on removal, when a federal question is presented by a complaint for a state declaratory judgment, but *Skelly Oil* would bar jurisdiction if the plaintiff had sought a federal declaratory judgment.

Food for Thought

How does the Court go about determining the "spirit" of *Skelly Oil*? Does the Court suggest here that state law cannot affect what kinds of cases come within the federal district courts' subject matter jurisdiction? That would be odd, since there are two ways state law does so routinely, one represented by *Smith*.

2. The question, then, is whether a federal district court could take jurisdiction of appellant's declaratory judgment claim had it been brought under 28 U.S.C.A. § 2201.[18] The application of *Skelly Oil* to such a suit is somewhat unclear. Federal courts have regularly taken original jurisdiction over declaratory judgment suits in which, if the declaratory judgment defendant brought a coercive action to enforce its rights, that suit would necessarily present a federal question.[19] Section 502(a)(3) of ERISA specifically grants trustees of ERISA-covered plans

17 It is not beyond the power of Congress to confer a right to a declaratory judgment in a case or controversy arising under federal law—within the meaning of the Constitution or of § 1331—without regard to *Skelly Oil*'s particular application of the well-pleaded complaint rule. The 1969 ALI report strongly criticized the *Skelly Oil* doctrine: "If no other changes were to be made in federal question jurisdiction, it is arguable that such language, and the historical test it seems to embody, should be repudiated." Nevertheless, Congress has declined to make such a change. At this point, any adjustment in the system that has evolved under the *Skelly Oil* rule must come from Congress.

18 It may seem odd that, for purposes of determining whether removal was proper, we analyze a claim brought under state law, in state court, by a party who has continuously objected to district court jurisdiction over its case, as if that party had been trying to get original federal-court jurisdiction all along. That irony, however, is a more-or-less constant feature of the removal statute, under which a case is removable if a federal district court could have taken jurisdiction had the same complaint been filed.

19 For instance, federal courts have consistently adjudicated suits by alleged patent infringers to

like CLVT a cause of action for injunctive relief when their rights and duties under ERISA are at issue, and that action is exclusively governed by federal law.[20] If CLVT could have sought an injunction under ERISA against application to it of state regulations that require acts inconsistent with ERISA,[21] does a declaratory judgment suit by the State "arise under" federal law?

We think not. We have always interpreted what Skelly Oil called "the current of jurisdictional legislation since the Act of March 3, 1875," with an eye to practicality and necessity. "What is needed is something of that common-sense accommodation of judgment to kaleidoscopic situations which characterizes the law in its treatment of problems of causation * * * a selective process which picks the substantial causes out of the web and lays the other ones aside." There are good reasons why the federal courts should not entertain suits by the States to declare the validity of their regulations despite possibly conflicting federal law. States are not significantly prejudiced by an inability to come to federal court for a declaratory judgment in advance of a possible injunctive suit by a person subject to federal regulation. They have a variety of means by which they can enforce their own laws in their own courts, and they do not suffer if the pre-emption questions such enforcement may raise are tested there.[22] The express grant of federal jurisdiction

Food for Thought

Isn't this an odd point for Justice Brennan to make? CLVT, not the state, sought federal adjudication here.

---

declare a patent invalid, on the theory that an infringement suit by the declaratory judgment defendant would raise a federal question over which the federal courts have exclusive jurisdiction. *See* E. Edelmann & Co. v. Triple-A Specialty Co., 88 F.2d 852 (7th Cir.1937). Taking jurisdiction over this type of suit is consistent with * * * dictum * * * in which we stated only that a declaratory judgment plaintiff could not get original federal jurisdiction if the anticipated lawsuit by the declaratory judgment defendant would *not* "arise under" federal law. It is also consistent with the nature of the declaratory remedy itself, which was designed to permit adjudication of either party's claims of right.

20 Section 502(a)(3) provides:

> [A civil action may be brought] by a participant, beneficiary, or fiduciary (A) to enjoin any act or practice which violates any provision of this subchapter or the terms of the plan, or (B) to obtain other appropriate equitable relief (i) to redress such violations or (ii) to enforce any provision of this subchapter * * *.

See also n.26, *infra* (federal jurisdiction over suits under § 502 is exclusive, and they are governed entirely by federal common law) * * * .

21 We express no opinion, however, whether a party in CLVT's position could sue under ERISA to enjoin or to declare invalid a state tax levy, despite the Tax Injunction Act, 28 U.S.C. § 1341. To do so, it would have to show either that state law provided no "speedy and efficient remedy" or that Congress intended § 502 of ERISA to be an exception to the Tax Injunction Act.

22 Indeed, as appellant's strategy in this case shows, they may often be willing to go to great lengths to avoid federal-court resolution of a pre-emption question. Realistically, there is little prospect that States will flood the federal courts with declaratory judgment actions; most questions will arise, as in this case, because a State has sought a declaration in state court and the defendant has removed the case to federal court. Accordingly, it is perhaps appropriate to note that considerations of comity make us reluctant to snatch cases which a State has brought from the courts of that State, unless some clear rule demands it.

in ERISA is limited to suits brought by certain parties, as to whom Congress presumably determined that a right to enter federal court was necessary to further the statute's purposes.[23] It did not go so far as to provide that any suit against such parties must also be brought in federal court when they themselves did not choose to sue. The situation presented by a State's suit for a declaration of the validity of state law is sufficiently removed from the spirit of necessity and careful limitation of district court jurisdiction that informed our statutory interpretation in Skelly Oil and Gully to convince us that, until Congress informs us otherwise, such a suit is not within the original jurisdiction of the United States district courts. Accordingly, the same suit brought originally in state court is not removable either.

B

CLVT also argues that appellant's "causes of action" are, in substance, federal claims. Although we have often repeated that "the party who brings a suit is master to decide what law he will rely upon," it is an independent corollary of the well-pleaded complaint rule that a plaintiff may not defeat removal by omitting to plead necessary federal questions in a complaint.

CLVT's best argument stems from our decision in Avco Corp. v. Aero Lodge No. 735 (1968). In that case, the petitioner filed suit in state court alleging simply that it had a valid contract with the respondent, a union, under which the respondent had agreed to submit all grievances to binding arbitration and not to cause or sanction any "work stoppages, strikes, or slowdowns." The petitioner further alleged that the respondent and its officials had violated the agreement by participating in and sanctioning work stoppages, and it sought temporary and permanent injunctions against further breaches. It was clear that, had petitioner invoked it, there would have been a federal cause of action under § 301 of the Labor Management Relations Act, 1947 (LMRA), and that, even in state court, any action to enforce an agreement within the scope of § 301 would be controlled by federal law. It was also clear, however, under the law in effect at the time, that independent limits on federal jurisdiction made it impossible for a federal court to grant the injunctive relief petitioner sought.

The Court of Appeals held, and we affirmed, that the petitioner's action "arose under" § 301, and thus could be removed to federal court, although the petitioner had undoubtedly pleaded an adequate claim for relief under the state law of contracts and had sought a remedy available only under state law. The necessary

23 *Cf.* nn.19, 20, *supra*. Alleged patent infringers, for example, have a clear interest in swift resolution of the federal issue of patent validity—they are liable for damages if it turns out they are infringing a patent, and they frequently have a delicate network of contractual arrangements with third parties that is dependent on their right to sell or license a product. Parties subject to conflicting state and federal regulatory schemes also have a clear interest in sorting out the scope of each government's authority, especially where they face a threat of liability if the application of federal law is not quickly made clear.

ground of decision was that the pre-emptive force of § 301 is so powerful as to displace entirely any state cause of action "for violation of contracts between an employer and a labor organization." Any such suit is purely a creature of federal law, notwithstanding the fact that state law would provide a cause of action in the absence of § 301. Avco stands for the proposition that if a federal cause of action completely pre-empts a state cause of action any complaint that comes within the scope of the federal cause of action necessarily "arises under" federal law.

CLVT argues by analogy that ERISA, like § 301, was meant to create a body of federal common law, and that "any state court action which would require the interpretation or application of ERISA to a plan document 'arises under' the laws of the United States." ERISA contains provisions creating a series of express causes of action in favor of participants, beneficiaries, and fiduciaries of ERISA-covered plans, as well as the Secretary of Labor.[26] It may be that, as with § 301 as interpreted in Avco, any state action coming within the scope of § 502(a) of ERISA would be removable to federal district court, even if an otherwise adequate state cause of action were pleaded without reference to federal law. It does not follow, however, that either of appellant's claims in this case comes within the scope of one of ERISA's causes of action.

The phrasing of § 502(a) is instructive. Section 502(a) specifies which persons—participants, beneficiaries, fiduciaries, or the Secretary of Labor—may bring actions for particular kinds of relief. It neither creates nor expressly denies any cause of action in favor of state governments, to enforce tax levies or for any other purpose. It does not purport to reach every question relating to plans covered by ERISA. Furthermore, ERISA makes clear that Congress did not intend to preempt entirely every state cause of action relating to such plans. With important, but express limitations, it states that "nothing in this subchapter shall be construed to exempt or relieve any person from any law of any State which regulates insurance, banking, or securities."

Food for Thought

Does this quotation prove too much? After all, *Franchise Tax* does not concern any of the three enumerated categories.

Against this background, it is clear that a suit by state tax authorities under a statute like § 18818 does not "arise under" ERISA. Unlike the contract rights at issue in Avco, the State's right to enforce its tax levies is not of central concern to the federal statute. For that

26 The statute further states that "the district courts of the United States shall have exclusive jurisdiction of civil actions under this subchapter brought by the Secretary or by a participant, beneficiary, or fiduciary," except for actions by a participant or beneficiary to recover benefits due, to enforce rights under the terms of a plan, or to clarify rights to future benefits, over which state courts have concurrent jurisdiction. In addition, ERISA's legislative history indicates that, in light of the Act's virtually unique pre-emption provision, "a body of Federal substantive law will be developed by the courts to deal with issues involving rights and obligations under private welfare and pension plans."

reason, as in *Gully*, on the face of a well-pleaded complaint there are many reasons completely unrelated to the provisions and purposes of ERISA why the State may or may not be entitled to the relief it seeks.[29] Furthermore, ERISA does not provide an alternative cause of action in favor of the State to enforce its rights, while § 301 expressly supplied the plaintiff in Avco with a federal cause of action to replace its pre-empted state contract claim. Therefore, even though the Court of Appeals may well be correct that ERISA precludes enforcement of the State's levy in the circumstances of this case, an action to enforce the levy is not itself pre-empted by ERISA.

Go Online

Where is the language in 29 U.S.C. § 185(a) (§ 301 of the Taft-Hartley Act) that creates a cause of action?

Once again, appellant's declaratory judgment cause of action presents a somewhat more difficult issue. The question on which a declaration is sought—that of the CLVT trustees' "power to honor the levies made upon them by the State of California,"—is undoubtedly a matter of concern under ERISA. It involves the meaning and enforceability of provisions in CLVT's trust agreement forbidding the trustees to assign or otherwise to alienate funds held in trust, and thus comes within the class of questions for which Congress intended that federal courts create federal common law. Under ERISA, a participant, beneficiary, or fiduciary of a plan covered by ERISA may bring a declaratory judgment action in federal court to determine whether the plan's trustees may comply with a state levy on funds held in trust. Nevertheless, CLVT's argument that appellant's second cause of action arises under ERISA fails for the second reason given above. ERISA carefully enumerates the parties entitled to seek relief under § 502; it does not provide anyone other than participants, beneficiaries, or fiduciaries with an express cause of action for a declaratory judgment on the issues in this case. A suit for similar relief by some other party does not "arise under" that provision.

IV

Our concern in this case is consistent application of a system of statutes conferring original federal-court jurisdiction, as they have been interpreted by this Court over many years. Under our interpretations, Congress has given the lower federal courts jurisdiction to hear, originally or by removal from a state court, only those cases in which a well-pleaded complaint establishes either that federal law creates the cause of action or that the plaintiff's right to relief necessarily depends on resolution of a substantial question of federal law. We hold that a suit by state

29 In theory (looking only at the complaint), it may turn out that the levy was improper under state law, or that in fact the defendant had complied with the levy. Furthermore, a levy on CLVT might be for something like property taxes on real estate it owned. CLVT's trust agreement authorizes its trustees to pay such taxes.

tax authorities both to enforce its levies against funds held in trust pursuant to an ERISA-covered employee benefit plan, and to declare the validity of the levies notwithstanding ERISA, is neither a creature of ERISA itself nor a suit of which the federal courts will take jurisdiction because it turns on a question of federal law. Accordingly, we vacate the judgment of the Court of Appeals and remand so that this case may be remanded to the Superior Court of the State of California for the County of Los Angeles.

It is so ordered.

Notes and Questions

1. The Court asserts that district courts should treat complaints resting on state declaratory judgment statutes as if they invoked the federal Declaratory Judgment Act, analyzing them under *Skelly Oil*. What reason does the Court offer for requiring this convoluted analytical procedure? Why did *Skelly Oil* articulate the technique it did? Was it a desire to limit the federal docket or was there another, more technical, reason? Do the assumptions that caused the *Skelly Oil* Court to decline jurisdiction apply with equal force when a state provision underlies a case?

2. a) Under ERISA, CLVT could have paid the disputed tax levy and then sought, essentially, replevin on the ground that ERISA preempted the state's power to tax. Clearly that would have been a federal question case under the established analysis. Moreover, CLVT could also have commenced an action seeking injunctive relief at the outset of the dispute, and that action would have been not merely federal, but exclusively federal under ERISA. Thus, if one is to look to the potential coercive action of the defendant in determining jurisdiction in a declaratory judgment case, as *Edelmann* suggested, the Franchise Tax Board's declaratory judgment action should have been maintainable in federal court. The Court cited *Edelmann* with approval, but failed to follow it. Why?

b) Moreover, if the Trust had proceeded to seek a declaratory judgment, under the state or federal provisions, *before* paying the disputed tax, that, too, would have been a federal question case under the *Skelly Oil* analysis. Thus, the result in *Franchise Tax* is anomalous, since the Trust would clearly have been able to proceed in federal court had it taken the initiative in the litigation. What rule causes this anomaly? Should the Court abandon the *Skelly Oil* approach in order to avoid results like this?

c) On the same day as *Franchise Tax*, the Court declared,

> A plaintiff who seeks injunctive relief from state regulation, on the ground that such regulation is pre-empted by a federal statute which, by virtue of the Su-

premacy Clause of the Constitution, must prevail, thus presents a federal question which the federal courts have jurisdiction under 28 U.S.C. § 1331 to resolve.

Shaw v. Delta Airlines, Inc., 463 U.S. 85, 96 n.14 (1983). Is there federal question jurisdiction if such a plaintiff only seeks declaratory relief? Suppose a state agency sued in state court seeking a declaration that the federal statute did not pre-empt. Would *Franchise Tax* prevent removal of the case as a federal question case?

d) In *Textron Lycoming Reciprocating Engine Division, AVCO Corp. v. United Automobile, Aerospace and Agricultural Implement Workers*, 523 U.S. 653 (1998), the Court cast some doubt on the analysis that Justice Brennan discussed in Note 19 and its accompanying text, at least limiting it to cases in which the defense itself, in addition to the anticipated suit by the opposing party, is federal. The Union sought a declaration that Textron's conduct in concluding a collective bargaining agreement amounted to fraud, making the contract voidable at the Union's option. It asserted jurisdiction under § 301(a) of the Labor Management Relations Act. The Court found that an action seeking to declare a contract voidable was not an action for violation of the contract as the statute requires and so refused jurisdiction.

> [I]n order to determine whether § 301(a) jurisdiction lies over the declaratory-judgment aspect of its suit, we [the Court] must look to the character of the threatened action to which its suit would interpose a defense, which in this case would be Textron's action for breach of the collective-bargaining agreement. It relies on our decision in *Skelly Oil*, which held that a declaratory judgment action asserting a federal defense to a nonfederal claim was not a "civil actio[n] arising under the * * * laws * * * of the United States" within the meaning of the federal question jurisdiction statute, 28 U.S.C. § 1331. This argument makes several assumptions that we do not think can be indulged.
>
> First, it assumes that facts which were the converse of *Skelly Oil*—*i.e.* a declaratory-judgment complaint raising a nonfederal defense to an anticipated federal claim—would confer § 1331 jurisdiction. That is not clear. It can be argued that anticipating a federal claim in a suit asserting a nonfederal defense no more effectively invokes § 1331 jurisdiction than anticipating a federal defense in a suit asserting a nonfederal claim. * * * Perhaps it was the purpose of the Declaratory Judgment Act to permit such anticipation, see *Franchise Tax Board v. [Construction] Laborers Vacation Trust*, 463 U.S. 1, 19 n.19 (1983), but *Skelly Oil* did not present that issue, and some of its language suggests that the declaratory-judgment plaintiff must himself have a federal claim. No decision of this Court has squarely confronted and explicitly upheld federal-question jurisdiction on the basis of the anticipated claim against which the declaratory-judgment plaintiff presents a nonfederal defense; and neither the Union nor the Government cites such a decision by any other federal court.[4]

4 In *Franchise Tax Board* we observed, with seeming approval, that "[f]ederal courts have regularly taken original jurisdiction over declaratory judgment suits in which, if the declaratory judgment defendant brought a coercive action to enforce its rights, that suit would necessarily present a federal question." The cases brought forward to support that observation, however, were suits by alleged patent infringers to declare a patent invalid, which of course themselves raise a federal question.

Query, however, whether the Court's limited view of the applicability of the technique of E. Edelmann Co. v. Triple-A Specialty Co. makes Justice Brennan's silent refusal to use it in *Franchise Tax Board* even more of a conundrum. The CLVT's anticipated suit under ERISA was federal—indeed, exclusively so, just as a patent case is. The Franchise Tax Board's defense to such an action would have been that ERISA did not pre-empt the state tax, clearly a federal matter just as much as an assertion by an alleged patent infringer of the invalidity of the patent. Instead of Edelmann being relegated to a footnote in *Franchise Tax*, should it have controlled the decision?

3. The technique of E. Edelmann Co. v. Triple-A Specialty Co. apparently is alive and well. In *Holmes Group, Inc. v. Vornado Air Circulation Systems Inc.*, 535 U.S. 826 (2002), the Supreme Court reviewed a case involving arising-under jurisdiction and the exclusivity of the Federal Circuit's jurisdiction over appeals in cases involving patent claims. The plaintiff sought a declaration of non-infringement of defendant's trade dress. The defendant filed a patent infringement counterclaim. The district court, the court of appeals, and the Supreme Court assumed without discussion that the district court had jurisdiction; the only jurisdictional dispute was over whether an appeal lay to the Federal Circuit or the Tenth Circuit from the decision of the district court in Kansas. The Court clearly indicated, however, that the defendant's federal counterclaim did not provide the foundation for the district court's jurisdiction. Perhaps the matter deserves more attention than the federal courts afforded it. In Skelly Oil, the Court looked to the plaintiff's hypothetical coercive action to evaluate the jurisdictional worthiness of the declaratory judgment action. In Holmes Group, what was the plaintiff's underlying coercive action, and why did it qualify for jurisdiction under § 1331? For that matter, what was the plaintiff's cause of action, irrespective of whether it qualified for federal question jurisdiction? Note that this is not a case where the defendant was threatening legal action against plaintiff's customers (as in American Well Works and Edelmann). Such conduct gives rise to claims of trade libel.

4. In light of the purposes of federal question jurisdiction, should a state or federal court adjudicate the federal issue *Franchise Tax* presents?

5. Apart from reflecting the problems declaratory judgment suits cause, *Franchise Tax* also involves issues of the effect of federal preemption on federal question jurisdiction. The *Franchise Tax* Court rejected the argument that the state law claims supported removal because ERISA preempted them. However, the Court reserved decision on whether ERISA preemption converted state-created causes of action "within the scope of § 502(a) of ERISA" into federal claims that would support removal. *Avco Corp. v. Machinists*, 390 U.S. 557 (1968), had held that § 301 of the Labor Management Relations Act had that effect on state claims for breaches of collective bargaining agreements. Four years after *Franchise Tax*, the Court ruled in *Metropolitan Life Ins. Co. v. Taylor*, 481 U.S. 58 (1987), that ERISA had the same effect on some state law claims. The Supreme Court upheld federal jurisdiction, finding that a suit by a beneficiary

seeking to recover benefits from a ERISA-covered plan falls directly under § 502. The Court noted that the language of ERISA's applicable jurisdictional provision closely paralleled the jurisdictional provision of the Labor Management Relations Act that led to Avco. Moreover, the Conference Report on ERISA had expressly stated that § 502 actions were to be regarded as arising under federal law in the same manner as those brought under § 301 of the Labor Management Relations Act. Thus, Congress had clearly shown its intent to make such claims removable. Taylor's claims for contract and tort damages were removable to federal court because ERISA had "convert[ed] an ordinary state common law complaint into one stating a federal claim for purposes of the well-pleaded complaint rule." Does *Taylor* overrule *Franchise Tax* by implication?

6. *Franchise Tax Board's* approval of Skelly Oil and "fidelity to its spirit" rests on a shaky foundation. Extensive research by Professors Doernberg and Mushlin indicates that Justice Frankfurter's underlying assumption that the Declaratory Judgment Act of 1934 was not intended to expand federal jurisdiction is unsound. Indeed, there is considerable evidence that Congress quite explicitly contemplated an increase of cases in the federal courts as a result of the Act. If Congress did intend an expansion of federal jurisdiction, what implications does that have for federal question jurisdiction in general and for the well-pleaded-complaint rule in particular?

For More Information

See Donald L. Doernberg & Michael B. Mushlin, *The Trojan Horse: How the Declaratory Judgment Act Created a Cause of Action and Expanded Federal Jurisdiction While the Supreme Court Wasn't Looking*, 36 U.C.L.A.L.REV. 529 (1989).

7. a) Some suggest that the Court's federal question jurisdiction jurisprudence needs to be overhauled. *See, e.g.*, William Cohen, *The Broken Compass: The Requirement that a Case Arise "Directly" under Federal Law*, 115 U.PA.L.REV. 890 (1967); AMERICAN LAW INSTITUTE, STUDY OF THE DIVISION OF JURISDICTION BETWEEN STATE AND FEDERAL COURTS (1969). Professor Cohen argues that no "single, all-purpose, neutral analytical concept" explains the Supreme Court decisions on statutory federal question jurisdiction. That should not be surprising. To some extent, the Court has balanced various pragmatic factors in determining whether a particular case warrants original federal court jurisdiction. He contends that the courts should not only engage in such pragmatic balancing but also should do so more openly. The factors he mentions include: "the extent of the caseload increase for federal trial courts if jurisdiction is recognized; the extent to which cases of this class will, in practice, turn on issues of state or federal law; the extent of the necessity for an expert federal tribunal to handle issues of federal law that do arise; the extent of the necessity for a sympathetic federal tribunal in cases of this class." Do the cases reflect such concerns? Should they?

b) Consider again the purposes of federal question jurisdiction. What sorts of circumstances should entitle litigants to take their disputes to the federal trial courts, not only in declaratory judgment cases, but generally? What are the factors that make federal adjudication desirable? In allocating types of cases to the federal courts, bear in mind both policy and practical limitations of the federal courts as a judicial system. To what extent should federalism compel a narrow federal judicial role, at least in cases with some state law components? To what extent should we keep groups of cases out of the federal courts because the federal system is comparatively small? If you were designing a federal question jurisdiction system within the limits of Article III, how would you proceed?

Chapter 4

Legislative Courts

A. Introduction

The Constitution establishes the limits of the federal judicial power and gives Congress discretion to create federal tribunals inferior to the Supreme Court. Additionally, Article III offers federal judges safeguards from interference by the legislature and executive. First, it provides that they shall have life tenure upon "good behavior." Federal judges can be removed from office only upon impeachment by the House of Representatives and conviction by the Senate for treason, bribery, or other high crimes and misdemeanors. Second, Article III prohibits reductions in their salaries while they are in office.

A literal interpretation of these provisions might suggest that if Congress creates a tribunal with the power to adjudicate federal cases, Article III would protect that court's judges, but these provisions have never been so interpreted. The first Congress, which included many former delegates to the Constitutional Convention, authorized Treasury Department officers to resolve some types of disputes, including claims to veteran's benefits, that were within Article III. Since then, Congress has often created non-Article III tribunals. When the judges of a federal tribunal do not enjoy the protections of Article III, the tribunal is often referred to as an "Article I" or "legislative" court.

The Supreme Court endorsed legislative courts early in the country's history. In *American Insurance Co. v. 356 Bales of Cotton,* 26 U.S. (1 Pet.) 511 (1828), the Court concluded that Congress could create territorial courts with judges not protected by Article III. The Court reasoned that in legislating for the territories Congress was exercising both state-like and national governmental powers. Consequently, territorial judges were analogous to state judges and were not entitled to the safeguards of Article III. Even today territorial district court judges exercise the same jurisdiction as other federal district judges, but serve only limited terms and are subject to removal by the President for cause.

The jurisdiction of many legislative courts is much more specialized than that of the territorial courts. The jurisdiction of the Tax Court, for example, consists primarily of deciding taxpayers' petitions for redetermination of deficiencies assessed by the Internal Revenue Service. Indeed, it is the only court with the power to review a determination of tax liability by the Service before the payment of the tax. Tax Court judges serve fifteen-year terms and can be removed from office for inefficiency, neglect of duty, or malfeasance. The courts of appeals, Article III courts, have jurisdiction over appeals from the Tax Court.

Modern administrative agencies also operate inconsistently with the literal language of Article III. Congress creates such agencies to administer various federal regulatory schemes. They often adjudicate disputes regarding the application of federal laws and regulations. *Crowell v. Benson*, 285 U.S. 22 (1932), upheld the right of the United States Employees' Compensation Commission to make initial factual determinations in disputes between employers and employees under a federal statutory scheme that required compensation for work-related injuries. The federal district courts could review the Commission's orders. The Supreme Court therefore found that the agency served as an adjunct to the Article III courts, and the scheme was not unconstitutional.

Congress has created Article I courts for several reasons: to keep the number of Article III federal judges small and the appointments prestigious, to limit the number of judges with life tenure and life-time employment, and to insure judicial expertise in specialized areas. This Chapter examines whether these goals are reconcilable with Article III and considers whether there are any limits on Congressional power to use Article I courts. Must their decisions be reviewable by an Article III court? Could every federal case initially be assigned to an administrative agency for fact-finding without violating Article III? Does broad congressional power to create Article I courts imply an inherent weakness of Article III courts?

B. Limits on Legislative Courts

Northern Pipeline Construction Co. v. Marathon Pipe Line Co.

Supreme Court of the United States, 1982.
458 U.S. 50.

> **Make the Connection**
>
> It is because of *Northern Pipeline* that bankruptcy courts must now make a distinction between "core" and "non-core" proceedings.

JUSTICE BRENNAN announced the judgment of the Court and delivered an opinion in which JUSTICE MARSHALL, JUSTICE BLACKMUN, and JUSTICE STEVENS joined.

The question presented is whether the assignment by Congress to bankruptcy judges of the jurisdiction granted in 28 U.S.C. § 1471 (1976 ed., Supp. IV) by § 241(a) of the Bankruptcy Act of 1978 violates Art. III of the Constitution.

I

A

In 1978, after almost 10 years of study and investigation, Congress enacted a comprehensive revision of the bankruptcy laws. The Bankruptcy Act of 1978 (Act) made significant changes in both the substantive and procedural law of bankruptcy. It is the changes in the latter that are at issue in this case.

Before the Act, federal district courts served as bankruptcy courts and employed a "referee" system. Bankruptcy proceedings were generally conducted before referees, except in those instances in which the district court elected to withdraw a case from a referee. The referee's final order was appealable to the district court. The bankruptcy courts were vested with "summary jurisdiction"—that is, with jurisdiction over controversies involving property in the actual or constructive possession of the court. And, with consent, the bankruptcy court also had jurisdiction over some "plenary" matters—such as disputes involving property in the possession of a third person.

The Act eliminates the referee system and establishes "in each judicial district, as an adjunct to the district court for such district, a bankruptcy court which shall be a court of record known as the United States Bankruptcy Court for the district." The judges of these courts are appointed to office for 14-year terms by the President, with the advice and consent of the Senate. They are subject to removal by the "judicial council of the circuit" on account of "incompetency, misconduct, neglect of duty or physical or mental disability." In addition, the salaries of the bankruptcy judges are set by statute and are subject to adjustment under the Federal Salary Act.

The jurisdiction of the bankruptcy courts created by the Act is much broader than that exercised under the former referee system. Eliminating the distinction between "summary" and "plenary" jurisdiction, the Act grants the new courts jurisdiction over all "civil proceedings arising under title 11 [the Bankruptcy title] or arising in or related to cases under title 11." This jurisdictional grant empowers bankruptcy courts to entertain a wide variety of cases involving claims that may affect the property of the estate once a petition has been filed under Title 11. Included within the bankruptcy courts' jurisdiction are suits to recover accounts, controversies involving exempt property, actions to avoid transfers and payments as preferences or fraudulent conveyances, and causes of action owned by the debtor at the time of the petition for bankruptcy. The bankruptcy courts can hear claims based on state law as well as those based on federal law.

The judges of the bankruptcy courts are vested with all of the "powers of a court of equity, law, and admiralty," except that they "may not enjoin another court or punish a criminal contempt not committed in the presence of the judge of the court or warranting a punishment of imprisonment." In addition to this broad grant of power, Congress has allowed bankruptcy judges the power to hold jury trials; to issue declaratory judgments; to issue writs of habeas corpus under certain circumstances; to issue all writs necessary in aid of the bankruptcy court's expanded jurisdiction; and to issue any order, process or judgment that is necessary or appropriate to carry out the provisions of Title 11.

The Act also establishes a special procedure for appeals from orders of bankruptcy courts. The circuit council is empowered to direct the chief judge of the circuit to designate panels of three bankruptcy judges to hear appeals. These panels have jurisdiction of all appeals from final judgments, orders, and decrees of bankruptcy courts, and, with leave of the panel, of interlocutory appeals. If no such appeals panel is designated, the district court is empowered to exercise appellate jurisdiction. The court of appeals is given jurisdiction over appeals from the appellate panels or from the district court. If the parties agree, a direct appeal to the court of appeals may be taken from a final judgment of a bankruptcy court.[5]

B

This case arises out of proceedings initiated in the United States Bankruptcy Court for the District of Minnesota after appellant Northern Pipeline Construction

5 Although no particular standard of review is specified in the Act, the parties in the present cases seem to agree that the appropriate one is the clearly-erroneous standard, employed in old Bankruptcy Rule 810 for review of findings of fact made by a referee.

Co. (Northern) filed a petition for reorganization in January 1980. In March 1980, Northern, pursuant to the Act, filed in that court a suit against appellee Marathon Pipe Line Co. (Marathon). Appellant sought damages for alleged breaches of contract and warranty, as well as for alleged misrepresentation, coercion, and duress. Marathon sought dismissal of the suit, on the ground that the Act unconstitutionally conferred Art. III judicial power upon judges who lacked life tenure and protection against salary diminution. The United States intervened to defend the validity of the statute.

The Bankruptcy Judge denied the motion to dismiss. But on appeal the District Court entered an order granting the motion, on the ground that "the delegation of authority in 28 U.S.C. § 1471 to the Bankruptcy Judges to try cases which are otherwise relegated under the Constitution to Article III judges" was unconstitutional. Both the United States and Northern filed notices of appeal in this Court. We noted probable jurisdiction.

II

A

Basic to the constitutional structure established by the Framers was their recognition that "[t]he accumulation of all powers, legislative, executive, and judiciary, in the same hands, whether of one, a few, or many, and whether hereditary, self-appointed, or elective, may justly be pronounced the very definition of tyranny." To ensure against such tyranny, the Framers provided that the Federal Government would consist of three distinct Branches, each to exercise one of the governmental powers recognized by the Framers as inherently distinct. "The Framers regarded the checks and balances that they had built into the tripartite Federal Government as a self-executing safeguard against the encroachment or aggrandizement of one branch at the expense of the other."

The Federal Judiciary was therefore designed by the Framers to stand independent of the Executive and Legislature—to maintain the checks and balances of the constitutional structure, and also to guarantee that the process of adjudication itself remained impartial. Hamilton explained the importance of an independent Judiciary:

> Periodical appointments, however regulated, or by whomsoever made, would, in some way or other, be fatal to [the courts'] necessary independence. If the power of making them was committed either to the Executive or legislature, there would be danger of an improper complaisance to the branch which possessed it; if to both, there would be an unwillingness to hazard the displeasure of either; if to the people, or to persons chosen by them for the special purpose, there would be too great a disposition to consult popularity, to justify a reliance that nothing would be consulted but the Constitution and the laws.

The Court has only recently reaffirmed the significance of this feature of the Framers' design: "A Judiciary free from control by the Executive and Legislature is essential if there is a right to have claims decided by judges who are free from potential domination by other branches of government."

As an inseparable element of the constitutional system of checks and balances, and as a guarantee of judicial impartiality, Art. III both defines the power and protects the independence of the Judicial Branch. It provides that "The judicial Power of the United States, shall be vested in one supreme Court, and in such inferior Courts as the Congress may from time to time ordain and establish." The inexorable command of this provision is clear and definite: The judicial power of the United States must be exercised by courts having the attributes prescribed in Art. III. Those attributes are also clearly set forth:

> The Judges, both of the supreme and inferior Courts, shall hold their Offices during good Behaviour, and shall, at stated Times, receive for their Services, a Compensation, which shall not be diminished during their Continuance in Office.

The "good Behaviour" Clause guarantees that Art. III judges shall enjoy life tenure, subject only to removal by impeachment. The Compensation Clause guarantees Art. III judges a fixed and irreducible compensation for their services. Both of these provisions were incorporated into the Constitution to ensure the independence of the Judiciary from the control of the Executive and Legislative Branches of government. * * * The Framers thus recognized:

> Next to permanency in office, nothing can contribute more to the independence of the judges than a fixed provision for their support * * * . In the general course of human nature, a power over a man's subsistence amounts to a power over his will.

In sum, our Constitution unambiguously enunciates a fundamental principle—that the "judicial Power of the United States" must be reposed in an independent Judiciary. It commands that the independence of the Judiciary be jealously guarded, and it provides clear institutional protections for that independence.

B

It is undisputed that the bankruptcy judges whose offices were created by the Bankruptcy Act of 1978 do not enjoy the protections constitutionally afforded to Art. III judges. The bankruptcy judges do not serve for life subject to their continued "good Behaviour." Rather, they are appointed for 14-year terms, and can be removed by the judicial council of the circuit in which they serve on grounds of "incompetency, misconduct, neglect of duty, or physical or mental disability." Second, the salaries of the bankruptcy judges are not immune from diminution by Congress. In short, there is no doubt that the bankruptcy judges created by the Act are not Art. III judges.

* * *

Appellants suggest two grounds for upholding the Act's conferral of broad adjudicative powers upon judges unprotected by Art. III. First, it is urged that "pursuant to its enumerated Article I powers, Congress may establish legislative courts that have jurisdiction to decide cases to which the Article III judicial power of the United States extends." Referring to our precedents upholding the validity of "legislative courts," appellants suggest that "the plenary grants of power in Article I permit Congress to establish non-Article III tribunals in 'specialized areas having particularized needs and warranting distinctive treatment,' " such as the area of bankruptcy law. Second, appellants contend that even if the Constitution does require that this bankruptcy-related action be adjudicated in an Art. III court, the Act in fact satisfies that requirement. "Bankruptcy jurisdiction was vested in the district court" of the judicial district in which the bankruptcy court is located, "and the exercise of that jurisdiction by the adjunct bankruptcy court was made subject to appeal as of right to an Article III court." Analogizing the role of the bankruptcy court to that of a special master, appellants urge us to conclude that this "adjunct" system established by Congress satisfies the requirements of Art. III. We consider these arguments in turn.

III

Congress did not constitute the bankruptcy courts as legislative courts. Appellants contend, however, that the bankruptcy courts could have been so constituted, and that as a result the "adjunct" system in fact chosen by Congress does not impermissibly encroach upon the judicial power. In advancing this argument, appellants rely upon cases in which we have identified certain matters that "Congress may or may not bring within the cognizance of [Art. III courts], as it may deem proper." But when properly understood, these precedents represent no broad departure from the constitutional command that the judicial power of the United States must be vested in Art. III courts.[15] Rather, they reduce to three narrow situations not subject to that command, each recognizing a circumstance in which the grant of power to the Legislative and Executive Branches was historically and constitutionally so exceptional that the congressional assertion of

15 Justice White's dissent finds particular significance in the fact that Congress could have assigned all bankruptcy matters to the state courts. But, of course, virtually all matters that might be heard in Art. III courts could also be left by Congress to state courts. This fact is simply irrelevant to the question before us. Congress has no control over state-court judges; accordingly the principle of separation of powers is not threatened by leaving the adjudication of federal disputes to such judges. The Framers chose to leave to Congress the precise role to be played by the lower federal courts in the administration of justice. But the Framers did not leave it to Congress to define the character of those courts—they were to be independent of the political branches and presided over by judges with guaranteed salary and life tenure.

a power to create legislative courts was consistent with, rather than threatening to, the constitutional mandate of separation of powers. These precedents simply acknowledge that the literal command of Art. III, assigning the judicial power of the United States to courts insulated from Legislative or Executive interference, must be interpreted in light of the historical context in which the Constitution was written, and of the structural imperatives of the Constitution as a whole.

Appellants first rely upon a series of cases in which this Court has upheld the creation by Congress of non-Art. III "territorial courts." This exception from the general prescription of Art. III dates from the earliest days of the Republic, when it was perceived that the Framers intended that as to certain geographical areas, in which no State operated as sovereign, Congress was to exercise the general powers of government. For example, in American Ins. Co. v. Canter, the Court observed that Art. IV bestowed upon Congress alone a complete power of government over territories not within the States that constituted the United States. The Court then acknowledged Congress' authority to create courts for those territories that were not in conformity with Art. III. Such courts were

> created in virtue of the general right of sovereignty which exists in the government, or in virtue of that clause which enables Congress to make all needful rules and regulations, respecting the territory belonging to the United States. The jurisdiction with which they are invested * * * is conferred by Congress, in the execution of those general powers which that body possesses over the territories of the United States. Although admiralty jurisdiction can be exercised in the states in those Courts, only, which are established in pursuance of the third article of the Constitution; the same limitation does not extend to the territories. In legislating for them, Congress exercises the combined powers of the general, and of a state government.

The Court followed the same reasoning when it reviewed Congress' creation of non-Art. III courts in the District of Columbia. It noted that there was in the District

> no division of powers between the general and state governments. Congress has the entire control over the district for every purpose of government; and it is reasonable to suppose, that in organizing a judicial department here, all judicial power necessary for the purposes of government would be vested in the courts of justice.

Appellants next advert to a second class of cases—those in which this Court has sustained the exercise by Congress and the Executive of the power to establish and administer courts-martial. The situation in these cases strongly resembles the situation with respect to territorial courts: It too involves a constitutional grant of power that has been historically understood as giving the political Branches of Government extraordinary control over the precise subject matter at issue. Article

I, § 8, cls. 13, 14, confer upon Congress the power "[t]o provide and maintain a Navy," and "[t]o make Rules for the Government and Regulation of the land and naval Forces." The Fifth Amendment, which requires a presentment or indictment of a grand jury before a person may be held to answer for a capital or otherwise infamous crime, contains an express exception for "cases arising in the land or naval forces." And Art. II, § 2, cl. 1, provides that "The President shall be Commander in Chief of the Army and Navy of the United States, and of the Militia of the several States, when called into the actual Service of the United States." Noting these constitutional directives, the Court in *Dynes v. Hoover* explained:

> These provisions show that Congress has the power to provide for the trial and punishment of military and naval offences in the manner then and now practiced by civilized nations; and that the power to do so is given without any connection between it and the 3d article of the Constitution defining the judicial power of the United States; indeed, that the two powers are entirely independent of each other.

Finally, appellants rely on a third group of cases, in which this Court has upheld the constitutionality of legislative courts and administrative agencies created by Congress to adjudicate cases involving "public rights."[18] The "public rights" doctrine was first set forth in *Murray's Lessee v. Hoboken Land & Improvement Co. (1856)*:

> [W]e do not consider congress can either withdraw from judicial cognizance any matter which, from its nature, is the subject of a suit at the common law, or in equity, or admiralty; nor, on the other hand, can it bring under the judicial power a matter which, from its nature, is not a subject for judicial determination. At the same time there are matters, involving public rights, which may be presented in such form that the judicial power is capable of acting on them, and which are susceptible of judicial determination, but which congress may or may not bring within the cognizance of the courts of the United States, as it may deem proper.

This doctrine may be explained in part by reference to the traditional principle of sovereign immunity, which recognizes that the Government may attach conditions to its consent to be sued. But the public-rights doctrine also draws upon the principle of separation of powers, and a historical understanding that certain prerogatives were reserved to the political Branches of Government. The doctrine extends only to matters arising "between the Government and persons subject to its authority in connection with the performance of the constitutional functions of the executive or legislative departments," and only to matters that historically could have been determined exclusively by those departments. The

18 Congress' power to create legislative courts to adjudicate public rights carries with it the lesser power to create administrative agencies for the same purpose, and to provide for review of those agency decisions in Art. III courts.

understanding of these cases is that the Framers expected that Congress would be free to commit such matters completely to nonjudicial executive determination, and that as a result there can be no constitutional objection to Congress' employing the less drastic expedient of committing their determination to a legislative court or an administrative agency.

The public-rights doctrine is grounded in a historically recognized distinction between matters that could be conclusively determined by the Executive and Legislative Branches and matters that are "inherently * * * judicial." For example, the Court in Murray's Lessee looked to the law of England and the States at the time the Constitution was adopted, in order to determine whether the issue presented was customarily cognizable in the courts. Concluding that the matter had not traditionally been one for judicial determination, the Court perceived no bar to Congress' establishment of summary procedures, outside of Art. III courts, to collect a debt due to the Government from one of its customs agents.[20] On the same premise, the Court held that the Court of Customs Appeals had been properly constituted by Congress as a legislative court:

> The full province of the court under the act creating it is that of determining matters arising between the Government and others in the executive administration and application of the customs laws * * * . The appeals include nothing which inherently or necessarily requires judicial determination, but only matters the determination of which may be, and at times has been, committed exclusively to executive officers.

The distinction between public rights and private rights has not been definitively explained in our precedents. Nor is it necessary to do so in the present cases, for it suffices to observe that a matter of public rights must at a minimum arise "between the government and others."

In contrast, "the liability of one individual to another under the law as defined" is a matter of private rights. Our precedents clearly establish that only controversies in the former category may be removed from Art. III courts and delegated to legislative courts or administrative agencies for their determination. Private-rights disputes, on the other hand, lie at the core of the historically recognized judicial power.

FYI

In Thomas v. Union Carbide and subsequent cases, the Court acknowledged that the "public rights" doctrine also extends to causes of action arising out of federal regulatory statutes.

20 Doubtless it could be argued that the need for independent judicial determination is greatest in cases arising between the Government and an individual. But the rationale for the public-rights line of cases lies not in political theory, but rather in Congress' and this Court's understanding of what power was reserved to the Judiciary by the Constitution as a matter of historical fact.

In sum, this Court has identified three situations in which Art. III does not bar the creation of legislative courts. In each of these situations, the Court has recognized certain exceptional powers bestowed upon Congress by the Constitution or by historical consensus. Only in the face of such an exceptional grant of power has the Court declined to hold the authority of Congress subject to the general prescriptions of Art. III.

We discern no such exceptional grant of power applicable in the cases before us. The courts created by the Bankruptcy Act of 1978 do not lie exclusively outside the States of the Federal Union, like those in the District of Columbia and the Territories. Nor do the bankruptcy courts bear any resemblance to courts-martial, which are founded upon the Constitution's grant of plenary authority over the Nation's military forces to the Legislative and Executive Branches. Finally, the substantive legal rights at issue in the present action cannot be deemed "public rights." Appellants argue that a discharge in bankruptcy is indeed a "public right," similar to such congressionally created benefits as "radio station licenses, pilot licenses, or certificates for common carriers" granted by administrative agencies. But the restructuring of debtor-creditor relations, which is at the core of the federal bankruptcy power, must be distinguished from the adjudication of state-created private rights, such as the right to recover contract damages that is at issue in this case. The former may well be a "public right," but the latter obviously is not. Appellant Northern's right to recover contract damages to augment its estate is "one of private right, that is, of the liability of one individual to another under the law as defined."

Recognizing that the present cases may not fall within the scope of any of our prior cases permitting the establishment of legislative courts, appellants argue that we should recognize an additional situation beyond the command of Art. III, sufficiently broad to sustain the Act. Appellants contend that Congress' constitutional authority to establish "uniform Laws on the subject of Bankruptcies throughout the United States," carries with it an inherent power to establish legislative courts capable of adjudicating "bankruptcy-related controversies."

* * *

Appellants' contention, in essence, is that pursuant to any of its Art. I powers, Congress may create courts free of Art. III's requirements whenever it finds that course expedient. This contention has been rejected in previous cases. Although the cases relied upon by appellants demonstrate that independent courts are not required for all federal adjudications, those cases also make it clear that where Art. III does apply, all of the legislative powers specified in Art. I and elsewhere are subject to it.

The flaw in appellants' analysis is that it provides no limiting principle. It thus threatens to supplant completely our system of adjudication in independent Art. III tribunals and replace it with a system of "specialized" legislative courts. True, appellants argue that under their analysis Congress could create legislative courts pursuant only to some "specific" Art. I power, and "only when there is a particularized need for distinctive treatment." They therefore assert that their analysis would not permit Congress to replace the independent Art. III Judiciary through a "wholesale assignment of federal judicial business to legislative courts." But these "limitations" are wholly illusory. For example, Art. I, § 8, empowers Congress to enact laws, *inter alia*, regulating interstate commerce and punishing certain crimes. Art. I, § 8, cls. 3, 6. On appellants' reasoning Congress could provide for the adjudication of these and "related" matters by judges and courts within Congress' exclusive control. The potential for encroachment upon powers reserved to the Judicial Branch through the device of "specialized" legislative courts is dramatically evidenced in the jurisdiction granted to the courts created by the Act before us. The broad range of questions that can be brought into a bankruptcy court because they are "related to cases under title 11" is the clearest proof that even when Congress acts through a "specialized" court, and pursuant to only one of its many Art. I powers, appellants' analysis fails to provide any real protection against the erosion of Art. III jurisdiction by the unilateral action of the political Branches. In short, to accept appellants' reasoning, would require that we replace the principles delineated in our precedents, rooted in history and the Constitution, with a rule of broad legislative discretion that could effectively eviscerate the constitutional guarantee of an independent Judicial Branch of the Federal Government.

* * *

In sum, Art. III bars Congress from establishing legislative courts to exercise jurisdiction over all matters related to those arising under the bankruptcy laws. The establishment of such courts does not fall within any of the historically recognized situations in which the general principle of independent adjudication commanded by Art. III does not apply. Nor can we discern any persuasive reason, in logic, history, or the Constitution, why the bankruptcy courts here established lie beyond the reach of Art. III.

IV

Appellants advance a second argument for upholding the constitutionality of the Act: that "viewed within the entire judicial framework set up by Congress," the bankruptcy court is merely an "adjunct" to the district court, and that the delegation of certain adjudicative functions to the bankruptcy court is accordingly consistent with the principle that the judicial power of the United States must be vested in Art. III courts. As support for their argument, appellants rely principally upon Crowell v. Benson and United States v. Raddatz, cases in which we approved the use of administrative agencies and magistrates as adjuncts to Art. III courts. The question to which we turn, therefore, is whether the Act has retained "the essential attributes of the judicial power," in Art. III tribunals.

The essential premise underlying appellants' argument is that even where the Constitution denies Congress the power to establish legislative courts, Congress possesses the authority to assign certain factfinding functions to adjunct tribunals. It is, of course, true that while the power to adjudicate "private rights" must be vested in an Art. III court,

> this Court has accepted factfinding by an administrative agency, * * * as an adjunct to the Art. III court, analogizing the agency to a jury or a special master and permitting it in admiralty cases to perform the function of the special master.

The use of administrative agencies as adjuncts was first upheld in Crowell v. Benson [in which the Court upheld an agency's power to make factual determinations for claims of injured employees, but had no power to enforce its orders, which were reviewable by Article III courts.] * * * Crowell involved the adjudication of congressionally created rights. But this Court has sustained the use of adjunct factfinders even in the adjudication of constitutional rights—so long as those adjuncts were subject to sufficient control by an Art. III district court. In United States v. Raddatz, the Court upheld the 1978 Federal Magistrates Act, which permitted district court judges to refer certain pretrial motions, including suppression motions based on alleged violations of constitutional rights, to a magistrate for initial determination. The Court observed that the magistrate's proposed findings and recommendations were subject to *de novo* review by the district court, which was free to rehear the evidence or to call for additional evidence. Moreover, it was noted that the magistrate considered motions only upon reference from the district court, and that the magistrates were appointed, and subject to removal, by the district court.[30] In short, the ultimate decisionmaking authority respecting all pretrial motions clearly remained with the district court. Under these circumstances, the Court held that the Act did not violate the constraints of Art. III.

Together these cases establish two principles that aid us in determining the extent to which Congress may constitutionally vest traditionally judicial functions in non-Art. III officers. First, it is clear that when Congress creates a substantive federal right, it possesses substantial discretion to prescribe the manner in which

---

30 Thus in Raddatz there was no serious threat that the exercise of the judicial power would be subject to incursion by other branches. "[T]he only conceivable danger of a 'threat' to the 'independence' of the magistrate comes from within, rather than without the judicial department."

that right may be adjudicated—including the assignment to an adjunct of some functions historically performed by judges. Thus Crowell recognized that Art. III does not require "all determinations of fact [to] be made by judges;" with respect to congressionally created rights, some factual determinations may be made by a specialized factfinding tribunal designed by Congress, without constitutional bar. Second, the functions of the adjunct must be limited in such a way that "the essential attributes" of judicial power are retained in the Art. III court. Thus in upholding the adjunct scheme challenged in Crowell, the Court emphasized that "the reservation of full authority to the court to deal with matters of law provides for the appropriate exercise of the judicial function in this class of cases." And in refusing to invalidate the Magistrates Act at issue in Raddatz, the Court stressed that under the congressional scheme " '[t]he authority—and the responsibility—to make an informed, final determination * * * remains with the judge;' " the statute's delegation of power was therefore permissible, since "the ultimate decision is made by the district court."

These two principles assist us in evaluating the "adjunct" scheme presented in these cases. Appellants assume that Congress' power to create "adjuncts" to consider all cases related to those arising under Title 11 is as great as it was in the circumstances of Crowell. But while Crowell certainly endorsed the proposition that Congress possesses broad discretion to assign factfinding functions to an adjunct created to aid in the adjudication of congressionally created statutory rights, Crowell does not support the further proposition necessary to appellants' argument—that Congress possesses the same degree of discretion in assigning traditionally judicial power to adjuncts engaged in the adjudication of rights not created by Congress. Indeed, the validity of this proposition was expressly denied in Crowell, when the Court rejected "the untenable assumption that the constitutional courts may be deprived in all cases of the determination of facts upon evidence even though a constitutional right may be involved," and stated that

> the essential independence of the exercise of the judicial power of the United States in the enforcement of constitutional rights requires that the Federal court should determine * * * an issue [of agency jurisdiction] upon its own record and the facts elicited before it.[34]

Appellants' proposition was also implicitly rejected in Raddatz. Congress' assignment of adjunct functions under the Federal Magistrates Act was substantially narrower than under the statute challenged in Crowell. Yet the Court's scrutiny of the adjunct scheme in Raddatz—which played a role in the adjudication of constitutional rights—was far stricter than it had been in Crowell. Critical to

---

34 Crowell's precise holding, with respect to the review of "jurisdictional" and "constitutional" facts that arise within ordinary administrative proceedings, has been undermined by later cases. But the general principle of Crowell—distinguishing between congressionally created rights and constitutionally recognized rights—remains valid.

the Court's decision to uphold the Magistrates Act was the fact that the ultimate decision was made by the district court.

Although Crowell and Raddatz do not explicitly distinguish between rights created by Congress and other rights, such a distinction underlies in part Crowell's and Raddatz's recognition of a critical difference between rights created by federal statute and rights recognized by the Constitution. Moreover, such a distinction seems to us to be necessary in light of the delicate accommodations required by the principle of separation of powers reflected in Art. III. The constitutional system of checks and balances is designed to guard against "encroachment or aggrandizement" by Congress at the expense of the other branches of government. But when Congress creates a statutory right, it clearly has the discretion, in defining that right, to create presumptions, or assign burdens of proof, or prescribe remedies; it may also provide that persons seeking to vindicate that right must do so before particularized tribunals created to perform the specialized adjudicative tasks related to that right. Such provisions do, in a sense, affect the exercise of judicial power, but they are also incidental to Congress' power to define the right that it has created. No comparable justification exists, however, when the right being adjudicated is not of congressional creation. In such a situation, substantial inroads into functions that have traditionally been performed by the Judiciary cannot be characterized merely as incidental extensions of Congress' power to define rights that it has created. Rather, such inroads suggest unwarranted encroachments upon the judicial power of the United States, which our Constitution reserves for Art. III courts.

We hold that the Bankruptcy Act of 1978 carries the possibility of such an unwarranted encroachment. Many of the rights subject to adjudication by the Act's bankruptcy courts, like the rights implicated in Raddatz, are not of Congress' creation. Indeed, the cases before us, which center upon appellant Northern's claim for damages for breach of contract and misrepresentation, involve a right created by state law, a right independent of and antecedent to the reorganization petition that conferred jurisdiction upon the Bankruptcy Court. Accordingly, Congress' authority to control the manner in which that right is adjudicated, through assignment of historically judicial functions to a non-Art. III "adjunct," plainly must be deemed at a minimum. Yet it is equally plain that Congress has vested the "adjunct" bankruptcy judges with powers over Northern's state-created right that far exceed the powers that it has vested in administrative agencies that adjudicate only rights of Congress' own creation.

Unlike the administrative scheme that we reviewed in Crowell, the Act vests all "essential attributes" of the judicial power of the United States in the "adjunct" bankruptcy court. First, the agency in Crowell made only specialized, narrowly confined factual determinations regarding a particularized area of law. In contrast, the subject-matter jurisdiction of the bankruptcy courts encompasses not only traditional matters of bankruptcy, but also "all civil proceedings arising under title 11 or arising in or related to cases under title 11." Second, while the agency in Crowell engaged in statutorily channeled factfinding functions, the bankruptcy courts exercise "all of the jurisdiction" conferred by the Act on the district courts. Third, the agency in Crowell possessed only a limited power to issue compensation orders pursuant to specialized procedures, and its orders could be enforced only by order of the district court. By contrast, the bankruptcy courts exercise all ordinary powers of district courts, including the power to preside over jury trials, the power to issue declaratory judgments, the power to issue writs of habeas corpus, and the power to issue any order, process, or judgment appropriate for the enforcement of the provisions of Title 11. Fourth, while orders issued by the agency in Crowell were to be set aside if "not supported by the evidence," the judgments of the bankruptcy courts are apparently subject to review only under the more deferential "clearly erroneous" standard. Finally, the agency in Crowell was required by law to seek enforcement of its compensation orders in the district court. In contrast, the bankruptcy courts issue final judgments, which are binding and enforceable even in the absence of an appeal. In short, the "adjunct" bankruptcy courts created by the Act exercise jurisdiction behind the facade of a grant to the district courts, and are exercising powers far greater than those lodged in the adjuncts approved in either Crowell or Raddatz.

We conclude that § 241(a) of the Bankruptcy Act of 1978 has impermissibly removed most, if not all, of "the essential attributes of the judicial power" from the Art. III district court, and has vested those attributes in a non-Art. III adjunct. Such a grant of jurisdiction cannot be sustained as an exercise of Congress' power to create adjuncts to Art. III courts.

V

Having concluded that the broad grant of jurisdiction to the bankruptcy courts * * * is unconstitutional, we must now determine whether our holding should be applied retroactively to the effective date of the Act. Our decision in Chevron Oil Co. v. Huson sets forth the three considerations recognized by our precedents as properly bearing upon the issue of retroactivity. They are, first, whether the holding in question "decid[ed] an issue of first impression whose resolution was not clearly foreshadowed" by earlier cases; second, "whether retrospective operation will further or retard [the] operation" of the holding in question; and third, whether retroactive application "could produce substantial inequitable results" in individual cases. In the present cases, all of these considerations militate against the retroactive application of our holding today. It is plain that Congress' broad grant of judicial power to non-Art. III bankruptcy judges presents an unprecedented question of interpretation of Art. III. It is equally plain that retroactive application would not further the operation of our holding, and would surely visit substantial injustice and hardship upon those litigants who relied upon the Act's vesting of jurisdiction in the bankruptcy courts. We hold, therefore, that our decision today shall apply only prospectively.

The judgment of the District Court is affirmed. However, we stay our judgment until October 4, 1982. This limited stay will afford Congress an opportunity to reconstitute the bankruptcy courts or to adopt other valid means of adjudication, without impairing the interim administration of the bankruptcy laws.

* * *

Note

A few years after *Northern Pipeline*, the Court decided *Thomas v. Union Carbide Agricultural Products Co.*, 473 U.S. 568 (1985). The Federal Insecticide, Fungicide, and Rodenticide Act, 7 U.S.C.A. § 136 *et seq.* (FIFRA), requires manufacturers to provide research data to the Environmental Protection Agency (EPA) concerning the health, safety, and environmental effects of products to be registered as pesticides. If an applicant seeks a new registration, permit, or use, FIFRA authorizes the EPA to consider other manufacturers' data, provided the applicant offers compensation to the original data supplier. Prior to 1978, if the parties were unable to agree on compensation, the EPA decided, subject to judicial review. Congress concluded that the EPA lacked the expertise necessary to determine proper compensation and that the burden of doing so impeded the registration process. Consequently, in 1978 Congress amended FIFRA to provide binding arbitration if the parties failed to agree. The arbitrator's decision is subject to judicial review only for fraud, misrepresentation, or other misconduct. Several large chemical companies challenged the constitutionality of the amendment. They claimed that the imposition of binding arbitration violated Article III because the arbitrators functioned as judicial officers without Article III protections and judicial review was so limited. The eight Justices who addressed the issue rejected the challenge.

The majority pointed out that *Northern Pipeline* did not limit the public rights doctrine to disputes between the federal government and private interests. If it had, the constitutionality of many administrative quasi-judicial activities with respect to wholly private disputes would be open to doubt. *Thomas* found that the doctrine reflects a pragmatic understanding that when Congress adopts a quasi-adjudicative method for resolving controversies that could otherwise be conclusively determined by the political branches, the danger of encroachment on the judicial power is reduced.

Specifically, the Court asserted that the federal right to compensation strongly resembled a public right, even if the United States was not a party. The unrestricted use of data was essential to safeguard public health and therefore served a public purpose. Congress could have authorized the EPA to impose fees on applicants using others' data and subsidized data suppliers. The Court thought that relying instead on arbitrators did not diminish the likelihood of decision-making free from political influence.

Moreover, the Court found that the "near disaster" of the previous scheme and concerns about the danger to public health caused by delays in the registration process had prompted Congress to adopt the arbitration system. It summarized its views thusly:

> Congress, acting for a valid legislative purpose pursuant to its powers under Article I, may create a seemingly "private" right that is so closely integrated into a public regulatory scheme as to be a matter appropriate for agency resolution with limited involvement by the Article III judiciary. To hold otherwise would be to erect a rigid and formalistic restraint on the ability of Congress to adopt innovative measures such as negotiation and arbitration with respect to rights created by a regulatory scheme.

Justice Brennan, the author of the plurality opinion in *Northern Pipeline*, concurred on behalf of three members of that group. He agreed with the majority that whether the government was a party did not determine whether a case fell within the public rights doctrine. Because the case involved a federal regulatory scheme that virtually occupied the field and included the active participation of a federal agency in resolving the dispute, he concluded that it was a public rights case.

C. The Modern Balancing Test

Commodity Futures Trading Commission v. Schor

Supreme Court of the United States, 1986.
478 U.S. 833.

JUSTICE O'CONNOR delivered the opinion of the Court.

The question presented is whether the Commodity Exchange Act (CEA or Act) empowers the Commodity Futures Trading Commission (CFTC or Commission) to entertain state law counterclaims in reparation proceedings and, if so, whether that grant of authority violates Article III of the Constitution.

I

The CEA broadly prohibits fraudulent and manipulative conduct in connection with commodity futures transactions. In 1974, Congress "overhaul[ed]" the Act in order to institute a more "comprehensive regulatory structure to oversee the volatile and esoteric futures trading complex." Congress also determined that the broad regulatory powers of the CEA were most appropriately vested in an agency which would be relatively immune from the "political winds that sweep Washington." It therefore created an independent agency, the CFTC, and entrusted to it sweeping authority to implement the CEA.

Among the duties assigned to the CFTC was the administration of a reparations procedure through which disgruntled customers of professional commodity brokers could seek redress for the brokers' violations of the Act or CFTC regulations. Thus, § 14 of the CEA provides that any person injured by such violations may apply to the Commission for an order directing the offender to pay reparations to the complainant and may enforce that order in federal district court. Congress intended this administrative procedure to be an "inexpensive and expeditious" alternative to existing fora available to aggrieved customers, namely, the courts and arbitration.

In conformance with the congressional goal of promoting efficient dispute resolution, the CFTC promulgated a regulation in 1976 which allows it to adjudicate counterclaims "aris[ing] out of the transaction or occurrence or series of transactions or occurrences set forth in the complaint." This permissive counterclaim rule leaves the respondent in a reparations proceeding free to seek relief against the reparations complainant in other fora.

The instant dispute arose in February 1980, when respondents Schor and Mortgage Services of America, Inc., invoked the CFTC's reparations jurisdiction by filing complaints against petitioner Conti Commodity Services, Inc. (Conti), a commodity futures broker, and Richard L. Sandor, a Conti employee. Schor had an account with Conti which contained a debit balance because Schor's net futures trading losses and expenses, such as commissions, exceeded the funds deposited in the account. Schor alleged that this debit balance was the result of Conti's numerous violations of the CEA.

Before receiving notice that Schor had commenced the reparations proceeding, Conti had filed a diversity action in Federal District Court to recover the debit balance. Schor counterclaimed in this action, reiterating his charges that the debit balance was due to Conti's violations of the CEA. Schor also moved on two separate occasions to dismiss or stay the District Court action, arguing that the continuation of the federal action would be a waste of judicial resources and an undue burden on the litigants in view of the fact that "[t]he reparations proceedings * * * will fully * * * resolve and adjudicate all the rights of the parties to this action with respect to the transactions which are the subject matter of this action."

Although the District Court declined to stay or dismiss the suit, Conti voluntarily dismissed the federal court action and presented its debit balance claim by way of a counterclaim in the CFTC reparations proceeding. Conti denied violating the CEA and instead insisted that the debit balance resulted from Schor's trading, and was therefore a simple debt owed by Schor.

After discovery, briefing, and a hearing, the Administrative Law Judge (ALJ) in Schor's reparations proceeding ruled in Conti's favor on both Schor's claims and Conti's counterclaims. After this ruling, Schor for the first time challenged the CFTC's statutory authority to adjudicate Conti's counterclaim. The ALJ rejected Schor's challenge, stating himself "bound by agency regulations and published agency policies." The Commission declined to review the decision and allowed it to become final, at which point Schor filed a petition for review with the Court of Appeals for the District of Columbia Circuit. Prior to oral argument, the Court of Appeals, ***sua sponte***, raised the question whether CFTC could constitutionally adjudicate Conti's counterclaims in light of Northern Pipeline Construction Co. v. Marathon Pipe Line Co., in which this Court held that "Congress may not vest in a non-Article III court the power to adjudicate, render final judgment, and issue binding orders in a traditional contract action arising under state law, without consent of the litigants, and subject only to ordinary appellate review." Thomas v. Union Carbide Agricultural Products Co. (Thomas).

> **FYI** A federal administrative law judge is not an Article III officer. There is neither life tenure nor salary protection.

After briefing and argument, the Court of Appeals upheld the CFTC's decision on Schor's claim in most respects, but ordered the dismissal of Conti's counterclaims on the ground that "the CFTC lacks authority (subject matter competence) to adjudicate" common law counterclaims. In support of this latter ruling, the Court of Appeals reasoned that the CFTC's exercise of jurisdiction over Conti's common law counterclaim gave rise to "[s]erious constitutional problems" under Northern Pipeline. The Court of Appeals therefore concluded that, under well-established principles of statutory construction, the relevant inquiry was whether the CEA was " 'fairly susceptible' of [an alternative] construction," such that Article III objections, and thus unnecessary constitutional adjudication, could be avoided.

After examining the CEA and its legislative history, the court concluded that Congress had no "clearly expressed" or "explicit" intention to give the CFTC constitutionally questionable jurisdiction over state common law counterclaims. The Court of Appeals therefore "adopt[ed] the construction of the Act that avoids significant constitutional questions," reading the CEA to authorize the CFTC to adjudicate only those counterclaims alleging violations of the Act or CFTC regulations. Because Conti's counterclaims did not allege such violations, the Court of Appeals held that the CFTC exceeded its authority in adjudicating those claims, and ordered that the ALJ's decision on the claims be reversed and the claims dismissed for lack of jurisdiction.

* * * This Court granted the CFTC's petition for certiorari, vacated the Court of Appeals' judgment, and remanded the case for further consideration in light of Thomas. * * *

On remand, the Court of Appeals reinstated its prior judgment. * * * We again granted certiorari and now reverse.

II

* * *

In view of the abundant evidence that Congress both contemplated and authorized the CFTC's assertion of jurisdiction over Conti's common law counterclaim, we conclude that the Court of Appeals' analysis is untenable. The canon of construction that requires courts to avoid unnecessary constitutional adjudication did not empower the Court of Appeals to manufacture a restriction on the CFTC's jurisdiction that was nowhere contemplated by Congress and to reject plain evidence of congressional intent because that intent was not specifically embodied in a statutory mandate. We therefore are squarely faced with the question whether the CFTC's assumption of jurisdiction over common law counterclaims violates Article III of the Constitution.

III

Food for Thought

Does the Court have any ascertainable standards for when federal courts may or must interpret statutes in such a way as to avoid constitutional questions?

Article III, § 1, directs that the "judicial Power of the United States shall be vested in one supreme Court and in such inferior Courts as the Congress may from time to time ordain and establish," and provides that these federal courts shall be staffed by judges who hold office during good behavior, and whose compensation shall not be diminished during tenure in office. Schor claims that these provisions prohibit Congress from authorizing the initial adjudication of common law counterclaims by the CFTC, an administrative agency whose adjudicatory officers do not enjoy the tenure and salary protections embodied in Article III.

Although our precedents in this area do not admit of easy synthesis, they do establish that the resolution of claims such as Schor's cannot turn on conclusory reference to the language of Article III. Rather, the constitutionality of a given congressional delegation of adjudicative functions to a non-Article III body must be assessed by reference to the purposes underlying the requirements of Article III. This inquiry, in turn, is guided by the principle that "practical attention to substance rather than doctrinaire reliance on formal categories should inform application of Article III."

A

Article III, § 1, serves both to protect "the role of the independent judiciary within the constitutional scheme of tripartite government," and to safeguard litigants' "right to have claims decided before judges who are free from potential domination by other branches of government." Although our cases have provided us with little occasion to discuss the nature or significance of this latter safeguard, our prior discussions of Article III, § 1's guarantee of an independent and impartial adjudication by the federal judiciary of matters within the judicial power of the United States intimated that this guarantee serves to protect primarily personal, rather than structural, interests.

Our precedents also demonstrate, however, that Article III does not confer on litigants an absolute right to the plenary consideration of every nature of claim by an Article III court. Moreover, as a personal right, Article III's guarantee of an impartial and independent federal adjudication is subject to waiver, just as are other personal constitutional rights that dictate the procedures by which civil and criminal matters must be tried. Indeed, the relevance of concepts of waiver to Article III challenges is demonstrated by our decision in Northern Pipeline, in which the absence of consent to an initial adjudication before a non-Article III tribunal was relied on as a significant factor in determining that Article III forbade such adjudication.

In the instant cases, Schor indisputably waived any right he may have possessed to the full trial of Conti's counterclaim before an Article III court. Schor expressly demanded that Conti proceed on its counterclaim in the reparations proceeding rather than before the District Court and was content to have the entire dispute settled in the forum he had selected until the ALJ ruled against him on all counts; it was only after the ALJ rendered a decision to which he objected that Schor raised any challenge to the CFTC's consideration of Conti's counterclaim.

Even were there no evidence of an express waiver here, Schor's election to forgo his right to proceed in state or federal court on his claim and his decision to seek relief instead in a CFTC reparations proceeding constituted an effective waiver. Three years before Schor instituted his reparations action, a private right of action under the CEA was explicitly recognized in the Circuit in which Schor and Conti filed suit in District Court. Moreover, at the time Schor decided to seek relief before the CFTC rather than in the federal courts, the CFTC's regulations made clear that it was empowered to adjudicate all counterclaims "aris[ing] out of the same transaction or occurrence or series of transactions or occurrences set forth in the complaint." Thus, Schor had the option of having the common law counterclaim against him adjudicated in a federal Article III court, but, with full knowledge that the CFTC would exercise jurisdiction over that claim, chose to avail himself of the quicker and less expensive procedure Congress had provided him. In such circumstances, it is clear that Schor effectively agreed to an adjudication by the CFTC of the entire controversy by seeking relief in this alternative forum.

B

As noted above, our precedents establish that Article III, § 1, not only preserves to litigants their interest in an impartial and independent federal adjudication of claims within the judicial power of the United States, but also serves as "an inseparable element of the constitutional system of checks and balances." Article III, § 1 safeguards the role of the Judicial Branch in our tripartite system by barring congressional attempts "to transfer jurisdiction [to non-Article III tribunals] for the purpose of emasculating" constitutional courts and thereby preventing "the encroachment or aggrandizement of one branch at the expense of the other." To the extent that this structural principle is implicated in a given case, the parties cannot by consent cure the constitutional difficulty for the same reason that the parties by consent cannot confer on federal courts subject-matter jurisdiction beyond the limitations imposed by Article III, § 2. When these Article III limitations are at issue, notions of consent and waiver cannot be dispositive because the limitations serve institutional interests that the parties cannot be expected to protect.

In determining the extent to which a given congressional decision to authorize the adjudication of Article III business in a non-Article III tribunal impermissibly threatens the institutional integrity of the Judicial Branch, the Court has declined to adopt formalistic and unbending rules. Although such rules might lend a greater degree of coherence to this area of the law, they might also unduly constrict Congress' ability to take needed and innovative action pursuant to its Article I powers. Thus, in reviewing Article III challenges, we have weighed a number of factors, none of which has been deemed determinative, with an eye to the practical effect that the congressional action will have on the constitutionally assigned role of the federal judiciary. Among the factors upon which we have focused are the extent to which the "essential attributes of judicial power" are reserved to Article III courts, and, conversely, the extent to which the non-Article III forum exercises the range of jurisdiction and powers normally vested only in Article III courts, the origins and importance of the right to be adjudicated, and the concerns that drove Congress to depart from the requirements of Article III.

An examination of the relative allocation of powers between the CFTC and Article III courts in light of the considerations given prominence in our precedents demonstrates that the congressional scheme does not impermissibly intrude on the province of the judiciary. The CFTC's adjudicatory powers depart from the traditional agency model in just one respect: the CFTC's jurisdiction over common law counterclaims. While wholesale importation of concepts of pendent or ancillary jurisdiction into the agency context may create greater constitutional difficulties, we decline to endorse an absolute prohibition on such jurisdiction out of fear of where some hypothetical "slippery slope" may deposit us. Indeed, the CFTC's exercise of this type of jurisdiction is not without precedent. Thus, in *RFC v. Bankers Trust Co. (1943)*, we saw no constitutional difficulty in the initial adjudication of a state law claim by a federal agency, subject to judicial review, when that claim was ancillary to a federal law dispute. Similarly, in *Katchen v. Landy (1966)*, this Court upheld a bankruptcy referee's power to hear and decide state law counterclaims against a creditor who filed a claim in bankruptcy when those counterclaims arose out of the same transaction. We reasoned that, as a practical matter, requiring the trustee to commence a plenary action to recover on its counterclaim would be a "meaningless gesture."

In the instant cases, we are likewise persuaded that there is little practical reason to find that this single deviation from the agency model is fatal to the congressional scheme. Aside from its authorization of counterclaim jurisdiction, the CEA leaves far more of the "essential attributes of judicial power" to Article III courts than did that portion of the Bankruptcy Act found unconstitutional in *Northern Pipeline*. The CEA scheme in fact hews closely to the agency model approved by the Court in *Crowell v. Benson (1932)*.

The CFTC, like the agency in *Crowell*, deals only with a "particularized area of law," whereas the jurisdiction of the bankruptcy courts found unconstitutional in *Northern Pipeline* extended to broadly "all civil proceedings arising under title 11 or arising in or related to cases under title 11." CFTC orders, like those of the agency in *Crowell*, but unlike those of the bankruptcy courts under the 1978 Act, are enforceable only by order of the district court. CFTC orders are also reviewed under the same "weight of the evidence" standard sustained in *Crowell*, rather than the more deferential standard found lacking in *Northern Pipeline*. The legal rulings of the CFTC, like the legal determinations of the agency in Crowell, are subject to de novo review. Finally, the CFTC, unlike the bankruptcy courts under the 1978 Act, does not exercise "all ordinary powers of district courts," and thus may not, for instance, preside over jury trials or issue writs of habeas corpus.

Of course, the nature of the claim has significance in our Article III analysis quite apart from the method prescribed for its adjudication. The counterclaim asserted in this litigation is a "private" right for which state law provides the rule of decision. It is therefore a claim of the kind assumed to be at the "core" of matters normally reserved to Article III courts. Yet this conclusion does not end our inquiry; just as this Court has rejected any attempt to make determinative for Article III purposes the distinction between public rights and private rights, there is no reason inherent in separation of powers principles to accord the state law character of a claim talismanic power in Article III inquiries.

We have explained that "the public rights doctrine reflects simply a pragmatic understanding that when Congress selects a quasi-judicial method of resolving matters that 'could be conclusively determined by the Executive and Legislative Branches,' the danger of encroaching on the judicial powers" is less than when private rights, which are normally within the purview of the judiciary, are relegated as an initial matter to administrative adjudication. Similarly, the state law character of a claim is significant for purposes of determining the effect that an initial adjudication of those claims by a non-Article III tribunal will have on the separation of powers for the simple reason that private, common law rights were historically the types of matters subject to resolution by Article III courts. The risk that Congress may improperly have encroached on the federal judiciary is obviously magnified when Congress "withdraw[s] from judicial cognizance any matter which, from its nature, is the subject of a suit at the common law, or in equity, or admiralty" and which therefore has traditionally been tried in Article III courts, and allocates the decision of those matters to a non-Article III forum of its own creation. Accordingly, where private, common law rights are at stake, our examination of the congressional attempt to control the manner in which those rights are adjudicated has been searching. In this litigation, however, "[l]ooking beyond form to the substance of what" Congress has done, we are persuaded that the congressional authorization of limited CFTC jurisdiction over a narrow class of common law claims as an incident to the CFTC's primary, and unchallenged, adjudicative function does not create a substantial threat to the separation of powers.

It is clear that Congress has not attempted to "withdraw from judicial cognizance" the determination of Conti's right to the sum represented by the debit balance in Schor's account. Congress gave the CFTC the authority to adjudicate such matters, but the decision to invoke this forum is left entirely to the parties and the power of the federal judiciary to take jurisdiction of these matters is unaffected. In such circumstances, separation of powers concerns are diminished, for it seems self-evident that just as Congress may encourage parties to settle a dispute out of court or resort to arbitration without impermissible incursions on the separation of powers, Congress may make available a quasi-judicial mechanism through which willing parties may, at their option, elect to resolve their differences. This is not to say, of course, that if Congress created a phalanx of non-Article III tribunals equipped to handle the entire business of the Article III courts without any Article III supervision or control and without evidence of valid and specific legislative necessities, the fact that the parties had the election to proceed in their forum of choice would necessarily save the scheme from constitutional attack. But this case obviously bears no resemblance to such a scenario, given the degree of judicial control saved to the federal courts, as well as the congressional purpose behind the jurisdictional delegation, the demonstrated need for the delegation, and the limited nature of the delegation.

When Congress authorized the CFTC to adjudicate counterclaims, its primary focus was on making effective a specific and limited federal regulatory scheme, not on allocating jurisdiction among federal tribunals. Congress intended to create an inexpensive and expeditious alternative forum through which customers could enforce the provisions of the CEA against professional brokers. Its decision to endow the CFTC with jurisdiction over such reparations claims is readily understandable given the perception that the CFTC was relatively immune from political pressures, and the obvious expertise that the Commission possesses in applying the CEA and its own regulations. This reparations scheme itself is of unquestioned constitutional validity. It was only to ensure the effectiveness of this scheme that Congress authorized the CFTC to assert jurisdiction over common law counterclaims. Indeed, as was explained above, absent the CFTC's exercise of that authority, the purposes of the reparations procedure would have been confounded.

It also bears emphasis that the CFTC's assertion of counterclaim jurisdiction is limited to that which is necessary to make the reparations procedure workable. The CFTC adjudication of common law counterclaims is incidental to, and completely dependent upon, adjudication of reparations claims created by federal law, and in actual fact is limited to claims arising out of the same transaction or occurrence as the reparations claim.

In such circumstances, the magnitude of any intrusion on the Judicial Branch can only be termed *de minimis*. Conversely, were we to hold that the Legislative Branch may not permit such limited cognizance of common law counterclaims at the election of the parties, it is clear that we would "defeat the obvious purpose of the legislation to furnish a prompt, continuous, expert and inexpensive method for dealing with a class of questions of fact which are peculiarly suited to examination and determination by an administrative agency specially assigned to that task." We do not think Article III compels this degree of prophylaxis.

* * *

C

> **FYI**
> "Prophylaxis" means intentionally applying a broad remedy in order to ensure that nothing is missed.

Schor asserts that Article III, § 1, constrains Congress for reasons of federalism, as well as for reasons of separation of powers. He argues that the state law character of Conti's counterclaim transforms the central question in this litigation from whether Congress has trespassed upon the judicial powers of the Federal Government into whether Congress has invaded the prerogatives of state governments.

At the outset, we note that our prior precedents in this area have dealt only with separation of powers concerns, and have not intimated that principles of federalism impose limits on Congress' ability to delegate adjudicative functions to non-Article III tribunals. This absence of discussion regarding federalism is particularly telling in Northern Pipeline, where the Court based its analysis solely on the separation of powers principles inherent in Article III despite the fact that the claim sought to be adjudicated in the bankruptcy court was created by state law.

Even assuming that principles of federalism are relevant to Article III analysis, however, we are unpersuaded that those principles require the invalidation of the CFTC's counterclaim jurisdiction. The sole fact that Conti's counterclaim is resolved by a federal rather than a state tribunal could not be said to unduly impair state interests, for it is established that a federal court could, without constitutional hazard, decide a counterclaim such as the one asserted here under its ancillary jurisdiction, even if an independent jurisdictional basis for it were lacking. Given that the federal courts can and do exercise ancillary jurisdiction over counterclaims such as the one at issue here, the question becomes whether the fact that a federal agency rather than a federal Article III court initially hears the state law claim gives rise to a cognizably greater impairment of principles of federalism.

Schor argues that those Framers opposed to diversity jurisdiction in the federal courts acquiesced in its inclusion in Article III only because they were assured that the federal judiciary would be protected by the tenure and salary provisions of Article III. He concludes, in essence, that to protect this constitutional compact, Article III should be read to absolutely preclude any adjudication of state law claims by federal decisionmakers that do not enjoy the Article III salary and tenure protections. We are unpersuaded by Schor's novel theory, which suffers from a number of flaws, the most important of which is that Schor identifies no historical support for the critical link he posits between the provisions of Article III that protect the independence of the federal judiciary and those provisions that define the extent of the judiciary's jurisdiction over state law claims.

The judgment of the Court of Appeals for the District of Columbia Circuit is reversed, and the cases remanded for further proceedings consistent with this opinion.

It is so ordered.

Notes and Questions

1. Would the result have been different if the statute required rather than permitted both the federal claims and the state law counterclaims to be asserted in the administrative proceedings? Absent waiver, how does a court determine if a legislative court violates a litigant's right to have a decision from a judge free from potential influence by the other branches of government?

2. In the federal courts, litigants cannot waive defects in subject matter jurisdiction. Are challenges based upon the lack of Article III safeguards "jurisdictional"?

3. Was CFTC jurisdiction over counterclaims necessary to the effectiveness of the statutory scheme? If so, why was the assertion of counterclaims permissive rather than compulsory?

4. How important are Congress's motives for departing from Article III? Would the result have differed if Congress enacted the scheme in part to reduce the power of the Article III courts?

5. The Court asserts that the state law character of a claim assigned to a legislative court indicates increased danger of encroachment on judicial power. Does it matter that state court judges do not enjoy the safeguards of Article III?

6. Must any adjudication by a legislative court be subject to review by an Article III court for the scheme to be constitutional? Does such review sufficiently protect the values underlying Article III? *See* Richard Fallon, *Of Legislative Courts, Administrative Agencies, and Article III*, 101 HARV. L.REV. 915 (1988) (answering both questions affirmatively).

D. Retrenchment?

Stern v. Marshall

131 S.Ct. 2594.
Supreme Court of the United States, 2011.

CHIEF JUSTICE ROBERTS delivered the opinion of the Court.

This "suit has, in course of time, become so complicated, that * * * no two * * * lawyers can talk about it for five minutes, without coming to a total disagreement as to all the premises. Innumerable children have been born into the cause: innumerable young people have married into it;" and, sadly, the original parties "have died out of it." A "long procession of [judges] has come in and gone out" during that time, and still the suit "drags its weary length before the Court."

Those words were not written about this case, see C. DICKENS, BLEAK HOUSE, in 1 WORKS OF CHARLES DICKENS 4–5 (1891), but they could have been. This is the second time we have had occasion to weigh in on this long-running dispute between Vickie Lynn Marshall and E. Pierce Marshall over the fortune of J. Howard Marshall II, a man believed to have been one of the richest people in Texas. The Marshalls' litigation has worked its way through state and federal courts in Louisiana, Texas, and California, and two of those courts—a Texas state probate court and the Bankruptcy Court for the Central District of California—have reached contrary decisions on its merits. The Court of Appeals below held that the Texas state decision controlled, after concluding that the Bankruptcy Court lacked the authority to enter final judgment on a counterclaim that Vickie brought against Pierce in her bankruptcy proceeding.[1] To determine whether the Court of Appeals was correct in that regard, we must resolve two issues: (1) whether the Bankruptcy Court had the statutory authority under 28 U.S.C. § 157(b) to issue a final judgment on Vickie's counterclaim; and (2) if so, whether conferring that authority on the Bankruptcy Court is constitutional.

Although the history of this litigation is complicated, its resolution ultimately turns on very basic principles. Article III, § 1, of the Constitution commands that "[t]he judicial Power of the United States, shall be vested in one supreme Court, and in such inferior Courts as the Congress may from time to time ordain and establish." That Article further provides that the judges of those courts shall hold their offices during good behavior, without diminution of salary. Those requirements of Article III were not honored here. The Bankruptcy Court in this case exercised the judicial power of the United States by entering final judgment on

1 Because both Vickie and Pierce passed away during this litigation, the parties in this case are Vickie's estate and Pierce's estate. We continue to refer to them as "Vickie" and "Pierce."

a common law tort claim, even though the judges of such courts enjoy neither tenure during good behavior nor salary protection. We conclude that, although the Bankruptcy Court had the statutory authority to enter judgment on Vickie's counterclaim, it lacked the constitutional authority to do so.

I

* * * Of current relevance are two claims Vickie filed in an attempt to secure half of J. Howard's fortune. Known to the public as Anna Nicole Smith, Vickie was J. Howard's third wife and married him about a year before his death. Although J. Howard bestowed on Vickie many monetary and other gifts during their courtship and marriage, he did not include her in his will. Before J. Howard passed away, Vickie filed suit in Texas state probate court, asserting that Pierce—J. Howard's younger son—fraudulently induced J. Howard to sign a living trust that did not include her, even though J. Howard meant to give her half his property. Pierce denied any fraudulent activity and defended the validity of J. Howard's trust and, eventually, his will.

After J. Howard's death, Vickie filed a petition for bankruptcy in the Central District of California. Pierce filed a complaint in that bankruptcy proceeding, contending that Vickie had defamed him by inducing her lawyers to tell members of the press that he had engaged in fraud to gain control of his father's assets. The complaint sought a declaration that Pierce's defamation claim was not dischargeable in the bankruptcy proceedings. Pierce subsequently filed a proof of claim for the defamation action, meaning that he sought to recover damages for it from Vickie's bankruptcy estate. Vickie responded to Pierce's initial complaint by asserting truth as a defense to the alleged defamation and by filing a counterclaim for tortious interference with the gift she expected from J. Howard. As she had in state court, Vickie alleged that Pierce had wrongfully prevented J. Howard from taking the legal steps necessary to provide her with half his property.

On November 5, 1999, the Bankruptcy Court issued an order granting Vickie summary judgment on Pierce's claim for defamation. On September 27, 2000, after a bench trial, the Bankruptcy Court issued a judgment on Vickie's counterclaim in her favor. The court later awarded Vickie over $400 million in compensatory damages and $25 million in punitive damages.

In post-trial proceedings, Pierce argued that the Bankruptcy Court lacked jurisdiction over Vickie's counterclaim. In particular, Pierce renewed a claim he had made earlier in the litigation, asserting that the Bankruptcy Court's authority over the counterclaim was limited because Vickie's counterclaim was not a "core proceeding" under 28 U.S.C. § 157(b)(2)(C). As explained below, bankruptcy courts may hear and enter final judgments in "core proceedings" in a bankruptcy case. In non-core proceedings, the bankruptcy courts instead submit proposed findings of fact and conclusions of law to the district court, for that court's review and issuance of final judgment. The Bankruptcy Court in this case concluded that Vickie's counterclaim was "a core proceeding" under § 157(b)(2)(C), and the court therefore had the "power to enter judgment" on the counterclaim under § 157(b)(1).

The District Court disagreed. It recognized that "Vickie's counterclaim for tortious interference falls within the literal language" of the statute designating certain proceedings as "core," but understood this Court's precedent to "suggest[ ] that it would be unconstitutional to hold that any and all counterclaims are core." The District Court accordingly concluded that a "counterclaim should not be characterized as core" when it "is only somewhat related to the claim against which it is asserted, and when the unique characteristics and context of the counterclaim place it outside of the normal type of set-off or other counterclaims that customarily arise."

Because the District Court concluded that Vickie's counterclaim was not core, the court determined that it was required to treat the Bankruptcy Court's judgment as "proposed[,] rather than final," and engage in an "independent review" of the record. Although the Texas state court had by that time conducted a jury trial on the merits of the parties' dispute and entered a judgment in Pierce's favor, the District Court declined to give that judgment preclusive effect and went on to decide the matter itself. Like the Bankruptcy Court, the District Court found that Pierce had tortiously interfered with Vickie's expectancy of a gift from J. Howard. The District Court awarded Vickie compensatory and punitive damages, each in the amount of $44,292,767.33.

The Court of Appeals reversed the District Court on a different ground, and we—in the first visit of the case to this Court—reversed the Court of Appeals on that issue. On remand from this Court, the Court of Appeals held that § 157 mandated "a two-step approach" under which a bankruptcy judge may issue a final judgment in a proceeding only if the matter both "meets Congress' definition of a core proceeding *and* arises under or arises in title 11," the Bankruptcy Code. The court also reasoned that allowing a bankruptcy judge to enter final judgments on all counterclaims raised in bankruptcy proceedings "would certainly run afoul" of this Court's decision in *Northern Pipeline*. With those concerns in mind, the court concluded that "a counterclaim under § 157(b)(2)(C) is properly a 'core' proceeding 'arising in a case under' the [Bankruptcy] Code only if the counterclaim is so closely related to [a creditor's] proof of claim that the resolution of the counterclaim is necessary to resolve the allowance or disallowance of the claim itself." ([I]nternal quotation marks omitted; second brackets added). The court ruled that Vickie's counterclaim did not meet that test. That holding made "the Texas probate court's judgment * * * the earliest final judgment entered on matters relevant to this proceeding," and therefore the Court of Appeals concluded that the District Court should have "afford[ed] preclusive effect" to the Texas "court's determination of relevant legal and factual issues."

We again granted certiorari.

II

A

With certain exceptions not relevant here, the district courts of the United States have "original and exclusive jurisdiction of all cases under title 11." Congress has divided bankruptcy proceedings into three categories: those that "aris[e] under title 11"; those that "aris[e] in" a Title 11 case; and those that are "related to a case under title 11." District courts may refer any or all such proceedings to the bankruptcy judges of their district, which is how the Bankruptcy Court in this case came to preside over Vickie's bankruptcy proceedings. District courts also may withdraw a case or proceeding referred to the bankruptcy court "for cause shown." Since Congress enacted the Bankruptcy Amendments and Federal Judgeship Act of 1984 (the 1984 Act), bankruptcy judges for each district have been appointed to 14–year terms by the courts of appeals for the circuits in which their district is located.

The manner in which a bankruptcy judge may act on a referred matter depends on the type of proceeding involved. Bankruptcy judges may hear and enter final judgments in "all core proceedings arising under title 11, or arising in a case under title 11." "Core proceedings include, but are not limited to" 16 different types of matters, including "counterclaims by [a debtor's] estate against persons filing claims against the estate." § 157(b)(2)(C).[3] Parties may appeal final

3 In full, § 157(b)(1)-(2) provides:

(1) Bankruptcy judges may hear and determine all cases under title 11 and all core proceedings arising under title 11, or arising in a case under title 11, referred under subsection (a) of this section, and may enter appropriate orders and judgments, subject to review under section 158 of this title.

(2) Core proceedings include, but are not limited to—

(A) matters concerning the administration of the estate;

(B) allowance or disallowance of claims against the estate or exemptions from property of the estate, and estimation of claims or interests for the purposes of confirming a plan under chapter 11, 12, or 13 of title 11 but not the liquidation or estimation of contingent or unliquidated personal injury tort or wrongful death claims against the estate for purposes of distribution in a case under title 11;

(C) counterclaims by the estate against persons filing claims against the estate;

(D) orders in respect to obtaining credit;

(E) orders to turn over property of the estate;

(F) proceedings to determine, avoid, or recover preferences;

(G) motions to terminate, annul, or modify the automatic stay;

(H) proceedings to determine, avoid, or recover fraudulent conveyances;

(I) determinations as to the dischargeability of particular debts;

judgments of a bankruptcy court in core proceedings to the district court, which reviews them under traditional appellate standards.

When a bankruptcy judge determines that a referred "proceeding * * * is not a core proceeding but * * * is otherwise related to a case under title 11," the judge may only "submit proposed findings of fact and conclusions of law to the district court." It is the district court that enters final judgment in such cases after reviewing *de novo* any matter to which a party objects.

B

[In this part of the opinion, the Court concluded that Vickie's counterclaim was a "core proceeding" within the meaning of § 157(b)(2)(C). The dissent agreed on this point.]

* * *

C

[The Court concluded that § 157(b)(5)'s specification that "[t]he district court shall order that personal injury tort and wrongful death claims shall be tried in the district court in which the bankruptcy case is pending, or in the district court in the district in which the claim arose" was not jurisdictional and that Pierce had consented to the bankruptcy court's adjudicating his defamation claim.]

* * *

Given Pierce's course of conduct before the Bankruptcy Court, we conclude that he consented to that court's resolution of his defamation claim (and forfeited any argument to the contrary). We have recognized "the value of waiver and forfeiture rules" in "complex" cases, and this case is no exception. In such cases, as here, the consequences of "a litigant * * * 'sandbagging' the court—remaining silent about his objection and belatedly raising the error only if the case does not conclude in his favor,"—can be particularly severe. If Pierce believed that the Bankruptcy Court lacked the authority to decide his claim for defamation, then

---

(J) objections to discharges;

(K) determinations of the validity, extent, or priority of liens;

(L) confirmations of plans;

(M) orders approving the use or lease of property, including the use of cash collateral;

(N) orders approving the sale of property other than property resulting from claims brought by the estate against persons who have not filed claims against the estate;

(O) other proceedings affecting the liquidation of the assets of the estate or the adjustment of the debtor-creditor or the equity security holder relationship, except personal injury tort or wrongful death claims; and

(P) recognition of foreign proceedings and other matters under chapter 15 of title 11.

he should have said so—and said so promptly. Instead, Pierce repeatedly stated to the Bankruptcy Court that he was happy to litigate there. We will not consider his claim to the contrary, now that he is sad.

III

Although we conclude that § 157(b)(2)(C) permits the Bankruptcy Court to enter final judgment on Vickie's counterclaim, Article III of the Constitution does not.

A

Article III, § 1, of the Constitution mandates that "[t]he judicial Power of the United States, shall be vested in one supreme Court, and in such inferior Courts as the Congress may from time to time ordain and establish." The same section provides that the judges of those constitutional courts "shall hold their Offices during good Behaviour" and "receive for their Services[ ] a Compensation[ ] [that] shall not be diminished" during their tenure.

As its text and our precedent confirm, Article III is "an inseparable element of the constitutional system of checks and balances" that "both defines the power and protects the independence of the Judicial Branch." Under "the basic concept of separation of powers * * * that flow[s] from the scheme of a tripartite government" adopted in the Constitution, "the 'judicial Power of the United States' * * * can no more be shared" with another branch than "the Chief Executive, for example, can share with the Judiciary the veto power, or the Congress share with the Judiciary the power to override a Presidential veto."

In establishing the system of divided power in the Constitution, the Framers considered it essential that "the judiciary remain[ ] truly distinct from both the legislature and the executive." As Hamilton put it, quoting Montesquieu, " 'there is no liberty if the power of judging be not separated from the legislative and executive powers.' "

We have recognized that the three branches are not hermetically sealed from one another, but it remains true that Article III imposes some basic limitations that the other branches may not transgress. Those limitations serve two related purposes. "Separation-of-powers principles are intended, in part, to protect each branch of government from incursion by the others. Yet the dynamic between and among the branches is not the only object of the Constitution's concern. The structural principles secured by the separation of powers protect the individual as well." *Bond v. United States (2011)*.

Article III protects liberty not only through its role in implementing the separation of powers, but also by specifying the defining characteristics of Article III judges. The colonists had been subjected to judicial abuses at the hand of the Crown, and the Framers knew the main reasons why: because the King of Great Britain "made Judges dependent on his Will alone, for the tenure of their offices, and the amount and payment of their salaries." The Declaration of Independence ¶ 11. The Framers undertook in Article III to protect citizens subject to the judicial power of the new Federal Government from a repeat of those abuses. By appointing judges to serve without term limits, and restricting the ability of the other branches to remove judges or diminish their salaries, the Framers sought to ensure that each judicial decision would be rendered, not with an eye toward currying favor with Congress or the Executive, but rather with the "[c]lear heads * * * and honest hearts" deemed "essential to good judges."

Article III could neither serve its purpose in the system of checks and balances nor preserve the integrity of judicial decisionmaking if the other branches of the Federal Government could confer the Government's "judicial Power" on entities outside Article III. That is why we have long recognized that, in general, Congress may not "withdraw from judicial cognizance any matter which, from its nature, is the subject of a suit at the common law, or in equity, or admiralty." When a suit is made of "the stuff of the traditional actions at common law tried by the courts at Westminster in 1789," and is brought within the bounds of federal jurisdiction, the responsibility for deciding that suit rests with Article III judges in Article III courts. The Constitution assigns that job—resolution of "the mundane as well as the glamorous, matters of common law and statute as well as constitutional law, issues of fact as well as issues of law"—to the Judiciary.

B

This is not the first time we have faced an Article III challenge to a bankruptcy court's resolution of a debtor's suit. In Northern Pipeline, we considered whether bankruptcy judges serving under the Bankruptcy Act of 1978—appointed by the President and confirmed by the Senate, but lacking the tenure and salary guarantees of Article III—could "constitutionally be vested with jurisdiction to decide [a] state-law contract claim" against an entity that was not otherwise part of the bankruptcy proceedings. The Court concluded that assignment of such state law claims for resolution by those judges "violates Art. III of the Constitution."

The plurality in Northern Pipeline recognized that there was a category of cases involving "public rights" that Congress could constitutionally assign to "legislative" courts for resolution. That opinion concluded that this "public rights" exception extended "only to matters arising between" individuals and the Government "in connection with the performance of the constitutional functions of the executive or legislative departments * * * that historically could have been determined exclusively by those" branches. A full majority of the Court, while not agreeing on the scope of the exception, concluded that the doctrine did not encompass adjudication of the state law claim at issue in that case.[5]

A full majority of Justices in Northern Pipeline also rejected the debtor's argument that the bankruptcy court's exercise of jurisdiction was constitutional because the bankruptcy judge was acting merely as an adjunct of the district court or court of appeals.

After our decision in Northern Pipeline, Congress revised the statutes governing bankruptcy jurisdiction and bankruptcy judges. In the 1984 Act, Congress provided that the judges of the new bankruptcy courts would be appointed by the courts of appeals for the circuits in which their districts are located. And, as we have explained, Congress permitted the newly constituted bankruptcy courts to enter final judgments only in "core" proceedings.

With respect to such "core" matters, however, the bankruptcy courts under the 1984 Act exercise the same powers they wielded under the Bankruptcy Act of 1978 (1978 Act). As in Northern Pipeline, for example, the newly constituted bankruptcy courts are charged under § 157(b)(2)(C) with resolving "[a]ll matters of fact and law in whatever domains of the law to which" a counterclaim may lead. As in Northern Pipeline, the new courts in core proceedings "issue final judgments, which are binding and enforceable even in the absence of an appeal." And, as in Northern Pipeline, the district courts review the judgments of the bankruptcy courts in core proceedings only under the usual limited appellate standards. That requires marked deference to, among other things, the bankruptcy judges' findings of fact.

C

Vickie and the dissent argue that the Bankruptcy Court's entry of final judgment on her state common law counterclaim was constitutional, despite the similarities between the bankruptcy courts under the 1978 Act and those exercising core jurisdiction under the 1984 Act. We disagree. It is clear that the Bankruptcy Court in this case exercised the "judicial Power of the United States" in purporting to resolve and enter final judgment on a state common law claim, just as the court did in Northern Pipeline. No "public right" exception excuses the failure to comply with Article III in doing so, any more than in Northern Pipeline. Vickie argues that this case is different because the defendant is a creditor in the bankruptcy. But the debtors' claims in the cases on which she relies were themselves federal claims under bankruptcy law, which would be completely resolved in the bankruptcy process of allowing or disallowing claims. Here Vickie's claim is a state law

5 The dissent is thus wrong in suggesting that less than a full Court agreed on the points pertinent to this case.

action independent of the federal bankruptcy law and not necessarily resolvable by a ruling on the creditor's proof of claim in bankruptcy. Northern Pipeline and our subsequent decision in Granfinanciera rejected the application of the "public rights" exception in such cases.

Nor can the bankruptcy courts under the 1984 Act be dismissed as mere adjuncts of Article III courts, any more than could the bankruptcy courts under the 1978 Act. The judicial powers the courts exercise in cases such as this remain the same, and a court exercising such broad powers is no mere adjunct of anyone.

1

Vickie's counterclaim cannot be deemed a matter of "public right" that can be decided outside the Judicial Branch. As explained above, in Northern Pipeline we rejected the argument that the public rights doctrine permitted a bankruptcy court to adjudicate a state law suit brought by a debtor against a company that had not filed a claim against the estate. Although our discussion of the public rights exception since that time has not been entirely consistent, and the exception has been the subject of some debate, this case does not fall within any of the various formulations of the concept that appear in this Court's opinions.

We first recognized the category of public rights in Murray's Lessee v. Hoboken Land & Improvement Co. (1856). That case involved the Treasury Department's sale of property belonging to a customs collector who had failed to transfer payments to the Federal Government that he had collected on its behalf. The plaintiff, who claimed title to the same land through a different transfer, objected that the Treasury Department's calculation of the deficiency and sale of the property was void, because it was a judicial act that could not be assigned to the Executive under Article III.

"To avoid misconstruction upon so grave a subject," the Court laid out the principles guiding its analysis. It confirmed that Congress cannot "withdraw from judicial cognizance any matter which, from its nature, is the subject of a suit at the common law, or in equity, or admiralty." The Court also recognized that "[a]t the same time there are matters, involving public rights, which may be presented in such form that the judicial power is capable of acting on them, and which are susceptible of judicial determination, but which congress may or may not bring within the cognizance of the courts of the United States, as it may deem proper."

As an example of such matters, the Court referred to "[e]quitable claims to land by the inhabitants of ceded territories" and cited cases in which land issues were conclusively resolved by Executive Branch officials. In those cases "it depends upon the will of congress whether a remedy in the courts shall be allowed at all," so Congress could limit the extent to which a judicial forum was available. The challenge in Murray's Lessee to the Treasury Department's sale of the collector's land likewise fell within the "public rights" category of cases, because it could only be brought if the Federal Government chose to allow it by waiving sovereign immunity. The point of Murray's Lessee was simply that Congress may set the terms of adjudicating a suit when the suit could not otherwise proceed at all.

Subsequent decisions from this Court contrasted cases within the reach of the public rights exception—those arising "between the Government and persons subject to its authority in connection with the performance of the constitutional functions of the executive or legislative departments"—and those that were instead matters "of private right, that is, of the liability of one individual to another under the law as defined." Crowell v. Benson (1932).[6]

Shortly after Northern Pipeline, the Court rejected the limitation of the public rights exception to actions involving the Government as a party. The Court has continued, however, to limit the exception to cases in which the claim at issue derives from a federal regulatory scheme, or in which resolution of the claim by an expert government agency is deemed essential to a limited regulatory objective within the agency's authority. In other words, it is still the case that what makes a right "public" rather than private is that the right is integrally related to particular federal government action.

Our decision in Thomas v. Union Carbide Agricultural Products Co., for example, involved a data-sharing arrangement between companies under a federal statute providing that disputes about compensation between the companies would be decided by binding arbitration. This Court held that the scheme did not violate Article III, explaining that "[a]ny right to compensation * * * results from [the statute] and does not depend on or replace a right to such compensation under state law."

Commodity Futures Trading Commission v. Schor concerned a statutory scheme that created a procedure for customers injured by a broker's violation of the fed-

---

6 Although the Court in Crowell went on to decide that the facts of the private dispute before it could be determined by a non-Article III tribunal in the first instance, subject to judicial review, the Court did so only after observing that the administrative adjudicator had only limited authority to make specialized, narrowly confined factual determinations regarding a particularized area of law and to issue orders that could be enforced only by action of the District Court. In other words, the agency in Crowell functioned as a true "adjunct" of the District Court. That is not the case here.

Although the dissent suggests that we understate the import of *Crowell* in this regard, the dissent itself recognizes—repeatedly—that Crowell by its terms addresses the determination of *facts* outside Article III. Crowell may well have additional significance in the context of expert administrative agencies that oversee particular substantive federal regimes, but we have no occasion to and do not address those issues today. The United States apparently agrees that any broader significance of Crowell is not pertinent in this case, citing to Crowell in its brief only once, in the last footnote, again for the limited proposition discussed above.

eral commodities law to seek reparations from the broker before the Commodity Futures Trading Commission (CFTC). A customer filed such a claim to recover a debit balance in his account, while the broker filed a lawsuit in Federal District Court to recover the same amount as lawfully due from the customer. The broker later submitted its claim to the CFTC, but after that agency ruled against the customer, the customer argued that agency jurisdiction over the broker's counterclaim violated Article III. This Court disagreed, but only after observing that (1) the claim and the counterclaim concerned a "single dispute"—the same account balance; (2) the CFTC's assertion of authority involved only "a narrow class of common law claims" in a " 'particularized area of law' "; (3) the area of law in question was governed by "a specific and limited federal regulatory scheme" as to which the agency had "obvious expertise"; (4) the parties had freely elected to resolve their differences before the CFTC; and (5) CFTC orders were "enforceable only by order of the district court." Most significantly, given that the customer's reparations claim before the agency and the broker's counterclaim were competing claims to the same amount, the Court repeatedly emphasized that it was "necessary" to allow the agency to exercise jurisdiction over the broker's claim, or else "the reparations procedure would have been confounded."

The most recent case in which we considered application of the public rights exception—and the only case in which we have considered that doctrine in the bankruptcy context since Northern Pipeline—is Granfinanciera (1989). In Granfinanciera we rejected a bankruptcy trustee's argument that a fraudulent conveyance action filed on behalf of a bankruptcy estate against a noncreditor in a bankruptcy proceeding fell within the "public rights" exception. We explained that, "[i]f a statutory right is not closely intertwined with a federal regulatory program Congress has power to enact, and if that right neither belongs to nor exists against the Federal Government, then it must be adjudicated by an Article III court." We reasoned that fraudulent conveyance suits were "quintessentially suits at common law that more nearly resemble state law contract claims brought by a bankrupt corporation to augment the bankruptcy estate than they do creditors' hierarchically ordered claims to a pro rata share of the bankruptcy res." As a consequence, we concluded that fraudulent conveyance actions were "more accurately characterized as a private rather than a public right as we have used those terms in our Article III decisions."[7]

Vickie's counterclaim—like the fraudulent conveyance claim at issue in Granfinanciera—does not fall within any of the varied formulations of the public rights exception in this Court's cases. It is not a matter that can be pursued only by grace

7 We noted that we did not mean to "suggest that the restructuring of debtor-creditor relations is in fact a public right." Our conclusion was that, "even if one accepts this thesis," Congress could not constitutionally assign resolution of the fraudulent conveyance action to a non-Article III court. Because neither party asks us to reconsider the public rights framework for bankruptcy, we follow the same approach here.

of the other branches, as in Murray's Lessee or one that "historically could have been determined exclusively by" those branches. The claim is instead one under state common law between two private parties. It does not "depend[ ] on the will of congress"; Congress has nothing to do with it.

In addition, Vickie's claimed right to relief does not flow from a federal statutory scheme * * * . It is not "completely dependent upon" adjudication of a claim created by federal law, as in Schor. And in contrast to the objecting party in Schor, Pierce did not truly consent to resolution of Vickie's claim in the bankruptcy court proceedings. He had nowhere else to go if he wished to recover from Vickie's estate.[8]

Furthermore, the asserted authority to decide Vickie's claim is not limited to a "particularized area of the law," as in Crowell, Thomas, and Schor. We deal here not with an agency but with a court, with substantive jurisdiction reaching any area of the *corpus juris*. This is not a situation in which Congress devised an "expert and inexpensive method for dealing with a class of questions of fact which are particularly suited to examination and determination by an administrative agency specially assigned to that task." The "experts" in the federal system at resolving common law counterclaims such as Vickie's are the Article III courts, and it is with those courts that her claim must stay.

The dissent reads our cases differently, and in particular contends that more recent cases view Northern Pipeline as " 'establish[ing] only that Congress may not vest in a non-Article III court the power to adjudicate, render final judgment, and issue binding orders in a traditional contract action arising under state law, without consent of the litigants, and subject only to ordinary appellate review.' " Just so: Substitute "tort" for "contract," and that statement directly covers this case.

We recognize that there may be instances in which the distinction between public and private rights—at least as framed by some of our recent cases—fails to provide concrete guidance as to whether, for example, a particular agency can adjudicate legal issues under a substantive regulatory scheme. Given the extent to which this case is so markedly distinct from the agency cases discussing the public rights exception in the context of such a regime, however, we do not in this opinion express any view on how the doctrine might apply in that different context.

---

8 Contrary to the claims of the dissent, Pierce did not have another forum in which to pursue his claim to recover from Vickie's prebankruptcy assets, rather than take his chances with whatever funds might remain after the Title 11 proceedings. Creditors who possess claims that do not satisfy the requirements for nondischargeability under 11 U.S.C. § 523 have no choice but to file their claims in bankruptcy proceedings if they want to pursue the claims at all. That is why, as we recognized in Granfinanciera, the notion of "consent" does not apply in bankruptcy proceedings as it might in other contexts.

What is plain here is that this case involves the most prototypical exercise of judicial power: the entry of a final, binding judgment *by a court* with broad substantive jurisdiction, on a common law cause of action, when the action neither derives from nor depends upon any agency regulatory regime. If such an exercise of judicial power may nonetheless be taken from the Article III Judiciary simply by deeming it part of some amorphous "public right," then Article III would be transformed from the guardian of individual liberty and separation of powers we have long recognized into mere wishful thinking.

2

Vickie and the dissent next attempt to distinguish Northern Pipeline and Granfinanciera on the ground that Pierce, unlike the defendants in those cases, had filed a proof of claim in the bankruptcy proceedings. Given Pierce's participation in those proceedings, Vickie argues, the Bankruptcy Court had the authority to adjudicate her counterclaim under our decisions in Katchen v. Landy (1966), and Langenkamp v. Culp (1990) (per curiam).

We do not agree. As an initial matter, it is hard to see why Pierce's decision to file a claim should make any difference with respect to the characterization of Vickie's counterclaim. " '[P]roperty interests are created and defined by state law,' and '[u]nless some federal interest requires a different result, there is no reason why such interests should be analyzed differently simply because an interested party is involved in a bankruptcy proceeding.' " Pierce's claim for defamation in no way affects the nature of Vickie's counterclaim for tortious interference as one at common law that simply attempts to augment the bankruptcy estate—the very type of claim that we held in Northern Pipeline and Granfinanciera must be decided by an Article III court.

Contrary to Vickie's contention, moreover, our decisions in Katchen and Langenkamp do not suggest a different result. Katchen permitted a bankruptcy referee acting under the Bankruptcy Acts of 1898 and 1938 (akin to a bankruptcy court today) to exercise what was known as "summary jurisdiction" over a voidable preference claim brought by the bankruptcy trustee against a creditor who had filed a proof of claim in the bankruptcy proceeding. A voidable preference claim asserts that a debtor made a payment to a particular creditor in anticipation of bankruptcy, to in effect increase that creditor's proportionate share of the estate. The preferred creditor's claim in bankruptcy can be disallowed as a result of the preference, and the amounts paid to that creditor can be recovered by the trustee.

Although the creditor in Katchen objected that the preference issue should be resolved through a "plenary suit" in an Article III court, this Court concluded that summary adjudication in bankruptcy was appropriate, because it was not possible for the referee to rule on the creditor's proof of claim without first resolving the voidable preference issue. There was no question that the bankruptcy referee could decide whether there had been a voidable preference in determining whether and to what extent to allow the creditor's claim. Once the referee did that, "nothing remains for adjudication in a plenary suit"; such a suit "would be a meaningless gesture." The plenary proceeding the creditor sought could be brought into the bankruptcy court because "the same issue [arose] as part of the process of allowance and disallowance of claims."

It was in that sense that the Court stated that "he who invokes the aid of the bankruptcy court by offering a proof of claim and demanding its allowance must abide the consequences of that procedure." In Katchen one of those consequences was resolution of the preference issue as part of the process of allowing or disallowing claims, and accordingly there was no basis for the creditor to insist that the issue be resolved in an Article III court. Indeed, the Katchen Court expressly noted that it "intimate[d] no opinion concerning whether" the bankruptcy referee would have had "summary jurisdiction to adjudicate a demand by the [bankruptcy] trustee for affirmative relief, all of the substantial factual and legal bases for which ha[d] not been disposed of in passing on objections to the [creditor's proof of] claim."

Our per curiam opinion in Langenkamp is to the same effect. We explained there that a preferential transfer claim can be heard in bankruptcy when the allegedly favored creditor has filed a claim, because *then* "the ensuing preference action by the trustee become[s] integral to the restructuring of the debtor-creditor relationship." If, in contrast, the creditor has not filed a proof of claim, the trustee's preference action does *not* "become[ ] part of the claims-allowance process" subject to resolution by the bankruptcy court.

In ruling on Vickie's counterclaim, the Bankruptcy Court was required to and did make several factual and legal determinations that were not "disposed of in passing on objections" to Pierce's proof of claim for defamation, which the court had denied almost a year earlier. There was some overlap between Vickie's counterclaim and Pierce's defamation claim that led the courts below to conclude that the counterclaim was compulsory, or at least in an "attenuated" sense related to Pierce's claim. But there was never any reason to believe that the process of adjudicating Pierce's proof of claim would necessarily resolve Vickie's counterclaim. The United States acknowledges the point.

The only overlap between the two claims in this case was the question whether Pierce had in fact tortiously taken control of his father's estate in the manner alleged by Vickie in her counterclaim and described in the allegedly defamatory statements. From the outset, it was clear that, even assuming the Bankruptcy Court would (as it did) rule in Vickie's favor on that question, the court could not enter judgment for Vickie unless the court additionally ruled on the questions whether Texas recognized tortious interference with an expected gift as a valid cause of action, what the elements of that action were, and whether those elements were met in this case. Assuming Texas accepted the elements adopted by other jurisdictions, that meant Vickie would need to prove, above and beyond Pierce's tortious interference, (1) the existence of an expectancy of a gift; (2) a reasonable certainty that the expectancy would have been realized but for the interference; and (3) damages. Also, because Vickie sought punitive damages in connection with her counterclaim, the Bankruptcy Court could not finally dispose of the case in Vickie's favor without determining whether to subject Pierce to the sort of "retribution," "punishment [,] and deterrence," those damages are designed to impose. There thus was never reason to believe that the process of ruling on Pierce's proof of claim would necessarily result in the resolution of Vickie's counterclaim.

In both Katchen and Langenkamp, moreover, the trustee bringing the preference action was asserting a right of recovery created by federal bankruptcy law. In Langenkamp, we noted that "the trustee instituted adversary proceedings under 11 U.S.C. § 547(b) to recover, as avoidable preferences," payments respondents received from the debtor before the bankruptcy filings. Vickie's claim, in contrast, is in no way derived from or dependent upon bankruptcy law; it is a state tort action that exists without regard to any bankruptcy proceeding.

In light of all the foregoing, we disagree with the dissent that there are no "relevant distinction[s]" between Pierce's claim in this case and the claim at issue in Langenkamp. We see no reason to treat Vickie's counterclaim any differently from the fraudulent conveyance action in *Granfinanciera*. *Granfinanciera's* distinction between actions that seek "to augment the bankruptcy estate" and those that seek "a pro rata share of the bankruptcy res" reaffirms that Congress may not bypass Article III simply because a proceeding may have *some* bearing on a bankruptcy case; the question is whether the action at issue stems from the bankruptcy itself or would necessarily be resolved in the claims allowance process. Vickie has failed to demonstrate that her counterclaim falls within one of the "limited circumstances" covered by the public rights exception, particularly given our conclusion that, "even with respect to matters that arguably fall within the scope of the 'public rights' doctrine, the presumption is in favor of Art. III courts."

3

Vickie additionally argues that the Bankruptcy Court's final judgment was constitutional because bankruptcy courts under the 1984 Act are properly deemed "adjuncts" of the district courts. We rejected a similar argument in *Northern Pipeline*, and our reasoning there holds true today.

To begin, as explained above, it is still the bankruptcy court itself that exercises the essential attributes of judicial power over a matter such as Vickie's counterclaim. The new bankruptcy courts, like the old, do not "ma[k]e only specialized, narrowly confined factual determinations regarding a particularized area of law" or engage in "statutorily channeled factfinding functions." Instead, bankruptcy courts under the 1984 Act resolve "[a]ll matters of fact and law in whatever domains of the law to which" the parties' counterclaims might lead.

In addition, whereas the adjunct agency in *Crowell v. Benson* "possessed only a limited power to issue compensation orders * * * [that] could be enforced only by order of the district court," a bankruptcy court resolving a counterclaim under 28 U.S.C. § 157(b)(2)(C) has the power to enter "appropriate orders and judgments"—including final judgments—subject to review only if a party chooses to appeal. It is thus no less the case here than it was in *Northern Pipeline* that "[t]he authority—and the responsibility—to make an informed, final determination * * * remains with" the bankruptcy judge, not the district court. Given that authority, a bankruptcy court can no more be deemed a mere "adjunct" of the district court than a district court can be deemed such an "adjunct" of the court of appeals. We certainly cannot accept the dissent's notion that judges who have the power to enter final, binding orders are the "functional [ ]" equivalent of "law clerks[ ] and the Judiciary's administrative officials." And even were we wrong in this regard, that would only confirm that such judges should not be in the business of entering final judgments in the first place.

It does not affect our analysis that, as Vickie notes, bankruptcy judges under the current Act are appointed by the Article III courts, rather than the President. If—as we have concluded—the bankruptcy court itself exercises "the essential attributes of judicial power [that] are reserved to Article III courts," it does not matter who appointed the bankruptcy judge or authorized the judge to render final judgments in such proceedings. The constitutional bar remains.

* * *

Article III of the Constitution provides that the judicial power of the United States may be vested only in courts whose judges enjoy the protections set forth in that Article. We conclude today that Congress, in one isolated respect, exceeded that limitation in the Bankruptcy Act of 1984. The Bankruptcy Court below lacked the constitutional authority to enter a final judgment on a state law counterclaim that is not resolved in the process of ruling on a creditor's proof of claim. Accordingly, the judgment of the Court of Appeals is affirmed.

It is so ordered.

JUSTICE SCALIA, concurring.

I agree with the Court's interpretation of our Article III precedents, and I accordingly join its opinion. I adhere to my view, however, that—our contrary precedents notwithstanding—"a matter of public rights * * * must at a minimum arise between the government and others."

The sheer surfeit of factors that the Court was required to consider in this case should arouse the suspicion that something is seriously amiss with our jurisprudence in this area. I count at least seven different reasons given in the Court's opinion for concluding that an Article III judge was required to adjudicate this lawsuit: that it was one "under state common law" which was "not a matter that can be pursued only by grace of the other branches"; that it was "not 'completely dependent upon' adjudication of a claim created by federal law"; that "Pierce did not truly consent to resolution of Vickie's claim in the bankruptcy court proceedings"; that "the asserted authority to decide Vickie's claim is not limited to a 'particularized area of the law' "; that "there was never any reason to believe that the process of adjudicating Pierce's proof of claim would necessarily resolve Vickie's counterclaim"; that the trustee was not "asserting a right of recovery created by federal bankruptcy law"; and that the Bankruptcy Judge "ha[d] the power to enter 'appropriate orders and judgments'—including final judgments—subject to review only if a party chooses to appeal."

Apart from their sheer numerosity, the more fundamental flaw in the many tests suggested by our jurisprudence is that they have nothing to do with the text or tradition of Article III. For example, Article III gives no indication that state-law claims have preferential entitlement to an Article III judge; nor does it make pertinent the extent to which the area of the law is "particularized." The multifactors relied upon today seem to have entered our jurisprudence almost randomly.

Leaving aside certain adjudications by federal administrative agencies, which are governed (for better or worse) by our landmark decision in *Crowell* * * * (1932), in my view an Article III judge is required in all federal adjudications, unless there is a firmly established historical practice to the contrary. For that reason—and not because of some intuitive balancing of benefits and harms—I agree that Article III judges are not required in the context of territorial courts, courts-martial, or true "public rights" cases. Perhaps historical practice permits non-Article III judges to process claims against the bankruptcy estate; the subject has not been briefed, and so I state no position on the matter. But Vickie points to no historical practice that authorizes a non-Article III judge to adjudicate a counterclaim of the sort at issue here.

JUSTICE BREYER, with whom JUSTICE GINSBURG, JUSTICE SOTOMAYOR, and JUSTICE KAGAN, join dissenting.

Pierce Marshall filed a claim in Federal Bankruptcy Court against the estate of Vickie Marshall. His claim asserted that Vickie Marshall had, through her lawyers, accused him of trying to prevent her from obtaining money that his father had wanted her to have; that her accusations violated state defamation law; and that she consequently owed Pierce Marshall damages. Vickie Marshall filed a compulsory counterclaim in which she asserted that Pierce Marshall had unlawfully interfered with her husband's efforts to grant her an *inter vivos* gift and that he consequently owed her damages.

The Bankruptcy Court adjudicated the claim and the counterclaim. In doing so, the court followed statutory procedures applicable to "core" bankruptcy proceedings. And ultimately the Bankruptcy Court entered judgment in favor of Vickie Marshall. The question before us is whether the Bankruptcy Court possessed jurisdiction to adjudicate Vickie Marshall's counterclaim. I agree with the Court that the bankruptcy statute, authorizes a bankruptcy court to adjudicate the counterclaim. But I do not agree with the majority about the statute's constitutionality. I believe the statute is consistent with the Constitution's delegation of the "judicial Power of the United States" to the Judicial Branch of Government. Art. III, § 1. Consequently, it is constitutional.

I

My disagreement with the majority's conclusion stems in part from my disagreement about the way in which it interprets, or at least emphasizes, certain precedents. In my view, the majority overstates the current relevance of statements this Court made in an 1856 case, Murray's Lessee v. Hoboken Land & Improvement Co., and it overstates the importance of an analysis that did not command a Court majority in Northern Pipeline Constr. Co. v. Marathon Pipe Line Co. (1982), and that was subsequently disavowed. At the same time, I fear the Court understates the importance of a watershed opinion widely thought to demonstrate the constitutional basis for the current authority of administrative agencies to adjudicate private disputes, namely, Crowell v. Benson (1932). And it fails to follow the analysis that this Court more recently has held applicable to the evaluation of claims of a kind before us here, * * * claims that a congressional delegation of adjudicatory authority violates separation-of-powers principles derived from Article III.

* * *

I believe we should put less weight than does the majority upon the statement in *Murray's Lessee* and the analysis followed by the *Northern Pipeline* plurality and instead should apply the approach this Court has applied in *Crowell*, *Thomas*, and *Schor*.

* * *

Notes and Questions

1. Is Vickie's counterclaim for tortious interference really a compulsory counterclaim under FED. R. CIV. P. 13(a)? Does it matter if it was compulsory? The majority finds that the Bankruptcy court lacks constitutional authority to adjudicate the claim. If the claim is "compulsory" within the meaning of Rule 13, doesn't that just mean that the Rule is unconstitutional as applied?

2. The real battle between majority and dissent revolves less around the convoluted facts of *Stern* than around the Justices' differences about the approach the Court should use in evaluating the constitutional legitimacy of legislative courts or of particular functions that Congress assigns to them. The majority appears to prefer a categorical approach, while Justice Breyer argues for a practical, balancing approach that sounds similar to Justice White's *Northern Pipeline* dissent. The majority relies heavily on *Northern Pipeline* (text at 377) and seeks to distinguish *Thomas* (text at 391-92, Note) and *Schor* (text at 392). Justice Breyer views those cases as having displaced the more rigid approach of *Northern Pipeline*. Who has the better of the argument? What are the possible consequences of accepting either approach?

3. The irony of the Court's reliance on *Boyd v. United States (1886)* is too rich to escape comment. *Boyd* invalidated a federal statute that authorized the federal courts to require production of evidence by the defendant in some criminal proceedings. The statute, said the Court, violated the defendant's Fourth and Fifth Amendment rights. In the course of that decision, Justice Bradley did pen the words that Chief Justice Roberts quotes. On the other hand, commentators have observed "that in most respects [*Boyd*] has little current vitality." WAYNE R. LAFAVE, JEROLD H. ISRAEL, NANCY J. KING & ORIN S. KERR, CRIMINAL PROCEDURE § 8.7, at 458 (5th ed. 2009). Others have been less circumspect. "*Boyd* in all its aspects has been overruled." James Boyd White, *Forgotten Points in the "Exclusionary Rule" Debate*, 81 MICH. L. REV. 1273, 1283 (1983). "*Boyd* is dead. But the Court refuses to take the final step of overruling it. Justice Brandeis once called *Boyd* 'a case that will be remembered as long as civil liberty lives in the United States.' At least it deserves a decent burial." Note, *The Life and Times of* Boyd v. United States (1886-1976), 76 MICH. L. REV. 184, 212 (1977).

The overruling to which Professor White referred has largely come at the hands of Justices substantially sharing Chief Justice Roberts's judicial philosophy.

E. Magistrate Judges as Adjuncts to the District Courts

The Federal Magistrates Act of 1968[1] replaced federal commissioners with magistrates and expanded their responsibilities. It gave them the powers and duties previously held by commissioners and also "such additional duties as are not inconsistent with the Constitution and laws of the United States." The Act presented a non-exhaustive list of "additional duties" that included serving as special masters, presiding over trials of minor criminal offenses with the consent of the accused, and assisting district judges in discovery and other pretrial proceedings. Thereafter, magistrates often conducted hearings and made recommendations to the district court. One provision authorized magistrates to conduct preliminary reviews of petitions for post-conviction relief, and a dispute about its meaning reached the Supreme Court.

Wingo v. Wedding, 418 U.S. 461 (1974), held that the Act authorized magistrates to recommend to district court judges whether to hold evidentiary hearings on habeas petitions, but did not authorize magistrates to conduct the hearings. Congress responded with the Federal Magistrates Act of 1976,[2] overruling *Wingo* by specifying that magistrates could hold the evidentiary hearings and then make recommendations to a district judge. The 1976 amendments also describe in greater detail the role magistrates should play in discovery and other pretrial proceedings. They authorize the district courts to refer to a magistrate for determination any pretrial matter except certain dispositive motions, such as motions for summary judgment or to suppress evidence. The district judge may reconsider the magistrate's decision on a non-dispositive pretrial matter if it is "clearly erroneous or contrary to the law." The court may also refer dispositive motions to a magistrate to conduct an evidentiary hearing, but after the hearing, the magistrate submits proposed findings of fact and a recommended disposition to the district judge. Any party may object to the proposed findings and recommendations; if someone does, the district court must make a de novo determination. Whether or not the parties file objections, the district court may accept, reject, or modify the magistrate's findings or recommendations.

---

1 Act of Oct. 17, 1968, Pub.L. No. 90-578, 82 Stat. 1107.

2 Act of Oct. 21, 1976, Pub.L. No. 94-577, 90 Stat. 2729.

Magistrates serve a fixed term of either eight or four years, subject to removal by the district's judges for several reasons, including incompetence. Their salaries can be reduced by act of Congress. Consequently, questions arose as to whether assigning those duties to magistrates violated Article III. In *United States v. Raddatz*, 447 U.S. 667 (1980), discussed in Northern Pipeline, the Supreme Court upheld the scheme.

Raddatz was charged with unlawfully receiving a firearm. He moved to suppress his incriminating statements. Over the defendant's objection, the district court referred the suppression motion to a magistrate for an evidentiary hearing. The magistrate conducted the hearing, made proposed findings of fact, and recommended that the motion be denied. The defendant objected. The district court reviewed the report, the transcript, and the objections, and heard oral argument before accepting the magistrate's recommendation. On appeal, the defendant argued that the procedure violated Article III. The Supreme Court pointed out that the district court had discretion to authorize the magistrate's hearing and that the entire process was under the district court's control. Because the responsibility and authority for final determination remained with the district judge, the Court found the statutory scheme did not violate Article III.

Raddatz did not end the controversy. The Federal Magistrate Act of 1979[3] again expanded the responsibilities of the magistrates, providing that magistrates specially designated by the district court could conduct all proceedings in civil matters and order entry of judgment, provided the parties consented to the reference. The Supreme Court has not discussed whether this delegation of authority to federal magistrates is constitutional, but the lower federal courts have.

Pacemaker Diagnostic Clinic v. Instromedix, Inc., 725 F.2d 537 (9th Cir. 1984) (en banc) is perhaps the leading case. Pacemaker alleged patent infringement by Instromedix, which counterclaimed to have the patent declared invalid. The parties consented to a trial before a magistrate, who found that the patent was valid and had not been infringed. Both parties appealed, and a court of appeals panel, ***sua sponte***, raised the constitutional issue. The panel found a constitutional problem, but the Ninth Circuit, en banc, reversed.

The majority began by asserting that Article III helps delineate the separation of powers and that the separation-of-powers issue has two components. One is the personal right of the litigant to have federal suits tried by Article III judges. The other component is the protection of the integrity and independence of the judiciary in the constitutional structure. The court pointed out that the Supreme Court had held that criminal defendants can waive fundamental constitutional

3 Act of Oct. 10, 1979, Pub.L. No. 96-82, 93 Stat. 643.

rights. Consequently, it thought it anomalous to hold that a litigant in a civil case cannot waive the personal right to an Article III judge.

Turning to the second component, the court concluded that the provision for trial by magistrate does not threaten the integrity or independence of Article III courts. The court did not see the political branches seeking to increase power at the expense of the judiciary. The judiciary maintains substantial control over the magistrate system generally and over cases where there has been references to magistrates for trial. Article III judges control selection and retention of magistrates. Consequently, magistrates are not dependent upon either of the political branches. The statute also authorizes the district court to revoke a reference upon a showing of good cause or extraordinary circumstances. Given these features, and the right of the parties to appeal to an Article III court, the Ninth Circuit found that the power over and the responsibility for such cases remains with the judiciary.

Judge Schroeder dissented vigorously, asserting that magistrates are not the independent decision-makers contemplated by Article III because they depend upon Article III judges for appointment and retention, and upon Congress for their salaries. Yet the provisions upheld by the court allow magistrates to review the constitutionality of actions of the political branches, lessening the judiciary's check upon them. The dissent also argued that the control the district judges have over magistrates destroys the independent decision-making contemplated by Article III. Such control creates a severe conflict of interest for the magistrate who may feel pressed to decide between what is right and what will please the district court. The litigants' consent is irrelevant to these issues because the federal judicial power is conferred and limited by Article III, not by the parties. Finally, Judge Schroeder asserted that in these circumstances, voluntary consent is illusory. Because of crowded dockets, district judges try to channel cases to magistrates, and at least some will try to pressure litigants to consent. Additionally, waiting for adjudication by an Article III judge will mean increased delay and expense and will induce some litigants to consent to trial by magistrates. For these reasons, the dissent concluded the scheme is unconstitutional.

Litigant consent was also an important factor in two Supreme Court cases dealing with magistrates. In *Gomez v. United States*, 490 U.S. 858 (1989), the Court held that the selection of a jury in a felony trial was not one of the "additional duties" a magistrate could receive over the defendant's objection. Focusing upon the language and legislative history of the statute, the Court concluded that Congress did not intend such assignments.

Nonetheless, *Peretz v. United States*, 501 U.S. 923 (1991), interpreted the Act to authorize such assignments *with* the consent of the defendant and held that that did not violate Article III. The Court read *Gomez* narrowly, motivated largely by a desire to interpret the statute to avoid a serious constitutional question. The holding in *Gomez* avoided the question of whether a defendant has a right to demand an Article III judge at every critical stage of a felony trial. In *Peretz*, the defendant's consent significantly changed the constitutional analysis, and the Court had "no trouble" finding no violation of Article III when the district judge permitted a magistrate to conduct *voir dire* with the defendant's consent. Felony defendants lose whatever protection the Constitution provides under Article III if they do not object. Citing Schor and cases where criminal defendants have waived other constitutional rights, *Peretz* held that the defendant had waived any personal right to an Article III judge.

In addition, the Court decided that the procedure did not damage the structural protection of the judiciary, pointing to factors very similar to those in *Pacemaker*. Article III judges appoint magistrates and can remove them. The district court has discretion to refer the matter to the magistrate and whether to empanel the jury selected under the magistrate's supervision. Thus, the Court found no danger that Congress was attempting to reduce the power of Article III courts.

The Court did concede that, unlike the provision of the Federal Magistrate Act that Raddatz upheld, the provision in *Peretz* did not expressly mandate *de novo* review of the magistrate's rulings during jury selection. *Peretz*, however, had not sought review of the magistrate's rulings. Raddatz, said the Court, establishes that to the extent Article III requires *de novo* review, the parties' failure to request it waives the requirement. Moreover, the Court observed that if a defendant does request review of a magistrate's ruling during jury selection, the statute does not preclude review; it merely does not require it.

In 1990 Congress changed the title "magistrate" to "magistrate judge." Judicial Improvement Act of 1990, Pub. L. No. 101-650, § 321, 104 Stat. 5089 (1990). However, the change in title did not prevent new controversies regarding what their duties should be and in what circumstances they could act. For example, in *Roell v. Withrow*, 538 U.S. 580 (2003), the Court faced the question of whether to infer a party's consent to having a magistrate judge conduct all proceedings and enter a judgment in a civil case from the party's litigation conduct. Though acknowledging that 28 U.S.C. § 636(c)(2) and FRCP 73(b) contemplated advance written consent by the parties, the majority concluded that the statute did not oust the magistrate judge of jurisdiction "so long as the parties have in fact voluntarily consented." The Court noted that interpreting the statute to require written consent as a prerequisite for a magistrate judge's jurisdiction would increase the risk of gamesmanship. A party could appear before a magistrate judge, try the case, and then await the outcome before deciding whether to raise the lack of written consent to vacate the judgment. Consequently, the Court held that "where the litigant or counsel was made aware of the need for consent and the right to refuse it, and still voluntarily appeared to try the case before the Magistrate Judge," there was the necessary consent to establish the magistrate judge's civil jurisdiction. The dissent argued that the majority's interpretation was inconsistent with the plain text of the statute and that its test for implied consent was "rife with ambiguities

---

Notes and Questions

1. Are the majority's or the dissent's arguments in *Pacemaker* more persuasive? Do *Schor* and *Peretz* indicate that *Pacemaker* is rightly or wrongly decided?

2. Does *Schor* necessarily lead to the result in *Peretz*? Is it distinguishable?

3. *Gonzalez v. United States*, 553 U.S. 242 (2008), filled in a gap *Gomez* and *Peretz* left. The former made clear the defendant's entitlement to have jury selection supervised by an Article III judge, while the latter allowed supervision by a magistrate judge *with* the defendant's consent. *Gonzalez*, in turn, may have broadened *Peretz* slightly by holding that counsel, not only the client, can expressly waive the Article III right. The Court analogized *Gonzalez* to *New York v. Hill*, 528 U.S. 110 (2000), in which the Court held that an attorney, even acting without indication of specific consent from the client, can waive the client's right to a speedy trial on the theory that "[s]cheduling matters are plainly among those for which agreement by counsel generally controls."

4. In *Elgin v. Department of the Treasury*, 132 S.Ct. 2126 (2012), the Court held that the Merit Systems Protection Board, had the authority to find facts in a case that could culminate in a challenge to the constitutionality of a statute, despite the fact that the Board could not decide the constitutional question itself. ""[W]e see nothing extraordinary in a statutory scheme that vests reviewable factfinding authority in a non-Article III entity that has jurisdiction over an action but cannot finally decide the legal question to which the facts pertain. Congress has authorized magistrate judges, for example, to conduct evidentiary hearings and make findings of fact relevant to dispositive pretrial motions, although they are powerless to issue a final ruling on such motions," wrote Justice Thomas for the majority, citing *Raddatz*. *Id.* at 2138.

Chapter 5

Federal Common Law

A. Introduction

The determination that a case should or may be heard in the federal courts settles only the question of forum. It does not simultaneously decide what body of law applies to each issue. The court still must choose between federal and state law, an inquiry commonly referred to as a vertical choice-of-law question. If the court decides to use state law (as is generally—but not always—the case for substantive issues in diversity cases), it then must decide which state's law to use, a horizontal choice-of-law question.[1]

Go Online

See, e.g., Banco Nacional de Cuba v. Sabbatino, 376 U.S. 398 (1964), discussed *infra* at 449-50.

It is important to realize from the start that choice-of-law inquiries require issue-by-issue analysis. Many cases involve both state and federal law; often state law applies to some issues and federal law to others. One common example occurs in the typical diversity case. After *Erie Railroad v. Tompkins* (1938), state law governs most substantive issues in diversity cases, but federal law will govern many procedural issues, particularly (but not exclusively) when the Federal Rules of Civil Procedure speak directly to the matter. It is not safe to assume that the subject matter jurisdiction provision that brings a claim into the federal courts simultaneously decides the law that applies to a particular issue relevant to that claim. At best it gives but a hint.

---

1 In many cases, where the dispute touches only one state, the answer may be clear, and the court may never articulate the horizontal choice-of-law inquiry. Other cases may involve many states, and the inquiry becomes considerably more complex. Erie Railroad v. Tompkins, 304 U.S. 64 (1938), involved both vertical and horizontal choice-of-law considerations. *Erie* is the progenitor of modern vertical choice-of-law principles. However, the final disposition of the case, which began in the Southern District of New York, depended also upon horizontal choice of law, and Pennsylvania substantive law ended up applying because the accident giving rise to the litigation had occurred in Pennsylvania. At the time, New York adhered to the *lex loci delicti commissi* approach of § 377 of the first Restatement of Conflict of Laws.

Although most first-year Civil Procedure courses cover *Erie*, many students emerge from the first year of law school with an inaccurate memory of it. One is apt to remember vaguely that Justice Brandeis, writing for the Court, said that there is no federal common law. He did not say that; he said instead that "[t]here is no federal *general* common law." (Emphasis added.) Justice Brandeis clearly did not contemplate the complete demise of federal common law since on the same day he wrote an opinion holding that federal common law applied to a dispute between states. Federal common law continues to exist and expand.

> **FYI**
>
> Until *Erie*, there were three sources of law in the United States: federal law, state law, and general law. The last was a hold-over from the common law's idea of natural law, a law governed by reason that existed independently of any sovereign. It was that body of law that *Swift v. Tyson* (1842) had authorized the federal courts to discern for themselves the common law principles to apply in diversity cases, rather than simply following the principles that the state courts had articulated. *Erie* rejected natural law theory in favor of legal positivism—the theory that law stems only from the definitive command of the sovereign, whether embodied in a constitution, in statutes or in principles of common law that the sovereign's judiciary recognized as authoritative.

This chapter explores the principles governing the creation of federal common law. The inquiry proceeds on several levels. First, consider whether state or federal law governs a particular issue. This is the vertical, or *Erie*, choice-of-law question. The answer depends partly on whether there is federal competence in the area, since the federal government has only delegated powers. If there is no federal competence, then clearly state law must govern—by default, as it were. If there is federal competence, and Congress has created a rule of decision applicable to the issue, then the Supremacy Clause requires federal law to control, displacing state law. But if there is federal competence, and Congress has not acted, is it appropriate for the federal courts to step in to make common law? The mere fact that the federal government can enter a substantive area is not equivalent to saying that it should or must do so. Perhaps only Congress should establish a federal presence in a substantive area. Some judges and commentators have suggested that,

> **Take Note**
>
> The ensuing discussion presumes familiarity with the early development of the *Erie* doctrine, particularly *Guaranty Trust Co. v. York*, 326 U.S. 99 (1945); *Byrd v. Blue Ridge Rural Elec. Co-op.*, 356 U.S. 525 (1958); *Hanna v. Plumer*, 380 U.S. 460 (1965); *Walker v. Armco Steel Corp.*, 446 U.S. 740 (1980); *Stewart Org. v. Ricoh Corp.*, 487 U.S. 22 (1988), and *Gasperini v. Center for the Humanities, Inc.*, 518 U.S. 415 (1996). For an excellent discussion of the *Erie* quatrain, see John Hart Ely, *The Irrepressible Myth of* Erie, 87 HARV.L.REV. 693 (1974).

attacking the institutional legitimacy of most judge-made federal law and thus greatly limiting its possible scope.

Even for those who accept the legitimacy of federal common law, there are limits. The federal courts could not, for example, create a national health care system out of whole cloth simply because they thought it a good idea and authority to create it could be found somewhere in the Constitution. On the other hand, if a dispute develops between two states over how to apportion water from an interstate stream, neither state can impose its law on the other. Moreover, there is a strong federal interest in peaceful resolution of the conflict. Consequently, relatively few may object to a federal court fashioning a rule of decision. These poles bound a vast spectrum of possible federal court activity; major amounts of judicial and scholarly time go into attempting to locate the federal courts' proper place on that spectrum.

Take Note

In considering the cases that follow, it is critically important to separate out the precise issue as to which the court must make a choice-of-law decision. Only by doing that will you be able to understand the arguments for and against creating federal common law.

Second, assuming federal common law should exist, how should the federal courts create it? Are the federal judges simply to make it up, as have common law judges for centuries, or are there resources available to today's federal judges to help decide complex questions that federal common law will govern? In the excerpt that follows Erie, Judge Friendly suggests that federal courts create common law in four distinct ways: "spontaneous generation, as in the case of government contracts or interstate controversies, implication of a private federal cause of action from a statute providing other sanctions, construing a jurisdictional grant as a command to fashion federal law, and the normal judicial filling in of statutory interstices." Given the proliferation of state laws, model codes and secondary scholarly sources, federal judges today operate in much less of a vacuum than did their predecessors, both here and in England.

B. The Cornerstone

Erie Railroad Co. v. Tompkins

Supreme Court of the United States, 1938.
304 U.S. 64.

MR. JUSTICE BRANDEIS delivered the opinion of the Court.

> **FYI**
> This statement was quite a shocking way for the Court to begin its opinion, because the parties had neither briefed nor argued that issue.

The question for decision is whether the oft-challenged doctrine of *Swift v. Tyson* shall now be disapproved. Tompkins, a citizen of Pennsylvania, was injured on a dark night by a passing freight train of the Erie Railroad Company while walking along its right of way at Hughestown in that State. He claimed that the accident occurred through negligence in the operation, or maintenance, of the train; that he was rightfully on the premises as licensee because on a commonly used beaten footpath which ran for a short distance alongside the tracks; and that he was struck by something which looked like a door projecting from one of the moving cars. To enforce that claim he brought an action in the federal court for southern New York, which had jurisdiction because the company is a corporation of that State. It denied liability; and the case was tried by a jury.

The Erie insisted that its duty to Tompkins was no greater than that owed to a trespasser. It contended, among other things, that its duty to Tompkins, and hence its liability, should be determined in accordance with the Pennsylvania law; that under the law of Pennsylvania, as declared by its highest court, persons who use pathways along the railroad right of way—that is a longitudinal pathway as distinguished from a crossing—are to be deemed trespassers; and that the railroad is not liable for injuries to undiscovered trespassers resulting from its negligence, unless it be wanton or wilful. Tompkins denied that any such rule had been established by the decisions of the Pennsylvania courts; and contended that, since there was no statute of the State on the subject, the railroad's duty and liability is to be determined in federal courts as a matter of general law.

The trial judge refused to rule that the applicable law precluded recovery. The jury brought in a verdict of $30,000; and the judgment entered thereon was affirmed by the Circuit Court of Appeals, which held that it was unnecessary to consider whether the law of Pennsylvania was as contended, because the question was one not of local, but of general, law and that

> upon questions of general law the federal courts are free, in the absence of a local statute, to exercise their independent judgment as to what the law is; and it is well settled that the question of the responsibility of a railroad for injuries caused by its servants is one of general law * * * .

The Erie had contended that application of the Pennsylvania rule was required, among other things, by § 34 of the Federal Judiciary Act of September 24, 1789, which provides: "The laws of the several States, except where the Constitution, treaties, or statutes of the United States otherwise require or provide, shall be regarded as rules of decisions in trials at common law, in the courts of the United States, in cases where they apply."

Because of the importance of the question whether the federal court was free to disregard the alleged rule of the Pennsylvania common law, we granted certiorari.

First. Swift v. Tyson held that federal courts exercising jurisdiction on the ground of diversity of citizenship need not, in matters of general jurisprudence, apply the unwritten law of the State as declared by its highest court; that they are free to exercise an independent judgment as to what the common law of the State is—or should be; and that, as there stated by Mr. Justice Story:

> the true interpretation of the thirty-fourth section limited its application to state laws strictly local, that is to say, to the positive statutes of the state, and the construction thereof adopted by the local tribunals, and to rights and titles to things having a permanent locality, such as the rights and titles to real estate, and other matters immovable and intraterritorial in their nature and character. It never has been supposed by us, that the section did apply, or was intended to apply, to questions of a more general nature, not at all dependent upon local statutes or local usages of a fixed and permanent operation, as, for example, to the construction of ordinary contracts or other written instruments, and especially to questions of general commercial law, where the state tribunals are called upon to perform the like functions as ourselves, that is, to ascertain upon general reasoning and legal analogies, what is the true exposition of the contract or instrument, or what is the just rule furnished by the principles of commercial law to govern the case.

The Court in applying the rule of § 34 to equity cases said: "The statute, however, is merely declarative of the rule which would exist in the absence of the statute." The federal courts assumed, in the broad field of "general law," the power to declare rules of decision which Congress was confessedly without power to enact as statutes.

Take Note!

This is the Court's first reference to whether the powers of the federal legislature and judiciary, with respect to substantive law, are co-extensive.

Doubt was repeatedly expressed as to the correctness of the construction given § 34, and as to the soundness of the rule which it introduced. But it was the more recent research of a competent scholar, who examined the original document, which established that the construction given to it by the Court was erroneous; and that the purpose of the section was merely to make certain that, in all matters except those in which some federal law is controlling, the federal courts exercising jurisdiction in diversity of citizenship cases would apply as their rules of decision the law of the State, unwritten as well as written.

Criticism of the doctrine became widespread after the decision of *Black & White Taxicab Co. v. Brown & Yellow Taxicab Co.* [1928]. There, Brown and Yellow, a Kentucky corporation owned by Kentuckians, and the Louisville and Nashville Railroad, also a Kentucky corporation, wished that the former should have the exclusive privilege of soliciting passenger and baggage transportation at the Bowling Green, Kentucky, railroad station; and that the Black and White, a competing Kentucky corporation, should be prevented from interfering with that privilege. Knowing that such a contract would be void under the common law of Kentucky, it was arranged that the Brown and Yellow reincorporate under the law of Tennessee, and that the contract with the railroad should be executed there. The suit was then brought by the Tennessee corporation in the federal court for western Kentucky to enjoin competition by the Black and White; an injunction issued by the District Court was sustained by the Court of Appeals; and this Court, citing many decisions in which the doctrine of *Swift v. Tyson* had been applied, affirmed the decree.

Second. Experience in applying the doctrine of *Swift v. Tyson*, had revealed its defects, political and social; and the benefits expected to flow from the rule did not accrue. Persistence of state courts in their own opinions on questions of common law prevented uniformity; and the impossibility of discovering a satisfactory line of demarcation between the province of general law and that of local law developed a new well of uncertainties.

On the other hand, the mischievous results of the doctrine had become apparent. Diversity of citizenship jurisdiction was conferred in order to prevent apprehended discrimination in state courts against those not citizens of the State. *Swift v. Tyson* introduced

Take Note!

You may wonder how it is that the state courts were able to persist in their own views, given the principle embodied in the Supremacy Clause. That is precisely the point. The Supremacy Clause makes federal law supreme. "General law" was not federal law; it was a sourceless common law that the Supremacy Clause did not embrace.

grave discrimination by non-citizens against citizens. It made rights enjoyed under the unwritten "general law" vary according to whether enforcement was sought in the state or in the federal court; and the privilege of selecting the court in which the right should be determined was conferred upon the non-citizen. Thus, the doctrine rendered impossible equal protection of the law. In attempting to promote uniformity of law throughout the United States, the doctrine had prevented uniformity in the administration of the law of the State.

The discrimination resulting became in practice far-reaching. This resulted in part from the broad province accorded to the so-called "general law" as to which federal courts exercised an independent judgment. In addition to questions of purely commercial law, "general law" was held to include the obligations under contracts entered into and to be performed within the State, the extent to which a carrier operating within a State may stipulate for exemption from liability for his own negligence or that of his employee; the liability for torts committed within the State upon persons resident or property located there, even where the question of liability depended upon the scope of a property right conferred by the State; and the right to exemplary or punitive damages. Furthermore, state decisions construing local deeds, mineral conveyances, and even devises of real estate were disregarded.

In part the discrimination resulted from the wide range of persons held entitled to avail themselves of the federal rule by resort to the diversity of citizenship jurisdiction. Through this jurisdiction individual citizens willing to remove from their own State and become citizens of another might avail themselves of the federal rule. And, without even change of residence, a corporate citizen of the State could avail itself of the federal rule by re-incorporating under the laws of another State, as was done in the *Taxicab* case.

The injustice and confusion incident to the doctrine of *Swift v. Tyson* have been repeatedly urged as reasons for abolishing or limiting diversity of citizenship jurisdiction. Other legislative relief has been proposed. If only a question of statutory construction were involved, we should not be prepared to abandon a doctrine so widely applied throughout nearly a century. But the unconstitutionality of the course pursued has now been made clear and compels us to do so.

Third. Except in matters governed by the Federal Constitution or by Acts of Congress, the law to be applied in any case is the law of the State. And whether the law of the State shall be declared by its Legislature in a statute or by its highest court in a decision is not a matter of federal concern. There is no federal general common law. Congress has no power to declare substantive rules of common law applicable in a State whether they be local in their nature or "general," be they commercial law or a part of the law of torts. And no clause in the Constitution purports to confer such a power upon the federal courts.

As stated by Mr. Justice Field:

> I am aware that what has been termed the general law of the country—which is often little less than what the judge advancing the doctrine thinks at the time should be the general law on a particular subject—has been often advanced in judicial opinions of this court to control a conflicting law of a State. I admit that learned judges have fallen into the habit of repeating this doctrine as a convenient mode of brushing aside the law of a State in conflict with their views. And I confess that, moved and governed by the authority of the great names of those judges, I have, myself, in many instances, unhesitatingly and confidently, but I think now erroneously, repeated the same doctrine. But, notwithstanding the great names which may be cited in favor of the doctrine, and notwithstanding the frequency with which the doctrine has been reiterated, there stands, as a perpetual protest against its repetition, the Constitution of the United States, which recognizes and preserves the autonomy and independence of the States—independence in their legislative and independence in their judicial departments. Supervision over either the legislative or the judicial action of the States is in no case permissible except as to matters by the Constitution specifically authorized or delegated to the United States. Any interference with either, except as thus permitted, is an invasion of the authority of the State and, to that extent, a denial of its independence.

Take Note!

This is the only mention in *Erie* of the substance/procedure distinction upon which the Court would rely in so many later cases, and it is an oblique mention at that. Note as well that the two preceding sentences make clear the co-extensiveness of congressional and federal judicial power with respect the the kinds of subjects with which the federal government may deal.

The fallacy underlying the rule declared in Swift v. Tyson is made clear by Mr. Justice Holmes. The doctrine rests upon the assumption that there is "a transcendental body of law outside of any particular State but obligatory within it unless and until changed by statute," that federal courts have the power to use their judgment as to what the rules of common law are; and that in the federal courts the parties are entitled to an independent judgment on matters of general law:

> but law in the sense in which courts speak of it today does not exist without some definite authority behind it. The common law so far as it is enforced in a State, whether called common law or not, is not the common law generally but the law of that State existing by the authority of that State without regard to what it may have been in England or anywhere else * * * .

[T]he authority and only authority is the State, and if that be so, the voice adopted by the State as its own [whether it be of its Legislature or of its Supreme Court] should utter the last word.

Take Note!

This is Justice Holmes's statement of the positivist thesis.

Thus the doctrine of Swift v. Tyson is, as Mr. Justice Holmes said, "an unconstitutional assumption of powers by courts of the United States which no lapse of time or respectable array of opinion should make us hesitate to correct." In disapproving that doctrine we do not hold unconstitutional § 34 of the Federal Judiciary Act of 1789 or any other Act of Congress. We merely declare that in applying the doctrine this Court and the lower courts have invaded rights which in our opinion are reserved by the Constitution to the several States.

Fourth. The defendant contended that by the common law of Pennsylvania as declared by its highest court the only duty owed to the plaintiff was to refrain from wilful or wanton injury. The plaintiff denied that such is the Pennsylvania law. In support of their respective contentions the parties discussed and cited many decisions of the Supreme Court of the State. The Circuit Court of Appeals ruled that the question of liability is one of general law; and on that ground declined to decide the issue of state law. As we hold this was error, the judgment is reversed and the case remanded to it for further proceedings in conformity with our opinion.

Take Note!

One is apt, perhaps because of Justice Brandeis's use of "merely," to read this sentence too quickly. To declare that the federal judiciary, led by the Supreme Court, has violated the Constitution for nigh unto a century is rather striking, is it not? By the way, what provisions of the Constitution does the Court think it has violated?

Reversed.

MR. JUSTICE BUTLER, concurring.

* * *

No constitutional question was suggested or argued below or here. And as a general rule, this Court will not consider any question not raised below and presented by the petition. Here it does not decide either of the questions presented but, changing the rule of decision in force since the foundation of the Government, remands the case to be adjudged according to a standard never before deemed permissible.

* * *

While amendments to § 34 have from time to time been suggested, the section stands as originally enacted. Evidently Congress has intended throughout the years that the rule of decision as construed should continue to govern federal courts in trials at common law. The opinion just announced suggests that Mr. Warren's research has established that from the beginning this Court has erroneously construed § 34. But that author's [article] does not purport to be authoritative and was intended to be no more than suggestive. The weight to be given to his discovery has never been discussed at this bar. Nor does the opinion indicate the ground disclosed by the research. In his dissenting opinion in the Taxicab case, Mr. Justice Holmes referred to Mr. Warren's work but failed to persuade the Court that "laws" as used in § 34 included varying and possibly ill-considered rulings by the courts of a State on questions of common law. It well may be that, if the Court should now call for argument of counsel on the basis of Mr. Warren's research, it would adhere to the construction it has always put upon § 34. Indeed, the opinion in this case so indicates. For it declares: "If only a question of statutory construction were involved, we should not be prepared to abandon a doctrine so widely applied throughout a century. But the unconstitutionality of the course pursued has now been made clear and compels us to do so." This means that, so far as concerns the rule of decision now condemned, the Judiciary Act of 1789, passed to establish judicial courts to exert the judicial power of the United States, and especially § 34 of that Act as construed, is unconstitutional; that federal courts are now bound to follow decisions of the courts of the State in which the controversies arise; and that Congress is powerless otherwise to ordain. It is hard to foresee the consequences of the radical change so made.

* * *

MR. JUSTICE REED.

I concur in the conclusion reached in this case, in the disapproval of the doctrine of Swift v. Tyson, and in the reasoning of the majority opinion except in so far as it relies upon the unconstitutionality of the "course pursued" by the federal courts.

The "doctrine of Swift v. Tyson," as I understand it, is that the words "the laws," as used in § 34, line one, of the Federal Judiciary Act of September 24, 1789, do not include in their meaning "the decisions of the local tribunals." Mr. Justice Story, in deciding that point, said: "Undoubtedly, the decisions of the local tribunals upon such subjects are entitled to, and will receive, the most deliberate attention and respect of this Court; but they cannot furnish positive rules, or conclusive authority, by which our own judgments are to be bound up and governed."

To decide the case now before us and to "disapprove" the doctrine of Swift v. Tyson requires only that we say that the words "the laws" include in their meaning the decisions of the local tribunals. As the majority opinion shows, by its reference to Mr. Warren's researches and the first quotation from Mr. Justice Holmes, that this Court is now of the view that "laws" includes "decisions," it is unnecessary to go further and declare that the "course pursued" was "unconstitutional," instead of merely erroneous.

The "unconstitutional" course referred to in the majority opinion is apparently the ruling in Swift v. Tyson that the supposed omission of Congress to legislate as to the effect of decisions leaves federal courts free to interpret general law for themselves. I am not at all sure whether, in the absence of federal statutory direction, federal courts would be compelled to follow state decisions. There was sufficient doubt about the matter in 1789 to induce the first Congress to legislate. No former opinions of this Court have passed upon it. Mr. Justice Holmes evidently saw nothing "unconstitutional" which required the overruling of Swift v. Tyson, for he said in the very opinion quoted by the majority, "I should leave Swift v. Tyson undisturbed * * * but I would not allow it to spread the assumed dominion into new fields." If the opinion commits this Court to the position that the Congress is without power to declare what rules of substantive law shall govern the federal courts, that conclusion also seems questionable. The line between procedural and substantive law is hazy, but no one doubts federal power over procedure. The Judiciary Article, 3, and the "necessary and proper" clause of Article 1, § 8, may fully authorize legislation, such as this section of the Judiciary Act.

* * *

Notes and Questions

1. If there were no Rules of Decision Act, how would the Court have decided *Erie*? Why? After *Erie,* what does the Rules of Decision Act do?

2. Suppose instead that the Rules of Decision Act made the opposite declaration: that in cases brought in the federal courts, federal law should be applied. Would that have caused any problems?

For More Information

To get an idea of the social and political context in which *Erie* and its progeny arose, see EDWARD R. PURCELL, BRANDEIS AND THE PROGESSIVE CONSTITUTION: ERIE, THE JUDICIAL POWER, AND THE POLITICS OF THE FEDERAL COURTS IN TWENTIETH CENTURY AMERICA (2000).

3. Justice Brandeis tells us that "[e]xcept in matters governed by the Federal Constitution or by Acts of Congress, the law to be applied in any case is the law of the State." A great debate rages around this aspect of *Erie.* The case raises two structural considerations. The first, discussed in most Civil Procedure courses, concerns federal-

ism: the appropriate demarcation of state versus federal power. *Erie* clearly increased state power when it repudiated the legitimacy of federal general common law.

The second concerns the allocation of federal power between Congress and the judiciary. Some scholars and judges argue that *Erie* also stands for the idea that the federal courts cannot create common law even in areas clearly within the constitutional competence of the federal government, on the theory that separation of powers allows only Congress to create federal law. This view has commanded increasing attention in recent decades. *See, e.g.*, George D. Brown, *Of Activism and Erie—The Implication Doctrine's Implication for the Nature and Role of the Federal Courts*, 69 IOWA L.REV. 617 (1984); Thomas Merrill, The *Common Law Powers of Federal Courts*, 52 U.CHI.L.REV. 1 (1985). Does Erie support that idea? Do you think that Justice Brandeis had that in mind?

4. If the separation-of-powers view is correct, how literally should one take it? In some areas Congress legislates in extraordinarily general terms. For example, the Sherman Antitrust Act merely prohibits "restraint of trade." Over the years, the federal courts have given extensive substantive content to that phrase. Is that practice illegitimate? If so, are there any disadvantages to returning to Congress the burden of defining an unacceptable restraint of trade?

Judicial lawmaking considerably antedates the Constitution. The Framers created a new government against the backdrop of hundreds of years of English common law. Is there any evidence that they intended to abandon that system? The new doctrine is rooted in the concept of separation of powers. What precisely does the Constitution say about separation of powers? What permits or justifies judge-made law?

5. Could Congress have passed a law that would have controlled the result in *Erie*? What part of the Constitution would allow it to do so? If Congress could not, what implications does that have for the separation-of-powers view of *Erie?* Suppose Congress could have legislated but did not. Is that significant in trying to understand Erie's message? What was the Court's view of Congress's power? Should we care?

6. Following *Erie*, there is no question that federal common law (not federal *general* common law) can exist. Concurring in *D'Oench, Duhme & Co. v.* FDIC, 315 U.S. 447, 469-70 (1942), Justice Jackson offered a concise explanation of why that is so:

> The federal courts have no general federal common law. * * * But this is not to say that whenever we have occasion to decide a federal question which cannot be answered from federal statutes alone we may not resort to all of the source materials of the common law, or that when we have fashioned an answer it does not become a part of the federal non-statutory or common law * * * . Were we bereft of the common law, our federal system would be impotent. This follows from the recognized futility of attempting all-complete statutory codes, and is apparent from the terms of the Constitution itself.

7. Professor Wilfred Ritz argued strongly that the *Erie* Court and most commentators on the Rules of Decision Act have badly misunderstood Congress's intent. He did not think the Act applied to diversity jurisdiction at all, basing his conclusion upon a variety of factors: the choice of language that refers to state law, the placement of the section in the Judiciary Act of 1789, the congressional debates on the Judiciary Act, and the general structure of state judicial systems at the time.

> [S]ufficient evidence [exists] to demonstrate that Section 34 could not possibly have been intended by Oliver Ellsworth and the other members of the Senate and the House of Representatives in the summer of 1789 to have performed the functions that Professors Warren and Goebel, Justices Story and Brandeis, and the Supreme Court majority in *Erie Railroad Co. v. Tompkins* have attributed to it. It would literally have been unthinkable for the members of the First Congress to have directed national courts sitting in diversity cases to apply the law of the states in which they sat. The necessary conceptual framework was only in the early stages of formation.
>
> * * *
>
> Section 34 is a direction to the national courts to apply American law, as distinguished from English law. American law is to be found in the "laws of the several states" viewed as a group of eleven states in 1789, and not viewed separately and individually. It is not a direction to apply the law of a particular state, for if it had been so intended, the section would have referred to the "laws of the respective states."
>
> * * *
>
> The section most probably was intended as a temporary measure to provide an applicable American law for national criminal prosecutions, should national criminal prosecutions be brought in the national courts, pending the time that Congress would provide by statute for the definition of national crimes.
>
> An alternative possibility, although less likely, is that the section was intended as a direction to the national courts to apply American law in all judicial proceedings at common law, both civil and criminal. This application would have included the diversity jurisdiction.
>
> The one thing that can be said with assurance is that Section 34 was not intended to apply exclusively to diversity proceedings; that it was not intended to direct the application of the law of particular states in diversity proceedings; and that it was not intended to apply to suits in equity. In short, on its historical basis, *Erie* is dead wrong.

WILFRED RITZ, REWRITING THE HISTORY OF THE JUDICIARY ACT OF 1789 79, 148 (1990). It seems unlikely that Professor Ritz's view will overcome the Court's commitment to *Erie* any time soon, considering it took ninety-six years for the Court to overrule Swift v. Tyson, but his work poses interesting questions. If *Erie*'s interpretation of the Rules of Decision Act is incorrect, what law should the federal courts apply in civil litigation?

Does Professor Ritz imply that Swift v. Tyson was decided correctly? Does *Erie*, even if incorrect about the Rules of Decision Act, have anything to say about the legitimacy of federal common law?

In Praise of Erie—and of the New Federal Common Law

Henry J. Friendly
39 N.Y.U.L.REV. 383, 405-07, 421-22 (1964) (footnotes omitted)[a]

[B]y banishing the spurious uniformity of Swift v. Tyson—what Mr. Justice Frankfurter was to call "the attractive vision of a uniform body of federal law" but a vision only—and by leaving to the states what ought be left to them, Erie led to the emergence of a federal decisional law in areas of national concern that is truly uniform because, under the supremacy clause, it is binding in every forum, and therefore is predictable and useful as its predecessor, more general in subject matter but limited to the federal courts, was not. The clarion yet careful pronouncement of Erie, "There is no federal general common law," opened the way to what, for want of a better term, we may call specialized federal common law. I doubt that we sufficiently realize how far this development has gone—let alone where it is likely to go.

Whatever promise Mr. Justice Story's aim to achieve uniformity through the persuasive force of Supreme Court decisions may have had in the fifth decade of the nineteenth century, at least as to commercial law, the prospect had faded long before the fourth decade of the twentieth. The growth of the country multiplied the nation's judicial business far beyond the capacity of any single court to preserve uniformity by the force of example. The trend to making law by statutes struck another blow. Story had excepted from the "general" law which federal courts were free to determine "the positive statutes of the state, and the construction thereof adopted by the local tribunals," as the language of the 34th section [of the Judiciary Act of 1789] rather clearly compelled. Since this exception was held to cover the construction of uniform statutes declaratory of the common law, including the Negotiable Instruments Law, Story's ideal was thereby frustrated in the very area for which it had been most pointedly designed. Finally the increased review of state action as a result of the Fourteenth Amendment and the explosion of federal legislation beginning with Roosevelt I required the Supreme Court to devote the bulk of its time to constitutional law and the interpretation of federal statutes, with the result that, as Judge A.N. Hand noted in 1930, "relatively few cases where rights under the Federal Constitution and statutes are not involved are likely to get beyond the Circuit Court of Appeals" and hence "there is much

---

a Reprinted by permission of New York University Law Review.

less chance than formerly of securing or even promoting uniformity through the decisions of the Supreme Court" on issues of "general law." Although the New York Court of Appeals might bow to the superior wisdom of the Supreme Court, speaking through a Mr. Justice Story, on a point of commercial law, one could hardly expect similar deference to a decision of three judges of an intermediate federal court of appeals.

Furthermore, whatever degree of uniformity was attained under *Swift v. Tyson*, reckonability was small. One trouble was that the body of federal "general" law was so meagre. Prediction at the planning stage was nigh impossible since a lawyer could rarely tell whether the issue would be litigated in a state court, where the governing rule was well established, or in a federal court, where it had not been. But the situation was not vastly better even when litigation had begun. On what basis could counsel soundly advise whether the highest court of a state would alter its views on a matter of "general" law to conform to those that had been later expressed by a federal court? In the converse situation, where the litigation was in federal court, how could he fairly prophesy, unless the Supreme Court had already spoken, whether the court would strike out for itself or follow the local view under the "deference" often accorded state decisions?

There was, to be sure, no logical contradiction between federal judges being free to make their own determinations of "general" common law for use only in the federal courts, and also "developing a uniform body of federal decisional rules" which because of their subject are binding in all courts. But the coincidence of the death of the first doctrine and the growth of the second would itself suggest that *Swift v. Tyson* had retarded the development of federal decisional law of the latter type; and other considerations strongly reinforce the inference from chronology alone. Since most cases relating to federal matters were in the federal courts and involved "general" law, the familiar rule of *Swift v. Tyson* usually gave federal judges all the freedom they required in pre-*Erie* days and made it unnecessary for them to consider a more esoteric source of power. *Per contra*, in the rare instance where the issue in such a case was of "local" law in the *Swift v. Tyson* sense, as when the United States was asserting proprietary rights, the Supreme Court seems to have been content to let state law prevail as a sort of quid pro quo, without inquiring whether this was a necessary choice or only a desirable one in the particular case. By focusing judicial attention on the nature of the right being enforced, *Erie* caused the principle of a specialized federal common law, binding in all courts because of its source, to develop within a quarter century into a powerful unifying force. Just as federal courts now conform to state decisions on issues properly for the states, state courts must conform to federal decisions in areas where Congress, acting within powers granted to it, has manifested, be it ever so lightly, an intention to that end. A psychiatrist might say that, having rid itself of subconscious feelings of guilt of federal poaching on state preserves, the Supreme Court became freer to insist on deference to federal decisions by the states where deference was due. As a perceptive judge remarked only three years after Erie, "Unto each Caesar, State or federal, is thus rendered that which properly belongs to that particular Caesar, supreme in its distinctive field."

* * *

So, as it seems to me, the Supreme Court in the years since *Erie*, has been forging a new centripetal tool incalculably useful to our federal system. It has employed a variety of techniques—spontaneous generation as in the cases of government contracts or interstate controversies, implication of a private federal cause of action from a statute providing other sanctions, construing a jurisdictional grant as a command to fashion federal law, and the normal judicial filling of statutory interstices. * * * Professor Gilmore thinks the Court has taken these giant steps "almost unconsciously." I doubt that, but it scarcely matters. What does matter is that a not insignificant part of Story's "general law" is already under the sway of the new type of federal common law and that many other parts can readily be brought there if Congress thinks this desirable. We might * * * consider that the Hegelian dialectic has been here at work—with *Swift v. Tyson* the thesis, *Erie* the antithesis, and the new federal common law the synthesis. In less grandiose terms, we can see in this development the thrust and counterthrust so often encountered in the legal as well as the political history of a country wisely addicted to the method of trial and error.

The complementary concepts—that federal courts must follow state decisions on matters of substantive law appropriately cognizable by the states whereas state courts must follow federal decisions on subjects within national legislative power where Congress has so directed—seem so beautifully simple, and so simply beautiful, that we must wonder why a century and a half were needed to discover them, and must wonder even more why anyone should want to shy away once the discovery was made. We may not yet have achieved the best of all possible worlds with respect to the relationship between state and federal law. But the combination of *Erie* with *Clearfield* and *Lincoln Mills* has brought us to a far, far better one than we have ever known before. It thus seems fitting, twenty-five years after the *Erie* decision, to lay this tribute at the feet of Mr. Justice Brandeis and his colleagues, and of the builders, most of them happily still with us, of the new federal common law.

C. Choosing the Applicable Law and Determining Its Content—Federal Interests or Lack Thereof

1. Spontaneous Generation

Clearfield Trust Co. v. United States

Supreme Court of the United States, 1943.
318 U.S. 363.

MR. JUSTICE DOUGLAS delivered the opinion of the Court.

On April 28, 1936, a check was drawn on the Treasurer of the United States through the Federal Reserve Bank of Philadelphia to the order of Clair A. Barner in the amount of $24.20. It was dated at Harrisburg, Pennsylvania, and was drawn for services rendered by Barner to the Works Progress Administration. The check was placed in the mail addressed to Barner at his address in Mackeyville, Pa. Barner never received the check. Some unknown person obtained it in a mysterious manner and presented it to the J.C. Penney Co. store in Clearfield, Pa., representing that he was the payee and identifying himself to the satisfaction of the employees of J.C. Penney Co. He endorsed the check in the name of Barner and transferred it to J.C. Penney Co. in exchange for cash and merchandise. Barner never authorized the endorsement nor participated in the proceeds of the check. J.C. Penney Co. endorsed the check over to the Clearfield Trust Co. which accepted it as agent for the purpose of collection and endorsed it as follows: "Pay to the order of Federal Reserve Bank of Philadelphia, Prior Endorsements Guaranteed." Clearfield Trust Co. collected the check from the United States through the Federal Reserve Bank of Philadelphia and paid the full amount thereof to J.C. Penney Co. Neither the Clearfield Trust Co. nor J.C. Penney Co. had any knowledge or suspicion of the forgery. Each acted in good faith. On or before May 10, 1936, Barner advised the timekeeper and the foreman of the W.P.A. project on which he was employed that he had not received the check in question. This information was duly communicated to other agents of the United States and on November 30, 1936, Barner executed an affidavit alleging that the endorsement of his name on the check was a forgery. No notice was given the Clearfield Trust Co. or J.C. Penney Co. of the forgery until January 12, 1937, at which time the Clearfield Trust Co. was notified. The first notice received by Clearfield Trust Co. that the United States was asking reimbursement was on August 31, 1937.

This suit was instituted in 1939 by the United States against the Clearfield Trust Co. * * * . The cause of action was based on the express guaranty of prior endorsements made by the Clearfield Trust Co. J.C. Penney Co. intervened as a defendant. The case was heard on complaint, answer and stipulation of facts. The District Court held that the rights of the parties were to be determined by the law of Pennsylvania and that since the United States unreasonably delayed in giving notice of the forgery to the Clearfield Trust Co., it was barred from recovery. It accordingly dismissed the complaint. On appeal the Circuit Court of Appeals reversed. * * *

We agree with the Circuit Court of Appeals that the rule of *Erie R. Co. v. Tompkins* does not apply to this action. The rights and duties of the United States on commercial paper which it issues are governed by federal rather than local law. When the United States disburses its funds or pays its debts, it is exercising a constitutional function or power. This check was issued for services performed under the Federal Emergency Relief Act of 1935. The authority to issue the check had its origin in the Constitution and the statutes of the United States and was in no way dependent on the laws of Pennsylvania or of any other state. The duties imposed upon the United States and the rights acquired by it as a result of the issuance find their roots in the same federal sources. In absence of an applicable Act of Congress it is for the federal courts to fashion the governing rule of law according to their own standards. * * *

Take Note!

What is the function of the sentence declaring that the check was an exercise of a "constitutional function or power"? What work does it do for the Court?

In our choice of the applicable federal rule we have occasionally selected state law. But reasons which may make state law at times the appropriate federal rule are singularly inappropriate here. The issuance of commercial paper by the United States is on a vast scale and transactions in that paper from issuance to payment will commonly occur in several states. The application of state law, even without the conflict of laws rules of the forum, would subject the rights and duties of the United States to exceptional uncertainty. It would lead to great diversity in results by making identical transactions subject to the vagaries of the laws of the several states. The desirability of a uniform rule is plain. And while the federal law merchant, developed for about a century under the regime of *Swift v. Tyson* represented general commercial law rather than a choice of a federal rule designed to protect a federal right, it nevertheless stands as a convenient source of reference for fashioning federal rules applicable to these federal questions.

Food for Thought

In what process does Justice Douglas sound like he's engaging here?

United States v. National Exchange Bank [1909] falls in that category. The Court held that the United States could recover as drawee from one who presented for payment a pension check on which the name of the payee had been forged, in spite of a protracted delay on the part of the United States in giving notice of the forgery. * * * The drawee, whether it be the United States or another, is not chargeable with the knowledge of the signature of the payee.

> **Take Note!**
>
> It is important to understand that Erie did not condemn as unwise all of the substantive rules that the federal courts created under Swift's regime; it instead limited the kinds of cases in which they could apply. In areas where there *is* federal competence, the Court has often referred to pre-Erie substantive principles to resolve issues.

The National Exchange Bank case went no further than to hold that prompt notice of the discovery of the forgery was not a condition precedent to suit. It did not reach the question whether lack of prompt notice might be a defense. We think it may. If it is shown that the drawee on learning of the forgery did not give prompt notice of it and that damage resulted, recovery by the drawee is barred. The fact that the drawee is the United States and the **laches** those of its employees are not material. The United States as drawee of commercial paper stands in no different light than any other drawee. As stated in United States v. National Exchange Bank, "The United States does business on business terms." It is not excepted from the general rules governing the rights and duties of drawees "by the largeness of its dealings and its having to employ agents to do what if done by a principal in person would leave no room for doubt." But the damage occasioned by the delay must be established and not left to conjecture. Cases such as Market St. Title & Trust Co. v. Chelten Trust Co. [a Pennsylvania Supreme Court case] place the burden on the drawee of giving prompt notice of the forgery—injury to the defendant being presumed by the mere fact of delay. But we do not think that he who accepts a forged signature of a payee deserves that preferred treatment. It is his neglect or error in accepting the forger's signature which occasions the loss. He should be allowed to shift that loss to the drawee only on a clear showing that the drawee's delay in notifying him of the forgery caused him damage. No such damage has been shown by Clearfield Trust Co. who so far as appears can still recover from J.C. Penney Co. The only showing on the part of the latter is contained in the stipulation to the effect that if a check cashed for a customer is returned unpaid or for reclamation a short time

> **What's That?**
>
> "Unreasonable delay in pursuing a right of claim—almost always an equitable one—in a way that prejudices the party against whom relief is sought.—Also termed *sleeping on rights*."

after the date on which it is cashed, the employees can often locate the person who cashed it. It is further stipulated that when J.C. Penney Co. was notified of the forgery in the present case none of its employees was able to remember anything about the transaction or check in question. The inference is that the more prompt the notice the more likely the detection of the forger. But that falls short of a showing that the delay caused a manifest loss. It is but another way of saying that mere delay is enough.

Affirmed.

Notes and Questions

1. On Justice Douglas's reasoning, does federal common law apply whenever the United States is a party and is exercising "a constitutional function"? What cases to which the United States is a party would that formulation exclude from the ambit of federal common law?

2. Why should federalism entitle the United States to have federal law applied? What is the constitutional authority upon which the Court relies? Resort to the Supremacy Clause begs the questions. That Clause by its terms applies when there is a clash between federal and state law; here the issue is whether there should be any federal law in the first place.

3. Should federal common law govern all or most issues in cases in which the federal government is a party?

4. If federal common law applies whenever the United States is a party and exercising a constitutional function, why does the Court bother to discuss the federal interest in uniformity? If the rule calling for federal common law is a *per se* rule, interest analysis should be irrelevant. If the rule is not absolute, when might the Court consider applying state law in cases to which the United States is a party?

5. How great is the federal interest in uniformity in *Clearfield*? If it is as palpable as the Court suggests, why did Congress not pass a statute embodying a uniform rule? Congress's failure to act poses some interesting problems. Suppose Congress considered such a rule, but the bill failed to pass. Should that affect the result in *Clearfield?* In connection with that problem, consider *Boyle v. United Technologies* at page 461.

6. In *Bank of America National Trust & Savings Association v. Parnell,* 352 U.S. 29 (1956), the United States had issued an early call for redemption of some bonds. Bank of America held some bonds that disappeared the day after the call. Four years later, Parnell cashed them at another bank. Bank of America brought a diversity action for

conversion against the individuals and banks involved in the presentment and payout. The critical issue was whether state or federal law should determine who had the burden of proof on the issue of respondents' good faith in presenting the bonds. The trial court charged the state rule, placing the burden on the presenters to "show[ ] that they acted innocently, honestly, and in good faith * * * ." The Third Circuit reversed in a four-to-three en banc decision, holding that *Clearfield* compelled use of a federal rule requiring Bank of America to show the presenters' lack of good faith.

The Supreme Court reversed, holding that federal law determined whether the bonds were overdue when presented but that state law prescribed the locus of the burden of proof on the issue of good faith in an action between private parties that did not affect the rights and duties of the United States. Justice Frankfurter, writing for the seven-to-two majority, sounded miffed at the Third Circuit's handling of the case, noting that "[t]he Court of Appeals misconceived the nature of this litigation in holding that the *Clearfield Trust* case controlled. * * * The basis for this decision was stated with unclouded explicitness * * * ." He then quoted *Clearfield's* discussion of the vast scale of United States' commercial paper operations and the uncertainty inherent in governing rights and obligations of the United States by state law. The Court allowed that a suit between private parties might nonetheless implicate federal interests properly governed by federal law, but elaborated only by saying that "[f]ederal law of course governs the interpretation of the nature of the rights and obligations created by the Government bonds themselves." Justices Black and Douglas dissented, believing the distinction between suits on government paper by the government versus by private parties to be untenable.

Suppose the majority agreed with the dissenters about the utility of a uniform rule in *Parnell*. Are there any impediments to the Court creating such a rule? Is there federal competence? If not, of course, the matter is simple, but if there is, consider the institutional legitimacy of the Court creating substantive rules in an area that Congress has not entered. Even if Justices Black and Douglas are correct about the difficulties caused by using state law, can one argue that state law must nonetheless govern? What might justify or compel such a position?

7. Lest one think that the United States being a party in an action involving a federal commercial transaction is sufficient to command the use of federal law for all issues, consider *United States v. Yazell*, 382 U.S. 341 (1966), in which the United States tried to recoup a Small Business Administration loan made to the Yazells. Texas then had a coverture law shielding a married woman's separate property from contractual alienation in the absence of a court order removing her disability to contract. The government argued that there was a federal interest in collecting the amount due and that such an interest justified having a federal common law rule apply to Mrs. Yazell's capacity to contract.

The Court disagreed. Justice Fortas emphasized that the SBA negotiated all loans individually and had hired local counsel to assist with the Yazells' loan. He noted that the SBA made no attempt to have Mrs. Yazell's disability removed and interpreted its inaction as willingness to operate under the restrictions of Texas law. He found no need for a uniform rule given the individual negotiation of loan contracts and then discussed federalism concerns:

> We do not here consider the question of the constitutional power of the Congress to override state law in these circumstances by direct legislation or by appropriate authorization to an administrative agency coupled with suitable implementing action by the agency. We decide only that this Court, in the absence of specific congressional action, should not decree in this situation that implementation of federal interests requires overriding the particular state rule involved here. Both theory and the precedents of this Court teach us solicitude for state interests, particularly in the field of family and family-property arrangements. They should be overridden by the federal courts only where clear and substantial interests of the National Government, which cannot be served consistently with respect for such state interests, will suffer major damage if the state law is applied.

Notwithstanding that obvious bow to state interests, the Court waffled on what it was actually doing:

> Generally, in the cases applying state law to limit or condition the enforcement of a federal right, the Court has insisted that the state law is being "adopted" as the federal rule. Even so, it has carefully pointed out that this theory would make it possible to "adopt," as the operative "federal" law, differing laws in the different States, depending upon the State where the relevant transaction takes place.
>
> Although it is unnecessary to decide in the present case whether the Texas law of coverture should apply ***ex proprio vigore***—on the theory that the contract here was made pursuant and subject to this provision of state law—or by "adoption" as a federal principle, it is clear that the state rule should govern.

Food for Thought

Why did Justice Fortas say it was unnecessary to decide the theory under which state law would govern the issue? In what sorts of cases would it be necessary? What difference does it make anyway?

a) Has Congress the authority to pass a statute to govern federal loan transactions? The Court suggested in a footnote that it could. If so, is it significant that Congress had not done so? If not, under what theory is there any federal power to make common law?

b) *Yazell* relied on 28 U.S.C.A. § 1345 for subject matter jurisdiction. That statute confers district court jurisdiction for any action in which the United States is a plaintiff. Does its existence shed any light on the choice-of-law decision? Perhaps Congress intended to signify a federal interest in the application (and development, if necessary) of federal law. But if that is what Congress intended, why did it not say so? Moreover, the jurisdiction § 1345 confers is not exclusive. That, too, may suggest either congressional indifference or inattention to the choice-of-law problem.

c) The majority opinion offered an early overview of the convergence of the federalism and separation-of-powers branches of the *Erie* doctrine. Justice Fortas contrasted Congress's constitutional power to override state concerns with the federal courts' far more limited power to subordinate state to federal interests. He noted that the courts can act only when absolutely necessary to preserve national interests. Congress's authority to act is in Article I, § 8, and Article VI, § 2 of the Constitution. Should the Court have identified the source of authority for the federal courts?

Justice Fortas also emphasized the federalism reasons for allowing state law to govern. If federal law is to displace state law, is it more legitimate for Congress or the federal courts to direct it? Should the criteria that each body might use to make such decisions be different? Why? If you conclude that federal displacement of state law is exclusively or predominantly within Congress's purview, then is the federal courts' role in this respect limited to supremacy inquiries?

8. On occasion, the Court has also recognized the need for federal common law, even in diversity cases. *Banco Nacional de Cuba v. Sabbatino*, 376 U.S. 398 (1964), arose out of what should have been a simple sugar sale between private entities. The seller conveyed the sugar to the buyer, who loaded it on a ship in Cuba. The Cuban government expropriated the sugar because United States nationals predominantly owned the corporate seller, but allowed the ship to sail when the seller agreed to remit the purchase price to Banco Nacional's predecessor in interest. Demand for payment duly occurred in New York. The buyer, rather than remitting the purchase price to Banco Nacional, gave it to Sabbatino, a temporary receiver of the seller's assets in New York. Banco Nacional brought a diversity action against the receiver and the buyer in the Southern District of New York.

The issue as to which the Court had to make a choice-of-law decision was the applicability of the act-of-state doctrine, which prohibits the courts of one country from questioning the legitimacy of acts of a nation within its own territory. The doctrine would have compelled the court to honor Cuba's claim to the proceeds, notwithstanding the expropriation. Under New York's view of international law, the seller was entitled to the proceeds. The district and circuit courts followed New York law, but the Supreme Court reversed.

The Court explained that it was necessary for uniform federal law to govern foreign relations cases. Thus, the states could not be left free to interpret international law, nor could federal courts sitting in diversity apply state variants. The act-of-state doctrine applied. Although Congress quickly passed a law establishing a different federal view of the doctrine's applicability, *Sabbatino* stands unchallenged for the proposition that federal common law governs the law of foreign relations in the absence of a federal statute.

Note that the Court's decision compelled use of federal law in Sabbatino, a diversity case, notwithstanding Erie. Sabbatino is a reminder that one cannot answer the choice-of-law inquiry based merely on the type of federal subject matter jurisdiction that the plaintiff invokes. The Court opined that it was highly unlikely that the Erie Court considered the sort of situation *Sabbatino* presented. Indeed, Erie is distinguishable on the basis of the Erie Court's approach. Justice Brandeis stated that there was no federal competence to prescribe the rule of tort law that would govern Erie. In Sabbatino, by contrast, there is clearly federal competence, both in Congress's power to regulate international commerce, art. I, § 8, cl. 3, and in the President's treaty power, art. II, § 2, cl. 2.

9. Intuitively, preemption and federal common law do not seem linked; one is likely instead to get caught up in the details of the particular competing schemes of substantive law. In fact, Congress rarely specifies that legislation preempts state law. For example, the Court has found preemption in the areas of alien registration, anti-subversive legislation, and food labeling. In such circumstances, the Court is making important decisions about the scope of federal law.

The law of preemption is itself federal, and the Supreme Court has created most of it. The Court has identified three types of preemption: explicit, by congressional occupation of the field, and by conflict between state and federal law. In the latter two categories, the federal law of preemption is judge-made, and the preemption inquiry involves balancing sensitive matters of federal and state concern.

Does Congress's occasionally specifying preemption suggest its intent that federal law *not* preempt state law in other circumstances? If so, the Court's actions fly in the face of congressional intent, raising severe separation-of-powers problems. Even if not, should the Court or the legislature decide whether federal law preempts state law in any particular situation?

The courts have recognized the similarity of the preemption inquiry to other areas of common law.[2] "To determine whether a provision of the bankruptcy code

---

2 Pennsylvania v. Nelson, 350 U.S. 497, 502, 504-05 (1956), articulated three criteria for the courts to use in deciding whether preemption was appropriate:

> First, "[t]he scheme of federal regulation [is] so pervasive as to make reasonable the inference that Congress left no room for the States to supplement it."
>
> * * *
>
> Second, the federal statutes "touch a field in which the federal interest is so dominant that the federal system [must] be assumed to preclude enforcement of state laws on the same subject."
>
> * * *
>
> Third, enforcement of state * * * acts presents a serious danger of conflict with the administration of the federal program.

This formulation resembles the three-part inquiry in *United States v. Kimbell Foods, Inc.* (following) that determines whether the courts should get the content of federal common law by reference to state law or from some other source. In *Nelson*, the emphasis seems much more on the federal interest than on the state's, but the pendulum may now be swinging the other way. In an echo of its growing

empowers the federal courts to create federal common law, we apply much the same analysis used to decide whether preemption is necessary." *Justice v. Valley National Bank,* 849 F.2d 1078, 1087 (8th Cir.1988) (citation omitted). The identity, of course, goes both ways. Accordingly, preemption raises the same institutional problems of federalism and separation of powers.

10. The federal courts were also active with respect to determining limitations periods for federal rights of action without congressionally specified limits until Congress created a default federal limitations provision in 28 U.S.C. § 1658 (1990) for federal claims created after the date of § 1658 for which Congress did not otherwise provide a limitation. That law, however, is more interstitial than the areas discussed above. The note on Filling in Statutory Interstices at page 553 focuses on this aspect of creating federal common law.

United States v. Kimbell Foods, Inc.

Supreme Court of the United States, 1979.
440 U.S. 715.

MR. JUSTICE MARSHALL delivered the opinion of the Court.

We granted certiorari in these cases to determine whether contractual liens arising from certain federal loan programs take precedence over private liens, in the absence of a federal statute setting priorities. To resolve this question, we must decide first whether federal or state law governs the controversies; and second, if federal law applies, whether this Court should fashion a uniform priority rule or incorporate state commercial law. We conclude that the source of law is federal, but that a national rule is unnecessary to protect the federal interests underlying the loan programs. Accordingly, we adopt state law as the appropriate federal rule for establishing the relative priority of these competing federal and private liens.

Take Note

Observe the sequence in which the Court considers the questions. That is always the sequence to follow, and it is important not to conflate the two questions.

---

reluctance to create common law generally, the Burger Court announced in New York State Dept. of Soc. Serv. v. Dublino, 413 U.S. 405 (1973), its presumption of state competence to legislate in the absence of some clear manifestation from Congress that it intends to preempt state action. Bear this in mind when considering the Court's treatment of implied-right-of-action cases arising under federal statutes, at pages 510-35.

I

A

No. 77-1359 involves two contractual security interests in the personal property of O.K. Super Markets, Inc. Both interests were perfected pursuant to Texas' Uniform Commercial Code (UCC). The United States' lien secures a loan guaranteed by the Small Business Administration (SBA). The private lien, which arises from security agreements that preceded the federal guarantee, secures advances respondent made after the federal guarantee.

In 1968, O.K. Super Markets borrowed $27,000 from Kimbell Foods, Inc. (Kimbell), a grocery wholesaler. Two security agreements identified the supermarket's equipment and merchandise as collateral. The agreements also contained a standard **"dragnet" clause** providing that this collateral would secure future advances from Kimbell to O.K. Super Markets. Kimbell properly perfected its security interests by filing financing statements with the Texas Secretary of State according to Texas law.

What's That?

A dragnet clause, also known as a "Mother Hubbard" clause or a "cross-collateral clause," makes collateral for one loan also collateral for future loans from the same lender. Black's Law Dictionary notes that it is sometimes referred to as an "anaconda clause."

In February 1969, O.K. Super Markets obtained a $300,000 loan from Republic National Bank of Dallas (Republic). The bank accepted as security the same property specified in Kimbell's 1968 agreements, and filed a financing statement with the Texas Secretary of State to perfect its security interest. The SBA guaranteed 90% of this loan under the Small Business Act, which authorizes such assistance but, with one exception, does not specify priority rules to govern the SBA's security interests.

O.K. Super Markets used the Republic loan proceeds to satisfy the remainder of the 1968 obligation and to discharge an indebtedness for inventory purchased from Kimbell on open account. Kimbell continued credit sales to O.K. Super Markets until the balance due reached $18,258.57 on January 15, 1971. Thereupon, Kimbell initiated state proceedings against O.K. Super Markets to recover this inventory debt.

Shortly before Kimbell filed suit, O.K. Super Markets had defaulted on the SBA-guaranteed loan. Republic assigned its security interest to the SBA in late December 1970, and recorded the assignment with Texas authorities on January 21, 1971. The United States then honored its guarantee and paid Republic $252,331.93 (90% of the outstanding indebtedness) on February 3, 1971. That same day, O.K. Super Markets, with the approval of its creditors, sold its equipment and inventory and placed the proceeds in escrow pending resolution of the competing claims to the funds. Approximately one year later, the state court entered judgment against O.K. Super Markets, and awarded Kimbell $24,445.37, representing the inventory debt, plus interest and attorney's fees.

Kimbell thereafter brought the instant action to foreclose on its lien, claiming that its security interest in the escrow fund was superior to the SBA's. The District Court held for the Government. On determining that federal law controlled the controversy, the court applied principles developed by this Court to afford federal statutory tax liens special priority over state and private liens where the governing statute does not specify priorities. Under these rules, the lien "first in time" is "first in right." However, to be considered first in time, the nonfederal lien must be "choate," that is, sufficiently specific, when the federal lien arises. A state-created lien is not choate until the "identity of the lienor, the property subject to the lien, and the amount of the lien are established." Failure to meet any one of these conditions forecloses priority over the federal lien, even if under state law the nonfederal lien was enforceable for all purposes when the federal lien arose.

Because Kimbell did not reduce its lien to judgment until February 1972, and the federal lien had been created either in 1969, when Republic filed its financing statement, or in 1971, when Republic recorded its assignment, the District Court concluded that respondent's lien was inchoate when the federal lien arose. Alternatively, the court held that even under state law, the SBA lien was superior to Kimbell's claim because the future advance clauses in the 1968 agreements were not intended to secure the debts arising from O.K. Super Market's subsequent inventory purchases.

The Court of Appeals reversed. It agreed that federal law governs the rights of the United States under its SBA loan program and that the "first in time, first in right" priority principle should control the competing claims. However, the court refused to extend the choateness rule to situations in which the Federal Government was not an involuntary creditor of tax delinquents, but rather a voluntary commercial lender. Instead, it fashioned a new federal rule for determining which lien was first in time, and concluded that "in the context of competing state security interests arising under the U.C.C.," the first to meet UCC perfection requirements achieved priority.[9]

The Court of Appeals then considered which lien qualified as first perfected. Disagreeing with the District Court, the court determined that, under Texas law, the 1968 security agreements covered Kimbell's future advances, and that the liens securing those advances dated from the filing of the security agreements before

9 In so holding, the Court of Appeals refused to formulate a federal doctrine of general applicability, "leav[ing] for another day" questions involving the priority of other nonfederal liens, such as state tax and mechanic's liens.

the federal lien arose. But the Court of Appeals did not adopt Texas law. Rather, it proceeded to decide whether the future advances should receive the same treatment under federal common law. After surveying three possible approaches,[10] the court held that Kimbell's future advances dated back to the 1968 agreements, and therefore took precedence over Republic's 1969 loan.

B

At issue in No. 77-1644 is whether a federal contractual security interest in a tractor is superior to a subsequent repairman's lien in the same property. From 1970 to 1972, Ralph Bridges obtained several loans from the Farmers Home Administration (FHA), under the Consolidated Farmers Home Administration Act of 1961. Like the Small Business Act, this statute does not establish rules of priority. To secure the FHA loans, the agency obtained a security interest in Bridges' crops and farm equipment, which it perfected by filing a standard FHA financing statement with Georgia officials on February 2, 1972. Bridges subsequently took his tractor to respondent Crittenden for repairs on numerous occasions, accumulating unpaid repair bills of over $1,600. On December 21, 1973, Bridges again had respondent repair the tractor, at a cost of $543.81. When Bridges could not pay the balance of $2,151.28, respondent retained the tractor and acquired a lien therein under Georgia law.

On May 1, 1975, after Bridges had filed for bankruptcy and had been discharged from his debts,[12] the United States instituted this action against Crittenden to obtain possession of the tractor. The District Court rejected the Government's claim that the FHA's security interest was superior to respondent's, and granted summary judgment for respondent on alternative grounds. First, it held that the agency had not properly perfected its security interest because the financing statement inadequately described the collateral. Second, it found that even if the description were sufficient, both federal and state law accorded priority to respondent's lien.

The Court of Appeals affirmed in part and reversed in part. It first ruled that "the rights and liabilities of the parties to a suit arising from FHA loan transactions must, under the rationale of the *Clearfield Trust* doctrine, be determined with reference to federal law." In fashioning a federal rule for assessing the sufficiency of the FHA's financing statement, the court elected to follow the Model UCC rather than

10 One approach afforded priority to liens intervening between execution of a security agreement covering future advances and extension of those advances. Another gave priority only to future advances made before the advancing creditor received actual notice of an intervening lien, while a third rule afforded priority regardless of actual notice. The court rejected the first option and found that Kimbell would prevail under either of the other two since it did not have notice of the SBA guarantee.

12 Bridges' bankruptcy did not affect the relative priority of the Government and respondent. The priority rights afforded the United States under § 64a of the Bankruptcy Act do not defeat valid preexisting liens.

to incorporate Georgia law. And, it determined that the description of the collateral was adequate under the Model UCC to perfect the FHA's security interest.

The Court of Appeals then addressed the priority question and concluded that neither state law nor the first-in-time, first-in-right and choateness doctrines were appropriate to resolve the conflicting claims. In their place, the court devised a special "federal commercial law rule," using the Model UCC and the Tax Lien Act of 1966 as guides. This rule would give priority to repairman's liens over the Government's previously perfected consensual security interests when the repairman continuously possesses the property from the time his lien arises. Applying its rule, the Court of Appeals concluded that Crittenden's lien for only the final $543.81 repair bill took precedence over the FHA's security interest.

II

This Court has consistently held that federal law governs questions involving the rights of the United States arising under nationwide federal programs. * * *

Guided by these principles, we think it clear that the priority of liens stemming from federal lending programs must be determined with reference to federal law. The SBA and FHA unquestionably perform federal functions within the meaning of *Clearfield*. Since the agencies derive their authority to effectuate loan transactions from specific Acts of Congress passed in the exercise of a "constitutional function or power," their rights, as well, should derive from a federal source. When Government activities "aris[e] from and bea[r] heavily upon a federal * * * program," the Constitution and Acts of Congress " 'require' otherwise than that state law govern of its own force." In such contexts, federal interests are sufficiently implicated to warrant the protection of federal law.

That the statutes authorizing these federal lending programs do not specify the appropriate rule of decision in no way limits the reach of federal law. It is precisely when Congress has not spoken " 'in an area comprising issues substantially related to an established program of government operation,' " that *Clearfield* directs federal courts to fill the interstices of federal legislation "according to their own standards."

Federal law therefore controls the Government's priority rights. The more difficult task, to which we turn, is giving content to this federal rule.

III

Controversies directly affecting the operations of federal programs, although governed by federal law, do not inevitably require resort to uniform federal rules. Whether to adopt state law or to fashion a nationwide federal rule is a matter of judicial policy "dependent upon a variety of considerations always relevant to the nature of the specific governmental interests and to the effects upon them of applying state law."[21]

Undoubtedly, federal programs that "by their nature are and must be uniform in character throughout the Nation" necessitate formulation of controlling federal rules. Conversely, when there is little need for a nationally uniform body of law, state law may be incorporated as the federal rule of decision. Apart from considerations of uniformity, we must also determine whether application of state law would frustrate specific objectives of the federal programs. If so, we must fashion special rules solicitous of those federal interests. Finally, our choice-of-law inquiry must consider the extent to which application of a federal rule would disrupt commercial relationships predicated on state law.

The Government argues that effective administration of its lending programs requires uniform federal rules of priority. It contends further that resort to any rules other than first in time, first in right and choateness would conflict with protectionist fiscal policies underlying the programs. We are unpersuaded that, in the circumstances presented here, nationwide standards favoring claims of the United States are necessary to ease program administration or to safeguard the Federal Treasury from defaulting debtors. Because the state commercial codes "furnish convenient solutions in no way inconsistent with adequate protection of the federal interest[s]," we decline to override intricate state laws of general applicability on which private creditors base their daily commercial transactions.

A

Incorporating state law to determine the rights of the United States as against private creditors would in no way hinder administration of the SBA and FHA loan programs. In *United States v. Yazell*, this Court rejected the argument, similar to the Government's here, that a need for uniformity precluded application of state coverture rules to an SBA loan contract. Because SBA operations were "specifically and in great detail adapted to state law," the federal interest in supplanting "important and carefully evolved state arrangements designed to serve multiple purposes" was minimal. Our conclusion that compliance with state law would produce no hardship on the agency was also based on the SBA's practice of "individually negotiat[ing] in painfully particularized detail" each loan transaction. These observations apply with equal force here and compel us again to reject

21 As explained by one commentator:

Whether state law is to be incorporated as a matter of federal common law * * * involves the * * * problem of the relationship of a particular issue to a going federal program. The question of judicial incorporation can only arise in an area which is sufficiently close to a national operation to establish competence in the federal courts to choose the governing law, and yet not so close as clearly to require the application of a single nationwide rule of substance.

generalized pleas for uniformity as substitutes for concrete evidence that adopting state law would adversely affect administration of the federal programs.

* * * FHA regulations expressly incorporate state law. They mandate compliance with state procedures for perfecting and maintaining valid security interests, and highlight those rules that differ from State to State. To ensure that employees are aware of new developments, the FHA also issues "State supplements" to "reflect any State statutory changes in its version of the UCC." Contrary to the Government's claim that the FHA complies only with state procedural rules, the agency's reliance on state law extends to substantive requirements as well. Indeed, applicable regulations suggest that state rules determine the priority of FHA liens when federal statutes or agency regulations are not controlling.

Thus, the agencies' own operating practices belie their assertion that a federal rule of priority is needed to avoid the administrative burdens created by disparate state commercial rules. The programs already conform to each State's commercial standards. By using local lending offices and employees who are familiar with the law of their respective localities, the agencies function effectively without uniform procedures and legal rules.

Nevertheless, the Government maintains that requiring the agencies to assess security arrangements under local law would dictate close scrutiny of each transaction and thereby impede expeditious processing of loans. We disagree. Choosing responsible debtors necessarily requires individualized selection procedures, which the agencies have already implemented in considerable detail. * * * Because each application currently receives individual scrutiny, the agencies can readily adjust loan transactions to reflect state priority rules, just as they consider other factual and legal matters before disbursing Government funds. As we noted in *United States v. Yazell*, these lending programs are distinguishable from "nationwide act[s] of the Federal Government, emanating in a single form from a single source." (Footnote omitted.) Since there is no indication that variant state priority schemes would burden current methods of loan processing, we conclude that considerations of administrative convenience do not warrant adoption of a uniform federal law.

B

The Government argues that applying state law to these lending programs would undermine its ability to recover funds disbursed and therefore would conflict with program objectives. In the Government's view, it is difficult "to identify a material distinction between a dollar received from the collection of taxes and a dollar returned to the Treasury on repayment of a federal loan." Therefore, the agencies conclude, just as "the purpose of the federal tax lien statute to insure prompt and certain collection of taxes" justified our imposition of the first-in-time and choateness doctrines in the tax lien context, the federal interest in recovering on loans compels similar legal protection of the agencies' consensual liens. * * *

That collection of taxes is vital to the functioning, indeed existence, of government cannot be denied. Congress recognized as much over 100 years ago when it authorized creation of federal tax liens. The importance of securing adequate revenues to discharge national obligations justifies the extraordinary priority accorded federal tax liens through the choateness and first-in-time doctrines. By contrast, when the United States operates as a moneylending institution under carefully circumscribed programs, its interest in recouping the limited sums advanced is of a different order. Thus, there is less need here than in the tax lien area to invoke protective measures against defaulting debtors in a manner disruptive of existing credit markets.

To equate tax liens with these consensual liens also misperceives the principal congressional concerns underlying the respective statutes. The overriding purpose of the tax lien statute obviously is to ensure prompt revenue collection. The same cannot be said of the SBA and FHA lending programs. They are a form of social welfare legislation, primarily designed to assist farmers and businesses that cannot obtain funds from private lenders on reasonable terms. We believe that had Congress intended the private commercial sector, rather than taxpayers in general, to bear the risks of default entailed by these public welfare programs, it would have established a priority scheme displacing state law. Far from doing so, both Congress and the agencies have expressly recognized the priority of certain private liens over the agencies' security interests, thereby indicating that the extraordinary safeguards applied in the tax lien area are unnecessary to maintain the lending programs.

The Government's ability to safeguard its interests in commercial dealings further reveals that the rules developed in the tax lien area are unnecessary here, and that state priority rules would not conflict with federal lending objectives.[37] The United States is an involuntary creditor of delinquent taxpayers, unable to control the factors that make tax collection likely. In contrast, when the United States acts as a lender or guarantor, it does so voluntarily, with detailed knowledge of the borrower's financial status. * * *

The Government nonetheless argues that its opportunity to evaluate the credit worthiness of loan applicants provides minimal safety. Because the SBA and FHA make loans only when private lenders will not, the United States believes that its security interests demand greater protection than ordinary commercial

37 We reject the Government's suggestion that the choateness and first-in-time doctrines are needed to prevent States from "undercutting" the agencies' liens by creating "arbitrary" rules. Adopting state law as an appropriate federal rule does not preclude federal courts from excepting local laws that prejudice federal interests. The issue here, however, involves commercial rules of general applicability, based on codes that are remarkably uniform throughout the Nation.

arrangements. We find this argument unconvincing. The lending agencies do not indiscriminately distribute public funds and hope that reimbursement will follow. SBA loans must be "of such sound value or so secured as reasonably to assure repayment." The FHA operates under a similar restriction. Both agencies have promulgated exhaustive instructions to ensure that loan recipients are financially reliable and to prevent improvident loans. The Government therefore is in substantially the same position as private lenders, and the special status it seeks is unnecessary to safeguard the public fisc. Moreover, Congress' admonitions to extend loans judiciously supports the view that it did not intend to confer special privileges on agencies that enter the commercial field. Accordingly, we agree with the Court of Appeals in [Kimbell Foods' case] that "[a]s a quasi-commercial lender, [the Government] does not require * * * the special priority which it compels as sovereign" in its tax-collecting capacity.

The Federal Tax Lien Act of 1966 provides further evidence that treating the United States like any other lender would not undermine federal interests. These amendments modified the Federal Government's preferred position under the choateness and first-in-time doctrines, and recognized the priority of many state claims over federal tax liens. In enacting this legislation, Congress sought to "improv[e] the status of private secured creditors" and prevent impairment of commercial financing transactions by "moderniz[ing] * * * the relationship of Federal tax liens to the interests of other creditors." This rationale has even greater force when the Government acts as a moneylender. We do not suggest that Congress' actions in the tax lien area control our choice of law in the commercial lien context. But in fashioning federal principles to govern areas left open by Congress, our function is to effectuate congressional policy. To ignore Congress' disapproval of unrestricted federal priority in an area as important to the Nation's stability as taxation would be inconsistent with this function. Thus, without a showing that application of state laws would impair federal operations, we decline to extend to new contexts extraordinary safeguards largely rejected by Congress.

C

In structuring financial transactions, businessmen depend on state commercial law to provide the stability essential for reliable evaluation of the risks involved. However, subjecting federal contractual liens to the doctrines developed in the tax lien area could undermine that stability. Creditors who justifiably rely on state law to obtain superior liens would have their expectations thwarted whenever a federal contractual security interest suddenly appeared and took precedence.

Because the ultimate consequences of altering settled commercial practices are so difficult to foresee, we hesitate to create new uncertainties, in the absence of careful legislative deliberation. Of course, formulating special rules to govern the priority of the federal consensual liens in issue here would be justified if necessary to vindicate important national interests. But neither the Government nor the Court of Appeals advanced any concrete reasons for rejecting well-established commercial rules which have proven workable over time. Thus, the prudent course is to adopt the readymade body of state law as the federal rule of decision until Congress strikes a different accommodation.

IV

Accordingly, we hold that, absent a congressional directive, the relative priority of private liens and consensual liens arising from these Government lending programs is to be determined under nondiscriminatory state laws. * * *

So ordered.

Notes and Questions

1. Justice Marshall begins by "conclud[ing] that the source of the law is federal." Why does federal law govern? Is this decision consistent with *United States v. Yazell*, discussed in note 7 at page 447-48? What view of *Yazell* does the *Kimbell Foods* Court seem to have?

2. In *Butner v. United States*, 440 U.S. 48 (1979), a trustee in bankruptcy and a second mortgagee each claimed rents owed the mortgagor during its bankruptcy before a foreclosure sale of the mortgaged property. The issue was whether a federal rule or state law should govern. In similar disputes, the Third and Seventh Circuits had adopted a federal rule giving the mortgagee an automatic security interest in rents upon default and before foreclosure. Five circuits referred to state law; some states accorded mortgagees an automatic security interest while others did not. The *Butner* Court ruled that state law (in that case North Carolina law) should govern. Under that law, a mortgagee was required to take affirmative steps after default to obtain a security interest.

Explaining its decision to endorse the approach of the circuit majority, the Court noted:

> The constitutional authority of Congress to establish "uniform Laws on the subject of Bankruptcies throughout the United States" would clearly encompass a federal statute defining the mortgagee's interest in the rents and profits earned by property in a bankrupt estate. But Congress has not chosen to exercise its power to fashion any such rule. The Bankruptcy Act does include provisions invalidating certain security interests as fraudulent, or as improper preferences over general creditors. Apart from these provisions, however, Congress has generally left the determination of property rights in the assets of a bankrupt's estate to state law.

Butner raises several questions, either alone or in combination with *Kimbell Foods* and Yazell.

a) Can Congress overrule the Court's decision in Butner? That is, is there federal competence in this area generally, or did the Court mandate the application of state law because it was constitutionally compelled to do so under Erie?

b) Assuming Butner addresses an area where there is federal competence, if Congress passed a statute embodying the rule that the Third and Seventh Circuits had used before Butner, would the Supreme Court be obligated to yield to that rule?

c) If the Supreme Court must yield to a statute creating a federal substantive rule for cases like Butner, does the absence of legislation connote Congress's intention that state law not be displaced? Suppose Congress passed a law asserting that state law should govern. Would that control, even if the Supreme Court later decided that the minority circuits had been correct all along and that there were powerful reasons of federal policy that required the protection of a federal substantive rule?

d) In Erie, the Court applied state law as a matter of constitutional compulsion; state law applied *because* it was state law, not because its content appealed to the Court as a rule of decision. *Kimbell Foods* explicitly adopted state law as the content of federal common law. Is the same true in *Butner*? Does it make any difference?

3. After *Kimbell Foods,* what are federal agencies to do in order to protect themselves? Must they now blindly enter commercial transactions and take their chances according to which state or states a particular transaction happens to touch? Does *Kimbell Foods* enshrine unpredictability?

4. The Court considered, but did not adopt, a uniform federal rule. If it had, federal uniformity would have been obtained at the expense of intrastate uniformity, since the uniform federal rule would have diverged from the state rules in at least some jurisdictions. What problems might that create?

Boyle v. United Technologies Corporation

Supreme Court of the United States, 1988.
487 U.S. 500.

JUSTICE SCALIA delivered the opinion of the Court.

This case requires us to decide when a contractor providing military equipment to the Federal Government can be held liable under state tort law for injury caused by a design defect.

I

On April 27, 1983, David A. Boyle, a United States Marine helicopter copilot, was killed when the CH-53D helicopter in which he was flying crashed off the coast of Virginia Beach, Virginia, during a training exercise. Although Boyle survived the impact of the crash, he was unable to escape from the helicopter and drowned. Boyle's father, petitioner here, brought this diversity action in Federal District Court against the Sikorsky Division of United Technologies Corporation (Sikorsky), which built the helicopter for the United States.

At trial, petitioner presented two theories of liability under Virginia tort law that were submitted to the jury. First, petitioner alleged that Sikorsky had defectively repaired a device called the servo in the helicopter's automatic flight control system, which allegedly malfunctioned and caused the crash. Second, petitioner alleged that Sikorsky had defectively designed the copilot's emergency escape system: the escape hatch opened out instead of in (and was therefore ineffective in a submerged craft because of water pressure), and access to the escape hatch handle was obstructed by other equipment. The jury returned a general verdict in favor of petitioner and awarded him $725,000 * * * .

The Court of Appeals reversed and remanded with directions that judgment be entered for Sikorsky. It found, as a matter of Virginia law, that Boyle had failed to meet his burden of demonstrating that the repair work performed by Sikorsky, as opposed to work that had been done by the Navy, was responsible for the alleged malfunction of the flight control system. It also found, as a matter of federal law, that Sikorsky could not be held liable for the allegedly defective design of the escape hatch because, on the evidence presented, it satisfied the requirements of the "military contractor defense," which the court had recognized the same day * * * .

* * *

II

Petitioner's broadest contention is that, in the absence of legislation specifically immunizing Government contractors from liability for design defects, there is no basis for judicial recognition of such a defense. We disagree. In most fields of activity, to be sure, this Court has refused to find federal preemption of state law in the absence of either a clear statutory prescription or a direct conflict between federal and state law. But we have held that a few areas, involving "uniquely federal interests," are so committed by the Constitution and laws of the United States to federal control that state law is preempted and replaced, where necessary, by federal law of a content prescribed (absent explicit statutory directive) by the courts—so-called "federal common law."

The dispute in the present case borders upon two areas that we have found to involve such "uniquely federal interests." We have held that obligations to and rights of the United States under its contracts are governed exclusively by federal law. The present case does not involve an obligation to the United States under its contract, but rather liability to third persons. That liability may be styled one in tort, but it arises out of performance of the contract—and traditionally has been regarded as sufficiently related to the contract that until 1962 Virginia would generally allow design defect suits only by the purchaser and those in privity with the seller.

Food for Thought

In light of what the Court did in *Kimbell Foods*, is this a strictly accurate characterization?

Another area that we have found to be of peculiarly federal concern, warranting the displacement of state law, is the civil liability of federal officials for actions taken in the course of their duty. We have held in many contexts that the scope of that liability is controlled by federal law. The present case involves an independent contractor performing its obligation under a procurement contract, rather than an official performing his duty as a federal employee, but there is obviously implicated the same interest in getting the Government's work done.[1]

We think the reasons for considering these closely related areas to be of "uniquely federal" interest apply as well to the civil liabilities arising out of the performance of federal procurement contracts * * * .

[I]t is plain that the Federal Government's interest in the procurement of equipment is implicated by suits such as the present one—even though the dispute is one between private parties. It is true that where "litigation is purely between private parties and does not touch the rights and duties of the United States," federal law does not govern. Thus for example, in *Miree v. Dekalb County*, which involved the question whether certain private parties could sue as third-party beneficiaries to an agreement between a municipality and the Federal Aviation Administration, we found that state law was not displaced because "the operations of the United States in connection with FAA grants such as these * * * would [not] be burdened" by allowing state law to determine whether third-party beneficiaries could sue, and because "any federal interest in the outcome of the [dispute] before us '[was] far too speculative, far too remote a possibility to justify the application of federal law to transactions essentially of local concern.' " But

1 The dissent misreads our discussion here to "intimat[e] that the immunity [of federal officials] * * * might extend * * * to nongovernment employees" such as a government contractor. But we do not address this issue, as it is not before us. We cite these cases merely to demonstrate that the liability of independent contractors performing work for the Federal Government, like the liability of federal officials, is an area of uniquely federal interest.

the same is not true here. The imposition of liability on Government contractors will directly affect the terms of Government contracts: either the contractor will decline to manufacture the design specified by the Government, or it will raise its price. Either way, the interests of the United States will be directly affected.

That the procurement of equipment by the United States is an area of uniquely federal interest does not, however, end the inquiry. That merely establishes a necessary, not a sufficient, condition for the displacement of state law.[3] Displacement will occur only where, as we have variously described, a "significant conflict" exists between an identifiable "federal policy or interest and the [operation] of state law," or the application of state law would "frustrate specific objectives" of federal legislation. The conflict with federal policy need not be as sharp as that which must exist for ordinary preemption when Congress legislates "in a field which the States have traditionally occupied." Or to put the point differently, the fact that the area in question is one of unique federal concern changes what would otherwise be a conflict that cannot produce preemption into one that can. But conflict there must be. In some cases, for example where the federal interest requires a uniform rule, the entire body of state law applicable to the area conflicts and is replaced by federal rules. *See, e.g.*, Clearfield Trust * * * . In others, the conflict is more narrow, and only particular elements of state law are superseded.

Food for Thought

Does the Court here eliminate the possibility of ever adopting state law as the content of federal common law? If there must be "significant conflict," how will adopting state law be able to alleviate the conflict? Keep this in mind when you read Semtek, the next principal case.

In Miree, the suit was not seeking to impose upon the person contracting with the Government a duty contrary to the duty imposed by the Government contract. Rather, it was the contractual duty *itself* that the private plaintiff (as third-party beneficiary) sought to enforce. Between Miree and the present case, it is easy to conceive of an intermediate situation, in which the duty sought to be imposed on the contractor is not identical to one assumed under the contract, but is also not contrary to any assumed. If, for example, the United States contracts for the purchase and installation of an air conditioning unit, specifying the cooling capacity but not the precise manner of construction, a state law imposing upon the manufacturer of such units a duty of care to include a certain safety feature

3 We refer here to the displacement of state law although it is possible to analyze it as the displacement of federal-law reference to state law for the rule of decision. Some of our cases appear to regard the area in which a uniquely federal interest exists as being entirely governed by federal law, with federal law deigning to "borro[w]," or "incorporat[e]" or "adopt" state law except where a significant conflict with federal policy exists. We see nothing to be gained by expanding the theoretical scope of the federal preemption beyond its practical effect, and so adopt the more modest terminology. If the distinction between displacement of state law and displacement of federal law's incorporation of state law ever makes a practical difference, it at least does not do so in the present case.

would not be a duty identical to anything promised the Government, but neither would it be contrary. The contractor could comply with both its contractual obligations and the state-prescribed duty of care. No one suggests that state law would generally be preempted in this context.

The present case, however, is at the opposite extreme from *Miree.* Here the state-imposed duty of care that is the asserted basis of the contractor's liability (specifically, the duty to equip helicopters with the sort of escape-hatch mechanism petitioner claims was necessary) is precisely contrary to the duty imposed by the Government contract (the duty to manufacture and deliver helicopters with the sort of escape-hatch mechanism shown by the specifications). Even in this sort of situation, it would be unreasonable to say that there is always a "significant conflict" between the state law and a federal policy or interest. If, for example, a federal procurement officer orders, by model number, a quantity of stock helicopters that happen to be equipped with escape hatches opening outward, it is impossible to say that the Government has a significant interest in that particular feature. That would be scarcely more reasonable than saying that a private individual who orders such a craft by model number cannot sue for the manufacturer's negligence because he got precisely what he ordered.

* * *

There is however, a statutory provision that demonstrates the potential for, and suggests the outlines of, "significant conflict" between federal interests and state law in the context of government procurement. In the Federal Tort Claims Act (FTCA), Congress authorized damages to be recovered against the United States for harm caused by the negligent or wrongful conduct of Government employees, to the extent that a private person would be liable under the law of the place where the conduct occurred. It excepted from this consent to suit, however, "[a]ny claim * * * based upon the exercise or performance or the failure to exercise or perform a discretionary function or duty on the part of a federal agency or an employee of the Government, whether or not the discretion involved be abused."

We think that the selection of the appropriate design for military equipment to be used by our Armed Forces is assuredly a discretionary function within the meaning of this provision. It often involves not merely engineering analysis but judgment as to the balancing of many technical, military, and even social considerations, including specifically the trade-off between greater safety and greater combat effectiveness. And we are further of the view that permitting "second-guessing" of these judgments, through state tort suits against contractors[,] would produce the same effect sought to be avoided by the FTCA exemption. The financial burden of judgments against the contractors would ultimately be passed through, substantially if not totally, to the United States itself, since defense contractors will predictably raise their prices to cover, or to insure against, contingent liability for the Government-ordered designs. To put the point differently: It makes little sense to insulate the Government against financial liability for the judgment that a particular feature of military equipment is necessary when the Government produces the equipment itself, but not when it contracts for the production. In sum, we are of the view that state law which holds Government contractors liable for design defects in military equipment does in some circumstances present a "significant conflict" with federal policy and must be displaced.

We agree with the scope of displacement adopted by the Fourth Circuit here * * * . Liability for design defects in military equipment cannot be imposed, pursuant to state law, when (1) the United States approved reasonably precise specifications; (2) the equipment conformed to those specifications; and (3) the supplier warned the United States about the dangers in the use of the equipment that were known to the supplier but not to the United States. The first two of these conditions assure that the suit is within the area where the policy of the "discretionary function" would be frustrated—*i.e.*, they assure that the design feature in question was considered by a Government officer, and not merely by the contractor itself. The third condition is necessary because, in its absence, the displacement of state tort law would create some incentive for the manufacturer to withhold knowledge of risks, since conveying that knowledge might disrupt the contract but withholding it would produce no liability. We adopt this provision lest our effort to protect discretionary functions perversely impede them by cutting off information highly relevant to the discretionary decision.

We have considered the alternative formulation of the Government contractor defense, urged upon us by petitioner * * * . That would preclude suit only if (1) the contractor did not participate, or participated only minimally, in the design of the defective equipment; *or* (2) the contractor timely warned the Government of the risks of the design and notified it of alternative designs reasonably known by it, *and* the Government, although forewarned, clearly authorized the contractor to proceed with the dangerous design. While this formulation may represent a perfectly reasonable tort rule, it is not a rule designed to protect the federal interest embodied in the "discretionary function" exemption. The design ultimately selected may well reflect a significant policy judgment by Government officials whether or not the contractor rather than those officials developed the design. In addition, it does not seem to us sound policy to penalize, and thus deter, active contractor participation in the design process, placing the contractor at risk unless it identifies all design defects.

III

* * *

[The majority decided that the Court of Appeals' opinion was ambiguous as to whether there was sufficient evidence to send the case to the jury under the correct view of the contractor's defense, and so remanded the case for determination of that question.]

JUSTICE BRENNAN, with whom JUSTICE MARSHALL and JUSTICE BLACKMUN join, dissenting.

Lieutenant David A. Boyle died when the CH-53D helicopter he was copiloting spun out of control and plunged into the ocean. We may assume, for purposes of this case, that Lt. Boyle was trapped under water and drowned because respondent United Technologies negligently designed the helicopter's escape hatch. We may further assume that any competent engineer would have discovered and cured the defects, but that they inexplicably escaped respondent's notice. Had respondent designed such a death trap for a commercial firm, Lt. Boyle's family could sue under Virginia tort law and be compensated for his tragic and unnecessary death. But respondent designed the helicopter for the Federal Government, and that, the Court tells us today, makes all the difference: Respondent is immune from liability so long as it obtained approval of "reasonably precise specifications"—perhaps no more than a rubberstamp from a federal procurement officer who might or might not have noticed or cared about the defects, or even had the expertise to discover them.

If respondent's immunity "bore the legitimacy of having been prescribed by the people's elected representatives," we would be duty bound to implement their will, whether or not we approved. *United States v. Johnson* (1987) (dissenting opinion of Scalia, J.). Congress, however, has remained silent—and conspicuously so, having resisted a sustained campaign by Government contractors to legislate for them some defense. The Court—unelected and unaccountable to the people—has unabashedly stepped into the breach to legislate a rule denying Lt. Boyle's family the compensation that state law assures them. This time the injustice is of this Court's own making.

Worse yet, the injustice will extend far beyond the facts of this case, for the Court's newly discovered Government contractor defense is breathtakingly sweeping. It applies not only to military equipment like the CH-53D helicopter, but (so far as

Food for Thought

Justice Brennan here cited six bills that failed to pass, two directly limiting government contractors' liability and four providing indemnity from the federal government. Witnesses in committee hearings suggested two reasons to refuse indemnity: its potential effect on the federal treasury and that it would remove a prime incentive for contractors to maintain high standards. In terms of the legitimacy of federal common law, does it make any difference which of those two reasons underlay Congress's inaction? Justice Scalia's majority opinion does not even acknowledge the bills' existence. Could the majority respond to that evidence and preserve the result in *Boyle*?

I can tell) to any made-to-order gadget that the Federal Government might purchase after previewing plans—from NASA's Challenger space shuttle to the Postal Service's old mail cars. The contractor may invoke the defense in suits brought not only by military personnel like Lt. Boyle, or Government employees, but by anyone injured by a Government contractor's negligent design, including, for example, the children who might have died had respondent's helicopter crashed on the beach. It applies even if the Government has not intentionally sacrificed safety for other interests like speed or efficiency, and, indeed, even if the equipment is not of a type that is typically considered dangerous; thus, the contractor who designs a Government building can invoke the defense when the elevator cable snaps or the walls collapse. And the defense is invocable regardless of how blatant or easily remedied the defect, so long as the contractor missed it and the specifications approved by the Government, however unreasonably dangerous, were "reasonably precise."

In my view, this Court lacks both authority and expertise to fashion such a rule, whether to protect the Treasury of the United States or the coffers of industry. Because I would leave that exercise of legislative power to Congress, where our Constitution places it, I would reverse the Court of Appeals and reinstate petitioner's jury award.

* * *

II

Congress has not decided to supersede state law here (if anything, it has decided not to) and the Court does not pretend that its newly manufactured "Government contractor defense" fits within any of the handful of "narrow areas" of "uniquely federal interests" in which we have heretofore done so. Rather, the Court creates a new category of "uniquely federal interests" out of a synthesis of two whose origins predate *Erie* itself: the interest in administering the "obligations to and rights of the United States under its contracts," and the interest in regulating the "civil liability of federal officials for actions taken in the course of their duty." This case is, however, simply a suit between two private parties. We have steadfastly declined to impose federal contract law on relationships that are collateral to a federal contract, or to extend the federal employee's immunity beyond federal employees. And the Court's ability to list two, or ten, inapplicable areas of "uniquely federal interest" does not support its conclusion that the liability of Government contractors is so "clear and substantial" an interest that this Court must step in lest state law does "major damage."

A

The proposition that federal common law continues to govern the "obligations to and rights of the United States under its contracts" is nearly as old as *Erie* itself. Federal law typically controls when the Federal Government is a party to a suit involving its rights or obligations under a contract * * * . But it is by now established that our power to create federal common law controlling the Federal Government's contractual rights and obligations does not translate into a power to prescribe rules that cover all transactions or contractual relationships collateral to Government contracts.

In *Miree v. DeKalb County,* for example, the county was contractually obligated under a grant agreement with the Federal Aviation Administration (FAA) to " 'restrict the use of land adjacent to * * * the Airport to activities and purposes compatible with normal airport operations including landing and takeoff of aircraft.' " At issue was whether the county breached its contractual obligation by operating a garbage dump adjacent to the airport, which allegedly attracted the swarm of birds that caused a plane crash. Federal common law would undoubtedly have controlled in any suit by the Federal Government to enforce the provision against the county or to collect damages for its violation. The diversity suit, however, was brought not by the Government, but by assorted private parties injured in some way by the accident. We observed that "the operations of the United States in connection with FAA grants such as these are undoubtedly of considerable magnitude," and that "the United States has a substantial interest in regulating aircraft travel and promoting air travel safety." Nevertheless, we held that state law should govern the claim because "only the rights of private litigants are at issue here," and the claim against the county "will have *no direct effect upon the United States or its treasury,*" (emphasis added).

Miree relied heavily on *Parnell* and *Wallis,* the former involving commercial paper issued by the United States and the latter involving property rights in federal land. In the former case, Parnell cashed certain government bonds that had been stolen from their owner, a bank. It is beyond dispute that federal law would have governed the United States' duty to pay the value bonds upon presentation; we held as much in *Clearfield Trust.* But the central issue in *Parnell,* a diversity suit, was whether the victim of the theft could recover the money paid to Parnell. That issue, we held, was governed by state law, because the "litigation [was] purely between private parties and [did] *not touch the rights and duties of the United States.*" ([E]mphasis added).

The same was true in *Wallis,* which also involved a Government contract—a lease issued by the United States to a private party under the Mineral Leasing Act of 1920—governed entirely by federal law. Again, the relationship at issue in this diversity case was collateral to the Government contract: It involved the validity of contractual arrangements between the lessee and other private parties, not between the lessee and the Federal Government. Even though a federal statute authorized certain assignments of lease rights, and imposed certain conditions on their validity, we held that state law, not federal common law, governed their validity because application of state law would present "no significant threat to any identifiable federal policy or interest."

Here, * * * a Government contract governed by federal common law looms in the background. But here, too, the United States is not a party to the suit and the suit neither "touch[es] the rights and duties of the United States," nor has a "direct effect upon the United States or its Treasury." The relationship at issue is at best collateral to the Government contract. We have no greater power to displace state law governing the collateral relationship in the Government procurement realm than we had to dictate federal rules governing equally collateral relationships in the areas of aviation, Government-issued commercial paper, or federal lands.

That the Government might "have to pay higher prices for what it orders if delivery in accordance with the contract exposes the seller to potential liability" does not distinguish this case. Each of the cases just discussed declined to extend the reach of federal common law despite the assertion of comparable interests that would have affected the terms of the Government contract—whether its price or its substance—just as "*directly*" (or indirectly). Third-party beneficiaries can sue under a county's contract with the FAA, for example, even though—as the Court's focus on the absence of "*direct* effect on the United States or its Treasury," (emphasis added), suggests—counties will likely pass on the costs to the Government in future contract negotiations. Similarly, we held that state law may govern the circumstances under which stolen federal bonds can be recovered, notwithstanding Parnell's argument that "the value of bonds to the first purchaser and hence their salability by the Government would be materially affected." As in each of the cases declining to extend the traditional reach of federal law of contracts beyond the rights and duties of the Federal Government, "any federal interest in the outcome of the question before us 'is far too speculative, far too remote a possibility to justify the application of federal law to transactions essentially of local concern.' "

B

Our "uniquely federal interest" in the tort liability of affiliates of the Federal Government is equally narrow * * * . Never before have we so much as intimated that the immunity (or the "uniquely federal interest" that justifies it) might extend beyond * * * to cover also nongovernment employees whose authority to act is independent of any source of federal law and that are as far removed from the "functioning of the Federal Government" as is a Government contractor.

The historical narrowness of the federal interest and the immunity is hardly accidental. A federal officer exercises statutory authority, which not only provides the necessary basis for the immunity in positive law, but also permits us confidently to presume that interference with the exercise of discretion undermines congressional will. In contrast, a Government contractor acts independently of any congressional enactment. Thus, immunity for a contractor lacks both the positive law basis and the presumption that it furthers congressional will.

Moreover, even within the category of congressionally authorized tasks, we have deliberately restricted the scope of immunity to circumstances in which "the contributions of immunity to effective government in particular contexts outweigh the perhaps recurring harm to individual citizens," because immunity "contravenes the basic tenet that individuals be held accountable for their wrongful conduct." The extension of immunity to Government contractors skews the balance we have historically struck. On the one hand, whatever marginal effect contractor immunity might have on the "effective administration of policies of government," its "harm to individual citizens" is more severe than in the Government-employee context. Our observation that "there are * * * other sanctions than civil tort suits available to deter the executive official who may be prone to exercise his functions in an unworthy and irresponsible manner," offers little deterrence to the Government contractor. On the other hand, a grant of immunity to Government contractors could not advance "the fearless, vigorous, and effective administration of policies of government" nearly as much as does the current immunity for Government employees. In the first place, the threat of a tort suit is less likely to influence the conduct of an industrial giant than that of a lone civil servant, particularly since the work of a civil servant is significantly less profitable, and significantly more likely to be the subject of a vindictive lawsuit. In fact, were we to take seriously the Court's assertion that contractors pass their costs—including presumably litigation costs—through, "substantially if not totally, to the United States," the threat of a tort suit should have only marginal impact on the conduct of Government contractors. More importantly, inhibition of the Government official who actually sets Government policy presents a greater threat to the "administration of policies of government," than does inhibition of a private contractor, whose role is devoted largely to assessing the technological feasibility and cost of satisfying the Government's predetermined needs. Similarly, unlike tort suits against Government officials, tort suits against Government contractors would rarely "consume time and energies" that "would otherwise be devoted to governmental service."

In short, because the essential justifications for official immunity do not support an extension to the Government contractor, it is no surprise that we have never extended it that far.

III

[T]he Court invokes the discretionary function exception of the Federal Tort Claims Act (FTCA). The Court does not suggest that the exception has any direct bearing here, for petitioner has sued a private manufacturer (not the Federal Government) under Virginia law (not the FTCA) * * * .

[T]he Court * * * reason[s] that federal common law must immunize Government contractors from state tort law to prevent erosion of the discretionary function exception's *policy* of foreclosing judicial " 'second-guessing' " of discretionary governmental decisions. The erosion the Court fears apparently is rooted not in a concern that suits against Government contractors will prevent them from designing, or the Government from commissioning the design of, precisely the product the Government wants, but in the concern that such suits might preclude the Government from purchasing the desired product at the price it wants: "The financial burden of judgments against the contractors," the Court fears, "would ultimately be passed through, substantially if not totally, to the United States itself."

Even granting the Court's factual premise, which is by no means self-evident, the Court cites no authority for the proposition that burdens imposed on Government contractors, but passed on to the Government, burden the Government in a way that justifies extension of its immunity. However substantial such indirect burdens may be, we have held in other contexts that they are legally irrelevant. * * *

Moreover, the statutory basis on which the Court's rule of federal common law totters is more unstable than any we have ever adopted. In the first place, we rejected an analytically similar attempt to construct federal common law out of the FTCA when we held that the Government's waiver of sovereign immunity for the torts of its employees does not give the Government an implied right of indemnity from them, even though * * * "[t]he financial burden placed on the United States by the Tort Claims Act [could conceivably be] so great that government employees should be required to carry part of the burden." So too here, the FTCA's retention of sovereign immunity for the Government's discretionary acts does not imply a defense for the benefit of contractors who participate in those acts, even though they might pass on the financial burden to the United States. In either case, the most that can be said is that the position "asserted, though the product of a law Congress passed, is a matter on which Congress has not taken a position."

Here, even that much is an overstatement, for the Government's immunity for discretionary functions is not even "a product of" the FTCA. Before Congress enacted the FTCA (when sovereign immunity barred any tort suit against the Federal Government) we perceived no need for a rule of federal common law to reinforce the Government's immunity by shielding also parties who might contractually pass costs on to it. Nor did we (or any other court of which I am aware) identify a special category of "discretionary" functions for which sovereign immunity was so crucial that a government contractor who exercised discretion should share the Government's immunity from state tort law.

* * * There is no more reason for federal common law to shield contractors now that the Government is liable for some torts than there was when the Government was liable for none * * * .

* * *

IV

At bottom, the Court's analysis is premised on the proposition that any tort liability indirectly absorbed by the Government so burdens governmental functions as to compel us to act when Congress has not. That proposition is by no means uncontroversial. The tort system is premised on the assumption that the imposition of liability encourages actors to prevent any injury whose expected cost exceeds the cost of prevention. If the system is working as it should, Government contractors will design equipment to avoid certain injuries (like the deaths of soldiers or Government employees), which would be certain to burden the Government. The Court therefore has no basis for its assumption that tort liability will result in a net burden on the Government (let alone a clearly excessive net burden) rather than a net gain.

Perhaps tort liability is an inefficient means of ensuring the quality of design efforts, but "[w]hatever the merits of the policy" the Court wishes to implement, "its conversion into law is a proper subject for congressional action, not for any creative power of ours." It is, after all, "Congress, not this Court or the other federal courts, [that] is the custodian of the national purse. By the same token [Congress] is the primary and most often the exclusive arbiter of federal fiscal affairs. And these comprehend, as we have said, securing the treasury or the Government against financial losses *however inflicted* * * * ." ([E]mphasis added).

Were I a legislator, I would probably vote against any law absolving multibillion dollar private enterprises from answering for their tragic mistakes, at least if that law were justified by no more than the unsupported speculation that their liability might ultimately burden the United States Treasury. Some of my colleagues here would evidently vote otherwise (as they have here), but that should not matter here. We are judges not legislators, and the vote is not ours to cast.

I respectfully dissent.

JUSTICE STEVENS, dissenting.

When judges are asked to embark on a lawmaking venture, I believe they should carefully consider whether they, or a legislative body, are better equipped to perform the task at hand. There are instances of so-called interstitial lawmaking that inevitably become part of the judicial process. But when we are asked to create an entirely new doctrine—to answer "questions of policy on which Congress has not spoken"—we have a special duty to identify the proper decisionmaker before trying to make the proper decision.

When the novel question of policy involves a balancing of the conflicting interests in the efficient operation of a massive governmental program and the protection of the rights of the individual—whether in the social welfare context, the civil service context, or the military procurement context—I feel very deeply that we should defer to the expertise of the Congress. * * * "The selection of that policy which is most advantageous to the whole involves a host of considerations that must be weighed and appraised. That function is more appropriately for those who write the laws, rather than for those who interpret them."

I respectfully dissent.

Notes and Questions

1. a) Suppose Congress had passed a statute saying that state law should govern claims against government contractors. Would the majority be able to reach the same result in *Boyle,* or would doing so pose insurmountable separation-of-powers problems?

b) Suppose instead that Congress passed a statute denying government contractors immunity from tort liability arising out of design or manufacturing defects. Would that preclude the result in *Boyle*?

4. Does the majority suggest that in any area that implicates the "interest in getting the Government's work done * * * " there is a unique federal interest that displaces state law? If so, is Justice Brennan correct that the majority displaces not merely state law but also Congress's function? If not, what are the express or implied boundaries of the decision?

5. Justice Scalia says federal common law is appropriate only when there is a unique federal interest and significant conflict between that interest and state law. Does this prove too much? The more significant the conflict, the more likely Congress was aware of it. Could congressional silence then signify that Congress did not want federal law to govern?

6. Would not the most conservative, judicially restrained course of action in *Boyle* have been to refuse the immunity, leaving the ensuing plaintiff's judgment as a spur to Congress to correct the situation if necessary (and to indemnify United Technologies in a private bill, if it saw fit)?

7. Justice Scalia argues with some force the analogy between *Boyle* and the Federal Torts Claims Act's exclusion of governmental liability in suits based on discretionary functions. Is there any difference between the government's waiver of sovereign immunity and a private contractor's liability for negligence? Is Justice Scalia saying that the government's sovereign immunity extends to those with whom the government contracts? Could even Congress do that?

8. a) In *United States v. Standard Oil Co.*, 332 U.S. 301 (1947), was an action by the United States to recover medical expenses and reimbursement for the pay of a soldier who suffered injury and incapacitation owing to Standard Oil's negligence. The Court refused to imply an action on behalf of the United States, leaving determination of federal fiscal policy to Congress, as "custodian of the national purse." Why did it not do so here? What distinguishes *Standard Oil* from *Boyle*? Arguably the impact on the federal treasury was far more direct in *Standard Oil*.

b) *In re "Agent Orange" Product Liability Litigation*, 635 F.2d 987 (2d Cir. 1980), involved consolidated actions by veterans against various American companies to recover for injuries from Agent Orange, a defoliant that defendants had supplied to the military. Plaintiffs urged the court to recognize a federal common law right to recover, arguing that *Clearfield* compelled it. The court responded:

> The present litigation is fundamentally different from * * * *Clearfield Trust* with respect to both uniformity interest and substantive interest in the content of the rules to be applied. Since this litigation is between private parties and no substantial rights or duties of the government hinge on its outcome, there is no federal interest in uniformity for its own sake.
>
> * * *
>
> Thus, the prospect of uniformity is insufficient reason to invoke federal common law in private litigation; and if federal common law were invoked, it would not ensure uniformity since frequently that law takes its substance from local law.
>
> The second fundamental difference between the present litigation and the *Clearfield Trust* type of case is that in the latter, the government's substantive interest in the litigation is essentially monothetic, in that it is concerned only with preserving the federal fisc, whereas here the government has two interests; and here the two interests have been placed in sharp contrast with one another. Thus, the government has an interest in the welfare of its veterans; they have given of themselves in the most fundamental way possible in the national interest. But the government also has an interest in the suppliers of its materiel; imposition, for example, of strict liability as contended for by plaintiffs would affect the government's ability to procure materiel without the exaction of significantly higher prices, or the attachment of onerous conditions, or the demand of indemnification or the like. * * * [U]nlike a simple uniformity interest, neither the government's interest in its veterans nor its interest in its suppliers is content-neutral. Each interest will be furthered only if the federal rule of law to be applied favors that particular group.

> The extent to which either group should be favored, and its welfare deemed "paramount" * * * is preeminently a policy determination of the sort reserved in the first instance for Congress. The welfare of veterans and that of military suppliers are clearly federal concerns which Congress should appropriately consider in the setting policy for the governance of the nation, and it is properly left to Congress in the first instance to strike the balance between the conflicting interests of the veterans and the contractors, and thereby identify federal policy.

The majority declined to create the common law cause of action. Since the plaintiffs had predicated jurisdiction on 28 U.S.C.A. § 1331 and, after the court's ruling, had no federal common law with which to present a federal question, the court dismissed the case for want of subject matter jurisdiction.

Chief Judge Feinberg dissented; he saw no federal interest conflict presenting a policy question more appropriately resolved by Congress:

> The allegedly conflicting federal interests are in the welfare of veterans and in the welfare of suppliers of war materiel. But that the plaintiff veterans and the defendant contractors have opposing interests in this litigation hardly means that the paramount federal interest is somehow divided or self-contradictory. The United States has a clear interest in the protection of its soldiers from harm caused by defective war materiel. What other interests does the United States arguably have that might conflict with this clear interest? One such interest might be in seeing that defendants, as suppliers of war materiel, are treated fairly. But that interest cannot be said to conflict with the government's interest in the safety of its soldiers. Another such interest might be in preventing defendants from being driven to bankruptcy by large damage awards to Agent Orange plaintiffs, who have already made claims assertedly greater than defendants' combined liquid assets. This, I take it, is what the majority means by its reference to the federal interest in the "welfare" of defendants. But this interest lies in the future, and in the realm of speculation. There will be time enough to deal with the potential impact of defendants' financial liability if and when they incur any, if it is truly in the interest of the United States to do so. By contrast, plaintiffs' injuries—assuming for the moment that plaintiffs have a viable cause of action—lie in large part in the present, and in the realm of the concrete. The conclusion seems inescapable to me that the United States' interest in the "welfare" of defendants cannot approach, either in magnitude or in quality, its interest in the welfare of the Agent Orange plaintiffs. In short, in the case before us the paramount interests of the United States are in the welfare of its veterans and in their fair and uniform treatment.

Is there a significant difference in approach between *Agent Orange* and *Boyle*? Confronted with possible policy conflicts, should the federal courts do their best to resolve them, leaving it to Congress to adjust the balance if the courts err, or should they effectively throw up their hands and refuse to displace state law by creating federal common law? Or can the approaches in *Agent Orange* and *Boyle* be harmonized? Are the cases sufficiently distinguishable so that creating federal common law in *Boyle* and refusing to do so in *Agent Orange* may both be proper? If so, what is the distinction? If not, which approach better reflects the proper role of the federal courts?

9. *Boyle* demonstrates the dispute over federal courts as common law courts that the separation-of-powers view of the Erie doctrine addresses. Justice Brennan argues strenuously that creating a defense in *Boyle* violates separation of powers. The five-member majority seems untroubled by either the abstract possibility that Congress could have acted in the area or by Congress's actual refusal to do so on six occasions. In *Cannon v. University of Chicago*, 441 U.S. 677 (1979), *infra* at 513, Justice Powell dissented on the ground that policy making should be left to the representative branches of government, not undertaken by the Court. Justice Powell had left the Court before *Boyle*. Justice Kennedy, who replaced him, voted with the majority. Would Justice Powell have joined the majority? That aside, should the federal courts ever make policy decisions, or should they leave them to the representative branches? If so, does that place an intolerable burden on the legislature to anticipate and keep up with every developing problem in modern society? If not, what principles distinguish legitimate judicial participation in or implementation of policy decisions from that which is illegitimate?

10. A unanimous Court reaffirmed the *Boyle* approach in *Atherton v. Federal Deposit Insurance Corporation*, 519 U.S. 213 (1997). The underlying issue was whether there should be a federal common law standard governing the standard of conduct governing officers and directors of federally chartered banks. Congress had specified that officials were liable for "gross negligence" or "similar conduct." The question was whether individual states could impose a stricter standard of conduct. Justice Breyer's opinion rehearsed the Court's post-Erie reluctance to create special federal rules of decision and echoed the separation-of-powers theme, noting that the decision to use latent federal power to displace state law "is primarily a decision for Congress." Harking back to a 1966 decision, the Court noted that " 'the guiding principle is that a significant conflict between some federal policy or interest and the use of state law * * * must first be specifically shown.' " Justice Breyer noted that such conflict is "normally" a precondition, citing, inter alia, Kimbell Foods. He did not explain when it might not be a precondition.

The opinion did not specify whether state law governed of its own force or because the Court adopted it as federal common law, though the former seems more likely. If that is so, has the Court repudiated at least some of Kimbell Foods? If not, has the Court altered the Kimbell Foods balancing test? Although the Court cited Kimbell Foods as a precedent for the significant-conflict standard, Justice Marshall's opinion is hardly the sort of ringing endorsement of that standard that either *Boyle* or Atherton represents.

Although *Boyle* and Atherton mention Kimbell Foods favorably, it is not so clear that they are compatible with it. Consider whether the Kimbell Foods Court actually found a significant conflict between state law and a federal policy or interest. If you think it did not, then why did the Court hold that federal law governed the disputed priority question? If there was a significant conflict, then how did *Kimbell Foods'* adoption of state law as the content of federal common law ameliorate the conflict?

* * *

The next case is procedurally complex, because there is litigation in two states, both in federal and state court. It will help you get a better picture of what was going on in the case if you make side-by-side timelines for the California and Maryland litigation. You do not need dates for each of the events that occurred, but it is helpful to be able to see the sequence of events at a glance.

Semtek International Incorporated v. Lockheed Martin Corporation

Supreme Court of the United States, 2001.
531 U.S. 497.

JUSTICE SCALIA delivered the opinion of the Court.

This case presents the question whether the claim-preclusive effect of a federal judgment dismissing a diversity action on statute-of-limitations grounds is determined by the law of the State in which the federal court sits.

I

Petitioner filed a complaint against respondent in California state court, alleging breach of contract and various business torts. Respondent removed the case to the United States District Court for the Central District of California on the basis of diversity of citizenship, and successfully moved to dismiss petitioner's claims as barred by California's 2-year statute of limitations. In its order of dismissal, the District Court, adopting language suggested by respondent, dismissed petitioner's claims "in [their] entirety on the merits and with prejudice." Without contesting the District Court's designation of its dismissal as "on the merits," petitioner appealed to the Court of Appeals for the Ninth Circuit, which affirmed the District Court's order. Petitioner also brought suit against respondent in the State Circuit Court for Baltimore City, Maryland, alleging the same causes of action, which were not

Practice Pointer

Considering the following procedural history of the case, how would you evaluate the job that the attorneys for both sides did? What might they have done differently?

time barred under Maryland's 3-year statute of limitations. Respondent sought injunctive relief against this action from the California federal court under the All Writs Act, 28 U.S.C. § 1651, and removed the action to the United States District Court for the District of Maryland on federal-question grounds (diversity grounds were not available because Lockheed "is a Maryland citizen"). The California federal court denied the relief requested, and the Maryland federal court remanded the case to state court because the federal question arose only by way of defense. Following a hearing, the Maryland state court granted respondent's motion to dismiss on the ground of res judicata. Petitioner then returned to the California federal court and the Ninth Circuit, unsuccessfully moving both courts to amend the former's earlier order so as to indicate that the dismissal was not "on the merits." Petitioner also appealed the Maryland trial court's order of dismissal to the Maryland Court of Special Appeals. The Court of Special Appeals affirmed, holding that, regardless of whether California would have accorded claim-preclusive effect to a statute-of-limitations dismissal by one of its own courts, the dismissal by the California federal court barred the complaint filed in Maryland, since the res judicata effect of federal diversity judgments is prescribed by federal law, under which the earlier dismissal was on the merits and claim preclusive. After the Maryland Court of Appeals declined to review the case, we granted certiorari.

Food for Thought

Consider Lockheed's request in light of 28 U.S.C. § 2283, which you will study in Chapter 8.

II

Petitioner contends that the outcome of this case is controlled by *Dupasseur v. Rochereau* (1875), which held that the res judicata effect of a federal diversity judgment "is such as would belong to judgments of the State courts rendered under similar circumstances," and may not be accorded any "higher sanctity or effect." Since, petitioner argues, the dismissal of an action on statute-of-limitations grounds by a California state court would not be claim preclusive, it follows that the similar dismissal of this diversity action by the California federal court cannot be claim preclusive. While we agree that this would be the result demanded by *Dupasseur*, the case is not dispositive because it was decided under the Conformity Act of 1872, which required federal courts to apply the procedural law of the forum State in nonequity cases. That arguably affected the outcome of the case.

Take Note!

The Rules Enabling Act of 1934 superseded the Conformity Act by ushering in the procedural era of the Federal Rules of Civil Procedure, which the Court promulgated in 1938, the year it decided *Erie*.

Respondent, for its part, contends that the outcome of this case is controlled by Federal Rule of Civil Procedure 41(b), which provides as follows:

> Involuntary Dismissal: Effect Thereof. For failure of the plaintiff to prosecute or to comply with these rules or any order of court, a defendant may move for dismissal of an action or of any claim against the defendant. Unless the court in its order for dismissal otherwise specifies, a dismissal under this subdivision and any dismissal not provided for in this rule, other than a dismissal for lack of jurisdiction, for improper venue, or for failure to join a party under Rule 19, operates as an adjudication upon the merits.

Since the dismissal here did not "otherwise specif[y]" (indeed, it specifically stated that it was "on the merits"), and did not pertain to the excepted subjects of jurisdiction, venue, or joinder, it follows, respondent contends, that the dismissal "is entitled to claim preclusive effect."

Implicit in this reasoning is the unstated minor premise that all judgments denominated "on the merits" are entitled to claim-preclusive effect. That premise is not necessarily valid. The original connotation of an "on the merits" adjudication is one that actually "pass[es] directly on the substance of [a particular] claim" before the court. That connotation remains common to every jurisdiction of which we are aware. ("The prototyp[ical] [judgment on the merits is] one in which the merits of [a party's] claim are in fact adjudicated [for or] against the [party] after trial of the substantive issues"). And it is, we think, the meaning intended in those many statements to the effect that a judgment "on the merits" triggers the doctrine of res judicata or claim preclusion.

But over the years the meaning of the term "judgment on the merits" "has gradually undergone change," and it has come to be applied to some judgments (such as the one involved here) that do *not* pass upon the substantive merits of a claim and hence do *not* (in many jurisdictions) entail claim-preclusive effect. That is why the Restatement of Judgments has abandoned the use of the term—"because of its possibly misleading connotations."

In short, it is no longer true that a judgment "on the merits" is necessarily a judgment entitled to claim-preclusive effect; and there are a number of reasons for believing that the phrase "adjudication upon the merits" does not bear that meaning in Rule 41(b). To begin with, Rule 41(b) sets forth nothing more than a default rule for determining the import of a dismissal (a dismissal is "upon the merits," with the three stated exceptions, unless the court "otherwise specifies"). This would be a highly peculiar context in which to announce a federally prescribed rule on the complex question of claim preclusion, saying in effect, "All federal dismissals (with three specified exceptions) preclude suit elsewhere, unless the court otherwise specifies."

And even apart from the purely default character of Rule 41(b), it would be peculiar to find a rule governing the effect that must be accorded federal judgments by other courts ensconced in rules governing the internal procedures of the rendering court itself. Indeed, such a rule would arguably violate the jurisdictional limitation of the Rules Enabling Act: that the Rules "shall not abridge, enlarge or modify any substantive right." In the present case, for example, if California law left petitioner free to sue on this claim in Maryland even after the California statute of limitations had expired, the federal court's extinguishment of that right (through Rule 41(b)'s mandated claim-preclusive effect of its judgment) would seem to violate this limitation.

Moreover, as so interpreted, the Rule would in many cases violate the federalism principle of *Erie R. Co. v. Tompkins* (1938), by engendering " 'substantial' variations [in outcomes] between state and federal litigation" which would "[l]ikely * * * influence the choice of a forum," *Hanna v. Plumer* (1965). With regard to the claim-preclusion issue involved in the present case, for example, the traditional rule is that expiration of the applicable statute of limitations merely bars the remedy and does not extinguish the substantive right, so that dismissal on that ground does not have claim-preclusive effect in other jurisdictions with longer, unexpired limitation periods. Out-of-state defendants sued on stale claims in California and in other States adhering to this traditional rule would systematically remove state-law suits brought against them to federal court—where, unless otherwise specified, a statute-of-limitations dismissal would bar suit everywhere.

Finally, if Rule 41(b) did mean what respondent suggests, we would surely have relied upon it in our cases recognizing the claim-preclusive effect of federal judgments in federal-question cases. Yet for over half a century since the promulgation of Rule 41(b), we have not once done so.

We think the key to a more reasonable interpretation of the meaning of "operates as an adjudication upon the merits" in Rule 41(b) is to be found in Rule 41(a), which, in discussing the effect of voluntary dismissal by the plaintiff, makes clear that an "adjudication upon the merits" is the opposite of a "dismissal without prejudice":

> Unless otherwise stated in the notice of dismissal or stipulation, the dismissal is without prejudice, except that a notice of dismissal operates as an adjudication upon the merits when filed by a plaintiff who has once dismissed in any court of the United States or of any state an action based on or including the same claim.

The primary meaning of "dismissal without prejudice," we think, is dismissal without barring the plaintiff from returning later, to the same court, with the same underlying claim. That will also ordinarily (though not always) have the consequence of not barring the claim from *other* courts, but its primary meaning relates to the dismissing court itself. Thus, Black's Law Dictionary defines "dismissed without prejudice" as "removed from the court's docket in such a way that the plaintiff may refile the same suit on the same claim," and defines "dismissal without prejudice" as "[a] dismissal that does not bar the plaintiff from refiling the lawsuit within the applicable limitations period."

We think, then, that the effect of the "adjudication upon the merits" default provision of Rule 41(b)—and, presumably, of the explicit order in the present case that used the language of that default provision—is simply that, unlike a dismissal "without prejudice," the dismissal in the present case barred refiling of the same claim in the United States District Court for the Central District of California. That is undoubtedly a necessary condition, but it is not a sufficient one, for claim-preclusive effect in other courts.[11]

Food for Thought

Does Justice Scalia's argument beg the question of why the Court, in promulgating Rule 41(b), used the phrase "on the merits" instead of "with prejudice," the direct opposite of the phrase in Rule 41(a), the immediately preceding subsection, upon which Justice Scalia relies for his arguably anti-textualist interpretation of Rule 41(b)? If the Court meant "with prejudice," why did it not say so directly? Perhaps one could argue that by eschewing the phrase "with prejudice," the Court did intend to convey different meaning.

III

Having concluded that the claim-preclusive effect, in Maryland, of this California federal diversity judgment is dictated neither by *Dupasseur v. Rochereau*, as petitioner contends, nor by Rule 41(b), as respondent contends, we turn to consideration of what determines the issue. Neither the Full Faith and Credit Clause nor the full faith and credit statute addresses the question. By their terms they govern the effects to be given only to state-court judgments (and, in the case of the statute, to judgments by courts of territories and possessions). And no other federal textual provision, neither of the Constitution nor of any statute, addresses the claim-preclusive effect of a judgment in a federal diversity action.

It is also true, however, that no federal textual provision addresses the claim-preclusive effect of a federal-court judgment in a federal-question case, yet we have long held that States cannot give those judgments merely whatever effect they would give their own judgments, but must accord them the effect that this Court prescribes. The reasoning of that line of cases suggests, moreover, that even when States are allowed to give federal judgments (notably, judgments in diversity

11 We do not decide whether, in a diversity case, a federal court's "dismissal upon the merits" (in the sense we have described), under circumstances where a state court would decree only a "dismissal without prejudice," abridges a "substantive right" and thus exceeds the authorization of the Rules Enabling Act. We think the situation will present itself more rarely than would the arguable violation of the Act that would ensue from interpreting Rule 41(b) as a rule of claim preclusion; and if it is a violation, [it] can be more easily dealt with on direct appeal.

cases) no more than the effect accorded to state judgments, that disposition is by direction of this Court, which has the last word on the claim-preclusive effect of *all* federal judgments * * * . In other words, in Dupasseur the State was allowed (indeed, required) to give a federal diversity judgment no more effect than it would accord one of its own judgments only because reference to state law was *the federal rule that this Court deemed appropriate*. In short, federal common law governs the claim-preclusive effect of a dismissal by a federal court sitting in diversity.

It is left to us, then, to determine the appropriate federal rule. And despite the sea change that has occurred in the background law since Dupasseur was decided—not only repeal of the Conformity Act but also the watershed decision of this Court in Erie—we think the result decreed by Dupasseur continues to be correct for diversity cases. Since state, rather than federal, substantive law is at issue there is no need for a uniform federal rule. And indeed, nationwide uniformity in the substance of the matter is better served by having the same claim-preclusive rule (the state rule) apply whether the dismissal has been ordered by a state or a federal court. This is, it seems to us, a classic case for adopting, as the federally prescribed rule of decision, the law that would be applied by state courts in the State in which the federal diversity court sits. As we have alluded to above, any other rule would produce the sort of "forum-shopping * * * and * * * inequitable administration of the laws" that Erie seeks to avoid, since filing in, or removing to, federal court would be encouraged by the divergent effects that the litigants would anticipate from likely grounds of dismissal.

Food for Thought

Remember that Justice Scalia was also the author of the majority opinion in Boyle v. United Technologies, *supra* at 461. Was it not he who declared that in order to have a federal common law rule, one first had to find that the area was one of "uniquely federal interest"? Was it not he who declared that there had to be "significant conflict" between the state and federal rules, in the statement, "[b]ut conflict there must be"? How good a job does he do identifying either of those requirements here?

This federal reference to state law will not obtain, of course, in situations in which the state law is incompatible with federal interests. If, for example, state law did not accord claim-preclusive effect to dismissals for willful violation of discovery orders, federal courts' interest in the integrity of their own processes might justify a contrary federal rule. No such conflict with potential federal interests exists in the present case. Dismissal of this state cause of action was decreed by the California federal court only because the California statute of limitations so required; and there is no conceivable federal interest in giving that time bar more effect in other courts than the California courts themselves would impose.

* * *

Because the claim-preclusive effect of the California federal court's dismissal "upon the merits" of petitioner's action on statute-of-limitations grounds is governed by a federal rule that in turn incorporates California's law of claim preclusion (the content of which we do not pass upon today), the Maryland Court of Special Appeals erred in holding that the dismissal necessarily precluded the bringing of this action in the Maryland courts. The judgment is reversed, and the case remanded for further proceedings not inconsistent with this opinion.

It is so ordered.

Notes and Questions

1. The Court notes Dupasseur as an example of a state giving a federal judgment the same effect as a state judgment, not more, because of the *Court's* direction. Is this incompatible with Justice Scalia's opening mention that the Court decided Dupasseur pursuant to the Conformity Act of 1872, which prescribed federal courts' use of state procedure? In other words, was it the Court's direction or Congress's that produced the result?

2. The Court asserts that because state law provides the rule of decision in *Semtek*, a diversity case, there is no need for a uniform federal rule of preclusion. Is the Court suggesting that the choice of preclusion law depends upon whether the claim being adjudicated reaches the court via federal-question or diversity jurisdiction? If so, why? Alternatively, is the determinative factor that "state, rather than federal, substantive law is at issue?" If so, why should that be determinative?

Is there a federal interest in having all federal judgments subject to the same preclusion rules? When federal courts exercise supplemental jurisdiction over state law claims, state law provides the rule of decision. Is there thus no need for uniform federal rules to govern the preclusive effect of a federal court's determination of supplemental state law claims? Or is there a federal interest in having all the claims determined by a court in a single judgment subject to the same preclusion rules?

3. *Empire Healthchoice Assurance, Inc. v. McVeigh*, 547 U.S. 677 (2006), demonstrated how difficult the Erie-choice-of-law question remains on the substantive side of the ledger. McVeigh was a federal employee covered by the Federal Employees Health Benefits Act of 1959 (FEHBA). The federal Office of Personnel Management (OPM) contracted with private carriers for them to provide health insurance plans, and McVeigh was an enrollee of the Empire Healthchoice Plan until his death. Premiums paid by the government and enrollees went into a special Treasury Department fund, from which the carriers paid benefits. McVeigh was badly injured in an accident, and over the course of the remaining four years of his life, received almost $160,000 in

benefits. The health insurance contract to which McVeigh was a party provided in part that if a covered individual wrongfully suffered illness or injury at the hands of another, the carrier was entitled to reimbursement of compensated expenses if there was a recovery from the tortfeasors on any basis ("lawsuit, settlement or otherwise"). (It provided alternatively that if the enrollee elected not to pursue a claim, the carrier was subrogated to the claim.) Reimbursement funds that the carriers received were redeposited in the fund.

McVeigh's surviving wife and child settled claims against the tortfeasors for more than $3,000,000. The carrier sought reimbursement and, when McVeigh's wife-administratrix rejected the claim, the carrier sued in the Southern District of New York. The defendant sought dismissal for lack of subject matter jurisdiction, arguing that the case was a simple contract dispute between two private parties. The district and circuit courts agreed, and the case made its way to the Supreme Court, which split five-to-four on the issue. Although the question on which the Court granted certiorari was whether there was jurisdiction under 28 U.S.C. § 1331, it turned entirely on whether federal or state law should govern the carrier's claim for reimbursement.

Empire's arguments were reminiscent of those heard in cases such as *Kimbell Foods* (*supra* at 451) and *Boyle v. United Technologies, Inc.* (*supra* at 461). It argued first that federal common law governed and second that the Empire Healthchoice Plan itself constituted federal law because it was a contract with the federal government. In support, Empire argued *à la Boyle* that because resolution of the dispute ultimately would affect the federal treasury and the cost of providing health insurance to federal employees, federal control and uniformity of rules governing reimbursement were essential.

Justice Ginsburg's majority opinion disagreed. The critical factor was Congress's intent to have federal law govern and although the contract that OPM negotiated with its carriers required reimbursement, FEHBA, the statute that authorized the contract contained no such provision. Thus, the majority declined to accept Empire's argument that the federal law created the right to reimbursement and therefore should govern reimbursement disputes.

The majority, adverting to *Boyle's* two-part test for creating federal common law , declined to find a significant conflict. It relied on the Second Circuit's majority and concurring opinions, both of which had made clear that the burden with respect to significant conflict rested on the party seeking the creation of federal common law—here Empire—and that there had been no showing of any conflict between New York law that would otherwise govern the reimbursement claim and the unique federal interest that Empire asserted.

In addition, the opinion noted that had Empire been subrogated to McVeigh's entitlement to sue, federal law clearly would not have governed the action. The tortfeasors were strangers to the contract negotiated by OPM with the carriers and to the agreement between the carriers and their insureds. Accordingly, none of those agreements, assuming *arguendo* that federal law governed any dispute connected with them, could apply to the tortfeasors, whose "liability, whether to the insured or the insurer, would be governed not by an agreement to which the tortfeasors are strangers, but by state law, and § 8902(m)(1) would have no sway."

> **Food for Thought**
>
> In the course of that argument, Justice Breyer cited Kimbell Foods. That was a curious case upon which to rely, was it not? After all, notwithstanding that the Court ruled that federal common law had to govern SBA and FHA loans' priority vis-à-vis other claims on the debtor, it adopted state law as the content of the federal common law. In the course of doing that, the Court rejected the government's argument that its interest in recoupment of funds required a uniform federal rule, noting that the purpose of the lending programs was not to generate revenue, but rather to provide federal support for people and businesses whom Congress had identified as in need of it. One might make the same argument in response to Justice Breyer. The purpose of the federal health insurance program is not to generate revenue. To be sure, to the extent that the program is able to recoup benefits payments, the fund is better able to make subsequent payments, but the government made the same argument with respect to the SBA and FHA programs in Kimbell Foods, to no avail.

Justice Breyer, writing for the four dissenters, dwelt on the pervasively federal nature of the entire health care program[3] and the fact that the contract under which the reimbursement entitlement arose was between a federal agency and the insurance carriers. In effect, he characterized the federal government as the real party in interest, the carrier merely being its agent with respect both to administering the health plans and to seeking reimbursement for payouts to enrollees who subsequently received compensation from tortfeasors. He relied heavily on Clearfield for its holding that federal law governed the United States' duties and rights with regard to federal commercial paper.

Note on Discerning the Content of State Law

Once a federal court has determined that state law governs an issue, because 1) Erie says it must as a matter of constitutional imperative, or 2) state law exists in an area of concurrent federal and state power and Congress has not displaced the state law, or 3) state law is to be adopted, as in Kimbell Foods, as the appropriate content of federal common law, the court must then determine what the state law

3 He characterized the matter as follows:

In sum, the statute is federal, the program it creates is federal, the program's beneficiaries are federal employees working throughout the country, the Federal Government pays all relevant costs, and the Federal Government receives all relevant payments. The private carrier's only role in this scheme is to administer the health benefits plan for the federal agency in exchange for a fixed service charge.

is. That is easy if there is a state statute directly on point or if the highest state court recently issued an opinion. For most cases, however, the federal court has a more difficult task at hand.

The Supreme Court has addressed this issue on several occasions. *Commissioner of Internal Revenue v. Bosch's Estate*, 387 U.S. 456 (1967), summarized the precepts that should guide federal judges. Justice Clark noted that *Erie* requires the federal courts to follow decisions of the highest state courts on issues properly governed by state law. The difficulty arises when the highest court has not spoken and the federal court confronts only lower state court decisions or no decisions at all. In such circumstances, the federal judge should accord some weight to decisions of inferior state courts, but they are not dispositive. Thus, the federal courts place themselves in the position of inferior state courts and apply essentially the same processes for determining unsettled questions of state law.[4]

---

2. Construing a Jurisdictional Grant as a Command to Create Federal Common Law

Textile Workers Union v. Lincoln Mills

Supreme Court of the United States, 1957.
353 U.S. 448.

MR. JUSTICE DOUGLAS delivered the opinion of the Court.

Petitioner-union entered into a collective bargaining agreement in 1953 with respondent-employer, the agreement to run one year and from year to year thereafter, unless terminated on specified notices. The agreement provided that there would be no strikes or work stoppages and that grievances would be handled pursuant to a specified procedure. The last step in the grievance procedure—a step that could be taken by either party—was arbitration.

This controversy involves several grievances that concern work loads and work assignments. The grievances were processed through the various steps in the grievance procedure and were finally denied by the employer. The union requested arbitration, and the employer refused. Thereupon the union brought this suit in the District Court to compel arbitration.

---

4 District court determinations of state law are subject to the normal appellate review process. In Salve Regina College v. Russell, 499 U.S. 225 (1991), the Court ruled that the circuit courts should not defer to district court determinations of state law, but instead should conduct their own *de novo* review of state law under the general principles for determining what state law is.

The District Court concluded that it had jurisdiction and ordered the employer to comply with the grievance arbitration provisions of the collective bargaining agreement. The Court of Appeals reversed by a divided vote. It held that, although the District Court had jurisdiction to entertain the suit, the court had no authority founded either in federal or state law to grant the relief. The case is here on a petition for a writ of certiorari which we granted because of the importance of the problem and the contrariety of views in the courts.

The starting point of our inquiry is § 301 of the Labor Management Relations Act of 1947, which provides:

> (a) Suits for violation of contracts between an employer and a labor organization representing employees in an industry affecting commerce as defined in this chapter, or between any such labor organizations, may be brought in any district court of the United States having jurisdiction of the parties, without respect to the amount in controversy or without regard to the citizenship of the parties.
>
> (b) Any labor organization which represents employees in an industry affecting commerce as defined in this chapter and any employer whose activities affect commerce as defined in this chapter shall be bound by the acts of its agents. Any such labor organization may sue or be sued as an entity and in behalf of the employees whom it represents in the courts of the United States. Any money judgment against a labor organization in a district court of the United States shall be enforceable only against the organization as an entity and against its assets, and shall not be enforceable against any individual member or his assets.

There has been considerable litigation involving § 301[,] and courts have construed it differently. There is one view that § 301(a) merely gives federal district courts jurisdiction in controversies that involve labor organizations in industries affecting commerce, without regard to diversity of citizenship or the amount in controversy. Under that view § 301(a) would not be the source of substantive law; it would neither supply federal law to resolve these controversies nor turn the federal judges to state law for answers to the questions. Other courts—the overwhelming number of them—hold that § 301(a) is more than jurisdictional—that it authorizes federal courts to fashion a body of federal law for the enforcement of these collective bargaining agreements and includes within that federal law specific performance of promises to arbitrate grievances under collective bargaining agreements. * * * That is our construction of § 301(a), which means that the agreement to arbitrate grievance disputes, contained in this collective bargaining agreement, should be specifically enforced.

From the face of the Act it is apparent that § 301(a) and § 301(b) supplement one another. Section 301(b) makes it possible for a labor organization, representing employees in an industry affecting commerce, to sue and be sued as an entity in the federal courts. Section 301(b) in other words provides the procedural remedy lacking at common law. Section 301(a) certainly does something more than that. Plainly, it supplies the basis upon which the federal district courts may take jurisdiction and apply the procedural rule of § 301(b). The question is whether § 301(a) is more than jurisdictional.

The legislative history of § 301 is somewhat cloudy and confusing. But there are a few shafts of light that illuminate our problem.

The bills, as they passed the House and the Senate, contained provisions which would have made the failure to abide by an agreement to arbitrate an unfair labor practice. This feature of the law was dropped in Conference. As the Conference Report stated, "Once parties have made a collective bargaining contract the enforcement of that contract should be left to the usual processes of the law and not to the National Labor Relations Board."

Food for Thought

Does this quotation prove too much? If it was so clear to the Senate that an aggrieved party should have "a right of action" in federal court, where is the "right of action"? The Conference Report referred only to "the usual processes of law." The usual processes of law with respect to contracts view contracts as matters of state law. If Congress wanted to federalize what otherwise would have been a state contract claim,—a fairly significant shift following *Erie*—why is the legislative history so "cloudy and confusing"?

Both the Senate and the House took pains to provide for "the usual processes of the law" by provisions which were the substantial equivalent of § 301(a) in its present form. Both the Senate Report and the House Report indicate a primary concern that unions as well as employees should be bound to collective bargaining contracts. But there was also a broader concern—a concern with a procedure for making such agreements enforceable in the courts by either party. At one point the Senate Report, states,

> We feel that the aggrieved party should also have a right of action in the Federal courts. Such a policy is completely in accord with the purpose of the Wagner Act which the Supreme Court declared was "to compel employers to bargain collectively with their employees to the end that an employment contract, binding on both parties, should be made * * * ."

Congress was also interested in promoting collective bargaining that ended with agreements not to strike.

* * *

Plainly the agreement to arbitrate grievance disputes is the *quid pro quo* for an agreement not to strike. Viewed in this light, the legislation does more than confer jurisdiction in the federal courts over labor organizations. It expresses a federal policy that federal courts should enforce these agreements on behalf of or against labor organizations and that industrial peace can be best obtained only in that way.

To be sure, there is a great medley of ideas reflected in the hearings, reports, and debates on this Act. Yet, to repeat, the entire tenor of the history indicates that the agreement to arbitrate grievance disputes was considered as *quid pro quo* of a no-strike agreement. And when in the House the debate narrowed to the question whether § 301 was more than jurisdictional, it became abundantly clear that the purpose of the section was to provide the necessary legal remedies. Section 302 of the House bill, the substantial equivalent of the present § 301, was being described by Mr. Hartley, the sponsor of the bill in the House:

> Mr. BARDEN. Mr. Chairman, I take this time for the purpose of asking the Chairman a question, and in asking the question I want it understood that it is intended to make a part of the record that may hereafter be referred to as history of the legislation.
>
> It is my understanding that section 302, the section dealing with equal responsibility under collective bargaining contracts in strike actions and proceedings in district courts contemplates not only the ordinary lawsuits for damages but also such other remedial proceedings, both legal and equitable, as might be appropriate in the circumstances; in other words, proceedings could, for example, be brought by the employers, the labor organizations, or interested individual employees under the Declaratory Judgments Act in order to secure declarations from the Court of legal rights under the contract.
>
> Mr. HARTLEY. The interpretation the gentleman has just given of that section is absolutely correct.

It seems, therefore, clear to us that Congress adopted a policy which placed sanctions behind agreements to arbitrate grievance disputes, by implication rejecting the common-law rule against enforcement of executory agreements to arbitrate. We would undercut the Act and defeat its policy if we read § 301 narrowly as only conferring jurisdiction over labor organizations.

The question then is, what is the substantive law to be applied in suits under § 301(a)? We conclude that the substantive law to apply in suits under § 301(a) is federal law, which the courts must fashion from the policy of our national labor laws. The Labor Management Relations Act expressly furnishes some substantive law. It points out what the parties may or may not do in certain situations. Other problems will lie in the penumbra of express statutory mandates. Some will lack express statutory sanction but will be solved by looking at the policy

Griswold reference

of the legislation and fashioning a remedy that will effectuate that policy. The range of judicial inventiveness will be determined by the nature of the problem. Federal interpretation of the federal law will govern, not state law. But state law, if compatible with the purpose of § 301, may be resorted to in order to find the rule that will best effectuate the federal policy. Any state law applied, however, will be absorbed as federal law and will not be an independent source of private rights.

It is not uncommon for federal courts to fashion federal law where federal rights are concerned. Congress has indicated by § 301(a) the purpose to follow that course here. There is no constitutional difficulty. Article III, § 2, extends the judicial power to cases "arising under * * * the Laws of the United States * * * ." The power of Congress to regulate these labor-management controversies under the Commerce Clause is plain. A case or controversy arising under § 301(a) is, therefore, one within the purview of judicial power as defined in Article III.

* * *

The judgment of the Court of Appeals is reversed and the cause is remanded to that court for proceedings in conformity with this opinion.

Reversed.

MR. JUSTICE FRANKFURTER, dissenting.

The Court has avoided the difficult problems raised by § 301 of the Taft-Hartley Act by attributing to the section an occult content. This plainly procedural section is transmuted into a mandate to the federal courts to fashion a whole body of substantive federal law appropriate for the complicated and touchy problems raised by collective bargaining. * * * I believe that § 301 cannot be so construed, even if constitutional questions cannot be avoided. But the Court has a "clear" and contrary conclusion emerge from the "somewhat," to say the least, "cloudy and confusing legislative history." This is more than can be fairly asked even from the alchemy of construction. Since the Court relies on a few isolated statements in the legislative history which do not support its conclusion, however favoringly read, I have deemed it necessary to set forth in an appendix the entire relevant legislative history of the Taft-Hartley Act and its predecessor, the Case Bill. This legislative history reinforces the natural meaning of the statute as an exclusively procedural provision, affording, that is, an accessible federal forum for suits on agreements between labor organizations and employers, but not enacting federal law for such suits.

[Justice Frankfurter's extended argument against § 301's legitimacy as a jurisdiction-conferring statute appears at page 294-302.]

* * *

One word more remains to be said. The earliest declaration of unconstitutionality of an act of Congress—by the Justices on circuit—involved a refusal by the Justices to perform a function imposed upon them by Congress because of the non-judicial nature of that function. Since then, the Court has many times declared legislation unconstitutional because it imposed on the Court powers or functions that were regarded as outside the scope of the "judicial power" lodged in the Court by the Constitution.

One may fairly generalize from these instances that the Court has deemed itself peculiarly qualified, with due regard to the contrary judgment of Congress, to determine what is meet and fit for the exercise of "judicial power" as authorized by the Constitution. Solicitude and respect for the confines of "judicial power," and the difficult problem of marking those confines, apply equally in construing precisely what duties Congress has cast upon the federal courts, especially when, as in this case, the most that can be said in support of finding a congressional desire to impose these "legislative" duties on the federal courts is that Congress did not mention the problem in the statute and that, insofar as purpose may be gathered from congressional reports and debates, they leave us in the dark.

The Court, however, sees no problem of "judicial power" in casting upon the federal courts, with no guides except "judicial inventiveness," the task of applying a whole industrial code that is as yet in the bosom of the judiciary. There are severe limits on "judicial inventiveness" even for the most imaginative judges. The law is not a "brooding omnipresence in the sky," and it cannot be drawn from there like nitrogen from the air. These problems created by the Court's interpretation of § 301 cannot

> be solved by resort to the established canons of construction that enable a court to look through awkward or clumsy expression, or language wanting in precision, to the intent of the legislature. For the vice of the statute here lies in the impossibility of ascertaining, by any reasonable test, that the legislature meant one thing rather than another * * * .

But the Court makes § 301 a mountain instead of a molehill and, by giving an example of "judicial inventiveness," it thereby solves all the constitutional problems that would otherwise have to be faced.

* * *

Notes and Questions

1. Justice Frankfurter has a point; surely if Congress intended to authorize the federal courts to fashion a vast body of substantive labor law, § 301 is a particularly backhanded manner of communicating that. Assuming that was Congress's intent, is the delegation permissible? May Congress assign such wide-ranging exercise of fundamentally legislative power to another branch, or does that circumvent the deliberately cumbersome process Article I prescribes for enacting a law? On the majority's theory of delegation, is there anything to stop Congress from assigning legislative power to the President, thus uniting in one branch a legislative process that the Framers prescribed should be separated into two?

2. If Justice Frankfurter is correct that there was no delegation, then can § 301 survive scrutiny under Article III? What is the constitutional basis for a purely jurisdictional statute that confers jurisdiction upon the district courts "without respect to the amount in controversy or without regard to the citizenship of the parties"? If such a statute seems plainly outside the ambit of Article III, § 2, perhaps Congress, presumptively aware of the Court's jurisdictional jurisprudence, would have been unlikely to enact a patently unconstitutional jurisdictional grant and so must have believed there was some "federal question" basis to labor law actions. But does that inference compel or even suggest the further inference that Congress intended to enlist the federal judiciary as additional lawmakers?

3. There is a middle possibility for *Lincoln Mills*. The cryptic reference in § 301 to "an industry affecting commerce" apparently refers to Congress's power to legislate under the Commerce Clause. This, in turn, raises the question of "protective jurisdiction." As Professor Redish points out, the theory exists in two forms, one that would allow a grant of jurisdiction to consider cases involving any area in which Congress can legislate, whether or not it already has, and the other requiring that Congress have already enacted " 'statutes expressing a national policy in the area concerned * * * .' " MARTIN H. REDISH, FEDERAL JURISDICTION: TENSIONS IN THE ALLOCATION OF JUDICIAL POWER 92 (2d ed. 1990) (quoting Paul J. Mishkin, *The Federal "Question" in the District Courts*, 53 Colum.L.Rev. 157, 195 (1953)). Is protective jurisdiction consistent with the jurisdictional theory of *Osborn*, text at 281 and *Verlinden B.V. v. Central Bank of Nigeria*, 461 U.S. 480 (1983), text at 314? If so, on which of the bases described above? If not, can one save the majority's opinion?

4. If the Court's reasoning is supportable, how can one determine which jurisdiction-conferring statutes are intended also as directions to the federal courts to create federal common law and which are not? Should the Court presume that whenever Congress grants jurisdiction but has not enacted a comprehensive legislative scheme, it intends the federal courts to step into the breach?

5. Not all directions to the federal courts to create common law come in jurisdictional statutes. Federal Rule of Evidence 501 provided:

> Except as otherwise required by the Constitution of the United States or provided by Act of Congress, or in rules prescribed by the Supreme Court pursuant to statutory authority, the privilege of a witness, person, government, State, or political subdivision thereof shall be governed by the principles of the common law as they may be interpreted by the courts of the United States in the light of reason and experience. However, in civil actions and proceedings, with respect to an element of a claim or defense as to which State law supplies the rule of decision, the privilege of a witness, person, government, State or political subdivision thereof shall be determined in accordance with State law.

Pursuant to that authorization, *Jaffee v. Redmond*, 518 U.S. 1 (1996) recognized a new psychotherapist-patient privilege. This, of course, raises the same delegation difficulties as are present in *Lincoln Mills*, but with an additional twist. The enabling statute that governs the Federal Rules of Evidence, 28 U.S.C. § 2072 (1994), is also the statute that governs the Federal Rules of Civil Procedure; rules proposed by the Supreme Court become effective if not disapproved by Congress by a date certain. See 28 U.S.C. § 2076 (1994). However, when the Court first proposed the Federal Rules of Evidence, the privilege provisions would have extended to documents or reports required by statute to be prepared and specifically recognized the following relationships as privileged: lawyer-client, psychotherapist-patient, husband-wife, and clergyman-congregant. Those proposals were sufficiently controversial that Congress disapproved them, substituted Rule 501 above, and further required affirmative approval of any subsequent modification of the rule governing privilege before it may go into effect: "Any such amendment [to the Federal Rules of Evidence] creating, abolishing, or modifying a privilege shall have no force and effect unless it shall be approved by act of Congress." Does Congress's restrictive reaction to the original proposals of privileges under the Federal Rules connote its own dissatisfaction with the delegation of common law lawmaking authority generally, or does it represent Congress's faith in its legitimacy? Is the procedure Congress prescribed subject to the same objections as the type of delegation the Court found in *Lincoln Mills*?

Food for Thought

Note that the limitations of the privileges prescribed by Rule 501 pose some interesting questions for the federal courts. Suppose, for example, that an individual brings a federal civil rights action against a state governmental actor and joins a parallel state claim with it, as happened in *Jaffee*. The defendant official may claim the new psychotherapist privilege, but state law may not recognize it. Does this mean that the court has to try the claims separately even though there is considerable overlap in their factual predicates? Or, if the claims may be tried together, should the court recognize the privilege?

6. In admiralty and antitrust law, the federal courts have been essentially unrestrained in creating common law. The only mention of admiralty or maritime law in the Constitution is in Article III, which allows federal jurisdiction over such cases. There is no corresponding grant of legislative power in Article I. Most (but not all) of the law of admiralty is judge-made.

No one has ever seriously questioned the federal courts' power to create such wide-ranging common law, though to be sure the source of authority for doing so is obscure. Justice Story argued in *DeLovio v. Boit*, 7 F. Cas. 418 (C.C.D.Mass.1815), that the constitutional grant of jurisdiction is an implicit command to the federal courts to create the needed body of law. Such a suggestion, however, proves too much. If the grant of admiralty jurisdiction empowers the federal court to create a law of admiralty, why does not the grant of diversity jurisdiction in the same sentence authorize the creation of a federal common law of the type that *Erie* condemned as unconstitutional? In *Southern Pacific Co. v. Jensen,* 244 U.S. 205 (1917), the Court observed that long-established practice confirmed that the federal courts had adopted the general maritime law and that the Constitution contemplated that they would. Whatever the underlying authority, the federal courts' practice of creating admiralty common law is well established and functions in service of policies of uniformity and strong federal interest that are easily understood..

> **FYI**
>
> Congress' power to legislate derives from the Necessary and Proper Clause—U.S. CONST. art. I, § 8, cl. 18. In *Southern Pacific Co. v. Jensen*, 244 U.S. 205, 214-15 (1917), the Court noted that the Necessary and Proper Clause empowers Congress to legislate with respect to all powers vested in any department of the federal government. Since Article III, § 2 brings admiralty cases within the judicial power, the Court reasoned that Congress could legislate in that area even without a specific Article I grant.

The basic statutes governing antitrust law, the Sherman Antitrust Act, 15 U.S.C.A. § 1 *et seq*. and the Clayton Act, 15 U.S.C.A. § 15, speak in very broad terms; the federal courts have developed most of the specific governing rules. Antitrust law stands on a footing different from admiralty law, however, because the antitrust statutes are interpreted as intentional, though implicit, delegations of law-making authority from Congress to the federal courts, much as the Court found in *Textile Workers Union v. Lincoln Mills.* The development of common law in this area is distinguishable from *Lincoln Mills* only because here there are at least some substantive statutory provisions expressing congressional goals, whereas in *Lincoln Mills* the statute purported only to be a jurisdictional grant. For institutional legitimacy purposes, does it make any difference whether the courts are trying to determine what Congress meant by "restraint of trade" or are themselves deciding what "restraint of trade" means?

3. Implying Private Rights of Action

The cases in this subsection challenge us to think about what it means to have a right. If law, whether at the constitutional or sub-constitutional level, forbids actions with respect to individuals in general or a subclass of individuals, does that create a "right"? Does or should the answer depend on whether there is any way for the beneficiary to seek legal enforcement? In the sphere of the law, can one meaningfully say that a right exists if there is no remedy for its violation?

Bivens v. Six Unknown Named Agents of Federal Bureau of Narcotics

Supreme Court of the United States, 1971.
403 U.S. 388.

MR. JUSTICE BRENNAN delivered the opinion of the Court.

The Fourth Amendment provides that: "The right of the people to be secure in their persons, houses, papers, and effects, against unreasonable searches and seizures, shall not be violated * * * ."

In *Bell v. Hood* we reserved the question whether violation of that command by a federal agent acting under color of his authority gives rise to a cause of action for damages consequent upon his unconstitutional conduct. Today we hold that it does.

This case has its origin in an arrest and search carried out on the morning of November 26, 1965. Petitioner's complaint alleged that on that day respondents, agents of the Federal Bureau of Narcotics acting under claim of federal authority, entered his apartment and arrested him for alleged narcotics violations. The agents manacled petitioner in front of his wife and children, and threatened to arrest the entire family. They searched the apartment from stem to stern. Thereafter, petitioner was taken to the federal courthouse in Brooklyn, where he was interrogated, booked, and subjected to a visual strip search.

On July 7, 1967, petitioner brought suit in Federal District Court. In addition to the allegations above, his complaint asserted that the arrest and search were effected without a warrant, and that unreasonable force was employed in making the arrest; fairly read, it alleges as well that the arrest was made without probable cause. Petitioner claimed to have suffered great humiliation, embarrassment, and mental suffering as a result of the agents' unlawful conduct, and sought $15,000 damages from each of them. The District Court, on respondents' motion, dismissed the complaint on the ground, *inter alia*, that it failed to state a cause of action. The Court of Appeals * * * affirmed on that basis. * * * We reverse.

I

Respondents do not argue that petitioner should be entirely without remedy for an unconstitutional invasion of his rights by federal agents. In respondents' view, however, the rights that petitioner asserts—primarily rights of privacy—are creations of state and not of federal law. Accordingly, they argue, petitioner may obtain money damages to redress invasion of these rights only by an action in tort, under state law, in the state courts. In this scheme the Fourth Amendment would serve merely to limit the extent to which the agents could defend the state law tort suit by asserting that their actions were a valid exercise of federal power: if the agents were shown to have violated the Fourth Amendment, such a defense would be lost to them and they would stand before the state law merely as private individuals. Candidly admitting that it is the policy of the Department of Justice to remove all such suits from the state to the federal courts for decision,[4] respondents nevertheless urge that we uphold dismissal of petitioner's complaint in federal court, and remit him to filing an action in the state courts in order that the case may properly be removed to the federal court for decision on the basis of state law.

We think that respondents' thesis rests upon an unduly restrictive view of the Fourth Amendment's protection against unreasonable searches and seizures by federal agents, a view that has consistently been rejected by this Court. Respondents seek to treat the relationship between a citizen and a federal agent unconstitutionally exercising his authority as no different from the relationship between two private citizens. In so doing, they ignore the fact that power, once granted, does not disappear like a magic gift when it is wrongfully used. An agent acting—albeit unconstitutionally—in the name of the United States possesses a far greater capacity for harm than an individual trespasser exercising no authority other than his own. Accordingly, as our cases make clear, the Fourth Amendment operates as a limitation upon the exercise of federal power regardless of whether the State in whose jurisdiction that power is exercised would prohibit or penalize the identical act if engaged in by a private citizen. It guarantees to citizens of the United States the absolute right to be free from unreasonable searches and seizures carried out by virtue of federal authority. And "where federally protected rights have been invaded, it has been the rule from the beginning that courts will be alert to adjust their remedies so as to grant the necessary relief."

First. Our cases have long since rejected the notion that the Fourth Amendment proscribes only such conduct as would, if engaged in by private persons, be

4 * * * In light of this, it is difficult to understand our Brother Blackmun's complaint that our holding today "opens the door for another avalanche of new federal cases." In estimating the magnitude of any such "avalanche," it is worth noting that a survey of comparable actions against state officers under 42 U.S.C. § 1983 found only 53 reported cases in 17 years (1951-1967) that survived a motion to dismiss. Increasing this figure by 900% to allow for increases in rate and unreported cases, every federal district judge could expect to try one such case every 13 years.

condemned by state law. * * * And our recent decisions regarding electronic surveillance have made it clear beyond peradventure that the Fourth Amendment is not tied to the niceties of local trespass laws. In light of these cases, respondents' argument that the Fourth Amendment serves only as a limitation on federal defenses to a state law claim, and not as an independent limitation upon the exercise of federal power, must be rejected.

> **FYI**
>
> Justice Brennan refers here to the line of cases best exemplified by Katz v. United States (1967), which ruled that the government violated the Fourth Amendment by wiretapping a public telephone booth, even though there was no trespassory intrusion.

Second. The interests protected by state laws regulating trespass and the invasion of privacy, and those protected by the Fourth Amendment's guarantee against unreasonable searches and seizures, may be inconsistent or even hostile. Thus, we may bar the door against an unwelcome private intruder, or call the police if he persists in seeking entrance. The availability of such alternative means for the protection of privacy may lead the State to restrict imposition of liability for any consequent trespass. A private citizen, asserting no authority other than his own, will not normally be liable in trespass if he demands, and is granted, admission to another's house. But one who demands admission under a claim of federal authority stands in a far different position. The mere invocation of federal power by a federal law enforcement official will normally render futile any attempt to resist an unlawful entry or arrest by resort to the local police; and a claim of authority to enter is likely to unlock the door as well. "In such cases there is no safety for the citizen, except in the protection of the judicial tribunals, for rights which have been invaded by the officers of the government, professing to act in its name. There remains to him but the alternative of resistance, which may amount to crime." Nor is it adequate to answer that state law may take into account the different status of one clothed with the authority of the Federal Government. For just as state law may not authorize federal agents to violate the Fourth Amendment, neither may state law undertake to limit the extent to which federal authority can be exercised. The inevitable consequence of this dual limitation on state power is that the federal question becomes not merely a possible defense to the state law action, but an independent claim both necessary and sufficient to make out the plaintiff's cause of action.

Third. That damages may be obtained for injuries consequent upon a violation of the Fourth Amendment by federal officials should hardly seem a surprising proposition. Historically, damages have been regarded as the ordinary remedy for an invasion of personal interests in liberty. Of course, the Fourth Amendment does not in so many words provide for its enforcement by an award of money damages for the consequences of its violation. But "it is * * * well settled that where legal rights have been invaded, and a federal statute provides for a general right to sue for such invasion, federal courts may use any available remedy to make good the wrong done." The present case involves no special factors counselling hesitation in the absence of affirmative action by Congress. We are not dealing with a question of "federal fiscal policy," as in *United States v. Standard Oil Co.* In that case we refused to infer from the Government-soldier relationship that the United States could recover damages from one who negligently injured a soldier and thereby caused the Government to pay his medical expenses and lose his services during the course of his hospitalization. Noting that Congress was normally quite solicitous where the federal purse was involved, we pointed out that "the United States [was] the party plaintiff to the suit. And the United States has power at any time to create the liability." Nor are we asked in this case to impose liability upon a congressional employee for actions contrary to no constitutional prohibition, but merely said to be in excess of the authority delegated to him by the Congress. Finally, we cannot accept respondents' formulation of the question as whether the availability of money damages is necessary to enforce the Fourth Amendment. For we have here no explicit congressional declaration that persons injured by a federal officer's violation of the Fourth Amendment may not recover money damages from the agents, but must instead be remitted to another remedy, equally effective in the view of Congress. The question is merely whether petitioner, if he can demonstrate an injury consequent upon the violation by federal agents of his Fourth Amendment rights, is entitled to redress his injury through a particular remedial mechanism normally available in the federal courts.

Food for Thought

To what federal statute does Justice Brennan refer here? Neither of the jurisdictional statutes under which this case might arise, 28 U.S.C. § 1331 and 28 U.S.C. § 1343, "provides for a general right to sue for such invasion * * * ."

Food for Thought

This sentence raises a welter of issues that are not immediately obvious. Does Congress have the power to declare that there should be no private right of action for constitutional violations? If Congress provides an alternative remedy that it thinks is "equally effective," what should happen if the Court disagrees about its effectiveness? Keep these matter in mind when you read *Schweiker v. Chilicky* at page 536.

"The very essence of civil liberty certainly consists in the right of every individual to claim the protection of the laws, whenever he receives an injury." Having concluded that petitioner's complaint states a cause of action under the Fourth Amendment, we hold that petitioner is entitled to recover money damages for any injuries he has suffered as a result of the agents' violation of the Amendment.

II

In addition to holding that petitioner's complaint had failed to state facts making out a cause of action, the District Court ruled that in any event respondents were immune from liability by virtue of their official position. This question was not passed upon by the Court of Appeals, and accordingly we do not consider it here. The judgment of the Court of Appeals is reversed and the case is remanded for further proceedings consistent with this opinion.

> **Food for Thought**
>
> The Constitution provides only one immunity: legislators' immunity in Article I, § 6, cl. 1. Could Congress immunize other officials from liability for constitutional violations? Can the Court?]

So ordered.

MR. JUSTICE HARLAN, concurring in the judgment.

My initial view of this case was that the Court of Appeals was correct in dismissing the complaint, but for reasons stated in this opinion I am now persuaded to the contrary. Accordingly, I join in the judgment of reversal.

* * *

I

I turn first to the contention that the constitutional power of federal courts to accord Bivens damages for his claim depends on the passage of a statute creating a "federal cause of action." Although the point is not entirely free of ambiguity, I do not understand either the Government or my dissenting Brothers to maintain that Bivens' contention that he is entitled to be free from the type of official conduct prohibited by the Fourth Amendment depends on a decision by the State in which he resides to accord him a remedy. Such a position would be incompatible with the presumed availability of federal equitable relief, if a proper showing can be made in terms of the ordinary principles governing equitable remedies. However broad a federal court's discretion concerning equitable remedies, it is absolutely clear—at least after *Erie R. Co. v. Tompkins*—that in a nondiversity suit a federal court's power to grant even equitable relief depends on the presence of a substantive right derived from federal law.

Thus the interest which Bivens claims—to be free from official conduct in contravention of the Fourth Amendment—is a federally protected interest.[3] Therefore, the question of judicial power to grant Bivens damages is

3 The Government appears not quite ready to concede this point. Certain points in the Government's argument seem to suggest that the "state-created right—federal defense" model reaches not only the question of the power to accord a federal damages remedy, but also the claim to any judicial

not a problem of the "source" of the "right"; instead, the question is whether the power to authorize damages as a judicial remedy for the vindication of a federal constitutional right is placed by the Constitution itself exclusively in Congress' hands.

II

The contention that the federal courts are powerless to accord a litigant damages for a claimed invasion of his federal constitutional rights until Congress explicitly authorizes the remedy cannot rest on the notion that the decision to grant compensatory relief involves a resolution of policy considerations not susceptible of judicial discernment. Thus, in suits for damages based on violations of federal statutes lacking any express authorization of a damage remedy, this Court has authorized such relief where, in its view, damages are necessary to effectuate the congressional policy underpinning the substantive provisions of the statute.

If it is not the nature of the remedy which is thought to render a judgment as to the appropriateness of damages inherently "legislative," then it must be the nature of the legal interest offered as an occasion for invoking otherwise appropriate judicial relief. But I do not think that the fact that the interest is protected by the Constitution rather than statute or common law justifies the assertion that federal courts are powerless to grant damages in the absence of explicit congressional action authorizing the remedy. Initially, I note that it would be at least anomalous to conclude that the federal judiciary—while competent to choose among the range of traditional judicial remedies to implement statutory and common-law policies, and even to generate substantive rules governing primary behavior in furtherance of broadly formulated policies articulated by statute or Constitution—is powerless to accord a damages remedy to vindicate social poli-

---

remedy in any court. Thus, we are pointed to Lasson's observation concerning Madison's version of the Fourth Amendment as introduced into the House: "The observation may be made that the language of the proposal did not purport to create the right to be secure from unreasonable search and seizures but merely stated it as a right which already existed." * * *

On this point, the choice of phraseology in the Fourth Amendment itself is singularly unpersuasive. The leading argument against a "Bill of Rights" was the fear that individual liberties not specified expressly would be taken as excluded. This circumstance alone might well explain why the authors of the Bill of Rights would opt for language which presumes the existence of a fundamental interest in liberty, albeit originally derived from the common law.

In truth, the legislative record as a whole behind the Bill of Rights is silent on the rather refined doctrinal question whether the framers considered the rights therein enumerated as dependent in the first instance on the decision of a State to accord legal status to the personal interests at stake. That is understandable since the Government itself points out that general federal-question jurisdiction was not extended to the federal district courts until 1875. The most that can be drawn from this historical fact is that the authors of the Bill of Rights assumed the adequacy of common-law remedies to vindicate the federally protected interest. One must first combine this assumption with contemporary modes of jurisprudential thought which appeared to link "rights" and "remedies" in a 1:1 correlation, before reaching the conclusion that the framers are to be understood today as having created no federally protected interests. And, of course, that would simply require the conclusion that federal equitable relief would not lie to protect those interests guarded by the Fourth Amendment. * * *

cies which, by virtue of their inclusion in the Constitution, are aimed predominantly at restraining the Government as an instrument of the popular will.

More importantly, the presumed availability of federal equitable relief against threatened invasions of constitutional interests appears entirely to negate the contention that the status of an interest as constitutionally protected divests federal courts of the power to grant damages absent express congressional authorization. Congress provided specially for the exercise of equitable remedial powers by federal courts, in part because of the limited availability of equitable remedies in state courts in the early days of the Republic. And this Court's decisions make clear that, at least absent congressional restrictions, the scope of equitable remedial discretion is to be determined according to the distinctive historical traditions of equity as an institution. The reach of a federal district court's "inherent equitable powers," is broad indeed; nonetheless, the federal judiciary is not empowered to grant equitable relief in the absence of congressional action extending jurisdiction over the subject matter of the suit.

> **FYI**
>
> Justice Harlan's reference here is apparently to the All Writs Act, 28 U.S.C. § 1651. The present statute originated in the Judiciary Act of 1789.

If explicit congressional authorization is an absolute prerequisite to the power of a federal court to accord compensatory relief regardless of the necessity or appropriateness of damages as a remedy simply because of the status of a legal interest as constitutionally protected, then it seems to me that explicit congressional authorization is similarly prerequisite to the exercise of equitable remedial discretion in favor of constitutionally protected interests. Conversely, if a general grant of jurisdiction to the federal courts by Congress is thought adequate to empower a federal court to grant equitable relief for all areas of subject-matter jurisdiction enumerated therein, then it seems to me that the same statute is sufficient to empower a federal court to grant a traditional remedy at law. Of course, the special historical traditions governing the federal equity system might still bear on the comparative appropriateness of granting equitable relief as opposed to money damages. That possibility, however, relates, not to whether the federal courts have the power to afford one type of remedy as opposed to the other, but rather to the criteria which should govern the exercise of our power. To that question, I now pass.

III

The major thrust of the Government's position is that, where Congress has not expressly authorized a particular remedy, a federal court should exercise its power to accord a traditional form of judicial relief at the behest of a litigant, who claims a constitutionally protected interest has been invaded, only where the remedy is "essential," or "indispensable for vindicating constitutional rights." While this "essentiality" test is most clearly articulated with respect to damages remedies, apparently the Government believes the same test explains the exercise of equitable remedial powers. It is argued that historically the Court has rarely exercised the power to accord such relief in the absence of an express congressional authorization and that "[i]f Congress had thought that federal officers should be subject to a law different than state law, it would have had no difficulty in saying so, as it did with respect to state officers * * * ." Although conceding that the standard of determining whether a damage remedy should be utilized to effectuate statutory policies is one of "necessity" or "appropriateness," the Government contends that questions concerning congressional discretion to modify judicial remedies relating to constitutionally protected interests warrant a more stringent constraint on the exercise of judicial power with respect to this class of legally protected interests.

These arguments for a more stringent test to govern the grant of damages in constitutional cases seem to be adequately answered by the point that the judiciary has a particular responsibility to assure the vindication of constitutional interests such as those embraced by the Fourth Amendment. To be sure, "it must be remembered that legislatures are ultimate guardians of the liberties and welfare of the people in quite as great a degree as the courts." But it must also be recognized that the Bill of Rights is particularly intended to vindicate the interests of the individual in the face of the popular will as expressed in legislative majorities; at the very least, it strikes me as no more appropriate to await express congressional authorization of traditional judicial relief with regard to these legal interests than with respect to interests protected by federal statutes.

The question then, is, as I see it, whether compensatory relief is "necessary" or "appropriate" to the vindication of the interest asserted. In resolving that question, it seems to me that the range of policy considerations we may take into account is at least as broad as the range of those a legislature would consider with respect to an express statutory authorization of a traditional remedy. In this regard I agree with the Court that the appropriateness of according Bivens compensatory relief does not turn simply on the deterrent effect liability will have on federal official conduct. Damages as a traditional form of compensation for invasion of a legally protected interest may be entirely appropriate even if no substantial deterrent effects on future official lawlessness might be thought to result. Bivens, after all, has invoked judicial processes claiming entitlement to compensation for injuries resulting from allegedly lawless official behavior, if those injuries are properly compensable in money damages. I do not think a court of law—vested with the power to accord a remedy—should deny him his relief simply because he cannot show that future lawless conduct will thereby be deterred.

And I think it is clear that Bivens advances a claim of the sort that, if proved, would be properly compensable in damages. The personal interests protected by the Fourth Amendment are those we attempt to capture by the notion of "privacy"; while the Court today properly points out that the type of harm which officials can inflict when they invade protected zones of an individual's life are [*sic*] different from the types of harm private citizens inflict on one another, the experience of judges in dealing with private trespass and false imprisonment claims supports the conclusion that courts of law are capable of making the types of judgment concerning causation and magnitude of injury necessary to accord meaningful compensation for invasion of Fourth Amendment rights.

On the other hand, the limitations on state remedies for violation of common-law rights by private citizens argue in favor of a federal damages remedy. The injuries inflicted by officials acting under color of law, while no less compensable in damages than those inflicted by private parties, are substantially different in kind, as the Court's opinion today discusses in detail. It seems to me entirely proper that these injuries be compensable according to uniform rules of federal law, especially in light of the very large element of federal law which must in any event control the scope of official defenses to liability. Certainly, there is very little to be gained from the standpoint of federalism by preserving different rules of liability for federal officers dependent on the State where the injury occurs.

Putting aside the desirability of leaving the problem of federal official liability to the vagaries of common-law actions, it is apparent that some form of damages is the only possible remedy for someone in Bivens' alleged position. It will be a rare case indeed in which an individual in Bivens' position will be able to obviate the harm by securing injunctive relief from any court. However desirable a direct remedy against the Government might be as a substitute for individual official liability, the sovereign still remains immune to suit. Finally, assuming Bivens' innocence of the crime charged, the "exclusionary rule" is simply irrelevant. For people in Bivens' shoes, it is damages or nothing.

> **FYI**
>
> Justice Harlan responds here to the argument that Chief Justice Burger's dissent makes below at page 506-07.

The only substantial policy consideration advanced against recognition of a federal cause of action for violation of Fourth Amendment rights by federal officials is the incremental expenditure of judicial resources that will be necessitated by this class of litigation. There is, however, something ultimately self-defeating about this argument. For if, as the Government contends, damages will rarely be realized by plaintiffs in these cases because of jury hostility, the limited resources of the official concerned, etc., then I am not ready to assume that there will be a significant increase in the expenditure of judicial resources on these claims. Few responsible lawyers and plaintiffs are likely to choose the course of litigation if the statistical chances of success are truly *de minimis*. And I simply cannot agree with my Brother Black that the possibility of "frivolous" claims—if defined simply as claims with no legal merit—warrants closing the courthouse doors to people in Bivens' situation. There are other ways, short of that, of coping with frivolous lawsuits.

On the other hand, if—as I believe is the case with respect, at least, to the most flagrant abuses of official power—damages to some degree will be available when the option of litigation is chosen, then the question appears to be how Fourth Amendment interests rank on a scale of social values compared with, for example, the interests of stockholders defrauded by misleading proxies. Judicial resources, I am well aware, are increasingly scarce these days. Nonetheless, when we automatically close the courthouse door solely on this basis, we implicitly express a value judgment on the comparative importance of classes of legally protected interests. And current limitations upon the effective functioning of the courts arising from budgetary inadequacies should not be permitted to stand in the way of the recognition of otherwise sound constitutional principles.

Of course, for a variety of reasons, the remedy may not often be sought. And the countervailing interests in efficient law enforcement of course argue for a protective zone with respect to many types of Fourth Amendment violations. But, while I express no view on the immunity defense offered in the instant case, I deem it proper to venture the thought that at the very least such a remedy would be available for the most flagrant and patently unjustified sorts of police conduct. Although litigants may not often choose to seek relief, it is important, in a civilized society, that the judicial branch of the Nation's government stand ready to afford a remedy in these circumstances. It goes without saying that I intimate no view on the merits of petitioner's underlying claim.

For these reasons, I concur in the judgment of the Court.

MR. CHIEF JUSTICE BURGER, dissenting.

I dissent from today's holding which judicially creates a damage remedy not provided for by the Constitution and not enacted by Congress. We would more surely preserve the important values of the doctrine of separation of powers—and perhaps get a better result—by recommending a solution to the Congress as the branch of government in which the Constitution has vested the legislative power. Legislation is the business of the Congress, and it has the facilities and competence for that task—as we do not.

* * *

> **FYI**
>
> *Weeks v. United States*, 232 U.S. 383 (1914), was the first case to order suppression of evidence seized by federal authorities in violation of the Fourth Amendment, a rule that the Court extended to the states in *Mapp v. Ohio*, 367 U.S. 643 (1961). That is the "exclusionary rule" or "suppression doctrine" that he argued against in *Bivens*, although since the federal agents had seized no evidence from Bivens, the Chief Justice's discussion was gratuitous.

[Chief Justice Burger's extended argument for overturning the exclusionary rule is omitted.]

* * *

The problems of both error and deliberate misconduct by law enforcement officials call for a workable remedy. Private damage actions against individual police officers concededly have not adequately met this requirement, and it would be fallacious to assume today's work of the Court in creating a remedy will really accomplish its stated objective. There is some validity to the claims that juries will not return verdicts against individual officers except in those unusual cases where the violation has been flagrant or where the error has been complete, as in the arrest of the wrong person or the search of the wrong house. * * * Jurors may well refuse to penalize a police officer at the behest of a person they believe to be a "criminal" and probably will not punish an officer for honest errors of judgment. In any event an actual recovery depends on finding nonexempt assets of the police officer from which a judgment can be satisfied.

I conclude, therefore, that an entirely different remedy is necessary but it is one that in my view is as much beyond judicial power as the step the Court takes today. Congress should develop an administrative or quasi-judicial remedy against the government itself to afford compensation and restitution for persons whose Fourth Amendment rights have been violated. The venerable doctrine of *respondeat superior* in our tort law provides an entirely appropriate conceptual basis for this remedy. * * * Such a statutory scheme would have the added advantage of providing some remedy to the completely innocent persons who are sometimes the victims of illegal police conduct—something that the suppression doctrine, of course, can never accomplish.

A simple structure would suffice. For example, Congress could enact a statute along the following lines:

(a) a waiver of sovereign immunity as to the illegal acts of law enforcement officials committed in the performance of assigned duties;

(b) the creation of a cause of action for damages sustained by any person aggrieved by conduct of governmental agents in violation of the Fourth Amendment or statutes regulating official conduct;

(c) the creation of a tribunal, quasi-judicial in nature or perhaps patterned after the United States Court of Claims, to adjudicate all claims under the statute;

(d) a provision that this statutory remedy is in lieu of the exclusion of evidence secured for use in criminal cases in violation of the Fourth Amendment; and

(e) a provision directing that no evidence, otherwise admissible, shall be excluded from any criminal proceeding because of violation of the Fourth Amendment.

I doubt that lawyers serving on such a tribunal would be swayed either by undue sympathy for officers or by the prejudice against "criminals" that has sometimes moved lay jurors to deny claims. In addition to awarding damages, the record of the police conduct that is condemned would undoubtedly become a relevant part of an officer's personnel file so that the need for additional training or disciplinary action could be identified or his future usefulness as a public official evaluated. Finally, appellate judicial review could be made available on much the same basis that it is now provided as to district courts and regulatory agencies. This would leave to the courts the ultimate responsibility for determining and articulating standards.

Once the constitutional validity of such a statute is established,[7] it can reasonably be assumed that the States would develop their own remedial systems on the federal model. Indeed there is nothing to prevent a State from enacting a comparable statutory scheme without waiting for the Congress. Steps along these lines would move our system toward more responsible law enforcement on the one hand and away from the irrational and drastic results of the suppression doctrine on the other. Independent of the alternative embraced in this dissenting opinion, I believe the time has come to re-examine the scope of the exclusionary rule and consider at least some narrowing of its thrust so as to eliminate the anomalies it has produced.

* * *

7 Any such legislation should emphasize the interdependence between the waiver of sovereign immunity and the elimination of the judicially created exclusionary rule so that if the legislative determination to repudiate the exclusionary rule falls, the entire statutory scheme would fall.

MR. JUSTICE BLACK, dissenting.

* * * There can be no doubt that Congress could create a federal cause of action for damages for an unreasonable search in violation of the Fourth Amendment. Although Congress has created such a federal cause of action against state officials acting under color of state law, it has never created such a cause of action against federal officials. If it wanted to do so, Congress could, of course, create a remedy against federal officials who violate the Fourth Amendment in the performance of their duties. But the point of this case and the fatal weakness in the Court's judgment is that neither Congress nor the State of New York has enacted legislation creating such a right of action. For us to do so is, in my judgment, an exercise of power that the Constitution does not give us.

Even if we had the legislative power to create a remedy, there are many reasons why we should decline to create a cause of action where none has existed since the formation of our Government. The courts of the United States as well as those of the States are choked with lawsuits. The number of cases on the docket of this Court have reached an unprecedented volume in recent years. A majority of these cases are brought by citizens with substantial complaints—persons who are physically or economically injured by torts or frauds or governmental infringement of their rights; persons who have been unjustly deprived of their liberty or their property; and persons who have not yet received the equal opportunity in education, employment, and pursuit of happiness that was the dream of our forefathers. Unfortunately, there have also been a growing number of frivolous lawsuits, particularly actions for damages against law enforcement officers whose conduct has been judicially sanctioned by state trial and appellate courts and in many instances even by this Court. My fellow Justices on this Court and our brethren throughout the federal judiciary know only too well the time-consuming task of conscientiously poring over hundreds of thousands of pages of factual allegations of misconduct by police, judicial, and corrections officials. Of course, there are instances of legitimate grievances, but legislators might well desire to devote judicial resources to other problems of a more serious nature.

We sit at the top of a judicial system accused by some of nearing the point of collapse. Many criminal defendants do not receive speedy trials and neither society nor the accused are assured of justice when inordinate delays occur. Citizens must wait years to litigate their private civil suits. Substantial changes in correctional and parole systems demand the attention of the lawmakers and the judiciary. If I were a legislator I might well find these and other needs so pressing as to make me believe that the resources of lawyers and judges should be devoted to them rather than to civil damage actions against officers who generally strive to perform within constitutional bounds. There is also a real danger that such suits might deter officials from the proper and honest performance of their duties.

All of these considerations make imperative careful study and weighing of the arguments both for and against the creation of such a remedy under the Fourth Amendment. I would have great difficulty for myself in resolving the competing policies, goals, and priorities in the use of resources, if I thought it were my job to resolve those questions. But that is not my task. The task of evaluating the pros and cons of creating judicial remedies for particular wrongs is a matter for Congress and the legislatures of the States. Congress has not provided that any federal court can entertain a suit against a federal officer for violations of Fourth Amendment rights occurring in the performance of his duties. A strong inference can be drawn from creation of such actions against state officials that Congress does not desire to permit such suits against federal officials. Should the time come when Congress desires such lawsuits, it has before it a model of valid legislation, 42 U.S.C. § 1983, to create a damage remedy against federal officers. Cases could be cited to support the legal proposition which I assert, but it seems to me to be a matter of common understanding that the business of the judiciary is to interpret the laws and not to make them.

I dissent.

MR. JUSTICE BLACKMUN, dissenting.

I, too, dissent. I do so largely for the reasons expressed in Chief Judge Lumbard's thoughtful and scholarly opinion for the Court of Appeals. But I also feel that the judicial legislation, which the Court by its opinion today concededly is effectuating, opens the door for another avalanche of new federal cases. * * * The Fourth Amendment was adopted in 1791, and in all the intervening years neither the Congress nor the Court has seen fit to take this step. I had thought that for the truly aggrieved person other quite adequate remedies have always been available. If not, it is the Congress and not this Court that should act.

Notes and Questions

1. The majority discusses a "dual limitation on state power" as "mak[ing] out the plaintiff's cause of action." Why should the states' inability either to authorize federal agents to violate federal law or to limit federal officials' exercise of authority give rise to a federal cause of action?

2. The majority opinion also mentions "special factors counseling hesitation * * * ," and lists some such factors. The phrase becomes particularly important in cases involving implication of private rights of action in constitutional provisions, especially *Schweiker v. Chilicky*, 487 U.S. 412 (1988), presented at page 536. Is the listing exhaustive and exclusive, or was Justice Brennan merely offering illustrative

examples? If the latter, on what principled basis can the Court recognize a new special factor?

3. Justice Harlan argues in part that the Court's established practice of implying private rights of action in federal statutes connotes the propriety of judicial authorization of a damages remedy for a constitutional violation. Has the Court's subsequent retreat from implying causes of action in statutes, exemplified by cases discussed later in this Chapter, undermined Justice Harlan's argument?

4. Chief Justice Burger, apart from his disapproval of the exclusionary rule, bases his dissent on separation of powers. Justice Black agrees that separation-of-powers concerns counsel against the Court creating the damages remedy. Where does the Constitution discuss separation of powers? Is it implicit in the constitutional scheme that Congress, in addition to being the body with the general legislative power of article I, § 8, is also the exclusive source of enforceability of the Bill of Rights?

6. Suppose Congress decided that the courts should not enforce the Bill of Rights at all. Accepting *arguendo* the Chief Justice's suggestion, if Congress declines to act, are executive violations of the Bill of Rights unredressable, making those provisions hortatory only?

> [A] right without a remedy is not a legal right; it is merely a hope or a wish * * * . In Hohfeldian terms, a right entails a correlative duty to act or refrain from acting for the benefit of another person. Unless a duty can be enforced, it is not really a duty; it is only a voluntary obligation that a person can fulfill or not at his whim.

Donald H. Zeigler, *Rights Require Remedies: A New Approach to the Enforcement of Rights in the Federal Courts*, 38 HASTINGS L.J. 665, 678 (1987). Professor Zeigler notes Justice Holmes's characterization of the problem: "Legal obligations that 'exist but cannot be enforced are ghosts that are seen in the law but that are elusive to the grasp.' "

7. Suppose, following *Bivens*, Congress were to enact a statute allowing only nominal damages against federal officials who violate the Fourth Amendment. What effect would or should the statute have on the judicially-created remedy?

Introductory Note on Implying Private Rights of Action in Federal Statutes

Statutes that create new rights or duties often fail to provide private rights of action to enforce them. Almost 300 years ago, the Chief Justice of the King's Bench observed: "If the plaintiff has a right, he must of necessity have a means to vindicate and maintain it, and a remedy if he is injured in the exercise or enjoyment of it; and indeed it is a vain thing to imagine a right without a remedy * * * ." *Ashby v. White*,

92 Eng.Rep. 126, 135-37 (K.B. 1703) (Holt, C.J., dissenting).[5] As Professor Zeigler noted, in the United States during the late nineteenth and early twentieth centuries, state courts routinely created private tort remedies for violations of statutory duties as long as "the statute was intended for the benefit of a class of persons of which the plaintiff was a member rather than for the public generally, and if the harm suffered was of a kind the statute generally was intended to prevent."[6]

Professor Zeigler[7] chronicled the development of implying remedies in statutes in the United States.

> Legislative intent played an important role in the early cases. The requirements that the statute be enacted for the plaintiff's benefit and aimed at preventing the sort of harm that actually occurred ensured that a private remedy was consistent with underlying legislative purposes. * * * [A] court would provide a private remedy even if the legislature was silent on the matter. A court would refuse a private remedy only if the legislature explicitly barred the remedy or made clear its intention to substitute other relief.
>
> Until quite recently, the federal courts generally followed traditional standards in providing remedies for violation of statutory duties. * * *
>
> After [*Texas & Pacific Railroad v.*] *Rigsby* [1916], the federal courts often allowed or "implied" remedies for violations of statutory duties when the statute did not explicitly authorize a private right of action.

This approach may have reached its high water mark in *J.I. Case Company v. Borak*, 377 U.S. 426 (1964). A unanimous Court implied a private right of action in the Securities Exchange Act for a stockholder seeking recission of a merger or damages because of a misleading proxy statement. The Court noted that although Congress had provided for direct enforcement of the Act only by the Securities Exchange Commission, "[t]o hold that derivative actions are not within the sweep of the section would therefore be tantamount to a denial of private relief. Private enforcement of the proxy rules provides a necessary supplement to Commission action." The Court defended its approach:

> We, therefore, believe that under the circumstances here it is the duty of the courts to be alert to provide such remedies as are necessary to make effective the congressional purpose. * * *
>
> When a federal statute condemns an act as unlawful, the extent and nature of the legal consequences of the condemnation, though left by the statute to judicial determination, are nevertheless federal questions, the answers to which are to be derived from the statute and the federal policy which it has adopted.

5 "Subsequently, * * * Chief Justice Holt's dissenting opinion was accepted by the House of Lords and judgment was entered for the plaintiff." Donald H. Zeigler, *Rights Require Remedies: A New Approach to the Enforcement of Rights in the Federal Courts*, 38 HASTINGS L.J. 665, 672 n.44 (1987).

6 *Id.* at 674.

7 *Id.* at 674-76.

Thus, the Court characterized itself as advancing or supporting the legislative policy represented by the statute.

Eleven years after *Borak*, *Cort v. Ash* (1975) reconsidered implied statutory rights of action in. When a shareholder commenced a derivative action premised on corporate directors' violations of a provision of the federal criminal code prohibiting corporate campaign contributions, the Court (again unanimous) declined to imply a private right of action. Justice Brennan announced a new, four-factor test:

> First, is the plaintiff "one of the class for whose *especial* benefit the statute was enacted," *Texas & Pacific R. Co. v. Rigsby*, 241 U.S. 33, 39 (1916) (emphasis supplied)—that is, does the statute create a federal right in favor of the plaintiff? Second, is there any indication of legislative intent, explicit or implicit, either to create such a remedy or to deny one? Third, is it consistent with the underlying purposes of the legislative scheme to imply such a remedy for the plaintiff? And finally, is the cause of action one traditionally relegated to state law, in an area basically the concern of the States, so that it would be inappropriate to infer a cause of action based solely on federal law?

Food for Thought

How does the *Cort* test differ from the Court's approach to statutory implication from the 1800's through *Borak* ?

Food for Thought

Given that Congress did articulate what Justice Brennan characterizes as a "secondary" goal, why is it unworthy of support through a private right of action? Should the Court refuse to support a goal unless it is Congress's "primary" goal? Can Congress have only one "primary" goal? Is it even self-evident that a private right of action would not further the primary goal of protecting federal elections?

The opinion is less than illuminating about why the Justices implied no action. Justice Brennan did note that Ash relied upon a criminal rather than civil statute and that it was thus difficult for him to show that he was a member of a benefited class apart from being a member of society generally, but Justice Brennan also noted that the Court had implied private rights of action in criminal statutes. He did not distinguish those cases. Second, he characterized the primary purpose of the statute as protection of federal election campaigns but acknowledged that protection of stockholders was a secondary concern. Nonetheless, the Court refused to effectuate that secondary purpose at the behest of one of its intended beneficiaries.

Notes and Questions

1. a) The fourth *Cort* criterion raises several interesting problems. Although the other criteria appear in the history of implying private rights of action in statutes, the fourth is new. What values does its introduction serve?

b) Is there not a Janus-like aspect to the fourth criterion? For most of the first century under the Constitution, federal power was extremely limited. Indeed, the Framers feared that the emerging national government would become too strong, hence the Constitution's plan of limited, enumerated powers for the federal government with the balance of governmental authority residing in the states. Only since about 1885 has the federal government expanded so that national regulation is common. In that light, cannot most issues be seen as "traditionally" relegated to state concern? Still, does the presence of a federal statute at least suggest a strong federal interest in the subject matter? These conflicting perspectives will be present most of the time.

c) The Court is less than consistent applying the fourth criterion to the facts of *Cort*. Having dismissed the "secondary" goal (corporate protection) for purposes of the second criterion, the Court resurrected it in discussing the fourth. In asking whether the statute is aimed primarily at an area of traditional state or federal concern, Justice Brennan concluded that state-chartered corporations are within the realm of state interest. Should he have asked instead whether protection of the federal electoral process is traditionally a matter of state or federal concern?

2. What should be the relationship of the *Cort* factors to each other? Does a negative answer to any one of them preclude an implied right of action? Should all the factors have equal weight?

Cannon v. University Of Chicago

Supreme Court of the United States, 1979.
441 U.S. 677.

MR. JUSTICE STEVENS delivered the opinion of the Court.

Petitioner's complaints allege that her applications for admission to medical school were denied by the respondents because she is a woman. Accepting the truth of those allegations for the purpose of its decision, the Court of Appeals held that petitioner has no right of action against respondents that may be asserted in a federal court. We granted certiorari to review that holding.

Only two facts alleged in the complaints are relevant to our decision. First, petitioner was excluded from participation in the respondents' medical education programs because of her sex. Second, these education programs were receiving federal financial assistance at the time of her exclusion. These facts, admitted *arguendo* by respondents' motion to dismiss the complaints, establish a violation of § 901(a) of Title IX of the Education Amendments of 1972 (hereinafter Title IX).[2]

That section, in relevant part, provides: "No person in the United States shall, on the basis of sex, be excluded from participation in, be denied the benefits of, or be subjected to discrimination under any education program or activity receiving Federal financial assistance * * * ." The statute does not, however, expressly authorize a private right of action by a person injured by a violation of § 901. For that reason, and because it concluded that no private remedy should be inferred, the District Court granted the respondents' motions to dismiss.

The Court of Appeals agreed that the statute did not contain an implied private remedy. Noting that § 902 of Title IX establishes a procedure for the termination of federal financial support for institutions violating § 901, the Court of Appeals concluded that Congress intended that remedy to be the exclusive means of enforcement. It recognized that the statute was patterned after Title VI of the Civil Rights Act of 1964 (hereinafter Title VI), but rejected petitioner's argument that Title VI included an implied private cause of action.

After the Court of Appeals' decision was announced, Congress enacted the Civil Rights Attorney's Fees Awards Act of 1976, which authorizes an award of fees to prevailing private parties in actions to enforce Title IX. The court therefore granted a petition for rehearing to consider whether, in the light of that statute, its original interpretation of Title IX had been correct. After receiving additional briefs, the court concluded that the 1976 Act was not intended to create a remedy that did not previously exist. The court also noted that the Department of Health, Education, and Welfare had taken the position that a private cause of action under

2 * * * [A]ll of the facts alleged in petitioner's complaints must be taken as true for purposes of review.

According to her complaints, petitioner was qualified to attend both of the respondent medical schools based on both objective (*i.e.*, grade-point average and test scores) and subjective criteria. In fact, both schools admitted some persons to the classes to which she applied despite the fact that those persons had less impressive objective qualifications than she did.

Both medical schools receive federal aid, and both have policies against admitting applicants who are more than 30 years old (petitioner was 39 years old at the time she applied), at least if they do not have advanced degrees. Northwestern Medical School absolutely disqualifies applicants over 35. These policies, it is alleged, prevented petitioner from being asked to an interview at the medical schools, so that she was denied even the opportunity to convince the schools that her personal qualifications warranted her admission in place of persons whose objective qualifications were better than hers. Because the incidence of interrupted higher education is higher among women than among men, it is further claimed, the age and advanced-degree criteria operate to exclude women from consideration even though the criteria are not valid predictors of success in medical schools or in medical practice. As such, the existence of the criteria either makes out or evidences a violation of the medical school's duty under Title IX to avoid discrimination on the basis of sex. * * *

Title IX should be implied, but the court disagreed with that agency's interpretation of the Act. In sum, it adhered to its original view.

> **Go Online**
>
> At first glance, the Seventh Circuit's conclusion may appear inexplicable, but the court explained its position at length, showing that the record is not so one-sided as Justice Stevens's summary may make it appear. Note that Justice Scalia's general disinclination to look at legislative history in construing statutes might well have cut in plaintiff's favor in this case.

The Court of Appeals quite properly devoted careful attention to this question of statutory construction. As our recent cases—particularly *Cort v. Ash*—demonstrate, the fact that a federal statute has been violated and some person harmed does not automatically give rise to a private cause of action in favor of that person. Instead, before concluding that Congress intended to make a remedy available to a special class of litigants, a court must carefully analyze the four factors that *Cort* identifies as indicative of such an intent. Our review of those factors persuades us, however, that the Court of Appeals reached the wrong conclusion and that petitioner does have a statutory right to pursue her claim that respondents rejected her application on the basis of her sex. After commenting on each of the four factors, we shall explain why they are not overcome by respondents' countervailing arguments.

I

First, the threshold question under *Cort* is whether the statute was enacted for the benefit of a special class of which the plaintiff is a member. That question is answered by looking to the language of the statute itself. Thus, the statutory reference to "any employee of any such common carrier" in the 1893 legislation requiring railroads to equip their cars with secure "grab irons or handholds," made "irresistible" the Court's earliest "inference of a private right of action"—in that case in favor of a railway employee who was injured when a grab iron gave way.

Similarly, it was statutory language describing the special class to be benefited by § 5 of the Voting Rights Act of 1965 that persuaded the Court that private parties within that class were implicitly authorized to seek a declaratory judgment against a covered State. The dispositive language in that statute—"no person shall be denied the right to vote for failure to comply with [a new state enactment covered by, but not approved under, § 5]"—is remarkably similar to the language used by Congress in Title IX.

The language in these statutes—which expressly identifies the class Congress intended to benefit—contrasts sharply with statutory language customarily found in criminal statutes, such as that construed in Cort, and other laws enacted for the protection of the general public. There would be far less reason to infer a private remedy in favor of individual persons if Congress, instead of drafting Title IX with an unmistakable focus on the benefited class, had written it simply as a ban on discriminatory conduct by recipients of federal funds or as a prohibition against the disbursement of public funds to educational institutions engaged in discriminatory practices.

Unquestionably, therefore, the first of the four factors identified in Cort favors the implication of a private cause of action. Title IX explicitly confers a benefit on persons discriminated against on the basis of sex, and petitioner is clearly a member of that class for whose special benefit the statute was enacted.

Second, the Cort analysis requires consideration of legislative history. We must recognize, however, that the legislative history of a statute that does not expressly create or deny a private remedy will typically be equally silent or ambiguous on the question. Therefore, in situations such as the present one "in which it is clear that federal law has granted a class of persons certain rights, it is not necessary to show an intention to *create* a private cause of action, although an explicit purpose to deny such cause of action would be controlling." Cort (emphasis in original). But this is not the typical case. Far from evidencing any purpose to deny a private cause of action, the history of Title IX rather plainly indicates that Congress intended to create such a remedy.

Food for Thought

As you will see when you read Justice Powell's dissent, this sentence may prove too much. If Congress so plainly intended to create a private right of action, Justice Powell asks with some force why the statute does not say so. As Justice Stevens points out later, however, Congress enacted Title IX in 1972, after J.I. Case Company v. Borak and before Cort v. Ash.

Title IX was patterned after Title VI of the Civil Rights Act of 1964. Except for the substitution of the word "sex" in Title IX to replace the words "race, color, or national origin" in Title VI, the two statutes use identical language to describe the benefited class. Both statutes provide the same administrative mechanism for terminating federal financial support for institutions engaged in prohibited discrimination. Neither statute expressly mentions a private remedy for the person excluded from participation in a federally funded program. The drafters of Title IX explicitly assumed that it would be interpreted and applied as Title VI had been during the preceding eight years. In 1972 when Title IX was enacted, the critical language in Title VI had already been construed as creating a private remedy. Most particularly, in 1967, a distinguished panel of the Court of Appeals for the Fifth Circuit squarely decided this issue in an opinion that was repeatedly cited with approval and never questioned during the ensuing five years. In addition, at least a dozen other federal courts reached similar conclusions in the same or related contexts during those years. It is always appropriate to assume that our elected representatives, like other citizens, know the law; in this case, because of their repeated references to Title VI and its modes of enforcement, we are especially justified in presuming both that those representatives were aware of the prior interpretation of Title VI and that that interpretation reflects their intent with respect to Title IX.

Food for Thought

Is Justice Stevens's view of the legislative background of Title IX reconcilable with the Seventh Circuit's canvass of the legislative history?

Moreover, in 1969, this Court had interpreted the comparable language in § 5 of the Voting Rights Act as sufficient to authorize a private remedy.[22] Indeed, during the period between the enactment of Title VI in 1964 and the enactment of Title IX in 1972, this Court had consistently found implied remedies—often in cases much less clear than this.[23] It was *after* 1972 that this Court decided *Cort v. Ash* and the other cases cited by the Court of Appeals in support of its strict construction of the remedial aspect of the statute. We, of course, adhere to the strict approach followed in our recent cases, but our evaluation of congressional action in 1972 must take into account its contemporary legal context. In sum, it is not only appropriate but also realistic to presume that Congress was thoroughly familiar with these unusually important precedents from this and other federal courts and that it expected its enactment to be interpreted in conformity with them.

It is not, however, necessary to rely on these presumptions. The package of statutes of which Title IX is one part also contains a provision whose language and history demonstrate that Congress itself understood Title VI, and thus its companion, Title IX, as creating a private remedy. Section 718 of the Education Amendments authorizes federal courts to award attorney's fees to the prevailing parties, other than the United States, in private actions brought against public educational agencies to enforce Title VI in the context of elementary and secondary education. The language of this provision explicitly presumes the availability of private suits to enforce Title VI in the education context. For many such suits, no express cause of action was then available; hence Congress must have assumed that one could be implied under Title VI itself. That assumption was made explicit during the debates on § 718. It was also aired during the debates on other provisions in the Education Amendments of 1972 and on Title IX itself, and is consistent with the Executive Branch's apparent understanding of Title VI at the time.

22 In fact, Congress enacted Title IX against a backdrop of three recently issued implied-cause-of-action decisions of this Court involving civil rights statutes with language similar to that in Title IX. In all three, a cause of action was found.

23 In the decade preceding the enactment of Title IX, the Court decided six implied-cause-of-action cases. In all of them a cause of action was found.

Finally, the very persistence—before 1972 and since, among judges and executive officials, as well as among litigants and their counsel, and even implicit in decisions of this Court—of the assumption that both Title VI and Title IX created a private right of action for the victims of illegal discrimination and the absence of legislative action to change that assumption provide further evidence that Congress at least acquiesces in, and apparently affirms, that assumption. We have no doubt that Congress intended to create Title IX remedies comparable to those available under Title VI and that it understood Title VI as authorizing an implied private cause of action for victims of the prohibited discrimination.

Third, under *Cort*, a private remedy should not be implied if it would frustrate the underlying purpose of the legislative scheme. On the other hand, when that remedy is necessary or at least helpful to the accomplishment of the statutory purpose, the Court is decidedly receptive to its implication under the statute.

Food for Thought

Why does the Court express the third criterion in disjunctive terms? What's the bottom line if that is the standard?

Title IX, like its model Title VI, sought to accomplish two related, but nevertheless somewhat different, objectives. First, Congress wanted to avoid the use of federal resources to support discriminatory practices; second, it wanted to provide individual citizens effective protection against those practices. Both of these purposes were repeatedly identified in the debates on the two statutes.

The first purpose is generally served by the statutory procedure for the termination of federal financial support for institutions engaged in discriminatory practices. That remedy is, however, severe and often may not provide an appropriate means of accomplishing the second purpose if merely an isolated violation has occurred.

In that situation, the violation might be remedied more efficiently by an order requiring an institution to accept an applicant who had been improperly excluded. Moreover, in that kind of situation it makes little sense to impose on an individual, whose only interest is in obtaining a benefit for herself, or on HEW, the burden of demonstrating that an institution's practices are so pervasively

FYI

It is important to understand that major research institutions, such as the University of Chicago and Northwestern University, annually receive many millions of federal dollars to support research. For example, for fiscal year 2009, United States universities received more than $50 *billion* in science and engineering research funds alone. Justice Stevens obliquely suggests that cutting off federal funding would so widely be perceived as overkill that the government would be loath to impose the penalty at all.

discriminatory that a complete cut-off of federal funding is appropriate. The award of individual relief to a private litigant who has prosecuted her own suit is not only sensible but is also fully consistent with—and in some cases even necessary to—the orderly enforcement of the statute.

The Department of Health, Education, and Welfare, which is charged with the responsibility for administering Title IX, perceives no inconsistency between the private remedy and the public remedy. On the contrary, the agency takes the unequivocal position that the individual remedy will provide effective assistance to achieving the statutory purposes. The agency's position is unquestionably correct.

Fourth, the final inquiry suggested by Cort is whether implying a federal remedy is inappropriate because the subject matter involves an area basically of concern to the States. No such problem is raised by a prohibition against invidious discrimination of any sort, including that on the basis of sex. Since the Civil War, the Federal Government and the federal courts have been the " '*primary* and powerful reliances' " in protecting citizens against such discrimination. *Steffel v. Thompson*, 415 U.S. 452, 464 (emphasis in original), quoting F. FRANKFURTER & J. LANDIS, THE BUSINESS OF THE SUPREME COURT 65 (1928). Moreover, it is the expenditure of federal funds that provides the justification for this particular statutory prohibition. There can be no question but that this aspect of the Cort analysis supports the implication of a private federal remedy.

In sum, there is no need in this case to weigh the four Cort factors; all of them support the same result. Not only the words and history of Title IX, but also its subject matter and underlying purposes, counsel implication of a cause of action in favor of private victims of discrimination.

II

Respondents' principal argument against implying a cause of action under Title IX is that it is unwise to subject admissions decisions of universities to judicial scrutiny at the behest of disappointed applicants on a case-by-case basis. They argue that this kind of litigation is burdensome and inevitably will have an adverse effect on the independence of members of university committees.

Take Note!

Here one can see the two faces of the fourth criterion. Even accepting Justice Stevens's assertion at face value, it may be laying it on a bit thick to assert that the federal government has been concerned with sex discrimination for so long. After all, women were not even permitted to vote in federal elections until ratification of the Nineteenth Amendment in 1920. Even the federal government's concern with race discrimination was, to many, difficult to perceive until at least a century after the Civil War. That aside, note the role of characterization in attempting to apply the fourth Cort criterion. Education has traditionally been an area of almost exclusive state, not federal, concern. What makes one characterization superior to (or more accurate than) another

This argument is not original to this litigation. It was forcefully advanced in both 1964 and 1972 by the congressional opponents of Title VI and Title IX, and squarely rejected by the congressional majorities that passed the two statutes. In short, respondents' principal contention is not a legal argument at all; it addresses a policy issue that Congress has already resolved.

History has borne out the judgment of Congress. Although victims of discrimination on the basis of race, religion, or national origin have had private Title VI remedies available at least since 1965, respondents have not come forward with any demonstration that Title VI litigation has been so costly or voluminous that either the academic community or the courts have been unduly burdened. Nothing but speculation supports the argument that university administrators will be so concerned about the risk of litigation that they will fail to discharge their important responsibilities in an independent and professional manner.

III

Respondents advance two other arguments that deserve brief mention. Starting from the premise that Title IX and Title VI should receive the same construction, respondents argue (1) that a comparison of Title VI with other Titles of the Civil Rights Act of 1964 demonstrates that Congress created express private remedies whenever it found them desirable; and (2) that certain excerpts from the legislative history of Title VI foreclose the implication of a private remedy.

Even if these arguments were persuasive with respect to Congress' understanding in 1964 when it passed Title VI, they would not overcome the fact that in 1972 when it passed Title IX, Congress was under the impression that Title VI could be enforced by a private action and that Title IX would be similarly enforceable. "For the relevant inquiry is not whether Congress correctly perceived the then state of the law, but rather what its perception of the state of the law was." But each of respondents' arguments is, in any event, unpersuasive.

* * *

IV

When Congress intends private litigants to have a cause of action to support their statutory rights, the far better course is for it to specify as much when it creates those rights. But the Court has long recognized that under certain limited circumstances the failure of Congress to do so is not inconsistent with an intent on its part to have such a remedy available to the persons benefited by its legislation. Title IX presents the atypical situation in which all of the circumstances that the Court has previously identified as supportive of an implied remedy are present. We therefore conclude that petitioner may maintain her lawsuit, despite the absence of any express authorization for it in the statute.

The judgment of the Court of Appeals is reversed, and the case is remanded for further proceedings consistent with this opinion.

It is so ordered.

MR. JUSTICE POWELL, dissenting.

[E]ven under the standards articulated in our prior decisions, it is clear that no private action should be implied here. It is evident from the legislative history reviewed in [Justice White's omitted] dissenting opinion that Congress did not intend to create a private action through Title IX of the Education Amendments of 1972. It also is clear that Congress deemed the administrative enforcement mechanism it did create fully adequate to protect Title IX rights. But as mounting evidence from the courts below suggests, and the decision of the Court today demonstrates, the mode of analysis we have applied in the recent past cannot be squared with the doctrine of the separation of powers. The time has come to reappraise our standards for the judicial implication of private causes of action.

Under Art. III, Congress alone has the responsibility for determining the jurisdiction of the lower federal courts. As the Legislative Branch, Congress also should determine when private parties are to be given causes of action under legislation it adopts. As countless statutes demonstrate, including Titles of the Civil Rights Act of 1964, Congress recognizes that the creation of private actions is a legislative function and frequently exercises it. When Congress chooses not to provide a private civil remedy, federal courts should not assume the legislative role of creating such a remedy and thereby enlarge their jurisdiction.

> **Take Note!**
>
> Justice Powell focuses quite specifically on legislation. Does that focus connote that he would not apply the same reasoning if a litigant asked the Court to imply a private right of action under a constitutional provision, as in *Bivens*?

The facts of this case illustrate the undesirability of this assumption by the Judicial Branch of the legislative function. Whether every disappointed applicant for admission to a college or university receiving federal funds has the right to a civil-court remedy under Title IX is likely to be a matter of interest to many of the thousands of rejected applicants. It certainly is a question of vast importance to the entire higher educational community of this country. But quite apart from the interests of the persons and institutions affected, respect for our constitutional system dictates that the issue should have been resolved by the elected representatives in Congress after public hearings, debate, and legislative decision. It is not a question properly to be decided by relatively uninformed federal judges who are isolated from the political process.

In recent history, the Court has tended to stray from the Art. III and separation-of-powers principle of limited jurisdiction. This, I believe, is evident from a review of the more or less haphazard line of cases that led to our decision in Cort v. Ash. The "four factor" analysis of that case is an open invitation to federal courts to legislate causes of action not authorized by Congress. It is an analysis not faithful to constitutional principles and should be rejected. Absent the most compelling evidence of affirmative congressional intent, a federal court should not infer a private cause of action.

> **Take Note!**
>
> Justice Powell joined the unanimous decision in Cort v. Ash.

I

The implying of a private action from a federal regulatory statute has been an exceptional occurrence in the past history of this Court. A review of those few decisions where such a step has been taken reveals in almost every case special historical circumstances that explain the result, if not the Court's analysis. These decisions suggest that the doctrine of implication applied by the Court today not only represents judicial assumption of the legislative function, but also lacks a principled precedential basis.

* * *

B

It was against this background of almost invariable refusal to imply private actions, absent a complete failure of alternative enforcement mechanisms and a clear expression of legislative intent to create such a remedy, that Cort v. Ash was decided. In holding that no private action could be brought to enforce a criminal statute, the Court referred to four factors said to be relevant to determining generally whether private actions could be implied. As Mr. Justice White suggests, these factors were meant only as guideposts for answering a single question, namely, whether Congress intended to provide a private cause of action. The conclusion in that particular case was obvious. But, as the opinion of the Court today demonstrates, the Cort analysis too easily may be used to deflect inquiry away from the intent of Congress, and to permit a court instead to substitute its own views as to the desirability of private enforcement.

Of the four factors mentioned in Cort, only one refers expressly to legislative intent. The other three invite independent judicial lawmaking. Asking whether a statute creates a right in favor of a private party, for example, begs the question at issue. What is involved is not the mere existence of a legal right, but a particular person's right to invoke the power of the courts to enforce that right. Determining whether a private action would be consistent with the "underlying purposes" of a legislative scheme permits a court to decide for itself what the goals of a scheme should be, and how those goals should be advanced. Finally, looking to state law for parallels to the federal right simply focuses inquiry on a particular policy consideration that Congress already may have weighed in deciding not to create a private action.

That the Cort analysis too readily permits courts to override the decision of Congress not to create a private action is demonstrated conclusively by the flood of lower-court decisions applying it. Although from the time Cort was decided until today this Court consistently has turned back attempts to create private actions, other federal courts have tended to proceed in exactly the opposite direction. In the four years since we decided Cort, no less than 20 decisions by the Courts of Appeals have implied private actions from federal statutes. It defies reason to believe that in each of these statutes Congress absentmindedly forgot to mention an intended private action. Indeed, the accelerating trend evidenced by these decisions attests to the need to re-examine the Cort analysis.

II

In my view, the implication doctrine articulated in Cort and applied by the Court today engenders incomparably greater problems than the possibility of occasionally failing to divine an unexpressed congressional intent. If only a matter of statutory construction were involved, our obligation might be to develop more refined criteria which more accurately reflect congressional intent. "But the unconstitutionality of the course pursued has now been made clear" and compels us to abandon the implication doctrine of Cort.

As the above-cited 20 decisions of the Courts of Appeals illustrate, Cort allows the Judicial Branch to assume policymaking authority vested by the Constitution in the Legislative Branch. It also invites Congress to avoid resolution of the often controversial question whether a new regulatory statute should be enforced through private litigation. Rather than confronting the hard political choices involved, Congress is encouraged to shirk its constitutional obligation and leave the issue to the courts to decide.[14] When this happens, the legislative process with its public scrutiny and participation has been bypassed, with attendant prejudice to everyone concerned. Because the courts are free to reach

14 Mr. Justice Rehnquist, perhaps considering himself temporarily bound by his position in University of California Regents v. Bakke, concurs in the Court's decision today. But writing briefly, he correctly observes "that Congress, at least during the period of the enactment of the several Titles of the Civil Rights Act tended to rely to a large extent on the courts to decide whether there should be a private right of action, rather than determining this question for itself * * *." It does not follow, however, that this Court is obliged to indulge Congress in its refusal to confront these hard questions. In my view, the very reasons advanced by Mr. Justice Rehnquist why "this Court in the future should be extremely reluctant to imply a cause of action" absent specific direction by Congress, apply to this case with special force.

a result different from that which the normal play of political forces would have produced, the intended beneficiaries of the legislation are unable to ensure the full measure of protection their needs may warrant. For the same reason, those subject to the legislative constraints are denied the opportunity to forestall through the political process potentially unnecessary and disruptive litigation. Moreover, the public generally is denied the benefits that are derived from the making of important societal choices through the open debate of the democratic process.

The Court's implication doctrine encourages, as a corollary to the political default by Congress, an increase in the governmental power exercised by the federal judiciary. The dangers posed by judicial arrogation of the right to resolve general societal conflicts have been manifest to this Court throughout its history.

* * *

It is true that the federal judiciary necessarily exercises substantial powers to construe legislation, including, when appropriate, the power to prescribe substantive standards of conduct that supplement federal legislation. But this power normally is exercised with respect to disputes over which a court already has jurisdiction, and in which the existence of the asserted cause of action is established. Implication of a private cause of action, in contrast, involves a significant additional step. By creating a private action, a court of limited jurisdiction necessarily extends its authority to embrace a dispute Congress has not assigned it to resolve.[17] This runs contrary to the established principle

Take Note!

Observe the similarity of Justice Powell's argument here with Justice Frankfurter's opinion for the Court in *Skelly Oil*. Justice Powell accuses the Court of expanding its own jurisdiction, not only in implied-right-of-action cases, but also in cases like *Smith v. Kansas City Title & Trust Co.* Justice Powell was in the majority in *Merrell Dow Pharmaceuticals v. Thompson* seven years after *Cannon*. Query whether he would have favored explicit adoption of Justice Holmes's law-that-creates-the-cause-of-action test from American Well Works. On the other hand, *Merrell Dow* explicitly recognized *Smith's* continuing force, and Justice Powell did not concur specially to distance himself from that position.

17 Because a private action implied from a federal statute has as an element the violation of that statute, the action universally has been considered to present a federal question over which a federal court has jurisdiction under 28 U.S.C. § 1331. Thus, when a federal court implies a private action from a statute, it necessarily expands the scope of its federal-question jurisdiction.

It is instructive to compare decisions implying private causes of action to those cases that have found nonfederal causes of action cognizable by a federal court under § 1331. *E.g.*, *Smith v. Kansas City Title & Trust Co.* Where a court decides both that federal-law elements are present in a state-law cause of action, and that these elements predominate to the point that the action can be said to present a "federal question" cognizable in federal court, the net effect is the same as implication of a private action directly from the constitutional or statutory source of the federal-law elements. To the extent an expansive interpretation of § 1331 permits federal courts to assume control over disputes which Congress did not consign to the federal judicial process, it is subject to the same criticisms of judicial implication of private actions discussed in the text.

that "[t]he jurisdiction of the federal courts is carefully guarded against expansion by judicial interpretation * * * " and conflicts with the authority of Congress under Art. III to set the limits of federal jurisdiction.

* * *

III

In sum, I believe the need both to restrain courts that too readily have created private causes of action, and to encourage Congress to confront its obligation to resolve crucial policy questions created by the legislation it enacts, has become compelling. Because the analysis suggested by *Cort* has proved inadequate to meet these problems, I would start afresh. Henceforth, we should not condone the implication of any private action from a federal statute absent the most compelling evidence that Congress in fact intended such an action to exist. Where a statutory scheme expressly provides for an alternative mechanism for enforcing the rights and duties created, I would be especially reluctant ever to permit a federal court to volunteer its services for enforcement purposes. Because the Court today is enlisting the federal judiciary in just such an enterprise, I dissent.

Notes and Questions

1. Is the majority opinion a straight application of the *Cort* test or does it subtly alter the four factors or the manner in which they apply? Is the majority as comfortable with implying rights of action as the Courts that decided *Cort v. Ash* and the cases preceding it appear to have been?

2. Justice Powell's dissent is the beginning of the Supreme Court's articulated interest in the separation-of-powers view of *Erie*. He begins by observing that implying private rights of action violates separation of powers. But he does suggest that in "compelling" circumstances, where congressional intent is clear, the courts may proceed. If his objection rests on the constitutional doctrine of separation of powers, how is an exception allowable? What evidence would he accept as sufficiently compelling?

3. Justice Powell attributes the federal courts' practice of implying private rights of action to cases where Congress "absentmindedly forgot" to include a private right of action. Is it not possible that Congress assumed that the courts would imply rights of action to provide remedies for substantive rights Congress created, as they traditionally had and as Justice Rehnquist pointed out in the language Justice Powell quotes in footnote 14? Perhaps Congress thought this fulfilled the courts' customary and proper role. On the other hand, perhaps that begs the question of whether that role is compatible with separation of powers.

4. Quoting Erie, Justice Powell asserts that implying a private right of action is unconstitutional. Upon which constitutional provisions does he rely? Is he perhaps guilty of the same sin as Justice Brandeis in Erie: failing to specify the particular constitutional language that prohibits the assailed practice?

5. Justice Powell argues that if the courts create private rights of action, the "intended beneficiaries of the legislation" may not receive as much protection as Congress intended, thus frustrating congressional intent. How might that happen?

6. The majority focuses on the relationship between Title VI and Title IX. Does Justice Powell's opinion suggest that the implied right of action in Title VI is also illegitimate? If so, how can he explain Congress's providing a statutory right to recover attorney's fees in Title VI actions? If not, how can he distinguish Title VI from Title IX for implication purposes?

7. Justice Powell is clearly troubled by the idea of federal judges being policy makers and sees implication of private rights of action as one way in which they do that. Is his objection constitutional or prudential?

Is it so clear that implying a private right of action makes policy? Perhaps the policy inheres in the right, not the availability of a particular remedy. Congressional policy against sex discrimination is certainly clear in Title IX. In what sense, then, does the Court make policy when it implies a private right of action to effectuate that congressional policy? Professor Doernberg has argued that "Judicial lethargy in the face of clearly expressed congressional policy may itself be an evisceration of the intent of the legislation, thus violating separation of powers." Donald L. Doernberg, *Juridical Chameleons in the "New Erie" Canal*, 1990 UTAH L.REV. 759, 803 n.235. *But see, e.g.*, Thomas W. Merrill, *The Judicial Prerogative*, 12 PACE L.REV. 327 (1992); Martin H. Redish, *Federal Common Law, Political Legitimacy, and the Interpretive Process: An "Institutionalist" Perspective*, 83 Nw.U.L.Rev. 761 (1989). It may make little sense to separate the right from the remedy when attempting to ascertain the underlying policy. One can argue that a "policy" underlies almost any decision, as opposed to a purely ministerial act, but then what does the word mean?

8. Is the Court using similar or different approaches to the implication question in Cannon and *Bivens*? To the extent they are similar, is that appropriate? To the extent that they are different, upon what is the difference founded? Why should they not be the same?

California v. Sierra Club

Supreme Court of the United States, 1981.
451 U.S. 287.

JUSTICE WHITE delivered the opinion of the Court.

Under review here is a decision of the Court of Appeals for the Ninth Circuit holding that private parties may sue under the Rivers and Harbors Appropriation Act of 1899 to enforce § 10 of that Act. An environmental organization and two private citizens (hereafter respondents), seek to enjoin the construction and operation of water diversion facilities which are part of the California Water Project (CWP). They rely upon § 10 of the Act, which prohibits "[t]he creation of any obstruction not affirmatively authorized by Congress, to the navigable capacity of any of the waters of the United States * * * ." Since the Act does not explicitly create a private enforcement mechanism, the initial question presented by these consolidated cases is whether such a private right of action can be implied on behalf of those allegedly injured by a claimed violation of § 10. Petitioner State of California also asks us to decide whether the Act requires permits for the state water allocation projects involved in these cases.

I

The California Water Project consists of a series of water storage and transportation facilities designed primarily to transport water from the relatively moist climate of northern California to the more arid central and southern portions of the State. The water which will be used by the CWP is initially stored behind dams on the Sacramento River and, as needed, released into the Sacramento-San Joaquin Delta. The CWP then diverts a quantity of this water from the Delta and directs it into canals and aqueducts which will carry it south. The project has both federal and state components. The federal component, the Central Valley Project, is designed in part to provide a constant source of water for irrigation to the Central Valley of California. Water for this project is diverted from the Delta by the Tracy Pumping Plant into the 115-mile Delta-Mendota Canal which transports the water to the Mendota Pool in California's Central Valley. The State Water Project supplies water to both central and southern California by way of the California Aqueduct. Water for this project is drawn from the Delta by the Delta Pumping Plant and deposited in the northern terminus of the California Aqueduct, through which it flows to its destinations in central and southern California.

Under the present system the quality of water captured in the north and released into the Delta may be degraded by intruding salt waters from the Pacific Ocean. As a consequence the water which is diverted from the Delta to the Delta-Mendota Canal or the California Aqueduct is potentially of a lesser quality than is the water which is transported to the Delta from storage facilities in the north and from there deposited in the Delta. The State of California has proposed the construction of a 42-mile Peripheral Canal along the eastern edge of the Delta area, which would avoid any mixing of the water from the north with the saline water of the Delta. Instead of depositing water in the Delta, the canal would carry high quality water directly to the Tracy and Delta Pumping Plants.

Respondents commenced the present action in 1971 in the United States District Court for the Northern District of California. Named as defendants were the various federal and state officials who administered the agencies responsible for overseeing the operation, construction, and regulation of the CWP facilities in question. Petitioner water agencies, which had contracted with the State for water from the Delta and which had incurred extensive financial obligations in reliance thereon, were permitted to intervene. The respondents alleged that present and proposed diversions of water from the Delta degraded the quality of Delta water, and that such diversion violated § 10 of the Rivers and Harbors Appropriation Act of 1899. They sought to enjoin further operation or construction of water diversion facilities until the consent of the Army Corps of Engineers was obtained as required by the Act.

proc. history

The District Court concluded that respondents could avail themselves of a "private cause of action" to enforce § 10 of the Act, and ruled on the merits that approval of the Corps of Engineers was required by § 10 for the Tracy and Delta Pumping Plants and the Peripheral Canal. The Court of Appeals for the Ninth Circuit agreed that a private cause of action to enforce the Act existed. It reversed the District Court as to the Tracy Pumping Plant, however, ruling that Congress has consented to its construction and operation. We granted petitions for certiorari filed by the water agencies and the State of California.

II

Cort v. Ash outlined a "preferred approach for determining whether a private right of action should be implied from a federal statute * * * ." This approach listed four factors thought to be relevant to the inquiry * * * . Combined, these four factors present the relevant inquiries to pursue in answering the recurring question of implied causes of action. Cases subsequent to *Cort* have explained that the ultimate issue is whether Congress intended to create a private right of action, but the four factors specified in *Cort* remain the "criteria through which this intent could be discerned."

Under *Cort*, the initial consideration is whether the plaintiff is a member of a class for " 'whose especial benefit the statute was enacted.' " Without analyzing either the language or legislative history of the Act, the Court of Appeals here concluded that the Act was designed for the especial benefit of private parties who may suffer "special injury" caused by an unauthorized obstruction to a navigable waterway. It was apparently reasoned that since Congress enacted a statute that forbids such obstructions in navigable waters, any person who would be "especially harmed" by an unauthorized obstruction was an especial beneficiary of the Act. But such a definition of "especial" beneficiary makes this factor meaningless. Under this view, a victim of any crime would be deemed an especial beneficiary of the criminal statute's proscription. *Cort* did not adopt such a broad-gauge approach. The question is not simply who would benefit from the Act, but whether Congress intended to confer federal rights upon those beneficiaries.

In ascertaining this intent, the first consideration is the language of the Act. Here, the statute states no more than a general proscription of certain activities; it does not unmistakably focus on any particular class of beneficiaries whose welfare Congress intended to further. Such language does not indicate an intent to provide for private rights of action. "There would be far less reason to infer a private remedy in favor of individual persons if Congress, instead of drafting Title IX (of the Education Amendments of 1972) with an unmistakable focus on the benefited class, had written it simply as a ban on discriminatory conduct by recipients of federal funds or as a prohibition against the disbursement of public funds to educational institutions engaged in discriminatory practices." Section 10 of the Rivers and Harbors Appropriation Act is the kind of general ban which carries with it no implication of an intent to confer rights on a particular class of persons.

Neither the Court of Appeals nor respondents have identified anything in the legislative history suggesting that § 10 was created for the especial benefit of a particular class. On the contrary, the legislative history supports the view that the Act was designed to benefit the public at large by empowering the Federal Government to exercise its authority over interstate commerce with respect to obstructions on navigable rivers caused by bridges and similar structures. In part, the Act was passed in response to this Court's decision in *Willamette Iron Bridge Co. v. Hatch*. There the Court held that there was no federal common law "which prohibits obstructions and nuisances in navigable rivers." Although *Willamette* involved private parties, the clear implication of the Court's opinion was that in the absence of specific legislation no party, including the Federal Government, would be empowered to take any action under federal law with respect to such obstructions. The Act was intended to enable the Secretary of War to take such action.[6] Congress was not concerned with the rights of individuals.

6 In addition, § 12 of the Act provides criminal penalties for violations of the provisions of various sections of the Act, including the provisions of § 10; and, § 17 of the Act provides that "[t]he Department of Justice shall conduct the legal proceedings necessary to enforce the provisions of [§ 10]." The creation of one explicit mode of enforcement is not dispositive of congressional intent with respect to other complementary remedies. However, here, considering the clear focus of the legislative history on the need to enable the Government to respond to obstructions in navigable waterways, the creation of this enforcement mechanism and the absence of the remedy sought by respondents, certainly reinforces the view that Congress was not concerned with private rights or remedies in designing this legislation.

It is not surprising, therefore, that there is no "indication of legislative intent, explicit or implicit, either to create such a remedy or to deny one." The Court of Appeals recognized as much: "The legislative history of the Rivers and Harbors Act of 1899 does not reflect a congressional intent either to afford a private remedy or to deny one." This silence on the remedy question serves to confirm that in enacting the Act, Congress was concerned not with private rights but with the Federal Government's ability to respond to obstructions on navigable waterways.

[T]he focus of the inquiry is on whether Congress intended to create a remedy. The federal judiciary will not engraft a remedy on a statute, no matter how salutary, that Congress did not intend to provide. Here consideration of the first two Cort factors is dispositive. The language of the statute and its legislative history do not suggest that the Act was intended to create federal rights for the especial benefit of a class of persons but rather that it was intended to benefit the public at large through a general regulatory scheme to be administered by the then Secretary of War. Nor is there any evidence that Congress anticipated that there would be a private remedy. This being the case, it is unnecessary to inquire further to determine whether the purpose of the statute would be advanced by the judicial implication of a private action or whether such a remedy is within the federal domain of interest. These factors are only of relevance if the first two factors give indication of congressional intent to create the remedy. There being no such indication, the judgment of the Court of Appeals must be reversed.

* * *

It is so ordered.

JUSTICE STEVENS, concurring.

In 1888 this Court reversed a decree enjoining the construction of a bridge over a navigable river. The Court's opinion in that case did not question the right of the private parties to seek relief in a federal court; rather, the Court held that no federal rule of law prohibited the obstruction of the navigable waterway. Congress responded to the Willamette case in the Rivers and Harbors Act of 1890 by creating a federal prohibition of such obstructions absent a permit from the Secretary of War. At the time the statute was enacted, I believe the lawyers in Congress simply assumed that private parties in a position comparable to that of the litigants in the Willamette case would have a remedy for any injury suffered by reason of a violation

Food for Thought

Indulging Justice Stevens's assumption that "the lawyers in Congress simply assumed," should one conclude that their understanding is the equivalent of congressional intent as the courts have used that term?

of the new federal statute. For at that time the implication of private causes of action was a well-known practice at common law and in American courts. Therefore, in my view, the Members of Congress merely assumed that the federal courts would follow the ancient maxim "***ubi jus, ibi remedium***" and imply a private right of action. Accordingly, if I were writing on a clean slate, I would hold that an implied remedy is available to respondents under this statute.

> Non constatjus civile a posteriori
>
> **It's Latin to Me!**
>
> "Where there is a right, there is a remedy."

The slate, however, is not clean. Because the problem of ascertaining legislative intent that is not expressed in legislation is often so difficult, the Court has wisely developed rules to guide judges in deciding whether a federal remedy is implicitly a part of a federal statute. In Cort v. Ash, all of my present colleagues subscribed to a unanimous formulation of those rules, and in Cannon v. University of Chicago, a majority of the Court joined my attempt to explain the application of those rules in that case. The Cort v. Ash analysis is therefore a part of our law.

* * * I believe the Court correctly concludes that application of the Cort v. Ash analysis indicates that no private cause of action is available. I think it is more important to adhere to the analytical approach the Court has adopted than to base my vote on my own opinion about what Congress probably assumed in 1890. I therefore join Justice White's opinion for the Court.

JUSTICE REHNQUIST, with whom THE CHIEF JUSTICE, JUSTICE STEWART, and JUSTICE POWELL join, concurring in the judgment.

I agree completely with the conclusion of the Court that in these cases "Congress was not concerned with the rights of individuals" and that "[i]t is not surprising, therefore, that there is no 'indication of legislative intent, explicit or implicit, either to create * * * a [private] remedy or to deny one.' "

I also agree with the Court's analysis where it says: "As recently emphasized, the focus of the inquiry is on whether Congress intended to create a remedy. The federal judiciary will not engraft a remedy on a statute, no matter how salutary, that Congress did not intend to provide." My only difference, and the difference which leads me to write this separate concurrence in the judgment, is that I think the Court's opinion places somewhat more emphasis on Cort v. Ash than is warranted in light of several more recent "implied right of action" decisions which limit it. These decisions make clear that the so-called Cort factors are merely guides in the central task of ascertaining legislative intent, that they are not of equal weight, and that in deciding an implied-right-of-action case courts need not mechanically trudge through all four of the factors when the dispositive question of legislative intent has been resolved. * * *

Notes and Questions

1. What becomes of the four Cort factors after *Sierra Club*? Are they still of any use, or has the Court retreated to asking simply whether Congress intended a private right of action to exist? If the Cort factors still exist, reconsider their relationship to each other. Are they of equal weight, or does one negative answer end the inquiry?

2. Justice Stevens's concurrence raises some interesting questions, not the least of which is why he is concurring rather than dissenting. He seems confident that Congress assumed that the federal courts would create a remedy of the type sought. Why does he not vote to create it? His answer is that the Court's newly-adopted analytical approach leads to the conclusion that no private right of action is appropriate. Consider, however, the anomaly his opinion leaves in its wake: the avowed purpose of the Court's analysis is to adhere to legislative intent. Justice Stevens finds that the Court's method of analysis does not lead to a result faithful to legislative intent, yet he applies it anyway. Does that not suggest that there is something wrong with the Court's analytical method, either in its declared purpose or in its application?

3. In *Thompson v. Thompson*, 484 U.S. 174 (1988), the plaintiff father sought declaratory and injunctive relief under the Parental Kidnapping Prevention Act (PKPA). The case involved conflicting child custody decrees from different states. The Supreme Court unanimously found that the PKPA could not support an implied cause of action.

The bulk of the analysis is unexceptional, tracking earlier cases and the Court's expression of primary (almost exclusive) reliance upon congressional intent. Because Congress had approached parental kidnapping as a full faith and credit problem, the Court refused to imply a right of action, since the Full Faith and Credit Clause itself creates no cause of action. Justice Marshall's opinion did note, however:

> Our focus on congressional intent does not mean that we require evidence that Members of Congress, in enacting the statute, actually had in mind the creation of a private cause of action. The implied cause of action doctrine would be a virtual dead letter were it limited to correcting drafting errors when Congress simply forgot to codify its evident intention to provide a cause of action.

Justice Scalia concurred in the judgment, and his separate opinion is a powerful echo of Justice Powell's Cannon dissent:

I write separately because in my view the Court is not being faithful to current doctrine in its dictum denying the necessity of an actual congressional intent to create a private right of action, and in referring to *Cort v. Ash* as though its analysis had not been effectively overruled by our later opinions. * * *

I am at a loss to imagine what congressional intent to create a private right of action might mean, if it does not mean that Congress had in mind the creation of a private right of action.

* * *

The Court's opinion exaggerates the difficulty of establishing an implied right when it surmises that "[t]he implied cause of action doctrine would be a virtual dead letter were it limited to correcting drafting errors * * * ." That statement rests upon the erroneous premise that one never implies anything except when he forgets to say it expressly.

* * *

It is, to be sure, not beyond imagination that in a particular case Congress may intend to create a private right of action, but choose to do so by implication. One must wonder, however, whether the good produced by a judicial rule that accommodates this remote possibility is outweighed by its adverse effects. An enactment by implication cannot realistically be regarded as the product of the difficult lawmaking process our Constitution has prescribed.

* * *

[A]s the likelihood that Congress would leave the matter to implication decreases, so does the justification for bearing the risk of distorting the constitutional process. A legislative act so significant, and so separable from the remainder of the statute, as the creation of a private right of action seems to me so implausibly left to implication that the risk should not be endured.

If we were to announce a flat rule that private rights of action will not be implied in statutes hereafter enacted, the risk that that course would occasionally frustrate genuine legislative intent would decrease from its current level of minimal to virtually zero.

* * *

If a change is to be made, we should get out of the business of implied private rights of action altogether.

Do Justices Powell's and Scalia's arguments that the Court ought never to imply causes of action in statutes put Congress on notice that implication is at least unlikely? If so, does a statute's silence take on additional meaning? Consider Note 4 below.

4. In *Karahalios v. National Federation of Federal Employees, Local 1263*, 489 U.S. 527 (1989), the plaintiff asked the Court to imply a private right of action in a statute,

this time the Civil Service Reform Act, for "breach by a union representing federal employees of its statutory duty of fair representation." The Court declined, noting that Congress had created an enforcement scheme in the Federal Labor Relations Authority. The plaintiff argued in vain that his action paralleled cases arising under the National Labor Relations Act, in which the Court had implied a private right of action. The Court distinguished those cases.

a) Of greater importance is the Court's treatment of the implication issue generally. Quoting its own cases from 1979 forward (including *Sierra Club* and *Thompson v. Thompson*), the Court said:

> The "ultimate issue is whether Congress intended to create a private cause of action." Unless such "congressional intent can be inferred from the language of the statute, the statutory structure, or some other source, the essential predicate for implication of a private remedy simply does not exist." It is also an "elemental canon" of statutory construction that where a statute expressly provides a remedy, courts must be especially reluctant to provide additional remedies. In such cases, "[i]n the absence of strong indicia of contrary congressional intent, we are compelled to conclude that Congress provided precisely the remedies it considered appropriate."

How does the Court's approach in *Karahalios* compare with its approach from the 1800's through Borak, Cort, and Cannon? Would the Borak Court have been more likely to imply a private right of action? If so, does the change in the Court's technique raise separation-of-powers issues?

b) The end of the *Karahalios* opinion discussed the significance of the Court's evolving technique of interpreting congressional intent.

> We therefore discern no basis for finding congressional intent to provide petitioner with a cause of action against the union. Congress undoubtedly was aware from our cases such as Cort v. Ash that the Court had departed from its prior standard for resolving a claim urging that an implied statutory cause of action should be recognized, and that such issues were being resolved by a straight-forward inquiry into whether Congress intended to provide a private cause of action. Had Congress intended the courts to enforce a federal employees union's duty of fair representation, we would expect to find some evidence of that intent in the statute or its legislative history. We find none.

The Court's reasoning is not without irony and perhaps not without problems. First, given the Justices' linking the changed approach manifested in Cort v. Ash with congressional awareness of the need to be explicit about private rights of action, has Cort sowed the seeds of its own destruction?

Second, before Cort v. Ash, Congress never suggested dissatisfaction with the Court's method of dealing with statutes that created new rights without explicitly creating remedies. Does Congress's apparent acquiescence connote that the Court should not have changed its technique? On the other hand, Congress has expressed no dissatisfaction with Cort v. Ash's technique, now established for nearly forty years.

Finally, from the nineteenth century to the present, the Court has discussed congressional intent in deciding whether to imply private rights of action in statutes. Is today's Court taking the same view of congressional intent as did its predecessors?

5. As the foregoing materials show, the Court has not been successful in limiting the inquiry in implied right of action cases solely to the second Cort criterion, which examines whether Congress intended to create the cause of action the plaintiff asserts. One scholar, a former author of this text has suggested that it is very difficult to decide whether a cause of action should be implied without considering the rights being asserted and the remedy sought. As a result, the first and third Cort criteria tend to creep back into the cases:

> The first Cort factor continues to be important because the Court must consider the purpose of a cause of action in deciding whether Congress intended to create it. A plaintiff does not come to court asserting a cause of action in the abstract. Instead, a plaintiff asserts that a particular federal statute grants a right that the defendant has violated, and asks the Court to imply a cause of action to enforce that right. The Court must then look at the provision and ask whether "the statute create[s] a federal right in favor of the plaintiff." It is almost impossible to answer the question of whether Congress intended to create a cause of action to enforce the right the plaintiff asserts without deciding whether a statute actually confers the right. Consequently, the first Cort factor continues to be central in implied right of action cases, even when the Court does not specifically identify it as such, but instead disguises it as an inquiry into the language of the statute or the legislative history.
>
> Similarly, it is very difficult for the Court to avoid considering the third Cort factor—"is it consistent with the underlying purposes of the legislative scheme to imply [a particular] remedy for the plaintiff?"—in deciding implied right of action cases. By definition, the statute does not explicitly create the cause of action, and the legislative history is silent as to whether Congress actually intended to create it. If a statutory provision appears to confer a right on the plaintiff, the Court would have difficulty deciding whether Congress wanted the right to be judicially enforceable without looking at whether it would foster or subvert the underlying statutory purposes to allow such lawsuits. Thus, unless the Court looks at the overall statutory purpose, it denies itself access to the information it needs to answer the question whether Congress intended to create the cause of action.

Donald H. Zeigler, *Rights, Rights of Action, and Remedies: An Integrated Approach*, 76 WASH. L. REV. 67, 110-111 (2001) (footnotes omitted).

The focus now returns to implication of private rights of action in constitutional provisions. In the years following *Bivens*, the Court had implied such rights on two other occasions, concerning the Fifth Amendment's Due Process Clause and the Eighth Amendment's Cruel and Unusual Punishments provision. In *Davis v. Passman* (1979), the Fifth Amendment case, the Court allowed an action by a former employee in the office of Congressman Otto Passman, who had fired her with the explicit statement that he wanted the position filled by a man. The majority opinion articulated a broad view of judicial power:

> [W]e presume that justiciable constitutional rights are to be enforced through the courts. And, unless such rights are to become merely precatory, the class of those litigants who allege that their own constitutional rights have been violated, and who at the same time have no effective means other than the judiciary to enforce these rights, must be able to invoke the existing jurisdiction of the courts for the protection of their justiciable constitutional rights.

In *Carlson v. Green* (1980), the Court implied a right of action in the Eighth Amendment in favor of an administratrix whose decedent had died in prison because of lack of appropriate medical care. The Court allowed the action against individual federal officers despite the fact that the administratrix also was entitled to seek relief from the government itself under the Federal Tort Claims Act.

As you read the following case, consider whether the Court's approach to implying private rights of action in constitutional provisions has been consistent since its initial venture in *Bivens*.

Schweiker v. Chilicky

Supreme Court of the United States, 1988.
487 U.S. 412.

JUSTICE O'CONNOR delivered the opinion of the Court.

This case requires us to decide whether the improper denial of Social Security disability benefits, allegedly resulting from violations of due process by government officials who administered the Federal Social Security program, may give rise to a cause of action for money damages against those officials. We conclude that such a remedy, not having been included in the elaborate remedial scheme devised by Congress, is unavailable.

I

A

Under Title II of the Social Security Act (Act), the Federal Government provides disability benefits to individuals who have contributed to the Social Security program and who, because of a medically determinable physical or mental impairment, are unable to engage in substantial gainful work. * * * Title II, which is administered in conjunction with state welfare agencies, provides benefits only while an individual's statutory disability persists. In 1980, Congress noted that existing administrative procedures provided for reexamination of eligibility "only under a limited number of circumstances." Congress responded by enacting legislation requiring that most disability determinations be reviewed at least once every three years. Although the statute did not require this program for "continuing disability review" (CDR) to become effective before January 1, 1982, the Secretary of Health and Human Services initiated CDR in March 1981.

The administration of the CDR program was at first modeled on the previous procedures for reexamination of eligibility. Under these procedures, an individual whose case is selected for review bears the burden of demonstrating the continuing existence of a statutory disability. The appropriate state agency performs the initial review, and persons who are found to have become ineligible are generally provided with administrative review similar to the review provided to new claimants. Under the original CDR procedures, benefits were usually terminated after a state agency found a claimant ineligible, and were not available during administrative appeals.

Finding that benefits were too often being improperly terminated by state agencies, only to be reinstated by a federal administrative law judge (ALJ), Congress enacted temporary emergency legislation in 1983. This law provided for the continuation of benefits, pending review by an ALJ, after a state agency determined that an individual was no longer disabled. In the Social Security Disability Benefits Reform Act of 1984 (1984 Reform Act), Congress extended this provision until January 1, 1988, and provided for a number of other significant changes in the administration of CDR * * * . In its final form, this legislation was enacted without a single opposing vote in either Chamber.

The problems to which Congress responded so emphatically were widespread. One of the cosponsors of the 1984 Reform Act, who had conducted hearings on the administration of CDR, summarized evidence from the General Accounting Office as follows:

> [T]he message perceived by the State agencies, swamped with cases, was to deny, deny, deny, and, I might add, to process cases faster and faster and faster. In the name of efficiency, we have scanned our computer terminals, rounded up the disabled workers in the country, pushed the discharge button, and let them go into a free [f]all toward economic chaos.

Other legislators reached similar conclusions. * * * Such conclusions were based, not only on anecdotal evidence, but on compellingly forceful statistics. The Social Security Administration itself apparently reported that about 200,000 persons were wrongfully terminated, and then reinstated, between March 1981 and April 1984. In the first year of CDR, half of those who were terminated appealed the decision, and "an amazing two-thirds of those who appealed were being reinstated."

Congress was also made aware of the terrible effects on individual lives that CDR had produced. The chairman of the Senate's Special Committee on Aging pointed out that "[t]he human dimension of this crisis—the unnecessary suffering, anxiety, and turmoil—has been graphically exposed by dozens of congressional hearings and in newspaper articles all across the country." Termination could also lead to the cut-off of Medicare benefits, so that some people were left without adequate medical care. There is little doubt that CDR led to many hardships and injuries that could never be adequately compensated.

B

Respondents are three individuals whose disability benefits under Title II were terminated pursuant to the CDR program in 1981 and 1982. Respondents Spencer Harris and Dora Adelerte appealed these determinations through the administrative process, were restored to disabled status, and were awarded full retroactive benefits. Respondent James Chilicky did not pursue these administrative remedies. Instead, he filed a new application for benefits about a year and a half after his benefits were stopped. His application was granted, and he was awarded one year's retroactive benefits; his application for the restoration of the other six months' benefits is apparently still pending. Because the terminations in these three cases occurred before the 1983 emergency legislation was enacted, respondents experienced delays of many months in receiving disability benefits to which they were entitled. All the respondents had been wholly dependent on their disability benefits, and all allege that they were unable to maintain themselves or their families in even a minimally adequate fashion after they were declared ineligible. Respondent James Chilicky was in the hospital recovering from open-heart surgery when he was informed that his heart condition was no longer disabling.

In addition to pursuing administrative remedies, respondents * * * filed this lawsuit * * * . They alleged that petitioners * * * had violated respondents' due process rights. The thrust of the complaint, which named petitioners in their official and individual capacities, was that petitioners had adopted illegal policies that led to the wrongful termination of benefits by state agencies. * * * Respondents sought injunctive and declaratory relief, and money damages for "emotional distress and for loss of food, shelter and other necessities proximately caused by [petitioners'] denial of benefits without due process."

* * *

The petition for certiorari presented one question: "Whether a *Bivens* remedy should be implied for alleged due process violations in the denial of social security disability benefits." We granted the petition, and now reverse.

II

A

* * *

In 1971, this Court held that the victim of a Fourth Amendment violation by federal officers acting under color of their authority may bring suit for money damages against the officers in federal court. The Court noted that Congress had not specifically provided for such a remedy and that "the Fourth Amendment does not in so many words provide for its enforcement by an award of money damages for the consequences of its violation." Nevertheless, finding "no special factors counselling hesitation in the absence of affirmative action by Congress," and "no explicit congressional declaration" that money damages may not be awarded, the majority relied on the rule that " 'where legal rights have been invaded, and a federal statute provides for a general right to sue for such invasion, federal courts may use any available remedy to make good the wrong done.' "

So-called "Bivens actions" for money damages against federal officers have subsequently been permitted under § 1331 for violations of the Due Process Clause of the Fifth Amendment, Davis v. Passman [1979], and the Cruel and Unusual Punishments Clause of the Eighth Amendment. Carlson v. Green [1980]. In each of these cases, as in Bivens itself, the Court found that there were no "special factors counselling hesitation in the absence of affirmative action by Congress," no explicit statutory prohibition against the relief sought, and no exclusive statutory alternative remedy.

Our more recent decisions have responded cautiously to suggestions that Bivens remedies be extended into new contexts. The absence of statutory relief for a constitutional violation, for example, does not by any means necessarily imply that courts should award money damages against the officers responsible for the violation. Thus, we refused—unanimously—to create a Bivens action for enlisted military personnel who alleged that they had been injured by the unconstitutional actions of their superior officers and who had no remedy against the Government itself:

> The special nature of military life—the need for unhesitating and decisive action by military officers and equally disciplined responses by enlisted personnel—would be undermined by a judicially created remedy exposing officers to personal liability at the hands of those they are charged to command * * * .

> Also, Congress, the constitutionally authorized source of authority over the military system of justice, has not provided a damages remedy for claims by military personnel that constitutional rights have been violated by superior officers. *Any action to provide a judicial response by way of such a remedy would be plainly inconsistent with Congress' authority in this field.*
>
> Taken together, the unique disciplinary structure of the Military Establishment and Congress' activity in the field constitute "special factors" which dictate that it would be inappropriate to provide enlisted military personnel a Bivens-type remedy against their superior officers.

([E]mphasis added; citation omitted). *See* also United States v. Stanley (1987) (disallowing Bivens actions by military personnel "whenever the injury arises out of activity 'incident to service' ").

> **FYI**
>
> Stanley involved an attempt by a former serviceman to recover damages for the Army's having secretly having administered LSD to him after he volunteered for what he was told was a chemical warfare testing program. The drug caused severe personality changes and led to the dissolution of his marriage. Stanley discovered the testing when the Army asked him to participate in a follow-up study. Justice O'Connor vigorously dissented from the Court's refusal to allow him to sue. *See infra* Note 1, at 549-50.

Similarly, [in Bush v. Lucas (1983)] we refused—again unanimously—to create a Bivens remedy for a First Amendment violation "aris[ing] out of an employment relationship that is governed by comprehensive procedural and substantive provisions giving meaningful remedies against the United States." In that case, a federal employee was demoted, allegedly in violation of the First Amendment, for making public statements critical of the agency for which he worked. He was reinstated through the administrative process, with retroactive seniority and full backpay, but he was not permitted to recover for any loss due to emotional distress or mental anguish, or for attorney's fees. Concluding that the administrative system created by Congress "provides meaningful remedies for employees who may have been unfairly disciplined for making critical comments about their agencies," the Court refused to create a Bivens action even though it assumed a First Amendment violation and acknowledged that "existing remedies do not provide complete relief for the plaintiff." The Court stressed that the case involved policy questions in an area that had received careful attention from Congress. Noting that the Legislature is far more competent than the Judiciary to carry out the necessary "balancing [of] governmental efficiency and the rights of employees," we refused to "decide whether or not it would be good policy to permit a federal employee to recover damages from a supervisor who has improperly disciplined him for exercising his First Amendment rights."

In sum, the concept of "special factors counselling hesitation in the absence of affirmative action by Congress" has proved to include an appropriate judicial deference to indications that congressional inaction has not been inadvertent. When the design of a government program suggests that Congress has provided what it considers adequate remedial mechanisms for constitutional violations that may occur in the course of its administration, we have not created additional *Bivens* remedies.

Food for Thought

Suppose Congress declared that there should be no remedy at all for a constitutional violation. Would (should) the *Chilicky* Court defer to Congress's judgment in such a case?

B

The administrative structure and procedures of the Social Security system, which affects virtually every American, "are of a size and extent difficult to comprehend." Millions of claims are filed every year under the Act's disability benefits programs alone, and these claims are handled under "an unusually protective [multi]-step process for the review and adjudication of disputed claims."

The steps provided for under Title II are essentially identical for new claimants and for persons subject to CDR. An initial determination of a claimant's eligibility for benefits is made by a state agency, under federal standards and criteria. Next, a claimant is entitled to *de novo* reconsideration by the state agency, and additional evidence may be presented at that time. If the claimant is dissatisfied with the state agency's decision, review may then be had by the Secretary of Health and Human Services, acting through a Federal ALJ; at this stage, the claimant is again free to introduce new evidence or raise new issues. If the claimant is still dissatisfied, a hearing may be sought before the Appeals Council of the Social Security Administration. Once these elaborate administrative remedies have been exhausted, a claimant is entitled to seek judicial review, including review of constitutional claims. The Act, however, makes no provision for remedies in money damages against officials responsible for unconstitutional conduct that leads to the wrongful denial of benefits. As respondents concede, claimants whose benefits have been fully restored through the administrative process would lack standing to invoke the Constitution under the statute's administrative review provision.

The case before us cannot reasonably be distinguished from *Bush v. Lucas*. Here, exactly as in *Bush*, Congress has failed to provide for "complete relief": respondents have not been given a remedy in damages for emotional distress or for other hardships suffered because of delays in their receipt of Social Security benefits. The creation of a *Bivens* remedy would obviously offer the prospect of relief for injuries that must now go unredressed. Congress, however, has not failed to provide meaningful safeguards or remedies for the rights of persons situated as respondents were. Indeed, the system for protecting their rights is, if anything, considerably more elaborate than the civil service system considered in Bush. The prospect of personal liability for official acts, moreover, would undoubtedly lead to new difficulties and expense in recruiting administrators for the programs Congress has established. Congressional competence at "balancing governmental efficiency and the rights of [individuals]" is no more questionable in the social welfare context than it is in the civil service context.

Congressional attention to problems that have arisen in the administration of CDR (including the very problems that gave rise to this case) has, moreover, been frequent and intense. Congress itself required that the CDR program be instituted. Within two years after the program began, Congress enacted emergency legislation providing for the continuation of benefits even after a finding of ineligibility by a state agency. Less than two years after passing that law, and fully aware of the results of extensive investigations of the practices that led to respondents' injuries, Congress again enacted legislation aimed at reforming the administration of CDR; that legislation again specifically addressed the problem that had provoked the earlier emergency legislation. At each step, Congress chose specific forms and levels of protection for the rights of persons affected by incorrect eligibility determinations under CDR. At no point did Congress choose to extend to any person the kind of remedies that respondents seek in this lawsuit. Thus, congressional unwillingness to provide consequential damages for unconstitutional deprivations of a statutory right is at least as clear in the context of this case as it was in Bush.

> **Food for Thought**
>
> When one side of the balance involves a constitutional right, what institution should have the final word on striking the balance? In this respect, consider City of Boerne v. Flores (1997), which you probably read in your Constitutional Law course. There the majority held the Religious Freedom Restoration Act (RFRA) unconstitutional because Congress attempted to define the scope of the First Amendment. Justice O'Connor dissented because she disagreed with the Court's previous decision that Congress passed RFRA to overcome. Had it not been for that disagreement, she said she would have joined the majority opinion.

Respondents nonetheless contend that Bush should be confined to its facts, arguing that it applies only in the context of what they call "the special nature of federal employee relations." Noting that the parties to this case did "not share the sort of close, collaborative, continuing juridical relationship found in the federal civil service," respondents suggest that the availability of Bivens remedies would create less "inconvenience" to the Social Security system than it would in the context of the civil service. The Solicitor General is less sanguine, arguing that the creation of Bivens remedy in this context would lead to "a complete disruption of [a] carefully crafted and constantly monitored congressional scheme."

We need not choose between these competing predictions, which have little bearing on the applicability of Bush to this case. The decision in Bush did not rest on this Court's belief that Bivens actions would be more disruptive of the civil service than they are in other contexts where they have been allowed, such as federal law enforcement agencies (*Bivens* itself) or the federal prisons. Rather, we declined in Bush " 'to create a new substantive legal liability * * * ' because we are convinced that Congress is in a better position to decide whether or not the public interest would be served by creating it." That reasoning applies as much, or more, in this case as it did in Bush itself.

Respondents also suggest that this case is distinguishable from Bush because the plaintiff in that case received compensation for the constitutional violation itself, while these respondents have merely received that to which they would have been entitled had there been no constitutional violation. ("Bush's reinstatement was a remedy for the alleged abuse, not just a restoration of something to which he was entitled * * * .") ([F]ailure to create a Bivens remedy "would give respondents precisely the same thing whether or not they were victims of constitutional deprivation and would thus leave respondents with no post-deprivation remedy at all for the constitutional violations they allege"). The Bush opinion, however, drew no distinction between compensation for a "constitutional wrong" and the restoration of statutory rights that had been unconstitutionally taken away. Nor did it suggest that such labels would matter. Indeed, the Court appeared to assume that civil service employees would get "precisely the same thing whether or not they were victims of constitutional deprivation." * * * Bush thus lends no support to the notion that statutory violations caused by unconstitutional conduct necessarily require remedies in addition to the remedies provided generally for such statutory violations. Here, as in Bush, it is evident that if we were "to fashion an adequate remedy for every wrong that can be proved in a case * * * [the complaining party] would obviously prevail." In neither case, however, does the presence of alleged unconstitutional conduct that is not separately remedied under the statutory scheme imply that the statute has provided "no remedy" for the constitutional wrong at issue.

* * *

In the end, respondents' various arguments are rooted in their insistent and vigorous contention that they simply have not been adequately recompensed for their injuries. * * *

We agree that suffering months of delay in receiving the income on which one has depended for the very necessities of life cannot be fully remedied by the "belated restoration of back benefits." The trauma to respondents, and thousands of others like them, must surely have gone beyond what anyone of normal sensibilities would wish to see imposed on innocent disabled citizens. Nor would we care to "trivialize" the nature of the wrongs alleged in this case. Congress, however, has addressed the problems created by state agencies' wrongful termination of disability benefits. Whether or not we believe that its response was the best response, Congress is the body charged with making the inevitable compromises required in the design of a massive and complex welfare benefits program. Congress has discharged that responsibility to the extent that it affects the case before us, and we see no legal basis that would allow us to revise its decision.

> **Take Note!**
>
> Does Justice O'Connor, perhaps inadvertently, connote that Congress is not composed of persons "of normal sensibilities"?

Because the relief sought by respondents is unavailable as a matter of law, the case must be dismissed. The judgment of the Court of Appeals to the contrary is therefore

Reversed.

JUSTICE BRENNAN, with whom JUSTICE MARSHALL and JUSTICE BLACKMUN join, dissenting.

Respondents are three individuals who, because they are unable to engage in gainful employment as a result of certain disabilities, rely primarily or exclusively on disability benefits awarded under Title II of the Social Security Act for their support and that of their families. Like hundreds of thousands of other such recipients, in the early 1980's they lost this essential source of income following state implementation of a federally mandated "continuing disability review" process (CDR), only to have an administrative law judge (ALJ) ultimately reinstate their benefits after appeal, or to regain them, as respondent James Chilicky did, by filing a new application for benefits. Respondents allege that the initial benefit termination resulted from a variety of unconstitutional actions taken by state and federal officials responsible for administering the CDR program. They further allege, and petitioners do not dispute, that as a result of these deprivations, which lasted from 7 to 19 months, they suffered immediate financial hardship, were unable to purchase food, shelter, and other necessities, and were unable to maintain themselves in even a minimally adequate fashion.

The Court today reaffirms the availability of a federal action for money damages against federal officials charged with violating constitutional rights. * * * Acknowledging that the trauma respondents and others like them suffered as a result of the allegedly unconstitutional acts of state and federal officials "must surely have gone beyond what anyone of normal sensibilities would wish to see imposed on innocent disabled citizens," the Court does not for a moment suggest that the retroactive award of benefits to which respondents were always entitled remotely approximates full compensation for such trauma. Nevertheless, it refuses to recognize a *Bivens* remedy here because the "design of [the disability insurance] program suggests that Congress has provided what it considers adequate remedial mechanisms for constitutional violations that may occur in the course of its administration."

I agree that in appropriate circumstances we should defer to a congressional decision to substitute alternative relief for a judicially created remedy. Neither the design of Title II's administrative review process, however, nor the debate surrounding its reform contain any suggestion that Congress meant to preclude recognition of a *Bivens* action for persons whose constitutional rights are violated by those charged with administering the program, or that Congress viewed this process as an adequate substitute remedy for such violations. Indeed, Congress never mentioned, let alone debated, the desirability of providing a statutory remedy for such constitutional wrongs. Because I believe legislators of "normal sensibilities" would not wish to leave such traumatic injuries unrecompensed, I find it inconceivable that Congress meant by mere silence to bar all redress for such injuries.

I

* * * Respondents allege that in the course of their review proceedings, state and federal officials violated their due process rights by judging their eligibility in light of impermissible quotas, disregarding dispositive favorable evidence, selecting biased physicians, purposely using unpublished criteria and rules inconsistent with statutory standards, arbitrarily reversing favorable decisions, and failing impartially to review adverse decisions.

* * *

Congress responded to the CDR crisis by establishing, for the first time, a statutory standard governing disability review. Designed primarily to end the practice of terminating benefits based on nothing more than a reassessment of old evidence under new eligibility criteria, the medical improvement standard permits the agency to terminate benefits only where substantial evidence demonstrates that one of four specific conditions is met. In addition to establishing these substantive eligibility criteria and directing SSA to revise certain others, Congress enacted several procedural reforms in order to protect recipients from future erroneous deprivations and to ensure that the review process itself would operate in a fairer and more humane manner. The most significant of these protections was a provision allowing recipients to elect to continue to receive benefit payments, subject to recoupment in certain circumstances, through appeal to a federal ALJ, the penultimate stage of administrative review.

II

A

In *Bivens* itself, we noted that, although courts have the authority to provide redress for constitutional violations in the form of an action for money damages, the exercise of that authority may be inappropriate where Congress has created another remedy that it regards as equally effective, or where "special factors counse[l] hesitation [even] in the absence of affirmative action by Congress." Among the "special factors" the Court divines today in our prior cases is "an appropriate deference to indications that congressional inaction has not been inadvertent." Describing congressional attention to the numerous problems the CDR process spawned as "frequent and intense," the Court concludes that the very design of that process "suggests that Congress has provided what it considers adequate remedial mechanisms for constitutional violations that may occur in the course of its administration." The cases setting forth the "special factors" analysis upon which the Court relies, however, reveal, by way of comparison, both the inadequacy of Title II's "remedial mechanism" and the wholly inadvertent nature of Congress' failure to provide any statutory remedy for constitutional injuries inflicted during the course of previous review proceedings.

In *Chappell v. Wallace*, where we declined to permit an action for damages by enlisted military personnel seeking redress from their superior officers for constitutional injuries, we noted that Congress, in the exercise of its "plenary constitutional authority over the military, has enacted statutes regulating military life, and has established a comprehensive internal system of justice to regulate military life * * * . The resulting system provides for the review and remedy of complaints and grievances such as [the equal protection claim] presented by respondents." That system not only permits aggrieved military personnel to raise constitutional challenges in administrative proceedings, it authorizes recovery of significant consequential damages, notably retroactive promotions. Similarly, in *Bush v. Lucas*, we concluded that, in light of the "elaborate, comprehensive scheme" governing federal employment relations, recognition of any supplemental judicial remedy for constitutional wrongs was inappropriate. Under that scheme—which Congress has "constructed step-by-step, with careful attention to conflicting policy considerations," over the course of nearly 100 years—"[c]onstitutional challenges * * * are fully cognizable" and prevailing employees are entitled not only to full backpay, but to retroactive promotions, seniority, pay raises, and accumulated leave. Indeed, Congress expressly "intended [to] put the employee 'in the same position he would have been in had the unjustified or erroneous personnel action not taken place.' "

> **Food for Thought**
>
> Does Justice Brennan concede too much here? What standards does he suggest for evaluating whether less than "full compensation for constitutional injuries" make judicial action appropriate?

It is true that neither the military justice system nor the federal employment relations scheme affords aggrieved parties full compensation for constitutional injuries; nevertheless, the relief provided in both is far more complete than that available under Title II's review process. Although federal employees may not recover damages for any emotional or dignitary harms they might suffer as a result of a constitutional injury, they, like their military counterparts, are entitled to redress for most economic consequential damages, including, most significantly, consequential damage to their Government careers. Here, by stark contrast, Title II recipients cannot even raise constitutional challenges to agency action in any of the four tiers of administrative review, and if they ultimately prevail on their eligibility claims in those administrative proceedings they can recover no consequential damages whatsoever. The only relief afforded persons unconstitutionally deprived of their disability benefits is retroactive payment of the very benefits they should have received all along. Such an award, of course, fails miserably to compensate disabled persons illegally stripped of the income upon which, in many cases, their very subsistence depends.[4]

The inadequacy of this relief is by no means a product of "the inevitable compromises required in the design of a massive and complex welfare benefits program." In *Chappell* and *Bush*, we dealt with elaborate administrative systems in which Congress anticipated that federal officials might engage in unconstitutional conduct, and in which it accordingly sought to afford injured persons a form of redress as complete as the Government's institutional concerns would allow.

Here, as the legislative history of the 1984 Reform Act makes abundantly clear, Congress did not attempt to achieve a delicate balance between the constitutional rights of Title II beneficiaries on the one hand, and administrative concerns on the other. Rather than fine-tuning "an elaborate remedial scheme that ha[d] been constructed step by step" over the better part of a century, Congress confronted a paralyzing breakdown in a vital social program, which it sought to rescue from near-total anarchy.

4 The legislative debate over the 1984 Reform Act is replete with anecdotal evidence of recipients who lost their cars and homes, and of some who may even have died as a result of benefit terminations.

Legislating in a near-crisis atmosphere, Congress saw itself as wrestling with the Executive Branch for control of the disability insurance program. It emphatically repudiated SSA's policy of restrictive, illiberal, and hasty benefit reviews, and adopted a number of prospective measures designed "to prevent further reckless reviews," * * * and to ensure that recipients dependent on disability benefits for their sustenance would be adequately protected in any future review proceedings.

At no point during the lengthy legislative debate, however, did any member of Congress so much as hint that the substantive eligibility criteria, notice requirements, and interim payment provisions that would govern future disability reviews adequately redressed the harms that beneficiaries may have suffered as a result of the unconstitutional actions of individual state and federal officials in past proceedings, or that the constitutional rights of those unjustly deprived of benefits in the past had to be sacrificed in the name of administrative efficiency or any other governmental interest. The Court today identifies no legislative compromise, "inevitable" or otherwise, in which lawmakers expressly declined to afford a remedy for such past wrongs. Nor can the Court point to any legislator who suggested that state and federal officials should be shielded from liability for any unconstitutional acts taken in the course of administering the review program, or that exposure to liability for such acts would be inconsistent with Congress' comprehensive and carefully crafted remedial scheme.

* * *

The mere fact, that Congress was aware of the prior injustices and failed to provide a form of redress for them, standing alone, is simply not a "special factor counselling hesitation" in the judicial recognition of a remedy. Inaction, we have repeatedly stated, is a notoriously poor indication of congressional intent, all the more so where Congress is legislating in the face of a massive breakdown calling for prompt and sweeping corrective measures. In 1984, Congress undertook to resuscitate a disability review process that had ceased functioning: that the prospective measures it prescribed to prevent future dislocations included no remedy for past wrongs in no way suggests a conscious choice to leave those wrongs unremedied.

B

Our decisions in *Chappell* and *Bush* reveal yet another flaw in the "special factors" analysis the Court employs today. In both those cases, we declined to legislate in areas in which Congress enjoys a special expertise that the judiciary clearly lacks.

* * *

Ignoring the unique characteristics of the military and civil service contexts that made judicial recognition of a *Bivens* action inappropriate in those cases, the Court today observes that "[c]ongressional competence at 'balancing governmental efficiency and the rights of [individuals]' is no more questionable in the social welfare context than it is in the civil service context * * * ." This observation, however, avails the Court nothing, for in *Bush* we declined to create a *Bivens* action for aggrieved federal employees not because Congress is simply competent to legislate in the area of federal employment relations, but because Congress is far more capable of addressing the special problems that arise in those relations than are courts. * * *

The Court's suggestion, therefore, that congressional authority over a given subject is itself a "special factor" that "counsel[s] hesitation [even] in the absence of affirmative action by Congress," is clearly mistaken. In *Davis v. Passman* we recognized a cause of action under the Fifth Amendment's Due Process Clause for a congressional employee who alleged that she had been discriminated against on the basis of her sex, even though Congress is competent to pass legislation governing the employment relations of its own Members. Likewise, in *Carlson v. Green* we created a *Bivens* action for redress of injuries flowing from the allegedly unconstitutional conduct of federal prison officials, notwithstanding the fact that Congress had expressly (and competently) provided a statutory remedy in the Federal Tort Claims Act for injuries inflicted by such officials. * * * [W]e permitted the claims because they arose in areas in which congressional competence is no greater than that of the courts, and in which, therefore, courts need not fear to tread even in the absence of congressional action.

The same is true here. Congress, of course, created the disability insurance program and obviously may legislate with respect to it. But unlike the military setting, where Congress' authority is plenary and entitled to considerable judicial deference, or the federal employment context, where Congress enjoys special expertise, social welfare is hardly an area in which the courts are largely incompetent to act. * * * In short, the social welfare context does not give rise to the types of concerns that make it an area where courts should refrain from creating a damages action even in the absence of congressional action.

* * *

Notes and Questions

1. *Chappell v. Wallace* and *United States v. Stanley* illustrate the Court's increasingly staunch resistance to implying private rights of action. In *Chappell*, cited with apparent approval even by Justice Brennan's dissent, enlisted servicemen sued superior

officers claiming that the defendants had discriminated against them by reason of race in making duty assignments, evaluations, and decisions about punishment. In a brief, unanimous opinion, the Court declined to recognize a private constitutional right of action for redress.

Stanley was, if anything, even more dramatic. In 1958, Stanley volunteered for what he was told was a chemical warfare testing program. The Army secretly administered LSD to him, which led to severe, permanent personality changes causing his release from service and dissolution of his marriage. In 1975, Stanley discovered the secret testing when the Army asked him to participate in a follow-up study. He brought a Bivens action alleging that the surreptitious dose of LSD violated his constitutional rights. A divided Court refused to allow a private right of action.

2. Justice O'Connor gives a dual picture of the remedial structure available to Chilicky. Analogizing *Schweiker* to Bush v. Lucas (1983), she first describes the structure as "comprehensive," but later recognizes that it is less effective than the damages remedy sought. Are those views reconcilable?

3. Would the Court have implied a private right of action if there had been no comprehensive scheme? If so, then Congress, by passing its remedial scheme, effectively limited the Fifth Amendment in *Schweiker* and the First Amendment in Bush. Is that proper? Are the questions of the available remedy and its substantive law source separate from the question of the substantive scope of constitutional amendments?

4. Is the majority's treatment of *Carlson v. Green*, 446 U.S. 14 (1980), persuasive? Justice O'Connor notes with respect to Carlson, that there was "no explicit statutory prohibition against the relief sought, and no exclusive statutory alternative remedy." Is that not true here? Or is Justice O'Connor saying that any congressionally provided remedy is exclusive whether Congress says it is or not? Justice Brennan, obviously, has a different view.

6. Justice Brennan disputes the majority's characterization of Congress as having carefully balanced or deliberately compromised the competing interests asserted in *Schweiker*. How direct an indication of congressional consideration of the constitutional issues ought the Court to require? If congressional silence about constitutional rights precludes implication of a remedy, has the standard for implying rights of action in constitutional provisions at least begun to merge with that for implying such rights in statutes? *See* George D. Brown, *Letting Statutory Tails Wag Constitutional Dogs—Have the* Bivens *Dissenters Prevailed?*, 64 IND.L.J. 263 (1989).

7. Is Congress's intention in creating its remedial scheme important? If the Court disagrees about the adequacy of relief, is it appropriate to supplement the congressional scheme? If not, then why does the Court not refrain from considering the merits

of the requested damages remedy? If so, under what theory does Congress achieve primacy in interpreting or balancing constitutional guarantees?

9. *Correctional Services Corp. v. Malesko*, 534 U.S. 61 (2001), seemed to add a new gloss to *Bivens* and *Chilicky*. Petitioner operated a halfway house on behalf of the federal Bureau of Prisons. Respondent, alleged that petitioner negligently injured him by failing to provide him with appropriate medication for his heart condition and by requiring him to walk up five flights of stairs on one occasion, resulting in a heart attack and other injury. He sued the corporation and the individual who had prevented him from using the elevator. The parties assumed that Malesko had alleged a violation of the Eighth Amendment. The district court dismissed the complaint with respect to the corporation, reading *FDIC v. Meyer* (1994), as holding that a *Bivens* action is available only against individuals. The Second Circuit reversed * * *, finding *Meyer* only declined to expand *Bivens* remedies to embrace federal agencies as well as federal agents. That court ruled that a remedy against a private entity should lie "to accomplish * * * the important *Bivens* goal of providing a remedy for constitutional violations."

The Supreme Court reversed, ruling five-to-four that the *Bivens* remedy does not extend to this action against a private entity acting under color of federal law. Chief Justice Rehnquist's opinion emphasized that the Court has recognized *Bivens* remedies only in situations where the plaintiff had no other avenue of relief. He then characterized Chilicky as rejecting even that basis for a *Bivens* remedy.

> We therefore rejected the claim that a *Bivens* remedy should be implied simply for want of any other means for challenging a constitutional deprivation in federal court. * * * So long as the plaintiff had an avenue for some redress, bedrock principles of separation of powers foreclosed judicial imposition of a new substantive liability.

Finally, the Chief Justice noted that *Meyer* had declared that " 'the purpose of *Bivens* is to deter the officer,' not the agency." The deterrent effect of a *Bivens* claim would be lost, the Court reasoned, if individuals could sue the agency rather than the agent. The Court also noted that "federal prisoners in private facilities enjoy a parallel tort remedy that is unavailable to prisoners housed in government facilities." Whereas the *Bivens* Court declined to make a new federal remedy conditional on the non-existence of state tort remedies, the *Malesko* majority did impose that limitation.

Food for Thought

If state prisoners were involved, do you suppose that the Court would have made the parallel argument? If so, does *Malesko* portend a narrower reading of *Monroe* and of § 1983?

Justice Stevens, writing for the four dissenters, viewed the case differently.

"[T]he question presented by this case is whether the Court should create an exception to the straightforward application of Bivens and Carlson, not whether it should extend our cases beyond their 'core premise.' " The dissenters read *Meyer* as a case limited to federal agencies. They also disputed the majority's assertion that alternative remedies were unavailable to Bivens and others similarly situated.

Is the majority correct that the primary purpose of the Bivens decision was to deter individual law enforcement officers from violating people's Fourth Amendment rights? What language in either Justice Brennan's majority or Justice Harlan's concurrence supports that assertion? Assuming that such deterrence was Bivens's primary purpose, should the majority Justices consider reevaluating their position on the availability of qualified immunity?

Is Justice Stevens a bit too casual in assuming congressional approval of the Bivens remedy (or approach)? Is it not possible that a disapproving Congress would nonetheless have eschewed an attempt to abolish the Bivens cause of action on the ground that the Court was construing the Fourth Amendment and that its decision was therefore not amenable to congressional alteration except by the amendment process of Article V? *Cf. City of Boerne v. Flores*, 521 U.S. 507 (1997). That aside, Congress may never have abolished the remedy, but it has not codified it either, nor has it legislated in any general way to provide individual remedies for constitutional violations at the hands of federal officials.

10. *Alexander v. Sandoval*, 532 U.S. 275 (2001), continued the Court's restrictive approach to implication. The case concerned a Title VI challenge to Alabama's English-only rule that prohibited administering examinations for drivers' licenses in any other language. Plaintiffs argued that the Alabama rule discriminated on the basis of national origin, in violation of a Department of Transportation regulation issued pursuant to § 602 of Title VI, which authorized DOT to effectuate the provisions of § 601. Plaintiffs asked the Court to imply a private right of action in § 602 to enforce the DOT regulations, but a five-to-four majority declined.

The majority assumed without deciding that even though § 601 prohibited only intentional discrimination, DOT had the authority to issue disparate-impact regulations under § 602. The issue then was whether the Court should imply a private right of action to enforce those regulations. Justice Scalia's opinion for the Court noted particularly the absence of rights-creating language in § 602, the fact that it addressed itself to federal agencies rather than to individuals, and § 602's provision of an enforcement mechanism that federal agencies, not individuals, can invoke. The Court, therefore, was unwilling to find congressional intent that there be a private right of action. In the course of the opinion, Justice Scalia recounted the Court's shift from the comparatively free-implication days preceding Cort v. Ash to the Justices' far more restrictive approach since 1975.

The four dissenting Justices focused on that shift as well, arguing that since Congress enacted Title VI before the Court's decision in Cort v. Ash, the majority should not apply the heightened standard for finding congressional intent that the Court began to develop more than a decade after Title VI became law. And so the battle continues.

A unanimous Court ruled in *Hui v. Castaneda*, 559 U.S. 799 (2010), that Federal Tort Claims Act § 233(a)'s making the FTCA the exclusive remedy for medical malpractice claims against Public Health Service personnel precluded the availability of a Bivens claim, despite 1) Congress having passed § 233(a) before Bivens, and 2) plaintiffs' claim that the state remedies to which FTCA remitted them were not as generous as a Bivens claim.

11. May a county that purchases pharmaceutical drugs from manufacturers that have contracted with the federal government as to permissible drug prices as a condition of being eligible for Medicaid payments sue the manufacturers for violating the contract? *Astra USA, Inc. v. Santa Clara County*, 131 S.Ct. 1342 (2011), holds that it cannot. The Court noted (and the County conceded) that Congress created no private right of action under the relevant statute, and it declined to allow the County to sue as a third-party beneficiary of the federal contract. For reasons similar to the Court's reasoning in *Chilicky*, text at 536, the Court declined to allow the action to go forward because it construed the statutory scheme as Congress's indication that it wanted the enforcement burden centralized in the federal government. Private actions, the Court reasoned, would undermine the enforcement scheme and pose a threat to the national uniformity that Congress desired.

---

4. Filling in Statutory Interstices

At the outset, one should remember that Judge Friendly referred to this technique of creating federal common law as "the *normal* judicial filling of statutory interstices." (Emphasis added.) Spontaneous generation, while certainly not unheard of, is comparatively rare. And although the Court has cut back dramatically on implying private rights of action in constitutional or statutory provisions and never has done much with construing jurisdictional grants as congressional commands to create common law, interstitial common law is, well, common.

When the courts spontaneously generate federal common law, there is no underlying statutory referent, and on the increasingly rare occasion that they imply a private right of action, the provision containing the underlying right simply does not address the existence *vel non* of a right of action even though it purports to create substantive rights. One might regard those forms of creating federal common law, as well as construing a jurisdictional grant as a congressional command to create common law, to be common law wholesale. Interstitial common law, on the other hand, is definitely retail, dealing essentially with omissions in detailed statutory schemes. Part of the courts' difficulty may be attempting to figure out whether the omission was intentional or inadvertent.

Creating interstitial common law is different from interpreting a statute. In the latter, the courts attribute meaning to particular words or phrases in a statute that, arguably at least, address the topic. In the typical interstitial common law situation, however, the underlying statute is utterly silent. For example, although the Supreme Court had implied private rights of action in § 10(b) of the Securities and Exchange Act of 1934 and Securities and Exchange Commission Rule 10b-5 for investors harmed by reliance on misrepresentations in securities offering memoranda, it had never made clear what limitation period should apply to such actions. The Court confronted that problem in *Lampf, Pleva, Lipkind, Prupis & Petigrow v. Gilbertson*, 501 U.S. 350 (1991), and its approach is revealing.

The district court, adhering to its circuit's expressed policy, applied the state limitation period applicable to the state law claim most closely analogous to the federal claim. In the district court's view, the analogous state law claim was common law fraud. Under state law the applicable limitations period for such claims was two years, but it included a discovery provision that could have extended prospective plaintiffs' time to sue. The district court dismissed the action on limitations grounds because it felt that the plaintiffs had sufficient notice of problems to give them "inquiry notice" of the fraud, and plaintiffs had not made inquiry sufficient to cause them to file within the basic two-year period. The court of appeals agreed with the district court's selection of the limitation period but reversed and remanded for consideration of unresolved issues of fact as to when the plaintiffs either did discover or reasonably could have discovered the alleged fraud.

In the Supreme Court, the plaintiff-respondents argued that the lower courts were correct in selecting the state limitations period. However, the petitioner contended that a federal law limitation should govern the claim and that the Court should use the limitations scheme that the 1934 Act created for the express causes of action that it contained. Those provisions require actions to be brought within one year of discovery (or reasonable discovery) but in no event more than three years after the actionable conduct. The Solicitor General appeared on behalf of the Securities and Exchange Commission and agreed that the applicable limitations period should come from federal law. Nonetheless, he asked the Court to apply a five-year period for a new cause of action that Congress had added to the statute after the *Lampf* litigation began, because it represented "Congress's most recent views on the accommodation of competing interests, provide[d] the closest federal analogy, and promise[d] to yield the best practical and policy results in 10b-5 litigation."

The Court splintered. Justice Blackmun wrote the Court's opinion except for a part that rehearsed the Court's long-standing practice of borrowing state limitations periods where Congress has not specified any. Despite recognizing that as the normal approach, Justice Blackmun pointed out that state-created limitations do not ordinarily reflect consideration of federal interests. "[W]hen the operation of a state limitations period would frustrate the policies embraced by the federal enactment, this Court has looked to federal law for a suitable period."

Justice Blackmun prescribed a hierarchical consideration of the question. "First, the court must determine whether a uniform statute of limitations is to be selected." He noted that federal claims often encompass matters that the states would treat under multiple limitations periods and acknowledged that the Court had occasionally chosen from among various state sources available in order to have a single limitation applicable to the federal claim. "Second, assuming a uniform limitations period is appropriate, the court must decide whether this period should be derived from a state or federal source." To the extent that the federal claim is one likely to touch multiple jurisdictions, that suggests the utility of a federal source in order to avoid forum shopping and extended litigation over limitations. Finally, Justice Blackmun cautioned that "even where geographic considerations counsel federal borrowing [i.e., borrowing from a federal source], the * * * presumption of state borrowing requires that a court determine that an analogous federal source truly affords a 'closer fit' with the cause of action * * * than does any available state-law source."

FYI

For example, a § 1983 action might rest on facts supporting state claims of trespass, assault and battery, conversion, or intentional infliction of emotional harm, each of which, under state law, might have a different limitation period.

Of course, the case before the Court presented a significant problem: "we are faced with the awkward task of discerning the limitations period that Congress intended courts to apply to a cause of action it really never knew existed." Justice Blackmun found succor in the original statute, in which Congress had created some explicit remedies and specified a limitation on them. "We can imagine no clearer indication of how Congress would have balanced the policy considerations implicit in any limitations provision than the balance struck by the same Congress in limiting similar and related protec-

Food for Thought

Is Justice Blackmun's comment strictly accurate? If the practice of implying private rights of action was as well established as Texas & Pacific R.R. v. Rigsby (pages 481, 482) suggests, perhaps Congress knew perfectly well that the claim would exist. Justice Blackmun thus may be assuming his conclusion.

tions." He adopted the one-and-three-year limitations scheme, rejecting the Government's argument for a five-year period on the ground that the part of the statute that contained it postdated the implied rights of action by nearly half a century and addressed itself only to insider trading.

Justice Scalia continued to bemoan the practice of implying rights of action, but grudgingly conceded that since the Court had created the *Lampf* claim so long ago, it had to answer the question presented. Though joining most of the majority opinion, he rejected Justice Blackmun's hierarchical approach, instead stating his preference for either borrowing an appropriate state limitations period or, if the state period was inconsistent with the federal statute's purposes, having no limitation at all. He acknowledged obliquely that having no limitation, while having the benefit of deterring courts from implying additional private rights of action, "would be highly unjust to those who must litigate past inventions." Consequently, he agreed with the other Justices making up the majority that "the most responsible approach, where the enactment that has been the occasion of our creation of a cause of action contains a limitations period for an analogous cause of action, is to use that."

Justice Stevens dissented. Given that the Court initially implied the private right of action more than forty years previously, when it was the practice to borrow state limitations periods for such actions because that was deemed to be the intent of Congress, he felt the Court should do nothing else in the absence of congressional action. In his view, creating limitations periods involved policy considerations better left to Congress. Moreover, he found nothing in the Securities and Exchange Act of 1934 leading him "to believe that Congress intended us to depart from our traditional rule and overrule four decades of established law."

Justice O'Connor also dissented. She agreed with Justice Blackmun that a uniform limitation period was appropriate, but disagreed with imposing the three-year period of repose in addition to the one-year discovery rule in *Lampf* itself. "In holding that respondents' suit is time barred under a limitations period that did not exist before today, the Court departs drastically from our established practice and inflicts an injustice on the respondents." She observed that the Court had not previously applied new limitations periods to the cases in which the Court announced them. When the plaintiffs filed suit the federal courts in that circuit had applied state law statutes of limitations for more than thirty years, and she argued that it was unfair to dismiss their claim because they did not predict the Court's subsequent decision.

Finally, Justice Kennedy dissented separately (though he had also joined Justice O'Connor's dissent). He agreed with the majority that since "§ 10(b) actions are implied under the 1934 Act, it makes sense for us to look to the limitations periods Congress established under the Act." Nonetheless, the Act made three different references to statutes of limitations, and the majority had rejected one. Justice Kennedy also opposed having a three-year repose period at all. He concluded that such an absolute time bar was "inconsistent with the practical realities of § 10(b) litigation and the congressional policies underlying that remedy." Victimized investors may be unable to discover fraudulent schemes within 3 years. "By adopting a 3-year period of repose, the Court makes a § 10(b) action all but a dead letter for injured investors who by no conceivable standard of fairness or practicality can be expected to file suit within three years after the violation occurred." He contended that "[t]he 1-year-from-discovery rule is sufficient to ensure a fair balancing between protecting the legitimate interests of aggrieved investors, yet preventing stale claims."

Lampf demonstrates the difficulties that the courts confront in having multiple sources at their disposal and no legislative guidance in choosing among them, although that assertion assuming its conclusion. Justice Blackmun and his colleagues felt quite comfortable in concluding that Congress did provide guidance in the 1934 Act. Does the Court's splintered approach in *Lampf* provide ammunition to those who believe that the federal courts are not equipped to be common law courts and should not try to be? Can one make principled distinctions among the Justices' approaches that *Lampf* exemplifies, or are they simply voting their own feelings and attempting, in a rather free-wheeling way, to identify and create good results in a way more commonly associated with legislatures?

Justice Blackmun's opinion in *Lampf* viewed borrowing state limitations periods as "derived from" the Rules of Decision Act. What does that mean? Does the Rules of Decision Act compel borrowing? If not, then why is it relevant? If so, how can one justify *Lampf*? Justice Stevens believed the Act "directed" the practice of borrowing state law. Does that belief explain his dissent?

If Congress intends by its silence to have state law govern, is it proper for the Court to decide that state law does not sufficiently protect federal interests? Suppose Congress created a substantive right and a right to sue upon it and specifically included a borrowing position in the new statute. Would it then be appropriate for the Court to conclude that Congress had underestimated the adverse impact of state limitations law on federal interests? In this connection, consider *Lampf's* conclusion that it is "inappropriate" to believe that Congress would have intended adoption of state law. If Congress's normal intention, manifested by silence, is that the federal courts adopt state law, does it seem the Court should conclude in a particular case that Congress did not so intend, without the statute bearing some evidence of that change of heart?

The majority relied on its conclusion that the federal rule is a "closer" analogy. Is that appropriate? Whatever happened to Boyle's and Atherton's requirement that there be a "significant conflict" between federal and state law before federal common law will displace state law? Given the underlying assumption of congressional intention with respect to limitations, does the significant-conflict test seem even more appropriate, or is the Boyle approach inapplicable when a federal court is filling statutory interstices?

Should one assume that Congress, had it thought explicitly about the question, would have selected the same limitations period for this claim as for other claims under the statute? If the claims are different and the remedies are different, is the assumption supportable? Note that in creating the insider-trading claim, Congress specified a different limitation.

The majority rejected the proffered analogy to § 20A of the Insider Trading Act, but perhaps overlooked the provision's greater significance. That statute explicitly recognized and obviously approved of the implied actions that the courts had recognized. Does this sort of congressional awareness and obvious acquiescence blunt the thrust of the Justices Powell's and Scalia's anti-implication positions?

Justice Scalia was careful to distinguish common law courts from federal tribunals. Is the distinction justified? As a matter of original intent (leaving aside the broad issue of whether that sort of approach is appropriate), what sorts of courts are the Framers likely to have contemplated?

The Court decided *James B. Beam Distilling Co. v. Georgia,* 501 U.S. 529 (1991), making the *Lampf* rule retroactive, the same day as *Lampf*. Thus, cases that had been timely when filed under the pre-*Lampf* rules became untimely, and the courts began to dismiss them. Within six months, Congress overruled Lampf for all then-pending cases by restoring state limitations periods for the implied right of action. Congress also included a provision that would have permitted plaintiffs whose cases had been dismissed pursuant to *Lampf* to refile, which raised severe separation-of-powers problems. *Plaut v. Spendthrift Farm, Inc.,* 514 U.S. 211 (1995), declared this aspect of the statute unconstitutional. For more extended discussion of *Plaut* and this part of the controversy, see pages 254-76.

Two things are notable. First, although the Court and Congress disagreed about the proper result in these circumstances, the process through which the majority arrived at its decision remains unquestioned. Congress did not dispute the Court's *technique* of balancing federal and state interests; it simply thought the Court had misunderstood the legislature's view of the federal interests involved. Second, the progression from *Lampf* through *Plaut* represents a kind of dialogue between Court and Congress with respect to the proper contours of the law. Even in *Lampf*, the Court tried to discern congressional intent. Congress corrected the Court, but did so in a way that intruded on the functioning of the judiciary as a separate branch, a misstep the Court quickly corrected. The result is that the congressionally preferred rule governs; the only real losers were those plaintiffs whose litigation (appeals included) ended in a final judgment of dismissal on limitations grounds in the six months between *Lampf* and the effective date of the statute.

Many federal statutes that create causes of action do not contain limitations periods. Until recently, a federal court confronted with such a case had three options: 1) inferring that Congress intended there to be no limitations period at all, 2) inferring that Congress intended the courts to borrow some state limitation to use as federal common law, or 3) inferring that Congress intended the federal courts to create a limitations period. The first and third approaches resulted in a uniform, nationwide policy. The second allowed the same generic cause of action to have different limitations in each state. In practice, the Justices at various times have used all three approaches, and each has its difficulties. Construing the sounds of congressional silence is a difficult enterprise.

County of Oneida v. Oneida Indian Nation (1985) considered the Oneidas' 1970 claim for return of lands conveyed to New York in 1795 in violation of a federal statute. The Court found that Congress intended that there be no limitations period. Justice Powell based his conclusion in part on separation of powers and his perception of congressional intent, and rejected the County's argument that the Court should borrow some state limitation. *See also, e.g., Occidental Life Insurance Co. v. EEOC (1977)* (holding that there is no limitation period governing the ability of the Equal Employment Opportunity Commission to commence a federal action against an employer).

Wilson v. Garcia (1985) exemplified the second option. There the Court confronted the question of the limitations period applicable to actions under the Civil Rights Act of 1871, 42 U.S.C.A. § 1983. A majority ruled that the personal injury limitations period of the state in which the action was brought govern such actions. The Court noted that "[w]hen Congress has not established a time limitation for a federal cause of action, the settled practice has been to adopt a local time limitation as federal law if it is not inconsistent with federal law or policy to do so." Having decided to borrow state law, the Court also had to choose a state limitations period. It rejected using the period that the state would apply to a state claim on identical facts, explaining that § 1983 claims are subject to such varied characterization that such a practice could lead to great uncertainty and to more than one limitations period applying to a single claim. (For example, on the facts in Wilson a state court could have used limitations periods relating to false arrest, false imprisonment, assault and battery, personal injuries, or an action arising under a statute.) The Court concluded that Congress probably would have considered a § 1983 claim most analogous to a claim for personal injuries and directed that each state's personal injury statute govern § 1983 claims brought in that state.

Finally, for some types of claims, the Court has felt that a single, nationwide limitations period is necessary. Sometimes the Court thinks either that state limitations periods are too restrictive to protect important federal interests properly or that using state laws would create unacceptable confusion. *DelCostello v. International Brotherhood of Teamsters* (1983), exemplified the first problem. It held that a uniform federal limitations period was necessary to protect fundamental federal labor relations policy in actions by employees against employers for breach of collective bargaining agreements and against unions for breach of the duty of fair representation.

Agency Holding Corp. v. Malley-Duff & Associates (1987), illustrated the second. There the Court insisted on a federal limitations period for a civil RICO action because the novel nature of the civil RICO claim, the unlikelihood of finding true analogs in state law, and the fact that such actions may touch many jurisdictions combined to make use of state limitations likely to produce only intolerable uncertainty and extended litigation. Again, the Court looked to the closest federal analogy.

In 1990, Congress limited the development of federal common law in this area. Title 28 U.S.C.A. § 1658 now provides that actions must be commenced within four years of accrual of a claim for any cause of action Congress creates after the effective date of § 1658 that does not otherwise contain a limitation period. Note, however, that Congress did not displace limitations periods adopted by the federal courts for statutory rights antedating 1990. The legislative history suggests that this grandfather treatment reflects Congress's disinclination to "disrupt the settled expectations of a great many parties." On the other hand, Congress could have applied the new limitation generally to all federal causes of action lacking individually-legislated limitations periods, irrespective of when Congress created the cause of action, exempting only cases in which a plaintiff's claim had accrued before the effective date of § 1658. Such an approach would have unified limitations treatment of federal claims without frustrating existing parties' (or potential parties') expectations. Notwithstanding § 1658, questions regarding appropriate limitations periods continue to arise with respect to federal statutes enacted before 1990, andhus, the inquiry continues closely to parallel that in substantive common law cases.

D. Concluding Note

Every federal common law case raises federalism and separation-of-powers concerns. In *Clearfield*, for example, the Court's decision to use a federal common law rule created during the reign of *Swift v. Tyson* displaced a contrary Pennsylvania rule, thus potentially raising the hackles of federalism. Should Congress have made that decision? Perhaps the courts' freely creating common law to protect court-perceived dominant federal interests implies that the representative branches are not up to the job. Those who view *Erie* as a separation-of-powers case argue that practice is illegitimate.

At the extreme, the separation-of-powers view of federal common law means that federal courts can never create common law, clearly something not contemplated by the *Erie* Court. Even Justice Powell, perhaps the Court's most ardent champion of that view, did not advocate so rigid an approach, for although he dissented in *Merrill Lynch, Pierce, Fenner & Smith v. Curran* (1982), he did note the possibility of implying a private right of action if there were " 'compelling evidence that Congress in fact intended such an action to exist.' " On the other hand, giving the federal courts effectively unfettered discretion to create common law in any area in which the Constitution permits the federal government to operate may well disrupt the balance of power among the branches of the federal government and has at least the appearance of being anti-majoritarian. Professor Redish, among others, has argued strongly that judicial law-making is incompatible with the nature of our democracy.

A middle position may be possible. Perhaps separation of powers allows the federal courts to create common law that implements policies declared in positive law by the representative branches. Thus, each rule of common law would have to find an anchor in legislation declaring or exemplifying the policy the common law rule serves. Implying a private right of action, as in *Cannon v. University of Chicago*, is then permissible because of the clear policy declaration in Title IX against sex discrimination. Creation of the federal contractors' immunity in *Boyle v. United Technologies*, however, is on considerably shakier ground because there is no apparent anchor in positive law.

For More Information

See, e.g., Martin H. Redish, *Federal Common Law, Political Legitimacy, and the Interpretive Process: An "Institutionalist" Perspective*, 83 NW.U.L.REV. 761 (1989); Martin H. Redish, *Abstention, Separation of Powers, and the Limits of the Judicial Function*, 94 YALE L.J. 71 (1984).

In 1992, the Association of American Law Schools' Section on Federal Courts considered more broadly the legitimacy of creating of federal common law. Pace Law Review published the papers as a symposium, beginning at 12 PACE L.REV. 227 (1992).

Note that the Court's recent emphasis on "significant conflict" as the only legitimate predicate for creating federal common law may, in different circumstances, leave the Justices more or less latitude for creating federal common law than having to find a policy anchor in positive law. *Boyle*, for example, has no such anchor, but the Court found significant conflict and proceeded to fashion federal common law. On the other hand, the Court might have found such an anchor in *United States v. Yazell* (in the federal government's authority to create loan programs through the Small Business Administration), but it found no significant conflict and therefore refused to create federal common law.

Scholars and judges will doubtless continue vigorously to debate the propriety of federal common law. *Erie* opened a Pandora's Box of a sort, but one that may have released something beneficial. The debate about federal common law is merely one aspect of the continuing debate about the contours of the federal system generally. It may be that the debate itself is valuable without any thought of an eventual resolution, because it keeps us keenly aware of the delicate balance that the federal system entails. That there are no easy answers (or, perhaps, any answers at all) may be the good news rather than the bad news.

Chapter 6

The Federal Forum, the Fourteenth Amendment, and Section 1983

A. Introduction

Earlier chapters explored the theme of federalism extensively. This chapter continues the focus on federalism, but in the context of state governments' relations with individuals and the federal courts' role in mediating those relationships. The Civil War and its aftermath provoked enormous change in the dynamics of these relationships, stimulated primarily by problems of African-Americans' attempts to become full, equal participants in American society. The most important statute addressing the problem is "the" Civil Rights Act of 1871, now codified at 42 U.S.C.A. § 1983.[1] In addition to its tremendous significance in real-world litigation, § 1983 is a unique intellectual vehicle for exploring the federal courts' functioning *vis-à-vis* the states and Congress. The themes of federalism and government accountability to its citizens surface repeatedly in civil rights cases.

1 The predecessor of § 1983 was not the only civil rights legislation passed by Congress during and just after Reconstruction. Congress also enacted measures that later became 42 U.S.C.A. §§ 1981, 1982, 1984 and 1985 on the civil side, and the predecessors of 18 U.S.C.A. §§ 241, 242 on the criminal side. All of these statutes were and are important, but none has the claim on history of § 1983. The Supreme Court has noted that of the five civil rights measures passed by Congress between 1866 and 1875, "[o]nly § 1 of the Act of April 20, 1871, presently codified as 42 U.S.C. § 1983, achieved measurable success in later years." Zwickler v. Koota, 389 U.S. 241, 247 n. 9 (1967).

B. Section 1983 as a Remedy for Violations of the Fourteenth Amendment

1. "Under Color of State Law"

Monroe v. Pape

Supreme Court of the United States, 1961.
365 U.S. 167.

MR. JUSTICE DOUGLAS delivered the opinion of the Court.

This case presents important questions concerning the construction of R.S. § 1979, 42 U.S.C. § 1983, which reads as follows:

> Every person who, under color of any statute, ordinance, regulation, custom, or usage, of any State or Territory, subjects, or causes to be subjected, any citizen of the United States or other person within the jurisdiction thereof to the deprivation of any rights, privileges, or immunities secured by the Constitution and laws, shall be liable to the party injured in an action at law, suit in equity, or other proper proceeding for redress.

> **FYI**
> Congress subsequently amended this statute to prohibit injunctions against state judges without a prior declaratory judgment having been issued.

The complaint alleges that 13 Chicago police officers broke into petitioners' home in the early morning, routed them from bed, made them stand naked in the living room, and ransacked every room, emptying drawers and ripping mattress covers. It further alleges that Mr. Monroe was then taken to the police station and detained on "open" charges for 10 hours, while he was interrogated about a two-day-old murder, that he was not taken before a magistrate, though one was accessible, that he was not permitted to call his family or attorney, that he was subsequently released without criminal charges being preferred against him. It is alleged that the officers had no search warrant and no arrest warrant and that they acted "under color of the statutes, ordinances, regulations, customs and usages" of Illinois and of the City of Chicago. Federal jurisdiction was asserted under R.S. § 1979, which we have set out above, and 28 U.S.C. § 1343 and 28 U.S.C. § 1331.

The City of Chicago moved to dismiss the complaint on the ground that it is not liable under the Civil Rights Acts nor for acts committed in performance of its governmental functions. All defendants moved to dismiss, alleging that the complaint alleged no cause of action under those Acts or under the Federal Constitution. The District Court dismissed the complaint. The Court of Appeals affirmed * * * .

I

* * *

Section 1979 came onto the books as § 1 of the Ku Klux Act of April 20, 1871. It was one of the means whereby Congress exercised the power vested in it by § 5 of the Fourteenth Amendment to enforce the provisions of that Amendment. Senator Edmunds, Chairman of the Senate Committee on the Judiciary, said concerning this section:

> The first section is one that I believe nobody objects to, as defining the rights secured by the Constitution of the United States when they are assailed by any State law or under color of any State law, and it is merely carrying out the principles of the civil rights bill, which has since become a part of the Constitution,

viz., the Fourteenth Amendment.

Its purpose is plain from the title of the legislation, "An Act to enforce the Provisions of the Fourteenth Amendment to the Constitution of the United States, and for other Purposes." Allegation of facts constituting a deprivation under color of state authority of a right guaranteed by the Fourteenth Amendment satisfies to that extent the requirement of R.S. § 1979. So far petitioners are on solid ground. For the guarantee against unreasonable searches and seizures contained in the Fourth Amendment has been made applicable to the States by reason of the Due Process Clause of the Fourteenth Amendment.

II

There can be no doubt at least since *Ex parte Virginia (1880)* that Congress has the power to enforce provisions of the Fourteenth Amendment against those who carry a badge of authority of a State and represent it in some capacity, whether they act in accordance with their authority or misuse it. The question with which we now deal is the narrower one of whether Congress, in enacting § 1979, meant to give a remedy to parties deprived of constitutional rights, privileges and immunities by an official's abuse of his position. We conclude that it did so intend.

It is argued that "under color of" enumerated state authority excludes acts of an official or policeman who can show no authority under state law, state custom, or state usage to do what he did. In this case it is said that these policemen, in breaking into petitioners' apartment, violated the Constitution and laws of Illinois. It is pointed out that under Illinois law a simple remedy is offered for that violation and that, so far as it appears, the courts of Illinois are available to give petitioners that full redress which the common law affords for violence done to a person; and it is earnestly argued that no "statute, ordinance, regulation, custom or usage" of Illinois bars that redress.

The Ku Klux Act grew out of a message sent to Congress by President Grant on March 23, 1871, reading:

> A condition of affairs now exists in some States of the Union rendering life and property insecure and the carrying of the mails and the collection of the revenue dangerous. The proof that such a condition of affairs exists in some localities is now before the Senate. That the power to correct these evils is beyond the control of State authorities I do not doubt; that the power of the Executive of the United States, acting within the limits of existing laws, is sufficient for present emergencies is not clear. Therefore, I urgently recommend such legislation as in the judgment of Congress shall effectually secure life, liberty, and property, and the enforcement of law in all parts of the United States * * * .

The legislation—in particular the section with which we are now concerned—had several purposes. There are threads of many thoughts running through the debates. One who reads them in their entirety sees that the present section had three main aims.

First, it might, of course, override certain kinds of state laws * * * .

Second, it provided a remedy where state law was inadequate. That aspect of the legislation was summed up as follows by Senator Sherman of Ohio:

> * * * [I]t is said the reason is that any offense may be committed upon a negro by a white man, and a negro cannot testify in any case against a white man, so that the only way by which any conviction can be had in Kentucky in those cases is in the United States courts, because the United States courts enforce the United States laws by which negroes may testify.

But the purposes were much broader. The *third* aim was to provide a federal remedy where the state remedy, though adequate in theory, was not available in practice. The opposition to the measure complained that "It overrides the reserved powers of the States," just as they argued that the second section of the bill "[absorbed] the entire jurisdiction of the States over their local and domestic affairs."

This Act of April 20, 1871, sometimes called "the third 'force bill,' " was passed by a Congress that had the Klan "particularly in mind." The debates are replete with references to the lawless conditions existing in the South in 1871.

There was available to the Congress during these debates a report, nearly 600 pages in length, dealing with the activities of the Klan and the inability of the state governments to cope with it. This report was drawn on by many of the speakers. It was not the unavailability of state remedies but the failure of certain States to enforce the laws with an equal hand that furnished the powerful momentum behind this "force bill."

* * *

While one main scourge of the evil—perhaps the leading one—was the Ku Klux Klan, the remedy created was not a remedy against it or its members but against those who representing a State in some capacity were unable or unwilling to enforce a state law * * * .

* * *

The debates were long and extensive. It is abundantly clear that one reason the legislation was passed was to afford a federal right in federal courts because, by reason of prejudice, passion, neglect, intolerance or otherwise, state laws might not be enforced and the claims of citizens to the enjoyment of rights, privileges, and immunities guaranteed by the Fourteenth Amendment might be denied by the state agencies.

* * *

Although the legislation was enacted because of the conditions that existed in the South at that time, it is cast in general language and is as applicable to Illinois as it is to the States whose names were mentioned over and again in the debates. It is no answer that the State has a law which if enforced would give relief. The federal remedy is supplementary to the state remedy, and the latter need not be first sought and refused before the federal one is invoked. Hence the fact that Illinois by its constitution and laws outlaws unreasonable searches and seizures is no barrier to the present suit in the federal court.

> **FYI**
> This is the federal criminal statute for prosecuting state officers' violations of federal rights, now codified at 18 U.S.C. Sec. 242.

We had before us in *United States v. Classic* (1941) § 20 of the Criminal Code, which provides a criminal punishment for anyone who "under color of any law, statute, ordinance, regulation, or custom" subjects any inhabitant of a State to the deprivation of "any rights, privileges, or immunities secured or protected by the Constitution or laws of the United States." * * * The right involved in the *Classic* case was the right of voters in a primary to have their votes counted. The laws of Louisiana required the defendants "to count the ballots, to record the result of the count, and to certify the result of the election." But according to the indictment they did not perform their duty. * * * [T]he Court ruled, "Misuse of power, possessed by virtue of state law and made possible only because the wrongdoer is clothed with the authority of state law, is action taken 'under color of' state law." * * *

That view of the meaning of the words "under color of" state law was reaffirmed in Screws v. United States (1945). The acts there complained of were committed by state officers in performance of their duties, *viz.*, making an arrest effective. It was urged there, as it is here, that "under color of" state law should not be construed to duplicate in federal law what was an offense under state law. It was said there, as it is here, that the ruling in the *Classic* case as to the meaning of "under color of" state law was not in focus and was ill-advised. It was argued there, as it is here, that "under color of" state law included only action taken by officials pursuant to state law. We rejected that view.

* * *

We conclude that the meaning given "under color of" law in the *Classic* case and in the Screws and Williams [v. United States (1951)] cases was the correct one; and we adhere to it.

In the Screws case we dealt with a statute that imposed criminal penalties for acts "wilfully" done. We construed that word in its setting to mean the doing of an act with "a specific intent to deprive a person of a federal right." We do not think that gloss should be placed on § 1979 which we have here. The word "wilfully" does not appear in § 1979. Moreover, § 1979 provides a civil remedy, while in the Screws case we dealt with a criminal law challenged on the ground of vagueness. Section 1979 should be read against the background of tort liability that makes a man responsible for the natural consequences of his actions.

Make the Connection

This means the federal prosecutor must prove that the defendant actually knew he or she was violating the victim's constitutional rights—that is, the prosecution must prove that the defendant knew constitutional law.

So far, then, the complaint states a cause of action. There remains to consider only a defense peculiar to the City of Chicago.

III

The City of Chicago asserts that it is not liable under § 1979. We do not stop to explore the whole range of questions tendered us on this issue at oral argument and in the briefs. For we are of the opinion that Congress did not undertake to bring municipal corporations within the ambit of § 1979.

When the bill that became the Act of April 20, 1871, was being debated in the Senate, Senator Sherman of Ohio proposed an amendment which would have made "the inhabitants of the county, city, or parish" in which certain acts of violence occurred liable "to pay full compensation" to the person damaged or his widow or legal representative. The amendment was adopted by the Senate. The House, however, rejected it. The Conference Committee reported another version. The House rejected the Conference report. In a second conference the Sherman amendment was dropped and in its place § 6 of the Act of April 20, 1871, was substituted. This new section, which is now 42 U.S.C.A. § 1986, dropped out all provision for municipal liability and extended liability in damages to "any person or persons, having knowledge that any" of the specified wrongs are being committed. Mr. Poland, speaking for the House Conferees about the Sherman proposal to make municipalities liable, said: "We informed the conferees on the part of the Senate that the House had taken a stand on that subject and would not recede from it; that that section imposing liability upon towns and counties must go out or we should fail to agree." The objection to the Sherman amendment stated by Mr. Poland was that "the House had solemnly decided that in their judgment Congress had no constitutional power to impose any obligation upon county and town organizations, the mere instrumentality for the administration of state law." The question of constitutional power of Congress to impose civil liability on municipalities was vigorously debated with powerful arguments advanced in the affirmative.

Much reliance is placed on the Act of February 25, 1871, entitled "An Act prescribing the Form of the enacting and resolving Clauses of Acts and Resolutions of Congress, and Rules for the Construction thereof." Section 2 of this Act provides that "the word 'person' may extend and be applied to bodies politic and corporate." It should be noted, however, that this definition is merely an allowable, not a mandatory, one. It is said that doubts should be resolved in favor of municipal liability because private remedies against officers for illegal searches and seizures are conspicuously ineffective, and because municipal liability will not only afford plaintiffs responsible defendants but cause those defendants to eradicate abuses that exist at the police level. We do not reach those policy considerations. Nor do we reach the constitutional question whether Congress has the power to make municipalities liable for acts of its officers that violate the civil rights of individuals.

The response of the Congress to the proposal to make municipalities liable for certain actions being brought within federal purview by the Act of April 20, 1871, was so antagonistic that we cannot believe that the word "person" was used in this particular Act to include them. Accordingly we hold that the motion to dismiss the complaint against the City of Chicago was properly granted. But since the complaint should not have been dismissed against the officials the judgment must be and is reversed.

Reversed.

> **Make the Connection**
>
> This is the part of Monroe that Department of Social Services v. Monell, the next principal case, overruled.

MR. JUSTICE HARLAN, whom MR. JUSTICE STEWART joins, concurring.

Were this case here as one of first impression, I would find the "under color of any statute" issue very close indeed. However, in Classic and Screws this Court considered a substantially identical statutory phrase to have a meaning which, unless we now retreat from it, requires that issue to go for the petitioners here.

From my point of view, the policy of *stare decisis*, as it should be applied in matters of statutory construction, and, to a lesser extent, the indications of congressional acceptance of this Court's earlier interpretation, require that it appear beyond doubt from the legislative history of the 1871 statute that Classic and Screws misapprehended the meaning of the controlling provision, before a departure from what was decided in those cases would be justified. Since I can find no such justifying indication in that legislative history, I join the opinion of the Court. However, what has been written on both sides of the matter makes some additional observations appropriate.

Those aspects of Congress' purpose which are quite clear in the earlier congressional debates, as quoted by my Brothers Douglas and Frankfurter in turn, seem to me to be inherently ambiguous when applied to the case of an isolated abuse of state authority by an official. One can agree with the Court's opinion that:

> It is abundantly clear that one reason the legislation was passed was to afford a federal right in federal courts because, by reason of prejudice, passion, neglect, intolerance or otherwise, state laws might not be enforced and the claims of citizens to the enjoyment of rights, privileges, and immunities guaranteed by the Fourteenth Amendment might be denied by the state agencies
> * * *

without being certain that Congress meant to deal with anything other than abuses so recurrent as to amount to "custom, or usage." One can agree with my Brother Frankfurter, in dissent, that Congress had no intention of taking over the whole field of ordinary state torts and crimes, without being certain that the enacting Congress would not have regarded actions by an official, made possible by his position, as far more serious than an ordinary state tort, and therefore as a matter of federal concern. If attention is directed at the rare specific references to isolated abuses of state authority, one finds them neither so clear nor so disproportionately divided between favoring the positions of the majority or the dissent as to make either position seem plainly correct.

* * *

The dissent considers that the "under color of" provision of § 1983 distinguishes between unconstitutional actions taken without state authority, which only the State should remedy, and unconstitutional actions authorized by the State, which the Federal Act was to reach. If so, then the controlling difference for the enacting legislature must have been either that the state remedy was more adequate for unauthorized actions than for authorized ones or that there was, in some sense, greater harm from unconstitutional actions authorized by the full panoply of state power and approval than from unconstitutional actions not so authorized or acquiesced in by the State. I find less than compelling the evidence that either distinction was important to that Congress.

I

If the state remedy was considered adequate when the official's unconstitutional act was unauthorized, why should it not be thought equally adequate when the unconstitutional act was authorized? For if one thing is very clear in the legislative history, it is that the Congress of 1871 was well aware that no action requiring state judicial enforcement could be taken in violation of the Fourteenth Amendment without that enforcement being declared void by this Court on direct review from the state courts. And presumably it must also have been understood that there would be Supreme Court review of the denial of a state damage remedy against an official on grounds of state authorization of the unconstitutional action. It therefore seems to me that the same state remedies would, with ultimate aid of Supreme Court review, furnish identical relief in the two situations * * * .

* * *

Since the suggested narrow construction of § 1983 presupposes that state measures were adequate to remedy unauthorized deprivations of constitutional rights and since the identical state relief could be obtained for state-authorized acts with the aid of Supreme Court review, this narrow construction would reduce the statute to having merely a jurisdictional function, shifting the load of federal supervision from the Supreme Court to the lower courts and providing a federal tribunal for fact findings in cases involving authorized action. Such a function could be justified on various grounds. It could, for example, be argued that the state courts would be less willing to find a constitutional violation in cases involving "authorized action" and that therefore the victim of such action would bear a greater burden in that he would more likely have to carry his case to this Court, and once here, might be bound by unfavorable state court findings. But the legislative debates do not disclose congressional concern about the burdens of litigation placed upon the victims of "authorized" constitutional violations contrasted to the victims of unauthorized violations. Neither did Congress indicate an interest in relieving the burden placed on this Court in reviewing such cases.

The statute becomes more than a jurisdictional provision only if one attributes to the enacting legislature the view that a deprivation of a constitutional right is significantly different from and more serious than a violation of a state right and therefore deserves a different remedy even though the same act may constitute both a state tort and the deprivation of a constitutional right. This view, by no means unrealistic as a common-sense matter, is, I believe, more consistent with the flavor of the legislative history than is a view that the primary purpose of the statute was to grant a lower court forum for fact findings.

* * *

In my view, these considerations put in serious doubt the conclusion that § 1983 was limited to state-authorized unconstitutional acts, on the premise that state remedies respecting them were considered less adequate than those available for unauthorized acts.

II

I think this limited interpretation of § 1983 fares no better when viewed from the other possible premise for it, namely that state-approved constitutional deprivations were considered more offensive than those not so approved. For one thing, the enacting Congress was not unaware of the fact that there was a substantial overlap between the protections granted by state constitutional provisions and those granted by the Fourteenth Amendment. Indeed one opponent of the bill, Senator Trumbull, went so far as to state in a debate with Senators Carpenter and Edmunds that his research indicated a complete overlap in every State, at least as to the protections of the Due Process Clause. Thus, in one very significant sense, there was no ultimate state approval of a large portion of otherwise authorized actions depriving a person of due-process rights. I hesitate to assume that the proponents of the present statute, who regarded it as necessary even though they knew that the provisions of the Fourteenth Amendment were self-executing, would have thought the remedies unnecessary whenever there were self-executing provisions of state constitutions also forbidding what the Fourteenth Amendment forbids. The only alternative is to disregard the possibility that a state court would find the action unauthorized on grounds of the state constitution. But if the defendant official is denied the right to defend in the federal court upon the ground that a state court would find his action unauthorized in the light of the state constitution, it is difficult to contend that it is the added harmfulness of state approval that justifies a different remedy for authorized than for unauthorized actions of state officers. Moreover, if indeed the legislature meant to distinguish between authorized and unauthorized acts and yet did not mean the statute to be inapplicable whenever there was a state constitutional provision which, reasonably interpreted, gave protection similar to that of a provision of the Fourteenth Amendment, would there not have been some explanation of this exception to the general rule? The fact that there is none in the legislative history at least makes more difficult a contention that these legislators were in fact making a distinction between use and misuse of state power.

* * *

These difficulties in explaining the basis of a distinction between authorized and unauthorized deprivations of constitutional rights fortify my view that the legislative history does not bear the burden which *stare decisis* casts upon it. For this reason and for those stated in the opinion of the Court, I agree that we should not now depart from the holdings of the *Classic* and *Screws* cases.

MR. JUSTICE FRANKFURTER, dissenting except insofar as the Court holds that this action cannot be maintained against the City of Chicago.

Abstractly stated, this case concerns a matter of statutory construction. So stated, the problem before the Court is denuded of illuminating concreteness and thereby of its far-reaching significance for our federal system. Again abstractly stated, this matter of statutory construction is one upon which the Court has already passed. But it has done so under circumstances and in settings that negative those considerations of social policy upon which the doctrine of *stare decisis*, calling for the controlling application of prior statutory construction, rests.

* * *

II

[Here Justice Frankfurter discusses the historical importance of protections against governmental overreaching by search and seizure.]

* * *

If the question whether due process forbids this kind of police invasion were before us in isolation, the answer would be quick. If, for example, petitioners had sought damages in the state courts of Illinois and if those courts had refused redress on the ground that the official character of the respondents clothed them with civil immunity, we would be faced with the sort of situation to which the language in the *Wolf* opinion was addressed: "we have no hesitation in saying that were a State affirmatively to sanction such police incursion into privacy it would run counter to the guaranty of the Fourteenth Amendment." If that issue is not reached in this case it is not because the conduct which the record here presents can be condoned. But by bringing their action in a Federal District Court petitioners cannot rest on the Fourteenth Amendment *simpliciter*. They invoke the protection of a specific statute by which Congress restricted federal judicial enforcement of its guarantees to particular enumerated circumstances. They must show not only that their constitutional rights have been infringed, but that they have been infringed "under color of [state] statute, ordinance, regulation, custom, or usage," as that phrase is used in the relevant congressional enactment.

III

* * *

Thus, although this Court has three times found that conduct of state officials which is forbidden by state law may be "under color" of state law for purposes of the Civil Rights Acts, it is accurate to say that that question has never received here the consideration which its importance merits. * * *

"The rule of *stare decisis,* though one tending to consistency and uniformity of decision, is not inflexible." It is true, of course, that the reason for the rule is more compelling in cases involving inferior law, law capable of change by Congress, than in constitutional cases, where this Court—although even in such cases a wise consciousness of the limitations of individual vision has impelled it always to give great weight to prior decisions—nevertheless bears the ultimate obligation for the development of the law as institutions develop.

* * *

IV

This case squarely presents the question whether the intrusion of a city policeman for which that policeman can show no such authority at state law as could be successfully interposed in defense to a state-law action against him, is nonetheless to be regarded as "under color" of state authority within the meaning of R.S. § 1979. Respondents, in breaking into the Monroe apartment, violated the laws of the State of Illinois. Illinois law appears to offer a civil remedy for unlawful searches; petitioners do not claim that none is available. Rather they assert that they have been deprived of due process of law and of equal protection of the laws under color of state law, although from all that appears the courts of Illinois are available to give them the fullest redress which the common law affords for the violence done them, nor does any "statute, ordinance, regulation, custom, or usage" of the State of Illinois bar that redress. Did the enactment by Congress of § 1 of the Ku Klux Act of 1871 encompass such a situation?

* * *

The general understanding of the legislators unquestionably was that, as amended, the Ku Klux Act did "not undertake to furnish redress for wrongs done by one person upon another in any of the States * * * in violation of their laws, unless he also violated some law of the United States, nor to punish one person for an ordinary assault and battery * * * ." Even those who—opposing the constitutional objectors—found sufficient congressional power in the Enforcement Clause of the Fourteenth Amendment to give this kind of redress, deemed inexpedient the exercise of any such power: "Convenience and courtesy to the States suggest a sparing use, and never so far as to supplant the State authorities except in cases of extreme necessity, and when the State governments criminally refuse or neglect those duties which are imposed upon them." Extreme Radicals, those who believed that the remedy for the oppressed Unionists in the South was a general expansion of federal judicial jurisdiction so that "loyal men could have the privilege of having their causes, civil and criminal, tried in the Federal courts," were disappointed with the Act as passed.

* * *

The Court now says, however, that "It was not the unavailability of state remedies but the failure of certain States to enforce the laws with an equal hand that furnished the powerful momentum behind this 'force bill.' " Of course, if the notion of "unavailability" of remedy is limited to mean an absence of statutory, paper right, this is in large part true. Insofar as the Court undertakes to demonstrate—as the bulk of its opinion seems to do—that § 1979 was meant to reach some instances of action not specifically authorized by the avowed, apparent, written law inscribed in the statute books of the States, the argument knocks at an open door. No one would or could deny this, for by its express terms the statute comprehends deprivations of federal rights under color of any "statute, ordinance, regulation, *custom, or usage*" of a State. (Emphasis added.) The question is, *what* class of cases other than those involving state statute law were meant to be reached. And, with respect to this question, the Court's conclusion is undermined by the very portions of the legislative debates which it cites. For surely the misconduct of individual municipal police officers, subject to the effective oversight of appropriate state administrative and judicial authorities, presents a situation which differs ***toto coelo*** from one in which "Immunity is given to crime, and the records of the public tribunals

> Non constat
> jus civile
> a posteriori
>
> **It's Latin to Me!**
>
> 'Literally "by the whole extent of the heavens'; as far as possible; diametrically

are searched in vain for any evidence of effective redress," or in which murder rages while a State makes "no successful effort to bring the guilty to punishment or afford protection or redress," or in which the "State courts * * * [are] unable to enforce the criminal laws * * * or to suppress the disorders existing," or in which, in a State's "judicial tribunals one class is unable to secure that enforcement of their rights and punishment for their infraction which is accorded to another," or "of * * * hundreds of outrages * * * not one [is] punished," or "the courts of the * * * States fail and refuse to do their duty in the punishment of offenders against the law," or in which a "class of officers charged under the laws with their administration permanently and as a rule refuse to extend [their] protection." These statements indicate that Congress—made keenly aware by the post-bellum conditions in the South that States through their authorities could sanction offenses against the individual by settled practice which established state law as truly as written codes—designed § 1979 to reach, as well, official conduct which, because engaged in "permanently and as a rule," or "systematically," came through acceptance by law-administering officers to constitute "custom, or usage" having the cast of law. They do not indicate an attempt to reach, nor does the statute by its terms include, instances of acts in defiance of state law and which no settled state practice, no systematic pattern of official action or inaction, no "custom, or usage, of any State," insulates from effective and adequate reparation by the State's authorities.

Rather, all the evidence converges to the conclusion that Congress by § 1979 created a civil liability enforceable in the federal courts only in instances of injury for which redress was barred in the state courts because some "statute, ordinance, regulation, custom, or usage" sanctioned the grievance complained of. This purpose, manifested even by the so-called "Radical" Reconstruction Congress in 1871, accords with the presuppositions of our federal system. The jurisdiction which Article III of the Constitution conferred on the national judiciary reflected the assumption that the state courts, not the federal courts, would remain the primary guardians of that fundamental security of person and property which the long evolution of the common law had secured to one individual as against other individuals. The Fourteenth Amendment did not alter this basic aspect of our federalism.

Its commands were addressed to the States. Only when the States, through their responsible organs for the formulation and administration of local policy, sought to deny or impede access by the individual to the central government in connection with those enumerated functions assigned to it,

Food for Thought

This is at the heart of the problem. The Fourteenth Amendment is indeed aimed at the States, not individuals. But a State is an incorporeal entity, capable of acting only through real people. Hence there will always be a problem of whether to assign responsibility to the individual alone, the State alone, or both.

or to deprive the individual of a certain minimal fairness in the exercise of the coercive forces of the State, or without reasonable justification to treat him differently than other persons subject to their jurisdiction, was an overriding federal sanction imposed. As between individuals, no corpus of substantive rights was guaranteed by the Fourteenth Amendment, but only "due process of law" in the ascertainment and enforcement of rights and equality in the enjoyment of rights and safeguards that the States afford. This was the base of the distinction between federal citizenship and state citizenship drawn by the *Slaughter-House Cases*. This conception begot the "State action" principle on which, from the time of the *Civil Rights Cases* this Court has relied in its application of Fourteenth Amendment guarantees. As between individuals, that body of mutual rights and duties which constitute the civil personality of a man remains essentially the creature of the legal institutions of the States.

But, of course, in the present case petitioners argue that the wrongs done them were committed not by individuals but by the police as state officials. There are two senses in which this might be true. It might be true if petitioners alleged that the redress which state courts offer them against the respondents is different than that which those courts would offer against other individuals, guilty of the same conduct, who were not the police. This is not alleged. It might also be true merely because the respondents are the police—because they are clothed with an appearance of official authority which is in itself a factor of significance in dealings between individuals. Certainly the night-time intrusion of the man with a star and a police revolver is a different phenomenon than the night-time intrusion of a burglar. The aura of power which a show of authority carries with it has been created by state government. For this reason the national legislature, exercising its power to implement the Fourteenth Amendment, might well attribute responsibility for the intrusion to the State and legislate to protect against such intrusion. The pretense of authority alone might seem to Congress sufficient basis for creating an exception to the ordinary rule that it is to the state tribunals that individuals within a State must look for redress against other individuals within that State. The same pretense of authority might suffice to sustain congressional legislation creating the exception. But until Congress has declared its purpose to shift the ordinary distribution of judicial power for the determination of causes between co-citizens of a State, this Court should not make the shift. Congress has not in § 1979 manifested that intention.

The unwisdom of extending federal criminal jurisdiction into areas of conduct conventionally punished by state penal law is perhaps more obvious than that of extending federal civil jurisdiction into the traditional realm of state tort law. But the latter, too, presents its problems of policy appropriately left to Congress. Suppose that a state legislature or the highest court of a State should determine that within its territorial limits no damages should be recovered in tort for pain and suffering, or for mental anguish, or that no punitive damages should be recoverable. Since the federal courts went out of the business of making "general law," such decisions of local policy have admittedly been the exclusive province of state lawmakers. Should the civil liability for police conduct which can claim no authority under local law, which is actionable as common-law assault or trespass in the local courts, comport different rules? Should an unlawful intrusion by a policeman in Chicago entail different consequences than an unlawful intrusion by a hoodlum? These are matters of policy in its strictly legislative sense, not for determination by this Court. And if it be, as it is, a matter for congressional choice, the legislative evidence is overwhelming that § 1979 is not expressive of that choice. Indeed, its precise limitation to acts "under color" of state statute, ordinance or other authority appears on its face designed to leave all questions of the nature and extent of liability of individuals to the laws of the several States except when a State seeks to shield those individuals under the special barrier of state authority. To extend Civil Rights Act liability beyond that point is to interfere in areas of state policymaking where Congress has not determined to interfere.

* * *

Relevant also are the effects upon the institution of federal constitutional adjudication of sustaining under § 1979 damage actions for relief against conduct allegedly violative of federal constitutional rights, but plainly violative of state law. Permitting such actions necessitates the immediate decision of federal constitutional issues despite the admitted availability of state-law remedies which would avoid those issues. This would make inroads, throughout a large area, upon the principle of federal judicial self-limitation which has become a significant instrument in the efficient functioning of the national judiciary. Self-limitation is not a matter of technical nicety, nor judicial timidity. It reflects the recognition that to no small degree the effectiveness of the legal order depends upon the infrequency with which it solves its problems by resorting to determinations of ultimate power. Especially is this true where the circumstances under which those ultimate determinations must be made are not conducive to the most mature deliberation and decision. If § 1979 is made a vehicle of constitutional litigation in cases where state officers have acted lawlessly at state law, difficult questions of the federal constitutionality of certain official practices—lawful perhaps in some States, unlawful in others—may be litigated between private parties without the participation of responsible state authorities which is obviously desirable to protect legitimate state interests, but also to better guide adjudication by competent record-making and argument.

* * *

Of course, if the States afford less protection against the police, as police, than against the hoodlum—if under authority of state "statute, ordinance, regulation, custom, or usage" the police are specially shielded—§ 1979 provides a remedy which dismissal of petitioners' complaint in the present case does not impair. Otherwise, the protection of the people from local delinquencies and shortcomings depends, as in general it must, upon the active consciences of state executives, legislators and judges. Federal intervention, which must at best be limited to securing those minimal guarantees afforded by the evolving concepts of due process and equal protection, may in the long run do the individual a disservice by deflecting responsibility from the state lawmakers, who hold the power of providing a far more comprehensive scope of protection. Local society, also, may well be the loser, by relaxing its sense of responsibility and, indeed, perhaps resenting what may appear to it to be outside interference where local authority is ample and more appropriate to supply needed remedies.

* * *

This meaning, no doubt, poses difficulties for the case-by-case application of § 1979. Manifestly the applicability of the section in an action for damages cannot be made to turn upon the actual availability or unavailability of a state-law remedy for each individual plaintiff's situation. Prosecution to adverse judgment of a state-court damage claim cannot be made prerequisite to § 1979 relief. In the first place, such a requirement would effectively nullify § 1979 as a vehicle for recovering damages. In the second place, the conclusion that police activity which violates state law is not "under color" of state law does not turn upon the existence of a state tort remedy. Rather, it recognizes the freedom of the States to fashion their own laws of torts in their own way under no threat of federal intervention save where state law makes determinative of a plaintiff's rights the particular circumstance that defendants are acting by state authority. Section 1979 was not designed to cure and level all the possible imperfections of local common-law doctrines, but to provide for the case of the defendant who can claim that some particular dispensation of state authority immunizes him from the ordinary processes of the law.

* * *

V

My Brother Harlan's concurring opinion deserves separate consideration. * * *

To ask why a Congress which legislated to reach a state officer enforcing an unconstitutional law or sanctioned usage did not also legislate to reach the same officer acting unconstitutionally without authority is to abstract this statute from its historical context. The legislative process of the ***post-bellum*** Congresses which enacted the several Civil Rights Acts was one of struggle and compromise in which the power of the National Government was expanded piece by piece against bitter resistance; the Radicals of 1871 had to yield ground and bargain over detail in order to keep the moderate Republicans in line. This was not an endeavor for achieving legislative patterns of analytically satisfying symmetry. It was a contest of large sallies and small retreats in which as much ground was occupied, at any time, as the temporary coalescences of forces strong enough to enroll a prevailing vote could agree upon. To assume that if Congress reached one situation it would also have reached another situation involving not dissimilar problems—assuming, *arguendo*, that the problems, viewed in intellectual abstraction, are not dissimilar—ignores the temper of the times which produced the Ku Klux Act. This approach would be persuasive only if the two situations, that of a state officer acting pursuant to state authority and that of a state officer acting without state authority, were so entirely similar that they would not, in 1871, have been perceived as two different situations at all * * * .

Non constat jus civile a posteriori

It's Latin to Me!

"*Post-bellum*" means after the Civil War. "*Ante-bellum*" means before the Civil War.

* * *

In truth, to deprecate the purposes of this 1871 statute in terms of analysis which refers to "merely * * * jurisdictional" effects, to "shifting the load of federal supervision," and to the "administrative burden on the Supreme Court," is to attribute twentieth century conceptions of the federal judicial system to the Reconstruction Congress. If today Congress were to devise a comprehensive scheme for the most effective protection of federal constitutional rights, it might conceivably think in terms of defining those classes of cases in which Supreme Court review of state-court decision was most appropriate, and those in which original federal jurisdiction was most appropriate, fitting all cases into one or the other category. The Congress of 1871 certainly did not think in such terms. Until 1875 there was no original "federal question" jurisdiction in the federal courts, and the ordinary mode of protection of federal constitutional rights was Supreme Court review. In light of the then prevailing notions of the appropriate relative spheres of jurisdiction of state and federal courts of first impression, any allowance of Federal District and Circuit Court competence to

FYI

Reconstruction lasted at least 12 years, by most accounts; thus, there were multiple Reconstruction Congresses.

adjudicate causes between co-citizens of a State was a very special case, a rarity. To ask why, when such a special case was created to redress deprivations of federal rights under authority of state laws which abridged those rights, a special case was not also created to cover other deprivations of federal rights whose somewhat similar nature might have made the same redress appropriate, disregards the dominant jurisdictional thought of the day and neglects consideration of the fact that redress in a federal trial court was then to be very sparingly afforded. To extend original federal jurisdiction only in the class of cases in which, constitutional violation being sanctioned by state law, state judges would be less likely than federal judges to be sympathetic to a plaintiff's claim, is a purpose quite consistent with the "overflowing protection of constitutional rights" which, assuredly, § 1979 manifests.

Finally, it seems not unreasonable to reject the suggestion that state-sanctioned constitutional violations are no more offensive than violations not sanctioned by the majesty of state authority. Degrees of offensiveness, perhaps, lie largely in the eye of the person offended, but is it implausible to conclude that there is something more reprehensible, something more dangerous, in the action of the custodian of a public building who turns out a Negro pursuant to a local ordinance than in the action of the same custodian who turns out the same Negro, in violation of state law, to vent a personal bias? Or something more reprehensible about the public officer who beats a criminal suspect under orders from the Captain of Detectives, pursuant to a systematic and accepted custom of third-degree practice, than about the same officer who, losing his temper, breaks all local regulations and beats the same suspect? If it be admitted that there is a significant difference between the situation of the individual injured by another individual and who, although the latter is an agent of the State, can claim from the State's judicial or administrative processes the same protection and redress against him as would be available against any other individual, and the situation of one who, injured under the sanction of a state law which shields the offender, is left alone and helpless in the face of the asserted dignity of the State, then, certainly, it was the latter of these two situations—that of the unprotected Southern Negroes and Unionists—about which Congress was concerned in 1871.

* * *

Notes and Questions

1. The *Monroe* Court's expansive interpretation of § 1983 sparked a debate that continues and touches upon federalism, separation of powers, and the content of various constitutional provisions, especially the Due Process Clause of Fourteenth

Amendment. Echoes of the debate between Justices Douglas and Harlan on one side and Justice Frankfurter on the other continue to reverberate in contemporary Supreme Court opinions, though not always with attribution.

2. The portion of *Monroe* that concerns the actions against the individual officers turns on the interpretation of the statutory language "under color of law." The events underlying § 1983 actions fall into three groups: actions authorized by the state, actions not authorized by the state but that do not violate state law, and actions in violation of state law. Even Justice Frankfurter seemed to agree that "under color of state law" includes actions authorized by state law. Should he have conceded that, or could he have taken the position that state judiciaries, bound by the Supremacy Clause, will give full scope to federal civil liberties provisions and are therefore competent to deal with state-authorized behaviors?

3. Another issue *Monroe* raised whether a prospective federal plaintiff must first exhaust any remedies available under state law. The Court noted that Congress meant to provide a federal remedy where state remedies, although adequate in theory, were not available in practice. From this premise the Court concluded that "[t]he federal remedy is supplementary to the state remedy," and no exhaustion of state remedies was required. The Court did not, however, address the question of whether a plaintiff who goes directly to federal court should have to make any showing of the *de jure or de facto* unavailability of an adequate state remedy. Would such a requirement have been practical?

5. When Congress passed the Civil Rights Act, there was no general federal question jurisdiction, although it was common for Congress to provide federal jurisdiction in individual statutes. Until 1875, only the predecessor of 28 U.S.C.A. § 1343, which was part of the 1871 statute, authorized federal jurisdiction for actions under the Civil Rights Act. Yet that statute did not make civil rights actions exclusively federal. Is that relevant in analyzing Congress's views on § 1983's place in the remedial scheme? Does it suggest that Justice Harlan is correct that the statute was not intended to have merely a jurisdiction-shifting effect? If so, does the possibility of a § 1983 action in the state courts suggest the irrelevance of the existence of state remedies?

6. a) Does a state official act "under color of" state law when he acts either *ultra vires* or in violation of state law? That question arose long before *Monroe* in *Home Telephone and Telegraph Co. v. City of Los Angeles*, 227 U.S. 278 (1913), in which the defendant city argued that until the challenged action received the state's imprimatur, it was not state action for Fourteenth Amendment purposes and hence could not support a federal claim. The Court strongly disapproved the argument, noting "its inherent unsoundness," "its destructive character," and "its departure from the substantially unanimous view which has prevailed from the beginning."

> [T]he proposition relied upon presupposes that the terms of the Fourteenth Amendment reach only acts done by State officers which are within the scope of the power conferred by the State. * * * In other words, the proposition is that the Amendment deals only with the acts of state officers within the strict scope of the public powers possessed by them and does not include an abuse of power by an officer as the result of a wrong done in excess of the power delegated. Here again the settled construction of the Amendment is that it presupposes the possibility of an abuse by a state officer or representative of the powers possessed and deals with such a contingency. * * * That is to say, the theory of the Amendment is that where an officer or other representative of a State in the exercise of the authority with which he is clothed misuses the power possessed to do a wrong forbidden by the Amendment, inquiry concerning whether the State has authorized the wrong is irrelevant and the Federal judicial power is competent to afford redress for the wrong by dealing with the officer and the result of his exertion of power.

How is the "under color of state law" issue in *Home Telegraph* different from the issue in *Monroe*? Do the defendants in *Monroe* challenge the holding of *Home Telegraph* or is their argument narrower? What is the relationship between the "under color of" state law requirement of § 1983 and the state action requirement of the Fourteenth Amendment? Should they be identical?

b) Do professionals employed by the state who owe independent duties to individuals act under color of state law when they breach those duties? In a series of cases involving physicians, the Supreme Court ruled that they do. *See O'Connor v. Donaldson*, 422 U.S. 563 (1975) (prison psychiatrist who also administered a state mental health institution was a state actor); *Estelle v. Gamble*, 429 U.S. 97 (1976) (prison doctor who ran the prison hospital was a state actor); *West v. Atkins*, 487 U.S. 42 (1988) (private physician under contract to care for prisoners was a state actor). However, in *Polk County v. Dodson*, 454 U.S. 312 (1981), the Court declined to extend that principle to public defenders. Is it tenable to treat government-employed physicians and lawyers differently in this context?

c) Are private individuals ever state actors? Yes, if they conspire with state officials. *See, e.g., Adickes v. S.H. Kress & Co.*, 398 U.S. 144 (1970); *Dennis v. Sparks*, 449 U.S. 24 (1980). This rule extends even to federal officials acting in concert with state officials, despite the fact that § 1983 does not reach federal conduct *simpliciter. See, e.g., Cabrera v. Martin*, 973 F.2d 735 (9th Cir. 1992).

7. Although one tends to think of § 1983 as being concerning only with violations of constitutional rights, the statute contains the words "and laws." In *Maine v. Thiboutot*, 448 U.S. 1 (1980), the Court gave that phrase an expansive reading, holding that it is available whenever the plaintiff alleges violation of any federal right. Subsequent cases, however, have greatly narrowed the effective scope of *Thiboutot*. For more recent restrictive cases, *see, e.g., Blessing v. Freestone*, 520 U.S. 329, 340 (1997) (plaintiff must allege violation of federal right, not merely a federal "law");. *Wilder*

v. Virginia Hospital Association, 496 U.S. 498 (1990) (§ 1983 available only when the statute relied upon creates a binding duty). *Middlesex County Sewerage Authority v. National Sea Clammers Association,* 453 U.S. 1 (1981) (holding that citizen suit provisions requiring 60 days notice to state and federal officials and to alleged violators, and authorizing only injunctive relief, precluded § 1983 actions for damages and injunctive relief without notice); *City of Rancho Palos Verdes v. Abrams,* 544 U.S. 113 (2005) ("[T]he provision of an express, private means of redress in the statute itself is ordinarily an indication that Congress did not intend to leave open a more expansive remedy under § 1983) * * * *But cf. Fitzgerald v. Barnstable School Committee,* 555 U.S. 246 (2009) (unanimously ruling that the Title IX implied right of action stemming from *Cannon* does not preclude an action under § 1983 relying on the Equal Protection Clause).

---

2. Municipalities as Defendants

Monell v. Department Of Social Services

Supreme Court of the United States, 1978.
436 U.S. 658.

MR. JUSTICE BRENNAN delivered the opinion of the Court.

Petitioners, a class of female employees of the Department of Social Services and of the Board of Education of the city of New York, commenced this action under 42 U.S.C. § 1983 in July 1971. The **gravamen** of the complaint was that the Board and the Department had as a matter of official policy compelled pregnant employees to take unpaid leaves of absence before such leaves were required for medical reasons. The suit sought injunctive relief and backpay for periods of unlawful forced leave. Named as defendants in the action were the Department and its Commissioner, the Board and its Chancellor, and the city of New York and its Mayor. In each case, the individual defendants were sued solely in their official capacities.

> **What's That?**
>
> "The substantial point or essence of a claim, grievance or complaint."

On cross-motions for summary judgment, the District Court for the Southern District of New York held moot petitioners' claims for injunctive and declaratory relief since the City of New York and the Board, after the filing of the complaint, had changed their policies relating to maternity leaves so that no pregnant employee would have to take leave unless she was medically unable to continue to perform her job. No one now challenges this conclusion. The court did conclude, however, that the acts complained of were unconstitutional. Nonetheless plaintiffs' prayers for backpay were denied because any such damages would come ultimately from the City of New York and, therefore, to hold otherwise would be to "circumven[t]" the immunity conferred on municipalities by *Monroe v. Pape* (1961).

On appeal, petitioners renewed their arguments that the Board of Education was not a "municipality" within the meaning of *Monroe v. Pape*, and that, in any event, the District Court had erred in barring a damages award against the individual defendants. The Court of Appeals for the Second Circuit rejected both contentions. The court first held that the Board of Education was not a "person" under § 1983 because "it performs a vital governmental function * * * , and, significantly, while it has the right to determine how the funds appropriated to it shall be spent * * * , it has no final say in deciding what its appropriations shall be." The individual defendants, however, were "persons" under § 1983, even when sued solely in their official capacities. Yet, because a damages award would "have to be paid by a city that was held not to be amenable to such an action in *Monroe v. Pape*," a damages action against officials sued in their official capacities could not proceed.

We granted certiorari in this case to consider "[w]hether local governmental officials and/or local independent school boards are "persons" within the meaning of 42 U.S.C. § 1983 when equitable relief in the nature of back pay is sought against them in their official capacities?"

Although, after plenary consideration, we have decided the merits of over a score of cases brought under § 1983 in which the principal defendant was a school board—and, indeed, in some of which § 1983 and its jurisdictional counterpart, 28 U.S.C. § 1343, provided the only basis for jurisdiction—we indicated last Term that the question presented here was open and would be decided "another day." That other day has come and we now overrule *Monroe v. Pape* insofar as it holds that local governments are wholly immune from suit under § 1983.

I

In *Monroe v. Pape*, we held that "Congress did not undertake to bring municipal corporations within the ambit of [§ 1983]." The sole basis for this conclusion was an inference drawn from Congress' rejection of the "Sherman amendment" to the bill which became the Civil Rights Act of 1871, the precursor of § 1983. The Amendment would have held a municipal corporation liable for damage done to the person or property of its inhabitants by *private* persons "riotously and tumultuously assembled." Although the Sherman amendment did not seek to amend § 1 of the Act, which is now § 1983, and although the nature of the obligation created by that amendment was vastly different from that created by § 1, the Court nonetheless concluded in *Monroe* that Congress must have meant to exclude municipal corporations from the coverage of § 1 because " 'the House [in voting against the Sherman amendment] had solemnly decided that in their judgment Congress had no constitutional power to impose any *obligation* upon county and town organizations, the mere instrumentality for the administration of state law.' " This statement, we thought, showed that Congress doubted its "constitutional power * * * to impose *civil liability* on municipalities," and that such doubt would have extended to any type of civil liability.

A fresh analysis of the debate on the Civil Rights Act of 1871, and particularly of the case law which each side mustered in its support, shows, however, that *Monroe* incorrectly equated the "obligation" of which Representative Poland spoke with "civil liability."

A. An Overview

There are three distinct stages in the legislative consideration of the bill which became the Civil Rights Act of 1871. On March 28, 1871, Representative Shellabarger, acting for a House select committee, reported H.R. 320, a bill "to enforce the provisions of the fourteenth amendment to the Constitution of the United States, and for other purposes." H.R. 320 contained four sections. Section 1, now codified as 42 U.S.C. § 1983, was the subject of only limited debate and was passed without amendment. Sections 2 through 4 dealt primarily with the "other purpose" of suppressing Ku Klux Klan violence in the Southern States. The wisdom and constitutionality of these sections—not § 1, now § 1983—were the subject of almost all congressional debate and each of these sections was amended. The House finished its initial debates on H.R. 320 on April 7, 1871, and one week later the Senate also voted out a bill. Again, debate on § 1 of the bill was limited and that section was passed as introduced.

Immediately prior to the vote on H.R. 320 in the Senate, Senator Sherman introduced his amendment. This was not an amendment to § 1 of the bill, but was to be added as § 7 at the end of the bill. Under the Senate rules, no discussion of the amendment was allowed and, although attempts were made to amend the amendment, it was passed as introduced. In this form, the amendment did not place liability on municipal corporations, but made any inhabitant of a municipality liable for damage inflicted by persons "riotously and tumultuously assembled."

The House refused to acquiesce in a number of amendments made by the Senate, including the Sherman amendment, and the respective versions of H.R. 320 were therefore sent to a conference committee. Section 1 of the bill, however, was not a subject of this conference since, as noted, it was passed *verbatim* as introduced in both Houses of Congress.

On April 18, 1871, the first conference committee completed its work on H.R. 320. The main features of the conference committee draft of the Sherman amendment were these: First, a cause of action was given to persons injured by

> any persons riotously and tumultuously assembled together * * * with intent to deprive any person of any right conferred upon him by the Constitution and laws of the United States, or to deter him or punish him for exercising such right, or by reason of his race, color, or previous condition of servitude * * * .

Second, the bill provided that the action would be against the county, city, or parish in which the riot had occurred and that it could be maintained by either the person injured or his legal representative. Third, unlike the amendment as proposed, the conference substitute made the government defendant liable on the judgment if it was not satisfied against individual defendants who had committed the violence. If a municipality were liable, the judgment against it could be collected

> by execution, attachment, mandamus, garnishment, or any other proceeding in aid of execution or applicable to the enforcement of judgments against municipal corporations; and such judgment [would become] a lien as well upon all moneys in the treasury of such county, city, or parish, as upon the other property thereof.

In the ensuing debate on the first conference report, which was the first debate of any kind on the Sherman amendment, Senator Sherman explained that the purpose of his amendment was to enlist the aid of persons of property in the enforcement of the civil rights laws by making their property "responsible" for Ku Klux Klan damage. Statutes drafted on a similar theory, he stated, had long been in force in England and were in force in 1871 in a number of States. Nonetheless there were critical differences between the conference substitute and extant state and English statutes: The conference substitute, unlike most state riot statutes, lacked a short statute of limitations and imposed liability on the government defendant whether or not it had notice of the impending riot, whether or not the municipality was authorized to exercise a police power, whether or not it exerted all reasonable efforts to stop the riot, and whether or not the rioters were caught and punished.

The first conference substitute passed the Senate but was rejected by the House. House opponents, within whose ranks were some who had supported § 1, thought the Federal Government could not, consistent with the Constitution, obligate municipal corporations to keep the peace if those corporations were neither so obligated nor so authorized by their state charters. And, because of this constitutional objection, opponents of the Sherman amendment were unwilling to impose damages liability for nonperformance of a duty which Congress could not require municipalities to perform. This position is reflected in Representative Poland's statement that is quoted in *Monroe*.

Because the House rejected the first conference report a second conference was called and it duly issued its report. The second conference substitute for the Sherman amendment abandoned municipal liability and, instead, made "any person or persons having knowledge [that a conspiracy to violate civil rights was afoot], and having power to prevent or aid in preventing the same," who did not attempt to stop the same, liable to any person injured by the conspiracy. The amendment in this form was adopted by both Houses of Congress and is now codified as 42 U.S.C. § 1986.

The meaning of the legislative history sketched above can most readily be developed by first considering the debate on the report of the first conference committee. This debate shows conclusively that the constitutional objections raised against the Sherman amendment—on which our holding in *Monroe* was based—would not have prohibited congressional creation of a civil remedy against state municipal corporations that infringed federal rights. Because § 1 of the Civil Rights Act does not state expressly that municipal corporations come within its ambit, it is finally necessary to interpret § 1 to confirm that such corporations were indeed intended to be included within the "persons" to whom that section applies.

* * *

C. Debate on § 1 of the Civil Rights Bill

From the foregoing discussion, it is readily apparent that nothing said in debate on the Sherman amendment would have prevented holding a municipality liable under § 1 of the Civil Rights Act for its own violations of the Fourteenth Amendment. The question remains, however, whether the general language describing those to be liable under § 1—"any person"—covers more than natural persons. An examination of the debate on § 1 and application of appropriate rules of construction show unequivocally that § 1 was intended to cover legal as well as natural persons.

Representative Shellabarger was the first to explain the function of § 1:

> [Section 1] not only provides a civil remedy for persons whose former condition may have been that of slaves, but also to all people where, under color of State law, they or any of them may be deprived of rights to which they are entitled under the Constitution by reason and virtue of their national citizenship.

By extending a remedy to all people, including whites, § 1 went beyond the mischief to which the remaining sections of the 1871 Act were addressed. Representative Shellabarger also stated without reservation that the constitutionality of § 2 of the Civil Rights Act of 1866 controlled the constitutionality of § 1 of the 1871 Act, and that the former had been approved by "the supreme courts of at least three States of this Union" and by Mr. Justice Swayne, sitting on circuit, who had concluded: " 'We have no doubt of the constitutionality of every provision of this act.' " Representative Shellabarger then went on to describe how the courts would and should interpret § 1:

> This act is remedial, and in aid of the preservation of human liberty and human rights. All statutes and constitutional provisions authorizing such statutes are liberally and beneficently construed. It would be most strange and, in civilized law, monstrous were this not the rule of interpretation. As has been again and again decided by your own Supreme Court of the United States, and everywhere else where there is wise judicial interpretation, the largest latitude consistent with the words employed is uniformly given in construing such statutes and constitutional provisions as are meant to protect and defend and give remedies for their wrongs to all the people * * * . Chief Justice Jay and also Story say: "Where a power is remedial in its nature there is much reason to contend that it ought to be construed liberally, and it is generally adopted in the interpretation of laws."

The sentiments expressed in Representative Shellabarger's opening speech were echoed by Senator Edmunds, the manager of H.R. 320 in the Senate:

> The first section is one that I believe nobody objects to, as defining the rights secured by the Constitution of the United States when they are assailed by any State law or under color of any State law, and it is merely carrying out the principles of the civil rights bill [of 1866], which have since become a part of the Constitution.
>
> [Section 1 is] so very simple and really reenact[s] the Constitution.

And he agreed that the bill "secure[d] the rights of white men as much as of colored men."

In both Houses, statements of the supporters of § 1 corroborated that Congress, in enacting § 1, intended to give a broad remedy for violations of federally protected civil rights. Moreover, since municipalities through their official acts could, equally with natural persons, create the harms intended to be remedied by § 1, and, further, since Congress intended § 1 to be broadly construed, there is no reason to suppose that municipal corporations would have been excluded from the sweep of § 1. One need not rely on this inference alone, however, for the debates show that Members of Congress understood "persons" to include municipal corporations.

II

Our analysis of the legislative history of the Civil Rights Act of 1871 compels the conclusion that Congress *did* intend municipalities and other local government units to be included among those persons to whom § 1983 applies. Local governing bodies, therefore, can be sued directly under § 1983 for monetary, declaratory, or injunctive relief where, as here, the action that is alleged to be unconstitutional implements or executes a policy statement, ordinance, regulation, or decision officially adopted and promulgated by that body's officers. Moreover, although the touchstone of the § 1983 action against a government body is an allegation that official policy is responsible for a deprivation of rights protected by the Constitution, local governments, like every other § 1983 "person," by the very terms of the statute, may be sued for constitutional deprivations visited pursuant to governmental "custom" even though such a custom has not received formal approval through the body's official decisionmaking channels. As Mr. Justice Harlan, writing for the Court, said in *Adickes v. S.H. Kress & Co. (1970)*: "Congress included customs and usages [in § 1983] because of the persistent and widespread discriminatory practices of state officials * * * . Although not authorized by written law, such practices of state officials could well be so permanent and well settled as to constitute a 'custom or usage' with the force of law."

On the other hand, the language of § 1983, read against the background of the same legislative history, compels the conclusion that *Congress* did not intend municipalities to be held liable unless action pursuant to official municipal policy of some nature caused a constitutional tort. In particular, we conclude that a municipality cannot be held liable solely because it employs a tortfeasor—or, in other words, a municipality cannot be held liable under § 1983 on a *respondeat superior* theory.

We begin with the language of § 1983 as originally passed:

> *[A]ny person who*, under color of any law, statute, ordinance, regulation, custom, or usage of any State, *shall subject, or cause to be subjected*, any person * * * to the deprivation of any rights, privileges, or immunities secured by the Constitution of the United States, shall, any such law, statute, ordinance, regulation, custom, or usage of the State to the contrary notwithstanding, be liable to the party injured in any action at law, suit in equity, or other proper proceeding for redress * * * .

The italicized language plainly imposes liability on a government that, under color of some official policy, "causes" an employee to violate another's constitutional rights. At the same time, that language cannot be easily read to impose liability vicariously on governing bodies solely on the basis of the existence of an employer-employee relationship with a tortfeasor. Indeed, the fact that Congress did specifically provide that A's tort became B's liability if B "caused" A to subject another to a tort suggests that Congress did not intend § 1983 liability to attach where such causation was absent.

Equally important, creation of a federal law of *respondeat superior* would have raised all the constitutional problems associated with the obligation to keep the peace, an obligation Congress chose not to impose because it thought imposition of such an obligation unconstitutional. To this day, there is disagreement about the basis for imposing liability on an employer for the torts of an employee when the sole nexus between the employer and the tort is the fact of the employer-employee relationship. Nonetheless, two justifications tend to stand out. First is the common-sense notion that no matter how blameless an employer appears to be in an individual case, accidents might nonetheless be reduced if employers had to bear the cost of accidents. Second is the argument that the cost of accidents should be spread to the community as a whole on an insurance theory.

The first justification is of the same sort that was offered for statutes like the Sherman amendment: "The obligation to make compensation for injury resulting from riot is, by arbitrary enactment of statutes, affirmatory law, and the reason of passing the statute is to secure a more perfect police regulation." This justification was obviously insufficient to sustain the amendment against perceived constitutional difficulties and there is no reason to suppose that a more general liability imposed for a similar reason would have been thought less constitutionally objectionable. The second justification was similarly put forward as a justification for the Sherman amendment: "we do not look upon [the Sherman amendment] as a punishment * * * . It is a mutual insurance." Again, this justification was insufficient to sustain the amendment.

We conclude, therefore, that a local government may not be sued under § 1983 for an injury inflicted solely by its employees or agents. Instead, it is when execution of a government's policy or custom, whether made by its lawmakers or by those whose edicts or acts may fairly be said to represent official policy, inflicts the injury that the government as an entity is responsible under § 1983. Since this case unquestionably involves official policy as the moving force of the constitutional violation found by the District Court, we must reverse the judgment below. In so doing, we have no occasion to address, and do not address, what the full contours of municipal liability under § 1983 may be. We have attempted only to sketch so much of the § 1983 cause of action against a local government as is apparent from the history of the 1871 Act and our prior cases, and we expressly leave further development of this action to another day.

* * *

IV

Since the question whether local government bodies should be afforded some form of official immunity was not presented as a question to be decided on this petition and was not briefed by the parties or addressed by the courts below, we express no views on the scope of any municipal immunity beyond holding that municipal bodies sued under § 1983 cannot be entitled to an absolute immunity, lest our decision that such bodies are subject to suit under § 1983 "be drained of meaning."

V

For the reasons stated above, the judgment of the Court of Appeals is

Reversed.

MR. JUSTICE POWELL, concurring.

I join the opinion of the Court, and express these additional views.

Few cases in the history of the Court have been cited more frequently than *Monroe v. Pape*, decided less than two decades ago. Focusing new light on 42 U.S.C. § 1983, that decision widened access to the federal courts and permitted expansive interpretations of the reach of the 1871 measure. But *Monroe* exempted local governments from liability at the same time it opened wide the courthouse door to suits against officers and employees of those entities—even when they act pursuant to express authorization. The oddness of this result, and the weakness of the historical evidence relied on by the *Monroe* Court in support of it, are well demonstrated by the Court's opinion today. Yet the gravity of overruling a part of so important a decision prompts me to write.

I

In addressing a complaint alleging unconstitutional police conduct that probably was unauthorized and actionable under state law, the *Monroe* Court treated the 42d Congress' rejection of the Sherman amendment as conclusive evidence of an intention to immunize local governments from all liability under the statute for constitutional injury. That reading, in light of today's thorough canvass of the legislative history, clearly "misapprehended the meaning of the controlling provision." In this case, involving formal, written policies of the Department of Social Services and the Board of Education of the city of New York that are alleged to conflict with the command of the Due Process Clause, the Court decides "not to reject [wisdom] merely because it comes late."

As the Court demonstrates, the Sherman amendment presented an extreme example of "riot act" legislation that sought to impose vicarious liability on government subdivisions for the consequences of private lawlessness. As such, it implicated concerns that are of marginal pertinence to the operative principle of § 1 of the 1871 legislation—now § 1983—that "any person" acting "under color of" state law may be held liable for affirmative conduct that "subjects, or causes to be subjected, any person * * * to the deprivation of any" federal constitutional or statutory right. Of the many reasons for the defeat of the Sherman proposal, none supports *Monroe's* observation that the 42d Congress was fundamentally "antagonistic," to the proposition that government entities and natural persons alike should be held accountable for the consequences of conduct directly working a constitutional violation. Opponents in the Senate appear to have been troubled primarily by the proposal's unprecedented lien provision, which would have exposed even property held for public purposes to the demands of § 1983 judgment lienors. The opposition in the House of Representatives focused largely on the Sherman amendment's attempt to impose a peacekeeping obligation on municipalities when the Constitution itself imposed no such affirmative duty and when many municipalities were not even empowered under state law to maintain police forces.

The Court correctly rejects a view of the legislative history that would produce the anomalous result of immunizing local government units from monetary liability for action directly causing a constitutional deprivation, even though such actions may be fully consistent with, and thus not remediable under, state law. No conduct of government comes more clearly within the "under color of" state law language of § 1983. It is most unlikely that Congress intended public officials acting under the command or the specific authorization of the government employer to be *exclusively* liable for resulting constitutional injury.

As elaborated in Part II of today's opinion, the rejection of the Sherman amendment can best be understood not as evidence of Congress' acceptance of a rule of absolute municipal immunity but as a limitation of the statutory ambit to actual wrongdoers, *i.e.*, a rejection of *respondeat superior* or any other principle of vicarious liability. Thus, it has been clear that a public official may be held liable in damages when his actions are found to violate a constitutional right and there is no qualified immunity. Today the Court recognizes that this principle also applies to a local government when implementation of its official policies or established customs inflicts the constitutional injury.

* * *

MR. JUSTICE REHNQUIST, with whom THE CHIEF JUSTICE joins, dissenting.

Seventeen years ago, in Monroe v. Pape, this Court held that the 42d Congress did not intend to subject a municipal corporation to liability as a "person" within the meaning of 42 U.S.C. § 1983. Since then, the Congress has remained silent, but this Court has reaffirmed that holding on at least three separate occasions. Today, the Court abandons this long and consistent line of precedents, offering in justification only an elaborate canvass of the same legislative history which was before the Court in 1961. Because I cannot agree that this Court is "free to disregard these precedents," which have been "considered maturely and recently" by this Court, I am compelled to dissent.

I

As this Court has repeatedly recognized, considerations of *stare decisis* are at their strongest when this Court confronts its previous constructions of legislation. In all cases, private parties shape their conduct according to this Court's settled construction of the law, but the Congress is at liberty to correct our mistakes of statutory construction, unlike our constitutional interpretations, whenever it sees fit. The controlling principles were best stated by Mr. Justice Brandeis:

> *Stare decisis* is usually the wise policy, because in most matters it is more important that the applicable rule of law be settled than that it be settled right. * * * This is commonly true even where the error is a matter of serious concern, provided correction can be had by legislation. But in cases involving the Federal Constitution, where correction through legislative action is practically impossible, this court has often overruled its earlier decisions.

Only the most compelling circumstances can justify this Court's abandonment of such firmly established statutory precedents. The best exposition of the proper burden of persuasion was delivered by Mr. Justice Harlan in Monroe itself:

> From my point of view, the policy of *stare decisis*, as it should be applied in matters of statutory construction, and, to a lesser extent, the indications of congressional acceptance of this Court's earlier interpretation, require that it appear *beyond doubt* from the legislative history of the 1871 statute that [*United States v.*] *Classic* and Screws [v. United States] misapprehended the meaning of the controlling provision, before a departure from what was decided in those cases would be justified." (Emphasis added).

The Court does not demonstrate that any exception to this general rule is properly applicable here. The Court's first assertion, that Monroe "was a departure from prior practice," is patently erroneous. * * *

Nor is there any indication that any later Congress has ever approved suit against any municipal corporation under § 1983. Of all its recent enactments, only the Civil Rights Attorney's Fees Awards Act of 1976 explicitly deals with the Civil Rights Act of 1871. The 1976 Act provides that attorney's fees may be awarded to the prevailing party "[i]n any action or proceeding to enforce a provision of sections 1981, 1982, 1983, 1985, and 1986 of this title." There is plainly no language in the 1976 Act which would enlarge the parties suable under those substantive sections; it simply provides that parties who are already suable may be made liable for attorney's fees. As the Court admits, the language in the Senate Report stating that liability may be imposed "whether or not the agency or government is a named party," suggests that Congress did not view its purpose as being in any way inconsistent with the well-known holding of Monroe.

The Court's assertion that municipalities have no right to act "on an assumption that they can violate constitutional rights indefinitely," is simply beside the point. Since Monroe, municipalities have had the right to expect that they would not be held liable retroactively for their officers' failure to predict this Court's recognition of new constitutional rights. No doubt innumerable municipal insurance policies and indemnity ordinances have been founded on this assumption, which is wholly justifiable under established principles of *stare decisis*. To obliterate those legitimate expectations without more compelling justifications than those advanced by the Court is a significant departure from our prior practice.

I cannot agree with Mr. Justice Powell's view that "[w]e owe somewhat less deference to a decision that was rendered without benefit of a full airing of all the relevant considerations." Private parties must be able to rely upon explicitly stated holdings of this Court without being obliged to peruse the briefs of the litigants to predict the likelihood that this Court might change its mind. To cast such doubt upon each of our cases, from Marbury v. Madison (1803) forward, in which the explicit ground of decision "was never actually briefed or argued," would introduce intolerable uncertainty into the law. Indeed, in Marbury itself, the argument of Charles Lee on behalf of the applicants—which, unlike the arguments in Monroe, is reproduced in the Reports of this Court where anyone can see it—devotes not a word to the question of whether this Court has the power to invalidate a statute duly enacted by the Congress. Neither this ground of decision nor any other was advanced by Secretary of State Madison, who evidently made no appearance. More recent landmark decisions of this Court would appear to be likewise vulnerable under my Brother Powell's analysis. In Mapp v. Ohio (1961), none of the parties requested the Court to overrule Wolf v. Colorado; it did so only at the request of an *amicus curiae*. That Marbury, *Mapp*, and countless other decisions retain their vitality despite their obvious flaws is a necessary by-product of the adversary system, in which both judges and the general public rely upon litigants to present "all the relevant considerations." While it undoubtedly has more latitude in the field of constitutional interpretation, this Court is surely not free to abandon settled statutory interpretation at any time a new thought seems appealing.

Thus, our only task is to discern the intent of the 42d Congress. That intent was first expounded in Monroe, and it has been followed consistently ever since. * * * In these circumstances, it cannot be disputed that established principles of *stare decisis* require this Court to pay the highest degree of deference to its prior holdings. Monroe may not be overruled unless it has been demonstrated "beyond doubt from the legislative history of the 1871 statute that [Monroe] misapprehended the meaning of the controlling provision." The Court must show not only that Congress, in rejecting the Sherman amendment, concluded that municipal liability was not unconstitutional, but also that, in enacting § 1, it intended to impose that liability. I am satisfied that no such showing has been made.

* * *

III

The decision in Monroe v. Pape was the fountainhead of the torrent of civil rights litigation of the last 17 years. Using § 1983 as a vehicle, the courts have articulated new and previously unforeseeable interpretations of the Fourteenth Amendment. At the same time, the doctrine of municipal immunity enunciated in Monroe has protected municipalities and their limited treasuries from the consequences of their officials' failure to predict the course of this Court's constitutional jurisprudence. None of the Members of this Court can foresee the practical consequences of today's removal of that protection. Only the Congress, which has the benefit of the advice of every segment of this diverse Nation, is equipped to consider the results of such a drastic change in the law. It seems all but inevitable that it will find it necessary to do so after today's decision.

I would affirm the judgment of the Court of Appeals.

Notes and Questions

1. a) *Monell* notes that there are at least three possible bases for municipal liability: liability for acts directly authorized by the municipality, liability for acts of municipal agents on a *respondeat superior* theory, and liability for the acts of private parties. The majority infers that because Congress rejected the last when it voted down the Sherman Amendment, it therefore rejected the second also. Does that conclusion follow?

b) With respect to *respondeat superior* liability, Justice Brennan resurrects the distinction between authorized and unauthorized acts that Justice Frankfurter urged in Monroe but that the Monroe majority (including Justice Brennan) rejected. Is the Court inconsistent or can you harmonize the two approaches? If the former, which approach should the Court embrace?

c) Shortly before *Monell*, the question of *respondeat superior* liability under § 1983 arose in a different context. The plaintiff class in *Rizzo v. Goode*, 423 U.S. 362 (1976), alleged widespread excessive use of force by Philadelphia police and challenged the city's lack of effective review procedures for citizen complaints. The primary defendants were the Mayor of Philadelphia, the City Police Commissioner, and the City Managing Director.

> The central thrust of [plaintiffs'] efforts * * * was to lay a foundation for equitable intervention, in one degree or another, because of an assertedly pervasive pattern of illegal and unconstitutional mistreatment by police officers. This mistreatment was said to have been directed at minority citizens in particular and against all Philadelphia residents in general.
>
> Hearing some 250 witnesses during 21 days of hearings, the District Court was faced with a staggering amount of evidence; each of the 40-odd incidents might alone have been the *pièce de résistance* of a short, separate trial.

But the Court denied equitable relief for several reasons. First, and most germane to *Monell*, the Court ruled that § 1983 liability required that the named defendants have played an active part in the constitutional deprivations, either directly or by establishing the policies and practices governing the offending police conduct. "As the facts developed, there was no affirmative link between the occurrence of the various incidents of police misconduct and the adoption of any plan or policy by petitioners—express or otherwise—showing their authorization or approval of such misconduct."

Thus, the majority insisted on a direct, causal connection between each defendant's performance of duty and the deprivation of constitutional rights. The multiple incidents cited by the plaintiffs did not establish the linkage required to cast highly-placed officials in liability. The Court distinguished cases that directly linked high officials to pervasive patterns of deprivation of constitutional rights and declined to read § 1983 to allow liability on the basis merely of failure to control or eliminate random police abuses.

The liability that the Rizzo plaintiffs sought to establish differs little in structure from *respondeat superior* liability. The only apparent difference is that the supervisory officials in Rizzo were not either the employers or the principals of the individual police officers; the city was. The Court's insistence on a direct, causal connection to establish individual liability compares closely with its insistence in *Monell* on finding a municipal statute, ordinance, custom, usage or policy in order to establish municipal liability.[2]

---

2 *Rizzo* is significant for two other reasons as well. First, the Court found equitable relief inappropriate on standing grounds, for reasons discussed in Chapter 1 at page 115. Second, the Court thought abstention under the doctrine of Younger v. Harris, 401 U.S. 37 (1971), was appropriate. Chapter 8 at page 870 discusses this aspect of Rizzo.

2. a) Is it significant that Congress did not repudiate *Monroe's* holding that municipalities were not § 1983 persons? Had Congress at least acquiesced in the conclusion? Justice Rehnquist's dissent seized upon Congress's inaction in the face of *Monroe* to argue that *Monroe* should be overruled only if the *Monroe* Court was wrong beyond doubt. Of course, time has an ironic way of affecting such arguments. The Congresses since *Monell* have not repudiated it, despite Justice Rehnquist's prediction that it was "all but inevitable that [Congress] would find it necessary to" address the problem of municipal liability in *Monell's* wake. *Monell's* life span now exceeds *Monroe's*. If municipal liability under § 1983 had again been an issue before the Court, should Chief Justice Rehnquist have abandoned his position *Monell*?

b) It is possible that Congress disagreed with *Monroe* but also felt it unnecessary to act. Between *Monroe* in 1961 and *Monell* in 1978, lower federal courts routinely implied rights of action against municipalities directly under the Fourteenth Amendment. *See, e.g., Turpin v. Mailet*, 579 F.2d 152, 164 n. 36 (2d Cir.1978) (en banc) ("Indeed, we are not aware of any federal Court of Appeals which has held that a damage action should not be implied from the fourteenth amendment where the municipality itself was responsible for the unconstitutional action.").

c) Assuming the Congresses from 1961 to 1978 either agreed with or acquiesced in *Monroe*, is that fact even relevant to a proper interpretation of § 1983, which the Congress of 1871 enacted? Should the Court as a general rule be concerned with congressional intent as an on-going matter, or only with the intent of the Congress that enacted the statute?

> **Make the Connection**
>
> There is an echo here of one of the questions that *Merrell Dow Pharmaceuticals, Inc. v. Thompson* raised. *See* footnote 8 at page 334.

3. What should be required to attribute an act to a municipality for purposes of establishing § 1983 liability? How much is necessary to establish municipal "custom or usage"? How can one demonstrate the existence of a municipal policy other than one declared in a statute or ordinance? The Court addressed these issues in a series of cases.

a) *Pembaur v. City of Cincinnati*, 475 U.S. 469 (1986), held that individuals with final authority over a particular matter may establish municipal policy for purposes of § 1983. The county prosecutor directed local police to serve a subpoena by breaking down the office door of a physician to serve patients thought to be evading service. Though there was no articulated policy to use forcible entry to serve subpoenas generally, the Court held the prosecutor's action sufficient to establish a policy. Thus, an individual decision can be a "policy" even if it is not of general application, and an isolated act may suffice for municipal liability. *But see Board of the County Commis-*

sioners v. Brown, at page 601. On the other hand, the Court distinguished between a policy-making body giving discretion to an official and the official having policy-making power. If this distinction seems difficult to administer, take comfort in the fact that the lower federal courts have not found it any easier. The circuits have, for example, split as to whether police chiefs and sheriffs, city managers, and judges are policy makers for purposes of § 1983.

In *City of St. Louis v. Praprotnik*, 485 U.S. 112 (1988), a plurality concluded that whether someone is a "policy maker" is a question of state law, not an issue of fact. A majority adopted that holding in *Jett v. Dallas Independent School District*, 491 U.S. 701 (1989). Thus, the issue of whether someone is a policy maker is for the court, not the jury. The broad statements of these decisions, however, do little to help the lower courts determine in particular cases whether an official is a policy maker under state law. What should be the *indicia* of policy making under state law? Does the Court's approach pave the way for officials' unconstitutional acts becoming unreachable?

b) A different question was bound to arise, and did, about when municipal failure to act constituted a policy. In *City of Canton v. Harris*, 489 U.S. 378 (1989), police arrested Geraldine Harris when she became upset after receiving a speeding ticket. When the police van arrived at the police station, she was sitting on the van's floor. Police asked if she needed medical attention, and she responded incoherently. After police took her inside the station, she twice slumped to the floor, and the police finally left her there to prevent her from falling again. They did not summon medical assistance. After an hour, they released her, whose family took her by ambulance to a hospital. Physicians diagnosed her as suffering from severe emotional ailments; she remained at the hospital for a week and thereafter received outpatient treatment for a year.

The plaintiff claimed that the City's policy of vesting complete discretion in police station commanders about when detainees should receive medical aid amounted to an actionable failure properly to train city employees. The City argued that it could be found liable only if the underlying policy itself were unconstitutional. The policy stated that a person needing medical care should be taken to a hospital, with the consent of the shift commander. The majority held that failure to train could support an action under § 1983, but "only where the failure to train amounts to deliberate indifference to the rights of persons with whom the police come into contact." The Court emphasized that random unconstitutional behavior by a single employee is not sufficient to cast the municipality in liability.

> Neither will it suffice to prove that an injury or accident could have been avoided if an officer had had better or more training, sufficient to equip him to avoid the particular injury-causing conduct. Such a claim could be made about almost any encounter resulting in injury, yet not condemn the adequacy of the [training] program * * * .

> Moreover, for liability to attach in this circumstance the identified deficiency in a city's training program must be closely related to the ultimate injury. Thus in the case at hand, respondent must still prove that the deficiency in training actually caused the police officers' indifference to her medical needs.

The Court then remanded the case for further proceedings.

How might a plaintiff be able to satisfy the Court's failure-to-train standard? Has the Court created an illusory possibility of successful suit, establishing a standard that all but the most dense municipal policy makers will be able to meet? If a municipality proceeds in the face of a known risk (a standard analogous to the *mens rea* of recklessness), is that deliberate indifference, or must a plaintiff show something akin to "knowledge"?

All of the cases in this mold are likely to be fact-intensive. As a practical matter, how can a plaintiff go about proving deliberate indifference? Is it the plaintiff's burden to rummage through the records of municipal proceedings to unearth evidence of municipal awareness of the risks of its training policy, or should the burden (at least of production) of showing the reasonableness of the training policy be placed in the first instance on the municipality? In this respect, consider the Court's views on executive immunities, at pages 621-42.

4. *Monell* left many unanswered questions, some of which later chapters discuss at length. First, is a state, rather than a political subdivision of a state, a "person" within the meaning of 42 U.S.C.A. § 1983? Similarly, are state-level officials § 1983 persons? One might have thought, given *Monell's* partial reliance on the Dictionary Act, that the Court had left the way open also for § 1983 suits against states, but the Court made clear in *Will v. Michigan Department of State Police*, 491 U.S. 58 (1989), that states (and state-level officials sued in their official capacities) are not "persons" within the meaning of § 1983, largely because of the Eleventh Amendment implications of the reverse position. "[I]n enacting § 1983, Congress did not intend to override well-established immunities or defenses under the common law * * * ." *See infra* at 698, Note 3 b).

Second, can local governmental units claim a qualified immunity from suit? *Owen v. City of Independence*, 445 U.S. 622 (1980), said no. The Court noted that the language of § 1983 makes no mention of immunities, but rather imposes liability on "every person" who violates an individual's rights under color of state law. The Justices did recognize that certain immunities were so well established at common law that "Congress would have specifically so provided had it wished their abrogation," and so viewed the statute as having incorporated those immunities. However, the Court held that there was no common law tradition of municipal immunity and that neither history nor policy justified creating one. In the process, the Court rejected the idea that municipalities, as arms of the state when acting in governmental capacities, shared the states' sovereign immunity, holding instead that the passage of § 1983 "abolished whatever vestige of the State's sovereign immunity the municipality possessed." Finally, the Justices refused to insulate municipalities even in cases where they exercised discretionary powers,

The third issue is whether a municipality is subject to punitive damages. *City of Newport v. Fact Concerts, Inc.*, 453 U.S. 247 (1981), answered negatively. The Court reasoned that a municipality cannot have malice independent of that of its officials, and that damages awarded for punitive purposes cannot sensibly be assessed against the municipality itself, particularly since the availability of punitive damages against officials *individually* will provide deterrence without subjecting local governments to potentially crippling awards.

Board of the County Commissioners v. Brown

Supreme Court of the United States, 1997.
520 U.S. 397.

JUSTICE O'CONNOR delivered the opinion of the Court.

Respondent Jill Brown brought a claim for damages against petitioner Bryan County under Rev. Stat. § 1979, 42 U.S.C. § 1983. She alleged that a county police officer used excessive force in arresting her, and that the county itself was liable for her injuries based on its sheriff's hiring and training decisions. She prevailed on her claims against the county following a jury trial, and the Court of Appeals for the Fifth Circuit affirmed the judgment against the county on the basis of the hiring claim alone. We granted certiorari. We conclude that the Court of Appeals' decision cannot be squared with our recognition that, in enacting § 1983, Congress did not intend to impose liability on a municipality unless *deliberate* action attributable to the municipality itself is the "moving force" behind the plaintiff's deprivation of federal rights.

holding

I

In the early morning hours of May 12, 1991, respondent Jill Brown and her husband were driving from Grayson County, Texas, to their home in Bryan County, Oklahoma. After crossing into Oklahoma, they approached a police checkpoint. Mr. Brown, who was driving, decided to avoid the checkpoint and return to Texas. After seeing the Browns' truck turn away from the checkpoint, Bryan County Deputy Sheriff Robert Morrison and Reserve Deputy Stacy Burns pursued the vehicle. Although the parties' versions of events differ, at trial both deputies claimed that their patrol car reached speeds in excess of 100 miles per hour. Mr. Brown testified that he was unaware of the deputies' attempts to overtake him. The chase finally ended four miles south of the police checkpoint.

After he got out of the squad car, Deputy Sheriff Morrison pointed his gun toward the Browns' vehicle and ordered the Browns to raise their hands. Reserve Deputy Burns, who was unarmed, rounded the corner of the vehicle on the passenger's side. Burns twice ordered respondent Jill Brown from the vehicle. When she did not exit, he used an "arm bar" technique, grabbing respondent's arm at the wrist and elbow, pulling her from the vehicle, and spinning her to the ground. Respondent's knees were severely injured, and she later underwent corrective surgery. Ultimately, she may need knee replacements.

Respondent sought compensation for her injuries under 42 U.S.C. § 1983 and state law from Burns, Bryan County Sheriff B.J. Moore, and the county itself. Respondent claimed, among other things, that Bryan County was liable for Burns' alleged use of excessive force based on Sheriff Moore's decision to hire Burns, the son of his nephew. Specifically, respondent claimed that Sheriff Moore had failed to adequately review Burns' background. Burns had a record of driving infractions and had pleaded guilty to various driving-related and other misdemeanors, including assault and battery, resisting arrest, and public drunkenness. Oklahoma law does not preclude the hiring of an individual who has committed a misdemeanor to serve as a peace officer. At trial, Sheriff Moore testified that he had obtained Burns' driving record and a report on Burns from the National Crime Information Center, but had not closely reviewed either. Sheriff Moore authorized Burns to make arrests, but not to carry a weapon or to operate a patrol car.

* * * Counsel for Bryan County stipulated that Sheriff Moore "was the policy maker for Bryan County regarding the Sheriff's Department." At the close of respondent's case and again at the close of all of the evidence, Bryan County moved for judgment as a matter of law. As to respondent's claim that Sheriff Moore's decision to hire Burns triggered municipal liability, the county argued that a single hiring decision by a municipal policymaker could not give rise to municipal liability under § 1983. The District Court denied the county's motions. * * *

To resolve respondent's claims, the jury was asked to answer several interrogatories. The jury concluded that Stacy Burns had arrested respondent without probable cause and had used excessive force, and therefore found him liable for respondent's injuries. It also found that the "hiring policy" and the "training policy" of Bryan County "in the case of Stacy Burns as instituted by its policymaker, B.J. Moore," were each "so inadequate as to amount to deliberate indifference to the constitutional needs of the Plaintiff." The District Court entered judgment for respondent on the issue of Bryan County's § 1983 liability. The county appealed on several grounds, and the Court of Appeals for the Fifth Circuit * * * held, among other things, that Bryan County was properly found liable under § 1983 based on Sheriff Moore's decision to hire Burns. The court addressed only those points that it thought merited review; it did not address the jury's determination of county liability based on inadequate training of Burns, nor do we. We granted certiorari to decide whether the county was properly held liable for respondent's injuries based on Sheriff Moore's single decision to hire Burns. We now reverse.

II

* * *

The parties join issue on whether, under *Monell* (1978) and subsequent cases, a single hiring decision by a county sheriff can be a "policy" that triggers municipal liability. Relying on our decision in *Pembaur* (1986), respondent claims that a single act by a decisionmaker with final authority in the relevant area constitutes a "policy" attributable to the municipality itself. So long as a § 1983 plaintiff identifies a decision properly attributable to the municipality, respondent argues, there is no risk of imposing *respondeat superior* liability. Whether that decision was intended to govern only the situation at hand or to serve as a rule to be applied over time is immaterial. Rather, under respondent's theory, identification of an act of a proper municipal decisionmaker is all that is required to ensure that the municipality is held liable only for its own conduct. The Court of Appeals accepted respondent's approach.

P's arg.

As our § 1983 municipal liability jurisprudence illustrates, however, it is not enough for a § 1983 plaintiff merely to identify conduct properly attributable to the municipality. The plaintiff must also demonstrate that, through its *deliberate* conduct, the municipality was the "moving force" behind the injury alleged. That is, a plaintiff must show that the municipal action was taken with the requisite degree of culpability and must demonstrate a direct causal link between the municipal action and the deprivation of federal rights.

Where a plaintiff claims that a particular municipal action *itself* violates federal law, or directs an employee to do so, resolving these issues of fault and causation is straightforward. Section 1983 itself "contains no state-of-mind requirement independent of that necessary to state a violation" of the underlying federal right. In any § 1983 suit, however, the plaintiff must establish the state of mind required to prove the underlying violation. Accordingly, proof that a municipality's legislative body or authorized decisionmaker has intentionally deprived a plaintiff of a federally protected right necessarily establishes that the municipality acted culpably. Similarly, the conclusion that the action taken or directed by the municipality or its authorized decisionmaker itself violates federal law will also determine that the municipal action was the moving force behind the injury of which the plaintiff complains.

Sheriff Moore's hiring decision was itself legal, and Sheriff Moore did not authorize Burns to use excessive force. Respondent's claim, rather, is that a single facially lawful hiring decision can launch a series of events that ultimately cause a violation of federal rights. Where a plaintiff claims that the municipality has not directly inflicted an injury, but nonetheless has caused an employee to do so, rigorous standards of culpability and causation must be applied to ensure that the municipality is not held liable solely for the actions of its employee.

In relying heavily on Pembaur, respondent blurs the distinction between § 1983 cases that present no difficult questions of fault and causation and those that do. To the extent that we have recognized a cause of action under § 1983 based on a single decision attributable to a municipality, we have done so only where the evidence that the municipality had acted and that the plaintiff had suffered a deprivation of federal rights also proved fault and causation. For example, [two cases] involved formal decisions of municipal legislative bodies. In Owen, the city council allegedly censured and discharged an employee without a hearing. In Fact Concerts, the city council canceled a license permitting a concert following a dispute over the performance's content. Neither decision reflected implementation of a generally applicable rule. But we did not question that each decision, duly promulgated by city lawmakers, could trigger municipal liability if the decision itself were found to be unconstitutional. Because fault and causation were obvious in each case, proof that the municipality's decision was unconstitutional would suffice to establish that the municipality itself was liable for the plaintiff's constitutional injury.

Similarly, Pembaur concerned a decision by a county prosecutor, acting as the county's final decisionmaker to direct county deputies to forcibly enter petitioner's place of business to serve *capiases* upon third parties. Relying on Owen (1980) and Newport (1981), we concluded that a final decisionmaker's adoption of a course of action "tailored to a particular situation and not intended to control decisions in later situations" may, in some circumstances, give rise to municipal liability under § 1983. In Pembaur, it was not disputed that the prosecutor had specifically directed the action resulting in the deprivation of petitioner's rights. The conclusion that the decision was that of a final municipal decisionmaker and was therefore properly attributable to the municipality established municipal liability. No questions of fault or causation arose.

Claims not involving an allegation that the municipal action itself violated federal law, or directed or authorized the deprivation of federal rights, present much more difficult problems of proof. That a plaintiff has suffered a deprivation of federal rights at the hands of a municipal employee will not alone permit an inference of municipal culpability and causation; the plaintiff will simply have shown that the *employee* acted culpably. We recognized these difficulties in Canton v. Harris (1989), where we considered a claim that inadequate training of shift supervisors at a city jail led to a deprivation of a detainee's constitutional rights. We held that, quite apart from the state of mind required to establish the underlying constitutional violation—in that case, a violation of due process—a plaintiff seeking to establish municipal liability on the theory that a facially lawful municipal action has led an employee to violate a plaintiff's rights must demonstrate that the municipal action was taken with "deliberate indifference" as to its known or obvious consequences. A showing of simple or even heightened negligence will not suffice.

Make the Connection

There are actually three potential mental culpability requirements to consider here. One is the mental culpability requirement for the underlying constitutional violation—each provision of the Bill of Rights or Fourteenth Amendment has its own. The second is the "delberate indifference" standard that the Court imposed on municipal *failure to act* cases under § 1983. The third is a general mental culpability requirement under § 1983, which the Court has thus far declined to impose, but which it could impose in the future.

We concluded in Canton that an "inadequate training" claim could be the basis for § 1983 liability in "limited circumstances." We spoke, however, of a deficient training "program," necessarily intended to apply over time to multiple employees. Existence of a "program" makes proof of fault and causation at least possible in an inadequate training case. If a program does not prevent constitutional violations, municipal decisionmakers may eventually be put on notice that a new program is called for. Their continued adherence to an approach that they know or should know has failed to prevent tortious conduct by employees may establish the conscious disregard for the consequences of their action—the "deliberate indifference"—necessary to trigger municipal liability. * * * In addition, the existence of a pattern of tortious conduct by inadequately trained employees may tend to show that the lack of proper training, rather than a one-time negligent administration of the program or factors peculiar to the officer involved in a particular incident, is the "moving force" behind the plaintiff's injury.

Before trial, counsel for Bryan County stipulated that Sheriff Moore "was the policy maker for Bryan County regarding the Sheriff's Department." Indeed, the county sought to avoid liability by claiming that its Board of Commissioners participated in no policy decisions regarding the conduct and operation of the office of the Bryan County Sheriff. Accepting the county's representations below, then, this case presents no difficult questions concerning whether Sheriff Moore has final authority to act for the municipality in hiring matters. Respondent does not claim that she can identify any pattern of injuries linked to Sheriff Moore's hiring practices. Indeed, respondent does not contend that Sheriff Moore's hiring practices are generally defective. The only evidence on this point at trial suggested that Sheriff Moore had adequately screened the backgrounds of all prior deputies he hired. Respondent instead seeks to trace liability to what can only be described as a deviation from Sheriff Moore's ordinary hiring practices. Where a claim of municipal liability rests on a single decision, not itself representing a violation of federal law and not directing such a violation, the danger that a municipality will be held liable without fault is high. Because the decision necessarily governs a single case, there can be no notice to the municipal decisionmaker, based on previous violations of federally protected rights, that his approach is inadequate. Nor will it be readily apparent that the municipality's action caused the injury in question, because the plaintiff can point to no other incident tending to make it more likely that the plaintiff's own injury flows from the municipality's action, rather than from some other intervening cause.

In Canton, we did not foreclose the possibility that evidence of a single violation of federal rights, accompanied by a showing that a municipality has failed to train its employees to handle recurring situations presenting an obvious potential for such a violation, could trigger municipal liability. * * * Respondent purports to rely on Canton, arguing that Burns' use of excessive force was the plainly obvious consequence of Sheriff Moore's failure to screen Burns' record. In essence, respondent claims that this showing of "obviousness" would demonstrate both that Sheriff Moore acted with conscious disregard for the consequences of his action and that the Sheriff's action directly caused her injuries, and would thus substitute for the pattern of injuries ordinarily necessary to establish municipal culpability and causation.

The proffered analogy between failure-to-train cases and inadequate screening cases is not persuasive. In leaving open in Canton the possibility that a plaintiff might succeed in carrying a failure-to-train claim without showing a pattern of constitutional violations, we simply hypothesized that, in a narrow range of circumstances, a violation of federal rights may be a highly predictable consequence of a failure to equip law enforcement officers with specific tools to handle recurring situations. The likelihood that the situation will recur and the predictability that an officer lacking specific tools to handle that situation will violate citizens' rights could justify a finding that policymakers' decision not to train the officer reflected "deliberate indifference" to the obvious consequence of the policymakers' choice—namely, a violation of a specific constitutional or statutory right. The high degree of predictability may also support an inference of causation—that the municipality's indifference led directly to the very consequence that was so predictable.

Where a plaintiff presents a § 1983 claim premised upon the inadequacy of an official's review of a prospective applicant's record, however, there is a particular danger that a municipality will be held liable for an injury not directly caused by a deliberate action attributable to the municipality itself. Every injury suffered at the hands of a municipal employee can be traced to a hiring decision in a "but-for" sense: But for the municipality's decision to hire the employee, the plaintiff would not have suffered the injury. To prevent municipal liability for a hiring decision from collapsing into *respondeat superior* liability, a court must carefully test the link between the policymaker's inadequate decision and the particular injury alleged.

In attempting to import the reasoning of Canton into the hiring context, respondent ignores the fact that predicting the consequence of a single hiring decision, even one based on an inadequate assessment of a record, is far more difficult than predicting what might flow from the failure to train a single law enforcement officer as to a specific skill necessary to the discharge of his duties. * * * "[D]eliberate indifference" is a stringent standard of fault, requiring proof that a municipal actor disregarded a known or obvious consequence of his action. Unlike the risk from a particular glaring omission in a training regimen, the risk from a single instance of inadequate screening of an applicant's background is not "obvious" in the abstract; rather, it depends upon the background of the applicant. A lack of scrutiny may increase the likelihood that an unfit officer will be hired, and that the unfit officer will, when placed in a particular position to affect the rights of citizens, act improperly. But that is only a generalized showing of risk. The fact that inadequate scrutiny of an applicant's background would make a violation of rights more *likely* cannot alone give rise to an inference that a policymaker's failure to scrutinize the record of a particular applicant produced a specific constitutional violation. After all, a full screening of an applicant's background might reveal no cause for concern at all; if so, a hiring official who failed to scrutinize the applicant's background cannot be said to have consciously disregarded an obvious risk that the officer would subsequently inflict a particular constitutional injury.

predictability

increasing probability not enough

We assume that a jury could properly find in this case that Sheriff Moore's assessment of Burns' background was inadequate. Sheriff Moore's own testimony indicated that he did not inquire into the underlying conduct or the disposition of any of the misdemeanor charges reflected on Burns' record before hiring him. But this showing of an instance of inadequate screening is not enough to establish "deliberate indifference." In layman's terms, inadequate screening of an applicant's record may reflect "indifference" to the applicant's background. For purposes of a legal inquiry into municipal liability under § 1983, however, that is not the *relevant* "indifference." A plaintiff must demonstrate that a municipal decision reflects deliberate indifference to the risk that a violation of a particular constitutional or statutory right will follow the decision. Only where adequate scrutiny of an applicant's background would lead a reasonable policymaker to conclude that the plainly obvious consequence of the decision to hire the applicant would be the deprivation of a third party's federally protected right can the official's failure to adequately scrutinize the applicant's background constitute "deliberate indifference."

Neither the District Court nor the Court of Appeals directly tested the link between Burns' actual background and the risk that, if hired, he would use excessive force. The District Court instructed the jury on a theory analogous to that reserved in Canton. The court required respondent to prove that Sheriff Moore's inadequate screening of Burns' background was "so likely to result in *violations of constitutional rights*" that the Sheriff could "reasonably [be] said to have been deliberately indifferent to the *constitutional needs* of the Plaintiff." The court also instructed the jury, without elaboration, that respondent was required to prove that the "inadequate hiring * * * policy directly caused the Plaintiff's injury."

As discussed above, a finding of culpability simply cannot depend on the mere probability that any officer inadequately screened will inflict any constitutional injury. Rather, it must depend on a finding that this officer was highly likely to inflict the *particular* injury suffered by the plaintiff. The connection between the background of the particular applicant and the specific constitutional violation alleged must be strong. What the District Court's instructions on culpability, and therefore the jury's finding of municipal liability, failed to capture is whether Burns' background made his use of excessive force in making an arrest a plainly obvious consequence of the hiring decision. The Court of Appeals' affirmance of the jury's finding of municipal liability depended on its view that the jury could have found that "inadequate screening of a *deputy* could likely result in the violation of *citizens' constitutional rights*." Beyond relying on a risk of violations of unspecified constitutional rights, the Court of Appeals also posited that Sheriff Moore's decision reflected indifference to "the public's welfare."

Even assuming without deciding that proof of a single instance of inadequate screening could ever trigger municipal liability, the evidence in this case was insufficient to support a finding that, in hiring Burns, Sheriff Moore disregarded a known or obvious risk of injury. To test the link between Sheriff Moore's hiring decision and respondent's injury, we must ask whether a full review of Burns' record reveals that Sheriff Moore should have concluded that Burns' use of excessive force would be a plainly obvious consequence of the hiring decision.[1] On

---

1 In suggesting that our decision complicates this Court's § 1983 municipal liability jurisprudence by altering the understanding of culpability, Justice Souter and Justice Breyer misunderstand our approach. We do not suggest that a plaintiff in an inadequate screening case must show a higher degree of culpability than the "deliberate indifference" required in Canton; we need not do so, because, as discussed below, respondent has not made a showing of deliberate indifference here. Furthermore, in assessing the risks of a decision to hire a particular individual, we draw no distinction between what is "so obvious" or "so likely to occur" and what is "plainly obvious." The difficulty with the lower courts' approach is that it fails to connect the background of the particular officer hired in this case to the particular constitutional violation the respondent suffered. Ensuring that lower courts

this point, respondent's showing was inadequate. To be sure, Burns' record reflected various misdemeanor infractions. Respondent claims that the record demonstrated such a strong propensity for violence that Burns' application of excessive force was highly likely. The primary charges on which respondent relies, however, are those arising from a fight on a college campus where Burns was a student. In connection with this single incident, Burns was charged with assault and battery, resisting arrest, and public drunkenness.[2] In January 1990, when he pleaded guilty to those charges, Burns also pleaded guilty to various driving-related offenses, including nine moving violations and a charge of driving with a suspended license. In addition, Burns had previously pleaded guilty to being in actual physical control of a vehicle while intoxicated.

[R]espondent's own expert witness testified that Burns' record reflected a single assault conviction. Petitioner has repeatedly so claimed. Respondent has not once contested this characterization. * * * Involvement in a single fraternity fracas does not demonstrate "a proclivity to violence against the person."

The fact that Burns had pleaded guilty to traffic offenses and other misdemeanors may well have made him an extremely poor candidate for reserve deputy. Had Sheriff Moore fully reviewed Burns' record, he might have come to precisely that conclusion. But unless he would necessarily have reached that decision *because* Burns' use of excessive force would have been a plainly obvious consequence of the hiring decision, Sheriff Moore's inadequate scrutiny of Burns' record cannot constitute "deliberate indifference" to respondent's federally protected right to be free from a use of excessive force.

Justice Souter's reading of the case is that the jury believed that Sheriff Moore in fact read Burns' entire record. That is plausible, but it is also irrelevant. It is not sufficient for respondent to show that Sheriff Moore read Burns' record and therefore hired Burns with knowledge of his background. Such a decision may reflect indifference to Burns' *record*, but what is required is deliberate indifference to a plaintiff's constitutional right. That is, whether Sheriff Moore failed to examine Burns' record, partially examined it, or fully examined it, Sheriff Moore's hiring decision could not have been "deliberately indifferent" unless in light of that record Burns' use of excessive force would have been a plainly obvious consequence of the hiring decision. Because there was insufficient evidence on which

---

link the background of the officer to the constitutional violation alleged does not complicate our municipal liability jurisprudence with degrees of "obviousness," but seeks to ensure that a plaintiff in an inadequate screening case establishes a policymaker's deliberate indifference—that is, conscious disregard for the known and obvious consequences of his actions.

2 Justice Souter implies that Burns' record reflected assault and battery charges arising from more than one incident. There has never been a serious dispute that a single misdemeanor assault and battery conviction arose out of a single campus fight. Nor did petitioner's expert testify that the record reflected any assault charge without a disposition, although Justice Souter appears to suggest otherwise.

a jury could base a finding that Sheriff Moore's decision to hire Burns reflected conscious disregard of an obvious risk that a use of excessive force would follow, the District Court erred in submitting respondent's inadequate screening claim to the jury.

III

Cases involving constitutional injuries allegedly traceable to an ill-considered hiring decision pose the greatest risk that a municipality will be held liable for an injury that it did not cause. In the broadest sense, every injury is traceable to a hiring decision. Where a court fails to adhere to rigorous requirements of culpability and causation, municipal liability collapses into *respondeat superior* liability. As we recognized in Monell and have repeatedly reaffirmed, Congress did not intend municipalities to be held liable unless *deliberate* action attributable to the municipality directly caused a deprivation of federal rights. A failure to apply stringent culpability and causation requirements raises serious federalism concerns, in that it risks constitutionalizing particular hiring requirements that States have themselves elected not to impose. Bryan County is not liable for Sheriff Moore's isolated decision to hire Burns without adequate screening, because respondent has not demonstrated that his decision reflected a conscious disregard for a high risk that Burns would use excessive force in violation of respondent's federally protected right. We therefore vacate the judgment of the Court of Appeals and remand this case for further proceedings consistent with this opinion.

It is so ordered.

JUSTICE SOUTER, with whom JUSTICE STEVENS and JUSTICE BREYER join, dissenting.

* * *

[T]here are * * * three alternatives discernible in our prior cases [for satisfying the requirement that municipalities are liable only when the acts complained of are pursuant to some municipal policy]. It is certainly met when the appropriate officer or entity promulgates a generally applicable statement of policy and the subsequent act complained of is simply an implementation of that policy. Monell exemplified these circumstances, where city agencies had issued a rule requiring pregnant employees to take unpaid leaves of absence before any medical need arose.

We have also held the policy requirement satisfied where no rule has been announced as "policy" but federal law has been violated by an act of the policymaker itself. In this situation, the choice of policy and its implementation are one, and the first or only action will suffice to ground municipal liability simply because it is the very policymaker who is acting. * * * It does not matter that the policymaker may have chosen "a course of action tailored [only] to a particular situation and not intended to control decisions in later situations"; if the decision to adopt that particular course of action is intentionally made by the authorized policymaker, "it surely represents an act of official government 'policy'" and "the municipality is equally responsible whether that action is to be taken only once or to be taken repeatedly."

We have, finally, identified a municipal policy in a third situation, even where the policymaker has failed to act affirmatively at all, so long as the need to take some action to control the agents of the Government "is so obvious, and the inadequacy [of existing practice] so likely to result in the violation of constitutional rights, that the policymake[r] * * * can reasonably be said to have been deliberately indifferent to the need." Where, in the most obvious example, the policymaker sits on his hands after repeated, unlawful acts of subordinate officers and that failure "evidences a 'deliberate indifference' to the rights of [the municipality's] inhabitants," the policymaker's toleration of the subordinates' behavior establishes a policy-in-practice just as readily attributable to the municipality as the one-act policy-in-practice described above. Such a policy choice may be inferred even without a pattern of acts by subordinate officers, so long as the need for action by the policymaker is so obvious that the failure to act rises to deliberate indifference.

Deliberate indifference is thus treated, as it is elsewhere in the law, as tantamount to intent, so that inaction by a policymaker deliberately indifferent to a substantial risk of harm is equivalent to the intentional action that setting policy presupposes. * * *

Under this prior law, Sheriff Moore's failure to screen out his 21-year-old great-nephew Burns on the basis of his criminal record, and the decision instead to authorize Burns to act as a deputy sheriff, constitutes a policy choice attributable to Bryan County under § 1983. There is no serious dispute that Sheriff Moore is the designated policymaker for implementing the sheriff's law enforcement powers and recruiting officers to exercise them, or that he "has final authority to act for the municipality in hiring matters." As the authorized policymaker, Sheriff Moore is the county for purposes of § 1983 municipal liability arising from the sheriff's department's exercise of law enforcement authority. * * * It was open to the jury to find that the sheriff knew of the record of his nephew's violent propensity, but hired him in deliberate indifference to the risk that he would use excessive force on the job, as in fact he later did. That the sheriff's act did not itself command or require commission of a constitutional violation (like the order to perform an unlawful entry and search in *Pembaur*) is not dispositive under § 1983, for we have expressly rejected the contention that "only unconstitutional policies are actionable" under § 1983, and have never suggested that liability under the statute is otherwise limited to policies that facially violate other federal law. The sheriff's policy choice creating a substantial risk of a constitutional violation therefore could subject the county to liability under existing precedent.[2]

II

At the level of theory, at least, the Court does not disagree, and it assumes for the sake of deciding the case that a single, facially neutral act of deliberate indifference by a policymaker could be a predicate to municipal liability if it led to an unconstitutional injury inflicted by subordinate officers. At the level of practice, however, the tenor of the Court's opinion is decidedly different: it suggests that the trial court insufficiently appreciated the specificity of the risk to which such indifference must be deliberate in order to be actionable; it expresses deep skepticism that such appreciation of risk could ever reasonably be attributed to the policymaker who has performed only a single unsatisfactory, but not facially unconstitutional, act; and it finds the record insufficient to make any such showing in this case. The Court is serially mistaken. This case presents no occasion to correct or refine the District Court's jury instructions on the degree of risk required for deliberate indifference; the Court's skepticism converts a newly-demanding formulation of the standard of fault into a virtually categorical impossibility of showing it in a case like this; and the record in this case is perfectly sufficient to support the jury's verdict even on the Court's formulation of the high degree of risk that must be shown.

* * *

B

The Court's skepticism that the modified standard of fault can ever be met in a single-act case of inadequate screening without a patently unconstitutional policy, both reveals the true value of the assumption that in theory there might be municipal liability in such a case, and dictates the result of the Court's review of the record in the case before us. It is skepticism gone too far.

It is plain enough that a facially unconstitutional policy is likely to produce unconstitutional injury, and obvious, too, that many facially neutral policy decisions evince no such clear portents. Written standards for hiring law enforcement personnel might be silent on the significance of a prior criminal record without justifying much worry about employing axe-murderers (who are unlikely to apply) or subjecting the public to attacks by someone with a 30-year-old assault conviction (who has probably grown up). But a policymaker need not mandate

2 Given the sheriff's position as law enforcement policymaker, it is simply off the point to suggest, as the Court does, that there is some significance in either the fact that Sheriff Moore's failure to screen may have been a "deviation" from his ordinary hiring practices or that a pattern of injuries resulting from his past practices is absent. Pembaur made clear that a single act by a designated policymaker is sufficient to establish a municipal policy, and *Canton* explained, as the Court recognizes, that evidence of a single violation of federal rights can trigger municipal liability under § 1983.

injury to be indifferent to its risk when obvious, and, because a particular hiring decision may raise a very high probability of harm down the line, it simply ignores the issue before us to lump together in one presumptively benign category every singular administrative act of a policymaker that does not expressly command or constitute unconstitutional behavior. Thus a decision to give law enforcement authority to a scofflaw who had recently engaged in criminal violence presents a very different risk from hiring someone who once drove an overweight truck. While the decision to hire the violent scofflaw may not entail harm to others as unquestionably as an order to "go out and rough-up some suspects," it is a long way from neutral in the risk it creates.

While the Court should rightly be skeptical about predicating municipal or individual liability merely on a failure to adopt a crime-free personnel policy or on a particular decision to hire a guilty trucker, why does it extend that valid skepticism to the quite unsound point of doubting liability for hiring the violent scofflaw? The Court says it fears that the latter sort of case raises a danger of liability without fault. But if the Court means fault generally (as distinct from the blame imputed on classic *respondeat superior* doctrine), it need only recall that whether a particular violent scofflaw is violent enough or scoffing enough to implicate deliberate indifference will depend on applying the highly demanding standard the Court announces: plainly obvious consequence of particular injury. It is the high threshold of deliberate indifference that will ensure that municipalities be held liable only for considered acts with substantial risks. That standard will distinguish single-act cases with only a mild portent of injury from single-act cases with a plainly obvious portent, and from cases in which the harm is only the latest in a series of injuries known to have followed from the policymaker's action. The Court has fenced off the slippery slope.

A second stated reason of the skeptical majority is that, because municipal liability under Monell cannot rest on *respondeat superior*, "a court must carefully test the link between the policymaker's inadequate decision and the particular injury alleged." But that is simply to say that the tortious act must be proximately caused by the policymaker. The policy requirement is the restriction that bars straightforward *respondeat superior* liability, and the need to "test the link" is merely the need to apply the law that defines what a cognizable link is. The restriction on imputed fault that saves municipalities from liability has no need of categorical immunization in single-act cases.

In short, the Court's skepticism is excessive in ignoring the fact that some acts of a policymaker present substantial risks of unconstitutional harm even though the acts are not unconstitutional *per se*. And the Court's purported justifications for its extreme skepticism are washed out by the very standards employed to limit liability.

* * *

III

The county escapes from liability through the Court's untoward application of an enhanced fault standard to a record of inculpatory evidence showing a contempt for constitutional obligations as blatant as the nepotism that apparently occasioned it. The novelty of this escape shows something unsuspected (by me, at least) until today. Despite arguments that Monell's policy requirement was an erroneous reading of § 1983, I had not previously thought that there was sufficient reason to unsettle the precedent of Monell. Now it turns out, however, that Monell is hardly settled. That being so, Justice Breyer's powerful call to reexamine § 1983 municipal liability afresh finds support in the Court's own readiness to rethink the matter.

I respectfully dissent.

JUSTICE BREYER, with whom JUSTICE STEVENS and JUSTICE GINSBURG join, dissenting.

In Monell, this Court said that municipalities cannot be held liable for constitutional torts under 42 U.S.C. § 1983 "on a *respondeat superior* theory," but they can be held liable "when execution of" a municipality's "policy or custom * * * inflicts the injury." That statement has produced a highly complex body of interpretive law. Today's decision exemplifies the law's complexity, for it distinguishes among a municipal action that "itself violates federal law," an action that "intentionally deprive[s] a plaintiff of a federally protected right," and one that "has caused an employee to do so." It then elaborates this Court's requirement that a consequence be "*so likely*" to occur that a policymaker could "*reasonably be said to have been deliberately indifferent*" with respect to it (emphasis added), with an admonition that the unconstitutional consequence must be "plainly obvious." The majority fears that a contrary view of prior precedent would undermine Monell's basic distinction. That concern, however, rather than leading us to spin ever finer distinctions as we try to apply Monell's basic distinction between liability that rests upon policy and liability that is vicarious, suggests that we should reexamine the legal soundness of that basic distinction itself.

I believe that the legal prerequisites for reexamination of an interpretation of an important statute are present here. The soundness of the original principle is doubtful. The original principle has generated a body of interpretive law that is so complex that the law has become difficult to apply. Factual and legal changes have divorced the law from the distinction's apparent original purposes. And there may be only a handful of individuals or groups that have significantly relied upon perpetuation of the original distinction. If all this is so, later law has made the original distinction, not simply wrong, but obsolete and a potential source of confusion.

First, consider Monell's original reasoning. The Monell "no vicarious liability" principle rested upon a historical analysis of § 1983 and upon § 1983's literal language—language that imposes liability upon (but only upon) any "person." * * * Essentially, the history on which Monell relied consists almost exclusively of the fact that the Congress that enacted § 1983 rejected an amendment (called the Sherman amendment) that would have made municipalities vicariously liable for the marauding acts of *private citizens*. That fact, as Justice Stevens and others have pointed out, does not argue against vicarious liability for the act of municipal employees—particularly since municipalities, at the time, were vicariously liable for many of the acts of their employees.

Without supporting history, it is difficult to find § 1983's words "[e]very person" inconsistent with *respondeat superior* liability. In 1871 "bodies politic and corporate," such as municipalities were "person[s]." Section 1983 requires that the "person" either "subjec[t]" or "caus[e]" a different person "to be subjected" to a "deprivation" of a right. As a purely linguistic matter, a municipality, which can act only through its employees, might be said to have "subject[ed]" a person or to have "cause[d]" that person to have been "subjected" to a loss of rights when a municipality's employee acts within the scope of his or her employment. Federal courts on occasion have interpreted the word "person" or the equivalent in other statutes as authorizing forms of vicarious liability.

Second, Monell's basic effort to distinguish between vicarious liability and liability derived from "policy or custom" has produced a body of law that is neither readily understandable nor easy to apply. Today's case provides a good example. The District Court in this case told the jury it must find (1) Sheriff Moore's screening "so *likely* to result in violations of constitutional rights" that he could "*reasonably [be] said to have been deliberately indifferent* to the constitutional needs of the Plaintiff" and (2) that the "inadequate hiring * * * policy directly caused the Plaintiff's injury." ([E]mphasis added). This instruction comes close to repeating this Court's language in Canton * * * .

The majority says that the District Court and the Court of Appeals did not look closely enough at the specific facts of this case. It also adds that the harm must be a "*plainly obvious consequence*" of the "decision to hire" Burns. But why elaborate Canton's instruction in this way? The Court's verbal formulation is slightly different; and that being so, a lawyer or judge will ignore the Court's precise words at his or her peril. Yet those words, while adding complexity, do not seem to reflect a difference that significantly helps one understand the difference between "vicarious" liability and "policy." Even if the Court means only that the record evidence does not meet Canton's standard, it will be difficult for juries, and for judges, to understand just why that is so. It will be difficult for them to apply today's elaboration of Canton—except perhaps in the limited context of police force hiring decisions that are followed by a recruit's unconstitutional conduct.

Consider some of the other distinctions that this Court has had to make as it has sought to distinguish liability based upon policymaking from liability that is "vicarious." It has proved necessary, for example, to distinguish further, between an exercise of *policymaking authority* and an exercise of *delegated discretionary policy-implementing authority*. Without some such distinction, "municipal liability [might] collaps[e] into *respondeat superior*," for the law would treat similarly (and hold municipalities responsible for) both a police officer's decision about how much force to use when making a particular arrest and a police chief's decision about how much force to use when making a particular *kind* of arrest. But the distinction is not a clear one. It requires federal courts to explore state and municipal law that distributes different state powers among different local officials and local entities. That law is highly specialized; it may or may not say just where policymaking authority lies, and it can prove particularly difficult to apply in light of the Court's determination that a decision can be "policymaking" even though it applies only to a single instance.

It is not surprising that results have sometimes proved inconsistent. * * *

Nor does the location of "policymaking" authority pose the only conceptually difficult problem. Lower courts must also ask decide whether a failure to make policy was "deliberately indifferent," rather than "grossly negligent." And they must decide, for example, whether it matters that some such failure occurred in the officer-training, rather than the officer-hiring, process.

Given the basic Monell principle, these distinctions may be necessary, for without them, the Court cannot easily avoid a "municipal liability" that "collaps[es] into *respondeat superior*." But a basic legal principle that requires so many such distinctions to maintain its legal life may not deserve such longevity.

Finally, relevant legal and factual circumstances may have changed in a way that affects likely reliance upon Monell's liability limitation. The legal complexity just described makes it difficult for municipalities to predict just when they will be held liable based upon "policy or custom." Moreover, their potential liability is, in a sense, greater than that of individuals, for they cannot assert the "qualified immunity" defenses that individuals may raise. Further, many States have statutes that appear to, in effect, mimic *respondeat superior* by authorizing indemnification of employees found liable under § 1983 for actions within the scope of their employment. These statutes—valuable to government employees as well as to civil rights victims—can provide for payments from the government that are similar to those that would take place in the absence of Monell's limitations. To the extent that they do so, municipal reliance upon the continuation of Monell's "policy" limitation loses much of its significance.

Any statement about reliance, of course, must be tentative, as we have not heard argument on the matter. We do not know the pattern of indemnification: how often, and to what extent, States now indemnify their employees, and which of their employees they indemnify. I also realize that there may be other reasons, constitutional and otherwise, that I have not discussed that argue strongly for reaffirmation of Monell's holding.

Nonetheless, for the reasons I have set forth, I believe the case for reexamination is a strong one. Today's decision underscores this need. Consequently, I would ask for further argument that would focus upon the continued viability of Monell's distinction between vicarious municipal liability and municipal liability based upon policy and custom.

Notes and Questions

1. The Court tries hard in *Brown* to enforce the mandate of Monell that municipalities are liable only for their own misconduct, not that of employees on a *respondeat superior* basis. To that end, it requires plaintiffs to make a two-part showing: 1) "that the municipal action was taken with the requisite degree of culpability"; that is, the conduct was "deliberate," and 2) the municipality was the "moving force" behind the injury; i.e. that there is "direct causal link between the municipal action and the deprivation of federal rights." Counsel for Bryan County stipulated that Sheriff Moore was the policy-maker for the County regarding the Sheriff's Department. Moore clearly acted intentionally in hiring Deputy Burns, and the plaintiff would not have suffered injury unless Moore had hired Burns. Why, then, does the Court conclude the plaintiff failed to make the required showing? What set of facts do you think would have persuaded the majority that the plaintiff satisfied its two-part test?

Los Angeles County v. Humphries, 131 S.Ct. 447 (2010), raised the question of whether Monell's and Brown's policy-or-custom requirements apply to actions seeking equitable rather than damages relief. A unanimous Court applied them. The plaintiffs had been investigated for child abuse, but they were exonerated. A state Child Abuse Central Index retained their names, however, and may retain them for at least ten years. The statute creating the index had no procedures for individuals to challenge their inclusion in the index, and neither the state nor the county had created any. The plaintiffs sought declaratory and injunctive relief establishing the entitlement of persons on the list to receive notice and a hearing. The Ninth Circuit overturned the district court's grant of summary judgment to defendant, finding that the plaintiffs were entitled to declaratory relief.

Referring to Monell, the Court noted that a municipality is "liable under § 1983 only for its own violations of federal law." Since Monell, and particularly in *Brown*, the Court has always discussed *respondeat superior* liability in terms of causation, and Humphries continued to do so.

> The language of § 1983 read in light of Monell's understanding of the legislative history explains why claims for prospective relief, like claims for money damages, fall within the scope of the "policy or custom" requirement. Nothing in the text of § 1983 suggests that the causation requirement contained in the statute should change with the form of relief sought.

Recall that the risk that concerned Justice O'Connor in *Brown* was "that a municipality will be held liable for an injury that it did not cause * * * . Where a court fails to adhere to rigorous requirements of culpability and causation, municipal liability collapses into *respondeat superior* liability."

Consider the implications of the Court's connecting causation and *respondeat superior* liability. Is the Court suggesting that garden-variety *respondeat superior* liability is liability without causation? Is there any circumstance in the law of torts where there is liability without causation? (There certainly are many instances of liability without fault.) Why are non-driving owners of motor vehicles generally liable in tort for the negligent driving of the persons to whom they have entrusted their vehicles but *not* liable if the driver was operating outside the scope of the owner's permission? Does *respondeat superior* liability rest on an implicit notion of causation by the principal?[3] If so, is there any reason to believe that the 1871 Congress intended to introduce a new, more restrictive theory of causation when it drafted § 1983? Congress's rejection of the Sherman Amendment is precisely congruent with *respondeat superior* theory then and now. It refused to make municipalities vicariously liable for the acts of persons not their agents (notably the Ku Klux Klan). Does the rejection of the Sherman Amendment offer any support for the idea that Congress intended to relieve municipalities of vicarious liability for the acts of their own agents within the scope of their agency?

2. The Court observes that in a single-case situation, there is no notice to the decisionmaker of the inadequacy of his approach. Yet, elsewhere in the opinion, Justice O'Connor notes that "[t]he fact that inadequate scrutiny of an applicant's background would make a violation of rights more likely cannot alone give rise to an inference that a policymaker's failure to scrutinize the record of a particular applicant produced a specific constitutional violation." She thus criticizes the plaintiff's argument as too general. Could not one level the same charge at the majority opinion? To borrow from Justice O'Connor, to say that there may be no predictability of inad-

3 Granted, it may include a more diluted idea of proximate causation than is normal, but recall that the whole idea of proximate causation reflects not the physical world's causes and effects, but rather policy considerations about when it is appropriate (dare one say "fair"?) to cast someone in liability. The law of torts recognizes *respondeat superior* liability precisely because in most circumstances it is fair to place the principal in the agent's shoes.

equacy in the general single-case situation "cannot alone * * * [avoid] to an inference that a policymaker's failure to scrutinize the record of a *particular* applicant produced a specific constitutional violation." (Emphasis added.) Cannot one argue that in this case, Sheriff Moore's possession of Burns's record should have put him on notice of the likelihood of constitutional violations involving improper use of force? Who, if not a sheriff, should be more aware of the importance of checking someone's criminal information history, particularly if it shows at least one crime of violence, before placing him in a position of significant power and trust that may require the use of state-sanctioned force? Does the Court recharacterize the plaintiff's argument fairly when it refers to lack of scrutiny of applicants' records as tending to promote hiring of unfit officers and denominates that as a "generalized showing of risk," or is it the Court that erects the straw man of generality and then strikes it down in the face of plaintiff's more specific argument?

3. Justice O'Connor concludes by declaring that the particular constitutional violation upon which a plaintiff bases a claim for relief must be a "plainly obvious consequence of the hiring decision," and that the evidence here was insufficient to permit a jury to reach that conclusion. How much evidence is enough to constitute a plainly obvious consequence? Did the Court substitute itself for the jury? Justice Souter sees this case in part as a proximate causation issue. Could a jury reasonably find on the facts of this case that Moore's decision not to look further into Burns's rap sheet proximately caused Brown's injury? Sheriff Moore did, after all, refuse to issue a firearm to Burns or to permit him to drive a police vehicle.

4. Does *Brown* announce a new standard for municipal liability? If so, how is it different from the previous one? How specific will a plaintiff have to be in pleading and proving that a municipal decision not itself illegal nonetheless should expose the municipality to liability?

5. Justice O'Connor posits that the consequences of a hiring decision are more difficult to predict than those of a failure-to-train decision with respect to a specific skill. Is the distinction maintainable, or is it just a matter of semantics? Certainly Ms. Brown could argue that one specific skill that a peace officer needs is the ability to restrain himself from using force inappropriately and that Burns's record forecast his inability to do so.

6. *Connick v. Thompson*, 131 S.Ct. 1350 (2011), demonstrates further just how difficult it is to establish a failure-to-train case. The New Orleans District Attorney's office prosecuted Thompson on unrelated charges of murder and attempted armed robbery. Prosecutors tried the robbery case first, although the crime had occurred second. They deliberately did not disclose to the defense the existence of fabric stained with the perpetrator's blood, which they had had tested for blood type, and they did not disclose the results either. This was a clear violation of *Brady v. Maryland* (1963), which District Attorney Connick conceded at the subsequent trial of Thompson's

§ 1983 action. The jury convicted Thompson. When the murder case came to trial, Thompson did not testify because of the attempted robbery conviction. The jury convicted him of murder, and the Court sentenced him to death. He spent the next eighteen years in state prisons, fourteen of them on death row.

When investigators for Thompson discovered the blood evidence shortly before his scheduled execution date, his attorney had Thompson's blood type tested. It differed from the perpetrator's of the attempted robbery. The district attorney's office moved to stay the execution and to vacate the attempt conviction. The Louisiana Court of Appeals reversed the murder conviction and ordered a new trial, on the ground that the attempt conviction had deprived Thompson of the right to testify in his own defense at the murder trial. On the retrial, the jury acquitted in about thirty-five minutes.

But there was more. Nine years after the original murder trial, one of the prosecutors, terminally ill, told a colleague that he had deliberately made the blood evidence unavailable to the defense. The prosecutor who received that information did nothing until after Thompson's investigator discovered the blood evidence five years after that; then he came forward. (The Louisiana Supreme Court later reprimanded him for his tardiness.)

But there was more. Prosecutors in the murder case had not disclosed to the defense police reports with the eyewitness's contemporaneous description of the killer, which differed substantially from Thompson's appearance.

Thompson's § 1983 action rested on Connick's failure to provide sufficient training to his junior prosecutors about the intricacies of the *Brady* requirements. The jury awarded Thompson $14 million dollars in damages. A divided Fifth Circuit affirmed.

The Supreme Court reiterated *Brown's* requirement that there ordinarily be a pattern of "similar constitutional violations." The majority declined to find a pattern in the fact that Louisiana courts had vacated four convictions from Connick's office because of *Brady* violations. "None of those cases involved failure to disclose blood evidence, a crime lab report, or physical or scientific evidence of any kind." Therefore, the Court said, the earlier incidents were not similar. Thompson had not argued the contrary, maintaining instead that the need for *Brady* training in general was so obvious that only deliberate indifference on the part of Connick could explain the lack of *Brady* training. The majority rejected the argument on the ground that attorneys undergo a rigorous process of training in law school and thereafter and so may be presumed to be sensitive to difficult legal questions of the type that *Brady* may present.

The dissent had a different view.

> Abundant evidence supported the jury's finding that additional *Brady* training was obviously necessary to ensure that *Brady* violations would not occur: (1) Con-

nick, the Office's sole policymaker, misunderstood Brady. (2) Other leaders in the Office, who bore direct responsibility for training less experienced prosecutors, were similarly uninformed about Brady. (3) Prosecutors in the Office received no Brady training. (4) The Office shirked its responsibility to keep prosecutors abreast of relevant legal developments concerning Brady requirements. As a result of these multiple shortfalls, it was hardly surprising that Brady violations in fact occurred, severely undermining the integrity of Thompson's trials * * * .

Connick was the Office's sole policymaker, and his testimony exposed a flawed understanding of a prosecutor's Brady obligations. First, Connick admitted to the jury that his earlier understanding of Brady, conveyed in prior sworn testimony, had been too narrow. Second, Connick confessed to having withheld a crime lab report "one time as a prosecutor and I got indicted by the U.S. Attorney over here for doing it." Third, even at trial Connick persisted in misstating Brady's requirements. For example, Connick urged that there could be no Brady violation arising out of "the inadvertent conduct of [an] assistant under pressure with a lot of case load." The court, however, correctly instructed the jury that, in determining whether there has been a *Brady* violation, the "good or bad faith of the prosecution does not matter."

After Thompson, is Connick on notice about the need for Brady training? If not, what would it take to satisfy the Court?

7. Justice Breyer's *Brown* dissent may be the most far-reaching opinion of all, calling for complete reevaluation of Monell's majority conclusion that § 1983 does not support any form of respondeat superior liability. Is he correct that the law that has sprung from this part of Monell is so hopelessly convoluted that reexamination makes sense? Does his opinion suggest that the questions in Notes 1(a, b) on page 596 of the text have taken on new life? How should the pattern of indemnification affect the debate about municipal liability? If indemnification is widespread, does that suggest that there is no need to expand municipal liability because successful plaintiffs already receive compensation from municipalities? Or would widespread indemnification indicate that *de facto* respondeat superior liability exists, and that municipality liability doctrine is therefore unnecessarily complex?

---

3. Officials' Immunities

Cases like Monell and Brown did not concern immunity individual officials might have for unlawful conduct while in office. Some immunities, such as those covering judges and other court officials, are well established. Others, concerning officials in the executive branch, are more problematic.

The Supreme Court discussed judicial immunity three times late in the twentieth century. In *Stump v. Sparkman*, 435 U.S. 349 (1978), the Court reaffirmed the traditional rule that judges enjoy absolute immunity for the performance of judicial acts unless there is a "clear absence of all jurisdiction" to perform the act in question. When Mrs. Sparkman was fifteen years old, her mother brought an *ex parte* proceeding to have her sterilized because she was "somewhat retarded."

> **FYI**
> There was neither complaint nor any other pleading.

The mother told the daughter that the operation was to remove her appendix. Stump, a state judge, approved the petition the same day, without a hearing, notice to the daughter, or appointment of a guardian *ad litem*. The daughter did not discover the truth until years later when she and her husband sought medical assistance for their inability to conceive. The Court ruled that the authority of the state court simply to consider the sterilization petition constituted a complete shield precluding any liability for the judge and denied plaintiffs' claim for damages under 42 U.S.C.A. § 1983. Judicial immunity rests on the notion that the proper administration of justice requires that judges feel free to perform their judicial duties without fear of personal consequences.

Pulliam v. Allen, 466 U.S. 522 (1984), demonstrated that there are some limits to absolute judicial immunity. A five-to-four Court held that absolute judicial immunity does not preclude injunctive relief and that Congress's intent to abrogate traditional immunities by passing 42 U.S.C.A. § 1988 (allowing victorious parties in civil rights actions to collect attorneys' fees) was sufficiently clear to permit awards of such fees against the state judge in Pulliam.

Finally, *Forrester v. White*, 484 U.S. 219 (1988), considered immunity when a judge acts in a non-judicial capacity. Forrester was a probation officer serving in White's court. White fired her because of her sex. The Court ruled that the judge's supervision of the court's probation officers was non-judicial in nature, so that he was entitled only to the qualified immunity applicable to executive officials under *Harlow v. Fitzgerald* (at page 626), not the absolute immunity that attends judicial decisions.

The Court has also been active with respect to prosecutors' immunity. *Imbler v. Pachtman*, 424 U.S. 409 (1976), reaffirmed prosecutors' absolute immunity from civil litigation concerning the initiation of prosecution or the presentation of the state's case because these activities are closely associated with the judicial portion of the criminal process and thus "quasi-judicial." Consequently, the Court has found that the policies supporting absolute immunity for judges also supported absolute immunity for prosecutors carrying out these functions. Note, however, that in *Mitchell v. Forsyth*, 472 U.S. 511 (1985), the Court denied absolute immunity to former Attorney General John Mitchell for ordering warrantless wiretaps. The Court distinguished between prosecutorial and other functions of the Attorney General, permitting absolute immunity only for the former, and denying absolute immunity to Mitchell as a cabinet officer.

Imbler involved a charge that the prosecutor in a prior criminal action had knowingly presented perjured testimony. The Court refused to allow the civil suit to proceed, but in *Burns v. Reed*, 500 U.S. 478 (1991), the Justices distinguished between conduct of litigation, still entitled to absolute immunity, and giving legal advice to the police during the course of their investigation. The latter, said the Court, entitles the prosecutor only to qualified immunity. In *Buckley v. Fitzsimmons*, 509 U.S. 259 (1993) the Court held that the *Imbler-Burns* analysis required only qualified immunity for prosecutors alleged to have manufactured evidence prior to the existence of probable cause and to have held an inflammatory press conference to influence the result of a trial, since neither action is part of a prosecutor's functioning as the state's advocate.

Kalina v. Fletcher, 522 U.S. 118 (1997), continued the *Imbler-Burns-Buckley* distinction between prosecutorial conduct in which the prosecutor acts as an officer of the court, for which there is absolute immunity, and conduct in which the prosecutor functions in some other capacity. The plaintiff alleged that the prosecutor violated his Fourth Amendment rights by personally attesting to false statements recited in a document filed with the court to procure an arrest warrant. The majority reasoned that no part of prosecutorial judgment could affect "the truth or falsity of the factual statements themselves. Testifying about facts is the function of the witness, not of the lawyer." Thus, the defendant was not entitled to absolute immunity. The absolute immunity for witnesses recognized in *Briscoe v. LaHue*, 460 U.S. 325 (1983), (holding trial witnesses absolutely immune from civil suits based on their testimony even if perjured) is limited to trial testimony. A state actor—even a prosecutor—who serves as a "complaining witness" by making statements to obtain an arrest warrant has only qualified immunity from damages liability.

Imbler noted that prosecutors might not be entitled to absolute immunity when acting in an administrative capacity, but left consideration of that issue to another day. That day came in 2009 in *Van de Kamp v. Goldstein*, 555 U.S. 335 (2009). A federal court granted Goldstein habeas corpus relief because his state court conviction rested in part on false testimony by a jailhouse informant. The federal court also found that prosecutors had improperly failed to tell Goldstein's attorney about potential impeachment information: that the informant had received reduced sentences for providing prosecutors with favorable testimony in other cases. Goldstein subsequently filed a § 1983 action against the former Los Angeles district attorney and his deputy, claiming they had failed properly to train and supervise prosecutors and to establish an information system containing impeachment about informants. The Court held the prosecutors absolutely immune because they were acting as attorneys in training and supervising other attorneys and because their actions affected prosecutorial functioning for specific trials.

The Court has long held that state legislators are absolutely immune from damages liability under § 1983 for acts within their legislative capacity. Such immunity is designed to preserve legislative independence and prevent the diversion of the legislators' time and energy from their legislative tasks. *Bogan v. Scott-Harris,* 523 U.S. 44 (1998), held that legislators are also absolutely immune from civil liability for acts performed in a legislative capacity, irrespective of their motive. Plaintiff claimed that the municipality eliminated a department (in which the plaintiff was the sole employee) because of racial animus and in retaliation for plaintiff's exercise of her First Amendment rights. Justice Thomas, writing for a unanimous Court, noted that "[w]hether an act is legislative turns on the nature of the act, rather than on the motive or intent of the official performing it."

The Court recognizes absolute immunity believing that Congress, in enacting § 1983, intended to retain common law immunities rather than eliminate them by implication. The Court often notes the policies that might have motivated Congress, particularly that if legislators, prosecutors, and judges are subject to liability arising out of the performance of their duties, they will be inhibited by fear of civil suits, whether well-founded or groundless. Is the price paid worth it, or, as Justice Harlan observed in Bivens, are there better ways to deal with frivolous lawsuits than by dismissing meritorious ones?

In 1996, Congress amended § 1983, which now reads as follows:

> Every person who, under color of any statute, ordinance, regulation, custom, or usage, of any State or Territory or the District of Columbia, subjects, or causes to be subjected, any citizen of the United States or other person within the jurisdiction thereof to the deprivation of any rights, privileges, or immunities secured by the Constitution and laws, shall be liable to the party injured in an action at law, suit in equity, or other proper proceeding for redress, except that in any action brought against a judicial officer for an act or omission taken in such officer's judicial capacity, injunctive relief shall not be granted unless a declaratory decree was violated or declaratory relief was unavailable. For the purposes of this section, any Act of Congress applicable exclusively to the District of Columbia shall be considered to be a statute of the District of Columbia.

42 U.S.C.A. § 1983 (2002). At the same time, Congress restricted the availability of attorney's fees by amending 42 U.S.C.A. § 1988(b) (Supp. 2002):

> In any action or proceeding to enforce a provision of sections 1981, 1981a, 1982, 1983, 1985, and 1986 of this title, * * * the court, in its discretion, may allow the prevailing party, other than the United States, a reasonable

> attorney's fee as part of the costs, except that in any action brought against a judicial officer for an act or omission taken in such officer's judicial capacity such officer shall not be held liable for any costs, including attorney's fees, unless such action was clearly in excess of such officer's jurisdiction.

These changes significantly alter the rule of Pulliam v. Allen, which permitted injunctive suits against judges notwithstanding their otherwise-existing absolute immunity and also permitted recovery of costs and fees by successful plaintiffs. New § 1983 does not, however, establish absolute judicial immunity against prospective relief suits; it instead requires that they begin as declaratory judgment actions, with the possibility of further relief to follow under the authority of 28 U.S.C. § 2202. It does, however, make the effort considerably more expensive for victorious plaintiffs by limiting the possibility of recovering expenses, and may thus, as a practical matter, have the effect of making Pulliam a dead letter.

Perhaps these changes are desirable because they lend support to judicial independence and, by analogy, to other factors typically discussed in the context of the qualified immunity the Court has recognized under § 1983, but they do not come without attendant social costs. Is it appropriate to spare judicial officers costs and fees in initial rounds of litigation? If so, do the arguments in favor of doing so hold equally well after a plaintiff, having obtained declaratory relief, must seek further, injunctive relief?

With respect to executive branch officials entitled to qualified immunity, the picture is somewhat murkier. The Court considered qualified immunity in the context of § 1983 in *Wood v. Strickland*, 420 U.S. 308 (1975). Students challenged the procedure used to expel them from a public high school for "spiking" the punch served at an extracurricular activity attended by parents and students. (As the Court noted, "[t]he punch was served at the meeting, without apparent effect.") All nine Justices agreed that school officials were entitled to a qualified immunity, but the Court split five to four on the nature of the immunity. The majority articulated a standard with both objective and subjective elements:

> Therefore, in the specific context of school discipline, we hold that a school board member is not immune from liability for damages under § 1983 if he knew or reasonably should have known that the action he took within his sphere of official responsibility would violate the constitutional rights of the student affected, or if he took the action with the malicious intention to cause a deprivation of constitutional rights or other injury to the student. That is not to say that school board members are "charged with predicting the future course of constitutional law." A compensatory award will be appropriate only if the school board member has acted with such an impermissible motivation or with such disregard of the student's clearly established constitutional rights that his action cannot reasonably be characterized as being in good faith.

The remaining four Justices, led by Justice Powell (a former member and chairman of the Richmond, Virginia, and Virginia State Boards of Education), concurred and dissented. Justice Powell lamented "impos[ing] a higher standard of care upon public school officials * * * than that heretofore required of any other official." He argued that the majority's concepts of "settled, indisputable law" and "unquestioned constitutional rights" were devoid of reasonably ascertainable meaning, leaving school officials to guess at the law at their peril and raising the possibility that well qualified individuals would hesitate to undertake public responsibilities as a result. "One need only look to the decisions of this Court—to our reversals, our recognition of evolving concepts, and our five-to-four splits—to recognize the hazard of even informed prophecy as to what are 'unquestioned constitutional rights.' " Instead, Justice Powell and his dissenting colleagues would have imposed a much more subjective standard: "whether in light of the discretion and responsibilities of his office, and under all of the circumstances as they appeared at the time, the officer acted reasonably and in good faith."[4] Nine years later, the Court reconsidered the qualified immunity doctrine *vis-à-vis* executive officials, and Justice Powell wrote the opinion for the Court.

Harlow v. Fitzgerald

Supreme Court of the United States, 1982.
457 U.S. 800.

JUSTICE POWELL delivered the opinion of the Court.

The issue in this case is the scope of the immunity available to the senior aides and advisers of the President of the United States in a suit for damages based upon their official acts.

I

In this suit for civil damages petitioners Bryce Harlow and Alexander Butterfield are alleged to have participated in a conspiracy to violate the constitutional and statutory rights of the respondent A. Ernest Fitzgerald. Respondent avers that petitioners entered the conspiracy in their capacities as senior White House aides to former President Richard M. Nixon.

* * *

4 One might ask, however, whether Justice Powell's concept of reasonableness differed at all from acting in good faith. If not, then he was merely being redundant. If so, however, then one must wonder how Justice Powell would have defined reasonableness and the extent to which it would have been distinct from the majority's "settled, indisputable law."

Petitioner Butterfield also is alleged to have entered the conspiracy not later than May 1969. Employed as Deputy Assistant to the President and Deputy Chief of Staff to H.R. Haldeman, Butterfield circulated a White House memorandum in that month in which he claimed to have learned that Fitzgerald planned to "blow the whistle" on some "shoddy purchasing practices" by exposing these practices to public view. Fitzgerald characterizes this memorandum as evidence that Butterfield had commenced efforts to secure Fitzgerald's retaliatory dismissal. As evidence that Butterfield participated in the conspiracy to conceal his unlawful discharge and prevent his reemployment, Fitzgerald cites communications between Butterfield and Haldeman in December 1969 and January 1970. After the President had promised at a press conference to inquire into Fitzgerald's dismissal, Haldeman solicited Butterfield's recommendations. In a subsequent memorandum emphasizing the importance of "loyalty," Butterfield counseled against offering Fitzgerald another job in the administration at that time.

For his part, Butterfield denies that he was involved in any decision concerning Fitzgerald's employment status until Haldeman sought his advice in December 1969—more than a month after Fitzgerald's termination had been scheduled and announced publicly by the Air Force. Butterfield states that he never communicated his views about Fitzgerald to any official of the Defense Department. He argues generally that nearly eight years of discovery have failed to turn up any evidence that he caused injury to Fitzgerald.

Together with their codefendant Richard Nixon, petitioners Harlow and Butterfield moved for summary judgment * * * . In denying the motion the District Court upheld the legal sufficiency of Fitzgerald's *Bivens* claim under the First Amendment and his "inferred" statutory causes of action under 5 U.S.C. § 7211 and 18 U.S.C. § 1505. The court found that genuine issues of disputed fact remained for resolution at trial. It also ruled that petitioners were not entitled to absolute immunity.

implied

* * *

II

* * *

Our decisions have recognized immunity defenses of two kinds. For officials whose special functions or constitutional status requires complete protection from suit, we have recognized the defense of "absolute immunity." The absolute immunity of legislators, in their legislative functions, and of judges, in their judicial functions now is well settled. Our decisions also have extended absolute immunity to certain officials of the Executive Branch. These include prosecutors and similar officials, executive officers engaged in adjudicative functions, and the President of the United States.

For executive officials in general, however, our cases make plain that qualified immunity represents the norm. In Scheuer v. Rhodes we acknowledged that high officials require greater protection than those with less complex discretionary responsibilities. Nonetheless, we held that a governor and his aides could receive the requisite protection from qualified or good-faith immunity. In Butz v. Economou (1978), we extended the approach of Scheuer to high federal officials of the Executive Branch. * * * [W]e explained that the recognition of a qualified immunity defense for high executives reflected an attempt to balance competing values: not only the importance of a damages remedy to protect the rights of citizens, but also "the need to protect officials who are required to exercise their discretion and the related public interest in encouraging the vigorous exercise of official authority." Without discounting the adverse consequences of denying high officials an absolute immunity from private lawsuits alleging constitutional violations * * * we emphasized our expectation that insubstantial suits need not proceed to trial:

> **FYI**
>
> This litigation grew out of the infamous "Kent State massacre" on May 4, 1970, when Ohio National Guardsmen shot and killed four unarmed students and wounded nine other unarmed people, some of whom were protesting the invasion of Cambodia by American forces and some of whom were merely observing.

> Insubstantial lawsuits can be quickly terminated by federal courts alert to the possibilities of artful pleading. Unless the complaint states a compensable claim for relief * * * , it should not survive a motion to dismiss. Moreover, the Court recognized in *Scheuer* that damages suits concerning constitutional violations need not proceed to trial, but can be terminated on a properly supported motion for summary judgment based on the defense of immunity * * * . In responding to such a motion, plaintiffs may not play dog in the manger; and firm application of the Federal Rules of Civil Procedure will ensure that federal officials are not harassed by frivolous lawsuits.

* * *

IV

Even if they cannot establish that their official functions require absolute immunity, petitioners assert that public policy at least mandates an application of the qualified immunity standard that would permit the defeat of insubstantial claims without resort to trial. We agree.

A

The resolution of immunity questions inherently requires a balance between the evils inevitable in any available alternative. In situations of abuse of office, an action for damages may offer the only realistic avenue for vindication of constitutional guarantees. It is this recognition that has required the denial of absolute immunity to most public officers. At the same time, however, it cannot be disputed seriously that claims frequently run against the innocent as well as the guilty—at a cost not only to the defendant officials, but to society as a whole. These social costs include the expenses of litigation, the diversion of official energy from pressing public issues, and the deterrence of able citizens from acceptance of public office. Finally, there is the danger that fear of being sued will "dampen the ardor of all but the most resolute, or the most irresponsible [public officials], in the unflinching discharge of their duties."

In identifying qualified immunity as the best attainable accommodation of competing values, we relied on the assumption that this standard would permit "[i]nsubstantial lawsuits [to] be quickly terminated." Yet petitioners advance persuasive arguments that the dismissal of insubstantial lawsuits without trial—a factor presupposed in the balance of competing interests struck by our prior cases—requires an adjustment of the "good faith" standard established by our decisions.

B

Qualified or "good faith" immunity is an affirmative defense that must be pleaded by a defendant official. Decisions of this Court have established that the "good faith" defense has both an "objective" and a "subjective" aspect. The objective element involves a presumptive knowledge of and respect for "basic, unquestioned constitutional rights." The subjective component refers to "permissible intentions." Characteristically the Court has defined these elements by identifying the circumstances in which qualified immunity would *not* be available. Referring both to the objective and subjective elements, we have held that qualified immunity would be defeated if an official "*knew or reasonably should have known* that the action he took within his sphere of official responsibility would violate the constitutional rights of the [plaintiff], or if he took the action *with the malicious intention* to cause a deprivation of constitutional rights or other injury * * * ." ([E]mphasis added).

The subjective element of the good-faith defense frequently has proved incompatible with our admonition in *Butz* that insubstantial claims should not proceed to trial. Rule 56 of the Federal Rules of Civil Procedure provides that disputed questions of fact ordinarily may not be decided on motions for summary judgment. And an official's subjective good faith has been considered to be a question of fact that some courts have regarded as inherently requiring resolution by a jury.

In the context of *Butz*' attempted balancing of competing values, it now is clear that substantial costs attend the litigation of the subjective good faith of government officials. Not only are there the general costs of subjecting officials to the risks of trial—distraction of officials from their governmental duties, inhibition of discretionary action, and deterrence of able people from public service. There are special costs to "subjective" inquiries of this kind. Immunity generally is available only to officials performing discretionary functions. In contrast with the thought processes accompanying "ministerial" tasks, the judgments surrounding discretionary action almost inevitably are influenced by the decisionmaker's experiences, values, and emotions. These variables explain in part why questions of subjective intent so rarely can be decided by summary judgment. Yet they also frame a background in which there often is no clear end to the relevant evidence. Judicial inquiry into subjective motivation therefore may entail broad-ranging discovery and the deposing of numerous persons, including an official's professional colleagues. Inquiries of this kind can be peculiarly disruptive of effective government.

Consistently with the balance at which we aimed in *Butz*, we conclude today that bare allegations of malice should not suffice to subject government officials either to the costs of trial or to the burdens of broad-reaching discovery. We therefore hold that government officials performing discretionary functions generally are shielded from liability for civil damages insofar as their conduct does not violate clearly established statutory or constitutional rights of which a reasonable person would have known.[30]

Reliance on the objective reasonableness of an official's conduct, as measured by reference to clearly established law, should avoid excessive disruption of government and permit the resolution of many insubstantial claims on summary judgment. On summary judgment, the judge appropriately may determine, not only the currently applicable law, but whether that law was clearly established at the time an action occurred. If the law at that time was not clearly established, an official could not reasonably be expected to anticipate subsequent legal developments, nor could he fairly be said to "know" that the law forbade conduct not previously identified as unlawful. Until this threshold immunity question is resolved, discovery should not be allowed. If the law was clearly established, the immunity defense ordinarily should fail, since a reasonably competent public

30 This case involves no issue concerning the elements of the immunity available to state officials sued for constitutional violations under 42 U.S.C. § 1983. We have found previously, however, that it would be "untenable to draw a distinction for purposes of immunity law between suits brought against state officials under § 1983 and suits brought directly under the Constitution against federal officials." Our decision in no way diminishes the absolute immunity currently available to officials whose functions have been held to require a protection of this scope.

official should know the law governing his conduct. Nevertheless, if the official pleading the defense claims extraordinary circumstances and can prove that he neither knew nor should have known of the relevant legal standard, the defense should be sustained. But again, the defense would turn primarily on objective factors.

* * *

V

The judgment of the Court of Appeals is vacated, and the case is remanded for further action consistent with this opinion.

So ordered.

JUSTICE BRENNAN, with whom JUSTICE MARSHALL, and JUSTICE BLACKMUN join, concurring.

I agree with the substantive standard announced by the Court today, imposing liability when a public-official defendant "knew or should have known" of the constitutionally violative effect of his actions. This standard would not allow the official who actually knows that he was violating the law to escape liability for his actions, even if he could not "reasonably have been expected" to know what he actually did know. Thus the clever and unusually well-informed violator of constitutional rights will not evade just punishment for his crimes. I also agree that this standard applies "across the board," to all "government officials performing discretionary functions." I write separately only to note that given this standard, it seems inescapable to me that some measure of discovery may sometimes be required to determine exactly what a public-official defendant did "know" at the time of his actions. * * *

Notes and Questions

1. Is *Harlow* inconsistent with *Wood v. Strickland* or do they present fundamentally different questions? How did Fitzgerald get into court? Does his basis for proceeding have any implications for the Court's role in evaluating the defendants' claims of immunity?

2. Justice Powell appears substantially to change his approach from the position he took in *Wood*. There he appeared to rely heavily on the concept of the actor's subjective good faith, whereas in *Harlow* he ostensibly creates an "primarily" objective standard. What explanation does he give for this change? What shortcoming of the subjective standard does he identify?

Ashcroft v. al-Kidd, 131 S.Ct. 2074 (2011), forcefully reiterated that there is no subjective component to the qualified immunity standard. Federal officials obtained a warrant for al-Kidd's arrest, representing to a Magistrate Judge that al-Kidd had information "crucial" to another terrorism case that would be unavailable if he left the country. They detained him as he sought to board an international flight. Attorney General Ashcroft had allegedly established a policy permitting the detention of terrorism suspects under the federal material-witness statute. The plaintiff argued that the prosecutors who secured the arrest warrant neither called him as a witness nor ever had intended to do so—that using the material-witness statute was merely a pretext. This, he claimed, violated his Fourth Amendment rights.

The issue for the Court was "whether a former Attorney General enjoys immunity from suit for allegedly authorizing federal prosecutors to obtain valid material-witness warrants for detention of terrorism suspects whom they would otherwise lack probable cause to arrest."[5] The Court emphasized that the Fourth Amendment reasonableness inquiry is itself objective. It relied upon *Whren v. United States* (1996) for the proposition that the arresting officer's subjective intent was irrelevant as long as there was a lawful basis for the action.[6] In other words, pretext did not matter if there was probable cause to proceed. al-Kidd attempted to distinguish *Whren* because there was no probable cause to arrest in his case, whereas there had been in *Whren*. The Court rejected that argument, asking only whether the issuance of the warrant, based on the information before the Magistrate Judge, was objectively reasonable. It declined to look behind the face of the warrant to inquire about the prosecutors' intentions, and it sharply criticized the Ninth Circuit for accepting al-Kidd's distinction of *Whren*.

The Court also dealt with *Harlow's* requirement that the underlying constitutional right be clearly established, and it was not gentle with the Ninth Circuit.

> The Court of Appeals also found clearly established law lurking in the broad "history and purposes of the Fourth Amendment." We have repeatedly told courts—and the Ninth Circuit in particular—not to define clearly established law at a high level of generality. The general proposition, for example, that an unreasonable search or seizure violates the Fourth Amendment is of little help in determining whether the violative nature of particular conduct is clearly established.

All Justices concurred in the result. Justice Kennedy's concurrence emphasized that the Court had not decided the merits of the Fourth Amendment issue that underlay al-Kidd's complaint. Justice Ginsburg questioned the Court's assumption that the

---

5 The Court found for Ashcroft on the basis of qualified immunity and therefore did not address the question of whether a prosecutor's absolute immunity applied in these circumstances.

6 In *Whren*, plainclothes officers became suspicious when Whren's vehicle idled at an intersection for an extended time and then turned without signaling and "sped off." They stopped Whren, ostensibly to warn him about the traffic offence, and saw plastic bags of crack cocaine in plain view. Whren argued that the reasonable police officer would not have stopped his vehicle. The Court held that as long as there was objective cause to do so, the fact that the officers might instead have been looking for drugs was immaterial.

warrant was valid at all, given that the officials seeking the warrant did not notify the Magistrate Judge "that al-Kidd's parents, wife and children were all citizens and residents of the United States." The officials also misrepresented that al-Kidd was traveling on a one-way, first-class ticket when he had a round-trip coach ticket. "Given these omissions and misrepresentations, there is strong cause to question the Court's opening assumption—a valid material-witness warrant—and equally strong reason to conclude that a merits determination was neither necessary nor proper." (Footnote omitted). Justice Sotomayor objected that the majority opinion "unnecessarily 'resolve[s] [a] difficult and novel questio[n] of constitutional * * * interpretation that will "have no effect on the outcome of the case." ' " (Quoting both the majority opinion in al-Kidd and the Court's opinion in *Pearson v. Callahan*, 555 U.S. 233 (2009)).

Do you find it curious that the Court insists that the official's state of mind is irrelevant to the immunity inquiry except in the failure-to-train cases, where the Court demands that the plaintiff prove the defendant official's "deliberate indifference" to the need for training? In addition to its statements in Brown, the Court also reemphasized that requirement in *Connick v. Thompson*, 131 S.Ct. 1350 (2011), *supra* at 619-21. Why is state of mind relevant in one context and not the other? Does the deliberate-indifference requirement in the failure-to-train cases open up the possibility for plaintiffs' discovery, a possibility that appeared to concern the Court in *Harlow v. Fitzgerald*?

3. Leaving to the side for a moment the issue of the appropriate standard for qualified immunity, what values is the Court seeking to serve? Is the goal of the Court's policy to do away with insubstantial claims or to ensure, to the extent possible, that public servants are not deterred from vigorously exercising the powers of their offices by concern over possible litigation?

4. Although the Court has extended qualified immunity to public officials confronting § 1983 actions, as in Wood and *Harlow*, it has refused other protections. *Leatherman v. Tarrant County Narcotics Intelligence and Coordination Unit*, 507 U.S. 163 (1993), declined to endorse any sort of heightened pleading standard for § 1983 cases against municipalities, Chief Justice Rehnquist holding that the ordinary pleading requirements of the Federal Rules of Civil Procedure apply, unmodified, to such cases.

In *Johnson v. Jones*, 515 U.S. 304 (1995), the Court unanimously declined to apply special appealability standards to § 1983 actions in which summary judgment is refused.

5. *Behrens v. Pelletier*, 516 U.S. 299 (1996), took another step down the *Mitchell v. Forsyth* path, holding that not only is "a district court's denial of a claim of qualified immunity, to the extent that it turns on an issue of law, * * * an appealable 'final decision' within the meaning of 28 U.S.C. § 1291," but also that a defendant might have more than one such interlocutory appeal. The defendant had sought summary judg-

ment on qualified immunity grounds immediately after the complaint was filed and again after discovery. The Ninth Circuit had declined to permit the second appeal, but the Supreme Court disagreed:

> * * * Mitchell clearly establishes that an order rejecting the defense of qualified immunity at either the dismissal stage or the summary-judgment stage is a "final" judgment subject to immediate appeal. Since an unsuccessful appeal from a denial of dismissal cannot possibly render the later denial of a motion for summary judgment any less "final," it follows that petitioner's appeal falls within § 1291 and dismissal was improper.

Ashcroft v. Iqbal, 556 U.S. 662 (2009), made interlocutory appeal of denial of a claim of qualified immunity easier by expanding the class of issues deemed issues of law. Iqbal, a Pakistani Muslim, was detained following the 9/11 attacks. He claimed he was designated a person "of high interest" and subjected to harsh detention conditions because of his race, religion, or national origin, in violation of the First and Fifth Amendments. He brought a *Bivens* action against many federal officials, including Attorney General Ashcroft and FBI Director Mueller, claiming Ashcroft was a principal architect of the detention of thousands of Muslims and that Mueller was "instrumental" in the adoption and execution of the detention policy. Ashcroft and Mueller moved to dismiss the complaint, challenging the sufficiency of Iqbal's pleadings on the ground that Iqbal failed to present sufficient allegations of their personal involvement in clearly established unconstitutional conduct. The District Court found the allegations sufficient under FED. R. CIV. P. 8(a) and denied the motion. The Court of Appeals affirmed.

Iqbal argued in the Supreme Court that the Court of Appeals lacked jurisdiction to hear the appeal. He argued that a qualified immunity appeal based solely on the complaint's failure to state a claim and not upon the ultimate issues involved in determining a qualified immunity defense is not a proper subject for an interlocutory appeal. The Court disagreed, holding that the sufficiency of plaintiff's allegations presented an issue of law for these purposes. Having decided that it had jurisdiction, the Court went on to impose heightened pleading standards in *Bivens* actions. The Court explicitly stated that its recent decision in *Bell Atlantic Corp. v. Twombly*, 550 U.S. 544 (2007), which imposed heightened pleading standards in antitrust cases, is not limited to those cases: "Our decision in *Twombly* expounded the pleading standard for 'all civil actions,' * * * and it applies to antitrust and discrimination suits alike." Consequently, *Iqbal* substantially undermines the impact of *Leatherman v. Tarrant County Narcotics Intelligence and Coordination Unit*, which explicitly declined to impose heightened pleading requirements in § 1983 actions against municipalities.

6. In *Richardson v. McKnight*, 521 U.S. 399 (1997), a 5-4 majority held that private employees of a company hired to perform a traditional state function are not entitled to the qualified immunity enjoyed by public officials, at least in the circum-

stances of that case. The majority consisted of Justice Breyer, who wrote the opinion, and Justices Stevens, O'Connor, Souter and Ginsburg. Justice Breyer rejected a purely functional approach to the immunity question, limiting such an approach to the type of immunity (absolute or qualified) that follows a judicial determination that there should be some immunity. Thus, he refused to recognize any immunity for privately employed prison guards working for a commercial prison management firm. Justice Breyer lauded the market as a control device that makes qualified immunity unnecessary. He argued that overly-aggressive guards unshielded by immunity will ultimately raise prison administration costs and force employers either to leave the market or to train guards to be less aggressive. (He also pointed out that prison management contracts typically are renewable over a relatively short period of time; companies whose personnel do not perform properly face nonrenewal.) In the majority's view, in effect, the combination of privatization and the availability of liability insurance eliminates the "performance-fear factor" that partially undergirds qualified immunity. Justice Breyer did offer three caveats that limit the opinion: the possibility that § 1983 does not reach these defendants at all, the narrowness of the fact pattern that generated the opinion, and the possibility of a good faith defense.

Justice Scalia, speaking for the four dissenters, was not persuaded. Primarily, he saw the matter turning on a purely functional analysis and therefore declined to distinguish privately employed guards from publicly employed guards. He also disparaged the market-pressure theory as illusory, arguing that the political process will interfere with market processes that might otherwise operate. Indeed, he argued that immunity as an incentive to discipline should be the key, though he did not make clear how affording immunity would pressure prison management companies to supervise and control their employees.

Note on Post-*Harlow* Developments

The Harlow Court plainly hoped to simplify qualified immunity law and make the defense easier to adjudicate. Unfortunately, however, Harlow raised more questions than it answered. The federal courts have struggled to answer those questions and to clarify how actions against government officials should proceed.

The Supreme Court subsequently attempted to clarify the proper sequence of inquiry when a defendant raises a qualified immunity defense. In *Wilson v. Layne*, 526 U.S. 603 (1999), and again in *Saucier v. Katz*, 533 U.S. 194 (2001), the Court held that a judge considering the defense must first determine whether the facts alleged would amount to a constitutional violation, and if so, whether the constitutional right was clearly established at the time of the alleged violation. Wilson stated that the purpose of deciding the constitutional question first was to spare a defendant not only unwarranted liability but also the unwarranted demands from defending drawn-out litigation. Saucier reiterated that the Harlow qualified immunity is an immunity from suit, not simply an immunity from liability. It resembles the double jeopardy protection in that it is an entitlement not to face judicial proceedings at all. Consequently, the defense should be resolved at the earliest possible stage of a litigation.

However, in *Pearson v. Callahan*, 555 U.S. 233 (2009), the Court retreated from *Saucier*'s inquiry prescription. Writing for a unanimous Court, Justice Alito acknowledged many lower courts' disapproval of the *Saucier* sequence, noting that it often required rulings on constitutional questions that lower courts might have avoided had they been able to consider whether the right asserted by the plaintiff was clearly established and thus imposed additional litigation costs on the parties and the judicial system. The Court did not exactly overrule *Saucier*; instead it made the *Saucier* sequence of inquiry optional rather than mandatory, in effect directing the lower courts to consider whichever branch of the inquiry seemed likely to dispose of the case more quickly.

Callahan admitted Bartholomew to his home and sold him a gram of methamphetamine. It turned out that Bartholomew was acting as a police informant and was wearing a wire. When Bartholomew gave police officers a prearranged signal, they entered, arrested Callahan and seized drugs, drug paraphernalia and the marked money with which Bartholomew had completed the purchase. The Utah trial court convicted Callahan. After the attorney general conceded the absence of exigent circumstances, a Utah appellate court overturned Callahan's conviction, rejecting the state's argument that the doctrine of inevitable discovery justified admission of the evidence.

Callahan brought a § 1983 action in federal court against the arresting officers. The district court granted the officers summary judgment based an qualified immunity, on the ground "that other courts had adopted the 'consent-once-removed' doctrine, which permits a warrantless entry by police officers into a home when consent to enter has already been granted to an undercover officer or [in the Sixth and Seventh Circuits only] informant who has observed contraband in plain view." No Utah court or federal court in the Tenth Circuit had ever commented on the doctrine. The district court, although believing the Supreme Court would ultimately reject consent-once-removed, ruled that the officers could reasonably have relied on the doctrine.

The Tenth Circuit reversed. First, it noted that decisions of the Supreme Court and the Tenth Circuit clearly established that warrantless home entries were unreasonable per se unless accompanied by exigent circumstances or consent of the occupant. Second, it refused to recognize the informant's consent to the police entry as authoritative. In a slightly different context, the court had ruled that "Tenth Circuit law provides that a mere transient guest, without a 'substantial interest in or common authority over the property,' cannot consent to the entry of others."[7] Finally, it rejected the relevance of the consent-once-removed doctrine: "The precedent of one circuit cannot rebut that the 'clearly established weight of authority' is as the Tenth Circuit and the Supreme Court have addressed it." It therefore found that the officers could not have reasonably believed that their conduct was lawful.

The Supreme Court reversed. Justice Alito implicitly ruled that the existence of consent-once-removed cases in other jurisdictions established uncertainty for Harlow purposes: "The officers here were entitled to rely on these cases, even though their own Federal Circuit had not yet ruled on 'consent-once-removed' entries." Should it matter whether the officers in question were even aware of those other cases? Can there be reliance without awareness?

Suppose the Utah courts and the Tenth Circuit had explicitly disapproved the consent-once-removed doctrine. Should the existence of contrary law in other jurisdictions entitle Utah officers to invoke Harlow immunity if they disregard their own courts' clear rulings? In other words, for Harlow purposes, can something be clearly established within one or more circuits even if other circuits take a different approach?

Now consider the Court's decision in *Camreta v. Greene*, 131 S.Ct. 2020 (2011). State officials had reason to believe that Greene's daughter had been the subject of sexual abuse by her father. They visited the child's public school and, with the cooperation of school officials, conducted a private interview with the child for a period alleged to be about two hours. During the course of the interview, the daughter made statements tending to incriminate her father. Her mother brought a federal action against state officials, alleging that they had violated her then-minor daughter's Fourth Amendment rights by interviewing her at her school without parental permission, exigent circumstances, a court order or a warrant. The district court granted summary judgment to the defendants on the ground of qualified immunity, also finding that the officials' actions were reasonable for Fourth Amendment purposes. The Ninth Circuit affirmed the grant of summary judgment but reversed the district court's ruling on the Fourth Amendment issue. Greene did not seek review of the Ninth Circuit's judgment. The officials, on the other hand, did, and the Supreme Court heard the case.

By the time the case came to the Court, the daughter had reached majority, left the public school system, and moved across the country. The Court found

7 The Tenth Circuit had ruled that the co-inhabitant of an apartment, not acting as an informant, could not consent to a search of the other tenant's private space, although he could consent to a search of common areas.

that the case had become moot. (Presumably, if Greene had sought review, hoping to preserve the claim for damages, the case would not have been moot.) The Court vacated the Ninth Circuit's finding on the Fourth Amendment issue. "In line with our normal practice when mootness frustrates a party's right to appeal, we vacate the part of the Ninth Circuit's opinion that decided the Fourth Amendment issue." This disposition has implications, not relevant here, with respect to advisory opinions, *see supra* at 25, standing, *see supra* at 36, and Supreme Court review of state court decisions, *see infra* at 905. For present purposes, consider what is left of Saucier v. Katz's sequence of inquiry in qualified immunity cases. Although the lower federal courts may (but no longer must) still adjudicate the substantive constitutional issues, what is the point of their doing so? If you were a federal judge, would the decision in Camreta incline you to engage in that analysis, or would you be more inclined simply to dispose of the case on immunity grounds if that was possible?

Justice Kennedy, joined by Justice Thomas, dissented. He objected to the Court's hearing an appeal from a party "that has already obtained the judgment it requested * * * ." The problem, as he saw it, lay with the Saucier sequence of inquiry, which he noted departed from

> conventional principles of case-or-controversy adjudication. This Court has given the Courts of Appeals "permission" to find constitutional violations when ordering dismissal or summary judgment based on qualified immunity. This invitation, as the Court is correct to note, was intended to produce binding constitutional holdings on the merits. The goal was to make dictum precedent, in order to hasten the gradual process of constitutional interpretation and alter the behavior of government defendants. The present case brings the difficulties of that objective into perspective. In express reliance on the permission granted in *Pearson*, the Court of Appeals went out of its way to announce what may be an erroneous interpretation of the Constitution; and, under our case law, the Ninth Circuit must give that dictum legal effect as precedent in future cases.
>
> In this way unnecessary merits decisions in qualified immunity cases could come to resemble declaratory judgments or injunctions. Indeed the United States as *amicus curiae* contends that the merits decision below "has an effect similar to an injunction or a declaratory judgment against the government as a whole." Today's opinion adopts that view, providing as relief the *vacatur* of "part of the Ninth Circuit's opinion"—namely, the part of the opinion that rules on the constitutional merits. For the first time, *obiter dictum* is treated not just as precedent for future cases but as a judgment in its own right.

Justice Kennedy was certainly not the first to object to the Saucier prescription. *See, e.g.*, Pierre N. Leval, *Judging Under the Constitution: Dicta About Dicta*, 81 N.Y.U. L. REV. 1249 (2006). What effect do you think Camreta will have, if any, on the development of constitutional interpretation?

The Court has addressed the central elements of the *Harlow* defense in several cases. *Hope v. Pelzer*, 536 U.S. 730 (2002), considered the circumstances in which a right should be considered clearly established. The Court held that judicial precedent directly on point was unnecessary as long as the defendants had "fair warning" their conduct was unlawful. Alabama had a practice of handcuffing prisoners to "hitching posts" as a disciplinary measure. Hope was handcuffed to a hitching post on two occasions, once for arguing with another inmate, and a second time for using vulgar language that led to a wrestling match with a guard. On the second occasion Hope was attached to the post for seven hours, shirtless in the hot sun, and denied water and toilet breaks. The Court of Appeals held that the use of the hitching post for punitive purposes violated the Eighth Amendment, but granted the defendants immunity because existing judicial precedent, while analogous, were not sufficiently similar to Hope's case. The Supreme Court reversed, holding that the defendants were not entitled to qualified immunity.

The Court began, as mandated in Saucier, by deciding whether Hope's allegations, if true, established a constitutional violation. The Court found the Eighth Amendment violation to be "obvious," and then moved to the question of whether the defendants' actions violated clearly established statutory or constitutional rights of which a reasonable person would have known. The Court rejected the Court of Appeals requirement that the facts of previous cases be "materially similar" to the plaintiff's case, stating "[t]his rigid gloss on the qualified immunity standard * * * is not consistent with our cases." While officials must be notice their conduct is unlawful, it is not necessary that the precise misconduct has been so adjudged, as long as the unlawfulness is apparent in light of pre-existing law. The Court then examined existing circuit case law and concluded that because other kinds of severe corporal punishment had been found unconstitutional, defendants should have known their treatment of Hope was unlawful.

Hope v. Pelzer relied heavily on *United States v. Lanier*, 520 U.S. 259 (1997), for its interpretation of "clearly established" law. Lanier involved charges pursuant to 18 U.S.C. § 242, the criminal counterpart of § 1983. The defendant judge, charged with sexual assaults, argued both that § 242's incorporation by reference of the state of federal constitutional law was impermissibly vague and that divergent views among the circuits meant that the right concerned could not be clearly established within the meaning of Harlow. The Court rejected the vagueness argument and ruled that its own cases do not represent the boundary of the relevant universe of decisional law, even when the circuits are not in agreement:

Although the Sixth Circuit was concerned, and rightly so, that disparate decisions in various Circuits might leave the law insufficiently certain even on a point widely considered, such a circumstance may be taken into account in deciding whether the warning is fair enough, without any need for a categorical rule that decisions of the Courts of Appeals and other courts are inadequate as a matter of law to provide it.

The Court also disapproved the defendant's argument that "clearly established" in the context of a criminal charge is a higher standard than in a civil suit, noting:

> the object of the "clearly established immunity standard is not different from that of "fair warning" as it relates to law "made specific" for the purpose of validly applying § 242. The fact that one has a civil and the other a criminal role is of no significance; both serve the same objective, and in effect the qualified immunity test is simply the adaptation of the fair warning standard to give officials (and, ultimately, governments) the same protection from civil liability and its consequences that individuals have traditionally possessed in the face of vague criminal statutes.

Does the Court's linkage of the due-process-notice standard from § 242 and the qualified immunity standard of clarity suggest at least the possibility that the Harlow immunity standard has become constitutional in stature? If so, what difference does it make? If not, why should the two rules not have the same hierarchical status?

While Hope and Lanier may appear pro-plaintiff, *Anderson v. Creighton*, 483 U.S. 635 (1987), and Saucier tilt toward defendants on the closely related question of whether a reasonable official must know merely the underlying constitutional rules or know that his conduct in a specific factual context is unlawful. These cases make clear the defense is lost only in the latter situation. The Creightons alleged that FBI agent Anderson and other state and federal law enforcement officials invaded their home without a warrant to search the home and without probable cause. The agents brandished weapons and terrorized the family while searching for a fugitive who was not there, and the agents found no evidence the fugitive had ever been there or that the Creightons or their three young daughters were involved in any type of criminal activity.

When the case reached the Supreme Court, only a Bivens claim against Anderson was at issue. Writing for the majority, Justice Scalia argued that "whether an official protected by qualified immunity may be held personally liable for an allegedly unlawful official action generally turns on the 'objective legal reasonableness' of the action * * * assessed in light of the legal rules that were 'clearly established' at the time it was taken." Justice Scalia warned against construing the concept of clearly established right too broadly, noting that if the right in this case were viewed as the Fourth Amendment's proscription against warrantless searches of a dwelling without probable cause, "the test of 'clearly established law' * * * applied at this level of generality * * * would bear no relationship to the 'objective legal reasonableness' that is the touchstone of Harlow." The Court continued:

> The contours of the right must be sufficiently clear that a reasonable official would understand that what he is doing violates that right. This is not to say that an official action is protected by qualified immunity unless the very action in question has previously been held unlawful, but it is to say that in light of pre-existing law the unlawfulness must be apparent.
>
> * * *
>
> The Court of Appeals specifically refused to consider the argument that it was not clearly established that the circumstances with which Anderson was confronted did not constitute probable cause and exigent circumstances. The previous discussion should make clear that this refusal was erroneous. It simply does not follow immediately from the conclusion that it was firmly established that warrantless searches not supported by probable cause and exigent circumstances violate the Fourth Amendment that Anderson's search was objectively legally unreasonable. We have recognized that it is inevitable that law enforcement officials will in some cases reasonably but mistakenly conclude that probable cause is present, and we have indicated that in such cases those officials—like other officials who act in ways they reasonably believe to be lawful—should not be held personally liable. The same is true of their conclusions regarding exigent circumstances.
>
> It follows from what we have said that the determination whether it was objectively legally reasonable to conclude that a given search was supported by probable cause of exigent circumstances will often require examination of the information possessed by the searching officials. * * * The relevant question in this case, for example is the objective (albeit fact-specific) question whether a reasonable officer could have believed Anderson's warrantless search to be lawful, in light of clearly established law and the information the searching officers possessed.

To what extent does Anderson imply that all applications of the Harlow immunity doctrine will now become fact based? Has the Court simply created a special rule for law enforcement officials, or has it performed a more general shift, perhaps opening the door to more discovery generally in cases dealing with immunity as the price of greater substantive protection under the immunity?

Safford Unified School District v. Redding, 557 U.S. 364 (2009), considered whether the law can be "clearly established" if lower court opinions evidence any disagreement about the proper application of a constitutional provision in a particular context. School officials searching for ibuprofen strip-searched thirteen year-old April Redding. The suspicion that Redding might be in possession of the pain medication was based, as Justice Ginsburg, concurring in part and dissenting in part, stated, "on the bare accusation of another student whose reliability the Assistant Principal had no reason to trust." After officials forced her to strip to her underwear, they told Redding to pull her bra out and to the side and shake it and to pull out the elastic on her underpants, thus exposing her breasts and pelvic area to scrutiny. All of the Justices save Justice Thomas agreed that the search violated the Fourth Amendment. Nonetheless, all Justices except Stevens and Ginsburg voted to grant school officials qualified immunity. The leading Supreme Court precedent on school searches, *New Jersey v. T.L.O.*, 469 U.S. 325 (1985), applied a "reasonable suspicion" standard and held that a school search "will be permissible in its scope when the measures adopted are reasonably related to the objectives of the search and not excessively intrusive in light of the age and sex of the student and the nature of the infraction." The Court cited several Court of Appeals decisions upholding strip searches under these standards and held these cases were "numerous enough, with well-reasoned majority and dissenting opinions," to "counsel doubt" about the clarity of the law and justify a grant of qualified immunity. Justice Stevens, dissenting on this point, said this case was one "in which clearly established law meets clearly outrageous conduct." He argued that Supreme Court precedent plainly outlawed the strip-search in this case and that "the clarity of a well-established right should not depend on whether jurists have misread our precedents."

The majority cautioned that disagreement in the lower courts would not necessarily warrant qualified immunity in all cases. "We do not suggest," the Court stated, "that entitlement to qualified immunity is the guaranteed product of disuniform views of the law in the other federal, or state, courts, and the fact that single judge, or even group of judges, disagrees about the contours of a right does not automatically render the law unclear if we have been clear." Does this disclaimer ring hollow given the grant of qualified immunity in this case?

Chapter 7

The Eleventh Amendment

A. Introduction

Few provisions of the Constitution so clearly reflect the federal-state sovereignty conflict as the Eleventh Amendment. *Chisholm v. Georgia*, (1793), in which the Supreme Court directed a state government to redeem a bond it had issued during the Revolution, almost instantly provoked a national outcry that caused speedy proposal and ratification of the Amendment. It was almost as if the states said in unison to the federal government, "You shall not call us to account for our debts in your courts." To some, *Chisholm* may have brought to life the fears, often expressed during the Constitutional Convention, that the central government would quickly seek to become dominant, destroying states' sovereignty. The colonial experience had sensitized the colonists to the problems of a strong and unresponsive central government. The Articles of Confederation reflected that sensitivity too well: they created so weak a central government that the nation was forced to discard it in only six years. In a very direct way, the Constitutional Convention and the document it created are products of that suspicion of national authority. So, too, is the Eleventh Amendment, and it is well to remember that it reflects, above all, a struggle between states and the federal government that continues unabated.

A cynic might say that the Amendment is deceptively simple and simply deceptive. There is more to it than meets the eye, but there is also less to it than meets the eye. This Chapter explores that apparent contradiction. Before undertaking *Hans v. Louisiana*, consider the Eleventh Amendment's wording: "The Judicial power of the United States shall not be construed to extend to any suit in law or equity, commenced or prosecuted against one of the United States by Citizens of another State, or by Citizens or Subjects of any Foreign State." What did those who wrote it intend to accomplish? Are the words they chose well-suited to that goal? Why did they not simply say that no individual could sue a state in a federal court? They did not say that, of course, and so it may not be too surprising to discover that states can, in some circumstances, be defendants in the federal courts. The cases that follow demonstrate the limits of that possibility and of the Eleventh Amendment.

> **FYI**
>
> That is not to say no one suggested it. Representative Theodore Sedgwick of Massachusetts, later to become Speaker of the House, proposed precisely such an amendment:
>
> No state shall be liable to be made a party defendant, in any of the judicial courts, established, or which shall be established under the authority of the United States, at the suit of any person or persons, whether a citizen or citizens, or a foreigner or foreigners, or of any body politic or corporate, whether within or without the United States.

B. The Basic Doctrine: More Than Meets the Eye

This is one of the foundational cases for the Court's current Eleventh Amendment jurisprudence. As you read Justice Bradley's opinion for the Court, pay careful attention to the actual basis for the decision, because there are at least four candidates. Is the Court holding that the Eleventh Amendment bars Hans's action? Is the Court holding that there is some sort of constitutionalized immunity for the states, not found in the Eleventh Amendment, that bars Hans's action? Is the Court holding that the states retain a common law immunity from suits by individuals that Congress might remove but has not? Is the Court holding that the federal courts lack jurisdiction for some other reason? What exactly that drives the decision here?

Hans v. Louisiana

Supreme Court of the United States, 1890.
134 U.S. 1.

[Hans, a citizen of Louisiana, sought payment on certain state bonds. He alleged that the Louisiana Constitution of 1874, as amended, declared the validity of the bonds and that the state should do nothing to impair them, but that a state constitution adopted five years later did exactly that. He also alleged that Louisiana had levied and collected taxes specifically for the payment of the bonds but had subsequently failed to use those revenues for their intended purpose. Hans sought recovery on the theory that Louisiana's 1879 con-

> **FYI**
>
> The 1874 Louisiana Constitution provided that "[t]o secure * * * payment, the judicial power shall be exercised when necessary." Should the Court have considered that language a waiver by Louisiana of its Eleventh Amendment or other sovereign immunity protection?

stitution and its refusal to disburse the tax revenues as above effected an impairment of contract within the meaning of Article I, § 10 of the United States Constitution. Louisiana successfully argued below that the Eleventh Amendment barred the action.]

MR. JUSTICE BRADLEY delivered the opinion of the court.

* * *

[T]he question is presented, whether a State can be sued in a Circuit Court of the United States by one of its own citizens upon a suggestion that the case is one that arises under the Constitution or laws of the United States. The ground taken is, that under the Constitution, as well as under the act of Congress passed to carry it into effect, a case is within the jurisdiction of the federal courts, without regard to the character of the parties, if it arises under the Constitution or laws of the United States, or, which is the same thing, if it necessarily involves a question under said Constitution or laws. The language relied on is that clause of the 3d article of the Constitution, which declares that "the judicial power of the United States shall extend to all cases in law and equity arising under this Constitution, the laws of the United States, and treaties made, or which shall be made, under their authority;" and the corresponding clause of the act conferring jurisdiction upon the Circuit Court * * * . It is said that these jurisdictional clauses make no exception arising from the character of the parties, and, therefore, that a State can claim no exemption from suit, if the case is really one arising under the Constitution, laws or treaties of the United States. It is conceded that where the jurisdiction depends alone upon the character of the parties, a controversy between a State and its own citizens is not embraced within it; but it is contended that though jurisdiction does not exist on that ground, it nevertheless does exist if the case itself is one which necessarily involves a federal question; and with regard to ordinary parties this is undoubtedly true. The question now to be decided is, whether it is true where one of the parties is a State, and is sued as a defendant by one of its own citizens.

Food for Thought

Why does Justice Bradley characterize *Hans* as a federal question case? Note that the Court never discusses the point. Would *Hans* be a federal question case today? What is the plaintiff's cause of action? What federal issue is involved in the case, and upon which constitutional provision does it draw?

That a State cannot be sued by a citizen of another State, or of a foreign state, on the mere ground that the case is one arising under the Constitution or laws of the United States, is clearly established by the decisions of this court in several recent cases. Those were cases arising under the Constitution of the United States, upon laws complained of as impairing the obligation of contracts, one of which was the constitutional amendment of Louisiana complained of in the present case. Relief was sought against state officers who professed to act in obedience to those laws. This court held that the suits were virtually against the States themselves and were consequently violative of the Eleventh Amendment of the Constitution, and could not be maintained. It was not denied that they presented cases arising under the Constitution; but, notwithstanding that, they were held to be prohibited by the amendment referred to.

In the present case the plaintiff in error contends that he, being a citizen of Louisiana, is not embarrassed by the obstacle of the Eleventh Amendment, inasmuch as that amendment only prohibits suits against a State which are brought by the citizens of another State, or by citizens or subjects of a foreign State. It is true, the amendment does so read: and if there were no other reason or ground for abating his suit, it might be maintainable; and then we should have this anomalous result, that in cases arising under the Constitution or laws of the United States, a State may be sued in the federal courts by its own citizens, though it cannot be sued for a like cause of action by the citizens of other States, or of a foreign state; and may be thus sued in the federal courts, although not allowing itself to be sued in its own courts. If this is the necessary consequence of the language of the Constitution and the law, the result is no less startling and unexpected than was the original decision of this court, that under the language of the Constitution and of the judiciary act of 1789, a State was liable to be sued by a citizen of another State, or of a foreign country. That decision was made in the case of *Chisholm v. Georgia*, and created such a shock of surprise throughout the country that, at the first meeting of Congress thereafter, the Eleventh Amendment to the Constitution was almost unanimously proposed, and was in due course adopted by the legislatures of the States. This amendment, expressing the will of the ultimate sovereignty of the whole country, superior to all legislatures and all courts, actually reversed the decision of the Supreme Court. It did not in terms prohibit suits by individuals against the States, but declared that the Constitution should not be construed

Food for Thought

Given this language, in reading the remainder of the Court's opinion try to pick out the "other reason or ground[s] for abating his suit * * * ."

Food for Thought

At what level of generality should one view *Chisholm*? Was it a "case against a state by an individual," or was it a "diversity case against a state by an individual," or was it a "diversity case sounding in contract against a state by an individual"? Keep this in mind when you read the excerpt from The FEDERALIST NO. 81 that Justice Bradley includes three paragraphs hence.

to import any power to authorize the bringing of such suits. * * * The Supreme Court had construed the judicial power as extending to such a suit, and its decision was thus overruled. * * * [O]n the succeeding day, the court delivered a unanimous opinion, "that the amendment being constitutionally adopted, there could not be exercised any jurisdiction, in any case, past or future, in which a State was sued by the citizens of another State, or by citizens or subjects of any foreign state."

> **Take Note**
>
> As you can see, the unanimous opinion in Hollingsworth v. Virginia (1798) hewed quite closely to the words of the Amendment.

This view of the force and meaning of the amendment is important. It shows that, on this question of the suability of the States by individuals, the highest authority of this country was in accord rather with the minority than with the majority of the court in the decision of the case of *Chisholm v. Georgia;* and this fact lends additional interest to the able opinion of Mr. Justice Iredell on that occasion. The other justices were more swayed by a close observance of the letter of the Constitution, without regard to former experience and usage; and because the letter said that the judicial power shall extend to controversies "between a State and citizens of another State;" and "between a State and foreign states, citizens or subjects," they felt constrained to see in this language a power to enable the individual citizens of one State, or of a foreign state, to sue another State of the Union in the federal courts. Justice Iredell, on the contrary, contended that it was not the intention to create new and unheard of remedies, by subjecting sovereign States to actions at the suit of individuals, (which he conclusively showed was never done before,) but only, by proper legislation, to invest the federal courts with jurisdiction to hear and determine controversies and cases, between the parties designated, that were properly susceptible of litigation in courts.

Looking back from our present standpoint at the decision in *Chisholm v. Georgia,* we do not greatly wonder at the effect which it had upon the country. Any such power as that of authorizing the federal judiciary to entertain suits by individuals against the States, had been expressly disclaimed, and even resented, by the great defenders of the Constitution whilst it was on its trial before the American people. As some of their utterances are directly pertinent to the question now under consideration, we deem it proper to quote them.

> **Food for Thought**
>
> In terms of federal subject matter jurisdiction, what sort of cases is Hamilton describing?

The eighty-first number of the Federalist, written by Hamilton, has the following profound remarks:

> It has been suggested that an assignment of the public securities of one State to the citizens of an-

other, would enable them to prosecute that State in the federal courts for the amount of those securities; a suggestion which the following considerations prove to be without foundation:

It is inherent in the nature of sovereignty not to be amenable to the suit of an individual without its consent. This is the general sense and the general practice of mankind; and the exemption, as one of the attributes of sovereignty, is now enjoyed by the government of every State in the Union. Unless, therefore, there is a surrender of this immunity in the plan of the convention, it will remain with the States, and the danger intimated must be merely ideal. The circumstances which are necessary to produce an alienation of state sovereignty were discussed in considering the article of taxation, and need not be repeated here. A recurrence to the principles there established will satisfy us, that there is no color to pretend that the state governments would, by the adoption of that plan, be divested of the privilege of paying their own debts in their own way, free from every constraint but that which flows from the obligations of good faith. The contracts between a nation and individuals are only binding on the conscience of the sovereign, and have no pretension to a compulsive force. They confer no right of action independent of the sovereign will. To what purpose would it be to authorize suits against States for the debts they owe? How could recoveries be enforced? It is evident that it could not be done without waging war against the contracting State; and to ascribe to the federal courts by mere implication, and in destruction of a pre-existing right of the state governments, a power which would involve such a consequence, would be altogether forced and unwarrantable.

Take Note

This phrase—"surrender of [the states'] immunity in the plan of the convention"—is one you will see often, and it is critically important. Consider the extent to which ratification of the Constitution either yielded or subordinated previously existing state authority to the new federal government.

The obnoxious clause to which Hamilton's argument was directed, and which was the ground of the objections which he so forcibly met, was that which declared that "the judicial power shall extend to all * * * controversies between a State and citizens of another State, * * * and between a State and foreign states, citizens or subjects." It was argued by the opponents of the Constitution that this clause would authorize jurisdiction to be given to the federal courts to entertain suits against a State brought by the citizens of another State, or of a foreign state. Adhering to the mere letter, it might be so; and so, in fact, the Supreme

Food for Thought

In this sentence, does Justice Bradley implicitly concede Hans's point that the Eleventh Amendment addresses itself only to diversity cases?

Court held in Chisholm v. Georgia; but looking at the subject as Hamilton did, and as Mr. Justice Iredell did, in the light of history and experience and the established order of things, the views of the latter were clearly right,—as the people of the United States in their sovereign capacity subsequently decided.

Food for Thought

Perhaps Justice Bradley's reference to "the subject" begs the question. Is "the subject" state sovereign immunity generally, or is it the availability of a particular type of federal jurisdiction? To be sure, states can make themselves immune to claims sounding in their own law. Can they do the same with respect to claims that federal law creates?

But Hamilton was not alone in protesting against the construction put upon the Constitution by its opponents. In the Virginia convention the same objections were raised by George Mason and Patrick Henry, and were met by Madison and Marshall as follows. Madison said:

> [Federal] jurisdiction in controversies between a State and citizens of another State is much objected to, and perhaps without reason. It is not in the power of individuals to call any State into court. The only operation it can have is that, if a State should wish to bring a suit against a citizen, it must be brought before the federal court.
>
> This will give satisfaction to individuals, as it will prevent citizens on whom a State may have a claim being dissatisfied with the state courts * * * . It appears to me that this [clause] can have no operation but this—to give a citizen a right to be heard in the federal courts; and if a State should condescend to be a party, this court may take cognizance of it.

Food for Thought

What language supports this assertion by Madison?

Marshall, in answer to the same objection, said:

> With respect to disputes between a State and the citizens of another State, its jurisdiction has been decried with unusual vehemence. I hope that no gentleman will think that a State will be called at the bar of the federal court * * * . It is not rational to suppose that the sovereign power should be dragged before a court.

Food for Thought

Is sovereignty "directional" in some sense? Can a state be a sovereign *vis-á-vis* the individual but not sovereign *vis-á-vis* the federal government? Within that division, can a state be sovereign *vis-á-vis* the federal government concerning matters of state law but not be sovereign concerning federal law matters because of supremacy?

The intent is to enable States to recover claims of individuals residing in other States * * * . But, say they, there will be partiality in it if a State cannot be defendant—if an individual cannot proceed to obtain judgment against a State, though he may be sued by a State. It is necessary to be so, and cannot be avoided. I see a difficulty in making a State defendant which does not prevent its being plaintiff.

It seems to us that these views of those great advocates and defenders of the Constitution were most sensible and just; and they apply equally to the present case as to that then under discussion. The letter is appealed to now, as it was then, as a ground for sustaining a suit brought by an individual against a State. The reason against it is as strong in this case as it was in that. It is an attempt to strain the Constitution and the law to a construction never imagined or dreamed of. Can we suppose that, when the Eleventh Amendment was adopted, it was understood to be left open for citizens of a State to sue their own state in the federal courts, whilst the idea of suits by citizens of other states, or of foreign states, was indignantly repelled? Suppose that Congress, when proposing the Eleventh Amendment, had appended to it a *proviso* that nothing therein contained should prevent a State from being sued by its own citizens in cases arising under the Constitution or laws of the United States: can we imagine that it would have been adopted by the States? The supposition that it would is almost an absurdity on its face.

> **Food for Thought**
>
> There is no question that *Chisholm* engendered outrage. There may be a question about whether *Chisholm* engendered outrage because of the judgment's source (the federal court) or its content (compelled repayment of debts from the Revolution).

The truth is, that the cognizance of suits and actions unknown to the law, and forbidden by the law, was not contemplated by the Constitution when establishing the judicial power of the United States. Some things, undoubtedly, were made justiciable which were not known as such at the common law; such, for example, as controversies between States as to boundary lines, and other questions admitting of judicial solution. * * *

The suability of a State without its consent was a thing unknown to the law. This has been so often laid down and acknowledged by courts and jurists that it is hardly necessary to be formally asserted. It was fully shown by an exhaustive examination of the old law by Mr. Justice Iredell in his opinion in *Chisholm v. Georgia*; and it has been conceded in every case since, where the question has, in any way been presented, even in the cases which have gone farthest in sustaining suits against the officers or agents of States. In all these cases the effort was to show, and the court held, that the suits were not against the State or the United States, but against the individuals; conceding that if they had been against either the State or the United States, they could not be maintained.

* * *

Undoubtedly a State may be sued by its own consent * * * . But this court decided that the State could repeal that law at any time; that it was not a contract within the terms of the constitution prohibiting the passage of state laws impairing the obligation of a contract. * * *

But besides the presumption that no anomalous and unheard-of proceedings or suits were intended to be raised up by the Constitution—anomalous and unheard of when the Constitution was adopted—an additional reason why the jurisdiction claimed for the Circuit Court does not exist, is the language of the act of Congress by which its jurisdiction is conferred. The words are these: "The circuit courts of the United States shall have original cognizance, concurrent with the courts of the several States, of all suits of a civil nature at common law or in equity, * * * arising under the Constitution or laws of the United States, or treaties," etc.—"Concurrent with the courts of the several States." Does not this qualification show that Congress, in legislating to carry the Constitution into effect, did not intend to invest its courts with any new and strange jurisdictions? The state courts have no power to entertain suits by individuals against a State without its consent. Then how does the Circuit Court, having only concurrent jurisdiction, acquire any such power? It is true that the same qualification existed in the judiciary act of 1789, which was before the court in *Chisholm v. Georgia*, and the majority of the court did not think that it was sufficient to limit the jurisdiction of the Circuit Court. Justice Iredell thought differently. In view of the manner in which that decision was received by the country, the adoption of the Eleventh Amendment, the light of history and the reason of the thing, we think we are at liberty to prefer Justice Iredell's views in this regard.

Some reliance is placed by the plaintiff upon the observations of Chief Justice Marshall, in *Cohens v. Virginia*. The Chief Justice was there considering the power of review exercisable by this court over the judgments of a state court, wherein it might be necessary to make the State itself a defendant in error. He showed that this power was absolutely necessary in order to enable the judiciary of the United States to take cognizance of all cases arising under the Constitution and laws of the United States. He also showed that making a State a defendant in error was entirely different from suing a State in an original action in prosecution of a demand against it, and was not within the meaning of the Eleventh Amendment; that the prosecution of a writ of error against a State was not the prosecution of a suit in the sense of that amendment, which had reference to the prosecution, by suit, of claims against a State. * * *

After * * * showing by incontestable argument that a writ of error to a judgment recovered by a State, in which the State is necessarily the defendant in error, is not a suit commenced or prosecuted against a State in the sense of the amendment, he added, that if the court were mistaken in this, its error did not affect that case, because the writ of error therein was not prosecuted by "a citizen of another State" or "of any foreign state," and so was not affected by the amendment; but was governed by the general grant of judicial power, as extending "to all cases arising under the Constitution or laws of the United States, without respect to parties."

It must be conceded that the last observation of the Chief Justice does favor the argument of the plaintiff. But the observation was unnecessary to the decision, and in that sense extra judicial, and though made by one who seldom used words without due reflection, ought not to outweigh the important considerations referred to which lead to a different conclusion. With regard to the question then before the court, it may be observed, that writs of error to judgments in favor of the crown, or of the State, had been known to the law from time immemorial; and had never been considered as exceptions to the rule, that an action does not lie against the sovereign.

* * *

It is not necessary that we should enter upon an examination of the reason or expediency of the rule which exempts a sovereign State from prosecution in a court of justice at the suit of individuals. * * * It is enough for us to declare its existence. The legislative department of a State represents its polity and its will; and is called upon by the highest demands of natural and political law to preserve justice and judgment, and to hold inviolate the public obligations. Any departure from this rule, except for reasons most cogent, (of which the legislature, and not the courts, is the judge,) never fails in the end to incur the odium of the world, and to bring lasting injury upon the State itself. But to deprive the legislature of the power of judging what the honor and safety of the State may require, even at the expense of a temporary failure to discharge the public debts, would be attended with greater evils than such failure can cause.

The judgment of the Circuit Court is

Affirmed.

MR. JUSTICE HARLAN concurring.

I concur with the court in holding that a suit directly against a State by one of its own citizens is not one to which the judicial power of the United States extends, unless the State itself consents to be sued. Upon this ground alone I assent to the judgment. But I cannot give my assent to many things said in the opinion. The comments made upon the decision in *Chisholm v. Georgia* do not meet my approval. They are not necessary to the determination of the present case. Besides, I am of opinion that the decision in that case was based upon a sound interpretation of the Constitution as that instrument then was.

Notes and Questions

1a) At the outset, *Hans* confronts the peculiar wording of the Eleventh Amendment. Scholars have echoed and expanded Hans's argument that the Amendment was intended to curtail only party-based jurisdiction. Judge Fletcher, for example, interprets the Eleventh Amendment purely as forbidding diversity cases against the states. Under his theory, any federal question case is maintainable against the states in the federal courts.

For More Information

See, e.g., William A. Fletcher, *A Historical Interpretation of the Eleventh Amendment: A Narrow Construction of an Affirmative Grant of Jurisdiction Rather Than a Prohibition Against Jurisdiction*, 35 STAN. L. REV. 1033 (1983); John J. Gibbons, *The Eleventh Amendment and State Sovereign Immunity: A Reinterpretation*, 83 COLUM. L. REV. 1889 (1983).

Yet, as the Court points out, to accept that argument is to ignore the Amendment's wording when a non-citizen of the defendant state brings a federal-question action. On the other hand, restricting the federal forum to federal question cases brought by a state's citizens would create the anomaly the *Hans* Court noted.

b) Does the Court's argument prove too much? Justice Bradley notes that if the Eleventh Amendment excludes only federal actions against states by non-residents, a resident may bring a federal question action against the state even though a non-resident with the same claim could not. If the anomaly is so plain, and if the Constitution's (and the Eleventh Amendment's) framers were so opposed to federal judicial power being exercised against the states, how did the literal effect of the language escape their attention?

c) Justice Bradley's argument leaves open the question about the Eleventh Amendment's wording that the Chapter introduction poses: if the drafters intended to preclude all individual actions against states in the federal courts, why did the Amendment not say something like that? It might have read, "The judicial power shall not be construed to extend to suits by individuals against one of the United States." What might have impelled the draftsmen to include wording that seems clearly not to rule out federal suits against a state by its own citizens?

3. a) Is the basis for the decision in *Hans* that the Amendment prohibits the federal courts from hearing the case, or that there is some other immunity doctrine of

like effect, or that there is a statutory basis for declining relief? What difference does it make?

b) What is the Hans Court's view of the Eleventh Amendment? Does it restrict the Constitution's jurisdictional scope for the federal courts, or is it an entitlement of the states individually? What difference does it make?

4. Is Hans predominantly a statutory interpretation case? Note the Court's reliance on the federal question jurisdiction statute's language regarding concurrent jurisdiction. The Court reads "concurrent with the courts of the several States" as expressing a limitation on the jurisdictional grant, *i.e.* that Congress intended to grant no jurisdiction broader than that already existing at the state level. Cannot the same language merely indicate that the grant of federal question jurisdiction was not intended to oust the state courts of jurisdiction that they had exercised for eighty-six years? Given the empty legislative history of the 1875 jurisdictional grant, is there any basis for preferring one interpretation over the other?

Take Note

Recall from page 305 that the legislative history of the original federal-question jurisdiction statute is extraordinarily brief.

5. The Court draws heavily upon Justice Iredell's dissenting opinion in Chisholm v. Georgia, yet it is far from clear that his dissent directly supports the Hans result, much less the more general rule now attributed to Hans. In Chisholm, plaintiff's attorney framed the issue as whether a state could be sued in the federal courts. Justice Iredell was at pains to limit the scope of the issue, though he recognized the difficulty of doing so.

> The particular question then before the Court is, will an action of *assumpsit* lie against a State? This particular question (abstracted from the general one, *viz.* Whether, a State can in any instance be sued?) I took the liberty to propose to the consideration of the Attorney-General * * * . I shall * * * confine myself, as much as possible, to the particular question before the Court, though every thing I have to say upon it will effect [*sic*] every kind of suit, the object of which is to compel the payment of money by a State.

Did Justice Iredell imply by omission that actions against a state for other than monetary relief may stand upon a different footing from cases seeking damages? He noted later that when the Constitution and the Eleventh Amendment were adopted, no individual could maintain an action against a state "for the recovery of money * * * ."

One can read much of Justice Iredell's opinion, however, to allow at least the possibility of federal question cases against states. His discussion of the division of sovereignty between states and federal government and the creation of concurrent judicial power is illuminating.

> Every State in the *Union* in every instance where its sovereignty has not been delegated to the *United States*, I consider to be as completely sovereign, as the *United States* are in respect to the powers surrendered. The *United States* are sovereign as to all the powers of Government actually surrendered: Each State in the *Union* is sovereign as to all the powers reserved. * * * Where certain parties are concerned, although the subject in controversy does not relate to any of the special objects of authority of the general government, wherein the separate sovereignties of the States are blended in one common mass of supremacy, yet the general Government has a Judicial Authority in regard to such subjects of controversy, and the Legislature of the *United States*, and their individual sovereignty is in this respect limited. But it is limited no farther than the necessary execution of such authority requires. The authority extends only to the decision of controversies in which a State is a party, and providing laws necessary for that purpose. That surely can refer only to such controversies in which a State *can* be a part; in respect to which, if any question arises, it can be determined, according to the principles I have supported, in no other manner than by a reference either to pre-existent laws, or laws passed under the Constitution and in conformity to it.

Would it be consistent with this view of state immunity to conclude that Congress could authorize federal actions against states concerning any federal power created by the Constitution? If Congress were to create a federal cause of action based on the Commerce Clause, is there anything in Justice Iredell's view of the relationship between states and the federal government that would preclude such a claim against a state in federal court?

6. There are at least four ways in which to read the Eleventh Amendment. First, it may create a general limitation on the subject matter jurisdiction of the federal courts, indicating that their jurisdiction never extends to cases in which a state is a defendant. Note particularly the introductory wording of the Amendment: "The judicial power shall not be construed * * * ." Second, it may constitutionalize a pre-existing common law immunity. Third, it may recognize a common law immunity neither based in nor abrogated by the Constitution or by act of Congress. For example, in *In re New York*, 256 U.S. 490, 497 (1921), the Court noted that the federal courts cannot entertain a suit by an out-of-stater "because of the Eleventh Amendment; and not even one brought by [a state's] own citizens, because of the fundamental rule of which the Amendment is but an exemplification." Fourth, it may constitute a simple limitation only on the diversity jurisdiction of the federal courts.

a) If the Amendment is a limitation on subject matter jurisdiction, why does the *Hans* Court emphasize that a state may not be sued "without its consent"? Parties cannot agree to subject matter jurisdiction that a court does not possess it under its constitutive law, can they?

b) With respect to the "fundamental rule" of state immunity exemplified by the Eleventh Amendment, is there not a substantial supremacy problem? Whence the fundamental rule? Article VI declares the Constitution and laws passed in conformity with it to be the supreme law. Why would an action based upon a federal statute and brought as a federal question case not prevail over a claim of pre-existing common law immunity?

7. Hans is clearly the engine that drives all of the Court's modern Eleventh Amendment jurisprudence. As you proceed through the following cases, keep in mind the role of Hans and its effect on the resolution of particular Eleventh Amendment controversies. Notice also that later Courts may have different views of exactly what Hans decided.

Go Online

For a particularly interesting look at Hans's place in American history of the time, see Edward A. Purcell, Jr., *The Particularly Dubious Case of* Hans v. Louisiana: *An Essay on Law, History, and "Federal Courts,"* 81 N.CAR.L.REV. 1927 (2003).

Giles v. Harris

Supreme Court of the United States, 1903.
189 U.S. 475.

MR. JUSTICE HOLMES delivered the opinion of the Court.

This is a bill in equity brought by a colored man, on behalf of himself "and on behalf of more than five thousand negroes, citizens of the county of Montgomery, Alabama, similarly situated and circumstanced as himself," against the board of registrars of that county. The prayer of the bill is in substance that the defendants may be required to enroll upon the voting lists the name of the plaintiff and of all other qualified members of his race who applied for registration before August 1, 1902, and were refused, and that certain sections of the constitution of Alabama * * * may be declared contrary to the Fourteenth and Fifteenth Amendments of the Constitution of the United States, and void.

The allegations of the bill may be summed up as follows. The plaintiff is subject to none of the disqualifications set forth in the constitution of Alabama and is entitled to vote,—entitled, as the bill plainly means, under the constitution as it is. He applied in March, 1902, for registration as a voter, and was refused arbitrarily on the ground of his color, together with large numbers of other duly qualified negroes, while all white men were registered. The same thing was done all over the State. Under § 187 of article 8 of the Alabama constitution[,] persons registered before January 1, 1903, remain electors for life unless they become disqualified by certain crimes, etc., while after that date severer tests come into play which would exclude, perhaps, a large part of the black race. Therefore, by the refusal, the plaintiff and the other negroes excluded were deprived not only of their votes at an election which has taken place since the bill was filed, but of the permanent advantage incident to registration before 1903. The white men generally are registered for good under the easy test and the black men are likely to be kept out in the future as in the past. This refusal to register the blacks was part of a general scheme to disfranchise them, to which the defendants and the State itself, according to the bill, were parties. The defendants accepted their office for the purpose of carrying out the scheme. The part taken by the State, that is, by the white population which framed the constitution, consisted in shaping that instrument so as to give opportunity and effect to the wholesale fraud which has been practised.

* * *

Perhaps it should be added to the foregoing statement that the bill was filed in September, 1902, and alleged the plaintiff's desire to vote at an election coming off in November. This election has gone by, so that it is impossible to give specific relief with regard to that. But we are not prepared to dismiss the bill or the appeal on the ground, because to be enabled to cast a vote in that election is not the whole object of the bill. It is not even the principal object of the relief sought by the plaintiff. The principal object of that is to obtain the permanent advantages of registration as of a date before 1903.

The certificate of the circuit judge raises the single question of the jurisdiction of the court. The plaintiff contends that this jurisdiction is given expressly by Rev. Stat. § 629, cl. 16, coupled with Rev. Stat. § 1979 [the predecessor of 42 U.S.C. § 1983], which provides that every person who, under color of a state "statute, ordinance, regulation, custom, or usage," "subjects, or causes to be subjected, any citizen of the United States or other person within the jurisdiction thereof to the deprivation of any rights, privileges, or immunities secured by the Constitution and laws, shall be liable to the party injured in an action at law, suit in equity, or other proper proceeding for redress."

We assume * * * that § 1979 has not been repealed, and that jurisdiction to enforce its provisions has not been taken away by any later act. But it is suggested that the Circuit Court was right in its ruling that it had no jurisdiction as a court of the United States, because the bill did not aver threatened damage to an amount exceeding two thousand dollars. It is true that * * * the Circuit Courts are given cognizance of suits of a civil nature, at common law or in equity, arising under the Constitution or laws of the United

Take Note

Until 1980, all of the predecessors of today's § 1331 had a monetary jurisdictional floor that tracked the amount in the diversity statute. When the Court announced *Giles v. Harris*, the amount was $2,000.

States, in which the matter in dispute exceeds the sum or value of two thousand dollars. We have recognized, too, that the deprivation of a man's political and social rights properly may be alleged to involve damage to that amount, capable of estimation in money. But, assuming that the allegation should have been made in a case like this, the objection to its omission was not raised in the Circuit Court, and as it could have been remedied by amendment, we think it unavailing. The certificate was made ***alio intuitu***. There is no pecuniary limit on appeals to this court under section 5 of the act of 1891, and we do not feel called upon to send the case back to the Circuit Court in order that it might permit the amendment. * * *

Food for Thought

Does Justice Holmes suggest here that either the parties or the court below waived any lack of subject matter jurisdiction relating to the amount in controversy?

It's Latin to Me!

"In a different view; with respect to another case or condition."

* * *

It seems to us impossible to grant the equitable relief which is asked. It will be observed in the first place that the language of § 1979 does not extend the sphere of equitable jurisdiction in respect of what shall be held an appropriate subject matter for that kind of relief. The words are "shall be liable to the party injured in an action at law, suit in equity, or other proper proceeding for redress." They allow a suit in equity only when that is the proper proceeding for redress, and they refer to existing standards to determine what is a proper proceeding. The traditional limits of proceedings in equity have not embraced a remedy for political wrongs. But we cannot forget that we are dealing with a new and extraordinary situation, and we are unwilling to stop short of the final considerations which seems to us to dispose of the case.

Food for Thought

The majority also characterized the rights that Giles sought to enforce as "political rights." Do you think the majority meant that Congress intended to erect a distinction between political rights and civil rights and to make only the latter enforceable through § 1983? Is the Fifteenth Amendment relevant to that question?

That aside, Justice Holmes asserts that any remedy for Giles must come through the political branches, not through the courts. Is Holmes saying by implication that such a remedy cannot depend on the judiciary for interpretation and enforcement? Could Giles have argued that the political branches had given him a remedy, in the form of the Fifteenth Amendment and the statutes upon which he relied?

The difficulties which we cannot overcome are two, and the first is this: The plaintiff alleges that the whole registration scheme of the Alabama constitution is a fraud upon the Constitution of the United States, and asks us to declare it void. But of course he could not maintain a bill for a mere declaration in the air. He does not try to do so, but asks to be registered as a party qualified under the void instrument. If then we accept the conclusion which it is the chief purpose of the bill to maintain, how can we make the court a party to the unlawful scheme by accepting it and adding another voter to its fraudulent lists? If a white man came here on the same general allegations, admitting his sympathy with the plan, but alleging some special prejudice that had kept him off the list, we hardly should think it necessary to meet him with a reasoned answer. But the relief cannot be varied because we think that in the future the particular plaintiff is likely to try to overthrow the scheme. If we accept the plaintiff's allegations for the purposes of his case, he cannot complain. We must accept or reject them. It is impossible simply to shut our eyes, put the plaintiff on the lists, be they honest or fraudulent, and leave the determination of the fundamental question for the future. If we have an opinion that the bill is right on its face, or if we are undecided, we are not at liberty to assume it to be wrong for the purposes of decision. It seems to us that unless we are prepared to say that it is wrong, that all its principal allegations are immaterial and that the registration plan of the Alabama constitution is valid, we cannot order the plaintiff's name to be registered. It is not an answer to say that if all the blacks who are qualified according to the letter of the instrument were registered, the fraud would be cured. In the first place, there is no probability that any way now is open by which more than a few could be registered, but if all could be the difficulty would not be overcome. If the sections of the constitution concerning registration were illegal in their inception, it would be a new doctrine in constitutional law that the original invalidity could be cured by an administration which defeated their intent. We express no opinion as to the alleged fact of their unconstitutionality beyond saying that we are not willing to assume that they are valid, in the face of the allegations and main object of the bill, for the purpose of granting the relief which it was necessary to pray in order that that object should be secured.

The other difficulty is of a different sort, and strikingly reinforces the argument that equity cannot undertake now, any more than it has in the past, to enforce political rights, and also the suggestion that state constitutions were not left unmentioned in § 1979 by accident. In determining whether a court of equity can take jurisdiction, one of the first questions is what it can do to enforce any order that it may make. This is alleged to be the conspiracy of a State, although the State is not and could not be made a party to the bill. *Hans v. Louisiana*. The Circuit Court has no constitutional power to control its action by any direct means. And if we leave the State out of consideration, the court has as little practical power to deal with the people of the State in a body. The bill imports that the great mass of the white population intends to keep the blacks from voting. To meet such an intent something more than ordering the plaintiff's name to be inscribed upon the lists of 1902 will be needed. If the conspiracy and the intent exist, a name on a piece of paper will not defeat them. Unless we are prepared to supervise the voting in that State by officers of the court, it seems to us that all that the plaintiff could get from equity would be an empty form. Apart from damages to the individual, relief from a great political wrong, if done, as alleged, by the people of a state and the State itself, must be given by them or by the legislative and political department of the Government of the United States.

Food for Thought

The Court seems to assume here that the state officials would ignore its judgment. Does that place the efficacy of the Fifteenth Amendment totally in the control of the majoritarian branches of the government? If not, how can enforcement occur? If so, how would the Court deal with the issue of constitutional provisions' entitlement (under Article V) *not* to be in those branches' control?

Decree affirmed.

MR. JUSTICE HARLAN dissenting.

By the final judgment in the Circuit Court the bill in this case was dismissed for want of jurisdiction to entertain it and for want of equity; and from that judgment the plaintiffs prayed and were allowed an appeal.

Subsequently an order was made by the Circuit Court certifying that the only question considered and decided was whether upon the bill and demurrer a case was presented of which it had jurisdiction under the Constitution and laws of the United States.

* * *

It is clear that under the act of 1888 a Circuit Court could not take original cognizance of a suit simply because it was one arising under the Constitution or laws of the United States. The value of the matter in dispute in such a case must exceed $2000, exclusive of interest and costs.

* * *

It seems to me that this question as to the value of the matter in dispute was sufficiently raised in the Circuit Court; for the demurrer to the bill was, in part, on the ground that the facts stated did not make a case "within the jurisdiction of the court." But, passing that view, I come to a more serious matter. In cases of which a Circuit Court may take original cognizance, the value of the matter in dispute—which is mentioned in the statute in advance of any reference to the nature of the subject of the action—is as essential to jurisdiction as is the nature of the subject of such dispute. And yet the court says that an objection that the record from the Circuit Court does not show an allegation as to value is unavailing here, even if such allegation ought to have been made. That is a new, and I take leave to say a startling, doctrine. Must not this court upon its own motion decline to pass upon,—indeed, has this court, strictly speaking, jurisdiction to consider and determine,—the merits of a case coming from the Circuit Court, unless it *affirmatively* appears *from the record* that the case is one of which that court could take cognizance?

* * *

The question of the jurisdiction of the Circuit Court under the acts of Congress, the one certified, is thus left in the air, and the case is examined and disposed of upon its merits just as if jurisdiction of the Circuit Court appeared upon the record. There is no claim that the essential fact of value appears anywhere in the record, either in the bill or otherwise. Consequently, as already said, this court is without power to consider the merits.

* * *

As these are my views as to the jurisdiction of this court, upon this record, I will not formulate and discuss my views upon the merits of this case. But to avoid misapprehension, I may add that my conviction is that upon the facts alleged in the bill (if the record showed a sufficient value of the matter in dispute) the plaintiff is entitled to relief in respect of his right to be registered as a voter. I agree with Mr. Justice Brewer that it is competent for the courts to give relief in such cases as this.

MR. JUSTICE BREWER, dissenting.

I am unable to concur in either the opinion or judgment in this case. The single question is whether the Circuit Court of the United States had jurisdiction.

* * *

Although the statute and * * * decisions thus expressly limit the range of inquiry on a certificate of jurisdiction to the question of jurisdiction, it is held that because there is a constitutional question shown in the pleadings, the certificate may be ignored and the entire case presented to this court for consideration. In other words, although the plaintiff, by his method of appeal, following the provisions of the statute, limited the inquiry to the matter of jurisdiction, this court will ignore such limit and treat the case as coming here on a general appeal, which he did not take. * * *

* * *

That the United States Circuit Court has jurisdiction of an action like this seems to me to result inevitably from prior decisions of this court.

* * *

It seems to me nothing need be added to these decisions, and unless they are to be considered as overruled they are decisive of this case.

Notes and Questions

1. Professor Richard Pildes has noted both Giles's importance and its obscurity. Noting what he called "the Supreme Court's removal of democracy from the agenda of constitutional law," Richard H. Pildes, *Democracy, Anti-Democracy and the Canon*, 17 CONST. COMMENT. 295, 296-98 (2000) (footnotes omitted), he went on to observe:

> If canonization requires a ready focal point, this is it for (anti-)democracy in American constitutional law. * * *
>
> *Giles* has been airbrushed out of the constitutional canon. It is surely one of the most momentous decisions in United States Supreme Court history and one of the most revealing. * * * *Giles* permits the virtual elimination of black citizens from political participation in the South. Yet while extensive attention is devoted to judicial validation of separate but equal segregation, none is devoted to this. Every law student knows *Plessy v. Ferguson*; virtually none know *Giles*. * * * Even the Soviets could admire this success at obscuring all traces of a prior political regime.

2. Justice Holmes's approach to subject matter jurisdiction is an eye opener. From their first year, law students learn that subject matter jurisdiction is always in issue and that the courts will examine it **sua sponte** if the parties do not raise it, and the Court had done so in four cases that antedated Giles. Notice that Justice Harlan chastised the majority for taking the position that "the objection * * * was not raised in the Circuit Court, and as it could have been remedied by amendment, we think it is unavailing." Why did the majority take this surprising approach?

Make the Connection

See, e.g., Louisville and Nashville Railroad Company v. Mottley, 211 U.S. 149 (1908) (at page 307); *Smith v. Kansas City Title & Trust Co.*, 255 U.S. 180 (1921) (at page 325). Cf. FED. R. CIV. P 12(h)(3) ("Whenever it appears by suggestion of the parties or otherwise that the court lacks jurisdiction of the subject matter, the court shall dismiss the action.").

3. The majority also argued that plaintiff's attack on the Alabama registration scheme in its entirety left him no platform upon which the Court could fashion relief even if it had no other problems with his request. Is that an accurate representation of the plaintiff's complaint? Was the plaintiff really attacking the structure of the scheme (with its grandfather clause and post-1902 requirements for becoming an elector) or was he attacking the race-based implementation of the scheme?

4. It is by now common to refer to the Civil War Amendments as self-executing. *See, e.g., City of Boerne v. Flores,* (1997) (Fourteenth Amendment); *South Carolina v. Katzenbach* (1966) (Fifteenth Amendment). Did *Giles* effectively take the position that the Amendments were not self-executing, at least with respect to the category of "political rights" that Justice Holmes recognized?

C. The Basic Doctrine: Less Than Meets the Eye

Ex Parte Young

Supreme Court of the United States, 1908.
209 U.S. 123.

[Justice Peckham delivered for the Court a statement of facts separate from the main body of the opinion. This is a summary of those facts.

The state of Minnesota passed some statutes severely restricting rates that railroads operating within the state could charge. The statutes prescribed extraordinarily severe penalties for their violation, including substantial fines and imprisonment of any person connected with a railroad who participated in any manner in charging rates exceeding the statutory authorizations.

Several railroads' shareholders commenced derivative actions in federal court, alleging that the Minnesota statutes were unconstitutional as confiscatory takings under the Fourteenth Amendment's Due Process Clause and as interferences with the Commerce Clause. In addition to joining the railroad corporations and their officers and directors as parties-defendant, the shareholders joined Edward T. Young, the Attorney General of Minnesota. In one of those derivative actions, the court granted injunctive relief against the railroad and its officials, ordering them not to comply with the new rate statutes, and against Young, ordering him to refrain from instituting any enforcement procedure under the challenged statutes. Young had appeared specially in the federal actions, objecting on Eleventh Amendment grounds to the court's jurisdiction.

The day after the court issued the preliminary injunction, Young filed a state mandamus proceeding against the railroad to compel it to comply with the new statutes. The federal court thereupon ordered Young to show cause why he should not be punished for contempt and, upon his reiteration of his Eleventh Amendment jurisdictional objection, found him in contempt and committed him to the custody of the United States marshal. He then applied to the United States Supreme Court for leave to file a petition for a writ of habeas corpus in the Supreme Court as an original proceeding. The Court granted leave and now reviews Young's petition.]

> **Food for Thought**
>
> Note the position in which a mandamus from the state court would have placed the railroad: compelled by the federal injunction not to comply with the rate statutes and by the state mandamus to comply. Could the federal court do anything in that circumstance? Consider 28 U.S.C. § 2283, the Anti-Injunction Act, discussed *infra* at 784-98.

MR. JUSTICE PECKHAM, after making the foregoing statement, delivered the opinion of the court:

* * *

The question of jurisdiction, whether of the circuit court or of this court, is frequently a delicate matter to deal with, and it is especially so in this case, where the material and most important objection to the jurisdiction of the circuit court is the assertion that the suit is, in effect, against one of the states of the Union. It is a question, however, which we are called upon, and which it is our duty to decide. * * *

It is insisted by the petitioner that there is no Federal question presented under the 14th Amendment, because there is no dispute as to the meaning of the Constitution, where it provides that no state shall deprive any person of life, liberty, or property without due process of law; nor deny to any person within its jurisdiction the equal protection of the laws; and whatever dispute there may be in this case is one of fact simply, whether the freight or passenger rates, as fixed by the legislature or by the railroad commission, are so low as to be confiscatory; and that is not a Federal question.

Jurisdiction is given to the circuit court in suits involving the requisite amount, arising under the Constitution or laws of the United States, and the question really to be determined under this objection is whether the acts of the legislature and the orders of the railroad commission, if enforced, would take property without due process of law; and although that question might incidentally involve a question of fact, its solution, nevertheless, is one which raises a Federal question * * *.

Another Federal question is the alleged unconstitutionality of these acts because of the enormous penalties denounced for their violation, which prevent the railway company, as alleged, or any of its servants or employees, from resorting to the courts for the purpose of determining the validity of such acts. * * *

Still another Federal question is urged, growing out of the assertion that the laws are, by their necessary effect, an interference with and a regulation of interstate commerce, the grounds for which assertion it is not now necessary to enlarge upon. The question is not, at any rate, frivolous.

We conclude that the circuit court had jurisdiction in the case before it, because it involved the decision of Federal questions arising under the Constitution of the United States.

[The Court analyzed the merits, finding the rate statutes unconstitutional.]

* * *

We have, therefore, upon this record, the case of an unconstitutional act of the state legislature and an intention by the attorney general of the state to endeavor to enforce its provisions, to the injury of the company * * * . The question that arises is whether there is a remedy that the parties interested may resort to, by going into a Federal court of equity, in a case involving a violation of the Federal Constitution, and obtaining a judicial investigation of the problem, and, pending its solution, obtain freedom from suits, civil or criminal, by a temporary injunction, and, if the question be finally decided favorably to the contention of the company, a permanent injunction restraining all such actions or proceedings.

This inquiry necessitates an examination of the most material and important objection made to the jurisdiction of the circuit court,—the objection being that the suit is, in effect, one against the state of Minnesota, and that the injunction issued against the attorney general illegally prohibits state action, either criminal or civil, to enforce obedience to the statutes of the state. This objection is to be considered with reference to the 11th and 14th Amendments to the Federal Constitution. * * *

Food for Thought

Is it significant that the Court considers the Eleventh Amendment objection only after having ruled on the merits?

The case before the circuit court proceeded upon the theory that the orders and acts heretofore mentioned would, if enforced, violate rights of the complainants protected by the latter amendment. We think that whatever the rights of complainants may be, they are largely founded upon that Amendment, but a decision of this case does not require an examination or decision of the question whether its adoption in any way altered or limited the effect of the earlier Amendment. We may assume that each exists in full force, and that we must give to the 11th Amendment all the effect it naturally would have, without cutting it down or rendering its meaning any more narrow than the language, fairly interpreted, would warrant. It applies to a suit brought against a state by one of its own citizens, as well as to a suit brought by a citizen of another state. Hans v. Louisiana (1890). It was adopted after the decision of this court in Chisholm v. Georgia (1793), where it was held that a state might be sued by a citizen of another state. Since that time there have been many cases decided in this court involving the 11th Amendment, among them being Osborn v. Bank of United States (1824), which held that the Amendment applied only to those suits in which the state was a party on the record. In the subsequent case of Sundry African Slaves v. Madrazo (1828), that holding was somewhat enlarged, and Chief Justice Marshall, delivering the opinion of the court, while citing *Osborn v. Bank of United States*, said that where the claim was made, as in the case then before the court, against the governor of Georgia as governor, and the demand was made upon him, not personally, but officially (for moneys in the treasury of the state and for slaves in possession of the state government), the state might be considered as the party on the record, and therefore the suit could not be maintained.

> **Take Note**
>
> The Court explicitly refuses to consider the interrelationship between the Eleventh and Fourteenth Amendments. It was not able, however, to avoid that question forever, as you will see in succeeding cases, particularly *Seminole Tribe of Florida v. Florida*, at page 721. Justice Harlan's dissent, at page 670, attempts to bring the question before the *Young* Court.

> **Take Note**
>
> Is that what Hans said? Upon which language in Justice Bradley's opinion for the Court do you think Justice Peckham relies? Three Justices from the Hans Court were also on the *Young* Court: Chief Justice Fuller, who was in the Hans majority, and Justices Brewer and Harlan, both of whom dissented in Hans. Perhaps it is significant that none of them said anything about this point.

Davis v. Gray (1872) reiterates the rule of *Osborn v. Bank of United States* so far as concerns the right to enjoin a state officer from executing a state law in conflict with the Constitution or a statute of the United States, when such execution will violate the rights of the complainant.

In Poindexter v. Greenhow (1885), it was adjudged that a suit against a tax collector who had refused coupons in payment of taxes, and, under color of a void law, was about to seize and sell the property of a taxpayer for nonpayment of his taxes, was a suit against him personally, as a wrongdoer, and not against the state.

Hagood v. Southern (1886) decided that the bill was, in substance, a bill for the specific performance of a contract between the complainants and the state of South Carolina; and, although the state was not in name made a party defendant, yet, being the actual party to the alleged contract the performance of which was sought, and the only party by whom it could be performed, the state was, in effect, a party to the suit, and it could not be maintained for that reason. The things required to be done by the actual defendants were the very things which, when done, would constitute a performance of the alleged contract by the state.

The cases upon the subject were reviewed, and it was held that a bill in equity brought against officers of a state, who, as individuals, have no personal interest in the subject-matter of the suit, and defend only as representing the state, where the relief prayed for, if done, would constitute a performance by the state of the alleged contract of the state, was a suit against the state.

* * *

The cases above cited do not include one exactly like this under discussion. They serve to illustrate the principles upon which many cases have been decided. We have not cited all the cases, as we have not thought it necessary. But the injunction asked for in the *Ayers* Case was to restrain the state officers from commencing suits under the act of May 12, 1887 (alleged to be unconstitutional), in the name of the state and brought to recover taxes for its use, on the ground that, if such suits were commenced, they would be a breach of a contract with the state. The injunction was declared illegal because the suit itself could not be entertained, as it was one against the state, to enforce its alleged contract. It was said, however, that, if the court had power to entertain such a suit, it would have power to grant the restraining order preventing the commencement of suits. It was not stated that the suit or the injunction was necessarily confined to a case of a threatened direct trespass upon or injury to property.

* * *

In *Smyth v. Ames* (1898) (another rate case), it was again held that a suit against individuals, for the purpose of preventing them, as officers of the state, from enforcing, by the commencement of suits or by indictment, an unconstitutional enactment, to the injury of the rights of the plaintiff, was not a suit against a state, within the meaning of the Amendment. [I]n answer to the objection that the suit was really against the state, it was said: "It is the settled doctrine of this court that a suit against individuals, for the purpose of preventing them, as officers of a state, from enforcing an unconstitutional enactment, to the injury of the rights of the plaintiff, is not a suit against the state within the meaning of that Amendment." The suit was to enjoin the enforcement of a statute of Nebraska because it was alleged to be unconstitutional, on account of the rates being too low to afford some compensation to the company, and contrary, therefore, to the 14th Amendment.

* * *

The various authorities we have referred to furnish ample justification for the assertion that individuals who, as officers of the state, are clothed with some duty in regard to the enforcement of the laws of the state, and who threaten and are about to commence proceedings, either of a civil or criminal nature, to enforce against parties affected an unconstitutional act, violating the Federal Constitution, may be enjoined by a Federal court of equity from such action.

* * *

The general discretion regarding the enforcement of the laws when and as he deems appropriate is not interfered with by an injunction which restrains the state officer from taking any steps towards the enforcement of an unconstitutional enactment, to the injury of complainant. In such case no affirmative action of any nature is directed, and the officer is simply prohibited from doing an act which he had no legal right to do. An injunction to prevent him from doing that which he has no legal right to do is not an interference with the discretion of an officer.

It is also argued that the only proceeding which the attorney general could take to enforce the statute, so far as his office is concerned, was one by mandamus, which would be commenced by the state, in its sovereign and governmental character, and that the right to bring such action is a necessary attribute of a sovereign government. It is contended that the complainants do not complain and they care nothing about any action which Mr. Young might take or bring as an ordinary individual, but that he was complained of as an officer, to whose discretion is confided the use of the name of the state of Minnesota so far as litigation is concerned, and that when or how he shall use it is a matter resting in his discretion and cannot be controlled by any court.

The answer to all this is the same as made in every case where an official claims to be acting under the authority of the state. The act to be enforced is alleged to be unconstitutional; and if it be so, the use of the name of the state to enforce an unconstitutional act to the injury of complainants is a proceeding without the authority of, and one which does not affect, the state in its sovereign or governmental capacity. It is simply an illegal act upon the part of a state official in attempting, by the use of the name of the state, to enforce a legislative enactment which is void because unconstitutional. If the act which the state attorney general seeks to enforce be a violation of the Federal Constitution, the officer, in proceeding under such enactment, comes into conflict with the superior authority of that Constitution, and he is in that case stripped of his official or representative character and is subjected in his person to the consequences of his individual conduct. The state has no power to impart to him any immunity from responsibility to the supreme authority of the United States. It would be an injury to complainant to harass it with a multiplicity of suits or litigation generally in an endeavor to enforce penalties under an unconstitutional enactment, and to prevent it ought to be within the jurisdiction of a court of equity. If the question of unconstitutionality, with reference, at least, to the Federal Constitution, be first raised in a Federal court, that court, as we think is shown by the authorities cited hereafter, has the right to decide it, to the exclusion of all other courts.

Take Note

There really are two theories competing for attention here. Can you spot both of them? Keep them in mind as you read the remainder of this chapter. Does it make any difference which theory is dominant?

* * *

It is further objected (and the objection really forms part of the contention that the state cannot be sued) that a court of equity has no jurisdiction to enjoin criminal proceedings, by indictment or otherwise, under the state law. This, as a general rule, is true. But there are exceptions. When such indictment or proceeding is brought to enforce an alleged unconstitutional statute, which is the subject-matter of inquiry in a suit already pending in a Federal court, the latter court, having first obtained jurisdiction over the subject-matter, has the right, in both civil and criminal cases, to hold and maintain such jurisdiction, to the exclusion of all other courts, until its duty is fully performed. But the Federal court cannot, of course, interfere in a case where the proceedings were already pending in a state court.

Where one commences a criminal proceeding who is already party to a suit then pending in a court of equity, if the criminal proceedings are brought to enforce the same right that is in issue before that court, the latter may enjoin such criminal proceedings * * * .

It is further objected that there is a plain and adequate remedy at law open to the complainants, and that a court of equity, therefore, has no jurisdiction in such case. It has been suggested that the proper way to test the constitutionality of the act is to disobey it, at least once, after which the company might obey the act pending subsequent proceedings to test its validity. But in the event of a single violation the prosecutor might not avail himself of the opportunity to make the test, as obedience to the law was thereafter continued, and he might think it unnecessary to start an inquiry. If, however, he should do so while the company was thereafter obeying the law, several years might elapse before there was a final determination of the question, and, if it should be determined that the law was invalid, the property of the company would have been taken during that time without due process of law, and there would be no possibility of its recovery.

Another obstacle to making the test on the part of the company might be to find an agent or employee who would disobey the law, with a possible fine and imprisonment staring him in the face if the act should be held valid. Take the passenger-rate act, for instance: A sale of a single ticket above the price mentioned in that act might subject the ticket agent to a charge of felony, and, upon conviction, to a fine of $5,000 and imprisonment for five years. It is true the company might pay the fine, but the imprisonment the agent would have to suffer personally. It would not be wonderful if, under such circumstances, there would not be a crowd of agents offering to disobey the law. The wonder would be that a single agent should be found ready to take the risk.

Take Note

Justice Peckham's double negative may obscure what he meant by "wonderful." He uses the word literally—"full of wonder," or "remarkable"—rather than in today's colloquial sense of "highly to be desired." The dilemma that the Court describes demonstrates why Congress, albeit not until 1934, passed the Declaratory Judgment Act.

* * *

There is nothing in the case before us that ought properly to breed hostility to the customary operation of Federal courts of justice in cases of this character.

The rule to show cause is discharged and the petition for writs of habeas corpus and certiorari is dismissed.

So ordered.

MR. JUSTICE HARLAN, dissenting:

* * *

Let it be observed that the suit instituted by Perkins and Shepard in the circuit court of the United States was, as to the defendant Young, one against him as, and only because he was, attorney general of Minnesota. No relief was sought against him individually, but only in his capacity as attorney general. And the manifest, indeed the avowed and admitted, object of seeking such relief, was to tie the hands of the state so that it could not in any manner or by any mode of proceeding, in its own courts, test the validity of the statutes and orders in question. It would therefore seem clear that within the true meaning of the 11th Amendment the suit brought in the Federal court was one, in legal effect, against the state,—as much so as if the state had been formally named on the record as a party,—and therefore it was a suit to which, under the Amendment, so far as the state or its attorney general was concerned, the judicial power of the United States did not and could not extend. If this proposition be sound it will follow,—indeed, it is conceded that if, so far as relief is sought against the attorney general of Minnesota, this be a suit against the state,—then, the order of the Federal court enjoining that officer from taking any action, suit, step, or proceeding to compel the railway company to obey the Minnesota statute was beyond the jurisdiction of that court and wholly void; in which case, that officer was at liberty to proceed in the discharge of his official duties as defined by the laws of the state, and the order adjudging him to be in contempt for bringing the mandamus proceeding in the state court was a nullity.

The fact that the Federal circuit court had, prior to the institution of the mandamus suit in the state court, preliminarily (but not finally) held the statutes of Minnesota and the orders of its railroad and warehouse commission in question to be in violation of the Constitution of the United States, was no reason why that court should have laid violent hands upon the attorney general of Minnesota, and by its orders have deprived the state of the services of its constitutional law officer in its own courts. Yet that is what was done by the Federal circuit court; for the intangible thing called a state, however extensive its powers, can never appear or be represented or known in any court in a litigated case, except by and through its officers. When, therefore, the Federal court forbade the defendant Young, as attorney general of Minnesota, from taking any action, suit, step, or proceeding whatever looking to the enforcement of the statutes in question, it said in effect to the state of Minnesota:

> [T]he Federal court adjudges that you, the state, although a sovereign for many important governmental purposes, shall not appear in your own courts, by your law officer, with the view of enforcing, or even for determining the validity of, the state enactments which the Federal court has, upon a preliminary hearing, declared to be in violation of the Constitution of the United States.

This principle, if firmly established, would work a radical change in our governmental system. It would inaugurate a new era in the American judicial system and in the relations of the national and state governments. It would enable the subordinate Federal courts to supervise and control the official action of the states as if they were "dependencies" or provinces. It would place the states of the Union in a condition of inferiority never dreamed of when the Constitution was adopted or when the 11th Amendment was made a part of the supreme law of the land. I cannot suppose that the great men who framed the Constitution ever thought the time would come when a subordinate Federal court, having no power to compel a state, in its corporate capacity, to appear before it as a litigant, would yet assume to deprive a state of the right to be represented in its own courts by its regular law officer. * * * Too little consequence has been attached to the fact that the courts of the states are under an obligation equally strong with that resting upon the courts of the Union to respect and enforce the provisions of the Federal Constitution as the supreme law of the land, and to guard rights secured or guaranteed by that instrument. We must assume—a decent respect for the states requires us to assume—that the state courts will enforce every right secured by the Constitution. If they fail to do so, the party complaining has a clear remedy for the protection of his rights; for he can come by writ of error, in an orderly, judicial way, from the highest court of the state to this tribunal for redress in respect of every right granted or secured by that instrument and denied by the state court.

Food for Thought

Does Justice Harlan here suggest that those who wrote and ratified the Eleventh Amendment intended to limit constitutional supremacy with respect to the states?

* * *

The essential and only question now before us or that need be decided is whether an order by the Federal court which prevents the state from being represented in its own courts, by its chief law officer, upon an issue involving the constitutional validity of certain state enactments, does not make a suit against the state within the meaning of the 11th Amendment. If it be a suit of that kind, then, it is conceded, the circuit court was without jurisdiction to fine and imprison the petitioner, and he must be discharged, whatever our views may be as to the validity of those state enactments. This must necessarily be so unless the Amendment has less force and a more restricted meaning now than it had at the time of its adoption, and unless a suit against the attorney general of a state, in his official capacity, is not one against a state under the 11th Amendment when its determination depends upon a question of constitutional power or right under the 14th Amendment. In that view I cannot concur. In my opinion the 11th Amendment has not been modified in the slightest degree as to its scope or meaning by the 14th Amendment, and a suit which, in its essence, is one against the state, remains one of that character and is forbidden even when brought to strike down a state statute alleged to be in violation of that clause of the 14th Amendment, forbidding the deprivation by a state of life, liberty, or property without due process of law.

* * *

* * * [T]o forbid the attorney general of a state (under the penalty of being punished as for contempt) from representing his state in suits of a particular kind, in its own courts, is to forbid the state itself from appearing and being heard in such suits. Neither the words nor the policy of the 11th Amendment will, under our former decisions, justify any order of a Federal court the necessary effect of which will be to exclude a state from its own courts. * * *

I dissent from the opinion and judgment.

Notes and Questions

1. Why does *Young* come out differently from Hans? If Hans had named the state treasurer instead of suing Louisiana, would it have made a difference? If the shareholders who brought the original action in *Young* had named Minnesota instead of its attorney general, would the case have followed Hans?

2. How does the *Young* Court read Hans? Was it an Eleventh Amendment case, an Article III constitutional immunity case, or an unabrogated-common-law immunity case, or a case turning purely on the Court's reading of the jurisdictional statute?

3. Note the mechanism that allows the federal proceeding against Young: he is "stripped" of his identity as an official of the state of Minnesota. Since the illegality strips Young of his official identity, how is there any basis under the Fourteenth Amendment for the shareholders' original suit? State action is a predicate for Fourteenth Amendment applicability. Where is the state action? Has the Court created a situation in which any unconstitutional action by a state official is not remediable because the state-action component no longer exists?

4. If the Court had upheld Young's claim, would the railroads and their shareholders have had no opportunity to challenge the rate statute other than by violating it and risking substantial penalties? Could the shareholders have brought a state action identical to the federal action?

a) Perhaps Minnesota would not have allowed such an action to proceed, but can a state court refuse to entertain a federal claim that is not exclusively federal? Should a state court be permitted to do so? Does the fact that until 1980 federal question cases, like diversity cases, were subject to a monetary jurisdictional floor suggest an answer?

A special problem exists if states refuse to entertain federal claims against the states themselves. At least in actions against non-state defendants, if the state closes its courts to federal claims, the federal courts may hear them; the same cannot be said for claims against the states. If the Eleventh Amendment prevents such actions in federal court, and the states can close their courts, what of the supposed supremacy of federal law?

> **FYI**
>
> *Testa v. Katt*, 330 U.S. 386 (1947), ruled that states cannot discriminatorily close their courts to federal claims. If a federal claim parallels a state claim (as, for example, a claim pursuant to the Civil Rights Act of 1871 (42 U.S.C. § 1983) may parallel a state tort claim) over which the state's courts have subject matter jurisdiction, the state may not keep the federal claim out. However, if the state does not permit a certain class of claims arising under state law, it may not have to entertain the class of cognate federal claims.

If a state maintains sovereign immunity against suit in its own courts, may it invoke the immunity in the face of a federal question action? One might have thought that the Supremacy Clause compelled a negative answer, but *Alden v. Maine*, 527 U.S. 706 (1999), held five-to-four that the sovereign immunity of states that the Eleventh Amendment reflects is substantive, not merely a forum immunity. The plaintiffs sought to recover from Maine based on violations of the federal Fair Labor Standards Act, which clearly applied to states. The majority held that Congress has no Article I power to compel the states (even if they are the proper subject of such legislation) to submit to adjudication of private suits in either state or federal court, relying on the constitutional structure that left the states intact as sovereigns in their own right. At the same time, the Court noted that

> The constitutional privilege of a State to assert its sovereign immunity in its own courts does not confer upon the State a concomitant right to disregard the Constitution or valid federal law. The States and their officers are bound by obligations imposed by the Constitution and by federal statutes that comport with the constitutional design. We are unwilling to assume the States will refuse to honor the Constitution or obey the binding laws of the United States. The good faith of the States thus provides an important assurance that "[t]his Constitution, and the Laws of the United States which shall be made in Pursuance thereof * * * shall be the supreme Law of the Land."

> **FYI**
>
> Note, however, that after the original disagreement about the Act's requirements, Maine began to comply. The dispute before the Court concerned only whether Maine should have to make the plaintiffs whole in light of the past transgressions.

The majority did not comment on the irony of its statement in light of the facts of the case before it, where the plaintiffs alleged precisely such a refusal. The Court did leave open the possibility that the United States, rather than private litigants, might be able to prosecute an enforcement action against Maine, but is

Alden's practical effect to leave individuals ostensibly protected by federal law with no way to enforce their entitlement *vis-à-vis* states or state agencies?

b) Assuming that the Young shareholders could have proceeded in state court, should they have been compelled to do so? If it is merely a matter of whether their claims were to be heard first in federal or state court, with possible United States Supreme Court review in either event, is the difference significant? This question goes to the heart of the parity debate, which raises several questions.

First, as an empirical matter, are the federal and state courts equal forums of justice on constitutional or other federal claims? Is there any way to determine this issue other than anecdotally? In laboratories one can set up "control cases," but in the judicial system that is rarely possible. If one could determine the question of parity as an empirical matter, and assuming that there is a demonstrable difference, is the difference something that the judicial system ought to acknowledge or are there unacceptable costs in conceding a lack of parity?

Food for Thought

Congress, at least, appears to harbor some doubts about parity. In 2005, it passed the Class Action Fairness Act, allowing removal of class actions involving at least $5,000,000 and having at least one plaintiff of diverse citizenship from one defendant (minimal diversity, also seen in the Federal Interpleader Act, 28 U.S.C. § 1335) from state to federal court. Congress acted to prevent plaintiff classes, particularly in mass tort cases, from seeking out favorable state courts ("magnet" jurisdictions) in which to bring claims.

Second, what weight should the plaintiff's choice of forum have in a case challenging official action? In most civil litigation, plaintiffs may choose among forums with jurisdiction over the subject matter and the parties, subject to removal, venue requirements, *forum non conveniens*, and transfer within the federal system, considerations that rarely, if ever, avail a *state* defendant anything. The Eleventh Amendment provides another forum-shifting device, one available exclusively to the states. Is it likely that the Congresses that enacted the Fourteenth Amendment, the Civil Rights Act of 1871, and 28 U.S.C. § 1331 contemplated that cases challenging state action on federal constitutional grounds should be brought only in the state court systems of which the Reconstruction Congresses had been so conspicuously suspicious? On the other hand, should the intentions of those nineteenth century Congresses have any weight in interpreting the Eleventh Amendment, enacted in the preceding century?

5. Justice Brennan called *Young* one of the most important constitutional cases of the century, undergirding most of the federal courts' involvement in civil rights in the twentieth century. Why did he have this view?

6. *Actions by States Against States*. The text of the Eleventh Amendment appears not to preclude suits for money damages in the federal courts by one state against

another. Nonetheless, the example of Hans v. Louisiana and the cases that have followed it cautions one not to place too much faith in the words themselves. *Kansas v. Colorado*, 533 U.S. 1 (2001), clarified the effect of the Eleventh Amendment on state-*versus*-state actions. If a state brings an action against another state acting only as a litigation front for individuals who retain effective control of the litigation, the Eleventh Amendment prevents the action. On the other hand, if the state is more than a nominal party and controls the litigation, the action may proceed, notwithstanding the state's intention to distribute the proceeds to individuals.

7. *Sub- and Extra-State Agencies—Municipalities*. In *Home Tel. and Tel. Co. v. City of Los Angeles*, 227 U.S. 278 (1913), the Court extended *Young*'s reasoning and echoed *Young*'s distinction between a litigant being a state for Eleventh Amendment purposes and acting under color of state law for Fourteenth Amendment purposes. Upon plaintiff's challenge to a municipal rate ordinance, the City argued that it was entitled to Eleventh Amendment protection and that its action did not become state action for Fourteenth Amendment purposes until the state had approved it, either legislatively or through judicial endorsement at the highest levels. The Court held that municipalities are not states for Eleventh Amendment purposes but are nonetheless state actors for Fourteenth Amendment purposes. The Court also found that municipal action not authorized by the state was state action for Fourteenth Amendment purposes. This aspect of the case anticipated the Douglas-Frankfurter debate in Monroe v. Pape, discussed throughout Chapter 6.

> **FYI**
>
> *Northern Ins. Co. v. Chatham County, Georgia*, 547 U.S. 189 (2006), reaffirmed that sub-state governments cannot avail themselves of the Eleventh Amendment's protection. In addition, a unanimous Court went further. The County did not rely on the Eleventh Amendment, but argued that it was the beneficiary of a "residual immunity" (in the words of the Court of Appeals) that common law had "carved out." The Supreme Court acknowledged that it had extended immunity on occasion to agencies acting as "an arm of the State," but held nonetheless that the County's concession that it was not an arm of the state for Eleventh Amendment purposes was dispositive as to whether it was an arm of the state for common law immunity purposes.

a) Home Telephone raises again questions of interpretive technique when dealing with materials more than a century old. Is it likely that those who passed the Eleventh Amendment so quickly after the shock of Chisholm v. Georgia contemplated that actions against states in the federal courts would not lie but that actions against state subdivisions would? Conversely, is it likely that the framers of the Fourteenth Amendment thought that it applied to states but not to municipalities?

With respect to the latter question, consider again the legislative history of § 1983. *Monell v. Department of Social Services*, 436 U.S. 658 (1978) (page 584) interpreted the rejection of the Sherman Amendment as Congress's unwillingness to impose new duties on state governmental subdivisions. Did the Fourteenth Amendment reflect the same understanding? If so, then what function was it to serve? If not, then was it § 1983 or the Amendment itself that imposed the "new duties" that some members of the House of Representatives thought inappropriate?

b) As a practical matter, what would have been the effect of accepting Los Angeles's argument that there was no state action until California had given the rate ordinance its *imprimatur*? What would have been the implications for the role of the inferior federal courts?

c) Does 28 U.S.C.A. § 1343 shed light on the likelihood that the Congress that enacted that jurisdictional statute and 42 U.S.C.A. § 1983 would have agreed with Los Angeles's interpretation of the state action requirement of the Fourteenth Amendment?

8. *Sub- and Extra-State Agencies—Multistate Agencies*. The Eleventh Amendment shields states from federal suit, but what about agencies formed by compacts among states with congressional consent pursuant to Article I, § 10, cl. 3? *Hess v. Port Auth. Trans-Hudson Corp.*, 513 U.S. 30 (1994), was the consolidation of two actions against PATH, a wholly-owned subsidiary of the Port Authority of New York and New Jersey, by employees injured on the job, and presented the issue of whether Eleventh Amendment immunity to federal suit extended to that bi-state agency. A five-to-four Court held that it did not. Justice Ginsburg's majority opinion and Justice O'Connor's dissent argued about the significance of the Port Authority's functional independence from the government of either state, given that each state appointed six commissioners, and the compact forbade Port Authority action if fewer than three commissioners from either state were present.

FYI

The Court relied in part on *Lake Country Estates, Inc. v. Tahoe Regional Planning Agency*, 440 U.S. 391 (1979), in which it had refused Eleventh Amendment immunity to a bi-state agency: "[u]nless there is good reason to believe that the States structured the new agency to enable it to enjoy the special constitutional protection of the States themselves, and that Congress concurred in that purpose."

a) Justice O'Connor also argued that *Hess* is incompatible with the Court's requiring either explicit congressional authorization of suits against the states in federal courts or explicit state consent to such suits to overcome the Eleventh Amendment. *See, e.g., Atascadero State Hospital v. Scanlon*, 473 U.S. 234 (1985), discussed in Note 6 at page 690 and Note 7 at page 699. Is it so obvious that the same standard ought to apply to a bi-state agency of limited purpose? The ostensible purpose of the Eleventh Amendment was to avoid interference with state governments in their sovereign capacities. Does a bi-state agency have a sovereign capacity, or is it more like a corporation simultaneously created by the laws of more than one state?

b) How could Justice Scalia join the dissenters? After all, the wording of the Eleventh Amendment is quite clear that it protects only "one of the United States." The Port Authority is not a state, and Justice Scalia has insisted on other occasions that when the words of a statutory provision are clear, resort to history, legislative or otherwise, is inappropriate. Has Justice Scalia ignored or forgotten his own counsel, or is the difference that the Court here deals with a constitutional rather than a statutory provision?

FYI

See, e.g., Pennsylvania v. Union Gas, 491 U.S. 1 (1989) ("It is our task, as I see it, not to enter the minds of the Members of Congress—who need have nothing in mind for their votes to be both lawful and effective—but rather to give fair and reasonable meaning to the text of the United States Code * * *.")

c) Given the majority's focus on the source of the funds to pay judgments (echoed in *Edelman v. Jordan*, 451 U.S. 651 (1974), at page 680), would you expect the Eleventh Amendment to bar a federal action nominally against a state agency if the federal government would entirely indemnify the state for any adverse judgment? In *Regents of the University of California v. Doe*, 519 U.S. 425 (1997), a unanimous Court held that the state retains its Eleventh Amendment immunity notwithstanding the federal government's undertaking. Is that result incompatible with the Court's analysis in *Hess*? If the money will not come from the state treasury, what purpose does the immunity serve? Is the purpose you identify not applicable in cases like where the money *does* come from the state treasury? In that respect, consider *Milliken v. Bradley*, discussed at page 689-90.

d) Several federal statutes channel funds to participating states to improve services to developmentally disabled individuals. One of the conditions of a state receiving such funds (and all do) is that the state create a "protection and advocacy" (P&A) system to enforce individuals' rights against the state. The entity the state creates for that purpose can be a state agency or a private nonprofit entity (at the state's option), but it must function independently of the state government, and federal law authorizes such entities to "pursue administrative, legal, and other remedies on behalf of protected individuals. The federal government also funds such entities. If the state elects to have a state agency perform the protection-and-advocacy function, does the Eleventh Amendment preclude an enforcement action by the agency against the state in federal court? A 6-2 Court held in *Virginia Office for Protection and Advocacy v. Stewart*, 131 S.Ct. 1632 (2011), that the Eleventh Amendment is no bar. (The state had conceded that a private entity would have been able to maintain the action.) Chief Justice Roberts's accusation that the majority authorized cannibalism or patricide by allowing a state agency to sue the state fell on deaf ears.

VOPA's effect on Eleventh Amendment jurisprudence generally is anything but clear, although on first glance the majority appeared to limit the scope of the states' sovereign immunity defense. None of the opinions pay much attention to the text. The Court's interpretation of this three-and-one-half line provision seems progressively to have elided more and more of its actual language. In Hans (at least as later Courts viewed it), the Court simply read the words "of another State" out of the Amendment, declining to ascribe any meaning to them, although not dealing with the question of why Congress might have included that phrase. In Seminole Tribe, (text at 721) the majority "explained" that the Amendment's words do not appear to contemplate federal question cases because no one was thinking about such cases.

Now comes VOPA, and the Amendment's two-fold reference to individuals seems also to have disappeared. However one might characterize agencies like VOPA, they certainly are neither "Citizens of another State, or * * * Citizens or Subjects of any Foreign State." Query whether the majority opinion presages a broader application of the Amendment's sovereign-immunity principle, unlimited by the newly-ignored text. Justice Scalia asserts that "there is no warrant in our cases for making the validity of an *Ex parte Young* action turn on the identity of the plaintiff." Perhaps so, but the Eleventh Amendment seems clearly to address plaintiffs' identity. Should that affect the Court's thinking?

Justice Scalia observed that since Hans, the Court has taken the position that "States entered the Union with their sovereign immunity intact, unlimited by Article III's jurisdictional grant." If one takes that language literally, it surely is a considerable overstatement. Article III, § 2 extends the judicial power to contests between states, and § 2 also vests original jurisdiction in the Supreme Court for any case "in which a State shall be a Party * * * ." Should that constitutional language inform the Court's view of the states' sovereign immunity?

The statutory foundation upon which the majority relied deserves some attention. The subsection that concerns the requirement of the state providing a P & A system reads: "[S]uch system shall * * * have the authority to * * * pursue legal, administrative, and other appropriate remedies and approaches * * * ." The following section of the statute reads, "Nothing in this subchapter shall preclude a [P & A] system from bringing a suit on behalf of individuals with developmental disabilities against a State, or an agency or instrumentality of a State." Do either of those sections unequivocally indicate that Congress intended to authorize *federal* actions against states? Does a state's acceptance of funds unequivocally indicate that the state has waived whatever immunity to federal suit it might otherwise have enjoyed?

The Eleventh Amendment cases taken as a whole reveal two emphases about its purpose. One, exemplified by Edelman v. Jordan, focuses on protecting state treasuries from private actions. The second, exemplified by Chief Justice Roberts's dissent in VOPA, focuses on the states' dignity interest as sovereigns in not being compelled to appear in the courts of another sovereign. If one were seeking a theory on which to limit or overrule Ex parte Young, which purpose would be better suited to the argument that Ex parte Young is either wrongly decided or has outlived its purpose?

8. It is easy to get so lost in the intricacies of the constitutional analysis in cases like Hans v. Louisiana and Ex parte Young that one overlooks their broader implications. On one level, they involve the amenability of states to suit in the federal courts as a matter of constitutional jurisprudence. On a wholly different level, however, they exemplify not just one but two power struggles that typify American society. The first pits the power of the central government against the individual states. The Eleventh Amendment is but one provision of the Constitution that seeks to address that balance, and Hans and Young reveal the federal judiciary's effort to understand the balance contemplated by the Constitution. The second struggle involves the power of government (here state government) over the individual. The Eleventh Amendment plays a part in that battle, too.

D. Extending and Cabining the Doctrine: The Limits of Limits

Edelman v. Jordan

Supreme Court of the United States, 1974.
415 U.S. 651.

MR. JUSTICE REHNQUIST delivered the opinion of the Court.

Respondent John Jordan filed a complaint in the United States District Court for the Northern District of Illinois, individually and as a representative of a class, seeking declaratory and injunctive relief against two former directors of the Illinois Department of Public Aid, the director of the Cook County Department of Public Aid, and the comptroller of Cook County. Respondent alleged that these state officials were administering the federal-state programs of Aid to the Aged, Blind, or Disabled (AABD) in a manner inconsistent with various federal regulations and with the Fourteenth Amendment to the Constitution.

AABD is one of the categorical aid programs administered by the Illinois Department of Public Aid pursuant to the Illinois Public Aid Code. Under the Social Security Act, the program is funded by the State and the Federal Governments. The Department of Health, Education, and Welfare (HEW), which administers these payments for the Federal Government, issued regulations prescribing maximum permissible time standards within which States participating in the program had to process AABD applications. Those regulations, originally issued in 1968, required, at the time of the institution of this suit, that eligibility determinations must be made by the States within 30 days of receipt of applications for aid to the aged and blind, and within 45 days of receipt of applications for aid to the disabled. For those persons found eligible, the assistance check was required to be received by them within the applicable time period.

During the period in which the federal regulations went into effect, Illinois public aid officials were administering the benefits pursuant to their own regulations as provided in the Categorical Assistance Manual of the Illinois Department of Public Aid. Respondent's complaint charged that the Illinois defendants, operating under those regulations, were improperly authorizing grants to commence only with the month in which an application was approved and not including prior eligibility months for which an applicant was entitled to aid under federal law. The complaint also alleged that the Illinois defendants were not processing the applications within the applicable time requirements of the federal regulations * * * . Such actions of the Illinois officials were alleged to violate federal law and deny the equal protection of the laws. Respondent's prayer requested declaratory and injunctive relief, and specifically requested "a permanent injunction enjoining the defendants to award to the entire class of plaintiffs all AABD benefits wrongfully withheld."

[T]he District Court declared § 4004 of the Illinois Manual to be invalid insofar as it was inconsistent with the federal regulations found in 45 C.F.R. § 206.10(a)(3), and granted a permanent injunction requiring compliance with the federal time limits for processing and paying AABD applicants. The District Court * * * also ordered the state officials to "release and remit AABD benefits wrongfully withheld to all applicants for AABD in the State of Illinois who applied between July 1, 1968 [the date of the federal regulations] and April 16, 1971 [the date of the preliminary injunction issued by the District Court] and were determined eligible * * * ."

On appeal to the * * * Seventh Circuit, the Illinois officials contended, *inter alia*, that the Eleventh Amendment barred the award of retroactive benefits * * * . The Court of Appeals rejected these contentions and affirmed the judgment of the District Court. * * * Because we believe the Court of Appeals erred in its disposition of the Eleventh Amendment claim, we reverse that portion of the Court of Appeals decision which affirmed the District Court's order that retroactive benefits be paid by the Illinois state officials.

* * *

The issue [of states' amenability to suit in the federal courts] was squarely presented to the Court in * * * in *Chisholm v. Georgia*. The decision in that case, that a State was liable to suit by a citizen of another State or of a foreign country, literally shocked the Nation. Sentiment for passage of a constitutional amendment to override the decision rapidly gained momentum, and five years after *Chisholm* the Eleventh Amendment was officially announced by President John Adams. * * *

While the Amendment by its terms does not bar suits against a State by its own citizens, this Court has consistently held that an unconsenting State is immune from suits brought in federal courts by her own citizens as well as by citizens of another State. It is also well established that even though a State is not named a party to the action, the suit may nonetheless be barred by the Eleventh Amendment. "[W]hen the action is in essence one for the recovery of money from the state, the state is the real, substantial party in interest and is entitled to invoke its sovereign immunity from suit even though individual officials are nominal defendants."

Thus the rule has evolved that a suit by private parties seeking to impose a liability which must be paid from public funds in the state treasury is barred by the Eleventh Amendment.

The Court of Appeals in this case, while recognizing that the *Hans* line of cases permitted the State to raise the Eleventh Amendment as a defense to suit by its own citizens, nevertheless concluded that the Amendment did not bar the award of retroactive payments of the statutory benefits found to have been wrongfully withheld * * * .

Petitioner concedes that *Ex parte Young* is no bar to that part of the District Court's judgment that prospectively enjoined petitioner's predecessors from failing to process applications within the time limits established by the federal regulations. Petitioner argues, however, that *Ex parte Young* does not extend so far as to permit a suit which seeks the award of an accrued monetary liability which must be met from the general revenues of a State, absent consent or waiver by the State of its Eleventh Amendment immunity, and that therefore the award of retroactive benefits by the District Court was improper.

Ex parte Young was a watershed case [that] * * * has permitted the Civil War Amendments to the Constitution to serve as a sword, rather than merely as a shield, for those whom they were designed to protect. But the relief awarded in *Ex parte Young* was prospective only; the Attorney General of Minnesota was enjoined to conform his future conduct of that office to the requirement of the Fourteenth Amendment. Such relief is analogous to that awarded by the District Court in the prospective portion of its order under review in this case.

But the retroactive portion of the District Court's order here, which requires the payment of a very substantial amount of money which that court held should have been paid, but was not, stands on quite a different footing. These funds will obviously not be paid out of the pocket of petitioner Edelman.

* * *

The funds to satisfy the award in this case must inevitably come from the general revenues of the State of Illinois, and thus the award resembles far more closely the monetary award against the State itself than it does the prospective injunctive relief awarded in *Ex parte Young*.

The Court of Appeals, in upholding the award in this case, held that it was permissible because it was in the form of "equitable restitution" instead of damages, and therefore capable of being tailored in such a way as to minimize disruptions of the state program of categorical assistance. But we must judge the award actually made in this case, and not one which might have been differently tailored in a different case, and we must judge it in the context of the important constitutional principle embodied in the Eleventh Amendment.[11]

We do not read *Ex parte Young* or subsequent holdings of this Court to indicate that any form of relief may be awarded against a state officer, no matter how closely it may in practice resemble a money judgment payable out of the state treasury, so long as the relief may be labeled "equitable" in nature. The Court's opinion in *Ex parte Young* hewed to no such line. * * *

As in most areas of the law, the difference between the type of relief barred by the Eleventh Amendment and that permitted under *Ex parte Young* will not in many instances be that between day and night. The injunction issued in *Ex parte Young* was not totally without effect on the State's revenues, since the state law which the Attorney General was enjoined from enforcing provided substantial monetary penalties against railroads which did not conform to its provisions. Later cases from this Court have authorized equitable relief which has probably had greater impact on state treasuries than did that awarded in *Ex parte Young*. * * * But the fiscal consequences to state treasuries in these cases were the necessary result of compliance with decrees which by their terms were prospective in nature. State officials, in order to shape their official conduct to the mandate

11 It may be true, as stated by our Brother Douglas in dissent, that "[m]ost welfare decisions by federal courts have a financial impact on the States." But we cannot agree that such a financial impact is the same where a federal court applies *Ex parte Young* to grant prospective declaratory and injunctive relief, as opposed to an order of retroactive payments as was made in the instant case. It is not necessarily true that "[w]hether the decree is prospective only or requires payments for the weeks or months wrongfully skipped over by the state officials, the nature of the impact on the state treasury is precisely the same." This argument neglects the fact that where the State has a definable allocation to be used in the payment of public aid benefits, and pursues a certain course of action such as the processing of applications within certain time periods as did Illinois here, the subsequent ordering by a federal court of retroactive payments to correct delays in such processing will invariably mean there is less money available for payments for the continuing obligations of the public aid system. * * *

of the Court's decrees, would more likely have to spend money from the state treasury than if they had been left free to pursue their previous course of conduct. Such an ancillary effect on the state treasury is a permissible and often an inevitable consequence of the principle announced in Ex parte Young.

But that portion of the District Court's decree which petitioner challenges on Eleventh Amendment grounds goes much further * * * . It requires payment of state funds, not as a necessary consequence of compliance in the future with a substantive federal-question determination, but as a form of compensation to those whose applications were processed on the slower time schedule at a time when petitioner was under no court-imposed obligation to conform to a different standard. While the Court of Appeals described this retroactive award of monetary relief as a form of "equitable restitution," it is in practical effect indistinguishable in many aspects from an award of damages against the State. It will to a virtual certainty be paid from state funds, and not from the pockets of the individual state officials who were the defendants in the action. It is measured in terms of a monetary loss resulting from a past breach of a legal duty on the part of the defendant state officials.

Food for Thought

Does the Court suggest here that a court-imposed obligation is more binding than an explicit federal statute?

* * *

Three fairly recent District Court judgments requiring state directors of public aid to make the type of retroactive payment involved here have been summarily affirmed by this Court notwithstanding Eleventh Amendment contentions made by state officers who were appealing from the District Court judgment. Shapiro v. Thompson is the only instance in which the Eleventh Amendment objection to such retroactive relief was actually presented to this Court in a case which was orally argued. The three-judge District Court in that case had ordered the retroactive payment of welfare benefits found by that court to have been unlawfully withheld because of residence requirements held violative of equal protection. This Court, while affirming the judgment, did not in its opinion refer to or substantively treat the Eleventh Amendment argument. Nor, of course, did the summary dispositions of the three District Court cases contain any substantive discussion of this or any other issues raised by the parties.

This case, therefore, is the first opportunity the Court has taken to fully explore and treat the Eleventh Amendment aspects of such relief in a

Food for Thought

Is it significant that the Court did not raise the Eleventh Amendment issue ***sua sponte***?

written opinion. *Shapiro v. Thompson* and these three summary affirmances obviously are of precedential value in support of the contention that the Eleventh Amendment does not bar the relief awarded by the District Court in this case. Equally obviously, they are not of the same precedential value as would be an opinion of this Court treating the question on the merits. Since we deal with a constitutional question, we are less constrained by the principle of *stare decisis* than we are in other areas of the law. Having now had an opportunity to more fully consider the Eleventh Amendment issue after briefing and argument, we disapprove the Eleventh Amendment holdings of those cases to the extent that they are inconsistent with our holding today.

The Court of Appeals held in the alternative that even if the Eleventh Amendment be deemed a bar to the retroactive relief awarded respondent in this case, the State of Illinois had waived its Eleventh Amendment immunity and consented to the bringing of such a suit by participating in the federal AABD program. The Court of Appeals relied upon our holdings in *Parden v. Terminal R. Co.* and *Petty v. Tennessee-Missouri Bridge Comm'n* and on the dissenting opinion of Judge Bright in *Employees v. Department of Public Health and Welfare*. While the holding in the latter case was ultimately affirmed by this Court, we do not think that the answer to the waiver question turns on the distinction between *Parden* and *Employees*. Both *Parden* and *Employees* involved a congressional enactment which by its terms authorized suit by designated plaintiffs against a general class of defendants which literally included States or state instrumentalities. Similarly, *Petty v. Tennessee-Missouri Bridge Comm'n* involved congressional approval, pursuant to the Compact Clause, of a compact between Tennessee and Missouri, which provided that each compacting State would have the power "to contract, to sue, and be sued in its own name." The question of waiver or consent under the Eleventh Amendment was found in those cases to turn on whether Congress had intended to abrogate the immunity in question, and whether the State by its participation in the program authorized by Congress had in effect consented to the abrogation of that immunity.

But in this case the threshold fact of congressional authorization to sue a class of defendants which literally includes States is wholly absent. Thus respondent is not only precluded from relying on this Court's holding in *Employees*, but on this Court's holdings in *Parden* and *Petty* as well.

The Court of Appeals held that as a matter of federal law Illinois had "constructively consented" to this suit by participating in the federal AABD program and agreeing to administer federal and state funds in compliance with federal law. Constructive consent is not a doctrine commonly associated with the surrender of constitutional rights, and we see no place for it here. In deciding whether a State has waived its constitutional protection under the Eleventh Amendment, we will find waiver only where stated "by the most express language or by such overwhelming implications from the text as [will] leave no room for any other reasonable construction." We see no reason to retreat from the Court's statement: "[W]hen we are dealing with the sovereign exemption from judicial interference in the vital field of financial administration a clear declaration of the state's intention to submit its fiscal problems to other courts than those of its own creation must be found."

The mere fact that a State participates in a program through which the Federal Government provides assistance for the operation by the State of a system of public aid is not sufficient to establish consent on the part of the State to be sued in the federal courts. And while this Court has, in cases such as *J.I. Case Co. v. Borak*, authorized suits by one private party against another in order to effectuate a statutory purpose, it has never done so in the context of the Eleventh Amendment and a state defendant. Since *Employees*, where Congress had expressly authorized suits against a general class of defendants and the only thing left to implication was whether the described class of defendants included States, was decided adversely to the putative plaintiffs on the waiver question, surely this respondent must also fail on that issue.

Our Brother Marshall argues in dissent, and the Court of Appeals held, that although the Social Security Act itself does not create a private cause of action, the cause of action created by 42 U.S.C. § 1983, coupled with the enactment of the AABD program, and the issuance by HEW of regulations which require the States to make corrective payments after successful "fair hearings" and provide for federal matching funds to satisfy federal court orders of retroactive payments, indicate that Congress intended a cause of action for public aid recipients such as respondent. It is, of course, true that * * * suits in federal court under § 1983 are proper to secure compliance with the provisions of the Social Security Act on the part of participating States. But it has not heretofore been suggested that § 1983 was intended to create a waiver of a State's Eleventh Amendment immunity merely because an action could be brought under that section against state officers, rather than against the State itself. Though a § 1983 action may be instituted by public aid recipients such as respondent, a federal court's remedial power, consistent with the Eleventh Amendment, is necessarily limited to prospective injunctive relief and may not include a retroactive award which requires the payment of funds from the state treasury.

Respondent urges that since the various Illinois officials sued in the District Court failed to raise the Eleventh Amendment as a defense to the relief sought by respondent, petitioner is therefore barred from raising the Eleventh Amendment defense in the Court of Appeals or in this Court. The Court of Appeals apparently felt the defense was properly presented, and dealt with it on the merits. We approve of this resolution, since it has been well settled * * * that the Eleventh

Amendment defense sufficiently partakes of the nature of a jurisdictional bar so that it need not be raised in the trial court * * * .

For the foregoing reasons we decide that the Court of Appeals was wrong in holding that the Eleventh Amendment did not constitute a bar to that portion of the District Court decree which ordered retroactive payment of benefits found to have been wrongfully withheld. The judgment of the Court of Appeals is therefore reversed and the cause remanded for further proceedings consistent with this opinion.

> **Food for Thought**
>
> Reconsider the Court's discussion of the four Supreme Court cases on which plaintiffs here relied, at pages 684-85.

So ordered.

MR. JUSTICE DOUGLAS, dissenting.

* * *

In this class action respondent sought to enforce against state aid officials of Illinois provisions of the Social Security Act known as the Aid to the Aged, Blind, or Disabled (AABD) program. The complaint alleges violations of the Equal Protection Clause of the Fourteenth Amendment and also violations of the Social Security Act. Hence § 1983 is satisfied ***in haec verba***, for a deprivation of "rights" which are "secured by the Constitution and laws" is alleged. The Court of Appeals, though ruling that the alleged constitutional violations had not occurred, sustained federal jurisdiction because federal "rights" were violated. The main issue tendered us is whether that ruling of the Court of Appeals is consistent with the Eleventh Amendment.

> **It's Latin to Me!**
>
> "In the same words; verbatim"

* * *

As the complaint in the instant case alleges violations by officials of Illinois of the Equal Protection Clause of the Fourteenth Amendment, it seems that the case is governed by *Ex parte Young* so far as injunctive relief is concerned. The main thrust of the argument is that the instant case asks for relief which if granted would affect the treasury of the State.

Most welfare decisions by federal courts have a financial impact on the States. Under the existing federal-state cooperative system, a state desiring to participate, submits a "state plan" to HEW for approval; once HEW approves the plan the State is locked into the cooperative scheme until it withdraws. * * * [T]he result in every welfare case coming here is to increase or reduce the financial responsibility of the participating State. In no case when the responsibility of the State is increased to meet the lawful demand of the beneficiary, is there any levy on state funds. Whether the decree is prospective only or requires payments for the weeks or months wrongfully skipped over by the state officials, the nature of the impact on the state treasury is precisely the same.

* * *

It is said however, that the Eleventh Amendment is concerned, not with immunity of States from suit, but with the jurisdiction of the federal courts to entertain the suit. The Eleventh Amendment does not speak of "jurisdiction"; it withholds the "judicial power" of federal courts "to any suit in law or equity * * * against one of the United States * * * ." If that "judicial power," or "jurisdiction" if one prefers that concept, may not be exercised even in "any suit in * * * equity" then *Ex parte Young* should be overruled. But there is none eager to take the step. Where a State has consented to join a federal-state cooperative project, it is realistic to conclude that the State has agreed to assume its obligations under that legislation. There is nothing in the Eleventh Amendment to suggest a difference between suits at law and suits in equity, for it treats the two without distinction. If common sense has any role to play in constitutional adjudication, once there is a waiver of immunity it must be true that it is complete so far as effective operation of the state-federal joint welfare program is concerned.

* * *

As the Court of Appeals in the instant case concluded, Illinois by entering into the joint federal-state welfare plan just as surely "[left] the sphere that is exclusively its own."

It is argued that participation in the program of federal financial assistance is not sufficient to establish consent on the part of the State to be sued in federal courts. But it is not merely participation which supports a finding of Eleventh Amendment waiver, but participation in light of the existing state of the law as exhibited in such decisions as *Shapiro v. Thompson*, which affirmed judgments ordering retroactive payment of benefits. Today's holding that the Eleventh Amendment forbids court-ordered retroactive payments, as the Court recognizes, necessitates an express overruling of several of our recent decisions. But it was against the background of those decisions that Illinois continued its participation in the federal program, and it can hardly be claimed that such participation was in ignorance of the possibility of court-ordered retroactive payments. The decision to participate against the background of precedent can only be viewed as a waiver of immunity from such judgments.

I would affirm the judgment of the Court of Appeals.

MR. JUSTICE BRENNAN, dissenting.

This suit is brought by Illinois citizens against Illinois officials. In that circumstance, Illinois may not invoke the Eleventh Amendment, since that Amendment bars only federal court suits against States by citizens of other States. Rather, the question is whether Illinois may avail itself of the nonconstitutional but ancient doctrine of sovereign immunity as a bar to respondent's claim for retroactive AABD payments. In my view Illinois may not assert sovereign immunity * * *: the States surrendered that immunity in Hamilton's words, "in the plan of the Convention," that formed the Union, at least insofar as the States granted Congress specifically enumerated powers.

I would affirm the judgment of the Court of Appeals.

Notes and Questions

1. What reading of *Hans* and the Eleventh Amendment does the Court adopt? Is it fair to say that *Hans* now stands for the proposition that the Eleventh Amendment prohibits federal question suits against the states, whether named or sued through their officials?

2. Should *Ex parte Young* have helped the plaintiffs here? The majority argues that the district court's judgment would have its impact only on the state. Yet, the injunction in *Young* affected only the state; Young had no personal interest in enforcing the rate statute. Should *Edelman* and *Young* come out the same way?

3. In *Edelman,* even the part of the lower court's decision that the majority approved would have a direct financial impact on the state. Why does that not violate the Eleventh Amendment? Is Justice Douglas's dissent correct that there is no principled distinction between a money judgment based on past conduct and a judgment that compels future disbursement of funds by ordering the state to behave in a certain way?

Milliken v. Bradley, 433 U.S. 267 (1977), approved a district court order that promised to force expenditure of millions of dollars of state funds in a school desegregation case. In dealing with the *Edelman* problem, the Court observed:

> The decree to share the future costs of educational components in this case fits squarely within the prospective-compliance exception reaffirmed by *Edelman.* That exception, which had its genesis in *Ex parte Young*, permits federal courts to enjoin state officials to conform their conduct to requirements of federal law, notwithstanding a direct and substantial impact on the state treasury. The order challenged here does no more than that. * * *

4. *Edelman* did not end the battle over Illinois's administration of this program. Several years later, the plaintiffs returned to the Supreme Court with a new judgment to protect. *Quern v. Jordan,* 440 U.S. 332 (1979), affirmed the Seventh Circuit's refusal to allow a federal court to order officials to notify recipients of AABD funds that officials had wrongfully withheld some funds, though it did allow an order requiring officials to notify recipients of the *possibility* of wrongful withholding and to supply a form to set a review process in motion.

Even that limited relief was narrower than might first appear. *Green v. Mansour,* 474 U.S. 64 (1985), disapproved so-called "notice relief," explaining that it had been allowed in *Quern* only because it was ancillary to prospective relief permitted under what the Court characterized as the narrow exception to states' sovereign immunity recognized by *Ex parte Young*.

5. *Edelman* distinguishes several cases, arguing that Congress intended in those cases to abrogate the states' immunity under the Eleventh Amendment and make them amenable to suit in the federal courts. How can Congress do that? If Congress, in setting up the AABD program, had provided that states could be sued in the federal courts in their own names, would the Court have honored that legislation or declared it unconstitutional as conflicting with the Eleventh Amendment?

6. *Atascadero State Hospital v. Scanlon*, 473 U.S. 234 (1985), demonstrated how rigorously the Court would examine claims of waiver of immunity or consent. Scanlon sought damages under the federal Rehabilitation Act of 1973. A section of the California Constitution provided: "Suits may be brought against the State in such manner and in such courts as shall be directed by law." The Court held the language insufficient to waive the state's Eleventh Amendment immunity: "in order for a state statute or constitutional provision to constitute a waiver of Eleventh Amendment immunity, it must specify the State's intention to subject itself to suit in federal court * * * ."

The Court also rejected the idea that the state consented by accepting federal funds under a statute that permitted suit against "any recipient." "The Act * * * falls short of manifesting a clear intent to condition participation in the programs funded under the Act on a State's consent to waive its constitutional immunity."

7. Is a case asserting all federal question claims, some running against a state and some against individuals, removable? If the state, as a defendant, consents to

or initiates removal, does that constitute consent to the federal forum that vitiates the Eleventh Amendment bar? *Wisconsin Department of Corrections v. Schacht*, 524 U.S. 381 (1998), confronted both questions. Justice Breyer's opinion for a unanimous Court held that "the presence in an otherwise removable case of a claim that the Eleventh Amendment may bar does not destroy removal jurisdiction that would otherwise exist." In the course of the discussion, the opinion considered whether the Amendment is an immunity or a component of subject matter jurisdiction, seeming to view it only as the former:

> The Eleventh Amendment, however, does not automatically destroy original jurisdiction. Rather, the Eleventh Amendment grants the State a legal power to assert a sovereign immunity defense should it choose to do so. The State can waive the defense. Nor need a court raise the defect on its own. Unless the State raises the matter, a court can ignore it. * * *
>
> * * *
>
> A State's proper assertion of an Eleventh Amendment bar after removal means that the federal court cannot hear the barred claim. But that circumstance does not destroy removal jurisdiction over the remaining claims in the case before us.

The Court's careful parsing of the sequence of events and its reliance on the fact that at the time of removal, the State had asserted no Eleventh Amendment immunity is perhaps surprising, given earlier treatments of the Amendment as a jurisdictional provision. If the Amendment provides only an immunity defense, does that have implications for cases like *Edelman* and *Pennhurst State School & Hospital v. Halderman*, *infra* at 757?

Justice Kennedy, although joining the Court's opinion with its apparent rejection of the waiver theory, also wrote separately to discuss waiver, noting that it should be considered "in some later case." He left little doubt, however, that he supported the waiver theory, effectively regarding the Eleventh Amendment as an affirmative defense under Rule 8(c). Is that a desirable change?

9. In *Lapides v. Board of Regents*, 535 U.S. 613 (2002), a unanimous Court took at least one step that Justice Kennedy had urged, holding that the state's decision to join in removal (necessary because under 28 U.S.C. § 1441(a) all defendants must agree for the case to be removable) constituted a waiver of the Eleventh Amendment protection. Thus, *Schacht*'s statement acknowledging the state's entitlement to raise its Eleventh Amendment claim subsequent to removal is no longer accurate.

Justice Breyer's opinion drew a careful distinction between litigation and non-litigation conduct as a source of Eleventh Amendment waiver. Whereas the Court will be extremely reluctant to infer waiver from non-litigation conduct, a state's voluntary invocation of federal jurisdiction will suffice. *Lapides* leaves some interesting questions in its wake, however. The Court emphasized that the case did not involve any federal claims against the state, having only state law claims to which the state had waived immunity state actions. The plaintiff had asserted a § 1983 claim for damages against the individual defendants, but the Court had previously held that states are not "persons" within the meaning of § 1983. If the plaintiff had joined a federal claim against the state, should not the state's removal still constitute a waiver of Eleventh Amendment immunity?

After *Lapides*, should a state's decision to eschew its Eleventh Amendment defense in the district court in favor of litigating on the merits represent an acceptance of federal jurisdiction no less significant than that in *Lapides* itself? If the Eleventh Amendment only bars the federal courts from exercising jurisdiction over suits against unconsenting states, do states really waive a limitation on the subject matter jurisdiction of the federal courts by consenting to suits, or is the limitation simply inapplicable to such suits? Does treating amenability to suit under the rubric of consent rather than waiver solve the problem or merely change the battleground?

Edelman demonstrated that the stripping theory of *Ex parte Young* would avail individual plaintiffs nothing if they sought damages, even if the damages were characterized as something else such as "equitable restitution." The successors to *Edelman* discussed in Note 4 show how rigorously the Court would enforce the prospective/retroactive distinction. In 1997, the Court decided that even some prospective relief was not exempted from the Eleventh Amendment's proscription.

Idaho v. Coeur d'Alene Tribe, 521 U.S. 261 (1997), involved a dispute between the Tribe and the state over Lake Coeur d'Alene and the water system of which it is a part. The Tribe claimed beneficial interest in the lake and its submerged lands, pursuant to an 1873 Executive Order establishing the Tribe's reservation and ownership by unextinguished aboriginal title. It sought declaratory and injunctive relief and associated costs and attorney's fees. A fractured Court decided that even though the Tribe sought only prospective relief, the Eleventh Amendment prevented the action.

There were three opinions. Justice Kennedy, whom the Chief Justice joined *in toto* and Justices O'Connor, Scalia and Thomas joined in part, held the Tribe's action to be "the functional equivalent of a quiet title action which [*sic*] implicates special sovereignty interests." Tracing the states' interests in their submerged lands back to colonial times, the majority effectively declared actions involving such land to be special cases, not appropriate for resolution under the usual Eleventh Amendment framework. Justices Souter, with whom Justices Stevens, Ginsburg and Breyer joined, dissented.

In a part of Justice Kennedy's opinion that only Chief Justice Rehnquist joined, Justice Kennedy argued that the availability of an action in the state courts should cut heavily against federal jurisdiction. Justice Kennedy characterized the *Ex parte Young* doctrine as having two primary applications: where no state forum is available and when "the case calls for an interpretation of federal law." He pointed out that the Idaho courts could have heard the Tribe's claim, and argued that there should be no assumption that federal issues necessarily called for federal court interpretation and suggested that the proper approach to the doctrine of *Ex parte Young* was a "case-by-case" balancing. As part of that balancing, heattempted to import into the jurisdictional analysis the far more restrictive "special factors counseling hesitation" that the Court has employed in determining whether to imply private rights of action in constitutional or statutory provisions.

Justices O'Connor, Scalia and Thomas declined to join those sections of Justice Kennedy's opinion. Justice O'Connor and her concurring colleagues rejected Justice Kennedy's attempt to reformulate *Ex parte Young* more generally. "This approach unnecessarily recharacterizes and narrows much of our *Young* jurisprudence."

Specifically, Justice O'Connor took issue with Justice Kennedy's assertion that unavailability of a state forum was a factor in *Ex parte Young* analysis, arguing that the Court had never articulated such a rationale. In addition, she objected to Justice Kennedy's downplaying of the importance of federal adjudication of important federal matters, highlighting the split between Justice Kennedy's approach and her own.

She argued that the availability of the federal forum under *Young* turned only on whether the relief sought was prospective or retroactive. Finally, she disputed Justice Kennedy's attempt to "import the inquiry employed in *Bivens* into our *Young* jurisprudence," although she acknowledged that *Seminole Tribe*, decided the year before, offered limited support for that notion.

Justice Souter's dissent argued that the case fell "squarely within the *Young* doctrine" and that Congress had imposed a jurisdictional obligation to hear such cases. He viewed *Seminole Tribe* (in which he also dissented) as leaving the basic structure of the *Young* doctrine intact, resting instead on the conclusion that in that particular circumstance there was an indication that Congress did not intend the *Young* doctrine to apply.[1]

---

1 Assuming that *Seminole Tribe* does reflect that view, it creates a problem that Justice Souter did not address in his *Coeur d'Alene* opinion. If *Young* stripping occurs because of supremacy, as Justice Peckham's opinion for the Court reflects and as the majority opinion in *Pennhurst State School & Hosp. v. Halderman (1984)* (*see infra* page 757) confirms, then why is it possible for Congress to declare that that constitutional interest should be disregarded in a particular case?

Justice Souter identified two points of commonality between Justices Kennedy and O'Connor with respect to the non-applicability of Ex parte Young. The first was the "functional equivalent" analysis that both subscribed on the basis that the Tribe's success "was an aspersion on the government's claim of title." Justice Souter raised two arguments. He argued first that the Framers could not have intended to leave the individual remediless in such circumstances, and second that logic was against the majority's view on this point, because all Young actions are the functional equivalent of actions against the state. This had the effect of pointing out the true fiction of Ex parte Young: not that an officer can simultaneously be the state (for Fourteenth Amendment purposes) and not be the state (for Eleventh Amendment purposes), but rather that in allowing the action to proceed against the officer, the federal courts are nonetheless not affecting the state.

Fitzpatrick v. Bitzer

Supreme Court of the United States, 1976.
427 U.S. 445.

MR. JUSTICE REHNQUIST delivered the opinion of the Court.

In the 1972 Amendments to Title VII of the Civil Rights Act of 1964, Congress, acting under § 5 of the Fourteenth Amendment, authorized federal courts to award money damages in favor of a private individual against a state government found to have subjected that person to employment discrimination on the basis of "race, color, religion, sex, or national origin." The principal question presented by these cases is whether, as against the shield of sovereign immunity afforded the State by the Eleventh Amendment * * * , Congress has the power to authorize federal courts to enter such an award against the State as a means of enforcing the substantive guarantees of the Fourteenth Amendment. The Court of Appeals for the Second Circuit held that the effect of * * * *Edelman* was to foreclose Congress' power. * * * . We reverse.

I

Petitioners in No. 75-251 sued in the United States District Court for the District of Connecticut on behalf of all present and retired male employees of the State of Connecticut. Their amended complaint asserted, *inter alia,* that certain provisions in the State's statutory retirement benefit plan discriminated against them because of their sex, and therefore contravened Title VII of the 1964 Act. Title VII, which originally did not include state and local governments, had in the interim been amended to bring the States within its purview.

The District Court held that the Connecticut State Employees Retirement Act violated Title VII's prohibition against sex-based employment discrimination.[3] It entered prospective injunctive relief in petitioners' favor against respondent state officials. Petitioners also sought an award of retroactive retirement benefits as compensation for losses caused by the State's discrimination, as well as "a reasonable attorney's fee as part of the costs." But the District Court held that both would constitute recovery of money damages from the State's treasury, and were therefore precluded by the Eleventh Amendment and by this Court's decision in *Edelman v. Jordan*.

On petitioners' appeal, the Court of Appeals affirmed in part and reversed in part. It agreed with the District Court that the action, "insofar as it seeks damages, is in essence against the state and as such is subject to the Eleventh Amendment." The Court of Appeals also found that under the 1972 Amendments to Title VII, "Congress intended to authorize a private suit for backpay by state employees against the state." Notwithstanding this statutory authority, the Court of Appeals affirmed the District Court and held that under *Edelman* a "private federal action for retroactive damages" is not a "constitutionally permissible method of enforcing Fourteenth Amendment rights." It reversed the District Court and remanded as to attorneys' fees, however, reasoning that such an award would have only an "ancillary effect" on the state treasury of the kind permitted under *Edelman*. The petition filed here by the state employees in No. 75-251 contends that Congress does possess the constitutional power under § 5 of the Fourteenth Amendment to authorize their Title VII damage action against the State. The state officials' cross-petition, No. 75-283, argues that under *Edelman* the Eleventh Amendment bars any award of attorneys' fees here because it would be paid out of the state treasury.

II

In *Edelman* this Court held that monetary relief awarded by the District Court to welfare plaintiffs, by reason of wrongful denial of benefits which had occurred previous to the entry of the District Court's determination of their wrongfulness, violated the Eleventh Amendment. Such an award was found to be indistinguishable from a monetary award against the State itself which had been prohibited in *Ford Motor Co. v. Department of Treasury* (1945). It was therefore controlled by that case rather than by *Ex parte Young*, which permitted suits against state officials to obtain prospective relief against violations of the Fourteenth Amendment. * * * We concluded that none of the statutes relied upon by plaintiffs in *Edelman* contained any authorization by Congress to join a State as defendant. The Civil Rights Act of 1871 had been held in *Monroe v. Pape* to exclude cities and other municipal corporations from its ambit; that being the case, it could not have been

3 Petitioners had also alleged that the retirement plan was contrary to the Equal Protection Clause of the Fourteenth Amendment, but in view of its ruling under Title VII the District Court found no reason to address the constitutional claim.

intended to include States as parties defendant. The provisions of the Social Security Act relied upon by plaintiffs were held by their terms not to "authorize suit against anyone," and they, too, were incapable of supplying the predicate for a claim of waiver on the part of the State. All parties in the instant litigation agree with the Court of Appeals that the suit for retroactive benefits by the petitioners is in fact indistinguishable from * * * Edelman, since what is sought here is a damages award payable to a private party from the state treasury.

Food for Thought

Two years after *Fitzpatrick*, the Court ruled in Monell that municipalities were indeed persons for § 1983 purposes. Nonetheless, the Court held in *Will v. Michigan Dept. of State Police*, 491 U.S. 58 (1989), that states were not.

Our analysis begins where Edelman ended, for in this Title VII case the "threshold fact of congressional authorization" to sue the State as employer is clearly present. This is, of course, the prerequisite found present in Parden and wanting in Employees. We are aware of the factual differences between the type of state activity involved in Parden and that involved in the present case, but we do not think that difference is material for our purposes. The congressional authorization involved in Parden was based on the power of Congress under the Commerce Clause; here, however, the Eleventh Amendment defense is asserted in the context of legislation passed pursuant to Congress' authority under § 5 of the Fourteenth Amendment.

FYI

This sentence is a bit misleading. The Court decided *Parden* on a waiver theory, not merely because Congress appeared to have contemplated such actions.

As ratified by the States after the Civil War, that Amendment quite clearly contemplates limitations on their authority.

* * *

The substantive provisions are by express terms directed at the States. Impressed upon them by those provisions are duties with respect to their treatment of private individuals. Standing behind the imperatives is Congress' power to "enforce" them "by appropriate legislation." The impact of the Fourteenth Amendment upon the relationship between the Federal Government and the States, and the reach of congressional power under § 5, were examined at length by this Court in Ex parte Virginia (1880). A state judge had been arrested and indicted under a federal criminal statute prohibiting the exclusion on the basis of race of any citizen from service as a juror in a state court. The judge claimed that the statute was beyond Congress' power to enact under either the Thirteenth or the Fourteenth Amendment. The Court first observed that these Amendments "were intended to be, what they really are, limitations of the power of the States and enlargements of the power of Congress." It then addressed the relationship between the language of § 5 and the substantive provisions of the Fourteenth Amendment:

> The prohibitions of the Fourteenth Amendment are directed to the States, and they are to a degree restrictions of State power. It is these which Congress is empowered to enforce, and to enforce against State action, however put forth, whether that action be executive, legislative, or judicial. Such enforcement is no invasion of State sovereignty. No law can be, which the people of the States have, by the Constitution of the United States, empowered Congress to enact * * * . Nor can [a state] deny to the general government the right to exercise all its granted powers, though they may interfere with the full enjoyment of rights she would have if those powers had not been thus granted. Indeed, every addition of power to the general government involves a corresponding diminution of the governmental powers of the States. It is carved out of them.

* * *

> [T]he Constitution now expressly gives authority for congressional interference and compulsion in the cases embraced within the Fourteenth Amendment. It is but a limited authority, true, extending only to a single class of cases; but within its limits it is complete.

Ex parte Virginia's early recognition of this shift in the federal-state balance has been carried forward by more recent decisions * * * .

* * *

It is true that none of these previous cases presented the question of the relationship between the Eleventh Amendment and the enforcement power granted to Congress under § 5 of the Fourteenth Amendment. But we think that the Eleventh Amendment, and the principle of state sovereignty which it embodies, * * * are necessarily limited by the enforcement provisions of § 5 of the Fourteenth Amendment. In that section Congress is expressly granted authority to enforce "by appropriate legislation" the substantive provisions of the Fourteenth Amendment, which themselves embody significant limitations on state authority. When Congress acts pursuant to § 5, not only is it exercising legislative authority that is plenary within the terms of the constitutional grant, it is exercising that authority under one section of a constitutional Amendment whose other sections by their own terms embody limitations on state authority. We think that Congress may, in determining what is "appropriate legislation" for the purpose of enforcing the provisions of the Fourteenth Amendment, provide for private suits against States or state officials which are constitutionally impermissible in other contexts.

* * *

The judgment in No. 75-251 is

Reversed.

The judgment in No. 75-283 is

Affirmed.

Notes and Questions

1. What reading of *Hans*, *Ex parte Young* and the Eleventh Amendment does the Court adopt?

2. *Fitzpatrick* is indeed an unusual case. In deciding that Congress can act under the Fourteenth Amendment to limit the ambit of the Eleventh, the Court recognized a significant shift of power from the states to the federal government. At the outset, the fact that Justice Rehnquist (hardly a proponent of expanded federal power at the expense of state governments) wrote the opinion deserves some thought. Why did he take the position he did?

3. a) The conclusion that Congress intended the Fourteenth Amendment to limit state power is not surprising. The Congress passed it in 1868, at the height of Radical Reconstruction. Does the Court hold that the Fourteenth Amendment itself limits the Eleventh Amendment? After *Fitzpatrick*, can any case asserting a due process violation be brought against a state in the federal courts? If not, how can the Court justify, on the wording of the Fourteenth Amendment and its legislative history, stopping short of that result? If so, is Edelman overruled *sub silentio*?

b) *Fitzpatrick*, and Monell's reinterpretation of § 1983 to include municipalities, raised the possibility that § 1983 actions in the federal courts could run also against the states themselves. Congress enacted § 1983 under § 5 of the Fourteenth Amendment, and pursuant to the Court's reasoning in *Fitzpatrick*, Congress could have abrogated the states' Eleventh Amendment immunity. But in *Quern v. Jordan*, 440 U.S. 332 (1979), the Court announced that it had not, because the Court did not think § 1983's legislative history clearly showed Congress's intent to limit the Eleventh Amendment. The debates on § 1983 did not mention the Eleventh Amendment, and the majority asserted that if the legislators had understood the Civil Rights Act to override the Eleventh Amendment, there would have been a major outcry. Was the majority assuming its conclusion?

Quern and Will do not mean that § 1983 is of no use against state officials. *Hafer v. Melo,* 502 U.S. 21 (1991), held that state officials sued in their individual capacities may be liable under § 1983, and that the predicate acts may be within or without their authority, provided only that the actions are taken under color of state law. After Hafer, what does Will accomplish? Has a potential § 1983 plaintiff lost anything as a result of Will that Hafer did not fully restore?

4. Do you think the Constitution-modifying effect of the Fourteenth Amendment applies only to the Eleventh Amendment or does it apply to other parts of the Constitution? Suppose, for example, Congress decides to attack the problem of "hate speech" by making it a criminal offense. If Congress finds the restriction necessary to secure due process and equal protection of the laws under the Fourteenth Amendment for groups that are the targets of hate speech, does that save it from constitutional infirmity on First Amendment grounds?

5. Is the *Ex parte Young* fiction necessary to the result in *Fitzpatrick*? If the plaintiffs in *Fitzpatrick* had joined the state of Connecticut as a defendant, would the Court have permitted the suit to proceed?

6. Does § 5 of the Fourteenth Amendment, as *Fitzpatrick* interprets it, effectively authorize Congress to amend the Constitution, or at least the Eleventh Amendment?

7. *Atascadero State Hospital v. Scanlon,* 473 U.S. 234 (1985), demonstrated that the Court will not lightly infer *Fitzpatrick* abrogation. Scanlon argued that when Congress specifically included states as recipients of federal funds under the Rehabilitation Act of 1973 and further provided for private actions against "any recipient" of such funds, it removed the states' Eleventh Amendment immunity to private enforcement actions. The majority disagreed, noting

> the requirement, well established in our cases, that Congress unequivocally express its intention to abrogate the Eleventh Amendment bar to suits against the States in federal court. We * * * affirm that Congress may abrogate the States' constitutionally secured immunity from suit in federal court only by making its intention unmistakably clear in the language of the statute.

Justice Brennan dissented, joined by three other Justices. He argued at length that the Court had taken a wrong turn with respect to the Eleventh Amendment in Hans and had continued to misunderstand the Amendment's place in the constitutional structure. According to him, the Amendment meant only to preserve in diversity actions a sovereign immunity defense to state-law claims that the states would have enjoyed in their own courts. His position, then and since, has failed to attract the crucial fifth vote.

8. In *Dellmuth v. Muth,* 491 U.S. 223 (1989), Muth sought damages from the Acting Secretary of Education of Pennsylvania for violations of the federal Education of the Handicapped Act. In a 5-4 decision, the Court upheld the state's Eleventh Amendment immunity claim, noting that Congress had not met *Atascadero*'s standard of explicitness.

> Legislative history generally will be irrelevant to a judicial inquiry into whether Congress intended to abrogate the Eleventh Amendment. If Congress' intention is "unmistakably clear in the language of the statute," recourse to legislative history will be unnecessary; if Congress' intention is not unmistakably clear, recourse to legislative history will be futile, because by definition the rule of *Atascadero* will not be met.

Justice Brennan, joined by Justices Blackmun, Marshall, and Stevens, dissented, predictably differing with the majority on the issue of the "unmistakability" of Congress's intent, but also noting the following:

> Congress has already had cause to complain of the Court's changing its interpretive rules in mid-course. After the Court held in *Atascadero* that § 504 of the Rehabilitation Act of 1973, * * * contained no "unmistakable language" abrogating Eleventh Amendment immunity, * * * Congress in 1986 enacted an amendment to the Act providing:
>
> A State shall not be immune under the Eleventh Amendment of the Constitution of the United States from suit in Federal court for a violation of [enumerated provisions of the Rehabilitation Act] or the provisions of any other Federal statute prohibiting discrimination by recipients of Federal financial assistance.
>
> Congress enacted this provision, the Senate Conference Report tells us, because "[t]he Supreme Court's decision [in *Atascadero*] misinterpreted congressional intent. Such a gap in Section 504 coverage was never intended. It would be inequitable for Section 504 to mandate state compliance with its provisions and yet deny litigants the right to enforce their rights in Federal courts when State or State agency actions are in issue."

Should the 1986 Congress's effort have precluded subsequent "misinterpretations" by the Court, or was it insufficiently specific about which statutes it

FYI

Congress had provided, *inter alia,* that "it is in the national interest that the Federal government assist State and local efforts to provide programs to meet the education needs of handicapped children in order to assure equal protection of the law," 20 U.S.C.A. § 1400(b)(9) (1982), and had authorized aggrieved parties to "bring a civil action * * * in any State court of competent jurisdiction or in a district court of the United States without regard to the amount in controversy." 20 U.S.C.A. § 1415(e)(2) (1982). Perhaps most important, a 1986 amendment stated that the Act's provision for a *reduction* of attorney's fees did not apply "if the court finds that the State or local educational agency unreasonably protracted the final resolution of the action or proceeding or there was a violation of this section." 20 U.S.C.A. § 1415(e)(4)(G) (1982 ed. Supp. V.)

included? Did the 1986 amendment implicitly express disapproval of the Court's new interpretive method? If so, should the Court accede, or is Congress stuck with the rules the Court has created?

a) Some commentators have been critical of this aspect of the Court's Eleventh Amendment jurisprudence. Professors Eskridge and Frickey, discussing the plethora of "clear statement" rules upon which the Court has increasingly insisted, note the following:

> Since *Atascadero*, the Court has stuck with this super-strong clear statement rule concerning congressional abrogation of Eleventh Amendment immunity and has applied a similarly strict approach to judging whether a state itself has waived its Eleventh Amendment rights. * * *

William N. Eskridge, Jr. & Philip P. Frickey, *Quasi-Constitutional Law: Clear Statement Rules As Constitutional Lawmaking*, 45 VAND.L.REV. 593, 621-22 (1992).[2] Professors Eskridge and Frickey go on to note that in the context of *Dellmuth*, the Court's approach has had a more profound effect on separation-of-powers concerns than one might appreciate at first glance.

> [T]he Court's new super-strong clear statement rules are extraordinarily countermajoritarian: they not only pose the possibility of ignoring legislative expectations, but they also make it quite hard for Congress to express its expectations even when it is focusing on the issue.
>
> But the decision was more than simply countermajoritarian. It suggested a certain judicial haughtiness and uncooperativeness that is surely inconsistent with the humble due process of lawmaking rationale for the Court's super-strong clear statement rules. For under the Supreme Court's prevailing Eleventh Amendment precedent in 1975, when Congress adopted the statute, the jurisdictional language covering actions against the states plus the specific legislative history were probably enough to rebut the presumption against congressional abrogation of the states' Eleventh Amendment immunity, and were perhaps even strong enough to satisfy a traditional clear statement rule. In 1985, of course, the Court changed its approach to the *Atascadero* super-strong clear statement rule.
>
> Given this shift, Congress in 1986 enacted the following statute: "A State shall not be immune under the Eleventh Amendment * * * from suit in Federal Court for a violation of [statutes protecting people with disabilities, including the EHA]." Congress complained that its intent in the Reha-

Make the Connection

This raises again the question of whether the Court's changing the rules should have retroactive effect on statutes enacted before the change.

2 Copyright © 1992 by the Vanderbilt Law Review. Reprinted by permission of Professor William N. Eskridge, Jr.

> bilitation Act had been thwarted by *Atascadero* and overrode that decision in a way expected to head off state immunity claims under other statutes protecting people with disabilities. Yet in *Dellmuth,* the Court not only held that the EHA of 1975 failed to abrogate state immunity, but cited as evidence the subsequent 1986 statute, which contained the requisite clear statement but did not apply to the case in question. Congress promptly overrode *Dellmuth* in 1990. What is most striking * * * is that it took Congress three statutes and fifteen years to accomplish what Congress probably thought it had done in 1975. That is extraordinarily countermajoritarian.

Id. at 638-40. When the Court deals with areas in which Congress has acted, are there separation-of-powers concerns that "counsel hesitation" in creating new rules of constitutional interpretation? Has the *Atascadero* approach effectively created a hierarchy of values with respect to federalism and separation of powers?

Since Atascadero and Dellmuth, Congress has demonstrated that it can be sufficiently clear. *See, e.g.,* Copyright Remedy Clarification Act of 1990, 17 U.S.C.A. § 511; Patent and Plant Variety Protection Clarification Act, 7 U.S.C.A. § 2570 (both specifically eliminating Eleventh Amendment protection). One might have anticipated that this would end the interbranch and intersovereign struggle in this respect, but it has not. The Court has responded by declaring substantive limitations on Congress's power.

College Savings Bank v. Florida Prepaid Postsecondary Education Expense Board, 527 U.S. 666 (1999), involved the Patent and Plant Variety Remedy Clarification Act. College Savings Bank alleged that Florida Prepaid had infringed the Bank's patent on a particular method of financing college educations. A five-to-four majority held that Congress's attempt to protect patents against state infringement by legislating pursuant to § 5 of the Fourteenth Amendment was unconstitutional because Congress had insufficient evidence that state infringement of patents was a national problem. The Court therefore ruled that the statute was not "appropriate legislation" within the meaning of § 5.[3]

---

3 In reaching this conclusion, the majority distinguished patent infringement by the states from constitutional violations by the states.

> [A] State's infringement of a patent, though interfering with a patent owner's right to exclude others, does not by itself violate the Constitution. Instead, only where the State provides no remedy, or only inadequate remedies, to injured patent owners for its infringement of their patent could a deprivation of property without due process result.

The Court thus echoed the question it posed in *Parratt v. Taylor* and related cases: "what process is due?" (In this case, of course, one might be skeptical of the state's ability (let alone its willingness) to provide a remedy for infringement, since patent cases are exclusively federal pursuant to 28 U.S.C. § 1338.) One might legitimately ask how intensively the Court plans to inject itself into the legislative process or, alternatively, what standard the majority will use to determine when Congress has heard "enough" testimony to justify its legislation.

Kimel v. Florida Board of Regents, 528 U.S. 62 (2000), confirmed that the Court will continue to take a critical view of § 5 legislation. The plaintiffs alleged that their state employers discriminated against them on the basis of age, in violation of the Age Discrimination in Employment Act. Although the Court acknowledged that Congress had been sufficiently explicit about abrogating Eleventh Amendment immunity, it nonetheless upheld the states' Eleventh Amendment challenge. Noting that age is not a suspect (or even quasi-suspect) classification, the Court went on to hold that under the rational-basis test, the presence of a class-based rationale for the classification took the case outside of the Fourteenth Amendment. The majority took the position that it was permissible to use age as a proxy for other characteristics (competence, energy, productivity) in which the state had a legitimate interest, even if the classification was probably not correct in the majority of cases.

Florida Prepaid and *Kimel* appeared to leave the door open for Congress to legislate provided that it assembled a better legislative record to show that it was addressing a national problem. Just as Congress had adapted to *Atascadero*'s clear-statement rule, it began to legislate in accord with the Court's new demand for more extensive legislative records. And, just as *Dellmuth* showed Congress that it is not as easy to make clear legislative statements as one might think, the Court demonstrated that it would take a rigorous view of whether the legislative record was sufficiently complete.

Take Note

The Court's approach raises fascinating questions about how rational a measuring device is if it malfunctions more often than not, but those are questions for the Constitutional Law course.

A related case, *Florida Prepaid Postsecondary Education Expense Board v. College Savings Bank*, 527 U.S. 627 (1999), arose in the context of the Trademark Remedy Clarification Act, which amended the Lanham Act to include states as permissible defendants in trademark actions. The same majority ruled there is no Fourteenth Amendment property interest at all in preventing a competitor from misrepresenting its own product to the detriment of one's trademark. The Court therefore held that Florida Prepaid's alleged misrepresentation did not deprive College Savings Bank of any Fourteenth Amendment property.

The Court's approach parallels *Paul v. Davis*, where the majority found no cognizable Fourteenth Amendment interest in protecting one's reputation from defamation by the state. That approach had the dual effect of making a § 1983 action unavailable (because there was no federal right upon which to base it) and of making the existence *vel non* of a state remedy irrelevant because there had been no Fourteenth Amendment deprivation for which the state might otherwise have had to provide due process.

Board of Trustees of the University of Alabama v. Garrett

Supreme Court of the United States, 2001.
531 U.S. 356.

CHIEF JUSTICE REHNQUIST delivered the opinion of the Court.

We decide here whether employees of the State of Alabama may recover money damages by reason of the State's failure to comply with the provisions of Title I of the Americans with Disabilities Act of 1990 (ADA or Act). We hold that such suits are barred by the Eleventh Amendment.

The ADA prohibits certain employers, including the States, from "discriminat[ing] against a qualified individual with a disability because of the disability of such individual in regard to job application procedures, the hiring, advancement, or discharge of employees, employee compensation, job training, and other terms, conditions, and privileges of employment." To this end, the Act requires employers to "mak[e] reasonable accommodations to the known physical or mental limitations of an otherwise qualified individual with a disability who is an applicant or employee, unless [the employer] can demonstrate that the accommodation would impose an undue hardship on the operation of the [employer's] business."

> [R]easonable accommodation may include—
>
> (A) making existing facilities used by employees readily accessible to and usable by individuals with disabilities; and (B) job restructuring, part-time or modified work schedules, reassignment to a vacant position, acquisition or modification of equipment or devices, appropriate adjustment or modifications of examinations, training materials or policies, the provision of qualified readers or interpreters, and other similar accommodations for individuals with disabilities.

The Act also prohibits employers from "utilizing standards, criteria, or methods of administration * * * that have the effect of discrimination on the basis of disability."

The Act defines "disability" to include "(A) a physical or mental impairment that substantially limits one or more of the major life activities of such individual; (B) a record of such an impairment; or (C) being regarded as having such an impairment." A disabled individual is otherwise "qualified" if he or she, "with or without reasonable accommodation, can perform the essential functions of the employment position that such individual holds or desires."

Respondent Patricia Garrett, a registered nurse, was employed as the Director of Nursing, OB/Gyn/Neonatal Services, for the University of Alabama in Birmingham Hospital. In 1994, Garrett was diagnosed with breast cancer and subsequently underwent a lumpectomy, radiation treatment, and chemotherapy. Garrett's treatments required her to take substantial leave from work. Upon returning to work in July 1995, Garrett's supervisor informed Garrett that she would have to give up her Director position. Garrett then applied for and received a transfer to another, lower paying position as a nurse manager.

Respondent Milton Ash worked as a security officer for the Alabama Department of Youth Services (Department). Upon commencing this employment, Ash informed the Department that he suffered from chronic asthma and that his doctor recommended he avoid carbon monoxide and cigarette smoke, and Ash requested that the Department modify his duties to minimize his exposure to these substances. Ash was later diagnosed with sleep apnea and requested, again pursuant to his doctor's recommendation, that he be reassigned to daytime shifts to accommodate his condition. Ultimately, the Department granted none of the requested relief. Shortly after Ash filed a discrimination claim with the Equal Employment Opportunity Commission, he noticed that his performance evaluations were lower than those he had received on previous occasions.

Garrett and Ash filed separate lawsuits in the District Court, both seeking money damages under the ADA. Petitioners moved for summary judgment, claiming that the ADA exceeds Congress' authority to abrogate the State's Eleventh Amendment immunity. In a single opinion disposing of both cases, the District Court agreed with petitioners' position and granted their motions for summary judgment. The cases were consolidated on appeal to the Eleventh Circuit. The Court of Appeals reversed, adhering to its intervening decision in *Kimel v. State Bd. of Regents* that the ADA validly abrogates the States' Eleventh Amendment immunity.

proc. history

* * *

I

The ultimate guarantee of the Eleventh Amendment is that nonconsenting States may not be sued by private individuals in federal court.

We have recognized, however, that Congress may abrogate the States' Eleventh Amendment immunity when it both unequivocally intends to do so and "act[s] pursuant to a valid grant of constitutional authority." The first of these requirements is not in dispute here. The question, then, is whether Congress acted within its constitutional authority by subjecting the States to suits in federal court for money damages under the ADA.

* * * Congress may subject nonconsenting States to suit in federal court when it does so pursuant to a valid exercise of its § 5 power. Our cases have

adhered to this proposition. Accordingly, the ADA can apply to the States only to the extent that the statute is appropriate § 5 legislation. Section 5 of the Fourteenth Amendment grants Congress the power to enforce the substantive guarantees contained in § 1 by enacting "appropriate legislation." Congress is not limited to mere legislative repetition of this Court's constitutional jurisprudence. "Rather, Congress' power 'to enforce' the Amendment includes the authority both to remedy and to deter violation of rights guaranteed thereunder by prohibiting a somewhat broader swath of conduct, including that which is not itself forbidden by the Amendment's text."

City of Boerne also confirmed, however, the long-settled principle that it is the responsibility of this Court, not Congress, to define the substance of constitutional guarantees. Accordingly, § 5 legislation reaching beyond the scope of § 1's actual guarantees must exhibit "congruence and proportionality between the injury to be prevented or remedied and the means adopted to that end."

> **Food for Thought**
>
> Consider this sentence in connection with the position that the Court had previously taken in Schweiker v. Chilicky, at page 536.

II

The first step in applying these now familiar principles is to identify with some precision the scope of the constitutional right at issue. Here, that inquiry requires us to examine the limitations § 1 of the Fourteenth Amendment places upon States' treatment of the disabled. As we did last Term in Kimel, we look to our prior decisions under the Equal Protection Clause dealing with this issue.

Under rational-basis review, where a group possesses "distinguishing characteristics relevant to interests the State has the authority to implement," a State's decision to act on the basis of those differences does not give rise to a constitutional violation. "Such a classification cannot run afoul of the Equal Protection Clause if there is a rational relationship between the disparity of treatment and some legitimate governmental purpose." Moreover, the State need not articulate its reasoning at the moment a particular decision is made. Rather, the burden is upon the challenging party to negative " 'any reasonably conceivable state of facts that could provide a rational basis for the classification.' "

rat'l basis

> **Food for Thought**
>
> How is it possible for a court to review the state's decision if the court does not know the reasons underlying it?

Thus, the result of Cleburne is that States are not required by the Fourteenth Amendment to make special accommodations for the disabled, so long as their actions toward such individuals are rational. They could quite hardheadedly—and perhaps hardheartedly—hold to job-qualification requirements which do not make allowance for the disabled. If special accommodations for the disabled are to be required, they have to come from positive law and not through the Equal Protection Clause.

III

Once we have determined the metes and bounds of the constitutional right in question, we examine whether Congress identified a history and pattern of unconstitutional employment discrimination by the States against the disabled. Just as § 1 of the Fourteenth Amendment applies only to actions committed "under color of state law," Congress' § 5 authority is appropriately exercised only in response to state transgressions. The legislative record of the ADA, however, simply fails to show that Congress did in fact identify a pattern of irrational state discrimination in employment against the disabled.

Respondents contend that the inquiry as to unconstitutional discrimination should extend not only to States themselves, but to units of local governments, such as cities and counties. All of these, they say, are "state actors" for purposes of the Fourteenth Amendment. This is quite true, but the Eleventh Amendment does not extend its immunity to units of local government. These entities are subject to private claims for damages under the ADA without Congress' ever having to rely on § 5 of the Fourteenth Amendment to render them so. It would make no sense to consider constitutional violations on their part, as well as by the States themselves, when only the States are the beneficiaries of the Eleventh Amendment.

Take Note!

Observe how in this situation the *Young* dichotomy cuts *against* relief.

Congress made a general finding in the ADA that "historically, society has tended to isolate and segregate individuals with disabilities, and, despite some improvements, such forms of discrimination against individuals with disabilities continue to be a serious and pervasive social problem." The record assembled by Congress includes many instances to support such a finding. But the great majority of these incidents do not deal with the activities of States.

Respondents in their brief cite half a dozen examples from the record that did involve States. * * *

Several of these incidents undoubtedly evidence an unwillingness on the part of state officials to make the sort of accommodations for the disabled required by the ADA. Whether they were irrational under our decision in *Cleburne* is more debatable * * * . But even if it were to be determined that each incident upon fuller examination showed unconstitutional action on the part of the State, these incidents taken together fall far short of even suggesting the pattern of unconstitutional discrimination on which § 5 legislation must be based. Congress, in enacting the ADA, found that "some 43,000,000 Americans have one or more physical or mental disabilities." In 1990, the States alone employed more than 4.5 million people. It is telling, we think, that given these large numbers, Congress assembled only such minimal evidence of unconstitutional state discrimination in employment against the disabled.

Justice Breyer maintains that Congress applied Title I of the ADA to the States in response to a host of incidents representing unconstitutional state discrimination in employment against persons with disabilities. A close review of the relevant materials, however, undercuts that conclusion. Justice Breyer's Appendix C consists not of legislative findings, but of unexamined, anecdotal accounts of "adverse, disparate treatment by state officials." Of course, as we have already explained, "adverse, disparate treatment" often does not amount to a constitutional violation where rational-basis scrutiny applies. These accounts, moreover, were submitted not directly to Congress but to the Task Force on the Rights and Empowerment of Americans with Disabilities, which made no findings on the subject of state discrimination in employment.[7] And, had Congress truly understood this information as reflecting a pattern of unconstitutional behavior by the States, one would expect some mention of that conclusion in the Act's legislative findings. There is none. Although Justice Breyer would infer from Congress' general conclusions regarding societal discrimination against the disabled that the States had likewise participated in such action, the House and Senate committee reports on the ADA flatly contradict this assertion. After describing the evidence presented to the Senate Committee on Labor and Human Resources and its subcommittee (including the Task Force Report upon which the dissent relies), the Committee's Report reached, among others, the following conclusion: "Discrimination still persists in such critical areas as *employment in the private sector,* public accommodations, public services, transportation, and telecommunications." ([E]mphasis added). The House Committee on Education and Labor, addressing the ADA's employment provisions, reached the same conclusion: "[A]fter extensive review and analysis over a number of Congressional sessions, * * * there exists a compelling need to establish a clear and comprehensive Federal prohibition of discrimination on the basis of disability in the areas of *employment in the private*

7 Only a small fraction of the anecdotes Justice Breyer identifies in his Appendix C relate to state discrimination against the disabled in employment. At most, somewhere around 50 of these allegations describe conduct that could conceivably amount to constitutional violations by the States, and most of them are so general and brief that no firm conclusion can be drawn. The overwhelming majority of these accounts pertain to alleged discrimination by the States in the provision of public services and public accommodations, which areas are addressed in Titles II and III of the ADA.

sector, public accommodations, public services, transportation and telecommunications." ([E]mphasis added). Thus, not only is the inference Justice Breyer draws unwarranted, but there is also strong evidence that Congress' failure to mention States in its legislative findings addressing discrimination in employment reflects that body's judgment that no pattern of unconstitutional state action had been documented. Even were it possible to squeeze out of these examples a pattern of unconstitutional discrimination by the States, the rights and remedies created by the ADA against the States would raise the same sort of concerns as to congruence and proportionality as were found in *City of Boerne*. For example, whereas it would be entirely rational (and therefore constitutional) for a state employer to conserve scarce financial resources by hiring employees who are able to use existing facilities, the ADA requires employers to "mak[e] existing facilities used by employees readily accessible to and usable by individuals with disabilities." The ADA does except employers from the "reasonable accommodatio[n]" requirement where the employer "can demonstrate that the accommodation would impose an undue hardship on the operation of the business of such covered entity." However, even with this exception, the accommodation duty far exceeds what is constitutionally required in that it makes unlawful a range of alternative responses that would be reasonable but would fall short of imposing an "undue burden" upon the employer. The Act also makes it the employer's duty to prove that it would suffer such a burden, instead of requiring (as the Constitution does) that the complaining party negate reasonable bases for the employer's decision.

The ADA also forbids "utilizing standards, criteria, or methods of administration" that disparately impact the disabled, without regard to whether such conduct has a rational basis. Although disparate impact may be relevant evidence of racial discrimination, such evidence alone is insufficient even where the Fourteenth Amendment subjects state action to strict scrutiny.

The ADA's constitutional shortcomings are apparent when the Act is compared to Congress' efforts in the Voting Rights Act of 1965 to respond to a serious pattern of constitutional violations. In *South Carolina v. Katzenbach* (1966), we considered whether the Voting Rights Act was "appropriate" legislation to enforce the Fifteenth Amendment's protection against racial discrimination in voting. Concluding that it was a valid exercise of Congress' enforcement power under § 2 of the Fifteenth Amendment, we noted that "[b]efore enacting the measure, Congress explored with great care the problem of racial discrimination in voting."

In that Act, Congress documented a marked pattern of unconstitutional action by the States. State officials, Congress found, routinely applied voting tests in order to exclude African-American citizens from registering to vote. * * *

The contrast between this kind of evidence, and the evidence that Congress considered in the present case, is stark. Congressional enactment of the ADA represents its judgment that there should be a "comprehensive national mandate for the elimination of discrimination against individuals with disabilities." Congress is the final authority as to desirable public policy, but in order to authorize private individuals to recover money damages against the States, there must be a pattern of discrimination by the States which violates the Fourteenth Amendment, and the remedy imposed by Congress must be congruent and proportional to the targeted violation. Those requirements are not met here, and to uphold the Act's application to the States would allow Congress to rewrite the Fourteenth Amendment law laid down by this Court in Cleburne. Section 5 does not so broadly enlarge congressional authority. The judgment of the Court of Appeals is therefore

Reversed.

JUSTICE BREYER, with whom JUSTICE STEVENS, JUSTICE SOUTER, and JUSTICE GINSBURG join, dissenting.

* * * In my view, Congress reasonably could have concluded that the remedy before us constitutes an "appropriate" way to enforce this basic equal protection requirement. And that is all the Constitution requires.

I

The Court says that its primary problem with this statutory provision is one of legislative evidence. * * * In fact, Congress compiled a vast legislative record documenting " 'massive, society-wide discrimination' " against persons with disabilities. In addition to the information presented at 13 congressional hearings and its own prior experience gathered over 40 years during which it contemplated and enacted considerable similar legislation, Congress created a special task force to assess the need for comprehensive legislation. That task force held hearings in every State, attended by more than 30,000 people, including thousands who had experienced discrimination first hand. The task force hearings, Congress' own hearings, and an analysis of "census data, national polls, and other studies" led Congress to conclude that "people with disabilities, as a group, occupy an inferior status in our society, and are severely disadvantaged socially, vocationally, economically, and educationally." As to employment, Congress found that "[t]wo-thirds of all disabled Americans between the age of 16 and 64 [were] not working at all," even though a large majority wanted to, and were able to, work productively. And Congress found that this discrimination flowed in significant part from "stereotypic assumptions" as well as "purposeful unequal treatment."

The powerful evidence of discriminatory treatment throughout society in general, including discrimination by private persons and local governments, implicates state governments as well, for state agencies form part of that same larger society. * * *

In any event, there is no need to rest solely upon evidence of discrimination by local governments or general societal discrimination. There are roughly 300 examples of discrimination by state governments themselves in the legislative record. I fail to see how this evidence "fall[s] far short of even suggesting the pattern of unconstitutional discrimination on which § 5 legislation must be based."

The congressionally appointed task force collected numerous specific examples, provided by persons with disabilities themselves, of adverse, disparate treatment by state officials. They reveal, not what the Court describes as "half a dozen" instances of discrimination, but hundreds of instances of adverse treatment at the hands of state officials—instances in which a person with a disability found it impossible to obtain a state job, to retain state employment, to use the public transportation that was readily available to others in order to get to work, or to obtain a public education, which is often a prerequisite to obtaining employment. State-imposed barriers also frequently made it difficult or impossible for people to vote, to enter a public building, to access important government services, such as calling for emergency assistance, and to find a place to live due to a pattern of irrational zoning decisions similar to the discrimination that we held unconstitutional in *Cleburne*.

As the Court notes, those who presented instances of discrimination rarely provided additional, independent evidence sufficient to prove in court that, in each instance, the discrimination they suffered lacked justification from a judicial standpoint. Perhaps this explains the Court's view that there is "minimal evidence of unconstitutional state discrimination." But a legislature is not a court of law. And Congress, unlike courts, must, and does, routinely draw general conclusions—for example, of likely motive or of likely relationship to legitimate need—from anecdotal and opinion-based evidence of this kind, particularly when the evidence lacks strong refutation. In reviewing § 5 legislation, we have never required the sort of extensive investigation of each piece of evidence that the Court appears to contemplate. Nor has the Court traditionally required Congress to make findings as to state discrimination, or to break down the record evidence, category by category.

Regardless, Congress expressly found substantial unjustified discrimination against persons with disabilities. Moreover, it found that such discrimination typically reflects "stereotypic assumptions" or "purposeful unequal treatment." In making these findings, Congress followed our decision in *Cleburne*, which established that not only discrimination against persons with disabilities that rests upon " 'a bare * * * desire to harm a politically unpopular group,' " violates the Fourteenth Amendment, but also discrimination that rests solely upon "negative attitude[s]," "fea[r],"or "irrational prejudice." Adverse treatment that rests upon such motives is unjustified discrimination in *Cleburne*'s terms.

The evidence in the legislative record bears out Congress' finding that the adverse treatment of persons with disabilities was often arbitrary or invidious in this sense, and thus unjustified. A complete listing of the hundreds of examples of discrimination by state and local governments that were submitted to the task force is set forth in Appendix C. Congress could have reasonably believed that these examples represented signs of a widespread problem of unconstitutional discrimination.

II

The Court's failure to find sufficient evidentiary support may well rest upon its decision to hold Congress to a strict, judicially created evidentiary standard, particularly in respect to lack of justification. * * *

The problem with the Court's approach is that neither the "burden of proof" that favors States nor any other rule of restraint applicable to *judges* applies to *Congress* when it exercises its § 5 power. "Limitations stemming from the nature of the judicial process * * * have no application to Congress." Oregon v. Mitchell (1970) (Brennan, White, and Marshall, JJ., concurring in part and dissenting in part). Rational-basis review—with its presumptions favoring constitutionality—is "a paradigm of *judicial* restraint." ([E]mphasis added). And the Congress of the United States is not a lower court.

Indeed, the Court in Cleburne drew this very institutional distinction. We emphasized that "courts have been very reluctant, as they should be in our federal system and with our respect for the separation of powers, to closely scrutinize legislative choices." Our invocation of judicial deference and respect for Congress was based on the fact that "[§]5 of the [Fourteenth] Amendment empowers *Congress* to enforce [the equal protection] mandate." ([E]mphasis added). Indeed, we made clear that the absence of a contrary congressional finding was critical to our decision to apply mere rational-basis review to disability discrimination claims—a "congressional direction" to apply a more stringent standard would have been "controlling." In short, the Court's claim that "to uphold the Act's application to the States would allow Congress to rewrite the Fourteenth Amendment law laid down by this Court in Cleburne," [is] repudiated by Cleburne itself.

There is simply no reason to require Congress, seeking to determine facts relevant to the exercise of its § 5 authority, to adopt rules or presumptions that reflect a court's institutional limitations. * * *

Moreover, unlike judges, Members of Congress are elected. When the Court has applied the majority's burden of proof rule, it has explained that we, *i.e.*, the courts, do not " 'sit as a superlegislature to judge the wisdom or desirability of legislative policy determinations.' " To apply a rule designed to restrict courts as if it restricted Congress' legislative power is to stand the underlying principle—a principle of judicial restraint—on its head. But without the use of this burden of proof rule or some other unusually stringent standard of review, it is difficult to see how the Court can find the legislative record here inadequate. * * *

III

The Court argues in the alternative that the statute's damages remedy is not "congruent" with and "proportional" to the equal protection problem that Congress found. The Court suggests that the Act's "reasonable accommodation" requirement, and disparate-impact standard, "far excee[d] what is constitutionally required." But we have upheld disparate-impact standards in contexts where they were not "constitutionally required."

And what is wrong with a remedy that, in response to unreasonable employer behavior, requires an employer to make accommodations that are reasonable? Of course, what is "reasonable" in the statutory sense and what is "unreasonable" in the constitutional sense might differ. In other words, the requirement may exceed what is necessary to avoid a constitutional violation. But it is just that power—the power to require more than the minimum that § 5 grants to Congress, as this Court has repeatedly confirmed. As long ago as 1880, the Court wrote that § 5 "brought within the domain of congressional power" whatever "tends to enforce submission" to its "prohibitions" and "to secure to all persons * * * the equal protection of the laws." More recently, the Court added that § 5's "draftsmen sought to grant to Congress, by a specific provision applicable to the Fourteenth Amendment, the same broad powers expressed in the Necessary and Proper Clause, Art. I, § 8, cl. 18."

In keeping with these principles, the Court has said that "[i]t is not for us to review the congressional resolution of * * * the various conflicting considerations—the risk or pervasiveness of the discrimination in governmental services * * *, the adequacy or availability of alternative remedies, and the nature and significance of the state interests that would be affected." "It is enough that we be able to perceive a basis upon which the Congress might resolve the conflict as it did." Nothing in the words "reasonable accommodation" suggests that the requirement has no "tend[ency] to enforce" the Equal Protection Clause, that it is an irrational way to achieve the objective, that it would fall outside the scope of the Necessary and Proper Clause, or that it somehow otherwise exceeds the bounds of the "appropriate."

* * *

IV

The Court's harsh review of Congress' use of its § 5 power is reminiscent of the similar (now-discredited) limitation that it once imposed upon Congress' Commerce Clause power. The legislation before us, however, does not discriminate against anyone, nor does it pose any threat to basic liberty. And it is difficult to understand why the Court, which applies "minimum 'rational-basis' review" to statutes that *burden* persons with disabilities, subjects to far stricter scrutiny a statute that seeks to *help* those same individuals.

I recognize nonetheless that this statute imposes a burden upon States in that it removes their Eleventh Amendment protection from suit, thereby subjecting them to potential monetary liability. Rules for interpreting § 5 that would provide States with special protection, however, run counter to the very object of the Fourteenth Amendment. By its terms, that Amendment prohibits *States* from denying their citizens equal protection of the laws. U.S. Const., Amdt. 14, § 1. Hence "principles of federalism that might otherwise be an obstacle to congressional authority are necessarily overridden by the power to enforce the Civil War Amendments 'by appropriate legislation.' Those Amendments were specifically designed as an expansion of federal power and an intrusion on state sovereignty."

* * *

For the reasons stated, I respectfully dissent.

Notes and Questions

1. a) Observe at the outset that majority and dissent disagree about the factual record that Congress assembled. Perhaps majority and dissent approach the problem differently. The majority refuses to approve legislation unless Congress has identified a widespread pattern of state discrimination *in employment cases*. The dissent, on the other hand, appears to have the view that a showing of pervasive state discrimination *against the disabled* in many areas, including but not limited to employment, allows Congress to infer that there may be a pattern of discrimination with respect to employment cases specifically. Which approach is better as a policy matter? Which is more faithful to the Fourteenth Amendment?

b) The Chief Justice rejects the respondents' arguments that the Court should consider evidence of sub-state government discrimination against disabled individuals, noting that the Eleventh Amendment does not protect local government units. Does that mean that a quantum of evidence that might satisfy the Court with respect to local government discrimination will not satisfy it with respect to state discrimination?

If that is so, the Eleventh Amendment seems to be modifying the Fourteenth Amendment by heightening the Court's "appropriateness" scrutiny. If earlier provisions of the Constitution can modify later ones in that way, then there seems to be no reason that Congress could not legislate under its Article I powers and curtail the states' Eleventh Amendment immunity, yet the Court (albeit by only a five-to-four margin) has rejected that possibility. See *Seminole Tribe v. Florida*, *infra* at 721. Should the Eleventh Amendment have anything to do with determining whether Fourteenth Amendment legislation is appropriate?

2. Does characterization become everything? If Congress's Fourteenth Amendment object is generally to deter or remedy government discrimination against disabled people, whether in the context of employment discrimination or access to public facilities or access to education, should that affect how the Court decides what evidence is relevant for congruence-and-proportionality purposes? Footnote 1 of the majority opinion separates Title I from Title II and declines to consider Title II questions because the parties did not focus on them. One might argue, however, that the parties' failure to brief and argue questions with respect to Title II is distinct from the evidence Congress had before it when it enacted the ADA, which is, after all, a single statute that seeks in different sections to affect different kinds of discriminatory conduct. When asking whether a statute satisfies the congruence-and-proportionality test, to what extent should the Court examine the evidence underlying the statute's subsections individually? To the extent that you think the Court's approach proper, consider whether Congress then is on notice to put diverse statutory goals into single sections of the law or, alternatively, how far the Court should go in breaking a statute down into its components. Instead of looking at employment discrimination, for example, the Court might have differentiated further between discrimination that runs against physical versus mental disabilities and then sought an extensive record with respect to each sub-category. Is there anything in the Fourteenth Amendment, particularly in the word "appropriate," that provides guidance on how searching the Court's scrutiny should be?

3. Justice Breyer argues that the majority is holding Congress to evidentiary standards that might be appropriate in a courtroom under a clear-and-convincing standard but are not properly applicable to the work of a legislature. He accuses the majority of abandoning the historical pattern of reviewing to see "whether Congress' likely conclusions were reasonable, not whether there was adequate evidentiary support in the record." Are the two as separable as Justice Breyer implies? How can one know whether a conclusion is reasonable without paying attention to the evidence upon which Congress reaches the conclusion?

4. One of the effects of the Court's jurisprudence in this area is to interpret § 5 of the Fourteenth Amendment to provide protection to the states against what the majority clearly sees as congressional overreaching. The Court reads the word "appropriate"

to be a limitation on Congress deliberately inserted to insulate the states from federal intrusion. Do you think that is what the 1868 Congress had in mind when it drafted what became the Fourteenth Amendment?

5. To what extent should the Court's scrutiny of "appropriateness" under the Fourteenth Amendment mirror its jurisprudence on what is "necessary and proper" under Art. I, § 8, cl. 18? The Court has typically been extremely deferential to Congress with respect to the latter. If the standard of review should be different, what in the Constitution and the theory of separation of powers accounts for the difference?

Irrespective of where one's sympathies lie in this debate, it is now clear that Congress must assemble a far more targeted and state-specific legislative record if it wishes to authorize federal suits against the states by individuals. Should the Court read the Eleventh Amendment to require Congress to go beyond the sort of record that ordinarily suffices to support legislation? Note, by the way, the metamorphosis in the Court's approach to such legislation. In the 1980s, in cases like *Atascadero State Hospital v. Scanlon*, the Court's focus was on whether Congress was sufficiently specific that states were subject to suit. Congress learned that lesson, and the Court has now shifted from requiring that sort of specificity in an area of legislative competence to viewing such competence as subdivided for Eleventh Amendment purposes. There is no suggestion in the *Garrett* majority opinion that Congress overstepped itself in applying the Americans with Disabilities Act to county and local governmental units. The legislative record apparently satisfied the normal rational-basis review. With respect to the states, however, the Court appears to have shifted its analysis from whether Congress has competence based on the area being regulated to whether Congress has competence based on the parties to be regulated. Do you think those who wrote the Eleventh Amendment saw it as a limitation on the scope of substantive legislation? In *Fitzpatrick v. Bitzer*, had Congress assembled the sort of legislative record that the Court now demands?

6. *Nevada Department of Human Resources v. Hibbs*, 538 U.S. 721 (2003), demonstrated that the Court's application of the *Garrett* rule to invalidate congressional attempts to subject the states to liability may not be as wide ranging as might have first appeared. The Court found that Congress, in passing The Family and Medical Leave Act (FMLA) of 1993 had assembled sufficient evidence of "the States' record of unconstitutional participation in, and fostering of, gender-based discrimination in the administration of leave benefits * * * to justify the enactment of prophylactic § 5 legislation." (Footnote omitted). The majority went on to find Congress's remedy congruent and proportional, and hence effective to overcome the Eleventh Amendment.

Justice Scalia dissented, arguing that the congressionally created remedy could not survive an Eleventh Amendment challenge by a state that had not itself engaged in gender discrimination. "The constitutional violation that is a prerequisite to 'prophylactic' congressional action to 'enforce' the Fourteenth Amendment is a violation by the State against which the enforcement action is taken." Justice Kennedy, joined by Justices Scalia and Thomas, wrote an extended dissent making two major points. First, he argued that FMLA is not an appropriate remedial statute within Congress's power under § 5 of the Fourteenth Amendment because it creates an entitlement, a new form of benefit program unrelated to Fourteenth Amendment concerns. He did not say that Congress could not create such an entitlement. In his view, Congress has ample power under the Commerce Clause (not § 5 of the Fourteenth Amendment) to do just what it did in FMLA. With respect to the Fourteenth Amendment, he suggested that Congress was effectively and impermissibly expanding the substantive content of the Equal Protection Clause, in violation of the doctrine of *City of Boerne v. Flores*.

It seems fair to say that the battle lines over *Garrett* invalidation are now relatively clear. The Justices will fight over the quantity of evidence and over its quality, specifically whether the evidence upon which Congress relies relates to the very same conduct that Congress attempts to address in a remedial statute. How much evidence of a widespread pattern of violations will suffice? For that matter, what is a pattern? Presumably if only one or two states are engaging unconstitutional behavior, that would not suffice. Suppose that Congress has evidence that thirty states are acting in a way that would justify legislation under § 5. May Congress then act? If it does, should the Court follow Justice Scalia's suggestion and only permit application of the statute to the thirty violators, or in the name of prophylaxis may Congress prohibit behavior that is not itself unconstitutional (as the Court has acknowledged Congress may do) and apply those prophylactic provisions to states not in violation of any constitutional provision?

With respect to an individual state, should the Court consider a statute unconstitutional as applied if a) Congress had no evidence that the state had ever acted unconstitutionally or b) if the plaintiff is unable to show that the state acted unconstitutionally either with respect to anyone or with respect to him?

Assuming that Congress has evidence of unconstitutional state behavior sufficient to support remedial legislation under § 5, does that legislation become unconstitutional as applied if a particular state ceases its unconstitutional behavior or on its face if the states as a whole no longer exhibit a pervasive pattern of constitutional violations? *See Shelby County, Ala. v. Holder*, 133 S.Ct. 2612 (2013).

7. *Tennessee v. Lane*, 541 U.S. 509 (2004), also upheld congressional action, this time concerning Title II of the Americans with Disabilities Act. Whereas Title I (involved in Garrett) concerned employment discrimination against individuals and involved equal protection only, Title II addressed access to public services, programs and activities.

> Respondents, both of whom are paraplegics who use wheelchairs for mobility, claimed that they were denied access to, and the services of, the state court system by reason of their disabilities. Lane alleged that he was compelled to appear to answer a set of criminal charges on the second floor of a county courthouse that had no elevator. At his first appearance, Lane crawled up two flights of stairs to get to the courtroom. When Lane returned to the courthouse for a hearing, he refused to crawl again or to be carried by officers to the courtroom; he consequently was arrested and jailed for failure to appear. Jones, a certified court reporter, alleged that she has not been able to gain access to a number of county courthouses, and, as a result, has lost both work and an opportunity to participate in the judicial process.

The majority ruled that because the access provisions of Title II implicated fundamental rights applicable to the states through the Fourteenth Amendment (including the Sixth Amendment's Confrontation Clause and fair-cross-section jury entitlement and the First Amendment's contemplation of public access to criminal proceedings), "the sheer volume of evidence demonstrating the nature and extent of unconstitutional discrimination against persons with disabilities in the provision of public services" meant Congress's Title II response was congruent and proportional and therefore satisfied the Court's test.

Thus, a two-tier analysis emerges. Congress can enact remedial legislation allowing damages for unconstitutional state conduct. Beyond that, Congress can enact what the Court has called prophylactic legislation that reaches conduct not itself unconstitutional but closely related to the unconstitutional conduct that Congress seeks to deter. Prophylactic legislation, however, must be "congruent and proportional" (under Boerne and *Garrett*) to the scope and breadth of constitutional violations by states. If Congress has not identified a pattern of state constitutional violations, then it cannot enact legislation prohibiting acts that are not unconstitutional under the Fourteenth Amendment.

Title II of the ADA continues to have some Eleventh Amendment teeth. In *United States v. Georgia*, 546 U.S. 151 (2006), the Court left the way open for a state prisoner to take advantage of the ADA's provisions. The Court quoted the statute's Eleventh Amendment abrogation provision: "[a] State shall not be immune under the eleventh amendment to the Constitution of the United States from an action in [a] Federal or State court of competent jurisdiction for a violation of this chapter." Justice Scalia's opinion for the Court noted that "We have accepted this * * * statement as an unequivocal expression of Congress's intent to abrogate state sovereign immunity."

The Court remanded , but before letting go, the Court remarked on congressional power under the Fourteenth Amendment and simultaneously signaled its interest in a future Eleventh Amendment issue.

> While the Members of this Court have disagreed regarding the scope of Congress's "prophylactic" enforcement powers under § 5 of the Fourteenth Amendment, no one doubts that § 5 grants Congress the power to "enforce * * * the provisions" of the Amendment by creating private remedies against the States for actual violations of those provisions. * * * This enforcement power includes the power to abrogate state sovereign immunity by authorizing private suits for damages against the States. Thus, insofar as Title II creates a private cause of action for damages against the States for conduct that actually violates the Fourteenth Amendment, Title II validly abrogates state sovereign immunity.

The Court pointedly suggested a line of inquiry to the lower courts on the remand:

> [T]he lower courts will be best situated to determine in the first instance, on a claim-by-claim basis, (1) which aspects of the State's alleged conduct violated Title II[,] (2) to what extent such misconduct also violated the Fourteenth Amendment[,] and (3) insofar as such misconduct violated Title II but did not violate the Fourteenth Amendment, whether Congress's purported abrogation of sovereign immunity as to that class of conduct is nevertheless valid.

Will it be possible for the Court simultaneously to reaffirm Congress's power to act prophylactically under the Fourteenth Amendment and to limit Congress's § 5 power to abrogate the states' Eleventh Amendment immunity? Certainly the Court's phrasing of the third issue suggests that it is entertaining that thought. Another way to look at this is to consider how closely linked § 5's grant of legislative power and § 1's recital of constitutional rights are. If § 5 permits Congress to enact prophylactic legislation, is there any textual basis for the Court to say that Congress may not, at the same time, expose the states to liability for violating that legislation? Conversely, if § 5 does not permit such abrogation, does that necessarily imply that prophylactic legislation is not "appropriate" within the meaning of § 5? Can legislation be "appropriate" for some purposes but not for others? How will the Court make the distinction?

CLICK FOR UPDATE
UPDATES FOUND ON PAGES 1191-1195

After *Fitzpatrick*, questions arose about whether Congress could limit states' Eleventh Amendment immunity under legislation-authorizing provisions other than Section 5 of the Fourteenth Amendment. A badly fractured Court held in *Pennsylvania v. Union Gas Company*, 491 U.S. 1 (1989), that the Commerce Clause also would support legislation explicitly authorizing suits in the federal courts against states. There was, however, no majority opinion on that issue. Four Justices, led by Justice Brennan, took the view that the Eleventh Amendment merely reflected common law sovereign immunity principles that antedated the Constitution and that Congress therefore could modify those principles. Justice Brennan argued that the states had ceded parts of their sovereignty to the federal government "in the plan of the Convention," and that Article I represented the end result of a zero-sum game, where each power granted to the federal government represented a diminution of state power. Moreover, he argued that the Eleventh Amendment constrained only judicial power, not federal legislative power.

> Because the Commerce Clause withholds power from the States at the same time as it confers it on Congress, and because the congressional power thus conferred would be incomplete without the authority to render States liable in damages, it must be that, to the extent that the States gave Congress the authority to regulate commerce, they also relinquished their immunity where Congress found it necessary, in exercising this authority, to render them liable.

In effect, Justice Brennan's group of four Justices found that the states had consented to be sued in the federal forum whenever Congress authorized such suits in exercise of its Article I powers.

Justice Stevens, though he joined Justice Brennan's opinion, also wrote a separate concurrence noting "the distinction between our two Eleventh Amendments." The first he saw as the party-based jurisdiction amendment that forbids plaintiffs from making states defendants in diversity cases. The second "is the defense of sovereign immunity that the Court has added to the text of the Amendment in cases like *Hans v. Louisiana*." That doctrine, he said, "is not a matter of Eleventh Amendment law at all, but rather is based on a prudential interest in federal-state comity and a concern for 'Our Federalism.' " Thus, he saw no reason why Congress, in the exercise of its Article I powers, could not overrule the Court's prudential doctrine of state sovereign immunity.

Justice Scalia and three other Justices dissented, arguing that the Eleventh Amendment postdated Article I and that Congress could not use Article I powers to modify the immunity it provided. Justice Scalia took direct issue with Justice Brennan's approach, particularly in its effect on *Hans*: "Better to overrule *Hans*, I should think, than to perpetuate the complexities that it creates but eliminate all its benefits to the federal system." Justice Scalia also predicted that *Union Gas* would not survive.

> The Court's holding today can be applauded only by those who think state sovereign immunity so constitutionally insignificant that *Hans* itself might as well be abandoned. It is only the Court's steadfast refusal to accept the fundamental structural importance of that doctrine, reflected in *Hans* and the other cases discussed above, that permits it to regard abrogation through Article I as an open question, and enables the plurality to fight the *Hans*-*Atascadero* battle all over again—but this time to win it—on the field of the Commerce Clause. It is a particularly unhappy victory, since instead of cleaning up the allegedly muddled Eleventh Amendment jurisprudence produced by *Hans*, the Court leaves that in place, and adds to the clutter the astounding principle that Article III limitations can be overcome by simply exercising Article I powers. It is an unstable victory as well, since that principle is too much at war with

itself to endure. We shall either overrule Hans in form as well as in fact, or return to its genuine meaning.

Justice White, the ninth Justice, voted for the result urged by Justice Brennan, but refused to join the opinion, noting "I concur in Justice Brennan's conclusion, but not his reasoning," and later, "I agree with the conclusion reached by Justice Brennan * * * that Congress has the authority under Article I to abrogate the Eleventh Amendment immunity of the States, although I do not agree with much of his reasoning." Justice White never, however, articulated his own basis for reaching the same conclusion or with what part of Justice Brennan's reasoning he disagreed. Thus, although the result in *Union Gas* was clear, there was no majority rationale on the critical constitutional point.

Food for Thought

(Should he have felt some obligation to do so, given that his was the crucial fifth vote on an important constitutional question?)

Justice Scalia was correct; the situation was inherently unstable. Six years after *Union Gas*, with four of the Justices who participated in that case and voted for the majority result (Justices Blackmun, Brennan, Marshall and White) having retired, the Court granted certiorari in a case raising the issue of whether Congress could limit the states' forum immunity when legislating under the Indian Commerce Clause of Article I. The next year, it issued its opinion.

Seminole Tribe v. Florida

Supreme Court of the United States, 1996.
517 U.S. 44.

CHIEF JUSTICE REHNQUIST delivered the opinion of the Court.

The Indian Gaming Regulatory Act provides that an Indian tribe may conduct certain gaming activities only in conformance with a valid compact between the tribe and the State in which the gaming activities are located. The Act, passed by Congress under the Indian Commerce Clause, imposes upon the States a duty to negotiate in good faith with an Indian tribe toward the formation of a compact and authorizes a tribe to bring suit in federal court against a State in order to compel performance of that duty. We hold that notwithstanding Congress' clear intent to abrogate the States' sovereign immunity, the Indian Commerce Clause does not grant Congress that power, and therefore § 2710(d)(7) cannot grant jurisdiction over a State that does not consent to be sued. We further hold that the doctrine of *Ex parte Young* may not be used to enforce § 2710(d)(3) against a state official.

I

The Act divides gaming on Indian lands into three classes—I, II, and III—and provides a different regulatory scheme for each class. * * * The Act provides that class III gaming is lawful only where it is: (1) authorized by an ordinance or resolution that (a) is adopted by the governing body of the Indian tribe, (b) satisfies certain statutorily prescribed requirements, and (c) is approved by the National Indian Gaming Commission; (2) located in a State that permits such gaming for any purpose by any person, organization, or entity; and (3) "conducted in conformance with a Tribal-State compact entered into by the Indian tribe and the State under paragraph (3) that is in effect."

The "paragraph (3)" to which the last prerequisite of § 2710(d)(1) refers is § 2710(d)(3), which describes the permissible scope of a Tribal-State compact and * * * describes the process by which a State and an Indian tribe begin negotiations toward a Tribal-State compact. * * *

The State's obligation to "negotiate with the Indian tribe in good faith," is made judicially enforceable by §§ 2710(d)(7)(A)(i) and (B)(i) * * *.

Sections 2710(d)(7)(B)(ii)-(vii) describe an elaborate remedial scheme designed to ensure the formation of a Tribal-State compact. A tribe that brings an action under § 2710(d)(7)(A)(i) must show that no Tribal-State compact has been entered and that the State failed to respond in good faith to the tribe's request to negotiate; at that point, the burden then shifts to the State to prove that it did in fact negotiate in good faith. If the district court concludes that the State has failed to negotiate in good faith toward the formation of a Tribal-State compact, then it "shall order the State and Indian tribe to conclude such a compact within a 60-day period." If no compact has been concluded 60 days after the court's order, then "the Indian tribe and the State shall each submit to a mediator appointed by the court a proposed compact that represents their last best offer for a compact." The mediator chooses from between the two proposed compacts the one "which best comports with the terms of [the Act] and any other applicable Federal law and with the findings and order of the court" and submits it to the State and the Indian tribe. If the State consents to the proposed compact within 60 days of its submission by the mediator, then the proposed compact is "treated as a Tribal-State compact entered into under paragraph (3)." If, however, the State does not consent within that 60-day period, then the Act provides that the mediator "shall notify the Secretary [of the Interior]" and that the Secretary "shall prescribe * * * procedures * * * under which class III gaming may be conducted on the Indian lands over which the Indian tribe has jurisdiction."

In September 1991, the Seminole Tribe of Indians, petitioner, sued the State of Florida and its Governor, Lawton Chiles, respondents. Invoking jurisdiction under 25 U.S.C. § 2710(d)(7)(A), as well as 28 U.S.C. §§ 1331 and 1362, petitioner alleged that respondents had "refused to enter into any negotiation for inclusion of [certain gaming activities] in a tribal-state compact," thereby violating the "requirement of good faith negotiation" contained in § 2710(d)(3). Respondents moved to dismiss the complaint, arguing that the suit violated the State's sovereign immunity from suit in federal court. The District Court denied respondents' motion, and the respondents took an interlocutory appeal of that decision.

The Court of Appeals for the Eleventh Circuit reversed the decision of the District Court, holding that the Eleventh Amendment barred petitioner's suit against respondents. Finding that it lacked subject-matter jurisdiction, the Eleventh Circuit remanded to the District Court with directions to dismiss petitioner's suit.

proc. history

[W]e granted certiorari in order to consider two questions: (1) Does the Eleventh Amendment prevent Congress from authorizing suits by Indian tribes against States for prospective injunctive relief to enforce legislation enacted pursuant to the Indian Commerce Clause? and (2) Does the doctrine of *Ex parte Young* permit suits against a State's governor for prospective injunctive relief to enforce the good faith bargaining requirement of the Act? We answer the first question in the affirmative, the second in the negative, and we therefore affirm the Eleventh Circuit's dismissal of petitioner's suit.

* * *

II

Petitioner argues that Congress through the Act abrogated the States' immunity from suit. In order to determine whether Congress has abrogated the States' sovereign immunity, we ask two questions: first, whether Congress has "unequivocally expresse[d] its intent to abrogate the immunity," and second, whether Congress has acted "pursuant to a valid exercise of power."

Atascadero

* * *

B

Having concluded that Congress clearly intended to abrogate the States' sovereign immunity through § 2710(d)(7), we turn now to consider whether the Act was passed "pursuant to a valid exercise of power." Before we address that question here, however, we think it necessary first to define the scope of our inquiry.

Petitioner suggests that one consideration weighing in favor of finding the power to abrogate here is that the Act authorizes only prospective injunctive relief rather than retroactive monetary relief. But we have often made it clear that the relief sought by a plaintiff suing a State is irrelevant to the question whether the suit is barred by the Eleventh Amendment. We think it follows *a fortiori* from this proposition that the type of relief sought is irrelevant to whether Congress has power to abrogate States' immunity. The Eleventh Amendment does not exist solely in order to "preven[t] federal court judgments that must be paid out of a State's treasury," it also serves to avoid "the indignity of subjecting a State to the coercive process of judicial tribunals at the instance of private parties."

Food for Thought

Does the Court here literally mean suing the state in its own name? Recall that in Edelman, where the plaintiff class named only state and municipal officials as defendants, the Court, noting that the relief granted by the district court would necessarily run against the state, treated the difference between injunctive and damages relief as not only relevant, but dispositive. Then-Justice Rehnquist wrote the Court's opinion in Edelman.

* * *

Thus our inquiry into whether Congress has the power to abrogate unilaterally the States' immunity from suit is narrowly focused on one question: Was the Act in question passed pursuant to a constitutional provision granting Congress the power to abrogate? Previously, in conducting that inquiry, we have found authority to abrogate under only two provisions of the Constitution. In Fitzpatrick, we recognized that the Fourteenth Amendment, by expanding federal power at the expense of state autonomy, had fundamentally altered the balance of state and federal power struck by the Constitution. * * * We held that through the Fourteenth Amendment, federal power extended to intrude upon the province of the Eleventh Amendment and therefore that § 5 of the Fourteenth Amendment allowed Congress to abrogate the immunity from suit guaranteed by that Amendment.

* * * In *Pennsylvania v. Union Gas Co.* [1989], a plurality of the Court found that the Interstate Commerce Clause, Art. I, § 8, cl. 3, granted Congress the power to abrogate state sovereign immunity, stating that the power to regulate interstate commerce would be "incomplete without the authority to render States liable in damages." Justice White added the fifth vote necessary to the result in that case, but wrote separately in order to express that he "[did] not agree with much of [the plurality's] reasoning."

* * *

Both parties make their arguments from the plurality decision in Union Gas, and we, too, begin there. We think it clear that Justice Brennan's opinion finds Congress' power to abrogate under the Interstate Commerce Clause from the

States' cession of their sovereignty when they gave Congress plenary power to regulate interstate commerce. Respondents' focus elsewhere is misplaced. While the plurality decision states that Congress' power under the Interstate Commerce Clause would be incomplete without the power to abrogate, that statement is made solely in order to emphasize the broad scope of Congress' authority over interstate commerce. Moreover, respondents' rationale would mean that where Congress has less authority, and the States have more, Congress' means for exercising that power must be greater. We read the plurality opinion to provide just the opposite. Indeed, it was in those circumstances where Congress exercised complete authority that Justice Brennan thought the power to abrogate most necessary.

Following the rationale of the *Union Gas* plurality, our inquiry is limited to determining whether the Indian Commerce Clause, like the Interstate Commerce Clause, is a grant of authority to the Federal Government at the expense of the States. The answer to that question is obvious. If anything, the Indian Commerce Clause accomplishes a greater transfer of power from the States to the Federal Government than does the Interstate Commerce Clause. * * *

Respondents * * * contend that if we find the rationale of the *Union Gas* plurality to extend to the Indian Commerce Clause, then "*Union Gas* should be reconsidered and overruled." Generally, the principle of *stare decisis*, and the interests that it serves, *viz.*, "the evenhanded, predictable, and consistent development of legal principles, * * * reliance on judicial decisions, and * * * the actual and perceived integrity of the judicial process," counsel strongly against reconsideration of our precedent. Nevertheless, we always have treated *stare decisis* as a "principle of policy," and not as an "inexorable command." "[W]hen governing decisions are unworkable or are badly reasoned, 'this Court has never felt constrained to follow precedent.' " Our willingness to reconsider our earlier decisions has been "particularly true in constitutional cases, because in such cases 'correction through legislative action is practically impossible.' "

The Court in *Union Gas* reached a result without an expressed rationale agreed upon by a majority of the Court. * * * Since it was issued, *Union Gas* has created confusion among the lower courts that have sought to understand and apply the deeply fractured decision.

The plurality's rationale also deviated sharply from our established federalism jurisprudence and essentially eviscerated our decision in *Hans*. It was well established in 1989 when *Union Gas* was decided that the Eleventh Amendment stood for the constitutional principle that state sovereign immunity limited the federal courts' jurisdiction under Article III. The text of the Amendment itself is clear enough on this point * * * .

* * *

The plurality's extended reliance upon our decision in Fitzpatrick v. Bitzer that Congress could under the Fourteenth Amendment abrogate the States' sovereign immunity was * * * misplaced. Fitzpatrick was based upon a rationale wholly inapplicable to the Interstate Commerce Clause, *viz.*, that the Fourteenth Amendment, adopted well after the adoption of the Eleventh Amendment and the ratification of the Constitution, operated to alter the pre-existing balance between state and federal power achieved by Article III and the Eleventh Amendment. As the dissent in *Union Gas* made clear, *Fitzpatrick* cannot be read to justify "limitation of the principle embodied in the Eleventh Amendment through appeal to antecedent provisions of the Constitution."

* * * *Union Gas* has proven to be a solitary departure from established law. Reconsidering the decision in *Union Gas*, we conclude that none of the policies underlying *stare decisis* require our continuing adherence to its holding. * * * We feel bound to conclude that *Union Gas* was wrongly decided and that it should be, and now is, overruled.

The dissent makes no effort to defend the decision in *Union Gas* but nonetheless would find congressional power to abrogate in this case. Contending that our decision is a novel extension of the Eleventh Amendment, the dissent chides us for "attend[ing]" to dicta. We adhere in this case, however, not to mere *obiter dicta*, but rather to the well-established rationale upon which the Court based the results of its earlier decisions. When an opinion issues for the Court, it is not only the result but also those portions of the opinion necessary to that result by which we are bound. For over a century, we have grounded our decisions in the oft-repeated understanding of state sovereign immunity as an essential part of the Eleventh Amendment. In *Principality of Monaco v. Mississippi*, the Court held that the Eleventh Amendment barred a suit brought against a State by a foreign state. Chief Justice Hughes wrote for a unanimous Court:

> * * * Manifestly, we cannot rest with a mere literal application of the words of § 2 of Article III, or assume that the letter of the Eleventh Amendment exhausts the restrictions upon suits against non-consenting States. Behind the words of the constitutional provisions are postulates which limit and control. There is the essential postulate that the controversies, as contemplated, shall be found to be of a justiciable character. There is also the postulate that States of the Union, still possessing attributes of sovereignty, shall be immune from suits, without their consent, save where there has been a "surrender of this immunity in the plan of the convention."

It is true that we have not had occasion previously to apply established

Food for Thought

Does Chief Justice Hughes connote here that the Constitution is not "the supreme Law of the Land" because there are extra-constitutional postulates that trump the Supremacy Clause?

Eleventh Amendment principles to the question whether Congress has the power to abrogate state sovereign immunity (save in Union Gas). But consideration of that question must proceed with fidelity to this century-old doctrine.

The dissent, to the contrary, disregards our case law in favor of a theory cobbled together from law review articles and its own version of historical events. The dissent cites not a single decision since Hans (other than Union Gas) that supports its view of state sovereign immunity, instead relying upon the now-discredited decision in Chisholm v. Georgia. Its undocumented and highly speculative extralegal explanation of the decision in Hans is a disservice to the Court's traditional method of adjudication.

The dissent mischaracterizes the Hans opinion. That decision found its roots not solely in the common law of England, but in the much more fundamental " 'jurisprudence in all civilized nations.' " The dissent's proposition that the common law of England, where adopted by the States, was open to change by the legislature, is wholly unexceptionable and largely beside the point: that common law provided the substantive rules of law rather than jurisdiction. It also is noteworthy that the principle of state sovereign immunity stands distinct from other principles of the common law in that only the former prompted a specific constitutional amendment.

Food for Thought

Is this the "other other reason or ground" to which the Hans Court referred at page 646?

Hans—with a much closer vantage point than the dissent—recognized that the decision in Chisholm was contrary to the well-understood meaning of the Constitution. The dissent's conclusion that the decision in Chisholm was "reasonable," certainly would have struck the Framers of the Eleventh Amendment as quite odd. The dissent's lengthy analysis of the text of the Eleventh Amendment is directed at a straw man—we long have recognized that blind reliance upon the text of the Eleventh Amendment is " 'to strain the Constitution and the law to a construction never imagined or dreamed of.' " The text dealt in terms only with the problem presented by the decision in Chisholm; in light of the fact that the federal courts did not have federal question jurisdiction at the time the Amendment was passed (and would not have it until 1875), it seems unlikely that much thought was given to the prospect of federal question jurisdiction over the States.

Food for Thought

If those who drafted and ratified the Eleventh Amendment were not thinking about federal-question jurisdiction, it is proper for the Court to apply the Amendment to a federal-question case?

* * *

In overruling *Union Gas* today, we reconfirm that the background principle of state sovereign immunity embodied in the Eleventh Amendment is not so ephemeral as to dissipate when the subject of the suit is an area, like the regulation of Indian commerce, that is under the exclusive control of the Federal Government. Even when the Constitution vests in Congress complete law-making authority over a particular area, the Eleventh Amendment prevents congressional authorization of suits by private parties against unconsenting States. The Eleventh Amendment restricts the judicial power under Article III, and Article I cannot be used to circumvent the constitutional limitations placed upon federal jurisdiction. Petitioner's suit against the State of Florida must be dismissed for a lack of jurisdiction.

III

Petitioner argues that we may exercise jurisdiction over its suit to enforce § 2710(d)(3) against the Governor notwithstanding the jurisdictional bar of the Eleventh Amendment. Petitioner notes that since our decision in *Ex parte Young* we often have found federal jurisdiction over a suit against a state official when that suit seeks only prospective injunctive relief in order to "end a continuing violation of federal law." The situation presented here, however, is sufficiently different from that giving rise to the traditional *Ex parte Young* action so as to preclude the availability of that doctrine.

Here, the "continuing violation of federal law" alleged by petitioner is the Governor's failure to bring the State into compliance with § 2710(d)(3). But the duty to negotiate imposed upon the State by that statutory provision does not stand alone. * * * Congress passed § 2710(d)(3) in conjunction with the carefully crafted and intricate remedial scheme set forth in § 2710(d)(7).

Where Congress has created a remedial scheme for the enforcement of a particular federal right, we have, in suits against federal officers, refused to supplement that scheme with one created by the judiciary. * * * Here, of course, the question is not whether a remedy should be created, but instead is whether the Eleventh Amendment bar should be lifted, as it was in *Ex parte Young*, in order to allow a suit against a state officer. Nevertheless, we think that the same general principle applies: therefore, where Congress has prescribed a detailed remedial scheme for the enforcement against a State of a statutorily created right, a court should hesitate before casting aside those limitations and permitting an action against a state officer based upon *Ex parte Young*.

Food for Thought

Compare and contrast *Seminole Tribe* and *Chilicky* with respect to the areas reflected in the attached chart.

Here, Congress intended § 2710(d)(3) to be enforced against the State in an action brought under § 2710(d)(7); the intricate procedures set forth in that provision show that Congress intended therein not only to define, but also significantly to limit, the duty imposed by § 2710(d)(3). By contrast with this quite modest set of sanctions, an action brought against a state official under *Ex parte Young* would expose that official to the full remedial powers of a federal court, including, presumably, contempt sanctions. If § 2710(d)(3) could be enforced in a suit under *Ex parte Young*, § 2710(d)(7) would have been superfluous; it is difficult to see why an Indian tribe would suffer through the intricate scheme of § 2710(d)(7) when more complete and more immediate relief would be available under *Ex parte Young*.[17]

Here, of course, we have found that Congress does not have authority under the Constitution to make the State suable in federal court under § 2710(d)(7). Nevertheless, the fact that Congress chose to impose upon the State a liability which is significantly more limited than would be the liability imposed upon the state officer under *Ex parte Young* strongly indicates that Congress had no wish to create the latter under § 2710(d)(3). Nor are we free to rewrite the statutory scheme in order to approximate what we think Congress might have wanted had it known that § 2710(d)(7) was beyond its authority. If that effort is to be made, it should be made by Congress, and not by the federal courts. We hold that *Ex parte Young* is inapplicable to petitioner's suit against the Governor of Florida, and therefore that suit is barred by the Eleventh Amendment and must be dismissed for a lack of jurisdiction.

Food for Thought

Given this assertion, might one argue that the Court has done exactly that with respect to the Eleventh Amendment and federal-question jurisdiction? *See supra* at 727.

* * *

The Eleventh Circuit's dismissal of petitioner's suit is hereby affirmed.

It is so ordered.

JUSTICE STEVENS, dissenting.

This case is about power—the power of the Congress of the United States to create a private federal cause of action against a State, or its Governor, for the violation of a federal right. In *Chisholm v. Georgia*, the entire Court—including Justice Iredell whose dissent provided the blueprint for the Eleventh Amend-

17 Contrary to the claims of the dissent, we do not hold that Congress cannot authorize federal jurisdiction under *Ex parte Young* over a cause of action with a limited remedial scheme. We find only that Congress did not intend that result in the Indian Gaming Regulatory Act. * * *

ment—assumed that Congress had such power. In Hans v. Louisiana— a case the Court purports to follow today—the Court again assumed that Congress had such power. In Fitzpatrick v. Bitzer and Pennsylvania v. Union Gas Co. the Court squarely held that Congress has such power. In a series of cases beginning with Atascadero State Hospital v. Scanlon, the Court formulated a special "clear statement rule" to determine whether specific Acts of Congress contained an effective exercise of that power. Nevertheless, in a sharp break with the past, today the Court holds that with the narrow and illogical exception of statutes enacted pursuant to the Enforcement Clause of the Fourteenth Amendment, Congress has no such power.

The importance of the majority's decision to overrule the Court's holding in Pennsylvania v. Union Gas Co. cannot be overstated. The majority's opinion * * * prevents Congress from providing a federal forum for a broad range of actions against States, from those sounding in copyright and patent law, to those concerning bankruptcy, environmental law, and the regulation of our vast national economy.

* * *

I

For the purpose of deciding this case, I can readily assume that Justice Iredell's dissent in Chisholm and the Court's opinion in Hans correctly stated the law that should govern our decision today. As I shall explain, both of those opinions relied on an interpretation of an Act of Congress rather than a want of congressional power to authorize a suit against the State.

In concluding that the federal courts could not entertain Chisholm's action against the State of Georgia, Justice Iredell relied on the text of the Judiciary Act of 1789, not the State's assertion that Article III did not extend the judicial power to suits against unconsenting States. Justice Iredell argued that, under Article III, federal courts possessed only such jurisdiction as Congress had provided, and that the Judiciary Act expressly limited federal-court jurisdiction to that which could be exercised in accordance with " 'the principles and usages of law.' " He reasoned that the inclusion of this phrase constituted a command to the federal courts to construe their jurisdiction in light of the prevailing common law, a background legal regime which he believed incorporated the doctrine of sovereign immunity.

Because Justice Iredell believed that the expansive text of Article III did not prevent Congress from imposing this common-law limitation on federal-court jurisdiction, he concluded that judges had no authority to entertain a suit against an unconsenting State. At the same time, although he acknowledged that the Constitution might allow Congress to extend federal-court jurisdiction to such an action, he concluded that the terms of the Judiciary Act of 1789 plainly had not done so. * * *

For Justice Iredell then, it was enough to assume that Article III permitted Congress to impose sovereign immunity as a jurisdictional limitation; he did not proceed to resolve the further question whether the Constitution went so far as to prevent Congress from withdrawing a State's immunity. Thus, it would be ironic to construe the *Chisholm* dissent as precedent for the conclusion that Article III limits Congress' power to determine the scope of a State's sovereign immunity in federal court.

* * * There is a special irony in the fact that the error committed by the *Chisholm* majority was its decision that this Court, rather than Congress, should define the scope of the sovereign immunity defense. That, of course, is precisely the same error the Court commits today.

* * *

Justice Brennan has persuasively explained that the Eleventh Amendment's jurisdictional restriction is best understood to apply only to suits premised on diversity jurisdiction, and Justice Scalia has agreed that the plain text of the Amendment cannot be read to apply to federal-question cases. Whatever the precise dimensions of the Amendment, its express terms plainly do not apply to all suits brought against unconsenting States. The question thus becomes whether the relatively modest jurisdictional bar that the Eleventh Amendment imposes should be understood to reveal that a more general jurisdictional bar implicitly inheres in Article III.

The language of Article III certainly gives no indication that such an implicit bar exists. That provision's text specifically provides for federal-court jurisdiction over all cases arising under federal law. Moreover, as I have explained, Justice Iredell's dissent argued that it was the Judiciary Act of 1789, not Article III, that prevented the federal courts from entertaining Chisholm's diversity action against Georgia. Therefore, Justice Iredell's analysis at least suggests that it was by no means a fixed view at the time of the founding that Article III prevented Congress from rendering States suable in federal court by their own citizens. In sum, little more than speculation justifies the conclusion that the Eleventh Amendment's express but partial limitation on the scope of Article III reveals that an implicit but more general one was already in place.

II

The majority appears to acknowledge that one cannot deduce from either the text of Article III or the plain terms of the Eleventh Amendment that the judicial power does not extend to a congressionally created cause of action against a State brought by one of that State's citizens. Nevertheless, the majority asserts that precedent compels that same conclusion. I disagree. * * * The majority suggests that by dismissing the suit, Hans effectively held that federal courts have no power to hear federal question suits brought by same-state plaintiffs.

Hans does not hold, however, that the Eleventh Amendment, or any other constitutional provision, precludes federal courts from entertaining actions brought by citizens against their own States in the face of contrary congressional direction. * * * Hans instead reflects, at the most, this Court's conclusion that, as a matter of federal common law, federal courts should decline to entertain suits against unconsenting States. Because Hans did not announce a constitutionally mandated jurisdictional bar, one need not overrule Hans, or even question its reasoning, in order to conclude that Congress may direct the federal courts to reject sovereign immunity in those suits not mentioned by the Eleventh Amendment. Instead, one need only follow it.

* * *

* * * Hans itself looked to see whether Congress had displaced the presumption that sovereign immunity obtains. Although the opinion did go to great lengths to establish the quite uncontroversial historical proposition that unconsenting States generally were not subject to suit, that entire discussion preceded the opinion's statutory analysis. Thus, the opinion's thorough historical investigation served only to establish a presumption against jurisdiction that Congress must overcome, not an inviolable jurisdictional restriction that inheres in the Constitution itself.

Indeed, the very fact that the Court characterized the doctrine of sovereign immunity as a "presumption" confirms its assumption that it could be displaced.

* * *

No one has ever suggested that Congress would be powerless to displace the other common-law immunity doctrines that this Court has recognized as appropriate defenses to certain federal claims such as the judicially fashioned *Bivens* remedy. Similarly, our cases recognizing qualified officer immunity in § 1983 actions rest on the conclusion that, in passing that statute, Congress did not intend to displace the common-law immunity

Take Note

Justice Stevens may be echoing a bit of sleight-of-hand jurisprudence by the Courts that recognized qualified immunity. Section 1983 *antedated* "the general jurisdictional statute" by four years. In 1866, Congress had enacted a special statute vesting federal subject matter jurisdiction in the federal trial courts for civil rights cases—today's 28 U.S.C. § 1343. Radical Reconstruction was nearing its peak as Congress battled President Johnson for control, he favoring a much more accommodating reconstruction than Congress. It is that Congress that the Court posits showed special solicitude for the immunity of state officials who had commited constitutional violations against the newly-recognized black citizenry.

that officers would have retained under suits premised solely on the general jurisdictional statute.

For that reason, the federal common law of officer immunity that Congress meant to incorporate, not a contrary state immunity, applies in § 1983 cases. There is no reason why Congress' undoubted power to displace those common-law immunities should be either greater or lesser than its power to displace the common-law sovereign immunity defense.

Some of our precedents do state that the sovereign immunity doctrine rests on fundamental constitutional "postulates" and partakes of jurisdictional aspects rooted in Article III. Most notably, that reasoning underlies this Court's holding in Principality of Monaco v. Mississippi.

Monaco is a most inapt precedent for the majority's holding today. That case barred a foreign sovereign from suing a State in an equitable state law action to recover payments due on State bonds. It did not, however, involve a claim based on federal law. Instead, the case concerned a purely state law question to which the State had interposed a federal defense. Thus, Monaco reveals little about the power of Congress to create a private federal cause of action to remedy a State's violation of federal law.

Take Note

Justice Stevens seems to be saying that *Monaco* is a post-Eleventh-Amendment version of Chisholm v. Georgia—a state claim to which Mississippi, unlike Georgia in Chisholm, had the defense that the Amendment provided.

* * *

Finally, the particular nature of the federal question involved in Hans renders the majority's reliance upon its rule even less defensible. Hans deduced its rebuttable presumption in favor of sovereign immunity largely on the basis of its extensive analysis of cases holding that the sovereign could not be forced to make good on its debts via a private suit. Because Hans * * * involved a suit that attempted to make a State honor its debt, its holding need not be read to stand even for the relatively limited proposition that there is a presumption in favor of sovereign immunity in all federal-question cases.

* * *

III

* * *

The fundamental error that continues to lead the Court astray is its failure to acknowledge that its modern embodiment of the ancient doctrine of sovereign immunity * * * rests rather on concerns of federalism and comity that merit respect but are nevertheless, in cases such as the one before us, subordinate to the plenary power of Congress.

IV

* * *

While I am persuaded that there is no justification for permanently enshrining the judge-made law of sovereign immunity, I recognize that federalism concerns—and even the interest in protecting the solvency of the States that was at work in *Chisholm* and *Hans*—may well justify a grant of immunity from federal litigation in certain classes of cases. Such a grant, however, should be the product of a reasoned decision by the policymaking branch of our Government. For this Court to conclude that time-worn shibboleths iterated and reiterated by judges should take precedence over the deliberations of the Congress of the United States is simply irresponsible.

* * *

For these reasons, as well as those set forth in Justice Souter's opinion, I respectfully dissent.

JUSTICE SOUTER, with whom JUSTICE GINSBURG and JUSTICE BREYER join, dissenting.

In holding the State of Florida immune to suit under the Indian Gaming Regulatory Act, the Court today holds for the first time since the founding of the Republic that Congress has no authority to subject a State to the jurisdiction of a federal court at the behest of an individual asserting a federal right. Although the Court invokes the Eleventh Amendment as authority for this proposition, the only sense in which that amendment might be claimed as pertinent here was tolerantly phrased by Justice Stevens in his concurring opinion in *Pennsylvania v. Union Gas*. There, he explained how it has come about that we have two Eleventh Amendments, the one ratified in 1795, the other (so-called) invented by the Court nearly a century later in *Hans*. Justice Stevens saw in that second Eleventh Amendment no bar to the exercise of congressional authority under the Commerce Clause in providing for suits on a federal question by individuals against a State, and I can only say that after my own canvass of the matter I believe he was entirely correct in that view, for reasons given below. His position, of course, was also the holding in *Union Gas*, which the Court now overrules and repudiates.

The fault I find with the majority today is not in its decision to reexamine *Union Gas*, for the Court in that case produced no majority for a single rationale supporting congressional authority. Instead, I part company from the Court because I am convinced that its decision is fundamentally mistaken, and for that reason I respectfully dissent.

I

It is useful to separate three questions: (1) whether the States enjoyed sovereign immunity if sued in their own courts in the period prior to ratification of the National Constitution; (2) if so, whether after ratification the States were entitled to claim some such immunity when sued in a federal court exercising jurisdiction either because the suit was between a State and a non-state litigant who was not its citizen, or because the issue in the case raised a federal question; and (3) whether any state sovereign immunity recognized in federal court may be abrogated by Congress.

The answer to the first question is not clear, although some of the Framers assumed that States did enjoy immunity in their own courts. The second question was not debated at the time of ratification, except as to citizen-state diversity jurisdiction; there was no unanimity, but in due course the Court in Chisholm v. Georgia answered that a state defendant enjoyed no such immunity. As to federal question jurisdiction, state sovereign immunity seems not to have been debated prior to ratification, the silence probably showing a general understanding at the time that the States would have no immunity in such cases.

The adoption of the Eleventh Amendment soon changed the result in *Chisholm*, not by mentioning sovereign immunity, but by eliminating citizen-state diversity jurisdiction over cases with state defendants. I will explain why the Eleventh Amendment did not affect federal question jurisdiction, a notion that needs to be understood for the light it casts on the soundness of *Hans*'s holding that States did enjoy sovereign immunity in federal question suits. The *Hans* Court erroneously assumed that a State could plead sovereign immunity against a noncitizen suing under federal question jurisdiction, and for that reason held that a State must enjoy the same protection in a suit by one of its citizens. The error of *Hans*'s reasoning is underscored by its clear inconsistency with the Founders' hostility to the implicit reception of common-law doctrine as federal law, and with the Founders' conception of sovereign power as divided between the States and the National Government for the sake of very practical objectives.

The Court's answer today to the third question is likewise at odds with the Founders' view that common law, when it was received into the new American legal systems, was always subject to legislative amendment. In ignoring the reasons for this pervasive understanding at the time of the ratification, and in holding that a nontextual common-law rule limits a clear grant of congressional power under Article I, the Court follows a course that has brought it to grief before in our history, and promises to do so again.

Beyond this third question that elicits today's holding, there is one further issue. To reach the Court's result, it must not only hold the *Hans* doctrine to be outside the reach of Congress, but must also displace the doctrine of *Ex parte Young* that an officer of the government may be ordered prospectively to follow federal law, in cases in which the government may not itself be sued directly. None of its reasons for displacing *Young*'s jurisdictional doctrine withstand scrutiny.

A

The doctrine of sovereign immunity comprises two distinct rules, which are not always separately recognized. The one rule holds that the King or the Crown, as the font of law, is not bound by the law's provisions; the other provides that the King or Crown, as the font of justice, is not subject to suit in its own courts. The one rule limits the reach of substantive law; the other, the jurisdiction of the courts. We are concerned here only with the latter rule, which took its common-law form in the high middle ages. * * *

* * *

Whatever the scope of sovereign immunity might have been in the Colonies * * * or during the period of Confederation, the proposal to establish a National Government under the Constitution drafted in 1787 presented a prospect unknown to the common law prior to the American experience: the States would become parts of a system in which sovereignty over even domestic matters would be divided or parcelled [*sic*] out between the States and the Nation, the latter to be invested with its own judicial power and the right to prevail against the States whenever their respective substantive laws might be in conflict. With this prospect in mind, the 1787 Constitution might have addressed state sovereign immunity by eliminating whatever sovereign immunity the States previously had, as to any matter subject to federal law or jurisdiction; by recognizing an analogue to the old immunity in the new context of federal jurisdiction, but subject to abrogation as to any matter within that jurisdiction; or by enshrining a doctrine of inviolable state sovereign immunity in the text, thereby giving it constitutional protection in the new federal jurisdiction.

The 1787 draft in fact said nothing on the subject, and it was this very silence that occasioned some, though apparently not widespread, dispute among the Framers and others over whether ratification of the Constitution would preclude a State sued in federal court from asserting sovereign immunity as it could have done on any matter of nonfederal law litigated in its own courts. As it has come down to us, the discussion gave no attention to congressional power under the proposed Article I but focused entirely on the limits of the judicial power provided in Article III. And although the jurisdictional bases together constituting the judicial power of the national courts under section 2 of Article III included questions arising under federal law and cases between States and individuals who are not citizens, it was only upon the latter citizen-state diversity provisions that preratification questions about state immunity from suit or liability centered.

[F]or now it is enough to say that there was no consensus on the issue. There was, on the contrary, a clear disagreement, which was left to fester during the ratification period, to be resolved only thereafter. One other point, however, was also clear: the debate addressed only the question whether ratification of the Constitution would, in diversity cases and without more, abrogate the state sovereign immunity or allow it to have some application. We have no record that anyone argued for the third option mentioned above, that the Constitution would affirmatively guarantee state sovereign immunity against any congressional action to the contrary. * * * It may have been reasonable to contend (as we will see that Madison, Marshall, and Hamilton did) that Article III would not alter States' pre-existing common-law immunity despite its unqualified grant of jurisdiction over diversity suits against States. But then, as now, there was no textual support for contending that Article III or any other provision would "constitutionalize" state sovereign immunity, and no one uttered any such contention.

* * *

C

The Eleventh Amendment, of course, repudiated *Chisholm* and clearly divested federal courts of some jurisdiction as to cases against state parties * * * . There are two plausible readings of this provision's text. Under the first, it simply repeals the Citizen-State Diversity Clauses of Article III for all cases in which the State appears as a defendant. Under the second, it strips the federal courts of jurisdiction in any case in which a state defendant is sued by a citizen not its own, even if jurisdiction might otherwise rest on the existence of a federal question in the suit. Neither reading of the Amendment, of course, furnishes authority for the Court's view in today's case, but we need to choose between the competing readings for the light that will be shed on the *Hans* doctrine and the legitimacy of inflating that doctrine to the point of constitutional immutability as the Court has chosen to do.

The history and structure of the Eleventh Amendment convincingly show that it reaches only to suits subject to federal jurisdiction exclusively under the Citizen-State Diversity Clauses. In precisely tracking the language in Article III providing for citizen-state diversity jurisdiction, the text of the Amendment does, after all, suggest to common sense that only the Diversity Clauses are being addressed. If the Framers had meant the Amendment to bar federal question suits as well, they could not only have made their intentions clearer very easily, but could simply have adopted the first post-*Chisholm* proposal, introduced in the House of Representatives by Theodore Sedgwick of Massachusetts on instructions from the Legislature of that Commonwealth. Its provisions would have had exactly that expansive effect:

> [N]o state shall be liable to be made a party defendant, in any of the judicial courts, established, or which shall be established under the authority of the United States, at the suit of any person or persons, whether a citizen or citizens, or a foreigner or foreigners, or of any body politic or corporate, whether within or without the United States.

With its references to suits by citizens as well as non-citizens, the Sedgwick amendment would necessarily have been applied beyond the Diversity Clauses, and for a reason that would have been wholly obvious to the people of the time. Sedgwick sought such a broad amendment because many of the States, including his own, owed debts subject to collection under the Treaty of Paris. Suits to collect such debts would "arise under" that Treaty and thus be subject to federal question jurisdiction under Article III. * * *

Congress took no action on Sedgwick's proposal, however, and the Amendment as ultimately adopted two years later could hardly have been meant to limit federal question jurisdiction, or it would never have left the states open to federal question suits by their own citizens. * * * If the Framers of the Eleventh Amendment had meant it to immunize States from federal question suits like those that might be brought to enforce the Treaty of Paris, they would surely have drafted the Amendment differently.

* * *

In sum, reading the Eleventh Amendment solely as a limit on citizen-state diversity jurisdiction has the virtue of coherence with this Court's practice, with the views of John Marshall, with the history of the Amendment's drafting, and with its allusive language. Today's majority does not appear to disagree, at least insofar as the constitutional text is concerned; the Court concedes, after all, that "the text of the Amendment would appear to restrict only the Article III diversity jurisdiction of the federal courts."

Thus, regardless of which of the two plausible readings one adopts, the further point to note here is that there is no possible argument that the Eleventh Amendment, by its terms, deprives federal courts of jurisdiction over all citizen lawsuits against the States. Not even the Court advances that proposition, and there would be no textual basis for doing so.[12] Because the plaintiffs in today's

12 The Court does suggest that the drafters of the Eleventh Amendment may not have had federal question jurisdiction in mind, in the apparent belief that this somehow supports its reading. The possibility, however, that those who drafted the Eleventh Amendment intended to deal "only with the problem presented by the decision in *Chisholm*" would demonstrate, if any demonstration beyond the clear language of the Eleventh Amendment were necessary, that the Eleventh Amendment was not

case are citizens of the State that they are suing, the Eleventh Amendment simply does not apply to them. We must therefore look elsewhere for the source of that immunity by which the Court says their suit is barred from a federal court.[13]

II

The obvious place to look elsewhere, of course, is *Hans v. Louisiana*, and *Hans* was indeed a leap in the direction of today's holding, even though it does not take the Court all the way. The parties in *Hans* raised, and the Court in that case answered, only what I have called the second question, that is, whether the Constitution, without more, permits a State to plead sovereign immunity to bar the exercise of federal question jurisdiction. Although the Court invoked a principle of sovereign immunity to cure what it took to be the Eleventh Amendment's anomaly of barring only those state suits brought by noncitizen plaintiffs, the *Hans* Court had no occasion to consider whether Congress could abrogate that background immunity by statute. Indeed (except in the special circumstance of Congress's power to enforce the Civil War Amendments), this question never came before our Court until *Union Gas*, and any intimations of an answer in prior cases were mere dicta. In *Union Gas* the Court held that the immunity recognized in *Hans* had no constitutional status and was subject to congressional abrogation. Today the Court overrules *Union Gas* and holds just the opposite. In deciding how to choose between these two positions, the place to begin is with *Hans*'s holding that a principle of sovereign immunity derived from the common law insulates a state from federal question jurisdiction at the suit of its own citizen. A

---

intended to address the broader issue of federal question suits brought by citizens. Moreover, the Court's point is built on a faulty foundation. The Court is simply incorrect in asserting that "the federal courts did not have federal question jurisdiction at the time the Amendment was passed." Article III, of course, provided for such jurisdiction, and early Congresses exercised their authority pursuant to Article III to confer jurisdiction on the federal courts to resolve various matters of federal law. In fact, only six years after the passage of the Eleventh Amendment, Congress enacted a statute providing for general federal question jurisdiction. It is, of course, true that this statute proved short-lived (it was repealed by the Act of Mar. 8, 1802, 2 Stat. 132), and that Congress did not pass another statute conferring general federal jurisdiction until 1875, but the drafters of the Eleventh Amendment obviously could not have predicted such things. The real significance of the 1801 act is that it demonstrates the awareness among the Members of the early Congresses of the potential scope of Article III. This, in combination with the pre-Eleventh Amendment statutes that conferred federal question jurisdiction on the federal courts, cast considerable doubt on the Court's suggestion that the issue of federal question jurisdiction never occurred to the drafters of the Eleventh Amendment; on the contrary, just because these early statutes underscore the early Congresses' recognition of the availability of federal question jurisdiction, the silence of the Eleventh Amendment is all the more deafening.

13 The majority chides me that the "lengthy analysis of the text of the Eleventh Amendment is directed at a straw man." But plain text is the Man of Steel in a confrontation with "background principle[s]" and " 'postulates which limit and control.' " An argument rooted in the text of a constitutional provision may not be guaranteed of carrying the day, but insubstantiality is not its failing. This is particularly true in construing the jurisdictional provisions of Art. III, which speak with a clarity not to be found in some of the more open-textured provisions of the Constitution. That the Court thinks otherwise is an indication of just how far it has strayed beyond the boundaries of traditional constitutional analysis.

critical examination of that case will show that it was wrongly decided, as virtually every recent commentator has concluded. It follows that the Court's further step today of constitutionalizing Hans's rule against abrogation by Congress compounds and immensely magnifies the century-old mistake of Hans itself and takes its place with other historic examples of textually untethered elevations of judicially derived rules to the status of inviolable constitutional law.

A

* * *

Justice Bradley's opinion did not purport to hold that the terms either of Article III or of the Eleventh Amendment barred the suit, but that the ancient doctrine of sovereign immunity that had inspired adoption of the Eleventh Amendment applied to cases beyond the Amendment's scope and otherwise within the federal question jurisdiction. * * *

Hans thus addressed the issue implicated (though not directly raised) in the preratification debate about the Citizen-State Diversity Clauses and implicitly settled by Chisholm: whether state sovereign immunity was cognizable by federal courts on the exercise of federal question jurisdiction. According to Hans, and contrary to Chisholm, it was. But that is all that Hans held. Because no federal legislation purporting to pierce state immunity was at issue, it cannot fairly be said that Hans held state sovereign immunity to have attained some constitutional status immunizing it from abrogation.

* * *

Although there was thus no anomaly to be cured by Hans, the case certainly created its own anomaly in leaving federal courts entirely without jurisdiction to enforce paramount federal law at the behest of a citizen against a State that broke it. It destroyed the congruence of the judicial power under Article III with the substantive guarantees of the Constitution, and with the provisions of statutes passed by Congress in the exercise of its power under Article I: when a State injured an individual in violation of federal law no federal forum could provide direct relief. Absent an alternative process to vindicate federal law John Marshall saw just what the consequences of this anomaly would be in the early Republic, and he took that consequence as good evidence that the Framers could never have intended such a scheme. * * * And yet that is just what Hans threatened to do.

How such a result could have been threatened on the basis of a principle not so much as mentioned in the Constitution is difficult to understand. But history provides the explanation. As I have already said, Hans was one episode in a long story of debt repudiation by the States of the former Confederacy after the end of Reconstruction. The turning point in the States' favor came with the Compromise of 1877, when the Republican party agreed effectively to end Reconstruction and to withdraw federal troops from the South in return for Southern acquiescence in the decision of the Electoral Commission that awarded the disputed 1876 presidential election to Rutherford B. Hayes. The troop withdrawal, of course, left the federal judiciary "effectively without power to resist the rapidly coalescing repudiation movement." Contract Clause suits like the one brought by Hans thus presented this Court with "a draconian choice between repudiation of some of its most inviolable constitutional doctrines and the humiliation of seeing its political authority compromised as its judgments met the resistance of hostile state governments." Indeed, Louisiana's brief in Hans unmistakably bore witness to this Court's inability to enforce a judgment against a recalcitrant State: "The solemn obligation of a government arising on its own acknowledged bond would not be enhanced by a judgment rendered on such bond. If it either could not or would not make provision for paying the bond, it is probable that it could not or would not make provision for satisfying the judgment." Given the likelihood that a judgment against the State could not be enforced, it is not wholly surprising that the Hans Court found a way to avoid the certainty of the State's contempt.

So it is that history explains, but does not honor, Hans. The ultimate demerit of the case centers, however, not on its politics but on the legal errors on which it rested. Before considering those errors, it is necessary to address the Court's contention that subsequent cases have read into Hans what was not there to begin with, that is, a background principle of sovereign immunity that is constitutional in stature and therefore unalterable by Congress.

* * *

III

Three critical errors in Hans weigh against constitutionalizing its holding as the majority does today. The first we have already seen: the Hans Court misread the Eleventh Amendment. It also misunderstood the conditions under which common-law doctrines were received or rejected at the time of the Founding, and it fundamentally mistook the very nature of sovereignty in the young Republic that was supposed to entail a State's immunity to federal question jurisdiction in a federal court. While I would not, as a matter of *stare decisis*, overrule Hans today, an understanding of its failings on these points will show how the Court today simply compounds already serious error in taking Hans the further step of investing its rule with constitutional inviolability against the considered judgment of Congress to abrogate it.

A

There is and could be no dispute that the doctrine of sovereign immunity that *Hans* purported to apply had its origins in the "familiar doctrine of the common law," "derived from the laws and practices of our English ancestors."[26] * * * Here, as in the mother country, it remained a common-law rule.

This fact of the doctrine's common-law status in the period covering the Founding and the later adoption of the Eleventh Amendment should have raised a warning flag to the *Hans* Court and it should do the same for the Court today. For although the Court has persistently assumed that the common law's presence in the minds of the early Framers must have functioned as a limitation on their understanding of the new Nation's constitutional powers, this turns out not to be so at all. One of the characteristics of the Founding generation, on the contrary, was its joinder of an appreciation of its immediate and powerful common-law heritage with caution in settling that inheritance on the political systems of the new Republic. It is not that the Framers failed to see themselves to be children of the common law * * * . But still it is clear that the adoption of English common law in America was not taken for granted, and that the exact manner and extent of the common law's reception were subject to careful consideration by courts and legislatures in each of the new States. An examination of the States' experience with common-law reception * * * demonstrate[s] that our history is entirely at odds with *Hans*'s resort to a common-law principle to limit the Constitution's contrary text.

* * *

2

While the States had limited their reception of English common law to principles appropriate to American conditions, the 1787 draft Constitution contained no provision for adopting the common law at all. This omission stood in sharp contrast to the state constitutions then extant, virtually all of which contained explicit provisions dealing with common-law reception. Since the experience in the States set the stage for thinking at the national level, this failure to address the notion of common-law reception could not have been inadvertent.

---

26 The Court seeks to disparage the common law roots of the doctrine, and the consequences of those roots which I outline by asserting that *Hans* "found its roots not solely in the common law of England, but in the much more fundamental ' "jurisprudence in all civilized nations." ' " The *Hans* Court, however, relied explicitly on the ground that a suit against the State by its own citizen was "not known * * * at the common law" and was not among the departures from the common law recognized by the Constitution. Moreover, *Hans* explicitly adopted the reasoning of Justice Iredell's dissent in *Chisholm*, and that opinion could hardly have been clearer in relying exclusively on the common law. * * *

* * *

B

Given the refusal to entertain any wholesale reception of common law, given the failure of the new Constitution to make any provision for adoption of common law as such, and given the protests already quoted that no general reception had occurred, the *Hans* Court and the Court today cannot reasonably argue that something like the old immunity doctrine somehow slipped in as a tacit but enforceable background principle. The evidence is even more specific, however, that there was no pervasive understanding that sovereign immunity had limited federal question jurisdiction.

1

* * *

The majority sees * * * chiefly in Hamilton's discussion of sovereign immunity in Federalist No. 81, an unequivocal mandate "which would preclude all federal jurisdiction over an unconsenting State." But there is no such mandate to be found.

[T]he immediate context of Hamilton's discussion in Federalist No. 81 has nothing to do with federal question cases. It addresses a suggestion "that an assignment of the public securities of one state to the citizens of another, would enable them to prosecute that state in the federal courts for the amount of those securities." Hamilton is plainly talking about a suit subject to a federal court's jurisdiction under the Citizen-State Diversity Clauses of Article III.

The general statement on sovereign immunity emphasized by the majority then follows, along with a reference back to Federalist No. 32. What Hamilton draws from that prior paper, however, is not a general conclusion about state sovereignty but a particular point about state contracts:

> A recurrence to the principles there established will satisfy us, that there is no colour to pretend that the state governments, would by the adoption of that plan, be divested of the privilege of paying their own debts in their own way, free from every constraint but that which flows from the obligations of good faith. The contracts between a nation and individuals are only binding on the conscience of the sovereign, and have no pretensions to a compulsive force. They confer no right of action independent of the sovereign will.

The most that can be inferred from this is, as noted above, that in diversity cases applying state contract law the immunity that a State would have enjoyed in its own courts is carried into the federal court. * * * No general theory of federal question immunity can be inferred from Hamilton's discussion of immunity in contract suits. But that is only the beginning of the difficulties that accrue to the majority from reliance on Federalist No. 81.

Hamilton says that a State is "not * * * amenable to the suit of an individual without its consent * * * [u]nless * * * there is a surrender of this immunity in the plan of the convention." He immediately adds, however, that "[t]he circumstances which are necessary to produce an alienation of state sovereignty, were discussed in considering the article of taxation, and need not be repeated here." The reference is to Federalist No. 32, also by Hamilton, which has this to say about the alienation of state sovereignty:

> [A]s the plan of the Convention aims only at a partial Union or consolidation, the State Governments would clearly retain all the rights of sovereignty which they before had and which were not by that act exclusively delegated to the United States. This exclusive delegation or rather this alienation of State sovereignty would only exist in three cases; where the Constitution in express terms granted an exclusive authority to the Union; where it granted in one instance an authority to the Union and in another prohibited the States from exercising the like authority; and where it granted an authority to the Union, to which a similar authority in the States would be absolutely and totally contradictory and repugnant. I use these terms to distinguish this last case from another which might appear to resemble it; but which would in fact be essentially different; I mean where the exercise of a concurrent jurisdiction might be productive of occasional interferences in the policy of any branch of administration, but would not imply any direct contradiction or repugnancy in point of constitutional authority.

* * *

The first embarrassment Hamilton's discussion creates for the majority turns on the fact that the power to regulate commerce with Indian Tribes has been interpreted as making "Indian relations * * * the exclusive province of federal law." * * * We have specifically held, moreover, that the states have no power to regulate gambling on Indian lands. In sum, since the States have no sovereignty in the regulation of commerce with the tribes, on Hamilton's view there is no source of sovereign immunity to assert in a suit based on congressional regulation of that commerce. If Hamilton is good authority, the majority of the Court today is wrong.

* * *

Thus, the Court's attempt to convert isolated statements by the Framers into answers to questions not before them is fundamentally misguided. The Court's difficulty is far more fundamental however, than inconsistency with a particular quotation, for the Court's position runs afoul of the general theory of sovereignty that gave shape to the Framers' enterprise. An enquiry into the development of that concept demonstrates that American political thought had so revolutionized the concept of sovereignty itself that calling for the immunity of a State as against the jurisdiction of the national courts would have been sheer illogic.

2

We said * * * that "the States entered the federal system with their sovereignty intact," but we surely did not mean that they entered that system with the sovereignty they would have claimed if each State had assumed independent existence in the community of nations, for even the Articles of Confederation allowed for less than that. * * * [I]t is clear that the act of ratification affected their sovereignty in a way different from any previous political event in America or anywhere else. For the adoption of the Constitution made them members of a novel federal system that sought to balance the States' exercise of some sovereign prerogatives delegated from their own people with the principle of a limited but centralizing federal supremacy.

As a matter of political theory, this federal arrangement of dual delegated sovereign powers truly was a more revolutionary turn than the late war had been. Before the new federal scheme appeared, 18th-century political theorists had assumed that "there must reside somewhere in every political unit a single, undivided, final power, higher in legal authority than any other power, subject to no law, a law unto itself." The American development of divided sovereign powers, which "shatter[ed] * * * the categories of government that had dominated Western thinking for centuries," was made possible only by a recognition that the ultimate sovereignty rests in the people themselves. The people possessing this plenary bundle of specific powers were free to parcel them out to different governments and different branches of the same government as they saw fit.

* * *

Given this metamorphosis of the idea of sovereignty in the years leading up to 1789, the question whether the old immunity doctrine might have been received as something suitable for the new world of federal question jurisdiction is a crucial one. The answer is that sovereign immunity as it would have been known to the Framers before ratification thereafter became inapplicable as a matter of logic in a federal suit raising a federal question. The old doctrine, after all, barred the involuntary subjection of a sovereign to the system of justice and law of which it was itself the font, since to do otherwise would have struck the common-law mind from the Middle Ages onward as both impractical and absurd. But the ratification demonstrated that state governments were subject to a superior regime of law in a judicial system established, not by the State, but by the people through a specific delegation of their sovereign power to a National Government that was paramount within its delegated sphere. When individuals sued States to enforce federal rights, the Government that corresponded to the "sovereign" in the traditional common-law sense was not the State but the National Government, and any state immunity from the jurisdiction of the Nation's courts would have required a grant from the true sovereign, the people, in their Constitution, or from the Congress that the Constitution had empowered.

* * *

This sketch of the logic and objectives of the new federal order is confirmed by what we have previously seen of the preratification debate on state sovereign immunity, which in turn becomes entirely intelligible both in what it addressed and what it ignored. It is understandable that reasonable minds differed on the applicability of the immunity doctrine in suits that made it to federal court only under the original Diversity Clauses, for their features were not wholly novel. While they were, of course, in the courts of the new and, for some purposes, paramount National Government, the law that they implicated was largely the old common law (and in any case was not federal law). It was not foolish, therefore, to ask whether the old law brought the old defenses with it. But it is equally understandable that questions seem not to have been raised about state sovereign immunity in federal question cases. The very idea of a federal question depended on the rejection of the simple concept of sovereignty from which the immunity doctrine had developed; under the English common law, the question of immunity in a system of layered sovereignty simply could not have arisen. The Framers' principal objectives in rejecting English theories of unitary sovereignty, moreover, would have been impeded if a new concept of sovereign immunity had taken its place in federal question cases, and would have been substantially thwarted if that new immunity had been held to be untouchable by any congressional effort to abrogate it.

Today's majority discounts this concern. Without citing a single source to the contrary, the Court dismisses the historical evidence regarding the Framers' vision of the relationship between national and state sovereignty, and reassures us that "the Nation survived for nearly two centuries without the question of the existence of [the abrogation] power ever being presented to this Court." But we are concerned here not with the survival of the Nation but the opportunity of its citizens to enforce federal rights in a way that Congress provides. * * * In the end, is it plausible to contend that the plan of the convention was meant to leave the National Government without any way to render individuals capable of enforcing their federal rights directly against an intransigent state?

Food for Thought

One may see in the majority's position a certain bifurcation of the concept of supremacy. Regarding the powers of the federal government *vis-à-vis* the states, supremacy is immutable. With respect to individuals' federal rights *vis-à-vis* state governments, however, it is a paper tiger.

C

The considerations expressed so far, based on text, *Chisholm*, caution in common-law reception, and sovereignty theory, have pointed both to the mistakes inherent in *Hans* and, even more strongly, to the error of today's holding. Although for reasons of *stare decisis* I would not today disturb the century-old precedent, I surely would not extend its error by placing the common-law immunity it mistakenly recognized beyond the power of Congress to abrogate. In doing just that, however, today's decision declaring state sovereign immunity itself immune from abrogation in federal question cases is open to a further set of objections peculiar to itself. For today's decision stands condemned alike by the Framers' abhorrence of any notion that such common-law rules as might be received into the new legal systems would be beyond the legislative power to alter or repeal, and by its resonance with this Court's previous essays in constitutionalizing common-law rules at the expense of legislative authority.

1

* * * Indeed, the Framers' very insistence that no common-law doctrine would be received by virtue of ratification was focused in their fear that elements of the common law might thereby have been placed beyond the power of Congress to alter by legislation.

* * *

Virtually every state reception provision, be it constitutional or statutory, explicitly provided that the common law was subject to alteration by statute. * * *

* * *

2

History confirms the wisdom of Madison's abhorrence of constitutionalizing common-law rules to place them beyond the reach of congressional amendment. The Framers feared judicial power over substantive policy and the ossification of law that would result from transforming common law into constitutional law, and their fears have been borne out every time the Court has ignored Madison's counsel on subjects that we generally group under economic and social policy. It is, in fact, remarkable that as we near the end of this century the Court should choose to open a new constitutional chapter in confining legislative judgments on these matters by resort to textually unwarranted common-law rules, for it was just this practice in the century's early decades that brought this Court to the nadir of competence that we identify with Lochner v. New York.

* * *

The majority today, indeed, seems to be going *Lochner* one better. When the Court has previously constrained the express Article I powers by resort to common-law or background principles, it has done so at least in an ostensible effort to give content to some other written provision of the Constitution, like the Due Process Clause, the very object of which is to limit the exercise of governmental power. Some textual argument, at least, could be made that the Court was doing no more than defining one provision that happened to be at odds with another. Today, however, the Court is not struggling to fulfill a responsibility to reconcile two arguably conflicting and Delphic constitutional provisions, nor is it struggling with any Delphic text at all. For even the Court concedes that the Constitution's grant to Congress of plenary power over relations with Indian tribes at the expense of any state claim to the contrary is unmistakably clear, and this case does not even arguably implicate a textual trump to the grant of federal question jurisdiction.

* * *

IV

The Court's holding that the States' Hans immunity may not be abrogated by Congress leads to the final question in this case, whether federal question jurisdiction exists to order prospective relief enforcing IGRA against a state officer, respondent Chiles, who is said to be authorized to take the action required by the federal law. * * * The answer to this question is an easy yes, the officer is subject to suit under the rule in Ex parte Young, and the case could, and should, readily be decided on this point alone.

A

* * *

It should be no cause for surprise that Young itself appeared when it did in the national law. It followed as a matter of course after the Hans Court's broad recognition of immunity in federal question cases, simply because "[r]emedies designed to end a continuing violation of federal law are necessary to vindicate the federal interest in assuring the supremacy of that law." Young provided, as it does today, a sensible way to reconcile the Court's expansive view of immunity expressed in Hans with the principles embodied in the Supremacy Clause and Article III.

* * *

B

* * * Once, then, the Eleventh Amendment was understood to forbid suit against a State *eo nomine*, the question arose "which suits against officers will be allowed and which will not be." * * * [No cases,] however, erase the fundamental principle of Osborn that sovereign immunity would not bar a suit against a state officer.

* * *

The doctrine we call Ex parte Young is nothing short of "indispensable to the establishment of constitutional government and the rule of law."

* * *

C

There is no question that by its own terms Young's indispensable rule authorizes the exercise of federal jurisdiction over respondent Chiles. Since this case does not, of course, involve retrospective relief, Edelman's limit is irrelevant, and there is no other jurisdictional limitation. * * *

No clear statement of intent to displace the doctrine of Ex parte Young occurs in IGRA, and the Court is instead constrained to rest its effort to skirt Young on a series of suggestions thought to be apparent in Congress's provision of "intricate procedures" for enforcing a State's obligation under the Act. The procedures are said to implicate a rule against judicial creativity in devising supplementary procedures; it is said that applying Young would nullify the statutory procedures;

Take Note!

Hasn't the majority just nullified those statutory procedures on constitutional grounds?

and finally the statutory provisions are said simply to reveal a congressional intent to preclude the application of *Young*.

1

The Court cites *Schweiker v. Chilicky* in support of refraining from what it seems to think would be judicial creativity in recognizing the applicability of *Young*. The Court quotes from *Chilicky* for the general proposition that when Congress has provided what it considers adequate remedial mechanisms for violations of federal law, this Court should not "creat[e]" additional remedies. * * *

Chilicky's remoteness from the point of this case is, however, apparent from its facts. In *Chilicky*, Congress had addressed the problem of erroneous denials of certain government benefits by creating a scheme of appeals and awards that would make a successful claimant whole for all benefits wrongly denied. The question was whether this Court should create a further remedy * * * for such harms as emotional distress, when the erroneous denial of benefits had involved a violation of procedural due process. The issue, then, was whether to create a supplemental remedy, backward-looking on the *Bivens* model, running against a federal official in his personal capacity, and requiring an affirmative justification (as *Bivens* does).

The *Bivens* issue in *Chilicky* * * * is different from the *Young* issue here in every significant respect. *Young* is not an example of a novel rule that a proponent has a burden to justify affirmatively on policy grounds in every context in which it might arguably be recognized; it is a general principle of federal equity jurisdiction that has been recognized throughout our history and for centuries before our own history began. *Young* does not provide retrospective monetary relief but allows prospective enforcement of federal law that is entitled to prevail under the Supremacy Clause. It requires, not money payments from a government employee's personal pocket, but lawful conduct by a public employee acting in his official capacity. *Young* would not function here to provide a merely supplementary regime of compensation to deter illegal action, but the sole jurisdictional basis for an Article III court's enforcement of a clear federal statutory obligation, without which a congressional act would be rendered a nullity in a federal court. One cannot intelligibly generalize from *Chilicky*'s standards for imposing the burden to justify a supplementary scheme of tort law, to the displacement of *Young*'s traditional and indispensable jurisdictional basis for ensuring official compliance with federal law when a State itself is immune from suit.

2

Next, the Court suggests that it may be justified in displacing *Young* because *Young* would allow litigants to ignore the "intricate procedures" of IGRA in favor of a menu of streamlined equity rules from which any litigant could order as he saw fit. But there is no basis in law for this suggestion, and the strongest authority to reject it. Young * * * stands for a jurisdictional rule by which paramount federal law may be enforced in a federal court by substituting a non-immune party (the state officer) for an immune one (the State itself). Young does no more and furnishes no authority for the Court's assumption that it somehow pre-empts procedural rules devised by Congress for particular kinds of cases that may depend on Young for federal jurisdiction.

If, indeed, the Court were correct in assuming that Congress may not regulate the procedure of a suit jurisdictionally dependent on Young, the consequences would be revolutionary, for example, in habeas law. It is well established that when a habeas corpus petitioner sues a state official alleging detention in violation of federal law and seeking the prospective remedy of release from custody, it is the doctrine identified in Ex parte Young that allows the petitioner to evade the jurisdictional bar of the Eleventh Amendment (or, more properly, the Hans doctrine). And yet Congress has imposed a number of restrictions upon the habeas remedy, and this Court has articulated several more. By suggesting that Ex parte Young provides a free-standing remedy not subject to the restrictions otherwise imposed on federal remedial schemes (such as habeas corpus), the Court suggests that a state prisoner may circumvent these restrictions by ostensibly bringing his suit under Young rather than 28 U.S.C. § 2254. The Court's view implies similar consequences under any number of similarly structured federal statutory schemes.

This, of course, cannot be the law, and the plausible rationale for rejecting the Court's contrary assumption is that Congress has just as much authority to regulate suits when jurisdiction depends on Young as it has to regulate when Young is out of the jurisdictional picture. If Young does not preclude Congress from requiring state exhaustion in habeas cases (and it clearly does not), then Young does not bar the application of IGRA's procedures when effective relief is sought by suing a state officer.

3

The Court's third strand of reasoning for displacing Ex parte Young is a supposed inference that Congress so intended. Since the Court rests this inference in large part on its erroneous assumption that the statute's procedural limitations would not be applied in a suit against an officer for which Young provided the jurisdictional basis, the error of that assumption is enough to show the unsoundness of any inference that Congress meant to exclude Young's application.

* * *

Finally, one must judge the Court's purported inference by stepping back to ask why Congress could possibly have intended to jeopardize the enforcement of the statute by excluding application of Young's traditional jurisdictional rule, when that rule would make the difference between success or failure in the federal court if state sovereign immunity was recognized. * * *

D

There is, finally, a response to the Court's rejection of Young that ought to go without saying. Our long-standing practice is to read ambiguous statutes to avoid constitutional infirmity. * * * Construing the statute to harmonize with Young, as it readily does, would have saved an act of Congress and rendered a discussion on constitutional grounds wholly unnecessary. This case should be decided on this basis alone.

* * *

Because neither text, precedent, nor history supports the majority's abdication of our responsibility to exercise the jurisdiction entrusted to us in Article III, I would reverse the judgment of the Court of Appeals.

Notes and Questions

1. The majority explicitly adopts Justice Scalia's view of antecedence from his dissent in *Union Gas*, accepting the proposition that since the Eleventh Amendment postdated the Commerce Clause, the latter cannot affect the states' immunity. Yet earlier in the opinion, the Chief Justice, noting the majority's refusal to limit its approach to the words of the Eleventh Amendment, observed that the Court has " 'understood the Eleventh Amendment to stand not so much for what it says, but for the presupposition * * * which it confirms.' " If indeed the Amendment merely confirmed a presupposition, does that not reintroduce the sequencing problem upon which Justice Brennan based his *Union Gas* conclusion: that the Commerce Clause in fact came after the sovereign immunity principle and therefore can modify it in much the same way as the Court (speaking through then-Justice Rehnquist) recognized for § 5 of the Fourteenth Amendment in *Fitzpatrick v. Bitzer*?

2. The historical debate between Chief Justice Rehnquist and Justice Souter about the intentions of those who wrote and ratified the Eleventh Amendment went to the heart of the Court's modern Eleventh Amendment jurisprudence. Justice Souter, picking up an argument line that Justice Brennan articulated at length in *Atascadero*, takes the diversity view of the Amendment. Chief Justice Rehnquist attempted to undermine Justice Souter's exclusive focus on *Chisholm* and the Eleventh Amendment

by arguing that the Eleventh Amendment was but a single manifestation of a generally accepted mosaic of sovereign immunity law. In effect, the Chief Justice accused the dissent of viewing *Chisholm* and the Amendment as if they existed in a vacuum rather than against the backdrop of general understanding of the immunity of governments to suit without their consent.

On the other hand, one might argue that it is the majority that is unrealistically isolated in its view. Consider that as of 1793 the states had just emerged from a colonial period during which they felt exploited and abused by the centralized power of the Crown. The first national government that they created, under the Articles of Confederation, proved so weak and ineffective that within six years the states convened the Constitutional Convention. Throughout the Convention and the ratification debates and conventions, the single greatest concern was the possibility of federal overreaching and subordination of the states. *Chisholm* came only five years after ratification and ignited a firestorm that resulted in the Eleventh Amendment. How likely is it that with *Chisholm* as a fresh example of their worst fears coming to pass, the states focused on the narrow diversity question *Chisholm* presented and left all other kinds of suits to the general understanding that had just failed to forestall *Chisholm* itself?

3. Note that the Court's (and the dissents') approach to the immunity question re-emphasizes the importance of determining the ground for the decision in *Hans v. Louisiana*. Was it, as Justice Peckham stated in *Ex parte Young*, a holding that the Eleventh Amendment itself precludes any federal action against an unconsenting state, or was it a recognition of an implicit Article III immunity, or was it a recognition of a common law sovereign immunity that Congress is free to alter in the exercise of its Article I powers but had not altered in *Hans*?

4. a) Two types of sovereign immunity compete for attention in cases like *Hans*, *Union Gas*, and *Seminole Tribe*. The Eleventh Amendment itself reflects a forum immunity. It clearly does not speak to whether individuals can sue the states in their own courts on federal claims. But governments often also assert substantive immunity that a cause of action simply does not lie against them irrespective of the forum. Although nothing in *Seminole Tribe* suggests that the losing plaintiff could not simply replicate its federal action in the Florida courts, *Alden v. Maine*, 527 U.S. 706 (1999), now demonstrates the impossibility of that course. *See supra* page 674. Is there then any way for Congress to provide for enforcement of the substantive state-tribe relationship scheme that IGRA reflects? If not, then what of the Supremacy Clause?

b) Distinguishing between forum sovereign immunity and substantive sovereign immunity may offer a new view of *Hans*. Is it possible that the Eleventh Amendment was intended to tell the federal courts only that they could not ignore a substantive sovereign immunity to state claims that would have precluded plaintiffs like Hans from maintaining the action in the state courts? This, of course, is merely a restatement of the party-based jurisdictional view of the Amendment, but it may have the advantage of explaining the wording of the Amendment without apparently doing violence to the Supremacy Clause. Does the disappearance of immunity on a supremacy-stripping view of Ex parte Young connote that the Eleventh Amendment should merely stand for the preservation of substantive sovereign immunity to state claims?

5. The Court's refusal to permit the plaintiff to proceed against state officials under the aegis of Ex parte Young surely is worth some attention. The Court imports the mode of analysis it employed in *Schweiker v. Chilicky* to reach the conclusion that the detailed congressional remedial scheme counsels against the Court permitting what it characterizes as "more complete and more immediate relief [than] would be available under Ex parte Young."

a) The Court thus views Ex parte Young as far more than a jurisdictional case for Eleventh Amendment purposes. Yet was it? Cannot one read Young merely to say that when a state officer acts incompatibly with federal law, he cannot claim the forum immunity of the Eleventh Amendment? Why should that conclusion necessarily have the additional effect of expanding the scope of relief otherwise available to the plaintiff but for the forum disqualification of the Eleventh Amendment? Is there anything in Young that would prevent a federal court, hearing an Indian Gaming Regulatory Act case against a state officer on the jurisdictional theory of Ex parte Young, from limiting relief to that specified in the Act?

b) In Chilicky, the Court essentially told Chilicky that it would not imply a private right of action on his behalf for relief exceeding that available under Congress's remedial scheme. Here, the plaintiff sought precisely the relief that Congress specified. Should that make a difference? (There is, of course, the great irony in *Seminole Tribe* of the Court refusing the Tribe relief by relying on the existence of a congressionally mandated remedial scheme that the Justices had just invalidated.)

For More Information

For an excellent discussion of the potential effects of *Seminole Tribe* on Ex parte Young, see Vicki C. Jackson, Seminole Tribe, *the Eleventh Amendment, and the Potential Evisceration of* Ex parte Young, 72 N.Y.U.L.Rev. 495 (1997), and David P. Currie, Ex parte Young *After* Seminole Tribe, 72 N.Y.U.L.Rev. 547 (1997).

6. Fundamentally, the majority seems to assume that the plan of the Convention reflected in the Eleventh Amendment was that the states should never be called to account in the federal courts at the behest of individuals. Yet clearly the Framers understood that states could be made defendants in the federal courts, since Article III explicitly provides state-state jurisdiction. Are those two positions incompatible?

One may be tempted to solve the apparent problem by arguing that federal courts cannot consider states as defendants except as specifically authorized by the Constitution. How, then, can one explain the federal government's ability to sue states in the federal courts? The Court has held that the Eleventh Amendment is unavailing against the United States as plaintiff. Is a state's sovereignty interest (or dignity) any more or less offended according to whether the plaintiff against it in a federal action is the federal government, a foreign government, another state, a citizen from another state, a citizen of the state, or a citizen or subject of another country?

7. Note that despite the departure of most of the Justices supporting the result in Union Gas, there still seem to have been four votes for overruling Hans v. Louisiana. The senior members of the *Seminole Tribe* Court were Chief Justice Rehnquist and Justices Stevens and O'Connor, two of whom strongly supported Hans. All have now left the Court, as has Justice Souter. Chief Justice Roberts and Justices Alito, Sotomayor and Kagan now occupy those four seats. It may be too soon to regard the book on Hans as closed.

8. After *Seminole Tribe*, one might have thought that the Eleventh Amendment barred any claim against a state sounding in Article I legislation. The impression was, however, at least temporarily misleading. In *Central Virginia Community College v. Katz*, 546 U.S. 356 (2006), a five-to-four majority ruled that Congress could also abrogate state immunity under the Bankruptcy Clause of Article I, § 4. Justice Stevens's opinion for the Court discussed at length the Framers' realization of the necessity for a uniform bankruptcy law that transcended state borders, lest bankruptcy relief awarded by a state availed the debtor nothing in any other state. He also noted that bankruptcy jurisdiction, "at its core, is *in rem*." That being the case, the majority argued that the bankruptcy court required plenary power over the debtor's estate, which in turn required being able to recover property of the bankrupt held by someone else. In effect, the majority said that bankruptcy was a special case, outside of the proscription of *Seminole Tribe* because the "States agreed in the plan of the Convention not to assert any sovereign immunity defense they might have had in proceedings brought pursuant to 'Laws on the subject of Bankruptcies.' "

Katz may be unstable. Justice O'Connor provided the majority's fifth vote shortly before her retirement. Justice Alito took her place, and it is difficult to glean his approach to Eleventh Amendment immunity from his circuit court opinions. As a Circuit Judge, he hewed closely to the Supreme Court's expressed doctrine without indicating whether he might harbor a more or less expansive view than the Court has articulated over the past thirty years. What he will do now that he is in a position to express his own view remains to be seen. In the end, Katz may rest on ground just as unstable as that under Pennsylvania v. Union Gas Co., which gave way to *Seminole Tribe* in only seven years.

E. The Eleventh Amendment and Supplemental Jurisdiction

Ex parte Young held that the Eleventh Amendment does not close the federal forum to actions against state officials for violation of the federal constitution. But what about a federal suits asserting state-law claims against state officials? Even before Ex parte Young, federal courts had routinely exercised supplemental (then "pendent") jurisdiction over such claims when they were brought with a related federal claim, and they continued to do so.

For More Information

See, e.g., Reagan v. Farmers' Loan & Trust, 154 U.S. 362, 390-91 (1894) (tortious conduct of state officials under color of state law not protected by Eleventh Amendment); *Johnson v. Lankford*, 245 U.S. 541 (1918) (same rule for claims that state officers violated state statutes).

The Court often decided such cases solely on the basis of the state law claim when by so doing it could avoid deciding a federal constitutional issue.

For More Information

See, e.g., Siler v. Louisville & Nashville R. Co., 213 U.S. 175, 193 (1909) (enjoining operation of state rate statute based on state law and declining to decide Fourteenth Amendment claim).

Given *Fitzpatrick v. Bitzer*'s 1976 ruling that Congress could remove the states' Eleventh Amendment immunity when legislating under the fifth section of the Fourteenth Amendment, the question of whether federal courts could continue to exercise supplemental jurisdiction over nonfederal claims was bound to arise again, and it did so in the following case. As you read the opinions, you will notice what one might describe as an "elevated level of rhetoric" between Justices Powell and Stevens. Consider what makes their feelings so intense.

Pennhurst State School & Hospital v. Halderman

Supreme Court of the United States, 1984.
465 U.S. 89.

JUSTICE POWELL delivered the opinion of the Court.

This case presents the question whether a federal court may award injunctive relief against state officials on the basis of state law.

I

This litigation, here for the second time, concerns the conditions of care at petitioner Pennhurst State School and Hospital, a Pennsylvania institution for the care of the mentally retarded. Although the litigation's history is set forth in detail in our prior opinion, it is necessary for purposes of this decision to review that history.

This suit originally was brought in 1974 by respondent Terri Lee Halderman, a resident of Pennhurst, in the District Court for the Eastern District of Pennsylvania. Ultimately, plaintiffs included a class consisting of all persons who were or might become residents of Pennhurst; the Pennsylvania Association for Retarded Citizens (PARC); and the United States. Defendants were Pennhurst and various Pennhurst officials; the Pennsylvania Department of Public Welfare and several of its officials; and various county commissioners, county mental retardation administrators, and other officials of five Pennsylvania counties surrounding Pennhurst. Respondents' amended complaint charged that conditions at Pennhurst violated the class members' rights under the Eighth and Fourteenth Amendments; § 504 of the Rehabilitation Act of 1973, the Developmentally Disabled Assistance and Bill of Rights Act, [42 U.S.C. § 6010] and the Pennsylvania Mental Health and Mental Retardation Act of 1966 (the "MH/MR Act"). Both damages and injunctive relief were sought.

In 1977, following a lengthy trial, the District Court rendered its decision. As noted in our prior opinion, the court's findings were undisputed: "Conditions at Pennhurst are not only dangerous, with the residents often physically abused or drugged by staff members, but also inadequate for the 'habilitation' of the retarded. Indeed, the court found that the physical, intellectual, and emotional skills of some residents have deteriorated at Pennhurst." The District Court held that these conditions violated each resident's right to "minimally adequate habilitation" under the Due Process Clause and the MH/MR Act, "freedom from harm" under the Eighth and Fourteenth Amendments, and "nondiscriminatory habilitation" under the Equal Protection Clause and § 504 of the Rehabilitation Act. Furthermore, the court found that "due process demands that if a state undertakes the habilitation of a retarded person, it must do so in the *least restrictive setting* consistent with that individual's habilitative needs." ([E]mphasis added). After concluding that the large size of Pennhurst prevented it from providing the necessary habilitation in the least restrictive environment, the court ordered "that immediate steps be taken to remove the retarded residents from Pennhurst." Petitioners were ordered "to provide suitable community living arrangements" for the class members, and the court appointed a Special Master "with the power and duty to plan, organize, direct, supervise and monitor the implementation of this and any further Orders of the Court."

3rd Cir.

The Court of Appeals for the Third Circuit affirmed most of the District Court's judgment. It agreed that respondents had a right to habilitation in the least restrictive environment, but it grounded this right solely on the "bill of rights" provision in the Developmentally Disabled Assistance and Bill of Rights Act. The court did not consider the constitutional issues or § 504 of the Rehabilitation Act, and while it affirmed the District Court's holding that the MH/MR Act provides a right to adequate habilitation, the court did not decide whether that state right encompassed a right to treatment in the least restrictive setting.

On the question of remedy, the Court of Appeals affirmed except as to the District Court's order that Pennhurst be closed. The court observed that some patients would be unable to adjust to life outside an institution, and it determined that none of the legal provisions relied on by plaintiffs precluded institutionalization. It therefore remanded for "individual determinations by the [District Court], or by the Special Master, as to the appropriateness of an improved Pennhurst for each such patient," guided by "a presumption in favor of placing individuals in [community living arrangements]."

* * *

SCOTUS

This Court reversed the judgment of the Court of Appeals, finding that 42 U.S.C. § 6010 did not create any substantive rights. We remanded the case to the Court of Appeals to determine if the remedial order could be supported on the basis of state law, the Constitution, or § 504 of the Rehabilitation Act. We also remanded for consideration of whether any relief was available under other provisions of the Developmentally Disabled Assistance and Bill of Rights Act.

Take Note!

Observe the Supreme Court's "charge" to the Third Circuit on remand.

On remand the Court of Appeals affirmed its prior judgment in its entirety. It determined that in a recent decision the Supreme Court of Pennsylvania had "spoken definitively" in holding that the MH/MR Act required the State to adopt the "least restrictive environment" approach for the care of the mentally retarded. The Court of Appeals concluded that this state statute fully supported its prior judgment, and therefore did not reach the remaining issues of federal law. It also rejected petitioners' argument that the Eleventh Amendment barred a federal court from considering this pendent state-law claim. The court noted that the Amendment did not bar a federal court from granting prospective injunctive relief against state officials on the basis of federal claims, and concluded that the same result obtained with respect to a pendent state-law claim. It reasoned that because *Siler v. Louisville & Nashville R. Co.*, an important case in the development of the doctrine of pendent jurisdiction, also involved state officials, "there cannot be * * * an Eleventh Amendment exception to that rule." Finally, the court rejected petitioners' argument that it should have abstained from deciding the state-law claim under principles of comity, and refused to consider petitioners' objections to the District Court's use of a special master. Three judges dissented in part, arguing that under principles of federalism and comity the establishment of a special master to supervise compliance was an abuse of discretion.

> **Take Note!**
>
> The Third Circuit explained its rejection of the Eleventh Amendment argument:
>
> > [T]he defendants urge that we may not rely on that Act as support for the order appealed from because the Eleventh Amendment is a bar to federal court consideration of that claim. The contention that neither the district court, this court, nor the Supreme Court has jurisdiction to consider plaintiffs' state law claims has not previously been advanced in this action, and from the dearth of authorities cited in its support, not previously advanced anywhere.
> >
> > * * *
> >
> > [E]ven if the Commonwealth's unique interpretation of the pendent jurisdiction rule as inapplicable to suits against state offers had any substance, the Court's express mandate that we reconsider the state law issue appears to preclude its adoption in this case by this court.

3rd Cir.

We granted certiorari and now reverse and remand.

II

Petitioners raise three challenges to the judgment of the Court of Appeals: (i) the Eleventh Amendment prohibited the District Court from ordering state officials to conform their conduct to state law; (ii) the doctrine of comity prohibited the District Court from issuing its injunctive relief; and (iii) the District Court abused its discretion in appointing two masters to supervise the decisions of state officials in implementing state law. We need not reach the latter two issues, for we find the Eleventh Amendment challenge dispositive.

A

* * *

The Amendment's language overruled the particular result in *Chisholm*, but this Court has recognized that its greater significance lies in its affirmation that the fundamental principle of sovereign immunity limits the grant of judicial authority in Art. III. Thus, in *Hans v. Louisiana* the Court held that, despite the limited terms of the Eleventh Amendment, a federal court could not entertain a suit brought by a citizen against his own State. After reviewing the constitutional debates concerning the scope of Art. III, the Court determined that federal jurisdiction over suits against unconsenting States "was not contemplated by the Constitution when establishing the judicial power of the United States." In short, the principle of sovereign immunity is a constitutional limitation on the federal judicial power established in Art. III:

> That a State may not be sued without its consent is a fundamental rule of jurisprudence having so important a bearing upon the construction of the Constitution of the United States that it has become established by repeated decisions of this court that *the entire judicial power granted by the Constitution does not embrace authority to entertain a suit brought by private parties against a State without consent given:* not one brought by citizens of another State, or by citizens or subjects of a foreign State, because of the Eleventh Amendment; and not even one brought by its own citizens, because of the fundamental rule of which the Amendment is but an exemplification.

([E]mphasis added).[8]

A sovereign's immunity may be waived, and the Court consistently has held that a State may consent to suit against it in federal court. We have insisted, however, that the State's consent be unequivocally expressed. Similarly, although Congress has power with respect to the rights protected by the Fourteenth Amendment to abrogate the Eleventh Amendment immunity, we have required an unequivocal expression of congressional intent to "overturn the constitutionally guaranteed immunity of the several States." Our reluctance to infer that a State's immunity from suit in the federal courts has been negated stems from recognition of the vital role of the doctrine of sovereign immunity in our federal system. A State's constitutional interest in immunity encompasses not merely whether it may be sued, but where it may be sued. As Justice Marshall well has noted, "[b]ecause of the problems of federalism inherent in making one sovereign appear against its will in the courts of the other, a restriction upon the exercise of the federal judicial power has long been considered to be appropriate in a case such as this." Accord-

8 The limitation deprives federal courts of any jurisdiction to entertain such claims, and thus may be raised at any point in a proceeding. "The Eleventh Amendment declares a policy and sets forth an explicit limitation on federal judicial power of such compelling force that this Court will consider the issue arising under this Amendment * * * even though urged for the first time in this Court."

ingly, in deciding this case we must be guided by "[t]he principles of federalism that inform Eleventh Amendment doctrine."

B

This Court's decisions thus establish that "an unconsenting State is immune from suits brought in federal courts by her own citizens as well as by citizens of another state." There may be a question, however, whether a particular suit in fact is a suit against a State. It is clear, of course, that in the absence of consent a suit in which the State or one of its agencies or departments is named as the defendant is proscribed by the Eleventh Amendment. This jurisdictional bar applies regardless of the nature of the relief sought. ("Expressly applying to suits in equity as well as at law, the Amendment necessarily embraces demands for the enforcement of equitable rights and the prosecution of equitable remedies when these are asserted and prosecuted by an individual against a State").

When the suit is brought only against state officials, a question arises as to whether that suit is a suit against the State itself. Although prior decisions of this Court have not been entirely consistent on this issue, certain principles are well established. The Eleventh Amendment bars a suit against state officials when "the state is the real, substantial party in interest." Thus, "[t]he general rule is that relief sought nominally against an officer is in fact against the sovereign if the decree would operate against the latter." And, as when the State itself is named as the defendant, a suit against state officials that is in fact a suit against a State is barred regardless of whether it seeks damages or injunctive relief.

The Court has recognized an important exception to this general rule: a suit challenging the constitutionality of a state official's action is not one against the State. * * * [In *Ex parte Young*,] [t]his Court held that the Eleventh Amendment did not prohibit issuance of an injunction. The theory of the case was that an unconstitutional enactment is "void" and therefore does not "impart to [the officer] any immunity from responsibility to the supreme authority of the United States." Since the State could not authorize the action, the officer was "stripped of his official or representative character and [was] subjected to the consequences of his official conduct."

While the rule permitting suits alleging conduct contrary to "the supreme authority of the United States" has survived, the theory of *Young* has not been provided an expansive interpretation. Thus, in *Edelman v. Jordan*, the Court emphasized that the Eleventh Amendment bars some forms of injunctive relief against state officials for violation of federal law. In particular, *Edelman* held that when a plaintiff sues a state official alleging a violation of federal law, the federal court may award an injunction that governs the official's future conduct, but not one that awards retroactive monetary relief. Under the theory of Young, such a suit would not be one against the State since the federal-law allegation would strip the state officer of his official authority. Nevertheless, retroactive relief was barred by the Eleventh Amendment.

III

With these principles in mind, we now turn to the question whether the claim that petitioners violated state law in carrying out their official duties at Pennhurst is one against the State and therefore barred by the Eleventh Amendment. Respondents advance two principal arguments in support of the judgment below. First, they contend that under the doctrine of Edelman v. Jordan, the suit is not against the State because the courts below ordered only prospective injunctive relief. Second, they assert that the state-law claim properly was decided under the doctrine of pendent jurisdiction. Respondents rely on decisions of this Court awarding relief against state officials on the basis of a pendent state-law claim.

A

We first address the contention that respondents' state-law claim is not barred by the Eleventh Amendment because it seeks only prospective relief as defined in Edelman v. Jordan. The Court of Appeals held that if the judgment below rested on federal law, it could be entered against petitioner state officials under the doctrine established in Edelman and Young even though the prospective financial burden was substantial and ongoing. The court assumed, and respondents assert, that this reasoning applies as well when the official acts in violation of state law. This argument misconstrues the basis of the doctrine established in Young and Edelman.

As discussed above, the injunction in Young was justified, notwithstanding the obvious impact on the State itself, on the view that sovereign immunity does not apply because an official who acts unconstitutionally is "stripped of his official or representative character." This rationale, of course, created the "well-recognized irony" that an official's unconstitutional conduct constitutes state action under the Fourteenth Amendment but not the Eleventh Amendment. Nonetheless, the Young doctrine has been accepted as necessary to permit the federal courts to vindicate federal rights and hold state officials responsible to "the supreme authority of the United States." As Justice Brennan has observed, "Ex parte Young was the culmination of efforts by this Court to harmonize the principles of the Eleventh Amendment with the effective supremacy of rights and powers secured elsewhere in the Constitution." Our decisions repeatedly have emphasized that the Young doctrine rests on the need to promote the vindication of federal rights.

The Court also has recognized, however, that the need to promote the supremacy of federal law must be accommodated to the constitutional immunity of the States. * * * Edelman's distinction between prospective and retroactive relief fulfills the underlying purpose of Ex parte Young while at the same time preserving to an important degree the constitutional immunity of the States.

This need to reconcile competing interests is wholly absent, however, when a plaintiff alleges that a state official has violated state law. In such a case the entire basis for the doctrine of Young and Edelman disappears. * * * [I]t is difficult to think of a greater intrusion on state sovereignty than when a federal court instructs state officials on how to conform their conduct to state law. Such a result conflicts directly with the principles of federalism that underlie the Eleventh Amendment. We conclude that Young and Edelman are inapplicable in a suit against state officials on the basis of state law.

Food for Thought

What is the principle of federalism to which Justice Powell refers? If it is the principle that the highest state court speaks ***ex cathedra*** (with final authority) on the interpretation of state law, did the Third Circuit's judgment in this case do violence to that principle? If that is not the operative principle, then what is?

B

The contrary view of Justice Stevens' dissent rests on fiction, is wrong on the law, and, most important, would emasculate the Eleventh Amendment. Under his view, an allegation that official conduct is contrary to a state statute would suffice to override the State's protection under that Amendment. The theory is that such conduct is contrary to the official's "instructions," and thus *ultra vires* his authority. Accordingly, official action based on a reasonable interpretation of any statute might, if the interpretation turned out to be erroneous, provide the basis for injunctive relief against the actors in their official capacities. In this case, where officials of a major state department, clearly acting within the scope of their authority, were found not to have improved conditions in a state institution adequately under state law, the dissent's result would be that the State itself has forfeited its constitutionally provided immunity.

The theory is out of touch with reality. The dissent does not dispute that the general criterion for determining when a suit is in fact against the sovereign is the effect of the relief sought. According to the dissent, the relief sought and ordered here—which in effect was that a major state institution be closed and smaller state institutions be created and expansively funded—did not operate against the State. This view would make the law a pretense. No other court or judge in the ten-year history of this litigation has advanced this theory. And the dissent's underlying view that the named defendants here were acting beyond and contrary to their authority cannot be reconciled with reality—or with the record. The District Court in this case held that the individual defendants "acted in the utmost good faith * * * *within the sphere of their official responsibilities,*" and therefore were entitled to immunity from damages. ([E]mphasis added). * * * As a result, all the relief ordered by the courts below was institutional and official in character. To the extent there was a violation of state law in this case, it is a case of the State itself not fulfilling its legislative promises.[17]

* * *

Thus, while there is language in the early cases that advances the authority-stripping theory advocated by the dissent, this theory had never been pressed as far as Justice Stevens would do in this case. And when the expansive approach of the dissent was advanced, this Court plainly and explicitly rejected it. In Larson v. Domestic & Foreign Commerce Corp., the Court was faced with the argument that an allegation that a government official committed a tort sufficed to distinguish the official from the sovereign. Therefore, the argument went, a suit for an injunction to remedy the injury would not be against the sovereign. The Court rejected the argument, noting that it would make the doctrine of sovereign immunity superfluous. A plaintiff would need only to "claim an invasion of his legal rights" in order to override sovereign immunity. In the Court's view, the argument "confuse[d] the doctrine of sovereign immunity with the requirement that a plaintiff state a cause of action." The dissent's theory suffers a like confusion. Under the dissent's view, a plaintiff would need only to claim a denial of rights protected or provided by statute in order to override sovereign immunity. Except in rare cases it would make the constitutional doctrine of sovereign immunity a nullity.

The crucial element of the dissent's theory was also the plaintiff's central contention in Larson. It is that "[a] sovereign, like any other principal, cannot authorize its agent to violate the law," so that when the agent does so he cannot be acting for the sovereign. * * * It is a view of agency law that the Court in Larson explicitly rejected. Larson thus made clear that, at least insofar as injunctive relief is sought, an error of law by state officers acting in their official capacities will not suffice to override the

Make the Connection

Which of the two possible bases for "stripping" that Young discussed underlies the Court's statement here?

17 The dissent appears to be confused about our argument here * * * . It is of course true, as the dissent says, that the finding below that petitioners acted in good faith and therefore were immune from damages does not affect whether an injunction might be issued against them by a court possessed of jurisdiction. The point is that the courts below did not have jurisdiction because the relief ordered so plainly ran against the State. * * * It is evident that the dissent would vest in federal courts authority, acting solely under state law, to ignore the sovereignty of the States that the Eleventh Amendment was adopted to protect. Article III confers no jurisdiction on this Court to strip an explicit Amendment of the Constitution of its substantive meaning.

Contrary to the dissent's view, an injunction based on federal law stands on very different footing, particularly in light of the Civil War Amendments. As we have explained, in such cases this Court is vested with the constitutional duty to vindicate "the supreme authority of the United States." There is no corresponding mandate to enforce state law.

sovereign immunity of the State where the relief effectively is against it. Any resulting disadvantage to the plaintiff was "outweigh[ed]" by "the necessity of permitting the Government to carry out its functions unhampered by direct judicial intervention." If anything, this public need is even greater when questions of federalism are involved.[23]

The dissent in Larson made many of the arguments advanced by Justice Stevens' dissent today, and asserted that many of the same cases were being overruled or ignored. Those arguments were rejected, and the cases supporting them are moribund.

The reason is obvious. Under the dissent's view of the *ultra vires* doctrine, the Eleventh Amendment would have force only in the rare case in which a plaintiff foolishly attempts to sue the State in its own name, or where he cannot produce some state statute that has been violated to his asserted injury. Thus, the *ultra vires* doctrine, a narrow and questionable exception, would swallow the general rule that a suit is against the State if the relief will run against it. That result gives the dissent no pause presumably because of its view that the Eleventh Amendment and sovereign immunity " 'undoubtedly ru[n] counter to modern democratic notions of the moral responsibility of the State.' " The dissent totally rejects the Eleventh Amendment's basis in federalism.

C

The reasoning of our recent decisions on sovereign immunity thus leads to the conclusion that a federal suit against state officials on the basis of state law contravenes the Eleventh Amendment when—as here—the relief sought and ordered has an impact directly on the State itself. In reaching a contrary conclusion, the Court of Appeals relied principally on a separate line of cases dealing with pendent jurisdiction. The crucial point for the Court of Appeals was that this Court has granted relief against state officials on the basis of a pendent state-law

23 As we have discussed, Edelman v. Jordan also shows that the broad *ultra vires* theory enunciated in Young and in some of the cases quoted by the dissent has been discarded. In Edelman, although the State officers were alleged to be acting contrary to law, and therefore should have been "stripped of their authority" under the theory of the dissent, we held the action to be barred by the Eleventh Amendment. The dissent attempts to distinguish Edelman on the ground that the retroactive relief there, unlike injunctive relief, does not run only against the agent. To say that injunctive relief against State officials acting in their official capacity does not run against the State is to resort to the fictions that characterize the dissent's theories. Unlike the English sovereign perhaps, an American State can act only through its officials. It is true that the Court in Edelman recognized that retroactive relief often, or at least sometimes, has a greater impact on the State treasury than does injunctive relief, but there was no suggestion that damages alone were thought to run against the State while injunctive relief did not.

* * * At bottom, the doctrine is based on the fiction of the Young opinion. The dissent's method is merely to take this fiction to its extreme. While the dissent's result may be logical, in the sense that it is difficult to draw principled lines short of that end, its view would virtually eliminate the constitutional doctrine of sovereign immunity. * * *

claim. We therefore must consider the relationship between pendent jurisdiction and the Eleventh Amendment.

This Court long has held generally that when a federal court obtains jurisdiction over a federal claim, it may adjudicate other related claims over which the court otherwise would not have jurisdiction. The Court also has held that a federal court may resolve a case solely on the basis of a pendent state-law claim, and that in fact the court usually should do so in order to avoid federal constitutional questions. But pendent jurisdiction is a judge-made doctrine inferred from the general language of Art. III. The question presented is whether this doctrine may be viewed as displacing the explicit limitation on federal jurisdiction contained in the Eleventh Amendment.

As the Court of Appeals noted, in *Siler* and subsequent cases concerning pendent jurisdiction, relief was granted against state officials on the basis of state-law claims that were pendent to federal constitutional claims. In none of these cases, however, did the Court so much as mention the Eleventh Amendment in connection with the state-law claim. Rather, the Court appears to have assumed that once jurisdiction was established over the federal-law claim, the doctrine of pendent jurisdiction would establish power to hear the state-law claims as well. The Court has not addressed whether that doctrine has a different scope when applied to suits against the State.

[Prior] cases thus did not directly confront the question before us. "[W]hen questions of jurisdiction have been passed on in prior decisions *sub silentio,* this Court has never considered itself bound when a subsequent case finally brings the jurisdictional issue before us." We therefore view the question as an open one.

As noted, the implicit view of these cases seems to have been that once jurisdiction is established on the basis of a federal question, no further Eleventh Amendment inquiry is necessary with respect to other claims raised in the case. This is an erroneous view and contrary to the principles established in our Eleventh Amendment decisions. * * * The Amendment * * * is a specific constitutional bar

Food for Thought

Does Justice Powell prove too much here? To the extent that the Eleventh Amendment is jurisdictional—and *Pennhurst* clearly views it as such—the prior Court's silence becomes almost deafening. As you know, the Court has regularly raised issues of subject matter jurisdiction on its own motion, as it did in *Mottley* and *Smith*. Does the Court's acceptance of jurisdiction in those prior cases say more than Justice Powell wants it to? For that matter, in light of the position the majority takes here, how can Justice Powell explain the terms of the Court's remand to the Third Circuit only three years before?

against hearing even federal claims that otherwise would be within the jurisdiction of the federal courts.

This constitutional bar applies to pendent claims as well. As noted above, pendent jurisdiction is a judge-made doctrine of expediency and efficiency derived from the general Art. III language conferring power to hear all "cases" arising under federal law or between diverse parties. The Eleventh Amendment should not be construed to apply with less force to this implied form of jurisdiction than it does to the explicitly granted power to hear federal claims. * * * If we were to hold otherwise, a federal court could award damages against a State on the basis of a pendent claim. Our decision in *Edelman v. Jordan* makes clear that pendent jurisdiction does not permit such an evasion of the immunity guaranteed by the Eleventh Amendment. We there held that "the District Court was correct in exercising pendent jurisdiction over [plaintiffs'] statutory claim," but then concluded that the Eleventh Amendment barred an award of retroactive relief on the basis of that pendent claim.

In sum, * * * neither pendent jurisdiction nor any other basis of jurisdiction may override the Eleventh Amendment. A federal court must examine each claim in a case to see if the court's jurisdiction over that claim is barred by the Eleventh Amendment. We concluded above that a claim that state officials violated state law in carrying out their official responsibilities is a claim against the State that is protected by the Eleventh Amendment. We now hold that this principle applies as well to state-law claims brought into federal court under pendent jurisdiction.

D

Respondents urge that application of the Eleventh Amendment to pendent state-law claims will have a disruptive effect on litigation against state officials. They argue that the "considerations of judicial economy, convenience, and fairness to litigants" that underlie pendent jurisdiction, counsel against a result that may cause litigants to split causes of action between state and federal courts. They also contend that the policy of avoiding unnecessary constitutional decisions will be contravened if plaintiffs choose to forgo their state-law claims and sue only in federal court or, alternatively, that the policy of *Ex parte Young* will be hindered if plaintiffs choose to forgo their right to a federal forum and bring all of their claims in state court. P's args

It may be that applying the Eleventh Amendment to pendent claims results in federal claims being brought in state court, or in bifurcation of claims. That is not uncommon in this area. Under *Edelman v. Jordan*, a suit against state officials for retroactive monetary relief, whether based on federal or state law, must be brought in state court. Challenges to the validity of state tax systems under 42 U.S.C. § 1983 also must be brought in state court. Under the abstention doctrine, unclear issues of state law commonly are split off and referred to the state courts.

In any case, the answer to respondents' assertions is that such considerations of policy cannot override the constitutional limitation on the authority of the federal judiciary to adjudicate suits against a State. That a litigant's choice of forum is reduced "has long been understood to be a part of the tension inherent in our system of federalism."

IV

Respondents contend that, regardless of the applicability of the Eleventh Amendment to their state claims against petitioner state officials, the judgment may still be upheld against petitioner county officials. We are not persuaded. Even assuming that these officials are not immune from suit challenging their actions under the MH/MR Act, it is clear that without the injunction against the state institutions and officials in this case, an order entered on state-law grounds necessarily would be limited. The relief substantially concerns Pennhurst, an arm of the State that is operated by state officials. Moreover, funding for the county mental retardation programs comes almost entirely from the State, and the costs of the masters have been borne by the State. Finally, the MH/MR Act contemplates that the state and county officials will cooperate in operating mental retardation programs. In short, the present judgment could not be sustained on the basis of the state-law obligations of petitioner county officials. Indeed, any relief granted against the county officials on the basis of the state statute would be partial and incomplete at best. Such an ineffective enforcement of state law would not appear to serve the purposes of efficiency, convenience, and fairness that must inform the exercise of pendent jurisdiction.

V

The Court of Appeals upheld the judgment of the District Court solely on the basis of Pennsylvania's MH/MR Act. We hold that these federal courts lacked jurisdiction to enjoin petitioner state institutions and state officials on the basis of this state law. The District Court also rested its decision on the Eighth and Fourteenth Amendments and § 504 of the Rehabilitation Act of 1973. On remand the Court of Appeals may consider to what extent, if any, the judgment may be sustained on these bases. The court also may consider whether relief may be granted to respondents under the Developmentally Disabled Assistance and Bill of Rights Act. The judgment of the Court of Appeals is reversed, and the case remanded for further proceedings consistent with this opinion.

It is so ordered.

JUSTICE STEVENS, with whom JUSTICE BRENNAN, JUSTICE MARSHALL, and JUSTICE BLACKMUN join, dissenting.

This case has illuminated the character of an institution. The record demonstrates that the Pennhurst State School and Hospital has been operated in violation of state law. In 1977, after three years of litigation, the District Court entered detailed findings of fact that abundantly support that conclusion. In 1981, after four more years of litigation, this Court ordered the United States Court of Appeals for the Third Circuit to decide whether the law of Pennsylvania provides an independent and adequate ground which can support the District Court's remedial order. The Court of Appeals, sitting en banc, unanimously concluded that it did. This Court does not disagree with that conclusion. Rather, it reverses the Court of Appeals because it did precisely what this Court ordered it to do; the only error committed by the Court of Appeals was its faithful obedience to this Court's command.

This remarkable result is the product of an equally remarkable misapplication of the ancient doctrine of sovereign immunity. In a completely unprecedented holding, today the Court concludes that Pennsylvania's sovereign immunity prevents a federal court from enjoining the conduct that Pennsylvania itself has prohibited. No rational view of the sovereign immunity of the States supports this result. To the contrary, the question whether a federal court may award injunctive relief on the basis of state law has been answered affirmatively by this Court many times in the past. Yet the Court repudiates at least 28 cases, spanning well over a century of this Court's jurisprudence, proclaiming instead that federal courts have no power to enforce the will of the States by enjoining conduct because it violates state law. This new pronouncement will require the federal courts to decide federal constitutional questions despite the availability of state-law grounds for decision, a result inimical to sound principles of judicial restraint. Nothing in the Eleventh Amendment, the conception of state sovereignty it embodies, or the history of this institution, requires or justifies such a perverse result.

* * *

II

The majority proceeds as if this Court has not had previous occasion to consider Eleventh Amendment argument made by petitioners, and contends that *Ex parte Young* has no application to a suit seeking injunctive relief on the basis of state law. That is simply not the case. The Court rejected the argument that the Eleventh Amendment precludes injunctive relief on the basis of state law twice only two Terms ago.

* * *

> [I]mmunity from suit is a high attribute of sovereignty—a prerogative of the State itself—which cannot be availed of by public agents when sued for their own torts. The Eleventh Amendment was not intended to afford them freedom from liability in any case where, under color of their office, they have injured one of the State's citizens. To grant them such immunity would be to create a privileged class free from liability for wrongs inflicted or injuries threatened * * * . Besides, neither a State nor an individual can confer upon an agent authority to commit a tort so as to excuse the perpetrator.
>
> In such cases the law of agency has no application—the wrongdoer is treated as a principal and individually liable for the damages inflicted and subject to injunction against the commission of acts causing irreparable injury.

Food for Thought

Upon what principle does Justice Stevens draw here?

The principles that were decisive in these cases are not confined to actions under state tort law. They also apply to claims that state officers have violated state statutes.

* * *

The Court also relies heavily on the fact that the District Court found petitioners immune from damages liability because they "acted in the utmost good faith * * * *within the sphere of their official responsibilities.*" This confuses two distinct concepts. An official can act in good faith and therefore be immune from damages liability despite the fact that he has done that which the law prohibits, a point recognized as recently as *Harlow v. Fitzgerald*. Nevertheless, good faith immunity from damage liability is irrelevant to the availability of injunctive relief. * * * Until today the rule has been simple: conduct that exceeds the scope of an official's lawful discretion is not conduct the sovereign has authorized and hence is subject to injunction. Whether that conduct also gives rise to damage liability is an entirely separate question.

III

On its face, the Eleventh Amendment applies only to suits against a State brought by citizens of other States and foreign nations. This textual limitation upon the scope of the states' immunity from suit in federal court was set aside in *Hans v. Louisiana*. * * * The Court stated that some of the arguments favoring sovereign immunity for the States made during the process of the Amendment's ratification had become a part of the judicial scheme created by the Constitution.

As a result, the Court concluded that the Constitution prohibited a suit by a citizen against his or her own state. When called upon to elaborate, the Court explained that the Eleventh Amendment did more than simply prohibit suits brought by citizens of one State against another State. Rather, it exemplified the broader and more ancient doctrine of sovereign immunity, which operates to bar a suit brought by a citizen against his own State without its consent.

The Court has subsequently adhered to this interpretation of the Eleventh Amendment. * * * Thus, under our cases it is the doctrine of sovereign immunity, rather than the text of the Amendment itself, which is critical to the analysis of any Eleventh Amendment problem.

The doctrine of sovereign immunity developed in England, where it was thought that the king could not be sued. However, common law courts, in applying the doctrine, traditionally distinguished between the king and his agents, on the theory that the king would never authorize unlawful conduct, and that therefore the unlawful acts of the king's officers ought not to be treated as acts of the sovereign.

* * *

The majority states that the holding of *Ex parte Young* is limited to cases in which relief is provided on the basis of federal law, and that it rests entirely on the need to protect the supremacy of federal law. That position overlooks the foundation of the rule of *Young* * * * and * * * [its] predecessors.

The *Young* Court distinguished between the State and its attorney general because the latter, in violating the Constitution, had engaged in conduct the sovereign could not authorize. The pivotal consideration was not that the conduct violated federal law, since nothing in the jurisprudence of the Eleventh Amendment permits a suit against a sovereign merely because federal law is at issue. Indeed, at least since *Hans v. Louisiana*, the law has been settled that the Eleventh Amendment applies even though the State is accused of violating the Federal Constitution. * * * It was clear until today that "the State [is not] divested of its immunity 'on the mere ground that the case is one arising under the Constitution or laws of the United States.' "

Food for Thought

Justice Stevens argues implicitly here (and explicitly later) that the *Young* distinction applies equally well to conduct that the sovereign *did not* authorize. Are you persuaded?

The pivotal consideration in Young was that it was not conduct of the sovereign that was at issue.[29] The rule that unlawful acts of an officer should not be attributed to the sovereign has deep roots in the history of sovereign immunity and makes Young reconcilable with the principles of sovereign immunity found in the Eleventh Amendment, rather than merely an unprincipled accommodation between federal and state interests that ignores the principles contained in the Eleventh Amendment.

This rule plainly applies to conduct of state officers in violation of state law. Young states that the significance of the charge of unconstitutional conduct is that it renders the state official's conduct "simply an illegal act," and hence the officer is not entitled to the sovereign's immunity. Since a state officer's conduct in violation of state law is certainly no less illegal than his violation of federal law, in either case the official, by committing an illegal act, is "stripped of his official or representative character."

* * *

[A]n illegal act strips the official of his state-law shield, thereby depriving the official of the sovereign's immunity. The majority criticizes this approach as being "out of touch with reality" because it ignores the practical impact of an injunction on the State though directed at its officers. Yet that criticism cannot account for Young, since an injunction has the same effect on the State whether it is based on federal or state law. Indeed, the majority recognizes that injunctions approved by Young "have an obvious impact on the State itself." In the final analysis the distinction between the State and its officers, realistic or not, is one firmly embedded in the doctrine of sovereign immunity. It is that doctrine and not any theory of federal supremacy which the Framers placed in the Eleventh Amendment and which this Court therefore has a duty to respect.

It follows that the basis for the Young rule is present when the officer sued has violated the law of the sovereign; in all such cases the conduct is of a type that would not be permitted by the sovereign and hence is not attributable to the sovereign under traditional sovereign immunity principles. In such a case, the sovereign's interest lies with those who seek to enforce its laws, rather than those who have violated them.

---

29 The distinction between the sovereign and its agents not only explains why the rationale of Ex parte Young and its predecessors is consistent with established sovereign immunity doctrine, but it also explains the critical difference between actions for injunctive relief and actions for damages recognized in Edelman v. Jordan. Since the damages remedy sought in that case would have required payment by the State, it could not be said that the action ran only against the agents of the State. Therefore, while the agents' unlawful conduct was considered *ultra vires* and hence could be enjoined, a remedy which did run against the sovereign and not merely its agent could not fit within the *ultra vires* doctrine and hence was impermissible. If damages are not sought from the State and the relief will run only against the state official, damages are a permissible remedy under the Eleventh Amendment.

* * *

The issuance of injunctive relief which enforces state laws and policies, if anything, enhances federal courts' respect for the sovereign prerogatives of the States. The majority's approach, which requires federal courts to ignore questions of state law and to rest their decisions on federal bases, will create more rather than less friction between the States and the federal judiciary.

Moreover, the majority's rule has nothing to do with the basic reason the Eleventh Amendment was added to the Constitution. There is general agreement that the Amendment was passed because the States were fearful that federal courts would force them to pay their Revolutionary War debts, leading to their financial ruin. Entertaining a suit for injunctive relief based on state law implicates none of the concerns of the Framers. Since only injunctive relief is sought there is no threat to the state treasury of the type that concerned the Framers, and if the State wishes to avoid the federal injunction, it can easily do so simply by changing its law. The possibility of States left helpless in the face of disruptive federal decrees which led to the passage of the Eleventh Amendment simply is not presented by this case. Indeed, the Framers no doubt would have preferred federal courts to base their decisions on state law, which the State is then free to reexamine, rather than forcing courts to decide cases on federal grounds, leaving the litigation beyond state control.

Take Note

This is another example of the importance of characterization. Justice Stevens ties the Eleventh Amendment closely to the issue of state war debts. Isn't it also possible that the states' concern was broader than that? Perhaps they were concerned with the entire spectre of the federal government being able to order large expenditures of money that the states might not be able to afford. More generally, how can we know at what level of generality to consider this or other questions?

In light of the preceding, it should come as no surprise that there is absolutely no authority for the majority's position that the rule of *Young* is inapplicable to violations of state law. The only cases the majority cites, for the proposition that *Young* is limited to the vindication of federal law do not consider the question whether *Young* permits injunctive relief on the basis of state law—in each of the cases the question was neither presented, briefed, argued nor decided. It is curious, to say the least, that the majority disapproves of reliance on cases in which the issue we face today was decided *sub silentio,* yet it is willing to rely on cases in which the issue was not decided at all. In fact, not only is there no precedent for the majority's position, but, as I have demonstrated in Part II, there is an avalanche of precedent squarely to the contrary.[38]

That the doctrine of sovereign immunity does not protect conduct which has been prohibited by the sovereign is clearly demonstrated by the case on which petitioners chiefly rely, Larson v. Domestic & Foreign Commerce Corp. The Larson opinion teaches that the actions of state officials are not attributable to the state—are *ultra vires*—in two different types of situations: (1) when the official is engaged in conduct that the sovereign has not authorized, and (2) when he has engaged in conduct that the sovereign has forbidden. A sovereign, like any other principal, cannot authorize its agent to violate the law. When an agent does so, his actions are considered *ultra vires* and he is liable for his own conduct under the law of agency. Both types of *ultra vires* conduct are clearly identified in Larson.

> There may be, of course, suits for specific relief against officers of the sovereign which are not suits against the sovereign. If the officer purports to act as an individual and not as an official, a suit directed against that action is not a suit against the sovereign. If the War Assets Administrator had completed a sale of his own personal home, he presumably could be enjoined from later conveying it to a third person. On a similar theory, *where the officer's powers are limited by statute, his actions beyond those limitations are considered individual and not sovereign actions.* The officer is not doing the business which the sovereign has empowered him to do *or he is doing it in a way that the sovereign has forbidden.* His actions are *ultra vires* his authority and therefore may be made the object of specific relief. It is important to note that in such cases the relief can be granted, without impleading the sovereign, only because of the officer's lack of delegated power. A claim of error in the exercise of that power is therefore not sufficient. And, since the jurisdiction of the court to hear the case may depend, as we have recently recognized, upon the decision which it ultimately reaches on the merits, it is necessary that the plaintiff set out in his complaint the statutory limitation on which he relies.

([E]mphasis supplied).

38 In addition to overruling the cases discussed in Part II, the majority's view that Young exists simply to ensure the supremacy of federal law indicates that a number of our prior cases, which held that the Eleventh Amendment may bar an action for injunctive relief even where the State has violated the Federal Constitution, *see, e.g.*, Alabama v. Pugh, were incorrectly decided. The Court can have no satisfactory explanation for *Pugh*, which held that even as to a federal constitutional claim, a suit may not be brought directly against a state even where it may be brought against its officials. On the majority's view, there is no basis for distinguishing between the state and its officials—as to both there is a need to vindicate the supremacy of federal law through the issuance of injunctive relief, and unless the officials are acting completely outside of their authority, they must be treated as is the state. However, Pugh can be explained simply by reference to Young's use of the *ultra vires* doctrine with respect to unconstitutional conduct by state officers—such conduct is not conduct by the sovereign because it could not be authorized by the sovereign, hence the officers are not entitled to the sovereign's immunity. A suit directly against the state cannot succeed because the *ultra vires* doctrine is unavailable without a state officer to which it can be applied. Pugh makes it clear that Young rests not on a need to vindicate federal law, but on the traditional distinction between the sovereign and its agents.

Larson thus clearly indicates that the immunity determination depends upon the merits of the plaintiff's claim. The same approach is employed by Young—the plaintiff can overcome the state official's immunity only by succeeding on the merits of its claim of unconstitutional conduct.

Following the two-track analysis of Larson, the cases considering the question whether the state official is entitled to the sovereign's immunity can be grouped into two categories. In cases like Larson, which usually involve the state functioning in its proprietary capacity, the *ultra vires* issue can be resolved solely by reference to the law of agency. Since there is no specific limitation on the powers of the officers other than the general limitations on their authority, the only question that need be asked is whether they have acted completely beyond their authority. But when the State has placed specific limitations on the manner in which state officials may perform their duties, as it often does in regulatory or other administrative contexts, the *ultra vires* inquiry also involves the question whether the officials acted in a way that state law forbids. No sovereign would authorize its officials to violate its own law, and if the official does so, then Larson indicates that his conduct is *ultra vires* and not protected by sovereign immunity.

* * *

In sum, a century and a half of this Court's Eleventh Amendment jurisprudence has established the following. A suit alleging that the official had acted within his authority but in a manner contrary to state statutes was not barred because the Eleventh Amendment prohibits suits against States; it does not bar suits against state officials for actions not permitted by the State under its own law. The sovereign could not and would not authorize its officers to violate its own law; hence an action against a state officer seeking redress for conduct not permitted by state law is a suit against the officer, not the sovereign. *Ex parte Young* concluded in as explicit a fashion as possible that unconstitutional action by state officials is not action by the State even if it purports to be authorized by state law, *because the federal Constitution strikes down the state law shield.* In the tort cases, if the plaintiff proves his case, there is by definition no state-law defense to shield the defendant. Similarly, *when the state officer violates a state statute, the sovereign has by definition erected no shield against liability.* These precedents make clear that there is no foundation for the contention that the majority embraces—that *Ex parte Young* authorizes injunctive relief against state officials only on the basis of federal law. To the contrary, *Young* is as clear as a bell: the Eleventh Amendment does not apply where there is no state-law shield. That simple principle should control this case.

IV

The majority's decision in this case is especially unwise in that it overrules a long line of cases in order to reach a result that is at odds with the usual practices of this Court. In one of the most respected opinions ever written by a Member of this Court, Justice Brandeis wrote:

> The Court [has] developed, for its own governance in the cases confessedly within its jurisdiction, a series of rules under which it has avoided passing upon a large part of all the constitutional questions pressed upon it for decision. They are:
>
> * * * The Court will not pass upon a constitutional question although properly presented by the record, if there is also present some other ground upon which the case may be disposed of. This rule has found most varied application. Thus, if a case can be decided on either of two grounds, one involving a constitutional question, the other a question of statutory construction or general law, the Court will decide only the latter.

The *Siler* case, cited with approval by Justice Brandeis in *Ashwander,* employed a remarkably similar approach to that used by the Court of Appeals in this case. The Court held that the plaintiff's claim * * * was sufficient to justify the assertion of federal jurisdiction over the case, but then declined to reach the federal question, deciding the case on the basis of state law instead:

> Where a case in this court can be decided without reference to questions arising under the Federal Constitution, that course is usually pursued and is not departed from without important reasons. In this case we think it much better to decide it with regard to the question of a local nature, involving the construction of the state statute and the authority therein given to the commission to make the order in question, rather than to unnecessarily decide the various constitutional questions appearing in the record.

The *Siler* principle has been applied on numerous occasions; when a suit against state officials has presented both federal constitutional questions and issues of state law, the Court has upheld injunctive relief on state-law grounds.

* * *

In fact, in this very case we applied the *Siler* rule by remanding the case to the Court of Appeals with explicit instructions to consider whether respondents were entitled to relief under state law.

* * *

In addition, application of the *Siler* rule enhances the decisionmaking autonomy of the States. *Siler* directs the federal court to turn first to state law, which the

State is free to modify or repeal. By leaving the policy determinations underlying injunctive relief in the hands of the State, the Court of Appeals' approach gives appropriate deference to established state policies.

In contrast, the rule the majority creates today serves none of the interests of the State. The majority prevents federal courts from implementing state policies through equitable enforcement of state law. Instead, federal courts are required to resolve cases on federal grounds that no state authority can undo. Leaving violations of state law unredressed and ensuring that the decisions of federal courts may never be reexamined by the States hardly comports with the respect for States as sovereign entities commanded by the Eleventh Amendment.

V

One basic fact underlies this case: far from immunizing petitioners' conduct, the State of Pennsylvania prohibited it. Respondents do not complain about the conduct of the State of Pennsylvania—it is Pennsylvania's commands which they seek to enforce. Respondents seek only to have Pennhurst run the way Pennsylvania envisioned that it be run. Until today, the Court understood that the Eleventh Amendment does not shield the conduct of state officers which has been prohibited by their sovereign.

Throughout its history this Court has derived strength from institutional self-discipline. Adherence to settled doctrine is presumptively the correct course. Departures are, of course, occasionally required by changes in the fabric of our society. When a court, rather than a legislature, initiates such a departure, it has a special obligation to explain and to justify the new course on which it has embarked. Today, however, the Court casts aside well settled respected doctrine that plainly commands affirmance of the Court of Appeals—the doctrine of the law of the case, the doctrine of *stare decisis* (the Court repudiates at least 28 cases), the doctrine of sovereign immunity, the doctrine of pendent jurisdiction, and the doctrine of judicial restraint. No sound reason justifies the further prolongation of this litigation or this Court's voyage into the sea of undisciplined lawmaking.

Food for Thought

To what institution does Justice Stevens refer here? To what institution did he refer "at the outset"?

As I said at the outset, this case has illuminated the character of an institution.

I respectfully dissent.

Notes and Questions

1. *Pennhurst* represents, first and foremost, a clash of theories underlying the idea that state officials can be sued in federal court pursuant to Ex parte Young. What are the two theories of state official liability competing in *Pennhurst?* Which does Young itself support better?

2. Note that the real issue in *Pennhurst* is far broader than the arcane question of whether pendent (now supplemental) jurisdiction extends to actions against state officials. The competing theories in *Pennhurst* connote vastly different views of the role of government *vis-à-vis* the individual. Which view gives the government more power and the individual less?

3. Note the effect of Justice Powell's view of Young on cases against state officials that present both federal and state claims. Plaintiffs have several choices. First, they may be able to litigate on two fronts, presenting state claims in state court and federal claims in federal court, thus incurring additional expense and inconvenience. But consider the effect of Migra v. Warren City School District Board of Education, discussed in Note 8 below, on that option. Second, they can present either their federal or state claims in the appropriate forum and abandon the other claims. Third, they may, unless the federal claims are within the exclusive jurisdiction of the federal courts, present all claims in the state courts. Are these options desirable? Perhaps more to the point, is Justice Powell telling us that the Constitution compels these options?

4. Does 28 U.S.C.A. § 1367, the statute codifying supplemental jurisdiction, affect the *Pennhurst* majority opinion?

5. Does Justice Stevens's dissent prove too much? He argues that the Court has long decided cases on non-constitutional and non-federal grounds when possible. Does that suggest that in cases against state officials involving federal and state questions, the federal courts might adjudicate only the state questions? Given that at least one aim of the Eleventh Amendment was to eliminate diversity jurisdiction against the states, (or was it?) should the federal courts adjudicate state claims to the exclusion of federal claims?

6. Both *Hans* and *Young* have a role in *Pennhurst.* Justice Powell characterizes *Young* as a narrow exception to the general rule of Eleventh Amendment immunity. Is that correct, or should we instead regard *Young* as the rule and the *Edelman* exclusion of damages as the exception?

7. *Pennhurst* is remarkable, among other things, for the level of rhetoric between the Justices. Why do you think the discussion was so heated? Feelings continued to run high on the Court for some time after *Pennhurst.* In *Atascadero State Hospital v. Scanlon*, 473 U.S. 234 (1985) (*supra* at pages 690, 699), decided the term after *Pennhurst*, Justice Stevens again dissented:

Because my decision to join Justice Brennan's dissent is a departure from the opinion I expressed in Florida Dept. of Health v. Florida Nursing Home Assn., a word of explanation is in order. As I then explained, notwithstanding my belief that Edelman v. Jordan was incorrectly decided, I then concluded that the doctrine of *stare decisis* required that Edelman be followed. Since then, however, the Court has not felt constrained by *stare decisis* in its expansion of the protective mantle of sovereign immunity, having repudiated at least 28 cases in its decision in *Pennhurst State School and Hospital v. Halderman* and additional study has made it abundantly clear that not only Edelman, but Hans v. Louisiana, as well, can properly be characterized as "egregiously incorrect." I am now persuaded that a fresh examination of the Court's Eleventh Amendment jurisprudence will produce benefits that far outweigh "the consequences of further unraveling the doctrine of *stare decisis*" in this area of the law.

8. In *Migra v. Warren City School District*, 465 U.S. 75 (1984), the defendant district offered a contract extension, and the plaintiff school supervisor accepted. Thereafter, the Board of Education voted not to renew the contract. Migra sued in state court, alleging breach of contract by the Board and wrongful interference with the contract by members of the Board, in their individual capacities but in conspiracy with each other. The Ohio court found for Migra on the breach of contract claim but declined to reach her claims against the individual Board members. The court ordered Migra's reinstatement and awarded compensatory damages. On Migra's motion, the court dismissed "without prejudice" the counts of her complaint relating to the liability of individual Board members.

Migra then commenced a federal action against the School District, the members of its Board, and the Superintendent. She pleaded claims under 42 U.S.C.A. §§ 1983, 1985 based on rights in the First, Fifth and Fourteenth Amendments, alleging that the Board attempted to terminate her contract because she participated, at the Board's request, in preparing a school desegregation plan. She sought injunctive relief and compensatory and punitive damages. The defendants pleaded res judicata, arguing that Migra could have litigated her federal claims in the state proceeding.

The Court rejected Migra's arguments that ordinary preclusion concepts should not apply to § 1983 actions, noting that Congress made no exception to the Full Faith and Credit Statute's requirement, 28 U.S.C.A. § 1738, that federal courts accord state court judgments the same preclusive effect as they would have in the rendering state.

a) Why did the plaintiff proceed as she did? If counsel had wanted to pursue the federal claim in federal court, why did the entire case not begin there initially? If you had been advising Ethel Migra, what would you have recommended?

b) Did the majority make much ado about nothing? It remanded the case for consideration of Ohio preclusion law. Does the Ohio trial court's dismissal of the individual and conspiracy claims without prejudice offer more than a clue? If dismissal without prejudice does not signify that the claim can be refiled, what does it mean? On the other hand, given that the plaintiff had never presented her federal claims to the state courts, but had used state analogs instead, would it still be possible for Ohio to rule that the federal claims, though perhaps not the state analogs, were precluded?

c) What is the effect of *Migra* and *Pennhurst* taken together? Is it significant that they were decided on the same day? Reconsider the options that a plaintiff with federal and state claims has, as discussed in note 3 above. Which of those is still a realistic possibility following *Migra*? Does it affect how you would advise a client?

Federal Maritime Commission v. South Carolina State Ports Authority, 535 U.S. 743 (2002), appears to have extended the states' immunity to federal proceedings in a new direction. The dispute revolved around the defendant Authority's (SCSPA) refusal to open Charleston's port facilities to a cruise ship that permitted gambling on board while in international waters. The company complained that the Authority discriminated in applying its anti-gambling policy, allowing ships from a rival company to use Charleston's berthing facilities.

The company alleged violations of the federal Shipping Act and took its complaint to the Federal Maritime Commission (FMC). FMC referred the complaint to an administrative law judge, who dismissed the complaint on Eleventh Amendment grounds, relying on *Seminole Tribe* for the conclusion that Congress's powerlessness to provide for federal court actions against states pursuant to its Article I powers connoted that FMC, created pursuant to those Article I powers, could not itself subject SCSPA to a federal proceeding at the behest of an individual.

The company did not appeal the ruling, but FMC reviewed it and reached the conclusion that sovereign immunity was not a bar to the proceeding. The Fourth Circuit overturned FMC's conclusion and ordered the case dismissed. The Supreme Court granted FMC's petition for certiorari and affirmed by the predictable five-to-four majority.

Justice Thomas's majority opinion made clear that the Court decided the case not on the basis of the Eleventh Amendment itself, but instead in service of "the sovereign immunity embedded in our constitutional structure and retained by the States when they joined the Union * * * ." It was necessary for him to do so because FMC clearly does not exercise Article III judicial power, and the Court has never pretended that the Eleventh Amendment addresses anything else. That being the case, the majority opinion was at pains to analogize the FMC proceeding to a traditional lawsuit, citing with approval the Fourth Circuit's observation that the proceeding "walks, talks, and squawks very much like a lawsuit."

The majority relied heavily on a carefully selected excerpt from Alexander Hamilton's The Federalist No. 81, in which he stated that "It is inherent in the nature of sovereignty not to be amenable to the suit of an individual without its consent." That sentiment, did not stand in isolation. The majority opinion in *Hans* reproduced much of Hamilton's discussion on the point (*see supra* page 647-48) and demonstrates clearly that he was speaking of the states' sovereign immunity with respect to actions on state debts, *i.e.* state-created contract actions. Lest there be any doubt, consider that the subject of The Federalist No. 81 was a general discussion of Article III, the organization of the Supreme Court and the possibility of having inferior federal courts. The sentence immediately before the quoted language in *Hans* reads: "Though it may rather be a digression from the immediate subject of this paper, I shall take occasion to mention here a supposition which has excited some alarm upon very mistaken grounds." At the conclusion of the aside, Hamilton said: "Let us resume the train of our observations."

It could hardly be clearer, as many distinguished scholars have pointed out, that Hamilton was addressing the possibility of diversity actions in the federal courts. Were that not the case, there would have been no reason to refer to an assignment of the debt to a non-citizen of the defendant state. Hamilton was talking about a state defense to a state claim. If the language (in context) to which Justice Thomas referred suggests anything, it suggests that the diversity interpretation of the Eleventh Amendment is right on target.

Justice Stevens's dissent rejected both of what he characterized as the majority's predicates for its decision. First, to the extent that the majority relied on *Alden v. Maine* and its mention of state dignity as a core value of the doctrine of sovereign immunity, he recalled Justice Souter's *Alden* dissent and continued the argument that neither history nor constitutional structure supported the idea of state immunity from federal law. Second, he disputed the idea that state dignity was a core value of the immunity doctrine that did exist, relying in part on Chief Justice Marshall's statement in *Cohens v. Virginia* (1821) that the Eleventh Amendment existed only to protect states from individual creditors and not to protect a dignity interest in not appearing in another sovereign's courts, for if it were, the Constitution would not have permitted suits against states by other states or by the federal government.

Justice Breyer also dissented, arguing that no constitutional text at all supported the Court's result, given that the Federal Maritime Commission was not a part of the judicial (or legislative) branch at all. He took the position that FMC was executing federal law, "in part by making rules or by adjudicating matters in dispute." For him, the determining factor was that "the Constitution created a Federal Government empowered to enact laws that would bind the States and it empowered that Federal Government to enforce those laws against the States.

It also left private individuals perfectly free to complain to the Federal Government about unlawful state activity, and it left the Federal Government free to take subsequent legal action."

More specifically, Justice Breyer asserted that the Court could not legitimately read the words "Judicial power" in the Eleventh Amendment to mean "executive power," though he did note with some acerbity that the Court had read "Citizens of another State" as if it said "citizen of the same State." He rejected a Tenth Amendment approach as well, since in his view the Constitution had delegated the power FMC exercised to the United States, and he accused the majority of reading into the Tenth Amendment a "hidden reservation" with respect to state sovereign immunity. Finally, he argued that the Court's underlying assumption—that state sovereign immunity survived the Constitutional Convention entirely intact—could not survive historical analysis. Moreover, he made clear that the dissenting Justices were not content to let the issue drop. "Today's decision reaffirms the need for continued dissent—unless the consequences of the Court's approach prove anodyne, as I hope, rather than randomly destructive, as I fear."

Finally, consider one additional point about *Federal Maritime Commission*. FMC argued that the action fell within the doctrine of *Ex parte Young* because even if resolved against the state, it would have no adverse impact on the state treasury. Justice Thomas's majority opinion recognized a hierarchy of values within the doctrine of sovereign immunity that the Court expounded, observing that protection of state treasuries was important but noting that "the doctrine's central purpose is to 'accord the States the respect owed them as' joint sovereigns." The Court juxtaposed that assertion with an observation that the federal government can still affect the states using its Article I legislative powers; it simply must enforce such regulations in its own name (including in federal lawsuits) rather than relying on litigation by private entities. This approach leaves several questions open.

First, if the core value of sovereign immunity doctrine is the states' dignity interest, why does a federal action by an individual seeking only injunctive relief (in the mold of *Ex parte Young*) not pose just as great a threat to the state's dignity as an action seeking damages? Second, why is the dignity interest subordinated if the plaintiff is the federal government or another state? Is the offense to a state's dignity interest determined by the forum in which the adjudication occurs or by the identity of the opposing party? Third, referring to the core concern with states' dignity interests, Justice Thomas noted that "[i]t is for this reason * * * that sovereign immunity applies regardless of whether a private plaintiff's suit is for monetary damages or some other type of relief." Does that statement lay groundwork for substantially limiting the doctrine of *Ex parte Young* or overturning it entirely?

Chapter 8

Refusing Jurisdiction: Abstention and Related Doctrines

A. Introduction

Sometimes a court having jurisdiction of the case and over all of the parties will nonetheless decline to hear it. The basic civil procedure concepts of *forum non conveniens* or transfer of venue are examples. More specialized examples include the federal courts' long-standing refusal to hear domestic relations or probate cases under their diversity jurisdiction. Some jurisdiction-declining rules are created by statute; others by the courts.

A set of doctrines and statutes relating particularly to federal courts has emerged over the two centuries since the Judiciary Act of 1789 created the inferior federal courts. The statutory provisions, which seek to serve the values of federalism, pose some intricate technical problems; the judge-made doctrines raise both substantial federalism and separation-of-powers questions. Section 1983 cases in particular exemplify the federal courts' continuing struggle to accommodate state interests, federal interests, separation-of-powers concerns, and individuals' constitutional rights to be free from government overreaching. The difficulty of this four-part balancing act is nowhere better illustrated than in the area of abstention.

All the statutory and common law rules in this area appear against a backdrop of serious issues about the propriety of federal courts refusing cases clearly within their jurisdiction. Nearly two centuries ago, Chief Justice John Marshall said, with characteristic understatement:

> It is most true that this Court will not take jurisdiction if it should not: but it is equally true, that it must take jurisdiction if it should. The judiciary cannot, as the legislature may, avoid a measure because it approaches the confines of the constitution. We cannot pass it by because it is doubtful. With whatever doubts, with whatever difficulties, a case may be attended, we must decide it, if it be brought before us. We have no more right to decline the exercise of jurisdiction which is given, than to usurp that which is not given. The one or the other would be treason to the constitution. Questions may occur which we would gladly avoid; but we cannot avoid them. All we can do is, to exercise our best judgment, and conscientiously to perform our duty.[1]

1 Cohens v. Virginia, 19 U.S. (6 Wheat.) 264, 404 (1821).

Whether or not those sentiments were ever the rule in the federal courts, they clearly are not today. In Marshall's terms, the Supreme Court and the inferior federal courts commit treason every day. When Congress has conferred jurisdiction, there is a substantial separation-of-powers question about the legitimacy of judge-made doctrines that implicitly treat jurisdictional statutes not as directives but as offers that can be refused. This section presents an overview of what Marshall might well have regarded as the federal courts' apostasy.

B. Congressional Doctrines Of Restraint

Atlantic Coast Line Railroad Company v. Brotherhood of Locomotive Engineers

Supreme Court of the United States, 1970.
398 U.S. 281.

MR. JUSTICE BLACK delivered the opinion of the Court.

Congress in 1793, shortly after the American Colonies became one united Nation, provided that in federal courts "a writ of injunction [shall not] be granted to stay proceedings in any court of a state." Although certain exceptions to this general prohibition have been added, that statute, directing that state courts shall remain free from interference by federal courts, has remained in effect until this time. Today that amended statute provides: "A court of the United States may not grant an injunction to stay proceedings in a State court except as expressly authorized by Act of Congress, or where necessary in aid of its jurisdiction, or to protect or effectuate its judgments." 28 U.S.C. § 2283. Despite the existence of this long standing prohibition, in this case a federal court did enjoin the petitioner, Atlantic Coast Line Railroad Co. (ACL), from invoking an injunction issued by a Florida state court which prohibited certain picketing by respondent Brotherhood of Locomotive Engineers (BLE). * * *

fed ct. told ACL it can't enforce state ct. injunction to stop BLE from picketing

In 1967 BLE began picketing the Moncrief Yard, a switching yard located near Jacksonville, Florida, and wholly owned and operated by ACL. As soon as this picketing began ACL went into federal court seeking an injunction. When the federal judge denied the request, ACL immediately went into state court and there succeeded in obtaining an injunction. No further legal action was taken in this dispute until two years later in 1969, after this Court's decision in *Brotherhood of Railroad Trainmen v. Jacksonville Terminal Co*. In that case the Court considered the validity of a state injunction against picketing by the BLE and other unions at the Jacksonville Terminal, located immediately next to Moncrief Yard. The Court reviewed the factual situation surrounding the Jacksonville Terminal picketing and concluded that the unions had a federally protected right to picket under the Railway Labor Act and that that right could not be interfered with by state court injunctions. Immediately after a petition for rehearing was denied in that case, the respondent BLE filed a motion in state court to dissolve the Moncrief Yard injunction, arguing that under the *Jacksonville Terminal* decision the injunction was improper. The state judge refused to dissolve the injunction, holding that this Court's *Jacksonville Terminal* decision was not controlling. The union did not elect to appeal that decision directly, but instead went back into the federal court and requested an injunction against the enforcement of the state court injunction. The District Judge granted the injunction and upon application a stay of that injunction, pending the filing and disposition of a petition for certiorari, was granted. The Court of Appeals summarily affirmed on the parties' stipulation, and we granted a petition for certiorari to consider the validity of the federal court's injunction against the state court.

In this Court the union contends that the federal injunction was proper either "to protect or effectuate" the District Court's denial of an injunction in 1967, or as "necessary in aid of" the District Court's jurisdiction. Although the questions are by no means simple and clear, and the decision is difficult, we conclude that the injunction against the state court was not justified under either of these two exceptions to the anti-injunction statute. We therefore hold that the federal injunction in this case was improper.

I

Before analyzing the specific legal arguments advanced in this case, we think it would be helpful to discuss the background and policy that led Congress to pass the anti-injunction statute in 1793. While all the reasons that led Congress to adopt this restriction on federal courts are not wholly clear, it is certainly likely that one reason stemmed from the essentially federal nature of our national government. When this Nation was established by the Constitution, each State surrendered only a part of its sovereign power to the national government. But those powers that were not surrendered were retained by the States and unless a State was restrained by "the supreme Law of the Land" as expressed in the Constitution, laws, or treaties of the United States it was free to exercise those retained powers as it saw fit. One of the reserved powers was the maintenance of state judicial systems for the decision of legal controversies. * * *

While the lower federal courts were given certain powers in the 1789 Act, they were not given any power to review directly cases from state courts, and they have not been given such powers since that time. Only the Supreme Court was authorized to review on direct appeal the decisions of state courts. Thus from the beginning we have had in this country two essentially separate legal systems. Each system proceeds independently of the other with ultimate review in this Court of the federal questions raised in either system. Understandably this dual court system was bound to lead to conflicts and frictions. Litigants who foresaw the possibility of more favorable treatment in one or the other system would predictably hasten to invoke the powers of whichever court it was believed would present the best chance of success. Obviously this dual system could not function if state and federal courts were free to fight each other for control of a particular case. Thus, in order to make the dual system work and "to prevent needless friction between state and federal courts," it was necessary to work out lines of demarcation between the two systems. Some of these limits were spelled out in the 1789 Act. Others have been added by later statutes as well as judicial decisions. The 1793 anti-injunction Act was at least in part a response to these pressures.

> **FYI**
>
> The Court has characterized federal habeas corpus review for state prisoners as reviewing the legality of the petitioner's being in custody, not a review of the underlying judicial decision. Is that distinction persuasive?

On its face the present Act is an absolute prohibition against enjoining state court proceedings, unless the injunction falls within one of three specifically defined exceptions. The respondents here have intimated that the Act only establishes a "principle of comity," not a binding rule on the power of the federal courts. The argument implies that in certain circumstances a federal court may enjoin state court proceedings even if that action cannot be justified by any of the three exceptions. We * * * hold that any injunction against state court proceedings otherwise proper under general equitable principles must be based on one of the specific statutory exceptions to § 2283 if it is to be upheld. Moreover since the statutory prohibition against such injunctions in part rests on the fundamental constitutional independence of the States and their courts the exceptions should not be enlarged by loose statutory construction. Proceedings in state courts should normally be allowed to continue unimpaired by intervention of the lower federal courts, with relief from error, if any, through the state appellate courts and ultimately this Court.

II

In this case the Florida Circuit Court enjoined the union's intended picketing, and the United States District Court enjoined the railroad "from giving effect to or availing [itself] of the benefits of" that state court order. Both sides agree that although this federal injunction is in terms directed only at the railroad it is an injunction "to stay proceedings in a State court." It is settled that the prohibition of § 2283 cannot be evaded by addressing the order to the parties or prohibiting utilization of the results of a completed state proceeding. * * *

Neither party argues that there is any express congressional authorization for injunctions in this situation and we agree with that conclusion. The respondent union does contend that the injunction was proper either as a means to protect or effectuate the District Court's 1967 order, or in aid of that court's jurisdiction. We do not think that either alleged basis can be supported.

A

The argument based on protecting the 1967 order is not clearly expressed, but in essence it appears to run as follows: In 1967 the railroad sought a temporary restraining order which the union opposed. In the course of deciding that request, the United States District Court determined that the union had a federally protected right to picket Moncrief Yard and that this right could not be interfered with by state courts. When the Florida Circuit Court enjoined the picketing, the United States District Court could, in order to protect and effectuate its prior determination, enjoin enforcement of the state court injunction. Although the record on this point is not unambiguously clear, we conclude that no such interpretation of the 1967 order can be supported.

When the railroad initiated the federal suit it filed a complaint with three counts, each based entirely on alleged violations of federal law. The first two counts alleged violations of the Railway Labor Act, and the third alleged a violation of that Act and the Interstate Commerce Act as well. Each of the counts concluded with a prayer for an injunction against the picketing. Although the union had not been formally served with the complaint and had not filed an answer, it appeared at a hearing on a motion for a temporary restraining order and argued against the issuance of such an order. The union argued that it was a party to a labor dispute with the FEC, that it had exhausted the administrative remedies required by the Railway Labor Act, and that it was thus free to engage in "self-help," or concerted economic activity. Then the union argued that such activity could not be enjoined by the federal court. In an attempt to clarify the basis of this argument the District Judge asked: "You are basing your case solely on the Norris-LaGuardia Act?" The union's lawyer replied: "Right. I think at this point of the argument, since Norris-LaGuardia is clearly in point here." At no point during the entire argument did either side refer to state law, the effects of that law on the picketing, or the possible preclusion of state remedies as a result of overriding federal law. The next day the District Court entered an order denying the requested restraining order. In relevant part that order included these conclusions of law:

> 3. The parties to the BLE-FEC "major dispute," having exhausted the procedures of the Railway Labor Act, are now free to engage in self-help. * * *
>
> 4. The conduct of the FEC pickets and that of the responding ACL employees are a part of the FEC-BLE major dispute. * * *
>
> 7. The Norris-LaGuardia Act and the Clayton Act are applicable to the conduct of the defendants here involved.

In this Court the union asserts that the determination that it was "free to engage in self-help" was a determination that it had a federally protected right to picket and that state law could not be invoked to negate that right. The railroad, on the other hand, argues that the order merely determined that the federal court could not enjoin the picketing, in large part because of the general prohibition in the Norris-LaGuardia Act against issuance by federal courts of injunctions in labor disputes. Based solely on the state of the record when the order was entered, we are inclined to believe that the District Court did not determine whether federal law precluded an injunction based on state law. Not only was that point never argued to the court, but there is no language in the order that necessarily implies any decision on that question. In short we feel that the District Court in 1967 determined that federal law could not be invoked to enjoin the picketing at Moncrief Yard, and that the union did have a right "to engage in self-help" as far as the federal courts were concerned. But that decision is entirely different from a decision that the Railway Labor Act precludes state regulation of the picketing as well, and this latter decision is an essential prerequisite for upholding the 1969 injunction as necessary "to protect or effectuate" the 1967 order. * * *

Any lingering doubts we might have as to the proper interpretation of the 1967 order are settled by references to the positions adopted by the parties later in the litigation. In response to the railroad's request for a temporary restraining order from the state court, the union referred to the prior federal litigation, noted that it was part of a "major dispute," that it was covered by § 20 of the Clayton Act and that "[l]abor activity which is within the Clayton Act is 'immunized trade union activities.' " At no point did the union appear to argue that the federal court had already determined that the railroad was precluded from obtaining an injunction under Florida law.

Similarly the union's arguments in 1969 indicate that the 1967 federal order did not determine whether federal law precluded resort to the state courts. When the union tried to dissolve the state court injunction, the argument was based entirely on the controlling effect of the *Jacksonville Terminal* decision on the picketing at Moncrief Yard. The union argued that this Court's "decision is squarely controlling upon [the Moncrief Yard] case which is identical in all material respects." Although the union again mentioned that the federal District Judge had determined in 1967 that it was free to engage in self-help, it never argued that the 1967 order had in effect held with respect to Moncrief Yard what this Court later held was the law with respect to the Jacksonville Terminal situation. The railroad argued that *Jacksonville Terminal* was not controlling, and the Florida judge agreed.[5]

Our reading of this record is not altered by the District Court's 1969 opinion issued when the injunction was granted two years after the 1967 order was entered. In that opinion the court said:

> In its Order of April 26, 1967, this Court found that Plaintiff's Moncrief Yard, the area in question, "is an integral and necessary part of [Florida East Coast Railway Company's] operations." * * * The Court concluded furthermore that Defendants herein "are now free to engage in self-help." * * * The injunction of the state court, if allowed to continue in force, would effectively nullify this Court's findings and delineation of rights of the parties. The categorization of Defendants' activities as "secondary" does not alter this state of affairs. * * * The prohibition of 28 U.S.C. § 2283, therefore, does not deprive this Court of jurisdiction to enter the injunction in this instance.

* * * We think the proper interpretation of that somewhat ambiguous passage can be reached only when it is considered in light of the arguments presented to the District Court by the union. In arguing that an injunction was necessary to protect the 1967 order, the union's lawyer said:

> Now, the basic finding [of that order] is that we are free to engage in such self-help as is permitted under the Railway Labor Act. Now, Your Honor, at that point, did not get to the question of how broad is this right, because the Norris-LaGuardia Act prevented Your Honor from issuing an injunction. Now, how broad, then, is that right? We know, from the [*Jacksonville Terminal*] decision. * * *

> **Practice Pointer**
>
> Can you see the mistake counsel made in thus framing the argument? Parse the sentences carefully.

* * * The lawyer then proceeded to argue that the *Jacksonville Terminal* case had clearly revealed that the right of self-help is beyond state court proscription in these circumstances. At no point during this hearing did the union try to argue, as it now appears to do, that the 1967 order itself had anticipated the *Jacksonville Terminal* decision. Rather the union appears to have argued that the decision of this Court in *Jacksonville Terminal* operated to define the scope of the right to self-help which the District Court had found the union entitled to exercise, and that the state court

5 For purposes of this case only, we will assume, without deciding, that the Florida Circuit Court's decision was wrong in light of our decision in *Jacksonville Terminal*.

injunction interfered with that right as so defined. Considered in this light we cannot agree with the dissenting view in this case that the District Court in 1967 "by necessary implication" decided that the union had a federally protected right to picket that "could not be subverted by resort to state proceedings." On the contrary, we read the quoted passage in the 1969 opinion as an indication that the District Court accepted the union's argument and concluded that the *Jacksonville Terminal* decision had amplified its 1967 order, and it was this amplification, rather than the original order itself, that required protection. Such a modification of an earlier order through an opinion in another case is not a "judgment" that can properly be protected by an injunction against state court proceedings.

This record, we think, conclusively shows that neither the parties themselves nor the District Court construed the 1967 order as the union now contends it should be construed. Rather we are convinced that the union in effect tried to get the Federal District Court to decide that the state court judge was wrong in distinguishing the *Jacksonville Terminal* decision. Such an attempt to seek appellate review of a state decision in the Federal District Court cannot be justified as necessary "to protect or effectuate" the 1967 order. The record simply will not support the union's contention on this point.

B

This brings us to the second prong of the union's argument in which it is suggested that even if the 1967 order did not determine the union's right to picket free from state interference, once the decision in *Jacksonville Terminal* was announced, the District Court was then free to enjoin the state court on the theory that such action was "necessary in aid of [the District Court's] jurisdiction." Again the argument is somewhat unclear, but it appears to go in this way: The District Court had acquired jurisdiction over the labor controversy in 1967 when the railroad filed its complaint, and it determined at that time that it did have jurisdiction. The dispute involved the legality of picketing by the union and the *Jacksonville Terminal* decision clearly indicated that such activity was not only legal, but was protected from state court interference. The state court had interfered with that right, and thus a federal injunction was "necessary in aid of its jurisdiction." For several reasons we cannot accept the contention.

First, a federal court does not have inherent power to ignore the limitations of § 2283 and to enjoin state court proceedings merely because those proceedings interfere with a protected federal right or invade an area preempted by federal law, even when the interference is unmistakably clear. * * * This conclusion is required because Congress itself set forth the only exceptions to the statute, and those exceptions do not include this situation. Second, if the District Court does have jurisdiction, it is not enough that the requested injunction is related to that jurisdiction, but it must be "necessary in aid of" that jurisdiction. While this language is admittedly broad, we conclude that it implies something similar to the concept of injunctions to "protect or effectuate" judgments. Both exceptions to the general prohibition of § 2283 imply that some federal injunctive relief may be necessary to prevent a state court from so interfering with a federal court's consideration or disposition of a case as to seriously impair the federal court's flexibility and authority to decide that case. Third, no such situation is presented here. Although the federal court did have jurisdiction of the railroad's complaint based on federal law, the state court also had jurisdiction over the complaint based on state law and the union's asserted federal defense as well. *Jacksonville Terminal*. * * * In short, the state and federal courts had concurrent jurisdiction in this case, and neither court was free to prevent either party from simultaneously pursuing claims in both courts. Therefore the state court's assumption of jurisdiction over the state law claims and the federal preclusion issue did not hinder the federal court's jurisdiction so as to make an injunction necessary to aid that jurisdiction. Nor was an injunction necessary because the state court may have taken action which the federal court was certain was improper under the *Jacksonville Terminal* decision. Again, lower federal courts possess no power whatever to sit in direct review of state court decisions. If the union was adversely affected by the state court's decision, it was free to seek vindication of its federal right in the Florida appellate courts and ultimately, if necessary, in this Court. * * * Unlike the Federal District Court, this Court does have potential appellate jurisdiction over federal questions raised in state court proceedings, and that broader jurisdiction allows this Court correspondingly broader authority to issue injunctions "necessary in aid of its jurisdiction."

III

This case is by no means an easy one. The arguments in support of the union's contentions are not insubstantial. But whatever doubts we may have are strongly affected by the general prohibition of § 2283. Any doubts as to the propriety of a federal injunction against state court proceedings should be resolved in favor of permitting the state courts to proceed in an orderly fashion to finally determine the controversy. The explicit wording of § 2283 itself implies as much, and the fundamental principle of a dual system of courts leads inevitably to that conclusion.

The injunction issued by the District Court must be vacated. Since that court has not yet proceeded to a final judgment in the case, the cause is remanded to it for further proceedings in conformity with this opinion.

Vacated and remanded.

MR. JUSTICE BRENNAN, with whom MR. JUSTICE WHITE joins, dissenting.

My disagreement with the Court in this case is a relatively narrow one. I do not disagree with much that is said concerning the history and policies underlying 28 U.S.C. § 2283. Nor do I dispute the Court's holding * * * that federal courts do not have authority to enjoin state proceedings merely because it is asserted that the state court is improperly asserting jurisdiction in an area preempted by federal law or federal procedures. Nevertheless in my view the District Court has discretion to enjoin the state proceedings in the present case because it acted pursuant to an explicit exception to the prohibition of § 2283, that is, "to protect or effectuate [the District Court's] judgments."

* * *

The thrust of the District Judge's order is that the procedures prescribed by the Railway Labor Act had been exhausted in relation to the BLE-FEC dispute, that BLE was therefore free to engage in self-help tactics, and that it was properly exercising this federal right when it engaged in the picketing that ACL sought to enjoin. This interpretation of the order is supported by the fact that the District Judge relied upon *Brotherhood of Locomotive Engineers v. Baltimore & Ohio R. Co.*, in which this Court held that the parties had exhausted all available procedures under the Railway Labor Act and thus were free to resort to self-help. Furthermore, the District Court invoked § 20 of the Clayton Act, which provides that certain union activities, including striking and peaceful picketing, shall not "be considered or held to be violations of any law of the United States."

Food for Thought

There are two ways to view the phrase "free to resort to self-help." It might mean either 1) that nothing in federal law provided a basis for enjoining self-help, or 2) that federal law contained an affirmative entitlement to engage in self-help with which state law was powerless to interfere. Given the posture of the case in the federal court in 1967, which alternative better describes what the district court thought it was doing?

Thus, contrary to petitioner's contention, the District Court obviously decided considerably more than the threshold question of whether the Norris-LaGuardia Act withdrew jurisdiction to grant federal injunctive relief in the circumstances of this case.

In my view, what the District Court decided in 1967 was that BLE had a federally protected right to picket at the Moncrief Yard and, by necessary implication, that this right could not be subverted by resort to state proceedings. I find it difficult indeed to ascribe to the District Judge the views that the Court now says he held, namely, that ACL, merely by marching across the street to the state court, could render wholly nugatory the District Judge's declaration that BLE had a federally protected right to strike at the Moncrief Yard.

Take Note!

Here Justice Brennan assumes his conclusion, does he not?

* * *

I believe that the Court has misinterpreted the argument of counsel in the lower courts. While I do not find the various proceedings below entirely free of confusion with respect to BLE's legal theory, there appear to be at least two strands to its argument. To be sure, BLE did contend, particularly in the state proceedings, that our decision in Jacksonville Terminal was controlling on the merits. As I read the record, however, BLE also argued that the state injunction should either be dissolved or enjoined so that it would not interfere with the federal court's 1967 decree. Thus, in moving for a preliminary injunction against the state court proceedings, BLE relied both upon Jacksonville Terminal and upon the power of the District Court to issue the injunction "to protect and effectuate the judgment of this Court dated April 26, 1967."

* * *

In sum, to the extent that the argument of counsel is an interpretive guide to what the District Court actually decided in its 1967 and 1969 orders, the Court's conclusion that the record "conclusively shows that neither the parties themselves nor the District Court construed the 1967 order" to preclude resort to state remedies to prohibit the Moncrief Yard picketing is wholly erroneous. And, quite apart from counsel's argument, it is apparent that the District Judge viewed his own 1967 order as delineating a federally protected right for the BLE picketing in question. Whether the District Court's anticipation of Jacksonville Terminal was correct in the circumstances of the present case is not now before us. But if the 1967 order is so understood, it is undeniably clear that the subsequent injunction against the state proceedings was both necessary and appropriate to preserve the integrity of the 1967 order.

* * * Unquestionably § 2283 manifests a general design on the part of Congress that federal courts not precipitately interfere with the orderly determination of controversies in state proceedings. However, this policy of nonintervention is by no means absolute, as the explicit exceptions in § 2283 make entirely clear. Thus, § 2283 itself evinces a congressional intent that resort to state proceedings not be permitted to undermine a prior judgment of a federal court. But that is exactly what has occurred in the present case. * * * .

Accordingly, I would affirm the judgment of the Court of Appeals sustaining the District Court's grant of injunctive relief against petitioner's giving effect to, or availing itself of, the benefit of the state court injunction.

Notes and Questions

1. Although Congress passed the original Anti-Injunction Act in 1793, there is little indication of a specific stimulus for it, unlike the Eleventh Amendment, which was a direct reaction to *Chisholm v. Georgia,* 2 U.S. (2 Dall.) 419 (1793). Professor Charles Warren suggested that *Chisholm* also underlay the Anti-Injunction Act, noting that Congress passed it only two weeks after *Chisholm*. This is at least questionable; *Chisholm* did not involve a federal injunction against a state proceeding, but rather a federal money judgment. Other scholars have argued that the statute was more likely stimulated by complaints from Justices about the rigors of circuit riding and was an effort to reduce the burdens on the federal judiciary. The Supreme Court has been less willing to speculate. "The precise origins of the legislation are shrouded in obscurity." *Mitchum v. Foster,* 407 U.S. 225, 232 (1972).

2. Although Justice Black spends much of the *Atlantic Coast Line* opinion discussing technical questions as to whether the case comes within various exceptions to the Anti-Injunction Act, it is clear that something more fundamental is bothering him. After *Jacksonville Terminal* in 1969, the union asked the state court to dissolve the Moncrief Yard injunction. When the state court refused, the union returned to federal court and asked that court to enjoin enforcement of the state injunction. What is it about this procedural posture that upsets Justice Black? When the district court issued the injunction, what role did it appear to be playing *vis-à-vis* the state trial court?

3. The Anti-Injunction Act expresses Congress's general policy against federal interference with state proceedings. It is important to consider separately the Act's three exceptions.

a) The "expressly authorized" exception seems straightforward, and indeed might be but for the Supreme Court's application of it. For example, the Federal Interpleader Act, 28 U.S.C.A. § 2361, specifically permits federal courts to enjoin competing state proceedings and to enjoin litigants from initiating potentially competing proceedings. The Court, however, has declined to require that Congress pass "read my lips" statutes that explicitly authorize an injunction against a state proceeding in order to invoke this exception to § 2283. *Amalgamated Clothing Workers v. Richman Brothers,* 348 U.S. 511 (1955), noted that a statute need not specifically refer to § 2283 to qualify as an express authorization.

The most famous decision regarding this exception is undoubtedly *Mitchum v. Foster*, 407 U.S. 225 (1972), which held that the Civil Rights Act of 1871, 42 U.S.C.A. § 1983, must be within the exception because the remedy Congress created "could be frustrated if the federal proceeding were not empowered to enjoin a state court proceeding." The Court elaborated its approach to the Anti-Injunction Act.

> Despite the seemingly uncompromising language of the anti-injunction statute prior to 1948, the Court soon recognized that exceptions must be made to its blanket prohibition if * * * other Acts of Congress were to be given their intended scope. So it was that, in addition to the bankruptcy law exception that Congress explicitly recognized in 1874, the Court through the years found that federal courts were empowered to enjoin state court proceedings, despite the anti-injunction statute, in carrying out the will of Congress under at least six other federal laws. These covered a broad spectrum of congressional action: (1) legislation providing for removal of litigation from state to federal courts, (2) legislation limiting the liability of ship owners, (3) legislation providing for federal interpleader actions, (4) legislation conferring federal jurisdiction over farm mortgages, (5) legislation governing federal habeas corpus proceedings, and (6) legislation providing for control of prices.
>
> In addition to the exceptions to the anti-injunction statute found to be embodied in these various Acts of Congress, the Court recognized other "implied" exceptions to the blanket prohibition of the anti-injunction statute. One was an "*in rem*" exception, allowing a federal court to enjoin a state court proceeding in order to protect its jurisdiction of a *res* over which it had first acquired jurisdiction. Another was a "relitigation" exception, permitting a federal court to enjoin relitigation in a state court of issues already decided in federal litigation. Still a third exception, more recently developed[,] permits a federal injunction of state court proceedings when the plaintiff in the federal court is the United States itself, or a federal agency asserting "superior federal interests."
>
> * * *
>
> [I]t is evident that in order to qualify under the "expressly authorized" exception of the anti-injunction statute, a federal law need not contain an express reference to that injunction statute. As the Court has said, "no prescribed formula is required; an authorization need not expressly refer to § 2283." Indeed, none of the previously recognized statutory exceptions contains any such reference. Secondly, a federal law need not expressly authorize an injunction of a state court proceeding in order to qualify as an exception. Three of the six previously recognized statutory exceptions contain no such authorization. Thirdly, it is clear that, in order to qualify as an "expressly authorized" exception to the anti-injunction statute, an Act of Congress must have created a specific and uniquely federal right or remedy, enforceable in a federal court of equity, that could be frustrated if the federal court were not empowered to enjoin a state court proceeding. This is not to say that in order to come within the exception an Act of Congress must, on its face and in every one of its provisions, be totally incompatible with the prohibition of the anti-injunction statute. The test, rather, is whether an Act of Congress,

> clearly creating a federal right or remedy enforceable in a federal court of equity, could be given its intended scope only by the stay of a state court proceeding.

Thus, after *Mitchum*, the way might have seemed open for the federal court in any action brought under § 1983 to enjoin pending state proceedings. However, the doctrine of *Younger* abstention, discussed later in this chapter, greatly blunts *Mitchum*'s effect.

Professor Redish strongly criticizes *Mitchum*, ridiculing the Court's reasoning. "In what may be one of the most bizarre contortions of Supreme Court analysis, the Court in *Mitchum* found section 1983 to be an 'implied' express exception (an oxymoron if ever there was one) * * * ." Martin H. Redish, *Abstention, Separation of Powers, and the Limits of the Judicial Function*, 94 YALE L.J. 71, 87 (1984). He does recognize, however, that the *Mitchum* interpretation seems firmly entrenched.

b) As Justice Black's opinion makes clear, the Court will narrowly construe the jurisdictional exception. Unless a state proceeding threatens in some sense to *defeat* federal jurisdiction, this exception does not apply. Thus, merely parallel litigation in the state courts is insufficient. Only where jurisdiction in one system is fatally incompatible with jurisdiction in the other may an injunction issue. It is well established, for example, that a federal or state court first obtaining jurisdiction by seizure of property may secure its jurisdiction by enjoining a court of the other system from hearing a case involving the same property. *Donovan v. City of Dallas*, 377 U.S. 408 (1964); *Toucey v. New York Life Insurance Co.*, 314 U.S. 118 (1941); *Kline v. Burke Construction Co.*, 260 U.S. 226 (1922).

c) The judgments exception is broader than the jurisdictional exception. The exception seeks to prevent harassment of successful federal litigants and to protect the finality of federal judgments. It permits the federal courts to issue injunctions to prevent the state courts from relitigating issues that have already been litigated and decided in federal court. In effect, it permits the federal courts to make sure that their judgments have preclusive effect.

Nonetheless, the Court continues to construe this exception, often referred to as the relitigation exception, quite strictly. *Smith v. Bayer*, 131 S.Ct. 2368 (2011), arose because of separate actions against Bayer, involving cholesterol-lowering medication. The first action (the McCollins action) was in federal court in Minnesota. McCollins sought class certification, but the court denied it on the ground that the common questions did not predominate over individual question. After the denial, two other consumers (the Smith action) commenced an action for the same relief in the state courts of West Virginia.[2] Bayer secured an injunction from the Minnesota district court (affirmed by the Eighth Circuit) to prevent the West Virginia action from going

2 Congress had not yet passed the Class Action Fairness Act when Smith sued, and since there were West Virginia citizens on both sides of the action, the case was not removable.

forward. Bayer's theory was that the injunction was necessary to protect the district court's judgment denying class certification. The case came to the Supreme Court on Smith's petition for certiorari.

The Court reversed for two reasons. "First, the issue presented in the state court was not identical to the one decided in the federal court." Although the texts of FED. R. CIV. P. 23 and West Virginia's Rule 23 are substantially identical, the Supreme Court noted that West Virginia's interpretation of its rule has diverged significantly from Federal Rule 23, and the West Virginia Supreme Court had made clear that it disagreed with the federal courts' interpretation of the Federal Rule's predominance requirement. The federal district court had taken the position that if each class plaintiff would have to submit individual evidence of injury and loss, the case failed the predominance test. West Virginia, by contrast, used a totality-of-the-circumstances balancing test. Said the Court, "A federal court and a state court apply different law. That means they decide distinct questions. The federal court's resolution of one issue does not preclude the state court's determination of another. It then goes without saying that the federal court may not issue an injunction." The astute reader will note that it did not go "without saying," which is why the Court had to step in to enforce the broad prohibition of the Anti-Injunction Act.

The Court also noted a conceptual problem with the lower courts' approach, finding that the Smith plaintiffs lacked sufficient connection to the McCollins action to be bound by its result. The lower courts had relied on the fact that Smith wanted to represent the very same class as had McCollins. That did not, however, suffice to bind Smith to the results of the McCollins litigation, largely because the district court had *refused* class certification. In effect, the Supreme Court told the lower federal courts that they could not have it both ways, first denying that there was a certifiable class and then seeking to bind "members" of the non-existent class to the results of litigation in which they had no part. Given the Court's ruling in *Phillips Petroleum Co. v. Shutts*, 472 U.S. 797 (1985) about the due process rights of unnamed plaintiff's in a class action maintained under Rule 23(b)(3), it would have been startling had the Court not ruled this way.

4. *County of Imperial v. Munoz*, 449 U.S. 54 (1980), affirmed that the Anti-Injunction Act does not prevent a federal constitutional challenge to a state statute, even a challenge seeking injunctive relief, merely because state litigation is pending between other parties. Thus, the Anti-Injunction Act has no effect upon a "stranger" to the pending state action. Does the Court's position have the potential of diminishing the protective function of the Act? If so, is that a problem the Court or Congress should address?

5. The Anti-Injunction Act's relationship with § 1983 raises questions about the role of congressional intent in the interpretation of statutes. At the outset, is it likely that the Congress that initially passed the Act would have intended unexpressed

exceptions? On the other hand, is it likely that the Reconstruction Congress that passed the Civil Rights Act of 1871 would have made access to the federal courts turn upon whether there was a pending state proceeding? Given that "[t]he very purpose of § 1983 was to interpose the federal courts between the States and the people as guardians of the people's federal rights * * *," *Mitchum v. Foster*, 407 U.S. 225, 242 (1972), is it likely that Congress would have left in place a statute that is premised upon deference to and respect for the state courts? On the other hand, Congress recodified the Act in 1948, specifically overruling the Court's declaration that a federal court could not enjoin a state proceeding to protect its own judgment. Why did it not make clear, one way or the other, whether the Civil Rights Act of 1871 was an exception to the prohibition?

6. Congress passed a much more specific prohibition of federal court interference with state government in the Johnson Act of 1934, 28 U.S.C.A. § 1342, which bars federal injunction of public utility rates. It provides some leeway to the federal courts, since it contains exceptions for cases where the state's order interferes with interstate commerce, where there has not been reasonable notice and an opportunity to be heard prior to setting the rate, and where there is no effective state court remedy.

7. In 1937, Congress passed the Tax Injunction Act, 28 U.S.C.A. § 1341, prohibiting federal judicial interference with the state *executive* function of collecting taxes as long as there is "a plain, speedy and efficient remedy" available in state court. The federalism implications of the Tax Injunction Act are too clear to require discussion, but it does present problems determining what is a tax, what qualifies as an effective state remedy, what federal court actions are unauthorized interference, and whether there are any other exceptions to the general noninterference policy Congress has expressed.

8. Both the Tax Injunction Act and the Johnson Act concern federal judicial interference with state executive functions. Does the fact that Congress specified these two situations connote that federal intervention in other situations is permissible?

For More Information

For an excellent discussion of these aspects of the statute, see ERWIN CHEMERINSKY, FEDERAL JURISDICTION § 11.3, at 753-64 (5th ed. 2007).

9. If you were designing a policy relating to the ability of federal or state courts directly to affect the operations of branches of the other system, how would you structure it?

C. Judicial Doctrines Of Restraint

1. Exhaustion

Monroe v. Pape, 365 U.S. 167 (1961) (*supra* at 564), held that litigants need not exhaust state judicial remedies before bringing an action in federal court under 42 U.S.C.A. § 1983. But what about state administrative remedies? The next case addresses that issue.

Patsy v. Board Of Regents

Supreme Court of the United States, 1982.
457 U.S. 496.

JUSTICE MARSHALL delivered the opinion of the Court.

This case presents the question whether exhaustion of state administrative remedies is a prerequisite to an action under 42 U.S.C. § 1983. Petitioner Georgia Patsy filed this action, alleging that her employer, Florida International University (FIU), had denied her employment opportunities solely on the basis of her race and sex. By a divided vote, the United States Court of Appeals for the Fifth Circuit found that petitioner was required to exhaust "adequate and appropriate" administrative remedies, and remanded the case to the District Court to consider the adequacy of the administrative procedures. We granted certiorari, and reverse the decision of the Court of Appeals.

I

Petitioner alleges that even though she is well qualified and has received uniformly excellent performance evaluations from her supervisors, she has been rejected for more than 13 positions at FIU. She further claims that FIU has unlawfully filled positions through intentional discrimination on the basis of race and sex. She seeks declaratory and injunctive relief or, in the alternative, damages.

* * *

The Court of Appeals reviewed numerous opinions of this Court holding that exhaustion of administrative remedies was not required, and concluded that these cases did not preclude the application of a "flexible" exhaustion rule. After canvassing the policy arguments in favor of an exhaustion requirement, the Court of Appeals decided that a § 1983 plaintiff could be required to exhaust administrative remedies if the following minimum conditions are met: (1) an orderly system of review or appeal is provided by statute or agency rule; (2) the agency can grant relief more or less commensurate with the claim; (3) relief is available within a reasonable period of time; (4) the procedures are fair, are not unduly burdensome, and are not used to harass or discourage those with legitimate claims; and (5) interim relief is available, in appropriate cases, to prevent irreparable injury and to preserve the plaintiff's rights during the administrative process. Where these minimum standards are met, a court must further consider the particular administrative scheme, the nature of the plaintiff's interest, and the values served by the exhaustion doctrine in order to determine whether exhaustion should be required. The Court of Appeals remanded the case to the District Court to determine whether exhaustion would be appropriate in this case.

II

The question whether exhaustion of administrative remedies should ever be required in a § 1983 action has prompted vigorous debate and disagreement. Our resolution of this issue, however, is made much easier because we are not writing on a clean slate. * * *

Beginning with *McNeese v. Board of Education* (1963), we have on numerous occasions rejected the argument that a § 1983 action should be dismissed where the plaintiff has not exhausted state administrative remedies. Respondent may be correct in arguing that several of these decisions could have been based on traditional exceptions to the exhaustion doctrine. Nevertheless, this Court has stated categorically that exhaustion is not a prerequisite to an action under § 1983, and we have not deviated from that position in the 19 years since *McNeese*. Therefore, we do not address the question presented in this case as one of first impression.

III

Respondent argues that we should reconsider these decisions and adopt the Court of Appeals' exhaustion rule. This Court has never announced a definitive formula for determining whether prior decisions should be overruled or reconsidered. However, in *Monell v. New York City Dept. of Social Services*, we articulated four factors that should be considered. Two of these factors—whether the decisions in question misconstrued the meaning of the statute as revealed in its legislative history and whether overruling these decisions would be inconsistent with more recent expressions of congressional intent—are particularly relevant to our decision today. Both concern legislative purpose, which is of paramount importance in the exhaustion context because Congress is vested with the power to prescribe the basic procedural scheme under which claims may be heard in federal courts. Of course, courts play an important role in determining the limits of an exhaustion requirement and may impose such a requirement even where Congress has not expressly so provided. However, the initial question whether exhaustion is required should be answered by reference to congressional intent;

and a court should not defer the exercise of jurisdiction under a federal statute unless it is consistent with that intent. Therefore, in deciding whether we should reconsider our prior decisions and require exhaustion of state administrative remedies, we look to congressional intent as reflected in the legislative history of the predecessor to § 1983 and in recent congressional activity in this area.

A

In determining whether our prior decisions misconstrued the meaning of § 1983, we begin with a review of the legislative history to § 1 of the Civil Rights Act of 1871, the precursor to § 1983. Although we recognize that the 1871 Congress did not expressly contemplate the exhaustion question, we believe that the tenor of the debates over § 1 supports our conclusion that exhaustion of administrative remedies in § 1983 actions should not be judicially imposed.

Take Note!

There would have been no reason for that Congress to have thought about exhaustion. The modern administrative state had not even begun to emerge in 1871.

The Civil Rights Act of 1871, along with the Fourteenth Amendment it was enacted to enforce, were crucial ingredients in the basic alteration of our federal system accomplished during the Reconstruction Era. During that time, the Federal Government was clearly established as a guarantor of the basic federal rights of individuals against incursions by state power. As we recognized in *Mitchum v. Foster,* "[t]he very purpose of § 1983 was to interpose the federal courts between the States and the people, as guardians of the people's federal rights—to protect the people from unconstitutional action under color of state law, 'whether that action be executive, legislative, or judicial.' "

At least three recurring themes in the debates over § 1 cast serious doubt on the suggestion that requiring exhaustion of state administrative remedies would be consistent with the intent of the 1871 Congress. First, in passing § 1, Congress assigned to the federal courts a paramount role in protecting constitutional rights.

* * *

A second theme in the debates further suggests that the 1871 Congress would not have wanted to impose an exhaustion requirement. A major factor motivating the expansion of federal jurisdiction through §§ 1 and 2 of the bill was the belief of the 1871 Congress that the state authorities had been unable or unwilling to protect the constitutional rights of individuals or to punish those who violated these rights. Of primary importance to the exhaustion question was the mistrust that the 1871 Congress held for the factfinding processes of state institutions. This Congress believed that federal courts would be less susceptible to local prejudice and to the existing defects in the factfinding processes of the state courts. This perceived defect in the States' factfinding processes is particularly relevant to the question of exhaustion of administrative remedies: exhaustion rules are often applied in deference to the superior factfinding ability of the relevant administrative agency.

A third feature of the debates relevant to the exhaustion question is the fact that many legislators interpreted the bill to provide dual or concurrent forums in the state and federal system, enabling the plaintiff to choose the forum in which to seek relief. * * *

This legislative history supports the conclusion that our prior decisions, holding that exhaustion of state administrative remedies is not a prerequisite to an action under § 1983, did not misperceive the statutory intent: it seems fair to infer that the 1871 Congress did not intend that an individual be compelled in every case to exhaust state administrative remedies before filing an action under § 1 of the Civil Rights Act. We recognize, however, that drawing such a conclusion from this history alone is somewhat precarious: the 1871 Congress was not presented with the question of exhaustion of administrative remedies, nor was it aware of the potential role of state administrative agencies. Therefore, we do not rely exclusively on this legislative history in deciding the question presented here. Congress addressed the question of exhaustion under § 1983 when it recently enacted 42 U.S.C. § 1997e. The legislative history of § 1997e provides strong evidence of congressional intent on this issue.

B

The Civil Rights of Institutionalized Persons Act was enacted primarily to ensure that the United States Attorney General has "legal standing to enforce existing constitutional rights and Federal statutory rights of institutionalized persons." In § 1997e, Congress also created a specific, limited exhaustion requirement for adult prisoners bringing actions pursuant to § 1983. Section 1997e and its legislative history demonstrate that Congress understood that exhaustion is not generally required in § 1983 actions, and that it decided to carve out only a narrow exception to this rule. A judicially imposed exhaustion requirement would be inconsistent with Congress' decision to adopt § 1997e and would usurp policy judgments that Congress has reserved for itself.

* * *

With the understanding that exhaustion generally is not required, Congress decided to adopt the limited exhaustion requirement of § 1997e in order to relieve the burden on the federal courts by diverting certain prisoner petitions back through state and local institutions, and also to encourage the States to develop appropriate grievance procedures. Implicit in this decision is Congress' conclusion that the no-exhaustion rule should be left standing with respect to other § 1983 suits.

A judicially imposed exhaustion requirement would also be inconsistent with the extraordinarily detailed exhaustion scheme embodied in § 1997e. Section 1997e carves out a narrow exception to the general no-exhaustion rule to govern certain prisoner claims, and establishes a procedure to ensure that the administrative remedies are adequate and effective. The exhaustion requirement is expressly limited to § 1983 actions brought by an adult convicted of a crime. * * * This detailed scheme is inconsistent with discretion to impose, on an *ad hoc* basis, a judicially developed exhaustion rule in other cases.

Congress hoped that § 1997e would improve prison conditions by stimulating the development of successful grievance mechanisms. To further this purpose, Congress provided for the deferral of the exercise of federal jurisdiction over certain § 1983 claims only on the condition that the state prisons develop adequate procedures. This purpose would be frustrated by judicial discretion to impose exhaustion generally: the States would have no incentive to adopt grievance procedures capable of certification, because prisoner § 1983 cases could be diverted to state administrative remedies in any event.

In sum, the exhaustion provisions of the Act make sense, and are not superfluous, only if exhaustion could not be required before its enactment and if Congress intended to carve out a narrow exception to this no-exhaustion rule. The legislative history of § 1997e demonstrates that Congress has taken the approach of carving out specific exceptions to the general rule that federal courts cannot require exhaustion under § 1983. It is not our province to alter the balance struck by Congress in establishing the procedural framework for bringing actions under § 1983.

C

Respondent and the Court of Appeals argue that exhaustion of administrative remedies should be required because it would further various policies. They argue that an exhaustion requirement would lessen the perceived burden that § 1983 actions impose on federal courts; would further the goal of comity and improve federal-state relations by postponing federal-court review until after the state administrative agency had passed on the issue; and would enable the agency, which presumably has expertise in the area at issue, to enlighten the federal court's ultimate decision.

As we noted earlier, policy considerations alone cannot justify judicially imposed exhaustion unless exhaustion is consistent with congressional intent. Furthermore, as the debates over incorporating the exhaustion requirement in § 1997e demonstrate, the relevant policy considerations do not invariably point in one direction, and there is vehement disagreement over the validity of the assumptions underlying many of them. The very difficulty of these policy considerations, and Congress' superior institutional competence to pursue this debate, suggest that legislative not judicial solutions are preferable.

Beyond the policy issues that must be resolved in deciding whether to require exhaustion, there are equally difficult questions concerning the design and scope of an exhaustion requirement. These questions include how to define those categories of § 1983 claims in which exhaustion might be desirable; how to unify and centralize the standards for judging the kinds of administrative procedures that should be exhausted; what tolling requirements and time limitations should be adopted;[17] what is the res judicata and collateral estoppel effect of particular administrative determinations; what consequences should attach to the failure to comply with procedural requirements of administrative proceedings; and whether federal courts could grant necessary interim injunctive relief and hold the action pending exhaustion, or proceed to judgment without requiring exhaustion even though exhaustion might otherwise be required, where the relevant administrative agency is either powerless or not inclined to grant such interim relief. These and similar questions might be answered swiftly and surely by legislation, but would create costly, remedy-delaying, and court-burdening litigation if answered incrementally by the judiciary in the context of diverse constitutional claims relating to thousands of different state agencies.

* * * After full debate and consideration of the various policy arguments, Congress adopted § 1997e, taking the largest class of § 1983 actions and constructing an exhaustion requirement that differs substantially from the * * * standard urged by respondent and adopted by the Court of Appeals. It is not for us to say whether Congress will or should create a similar scheme for other categories of § 1983 claims or whether Congress will or should adopt an altogether different exhaustion requirement for nonprisoner § 1983 claims.[19]

17 Unless the doctrine that statutes of limitations are not tolled pending exhaustion were overruled, a judicially imposed exhaustion requirement might result in the effective repeal of § 1983. Congress avoided this problem in § 1997e by directing the court to merely continue the case for a period not to exceed 90 days.

19 The question was posed from the bench at oral argument whether the Eleventh Amendment might bar this suit on the ground that the Board of Regents is an arm of the State for purposes of the Eleventh Amendment. The District Court dismissed this action on the pleadings, and no Eleventh Amendment issue had been raised. The Board of Regents first raised this issue in its brief to the original panel on appeal, but did not argue it in its brief on rehearing en banc. Neither the original panel nor the en banc court addressed this issue. Although the State mentioned a possible Eleventh Amendment defense in its response in opposition to the petition for certiorari, it did not brief the issue

IV

Based on the legislative histories of both § 1983 and § 1997e, we conclude that exhaustion of state administrative remedies should not be required as a prerequisite to bringing an action pursuant to § 1983. We decline to overturn our prior decisions holding that such exhaustion is not required. The decision of the Court of Appeals is reversed, and the case is remanded for proceedings consistent with this opinion.

It is so ordered.

JUSTICE WHITE, concurring in part.

I fully agree with the Court that our frequent and unequivocal statements on exhaustion cannot be explained or distinguished away as the Fifth Circuit attempted to do. Our precedents and the legislative history are sufficient to support reversal, and I accordingly join the judgment in all but Part III-B of the opinion of the Court.

In Part III-B, the Court unnecessarily and unwisely ventures further to find support where none may be had. The wisdom of a general no-exhaustion rule in § 1983 suits was not at issue when Congress considered and passed the Civil Rights of Institutionalized Persons Act. As Justice Powell persuasively points out in his dissenting opinion, and as reflected in the title of the Act, congressional attention was narrowly focused on procedures concerning the legal rights of prisoners and other institutionalized persons. Unsurprisingly, the legislation which emerged addressed only the specific problem under investigation; it indicates neither approval of a no-exhaustion rule nor an intent to preclude us from reconsidering the issue.

* * * To be sure, exhaustion is a statutory issue and the dispositive word on the matter belongs to Congress. It does not follow, however, that, were the issue not foreclosed by earlier decisions, we would be institutionally incompe-

or press it at oral argument. Indeed, counsel for respondent urged that we affirm the Court of Appeals solely on its exhaustion holding. We have noted that "the Eleventh Amendment defense sufficiently partakes of the nature of a jurisdictional bar" that it may be raised by the State for the first time on appeal. However, because of the importance of state law in analyzing Eleventh Amendment questions and because the State may, under certain circumstances, waive this defense, we have never held that it is jurisdictional in the sense that it must be raised and decided by this Court on its own motion. Where, as here, the Board of Regents expressly requested that we address the exhaustion question and not pass on its potential Eleventh Amendment immunity, and, as a consequence, the parties have not briefed the issue, we deem it appropriate to address the issue that was raised and decided below and vigorously pressed in this Court. Nothing in this opinion precludes the Board of Regents from raising its Eleventh Amendment claim on remand. The District Court is in the best position to address in the first instance the competing questions of fact and state law necessary to resolve the Eleventh Amendment issue, and at this stage it has the discretion to permit amendments to the pleadings that might cure any potential Eleventh Amendment problems.

tent to formulate an exhaustion rule. The lack of an exhaustion requirement in § 1983 actions is itself an exception to the general rule, judicially formulated, that exhaustion of administrative remedies is required in a civil action. Unlike other statutory questions, exhaustion is "a rule of judicial administration," and unless Congress directs otherwise, rightfully subject to crafting by judges. Our resolution of this case as governed by *stare decisis,* reinforced by the legislative history of § 1983, should not be taken as undercutting the general exhaustion principle of long standing. The result today is also fully consistent with our decisions that a defendant in a civil or administrative enforcement proceeding may not enjoin and sidetrack that proceeding by resorting to a § 1983 action in federal court, and that a federal action should be stayed pending determination of state-law issues central to the constitutional dispute. On this understanding, I join all but Part III-B of the opinion of the Court.*

JUSTICE POWELL, with whom THE CHIEF JUSTICE joins as to Part II, dissenting.

The Court holds that the limitations on federal judicial power embodied in the Eleventh Amendment and in the doctrine of sovereign immunity are not jurisdictional. I consider this holding to be a serious departure from established constitutional doctrine.

I dissent also from the Court's rejection of the rule of "flexible" exhaustion of state administrative remedies developed and stated persuasively by the Court of Appeals for the Fifth Circuit, sitting en banc. In disagreeing with the 17 judges of the Court of Appeals who adopted the flexible exhaustion principle, this Court places mistaken reliance on the Civil Rights of Institutionalized Persons Act. I disagree with both portions of the Court's holding and therefore dissent.

* * *

II. Exhaustion of Remedies.

In view of my belief that this case should be dismissed on jurisdictional grounds, I address the exhaustion question only briefly. Seventeen judges joined in the Court of Appeals' persuasive opinion adopting a rule of "flexible" exhaus-

---

* In my view, this case does not present a serious Eleventh Amendment issue. The Florida statute authorizing suits against the Board of Regents is clear on its face. I see no reason to read a broad waiver to sue and be sued in "all courts of law and equity" as meaning all but federal courts. Nor am I aware of anything in Florida law that suggests a more limited meaning was intended than indicated by the unequivocal terms of the statute. Certainly, none of our cases have gone so far as to hold that federal courts must be expressly mentioned for an effective Eleventh Amendment waiver. The statutes at issue in cases recited by Justice Powell presented more equivocal embodiments of state intent. * * * Thus, while I do not object to the Court's leaving the Eleventh Amendment issue for further consideration by the lower courts—at least where, as here, there is no logical priority in resolving Eleventh Amendment immunity before exhaustion—I find the issue sufficiently clear to be answered here and now. The statute means what it says.

tion of administrative remedies in § 1983 suits. Other Courts of Appeals have adopted a similar rule. The opinion for the en banc court carefully reviewed the exhaustion doctrine in general and as applied to § 1983 actions. It found that the prior decisions of this Court did not clearly decide the question. And it concluded that the exhaustion of adequate and appropriate state administrative remedies would promote the achievement of the rights protected by § 1983.

I agree with the Court of Appeals' opinion. The requirement that a § 1983 plaintiff exhaust adequate state administrative remedies was the accepted rule of law until quite recently. The rule rests on sound considerations. It does not defeat federal-court jurisdiction, it merely defers it. It permits the States to correct violations through their own procedures, and it encourages the establishment of such procedures. It is consistent with the principles of comity that apply whenever federal courts are asked to review state action or supersede state proceedings.

Moreover, and highly relevant to the effective functioning of the overburdened federal court system, the rule conserves and supplements scarce judicial resources. In 1961, the year that *Monroe v. Pape* was decided, only 270 civil rights actions were begun in the federal district courts. In 1981, over 30,000 such suits were commenced. The result of this unprecedented increase in civil rights litigation is a heavy burden on the federal courts to the detriment of all federal-court litigants, including others who assert that their constitutional rights have been infringed.

* * *

The Court seeks to support its no-exhaustion rule with indications of congressional intent. Finding nothing directly on point in the history of the Civil Rights Act itself, the Court places primary reliance on the recent Civil Rights of Institutionalized Persons Act. This legislation was designed to authorize the Attorney General to initiate civil rights actions on behalf of institutionalized persons. The Act also placed certain limits on the existing authority of the Attorney General to intervene in suits begun by institutionalized persons. In addition, in § 1997e, the Act sets forth an exhaustion requirement but only for § 1983 claims brought by prisoners.

On the basis of the exhaustion provision in § 1997e, and remarks primarily by Representative Kastenmeier, the Court contends that Congress has endorsed a general no-exhaustion rule. The irony in this reasoning should be obvious. A principal concern that prompted the Department of Justice to support, and the Congress to adopt, § 1997e was the vast increase in § 1983 suits brought by state prisoners in federal courts. * * * It was primarily this problem that prompted enactment of § 1997e.

* * *

In short, in enacting the Civil Rights of Institutionalized Persons Act Congress was focusing on the powers of the Attorney General, and the particular question of prisoners' suits, not on the general question of exhaustion in § 1983 actions. Also revealing as to the limited purpose of § 1997e is Congress' consistent refusal to adopt legislation imposing a general no-exhaustion requirement. Thus, for example, in 1979, a bill was introduced into the Senate providing: "No court of the United States shall stay or dismiss any civil action brought under this Act on the ground that the party bringing such action failed to exhaust the remedies available in the courts or the administrative agencies of any State." The bill was never reported out of committee.

The requirement that plaintiffs exhaust available and adequate administrative remedies—subject to well-developed exceptions—is firmly established in virtually every area of the law. This is dictated in § 1983 actions by common sense, as well as by comity and federalism, where adequate state administrative remedies are available.

If the exhaustion question were properly before us, I would affirm the Court of Appeals.

Take Note

In Boyle v. United Technologies, *supra* at 461, Justice Brennan's dissent relied in part on six bills that would have effectively controlled the result of that case, none of which passed. The majority did not even mention the argument. What is the significance of Congress's failure to proceed on the bill? Did it decline to proceed because it disagreed with the no-exhaustion requirement, or because it recognized that such a statute would be merely declaratory of extant law?

Notes and Questions

1. a) *Patsy* remains substantially unchallenged as federal law, despite Justice Powell's dissent. *See, e.g., Wilder v. Virginia Hospital Association,* 496 U.S. 498 (1990), reaffirming the absence of an exhaustion requirement for § 1983 cases. Chief Justice Rehnquist, joined by Justices O'Connor, Scalia and Kennedy, dissented on another point but did not challenge the majority's reading of *Patsy.*

b) Does *Patsy* govern only federal § 1983 actions, or does it apply as well to § 1983 actions brought in state court? If the former, then an exhaustion requirement is more a function of the court system than of the cause of action. If the latter, there may be significant federalism problems inherent in the federal government telling the states that they cannot indulge their own exhaustion-of-administrative-remedy requirements if a § 1983 case appears in their courts. If state courts were allowed to require exhaustion of administrative remedies in § 1983 actions, would they be likely to do so? If states did impose such a requirement, what impact would that have on plaintiffs' choice of forum?

2. The majority argues that distrust of state fact-finding procedures also underlay the passage of § 1983 and counsels against an exhaustion requirement because of the possible res judicata effect of administrative findings. The Court might achieve the same result by demanding exhaustion but allowing trial *de novo* in the district court if the § 1983 plaintiff was not satisfied with the result of the administrative proceeding. What is the drawback of this solution?

3. a) Justice Powell argues there should be an exhaustion requirement in § 1983 cases. Would it be legitimate for the Court to impose one? Is Justice Powell's position here inconsistent with his argument in *Cannon v. University of Chicago,* 441 U.S. 677 (1979), that the Court should not create federal common law to supplement congressional statutes? After all, Congress has not suggested an exhaustion requirement for civil rights cases.

b) Is it likely that the Congress that created § 1983 or the earlier Congress that enacted 28 U.S.C.A. § 1343 (the civil rights jurisdictional statute that dispensed with the general federal question jurisdiction statute's monetary floor) intended that civil rights plaintiffs, having thus been given a way to avoid state judicial processes, should nonetheless be required to submit to state administrative processes as a condition precedent to invoking the aid of the federal courts?

4. The dissent argues that an exhaustion requirement would encourage the states to develop sound administrative procedures. Would such procedures ultimately result in fewer federal lawsuits? One might argue that the absence of an exhaustion requirement provides more encouragement to develop sound administrative remedies, since in order to avoid federal court "interference," the states must now develop administrative procedures attractive enough to induce potential federal plaintiffs to forgo or defer going to federal court. Is this a realistic argument?

5. The majority says that "[b]eginning with *McNeese v. Board of Education* (1963), we have on numerous occasions rejected the argument that a § 1983 action should be dismissed where the plaintiff has not exhausted state administrative remedies * * * , and we have not deviated from that position in the 19 years since *McNeese*." In the full opinion, the majority cites several cases in the *McNeese* line. Why did the Court of Appeals impose an exhaustion requirement in the face of all this controlling precedent? Why does the Court choose to write a full opinion instead of summarily reversing? Is it possible that the picture was not as clear as the majority argues?

6. The Eleventh Amendment battle among the Justices emerges clearly in *Patsy.* Note the dispute about whether the Amendment is jurisdictional, whether it is waivable, and what is required to waive its protection if a state wishes to do so. Justice White's position is particularly interesting. His footnote rejecting an Eleventh Amendment problem argues that "[t]he statute means what it says." Yet, only three years after *Patsy,* Justice White joined the majority in *Atascadero State Hospital v. Scanlon,* 473 U.S. 234 (1985), holding that California had not waived its Eleventh Amendment immunity despite an apparent California constitutional waiver: "[s]uits may be brought against the State in such manner and in such courts as shall be directed by law." Are his positions inconsistent?

7. Remember that although the Court has construed § 1983 not to require exhaustion, other statutes may impose an exhaustion requirement with respect to particular kinds of suits. In *Woodford v. Ngo*, 548 U.S. 81 (2006), the Court ruled that the Prison Litigation Reform Act, 110 Stat. 1321-71, as amended, 42 U.S.C. §§ 1997e *et seq.* is in that category. The Act provides, *inter alia*: "No action shall be brought with respect to prison conditions under section 1983 of this title, or any other Federal law, by a prisoner confined in any jail, prison, or other correctional facility until such administrative remedies as are available are exhausted." Ngo challenged certain administrative actions taken against him by prison officials, actions that he alleged prevented him from participating in religious observances as a Catholic, but he did not file his prison grievance until more than fifteen days later, too late under prison rules. Ngo was unsuccessful in pursuing appellate administrative remedies in the California prison system and thereafter initiated a § 1983 action against the officials. The Court ruled that the PLRA precluded his action, construing the statutory requirement to require "proper" exhaustion, not simply, as Ngo and the dissenters argued, refraining from filing a federal action while administrative remedies remain available.

Justice Stevens, joined by Justices Souter and Ginsburg, dissented. He argued that if the state imposed a fifteen-day statute of limitations on an individual's entitlement to seek vindication of federal constitutional rights against state officials, it "would obviously be unenforceable in a federal court." In his view, the prison's fifteen-day rule effectively accomplished the same thing, and he was loath to conclude that Congress meant to enable states so to limit the time for asserting federal constitutional rights. He also suggested that if Congress had so intended, it would raise constitutional problems under the First Amendment's Petition Clause.

2. Abstention: The *Pullman* Doctrine

Railroad Commission v. Pullman Co.

Supreme Court of the United States, 1941.
312 U.S. 496.

MR. JUSTICE FRANKFURTER delivered the opinion of the Court.

In those sections of Texas where the local passenger traffic is slight, trains carry but one sleeping car. These trains, unlike trains having two or more sleepers, are without a Pullman conductor; the sleeper is in charge of a porter who is subject to the train conductor's control. As is well known, porters on Pullmans are colored and conductors are white. Addressing itself to this situation, the Texas Railroad Commission after due hearing ordered that "no sleeping car shall be operated on any line of railroad in the State of Texas * * * unless such cars are continuously in the charge of an employee * * * having the rank and position of Pullman conductor." Thereupon, the Pullman Company and the railroads affected brought this action in a federal district court to enjoin the Commission's order. Pullman porters were permitted to intervene as complainants, and Pullman conductors entered the litigation in support of the order. Three judges having been convened, the court enjoined enforcement of the order. From this decree, the case came here directly.

The Pullman Company and the railroads assailed the order as unauthorized by Texas law as well as violative of the Equal Protection, the Due Process and the Commerce Clauses of the Constitution. The intervening porters adopted these objections but mainly objected to the order as a discrimination against Negroes in violation of the Fourteenth Amendment.

P's args

The complaint of the Pullman porters undoubtedly tendered a substantial constitutional issue. It is more than substantial. It touches a sensitive area of social policy upon which the federal courts ought not to enter unless no alternative to its adjudication is open. Such constitutional adjudication plainly can be avoided if a definitive ruling on the state issue would terminate the controversy. It is therefore our duty to turn to a consideration of questions under Texas law.

The Commission found justification for its order in a Texas statute which we quote in the margin.[1] It is common ground that if the order is within the

1 VERNON'S ANNO. TEXAS CIVIL STATUTES, art. 6445:

* * * [I]t is hereby made the duty of the said Commission to adopt all necessary rates, charges and regulations, to govern and regulate such railroads, persons, associations and corporations, and to correct abuses and prevent unjust discrimination in the rates, charges and tolls of such railroads, persons, associations and corporations * * * ., and to * * * prevent any and all other abuses in the conduct of their business and to do and perform such other duties and details in connection therewith as may be provided by law.

state law issue

Commission's authority its subject matter must be included in the Commission's power to prevent "unjust discrimination * * * and to prevent any and all other abuses" in the conduct of railroads. Whether arrangements pertaining to the staffs of Pullman cars are covered by the Texas concept of "discrimination" is far from clear. What practices of the railroads may be deemed to be "abuses" subject to the Commission's correction is equally doubtful. Reading the Texas statutes and the Texas decisions as outsiders without special competence in Texas law, we would have little confidence in our independent judgment regarding the application of that law to the present situation. The lower court did deny that the Texas statutes sustained the Commission's assertion of power. And this represents the view of an able and experienced circuit judge of the circuit which includes Texas and of two capable district judges trained in Texas law. Had we or they no choice in the matter but to decide what is the law of the state, we should hesitate long before rejecting their forecast of Texas law. But no matter how seasoned the judgment of the district court may be, it cannot escape being a forecast rather than a determination. The last word on the meaning of Article 6445 of the Texas Civil Statutes, and therefore the last word on the statutory authority of the Railroad Commission in this case, belongs neither to us nor to the district court but to the supreme court of Texas. In this situation a federal court of equity is asked to decide an issue by making a tentative answer which may be displaced tomorrow by a state adjudication. The reign of law is hardly promoted if an unnecessary ruling of a federal court is thus supplanted by a controlling decision of a state court. The resources of equity are equal to an adjustment that will avoid the waste of a tentative decision as well as the friction of a premature constitutional adjudication.

An appeal to the chancellor, as we had occasion to recall only the other day, is an appeal to the "exercise of the sound discretion, which guides the determination of courts of equity." The history of equity jurisdiction is the history of regard for public consequences in employing the extraordinary remedy of the injunction. There have been as many and as variegated applications of this supple principle as the situations that have brought it into play. Few public interests have a higher claim upon the discretion of a federal chancellor than the avoidance of needless friction with state policies * * * or the final authority of a state court to interpret doubtful regulatory laws of the state. These cases reflect a doctrine of abstention appropriate to our federal system whereby the federal courts, "exercising a wise discretion," restrain their authority because of "scrupulous regard for the rightful independence of the state governments" and for the smooth working of the federal judiciary * * *. This use of equitable powers is a contribution of the courts in furthering the harmonious relation between state and federal authority without the need of rigorous congressional restriction of those powers.

Regard for these important considerations of policy in the administration of federal equity jurisdiction is decisive here. If there was no warrant in state law for the Commission's assumption of authority there is an end of the litigation; the constitutional issue does not arise. The law of Texas appears to furnish easy and ample means for determining the Commission's authority. Article 6453 of the Texas Civil Statutes gives a review of such an order in the state courts. Or, if there are difficulties in the way of this procedure of which we have not been apprised, the issue of state law may be settled by appropriate action on the part of the State to enforce obedience to the order. In the absence of any showing that these obvious methods for securing a definitive ruling in the state courts cannot be pursued with full protection of the constitutional claim, the district court should exercise its wise discretion by staying its hands.

We therefore remand the cause to the district court, with directions to retain the bill pending a determination of proceedings, to be brought with reasonable promptness, in the state court in conformity with this opinion.

Reversed and remanded.

Notes and Questions

1. The Court does not explicitly state the criteria for *Pullman* abstention, but the opinion implies three criteria the federal courts should use to decide whether to hear a case or to send the parties to state court for adjudication of state issues before considering whether to decide the federal issues at all. What are the criteria?

2. *Pullman* attempts to accommodate three important and potentially conflicting principles: 1) federal courts should decide cases within their jurisdiction; 2) courts should avoid adjudication of constitutional questions when possible; and 3) conflict between the federal and state systems should be minimized. The first principle would have warmed Chief Justice Marshall's heart (see the introduction at page 783), and the second echoes Justice Brandeis's famous admonition in *Ashwander v. TVA*, 297 U.S. 288, 346, (1936) (Brandeis, J., concurring). A federal court can accommodate the first two principles by deciding the state law issue itself in a way that avoids the need to consider the federal constitutional question. But would that course of action also accommodate the third principle, or would it increase federal-state friction?

3. Should the federal court abstain under *Pullman* whenever there is a state statute of arguably uncertain meaning or application involved? Consider the following.

a) A state statute imposes on public school teacher a duty to "by precept and example promote respect for the flag and the institutions of the United States of America * * * ." A group of teachers files a federal action seeking a declaration that the statute violates their rights under the First and Fourteenth Amendments. Should the district court abstain? Consider first what specific constitutional entitlements the teachers might argue the statute infringes and then what the state courts might do to ameliorate the asserted constitutional infirmities.

b) A state statute makes it a crime to distribute in quantity any written material relating to an election campaign or issue unless the name and address of the person behind the distribution appears. Individuals wishing anonymously to hand out leaflets critical of a congressman seeking re-election bring a federal challenge to the statute on First and Fourteenth Amendment grounds. Should the district court abstain?

4. a) Federal courts abstain in *Pullman* situations to seek state court clarification of unclear provisions of state law, but they do not abstain in ordinary diversity cases when state law is unclear. Congress has not authorized abstention in either circumstance. Is the Court's decision to abstain in one circumstance but not the other justifiable? What would be the effect on diversity jurisdiction if federal courts routinely abstained when state law was unclear, sending the litigants back to state court? *Pullman* situations, of course, involve the additional goal of avoiding decision of a federal constitutional question. Is that goal important enough to justify abstaining in *Pullman* situations but not in diversity cases?

b) Even if abstention is inappropriate in diversity cases, should the federal courts adopt a more general abstention doctrine for cases coming under the courts' federal question jurisdiction that also involve unsettled questions of state law? If they do, what would be the effect on the exercise of federal question jurisdiction? Should the decision to abstain depend on whether the state court that would hear the case would be deciding questions of its own state's law or the law of some other state because of the forum's horizontal choice-of-law approach?

c) One reason federal courts exercise supplemental jurisdiction over state claims that are related to a plaintiff's federal claims is to avoid discrimination against the federal courts. Because state and federal courts usually have concurrent jurisdiction over federal claims, state courts can hear federal and state claims together. Supplemental jurisdiction allows federal courts to do the same. Without supplemental jurisdiction, a plaintiff who wants to try her federal claim in federal court would be required to bring two actions to present all her claims to courts, thus creating a disincentive to use the federal forum. *Pullman* abstention creates an even greater disincentive. Not only are two lawsuits required, but the plaintiff cannot obtain a federal ruling until the state courts have ruled on the meaning of state law. Why do you think the Court took such different approaches in the supplemental jurisdiction and abstention contexts?

5. Does a court construing a statute have any obligation to interpret it to avoid constitutional infirmity? Does it matter whether it is a state or federal court that is acting?

6. There may be a second way to avoid a federal constitutional question. The state constitution may have a provision that could be interpreted in a way that would avoid the need to decide the federal constitutional question. Should the federal court abstain to allow the state courts the opportunity to dispose of the case under the state constitution? Should the answer turn on whether the federal constitutional provision is one that is widely applied, such as the First Amendment or the Due Process Clause, and the state constitutional provision substantially mirrors the federal provision? If federal courts abstained in such cases, would they abstain more often or less often than they presently abstain? Note that while abstention in such cases would avoid decision of a federal constitutional issue, it would not avoid decision of a state constitutional issue. Thus, the general goal of avoiding decision of constitutional issues would be only partly achieved. Is it better to avoid decision of federal than state constitutional issues, or should decision of both be avoided equally when possible?

7. The Court has modified the third Pullman criterion. In place of the requirement that "a definitive ruling on the state issue would terminate the controversy," *Harrison v. NAACP*, 360 U.S. 167 (1959), decided by a five-to-four vote, found abstention appropriate where "construction by the [state] courts * * * might avoid in whole or in part the necessity for federal constitutional adjudication, or at least materially change the nature of the problem." The dissenters decried what they saw as the expansion of Pullman abstention with the concomitant effect of delaying resolution of the dispute that the plaintiff organization had brought to the courts; indeed, Justice Douglas suggested that *Pullman* abstention had reached the status of "a delaying tactic." Is the Harrison modification sound as a policy matter, or does it make it too easy for the federal courts to perceive a lurking state issue that requires resort to the state courts? Should any statute subject to some interpretation rather than being totally unambiguous provide a predicate for abstention?

Bellotti v. Baird I, 428 U.S. 132 (1976), demonstrates how the modified abstention doctrine works and how developments in state procedural law may affect it. Massachusetts enacted a statute restricting the ability of unmarried women under the age of eighteen to get abortions. Plaintiffs, a group consisting of physicians, counselors and counseling groups, four pregnant, and unmarried minors, filed a class action challenging the statute's restrictions as inconsistent with *Roe v. Wade* (1973). The parties disputed, inter alia, whether the parental notification provisions of the statute meant that the parents had an effective veto and whether a woman could seek judicial authorization for an abortion without first consulting her parents. The majority, in an opinion by Justice Blackmun, who wrote *Roe*, remanded the case to the district court with directions that it certify questions on the statute's interpretation to the Supreme

Judicial Court of Massachusetts rather than immediately addressing plaintiffs' constitutional challenges.[3] The Court rejected plaintiffs' argument that the state court would inevitably interpret the statute to include a parental veto.

The Massachusetts statute was complex and contained many ambiguities. The district court certified nine questions, and the Supreme Judicial Court returned narrative answers that the United States Supreme Court summarized in a later ruling in the same case. *See Bellotti v. Baird II*, 443 U.S. 622 (1979). Certification is meant to speed up adjudication by providing an efficient way to clarify the meaning of state law. As the *Bellotti* decisions demonstrate, speed is a relative concept. *Bellotti I* began on October 30, 1974, and the district judge issued a temporary order restraining enforcement of the statute. On November 13, 1974, Massachusetts moved alternatively for dismissal, summary judgment, or abstention on *Pullman* grounds; the plaintiffs cross-moved for a preliminary injunction. On April 28, 1975, a three-judge district court declared the statute unconstitutional and enjoined its enforcement, prompting the appeal that the United States Supreme Court decided on July 1, 1976. Justice Brennan, as Circuit Justice, issued an order on July 30, 1976, restraining enforcement until the certification of state law questions to the Massachusetts courts was completed. The district court certified its questions to the Supreme Judicial Court of Massachusetts, which responded on January 25, 1977. The district court issued its final opinion on February 10, 1977, holding part of the statute unconstitutional and enjoining enforcement. Finally, on July 2, 1979, *Bellotti II* affirmed the district court's decision to enjoin operation of the statute permanently.

Thus, nearly five years elapsed between the initial challenge and the Supreme Court ruling that ended the case. From the time the Supreme Court ordered abstention in 1976 to the district court's receipt of the response to the certified questions and consequent opinion, more than seven months elapsed. While these time periods are not particularly long in the American legal system of the late twentieth century, in the context of a woman seeking abortion, both are obviously too long to permit effective protection of that right without temporary injunctive relief. Such relief was forthcoming in *Bellotti;* in other cases, involving abortion or other issues for which timing is critical, it might not be. Should the availability of temporary relief affect the decision to abstain?

8. *Arizonans for Official English v. Arizona*, 520 U.S. 43 (1997), offers a new view of Pullman abstention and of the relationship of the inferior federal courts to the state courts as authoritative interpreters of state law. Justice Ginsburg's opinion for the

3 Although certification statutes were comparatively rare when *Bellotti* was decided, now almost all states and the District of Columbia have them. The procedures under the statutes vary somewhat, but the basic process is the same. The statutes authorize a federal judge faced with an unclear provision of state law to certify questions about the meaning of the law to the state Supreme Court. When the state high court answers the questions, the federal judge can then proceed to decide the case, armed (at least in theory) with a clear understanding of state law.

Court vacated the decision below on the ground of mootness. In the course of the discussion, however, the Court criticized the district court that had found Arizona's "official English" statute facially overbroad. Noting *Pullman* abstention's drawbacks—delay and expense—Justice Ginsburg took the lower courts to task for producing effectively the same result by eschewing Arizona's certification procedure, which Arizona's Attorney General had asked the district court to invoke. The Court clearly suggests that the lower courts govern their discretion to seek certification according to the standard formerly associated with *Pullman*: whether interpretation of the state law "would avoid or substantially modify the federal constitutional challenge * * * ." One might conclude from this that where a state certification procedure exists, a court should use that procedure rather than send the parties to a state trial court to begin the cumbersome process of obtaining a ruling from the trial court, an intermediate appellate court, and finally the state Supreme Court. Given the Court's endorsement of certification and criticism of the delay and expense inherent in the process prescribed in *Pullman*, might the Court regard that process as an abuse of discretion if the district court selected it in preference to certification? Or is there some residual use to the *Pullman* process for which certification cannot substitute?

One might have thought that *Pullman* would wither on the vine in the face of the proliferation of state certification statutes, but it has not. Although almost all states now have certification statutes, their terms differ markedly. Nineteen states allow certification from any federal court and from any state court of last resort. Eighteen states will accept certification from any federal court but not from state courts, and eleven states, including California, Florida, Illinois, New York, Pennsylvania and Texas permit certification only from federal appellate courts. To the extent that federal district courts cannot certify questions of state law, *Pullman* abstention remains alive and well.

Note on Post-Abstention Procedure and Tactics

When the federal court decides that *Pullman* abstention is appropriate, consider what it and the parties should do. *Pullman* says the lower federal court should jurisdiction pending the plaintiff's resort to the state courts, a procedure that the Court later described as "the better practice," while noting that on occasion it had ordered dismissal rather than retention of jurisdiction.

The parties' task is more difficult. The federal plaintiff presumably should begin a state action seeking construction of the statute. At the outset, should the plaintiff merely argue the statutory construction issue? In *Government and Civil Employees Organizing Committee, CIO v. Windsor*, 353 U.S. 364 (1957), the courts twice ordered abstention. An organization of public employees challenged a state statute forbidding them union membership, arguing that it violated the First and

Fourteenth Amendments. The district court abstained because it appeared possible for the state courts to find that the organization was not a union within the meaning of the statute. Plaintiffs thereupon sought a construction of the statute from the state courts but did not mention any federal constitutional claims. Upon the state courts' determination that plaintiffs were subject to the statute, they returned to federal court. The Supreme Court then ordered abstention on the ground that the state court, had it known of the federal constitutional objections, might have construed the statute differently.

Suppose that after abstention, a plaintiff, fortified by her understanding of *Windsor,* argues both state law claims and federal constitutional claims in the state court. If the state court rules against her on all grounds, the doctrine of res judicata precludes her successful return to the federal forum. Once the state court has ruled, is not the plaintiff's proper avenue of redress an appeal to the United States Supreme Court? This would put the plaintiff in a *Pullman* case in a difficult spot. Failure to mention the federal claims to the state court begets renewed abstention under *Windsor.* Presenting the federal claims to the state court threatens to prevent return to the federal district court because of res judicata. *Cf. Migra v. Warren City School District Board of Education,* 465 U.S. 75 (1984) (failure to litigate § 1983 claim in state court with transactionally-related state contract claim precludes subsequent litigation in federal court if the state would preclude subsequent litigation).

The Supreme Court addressed this dilemma in *England v. Louisiana State Board of Medical Examiners,* 375 U.S. 411 (1964). Plaintiff chiropractors sought a federal determination that the educational requirements of the Louisiana Medical Practice Act were unconstitutional as applied to them. The district court, noting that Louisiana might construe the statute as not applicable to plaintiffs, abstained "until the courts of the State of Louisiana shall have been afforded an opportunity to determine the issues here presented, and retaining jurisdiction to take such steps as may be necessary for the just disposition of the litigation should anything prevent a prompt state court determination." The plaintiffs then proceeded in the Louisiana courts, where, in the words of the United States Supreme Court, they "unreservedly submitted for decision, and briefed and argued, their contention that the Act, if applicable to chiropractors, violated the Fourteenth Amendment." The Louisiana courts ruled against plaintiffs on all grounds.

Plaintiffs did not seek Supreme Court review of the Louisiana decision. Instead, they returned to the district court, where defendants moved to dismiss because the district court could not properly sit in review of the state courts. Plaintiffs countered that they had submitted their claims to the Louisiana courts because *Windsor* required them to do so; indeed, the district court had noted that as the correct procedure, and the Supreme Court observed that commentators had read *Windsor* the same way.

The confusion *Windsor* engendered was obvious; the Court refused to keep the plaintiffs out of federal court.

> There are fundamental objections to any conclusion that a litigant who has properly invoked the jurisdiction of a Federal District Court to consider federal constitutional claims can be compelled, without his consent and through no fault of his own, to accept instead a state court's determination of those claims. Such a result would be at war with the unqualified terms in which Congress, pursuant to constitutional authorization, has conferred specific categories of jurisdiction upon the federal courts, and with the principle that "When a Federal court is properly appealed to in a case over which it has by law jurisdiction, it is its duty to take such jurisdiction * * * . The right of a party plaintiff to choose a Federal court where there is a choice cannot be properly denied." Nor does anything in the abstention doctrine require or support such a result. Abstention is a judge-fashioned vehicle for according appropriate deference to the "respective competence of the state and federal court systems." Its recognition of the role of state courts as the final expositors of state law implies no disregard for the primacy of the federal judiciary in deciding questions of federal law. Accordingly, we have on several occasions explicitly recognized that abstention "does not, of course, involve the abdication of federal jurisdiction, but only the postponement of its exercise."
>
> It is true that, after a post-abstention determination and rejection of his federal claims by the state courts, a litigant could seek direct review in this Court. But such review, even when available by appeal rather than only by discretionary writ of certiorari, is an inadequate substitute for the initial District Court determination * * * to which the litigant is entitled in the federal courts. This is true as to issues of law; it is especially true as to issues of fact. Limiting the litigant to review here would deny him the benefit of a federal trial court's role in constructing a record and making fact findings. How the facts are found will often dictate the decision of federal claims. Thus in cases where, but for the application of the abstention doctrine, the primary fact determination would have been by the District Court, a litigant may not be unwillingly deprived of that determination. The possibility of appellate review by this Court of a state court determination may not be substituted, against a party's wishes, for his right to litigate his federal claims fully in the federal courts.

To ensure the party's right to return to federal court, the Court clarified *Windsor*. That case did not mean a party had to litigate his federal claims in state court, "but only that he must inform those courts of what his federal claims are, so that the state statute may be construed 'in light' of those claims." To preserve the right to return, a litigant should "inform the state courts that he is exposing his federal claims there only for the purpose of complying with *Windsor*, and that he intends, should the state courts hold against him on the question of state law, to return to the District Court for disposition of his federal contentions." The Court also realized a party might want to litigate the entire case in state court to save time and expense. In that event, the party cannot return to federal court.

England may not have been the beacon of clarity that the Court wished. The Court itself recognized that a party may have trouble in the "heat of litigation" merely stating, but not asserting or arguing, the federal constitutional claim. If a party "can persuade the state court that application of the statute to him would offend the Federal Constitution, he will ordinarily have persuaded it that the statute should not be construed as applicable to him." If the party crosses the line, however, return to federal court will likely be foreclosed. *San Remo Hotel v. City and County of San Francisco*, 545 U.S. 323 (2005), provides an example. San Francisco imposed restrictions on conversion of hotel units into tourist units because of the "severe shortage" of affordable rental units for elderly, disabled, and low-income persons. In state administrative proceedings, the Hotel claimed these restrictions were unconstitutional and improperly applied to it. After losing, the Hotel filed a state petition for writ of administrative mandamus, which lay dormant for several years.

The Hotel then began a federal suit claiming the City's actions denied due process and constituted an unlawful taking. The district court granted summary judgment for the City. Perhaps sensing it would not succeed on appeal to the Ninth Circuit, the Hotel took "the unusual position" that the court should abstain under *Pullman* "because a return to state court could conceivably moot the remaining federal questions." The Ninth Circuit obliged, reminding the Hotel to make the appropriate *England* reservation. When the Hotel reactivated the state court action, however, it did not limit itself to the issues asserted in the mandamus petition. Instead, it argued the broader federal constitutional claims. The Court held that "[b]y broadening their state action beyond the mandamus petition to include their "substantially advances" claims, petitioner effectively asked the state court to resolve the same federal issues it asked it to reserve. *England* does not support the exercise of any such right."

The *England* Court also recognized that even if a party does not seek a decision on the federal court claim in state court, a state court may nonetheless decide it. While such action muddies the waters, an early, clearly-stated *England* reservation will nonetheless allow a return to federal court. Confusion may also arise because *England* specifically stated that "an explicit reservation is not indispensable" as long as the record makes clear plaintiff did not attempt to actively present the federal claims in state court. When there is no express reservation, confusion is bound to arise over whether the litigant's actions in the state courts are incompatible with returning to federal court.

After *Pullman* abstention, suppose a state court declines to adjudicate because it is being asked for an advisory opinion. Texas had a rule prohibiting its courts from hearing a case that remained on a federal court's docket. In *Harris County Commissioners Court v. Moore,* 420 U.S. 77 (1975), the Court directed dismissal so that the state could rule without the shadow of the federal court over it. The Supreme Court explained that upon conclusion of the state litigation, the plaintiff could refile in federal court. Professor Chemerinsky asks rhetorically whether the Supreme Court's attempt to circumvent the states' advisory-opinion rules truly addresses the states' concerns. *See* ERWIN CHEMERINSKY, FEDERAL JURISDICTION § 12.3, at 811-12 (5th ed. 2007). Does referring a case to a state court make the dispute any less real or the state court's decision any less potentially dispositive of the dispute than if the case were pending in the state system?

Suppose a prospective plaintiff anticipates a *Pullman* abstention problem and, to save time, commences his litigation in the state court, mentioning his constitutional concerns but making an explicit *England* reservation of the federal constitutional issues for later federal decision. If the state court decides the case, including the federal issues, can the plaintiff nonetheless go to federal court, or will he run into insurmountable res judicata problems? *Cf. Migra v. Warren City School District Board of Education,* 465 U.S. 75 (1984), noted in Chapter 7 at pages 779-80. If so, would the plaintiff do better to begin in federal court and seek abstention so that a state ruling on the state issues may be obtained?

3. Abstention: The Doctrine of *Younger v. Harris*

Younger v. Harris

Supreme Court of the United States, 1971.
401 U.S. 37.

MR. JUSTICE BLACK delivered the opinion of the Court.

Appellee, John Harris, Jr., was indicted in a California state court, charged with violation of the California Penal Code §§ 11400 and 11401, known as the California Criminal Syndicalism Act * * * . He then filed a complaint in the Federal District Court, asking that court to enjoin the appellant, Younger, the District Attorney of Los Angeles County, from prosecuting him, and alleging that the prosecution and even the presence of the Act inhibited him in the exercise of his rights of free speech and press, rights guaranteed him by the First and Fourteenth Amendments. Appellees Jim Dan and Diane Hirsch intervened as plaintiffs in the suit, claiming that the prosecution of Harris would inhibit them as members of the Progressive Labor Party from peacefully advocating the program of their party, which was to replace capitalism with socialism and to abolish the profit system of production in this country. Appellee Farrell Broslawsky, an instructor in history at Los Angeles Valley College, also intervened claiming that the prosecution of Harris made him uncertain as to whether he could teach about the doctrines of Karl Marx or read from the Communist Manifesto as part of his class work. All claimed that unless the United States court restrained the state prosecution of Harris each would suffer immediate and irreparable injury. A three-judge Federal District Court, convened pursuant to 28 U.S.C. § 2284, held that it had jurisdiction and power to restrain the District Attorney from prosecuting, held that the State's Criminal Syndicalism Act was void for vagueness and overbreadth in violation of the First and Fourteenth Amendments, and accordingly restrained the District Attorney from "further prosecution of the currently pending action against plaintiff Harris for alleged violation of the Act."

> **FYI**
>
> In 1913, Congress enacted the Three-Judge-Court Act, most recently appearing at 28 U.S.C. § 2284. A predecessor in 1910 was a bit narrower than the later law, but both were congressional reactions to *Ex parte Young*'s (1908) holding that a district court could proceed against a state official alleged to be acting unlawfully, notwithstanding the Eleventh Amendment. It is noteworthy that Congress did not disapprove *Ex parte Young*; rather it acted to take such cases out of the control of a single district judge, placing them in control of a collegial court consisting of two district and one circuit judge. Beginning in 1976, Congress has cut back on the kinds of cases qualifying for three-judge courts.

* * * [W]e have concluded that the judgment of the District Court, enjoining appellant Younger from prosecuting under these California statutes, must be reversed as a violation of the national policy forbidding federal courts to stay or enjoin pending state court proceedings except under special circumstances. We express no view about the circumstances under which federal courts may act when there is no prosecution pending in state courts at the time the federal proceeding is begun.

I

Appellee Harris has been indicted, and was actually being prosecuted by California for a violation of its Criminal Syndicalism Act at the time this suit was filed. He thus has an acute, live controversy with the State and its prosecutor. But none of the other parties plaintiff in the District Court, Dan, Hirsch, or Broslawsky, has such a controversy. None has been indicted, arrested, or even threatened by the prosecutor.

* * *

Since Harris is actually being prosecuted under the challenged laws, however, we proceed with him as a proper party.

II

Since the beginning of this country's history Congress has, subject to few exceptions, manifested a desire to permit state courts to try state cases free from interference by federal courts. * * * During all this lapse of years from 1793 to 1970 the statutory exceptions to the 1793 congressional enactment have been only three; (1) "except as expressly authorized by Act of Congress"; (2) "where necessary in aid of its jurisdiction"; and (3) "to protect or effectuate its judgments." In addition, a judicial exception to the long-standing policy evidenced by the statute has been made where a person about to be prosecuted in a state court can show that he will, if the proceeding in the state court is not enjoined, suffer irreparable damages.

The precise reasons for this long-standing public policy against federal court interference with state court proceedings have never been specifically identified but the primary sources of the policy are plain. One is the basic doctrine of equity jurisprudence that courts of equity should not act, and particularly should not act to restrain a criminal prosecution, when the moving party has an adequate remedy at law and will not suffer irreparable injury if denied equitable relief. The doctrine may originally have grown out of circumstances peculiar to the English judicial system and not applicable in this country, but its fundamental purpose of restraining equity jurisdiction within narrow limits is equally important under our Constitution, in order to prevent erosion of the role of the jury and avoid a duplication of legal proceedings and legal sanctions where a single suit would be adequate to protect the rights asserted. This underlying reason for restraining courts of equity from interfering with criminal prosecutions is reinforced by an even more vital consideration, the notion of "comity," that is, a proper respect for state functions, a recognition of the fact that the entire country is made up of a Union of separate state governments, and a continuance of the belief that the National Government will fare best if the States and their institutions are left free to perform their separate functions in their separate ways. This, perhaps for lack of a better and clearer way to describe it, is referred to by many as "Our Federalism," and one familiar with the profound debates that ushered our Federal Constitution into existence is bound to respect those who remain loyal to the ideals and dreams of "Our Federalism." The concept does not mean blind deference to "States' Rights" any more than it means centralization of control over every important issue in our National Government and its courts. The Framers rejected both these courses. What the concept does represent is a system in which there is sensitivity to the legitimate interests of both State and National Governments, and in which the National Government, anxious though it may be to vindicate and protect federal rights and federal interests, always endeavors to do so in ways that will not unduly interfere with the legitimate activities of the States. It should never be forgotten that this slogan, "Our Federalism," born in the early struggling days of our Union of States, occupies a highly important place in our Nation's history and its future.

This brief discussion should be enough to suggest some of the reasons why it has been perfectly natural for our cases to repeat time and time again that the normal thing to do when federal courts are asked to enjoin pending proceedings in state courts is not to issue such injunctions. In *Fenner v. Boykin* (1926), suit had been brought in the Federal District Court seeking to enjoin state prosecutions under a recently enacted state law that allegedly interfered with the free flow of interstate commerce. The Court, in a unanimous opinion made clear that such a suit, even with respect to state criminal proceedings not yet formally instituted, could be proper only under very special circumstances:

> *Ex parte Young* and following cases have established the doctrine that, when absolutely necessary for protection of constitutional rights, courts of the United States have power to enjoin state officers from instituting criminal actions. But this may not be done, except under extraordinary circumstances, where the danger of irreparable loss is both great and immediate. Ordinarily, there should be no interference with such officers; primarily, they are charged with the duty of prosecuting offenders against the laws of the state, and must decide when and how this is to be done. The accused should first set up and rely upon his defense in the state courts, even though this involves a challenge of the validity of some statute, unless it plainly appears that this course would not afford adequate protection.

These principles * * * have been repeatedly followed and reaffirmed in other cases involving threatened prosecutions.

In all of these cases the Court stressed the importance of showing irreparable injury, the traditional prerequisite to obtaining an injunction. In addition, however, the Court also made clear that in view of the fundamental policy against federal interference with state criminal prosecutions, even irreparable injury is insufficient unless it is "both great and immediate." Certain types of injury, in particular, the cost, anxiety, and inconvenience of having to defend against a single criminal prosecution, could not by themselves be considered "irreparable" in the special legal sense of that term. Instead, the threat to the plaintiff's federally protected rights must be one that cannot be eliminated by his defense against a single criminal prosecution.

This is where the law stood when the Court decided *Dombrowski v. Pfister* (1965), and held that an injunction against the enforcement of certain state criminal statutes could properly issue under the circumstances presented in that case. * * * The appellants in *Dombrowski* had offered to prove that their offices had been raided and all their files and records seized pursuant to search and arrest warrants that were later summarily vacated by a state judge for lack of probable cause. They also offered to prove that despite the state court order quashing the warrants and suppressing the evidence seized, the prosecutor was continuing to threaten to initiate new prosecutions of appellants under the same statutes, was holding public hearings at which photostatic copies of the illegally seized documents were being used, and was threatening to use other copies of the illegally seized documents to obtain grand jury indictments against the appellants on charges of violating the same statutes. These circumstances, as viewed by the Court sufficiently establish the kind of irreparable injury, above and beyond that associated with the defense of a single prosecution brought in good faith, that had always been considered sufficient to justify federal intervention. * * *

> But the allegations in this complaint depict a situation in which defense of the State's criminal prosecution will not assure adequate vindication of constitutional rights. They suggest that a substantial loss of or impairment of freedoms of expression will occur if appellants must await the state court's disposition and ultimate review in this Court of any adverse determination. These allegations, if true, clearly show irreparable injury.

* * * And the Court made clear that even under these circumstances the District Court issuing the injunction would have continuing power to lift it at any time and remit the plaintiffs to the state courts if circumstances warranted * * * .

It is against the background of these principles that we must judge the propriety of an injunction under the circumstances of the present case. Here a proceeding was already pending in the state court, affording Harris an opportunity to raise his constitutional claims. There is no suggestion that this single prosecution against Harris is brought in bad faith or is only one of a series of repeated prosecutions to which he will be subjected. In other words, the injury that Harris faces is solely "that incidental to every criminal proceeding brought lawfully and in good faith," and therefore under the settled doctrine we have already described he is not entitled to equitable relief "even if such statutes are unconstitutional."

* * * It is undoubtedly true, as the Court stated in *Dombrowski*, that "[a] criminal prosecution under a statute regulating expression usually involves imponderables and contingencies that themselves may inhibit the full exercise of First Amendment freedoms." But this sort of "chilling effect," as the Court called it, should not by itself justify federal intervention. In the first place, the chilling effect cannot be satisfactorily eliminated by federal injunctive relief. * * * The chilling effect can, of course, be eliminated by an injunction that would prohibit any prosecution whatever for conduct occurring prior to a satisfactory rewriting of the statute. But the States would then be stripped of all power to prosecute even the socially dangerous and constitutionally unprotected conduct that had been covered by the statute, until a new statute could be passed by the state

legislature and approved by the federal courts in potentially lengthy trial and appellate proceedings. * * *

Moreover, the existence of a "chilling effect," even in the area of First Amendment rights, has never been considered a sufficient basis, in and of itself, for prohibiting state action. Where a statute does not directly abridge free speech, but—while regulating a subject within the State's power—tends to have the incidental effect of inhibiting First Amendment rights, it is well settled that the statute can be upheld if the effect on speech is minor in relation to the need for control of the conduct and the lack of alternative means for doing so. Just as the incidental "chilling effect" of such statutes does not automatically render them unconstitutional, so the chilling effect that admittedly can result from the very existence of certain laws on the statute books does not in itself justify prohibiting the State from carrying out the important and necessary task of enforcing these laws against socially harmful conduct that the State believes in good faith to be punishable under its laws and the Constitution.

Beyond all this is another, more basic consideration. Procedures for testing the constitutionality of a statute "on its face" in the manner apparently contemplated by *Dombrowski*, and for then enjoining all action to enforce the statute until the State can obtain court approval for a modified version, are fundamentally at odds with the function of the federal courts in our constitutional plan. The power and duty of the judiciary to declare laws unconstitutional is in the final analysis derived from its responsibility for resolving concrete disputes brought before the courts for decision; a statute apparently governing a dispute cannot be applied by judges, consistently with their obligations under the Supremacy Clause, when such an application of the statute would conflict with the Constitution. But this vital responsibility, broad as it is, does not amount to an unlimited power to survey the statute books and pass judgment on laws before the courts are called upon to enforce them. Ever since the Constitutional Convention rejected a proposal for having members of the Supreme Court render advice concerning pending legislation it has been clear that, even when suits of this kind involve a "case or controversy" sufficient to satisfy the requirements of Article III of the Constitution, the task of analyzing a proposed statute, pinpointing its deficiencies, and requiring correction of these deficiencies before the statute is put into effect, is rarely if ever an appropriate task for the judiciary. The combination of the relative remoteness of the controversy, the impact on the legislative process of the relief sought, and above all the speculative and amorphous nature of the required line-by-line analysis of detailed statutes ordinarily results in a kind of case that is wholly unsatisfactory for deciding constitutional questions, whichever way they might be decided. In light of this fundamental conception of the Framers as to the proper place of the federal courts in the governmental processes of passing and enforcing laws, it can seldom be appropriate for these courts to exercise any such power of prior approval or veto over the legislative process.

For these reasons, fundamental not only to our federal system but also to the basic functions of the Judicial Branch of the National Government under our Constitution, we hold that the Dombrowski decision should not be regarded as having upset the settled doctrines that have always confined very narrowly the availability of injunctive relief against state criminal prosecutions. We do not think that opinion stands for the proposition that a federal court can properly enjoin enforcement of a statute solely on the basis of a showing that the statute "on its face" abridges First Amendment rights. There may, of course, be extraordinary circumstances in which the necessary irreparable injury can be shown even in the absence of the usual prerequisites of bad faith and harassment. For example, * * * "[i]t is of course conceivable that a statute might be flagrantly and patently violative of express constitutional prohibitions in every clause, sentence and paragraph, and in whatever manner and against whomever an effort might be made to apply it." Other unusual situations calling for federal intervention might also arise, but there is no point in our attempting now to specify what they might be. It is sufficient for purposes of the present case to hold, as we do, that the possible unconstitutionality of a statute "on its face" does not in itself justify an injunction against good-faith attempts to enforce it, and that appellee Harris has failed to make any showing of bad faith, harassment, or any other unusual circumstance that would call for equitable relief. Because our holding rests on the absence of the factors necessary under equitable principles to justify federal intervention, we have no occasion to consider whether 28 U.S.C. § 2283, which prohibits an injunction against state court proceedings "except as expressly authorized by Act of Congress" would in and of itself be controlling under the circumstances of this case.

The judgment of the District Court is reversed, and the case is remanded for further proceedings not inconsistent with this opinion.

Reversed.

Notes and Questions

1. As Justice Black notes, this abstention doctrine did not originate with *Younger.* The Court mentions two of its antecedents: *Douglas v. City of Jeannette,* 319 U.S. 157 (1943), and *Fenner v. Boykin,* 271 U.S. 240 (1926). In fact, the Court's first consider-

ation of the propriety of federal intervention in state criminal proceedings came in *In re Sawyer,* 124 U.S. 200 (1888). Today the doctrine is universally referred to as *Younger* abstention.

> **FYI**
>
> For a history of its development up to *Younger*, see Donald H. Zeigler, *An Accommodation of the* Younger *Doctrine and the Duty of the Federal Courts to Enforce Safeguards in the State Criminal Process*, 125 U. PA. L. REV. 266 (1976).

Younger, however, worked a major change in the doctrine, though hardly one to which Justice Black called much attention. Note that the Court's discussion of Fenner v. Boykin makes clear that the doctrine there applied to an attempt to enjoin *threatened* prosecutions. Fenner did not involve pending criminal prosecutions. In fact, from In re Sawyer until *Younger,* the rule of restraint applied only in the context of threatened, not pending actions. Recall that in Ex parte Young, the Court said in *dictum,* connoting that it was stating the obvious, "[b]ut the Federal court cannot, of course, interfere in a case where the proceedings were already pending in a state court." *Ex parte Young,* 209 U.S. 123, 169 (1908). Thus, before *Younger,* long-standing federal policy barred any federal intervention in a pending state criminal proceeding and permitted equitable relief against threatened state proceedings only in the "extraordinary circumstances" referred to in Fenner.

Younger changed that structure dramatically. Near the outset of the opinion, the Court notes that it is reversing the judgment below because it violates the "national policy forbidding federal courts to stay or enjoin *pending* state court proceedings except under special circumstances," (emphasis added), and goes on to say that "[w]e express no view about the circumstances under which federal courts may act when there is no prosecution pending in state courts at the time the federal proceeding is begun." This is serious business, and one might view it as a *de facto* overruling of Fenner v. Boykin, despite Justice Black's citation of that case with obvious approval. Before *Younger,* federal intervention in pending state criminal prosecutions was substantially impossible, and federal action against threatened state prosecutions was extremely difficult to secure. After *Younger,* intervention in pending state criminal proceedings was possible, though extremely difficult to secure, and the Court, despite its protest, seemed to be signaling increased possibilities of federal judicial action with respect to threatened state criminal proceedings.

2. The Court rarely decides cases in a vacuum, political *or* doctrinal. *Younger* has an almost symbiotic relationship with *Mitchum v. Foster,* 407 U.S. 225 (1972), decided the year after *Younger.* Mitchum, (*see also* 795) held that 42 U.S.C. § 1983 is a congressionally-authorized exception to 28 U.S.C. § 2283, which bans federal courts from staying state court proceedings except in very limited circumstances. Without *Younger,* Mitchum potentially would have opened the federal courts to thousands of

lawsuits by state criminal defendants claiming violation of federal constitutional rights. Mitchum made it impossible for the Court to reach a compromise allowing federal court intervention in extreme cases while denying it in ordinary ones. Section 1983 was either an exception to § 2283 or it was not. If it was, the doors to the federal courthouse were flung open. If not, they were shut tight. The combination of *Younger* and Mitchum did leave the federal courts able to stay pending state civil proceedings.

For More Information

See Ann Althouse, *The Humble and the Treasonous: Judge-Made Jurisdiction Law*, 40 CASE W. RES. L. REV. 1035, 1041-44 (1990).

Trading away authority to enjoin criminal proceedings to gain power to enjoin civil proceedings may be desirable, but *Younger's* dramatic expansion into the civil area after 1971, described below, removes some of the benefit of the bargain that Professor Althouse argues the Court struck in 1971 and 1972.

In Mitchum, the unanimous seven-Member Court[4] explicitly discussed the relationship among *Younger*, the Anti-Injunction Act, and § 1983. First, unless the *Younger* Court had viewed § 1983 as an "expressly authorized" exception to the Act, it could have easily and quickly decided *Younger* without discussion of "Our Federalism." Second, if the Anti-Injunction Act applied to § 1983 cases, federal intervention would be impossible even in the extraordinary circumstances *Younger* apparently contemplated, necessitating at least partial overruling of *Younger*. Finally, the legislative debate on § 1983 clearly contemplated the possibility of the Civil Rights Act undergirding federal interference with state proceedings in any branch of state government. As the Court observed, even

> [t]hose who opposed the Act of 1871 clearly recognized that the proponents were extending federal power in an attempt to remedy the state courts' failure to secure federal rights. The debate was not about whether the predecessor of § 1983 extended to actions of state courts, but whether this innovation was necessary or desirable.

At the same time, Mitchum endorsed *Younger* abstention. "[W]e do not question or qualify in any way the principles of comity, equity, and federalism that must restrain a federal court when asked to enjoin a state court proceeding. These principles, in the context of state criminal prosecutions, were canvassed at length last Term in *Younger v. Harris* * * * ." In what sense is the Court's position in Mitchum inherently inconsistent with its views only a year earlier in *Younger*?

3. *Younger* abstention represents a clash between two of the dominant themes of federal courts jurisprudence: federalism and separation of powers. The federalism

---

4 Justices Powell and Rehnquist were appointed too late to participate.

aspects of the doctrine are clear; in all but extreme cases the states are free to enforce their statutes without federal interference until state proceedings end. On the other hand, there are some unavoidable separation-of-powers problems. There are two authorizations of federal jurisdiction for cases such as Harris's: the general federal-question statute, 28 U.S.C.A. § 1331, and the civil rights jurisdiction statute, 28 U.S.C.A. § 1343. Professor Martin Redish argues strongly that Younger violates separation of powers, particularly in light of the congressional intent underlying § 1983 that the Court so clearly recognized in *Mitchum*.

For More Information

Martin H. Redish, *Abstention, Separation of Powers, and the Limits of the Judicial Function*, 94 YALE L.J. 71 (1984). *But see* Michael Wells, *Why Professor Redish Is Wrong About Abstention*, 19 GA.L.REV. 1097 (1985).

4. Justice Black discusses *Dombrowski v. Pfister*, 380 U.S. 479 (1965), at some length, distinguishing it from *Younger*. *Younger* does not explicitly overrule *Dombrowski*, but what is left of *Dombrowski* after *Younger*? Has it been limited to its facts? Suppose in *Dombrowski* there had been no prior state dismissals. Would the *Younger* Court have allowed federal intervention? Suppose instead that plaintiffs offer to prove that the state prosecution is in retaliation for the exercise of constitutional rights. Does *Younger* permit federal injunctive relief? Does it even permit plaintiffs an evidentiary presentation on the issue?

For More Information

Professor Wingate has addressed some of these questions. C. Keith Wingate, *The Bad Faith Harassment Exception to the* Younger *Doctrine: Exploring the Empty Universe*, 5 REV. LITIG. 123 (1986).

5. a) *Younger* bars an injunction against a state criminal proceeding unless the plaintiff can demonstrate that he will suffer "irreparable injury." While Justice Black does not define irreparable injury, he does say that it is *not* the "cost, anxiety, and inconvenience of having to defend against a single criminal prosecution." Indeed, he speaks of this burden as if it is a comparatively minor aggravation that the good citizen should have to bear. Should the individual prosecuted for a crime under a statute that he alleges is unconstitutional be required to endure the wrenching experience of a criminal proceeding without hope of federal review of his constitutional claim until he has pursued his defense, if necessary, through several levels of state courts, has encumbered assets to post bail, has been held up to the community as a criminal, and perhaps has been imprisoned following conviction pending appeal? On the other hand, how would it affect *Younger* abstention to regard the burden of defending as irreparable injury?

b) Given the limited number of cases the Court hears each year, the practical effect of *Younger* abstention for most cases is that the state courts have not only the first but also the last word on the federal constitutional issues. When the Court decided *Younger*, federal habeas corpus review was considerably more available to test prisoners' constitutional claims than is now the case. *See generally* Chapter 11. Should the Court re-evaluate *Younger* abstention in light of the current restricted scope of federal habeas review?

c) The Court has taken varying positions about the "cost, anxiety, and inconvenience" of litigation. In the area of official immunities, the Justices have felt that litigation is so burdensome that they were justified in creating federal common law to prevent litigation of all but the clearest abuses of power. *See Harlow v. Fitzgerald*, 457 U.S. 800 (1982), *supra* at 626. True, the *Harlow* Court was concerned with interference with governmental processes, a factor not present when an individual is prosecuted for a crime. On the other hand, it is also true that an official sued for violation of constitutional rights has at his back the defensive resources of the government and may be indemnified in the event of an adverse judgment.

6. In addition to irreparable injury, a plaintiff seeking to avoid abstention must show there is no adequate state remedy for vindicating the plaintiff's federal claim. The Court has made clear that any theoretically available state remedy will suffice for *Younger* abstention purposes and that the federal courts have no obligation to evaluate the effectiveness of potential state remedies. *See O'Shea v. Littleton*, 414 U.S. 488 (1974). As Professor Owen Fiss has noted, the "adequacy of [the] alternative remedies [in *O'Shea*] was evidently to be presumed from the very fact that Justice White was able to think of them." Moreover, the presumption of adequacy is essentially irrebuttable. If a federal court dismisses because of *Younger*, litigants cannot return to federal court to show that the judge guessed wrong and that state remedies were unavailing. On occasion, the Court has found there is no adequate remedy at law when state remedies are not even theoretically available or when the plaintiffs can make a clear case the state tribunal will be biased against them.

a) *Gerstein v. Pugh*, 420 U.S. 103 (1975), provides an example of the first circumstance. The plaintiff class challenged Florida's procedure in criminal cases generally.

> In Florida, indictments are required only for prosecution of capital offenses. Prosecutors may charge all other crimes by information, without a prior preliminary hearing and without obtaining leave of court. At the time respondents were arrested, a Florida rule seemed to authorize adversary preliminary hearings to test probable cause for detention in all cases. But the Florida courts had held that the filing of an information foreclosed the suspect's right to a preliminary hearing. They had also held that habeas corpus could not be used, except perhaps in exceptional circumstances, to test the probable cause for detention under an information. The only possible methods for obtaining a judicial determination of probable cause were a special statute allowing a preliminary hearing after

> 30 days, and arraignment, which the District Court found was often delayed a month or more after arrest. As a result, a person charged by information could be detained for a substantial period solely on the decision of a prosecutor.

Plaintiffs argued that they had a constitutional right to a probable cause hearing before imposition of more pretrial detention than necessarily incident to an arrest. They sought declaratory and injunctive relief compelling such hearings. Notwithstanding the pending criminal cases against the members of the plaintiff class, the Supreme Court held abstention inappropriate because there was no Florida procedure to challenge the propriety of the pretrial detention. Thus, complete unavailability of a state procedure for raising federal constitutional claims may undercut *Younger* abstention.

b) The Court has also forsworn abstention where the federal plaintiff demonstrates bias in state proceedings otherwise theoretically adequate for raising the federal issues. *See Gibson v. Berryhill,* 411 U.S. 564 (1973). The plaintiffs, licensed optometrists, sought to enjoin hearings charging them with unprofessional conduct by reason of their employment with a corporation. They argued that because the members of the state board of optometry had a pecuniary interest in the outcome, abstention was not warranted. The Court agreed.

7. The Court notes an apparent exception (without examples) to the Younger doctrine if a state statute is "flagrantly and patently violative of express constitutional provisions in every clause, sentence and paragraph." Are equity, comity and federalism of any less force then? How is such a case distinguishable in any principled way from one in which the statute is "merely" unconstitutional? Moreover, if the statute is so demonstrably unconstitutional, should not the presumption of the state courts' ability to handle the constitutional issue be stronger rather than weaker?

Trainor v. Hernandez, 431 U.S. 434 (1977), provided an example of what would *not* satisfy this exception. Plaintiffs were public assistance recipients. In state court, Illinois sued to recover payments allegedly wrongfully received and, pursuant to a 100-year old state statute, attached some of plaintiffs' assets. Plaintiffs then sued in federal court, claiming the Illinois statute provided none of the procedural safeguards the Court had held the Due Process Clause to require in four recent cases. The district court found the Illinois procedure clearly unconstitutional, but the Supreme Court reversed, finding that the Illinois scheme was, in some sense, not unconstitutional enough to qualify under the "patently violative" exception. Justice Stevens dissented.

> [T]he Court finds a meaningful difference between a state procedure which is "patently and flagrantly violative of the Constitution" and one that is "flagrantly and patently violative of express constitutional prohibitions in every clause, sentence and paragraph, and in whatever manner and against whomever an effort might be made to apply it." * * *
>
> The District Court found the Illinois attachment procedure "patently and flagrantly violative of the constitution." This Court, on the other hand, writes:

> It is urged that this case comes within the exception that we said in *Younger* might exist where a state statute is "flagrantly and patently violative of express constitutional prohibitions in every clause, sentence and paragraph, and in whatever manner and against whomever an effort might be made to apply it." Even if such a finding was made below, *which we doubt*, it would not have been warranted in light of our cases. (Emphasis added).

Since there is no doubt whatsoever as to what the District Court actually said, this Court's expression of doubt can only refer to its uncertainty as to whether a finding that the crux of the statute is patently and flagrantly unconstitutional is sufficient to satisfy the requirement that the statute be patently and flagrantly unconstitutional "in every clause, sentence and paragraph * * * ." It is, therefore, appropriate to consider what is left of this exception to the *Younger* doctrine after today's decision.

The source of this exception is the passage Mr. Justice Black had written some years earlier in Watson v. Buck, a case which involved a complicated state antitrust Act. On the basis of its conclusion that certain sections were unconstitutional, a three-judge District Court had enjoined enforcement of the entire Act. This Court reversed, holding: first, that the invalidity of a part of a statute would not justify an injunction against the entire Act; and second, that in any event the eight sections in question were valid.

* * *

When he wrote the Court's opinion in *Younger,* Mr. Justice Black quoted * * * from the Watson case as an example of a situation in which it would be appropriate for a federal court to enjoin a pending state criminal prosecution. He did not, however, imply that his earlier language rigidly defined the boundaries of one kind of exception from the equitable rationale underlying the *Younger* decision itself.

> **FYI**
>
> In Watson v. Buck, although the Court denied relief, Justice Black's opinion for the unanimous Court contained the following language:
>
> It is of course conceivable that a statute might be flagrantly and patently violative of express constitutional prohibitions in every clause, sentence and paragraph, and in whatever manner and against whomever an effort might be made to apply it. It is sufficient to say that the statutes before us are not of this type.

Today the Court seems to be saying that the "patently and flagrantly unconstitutional" exception to *Younger*-type abstention is unavailable whenever a statute has a legitimate title, or a legitimate severability clause, or some other equally innocuous provision. If this is a fair reading of the Court's opinion, the Court has given Mr. Justice Black's illustrative language definitional significance. In effect, this treatment preserves an illusion of flexibility in the application of a *Younger*-type abstention, but it actually eliminates one of the exceptions from the doctrine. * * * More importantly, the Court has never explained why all sections of any statute must be considered invalid in order to justify an injunction against a portion that is itself flagrantly unconstitutional. Even if this Court finds the constitutional issue less clear than did the District Court, I do not understand what governmental interest is served by refusing to address the merits at this stage of the proceedings.

8. One of the premises of *Younger* abstention is that the state courts are as able as federal courts to determine federal constitutional claims. That leaves aside the question of whether state courts are equally hospitable to federal claims, particularly when the claims involve possible invalidation of state statutes. Scholars have long debated the supposition of parity. It is ironic, perhaps, that the Court has been eager to presume the states' expertise on matters of state law, but has not been willing to presume corresponding expertise of the federal courts with respect to federal law. *See generally* Burt Neuborne, *The Myth of Parity*, 90 HARV.L.REV. 1105 (1977); Symposium, *Federalism and Parity*, 71 B.U.L.REV. 593 (1991).

9. Is *Younger* a prudential doctrine or constitutionally compelled? For an argument that it is the latter, see Calvin R. Massey, *Abstention and the Constitutional Limits of the Judicial Power of the United States*, 1991 B.Y.U.L.REV. 811.

a) If it is prudential only, then is not the Court violating separation of powers by rejecting what it implicitly treats as an offer of jurisdiction by Congress rather than a command to exercise jurisdiction? In Professor Redish's terms, is it legitimate for the Court, a designedly counter-majoritarian branch of government, to make policy decisions about the wisdom of exercising federal jurisdiction that Congress has conferred? *Younger* abstention is a judicially-created doctrine that effectively overrides legislation conferring jurisdiction, or at least creates judicial exceptions to it. Yet the Court and its members have often inveighed against the propriety of courts considering other than the constitutionality of legislation. The abstention doctrines in particular deal with the day-to-day balance of power between state and federal governments. If the *Younger* doctrine is prudential, then the Court has imposed its vision of what the balance should be. Can Congress remedy the situation if it feels the Court has struck an improper balance?

Arguably, Congress has attempted to remedy the situation, at least if one takes Mitchum v. Foster seriously. Mitchum held, however questionably, that Congress intended § 1983 cases to fall within the "expressly authorized" exception of the Anti-Injunction Act. Should that statutory determination of federal policy overcome the federal common law that the Court has created in *Younger*? If so, can *Younger* apply at all to § 1983 cases? If not, then is a federal court's power to determine the propriety of equitable relief hierarchically superior to Congress's legislative power?

b) If the doctrine is constitutionally compelled, several problems arise. First, if *Younger* is a constitutional matter, then should the Court have examined whether the Anti-Injunction Act precluded Harris's action? The Court explicitly did not decide on that basis. Under the Ashwander principle of avoiding constitutional decisions, should it have?

Second, if the Constitution compels *Younger* abstention, is *Younger* abstention waivable? The Court has suggested that judges cannot raise it ***sua sponte***. *Swisher v. Brady*, 438 U.S. 204, 213 n.11 (1978). That the doctrine is effectively waivable does not necessarily mean that it lacks constitutional stature; many constitutional rights are waivable. On the other hand, given that *Younger* abstention now applies to a vast range of proceedings other than purely criminal matters, and given that the purpose of the doctrine is to safeguard the values of federalism, "it is unclear why consent of the *parties* is sufficient to justify interference." ERWIN CHEMERINSKY, FEDERAL JURISDICTION § 13.4, at 863 (5th ed. 2007).

Third, what is the precise constitutional basis for the tripartite predicate for the *Younger* doctrine—equity, comity and federalism? One can infer principles of federalism (and perhaps comity) from the constitutional structure that establishes the dual government system. Perhaps the only specific reservation in the name of federalism is the Tenth Amendment. It is a great stretch, however, to read the Tenth Amendment as a specific constitutional prohibition of federal injunctions of state proceedings in areas of admitted federal competence. Principles of equity are even more difficult to locate in the Constitution.

Fourth, if *Younger* is constitutionally compelled then its clash with the jurisdiction statutes (28 U.S.C.A. §§ 1331, 1343) is all the more apparent. Should the Court either explicitly construe those statutes not to apply when *Younger* abstention is appropriate or declare those statutes unconstitutional as applied when *Younger* confronts them?

10. *Younger* was only one case of a group now known as the *Younger* sextet, all decided the same day. In *Samuels v. Mackell*, 401 U.S. 66 (1971), the Court extended *Younger's* prohibition to requests for declaratory relief only, noting:

> [O]rdinarily a declaratory judgment will result in precisely the same interference with and disruption of state proceedings that the longstanding policy limiting injunctions was designed to avoid. This is true for at least two reasons. In the first place, the Declaratory Judgment Act provides that after a declaratory judgment is issued the district court may enforce it by granting "[f]urther necessary or proper relief," and therefore a declaratory judgment issued while state proceedings are pending might serve as the basis for a subsequent injunction against those proceedings to "protect or effectuate" the declaratory judgment, and thus result in a clearly improper interference with the state proceedings. Secondly, even if the declaratory judgment is not used as a basis for actually issuing an injunction, the declaratory relief alone has virtually the same practical impact as a formal injunction would. As we said in the *Wycoff* case:
>
> > Is the declaration contemplated here to be res judicata, so that the [state court] cannot hear evidence and decide any matter for itself? If so, the federal court has virtually lifted the case out of the State [court] before it could be heard. If not, the federal judgment serves no useful purpose as a final determination of rights.

> We therefore hold that, in cases where the state criminal prosecution was begun prior to the federal suit, the same equitable principles relevant to the propriety of an injunction must be taken into consideration by federal district courts in determining whether to issue a declaratory judgment, and that where an injunction would be impermissible under these principles, declaratory relief should ordinarily be denied as well.

Interestingly, Samuels expressed the same reservation about relief in the absence of a pending proceeding as had *Younger:* "We, of course, express no views on the propriety of declaratory relief when no state proceeding is pending at the time the federal suit is begun."

The Court also decided that a federal court cannot order suppression of evidence in a pending state criminal proceeding because such an order might terminate the prosecution as effectively as an injunction. *Perez v. Ledesma,* 401 U.S. 82 (1971). In *Boyle v. Landry,* 401 U.S. 77 (1971), the Court reversed and remanded with directions to dismiss on the ground that the plaintiffs had not shown even a threatened prosecution and therefore could not show irreparable harm.

a) Is the Court's position in Samuels tantamount to saying that the Declaratory Judgment Act, 28 U.S.C.A. §§ 2201-2202, was not intended to apply to state criminal proceedings? Refusal to grant equitable relief is usually justified by the argument that legal relief is available, not by any concept that some other court may be able to decide the same issue as that presented to the court sitting in equity. "It was never a doctrine of equity that a federal court should exercise its judicial discretion to dismiss a suit merely because a state court could entertain it." *Alabama Public Service Commission v. Southern Railway,* 341 U.S. 341, 361 (1951). Leaving comity aside, in light of the Court's confident pronouncement in 1951, is there any reason the federal courts should not issue a declaratory judgment in a *Samuels* situation?

b) The Court noted that it might allow declaratory relief where it would not allow injunctive relief. Since Samuels took some pains to demonstrate the unity of effect of declaratory and injunctive relief on state proceedings, how is it possible that one is permissible and the other not? In what sort of case would the Court permit declaratory, but not injunctive, relief because of *Younger*? The next case addresses that question.

Steffel v. Thompson

Supreme Court of the United States, 1974.
415 U.S. 452.

MR. JUSTICE BRENNAN delivered the opinion of the Court.

* * * This case presents the important question reserved in *Samuels v. Mackell*, whether declaratory relief is precluded when a state prosecution has been threatened, but is not pending, and a showing of bad-faith enforcement or other special circumstances has not been made.

Petitioner, and others, filed a complaint in the District Court for the Northern District of Georgia, invoking the Civil Rights Act of 1871 * * * . The complaint requested a declaratory judgment that GA. CODE ANN. § 26-1503 (1972) was being applied in violation of petitioner's First and Fourteenth Amendment rights, and an injunction restraining respondents * * * from enforcing the statute so as to interfere with petitioner's constitutionally protected activities.

The parties stipulated to the relevant facts: On October 8, 1970, while petitioner and other individuals were distributing handbills protesting American involvement in Vietnam on an exterior sidewalk of the North DeKalb Shopping Center, shopping center employees asked them to stop handbilling and leave. They declined to do so, and police officers were summoned. The officers told them that they would be arrested if they did not stop handbilling. The group then left to avoid arrest. Two days later petitioner and a companion returned to the shopping center and again began handbilling. The manager of the center called the police, and petitioner and his companion were once again told that failure to stop their handbilling would result in their arrests. Petitioner left to avoid arrest. His companion stayed, however, continued handbilling, and was arrested and subsequently arraigned on a charge of criminal trespass * * * . Petitioner alleged in his complaint that, although he desired to return to the shopping center to distribute handbills, he had not done so because of his concern that he, too, would be arrested * * * ; the parties stipulated that, if petitioner returned and refused upon request to stop handbilling, a warrant would be sworn out and he might be arrested and charged with a violation of the Georgia statute.

After hearing, the District Court denied all relief and dismissed the action, finding that "no meaningful contention can be made that the state has [acted] or will in the future act in bad faith," and therefore "the rudiments of an active controversy between the parties * * * [are] lacking." Petitioner appealed only from the denial of declaratory relief. The Court of Appeals for the Fifth Circuit, one judge concurring in the result, affirmed the District Court's judgment refusing declaratory relief. * * *

We granted certiorari and now reverse.

I

standing

At the threshold we must consider whether petitioner presents an "actual controversy," a requirement imposed by art. III of the Constitution and the express terms of the Federal Declaratory Judgment Act, 28 U.S.C. § 2201.

Petitioner has alleged threats of prosecution that cannot be characterized as "imaginary or speculative." He has been twice warned to stop handbilling that he claims is constitutionally protected and has been told by the police that if he again handbills at the shopping center and disobeys a warning to stop he will likely be prosecuted. The prosecution of petitioner's handbilling companion is ample demonstration that petitioner's concern with arrest has not been "chimerical." In these circumstances, it is not necessary that petitioner first expose himself to actual arrest or prosecution to be entitled to challenge a statute that he claims deters the exercise of his constitutional rights. Moreover, petitioner's challenge is to those specific provisions of state law which have provided the basis for threats of criminal prosecution against him.

Nonetheless, there remains a question as to the continuing existence of a live and acute controversy that must be resolved on the remand we order today. * * * Here, petitioner's complaint indicates that his handbilling activities were directed "against the war in Vietnam and the United States foreign policy in Southeast Asia." Since we cannot ignore the recent developments reducing the Nation's involvement in that part of the world, it will be for the District Court on remand to determine if subsequent events have so altered petitioner's desire to engage in handbilling at the shopping center that it can no longer be said that this case presents "a substantial controversy, between parties having adverse legal interests, of sufficient immediacy and reality to warrant the issuance of a declaratory judgment."

> **FYI**
>
> By the time the Supreme Court heard this case, four years had passed since the underlying fact pattern had arisen. The United States' involvement in Viet Nam was clearly coming to an end. Thus, although the Court clearly felt that originally Steffel had presented a justiciable controversy, it was no longer confident that it did. Since the district court had ruled on justiciability only at the outset of the original case, the Supreme Court was unwilling to be the first court to consider justiciability in light of the changed facts. If the case-or-controversy requirement goes to the federal courts' subject matter jurisdiction, should the Court have remanded for determination of that question?

II

We now turn to the question of whether the District Court and the Court of Appeals correctly found petitioner's request for declaratory relief inappropriate.

* * *

Neither Younger nor Samuels * * * decided the question whether federal intervention might be permissible in the absence of a pending state prosecution. * * *

These reservations anticipated the Court's recognition that the relevant principles of equity, comity, and federalism "have little force in the absence of a pending state proceeding." When no state criminal proceeding is pending at the time the federal complaint is filed, federal intervention does not result in duplicative legal proceedings or disruption of the state criminal justice system; nor can federal intervention, in that circumstance, be interpreted as reflecting negatively upon the state court's ability to enforce constitutional principles. In addition, while a pending state prosecution provides the federal plaintiff with a concrete opportunity to vindicate his constitutional rights, a refusal on the part of the federal courts to intervene when no state proceeding is pending may place the hapless plaintiff between the Scylla of intentionally flouting state law and the Charybdis of foregoing what he believes to be constitutionally protected activity in order to avoid becoming enmeshed in a criminal proceeding.

When no state proceeding is pending and thus considerations of equity, comity, and federalism have little vitality, the propriety of granting federal declaratory relief may properly be considered independently of a request for injunctive relief. Here, the Court of Appeals held that, because injunctive relief would not be appropriate since petitioner failed to demonstrate irreparable injury—a traditional prerequisite to injunctive relief—it followed that declaratory relief was also inappropriate. Even if the Court of Appeals correctly viewed injunctive relief as inappropriate—a question we need not reach today since petitioner has abandoned his request for that remedy—the court erred in treating the requests for injunctive and declaratory relief as a single issue.

* * *

The subject matter jurisdiction of the lower federal courts was greatly expanded in the wake of the Civil War. A pervasive sense of nationalism led to enactment of the Civil Rights Act of 1871, empowering the lower federal courts to determine the constitutionality of actions, taken by persons under color of state law, allegedly depriving other individuals of rights guaranteed by the Constitution and federal law.[13] Four years later, in the Judiciary Act of March 3, 1875, Congress conferred upon the lower federal courts, for but the second time in their nearly century-old history, general federal question jurisdiction subject only to a jurisdictional-amount requirement. With this latter enactment, the lower

13 Sensitiveness to "states' rights", fear of rivalry with state courts and respect for state sentiment, were swept aside by the great impulse of national feeling born of the Civil War. Nationalism was triumphant; in national administration was sought its vindication. The new exertions of federal power were no longer trusted to the enforcement of state agencies.

F. FRANKFURTER & J. LANDIS, THE BUSINESS OF THE SUPREME COURT 64 (1928).

federal courts "ceased to be restricted tribunals of fair dealing between citizens of different states and became the *primary* and powerful reliances for vindicating every right given by the Constitution, the laws, and treaties of the United States." F. FRANKFURTER & J. LANDIS, THE BUSINESS OF THE SUPREME COURT 65 (1928) (emphasis added). These two statutes, together with the Court's decision in *Ex parte Young*—holding that state officials who threaten to enforce an unconstitutional state statute may be enjoined by a federal court of equity and that a federal court may, in appropriate circumstances, enjoin future state criminal prosecutions under the unconstitutional Act—have "established the modern framework for federal protection of constitutional rights from state interference."

A "storm of controversy" raged in the wake of *Ex parte Young*, focusing principally on the power of a single federal judge to grant ex parte interlocutory injunctions against the enforcement of state statutes. This uproar was only partially quelled by Congress' passage of legislation requiring the convening of a three-judge district court before a preliminary injunction against enforcement of a state statute could issue, and providing for direct appeal to this Court from a decision granting or denying such relief. From a State's viewpoint the granting of injunctive relief—even by these courts of special dignity—"rather clumsily" crippled state enforcement of its statutes pending further review. Furthermore, plaintiffs were dissatisfied with this method of testing the constitutionality of state statutes, since it placed upon them the burden of demonstrating the traditional prerequisites to equitable relief—most importantly, irreparable injury.

To dispel these difficulties, Congress in 1934 enacted the Declaratory Judgment Act. That Congress plainly intended declaratory relief to act as an alternative to the strong medicine of the injunction and to be utilized to test the constitutionality of state criminal statutes in cases where injunctive relief would be unavailable is amply evidenced by the legislative history of the Act * * * .

* * *

First, as Congress recognized in 1934, a declaratory judgment will have a less intrusive effect on the administration of state criminal laws. As was observed in *Perez v. Ledesma* (separate opinion of Brennan, J.):

> Of course, a favorable declaratory judgment may nevertheless be valuable to the plaintiff though it cannot make even an unconstitutional statute disappear. A state statute may be declared unconstitutional *in toto*—that is, incapable of having constitutional applications; or it may be declared unconstitutionally vague or overbroad—that is, incapable of being constitutionally applied to the full extent of its purport. In either case, a federal declaration of unconstitutionality reflects the opinion of the federal court that the statute cannot be fully enforced. If a declaration of total unconstitutionality is af-

firmed by this Court, it follows that this Court stands ready to reverse any conviction under the statute. If a declaration of partial unconstitutionality is affirmed by this Court, the implication is that this Court will overturn particular applications of the statute, but that if the statute is narrowly construed by the state courts it will not be incapable of constitutional applications. Accordingly, the declaration does not necessarily bar prosecutions under the statute, as a broad injunction would. Thus, where the highest court of a State has had an opportunity to give a statute regulating expression a narrowing or clarifying construction but has failed to do so, and later a federal court declares the statute unconstitutionally vague or overbroad, it may well be open to a state prosecutor, after the federal court decision, to bring a prosecution under the statute if he reasonably believes that the defendant's conduct is not constitutionally protected and that the state courts may give the statute a construction so as to yield a constitutionally valid conviction. Even where a declaration of unconstitutionality is not reviewed by this Court, the declaration may still be able to cut down the deterrent effect of an unconstitutional state statute. The persuasive force of the court's opinion and judgment may lead state prosecutors, courts, and legislators to reconsider their respective responsibilities toward the statute. Enforcement policies or judicial construction may be changed, or the legislature may repeal the statute and start anew. Finally, the federal court judgment may have some res judicata effect, though this point is not free from difficulty and the governing rules remain to be developed with a view to the proper workings of a federal system. What is clear, however, is that even though a declaratory judgment has "the force and effect of a final judgment," 28 U.S.C. § 2201, it is a much milder form of relief than an injunction. Though it may be persuasive, it is not ultimately coercive; noncompliance with it may be inappropriate, but is not contempt.

Second, engrafting upon the Declaratory Judgment Act a requirement that all of the traditional equitable prerequisites to the issuance of an injunction be satisfied before the issuance of a declaratory judgment is considered would defy Congress' intent to make declaratory relief available in cases where an injunction would be inappropriate. * * *

The only occasions where this Court has disregarded these "different considerations" and found that a preclusion of injunctive relief inevitably led to a denial of declaratory relief have been cases in which principles of federalism militated altogether against federal intervention in a class of adjudications. In the instant case principles of federalism not only do not preclude federal intervention, they compel it. Requiring the federal courts totally to step aside when no state criminal prosecution is pending against the federal plaintiff would turn federalism on its head. When federal claims are premised on 42 U.S.C. § 1983 and 28 U.S.C. § 1343(3)—as they are here—we have not required exhaustion of state judicial or administrative remedies, recognizing the paramount role Congress has assigned to the federal courts to protect constitutional rights. But exhaustion of state remedies is precisely what would be required if both federal injunctive and declaratory relief were unavailable in a case where no state prosecution had been commenced.

III

Respondents, however, * * * argue that, although it may be appropriate to issue a declaratory judgment when no state criminal proceeding is pending and the attack is upon the facial validity of a state criminal statute, such a step would be improper where, as here, the attack is merely upon the constitutionality of the statute as applied, since the State's interest in unencumbered enforcement of its laws outweighs the minimal federal interest in protecting the constitutional rights of only a single individual. We reject the argument.

* * *

Indeed, the State's concern with potential interference in the administration of its criminal laws is of lesser dimension when an attack is made upon the constitutionality of a state statute as applied. A declaratory judgment of a lower federal court that a state statute is invalid *in toto*—and therefore incapable of any valid application—or is overbroad or vague—and therefore no person can properly be convicted under the statute until it is given a narrowing or clarifying construction—will likely have a more significant potential for disruption of state enforcement policies than a declaration specifying a limited number of impermissible applications of the statute. While the federal interest may be greater when a state statute is attacked on its face, since there exists the potential for eliminating any broad-ranging deterrent effect on would-be actors, we do not find this consideration controlling. The solitary individual who suffers a deprivation of his constitutional rights is no less deserving of redress than one who suffers together with others.[21]

We therefore hold that, regardless of whether injunctive relief may be appropriate, federal declaratory relief is not precluded when no state prosecution is pending and a federal plaintiff demonstrates a genuine threat of enforcement of a disputed state criminal statute, whether an attack is made on the constitutionality of the statute on its face or as applied. The judgment of the Court of Appeals is reversed, and the case is remanded for further proceedings consistent with this opinion.

It is so ordered.

21 Abstention, a question "entirely separate from the question of granting declaratory or injunctive relief," might be more appropriate when a challenge is made to the state statute as applied, rather than upon its face, since the reach of an uncertain state statute might, in that circumstance, be more susceptible of a limiting or clarifying construction that would avoid the federal constitutional question.

MR. JUSTICE REHNQUIST, with whom THE CHIEF JUSTICE joins, concurring.

I concur in the opinion of the Court. Although my reading of the legislative history of the Declaratory Judgment Act of 1934 suggests that its primary purpose was to enable persons to obtain a definition of their rights before an actual injury had occurred, rather than to palliate any controversy arising from *Ex parte Young*, Congress apparently was aware at the time it passed the Act that persons threatened with state criminal prosecutions might choose to forgo the offending conduct and instead seek a federal declaration of their rights. Use of the declaratory judgment procedure in the circumstances presented by this case seems consistent with that congressional expectation.

If this case were the Court's first opportunity to deal with this area of law, I would be content to let the matter rest there. But, as our cases abundantly illustrate, this area of law is in constant litigation, and it is an area through which our decisions have traced a path that may accurately be described as sinuous. Attempting to accommodate the principles of the new declaratory judgment procedure with other more established principles—in particular a proper regard for the relationship between the independent state and federal judiciary systems—this Court has acted both to advance and to limit the Act. Because the opinion today may possibly be read by resourceful counsel as commencing a new and less restrictive curve in this path of adjudication, I feel it is important to emphasize what the opinion does and does not say.

To begin with, it seems appropriate to restate the obvious: the Court's decision today deals only with declaratory relief and with threatened prosecutions. The case provides no authority for the granting of any injunctive relief nor does it provide authority for the granting of any relief at all when prosecutions are pending. The Court quite properly leaves for another day whether the granting of a declaratory judgment by a federal court will have any subsequent res judicata effect or will perhaps support the issuance of a later federal injunction.

But since possible resolutions of those issues would substantially undercut the principles of federalism reaffirmed in *Younger v. Harris*, and preserved by the decision today, I feel it appropriate to add a few remarks.

Food for Thought

Does Justice Rehnquist suggest here that a federal declaratory judgment might have *no* res judicata effect? Early opponents of the declaratory judgment device, including the Supreme Court itself, objected that it represented an advisory opinion. On the other hand, if such a judgment does have res judicata effect, is it simply a step toward obtaining injunctive relief, allowing a plaintiff to accomplish in two steps what the *Younger* doctrine suggests he should rarely be able to accomplish in one?

First, the legislative history of the Declaratory Judgment Act and the Court's opinion in this case both recognize that the declaratory judgment procedure is an alternative to pursuit of the arguably illegal activity.[1] There is nothing in the Act's history to suggest that Congress intended to provide persons wishing to violate state laws with a federal shield behind which they could carry on their contemplated conduct. Thus I do not believe that a federal plaintiff in a declaratory judgment action can avoid, by the mere filing of a complaint, the principles so firmly expressed in *Samuels*. The plaintiff who continues to violate a state statute after the filing of his federal complaint does so both at the risk of state prosecution and at the risk of dismissal of his federal lawsuit. For any arrest prior to resolution of the federal action would constitute a pending prosecution and bar declaratory relief under the principles of *Samuels*.

> **Take Note**
>
> Justice Rehnquist anticipates here the issue that the Court would confront in *Hicks v. Miranda*, the next case in this Chapter.

Second, I do not believe that today's decision can properly be raised to support the issuance of a federal injunction based upon a favorable declaratory judgment.[2] The Court's description of declaratory relief as "a milder alternative to the injunction remedy," having a "less intrusive effect on the administration of state criminal laws" than an injunction, indicates to me critical distinctions which make declaratory relief appropriate where injunctive relief would not be. It would all but totally obscure these important distinctions if a successful application for declaratory relief came to be regarded, not as the conclusion of lawsuit, but as a giant step toward obtaining an injunction against a subsequent criminal prosecution. The availability of injunctive relief must be considered with an eye toward the important policies of federalism which this Court has often recognized.

---

1 The report accompanying the Senate version of the bill stated:

> The procedure has been especially useful in avoiding the necessity, now so often present, of having to act at one's peril or to act on one's own interpretation of his rights, or abandon one's rights because of a fear of incurring damages. So now it is often necessary, in the absence of the declaratory judgment procedure, to violate or purport to violate a statute in order to obtain a judicial determination of its meaning or validity * * * . Persons now often have to act at their peril, a danger which could be frequently avoided by the ability to sue for a declaratory judgment as to their rights or duties.

Petitioner in this case, of course, did cease his handbilling activities after the warning of arrest.

2 In *Samuels v. Mackell*, the Court expressed concern that a declaratory judgment issued while a state prosecution was pending "might serve as the basis for a subsequent injunction against those proceedings * * * ." The Court recognized that this chain of litigation would "result in a clearly improper interference with the state proceedings." I believe that such improper interference would be present even though the declaratory judgment itself were issued prior to the time of the federal plaintiff's arrest.

If the rationale of cases such as Younger and Samuels turned in any way upon the relative ease with which a federal district court could reach a conclusion about the constitutionality of a challenged state statute, a preexisting judgment declaring the statute unconstitutional as applied to a particular plaintiff would, of course, be a factor favoring the issuance of an injunction as "further relief" under the Declaratory Judgment Act. But, except for statutes that are "flagrantly and patently violative of express constitutional prohibitions in every clause, sentence and paragraph * * * ," the rationale of those cases has no such basis. Their direction that federal courts not interfere with state prosecutions does not vary depending on the closeness of the constitutional issue or on the degree of confidence which the federal court possesses in the correctness of its conclusions on the constitutional point. Those decisions instead depend upon considerations relevant to the harmonious operation of separate federal and state court systems, with a special regard for the State's interest in enforcing its own criminal laws, considerations which are as relevant in guiding the action of a federal court which has previously issued a declaratory judgment as they are in guiding the action of one which has not. While the result may be that injunctive relief is not available as "further relief" under the Declaratory Judgment Act in this particular class of cases whereas it would be in similar cases not involving considerations of federalism, this would be no more a ***pro tanto*** repeal of that provision of the Declaratory Judgment Act than was Younger a *pro tanto* repeal of the All Writs Act, 28 U.S.C. § 1651.

A declaratory judgment is simply a statement of rights, not a binding order supplemented by continuing sanctions. State authorities may choose to be guided by the judgment of a lower federal court, but they are not compelled to follow the decision by threat of contempt or other penalties. If the federal plaintiff pursues the conduct for which he was previously threatened with arrest and is in fact arrested, he may not return the controversy to federal court, although he may, of course, raise the federal declaratory judgment in the state court for whatever value it may prove to have. In any event, the defendant at that point is able to present his case for full consideration by a state court charged, as are the federal courts, to preserve the defendant's constitutional rights. Federal interference with this process would involve precisely the same concerns discussed in Younger and recited in the Court's opinion in this case.

Third, attempts to circumvent Younger by claiming that enforcement of a statute declared unconstitutional by a federal court is *per se* evidence of bad faith should not find support in the Court's decision in this case.

If the declaratory judgment remains, as I think the Declaratory Judgment Act intended, a simple declaration of rights without more, it will not be used merely as a dramatic tactical maneuver on the part of any state defendant seeking extended delays. Nor will it force state officials to try cases time after time, first in the federal courts and then in the state courts. I do not believe Congress desired such unnecessary, results, and I do not think that today's decision should be read to sanction them. Rather the Act, and the decision, stand for the sensible proposition that both a potential state defendant, threatened with prosecution but not charged, and the State itself, confronted by a possible violation of its criminal laws, may benefit from a procedure which provides for a declaration of rights without activation of the criminal process. If the federal court finds that the threatened prosecution would depend upon a statute it judges unconstitutional, the State may decide to forgo prosecution of similar conduct in the future, believing the judgment persuasive. Should the state prosecutors not find the decision persuasive enough to justify forbearance, the successful federal plaintiff will at least be able to bolster his allegations of unconstitutionality in the state trial with a decision of the federal district court in the immediate locality. The state courts may find the reasoning convincing even though the prosecutors did not. Finally, of course, the state legislature may decide, on the basis of the federal decision, that the statute would be better amended or repealed. All these possible avenues of relief would be reached voluntarily by the States and would be completely consistent with the concepts of federalism discussed above. Other more intrusive forms of relief should not be routinely available.

These considerations should prove highly significant in reaching future decisions based upon the decision rendered today. For the present it is enough to say, as the Court does, that petitioner, if he successfully establishes the existence of a continuing controversy on remand, may maintain an action for a declaratory judgment in the District Court.

Food for Thought

In light of this paragraph, it may now be appropriate to ask how the declaratory judgment that Justice Rehnquist describes would be different from the advice that then-Secretary of State Thomas Jefferson sought from the Court and that Chief Justice Jay declined to give. *See supra* at 25-26.

Notes and Questions

1. The unanimous decision in *Steffel* may seem generous to potential § 1983 plaintiffs, but it poses substantial practical problems. The potential plaintiff must avoid actual arrest at all costs. Nonetheless, the threat of arrest must be sufficiently real to present a genuine case or controversy. Steffel was fortunate that his unnamed colleague's persistence provided a control case. Suppose the unnamed colleague had not been there or had desisted with Steffel when they were threatened with arrest.

Would the Court still have allowed Steffel to proceed? Suppose they had both desisted on the first occasion rather than returning to be warned a second time. Would that have affected the existence of a justiciable case?

Should any explicit threat be required? There are no empirical data available, but it may be unusual for police confronted with what they believe to be a violation, even a non-violent one, first to warn and only then to arrest if the conduct is not discontinued. Certainly there is no constitutional compulsion for them to do so. Thus, a potential federal plaintiff's ability to avoid the Scylla-Charybdis dilemma to which Justice Brennan referred may be limited as a practical matter by his luck in encountering a police officer at least as interested in negotiation as in arrest.

2. The Court notes that Congress intended the Declaratory Judgment Act to be available for challenging state criminal statutes. Does that undercut the rationale for *Samuels v. Mackell*? If Congress intended the Declaratory Judgment Act to be used even when a state criminal proceeding was already pending, then is *Samuels* a usurpation, exalting the judicial power to make common law over the congressional power to enact statutes? If Congress did not so intend, is it relevant to inquire how much of a threat of arrest or prosecution Congress thought should justify a declaratory judgment, or is that matter partially or entirely beyond Congress's control?

3. Justice Rehnquist's concurrence raises several interesting questions, having to do both with federalism and separation of powers.

a) He notes that the Court has attempted to reconcile what he calls the "new declaratory judgment procedure with other more established principles" involving primarily federalism. Does he imply that it is peculiarly the function of the federal courts to define what constitutes a "proper regard for the relationship between the independent state and federal judiciary systems"? Suppose the federal courts and Congress differ about what constitutes proper regard. Whose view should prevail?

b) In conjunction with that discussion, Justice Rehnquist notes that the Court has on occasion limited the reach of the Declaratory Judgment Act. Why is it permissible for the Court to do that?

c) [I]f the effect of declaratory relief is as limited as Justice Rehnquist argues, then is there not less justification for the Court's decision in *Samuels v. Mackell*? But the Court decided *Samuels* on premises directly contradicting Justice Rehnquist's arguments, relying on the possibility of further relief in support of the declaratory judgment that would be as intrusive as an injunction. "Ordinarily, * * * the practical effect of the two forms of relief will be virtually identical * * * ."

4. *Steffel* left open the question of whether plaintiffs threatened with prosecution under an allegedly unconstitutional statute may seek injunctive relief. The Court

answered affirmatively, though perhaps not expansively, in *Doran v. Salem Inn, Inc.*, 422 U.S. 922 (1975). A town in New York passed an ordinance prohibiting topless dancing. Three bars sued in federal court to enjoin enforcement. The district court denied an order temporarily restraining enforcement, but set a hearing date for the plaintiffs' motion for a preliminary injunction. In the interim, one bar resumed its activities and received criminal summonses. The district and circuit courts granted preliminary injunctive relief to all three bars. The Supreme Court affirmed in part and reversed in part. With respect to the bar being prosecuted, the Court held that traditional *Younger* principles precluded either declaratory or injunctive relief. With respect to the other two bars, however, the Court affirmed the preliminary injunction, noting that "they were assuredly entitled to declaratory relief, and since we have previously recognized that '[o]rdinarily * * * the practical effect of [injunctive and declaratory] relief will be virtually identical,' * * * we think that [the two plaintiffs not being prosecuted] were entitled to have their claims for preliminary injunctive relief considered without regard to *Younger*'s restrictions." In the year between *Steffel* and *Doran*, Justice Rehnquist seemed to have forgotten his previously-argued position about the impotence of declaratory relief.

Doran may be a very limited case. The circumstances strongly parallel those in *Steffel*: both involved multiple actors some of whom were subsequently charged and some of whom were not. It is not clear, as it was not in *Steffel*, whether the Court would permit an action if there were not such clear proof of a threat of prosecution.

In *Wooley v. Maynard*, 430 U.S. 705 (1977), the Court approved permanent injunctive relief on behalf of an individual threatened with repeated prosecutions. Plaintiff Maynard obscured the New Hampshire state motto, "Live Free or Die," on his license plate. Within a five week period, he was convicted three times of violating a New Hampshire statute that forbade obscuring any letters on a license plate. Though Maynard had not pursued his state appellate remedies, the Court permitted relief, noting that although *Younger* might preclude an attempt to interfere with on-going prosecutions and might therefore require exhaustion of state remedies with respect to the convictions entered, Maynard did not challenge those convictions, but sought instead only to enjoin future prosecutions. The Court also affirmed the district court's conclusion that declaratory relief was insufficient protection for Maynard in view of the repeated prosecutions.

In the following case it will help you to understand the relationship between the federal and state judicial proceedings if you make a two-track time line, showing the events in each court system side by side. Fill in the events with their dates as you come to them in Justice White's opinion.

Hicks v. Miranda

Supreme Court of the United States, 1975.
422 U.S. 332.

MR. JUSTICE WHITE delivered the opinion of the Court.

* * *

I

On November 23 and 24, 1973, pursuant to four separate warrants issued *seriatim*, the police seized four copies of the film "Deep Throat," each of which had been shown at the Pussycat Theatre in Buena Park, Orange County, Cal. On November 26 an eight-count criminal misdemeanor charge was filed in the Orange County Municipal Court against two employees of the theater, each film seized being the subject matter of two counts in the complaint. Also on November 26, the Superior Court of Orange County ordered appellees to show cause why "Deep Throat" should not be declared obscene, an immediate hearing being available to appellees, who appeared that day, objected on state-law grounds to the court's jurisdiction to conduct such a proceeding, purported to "reserve" all federal questions, and refused further to participate.

> **Take Note!**
>
> It is not clear, but appellees may have been attempting to create a variant to the procedure the Supreme Court had prescribed for preserving the possibility of federal district court review of the federal issues in a *Pullman* abstention situation. *See supra* at 817. On the other hand, the cases seem quite distinguishable; here the dispute began in the state courts.

Thereupon, on November 27 the Superior Court held a hearing, viewed the film, took evidence, and then declared the movie to be obscene and ordered seized all copies of it that might be found at the theater. This judgment and order were not appealed by appellees.

Instead, on November 29, they filed this suit in the District Court against appellants * * *. The complaint recited the seizures and the proceedings in the Superior Court, stated that the action was for an injunction against the enforcement of the California obscenity statute, and prayed for judgment declaring the obscenity statute unconstitutional, and for an injunction ordering the return of all copies of the film but permitting one of the films to be duplicated before its return.

A temporary restraining order was requested and denied, the District Judge finding the proof of irreparable injury to be lacking and an insufficient likelihood of prevailing on the merits to warrant an injunction. He requested the convening of a three-judge court, however, to consider the constitutionality of the statute. Such a court was then designated on January 8, 1974.

Service of the complaint was completed on January 14, 1974, and answers and motions to dismiss, as well as a motion for summary judgment, were filed by appellants. Appellees moved for a preliminary injunction. None of the motions was granted and no hearings held, all of the issues being ordered submitted on briefs and affidavits. The Attorney General of California also appeared and urged the District Court to follow People v. Enskat, which, after Miller v. California (1973) (*Miller I*), had upheld the California obscenity statute.

Meanwhile, on January 15, the criminal complaint pending in the Municipal Court had been amended by naming appellees as additional parties defendant and by adding four conspiracy counts, one relating to each of the seized films. Also, on motions of the defendants in that case, two of the films were ordered suppressed on the ground that the two search warrants for seizing "Deep Throat" last issued, one on November 23 and the other on November 24, did not sufficiently allege that the films to be seized under those warrants differed from each other and from the films previously seized, the final two seizures being said to be invalid multiple seizures. Immediately after this order, which was later appealed and reversed, the defense and the prosecution stipulated that for purposes of the trial, which was expected to be forthcoming, the four prints of the film would be considered identical and only one copy would have to be proved at trial.

On June 4, 1974, the three-judge court issued its judgment and opinion declaring the California obscenity statute to be unconstitutional for failure to satisfy the requirements of Miller I and ordering appellants to return to appellees all copies of "Deep Throat" which had been seized as well as to refrain from making any additional seizures. Appellants' claim that Younger v. Harris and Samuels v. Mackell required dismissal of the case was rejected, the court holding that no criminal charges were pending in the state court against appellees and that in any event the pattern of search warrants and seizures demonstrated bad faith and harassment on the part of the authorities, all of which relieved the court from the strictures of Younger v. Harris and its related cases.

Appellants filed various motions for rehearing, to amend the judgment, and for relief from judgment, also later calling the court's attention to two developments they considered important: First, the dismissal on July 25, 1974, "for want of a substantial federal question" of the appeal in Miller v. California (*Miller II*), from a judgment of the Superior Court, Appellate Department, Orange County, California, sustaining the constitutionality of the very California obscenity statute which the District Court had declared unconstitutional; second, the reversal by the Superior Court, Appellate Department, of the suppression order which had been issued in the criminal case pending in the Municipal Court, the *per curiam* reversal saying the "requisite prompt adversary determination of obscenity under *Heller v. New York* * * * has been held."

On September 30, the three-judge court denied appellants' motions, reaffirmed its June 4 *Younger v. Harris* ruling and, after concluding it was not bound by the dismissal of *Miller II*, adhered to its judgment that the California statute was invalid under the Federal Constitution. * * * Appeals were taken to this Court from both the judgment of June 4 and the amended judgment of September 30. We postponed further consideration of our jurisdiction to the consideration of the merits of the case.

* * *

III

The District Court committed error in reaching the merits of this case despite the appellants' insistence that it be dismissed under *Younger v. Harris* and *Samuels v. Mackell*. When they filed their federal complaint, no state criminal proceedings were pending against appellees by name; but two employees of the theater had been charged and four copies of "Deep Throat" belonging to appellees had been seized, were being held, and had been declared to be obscene and seizable by the Superior Court. Appellees had a substantial stake in the state proceedings, so much so that they sought federal relief, demanding that the state statute be declared void and their films be returned to them. Obviously, their interests and those of their employees were intertwined; and, as we have pointed out, the federal action sought to interfere with the pending state prosecution. Absent a clear showing that appellees, whose lawyers also represented their employees, could not seek the return of their property in the state proceedings and see to it that their federal claims were presented there, the requirements of *Younger v. Harris* could not be avoided on the ground that no criminal prosecution was pending against appellees on the date the federal complaint was filed. The rule in *Younger v. Harris* is designed to "permit state courts to try state cases free from interference by federal courts," particularly where the party to the federal case may fully litigate his claim before the state court. Plainly, "[t]he same comity considerations apply" where the interference is sought by some, such as appellees, not parties to the state case.

pending state ct. prosc. against employees

What is more, on the day following the completion of service of the complaint, appellees were charged along with their employees in Municipal Court. Neither *Steffel v. Thompson*

Food for Thought

In such a situation, how is a non-party supposed to protect its rights? Should the Court have denied relief to Steffel on the ground that it would interfere with the prosecution of his companion? Suppose Steffel had hired the companion to assist him in handing out the leaflets?

nor any other case in this Court has held that for Younger v. Harris to apply, the state criminal proceedings must be pending on the day the federal case is filed. Indeed, the issue has been left open; and we now hold that where state criminal proceedings are begun against the federal plaintiffs after the federal complaint is filed but before any proceedings of substance on the merits have taken place in the federal court, the principles of Younger v. Harris should apply in full force.

> **Take Note!**
>
> Compare the Court's statement here with its previous position on sequencing, expressed in Ex parte Young at page 663.

Here, appellees were charged on January 15, prior to answering the federal case and prior to any proceedings whatsoever before the three-judge court. Unless we are to trivialize the principles of Younger v. Harris, the federal complaint should have been dismissed on the appellants' motion absent satisfactory proof of those extraordinary circumstances calling into play one of the limited exceptions to the rule of Younger v. Harris and related cases.

The District Court concluded that extraordinary circumstances had been shown in the form of official harassment and bad faith, but this was also error. The relevant findings of the District Court were vague and conclusory. There were references to the "pattern of seizure" and to "the evidence brought to light by the petition for rehearing"; and the unexplicated conclusion was then drawn that "regardless of the nature of any judicial proceeding," the police were bent on banishing "Deep Throat" from Buena Park. Yet each step in the pattern of seizures condemned by the District Court was authorized by judicial warrant or order; and the District Court did not purport to invalidate any of the four warrants, in any way to question the propriety of the proceedings in the Superior Court,[20] or even to mention the reversal of the suppression order in the Appellate Department of that court. Absent at least some effort by the District Court to impeach the entitlement of the prosecuting officials to rely on repeated judicial authorization for their conduct, we cannot agree that bad faith and harassment were made out. Indeed, such conclusion would not necessarily follow even if it were shown that the state courts were in error on some one or more issues of state or federal law.

In the last analysis, it seems to us that the District Court's judgment rests almost entirely on its conclusion that the California obscenity statute was uncon-

---

20 It has been noted that appellees did not appeal the Superior Court's order of November 27, 1973, declaring "Deep Throat" obscene and ordering all copies of it seized. It may be that under Huffman v. Pursue, Ltd., 420 U.S. 592 (1975), the failure of appellees to appeal the Superior Court order of November 27, 1973, would itself foreclose resort to federal court, absent extraordinary circumstances bringing the case within some exception to Younger v. Harris. Appellees now assert, seemingly contrary to their prior statement before Judge Ferguson, that the November 27 order was not appealable. In view of our disposition of the case, we need not pursue the matter further.

stitutional and unenforceable. But even assuming that the District Court was correct in its conclusion, the statute had not been so condemned in November 1973, and the District Court was not entitled to infer official bad faith merely because it—the District Court—disagreed with *People v. Enskat*. Otherwise, bad faith and harassment would be present in every case in which a state statute is ruled unconstitutional, and the rule of Younger v. Harris would be swallowed up by its exception. The District Court should have dismissed the complaint before it and we accordingly reverse its judgment.

So ordered.

Mr. Justice Stewart, with whom Mr. Justice Douglas, Mr. Justice Brennan, and Mr. Justice Marshall join, dissenting.

* * *

In Steffel v. Thompson, the Court unanimously held that the principles of equity, comity, and federalism embodied in Younger v. Harris and Samuels v. Mackell do not preclude a federal district court from entertaining an action to declare unconstitutional a state criminal statute when a state criminal prosecution is threatened but not pending at the time the federal complaint is filed. Today the Court holds that the Steffel decision is inoperative if a state criminal charge is filed at any point after the commencement of the federal action "before any proceedings of substance on the merits have taken place in the federal court." Any other rule, says the Court, would "trivialize" the principles of Younger v. Harris. I think this ruling "trivializes" Steffel, decided just last Term, and is inconsistent with those same principles of equity, comity, and federalism.[1]

Food for Thought

Instead of denying the request for a temporary restraining order, as the footnote recites, suppose the district judge had granted the order. Would that change the majority's position? If appellees had instead had moved for a preliminary injunction, and the court had convened a hearing to take testimony and then denied the motion, would that change the majority's position? Suppose instead that the court granted the motion for the preliminary injunction. Would the state's filing criminal charges the next day replicate the situation in Ex parte Young?

1 There is the additional difficulty that the precise meaning of the rule the Court today adopts is a good deal less than apparent. What are "proceedings of substance on the merits"? Presumably, the proceedings must be both "on the merits" and "of substance." Does this mean, then, that months of discovery activity would be insufficient, if no question on the merits is presented to the court during that time? What proceedings "on the merits" are sufficient is also unclear. An application for a temporary restraining order or a preliminary injunction requires the court to make an assessment about the likelihood of success on the merits. Indeed, in this case, appellees filed an application for a temporary restraining order along with six supporting affidavits on November 29, 1973. Appellants responded on December 3, 1973, with six affidavits of their own as well as additional documents. On December 28, 1973, Judge Lydick denied the request for a temporary restraining order, in part because appellees

There is, to be sure, something unseemly about having the applicability of the *Younger* doctrine turn solely on the outcome of a race to the courthouse. The rule the Court adopts today, however, does not eliminate that race; it merely permits the State to leave the mark later, run a shorter course, and arrive first at the finish line. This rule seems to me to result from a failure to evaluate the state and federal interests as of the time the state prosecution was commenced.

As of the time when its jurisdiction is invoked in a *Steffel* situation, a federal court is called upon to vindicate federal constitutional rights when no other remedy is available to the federal plaintiff. The Court has recognized that at this point in the proceedings no substantial state interests counsel the federal court to stay its hand. * * *

Consequently, we concluded [in *Steffel*] that "[r]equiring the federal courts totally to step aside when no state criminal prosecution is pending against the federal plaintiff would turn federalism on its head." In such circumstances, "the opportunity for adjudication of constitutional rights in a federal forum, as authorized by the Declaratory Judgment Act, becomes paramount."

The duty of the federal courts to adjudicate and vindicate federal constitutional rights is, of course, shared with state courts, but there can be no doubt that the federal courts are "the primary and powerful reliances for vindicating every right given by the Constitution, the laws, and treaties of the United States." The statute under which this action was brought, 42 U.S.C. § 1983, established in our law "the role of the Federal Government as a guarantor of basic federal rights against state power." Indeed, "[t]he very purpose of § 1983 was to interpose the federal courts between the States and the people." And this central interest of a federal court as guarantor of constitutional rights is fully implicated from the moment its jurisdiction is invoked. How, then, does the subsequent filing of a state criminal charge change the situation from one in which the federal court's dismissal of the action under *Younger* principles "would turn federalism on its head" to one in which failure to dismiss would "trivialize" those same principles?

A State has a vital interest in the enforcement of its criminal law, and this Court has said time and again that it will sanction little federal interference with that important state function. But there is nothing in our decision in *Steffel* that requires a State to stay its hand during the pendency of the federal litigation. If, in the interest of efficiency, the State wishes to refrain from actively prosecuting the criminal charge pending the outcome of the federal declaratory judgment suit,

---

"have failed totally to make that showing of * * * likelihood of prevailing on the merits needed to justify the issuance of a temporary restraining order." These proceedings, the Court says implicitly, were not sufficient to satisfy the test it announces. Why that should be, even in terms of the Court's holding, is a mystery.

it may, of course, do so. But no decision of this Court requires it to make that choice.

The Court today, however, goes much further than simply recognizing the right of the State to proceed with the orderly administration of its criminal law; it ousts the federal courts from their historic role as the "primary reliances" for vindicating constitutional freedoms. This is no less offensive to "Our Federalism" than the federal injunction restraining pending state criminal proceedings condemned by *Younger v. Harris*. The concept of federalism requires "sensitivity to the legitimate interests of *both* State and National Governments." ([E]mphasis added). *Younger v. Harris* and its companion cases reflect the principles that the federal judiciary must refrain from interfering with the legitimate functioning of state courts. But surely the converse is a principle no less valid.

The Court's new rule creates a reality which few state prosecutors can be expected to ignore. It is an open invitation to state officials to institute state proceedings in order to defeat federal jurisdiction. One need not impugn the motives of state officials to suppose that they would rather prosecute a criminal suit in state court than defend a civil case in a federal forum. Today's opinion virtually instructs state officials to answer federal complaints with state indictments. Today, the State must file a criminal charge to secure dismissal of the federal litigation; perhaps tomorrow an action "akin to a criminal proceeding" will serve the purpose, and the day may not be far off when any state civil action will do.

The doctrine of *Younger v. Harris* reflects an accommodation of competing interests. The rule announced today distorts that balance beyond recognition.

Notes and Questions

1. *Younger v. Harris* held that a federal court could not enjoin a pending state criminal proceeding in the absence of special circumstances. Before *Hicks*, a state criminal proceeding was not considered "pending" for *Younger* purposes unless criminal charges were filed against the plaintiff before he began the federal action. After *Hicks*, a state criminal proceeding may be considered pending, thus triggering *Younger* abstention, even if state charges come after the federal suit. How long after initiation of the federal suit does a state prosecutor have to defeat federal jurisdiction by filing state criminal charges?

a) What is a federal proceeding "of substance on the merits"? In *Hicks*, state criminal charges were filed against the appellees on January 15, 1974, more than six weeks after the federal complaint was filed. What federal proceedings had occurred before January 15, and what papers had the parties filed? Why were these proceedings not "of substance on the merits"? Should determination of whether a proceeding of substance on the merits has occurred depend on whether the court grants or denies plaintiff's TRO motion? Does a difference in outcome mean the proceeding somehow has more or less substance?

b) In *Hawaii Housing Authority v. Midkiff*, 467 U.S. 229 (1984), the Court sidestepped the question of whether the grant of a TRO is a proceeding of substance on the merits, but held that granting a preliminary injunction is. "A federal court action in which a preliminary injunction is granted has proceeded well beyond the 'embryonic state,' and considerations of economy, equity, and federalism counsel against Younger abstention at that point." Suppose the federal court denied the preliminary injunction. Would that alter the result for Younger abstention purposes?

c) Suppose the plaintiff seeks neither a TRO nor a preliminary injunction, and the federal suit proceeds. *Hicks* and Hawaii Housing Authority give no guidance as to what other pretrial proceedings constitute proceedings of substance on the merits. Pretrial conferences under FED.R.CIV.P. 16, discovery, denial of motions for summary judgment or for failure to state a claim upon which relief may be granted, all might or might not qualify. If the prosecutor can wait until the federal case is far along to decide whether to file criminal charges, the prosecutor has an opportunity to evaluate the federal case, staying with it if a win looks likely or aborting it if not.

2. In *Hicks,* the practical effect of commencement of the prosecution six weeks after Miranda filed his federal action was to cut off his right to proceed in federal court. In other circumstances, however, the Court has recognized "the old and well-established judicially-declared rule that state courts are completely without power to restrain federal-court proceedings in *in personam* actions * * * ." *Donovan v. City of Dallas,* 377 U.S. 408 (1964). The Court also noted that Congress has authorized federal restraint of state proceedings in the limited circumstances described by the Anti-Injunction Act, but observed that Congress has done nothing to alter the rule against state-issued injunctions. Does not the result in *Hicks* have the same effect as a state injunction against a federal action? Does *Hicks* overrule *Donovan* in that respect, at least by implication?

3. Justice Rehnquist strongly foreshadowed *Hicks* in his *Steffel* concurrence when he argued that a federal plaintiff seeking a declaratory judgment could not with impunity continue to violate the state statute. "[A]ny arrest prior to resolution of the federal action would constitute a pending prosecution and bar declaratory relief under the principles of Samuels." The Court only a year later adopted much of Justice Rehnquist's idea, though *Hicks* contains a major variation. Under Justice Rehnquist's formulation, the federal proceeding apparently would have to go to judgment in order to survive the commencement of a state proceeding; *Hicks* requires only that there

have been "proceedings of substance." Thus, what on first reading may have seemed a restrictive standard in *Hicks* may actually represent a compromise between Justice Rehnquist and other members of the *Hicks* majority. The ultimate paragraph of Justice White's Steffel concurrence (articulating that the federal action be "sufficiently far along") sounds much like the opinion he wrote for the Court in *Hicks*, supports that theory.

Justice Rehnquist's formulation leaves another question in its wake. He contemplates a plaintiff who, after filing his federal action, resumes his putatively illegal activity and then is prosecuted. Justice Rehnquist has little sympathy for such an individual and sounds almost as if he resents the impatience he sees in such a course of conduct. Steffel was threatened with prosecution and desisted in favor of filing a federal action, while his companion persisted and was arrested. Suppose Steffel had not resumed his activity during the pendency of the federal action, but that the Georgia police had later arrested him for his conduct before the warning and the arrest of his companion. In Justice Rehnquist's view, would the commencement of that state prosecution serve as a predicate for dismissal of the federal action on the authority of Younger and *Hicks*? Should it?

4. Does *Hicks* ultimately reduce or increase federal-state friction?

5. In the mid-1970's the Younger doctrine was expanding on two fronts. One, exemplified in *Hicks,* involves the temporal relationship of federal and state proceedings. All of the cases before *Hicks* involved federal actions begun after state proceedings. But, in *Hicks,* the Court, following several broad hints that it would do so, began to consider whether a later-commenced state proceeding could cut off a federal action. The other, initiated by Huffman v. Pursue, Ltd., the following case, concerns the *type* of state proceeding that qualifies for Younger deference.

Huffman v. Pursue, Ltd.

Supreme Court of the United States, 1975.
420 U.S. 592.

MR. JUSTICE REHNQUIST delivered the opinion of the Court.

This case requires that we decide whether our decision in Younger v. Harris bars a federal district court from intervening in a state civil proceeding such as this, when the proceeding is based on a state statute believed by the district court to be unconstitutional. * * * [W]e * * * conclude that in the circumstances presented here the principles of Younger are applicable even though the state proceeding is civil in nature.

I

Appellants are the sheriff and prosecuting attorney of Allen County, Ohio. This case arises from their efforts to close the Cinema I Theatre, in Lima, Ohio. Under the management of both its current tenant, appellee Pursue, Ltd., and appellee's predecessor, William Dakota, the Cinema I has specialized in the display of films which may fairly be characterized as pornographic, and which in numerous instances have been adjudged obscene after adversary hearings.

Appellants sought to invoke the Ohio public nuisance statute against appellee. [It] provides that a place which exhibits obscene films is a nuisance, [and] requires closure for up to a year of any place determined to be a nuisance. The statute also provides for preliminary injunctions pending final determination of status as a nuisance, for sale of all personal property used in conducting the nuisance, and for release from a closure order upon satisfaction of certain conditions (including a showing that the nuisance will not be reestablished).

Appellants instituted a nuisance proceeding in the Court of Common Pleas of Allen County against appellee's predecessor, William Dakota. During the course of the somewhat involved legal proceedings which followed, the Court of Common Pleas reviewed 16 movies which had been shown at the theater. The court rendered a judgment that Dakota had engaged in a course of conduct of displaying obscene movies at the Cinema I, and that the theater was therefore to be closed, "for any purpose for a period of one year unless sooner released by Order of [the] Court pursuant to defendant-owners fulfilling the requirements provided in Section 3767.04 of the Revised Code of Ohio." The judgment also provided for the seizure and sale of personal property used in the theater's operations.

Appellee, Pursue, Ltd., had succeeded to William Dakota's leasehold interest in the Cinema I prior to entry of the state-court judgment. Rather than appealing that judgment within the Ohio court system, it immediately filed suit in the United States District Court for the Northern District of Ohio. The complaint was based on 42 U.S.C. § 1983 and alleged that appellants' use of Ohio's nuisance statute constituted a deprivation of constitutional rights under the color of state law. It sought injunctive relief and a declaratory judgment that the statute was unconstitutional and unenforceable. * * * The District Court concluded that while the statute was not vague, it did constitute an overly broad prior restraint on First Amendment rights insofar as it permanently or temporarily prevented the showing of films which had not been adjudged obscene in prior adversary hearings. Fashioning its remedy to match the perceived constitutional defect, the court permanently enjoined the execution of that portion of the state court's judgment that closed the Cinema I to films which had not been adjudged obscene. The judgment and opinion of the District Court give no indication that it considered whether it should have stayed its hand in deference to the principles of federalism which find expression in *Younger v. Harris*.

On this appeal, appellants raise the *Younger* problem, as well as a variety of constitutional and statutory issues. We need consider only the applicability of *Younger*.

* * *

III

The seriousness of federal judicial interference with state civil functions has long been recognized by this Court. We have consistently required that when federal courts are confronted with requests for such relief, they should abide by standards of restraint that go well beyond those of private equity jurisprudence. For example, *Massachusetts State Grange v. Benton (1926)* involved an effort to enjoin the operation of a state daylight savings act. Writing for the Court, Mr. Justice Holmes cited *Fenner v. Boykin* and emphasized a rule that "should be very strictly observed," "that no injunction ought to issue against officers of a State clothed with authority to enforce the law in question, unless in a case reasonably free from doubt and when necessary to prevent great and irreparable injury."

Although Mr. Justice Holmes was confronted with a bill seeking an injunction against state executive officers, rather than against state judicial proceedings, we think that the relevant considerations of federalism are of no less weight in the latter setting. If anything, they counsel more heavily toward federal restraint, since interference with a state judicial proceeding prevents the state not only from effectuating its substantive policies, but also from continuing to perform the separate function of providing a forum competent to vindicate any constitutional objections interposed against those policies. Such interference also results in duplicative legal proceedings, and can readily be interpreted "as reflecting negatively upon the state courts' ability to enforce constitutional principles."

The component of *Younger* which rests upon the threat to our federal system is thus applicable to a civil proceeding such as this quite as much as it is to a criminal proceeding. *Younger* however, also rests upon the traditional reluctance of courts of equity, even within a unitary system, to interfere with a criminal prosecution. Strictly speaking, this element of *Younger* is not available to mandate federal restraint in civil cases. But whatever may be the weight attached to this factor in civil litigation involving private parties, we deal here with a state proceeding which in important respects is more akin to a criminal prosecution than are most civil cases. The State is a party to the Court of Common Pleas proceeding, and the proceeding is both in aid of and closely related to criminal statutes which prohibit the dissemination of obscene materials. Thus, an offense to the State's interest in the nuisance litigation is likely to be every bit as great as it would be were this a criminal proceeding. Similarly, while in this case the District Court's injunction has not directly disrupted Ohio's criminal justice system, it has disrupted that State's efforts to protect the very interests which underlie its criminal laws and to obtain compliance with precisely the standards which are embodied in its criminal laws.

IV

In spite of the critical similarities between a criminal prosecution and Ohio nuisance proceedings, appellee nonetheless urges that there is also a critical difference between the two which should cause us to limit *Younger* to criminal proceedings. This difference, says appellee, is that whereas a state-court criminal defendant may, after exhaustion of his state remedies, present his constitutional claims to the federal courts through habeas corpus, no analogous remedy is available to one, like appellee, whose constitutional rights may have been infringed in a state proceeding which cannot result in custodial detention or other criminal sanction.

theatre's arg.

A civil litigant may, of course, seek review in this Court of any federal claim properly asserted in and rejected by state courts. Moreover, where a final decision of a state court has sustained the validity of a state statute challenged on federal constitutional grounds, an appeal to this Court lies as a matter of right. Thus, appellee in this case was assured of eventual consideration of its claim by this Court. But quite apart from appellee's right to appeal had it remained in state court, we conclude that it should not be permitted the luxury of federal litigation of issues presented by ongoing state proceedings, a luxury which, as we have already explained, is quite costly in terms of the interests which *Younger* seeks to protect.

Take Note

Congress amended 28 U.S.C. § 1257 in 1988, entirely eliminating review by appeal in the Supreme Court except for a few kinds of cases that Congress has directed (28 U.S.C. § 2284) be tried by three-judge district courts. As a general matter, the Court now hears appellate cases only through the discretionary device of certiorari.

Appellee's argument, that because there may be no civil counterpart to federal habeas it should have contemporaneous access to a federal forum for its federal claim, apparently depends on the unarticulated major premise that every litigant who asserts a federal claim is entitled to have it decided on the merits by a federal, rather than a state, court. We need not consider the validity of this premise in order to reject the result which appellee seeks. Even assuming, *arguendo,* that litigants are entitled to a federal forum for the resolution of all federal issues, that entitlement is most appropriately asserted by a state litigant when he seeks to relitigate a federal issue adversely determined in completed state court proceedings. We do not understand why the federal forum must be available prior to completion of the state proceedings in which the federal issue arises, and the considerations canvassed in *Younger* militate against such a result.

The issue of whether federal courts should be able to interfere with ongoing state proceedings is quite distinct and separate from the issue of whether litigants are entitled to subsequent federal review of state-court dispositions of federal questions. *Younger* turned on considerations of comity and federalism peculiar to the fact that state proceedings were pending; it did not turn on the fact that in any event a criminal defendant could eventually have obtained federal habeas consideration of his federal claims. The propriety of federal-court interference with an Ohio nuisance proceeding must likewise be controlled by application of those same considerations of comity and federalism.

* * *

V

Appellee contends that even if *Younger* is applicable to civil proceedings of this sort, it nonetheless does not govern this case because at the time the District Court acted there was no longer a "pending state court proceeding" as that term is used in *Younger. Younger* and subsequent cases such as *Steffel* have used the term "pending proceeding" to distinguish state proceedings which have already commenced from those which are merely incipient or threatened. Here, of course, the state proceeding had begun long before appellee sought intervention by the District Court. But appellee's point, we take it, is not that the state proceeding had not begun, but that it had ended by the time its District Court complaint was filed.

Appellee apparently relies on the facts that the Allen County Court of Common Pleas had already issued its judgment and permanent injunction when this action was filed, and that no appeal from that judgment has ever been taken to Ohio's appellate courts. As a matter of state procedure, the judgment presumably became final, in the sense of being nonappealable, at some point after the District Court filing, possibly prior to entry of the District Court's own judgment, but surely after the single judge stayed the state court's judgment. We need not, however, engage in such inquiry. For regardless of when the Court of Common Pleas' judgment became final, we believe that a necessary concomitant of *Younger* is that a party in appellee's posture must exhaust his state appellate remedies before seeking relief in the District Court, unless he can bring himself within one of the exceptions specified in Younger.

> **Food for Thought**
>
> If respondents had appealed through the Ohio Supreme Court and lost, how could they have gotten into the federal district court? The inferior federal courts cannot sit in review of state court judgments, pursuant to the *Rooker-Feldman* doctrine, which Chapter 10 discusses.

Virtually all of the evils at which Younger is directed would inhere in federal intervention prior to completion of state appellate proceedings, just as surely as they would if such intervention occurred at or before trial. Intervention at the later stage is if anything more highly duplicative, since an entire trial has already taken place, and it is also a direct aspersion on the capabilities and good faith of state appellate courts. Nor, in these state-initiated nuisance proceedings, is federal intervention at the appellate stage any the less a disruption of the State's efforts to protect interests which it deems important. Indeed, it is likely to be even more disruptive and offensive because the State has already won a *nisi prius* determination that its valid policies are being violated in a fashion which justifies judicial abatement.

Federal post-trial intervention, in a fashion designed to annul the results of a state trial, also deprives the States of a function which quite legitimately is left to them, that of overseeing trial court dispositions of constitutional issues which arise in civil litigation over which they have jurisdiction. We think this consideration to be of some importance because it is typically a judicial system's appellate courts which are by their nature a litigant's most appropriate forum for the resolution of constitutional contentions. Especially is this true when, as here, the constitutional issue involves a statute which is capable of judicial narrowing. In short, we do not believe that a State's judicial system would be fairly accorded the opportunity to resolve federal issues arising in its courts if a federal district court were permitted to substitute itself for the State's appellate courts. We therefore hold that Younger standards must be met to justify federal intervention in a state judicial proceeding as to which a losing litigant has not exhausted his state appellate remedies.[21]

---

21 By requiring exhaustion of state appellate remedies for the purposes of applying Younger we in no way undermine Monroe v. Pape. There we held that one seeking redress under 42 U.S.C. § 1983 for a deprivation of federal rights need not first initiate state proceedings based on related state causes of action. Monroe v. Pape had nothing to do with the problem presently before us, that of the deference to be accorded state proceedings which have already been initiated and which afford a competent tribunal for the resolution of federal issues. Our exhaustion requirement is likewise not inconsistent with * * * cases * * * [that] expressed the doctrine that a federal equity plaintiff challenging state administrative action need not have exhausted his state judicial remedies. Those cases did not deal with situations in which the state judicial process had been initiated.

* * *

The District Court should not have entertained this action, seeking pre-appeal interference with a state judicial proceeding, unless appellee established that early intervention was justified under one of the exceptions recognized in Younger.[22]

VI

* * *

We therefore think that this case is appropriate for remand so that the District Court may consider whether irreparable injury can be shown * * * and if so, whether that injury is of such a nature that the District Court may assume jurisdiction under an exception to the policy against federal judicial interference with state court proceedings of this kind. The judgment of the District Court is vacated and the cause is remanded for further proceedings consistent with this opinion.

It is so ordered.

MR. JUSTICE BRENNAN, with whom MR. JUSTICE DOUGLAS and MR. JUSTICE MARSHALL join, dissenting.

I dissent. The treatment of the state civil proceeding as one "in aid of and closely related to criminal statutes" is obviously only the first step toward extending to state civil proceedings generally the holding of Younger v. Harris that federal courts should not interfere with pending state criminal proceedings except under extraordinary circumstances. Similarly, today's holding that the plaintiff in an action under 42 U.S.C. § 1983 may not maintain it without first exhausting state appellate procedures for review of an adverse state trial court decision is but an obvious first step toward discard of heretofore settled law that such actions may be maintained without first exhausting state judicial remedies.

Food for Thought

In a footnote, Justice Brennan pointed out that the appellants had not raised Younger abstention in the district court and notes that the Court had previously treated Younger abstention as waivable. What are the implications of the Court's reaching the issue here?

* * *

22 While appellee had the option to appeal in state courts at the time it filed this action, we do not know for certain whether such remedy remained available at the time the District Court issued its permanent injunction, or whether it remains available now. In any event, appellee may not avoid the standards of Younger by simply failing to comply with the procedures of perfecting its appeal within the Ohio judicial system.

[T]oday's extension of Younger v. Harris turns the clock back and portends once again the resuscitation of the literal command of the 1793 Anti-Injunction Act—that the state courts should be free from interference by federal injunction even in civil cases. This not only would overrule some 18 decades of this Court's jurisprudence but would heedlessly flout Congress' evident purpose in enacting the 1948 amendment to acquiesce in that jurisprudence.

The extension also threatens serious prejudice to the potential federal-court plaintiff not present when the pending state proceeding is a criminal prosecution. That prosecution does not come into existence until completion of steps designed to safeguard him against spurious prosecution—arrest, charge, information, or indictment. In contrast, the civil proceeding, as in this case, comes into existence merely upon the filing of a complaint, whether or not well founded. To deny by fiat of this Court the potential federal plaintiff a federal forum in that circumstance is obviously to arm his adversary (here the public authorities) with an easily wielded weapon to strip him of a forum and a remedy that federal statutes were enacted to assure him. The Court does not escape this consequence by characterizing the state civil proceeding involved here as "in aid of and closely related to criminal statutes." The nuisance action was brought into being by the mere filing of the complaint in state court, and the untoward consequences for the federal plaintiff were thereby set in train without regard to the connection, if any, of the proceeding to the State's criminal laws.

Even if the extension of Younger v. Harris to pending state civil proceedings can be appropriate in any case, and I do not think it can be, it is plainly improper in the case of an action by a federal plaintiff, as in this case, grounded upon 42 U.S.C. § 1983. That statute serves a particular congressional objective long recognized and enforced by the Court. Today's extension will defeat that objective. * * *

Consistently with this congressional objective of the 1871 and 1875 Acts we held in Monroe v. Pape that a federal plaintiff suing under § 1983 need not exhaust state administrative or judicial remedies before filing his action under § 1983 in federal district court. * * * The extension today of Younger v. Harris to require exhaustion in an action under § 1983 drastically undercuts Monroe v. Pape and its numerous progeny—the mere filing of a complaint against a potential § 1983 litigant forces him to exhaust state remedies.

Mitchum v. Foster, holding that actions under § 1983 are excepted from the operation of the federal anti-injunction statute is also undercut by today's extension of Younger. Mitchum canvassed the history of § 1983 and concluded that it extended "federal power in an attempt to remedy the state courts' failure to secure federal rights." Mitchum prompted the comment that if Younger v. Harris were extended to civil cases, "much of the rigidity of section 2283 would be reintroduced, the significance of Mitchum for those seeking relief from state civil proceedings would largely be destroyed, and the recognition of section 1983 as an exception to the Anti-Injunction Statute would have been a Pyrrhic victory." Today's decision fulfills that gloomy prophecy. I therefore dissent from the remand and would reach the merits.

Notes and Questions

1. How does *Huffman* extend the Younger doctrine? Is the extension substantial or modest? How many cases will it affect?

2. In light of its discussion of the federalism interests Younger abstention serves (and note that comity seems to be subsumed as a particular sort of federalism interest), why does the majority feel it necessary to emphasize how closely the state proceedings in *Huffman* are allied to criminal proceedings? Is there anything about criminal proceedings that places them, arguably, in a different light for Younger purposes than ordinary civil proceedings to which the state is a party?

3. Appellee Pursue lost the nuisance action in the Court of Common Pleas. The state court ordered the theater closed for one year and seizure and sale of certain personal property used in the theater's operation. Pursue then began the federal litigation. Because the state action was over, Pursue argued there was no pending state proceeding, as Younger abstention requires. Pursue sought a declaratory judgment that the Ohio nuisance statute was unconstitutional and an injunction against its enforcement. What role was Pursue asking the federal court to play? What is wrong with that? Is Pursue's choice of the federal forum reminiscent of the union's return to federal court in *Atlantic Coast Line R.R. Co. v. Brotherhood of Locomotive Engineers* (page 784) after the state trial judge refused the union's request to dissolve the injunction prohibiting picketing?

4. Justice Brennan's dissent raises some substantial questions about the effect of Younger abstention generally, but also poses some problems about his own positions.

a) Primarily, as he points out, *Mitchum v. Foster* seems to have been overruled as a practical matter. Though the Court may not have reversed its view of § 1983 as an exception to the Anti-Injunction Act, after Younger's extension to civil matters, of what use is Mitchum to a litigant who wishes a federal court to enjoin a state court proceeding?

b) Justice Brennan may, however, make a bit too much out of *Huffman's* effect on Monroe v. Pape. There may be many cases in which a potential plaintiff has a choice of remedies—traditional state tort remedies, for example, or an action under § 1983. Where the injured individual would be the plaintiff either in state or federal court, *Huffman* in no sense diminishes his prospect of securing a federal forum. On the other hand, where the prospective federal plaintiff is the defendant in the state court, *Huffman* seems to prevent him from pursuing his federal claim in federal court. Bear in mind, however, that while Mitchum dealt with forum-selection, Monroe is concerned directly with the existence *vel non* of a cause of action under § 1983, not with the court in which the plaintiff may sue. A prospective § 1983 plaintiff who is the defendant in a state court proceeding (civil or criminal) may still file a § 1983 claim in a state proceeding. That result is at least consistent with Monroe.

c) The Justice argues that deference to state criminal proceedings may be justified because the procedural protections afforded the defendant in a criminal action are greater than those in a civil proceeding. Of course, part of the reason for that is that the penalties in a criminal proceeding are so much greater. Yet Justice Brennan does not seem to consider that the lesser threat to the defendant in a civil proceeding may justify greater, not less, state autonomy in evaluating constitutional questions. In any event, why does the permissibility of Younger abstention depend on the existence or non-existence of pre-judicial protections for the state defendant?

d) Justice Brennan also argues that Younger abstention is never appropriate in civil proceedings, particularly when the federal plaintiff states a § 1983 claim. Does his rationale also suggest that he should oppose Younger abstention even with respect to criminal proceedings when the federal challenge relies upon § 1983 (as it virtually always does)? Justice Brennan concurred in Younger. Is his position there reconcilable with his dissent here?

5. The majority observes that the district court never considered Younger abstention, implying that the court was derelict. On the other hand, as Justice Brennan points out, Ohio did not raise the abstention issue until the case reached the Supreme Court. Does that suggest both that Younger abstention is, in some sense, an issue having to do with subject matter jurisdiction and that it cannot be waived through failure to raise it? Each suggestion raises problems.

a) If the doctrine is an aspect of subject matter jurisdiction, what of the fact that it is apparently at odds with the subject matter jurisdiction conferred by Congress? Clearly, there are other judge-made subject matter jurisdiction doctrines, most notably the well-pleaded complaint rule and the complete diversity rule, but those at least purport to be constructions of congressional intent in enacting (and recodifying) 28 U.S.C.A. §§ 1331, 1332. *Younger* abstention, by contrast, seems to be at war with two jurisdictional statutes (28 U.S.C.A. §§ 1331, 1343) and a statute creating a federal cause of action (42 U.S.C.A. § 1983) that the Court ruled was specifically designed to permit interference with state proceedings. *See Mitchum v. Foster,* 407 U.S. 225 (1972). Mitchum is discussed at pages 795-96 and 828-29. Does the Court's interpretation of Younger as quasi-jurisdictional substantially intensify the separation-of-powers problems that seem in any event to inhere in abstention doctrines?

b) Should the Court take the position, even implicitly, that Younger protection is not waivable? Suppose the state wants the federal issues litigated in federal court in order to have a federal *imprimatur* of constitutionality on a challenged statute. In some ways, Younger abstention operates similarly to a doctrine of personal jurisdiction, limiting the forums in which an non-consenting party can be forced to appear. Defendants who fail to raise defects in personal jurisdiction at the outset of the proceedings waive them. Should Younger abstention work similarly?

6. Could *Huffman* have controlled the result in Hicks v. Miranda? The Court cited *Huffman* in note 20 of Hicks. Should the Court have relied upon *Huffman* in order to avoid creating new doctrine in Hicks?

7. *Huffman* represents the modern Younger doctrine's first attempt to protect noncriminal pending state proceedings. The majority seems to recognize how great an extension is involved, because Justice Rehnquist refers to Younger and "its civil counterpart which we apply today," implicitly acknowledging that new doctrine has been created rather than old doctrine applied. The dissent's prediction of continuing expansion was to be borne out over the following fifteen years. Indeed, Professors Soifer and Macgill have referred to *Huffman* as "Our Federalism's great leap forward."

For More Information

See Aviam Soifer & H.C. Macgill, *The* Younger *Doctrine: Reconstructing Reconstruction,* 55 TEX. L. REV. 1141, 1173 (1977).

a) *Trainor v. Hernandez,* 431 U.S. 434 (1977) (also discussed at pages 832-34), held that Younger principles apply with respect to any state judicial proceeding to which the state is a party. A state civil fraud proceeding sought to recover benefits allegedly wrongfully paid. The Illinois courts issued an attachment order directed at some of the respondents' assets, and the respondents commenced a federal action challenging the constitutionality of the attachment statute. In overturning the district court's grant of relief, the Supreme Court drew upon *Huffman* and made clear that any enforcement proceeding brought by the state qualifies for Younger abstention, irrespective of any formal linkage with criminal statutes.

b) *Juidice v. Vail,* 430 U.S. 327 (1977), extended Younger to a case not involving the state as a party in its sovereign capacity seeking to vindicate important state interests. Judgment creditors obtained contempt citations against their judgment debtors. The debtors brought a federal action arguing that the state's contempt proceedings violated their due process rights. Although the case involved only private parties, the Court held that the state's special interest in the integrity of its judicial proceedings, particularly with respect to contempt, compelled Younger abstention.

c) *Moore v. Sims*, 442 U.S. 415 (1979), extended Younger to another purely civil proceeding. Texas authorities seized the Sims children on suspicion that the parents were abusive. The parents brought a federal action challenging the Texas procedures, including an allegation that it was not possible for them to obtain a prompt hearing in the state proceedings to recover their children. The district court specifically found that the Texas procedure provided no single forum for timely adjudication of the parents' constitutional claims—that is, that there was no adequate remedy at law. A five-to-four majority reversed. Justice Rehnquist noted that Younger abstention was clearly applicable to any civil case in which substantial state interests were involved and further stated that "abstention is appropriate unless state law clearly bars the interposition of the constitutional claim." *Moore*'s tangled procedural history demonstrates how difficult it will be to demonstrate that state remedies are inadequate.

> **For More Information**
>
> The procedural history of the case appears in Sims v. State Department of Public Welfare, 438 F.Supp. 1179, 1183-85 (S.D.Tex. 1977), *rev'd sub nom. Moore v. Sims*, 442 U.S. 415 (1979) (footnotes omitted). Note that it consumes nearly two full pages in Federal Supplement.

The dissenting Justices argued that the proceedings in the Texas state courts demonstrated that there was no adequate remedy at law. Some commentators have not been kind to the Court either.

> The Court does not suggest that the course of action pursued by the plaintiffs in seeking return of their children was unreasonable, but only that it indicated insufficient diligence. It is not clear why the many apparently reasonable actions taken by plaintiffs fail to evidence diligent pursuit of state court opportunities, nor is it clear why the Court would have found the question of adequacy "closer" had plaintiffs taken further steps which were likely to be equally inefficacious. Moreover, the Court explains away the delay, confusion, and irregularities in the state's actions as "the predictable byproduct of a new statutory scheme." The Court, however, does not afford the plaintiffs the same consideration when evaluating their actions which were taken pursuant to the same "new statutory scheme."
>
> By holding that state remedies in *Sims* were adequate to vindicate the plaintiffs' claims, the Court actually may be modifying the adequacy standard. Henceforth, the mere theoretical existence of a state remedy may bar federal relief, no matter how impractical or inadequate such a remedy would be in practice. As Justice Stevens noted in his dissent in *Trainor v. Hernandez*: "Thirty years ago Mr. Justice Rutledge characterized a series of Illinois procedures which effectively foreclosed consideration of the merits of federal constitutional claims as a 'procedural laby-

> rinth * * * made up entirely of blind alleys.' *Marino v. Ragan*, 332 U.S. 561, 567." Texas parents could appropriately apply that characteristic to the state remedies which the Court certifies as adequate in *Moore v. Sims*.

Note, Moore v. Sims: *A Further Expansion of the* Younger *Abstention Doctrine*, 1 PACE L.REV. 149, 177-78 (1980).

d) The Court has also extended Younger to state administrative proceedings, noting in *Ohio Civil Rights Commission v. Dayton Christian Schools, Inc.*, 477 U.S. 619 (1986), that past cases suggested that administrative proceedings "judicial in nature" and in which the federal plaintiff "would have a full and fair opportunity to litigate his constitutional claim" qualified for Younger abstention. The Justices thus rebuffed Dayton Christian's claim of First Amendment exemption from the state administrative proceeding investigating a claim of sex discrimination filed against Dayton Christian by a former employee. In the course of its opinion, however, the Court subtly shifted the nature of the balance with which Younger abstention deals. In prior cases, the focus was on the state's interest in not having its process interrupted by intrusive federal adjudication. In *Dayton Christian*, on the other hand, then-Justice Rehnquist found "that the elimination of prohibited sex discrimination is a sufficiently important state interest to bring the present case within the ambit * * * " of prior *Younger* decisions. Parallel reasoning in Younger itself would have had the Court discussing not California's interest in having its criminal process go forward without federal interruption, but rather California's substantive interest in avoiding criminal syndicalism. Similarly, in *Steffel v. Thompson*, the Court would not have focused on the absence of a pending state proceeding with respect to Steffel, but would instead have examined Georgia's interest in combating criminal trespass. Is the shift in emphasis desirable? Does it make abstention more or less likely in the general case?

Middlesex County Ethics Committee v. Garden State Bar Assn., 457 U.S. 423 (1982), which Justice Rehnquist cited in *Dayton Christian*, involved an attorney brought up on disciplinary charges of conduct "prejudicial to the administration of justice" after publicly criticizing a state judge. The attorney filed a federal action attacking the constitutionality of both the regulations under which he was being prosecuted and the proceedings of the Ethics Committee itself. The Court affirmed the district court's decision to abstain. Yet Middlesex is not as broad as Dayton Christian; the Court emphasized the intimate connection between attorney disciplinary proceedings and the functioning of the state court system. As Dean Chemerinsky notes,

> [B]y itself, the *Middlesex County* decision might be viewed as a narrow expansion of *Younger* abstention principles because bar disciplinary proceedings are a part of the state judicial system. A distinction might be drawn between administrative matters that are handled pursuant to authority delegated by the state judiciary and those that are pending in other state agencies. *Younger* abstention, based on deference to the state judiciary, would be applied to the former, which is a part of the court system, but not the latter.

ERWIN CHEMERINSKY, FEDERAL JURISDICTION § 13.3.4, at 852 (5th ed. 2007). *Dayton Christian* clearly signals the rejection of the proposed distinction.

Note on Other Developments in Younger Abstention

a) *Dayton Christian* and the cases upon which it relied took the *Younger* doctrine out of the area of strictly judicial proceedings. Yet the Court's exploration of the doctrine's applicability to non-judicial matters did not begin with the administrative agency cases. Two cases in the mid-1970's suggested that *Younger* abstention might be appropriate with respect to executive actions.

In *O'Shea v. Littleton*, 414 U.S. 488 (1974), a coalition of individuals in Cairo, Illinois, brought a civil rights action against the county attorney, his investigator, the local magistrate and the local circuit judge, alleging that their administration of the criminal laws in Cairo was discriminatory against black citizens and was designed to curtail or burden their exercise of First Amendment rights. The Court invoked *Younger* abstention, noting in part that "recognition of the need for a proper balance in the concurrent operation of federal and state courts counsels restraint against the issuance of injunctions against state officers engaged in the administration of the State's criminal laws." Similarly, in *Rizzo v. Goode*, 423 U.S. 362 (1976), *see supra* at page 597, individuals and community groups charged that Philadelphia police systematically deprived blacks of their constitutional rights and that the department, through labyrinthine and unresponsive civilian complaint processes, deliberately refused to take appropriate disciplinary action. The Court directed abstention, noting that the federalism values that *Younger* sought to protect were heavily implicated. Neither *O'Shea* nor *Rizzo*, however, has led to a more generalized application of *Younger* outside of adjudicative proceedings, where there is an on-going state proceeding in which the plaintiff can raise his constitutional claims.

b) The *Younger* doctrine's expansion in the judicial context was not quite complete with the decision in *Dayton Christian*. *Pennzoil Company v. Texaco, Inc.*, 481 U.S. 1 (1987), applied *Younger* for the first time to a controversy entirely between private parties not involving the state's contempt power. The case is well-known because of its size; Pennzoil won a verdict in the Texas state courts against Texaco for the latter's tortious interference with a contract for the purchase of stock by Pennzoil from Getty Oil. The original verdict exceeded ten billion dollars, and accumulated prejudgment interest brought the figure to nearly thirteen billion. Under Texas law, the losing party was required to post a bond for the amount of the judgment in order to have execution of the judgment stayed pending appeal. Texaco sued in the United States District Court for the Southern District of New

York, seeking an injunction preventing Pennzoil from taking any steps to enforce the judgment, claiming that the Texas procedures for securing a stay of execution pending appeal were unconstitutional because of the bond requirement. The lower courts granted relief, but the Supreme Court unanimously reversed.

The case generated a majority opinion and five concurrences. The majority found that Texaco had failed to establish that its constitutional objection to the Texas procedure could not be heard in the state courts, particularly because of Texas' "open courts" statute declaring the availability of Texas judicial procedure to every aggrieved litigant. The majority also found a significant state interest in the regular administration of its appellate judicial system without interference from the federal courts, despite Texas' express representation to the Court of Appeals that it had "no interest in the outcome of the state-court adjudication underlying this cause" other than its fair adjudication. Justices Brennan and Marshall argued that Younger abstention was, therefore, inappropriate. Justice Brennan found Texaco's Fourteenth Amendment claim without merit, a conclusion with which Justice Marshall concurred but would not have reached. Justice Marshall argued that although abstention was not appropriate, the federal courts had no jurisdiction because of the *Rooker-Feldman* doctrine (*see infra* Chapter 10) that prohibits inferior federal courts from sitting in appellate review of state courts. Justice Scalia took issue with Justice Marshall's application of the *Rooker-Feldman* doctrine; in Justice Scalia's view the federal courts were not being asked to answer any question presented to or decided by the state courts, making *Rooker-Feldman* inapplicable and Younger appropriate.

Justices Blackmun and Stevens, each writing a concurring opinion, agreed that state action was involved for purposes of Texaco's § 1983 action, on the theory that Pennzoil's invocation of Texas's judgment-enforcement power effectively made Pennzoil a state actor. Justice Blackmun, however, thought Younger abstention inappropriate because Texaco had no adequate remedy at law because of its inability to be heard in the Texas courts without posting the bond. He would have, however, ordered abstention under *Pullman* so that Texas could construe its statute in light of Texaco's due process argument. Justice Stevens, by contrast, found Texaco's due process argument without merit, arguing that nothing in Texas law prevented Texaco from appealing and that the company sought only to avoid untoward business effects that would arise either from allowing execution to begin or from posting a bond to stay execution. In either event, Justice Stevens noted, Texaco's appeal in the Texas courts could go forward unhindered. For him, the true constitutional question presented by the case was whether Texas was constitutionally required to stay execution pending appeal, and that idea he rejected.

The five-member majority's reliance on Younger for the result in *Pennzoil* seemed to extend the doctrine to its greatest possible scope. *Pennzoil* is the first case in which the Court applied Younger to litigation between private parties where there was no particular state enforcement interest, such as with the contempt proceeding in *Juidice v. Vail*. Scholars wondered whether Younger had, in effect, become illimitable when there was any pending state proceeding of any sort. *See, e.g.*, Timothy Kin Lee Hui, Note, *The Ultimate Expansion of the* Younger *Doctrine*: Pennzoil Co. v. Texaco, Inc., 41 SW.L.J. 1055 (1987); Howard B. Stravitz, Younger *Abstention Reaches a Civil Maturity*, 57 FORDHAM L. REV. 997 (1989). As the New Orleans Public Service case was to show, however, reports of the death of federal litigation were somewhat exaggerated.

c) In the early 1970's, New Orleans Public Service, Inc. (NOPSI), a local power company, entered into a plan to construct a nuclear power facility in two parts. As a result of lower-than-expected consumer demand and great cost over-runs, the second part of the project was eventually abandoned, leaving behind the question of who was to pay for the first part. Although the Federal Energy Regulatory Commission (FERC) allocates costs and sets rates to be paid by members of "power pools" involved in such projects, local bodies (in this case the New Orleans City Council) have authority with respect to what part of allocated costs may be passed on to consumers and what part must be absorbed by company shareholders.

NOPSI disputed the Council's limited authorization for passing on the project costs. NOPSI sought an additional rate increase, which the Council denied. Thereafter the Council initiated an investigation into the "prudence" of NOPSI's participation in the project. Finally, the Council completed its prudence review and required the company to absorb approximately $135 million of the costs allocated by FERC. NOPSI, having unsuccessfully sought to challenge the Council's action on two previous occasions in federal court, returned to it, arguing there that an earlier Supreme Court decision pre-empted a state inquiry into the prudence of a utility's decision to participate in such a project. Anticipating the possibility of abstention, NOPSI also petitioned a Louisiana court for review of the Council's rate order and also informed the state court of NOPSI's intention to raise its federal pre-emption claim if the federal court again abstained. The district court abstained, and the Fifth Circuit affirmed.

The Supreme Court reversed. *New Orleans Public Service, Inc. v. Council of City of New Orleans*, 491 U.S. 350 (1989). Although it declined NOPSI's request to rule that Younger abstention is inappropriate when the underlying federal question is pre-emption, Justice Scalia's opinion for the Court held, nonetheless, that the pending Louisiana court action did not implicate Younger abstention. "[I]t has never been suggested that Younger requires abstention in deference to a state judicial proceeding reviewing legislative or executive action. Such a broad abstention requirement would make a mockery of the rule that only exceptional circumstances justify a federal court's refusal to decide a case in deference to the

States." The Council argued that the Louisiana action was a mere extension of the Council's own proceedings, and that the whole should be treated as a unitary proceeding much as trial and appellate proceedings otherwise are for Younger purposes. Again the Court balked:

> Respondents' case for abstention still requires, however, that the *Council proceeding* be the sort of proceeding entitled to Younger treatment. We think it is not. While we have expanded Younger beyond criminal proceedings, and even beyond proceedings in courts, we have never extended it to proceedings that are not "judicial in nature." * * * The Council's proceedings in the present case were not judicial in nature.

Canvassing cases dating back to 1908, Justice Scalia concluded that "the Council's proceedings here were plainly legislative" and did not compel or justify federal abstention. Justice Scalia divided the Louisiana proceedings, however, ruling that the legislative process had to come to an end to permit federal intervention. That, he argued, had happened when the Council issued its final order. The ensuing Louisiana judicial review was "not an extension of the legislative process," so "NOPSI's pre-emption claim was ripe for federal review when the Council's rate order was entered."

Perhaps the most significant part of Justice Scalia's opinion discusses abstention more generally.

> Before proceeding to the merits of the abstention issues, it bears emphasis that the Council does not dispute the District Court's jurisdiction to decide NOPSI's pre-emption claim. Our cases have long supported the proposition that federal courts lack the authority to abstain from the exercise of jurisdiction that has been conferred. For example: "We have no more right to decline the exercise of jurisdiction which is given, than to usurp that which is not given. The one or the other would be treason to the Constitution." * * * Underlying these assertions is the undisputed constitutional principle that Congress, and not the judiciary, defines the scope of federal jurisdiction within the constitutionally permissible bounds.
>
> That principle does not eliminate, however, and the categorical assertions based upon it do not call into question, the federal courts' discretion in determining whether to grant certain types of relief—a discretion that was part of the common-law background against which the statutes conferring jurisdiction were enacted. Thus, there are some classes of cases in which the withholding of authorized equitable relief because of undue interference with state proceedings is "the normal thing to do." We have carefully defined, however, the areas in which such "abstention" is permissible, and it remains " 'the exception, not the rule.' " As recently as last Term we described the federal courts' obligation to adjudicate claims within their jurisdiction as " 'virtually unflagging.' "

It seems fair to say that Justice Scalia is at least uncomfortable with abstention because of its separation-of-powers overtones and, although there were several concurring opinions, none directly challenged this part of the Court's opinion.

Notes and Questions

1. For those who thought Younger abstention a juggernaut, NOPSI must have been something of a shock. It is not hard to visualize the Court writing an opinion coming out the other way. Perhaps an even greater shock is the revelation of what apparently has begun to trouble the Court about its abstention jurisprudence: separation of powers.

Professor George Brown sees NOPSI as a collision between the twin themes of federalism and separation of powers and, indeed, sums up much of the basic conflict over abstention, federal common law, and federalism.

> Younger is different because serious questions of authority and legitimacy are present. The federal plaintiff comes to the district court armed with a federal cause of action—section 1983 plus an underlying provision of federal law, usually the Constitution—and a valid grant of jurisdiction authorizing the tribunal to hear the case. To send her packing, the Court interposes neither the Constitution nor statutory interpretation, but its own notions of comity and federalism. It seems to be flouting the will of Congress in an area over which Congress has clear authority: the jurisdiction of the federal courts. This step is surprising for a Court that often emphasizes the authority of Congress over federal jurisdiction and is generally deferential to the legislative branch.
>
> Younger abstention can thus be viewed solely as a separation of powers issue. It is a separation of powers problem in the literal sense that the Court is making law regarding federal jurisdiction that seems at odds with congressional statutes on the subject. It is also a separation of powers problem in a broader, structural sense. Even if specific legislative language does not resolve all jurisdictional questions, for the Court to develop a body of jurisdictional law is to exceed the judiciary's constitutional bounds and trespass on the legislature's domain. If either of these forms of the critique is valid, the logic of the Court's general position of deference to Congress would require the federalism-based, judge-made doctrine of Younger to yield. The critique emerges not as another argument but as an end to an argument.
>
> So far the Court has largely dealt with the separation of powers problem by ignoring it. The Younger cases say little about the source of the Court's authority to renounce jurisdiction based on notions of comity and federalism. How to reconcile this renunciation with federal statutory law is discussed even less. Recent abstention cases suggest, however, that the Court is aware of the separation of pow-

ers problem and deeply troubled by it. The Court increasingly has invoked the "virtually unflagging obligation" of the federal courts to exercise the jurisdiction conferred upon them. In *New Orleans Public Service Inc. (NOPSI) v. City Council*, the Court went so far as to state that "[o]ur cases have long supported the proposition that federal courts lack the authority to abstain from the exercise of the jurisdiction that has been conferred." It then reversed a lower court's plausible application of *Younger* to state administrative proceedings. *Younger* is anything but dead, as the 1987 decision in *Pennzoil Co. v. Texaco*, shows; but the notion of a "virtually unflagging obligation" of a federal court to exercise the jurisdiction granted cuts against the doctrine.

George D. Brown, *When Federalism and Separation of Powers Collide—Rethinking* Younger *Abstention*, 59 GEO.WASH.L.REV. 114, 116-17 (1990) (footnotes omitted).

2. Having expressed separation-of-powers reservations about abstention, the Court was unwilling completely to abandon it. The Court attempted to deal with the separation-of-powers problem by recharacterizing abstention not as a refusal to exercise jurisdiction conferred by Congress but rather as a paradigmatically judicial selection of appropriate remedies. Is that persuasive?

3. Justice Scalia notes that *Younger* abstention has "never" been applied to non-judicial proceedings. Is that statement reconcilable with *O'Shea* and *Rizzo*, or is it an acknowledgement of the Court's repudiation or at least abandonment of its dictum in *Rizzo*? Are *Rizzo* and *O'Shea* on the same footing with respect to *Younger* abstention?

4. Justice Scalia's emphatic assertion of the exceptional nature of the abstention doctrines may be difficult to accept at face value, given particularly the *Younger* doctrine's dramatic expansion after 1971. On the other hand, perhaps *NOPSI* foretells a reversal of the Court's recent approach to abstention and a re-evaluation of the balance between separation of powers and federalism. To the extent that Professor Brown is correct, does the Constitution resolve the battle between federalism and separation of powers? If so, how? If not, then is the Court, despite the efforts of many of the Justices over the past several decades to avoid judicial policy-making, cast unavoidably in that role? On what basis should the Court decide how to resolve the conflict?

4. *Burford* and *Thibodaux* Abstention

Burford v. Sun Oil Co.

Supreme Court of the United States, 1943.
319 U.S. 315.

MR. JUSTICE BLACK delivered the opinion of the Court.

In this proceeding brought in a federal district court, the Sun Oil Co. attacked the validity of an order of the Texas Railroad Commission granting the petitioner Burford a permit to drill four wells on a small plot of land in the East Texas oil field. Jurisdiction of the federal court was invoked because of the diversity of citizenship of the parties, and because of the Companies' contention that the order denied them due process of law. * * *

Although a federal equity court does have jurisdiction of a particular proceeding, it may, in its sound discretion, whether its jurisdiction is invoked on the ground of diversity of citizenship or otherwise, "refuse to enforce or protect legal rights, the exercise of which may be prejudicial to the public interest"; for it "is in the public interest that federal courts of equity should exercise their discretionary power with proper regard for the rightful independence of state governments in carrying out their domestic policy." While many other questions are argued, we find it necessary to decide only one: Assuming that the federal district court had jurisdiction, should it, as a matter of sound equitable discretion, have declined to exercise that jurisdiction here?

The order under consideration is part of the general regulatory system devised for the conservation of oil and gas in Texas, an aspect of "as thorny a problem as has challenged the ingenuity and wisdom of legislatures." The East Texas field, in which the Burford tract is located, is one of the largest in the United States. It is approximately forty miles long and between five and nine miles wide, and over 26,000 wells have been drilled in it. Oil exists in the pores and crevices of rocks and sand and moves through these channels. A large area of this sort is called a pool or reservoir and the East Texas field is a giant pool. The chief forces causing oil to move are gas and water, and it is essential that the pressures be maintained at a level which will force the oil through wells to the surface. As the gas pressure is dissipated, it becomes necessary to put the well "on the pump" at great expense; and the sooner the gas from a field is exhausted, the more oil is irretrievably lost. Since the oil moves through the entire field, one operator can not only draw the oil from under his own surface area, but can also, if he is advantageously located, drain oil from the most distant parts of the reservoir. The practice of attempting to drain oil from under the surface holdings of others leads to offset wells and other wasteful practices; and this problem is increased by the fact that the surface rights are split up into many small tracts. There are approximately nine hundred operators in the East Texas field alone.

For these, and many other reasons based on geologic realities, each oil and gas field must be regulated as a unit for conservation purposes. The federal government, for the present at least, has chosen to leave the principal regulatory responsibility with the states, but does supplement state control. While there is no question of the constitutional power of the State to take appropriate action to protect the industry and protect the public interest, the State's attempts to control the flow of oil and at the same time protect the interest of the many operators have from time to time been entangled in geological-legal problems of novel nature.

Texas interests in this matter are more than that very large one of conserving gas and oil, two of our most important natural resources. It must also weigh the impact of the industry on the whole economy of the state and must consider its revenue, much of which is drawn from taxes on the industry and from mineral lands preserved for the benefit of its educational and eleemosynary institutions. To prevent "past, present, and imminent evils" in the production of natural gas, a statute was enacted "for the protection of public and private interests against such evils by prohibiting waste and compelling ratable production." The primary task of attempting adjustment of these diverse interests is delegated to the Railroad Commission which Texas has vested with "broad discretion" in administering the law.

The Commission, in cooperation with other oil producing states, has accepted State oil production quotas and has undertaken to translate the amount to be produced for the State as a whole into a specific amount for each field and for each well. These judgments are made with due regard for the factors of full utilization of the oil supply, market demand, and protection of the individual operators, as well as protection of the public interest. As an essential aspect of the control program, the State also regulates the spacing of wells. The legislature has disavowed a purpose of requiring that "the separately owned properties in any pool [should] be unitized under one management, control or ownership" and the Commission must thus work out the difficult spacing problem with due regard for whatever rights Texas recognizes in the separate owners to a share of the common reservoir. At the same time it must restrain waste, whether by excessive production or by the unwise dissipation of the gas and other geologic factors that cause the oil to flow.

Since 1919 the Commission has attempted to solve this problem by its Rule 37. The rule provides for certain minimum spacing between wells, but also allows exceptions where necessary "to prevent waste or to prevent the confiscation of property." The prevention of confiscation is based on the premises that, insofar as these privileges are compatible with the prevention of waste and the achievement of conservation, each surface owner should be permitted to withdraw the oil under his surface area, and that no one else can fairly be permitted to drain his oil away. Hence the Commission may protect his interest either by adjusting his amount of production upward, or by permitting him to drill additional wells. * * *

Additional wells may be required to prevent waste as has been noticed, where geologic circumstances require immediate drilling: "The term 'waste,' as used in oil and gas Rule 37, undoubtedly means the ultimate loss of oil. If a substantial amount of oil will be saved by the drilling of a well that otherwise would ultimately be lost, the permit to drill such well may be justified under one of the exceptions provided in Rule 37 to prevent waste."

The delusive simplicity with which these principles of exception to Rule 37 can be stated should not obscure the actual nonlegal complexities involved in their application. While the surface holder may, subject to qualifications noted, be entitled under current Texas law to the oil under his land, there can be no absolute certainty as to how much oil actually is present, and since the waste and confiscation problems are as a matter of physical necessity so closely interrelated, decision of one of the questions necessarily involves recognition of the other. The sheer quantity of exception cases makes their disposition of great public importance. It is estimated that over two-thirds of the wells in the East Texas field exist as exceptions to the rule, and since each exception may provoke a conflict among the interested parties, the volume of litigation arising from the administration of the rule is considerable. The instant case arises from just such an exception. It is not peculiar that the state should be represented here by its Attorney General, for cases like this, involving "confiscation," are not mere isolated disputes between private parties. Aside from the general principles which may evolve from these proceedings, the physical facts are such that an additional permit may affect pressure on a well miles away. The standards applied by the Commission in a given case necessarily affect the entire state conservation system. Of far more importance than any other private interest is the fact that the over-all plan of regulation, as well as each of its case by case manifestations, is of vital interest to the general public which must be assured that the speculative interests of individual tract owners will be put aside when necessary to prevent the irretrievable loss of oil in other parts of the field. The Commission in applying the statutory standards of course considers the Rule 37 cases as a part of the entire conservation program with implications to the whole economy of the state.

With full knowledge of the importance of the decisions of the Railroad Commission both to the State and to the oil operators, the Texas legislature has established a system of thorough judicial review by its own State courts. * * *

While the constitutional power of the Commission to enforce Rule 37 or to make exceptions to it is seldom seriously challenged, the validity of particular orders from the standpoint of statutory interpretation may present a serious problem, and a substantial number of such cases have been disposed of by the Texas courts which alone have the power to give definite answers to the questions of State law posed in these proceedings.

In describing the relation of the Texas court to the Commission no useful purpose will be served by attempting to label the court's position as legislative, or judicial—suffice it to say that the Texas courts are working partners with the Railroad Commission in the business of creating a regulatory system for the oil industry. The Commission is charged with principal responsibility for fact finding and for policy making and the courts expressly disclaim the administrative responsibility, but on the other hand, the orders of the Commission are tested for "reasonableness" by trial *de novo* before the court, and the Court may on occasion make a careful analysis of all the facts of the case in reversing a Commission order. The court has fully as much power as the Commission to determine particular cases, since after trial *de novo* it can either restrain the leaseholder from proceeding to drill, or, if the case is appropriate, can restrain the Commission from interfering with the leaseholder. The court may even formulate new standards for the Commission's administrative practice and suggest that the Commission adopt them. * * *

To prevent the confusion of multiple review of the same general issues, the legislature provided for concentration of all direct review of the Commission's orders in the State district courts of Travis County. The Texas courts have authoritatively declared the purpose of this restriction: "If an order of the commission, lawful on its face, can be collaterally attacked in the various courts and counties of the state on grounds such as those urged in the instant case, interminable confusion would result." To permit various state courts to pass upon the Commission's rules and orders,

> would lead to intolerable confusion. If all district courts of this state had jurisdiction of such matters, different courts of equal dignity might reach different and conflicting conclusions as to the same rule. Manifestly, the jurisdictional provision under discussion was incorporated in the act for the express purpose of avoiding such confusion.

Time and experience, say the Texas courts, have shown the wisdom of this rule. Concentration of judicial supervision of Railroad Commission orders permits the state courts, like the Railroad Commission itself, to acquire a specialized knowledge which is useful in shaping the policy of regulation of the ever-changing demands in this field. At the present time, less than ten per cent of these cases come before the federal district court.

The very "confusion" which the Texas legislature and Supreme Court feared might result from review by many state courts of the Railroad Commission's orders has resulted from the exercise of federal equity jurisdiction. As a practical matter, the federal courts can make small contribution to the well organized system of regulation and review which the Texas statutes provide. Texas courts can give fully as great relief, including temporary restraining orders, as the federal courts. Delay, misunderstanding of local law, and needless federal conflict with the State policy, are the inevitable product of this double system of review. The most striking example of misunderstanding has come where the federal court has flatly disagreed with the position later taken by a State court as to State law. In those cases, the federal court attributed a given meaning to the state statute which went to the heart of the control program. The Court of Civil Appeals disagreed, but before ultimate review could be had either in Texas or here, the legislature amended its statutes so that the cases became moot. Had the Texas Civil Appeals decision come first, it would have been unnecessary to make the changes which were made in an effort to stay within the limit thought by the Governor of Texas to have been set by the tone of the federal court's opinion. The Texas legislature later changed the law back to its original state, as clear an example of waste motion as can be imagined. The federal court has been called upon constantly to determine whether the Railroad Commission has acted within the scope of statutory authority, while the important constitutional issues have, as the federal court has repeatedly said, been fairly well settled from the beginning.

These federal court decisions on state law have created a constant task for the Texas Governor, the Texas legislature, and the Railroad Commission. The Governor of Texas, as has been noted above, felt called upon to forge his oil program in the light of the remotest inferences of federal court opinions. In one instance he thought it necessary to declare martial law. Special sessions of the legislature have been occupied with consideration of federal court decisions. Legislation passed under the circumstances of the strain and doubt created by these decisions was necessarily unsatisfactory. The Railroad Commission has had to adjust itself to the permutations of the law as seen by the federal courts. * * *

As has been noted the federal court cases have dealt primarily with the interpretation of state law, some of it state law fairly remote from oil and gas problems. The instant case raised a number of problems of no general significance on which a federal court can only try to ascertain state law. For example, we are asked to determine whether a previous Travis county district court decision makes this case *res adjudicata* and whether another case pending in Travis county deprived the Commission of jurisdiction to consider Burford's application. The existence of these problems throughout the oil regulatory field creates a further possibility of serious delay which can injure the conservation program, for under our decision in *Railroad Commission v. Pullman Co.*, it may be necessary to stay federal action pending authoritative determination of the difficult state questions.

The conflict between federal courts and Texas has lessened appreciably in recent years primarily as a result of the decisions in the *Rowan & Nichols* case. In those cases we assumed that the principal issue in the review of Railroad Commission orders was whether the Commission had confined itself within the boundaries of due process of law, and held that any special relief provided by state statutes must be pursued in a state court. It is now argued that under the decision of the Texas Supreme Court in *Railroad Commission v. Shell Oil Co.*, the courts, whether federal or state, are required to review the Commission's order not for constitutional validity, but for compliance with a standard of "reasonableness" under the state statute which, it is said, is different from the constitutional standard of due process.

The whole cycle of federal-state conflict cannot be permitted to begin again by acceptance of this view. Insofar as we have discretion to do so, we should leave these problems of Texas law to the State court where each may be handled as "one more item in a continuous series of adjustments."

These questions of regulation of the industry by the State administrative agency, whether involving gas or oil prorationing programs or Rule 37 cases, so clearly involves basic problems of Texas policy that equitable discretion should be exercised to give the Texas courts the first opportunity to consider them.

* * *

The state provides a unified method for the formation of policy and determination of cases by the Commission and by the state courts. The judicial review of the Commission's decisions in the state courts is expeditious and adequate. Conflicts in the interpretation of state law, dangerous to the success of state policies, are almost certain to result from the intervention of the lower federal courts. On the other hand, if the state procedure is followed from the Commission to the State Supreme Court, ultimate review of the federal questions is fully preserved here. Under such circumstances, a sound respect for the independence of state action requires the federal equity court to stay its hand.

The decision of the Circuit Court of Appeals is reversed and the judgment of the District Court dismissing the complaint is affirmed for the reasons here stated.

It is so ordered.

MR. JUSTICE FRANKFURTER, joined by MR. JUSTICE ROBERTS and MR. JUSTICE REED, dissenting. THE CHIEF JUSTICE expresses no views as to the desirability, as a matter of legislative policy, of retaining the diversity jurisdiction. In all other respects he concurs in the opinion * * * .

To deny a suitor access to a federal district court under the circumstances of this case is to disregard a duty enjoined by Congress and made manifest by the whole history of the jurisdiction of the United States courts based upon diversity of citizenship between parties. For I am assuming that law declared by this Court, in contradistinction to law declared by Congress, is something other than the manipulation of words to formulate a predetermined result. Judicial law to me implies at least some continuity of intellectual criteria and procedures in dealing with recurring problems.

I believe it to be wholly accurate to say that throughout our history it has never been questioned that a right created by state law and enforceable in the state courts can also be enforced in the federal courts where the parties to the controversy are citizens of different states. The reasons which led Congress to grant such jurisdiction to the federal courts are familiar. It was believed that, consciously or otherwise, the courts of a state may favor their own citizens. Bias against outsiders may become embedded in a judgment of a state court and yet not be sufficiently apparent to be made the basis of a federal claim. To avoid possible discriminations of this sort, so the theory goes, a citizen of a state other than that in which he is suing or being sued ought to be able to go into a wholly impartial tribunal, namely, the federal court sitting in that state. Thus, the basic premise of federal jurisdiction based upon diversity of the parties' citizenship is that the federal courts should afford remedies which are coextensive with rights created by state law and enforceable in state courts.

That is the theory of diversity jurisdiction. Whether it is a sound theory, whether diversity jurisdiction is necessary or desirable in order to avoid possible unfairness by state courts, state judges and juries, against outsiders, whether the federal courts ought to be relieved of the burden of diversity litigation,—these are matters which are not my concern as a judge. They are the concern of those whose business it is to legislate, not mine. I speak as one who has long favored the entire abolition of diversity jurisdiction. But I must decide this case as a judge and not as a legislative reformer.

Aside from the Johnson Act, the many powerful and persistent legislative efforts to abolish or restrict diversity jurisdiction have ever since the Civil War been rejected by Congress. Again and again legislation designed to make inroads upon diversity jurisdiction has been proposed to Congress, and on each occasion Congress has deliberately refused to act. * * * We are dealing, then, not with a jurisdiction evolved and shaped by the courts but rather with one explicitly conferred and undeviatingly maintained by Congress.

The only limitations upon the exercise of diversity jurisdiction—apart from that which Congress made in the Johnson Act—are, broadly speaking, those illustrated by *Railroad Comm. v. Rowan & Nichols Oil Co.* In *Rowan & Nichols* the claim based upon state law was derived from a statute requiring proration on a "reasonable basis," and it was not clear from the decisions of the state courts whether such courts might exercise an independent judgment as to what was "reasonable." And in *Pullman* it was also "far from clear" whether state law, as authoritatively defined by the local courts, might not displace the federal questions raised by the bill. Where the controlling state law is so undefined that a federal court attempting to apply such law would be groping utterly in the dark—where "no matter how seasoned the judgment of the district court may be, it cannot escape being a forecast rather than a determination"—a court of equity may "avoid the waste of a tentative decision." * * * Under such circumstances it [is] an affirmation and not a denial of federal jurisdiction * * * to hold the bill pending a seasonable determination of the local issues in a proceeding to be brought in the state courts.

If, in a case of this sort, the state right sought to be enforced in the federal courts depended upon a "forecast rather than a determination" of state law, if the federal court was practically impotent to enforce state law because of its inability to fathom the complexities, legal or factual, of local law, the rule of *Rowan & Nichols* would be applicable. In such a situation the line of demarcation between what belongs to the state administrative body and what to its courts should not be drawn by the federal courts. If it could be shown that the circumstances of this case warranted the application of such a doctrine of abstention, I would gladly join in the decision of the Court. But such a showing has not been attempted, nor, I believe, could it be made.

* * *

It is true that Texas law governing review of Commission orders under Rule 37 has not always been clear and certain, and that there may be parts of the statute and some of the Railroad Commission's Rules, with which we are not now concerned, which, like other legal materials, are not as clear as they might be. But, in a series of recent decisions, the Supreme Court of Texas has not only given precision to the concepts of "waste" and "confiscation of property" employed in Rule 37, it has also defined with clarity the scope of judicial review of Commission action. * * *

In other words, as the Circuit Court of Appeals has said in this case, "We now know the legal requisites of orders and regulations of the Railroad Commission under the conservation laws of Texas."

* * *

And so, the case really reduces itself to this: in the actual application of the standards governing judicial review of Commission orders allowing exceptions under Rule 37—standards which today have been authoritatively and precisely defined—a different result may be obtained if suit is brought in the federal rather than the state courts. And why? Because federal judges are less competent and less fair than state judges in applying the rules that are binding upon both? If this were true here, it would be equally true as applied to almost all types of litigation brought into federal courts to enforce state-created rights. The explanation may perhaps lie in the realm of what has sometimes been called "psychological jurisprudence." In the assessment of evidence and the other elements which enter into a judicial judgment, a federal judge may make judgments different from those which a state judge may make. Federal judges are perhaps to be regarded as men apart—judges who cannot be trusted to judge fairly and impartially. But if this be our premise, why should it not follow that the federal courts are, because of their putative bias, to be denied the right to hear insurance cases, or cases involving controversies between debtors and creditors, landlords and tenants, employers and employees, and all the other complicated controversies arising out of the local law of the forty-eight states?

It is the essence of diversity jurisdiction that federal judges and juries should pass on asserted claims because the result might be different if they were decided by a state court. There may be excellent reasons why Congress should abolish diversity jurisdiction. But, with all deference, it is not a defensible ground for having this Court by indirection abrogate diversity jurisdiction when, as a matter of fact, Congress has persistently refused to restrict such jurisdiction except in the limited area occupied by the Johnson Act. The Congressional premise of diversity jurisdiction is that the possibility of unfairness against outside litigants is to be avoided by providing the neutral forum of a federal court. The Court today is in effect withdrawing this grant of jurisdiction in order to avoid possible unfairness against state interests in the federal courts. That which Congress created to assure impartiality of adjudication is now destroyed to prevent what is deemed to be hostility and bias in adjudication.

Of course, the usual considerations governing the exercise of equity jurisdiction are equally applicable to suits in the federal courts where jurisdiction depends upon the diversity of the parties' citizenship. The chancellor certainly must balance the equities before granting relief; he should stay his hand where another court seized of the controversy can do justice to the claims of the parties; he may refuse equitable relief where the asserted right is doubtful because of the substantive law which he must find as declared by the state. But it is too late in the day to suggest that the chancellor may act on whimsical or purely personal considerations or on private notions of policy regarding the particular suit. It is not for us to say that litigation affecting state laws and state policies ought to be tried only in the state courts. Congress has chosen to confer diversity jurisdiction upon the federal courts. It is not for us to reject that which Congress has made the law of the land simply because of our independent conviction that such legislation is unwise.

* * *

The opinion of the Court cuts deep into our judicial fabric. The duty of the judiciary is to exercise the jurisdiction which Congress has conferred. What the Court is doing today I might wholeheartedly approve if it were done by Congress. But I cannot justify translation of the circumstance of my membership on this Court into an opportunity of writing my private view of legislative policy into law and thereby effacing a far greater area of diversity jurisdiction than Senator Norris, as chairman of the Senate Judiciary Committee, was ever able to persuade Congress itself to do.

Notes and Questions

1. A combination of several factors persuaded the Court to abstain in *Burford*. What are they? It seems unlikely that all of these factors will be present in very many cases, which suggests that *Burford* abstention should be rare. On the other hand, what is the danger in opening the abstention door in this way?

2. Did the decision to abstain in *Burford* avoid "needless friction with state policies"? Justice Frankfurter, of course, regards the majority as illegitimately creating needless friction with congressional policy. He was in the majority in *Douglas v. City of Jeanette* (1943), one of *Younger*'s principal forebears, and so presumably would have approved of *Younger* abstention.

3. Sun Oil Company's complaint invoked federal question jurisdiction as well as diversity jurisdiction. In deciding the case, does the Court assume that both grounds for jurisdiction exist? Would abstention be more or less justified in the absence of a substantial federal question? Why does Justice Frankfurter's dissent discuss the policies underlying diversity jurisdiction at length but make no mention of those supporting federal question jurisdiction?

4. Would abstention under *Pullman* or *Younger* have been appropriate?

5. In *Alabama Public Service Comm. v. Southern Railway Co.*, 341 U.S. 341 (1951), appeared to expand *Burford*. Southern Railway sued in federal court to enjoin the Alabama Public Service Commission and the Attorney General of Alabama from enforcing state laws prohibiting the discontinuance of railroad service. Southern had petitioned the Commission for permission to discontinue the service, but the Commission denied the application, concluding that there was a public need for continued service and that the railroad had not attempted to reduce its losses by using cheaper operating methods. Southern's complaint alleged both that requiring it to continue to operate

the trains at a financial loss constituted confiscation of property in contravention of the Due Process Clause of the Fourteenth Amendment and that there was diversity of citizenship. Alabama law allowed an appeal from any order of the Commission to the Circuit Court of Montgomery County and thereafter to the state supreme court.

The Court cited *Burford* and listed several factors in support of abstention. The case involved "the essentially local problem of balancing the loss to the railroad from continued operation of trains * * * with the public need for that service." In addition, Alabama had concentrated judicial review of Commission orders in the circuit court of Montgomery County, and appellate review of circuit court decisions was relatively broad. The Court concluded with a sweeping endorsement of abstention:

> As adequate state court review of an administrative order based upon predominantly local factors is available to appellee, intervention of a federal court is not necessary for protection of federal rights. Equitable relief may be granted only when the District Court * * * is convinced that the asserted federal right cannot be preserved except by granting the "extraordinary relief of an injunction in the federal courts."

Alabama Public Service bears only a superficial resemblance to *Burford*. Which of the factors present in *Burford* are missing?

6. In *McNeese v. Board of Education*, 373 U.S. 668 (1963), a group of African-American school children sued in an Illinois federal court alleging that officials at the school they attended segregated white and African-American students. Illinois law provided that residents of a school district, if they met certain conditions, could file a complaint with the Superintendent of Public Instruction alleging racial segregation. If, after a hearing, the Superintendent determined the allegations were true, he was to request the state Attorney General to bring suit. The state courts could review the Superintendent's final decision. The Supreme Court noted that there was "no underlying issue of state law controlling" in the case nor was "the federal right in any way entangled in a skein of state law that must be untangled before the federal court can proceed." Additionally, the Court concluded that it was not clear that the state administrative remedy was adequate to preclude the plaintiffs from seeking federal court relief before invoking it. Consequently, the majority rejected the dissent's call for *Burford* abstention.

Zablocki v. Redhail, 434 U.S. 374 (1978), was a class action in federal court challenging the constitutionally of a state statute requiring minors' non-custodial parents subject to support orders to obtain a court order allowing them to marry. The statute required that in order to obtain permission to marry, such parents had to demonstrate that they were complying with their support obligation and that their children were not nor were not likely thereafter to become public charges. The Court rejected *Burford* abstention, declaring that "unlike *Burford*" the case did not involve "complex issues of state law, resolution of which would be 'disruptive of state efforts to establish a coherent policy with respect to a matter of substantial public concern.' " After *McNeese* and *Zablocki*, most scholars concluded that *Alabama Public Service Commission* did not portend the broad expansion of the *Burford* doctrine that some of its language may have indicated.

7. Reread the discussion of *New Orleans Public Service, Inc., v. Council of City of New Orleans*, 491 U.S. 350 (1989), at pages 872-74. Was *Burford* abstention appropriate? The Supreme Court held that it was not. The plaintiff's primary claim was that federal law required the Council to reimburse for wholesale costs that had been allocated by the federal agency. The Court distinguished that claim from one "that a state agency had misapplied its lawful authority or has failed to take into consideration or properly weigh relevant state-law factors." Federal adjudication of the plaintiff's preemption claim would not "disrupt the State's attempt to ensure uniformity in the treatment of an 'essentially local problem.' " The Court refused to view *Burford* as requiring abstention in every case where a complex state administrative process exists or where there is potential for conflict with state regulatory policy.

Plaintiff's alternative claim was that the rate order's nominal basis was a pretext for the Council's determination that the original investment was unwise. The Court acknowledged that adjudication of the pretext claim would require "an inquiry into industry practice, wholesale rates, and power availability," but concluded that because "wholesale electricity is not bought and sold within a predominantly local market," federal adjudication would not disrupt state resolution of local policies. Does *New Orleans Public Service* make the scope of the *Burford* doctrine relatively clear?

8. In the same year as *Burford*, abstention issues arose in a diversity case involving no federal issues at all but where state law was unclear. The Court refused abstention, in an opinion by Chief Justice Stone. *Meredith v. City of Winter Haven*, 320 U.S. 228, 234-35 (1943).

> The diversity jurisdiction was not conferred for the benefit of the federal courts or to serve their convenience. Its purpose was generally to afford to suitors an opportunity in such cases, at their option, to assert their rights in the federal rather than in the state courts. In the absence of some recognized public policy or defined principle guiding the exercise of the jurisdiction conferred, which would in exceptional cases warrant its non-exercise, it has from the first been deemed to be the duty of the federal courts, if their jurisdiction is properly invoked, to decide questions of state law whenever necessary to the rendition of a judgment. When such exceptional circumstances are not present, denial of that opportunity by the federal courts merely because the answers to the questions of state law are difficult or uncertain or have not yet been given by the highest court of the state, would thwart the purpose of the jurisdictional act.
>
> The exceptions relate to the discretionary powers of courts of equity. An appeal to the equity jurisdiction conferred on federal district courts is an appeal to the sound discretion which guides the determinations of courts of equity. Exercise

> of that discretion by those, as well as by other courts having equity powers, may require them to withhold their relief in furtherance of a recognized, defined public policy.

The Chief Justice canvassed the justifications for abstention and concluded that none of them applied to pure diversity cases that merely presented difficult or unsettled questions of state law.

9. *Quackenbush v. Allstate Insurance Company*, 517 U.S. 706 (1996), raised the question of whether *Burford* abstention was appropriate in common-law damages actions. The Court's opinion subdivided abstention into dismissal-abstention and stay-abstention, and held that dismissal-abstention was not proper in cases seeking non-discretionary relief. However, the Court did allow that the district courts might stay adjudication of some such cases, particularly state litigation was already pending and they involved areas of intense state concern or thorny questions of state law. (This is similar to *Pullman* abstention, except that *Quackenbush* did not involve any federal constitutional question, as the *Pullman* cases do).

There are some interesting things about the opinion. First, the Court noted that the abstention doctrines were rooted in common law and the normal discretion of courts of equity, which connotes that they are not constitutionally compelled. Second, the opinion contained the following language: "Unlike the outright dismissal or remand of a federal suit, * * * an order merely staying the action 'does not constitute abnegation of judicial duty. On the contrary, it is a wise and productive discharge of it.' " This is a remarkable characterization, is it not? It seems to lend fuel to Professor Redish's argument (*supra* at 830) that the abstention doctrines generally violate separation of powers.

Quackenbush raises some problems, however. Suppose a plaintiff seeks both damages and injunctive relief. If the case meets the other criteria for this type of *Burford* abstention, what should the district court do? Under *Burford*, it apparently can dismiss the equitable part of the case, but *Quackenbush* appears to forbid that disposition of the damages portion. Should or can the district court bifurcate the case, or should the presence of the damages portion of the case cut strongly against *Burford* abstention for the equitable part?

Justice Frankfurter, who dissented in *Burford*, wrote for the Court in *Louisiana Power & Light Co. v. City of Thibodaux*, 360 U.S. 25 (1959), and found abstention warranted in a case challenging the City's use of eminent domain against petitioner's property. Petitioner removed on the basis of diversity and claimed that the City lacked the power of eminent domain. State law on the question was not clear. The district court stayed its proceeding ***sua sponte*** to give the state supreme court an opportunity to decide the issue, but the Court of Appeals vacated the stay . The Supreme Court reversed and reinstated the stay. The Court pointed to the special nature of eminent domain proceedings, intimately involved with "sovereign prerogative," asserting that "[t]he considerations that prevailed in conventional equity suits for avoiding the hazards of serious disruption by federal court of state government or needless friction between state and federal authorities are similarly appropriate in a state eminent domain proceeding brought in, or removed to, a federal court." The Court also noted the quandary that faced the district court given the uncertainty of state law. The Court distinguished *Meredith* as a declination of jurisdiction and dismissal, whereas the district court in *Thibodaux* had merely stayed its proceedings to obtain an authoritative ruling on the state law issue from the state court.

Why was the *Pullman* doctrine inapplicable in *Thibodaux*? Was the rationale for abstention in *Thibodaux* analogous to the rationale for abstention in *Burford*? Was Justice Frankfurter's opinion in *Thibodaux* inconsistent with his dissent in *Burford*?

The same day as *Thibodaux*, the Court rejected a district court's decision to abstain in a case involving a state's eminent domain power in *County of Allegheny v. Frank Mashuda Co.*, 360 U.S. 185 (1959). The County initiated eminent domain proceedings to appropriate plaintiffs' property. A state-court-appointed board assessed the damages owing to plaintiffs, and both sides appealed the board's damages assessment to the state court as provided by state law. The state court proceeding was pending. Plaintiffs then sued in federal court on the basis of diversity, alleging that after the County took possession of the property, it leased it to a private company for a private purpose. State law clearly prohibited taking private property under eminent domain for a private use. Plaintiffs therefore sought a judgment of ouster and damages against the County. The district court dismissed on the ground that federal court interference with state condemnation proceedings was inappropriate. The Supreme Court held that the case presented no exceptional circumstances justifying abstention, declaring "the fact that a case concerns a State's power of eminent domain no more justifies abstention than the fact that it involves any other issue related to sovereignty."

Of course, one distinction between *Thibodaux* and *Frank Mashuda* is that the state law was unclear in *Thibodaux* where the Court upheld abstention, but was clear in *Frank Mashuda*, where the Court rejected it. Was there another distinction between the two cases? Only two justices voted in the majority in both cases, Justices Stewart and Whittaker. Justice Stewart's concurring opinion in *Thibodaux* explains his votes by asserting that in *Frank Mashuda* the Court held it was error for the lower court to dismiss and because the state law was clear there was no reason for the court not to adjudicate the claim promptly. Justice Whittaker was silent. Thus, it is less than crystal clear when abstention under *Thibodaux* is appropriate. Do you think *Thibodaux* abstention is limited to eminent domain cases or are there other state interests sufficiently important to support it?

5. *Colorado River* Abstention

Colorado River Water Conservation District v. United States

Supreme Court of the United States, 1976.
424 U.S. 800.

MR. JUSTICE BRENNAN delivered the opinion of the Court.

The McCarran Amendment provides that "consent is hereby given to join the United States as a defendant in any suit (1) for the adjudication of rights to the use of water of a river system or other source, or (2) for the administration of such rights, where it appears that the United States is the owner of or is in the process of acquiring water rights by appropriation under State law, by purchase, by exchange, or otherwise, and the United States is a necessary party to such suit." The questions presented by this case concern the effect of the McCarran Amendment upon the jurisdiction of the federal district courts under 28 U.S.C. § 1345 over suits for determination of water rights brought by the United States as trustee for certain Indian tribes and as owner of various non-Indian Government claims.

I

It is probable that no problem of the Southwest section of the Nation is more critical than that of scarcity of water. As southwestern populations have grown, conflicting claims to this scarce resource have increased. To meet these claims, several Southwestern States have established elaborate procedures for allocation of water and adjudication of conflicting claims to that resource. In 1969, Colorado enacted its Water Rights Determination and Administration Act in an effort to revamp its legal procedures for determining claims to water within the State.

Under the Colorado Act, the State is divided into seven Water Divisions, each Division encompassing one or more entire drainage basins for the larger rivers in Colorado. Adjudication of water claims within each Division occurs on a continuous basis. Each month, Water Referees in each Division rule on applications for water rights filed within the preceding five months or refer those applications to the Water Judge of their Division. Every six months, the Water Judge passes on referred applications and contested decisions by Referees. A State Engineer and engineers for each Division are responsible for the administration and distribution of the waters of the State according to the determinations in each Division.

Colorado applies the doctrine of prior appropriation in establishing rights to the use of water. Under that doctrine, one acquires a right to water by diverting it from its natural source and applying it to some beneficial use. Continued beneficial use of the water is required in order to maintain the right. In periods of shortage, priority among confirmed rights is determined according to the date of initial diversion.

The reserved rights of the United States extend to Indian reservations and other federal lands, such as national parks and forests. The reserved rights claimed by the United States in this case affect waters within Colorado Water Division No. 7. On November 14, 1972, the Government instituted this suit in the United States District Court for the District of Colorado, invoking the court's jurisdiction under 28 U.S.C. § 1345. The District Court is located in Denver, some 300 miles from Division 7. The suit, against some 1,000 water users, sought declaration of the Government's rights to waters in certain rivers and their tributaries located in Division 7. In the suit, the Government asserted reserved rights on its own behalf and on behalf of certain Indian tribes, as well as rights based on state law. It sought appointment of a water master to administer any waters decreed to the United States. Prior to institution of this suit, the Government had pursued adjudication of non-Indian reserved rights and other water claims based on state law in Water Divisions 4, 5, and 6, and the Government continues to participate fully in those Divisions.

Shortly after the federal suit was commenced, one of the defendants in that suit filed an application in the state court for Division 7, seeking an order directing service of process on the United States in order to make it a party to proceedings in Division 7 for the purpose of adjudicating all of the Government's claims, both state and federal. On January 3, 1973, the United States was served pursuant to authority of the McCarran Amendment. Several defendants and intervenors in the federal proceeding then filed a motion in the District Court to dismiss on the ground that under the Amendment, the court was without jurisdiction to determine federal water rights. Without deciding the jurisdictional question, the District Court, on June 21, 1973, granted the motion in an unreported oral opinion stating that the doctrine of abstention required deference to the proceedings in Division 7. On appeal, the Court of Appeals for the Tenth Circuit reversed, holding that the suit of the United States was within district-court jurisdiction under 28 U.S.C. § 1345, and that abstention was inappropriate. We granted certiorari to consider the important questions of whether the McCarran Amendment terminated jurisdiction of federal courts to adjudicate federal water rights and whether, if that jurisdiction was not terminated, the District Court's dismissal in this case was nevertheless appropriate. We reverse.

II

We first consider the question of district-court jurisdiction under 28 U.S.C. § 1345. That section provides that the district courts shall have original jurisdiction over all civil actions brought by the Federal Government "[e]xcept as otherwise provided by Act of Congress." It is thus necessary to examine whether the McCarran Amendment is such an Act of Congress excepting jurisdiction under § 1345.

* * *

In view of the McCarran Amendment's language and legislative history, controlling principles of statutory construction require the conclusion that the Amendment did not constitute an exception "provided by Act of Congress" that repealed the jurisdiction of district courts under § 1345 to entertain federal water suits. * * * Accordingly, we hold that the McCarran Amendment in no way diminished federal-district-court jurisdiction under § 1345 and that the District Court had jurisdiction to hear this case.[15]

district ct. had jurisdiction

III

We turn next to the question whether this suit nevertheless was properly dismissed in view of the concurrent state proceedings in Division 7.

* * *

B

Next, we consider whether the District Court's dismissal was appropriate under the doctrine of abstention. We hold that the dismissal cannot be supported under that doctrine in any of its forms.

dismissal not ok under abstention

Abstention from the exercise of federal jurisdiction is the exception, not the rule.

> The doctrine of abstention, under which a District Court may decline to exercise or postpone the

Take Note!

Justice Brennan speaks as though there is but a single abstention doctrine, which presumably comes in several flavors: *Pullman*, *Younger*, *Burford* and *Thibodaux*. Conceptually, it may make them easier to understand to view them separately, because the criteria for invoking them differ substantially. On the other hand, all versions of abstention present essentially the same separation-of-powers questions.

15 The District Court also would have had jurisdiction of this suit under the general federal-question jurisdiction of 28 U.S.C. § 1331. * * * [T]he McCarran Amendment did not affect jurisdiction under § 1331 either.

> exercise of its jurisdiction, is an extraordinary and narrow exception to the duty of a District Court to adjudicate a controversy properly before it. Abdication of the obligation to decide cases can be justified under this doctrine only in the exceptional circumstances where the order to the parties to repair to the state court would clearly serve an important countervailing interest.

"[I]t was never a doctrine of equity that a federal court should exercise its judicial discretion to dismiss a suit merely because a State court could entertain it." Our decisions have confined the circumstances appropriate for abstention to three general categories.

(a) Abstention is appropriate "in cases presenting a federal constitutional issue which might be mooted or presented in a different posture by a state court determination of pertinent state law." This case, however, presents no federal constitutional issue for decision.

(b) Abstention is also appropriate where there have been presented difficult questions of state law bearing on policy problems of substantial public import whose importance transcends the result in the case then at bar. *Louisiana Power & Light Co. v. City of Thibodaux*, for example, involved such a question * * * concern[ing] the scope of the eminent domain power of municipalities under state law. * * * In some cases, however, the state question itself need not be determinative of state policy. It is enough that exercise of federal review of the question in a case and in similar cases would be disruptive of state efforts to establish a coherent policy with respect to a matter of substantial public concern. In *Burford v. Sun Oil Co.*, for example, the Court held that a suit seeking review of the reasonableness under Texas state law of a state commission's permit to drill oil wells should have been dismissed by the District Court. The reasonableness of the permit in that case was not of transcendent importance, but review of reasonableness by the federal courts in that and future cases, where the State had established its own elaborate review system for dealing with the geological complexities of oil and gas fields, would have had an impermissibly disruptive effect on state policy for the management of those fields.[21]

The present case clearly does not fall within this second category of abstention. While state claims are involved in the case, the state law to be applied appears to be settled. No questions bearing on state policy are presented for deci-

---

21 We note that *Burford v. Sun Oil Co.*, and *Alabama Pub. Serv. Comm'n v. Southern R. Co.*, differ from *Louisiana Power & Light Co. v. City of Thibodaux*, and *County of Allegheny v. Frank Mashuda Co.*, in that the former two cases, unlike the latter two, raised colorable constitutional claims and were therefore brought under federal-question, as well as diversity jurisdiction. While abstention in *Burford* and *Alabama Public Service* had the effect of avoiding a federal constitutional issue, the opinions indicate that this was not an additional ground for abstention in those cases. We have held, of course, that the opportunity to avoid decision of a constitutional question does not alone justify abstention by a federal court. Indeed, the presence of a federal basis for jurisdiction may raise the level of justification needed for abstention.

sion. Nor will decision of the state claims impair efforts to implement state policy as in *Burford*. To be sure, the federal claims that are involved in the case go to the establishment of water rights which may conflict with similar rights based on state law. But the mere potential for conflict in the results of adjudications, does not, without more, warrant staying exercise of federal jurisdiction. * * * The potential conflict here, involving state claims and federal claims, would not be such as to impair impermissibly the State's effort to effect its policy respecting the allocation of state waters. Nor would exercise of federal jurisdiction here interrupt any such efforts by restraining the exercise of authority vested in state officers.

(c) Finally, abstention is appropriate where, absent bad faith, harassment, or a patently invalid state statute, federal jurisdiction has been invoked for the purpose of restraining state criminal proceedings, state nuisance proceedings antecedent to a criminal prosecution, which are directed at obtaining the closure of places exhibiting obscene films, or collection of state taxes. Like the previous two categories, this category also does not include this case. We deal here neither with a criminal proceeding, nor such a nuisance proceeding, nor a tax collection. We also do not deal with an attempt to restrain such actions or to seek a declaratory judgment as to the validity of a state criminal law under which criminal proceedings are pending in a state court.

C

Although this case falls within none of the abstention categories, there are principles unrelated to considerations of proper constitutional adjudication and regard for federal-state relations which govern in situations involving the contemporaneous exercise of concurrent jurisdictions, either by federal courts or by state and federal courts. These principles rest on considerations of "[w]ise judicial administration, giving regard to conservation of judicial resources and comprehensive disposition of litigation." Generally, as between state and federal courts, the rule is that "the pendency of an action in the state court is no bar to proceedings concerning the same matter in the Federal court having jurisdiction * * * ." As between federal district courts, however, though no precise rule has evolved, the general principle is to avoid duplicative litigation. This difference in general approach between state-federal concurrent jurisdiction and wholly federal concurrent jurisdiction stems from the virtually unflagging obligation of the federal courts to exercise the jurisdiction given them. Given this obligation, and the absence of weightier considerations of constitutional adjudication and state-federal relations, the circumstances permitting the dismissal of a federal suit due to the presence of a concurrent state proceeding for reasons of wise judicial administration are considerably more limited than the circumstances appropriate for abstention. The former circumstances, though exceptional, do nevertheless exist.

It has been held, for example, that the court first assuming jurisdiction over property may exercise that jurisdiction to the exclusion of other courts. This has been true even where the Government was a claimant in existing state proceedings and then sought to invoke district-court jurisdiction under the jurisdictional provision antecedent to 28 U.S.C. § 1345. In assessing the appropriateness of dismissal in the event of an exercise of concurrent jurisdiction, a federal court may also consider such factors as the inconvenience of the federal forum, the desirability of avoiding piecemeal litigation, and the order in which jurisdiction was obtained by the concurrent forums. No one factor is necessarily determinative; a carefully considered judgment taking into account both the obligation to exercise jurisdiction and the combination of factors counselling against that exercise is required. Only the clearest of justifications will warrant dismissal.

Turning to the present case, a number of factors clearly counsel against concurrent federal proceedings. The most important of these is the McCarran Amendment itself. The clear federal policy evinced by that legislation is the avoidance of piecemeal adjudication of water rights in a river system. This policy is akin to that underlying the rule requiring that jurisdiction be yielded to the court first acquiring control of property, for the concern in such instances is with avoiding the generation of additional litigation through permitting inconsistent dispositions of property. This concern is heightened with respect to water rights, the relationships among which are highly interdependent. Indeed, we have recognized that actions seeking the allocation of water essentially involve the disposition of property and are best conducted in unified proceedings. The consent to jurisdiction given by the McCarran Amendment bespeaks a policy that recognizes the availability of comprehensive state systems for adjudication of water rights as the means for achieving these goals.

Food for Thought

Recall that the Court had already found that the McCarran Amendment *did not* limit federal court jurisdiction. Is the majority now importing such a McCarran-based limitation through the back door?

As has already been observed, the Colorado Water Rights Determination and Administration Act established such a system for the adjudication and management of rights to the use of the State's waters. As the Government concedes and as this Court recognized in Eagle County and Water Div. 5, the Act established a single continuous proceeding for water rights adjudication which antedated the suit in District Court. That proceeding "reaches all claims, perhaps month by month but inclusively in the totality." Additionally, the responsibility of managing the State's waters, to the end that they be allocated in accordance with adjudicated water rights, is given to the State Engineer.

Beyond the congressional policy expressed by the McCarran Amendment and consistent with furtherance of that policy, we also find significant (a) the apparent absence of any proceedings in the District Court, other than the filing of the complaint, prior to the motion to dismiss, (b) the extensive involvement of state water rights occasioned by this suit naming 1,000 defendants, (c) the 300-mile distance between the District Court in Denver and the court in Division 7, and (d) the existing participation by the Government in Division 4, 5, and 6 proceedings. We emphasize, however, that we do not overlook the heavy obligation to exercise jurisdiction. We need not decide, for example, whether, despite the McCarran Amendment, dismissal would be warranted if more extensive proceedings had occurred in the District Court prior to dismissal, if the involvement of state water rights were less extensive than it is here, or if the state proceeding were in some respect inadequate to resolve the federal claims. But the opposing factors here, particularly the policy underlying the McCarran Amendment, justify the District Court's dismissal in this particular case.

Take Note!

Note the echo of the abstention discussion in *Hicks v. Miranda*, page 849, a decision from which Justice Brennan dissented. Is he simply recognizing *Hicks*'s precedential status or has he changed his view?

Take Note!

It is a remarkably ironic for Justice Brennan to be making this particular point, is it not? Recall his general position with respect to courts' exercise of personal jurisdiction. It was he, after all, who found Florida jurisdiction over the Michigan defendants in *Burger King Corp. v. Rudzewicz* (1985), despite the much greater distance between the two possible forums in that case.

The judgment of the Court of Appeals is reversed and the judgment of the District Court dismissing the complaint is affirmed for the reasons here stated.

It is so ordered.

MR. JUSTICE STEWART, with whom MR. JUSTICE BLACKMUN and MR. JUSTICE STEVENS concur, dissenting.

The Court says that the United States District Court for the District of Colorado clearly had jurisdiction over this lawsuit. I agree. The Court further says that the McCarran Amendment "in no way diminished" the District Court's jurisdiction. I agree. The Court also says that federal courts have a "virtually unflagging obligation * * * to exercise the jurisdiction given them." I agree. And finally, the Court says that nothing in the abstention doctrine "in any of its forms" justified the District Court's dismissal of the Government's complaint. I agree.

These views would seem to lead ineluctably to the conclusion that the District Court was wrong in dismissing the complaint. Yet the Court holds that the order of dismissal was "appropriate." With that conclusion I must respectfully disagree.

In holding that the United States shall not be allowed to proceed with its lawsuit, the Court relies principally on cases reflecting the rule that where "control of the property which is the subject of the suit (is necessary) in order to proceed with the cause and to grant the relief sought, the jurisdiction of one court must of necessity yield to that of the other." But, as those cases make clear, this rule applies only when exclusive control over the subject matter is necessary to effectuate a court's judgment. Here the federal court did not need to obtain *in rem* or *quasi in rem* jurisdiction in order to decide the issues before it. The court was asked simply to determine as a matter of federal law whether federal reservations of water rights had occurred, and, if so, the date and scope of the reservations. The District Court could make such a determination without having control of the river.

The rule invoked by the Court thus does not support the conclusion that it reaches. In the *Princess Lida [1939]* case, for example, the reason for the surrender of federal jurisdiction over the administration of a trust was the fact that a state court had already assumed jurisdiction over the trust estate. But the Court in that case recognized that this rationale "ha[d] no application to a case in a federal court * * * wherein the plaintiff seeks merely an adjudication of his right or his interest as a basis of a claim against a fund in the possession of a state court * * * ." The Court stressed that "[n]o question is presented in the federal court as to the right of any person to participate in the res or as to the quantum of his interest in it." * * *

The precedents cited by the Court thus not only fail to support the Court's decision in this case, but expressly point in the opposite direction. The present suit, in short, is not analogous to the administration of a trust, but rather to a claim of a "right to participate," since the United States in this litigation does not ask the court to control the administration of the river, but only to determine its specific rights in the flow of water in the river. This is an almost exact analogue to a suit seeking a determination of rights in the flow of income from a trust.

The Court's principal reason for deciding to close the doors of the federal courthouse to the United States in this case seems to stem from the view that its decision will avoid piecemeal adjudication of water rights.[6] To the extent that

6 The Court lists four other policy reasons for the "appropriateness" of the District Court's dismissal of this lawsuit. All of those reasons are insubstantial. First, the fact that no significant proceedings had yet taken place in the federal court at the time of the dismissal means no more than that the federal court was prompt in granting the defendants' motion to dismiss. At that time, of course, no proceedings involving the Government's claims had taken place in the state court either. Second, the

this view is based on the special considerations governing *in rem* proceedings, it is without precedential basis, as the decisions discussed above demonstrate. To the extent that the Court's view is based on the realistic practicalities of this case, it is simply wrong, because the relegation of the Government to the state courts will not avoid piecemeal litigation.

The Colorado courts are currently engaged in two types of proceedings under the State's water-rights law. First, they are processing new claims to water based on recent appropriations. Second, they are integrating these new awards of water rights with all past decisions awarding such rights into one all-inclusive tabulation for each water source. The claims of the United States that are involved in this case have not been adjudicated in the past. Yet they do not involve recent appropriations of water. In fact, these claims are wholly dissimilar to normal state water claims, because they are not based on actual beneficial use of water but rather on an intention formed at the time the federal land use was established to reserve a certain amount of water to support the federal reservations. The state court will, therefore, have to conduct separate proceedings to determine these claims. And only after the state court adjudicates the claims will they be incorporated into the water source tabulations. If this suit were allowed to proceed in federal court the same procedures would be followed, and the federal court decree would be incorporated into the state tabulation, as other federal court decrees have been incorporated in the past. Thus, the same process will occur regardless of which forum considers these claims. Whether the virtually identical separate proceedings take place in a federal court or a state court, the adjudication of the claims will be neither more nor less "piecemeal." Essentially the same process will be followed in each instance.

As the Court says, it is the virtual "unflagging obligation" of a federal court to exercise the jurisdiction that has been conferred upon it. Obedience to that obligation is particularly "appropriate" in this case, for at least two reasons.

First, the issues involved are issues of federal law. A federal court is more likely than a state court to be familiar with federal water law and to have had experience in interpreting the relevant federal statutes, regulations, and Indian treaties. Moreover, if tried in a federal court, these issues of federal law will be

---

geographic distance of the federal court from the rivers in question is hardly a significant factor in this age of rapid and easy transportation. Since the basic issues here involve the determination of the amount of water the Government intended to reserve rather than the amount it actually appropriated on a given date, there is little likelihood that live testimony by water district residents would be necessary. In any event, the Federal District Court in Colorado is authorized to sit at Durango, the headquarters of Water Division 7. Third, the Government's willingness to participate in some of the state proceedings certainly does not mean that it had no right to bring this action, unless the Court has today unearthed a new kind of waiver. Finally, the fact that there were many defendants in the federal suit is hardly relevant. It only indicates that the federal court had all the necessary parties before it in order to issue a decree finally settling the Government's claims. * * *

reviewable in a federal appellate court, whereas federal judicial review of the state courts' resolution of issues of federal law will be possible only on review by this Court in the exercise of its certiorari jurisdiction.

Second, some of the federal claims in this lawsuit relate to water reserved for Indian reservations. It is not necessary to determine that there is no state-court jurisdiction of these claims to support the proposition that a federal court is a more appropriate forum than a state court for determination of questions of life-and-death importance to Indians. This Court has long recognized that " '[t]he policy of leaving Indians free from state jurisdiction and control is deeply rooted in the Nation's history.' "

The Court says that "[o]nly the clearest of justifications will warrant dismissal" of a lawsuit within the jurisdiction of a federal court. In my opinion there was no justification at all for the District Court's order of dismissal in this case.

I would affirm the judgment of the Court of Appeals.

Notes and Questions

1. As a preliminary consideration, note the Court's observation that there is no indication, either textual or historical, that Congress intended the McCarran Amendment to limit federal jurisdiction. Justice Brennan quoted *Rosecrans v. United States*, 165 U.S. 257, 262 (1897): "When there are statutes clearly defining the jurisdiction of the courts the force and effect of such provisions should not be disturbed by a mere implication flowing from subsequent legislation." He also quoted *Morton v. Mancari*, 417 U.S. 535, 550 (1974), a case decided after Chief Justice Burger and Justices Powell and Rehnquist had joined the Court: "In the absence of some affirmative showing of an intention to repeal, the only permissible justification for a repeal by implication is when the earlier and later statutes are irreconcilable."

2. Justice Brennan implies that what is happening in *Colorado River* is different from abstention when he says, "the circumstances permitting the dismissal of a federal suit due to the presence of a concurrent state proceeding for reasons of wise judicial administration are considerably more limited than the circumstances appropriate for abstention." Why does he characterize *Colorado River* as something other than abstention?

3. Justice Brennan identifies four factors that federal courts should consider in deciding whether interests in wise judicial administration should override the duty to exercise jurisdiction. What are the factors? He states that "[n]o one factor is necessar-

ily determinative" and that "[o]nly the clearest of justifications will warrant dismissal." Does that mean dismissal is appropriate only if all of the factors favor that outcome? Finally, how do the Colorado River factors compare with the factors Pullman, Burford, Thibodaux and Younger abstention use?

4. Does the majority's view of the purpose of the McCarran Amendment prove too much? If Congress passed the Amendment because of concerns about piecemeal litigation and intended the federal courts to yield to avoid duplicative litigation, why did it not simply say so? Should its silence be construed to mean that it did not intend the federal courts to forswear their power under Article III and the statutory predicate for jurisdiction?

5. There are three other *Colorado River* cases of some import. *Will v. Calvert Fire Insurance Co.*, 437 U.S. 655 (1978), clearly caused more problems than it solved. The Court split four-four-one, with Justice Rehnquist writing a plurality opinion that allowed abstention and stated that "a district court is under no compulsion to exercise * * * jurisdiction where the controversy may be settled more expeditiously in state court." Justice Blackmun concurred based on *Colorado River* principles, but he could not agree with the Rehnquist plurality that the district courts had such broad discretion to abstain. Justice Brennan led a four-member group in dissent, arguing that the analytical framework of *Colorado River* did not permit the wide-ranging discretion visualized by Justice Rehnquist and that abstention was inappropriate on the facts. Nonetheless, "[a]fter *Calvert,* many lower courts believed they had increased authority to abstain to avoid duplicating state court proceedings." ERWIN CHEMERINSKY, FEDERAL JURISDICTION § 14.2, at 848 (5th ed. 2007) (citing Note, *Abstention and Mandamus After* Will v. Calvert Fire Insurance Co., 54 CORNELL L.REV. 566, 585 (1979)).

But then, in *Moses H. Cone Memorial Hospital v. Mercury Construction Corporation*, 460 U.S. 1 (1983), the Court seemed to retreat substantially from the position taken by the *Calvert* plurality. The defendant Hospital and the plaintiff disputed amounts due under a construction contract and disputed also the availability of arbitration. The Hospital conceded that the contract provided for arbitration but argued that the arbitration clause had become ineffective because of Mercury's actions. When negotiations broke down, the Hospital sought a state court declaration of non-arbitrability and non-liability. The Hospital later obtained an *ex parte* injunction prohibiting Mercury from "taking any steps toward arbitration." When the injunction was dissolved, Mercury filed in federal court, seeking to compel arbitration. The district court abstained, but an en banc Court of Appeals reversed.

Justice Brennan wrote for a Court unanimous in the view that *Colorado River* abstention was inappropriate. He again stressed the unusual nature of abstention and noted that the *Colorado River* factors were not to be used as a checklist, but were rather simply factors whose weight in any particular case might vary widely in a balancing "heavily weighted in favor of the exercise of jurisdiction." Justice Brennan found no "exceptional circumstances" in Moses Cone that justified abstention. Moreover, he placed heavy emphasis on "the fact that federal law provides the rule of decision on the merits * * * "—whether arbitration could be compelled under the United States Arbitration Act—a new factor in the *Colorado River* analysis. The Court's disinclination to abstain was undiminished by the fact that the state proceeding had been commenced first; echoing *Hicks v. Miranda,* 422 U.S. 332 (1975) (page 849), the majority cautioned: "priority should not be measured exclusively by which complaint was filed first, but rather in terms of how much progress has been made in the two actions."

The Court also focused again on the separation-of-powers implications of abstention.

> This refusal to proceed was plainly erroneous in view of Congress' clear intent, in the Arbitration Act, to move the parties to an arbitrable dispute out of court and into arbitration as quickly and easily as possible. The Act provides two parallel devices for enforcing an arbitration agreement: a stay of litigation in any case raising a dispute referable to arbitration and an affirmative order to engage in arbitration. Both of these sections call for an expeditious and summary hearing, with only restricted inquiry into factual issues. Assuming that the state court would have granted prompt relief to Mercury under the Act, there still would have been an inevitable delay as a result of the District Court's stay. The stay thus frustrated the statutory policy of rapid and unobstructed enforcement of arbitration agreements.

Does the Court's reasoning also, perhaps unintentionally, provide some ammunition against the invocation of other forms of abstention?

Moses Cone demonstrates the limited nature of *Colorado River* abstention, but it also leaves some questions unanswered. It certainly is not clear what factors qualify as sufficiently "exceptional" to justify abstention. In addition, although the presence of a federal issue weighs heavily on the side of exercising federal jurisdiction, the Court stopped short of saying that it ends the abstention inquiry—indeed, doing so would have overruled *Colorado River* at least by implication. Moreover, to the extent that a federal issue makes abstention less likely, is the Court implying a lack of confidence in state court competence to deal with federal issues, or is it merely giving more weight to the plaintiff's choice of forum in this context than it has in some other types of abstention? If the former, why should the Court have less confidence here than in other abstention situations? If the latter, why is the plaintiff's forum choice entitled to additional weight here?

Wilton v. Seven Falls Company (1995), suggests that there may be special abstention rules for declaratory judgment cases. The matter arose out of a dispute over some Texas land that contained oil and gas reserves. The Hill Group (one of the disputants) asked London Underwriters, its insurer, to defend and indemnify it, but London Underwriters refused. The Hill Group subsequently lost a $100 million judgment in Texas state court. After receiving notice of the verdict from the Hill Group, London Underwriters filed a federal declaratory judgment action based on diversity jurisdiction seeking a determination that its policies did not cover the Hill Group for the Texas judgment. After discussions with the Hill Group, London Underwriters withdrew the action on the condition that the Hill Group give at least two weeks notice if it planned to sue on the policy. When it received the notice, London Underwriters refiled the federal action. Four weeks later, the Hill Group sued in state court, joining parties whose presence made removal impossible. The Hill Group subsequently moved to dismiss or stay the federal action. The Supreme Court endorsed abstention.

The Court emphasized that London Underwriters sought only declaratory relief, characterizing it as a discretionary remedy, with the clear implication that abstention's appropriateness may turn on the type of relief demanded. Perhaps the Court's argument proves too much, though. Injunctive relief is discretionary also. Should the district courts abstain from deciding federal actions seeking injunctive relief if the federal defendant later files a state action seeking damages?

Finally, the Court roundly criticized London Underwriters for forum shopping. That is a bit odd, for certainly the Court might have leveled the same charge at the Hill Group. After all, London Underwriters chose the federal forum initially. Is every diversity action plaintiff guilty of forum shopping? Moreover, what's wrong with that? The *Erie* Court disapproved forum shopping where it would determine the outcome of the case because of the law the court would apply, but the development of the *Erie* doctrine appears to have pulled the argument's teeth. (London Underwriters, by the way, accused the Hill Group of forum shopping because of the addition of parties (none insured by London Underwriters) who destroyed diversity and thereby rendered the Texas action non-removable.)

Wilton adds a new twist to the idea underlying *Hicks v. Miranda*. The state court action in *Wilton* began almost four months after the original federal declaratory judgment action and more than one month after commencement of the second. Note that here a later-filed state proceeding was able effectively to cut off a federal court proceeding, just as happened in *Hicks*. Here, as there, there had not been "proceedings of substance on the merits," but in contrast to *Hicks*, the absence of such proceedings may have occurred only because the insured persuaded the insurer to withdraw the original action. Should the parties' agreement have affected the Court's willingness to endorse the stay?

Does any federal declaratory judgment action concerning questions of state law now become an endangered species subject to stay or dismissal (and note that because of res judicata and 28 U.S.C. § 1738 there is little practical difference between them) as a result of a later-filed state action (*à la* Hicks) brought by the declaratory judgment defendant? If so, should the Court extend this vulnerability of federal actions even to coercive cases turning upon state law, thus imperiling diversity jurisdiction more generally? If not, how can the Court distinguish cases like Wilton?

One of Congress's primary purposes in passing the Declaratory Judgment Act was to give potential defendants in unfiled but threatened coercive actions a means to precipitate resolution of the dispute. Congress particularly focused on the plight of the alleged patent infringer, but insurance coverage disputes present a similar, if slightly less compelling, question. The alleged patent infringer threatened with suit by the patentee faces the undesirable choice of continuing to market its own device, possibly running up ever-increasing damages if it eventually is unable to prevail in a patent infringement action, or discontinuing its conduct, possibly foregoing substantial profits to which it may have been fully entitled because of unpatentability of the patentee's original device, non-infringement by the alleged infringer's device, or some other reason. In insurance coverage disputes, the insurer does not face a real prospect either of mounting damages or of erroneously discontinuing perfectly lawful, profitable conduct. It does, however, face the dilemma of maintaining its position and losing the opportunity to control the underlying liability litigation or of abandoning its position and providing a defense, with all of the expense that that entails, in a circumstance in which the policy in fact provides no coverage. After *Wilton*, the Declaratory Judgment Act may still have the effect of precipitating judicial resolution of disputes, but not in the form Congress envisioned; the Act may now merely act as a prod to the declaratory judgment defendant to begin its own action.

It is difficult to know whether Wilton has greater implications for abstention or for the declaratory judgment remedy. As the majority conceded, the case has none of the traditional indicia of abstention, and the Court explicitly refused to abstain under the *Colorado River* doctrine because London Underwriters sought no coercive relief. There are indications that the absence of federal issues motivated the Court. On the other hand, there are no federal issues in diversity cases generally. Could Wilton foreshadow a more generalized abstention doctrine in diversity cases? That would present significant separation-of-powers issues given the command of 28 U.S.C.A. § 1332. Then, too, would those issues be any more nettlesome than when the courts abstain in federal question cases under § 1331? The Court's opinion explicitly declined to speculate.

Chapter 9

Supreme Court Review of State Decisions

A. Introduction

It is now so common for the Supreme Court to review state court decisions that the phenomenon draws virtually no notice, but it was not always so. Early in the republic's history, the fledgling federal government faced many state challenges to national authority. *Martin v. Hunter's Lessee*, 14 U.S. (1 Wheat.) 304 (1816), a staple of Constitutional Law courses, was one directed at the Supreme Court. The Virginia Court of Appeals asserted that the United States Supreme Court could not review state court judgments because it would infringe state sovereignty. This challenge and the Court's emphatic rejection of it exemplify the tension of federalism. The Supreme Court derives its power to review state judgments from a combination of article III and the Supremacy Clause. Although that power is now well established, the clash between federal and state sovereignty stands out in bold relief every time the Court does so. Although *Hunter's Lessee* seemed to resolve whether the states could resist judgments of the Supreme Court, in 1986, then-Attorney General Edwin Meese, Jr., asserted that the Supreme Court does not declare the meaning of the Constitution in any way binding persons not before the Court. Thus, he suggested that declarations of constitutional principle by the Court did not mean that non-parties to the case should alter their behavior accordingly. If that were taken seriously, consider its effect in the context of school desegregation, prayer in schools, search and seizure cases, or almost any other area in which the Court reviews governmental conduct and declares constitutional principle. Consider more generally its implications for *stare decisis*.

There was little debate in the Constitutional Convention about the federal power to review state court decisions. No doubt this is largely owing to the nature of the debate about the federal judicial system generally. Although the Framers agreed there should be a national court at the apex of the judicial system, the Anti-Federalists argued against having any inferior federal courts. They were concerned that an extensive national court system would siphon off too much power from the states and argued that inferior federal courts were unnecessary because the Supreme Court could review state court decisions of federal law. They could hardly have argued in the next breath that there was no Supreme Court power to review state court decisions. A compromise finally resolved the dispute, permitting inferior federal courts to exist only if the people's and states' representatives[1] in Congress created them. *See* U.S. CONST. art. I, § 8, cl. 9 and art. III, § 1.

Howell v. Mississippi, 543 U.S. 440 (2005), reaffirmed the well-established rule that the Supreme Court will not decide a federal issue unless it was fairly presented to the state courts. As in earlier cases, the Court declined to decide whether this rule is jurisdictional or merely prudential. In *Cardinale v. Louisiana*, 394 U.S. 437 (1969), Justice White discussed the policies underlying the rule:

> Questions not raised below are those on which the record is very likely to be inadequate, since it certainly was not compiled with those questions in mind. And in a federal system it is important that state courts be given the first opportunity to consider the applicability of state statutes in light of constitutional challenge, since the statutes may be construed in a way which saves their constitutionality.

The collision between federal and state power may be sharper in this area than in many others. When the federal courts review state legislative or executive action, they act on institutions that do not consider issues from a judicial perspective. Review does not reflect on the competence of those branches to carry out their particular functions, but Supreme Court review of a state court decision may connote that the state judicial system is not up to the adjudicative job, despite the fact that the state judges are themselves sworn to uphold the federal constitution and laws as well as their own, a phenomenon given substantial weight by the Supreme Court in other contexts. For example, the Court routinely asserts in abstention cases that state judges are presumed as dedicated as federal judges to the proper interpretation and application of federal law. *See, e.g., Trainor v. Hernandez*, 431 U.S. 434, 443 (1977) (reaffirming " 'the principle that state courts have the solemn responsibility equally with the federal courts' to safeguard constitutional rights * * * ") (quoting *Steffel v. Thompson*, 415 U.S. 452, 460-61 (1974)).

There are three statutory prerequisites for Supreme Court review, which 28 U.S.C. § 1257 authorizes. First, the Court can review only cases containing federal issues. Second, Congress has specified that the Court can review only "final" judgments from the state courts. As the law has developed, however, "finality" is as protean a term as any to be found in the law. Third, Congress has specified that only judgments coming from "the highest court * * * of a State in which a decision could be had" are reviewable. This does not mean that the Supreme Court can review cases only from the highest state court. Many states restrict appellate jurisdiction; often cases cannot reach the highest state court. They may nonethe-

1 Recall that until the Seventeenth Amendment, state legislatures chose senators, who were perceived to represent the states directly, not the populace.

less qualify for Supreme Court review. Perhaps the most famous example is *Thompson v. City of Louisville*, 362 U.S. 199 (1960). Upon defendant's conviction for disorderly conduct in the Louisville Police Court, no appeal lay to any Kentucky court, so Thompson was able to appeal directly to the United States Supreme Court. Although the "size" of the jump was unusual, the phenomenon is not.

What is the scope of Supreme Court review? In a case with federal and state issues, which should the Supreme Court review: the federal issues only or all of the issues? Note that Supreme Court adjudication of the state law issues might intensify federal-state friction.

In addition, can the state courts do anything to insulate their decisions from Supreme Court review? The Supreme Court has developed a complex body of doctrine that gives the states substantial latitude to make judgments effectively unreviewable. For example, state courts may decide state issues in a way that makes federal law irrelevant to the disposition of the case. If deciding the federal issue cannot affect the outcome of the case, the Supreme Court generally refuses review.

Finally, remember that there are other federal doctrines and rules that may limit or prevent Supreme Court review of state court decisions, such as standing, ripeness, mootness and the political question doctrine (discussed in detail in Chapter 1). These federal doctrines do not necessarily bind the state courts.

For More Information

See, e.g., *State v. Marsala*, 579 A.2d 58 (Conn. 1990) (rejecting the good-faith exception to the Fourth Amendment's warrant requirement announced in *United States v. Leon*, 468 U.S. 897 (1984)); *People v. Bigelow*, 488 N.E.2d 451 (N.Y. 1985) (same); *Commonwealth v. Blood*, 507 N.E.2d 1029 (Mass. 1987) ("We have often recognized that art. 14 of the Declaration of Rights does, or may, afford more substantive protection to individuals than that which prevails under the Constitution of the United States.") (rejecting the one-party-consent rule for electronic searches of *United States v. Caceres*, 440 U.S. 741 (1979) and *United States v. White*, 401 U.S. 745 (1971)); *State v. Kimbro*, 496 A.2d 498 (Conn. 1985) (rejecting the totality-of-the-circumstances test of *Illinois v. Gates*, 462 U.S. 213 (1983) and adopting as state law the *Aguilar-Spinelli* test formerly used as federal law); *People v. Griminger*, 524 N.E.2d 409 (N.Y. 1988) (same). Justice Brennan specifically suggested that states consider further development of state constitutional law. *See* William J. Brennan, *The Bill of Rights and the States: The Revival of State Constitutions as Guardians of Individual Rights*, 61 N.Y.U. L. REV. 535 (1986). On the other hand, such decisions are not unreviewable in any quarter. In California, the proliferation of state constitutional decisions caused voters to pass a referendum measure requiring state courts to construe California law congruently with federal law with respect to the admissibility of evidence in criminal proceedings. *See* CAL. CONST. art. I, § 28(d).

B. Preliminary Jurisdictional Considerations

Note that 28 U.S.C.A. § 1257, which governs Supreme Court review of state court decisions, now allows review only by writ of certiorari. This is the latest stage in two centuries of change. Review in the Supreme Court was originally only by writ of error, which required Supreme Court review of the case (review "as of right"), as contrasted with the writ of certiorari, which gives the Court discretion on whether to accept the case for review. The Judiciary Act of 1789 allowed review only in three circumstances.[2] The first two were: 1) when a state court invalidated a federal statute, treaty or authority, and 2) when a state court upheld state law in the face of a supremacy challenge. By clear implication, the Supreme Court could not review cases where federal law was upheld or state laws stricken, apparently on the theory that review was unnecessary to protect federal interests. The third category allowed review

> where is drawn in question the construction of any clause of the Constitution, or of a treaty or statute of the Constitution, or of a treaty or statute of, or commission held under the United States, and the decision is against the title, right, privilege or exemption specially set up or claimed by either party * * * .

In short, this category involved the bulk of federal question cases. Note, however, that review of federal questions in the Supreme Court was not subject to the well-pleaded complaint rule, as original and removal jurisdiction now are in the district court; the statute specifically provided that either party could raise the federal matter. Accordingly, a federal question arising anywhere in a case qualified the case for eventual Supreme Court review. Why do you think the Court does not apply the *Mottley* rule in this context? Recall the practical reasons for the *Mottley* rule in cases the federal courts heard after enactment of the general federal-question statute in 1875. Do they apply to review under § 1257? In addition, if the *Mottley* rule did apply, how would that affect the Supreme Court' ability to promote the uniformity of federal law?

In 1914, Congress provided review by certiorari for cases that were the converse of the three original categories: those where the state court had decided *in favor of* federal law by refusing to declare federal law unconstitutional, by invalidating a state statute on supremacy grounds, or by upholding a claimed federal

2 The Judiciary Act language authorizing Supreme Court review of state court decisions appears at the beginning of *Murdock v. City of Memphis*, at page 910.

right or construction. Certiorari is wholly discretionary. In 1916, all federal question cases (the old category 3 from the Judiciary Act of 1789) were moved from the writ of error category into the certiorari category, irrespective of whether the state court decided for or against the claimed federal entitlement. In 1928, Congress substituted review by appeal (which also provided review as of right) for review by writ of error, a structure that lasted until the latest revision of § 1257 in 1988, when Congress eliminated all review as of right in favor of review by certiorari.

Review by appeal no longer exists, but it commands one last bit of attention. Although cases reviewable by appeal or writ of error were entitled to review "as of right," they did not all receive full hearings. Often the Court summarily affirmed or dismissed the appeal without hearing oral argument or even getting briefs from the parties beyond those seeking the appellate review. Such dismissals were "for want of a substantial federal question" and operated as decisions on the merits, unlike denials of certiorari.[3] For example, in *Zucht v. King*, 260 U.S. 174 (1922), a challenge to a San Antonio ordinance requiring children in public schools to be vaccinated, the Court dismissed a writ of error because, "[l]ong before this suit was instituted, *Jacobson v. Massachusetts* [1905] had settled that it is within the police power of a state to provide for compulsory vaccination." The Court thus declared the federal issue that Zucht presented "insubstantial" and dismissed the case without a full appeal.

Section 1257's terms did limit appeal as of right to cases presenting a substantial federal issue. Did the substantiality requirement give the Court unauthorized power summarily to dismiss any case where the appellant sought to overturn existing precedent? Could the Court have turned aside review of the state court challenge to *Plessy v. Ferguson*, 163 U.S. 537 (1896), that was included in the four cases consolidated for review as *Brown v. Board of Education*, 347 U.S. 483 (1954)? What important practical reason underlay imposition of the substantiality requirement?

---

3 In practice, it mattered little whether review was by appeal (as of right) or by certiorari (discretionary). Statistically, the odds of getting full review by appeal were only slightly better than those for certiorari. But summary decisions on the merits have precedential effect; denials of certiorari do not, although that difference was muted by the Court's assertion in Edelman v. Jordan, 415 U.S. 651, 670-71 (1974), that summary dispositions lack the *stare decisis* impact of full hearings.

Murdock v. City of Memphis

Supreme Court of the United States, 1875.
87 U.S. (20 Wall.) 590.

THE TWENTY-FIFTH SECTION OF THE ACT OF 1789.

That a final judgment or decree in any suit, in the highest court *of law or equity* of a State in which a decision in the suit could be had, where is drawn in question the validity of a treaty or statute of, or an authority exercised under the United States, and the decision is against their validity; or where is drawn in question the validity of a statute of, or an authority exercised under any State, on the ground of their being repugnant to the Constitution, treaties, or laws of the United States, and the decision is in favor of such their validity, *or where is drawn in question the construction of any clause* of the Constitution, or of a treaty or statute of, or commission held under the United States, and the decision is against the title, right, privilege or *exemption* specially set up or claimed by either party, under such clause of the said Constitution, treaty, statute, or commission, may be reexamined and reversed or affirmed in the Supreme Court of the United States upon a writ of error, the citation being signed by the chief justice, or judge, or chancellor of the court rendering or passing the judgment or decree complained of, or by a justice of the Supreme Court of the United States, in the same manner and under the same regulations, and the writ shall have the same effect as if the judgment or decree complained of had been rendered or passed in a *Circuit Court*, and the proceeding upon the reversal shall also be the same, except that the Supreme Court, *instead of remanding*

THE SECOND SECTION OF THE ACT OF 1867.

That a final judgment or decree in any suit in the highest court of a State in which a decision in the suit could be had, where is drawn in question the validity of a treaty or statute of or an authority exercised under the United States, and the decision is against their validity, or where is drawn in question the validity of a statute of or an authority exercised under any State, on the ground of their being repugnant to the Constitution, treaties, or laws of the United States, and the decision is in favor of such their validity, or where any title, right, privilege, or *immunity is claimed* under the Constitution, or any treaty or statute of, or commission held, or *authority exercised*, under the United States, and the decision is against the title, right, privilege, or immunity specially set up or claimed by either party under such Constitution, treaty, statute, commission, or *authority,* may be re-examined and reversed or affirmed in the Supreme Court of the United States, upon a writ of error, the citation being signed by the chief justice, or judge, or chancellor of the court rendering or passing the judgment or decree complained of, or by a justice of the Supreme Court of the United States, in the same manner, and under the same regulations, and the writ shall have the same effect as if the judgment or decree complained of had been rendered or passed *in a court of the United States;* and the proceeding *the cause for a final decision, as before provided, may at their discretion, if the cause shall have been once remanded before, proceed to a final decision of the same and award execution. But no other error shall be assigned or regarded as a ground of reversal in any such case as aforesaid than such as appears on the face of the record and immediately respects the before-mentioned questions of validity or construction of the said Constitution, treaties, statutes, commissions, or authorities in dispute.*

upon the reversal shall also be the same, *except that the Supreme Court may, at their discretion, proceed to a final decision of the same, and award execution or remand the same to an inferior court.*

Murdock filed a bill in one of the courts of chancery of Tennessee, against the city of Memphis, in that State. The bill and its exhibits made this case:

In July, 1844,—Congress having just previously authorized the establishment of a naval depot in that city, and appropriated a considerable sum of money for the purpose—the ancestors of Murdock—by ordinary deed of bargain and sale, without any covenants or declaration of trust on which the land was to be held by the city, but referring to the fact of "the location of the naval depot lately established by the United States at said town"—conveyed to the city certain land described in and near its limits "for the location of the naval depot aforesaid."

By the same instrument (a quadrupartite one) both the grantors and the city conveyed the same land to one Wheatley, in fee, in trust for the grantors and their heirs, "in case the same shall not be appropriated by the United States for that purpose."

On the 14th of September, 1844, the city of Memphis, in consideration of the sum of $20,000 paid by the United States, conveyed the said land to the United States with covenant of general warranty; there being, however, in this deed to the United States no designation of any purpose to which the land was to be applied, nor any conditions precedent or subsequent, or of any kind whatsoever.

The United States took possession of the land for the purpose of the erection of a naval depot upon it, erected buildings, and made various expenditures and improvements for the said purpose; but in about ten years after, by an act of August 5th, 1854, transferred the land back to the city. The act was in these words: "All the grounds and appurtenances thereunto belonging, known as the Memphis Navy Yard, in Shelby County, Tennessee, be, and the same is hereby, ceded to the mayor and aldermen of the city of Memphis, *for the use and benefit of said city.*"

There was no allegation in the bill that the city was in any way instrumental in procuring this transfer or the abandonment of the site as a naval depot; on the contrary, it is averred that the city authorities endeavored to prevent both.

The bill charged that by the failure of the United States to appropriate the land for a naval depot, and the final abandonment by the United States of any intention to do so, the land came within the clause of the deed of July, 1844, conveying it to Wheatley in trust; or if not, that it was held by the city in trust for the original grantors, and the prayer sought to subject it to said trusts.

The answer, denying the construction put upon the deed of 1844, which established a trust, asserted that the land had been appropriated by the United States as a naval depot within the meaning and intent of the deed of July, 1844, and that the subsequent perpetual occupation of it was not a condition subsequent; and consequently that the abandonment of it as a naval depot was not a breach of a condition such as divested the title so conveyed by the deed.

It pleaded the statute of limitations. It also demurred to the bill as seeking to enforce a forfeiture for breach of condition subsequent.

The court sustained the demurrer, and also decreed that the city had a perfect title to the property against the complainants both under the act of Congress and the statute of limitations, and dismissed the bill. The Supreme Court of Tennessee affirmed this decree.

That court was also of opinion, and so declared itself to be, that the act of Congress "cedes the property in controversy in this cause to the mayor and aldermen of the city of Memphis, for the use of the city only, and not in trust for the complainant; and that the complainant takes no benefit under the said act."

The complainant thereupon sued out a writ of error to this court.

* * *

MR. JUSTICE MILLER (now, January 11th, 1875) delivered the opinion of the court.

In the year 1867 Congress passed an act, approved February 5th, entitled an act to amend "An act to establish the judicial courts of the United States, approved September the 24th, 1789." * * * The second section was a reproduction, with some changes, of the twenty-fifth section of the act of 1789, to which, by its title, the act of 1867 was an amendment, and it related to the appellate jurisdiction of this court over judgments and decrees of State courts.

* * *

[T]he proposition has been urged upon the court that the latter act worked a total repeal of the twenty-fifth section of the former, and introduced a rule for the action of this court in the class of cases to which they both referred, of such extended operation and so variant from that which had governed it heretofore that the subject received the serious consideration of the court. * * *

The proposition is that by a fair construction of the act of 1867 this court must, when it obtains jurisdiction of a case decided in a State court, by reason of one of the questions stated in the act, proceed to decide every other question which the case presents which may be found necessary to a final judgment on the whole merits. * * *

When the case * * * came on to be argued, it was insisted by counsel for defendants in error that none of the questions were involved in the case necessary to give jurisdiction to this court, either under the act of 1789 or of 1867, and that if they were, there were other questions exclusively of State court cognizance which were sufficient to dispose of the case, and that, therefore, the writ of error should be dismissed.

Counsel for plaintiffs in error, on the other hand, argued that not only was there a question in the case decided against them which authorized the writ of error from this court under either act, but that this court having for this reason obtained jurisdiction of the case, should re-examine all the questions found in the record, though some of them might be questions of general common law or equity, or raised by State statutes, unaffected by any principle of Federal law, constitutional or otherwise.

When, after argument, the court came to consider the case in consultation, it was found that it could not be disposed of without ignoring or deciding some of these propositions, and it became apparent that the time had arrived when the court must decide upon the effect of the act of 1867 on the jurisdiction of this court as it had been supposed to be established by the twenty-fifth section of the act of 1789.

* * *

The questions propounded by the court for discussion by counsel were these:

1. Does the second section of the act of February 5th, 1867, repeal all or any part of the twenty-fifth section of the act of 1789, commonly called the Judiciary Act?

2. Is it the true intent and meaning of the act of 1867, above referred to, that when this court has jurisdiction of a case, by reason of any of the questions therein

mentioned, it shall proceed to decide all the questions presented by the record which are necessary to a final judgment or decree?

3. If this question be answered affirmatively, does the Constitution of the United States authorize Congress to confer such a jurisdiction on this court?

1. The act of 1867 has no repealing clause nor any express words of repeal. If there is any repeal, therefore, it is one of implication * * * .

* * *

The * * * twenty-fifth section of the act of 1789 is technically repealed, and * * * the second section of the act of 1867 has taken its place. What of the statute of 1789 is embraced in that of 1867 is of course the law now and has been ever since it was first made so. What is changed or modified is the law as thus changed or modified. That which is omitted ceased to have any effect from the day that the substituted statute was approved.

* * *

2. The affirmative of the second question propounded above is founded upon the effect of the omission or repeal of the last sentence of the twenty-fifth section of the act of 1789. That clause in express terms limited the power of the Supreme Court in reversing the judgment of a State court, to errors apparent on the face of the record and which respected questions, that for the sake of brevity, though not with strict verbal accuracy, we shall call Federal questions, namely, those in regard to the validity or construction of the Constitution, treaties, statutes, commissions, or authority of the Federal government.

The argument may be thus stated: 1. That the Constitution declares that the judicial power of the United States shall extend to cases of a character which includes the questions described in the section, and that by the word case, is to be understood all of the case in which such a question arises. 2. That by the fair construction of the act of 1789 in regard to removing those cases to this court, the power and the duty of re-examining the whole case would have been devolved on the court, but for the restriction of the clause omitted in the act of 1867; and that the same language is used in the latter act regulating the removal, but omitting the restrictive clause. And, 3. That by re-enacting the statute in the same terms as to the removal of cases from the State courts, without the restrictive clause, Congress is to be understood as conferring the power which the clause prohibited.

We will consider the last proposition first.

What were the precise motives which induced the omission of this clause it is impossible to ascertain with any degree of satisfaction. In a legislative body like Congress, it is reasonable to suppose that among those who considered this matter at all, there were varying reasons for consenting to the change. No doubt there were those who, believing that the Constitution gave no right to the Federal judiciary to go beyond the line marked by the omitted clause, thought its presence or absence immaterial; and in a revision of the statute it was wise to leave it out, because its presence implied that such a power was within the competency of Congress to bestow. There were also, no doubt, those who believed that the section standing without that clause did not confer the power which it prohibited, and that it was, therefore, better omitted. It may also have been within the thought of a few that all that is now claimed would follow the repeal of the clause. But if Congress, or the framers of the bill, had a clear purpose to enact affirmatively that the court *should consider* the class of errors which that clause forbid, nothing hindered that they should say so in positive terms; and in reversing the policy of the government from its foundation in one of the most important subjects on which that body could act, it is reasonably to be expected that Congress would use plain, unmistakable language in giving expression to such intention.

There is, therefore, no sufficient reason for holding that Congress, by repealing or omitting this restrictive clause, intended to enact affirmatively the thing which that clause had prohibited.

* * *

Food for Thought

Does the Court mean that the legislative action repealing the limitation had no effect at all on the meaning of the statute? That would conflict with one of the best known canons of statutory construction.

If the invariable effect of a writ of error to a Circuit Court of the United States is to require of this court to examine and pass upon all the errors of the inferior court, and if re-examination of the judgment of the court in the same manner and under the same regulations, means that in the re-examination everything is to be considered which could be considered in [a writ to the Circuit Court, and nothing else, then the inference] which is drawn from these premises would seem to be correct.

* * *

There is, therefore, nothing in the language of the act, as far as we have criticized it, which in express terms defines the extent of the re-examination which this court shall give to such cases.

But we have not yet considered the most important part of the statute, namely, that which declares that it is only upon the existence of certain questions in the case that this court can entertain jurisdiction at all. Nor is the mere existence of such a question in the case sufficient to give jurisdiction—the question must have been *decided* in the State court. Nor is it sufficient that such a question was raised and was decided. It must have been decided in a certain way, that is, against the right set up under the Constitution, laws, treaties, or authority of the United States. The Federal question may have been erroneously decided. It may be quite apparent to this court that a wrong construction has been given to the Federal law, but if the right claimed under it by plaintiff in error has been conceded to him, this court cannot entertain jurisdiction of the case, so very careful is the statute, both of 1789 and of 1867, to narrow, to limit, and define the jurisdiction which this court exercises over the judgments of the State courts. Is it consistent with this extreme caution to suppose that Congress intended, when those cases came here, that this court should not only examine those questions, but all others found in the record—questions of common law, of State statutes, of controverted facts, and conflicting evidence? Or is it the more reasonable inference that Congress intended that the case should be brought here that *those questions* might be decided and *finally* decided by the court established by the Constitution of the Union, and the court which has always been supposed to be not only the most appropriate but the only proper tribunal for their final decision? No such reason nor any necessity exists for the decision by this court of other questions in those cases. The jurisdiction has been exercised for nearly a century without serious inconvenience to the due administration of justice. The State courts are the appropriate tribunals, as this court has repeatedly held, for the decision of questions arising under their local law, whether statutory or otherwise. And it is not lightly to be presumed that Congress acted upon a principle which implies a distrust of their integrity or of their ability to construe those laws correctly.

> **Take Note!**
>
> Pay particular attention, here and later in the opinion, to the sequence of inquiry that the Court specifies with respect to cases coming from the state courts.

Let us look for a moment into the effect of the proposition contended for upon the cases as they come up for consideration in the conference-room. If it is found that no such question is raised or decided in the court below, then all will concede that it must be dismissed for want of jurisdiction. But if it is found that the Federal question was raised and was decided against the plaintiff in error, then the first duty of the court obviously is to determine whether it was correctly decided by the State court. Let us suppose that we find that the court below was right in its decision on that question. What, then, are we to do? Was it the intention of Congress to say that while you can only bring the case here on account of this question, yet when it is here, though it may turn out that the plaintiff in error was wrong on that question, and the judgment of the court below was right, though he has wrongfully dragged the defendant into this court by the allegation of an error which did not exist, and without which the case could not rightfully be here, he can still insist on an inquiry into all the other matters which were litigated in the case? This is neither reasonable nor just.

In such case both the nature of the jurisdiction conferred and the nature and fitness of things demand that, no error being found in the matter which authorized the re-examination, the judgment of the State court should be affirmed, and the case remitted to that court for its further enforcement.

The whole argument we are combating, however, goes upon the assumption that when it is found that the record shows that one of the questions mentioned has been decided against the claim of the plaintiff in error, this court has jurisdiction, and that jurisdiction extends to the whole case. We are of opinion that upon a fair construction of the whole language of the section the jurisdiction conferred is limited to the decision of the questions mentioned in the statute, and, as a necessary consequence of this, to the exercise of such powers as may be necessary to cause the judgment in that decision to be respected.

Make the Connection

Note the similarity of the argument here to the one the Court accepted in *United Mine Workers v. Gibbs* (1966), approving the exercise of pendent (now supplemental) jurisdiction. Congress adopted the same approach when it codified supplemental jurisdiction in 28 U.S.C. § 1367.

We will now advert to one or two considerations apart from the mere language of the statute, which seem to us to give additional force to this conclusion.

It has been many times decided by this court, on motions to dismiss this class of cases for want of jurisdiction, that if it appears from the record that the plaintiff in error raised and presented to the court by pleadings, prayer for instruction, or other appropriate method, one of the questions specified in the statute, and the court ruled against him, the jurisdiction of this court attached, and we must hear the case on its merits. Heretofore these merits have been held to be to determine whether the propositions of law involved in the specific Federal question were rightly decided, and if not, did the case of plaintiff in error, on the pleadings and evidence, come within the principle ruled by this court. This has always been held to be the exercise of the jurisdiction and re-examination of the case provided by the statute. But if when we once get jurisdiction, everything in the case is open to re-examination, it follows that every case tried in any State court, from that of a justice of the peace to the highest court of the State, may be brought to this court for final decision on all the points involved in it.

* * *

The twenty-fifth section of the act of 1789 has been the subject of innumerable decisions, some of which are to be found in almost every volume of the reports from that year down to the present. These form a system of appellate jurisprudence relating to the exercise of the appellate power of this court over the courts of the States. That system has been based upon the fundamental principle that this jurisdiction was limited to the correction of errors relating solely to Federal law. And though it may be argued with some plausibility that the reason of this is to be found in the restrictive clause of the act of 1789, which is omitted in the act of 1867, yet an examination of the cases will show that it rested quite as much on the conviction of this court that without that clause and on general principles the jurisdiction extended no further. It requires a very bold reach of thought, and a readiness to impute to Congress a radical and hazardous change of a policy vital in its essential nature to the independence of the State courts, to believe that that body contemplated, or intended, what is claimed, by the mere omission of a clause in the substituted statute, which may well be held to have been superfluous, or nearly so, in the old one.

Food for Thought

On what was Congress focusing most of its attention in 1867?

Another consideration, not without weight in seeking after the intention of Congress, is found in the fact that where that body has clearly shown an intention to bring the whole of a case which arises under the constitutional provision as to its subject-matter under the jurisdiction of a Federal court, it has conferred its cognizance on Federal courts of original jurisdiction and not on the Supreme Court.

* * *

And we think it equally clear that it has been the counterpart of the same policy to vest in the Supreme Court, as a court of *appeal* from the State courts, a jurisdiction limited to the questions of a Federal character which might be involved in such cases.

* * *

There may be some plausibility in the argument that these rights cannot be protected in all cases unless the Supreme Court has final control of the whole case. But the experience of eighty-five years of the administration of the law under the opposite theory would seem to be a satisfactory answer to the argument. It is not to be presumed that the State courts, where the rule is clearly laid down to them on the Federal question, and its influence on the case fully seen, will disregard or overlook it, and this is all that the rights of the party claiming under it require. Besides, by the very terms of this statute, when the Supreme Court is of opinion that the question of Federal law is of such relative importance to the whole case that it should control the final judgment, that court is authorized to render such judgment and enforce it by its own process. It cannot, therefore, be maintained that it is in any case necessary for the security of the rights claimed under the Constitution, laws, or treaties of the United States that the Supreme Court should examine and decide other questions not of a Federal character.

And we are of opinion that the act of 1867 does not confer such a jurisdiction.

This renders unnecessary a decision of the question whether, if Congress had conferred such authority, the act would have been constitutional. It will be time enough for this court to inquire into the existence of such a power when that body has attempted to exercise it in language which makes such an intention so clear as to require it.

* * *

It is proper, in this first attempt to construe this important statute as amended, to say a few words on another point. What shall be done by this court when the question has been found to exist in the record, and to have been decided against the plaintiff in error, and *rightfully* decided, we have already seen, and it presents no difficulties.

But when it appears that the Federal question was decided erroneously against the plaintiff in error, we must then reverse the case undoubtedly, if there are no other issues decided in it than that. It often has occurred, however, and will occur again, that there are other points in the case than those of Federal cognizance, on which the judgment of the court below may stand; those points being of themselves sufficient to control the case.

Or it may be, that there are other issues in the case, but they are not of such controlling influence on the whole case that they are alone sufficient to support the judgment.

It may also be found that notwithstanding there are many other questions in the record of the case, the issue raised by the Federal question is such that its decision must dispose of the whole case.

In the two latter instances there can be no doubt that the judgment of the State court must be reversed, and under the new act this court can either render the final judgment or decree here, or remand the case to the State court for that purpose.

But in the other cases supposed, why should a judgment be reversed for an error in deciding the Federal question, if the same judgment must be rendered on the other points in the case? And why should this court reverse a judgment which is right on the whole record presented to us; or where the same judgment will be rendered by the court below, after they have corrected the error in the Federal question?

We have already laid down the rule that we are not authorized to examine these other questions for the purpose of deciding whether the State court ruled correctly on them or not. We are of opinion that on these subjects not embraced in the class of questions stated in the statute, we must receive the decision of the State courts as conclusive.

> **Take Note**
>
> This is the Court's recognition that state courts speak ***ex cathedra*** with respect to the meaning, interpretation and application of state law.

But when we find that the State court has decided the Federal question erroneously, then to prevent a useless and profitless reversal, which can do the plaintiff in error no good, and can only embarrass and delay the defendant, we must so far look into the remainder of the record as to see whether the decision of the Federal question alone is sufficient to dispose of the case, or to require its reversal; or on the other hand, whether there exist other matters in the record actually decided by the State court which are sufficient to maintain the judgment of that court, notwithstanding the error in deciding the Federal question. In the latter case the court would not be justified in reversing the judgment of the State court.

But this examination into the points in the record other than the Federal question is not for the purpose of determining whether they were correctly or erroneously decided, but to ascertain if any such have been decided, and their sufficiency to maintain the final judgment, as decided by the State court.

Beyond this we are not at liberty to go, and we can only go this far to prevent the injustice of reversing a judgment which must in the end be reaffirmed, even in this court, if brought here again from the State court after it has corrected its error in the matter of Federal law.

> **Take Note!**
>
> Justice Miller appears to get a bit lost in his own argument here. After correction of the federal error, how could the case again reach the Supreme Court under either statute?

Finally, we hold the following propositions on this subject as flowing from the statute as it now stands:

1. That it is essential to the jurisdiction of this court over the judgment of a State court, that it shall appear that one of the questions mentioned in the act must have been raised, and presented to the State court.

2. That it must have been decided by the State court, or that its decision was necessary to the judgment or decree, rendered in the case.

3. That the decision must have been against the right claimed or asserted by plaintiff in error under the Constitution, treaties, laws, or authority of the United States.

4. These things appearing, this court has jurisdiction and must examine the judgment so far as to enable it to decide whether this claim of right was correctly adjudicated by the State court.

5. If it finds that it was rightly decided, the judgment must be affirmed.

6. If it was erroneously decided against plaintiff in error, then this court must further inquire, whether there is any other matter or issue adjudged by the State court, which is sufficiently broad to maintain the judgment of that court, notwithstanding the error in deciding the issue raised by the Federal question. If this is found to be the case, the judgment must be affirmed without inquiring into the soundness of the decision on such other matter or issue.

7. But if it be found that the issue raised by the question of Federal law is of such controlling character that its correct decision is necessary to any final judgment in the case, or that there has been no decision by the State court of any other matter or issue which is sufficient to maintain the judgment of that court without regard to the Federal question, then this court will reverse the judgment of the State court, and will either render such judgment here as the State court should have rendered, or remand the case to that court, as the circumstances of the case may require.

Applying the principles here laid down to the case now before the court, we are of opinion that this court has jurisdiction, and that the judgment of the Supreme Court of Tennessee must be affirmed.

* * *

The plaintiffs in error, by their bill, allege that the title was originally conveyed to the city of Memphis, in trust, for certain purposes, including that of having a navy yard built on it by the United States; that when the title reverted to the city by reason of the abandonment of the place as a navy yard by the United States, and the act of Congress aforesaid, the city received the title in trust for the original grantors, who are the plaintiffs, or who are represented by plaintiffs. A demurrer to the bill was filed. Also an answer denying the trust and pleading the statute of limitations. On the hearing the bill was dismissed, and this decree was affirmed by the Supreme Court of the State. The complainants, in their bill, and throughout the case, insisted that the effect of the act of 1854 was to vest the title in the mayor or aldermen of the city in trust for them.

* * *

But we need not consume many words to prove that neither by the deed of the city to the United States, which is an ordinary deed of bargain and sale for a valuable consideration, nor from anything found in the act of 1854, is there any such trust to be inferred. The act, so far from recognizing or implying any such trust, cedes the property to the mayor and aldermen *for the use of the city.* We are, therefore, of opinion that this, the only Federal question in the case, was rightly decided by the Supreme Court of Tennessee.

But conceding this to be true, the plaintiffs in error have argued that the court having jurisdiction of the case must now examine it upon all the questions which affect its merits; and they insist that the conveyance by which the city of Memphis received the title previous to the deed from the city to government, and the circumstances attending the making of the former deed are such, that when the title reverted to the city, a trust was raised for the benefit of plaintiffs.

After what has been said in the previous part of this opinion, we need discuss this matter no further. The claim of right here set up is one to be determined by the general principles of equity jurisprudence, and is unaffected by anything found in the Constitution, laws, or treaties of the United States. Whether decided well or otherwise by the State court, we have no authority to inquire. According to the principles we have laid down as applicable to this class of cases, the judgment of the Supreme Court of Tennessee must be

Affirmed.

MR. JUSTICE CLIFFORD, with whom concurred MR. JUSTICE SWAYNE, dissenting:

I dissent from so much of the opinion of the court as denies the jurisdiction of this court to determine the whole case, where it appears that the record presents a Federal question and that the Federal question was erroneously decided to the prejudice of the plaintiff in error; as in that state of the record it is, in my judgment, the duty of this court, under the recent act of Congress, to decide the whole merits of the controversy, and to affirm or reverse the judgment of the State court. Tested by the new law it would seem that it must be so, as this court cannot in that state of the record dismiss the writ of error, nor can the court reverse the judgment without deciding every question which the record presents.

Where the Federal question is rightly decided the judgment of the State court may be affirmed, upon the ground that the jurisdiction does not attach to the other questions involved in the merits of the controversy; but where the Federal question is erroneously decided the whole merits must be decided by this court, else the new law, which it is admitted repeals the twenty-fifth section of the Judiciary Act, is without meaning, operation, or effect, except to repeal the prior law.

Sufficient proof of the fact that the new law was not intended to be without meaning and effective operation is found in the fact that the provision in the old law which restricts the right of the plaintiff in error or appellant to assign for error any matter except such as respects one of the Federal questions enumerated in the twenty-fifth section of the Judiciary Act, is wholly omitted in the new law.

MR. JUSTICE BRADLEY, dissenting:

I feel obliged to dissent from the conclusion to which a majority of the court has come on the public question in this cause, but shall content myself with stating briefly the grounds of that dissent, without entering into any prolonged argument on the subject.

* * *

[S]upposing, as the majority of the court holds, that it has jurisdiction, I cannot concur in the conclusion that we can only decide the Federal question raised by the record. If we have jurisdiction at all, in my judgment we have jurisdiction of the *case*, and not merely of a *question* in it. The act of 1867, and the twenty-fifth section of the Judiciary Act both provide that a final judgment or decree in any suit in the highest court of a State, where is drawn in question certain things relating to the Constitution or laws of the United States, or to rights or immunities claimed under the United States, and the decision is adverse to such Constitution, laws, or rights, may be re-examined and reversed or affirmed in the Supreme Court of the United States upon a writ of error. Had the original act stopped here there could have been no difficulty. This act derives its authority and is intended to carry into effect, at least in part, that clause of the Constitution which declares that the judicial power shall extend to all cases, in law and equity, arising under this Constitution, the laws of the United States, and treaties made under their authority—not to all *questions,* but to all *cases.* This word "cases," in the residue of the section, has frequently been held to mean suits, actions, embracing the whole cases, not mere questions in them; and that is undoubtedly the true construction. The Constitution, therefore, would have authorized a revision by the judiciary of the United States of all *cases* decided in State courts in which questions of United States law of Federal rights are necessarily involved. Congress in carrying out that clause could have so ordained. And the law referred to, had it stopped at the point to which I have quoted it above, would clearly have been understood as so ordaining. But the twenty-fifth section of the Judiciary Act went on to declare that in such cases no other error should be assigned or regarded as a ground of reversal than such as immediately respected the question referred to as the ground of jurisdiction. It having been early decided that Congress had power to regulate the exercise of the appellate jurisdiction of the Supreme Court, the court has always considered itself bound by this restriction, and as authorized to reverse judgments of State courts only for errors in deciding the Federal questions involved therein.

Now, Congress, in the act of 1867, when revising the twenty-fifth section of the Judiciary Act, whilst following the general frame and modes of expression of that section, omitted the clause above referred to, which restricted the court to a consideration of the Federal questions. This omission cannot be regarded as having no meaning. The clause by its presence in the original act meant something, and effected something. It had the effect of restricting the consideration of the court to a certain class of questions as a ground of reversal, which restriction would not have existed without it. The omission of the clause, according to a well-settled rule of construction, must necessarily have the effect of removing the restriction which it effected in the old law.

In my judgment, therefore, if the court had jurisdiction of the case, it was bound to consider not only the Federal question raised by the record, but the whole case. As the court, however, has decided otherwise, it is not proper that I should express any opinion on the merits.

Notes and Questions

1. All of the questions this case raises turn on Congress's intent in deleting the final sentence of § 25 of the Judiciary Act of 1789, which clearly limited review to matters of federal law. Consider whether the Court's assignment of meaning (or, rather, lack of meaning) to the deletion is historically sound. After all, the amendment did not occur in a vacuum; it came in 1867, when Reconstruction was at its peak. Federal distrust of the reconstituted Southern governments was enormous. The elections of 1866 completely repudiated President Andrew Johnson's efforts at moderate reconstruction; Radical Republicans swept into office. Although the Radical Republicans did not agree as to all particulars, "they did all agree * * * that the existing state governments in the South—with the exception of Tennessee's—must be set aside and replaced for the time being by direct federal rule." ERIC L. MCKITRICK, ANDREW JOHNSON AND RECONSTRUCTION 456 (1960). There were frequent reports of miscarriages of justice in southern courts. The amendment to the 1789 Act passed in February 1867 while Congress debated establishing military reconstruction in the South. Although Justice Miller asserts that "it is not lightly to be presumed that Congress acted upon a

principle which implies a distrust of [state courts'] integrity[,] * * *" given the times, the Court's view of Congress's likely intent is at least questionable.

2. Suppose the 1789 Act had not contained the sentence Congress struck in 1867. Would the Court still have ruled that Congress should "use plain, unmistakable language * * *" to allow review of state law issues?

3. *Murdock* declined to consider whether Congress could constitutionally extend the Supreme Court's jurisdiction to all issues raised in an appeal. Has Congress the power to do that? Consider the following arguments pro and con:

> One can make a very strong affirmative argument. The Supreme Court says that the arising under jurisdiction [of Article III] is coextensive in the original, removal, and appellate modes. In *Martin v. Hunter's Lessee* [1816], the Court said that the difference between removal and appellate jurisdiction was merely one of timing. When an action is removed to a lower federal court, the court adjudicates the entire case, not just the federal issue involved. If all issues can be adjudicated in a removed case, and removal and appellate jurisdiction are coextensive, then the Supreme Court should be able to hear all issues in cases on appeal.
>
> Moreover, in discussing the arising under jurisdiction, the Court refers uniformly to "cases," rather than to "issues" or "claims." This suggests that once jurisdiction over a case attaches, the federal courts have authority to decide the entire case, and not just the federal issues therein. The Court made this inference explicit in *Osborn v. Bank of United States* [1824] and *Tennessee v. Davis* [1879]. In discussing the original jurisdiction, the *Osborn* Court asserted that once federal jurisdiction attached, "then all the other questions must be decided as incidental to this, which gives that jurisdiction." The Court reasoned that because so few cases involve only federal issues, to hold otherwise would effectively cripple the original jurisdiction of the lower federal courts. In discussing the removal jurisdiction, the *Davis* Court stated: "Nor is it any objection that questions are involved which are not at all of a Federal character. If one of the latter exist, if there be a single such ingredient in the mass, it is sufficient."
>
> * * *
>
> In sum, one can make a very strong argument that Congress could constitutionally extend jurisdiction to all issues in an appeal. One counterargument has some merit, however. The states' highest courts are supposed to have the final word on the meaning of state law. If the Supreme Court takes a case on appeal from a state's high court and reverses based on a different interpretation of state law, state authority plainly is compromised. Of course, the federal courts (including the Supreme Court) decide issues of state law when exercising supplemental jurisdiction and in diversity cases, and they sometimes decide wrongly. The state courts are not bound in later cases by these misreadings of state law. Presumably, the state courts also could ignore misinterpretations by the Supreme Court in cases heard on appeal from the state courts. Nonetheless, the federal-state conflict seems potentially more acute in an appeal, because the Supreme Court might tell a state's high court that it is misinterpreting state law in the very case both courts are hearing.

Donald H. Zeigler, *Twins Separated at Birth: A Comparative History of the Civil and Criminal Arising Under Jurisdiction of the Federal Courts and Some Proposals for Change*, 19 VT. L. REV. 673, 729-30 n.285 (1995) (citations omitted or modified).

4. Congress originally required not only that a federal question be present, but also that the state court have decided the federal question in a way that would have a direct, adverse effect on federal interests if the state court had erred. Congress provided no review, however, when the state court upheld a federal law or overturned a state law in the face of a federal law challenge. What if the state court interpreted federal law too broadly? Since the balance of federal and state power constantly affects delicate federalism interests, there may be a federal interest in not having state courts give federal rights unintended scope. Perhaps this is why Congress removed these limitations on the Court's appellate jurisdiction in 1914.

5. a) Consider numbers four, five, and six of Justice Miller's list of propositions. If the state court decided an issue of federal law, he asserts that the Supreme Court must decide whether the state court decided the issue correctly. If it did, the Supreme Court should affirm. If the state court decided incorrectly, then the Supreme Court should see whether the state court also decided some issue of state law that requires affirmance "notwithstanding the error in deciding the issue raised by the federal question." If this is so, the Court should affirm without reviewing the state court decision on the state law issue. Is this not an inefficient procedure? If state law will control the decision in any event, why should the Court gratuitously decide whether the state court erred on the non-controlling federal issue? What would be a better way to proceed?

b) In accord with Justice Miller's propositions, the Court examines whether the Tennessee courts properly construed the federal statute that reconveyed the land to Memphis. The Court concludes the Tennessee courts decided the federal issue correctly and therefore affirms without reviewing any state law questions. What, then, is the weight of propositions six and seven, which explain how the Court should proceed when a state court wrongly decides the federal issue?

c) One intriguing question about *Murdock* is whether expiration of the statute of limitations would have required affirmance even if the state courts had decided the federal question wrongly. The answer lies in the opinions of the Justices of the Tennessee Supreme Court. The majority ruled for the City on the federal issue and then said: "The views we have expressed render it unnecessary to express an opinion as to many points raised in argument." Dissenting, Justice Hawkins made it plain that the court did not decide the limitations question. He would have ruled for the complainants on the federal issue, which, he said, would have made it necessary to reach the limitations question, but since the majority ruled against the complainants on the merits, he agreed it was not necessary to reach it. *Murdock v. The Mayor and Aldermen of Memphis*, 47 Tenn. 483, 507-08 (1870). Even if the Tennessee Supreme Court had decided the federal issue erroneously, its determination to decide the case on the federal question and not on that statute of limitations ground would have brought it within the rule discussed in Orr v. Orr (1979), *infra* at 983, where the Court held that its jurisdiction is secure if the state court actually decides a case on the federal issue, even though it might have disposed of the case on state law grounds.

Camreta v. Greene, 131 S.Ct. 2020 (2011), although involving review of a federal, not a state, decision, may nonetheless have subtle implications for Supreme Court review of state court decisions. Camreta declared that the Court could review "a lower court's constitutional ruling at the behest of a government official granted immunity." The Court explained that the purpose of allowing such review was to prevent a possibly erroneous constitutional ruling from affecting future official conduct by causing officials to change a method of operating that might be entirely lawful.

Consider Camreta's implications with respect to the adequate-and-independent-state-ground rule. If the Court is concerned about the accumulation of erroneous constitutional precedent, would it be able to review a state court's "constitutional ruling" even if doing so would not affect the outcome of the case? Camreta was an official-immunity case in which the federal circuit court found a Fourth Amendment violation but affirmed a summary judgment for the defendant officials on the ground that they enjoyed qualified immunity. If Camreta had been in the state court system, could the Court have reviewed? One distinction from the other cases in this Chapter, of course, is that immunity is a federal, not state, ground. Suppose, however, that the state court ruled on the Fourth Amendment issue in favor of the plaintiff but then ordered the case dismissed based on some state-law ground (perhaps that the plaintiff had settled a case arising from the same incident with another state official and that part of the settlement was a covenant not to sue additional officials). Should the Supreme Court be able to review the constitutional ruling? Can the Court review in that circumstance? If so, then what is the status of the adequate-and-independent-state-ground rule? If not, then how are the officials who lost on the constitutional point to conduct themselves in future? If they continue the challenged conduct, they may be subject to liability. If they modify their conduct to conform with the state court's constitutional interpretation, they may be less able to carry out their duties effectively.

d) What is the status of the rule that the Supreme Court will not reverse a state court judgment based on an erroneous interpretation of federal law if there is a state law ground sufficient to maintain the judgment notwithstanding the state court's error? Is the rule a constitutional imperative, a statutory prescription, or a prudential rule of the Court's own making? If the first, what provision of the Article III prevents the Court from ruling on the disputed federal issue? If the second, what part of the statute authorizing review dictates the rule the Court announces? If the last, what is the source of authority for the Court to prescribe such a rule?

C. Insulating State Decisions From Supreme Court Review

1. With Substantive Law

a. Adequacy, Independence and Certainty

Fox Film Corp. v. Muller

Supreme Court of the United States, 1935.
296 U.S. 207.

MR. JUSTICE SUTHERLAND delivered the opinion of the Court.

This is an action brought in a Minnesota state court of first instance by the Film Corporation against Muller, to recover damages for an alleged breach of two contracts by which Muller was licensed to exhibit certain moving picture films belonging to the corporation. Muller answered, setting up the invalidity of the contracts under the Sherman Anti-trust Act. It was and is agreed that these contracts are substantially the same as the one involved in *United States v. Paramount Famous Lasky Corp.*, 34 F.2d 984, *aff'd* 282 U.S. 30; that petitioner was one of the defendants in that action; and that the "arbitration clause," paragraph 18 of each of the contracts sued upon, is the same as that held in that case to be invalid. In view of the disposition which we are to make of this writ, it is not necessary to set forth the terms of the arbitration clause or the other provisions of the contract.

The court of first instance held that each contract sued upon violated the Sherman Anti-trust Act, and dismissed the action. In a supplemental opinion that court put its decision upon the grounds, first, that the arbitration plan is so connected with the remainder of the contract that the entire contract is tainted, and, second, that the contract violates the Sherman Anti-trust law. The state supreme court affirmed. * * *

In its opinion, the state supreme court, after a statement of the case, said: "The question presented on this appeal is whether the arbitration clause is severable from the contract, leaving the remainder of the contract enforceable, or not severable, permeating and tainting the whole contract with illegality and making it void."

That court then proceeded to refer to and discuss a number of decisions of state and federal courts, some of which took the view that the arbitration clause was severable, and others that it was not severable, from the remainder of the contract. After reviewing the opinion and decree of the federal district court in the *Paramount* case, the lower court reached the conclusion that the holding of the federal court was that the entire contract was illegal; and upon that view and upon what it conceived to be the weight of authority, held the arbitration plan was inseparable from the other provisions of the contract. Whether this conclusion was right or wrong we need not determine. It is enough that it is, at least, not without fair support.

Respondent contends that the question of severability was alone decided and that no federal question was determined by the lower court. This contention petitioner challenges, and asserts that a federal question was involved and decided. We do not attempt to settle the dispute; but, assuming for present purposes only that petitioner's view is the correct one, the case is controlled by the settled rule that where the judgment of a state court rests upon two grounds, one of which is federal and the other non-federal in character, our jurisdiction fails if the non-federal ground is independent of the federal ground and adequate to support the judgment. This rule had become firmly fixed * * * and has been reiterated in a long line of cases since that time.

Whether the provisions of a contract are non-severable, so that if one be held invalid the others must fall with it, is clearly a question of general and not of federal law. The invalidity of the arbitration clause which the present contracts embody is conceded. It was held invalid by the federal district court in the *Paramount* case, and its judgment was affirmed here. The question, therefore, was foreclosed; and was not the subject of controversy in the state courts. In that situation, the primary question to be determined by the court below was whether the concededly invalid clause was separable from the other provisions of the contract. The ruling of the state supreme court that it was not, is sufficient to conclude the case without regard to the determination, if, in fact, any was made, in respect of the federal question. It follows that the non-federal ground is adequate to sustain the judgment.

> **Take Note**
>
> *Fox Film* antedated *Erie*. Note the Court's distinction between general law and federal law. *Swift v. Tyson* had authorized the lower federal courts to declare their own rules of general law, but because such rules were not federal law, supremacy did not compel the state courts to follow those rules. That is what led to Justice Brandeis's plaintive observation about "persistence of state courts in their own opinions on questions of [general] common law prevented uniformity."

The rule announced * * * to the effect that our jurisdiction attaches where the non-federal ground is so interwoven with the other as not to be an independent matter, does not apply. The construction put upon the contracts did not constitute a preliminary step which simply had the effect of bringing forward for determination the federal question, but was a decision which automatically took the federal question out of the case if otherwise it would be there. The non-federal question in respect of the construction of the contracts, and the federal question in respect of their validity under the Anti-trust Act, were clearly independent of one another. The case, in effect, was disposed of before the federal question said to be involved was reached. A decision of that question then became unnecessary; and whether it was decided or not, our want of jurisdiction is clear.

Writ dismissed for want of jurisdiction.

Notes and Questions

1. Justice Sutherland notes that the parties agree that the contracts in *Fox Film* and *Paramount* are identical. Moreover, he notes that Fox Film is not challenging the ruling in *Paramount*. What, then, is the federal question that Fox Film insists is present for decision?

2. Recall that *Murdock* said that the Court would first determine whether the state court correctly decided the federal issue and, if it did not, then determine whether the state court's decision of state issues would nonetheless require affirmance. Does the Court follow that sequence in *Fox*?

4. a) The Court dismisses the writ of certiorari for "want of jurisdiction." Why does an adequate and independent state ground for the decision below mean that the Court lacks jurisdiction? What constitutional or statutory provisions preclude jurisdiction?

b) Note that the issues here involve substantive law. Keep in mind your answer to the preceding part of this note when you read *Herndon v. Georgia*, *infra* at 972, to see whether the same rationale applies when the asserted state ground for decision is procedural rather than substantive.

Delaware v. Prouse

Supreme Court of the United States, 1979.
440 U.S. 648.

MR. JUSTICE WHITE delivered the opinion of the Court.

The question is whether it is an unreasonable seizure under the Fourth and Fourteenth Amendments to stop an automobile, being driven on a public highway, for the purpose of checking the driving license of the operator and the registration of the car, where there is neither probable cause to believe nor reasonable suspicion that the car is being driven contrary to the laws governing the operation of motor vehicles or that either the car or any of its occupants is subject to seizure or detention in connection with the violation of any other applicable law.

I

At 7:20 p.m. on November 30, 1976, a New Castle County, Delaware, patrolman in a police cruiser stopped the automobile occupied by respondent. The patrolman smelled marihuana smoke as he was walking toward the stopped vehicle, and he seized marihuana in plain view on the car floor. Respondent was subsequently indicted for illegal possession of a controlled substance. At a hearing on respondent's motion to suppress the marihuana seized as a result of the stop, the patrolman testified that prior to stopping the vehicle he had observed neither traffic or equipment violations nor any suspicious activity, and that he made the stop only in order to check the driver's license and registration. The patrolman was not acting pursuant to any standards, guidelines, or procedures pertaining to document spot checks, promulgated by either his department or the State Attorney General. Characterizing the stop as "routine," the patrolman explained, "I saw the car in the area and wasn't answering any complaints, so I decided to pull them off." The trial court granted the motion to suppress, finding the stop and detention to have been wholly capricious and therefore violative of the Fourth Amendment.

The Delaware Supreme Court affirmed, noting first that "[t]he issue of the legal validity of systematic, roadblock-type stops of a number of vehicles for license and vehicle registration check is *not* now before the Court." The court held that "a random stop of a motorist in the absence of specific articulable facts which justify the stop by indicating a reasonable suspicion that a violation of the law has occurred is constitutionally impermissible and violative of the Fourth and Fourteenth Amendments to the United States Constitution." We granted certiorari to resolve the conflict between this decision, which is in accord with decisions in five other jurisdictions, and the contrary determination in six jurisdictions that the Fourth Amendment does not prohibit the kind of automobile stop that occurred here.

II

Because the Delaware Supreme Court held that the stop at issue not only violated the Federal Constitution but also was impermissible under art. I, § 6, of the Delaware Constitution, it is urged that the judgment below was based on an independent and adequate state ground and that we therefore have no jurisdiction in this case. At least, it is suggested, the matter is sufficiently uncertain that we should remand for clarification as to the ground upon which the judgment rested. Based on our reading of the opinion, however, we are satisfied that even if the State Constitution would have provided an adequate basis for the judgment, the Delaware Supreme Court did not intend to rest its decision independently on the State Constitution and that we have jurisdiction of this case.

As we understand the opinion below, art. I, § 6, of the Delaware Constitution will automatically be interpreted at least as broadly as the Fourth Amendment;[4] that is, every police practice authoritatively determined to be contrary to the Fourth and Fourteenth Amendments will, without further analysis, be held to be contrary to art. I, § 6. This approach, which is consistent with previous opinions of the Delaware Supreme Court,[5] was followed in this case. The court analyzed the various decisions interpreting the Federal Constitution, concluded that the Fourth Amendment foreclosed spot checks of automobiles, and summarily held that the State Constitution was therefore also infringed. This is one of those cases where "at the very least, the [state] court felt compelled by what it understood to be federal constitutional considerations to construe * * * its own law in the manner it did." Had state law not been mentioned at all, there would be no question about our jurisdiction, even though the state Consti-

Food for Thought

Is this at all surprising? Suppose Delaware took the position that police actions that violated the Fourth and Fourteenth Amendments were nonetheless permissible under the Delaware Constitution. What would be the effect of such a ruling?]

---

4 The court stated: "The Delaware Constitution Article I, § 6 is substantially similar to the Fourth Amendment and a violation of the latter is necessarily a violation of the former." 382 A.2d at 1362, citing State v. Moore, 55 Del. 356, 187 A.2d 807 (1963).

Moore was decided less than two years after Mapp v. Ohio, 367 U.S. 643 (1961), applied to the States the limitations previously imposed only on the Federal Government. In setting forth the approach reiterated in the opinion below, *Moore* noted not only the common purposes and wording of the Fourth Amendment and the state constitutional provision, but also the overriding effect of the former.

5 We have found only one case decided after *State v. Moore* in which the court relied solely on state law in upholding the validity of a search or seizure, and that case involved not only DEL. CONST. art. I, § 6, but also state statutory requirements for issuance of a search warrant. Moreover, every case holding a search or seizure to be contrary to the state constitutional provision relies on cases interpreting the Fourth Amendment and simultaneously concludes that the search or seizure is contrary to that provision.

tution might have provided an independent and adequate state ground. The same result should follow here where the state constitutional holding depended upon the state court's view of the reach of the Fourth and Fourteenth Amendments. If the state court misapprehended federal law, "[i]t should be freed to decide * * * these suits according to its own local law."

* * *

VII

Accordingly, we hold that except in those situations in which there is at least articulable and reasonable suspicion that a motorist is unlicensed or that an automobile is not registered, or that either the vehicle or an occupant is otherwise subject to seizure for violation of law, stopping an automobile and detaining the driver in order to check his driver's license and the registration of the automobile are unreasonable under the Fourth Amendment. This holding does not preclude the State of Delaware or other States from developing methods for spot checks that involve less intrusion or that do not involve the unconstrained exercise of discretion. Questioning of all oncoming traffic at roadblock-type stops is one possible alternative. We hold only that persons in automobiles on public roadways may not for that reason alone have their travel and privacy interfered with at the unbridled discretion of police officers. The judgment below is affirmed.

So ordered.

Notes and Questions

1. The Delaware Supreme Court's remark about the relative scope of the Fourth Amendment and the Delaware constitutional provision does no more than confirm federal supremacy. Why does the Delaware court's statement of the obvious lend support to the Supreme Court's position?

2. a) Is the Court implicitly saying that the Delaware Supreme Court would have been better off to have written the very same opinion but without reference to federal law if it wanted Delaware law to control the case?

b) Is there any way for a state court to cite federal and state constitutions and still use the adequate and independent state ground rule to insulate its decision from Supreme Court review?

c) If state law provides a complete ground for decision, why would a state court ever cite apparently superfluous federal law?

3. Suppose the Supreme Court decided that the police conduct in *Prouse* did not violate the Fourth Amendment. Should the Court then remand to the trial court, or should the Delaware Supreme Court have an opportunity to construe the Delaware Constitution more broadly than the Fourth Amendment, obviating the need for a trial?

Minnesota v. National Tea Co.

Supreme Court of the United States, 1940.
309 U.S. 551.

MR. JUSTICE DOUGLAS delivered the opinion of the Court.

In 1933 Minnesota enacted a chain store tax[,] one item of which was a tax on gross sales. The gross sales tax was graduated * * *. Respondents (chain stores conducting retail businesses in Minnesota) paid under protest the gross sales tax demanded by the Minnesota Tax Commission for the years 1933 and 1934 and thereafter sued in the state court for refunds. Judgments granting refunds were affirmed by the Supreme Court of Minnesota. * * *

At the threshold * * * we are met with a question which is decisive of the present petition. That is the question of jurisdiction.

The Supreme Court of Minnesota discussed not only the equal protection clause of the Fourteenth Amendment of the federal constitution but also art. 9, § 1 of the Minnesota constitution which provides: "Taxes shall be uniform upon the same class of subjects * * * ." It said that "these provisions of the Federal and State Constitutions impose identical restrictions upon the legislative power of the state in respect to classification for purposes of taxation." It stated that the "question is * * * whether the imposition of a graduated gross sales tax upon all those engaged in conducting chain stores is discriminatory as between such owners, thus violating the constitutional requirement of uniformity." It quoted the conclusion of the lower Minnesota court that the statute violated both the federal and the state constitution. It then adverted briefly to three of its former decisions which had interpreted art. 9, § 1 of the Minnesota constitution and quoted from one of them.[3] It merely added: "So much for our own cases"; and proceeded at once to a discussion of cases based solely on the Fourteenth Amendment of the federal constitution. While its discussion of art. 9, § 1 of the Minnesota constitution was in general terms, its analysis of the Fourteenth Amendment was specifically related to chain store taxation. It distinguished decisions of this Court which held that the number of stores in a given chain affords an appropriate basis for classification for imposition of progressively higher taxes. It then stated that the "precise question here presented" had been directly passed upon adversely to the state's contention in five cases. It added that the tax here involved was on all fours with that struck down by this Court. * * * And it concluded with the following statement:

> We think the five cases to which we have referred have so definitely and finally disposed of the legal problem presented as to make it needless for us to analyze or discuss the great number of other tax cases where the same constitutional question was involved. These being the only cases to which our attention has been called *directly deciding the question presented* we are of opinion that we should follow them and *that it is our duty so to do.* [Italics added.]

Respondents contend that the court held the statute invalid for violation not only of the federal constitution but also of the state constitution. Hence they seek to invoke the familiar rule that where a judgment of a state court rests on two grounds, one involving a federal question and the other not, this Court will not take jurisdiction. In support of this position they point to the court's discussion of the Minnesota constitution and to the fact that the syllabus states that such a tax is violative of both the federal and state constitutions. But as to the latter we are not referred to any Minnesota authority which, as in some states, makes the syllabi the law of the case. And as to the former the opinion is quite inconclusive. For the opinion as a whole leaves the impression that the court probably felt constrained to rule as it did because of the five decisions which it cited and which held such gross sales taxes unconstitutional by reason of the Fourteenth Amendment. That is at least the meaning, if the words used are taken literally. For if, as stated by the court, the "precise question here presented" was ruled by those five cases, that question was a federal one. And in that connection it is perhaps significant that

3 This reference to Minnesota constitutional law was limited to the following:

Our cases hold (and that is the general rule) that the legislature

> has a wide discretion in classifying property for the purposes of taxation, but the classification must be based on differences which furnish a reasonable ground for making a distinction between the several classes. The differences must not be so wanting in substance that the classification results in permitting one to escape a burden imposed on another under substantially similar circumstances and conditions. The rule of uniformity, established by the Constitution, requires that all similarly situated shall be treated alike.
>
> * * *

the court stated not only that it "should follow" those decisions but that "it is our duty so to do."

Enough has been said to demonstrate that there is considerable uncertainty as to the precise grounds for the decision. That is sufficient reason for us to decline at this time to review the federal question asserted to be present, consistently with the policy of not passing upon questions of a constitutional nature which are not clearly necessary to a decision of the case.

But that does not mean that we should dismiss the petition. This Court has frequently held that in the exercise of its appellate jurisdiction it has the power not only to correct errors of law in the judgment under review but also to make such disposition of the case as justice requires. That principle has been applied to cases coming from state courts where supervening changes had occurred since entry of the judgment, where the record failed adequately to state the facts underlying a decision of the federal question, and where the grounds of the state decision were obscure. That principle was also applied where it was said:

> * * * if the state court did in fact intend alternatively to base its decision upon the state statute and upon an immunity it thought granted by the Constitution as interpreted by this Court, these two grounds are so interwoven that we are unable to conclude that the judgment rests upon an independent interpretation of the state law.

The procedure in those cases was to vacate the judgment and to remand the cause for further proceedings, so that the federal question might be dissected out or the state and federal questions clearly separated.

In this type of case we deem it essential that this procedure be followed. It is possible that the state court employed the decisions under the federal constitution merely as persuasive authorities for its independent interpretation of the state constitution. If that were true, we would have no jurisdiction to review. On the other hand we cannot be content with a dismissal of the petition where there is strong indication, as here, that the federal constitution as judicially construed controlled the decision below.

If a state court merely said that the Fourteenth Amendment, as construed by this Court, is the "supreme law of the land" to which obedience must be given, our jurisdiction would seem to be inescapable. And that would follow though the state court might have given, if it had chosen, a different construction to an identical provision in the state constitution. But the Minnesota Supreme Court did not take such an unequivocal position. On the other hand, it did not declare its independence of the decisions of this Court, when the state constitutional provision avowedly had identity of scope with the relevant clause of the Fourteenth Amendment. * * * .

It is important that this Court not indulge in needless dissertations on constitutional law. It is fundamental that state courts be left free and unfettered by us in interpreting their state constitutions. But it is equally important that ambiguous or obscure adjudications by state courts do not stand as barriers to a determination by this Court of the validity under the federal constitution of state action. Intelligent exercise of our appellate powers compels us to ask for the elimination of the obscurities and ambiguities from the opinions in such cases. Only then can we ascertain whether or not our jurisdiction to review should be invoked. Only by that procedure can the responsibility for striking down or upholding state legislation be fairly placed. For no other course assures that important federal issues, such as have been argued here, will reach this Court for adjudication; that state courts will not be the final arbiters of important issues under the federal constitution; and that we will not encroach on the constitutional jurisdiction of the states. This is not a mere technical rule nor a rule for our convenience. It touches the division of authority between state courts and this Court and is of equal importance to each. Only by such explicitness can the highest courts of the states and this Court keep within the bounds of their respective jurisdictions.

For these reasons we vacate the judgment of the Supreme Court of Minnesota and remand the cause to that court for further proceedings.

Judgment vacated.

MR. CHIEF JUSTICE HUGHES, dissenting:

I think that sound principle governing the exercise of our jurisdiction requires the dismissal of the writ. I see no reason to doubt that the Supreme Court of Minnesota held that the tax in question was laid in violation of the uniformity clause of the State Constitution. Not only is that shown, as it seems to me, from the court's discussion of that question, but it conclusively appears from the syllabus which definitely states that the tax is "violative of art. 9, § 1, of our state constitution." Minnesota requires that in all cases decided by the Supreme Court it shall give its decision in writing, "together with headnotes, briefly stating the points decided." In obedience to the statute, the court has thus given explicitly in its syllabus its own deliberate construction of what it has decided.

The decision thus rested upon an adequate non-federal ground and in accordance with long-established doctrine we are without jurisdiction.

This is not a case where the record leaves us in uncertainty as to what has actually been determined by the state court. Nor have there been supervening changes since the entry of the judgment. I find no warrant for vacating the judgment on either of these grounds.

The fact that provisions of the state and federal constitutions may be similar or even identical does not justify us in disturbing a judgment of a state court which adequately rests upon its application of the provision of its own constitution. That the state court may be influenced by the reasoning of our opinions makes no difference. The state court may be persuaded by majority opinions in this Court or it may prefer the reasoning of dissenting judges, but the judgment of the state court upon the application of its own constitution remains a judgment which we are without jurisdiction to review. Whether in this case we thought that the state tax was repugnant to the federal constitution or consistent with it, the judgment of the state court that the tax violated the state constitution would still stand. It cannot be supposed that the Supreme Court of Minnesota is not fully conscious of its independent authority to construe the constitution of the State, whatever reasons it may adduce in so doing. As the Minnesota court said in [another case], after referring to the question presented under the federal constitution, "Our interpretation of our own constitution is of course final."

Take Note

N.B. Chief Justice Hughes's restatement of the ***ex cathedra*** principle.

* * *

Notes and Questions

1. Are *Prouse* and *National Tea* distinguishable? How do the federal and state constitutional provisions compare to each other in each case? Are they more similar in one case than in the other? In which case is the Court better able to determine whether the state court based its ruling on an adequate and independent state ground? How does the answer to that question help to explain the different outcomes?

2. Might Chief Justice Hughes also have rested his dissent on the ground that the party invoking federal jurisdiction always has the burden of demonstrating its existence, and that even in the eyes of the majority Minnesota had failed to do that?

Michigan v. Long

Supreme Court of the United States, 1983.
463 U.S. 1032.

JUSTICE O'CONNOR delivered the opinion of the Court.

In *Terry v. Ohio* we upheld the validity of a protective search for weapons in the absence of probable cause to arrest because it is unreasonable to deny a police officer the right "to neutralize the threat of physical harm," when he possesses an articulable suspicion that an individual is armed and dangerous. We did not, however, expressly address whether such a protective search for weapons could extend to an area beyond the person in the absence of probable cause to arrest. In the present case, respondent David Long was convicted for possession of marihuana found by police in the passenger compartment and trunk of the automobile that he was driving. The police searched the passenger compartment because they had reason to believe that the vehicle contained weapons potentially dangerous to the officers. We hold that the protective search of the passenger compartment was reasonable under the principles articulated in *Terry* and other decisions of this Court. We also examine Long's argument that the decision below rests upon an adequate and independent state ground, and we decide in favor of our jurisdiction.

* * *

II

Before reaching the merits, we must consider Long's argument that we are without jurisdiction to decide this case because the decision below rests on an adequate and independent state ground. The court below referred twice to the State Constitution in its opinion, but otherwise relied exclusively on federal law.[3] Long argues that the Michigan courts have provided greater protection from searches and seizures under the State Constitution than is afforded under the Fourth Amendment, and the references to the State Constitution therefore establish an adequate and independent ground for the decision below.

It is, of course, "incumbent upon this Court * * * to ascertain for itself * * * whether the asserted non-federal ground independently and adequately supports the judgment." Although we have announced a number of principles in order

3 On the first occasion, the court merely cited in a footnote both the State and Federal Constitutions. On the second occasion, at the conclusion of the opinion, the court stated: "We hold, therefore, that the deputies' search of the vehicle was proscribed by the Fourth Amendment to the United States Constitution and art. 1, § 11 of the Michigan Constitution."

to help us determine whether various forms of references to state law constitute adequate and independent state grounds,[4] we openly admit that we have thus far not developed a satisfying and consistent approach for resolving this vexing issue. In some instances, we have taken the strict view that if the ground of decision was at all unclear, we would dismiss the case. In other instances, we have vacated or continued a case in order to obtain clarification about the nature of a state court decision. In more recent cases, we have ourselves examined state law to determine whether state courts have used federal law to guide their application of state law or to provide the actual basis for the decision that was reached. In *Oregon v. Kennedy,* we rejected an invitation to remand to the state court for clarification even when the decision rested in part on a case from the state court, because we determined that the state case itself rested upon federal grounds. We added that "[e]ven if the case admitted of more doubt as to whether federal and state grounds for decision were intermixed, the fact that the state court relied to the extent it did on federal grounds requires us to reach the merits."

This ad hoc method of dealing with cases that involve possible adequate and independent state grounds is antithetical to the doctrinal consistency that is required when sensitive issues of federal-state relations are involved. Moreover, none of the various methods of disposition that we have employed thus far recommends itself as the preferred method that we should apply to the exclusion of others, and we therefore determine that it is appropriate to reexamine our treatment of this jurisdictional issue in order to achieve the consistency that is necessary.

The process of examining state law is unsatisfactory because it requires us to interpret state laws with which we are generally unfamiliar, and which often, as in this case, have not been discussed at length by the parties. Vacation and continuance for clarification have also been unsatisfactory both because of the delay and decrease in efficiency of judicial administration, and, more important, because these methods of disposition place significant burdens on state courts to demon-

---

4 For example, we have long recognized that "where the judgment of a state court rests upon two grounds, one of which is federal and the other non-federal in character, our jurisdiction fails if the non-federal ground is independent of the federal ground and adequate to support the judgment." We may review a state case decided on a federal ground even if it is clear that there was an available state ground for decision on which the state court could properly have relied. Also, if, in our view, the state court " 'felt compelled by what it understood to be federal constitutional considerations to construe * * * its own law in the manner it did,' " then we will not treat a normally adequate state ground as independent, and there will be no question about our jurisdiction.

Finally, "where the non-federal ground is so interwoven with the [federal ground] as not to be an independent matter, or is not of sufficient breadth to sustain the judgment without any decision of the other, our jurisdiction is plain."

strate the presence or absence of our jurisdiction. Finally, outright dismissal of cases is clearly not a panacea because it cannot be doubted that there is an important need for uniformity in federal law, and that this need goes unsatisfied when we fail to review an opinion that rests primarily upon federal grounds and where the independence of an alleged state ground is not apparent from the four corners of the opinion. We have long recognized that dismissal is inappropriate "where there is strong indication * * * that the federal constitution as judicially construed controlled the decision below."

Take Note

Justice O'Connor suggests that it is improper for the Supreme Court to do that, does she not?

Respect for the independence of state courts, as well as avoidance of rendering advisory opinions, have been the cornerstones of this Court's refusal to decide cases where there is an adequate and independent state ground. It is precisely because of this respect for state courts, and this desire to avoid advisory opinions, that we do not wish to continue to decide issues of state law that go beyond the opinion that we review, or to require state courts to reconsider cases to clarify the grounds of their decisions. Accordingly, when, as in this case, a state court decision fairly appears to rest primarily on federal law, or to be interwoven with the federal law, and when the adequacy and independence of any possible state law ground is not clear from the face of the opinion, we will accept as the most reasonable explanation that the state court decided the case the way it did because it believed that federal law required it to do so. If a state court chooses merely to rely on federal precedents as it would on the precedents of all other jurisdictions, then it need only make clear by a plain statement in its judgment or opinion that the federal cases are being used only for the purpose of guidance, and do not themselves compel the result that the court has reached. In this way, both justice and judicial administration will be greatly improved. If the state court decision indicates clearly and expressly that it is alternatively based on bona fide separate, adequate, and independent grounds, we, of course, will not undertake to review the decision.

Take Note!

Whatever happened to Justice O'Connor's desire to avoid "plac[ing] significant burdens on state courts to demonstrate the presence or absence of our jurisdiction"? Has Justice O'Connor ended that burden or merely shifted it ahead in time?

This approach obviates in most instances the need to examine state law in order to decide the nature of the state court decision, and will at the same time avoid the danger of our rendering advisory opinions.[6] It also avoids the unsatisfactory and intrusive practice of requiring state courts to clarify their decisions to the satisfaction of this Court. We believe that such an approach will provide state judges with a clearer opportunity to develop state jurisprudence unimpeded by federal interference, and yet will preserve the integrity of federal law. "It is fundamental that state courts be left free and unfettered by us in interpreting their state constitutions. But it is equally important that ambiguous or obscure adjudications by state courts do not stand as barriers to a determination by this Court of the validity under the federal constitution of state action."

Food for Thought

Will it really? Suppose the Court's assumption that there is no adequate and independent state ground is wrong in a particular case.

The principle that we will not review judgments of state courts that rest on adequate and independent state grounds is based, in part, on "the limitations of our own jurisdiction."[7] The jurisdictional concern is that we not "render an advisory opinion, and if the same judgment would be rendered by the state court after we corrected its views of federal laws, our review could amount to nothing more than an advisory opinion." Our requirement of a "plain statement" that a decision rests upon adequate and independent state grounds does not in any way authorize the rendering of advisory opinions. Rather, in determining, as we must, whether we have jurisdiction to review a case that is alleged to rest on adequate and independent state grounds, we merely assume that there are no such grounds when it is not clear from the opinion itself that the state court relied upon an adequate and independent state ground and when it fairly appears that the state court rested its decision primarily on federal law.[8]

---

6 There may be certain circumstances in which clarification is necessary or desirable, and we will not be foreclosed from taking the appropriate action.

7 In Herb v. Pitcairn, the Court also wrote that it was desirable that state courts "be asked rather than told what they have intended." It is clear that we have already departed from that view in those cases in which we have examined state law to determine whether a particular result was guided or compelled by federal law. Our decision today departs further from Herb insofar as we disfavor further requests to state courts for clarification, and we require a clear and express statement that a decision rests on adequate and independent state grounds. However, the "plain statement" rule protects the integrity of state courts for the reasons discussed above. * * *

8 It is not unusual for us to employ certain presumptions in deciding jurisdictional issues. For instance, although the petitioner bears the burden of establishing our jurisdiction, we have held that the party who alleges that a controversy before us has become moot has the "heavy burden" of establishing that we lack jurisdiction. That is, we presume in those circumstances that we have jurisdiction until some party establishes that we do not for reasons of mootness.

We also note that the rule that we announce today was foreshadowed by our opinions in Delaware v. Prouse, 440 U.S. 648 (1979), and Zacchini v. Scripps-Howard Broadcasting Co., 433 U.S. 562 (1977). In these cases, the state courts relied on both state and federal law. We determined that we had jurisdiction to decide the cases because our reading of the opinions led us to conclude that each

Our review of the decision below under this framework leaves us unconvinced that it rests upon an independent state ground. Apart from its two citations to the State Constitution, the court below relied *exclusively* on its understanding of Terry and other federal cases. Not a single state case was cited to support the state court's holding that the search of the passenger compartment was unconstitutional.[9] Indeed, the court declared that the search in this case was unconstitutional because "[t]he Court of Appeals erroneously applied the principles of Terry v. Ohio * * * to the search of the interior of the vehicle in this case." The references to the State Constitution in no way indicate that the decision below rested on grounds in any way *independent* from the state court's interpretation of federal law. Even if we accept that the Michigan Constitution has been interpreted to provide independent protection for certain rights also secured

Food for Thought

With respect to the Court's footnote's reference to mootness, there is a distinction, is there not? Once jurisdiction has attached, it may be permissible to require a party who wants to defeat it because of changed circumstances to bear the burden of showing its disappearance; that is a far different thing from presuming the existence of jurisdiction in the first place. Note that at every level of federal court, the party who invokes the court's jurisdiction bears the burden of demonstrating its existence, whether one is talking about the plaintiff's burden under Rule 8(a)(1) for a case begun in federal court, the defendant's burden under 28 U.S.C. § 1446(a), or an appealing party's burden to demonstrate appellate court jurisdiction under 28 U.S.C. §§ 1291, 1254 or 1257.

---

court "felt compelled by what it understood to be federal constitutional considerations to construe and apply its own law in the manner it did." In Delaware, we referred to prior state decisions that confirmed our understanding of the opinion in that case, but our primary focus was on the face of the opinion. In Zacchini, we relied entirely on the syllabus and opinion of the state court.

In dissent, Justice Stevens proposes the novel view that this Court should never review a state court decision unless the Court wishes to vindicate a federal right that has been endangered. The rationale of the dissent is not restricted to cases where the decision is arguably supported by adequate and independent state grounds. Rather, Justice Stevens appears to believe that even if the decision below rests exclusively on federal grounds, this Court should not review the decision as long as there is no federal right that is endangered.

The state courts handle the vast bulk of all criminal litigation in this country. In 1982, more than 12 million criminal actions (excluding juvenile and traffic charges) were filed in the 50 state court systems and the District of Columbia. By comparison, approximately 32,700 criminal suits were filed in federal courts during that same year. The state courts are required to apply federal constitutional standards, and they necessarily create a considerable body of "federal law" in the process. It is not surprising that this Court has become more interested in the application and development of federal law by state courts in the light of the recent significant expansion of federally created standards that we have imposed on the States.

9 At oral argument, Long argued that the state court relied on its decision in *People v. Reed*. However, the court cited that case only in the context of a statement that the State did not seek to justify the search in this case "by reference to other exceptions to the warrant requirement." The court then noted that *Reed* held that " '[a] warrantless search and seizure is unreasonable per se and violates the Fourth Amendment of the United States Constitution and Art. 1, § 11 of the state constitution unless shown to be within one of the exceptions to the rule.' "

under the Fourth Amendment, it fairly appears in this case that the Michigan Supreme Court rested its decision primarily on federal law.

Rather than dismissing the case, or requiring that the state court reconsider its decision on our behalf solely because of a mere possibility that an adequate and independent ground supports the judgment, we find that we have jurisdiction in the absence of a plain statement that the decision below rested on an adequate and independent state ground. It appears to us that the state court "felt compelled by what it understood to be federal constitutional considerations to construe * * * its own law in the manner it did." *Zacchini v. Scripps-Howard Broadcasting Co.*[10]

* * *

[The Court's discussion of the merits of the Fourth Amendment issue is omitted. The majority ruled that the police conduct did not violate Long's Fourth Amendment rights.]

V

The judgment of the Michigan Supreme Court is reversed, and the case is remanded for further proceedings not inconsistent with this opinion.

It is so ordered.

JUSTICE STEVENS, dissenting.

The jurisprudential questions presented in this case are far more important than the question whether the Michigan police officer's search of respondent's car violated the Fourth Amendment. The case raises profoundly significant questions concerning the relationship between two sovereigns—the State of Michigan and the United States of America.

The Supreme Court of the State of Michigan expressly held "that the deputies' search of the vehicle was proscribed by the Fourth Amendment to the United States Constitution and *art. 1, § 11 of the Michigan Constitution.*" ([E]mphasis added.) The state law ground is clearly adequate to support the judgment, but the question whether it is independent of the Michigan Supreme Court's under-

10 There is nothing unfair about requiring a plain statement of an independent state ground in this case. Even if we were to rest our decision on an evaluation of the state law relevant to Long's claim, as we have sometimes done in the past, our understanding of Michigan law would also result in our finding that we have jurisdiction to decide this case. Under state search-and-seizure law, a "higher standard" is imposed under art. 1, § 11, of the 1963 Michigan Constitution. If, however, the item seized is, *inter alia*, a "narcotic drug * * * seized by a peace officer outside the curtilage of any dwelling house in this state," art. 1, § 11, of the 1963 Michigan Constitution, then the seizure is governed by a standard identical to that imposed by the Fourth Amendment. * * *

standing of federal law is more difficult. Four possible ways of resolving that question present themselves: (1) asking the Michigan Supreme Court directly, (2) attempting to infer from all possible sources of state law what the Michigan Supreme Court meant, (3) presuming that adequate state grounds are independent unless it clearly appears otherwise, or (4) presuming that adequate state grounds are not independent unless it clearly appears otherwise. This Court has, on different occasions, employed each of the first three approaches; never until today has it even hinted at the fourth. In order to "achieve the consistency that is necessary," the Court today undertakes a reexamination of all the possibilities. It rejects the first approach as inefficient and unduly burdensome for state courts, and rejects the second approach as an inappropriate expenditure of our resources. Although I find both of those decisions defensible in themselves, I cannot accept the Court's decision to choose the fourth approach over the third—to presume that adequate state grounds are intended to be dependent on federal law unless the record plainly shows otherwise. I must therefore dissent.

If we reject the intermediate approaches, we are left with a choice between two presumptions: one in favor of our taking jurisdiction, and one against it. Historically, the latter presumption has always prevailed. * * *

The Court today points out that in several cases we have weakened the traditional presumption by using the other two intermediate approaches identified above. Since those two approaches are now to be rejected, however, I would think that *stare decisis* would call for a return to historical principle. Instead, the Court seems to conclude that because some precedents are to be rejected, we must overrule them all.

Even if I agreed with the Court that we are free to consider as a fresh proposition whether we may take presumptive jurisdiction over the decisions of sovereign States, I could not agree that an expansive attitude makes good sense. It appears to be common ground that any rule we adopt should show "respect for state courts, and [a] desire to avoid advisory opinions." And I am confident that all Members of this Court agree that there is a vital interest in the sound management of scarce federal judicial resources. All of those policies counsel against the exercise of federal jurisdiction. They are fortified by my belief that a policy of judicial restraint—one that allows other decisional bodies to have the last word in legal interpretation until it is truly necessary for this Court to intervene—enables this Court to make its most effective contribution to our federal system of government.

The nature of the case before us hardly compels a departure from tradition. These are not cases in which an American citizen has been deprived of a right secured by the United States Constitution or a federal statute. Rather, they are cases in which a state court has upheld a citizen's assertion of a right, finding the citizen to be protected under both federal and state law. The complaining party is an officer of the State itself, who asks us to rule that the state court interpreted federal rights too broadly and "overprotected" the citizen.

Such cases should not be of inherent concern to this Court. The reason may be illuminated by assuming that the events underlying this case had arisen in another country, perhaps the Republic of Finland. If the Finnish police had arrested a Finnish citizen for possession of marihuana, and the Finnish courts had turned him loose, no American would have standing to object. If instead they had arrested an American citizen and acquitted him, we might have been concerned about the arrest but we surely could not have complained about the acquittal, even if the Finnish court had based its decision on its understanding of the United States Constitution. That would be true even if we had a treaty with Finland requiring it to respect the rights of American citizens under the United States Constitution. We would only be motivated to intervene if an American citizen were unfairly arrested, tried, and convicted by the foreign tribunal.

In this case the State of Michigan has arrested one of its citizens and the Michigan Supreme Court has decided to turn him loose. The respondent is a United States citizen as well as a Michigan citizen, but since there is no claim that he has been mistreated by the State of Michigan, the final outcome of the state processes offended no federal interest whatever. Michigan simply provided greater protection to one of its citizens than some other State might provide or, indeed, than this Court might require throughout the country.

* * *

Until recently we had virtually no interest in cases of this type. Thirty years ago, this Court reviewed only one. Indeed, that appears to have been the only case during the entire 1953 Term in which a State even sought review of a decision by its own judiciary. Fifteen years ago, we did not review any such cases, although the total number of requests had mounted to three. Some time during the past decade, perhaps about the time of the 5-to-4 decision in *Zacchini v. Scripps-Howard Broadcasting Co.*, our priorities shifted. The result is a docket swollen with requests by States to reverse judgments that their courts have rendered in favor of their citizens. I am confident that a future Court will recognize the error of this allocation of resources. When that day comes, I

Food for Thought

Does Justice Stevens look only at one side of the balance here? Why are not the states entitled just as much as individuals to a correct, authoritative interpretation of federal law? After all, if the Michigan Supreme Court interpreted the Fourth Amendment too broadly, one might view that as upsetting the federal-state power balance. If the interests of federalism, presumably shared by the federal government and the states, call for a proper balance (whatever that might be), why should a state court's error not be a matter of concern to the Supreme Court?

think it likely that the Court will also reconsider the propriety of today's expansion of our jurisdiction.

The Court offers only one reason for asserting authority over cases such as the one presented today: "an important need for uniformity in federal law [that] goes unsatisfied when we fail to review an opinion that rests primarily upon federal grounds and where the independence of an alleged state grounds is not apparent from the four corners of the opinion." Of course, the supposed need to "review an opinion" clashes directly with our oft-repeated reminder that "our power is to correct wrong judgments, not to revise opinions." The clash is not merely one of form: the "need for uniformity in federal law" is truly an ungovernable engine. That same need is no less present when it is perfectly clear that a state ground is both independent and adequate. * * * We do not sit to expound our understanding of the Constitution to interested listeners in the legal community; we sit to resolve disputes. If it is not apparent that our views would affect the outcome of a particular case, we cannot presume to interfere.[4]

Finally, I am thoroughly baffled by the Court's suggestion that it must stretch its jurisdiction and reverse the judgment of the Michigan Supreme Court in order to show "[r]espect for the independence of state courts." Would we show respect for the Republic of Finland by convening a special sitting for the sole purpose of declaring that its decision to release an American citizen was based upon a misunderstanding of American law?

I respectfully dissent.

---

4 In this regard, one of the cases overruled today deserves comment. In Minnesota v. National Tea Co., the Court considered a case much like this one—the Minnesota Supreme Court had concluded that both the Fourteenth Amendment to the United States Constitution and art. 9, § 1, of the Minnesota Constitution prohibited a graduated income tax on chain store income. The state court stated that "th[e] provisions of the Federal and State Constitutions impose identical restrictions upon the legislative power of the state in respect to classification for purposes of taxation," and "then adverted briefly to three of its former decisions which had interpreted" the state provision. It then proceeded to conduct a careful analysis of the Federal Constitution. It could justly be said that the decision rested primarily on federal law. * * *

Today's Court rejects that approach as intruding unduly on the state judicial process. One might therefore expect it to turn to Chief Justice Hughes' dissenting opinion in National Tea. In a careful statement of the applicable principles, he made an observation that I find unanswerable:

> The fact that provisions of the state and federal constitutions may be similar or even identical does not justify us in disturbing a judgment of a state court which adequately rests upon its application of the provisions of its own constitution. That the state court may be influenced by the reasoning of our opinions makes no difference. The state court may be persuaded by majority opinions in this Court or it may prefer the reasoning of dissenting judges, but the judgment of the state court upon the application of its own constitution remains a judgment which we are without jurisdiction to review. Whether in this case we thought that the state tax was repugnant to the federal constitution or consistent with it, the judgment of the state court that the tax violated the state constitution would still stand. * * *

Notes and Questions

1. The majority and the dissent agree that the Supreme Court has used three different approaches when it is unclear from the face of an opinion whether the state court decision rests on an adequate and independent state ground. The majority rejects the traditional approaches and adopts a new one. Justice O'Connor then asserts that the new standard will "avoid the danger of our rendering advisory opinions." One might argue, however, that advisory opinions are more likely under the new standard than under any of the traditional approaches. Why?

2. In footnote 6, Justice O'Connor holds open the possibility of the Court using the National Tea approach to seek clarification in appropriate circumstances. The Court followed this course in *Bush v. Palm Beach County Canvassing Board,* 531 U.S. 70 (2000). Then-Governor George W. Bush sought review in the United States Supreme Court of an order of the Florida Supreme Court interpreting Florida election statutes to permit manual recounts of ballots and extending the time in which such recounts could occur beyond the time that the Florida Secretary of State had determined. Bush argued that the Florida decision ran afoul of two federal constitutional provisions. A *per curiam* Court concluded that

> After reviewing the opinion of the Florida Supreme Court, we find "that there is considerable uncertainty as to the precise grounds for the decision." *Minnesota v. National Tea Co.*, 309 U.S. 551, 555 (1940). This is sufficient reason for us to decline at this time to review the federal questions asserted to be present. * * *
>
> The judgment of the Supreme Court of Florida is therefore vacated, and the case is remanded for further proceedings not inconsistent with this opinion.

Why do you think the Court chose to follow the National Tea approach? Did the Court suspect there might be an adequate and independent state ground, or was it just uncertain how the Florida Supreme Court decided the federal law issues or how it gauged the impact of federal law on state law? Bush v. Palm Beach's more famous sibling, *Bush v. Gore*, 531 U.S. 98 (2000), shows the Court was not reluctant to enter this particular political thicket. One hopes that the 2000 federal election dispute is *sui generis*. If so, Bush v. Palm Beach may tell us little about whether the National Tea approach is staging a comeback.

3. a) Justice O'Connor asserts that the Court itself has the responsibility to determine whether a state judgment rests on an adequate and independent state ground. Is the new *Michigan v. Long* approach adequate to fulfill that responsibility? Are any of the traditional approaches likely to do a better job?

b) Chief Justice Burger, Justice Powell and then-Justice Rehnquist all join Justice O'Connor's opinion. These Justices generally favor narrow construction of federal jurisdictional statutes, yet here they embrace a rule that seems to expand the Supreme Court's jurisdiction. Why?

4. In *Caldwell v. Mississippi*, 472 U.S. 320 (1985), the Court applied *Long* to a case involving the adequacy and independence of a state procedural ground, presuming in the absence of a clear statement of reliance on state law that federal law drove the state decision. Is the effect of the *Long* presumption the same when the underlying state ground is procedural as when it is substantive? Consider Herndon v. Georgia and Henry v. Mississippi, at pages 972-98.

5. Justice Stevens asserts there is no federal interest in reviewing cases when state courts may have construed federal rights too broadly.

a) Does his approach raise questions reminiscent of the separation-of-powers view of the Erie doctrine about the proper role of the Supreme Court? He seems to engage in some sort of interest analysis or balancing to determine whether to exercise jurisdiction, asserting that where the only danger is overbroad construction of federal rights, the Court ought to decline jurisdiction. Would that be appropriate or an abdication (or nullification) of reviewing power conferred by Congress? Suppose, as Justice O'Connor suggests, a state court decided a criminal case clearly and exclusively on the basis of its perception of federal constitutional law, vacating a conviction in all other respects proper. Does Justice Stevens truly mean the Court lacks jurisdiction to review that decision?

b) Justice Stevens has stuck to his guns on this issue. In *Brigham City v. Stuart*, 547 U.S. 398, 407-09 (2006) (Stevens, J., concurring) (footnote omitted), he reiterated his *Long* argument regarding the impropriety of the Court taking the case for review:

> This is an odd flyspeck of a case. The charges that have been pending against respondents for the past six years are minor offenses—intoxication, contributing to the delinquency of a minor, and disorderly conduct—two of which could have been proved by evidence that was gathered by the responding officers before they entered the home. The maximum punishment for these crimes ranges between 90 days and 6 months in jail. And the Court's unanimous opinion restating well-settled rules of federal law is so clearly persuasive that it is hard to imagine the outcome was ever in doubt.
>
> Under these circumstances, the only difficult question is which of the following is the most peculiar: (1) that the Utah trial judge, the intermediate state appellate court, and the Utah Supreme Court all found a Fourth Amendment violation on these facts; (2) that the prosecution chose to pursue this matter all the way to the United States Supreme Court; or (3) that this Court voted to grant the petition for a writ of certiorari.
>
> * * *
>
> The Utah Supreme Court * * * has made clear that the Utah Constitution provides greater protection to the privacy of the home than does the Fourth Amendment. And it complained in this case of respondents' failure to raise or

> adequately brief a state constitutional challenge, thus preventing the state courts from deciding the case on anything other than Fourth Amendment grounds. "[S]urpris[ed]" by "[t]he reluctance of litigants to take up and develop a state constitutional analysis," the court expressly invited future litigants to bring challenges under the Utah Constitution to enable it to fulfill its "responsibility as guardians of the individual liberty of our citizens" and "undertak[e] a principled exploration of the interplay between federal and state protections of individual rights." The fact that this admonishment and request came from the Utah Supreme Court in this very case * * * indicates that the Utah Supreme Court would probably adopt the same rule as a matter of state constitutional law that we reject today under the Federal Constitution.
>
> Whether or not that forecast is accurate, I can see no reason for this Court to cause the Utah courts to redecide the question as a matter of state law. Federal interests are not offended when a single State elects to provide greater protection for its citizens than the Federal Constitution requires.

Does Justice Stevens undermine his own argument with respect to this particular case? He concedes that the Utah Supreme Court did not rule on the basis of the Utah Constitution. That being the case, should he concern himself with what that court might have done if Stuart's attorney had argued the case differently? Note that, in contrast to Long, this was not a case in which Justice Stevens could have argued for a remand for clarification of the basis for the state court's decision (a procedure that Long disapproved anyway), because the ground for the decision was apparent.

In *Kansas v. Marsh*, 548 U.S. 163 (2006), the Kansas Supreme Court had found a part of the capital sentencing statute to be facially unconstitutional under the Eighth and Fourteenth Amendments and had reversed Marsh's capital murder conviction and remanded for a new trial. The Supreme Court reviewed the case (raising finality questions discussed *infra* at page 999) and reversed.

> Undeterred, Justice Stevens continued the battle.
>
> [T]he State of Kansas petitioned us to review a ruling of its own Supreme Court on the grounds that the Kansas court had granted more protection to a Kansas litigant than the Federal Constitution required. A policy of judicial restraint would allow the highest court of the State to be the final decisionmaker in a case of this kind.

Of course, by phrasing the matter in this way, Justice Stevens also makes clear that the Kansas court granted *less* protection to a Kansas litigant's—the state's—position by its misinterpretation of the Constitution. It seems appropriate at least to wonder why only one of the two litigants in cases like this is entitled to an authoritative reading of federal law.

So it seemed to Justice Scalia. "While it might be appropriate for Congress to place such a thumb on the scales of our power to review, it seems to me a peculiar mode of decisionmaking for judges sworn to 'impartially discharge * * * all the duties' of their office." In addition, Justice Scalia identified federalism interests that he felt Justice Stevens's approach overlooked.

> When state courts erroneously invalidate actions taken by the people of a State (through initiative or through normal operation of the political branches of their state government) on *state-law* grounds, it is generally none of our business; and our displacing of those judgments would indeed be an intrusion upon state autonomy. But when state courts erroneously invalidate such actions because they believe federal law requires it—and *especially* when they do so because they believe the Federal *Constitution* requires it—review by this Court, far from *undermining* state autonomy, is the only possible way to *vindicate* it. When a federal constitutional interdict against the duly expressed will of the people of a State is erroneously pronounced by a State's highest court, no authority in the State—not even a referendum agreed to by all its citizens—can undo the error. Thus, a general presumption against such review displays not respect for the States, but a complacent willingness to allow judges to strip the people of the power to govern themselves. When we correct a state court's federal errors, *we return power to the State, and to its people.*

Who has the better side of this debate? Justice Stevens, repeating his own question from an earlier case, asked "what harm would have been done to the administration of justice by state courts if the [Kansas] court had been left undisturbed in its determination[?]" Is he taking the position that overturning a criminal conviction based on a misinterpretation of the Constitution is harmless error?

6. In a case decided the same day as *Long*, the Oregon Supreme Court either responded to or anticipated the Court's invitation to be specific:

> This court like others has high respect for the opinions of the Supreme Court, particularly when they provide insight into the origins of provisions common to the state and federal bills of rights rather than only a contemporary "balance" of pragmatic considerations about which reasonable people may differ over time and among the several states. It is therefore to be expected that counsel and courts often will refer to federal decisions, or to commentary based on such decisions, even in debating an undecided issue under state law. Lest there be any doubt about it, when this court cites federal opinions in interpreting a provision of Oregon law, it does so because it finds the views there expressed persuasive, not because it considers itself bound to do so by its understanding of federal doctrines.

State v. Kennedy, 666 P.2d 1316, 1321 (Or. 1983). Is there a difference between a state following federal constitutional interpretation when construing its own constitution because the state feels compelled to do so and a state following the federal lead because it recognizes it as good policy? If so, should that make a difference in the way the Court decides cases like *Michigan v. Long* or *Delaware v. Prouse*?

7. a) In what must surely be one of the most famous concurring opinions in Court history, Justice Brandeis set forth his understanding of the Court's obligations when confronted with constitutional questions:

> The Court [has] developed, for its own governance in the cases confessedly within its jurisdiction, a series of rules under which it has avoided passing upon a large part of all the constitutional questions pressed upon it for decision. They are:
>
> * * *
>
> 2. The Court will not "anticipate a question of constitutional law in advance of the necessity of deciding it." "It is not the habit of the court to decide questions of a constitutional nature unless absolutely necessary to a decision of the case." * * *
>
> 4. The Court will not pass upon a constitutional question although properly presented by the record, if there is also present some other ground upon which the case may be disposed of. This rule has found most varied application. Thus, if a case can be decided on either of two grounds, one involving a constitutional question, the other a question of statutory construction or general law, the Court will decide only the latter. Appeals from the highest court of a state challenging its decision of a question under the Federal Constitution are frequently dismissed because the judgment can be sustained on an independent state ground.

Ashwander v. TVA, 297 U.S. 288, 346-47 (1936) (Brandeis, J., concurring). There the Court confronted a challenge to a federal statute, and separation-of-powers considerations heavily influenced the concurrence. Nonetheless, do not those principles, which the Court cites approvingly in many contexts, suggest some difficulty with the new approach *Long* articulates? Where the grounds of the state court's decision are at least arguably unclear, does the Court risk unnecessary constitutional decisions by proceeding?

b) On the other hand, in cases like *Prouse* or *Long*, the state court has already made a constitutional decision that is necessary to resolve the controversy. Assuming *arguendo* that the *Ashwander* principles apply to Supreme Court review of state court decisions, do they apply with equal force when declining jurisdiction merely substitutes a state constitutional decision for a federal one? In another context, the federal courts have not held back. The doctrine of *Railroad Commission v. Pullman Co.*, 312 U.S. 496 (1941) (at pages 811-21), requires federal courts to abstain from deciding a federal constitutional challenge to a state statute if construing the statute may obviate or substantially modify the constitutional issue. Nonetheless, the Court has held that abstention is inappropriate in favor of a state constitutional provision that mirrors the federal provision. *See, e.g., Wisconsin v. Constantineau*, 400 U.S. 433 (1971); *Zwickler v. Koota*, 389 U.S. 241 (1967). Perhaps the Court's willingness to proceed with federal constitutional adjudication supports Justice O'Connor's position that the state courts should have the burden of stating clearly their reliance on state constitutional grounds.

b. Limits: Of State Incorporation of Federal and Federal Incorporation of State Law

Standard Oil v. Johnson

Supreme Court of the United States, 1942.
316 U.S. 481.

MR. JUSTICE BLACK delivered the opinion of the Court.

The California Motor Vehicle Fuel License Tax Act imposes a license tax, measured by gallonage, on the privilege of distributing any motor vehicle fuel. Section 10 states that the Act is inapplicable "to any motor vehicle fuel sold to the government of the United States or any department thereof for official use of said government." The appellant, a "distributor" within the meaning of the Act, sold gasoline to the United States Army Post Exchanges in California. The State levied a tax, and the appellant paid it under protest. The appellant then filed this suit in the Superior Court of Sacramento County seeking to recover the payment on two grounds: (1) that sales to the Exchanges were exempt from tax under § 10; (2) that, if construed and applied to require payment of the tax on such sales, the Act would impose a burden upon instrumentalities or agencies of the United States contrary to the Federal Constitution. Holding against the appellant on both grounds, the trial court rendered judgment for the State. The Supreme Court of California affirmed * * * . Since validity of the state statute as construed was drawn in question on the ground of its being repugnant to the Constitution, we think the case is properly here on appeal * * * .

Since § 10 of the California Act made the tax inapplicable "to any motor vehicle fuel sold to the government of the United States or any department thereof," it was necessary for the Supreme Court of California to determine whether the language of this exemption included sales to post exchanges. If the court's construction of § 10 of the Act had been based purely on local law, this construction would have been conclusive, and we should have to determine whether the statute so construed and applied is repugnant to the Federal Constitution. But in deciding that post exchanges were not "the government of the United States or any department thereof," the court did not rely upon the law of California. On the contrary, it relied upon its determination concerning the relationship between post exchanges and the Government of the United States, a relationship which is controlled by federal law. For post exchanges operate under regulations of the Secretary of War pursuant to federal authority. These regulations and the practices under them establish the relationship between the post exchange and the United States Government, and together with the relevant statutory and constitutional provisions from which they derive, afford the data upon which the legal status of the post exchange may be determined. It was upon a determination of a federal question, therefore, that the Supreme Court of California rested its conclusion that, by § 10, sales to post exchanges were not exempted from the tax. Since this determination of a federal question was by a state court, we are not bound by it. We proceed to consider whether it is correct.

* * *

[The Court concluded that the California Supreme Court was incorrect.]

Whether the California Supreme Court would have construed the Motor Vehicle Fuel License Act as applicable to post exchanges if it had decided the issue of legal status of post exchanges in accordance with this opinion, we have no way of knowing. Hence, a determination here of the constitutionality of such an application of the Act is not called for by the state of the record. Accordingly, we reverse the judgment and remand the cause to the court below for further proceedings not inconsistent with this opinion.

Reversed.

Notes and Questions

1. Following the decision, could the California legislature amend its statute explicitly to exclude post exchanges from favored tax treatment? If it did so, would that cause further sales of fuel to the post exchanges to be subject to the tax, or would it merely change the nature of the question facing the Supreme Court?

2. By structuring the inquiry as it does, the Court manages to avoid adjudicating the constitutionality of the California statute. Are there other values served by the Court's review of California's understanding of the federal law incorporated into the state statute?

3. Suppose California interpreted federal law too broadly. Should the Supreme Court still review, or should it adopt Justice Stevens's philosophy from *Michigan v. Long* that the federal government has no need to limit an overbroad deference to federal interests, real or imaginary?

4. Reread Note 2 following *Michigan v. Long*, at page 948. In discussing its power to review the Florida decision, the Court said:

> As a general rule, this Court defers to a state court's interpretation of a state statute. But in the case of a law enacted by a state legislature applicable not only to elections to state offices, but also to the selection of Presidential electors, the legislature is not acting solely under the authority given it by the people of the State, but by virtue of a direct grant of authority made under Art. II, § 1, cl. 2, of the United States Constitution.

As an aside, is the Court entirely accurate in characterizing its normal approach as "*deferring*" to state courts? *Murdock v. Memphis* appears to stand for the proposition that on appeals from state courts, those courts speak with final authority on the *meaning* of state law, and the Supreme Court is without power to review such determinations except for constitutional infirmity. Is the Court suggesting that its deference is a matter of policy more than of jurisdiction? As in *Standard Oil v. Johnson*, since the proper interpretation of state law depended on the meaning of federal law incorporated in federal law, either explicitly or by necessary implication, the Supreme Court had authority to review the federal issues.

5. *Reconstruction Finance Corporation v. Beaver County*, 328 U.S. 204 (1946), presented the converse of *Standard Oil*. The County taxed machinery in a defense plant RFC, a federal corporation, operated. A federal statute prohibited state taxation of the corporation's personal property but did not define personal property, leaving state definitions to fill the vacuum. The Pennsylvania Supreme Court upheld the tax on the theory that the machinery was real, not personal, property.

The United States Supreme Court affirmed, accepting Pennsylvania's definition of personal property. Notice the importance of the *Erie* choice-of-law question. Congress used the term "real property" but did not define it. This implicitly raised the question of whether state or federal law should give content to the term. The Court reasoned that Congress knew and intended that state definitions would apply. (Is it likely that Congress even thought about this sort of problem?) The Court, however, did not give the states ***carte blanche***; it held that the state rules could be adopted as the content of federal common law as long as the state law did not discriminate against the federal government (which presumably would take the matter outside of the intent of Congress) or patently run counter to the federal Act.

Reconstruction Finance is important as a matter of federal common law, but it also significant for Supreme Court review. Ordinarily, state courts speak with final authority on matters of state law; thus the Supreme Court cannot review. *Reconstruction Finance* cautions that when state law has been adopted as federal common law, state-court authoritativeness is compromised, though not discarded entirely.

Thus, in *Standard Oil*, the federal government gets the last word on federal law incorporated in state law, and, in *Reconstruction Finance*, the states usually, but not always, get the last word on state law incorporated in federal law. This arrangement is not quite symmetrical; there are no conditions on the federal government's ability to impose its own view of federal law used by the states. What accounts for the asymmetry?

---

c. Limits: Supreme Court Review of Findings of Fact

Ward v. Board Of County Commissioners

Supreme Court of the United States, 1920.
253 U.S. 17.

MR. JUSTICE VAN DEVANTER delivered the opinion of the Court.

This is a proceeding by and on behalf of Coleman J. Ward and sixty-six other Indians to recover moneys alleged to have been coercively collected from them by Love County, Oklahoma, as taxes on their allotments, which under the laws and Constitution of the United States were nontaxable. The county commissioners disallowed the claim and the claimants appealed to the district court of the county. There the claimants' petition was challenged by a demurrer, which was overruled and the county elected not to plead further. A judgment for the claimants followed, and this was reversed by the Supreme Court. The case is here on writ of certiorari.

The claimants, who were members of the Choctaw Tribe and wards of the United States, received their allotments out of the tribal domain under a congressional enactment of 1898, which subjected the right of alienation to certain restrictions and provided that "the lands allotted shall be nontaxable while the title remains in the original allottee, but not to exceed twenty-one years from date of patent." * * * In the act of 1906, enabling Oklahoma to become a state, Congress made it plain that no impairment of the rights of property pertaining to the Indians was intended, * * * and the state included in its Constitution a provision exempting from taxation "such property as may be exempt by reason of treaty stipulations, existing between the Indians and the United States government, or by federal laws, during the force and effect of such treaties or federal laws." * * * Afterwards Congress, by an act of 1908, removed the restrictions on alienation as to certain classes of allottees, including the present claimants, and declared that all land from which the restrictions were removed "shall be subject to taxation, * * * as though it were the property of other persons than allottees."

Following the last enactment the officers of Love and other counties began to tax the allotted lands from which restrictions on alienation were removed, and this met with pronounced opposition on the part of the Indian allottees, who insisted, as they had been advised, that the tax exemption was a vested property right which could not be abrogated or destroyed consistently with the Constitution of the United States. Suits were begun in the state courts to maintain the exemption and enjoin the threatened taxation, one of the suits being prosecuted by some 8,000 allottees against the officers of Love and other counties. The suits were resisted, and the state courts, being of opinion that the exemption had been repealed by Congress, sustained the power to tax. The cases were then brought here, and this court held that the exemption was a vested property right which Congress could not repeal consistently with the Fifth Amendment, that it was binding on the taxing authorities in Oklahoma, and that the state courts had erred in refusing to enjoin them from taxing the lands.

While those suits were pending the officers of Love County, with full knowledge of the suits, and being defendants in one, proceeded with the taxation of the allotments, demanded of these claimants that the taxes on their lands be paid to the county, threatened to advertise and sell the lands unless the taxes were paid, did advertise and sell other lands similarly situated, and caused these claimants to believe that their lands would be sold if the taxes were not paid. So, to prevent such a sale and to avoid the imposition of a penalty of eighteen per cent., for which the local statute provided, these claimants paid the taxes. They protested and objected at the time that the taxes were invalid, and the county officers knew that all the allottees were pressing the objection in the pending suits.

As a conclusion from these facts the claimants asserted that the taxes were collected by Love County by coercive means, that their collection was in violation of a right arising out of a law of Congress and protected by the Constitution of the United States, and that the county was accordingly bound to repay the moneys thus collected. The total amount claimed is $7,833.35, aside from interest.

* * *

In reversing the judgment which the district court had given for the claimants the [state] Supreme Court held, first, that the taxes were not collected by coercive means, but were paid voluntarily * * *.

The county challenges our jurisdiction by a motion to dismiss the writ of certiorari and by way of supporting the motion insists that the Supreme Court put its judgment entirely on independent nonfederal grounds which were broad enough to sustain the judgment.

As these claimants had not disposed of their allotments and twenty-one years had not elapsed since the date of the patents, it is certain that the lands were nontaxable. * * * This being so, the state and all its agencies and political subdivisions were bound to give effect to the exemption. It operated as a direct restraint on Love County, no matter what was said in local statutes. The county did not respect it, but, on the contrary, assessed the lands allotted to these claimants, placed them on the county tax roll, and there charged them with taxes like other property. * * * Payment of all the taxes was demanded by the county, and all were paid to it in the circumstances already narrated.

We accept so much of the [state] Supreme Court's decision as held that, if the payment was voluntary, the moneys could not be recovered back in the absence of a permissive statute, and that there was no such statute. But we are unable to accept its decision in other respects.

The right to the exemption was a federal right, and was specially set up and claimed as such in the petition. Whether the right was denied, or not given due recognition, by the Supreme Court is a question as to which the claimants were entitled to invoke our judgment, and this they have done in the appropriate way. It therefore is within our province to inquire not only whether the right was denied in express terms, but also whether it was denied in substance and effect, as by putting forward nonfederal grounds of decision that were without any fair or substantial support. Of course, if nonfederal grounds, plainly untenable, may be thus put forward successfully, our power to review easily may be avoided. With this qualification, it is true that a judgment of a state court, which is put on independent nonfederal grounds broad enough to sustain it, cannot be reviewed by us. But the qualification is a material one and cannot be disregarded without neglecting or renouncing a jurisdiction conferred by law and designed to protect and maintain the supremacy of the Constitution and the laws made in pursuance thereof.

The facts set forth in the petition, all of which were admitted by the demurrer whereon the county elected to stand, make it plain, as we think, that the finding or decision that the taxes were paid voluntarily was without any fair or substantial support. The claimants were Indians just emerging from a state of dependency and wardship. Through the pending suits and otherwise they were objecting and protesting that the taxation of their lands was forbidden by a law of Congress. But, notwithstanding this, the county demanded that the taxes be paid, and by threatening to sell the lands of these claimants and actually selling other lands similarly situated made it appear to the claimants that they must choose between paying the taxes and losing their lands. To prevent a sale and to avoid the imposition of a penalty of eighteen per cent. they yielded to the county's demand and paid the taxes, protesting and objecting at the time that the same were illegal. The moneys thus collected were obtained by coercive means—by compulsion. The county and its officers reasonably could not have regarded it otherwise; much less the Indian claimants.

* * *

To say that the county could collect these unlawful taxes by coercive means and not incur any obligation to pay them back is nothing short of saying that it could take or appropriate the property of these Indian allottees arbitrarily and without due process of law. Of course this would be in contravention of the Fourteenth Amendment * * * .

* * *

Motion to dismiss denied.

Judgment reversed.

Notes and Questions

1. How much latitude should the Supreme Court have to ignore state court findings of fact? Is it enough for the Court merely to disagree about the inferences to be made from the record, or must the Court be willing to rule that the state courts' findings were, in effect, a sham designed to circumvent Supreme Court review?

2. With respect to the standard of review, consider *Thompson v. City of Louisville*, 362 U.S. 199 (1960). The Court reversed the defendant's conviction for disorderly conduct and loitering on the ground that the conviction was "so totally devoid of evidentiary support as to render [it] unconstitutional * * * ." Had *Ward* adopted the same standard? The *Thompson* Court insisted that the case was not one of evidentiary insufficiency, but instead involved whether there was any evidence at all to support the conviction. Should one view *Ward* differently because it involves only the question of whether the tax payments were made "voluntarily"? *Thompson* was a due process case, not involving Supreme Court review of a purportedly adequate and independent state ground. Should the difference in characterization determine the standard applied?

3. Note that this area magnifies the federalism problems inherent in Supreme Court review of state court decisions. It is one thing for the Court to reverse a state decision because the state courts misapprehend the meaning or application of federal law to a complex matter; it is quite another for the Court to tell the state court that it did not realistically evaluate the facts. Should the Court do that? If so, what standards should govern when the practice is permissible? Bear in mind the obvious desirability of keeping overt clashes between state and federal courts to a minimum. If not, what can be done about a state court decision that, while careful, is manifestly disingenuous?

Fiske v. Kansas

Supreme Court of the United States, 1927.
274 U.S. 380.

MR. JUSTICE SANFORD delivered the opinion of the Court.

The plaintiff in error was tried and convicted in the District Court of Rice County, Kansas, upon an information charging him with violating the Criminal Syndicalism Act of that State * * * . The judgment was affirmed by the Supreme Court of the State, * * * .

The only substantial Federal question presented to and decided by the State court, and which may therefore be re-examined by this Court, is whether the Syndicalism Act as applied in this case is repugnant to the due process clause of the Fourteenth Amendment.

The relevant provisions of the Act are:

> Section 1. "Criminal syndicalism" is hereby defined to be the doctrine which advocates crime, physical violence, arson, destruction of property, sabotage, or other unlawful acts or methods, as a means of accomplishing or effecting industrial or political ends, or as a means of effecting industrial or political revolution, or for profit. * * *
>
> Sec. 3. Any person who, by word of mouth, or writing, advocates, affirmatively suggests or teaches the duty, necessity, propriety or expediency of crime, criminal syndicalism, or sabotage, * * * is guilty of a felony. * * *

The information charged that the defendant did

> by word of mouth and by publicly displaying and circulating certain books and pamphlets and written and printed matter, advocate, affirmatively suggest and teach the duty, necessity, propriety and expediency of crime, criminal syndicalism, and sabotage by * * * knowingly and feloniously persuading, inducing and securing [certain persons] to sign an application for membership in * * * and by issuing to [them] membership cards [in a certain Workers' Industrial Union,] a branch of and component part of the Industrial Workers of the World organization, said defendant then and there knowing that said organization unlawfully teaches, advocates and affirmatively suggests:
>
> > That the working class and the employing class have nothing in common, and that there can be no peace so long as hunger and want are found among millions of working people and the few who make up the employing class have all the good things of life. [And that] Between these two classes a struggle must go on until the workers of the World organize as a class, take possession of the earth and the machinery of production and abolish the wage system. [And that]: Instead of the

> conservative motto, "A fair day's wages for a fair day's work," we must inscribe on our banner the revolutionary watchword, "Abolition of the wage system." By organizing industrially we are forming the structure of the new society within the shell of the old.

The defendant moved to quash the information as insufficient, for the reason, among others, that it failed to specify the character of the organization in which he was alleged to have secured members. This was overruled.

On the trial the State offered no evidence as to the doctrines advocated, suggested or taught by the Industrial Workers of the World organization other than a copy of the preamble to the constitution of that organization containing the language set forth and quoted in the information. The defendant, who testified in his own behalf, stated that he was a member of that organization and understood what it taught; that while it taught the matters set forth in this preamble it did not teach or suggest that it would obtain industrial control in any criminal way or unlawful manner, but in a peaceful manner; that he did not believe in criminal syndicalism or sabotage, and had not at any time advocated, suggested or taught the duty, necessity, propriety and expediency of crime, criminal syndicalism or sabotage, and did not know that they were advocated, taught or suggested by the organization; and that in taking the applications for membership in the organization, which contained the preamble to the constitution, he had explained the principles of the organization so far as he knew them by letting the applicants read this preamble.

The jury was instructed that before the defendant could be convicted they must be satisfied from the evidence, beyond a reasonable doubt, that the Industrial Workers of the World was an organization that taught criminal syndicalism as defined by the Syndicalism Act.

The defendant moved in arrest of judgment upon the ground, among others, that the evidence and the facts stated did not constitute a public offense and substantiate the charges alleged in the information. And he also moved for a new trial upon the grounds, among others, that the verdict was contrary to the law and the evidence and wholly unsupported by the evidence. Both of these motions were overruled.

On the appeal to the Supreme Court of the State, among the errors assigned were, generally, that the court erred in overruling his motions to quash the information, his demurrer to the evidence—which does not appear in the record—and his motions in arrest of judgment and for a new trial; and specifically, that the "court erred in refusing to quash the information, in overruling the demurrer to the evidence, and in overruling the motion in arrest of judgment, because the information and the cause of action attempted to be proved were based upon" the

Kansas Syndicalism Act, "which, in so far as it sustains this prosecution is in violation * * * of the Constitution of the United States and especially of the Fourteenth Amendment" including the due process clause thereof.

The Supreme Court of the State, in its opinion, said:

> The information does not in set phrase allege that the association known as the Industrial Workers of the World advocates, affirmatively suggests or teaches criminal syndicalism, but when read as a whole it clearly signifies this, and also that the language quoted (which the evidence shows to be taken from the preamble of the constitution of that organization) was employed to express that doctrine * * * . The language quoted from the I.W.W. preamble need not—in order to sustain the judgment—be held necessarily and as a matter of law, to advocate, teach or even affirmatively suggest physical violence as a means of accomplishing industrial or political ends. It is open to that interpretation and is capable of use to convey that meaning * * * . The jury were not required to accept the defendant's testimony as a candid and accurate statement. There was room for them to find, as their verdict shows they did, that the equivocal language of the preamble and of the defendant in explaining it to his prospects was employed to convey and did convey the sinister meaning attributed to it by the state. A final contention is that the statute * * * is obnoxious to the due process of law clause of the Fourteenth Amendment to the Federal Constitution. Statutes penalizing the advocacy of violence in bringing about governmental changes do not violate constitutional guarantees of freedom of speech.

A decision of a State court applying and enforcing a State statute of general scope against a particular transaction as to which there was a distinct and timely insistence that if so applied, the statute was void under the Federal Constitution, necessarily affirms the validity of the statute as so applied, and the judgment is, therefore, reviewable by writ of error * * * . The inquiry then is whether the statute is constitutional as applied and enforced in respect of the situation presented.

And this Court will review the finding of facts by a State court where a Federal right has been denied as the result of a finding shown by the record to be without evidence to support it; or where a conclusion of law as to a Federal right and a finding of fact are so intermingled as to make it necessary, in order to pass upon the Federal question, to analyze the facts.

Here the State court held the Syndicalism Act not to be repugnant to the due process clause as applied in a case in which the information in effect charged the defendant with violation of the Act in that he had secured members in an organization which taught, advocated and affirmatively suggested the doctrines set forth in the extracts from the preamble to its constitution, and in which there was no evidence that the organization, taught, advocated or suggested any other doctrines. No substantial inference can, in our judgment, be drawn from the language of this preamble, that the organization taught, advocated or suggested the duty, necessity, propriety, or expediency of crime, criminal syndicalism, sabotage, or other unlawful acts or methods. There is no suggestion in the preamble that the industrial organization of workers as a class for the purpose of getting possession of the machinery of production and abolishing the wage system, was to be accomplished by any other than lawful methods; nothing advocating the overthrow of the existing industrial or political conditions by force, violence or unlawful means. And standing alone, as it did in this case, there was nothing which warranted the court or jury in ascribing to this language, either as an inference of law or fact, "the sinister meaning attributed to it by the state." In this respect the language of the preamble is essentially different from that of the manifesto involved in *Gitlow v. New York* [1925], and lacks the essential elements which brought that document under the condemnation of the law. And it is not as if the preamble were shown to have been followed by further statements or declarations indicating that it was intended to mean, and to be understood as advocating, that the ends outlined therein would be accomplished or brought about by violence or other related unlawful acts or methods.

The result is that the Syndicalism Act has been applied in this case to sustain the conviction of the defendant, without any charge or evidence that the organization in which he secured members advocated any crime, violence or other unlawful acts or methods as a means of effecting industrial or political changes or revolution. Thus applied the Act is an arbitrary and unreasonable exercise of the police power of the State, unwarrantably infringing the liberty of the defendant in violation of the due process clause of the Fourteenth Amendment. The judgment is accordingly reversed, and the case is remanded for further proceedings not inconsistent with this opinion.

Reversed.

Notes and Questions

1. a) What scope of review of facts does the Court describe? When will the Court review the facts and permit itself to make findings at variance with those below? Of the patterns that that the Court says justify Supreme Court review of the facts, into which does *Fiske* fit?

b) How does the standard the Court suggests compare with the standard for granting judgment as a matter of law following a jury verdict? Should the Court review the facts only when it is persuaded that no rational finder of fact could have concluded as the court or jury did below, or is some more relaxed standard appropriate? If so, what standard? If not, then should Supreme Court review of the facts be available only if the party seeking review timely made and preserved a motion for judgment as a matter of law?

2. Whenever the Court is prepared to examine the factual record, should it merely indicate its dissatisfaction with the fact-finding below and remand for further consideration of the facts? Or should the Court feel free to substitute its own findings based on the record for those certified by the highest state court?

The following case is an outgrowth of Powell v. Alabama, 287 U.S. 45 (1932), the first case in which the Supreme Court announced a constitutional right to appointed counsel for indigent defendants facing capital charges. The Court expanded that holding in Gideon v. Wainwright, 372 U.S. 335 (1963), to apply to all felonies.

Norris v. Alabama

Supreme Court of the United States, 1935.
294 U.S. 587.

MR. CHIEF JUSTICE HUGHES delivered the opinion of the Court.

Petitioner, Clarence Norris, is one of nine negro boys who were indicted in March, 1931, in Jackson county, Ala., for the crime of rape. On being brought to trial in that county, eight were convicted. The Supreme Court of Alabama reversed the conviction of one of these and affirmed that of seven, including Norris. This Court reversed the judgments of conviction upon the ground that the defendants had been denied due process of law in that the trial court had failed in the light of the circumstances disclosed, and of the inability of the defendants at that time to obtain counsel, to make an effective appointment of counsel to aid them in preparing and presenting their defense.

After the remand, a motion for change of venue was granted and the cases were transferred to Morgan county. Norris was brought to trial in November, 1933. At the outset, a motion was made on his behalf to quash the indictment upon the ground of the exclusion of negroes from juries in Jackson county where the indictment was found. A motion was also made to quash the trial venire in Morgan county upon the ground of the exclusion of negroes from juries in that county. In relation to each county, the charge was of long-continued, systematic, and arbitrary exclusion of qualified negro citizens from service on juries, solely because of their race and color, in violation of the Constitution of the United States. The state joined issue on this charge and after hearing the evidence, which we shall presently review, the trial judge denied both motions, and exception was taken. The trial then proceeded and resulted in the conviction of Norris who was sentenced to death. On appeal, the Supreme Court of the state considered and decided the federal question which Norris had raised and affirmed the judgment. We granted a writ of certiorari.

First. There is no controversy as to the constitutional principle involved. That principle, long since declared, was not challenged, but was expressly recognized, by the Supreme Court of the state. Summing up precisely the effect of earlier decisions, this Court thus stated the principle in relation to exclusion from service on grand juries:

> Whenever by any action of a state, whether through its Legislature, through its courts, or through its executive or administrative officers, all persons of the African race are excluded, solely because of their race or color, from serving as grand jurors in the criminal prosecution of a person of the African race, the equal protection of the laws is denied to him, contrary to the Fourteenth Amendment of the Constitution of the United States.

* * * The principle is equally applicable to a similar exclusion of negroes from service on petit juries. * * * And although the state statute defining the qualifications of jurors may be fair on its face, the constitutional provision affords protection against action of the state through its administrative officers in effecting the prohibited discrimination. * * *

The question is of the application of this established principle to the facts disclosed by the record. That the question is one of fact does not relieve us of the duty to determine whether in truth a federal right has been denied. When a federal right has been specially set up and claimed in a state court, it is our province to inquire not merely whether it was denied in express terms but also whether it was denied in substance and effect. If this requires an examination of evidence, that examination must be made. Otherwise, review by this Court would fail of its purpose in safeguarding constitutional rights. Thus, whenever a conclusion of law of a state court as to a federal right and findings of fact are so intermingled that the latter control the former, it is incumbent upon us to analyze the facts in order that the appropriate enforcement of the federal right may be assured. * * *

Second. The evidence on the motion to quash the indictment. In 1930, the total population of Jackson county, where the indictment was found, was 36,881, of whom 2,688 were negroes. The male population over twenty-one years of age numbered 8,801, and of these 666 were negroes.

The qualifications of jurors were thus prescribed by the state statute:

> The jury commission shall place on the jury roll and in the jury box the names of all male citizens of the county who are generally reputed to be honest and intelligent men, and are esteemed in the community for their integrity, good character and sound judgment, but no person must be selected who is under twenty-one or over sixty-five years of age, or, who is an habitual drunkard, or who, being afflicted with a permanent disease or physical weakness is unfit to discharge the duties of a juror, or who cannot read English, or who has ever been convicted of any offense involving moral turpitude. If a person cannot read English and has all the other qualifications prescribed herein and is a freeholder or householder, his name may be placed on the jury roll and in the jury box.

* * *

Defendant adduced evidence to support the charge of unconstitutional discrimination in the actual administration of the statute in Jackson county. The testimony, as the state court said, tended to show that "in a long number of years no negro had been called for jury service in that county." It appeared that no negro had served on any grand or petit jury in that county within the memory of witnesses who had lived there all their lives. Testimony to that effect was given by men whose ages ran from fifty to seventy-six years. Their testimony was uncontradicted. It was supported by the testimony of officials. The clerk of the jury commission and the clerk of the circuit court had never known of a negro serving on a grand jury in Jackson county. The court reporter, who had not missed a session in that county in twenty-four years, and two jury commissioners testified to the same effect. One of the latter, who was a member of the commission which made up the jury roll for the grand jury which found the indictment, testified that he had "never known of a single instance where any negro sat on any grand or petit jury in the entire history of that county."

That testimony in itself made out a *prima facie* case of the denial of the equal protection which the Constitution guarantees * * * . The case thus made was supplemented by direct testimony that specified negroes, thirty or more in number, were qualified for jury service. Among these were negroes who were members of school boards, or trustees, of colored schools, and property owners and householders. It also appeared that negroes from that county had been called for jury service in the federal court. Several of those who were thus described as qualified were witnesses. While there was testimony which cast doubt upon the qualifications of some of the negroes who had been named, and there was also general testimony by the editor of a local newspaper who gave his opinion as to the lack of "sound judgment" of the "good negroes" in Jackson county, we think that the definite testimony as to the actual qualifications of individual negroes, which was not met by any testimony equally direct, showed that there were negroes in Jackson county qualified for jury service.

The question arose whether names of negroes were in fact on the jury roll. The books containing the jury roll for Jackson county for the year 1930-31 were produced. They were produced from the custody of a member of the jury commission which, in 1931, had succeeded the commission which had made up the jury roll from which the grand jury in question had been drawn. On the pages of this roll appeared the names of six negroes. They were entered, respectively, at the end of the precinct lists which were alphabetically arranged. The genuineness of these entries was disputed. It appeared that after the jury roll in question had been made up, and after the new jury commission had taken office, one of the new commissioners directed the new clerk to draw lines after the names which had been placed on the roll by the preceding commission. These lines, on the pages under consideration, were red lines, and the clerk of the old commission testified that they were not put in by him. The entries made by the new clerk, for the new jury roll, were below these lines.

The names of the six negroes were in each instance written immediately above the red lines. An expert of long experience testified that these names were superimposed upon the red lines, that is, that they were written after the lines had been drawn. The expert was not cross-examined and no testimony was introduced to contradict him.[1] In denying the motion to quash, the trial judge expressed the view that he would not "be authorized to presume that somebody had committed a crime" or to presume that the jury board "had been unfaithful to their duties and allowed the books to be tampered with." His conclusion was that names of negroes were on the jury roll.

We think that the evidence did not justify that conclusion. The Supreme Court of the state did not sustain it. That court observed that the charge that the names of negroes were fraudulently placed on the roll did not involve any member of the jury board, and that the charge "was, by implication at least, laid at the door of the clerk of the board." The court, reaching its decision irrespective of that question, treated that phase of the matter as "wholly immaterial" and hence passed it by "without any expression of opinion thereon."

The state court rested its decision upon the ground that even if it were assumed that there was no name of a negro on the jury roll, it was not established that race or color caused the omission. The court pointed out that the statute fixed a high standard of qualifications for jurors * * * and that the jury commission was vested with a wide discretion. The court adverted to the fact that more white citizens possessing age qualifications had been omitted from the jury

1 The books containing the jury roll in question were produced on the argument at this bar and were examined by the Court.

roll than the entire negro population of the county, and regarded the testimony as being to the effect that "the matter of race, color, politics, religion or fraternal affiliations" had not been discussed by the commission and had not entered into their consideration, and that no one had been excluded because of race or color.

The testimony showed the practice of the jury commission. One of the commissioners who made up the jury roll in question, and the clerk of that commission, testified as to the manner of its preparation. The other two commissioners of that period did not testify. It was shown that the clerk, under the direction of the commissioners, made up a preliminary list which was based on the registration list of voters, the polling list and the tax list, and apparently also upon the telephone directory. The clerk testified that he made up a list of all male citizens between the ages of twenty-one and sixty-five years without regard to their status or qualifications. The commissioner testified that the designation "col." was placed after the names of those who were colored. In preparing the final jury roll, the preliminary list was checked off as to qualified jurors with the aid of men whom the commissioners called in for that purpose from the different precincts. And the commissioner testified that in the selections for the jury roll no one was "automatically or systematically" excluded, or excluded on account of race or color; that he "did not inquire as to color," that was not discussed.

But, in appraising the action of the commissioners, these statements cannot be divorced from other testimony. As we have seen, there was testimony, not overborne or discredited, that there were in fact negroes in the county qualified for jury service. That testimony was direct and specific. After eliminating those persons as to whom there was some evidence of lack of qualifications, a considerable number of others remained. The fact that the testimony as to these persons, fully identified, was not challenged by evidence appropriately direct, cannot be brushed aside. There is no ground for an assumption that the names of these negroes were not on the preliminary list. The inference to be drawn from the testimony is that they were on that preliminary list, and were designated on that list as the names of negroes, and that they were not placed on the jury roll. There was thus presented a test of the practice of the commissioners. Something more than mere general asseverations was required. Why were these names excluded from the jury roll? Was it because of the lack of statutory qualifications? Were the qualifications of negroes actually and properly considered?

The testimony of the commissioner on this crucial question puts the case in a strong light. That testimony leads to the conclusion that these or other negroes were not excluded on account of age, or lack of esteem in the community for integrity and judgment, or because of disease or want of any other qualification.

The commissioner's answer to specific inquiry upon this point was that negroes were "never discussed." We give in the margin quotations from his testimony.[2]

We are of the opinion that the evidence required a different result from that reached in the state court. We think that the evidence that for a generation or longer no negro had been called for service on any jury in Jackson county, that there were negroes qualified for jury service, that according to the practice of the jury commission their names would normally appear on the preliminary list of male citizens of the requisite age but that no names of negroes were placed on the jury roll, and the testimony with respect to the lack of appropriate consideration of the qualifications of negroes, established the discrimination which the Constitution forbids. The motion to quash the indictment upon that ground should have been granted.

evidence

Third. The evidence on the motion to quash the trial venire. The population of Morgan county, where the trial was had, was larger than that of Jackson county, and the proportion of negroes was much greater. The total population of Morgan county in 1930 was 46,176, and of this number 8,311 were negroes.

---

2 Q. Did you ever exclude from the jury rolls any negroes because you found first, he was a man under twenty-one years old or over sixty-five, and he was excluded by reason of his age; secondly because he was a person who wasn't esteemed in the community for being a decent and honorable citizen, for good sound common sense and judgment, did you ever see or hear of them not going to take that negro because he wasn't esteemed in the community for good sense and judgment?

A. No, sir.

Q. Did you ever have occasion to say, I can't take that negro because he is a fellow that has a disease which may affect or does affect, his mentality, did you ever say that to yourself, with reference to any particular negro?

A. No, sir, negroes was never discussed.

Q. Did you ever say to yourself as a jury commissioner in compiling those lists, I am not going to take that negro because he has been convicted before of a crime involving moral turpitude, have you ever excluded a negro on that ground, did you ever find any negro that came within that category, under your personal knowledge in Jackson County?

A. I couldn't recall any, no, sir, I don't know.

Q. Have you ever known of any negro in Jackson County who was excluded by reason of the fact that he could not read English, and that negro at the same time wasn't a free holder or house holder, did you ever say I can't take that negro because he is prohibited under the rules from serving by reason of that provision?

A. No, sir.

Q. Or anybody in your presence?

A. It never was discussed.

Q. You had been a jury commissioner how long?

A. I was on it under Bibb Graves administration, 1928, 1929, 1930.

Q. Three years?

A. Yes, sir.

Q. And you never had occasion to exclude any negro in Jackson County by reason of the disqualifying provisions I have just called to your attention?

A. Not to my personal knowledge, no, sir.

Within the memory of witnesses, long resident there, no negro had ever served on a jury in that county or had been called for such service. Some of these witnesses were over fifty years of age and had always lived in Morgan county. Their testimony was not contradicted. A clerk of the circuit court, who had resided in the county for thirty years, and who had been in office for over four years, testified that during his official term approximately 2,500 persons had been called for jury service and that not one of them was a negro; that he did not recall "ever seeing any single person of the colored race serve on any jury in Morgan County."

There was abundant evidence that there were a large number of negroes in the county who were qualified for jury service. Men of intelligence, some of whom were college graduates, testified to long lists (said to contain nearly 200 names) of such qualified negroes, including many business men, owners of real property and householders. When defendant's counsel proposed to call many additional witnesses in order to adduce further proof of qualifications of negroes for jury service, the trial judge limited the testimony, holding that the evidence was cumulative.

We find no warrant for a conclusion that the names of any of the negroes as to whom this testimony was given, or of any other negroes, were placed on the jury rolls. No such names were identified. The evidence that for many years no negro had been called for jury service itself tended to show the absence of the names of negroes from the jury rolls, and the state made no effort to prove their presence. The trial judge limited the defendant's proof "to the present year, the present jury roll." The sheriff of the county, called as a witness for defendants, scanned the jury roll and after "looking over every single name on that jury roll, from A to Z," was unable to point out "any single negro on it."

For this long-continued, unvarying, and wholesale exclusion of negroes from jury service we find no justification consistent with the constitutional mandate. We have carefully examined the testimony of the jury commissioners upon which the state court based its decision. One of these commissioners testified in person and the other two submitted brief affidavits. By the state act * * * in force at the time the jury roll in question was made up, the clerk of the jury board was required to obtain the names of all male citizens of the county over twenty-one and under sixty-five years of age, and their occupation, place of residence, and place of business * * * . The qualifications of those who were to be placed on the jury roll were the same as those prescribed by the earlier statute which we have already quoted * * * . The member of the jury board, who testified orally, said that a list was made up which included the names of all male citizens of suitable age; that black residents were not excluded from this general list; that in compiling the jury roll he did not consider race or color; that no one was excluded for that reason; and that he had placed on the jury roll the names of persons possessing the qualifications under the statute. The affidavits of the other members of the board contained general statements to the same effect.

gov't's evidence

We think that this evidence failed to rebut the strong *prima facie* case which defendant had made. That showing as to the long-continued exclusion of negroes from jury service, and as to the many negroes qualified for that service, could not be met by mere generalities. If, in the presence of such testimony as defendant adduced, the mere general assertions by officials of their performance of duty were to be accepted as in adequate justification for the complete exclusion of negroes from jury service, the constitutional provision—adopted with special reference to their protection—would be but a vain and illusory requirement. The general attitude of the jury commissioner is shown by the following extract from his testimony:

> I do not know of any negro in Morgan County over twenty-one and under sixty-five who is generally reputed to be honest and intelligent and who is esteemed in the community for his integrity, good character and sound judgment, who is not an habitual drunkard, who isn't afflicted with a permanent disease or physical weakness which would render him unfit to discharge the duties of a juror, and who can read English, and who has never been convicted of a crime involving moral turpitude.

In the light of the testimony given by defendant's witnesses, we find it impossible to accept such a sweeping characterization of the lack of qualifications of negroes in Morgan county. It is so sweeping, and so contrary to the evidence as to the many qualified negroes, that it destroys the intended effect of the commissioner's testimony.

In *Neal v. Delaware*, decided over fifty years ago, this Court observed that it was a "violent presumption," in which the state court had there indulged, that the uniform exclusion of negroes from juries, during a period of many years, was solely because, in the judgment of the officers, charged with the selection of grand and petit jurors, fairly exercised, "the black race in Delaware were utterly disqualified by want of intelligence, experience, or moral integrity, to sit on juries." Such a presumption at the present time would be no less violent with respect to the exclusion of the negroes of Morgan county. And, upon the proof contained in the record now before us, a conclusion that their continuous and total exclusion from juries was because there were none possessing the requisite qualifications, cannot be sustained.

We are concerned only with the federal question which we have discussed, and in view of the denial of the federal right suitably asserted, the judgment must be reversed and the cause remanded for further proceedings not inconsistent with this opinion.

It is so ordered.

Notes and Questions

1. Does the Court implicitly take the position that a witness can be incredible as a matter of law, thus allowing appellate review of what otherwise is a matter only for the fact-finder?

2. Chief Justice Hughes describes an apparently broad standard for allowing review of facts found in the state courts. Ordinarily do not the facts of a case control the success or failure of assertions of rights, federal or otherwise? Has the Court just described a standard of review without effective limitation?

3. Should the Court regularly review the facts to see whether they are fairly supported by the record? If not, cannot the lower courts effectively prevent Supreme Court review by manipulating the facts? Ward v. Love County, of course, suggests that there are limits to the Court's patience with lower court dissembling. But does Ward merely suggest that the state courts must be a bit subtle about insulating the record?

---

2. With Procedural Law

Herndon v. Georgia

Supreme Court of the United States, 1935.
295 U.S. 441.

MR. JUSTICE SUTHERLAND delivered the opinion of the Court.

Appellant was sentenced to a term of imprisonment upon conviction by a jury in a Georgia court of first instance of an attempt to incite insurrection by endeavoring to induce others to join in combined resistance to the authority of the state to be accomplished by acts of violence, in violation of § 56 of the Penal Code of Georgia.[1] The supreme court of the state affirmed the judgment. On this appeal, the statute is assailed as contravening the due process clause of the Fourteenth Amendment in certain designated particulars. We find it unnecessary to review the points made, since this court is without jurisdiction for the reason that no federal question was seasonably raised in the court below or passed upon by that court.

---

1 "§ 56. Any attempt, by persuasion or otherwise, to induce others to join in any combined resistance to the lawful authority of the State shall constitute an attempt to incite insurrection."

"Insurrection" is defined by the preceding section. "§ 55. Insurrection shall consist in any combined resistance to the lawful authority of the State, with intent to the denial thereof, when the same is manifested, or intended to be manifested, by acts of violence."

It is true that there was a preliminary attack upon the indictment in the trial court on the ground, among others, that the statute was in violation "of the Constitution of the United States," and that this contention was overruled. But, in addition to the insufficiency of the specification, the adverse action of the trial court was not preserved by exceptions ***pendente lite*** or assigned as error in due time in the bill of exceptions, as the settled rules of the state practice require. In that situation, the state supreme court declined to review any of the rulings of the trial court in respect of that and other preliminary issues; and this determination of the state court is conclusive here.

The federal question was never properly presented to the state supreme court unless upon motion for rehearing; and that court then refused to consider it. The long-established general rule is that the attempt to raise a federal question after judgment, upon a petition for rehearing, comes too late, unless the court actually entertains the question and decides it.

Petitioner, however, contends that the present case falls within an exception to the rule—namely, that the question respecting the validity of the statute as applied by the lower court first arose from its unanticipated act in giving to the statute a new construction which threatened rights under the Constitution. There is no doubt that the federal claim was timely if the ruling of the state court could not have been anticipated and a petition for rehearing presented the first opportunity for raising it. The whole point, therefore, is whether the ruling here assailed should have been anticipated.

The trial court instructed the jury that the evidence would not be sufficient to convict the defendant if it did not indicate that his advocacy would be acted upon immediately; and that—"In order to convict the defendant, * * * it must appear clearly by the evidence that immediate serious violence against the State of Georgia was to be expected or was advocated." Petitioner urges that the question presented to the state supreme court was whether the evidence made out a violation of the statute as thus construed by the trial court, while the supreme court construed the statute as not requiring that an insurrection should follow instantly or at any given time, but that "it would be sufficient that he [the defendant] intended it to happen at any time, as a result of his influence, by those whom he sought to incite," and upon that construction determined the sufficiency of the evidence against the defendant. If that were all, the petitioner's contention that the federal question was raised at the earliest opportunity well might be sustained; but it is not all.

Make the Connection

Any statute criminalizing speech invites a First Amendment challenge. Think back to your Constitutional Law course. What test was the trial court giving to the jury?

The verdict of the jury was returned on January 18, 1933, and judgment immediately followed. On July 5, 1933, the trial court overruled a motion for new trial. The original opinion was handed down and the judgment of the state supreme court entered May 24, 1934, the case having been in that court since the preceding July.

On March 18, 1933, several months prior to the action of the trial court on the motion for new trial, the state supreme court had decided Carr v. State. In that case § 56 of the Penal Code, under which it arose, was challenged as contravening the Fourteenth Amendment. The court in substance construed the statute as it did in the present case. In the course of the opinion it said:

> It [the state] can not reasonably be required to defer the adoption of measures for its own peace and safety until the revolutionary utterances lead to actual disturbances of the public peace or imminent and immediate danger of its own destruction; but it may, in the exercise of its judgment, suppress the threatened danger in its incipiency * * * .
>
>> Manifestly, the legislature has authority to forbid the advocacy of a doctrine designed and intended to overthrow the government, without waiting until there is a present and imminent danger of the success of the plan advocated. If the State were compelled to wait until the apprehended danger became certain, then its right to protect itself would come into being simultaneously with the overthrow of the government, when there would be neither prosecuting officers nor courts for the enforcement of the law.

The language contained in the subquotation is taken from People v. Lloyd [an Illinois case] and is quoted with approval by this court in Gitlow v. New York.

In the present case, following the language quoted at an earlier point in this opinion to the effect that it was sufficient if the defendant intended an insurrection to follow *at any time*, etc., the court below, in its original opinion, added—"It was the intention of this law to arrest at its incipiency any effort to overthrow the state government, where it takes the form of an actual attempt to incite others to insurrection." The phrase "at any time" is not found in the foregoing excerpt from the Carr case, but it is there in effect, when the phrase is given the meaning disclosed by the context, as that meaning is pointed out by the court below in its opinion denying the motion for a rehearing, when it said that the phrase was necessarily intended to mean within a reasonable time—"that is, within such time as one's persuasion or other adopted means might reasonably be expected to be directly operative in causing an insurrection."

Appellant, of course, cannot plead ignorance of the ruling in the *Carr* case, and was therefore bound to anticipate the probability of a similar ruling in his own case, and preserve his right to a review here by appropriate action upon the original hearing in the court below. It follows that his contention that he raised the federal question at the first opportunity is without substance, and the appeal must be dismissed for want of jurisdiction.

Dismissed.

MR. JUSTICE CARDOZO, dissenting.

The appellant has been convicted of an attempt to incite insurrection in violation of § 56 of the Penal Code of Georgia. He has been convicted after a charge by the trial court that to incur a verdict of guilt he must have advocated violence with the intent that his advocacy should be acted on immediately and with reasonable grounds for the expectation that the intent would be fulfilled. The appellant did not contend then, nor does he contend now, that a statute so restricted would involve an unconstitutional impairment of freedom of speech. However, upon appeal from the judgment of conviction the Supreme Court of Georgia repudiated the construction adopted at the trial and substituted another. Promptly thereafter the appellant moved for a rehearing upon the ground that the substituted meaning made the statute unconstitutional, and in connection with that motion invoked the protection of the Fourteenth Amendment. A rehearing was denied with an opinion which again construed the statute and again rejected the construction accepted in the court below. Now in this court the appellant renews his plaint that the substituted meaning makes the statute void. By the judgment just announced the court declines to hear him. It finds that he was tardy in asserting his privileges and immunities under the Constitution of the United States, and disclaiming jurisdiction dismisses his appeal.

I hold the view that the protection of the Constitution was seasonably invoked and that the court should proceed to an adjudication of the merits. Where the merits lie I do not now consider, for in the view of the majority the merits are irrelevant. My protest is confined to the disclaimer of jurisdiction. The settled doctrine is that when a constitutional privilege or immunity has been denied for the first time by a ruling made upon appeal, a litigant thus surprised may challenge the unexpected ruling by a motion for rehearing, and the challenge will be timely. Within that settled doctrine the cause is rightly here.

Though the merits are now irrelevant, the controversy must be so far explained as to show how a federal

Take Note

Here Justice Cardozo joins issue with the majority on whether Herndon was "surprised" by the Georgia Supreme Court's ruling on his initial appeal. The majority does not necessarily dispute that Herndon was surprised but relies instead on whether, even if he was surprised, his surprise was justifiable. Justice Cardozo turns to that issue next.

question has come into the record. The appellant insists that words do not amount to an incitement to revolution, or to an attempt at such incitement, unless they are of such a nature and are used in such circumstances as to create "a clear and present danger" (Schenck v. United States [1919]) of bringing the prohibited result to pass. He insists that without this limitation a statute so lacking in precision as the one applied against him here is an unconstitutional restraint upon historic liberties of speech. For present purposes it is unimportant whether his argument be sound or shallow. At least it has color of support in words uttered from this bench, and uttered with intense conviction. The court might be unwilling, if it were to pass to a decision of the merits, to fit the words so uttered within the framework of this case. What the appellant is now asking of us is an opportunity to be heard. That privilege is his unless he has thrown it away by silence and acquiescence when there was need of speech and protest.

We are told by the state that the securities of the Constitution should have been invoked upon the trial. The presiding judge should have been warned that a refusal to accept the test of clear and present danger would be a rejection of the restraints of the Fourteenth Amendment. But the trial judge had not refused to accept the test proposed; on the contrary, he had accepted it and even gone a step beyond. In substance he had charged that even a present "danger" would not suffice, if there was not also an expectation, and one grounded in reason, that the insurrection would begin at once. It is novel doctrine that a defendant who has had the benefit of all he asks, and indeed of a good deal more, must place a statement on the record that if some other court at some other time shall read the statute differently, there will be a denial of liberties that at the moment of the protest are unchallenged and intact. Defendants charged with crime are as slow as are men generally to borrow trouble of the future.

> **Ethical Issue**
>
> If Justice Cardozo's characterization is correct, what was the majority saying defense counsel should have done at trial when the court charged the jury? Whether counsel had followed that course of action or not, does the matter raise ethical problems?

We are told, however, that protest, even if unnecessary at the trial, should have been made by an assignment of error or in some other appropriate way in connection with the appeal, and this for the reason that by that time, if not before, the defendant was chargeable with knowledge as a result of two decisions of the highest court of Georgia that the statute was destined to be given another meaning. The decisions relied upon are Carr v. State (No. 1) and Carr v. State (No. 2). The first of these cases was decided in November, 1932, before the trial of the appellant, which occurred in January, 1933. The second was decided in March, 1933, after the appellant had been convicted, but before the denial or submission of his motion for a new trial. Neither is decisive of the question before us now.

Carr v. State, No. 1, came up on demurrer to an indictment. The prosecution was under § 58 of the Penal Code, which makes it a crime to circulate revolutionary documents.* All that was held was that upon the face of the indictment there had been a wilful incitement to violence, sufficient, if proved, to constitute a crime. The opinion contains an extract covering about four pages from the opinion of this court in Gitlow v. New York [1925]. Imbedded in that long quotation are the words now pointed to by the state as decisive of the case at hand. * * * "The immediate danger is none the less real and substantial, because the effect of a given utterance cannot be accurately foreseen." A state

> cannot reasonably be required to defer the adoption of measures for its own peace and safety until the revolutionary utterances lead to actual disturbances of the public peace or imminent and immediate danger of its own destruction; but it may, in the exercise of its judgment, suppress the threatened danger in its incipiency.

To learn the meaning of these words in their application to the Georgia statute we must read them in their setting. Sanford, J., had pointed out that the statute then before him, the New York criminal anarchy act, forbade the teaching and propagation by spoken word or writing of a particular form of doctrine, carefully defined and after such definition denounced on reasonable grounds as fraught with peril to the state. There had been a determination by the state through its legislative body that such utterances "are so inimical to the general welfare and involve such danger of substantive evil that they may be penalized in the exercise of its police power." In such circumstances "the question whether any specific utterance coming within the prohibited class is likely, in and of itself, to bring about the substantive evil, is not open to consideration. It is sufficient that the statute itself be constitutional and that the use of the language comes within its prohibition." In effect the words had been placed upon an expurgatory index. At the same time the distinction was sharply drawn between statutes condemning utterances identified by a description of their meaning and statutes condemning them by reference to the results that they are likely to induce.

> It is clear that the question in such cases [*i.e.* where stated doctrines are denounced] is entirely different from that involved in those cases where the statute merely prohibits certain acts involving the danger of substantive evil,

* "§ 58. If any person shall bring, introduce, print, or circulate, or cause to be introduced, circulated, or printed, or aid or assist, or be in any manner instrumental in bringing, introducing, circulating, or printing within this State any paper, pamphlet, circular, or any writing, for the purpose of inciting insurrection, riot, conspiracy, or resistance against the lawful authority of the State, or against the lives of the inhabitants thereof, or any part of them, he shall be punished by confinement in the penitentiary for not less than five nor longer than twenty years."

> without any reference to language itself, and it is sought to apply its provisions to language used by the defendant for the purpose of bringing about the prohibited results.

The effect of all this was to leave the question open whether in cases of the second class, in cases, that is to say, where the unlawful quality of words is to be determined not upon their face but in relation to their consequences, the opinion in *Schenck v. United States*, supplies the operative rule. The conduct charged to this appellant—in substance an attempt to enlarge the membership of the Communist party in the city of Atlanta—falls, it will be assumed, within the second of these groupings, but plainly is outside the first. There is no reason to believe that the Supreme Court of Georgia, when it quoted from the opinion in Gitlow's case, rejected the restraints which the author of that opinion had placed upon his words. For the decision of the case before it there was no need to go so far. Circulation of documents with intent to incite to revolution had been charged in an indictment. The state had the power to punish such an act as criminal, or so the court had held. How close the nexus would have to be between the attempt and its projected consequences was matter for the trial.

Carr v. State, No. 2, like the case under review, was a prosecution under Penal Code, § 56 (not § 58), and like *Carr v. State, No. 1*, came up on demurrer. All that the court held was that when attacked by demurrer the indictment would stand. This appears from the headnote, drafted by the court itself. After referring to this headnote, the court states that it may be "useful and salutary" to repeat what it had written in *Carr v. State, No. 1*. Thereupon it quotes copiously from its opinion in that case including the bulk of the same extracts from *Gitlow v. New York*. The extracts show upon their face that they have in view a statute denouncing a particular doctrine and prohibiting attempts to teach it. They give no test of the bond of union between an idea and an event.

What has been said as to the significance of the opinions in the two cases against Carr has confirmation in what happened when appellant was brought to trial. The judge who presided at that trial had the first of those opinions before him when he charged the jury, or so we may assume. He did not read it as taking from the state the burden of establishing a clear and present danger that insurrection would ensure as a result of the defendant's conduct. This is obvious from the fact that in his charge he laid that very burden on the state with emphasis and clarity. True, he did not have before him the opinion in prosecution No. 2, for it had not yet been handed down, but if he had seen it, he could not have gathered from its quotation of the earlier case that it was announcing novel doctrine.

From all this it results that Herndon, this appellant, came into the highest court of Georgia without notice that the statute defining his offense was to be given a new meaning. There had been no rejection, certainly no unequivocal rejection, of the doctrine of Schenck v. United States, which had been made the law of the case by the judge presiding at his trial. For all that the record tells us, the prosecuting officer acquiesced in the charge, and did not ask the appellate court to apply a different test. In such a situation the appellant might plant himself as he did on the position that on the case given to the jury his guilt had not been proved: He was not under a duty to put before his judges the possibility of a definition less favorable to himself, and make an argument against it, when there had been no threat of any change, still less any forecast of its form or measure. He might wait until the law of the case had been rejected by the reviewing court before insisting that the effect would be an invasion of his constitutional immunities. If invasion should occur, a motion for rehearing diligently pressed thereafter would be seasonable notice. * * * It is the doctrine that must prevail if the great securities of the Constitution are not to be lost in a web of procedural entanglements.

Ethical Issue

When, if ever, is counsel obligated to bring unfavorable material to the court's attention? Is Justice Cardozo saying that counsel never should do that?

New strength is given to considerations such as these when one passes to a closer view of just what the Georgia court did in its definition of the statute. We have heard that the meaning had been fixed by what had been held already in Carr v. State [No. 1], and that thereby the imminence of the danger had been shown to be unrelated to innocence or guilt. But if that is the teaching of those cases, it was discarded by the very judgment now subjected to review. True, the Georgia court, by its first opinion in the case at hand, did prescribe a test that, if accepted, would bar the consideration of proximity in time. "It is immaterial whether the authority of the state was in danger of being subverted or that an insurrection actually occurred or was impending." "Force must have been contemplated, but * * * the statute does not include either its occurrence or its imminence as an ingredient of the particular offense charged." It would not be "necessary to guilt that the alleged offender should have intended that an insurrection should follow instantly, or at any given time, but it would be sufficient that he intended it to happen at any time, as a result of his influence, by those whom he sought to incite." On the motion for a rehearing the Georgia court repelled with a little heat the argument of counsel that these words were to be taken literally, without "the usual reasonable implications." "The phrase 'at any time,' as criticized in the motion for rehearing, was not intended to mean at any time in the indefinite future, or at any possible later time, however remote." "On the contrary the phrase 'at any time' was necessarily intended, and should have been understood, to mean within a reasonable time; that is, within such time as one's persuasion or other adopted means might reasonably be expected to be directly operative in causing an insurrection." "Under the statute as thus interpreted, we say, as before, that the evidence was sufficient to authorize the conviction."

Here is an unequivocal rejection of the test of clear and present danger, yet a denial also of responsibility without boundaries in time. True, in this rejection, the court disclaimed a willingness to pass upon the question as one of constitutional law, assigning as a reason that no appeal to the Constitution had been made upon the trial or then considered by the judge. Such a rule of state practice may have the effect of attaching a corresponding limitation to the jurisdiction of this court where fault can fairly be imputed to an appellant for the omission to present the question sooner. No such consequence can follow where the ruling of the trial judge has put the Constitution out of the case and made an appeal to its provisions impertinent and futile. In such circumstances, the power does not reside in a state by any rule of local practice to restrict the jurisdiction of this court in the determination of a constitutional question brought into the case thereafter. If the rejection of the test of clear and present danger was a denial of fundamental liberties, the path is clear for us to say so.

What was brought into the case upon the motion for rehearing was a standard wholly novel, the expectancy of life to be ascribed to the persuasive power of an idea. The defendant had no opportunity in the state court to prepare his argument accordingly. He had no opportunity to argue from the record that guilt was not a reasonable inference, or one permitted by the Constitution, on the basis of that test any more than on the basis of others discarded as unfitting. The argument thus shut out is submitted to us now. Will men "judging in calmness" (Brandeis, J.) say of the defendant's conduct as shown forth in the pages of this record that it was an attempt to stir up revolution through the power of his persuasion and within the time when that persuasion might be expected to endure? If men so judging will say yes, will the Constitution of the United States uphold a reading of the statute that will lead to that response? Those are the questions that the defendant lays before us after conviction of a crime punishable by death in the discretion of the jury. I think he should receive an answer.

Notes and Questions

1. *Herndon* makes clear that procedural default in state court, such as failure to raise a federal issue in a timely manner, can constitute an adequate and independent state ground barring Supreme Court review of the federal issue. This bar does not apply if the state court actually decides the federal issue notwithstanding the procedural default. *See* Note on *Orr v. Orr* at page 983. It may also not apply if the state

court gives a new interpretation to a state statute that raises a federal issue for the first time. If the party seeking United States Supreme Court review could not have anticipated the new interpretation, then an objection based on federal law is timely made, and the Supreme Court may hear it. "The whole point, therefore," says Justice Sutherland, "is whether the ruling here assailed should have been anticipated."

It is difficult to understand the battle between Justices Sutherland and Cardozo on this question without understanding more fully what the two *Carr* cases were about. Justice Cardozo points out that *Carr v. State (No. 1)*, 166 S.E. 827 (Ga. 1932), decided before Herndon's trial, involved a different statute from the one in *Herndon*. The Georgia Supreme Court heard the case on appeal from the trial court's overruling of a demurrer to the indictment that argued, *inter alia,* that the statute was void for vagueness and violated both the free speech provision of the Georgia Civil Code and the due process and privileges-and-immunities provisions of the Fourteenth Amendment.

The Georgia Supreme Court quoted from *Gitlow v. New York*, 268 U.S. 652 (1925), four and one-half pages discussing the difference between abstract advocacy of the doctrine of forcible overthrow of the government and advocacy of concrete action directed to that end. The Supreme Court had noted that the state "cannot reasonably be required to defer the adoption of measures for its own peace and safety until the revolutionary utterances lead to actual disturbances of the public peace or imminent and immediate danger of its own destruction; but it may, in the exercise of its judgment, suppress the threatened danger in its incipiency." Gitlow did not, however, explicitly repudiate the clear-and-present-danger test of *Schenck v. United States,* 249 U.S. 47 (1919), instead finding it inapplicable on the facts. *Gitlow* seemed to say that *Schenck* applied only when the legislature had not prohibited particular utterances but had sought instead only to prohibit certain acts without focusing on speech that might stimulate or accompany such acts. JOHN E. NOWAK & RONALD D. ROTUNDA, CONSTITUTIONAL LAW § 16.13(c), at 1294 (8th ed. 2010). The Georgia Supreme Court held that the indictment in *Carr I* was sufficient to withstand the demurrer.

Justice Cardozo argued that *Carr I* did not clearly announce a First Amendment standard different from *Schenck*. Certainly the opinion focused on the difference between doctrinal advocacy in principle and advocacy intended to spur people to action, not on the related but separate question of the temporal connection between advocacy and event that *Schenck* addressed. Moreover, the *Carr I* statute was far more specific about the precise prohibited speech (and thus within *Gitlow* and outside of *Schenck*) than the *Herndon* statute. *Carr I* was far from clear that it repudiated *Schenck* for all purposes, and it requires some stretching to conclude that even if the Georgia Supreme Court intended repudiation with respect to the statute involved in *Carr I,* that would also have been its intention in construing a different statute.

Carr v. State (No. 2), 169 S.E. 201 (Ga. 1933), came down after Herndon's trial, but before the trial court considered his motion for a new trial. Although *Carr II* at least concerned the same statute as *Herndon,* there the repudiation of *Schenck* is even less clear. The Georgia Supreme Court did, however, say that "[t]here is no constitutional right to advocate the overthrow of this government by force," apparently eschewing any requirement of a likely temporal connection between advocacy and event. The Georgia court also implied that it thought the immediacy of the connection between advocacy and event was less important than had the Court in *Schenck*.

What should Herndon have done then? The trial court had apparently adopted a view of the statute that satisfied *Schenck*. In his motion for a new trial should the defendant have urged the trial court, in reliance on *Carr II,* to adopt a broader view of § 56 that would make it easier to convict him on retrial? Is that a realistic position to expect counsel to take?

2. This aspect of *Herndon* raises an interesting ethical question concerning the obligation of counsel to be candid with the court. Counsel has an obligation to notify the court that it is proceeding upon a manifestly erroneous view of the law in contravention of clear authority, even if the court's error helps counsel's client. How far does that obligation extend? How "manifest" must the court's error be in order to bring to bear counsel's ethical obligation? Note the conflict here between counsel's obligation zealously to represent the client's interests and the obligation to deal candidly with the court. To be sure, counsel cannot conceal from the court a case on all fours and incompatible with the client's position. Does that mean, however, that candor requires counsel to raise and then rebut all arguments that might reasonably be made against the client's position?

3. As a practical matter, even if counsel had so informed the trial court, would it have made any difference? Upon hearing counsel's argument that the Georgia Supreme Court's interpretation of § 56 in *Carr II* was unconstitutional, could the trial court have invalidated the statute or reinterpreted it? Was the Georgia Supreme Court saying to Herndon that it was his obligation futilely to raise the constitutional point in the trial court to preserve it for review by the Georgia Supreme Court? What does such a course gain?

4. The fact that the Georgia Supreme Court announced a further clarification of the state statute on the motion for rehearing strengthens Justice Cardozo's argument that the *Carr* cases had not announced a clear change in the law. What was the clarification? How did that affect Herndon's ability to have made a coherent objection to the state statute in the trial court?

5. *Herndon* is the first case in this chapter in which a *procedural* default is asserted as an adequate and independent state ground precluding Supreme Court

review. Justice Sutherland says the Court lacks jurisdiction to review. Why is that so? The adequate-and-independent-state-ground rule operates differently depending on whether the state ground alleged to bar Supreme Court review is substantive or procedural. *Henry v. Mississippi*, which appears immediately following the note on *Orr v. Orr*, explores the difference.

NOTE ON ORR V. ORR, 440 U.S. 268 (1979).

Orr demonstrates that only a state ground upon which the state court actually relies precludes review by the United States Supreme Court. The appellant in *Orr* was a husband who, as a part of a divorce proceeding in Alabama, had agreed to pay alimony. When he fell into arrears, his former wife began a contempt proceeding. The defendant argued that Alabama's statute, which allowed alimony only to wives, violated the Equal Protection Clause.

The Court considered three preliminary issues. First, the Justices inquired whether the husband had standing despite having requested no alimony from the wife; they held that he did. Second, the Court asked whether the challenge was timely, since he had never raised the constitutional question in the initial divorce proceeding. The Court noted that the timing issue might have provided an adequate and independent state (procedural) ground, but the wife had never raised it, and the Alabama Supreme Court had decided the husband's claim on its merits. "[T]he elementary rule is that it is irrelevant to inquire * * * *when* a Federal question was raised in a court below when it appears that such a question was actually considered and decided." (Emphasis added). Third, the Court considered whether the husband should be bound, as a matter of state contract law, by his stipulation to pay alimony. That could have constituted an adequate and independent state substantive ground, but since the objection was neither raised nor relied upon in the Alabama courts, the Supreme Court refused to consider it.

> Where a state court does not decide against a petitioner or appellant upon an independent state ground, but deeming the federal question before it, actually entertains and decides that question adversely to the federal right asserted, this Court has jurisdiction to review the judgment if, as here, it is a final judgment. We cannot refuse jurisdiction because the state court might have based its decision, consistently with the record, upon an independent and adequate non-federal ground.

A party may thus be saved from his (or his attorney's) folly if the highest state court bypasses potentially adequate and independent state grounds and decides the federal issues presented.

Henry v. Mississippi

Supreme Court of the United States, 1965.
379 U.S. 443.

MR. JUSTICE BRENNAN delivered the opinion of the Court.

Petitioner was convicted of disturbing the peace, by indecent proposals to and offensive contact with an 18-year-old hitchhiker to whom he is said to have given a ride in his car. The trial judge charged the jury that "you cannot find the defendant guilty on the unsupported and uncorroborated testimony of the complainant alone." The petitioner's federal claim derives from the admission of a police officer's testimony, introduced to corroborate the hitchhiker's testimony. The Mississippi Supreme Court held that the officer's testimony was improperly admitted as the fruit of "an unlawful search and was in violation of § 23, Miss. Constitution 1890." The tainted evidence tended to substantiate the hitchhiker's testimony by showing its accuracy in a detail which could have been seen only by one inside the car. In particular, it showed that the right-hand ash tray of the car in which the incident took place was full of Dentyne chewing gum wrappers, and that the cigarette lighter did not function. The police officer testified that after petitioner's arrest he had returned to the petitioner's house and obtained the permission of petitioner's wife to look in petitioner's car. The wife provided the officer with the keys * * * . He testified that he tried the lighter and it would not work, and also that the ashtray "was filled with red dentyne chewing gum wrappers."

The Mississippi Supreme Court first filed an opinion which reversed petitioner's conviction and remanded for a new trial. The court held that the wife's consent to the search of the car did not waive petitioner's constitutional rights, and noted that the "[t]estimony of the State's witness * * * is, in effect, uncorroborated without the evidence disclosed by the inspection of defendant's automobile." Acting in the belief that petitioner had been represented by nonresident counsel unfamiliar with local procedure, the court reversed despite petitioner's failure to comply with the Mississippi requirement that an objection to illegal evidence be made at the time it is introduced. The court noted that petitioner had moved for a directed verdict at the close of the State's case, assigning as one ground the use of illegally obtained evidence; it did not mention petitioner's renewal of his motion at the close of all evidence.

After the first opinion was handed down, the State filed a Suggestion of Error, pointing out that petitioner was in fact represented at his trial by competent local counsel, as well as by out-of-state lawyers. Thereupon the Mississippi Supreme Court withdrew its first opinion and filed a new opinion in support of a judgment affirming petitioner's conviction. The new opinion is identical with the first save for the result, the statement that petitioner had local counsel, and the discussion of the effect of failure for whatever reason to make timely objection to the evidence[:] "In such circumstances, even if honest mistakes of counsel in respect to policy or strategy or otherwise occur, they are binding upon the client as a part of the hazards of courtroom battle." Moreover, the court reasoned, petitioner's cross-examination of the State's witness before the initial motion for directed verdict, and introduction of other evidence of the car's interior appearance afterward, "cured" the original error and estopped petitioner from complaining of the tainted evidence. * * * We vacate the judgment of conviction and remand for a hearing on the question whether the petitioner is to be deemed to have knowingly waived decision of his federal claim when timely objection was not made to the admission of the illegally seized evidence.

It is, of course, a familiar principle that this Court will decline to review state court judgments which rest on independent and adequate state grounds, even where these judgments also decide federal questions. The principle applies not only in cases involving state substantive grounds, but also in cases involving state procedural grounds. But it is important to distinguish between state substantive grounds and state procedural grounds. Where the ground involved is substantive, the determination of the federal question cannot affect the disposition if the state court decision on the state law question is allowed to stand. Under the view taken in *Murdock* of the statutes conferring appellate jurisdiction on this Court, we have no power to revise judgments on questions of state law. Thus, the adequate nonfederal ground doctrine is necessary to avoid advisory opinions.

These justifications have no application where the state ground is purely procedural. A procedural default which is held to bar challenge to a conviction in state courts, even on federal constitutional grounds, prevents implementation of the federal right. Accordingly, we have consistently held that the question of when and how defaults in compliance with state procedural rules can preclude our consideration of a federal question is itself a federal question. As Mr. Justice Holmes said:

> When as here there is a plain assertion of federal rights in the lower court, local rules as to how far it shall be reviewed on appeal do not necessarily prevail. * * * Whether the right was denied or not given due recognition by the [state court] * * * is a question as to which the plaintiffs are entitled to invoke our judgment.

Only last Term, we reaffirmed this principle, holding that a state appellate court's refusal, on the ground of mootness, to consider a federal claim, did not preclude our independent determination of the question of mootness; that is itself a question of federal law which this Court must ultimately decide. These cases settle the proposition that a litigant's procedural defaults in state proceedings do not prevent vindication of his federal rights unless the State's insistence on compliance with its procedural rule serves a legitimate state interest. In every case we must inquire whether the enforcement of a procedural forfeiture serves such a state interest. If it does not, the state procedural rule ought not be permitted to bar vindication of important federal rights.[3]

The Mississippi rule requiring contemporaneous objection to the introduction of illegal evidence clearly does serve a legitimate state interest. By immediately apprising the trial judge of the objection, counsel gives the court the opportunity to conduct the trial without using the tainted evidence. If the objection is well taken the fruits of the illegal search may be excluded from jury consideration, and a reversal and new trial avoided. But on the record before us it appears that this purpose of the contemporaneous-objection rule may have been substantially served by petitioner's motion at the close of the State's evidence asking for a directed verdict because of the erroneous admission of the officer's testimony. For at this stage the trial judge could have called for elaboration of the search and seizure argument and, if persuaded, could have stricken the tainted testimony or have taken other appropriate corrective action. For example, if there was sufficient competent evidence without this testimony to go to the jury, the motion for a directed verdict might have been denied, and the case submitted to the jury with a properly worded appropriate cautionary instruction. In these

Food for Thought

How rigorous does the legitimate-state-interest test sound? Note Justice Brennan's assertion that the Court must apply it on a case-by-case basis. Does this mean that one cannot determine whether a general procedural rule—here the contemporaneous-objection rule—"serves a legitimate state interest" without knowing how it was applied?

Take Note!

Once Justice Brennan declares (without reference to the particular case) that the Mississippi rule "clearly does serve a legitimate state interest," should he have dismissed the appeal because there was an adequate and independent state procedural ground?

Food for Thought

After the jury has heard the tainted evidence, would it do any good to strike the testimony? Can a judge unring the bell? That aside, what "other appropriate corrective action" do you think Justice Brennan contemplates?

3 This will not lead inevitably to a plethora of attacks on the application of state procedural rules; where the state rule is a reasonable one and clearly announced to defendant and counsel, application of the waiver doctrine will yield the same result as that of the adequate nonfederal ground doctrine in the vast majority of cases.

circumstances, the delay until the close of the State's case in presenting the objection cannot be said to have frustrated the State's interest in avoiding delay and waste of time in the disposition of the case. If this is so, and enforcement of the rule here would serve no substantial state interest, then settled principles would preclude treating the state ground as adequate; giving effect to the contemporaneous-objection rule for its own sake "would be to force resort to an arid ritual of meaningless form."

We have no reason, however, to decide that question now or to express any view on the merits of petitioner's substantial constitutional claim. For even assuming that the making of the objection on the motion for a directed verdict satisfied the state interest served by the contemporaneous-objection rule, the record suggests a possibility that petitioner's counsel deliberately bypassed the opportunity to make timely objection in the state court, and thus that the petitioner should be deemed to have forfeited his state court remedies. Although the Mississippi Supreme Court characterized the failure to object as an "honest mistake," the State, in the brief in support of its Suggestion of Error in the Supreme Court of Mississippi asserted its willingness to agree that its Suggestion of Error "should not be sustained if either of the three counsel [for petitioner] participating in this trial would respond hereto with an affidavit that he did not know that at some point in a trial in criminal court in Mississippi that an objection to such testimony must have been made." The second opinion of the Mississippi Supreme Court does not refer to the State's proposal and thus it appears that the Court did not believe that the issue was properly presented for decision. Another indication of possible waiver appears in an affidavit attached to the State's brief in this Court; there, the respondent asserted that one of petitioner's lawyers stood up as if to object to the officer's tainted testimony, and was pulled down by co-counsel. Again, this furnishes an insufficient basis for decision of the waiver questions at this time. But, together with the proposal in the Suggestion of Error, it is enough to justify an evidentiary hearing to determine whether petitioner "after consultation with competent counsel or otherwise, understandingly and knowingly forewent the privilege of seeking to vindicate his federal claims in the state courts, whether for strategic, tactical, or any other reasons that can fairly be described as the deliberate by-passing of state procedures * * * ."

Food for Thought

How would such an evidentiary hearing proceed? Whom would the prosecution call as witnesses?

The evidence suggests reasons for a strategic move. Both the complaining witness and the police officer testified that the cigarette lighter in the car did not work. After denial of its motion for a directed verdict the defense called a mechanic who had repaired the cigarette lighter. The defense might have planned to allow the complaining witness and the officer to testify that the cigarette lighter did not work, and then, if the motion for directed verdict were not granted, to discredit both witnesses by showing that it did work, thereby persuading the jury to acquit. Or, by delaying objection to the evidence, the defense might have hoped to invite error and lay the foundation for a subsequent reversal. If either reason motivated the action of petitioner's counsel, and their plans backfired, counsel's deliberate choice of the strategy would amount to a waiver binding on petitioner and would preclude him from a decision on the merits of his federal claim either in the state courts or here. Although trial strategy adopted by counsel without prior consultation with an accused will not, where the circumstances are exceptional, preclude the accused from asserting constitutional claims, we think that the deliberate bypassing by counsel of the contemporaneous-objection rule as a part of trial strategy would have that effect in this case.

> **Food for Thought**
>
> Remember that Mississippi law forbade conviction without corroborating evidence. Since the officer's testimony was the only corroborating evidence the state offered, what tactical gain is there from not seeking to prevent the officer from testifying? That is not to say that other cases might not present such tactical temptations, but does *this* case?

Only evidence extrinsic to the record before us can establish the fact of waiver, and the State should have an opportunity to establish that fact. * * * [A] dismissal on the basis of an adequate state ground would not end this case; petitioner might still pursue vindication of his federal claim in a federal habeas corpus proceeding in which the procedural default will not alone preclude consideration of his claim, at least unless it is shown that petitioner deliberately bypassed the orderly procedure of the state courts.[a]

Of course, in so remanding we neither hold nor even remotely imply that the State must forgo insistence on its procedural requirements if it finds no waiver. Such a finding would only mean that petitioner could have a federal court apply settled principles to test the effectiveness of the procedural default to foreclose consideration of his constitutional claim. If it finds the procedural default ineffective, the federal court will itself decide the merits of his federal claim, at least so long as the state court does not wish to do so. By permitting the Mississippi courts to make an initial determination of waiver, we serve the causes of efficient administration of criminal justice, and of harmonious federal-state judicial relations. Such a disposition may make unnecessary the processing of the case through federal courts already laboring under congested dockets, or it may make

---

a [AUTHORS' NOTE] The Court has since overruled the standard for review on habeas corpus expressed here. *See* Coleman v. Thompson, 501 U.S. 722 (1991), presented at page 1163 in Chapter 11.

unnecessary the relitigation in a federal forum of certain issues. * * * Therefore, the judgment is vacated and the case is remanded to the Mississippi Supreme Court for further proceedings not inconsistent with this opinion.

It is so ordered.

MR. JUSTICE BLACK, dissenting.

Petitioner contends that his conviction was based in part on evidence obtained by an allegedly unlawful search in violation of the United States Constitution. I would decide this federal question here and now. I do not believe that the Mississippi procedural trial rule relied on by the State can shut off this Court's review, nor do I find a particle of support for the Court's suggestion that petitioner knowingly waived his right to have this constitutional question decided by the state trial court.

As far as the issue of waiver is concerned, I agree with the Mississippi Supreme Court, which considered the failure to object one of the "honest mistakes" which any lawyer might make, since I believe that the record is completely barren of evidence to support a finding of a conscious and intentional waiver of petitioner's due process right to have the trial court decide whether evidence used against him had been unconstitutionally seized. Therefore I would not remand for a hearing by the State Supreme Court or the trial court on the issue of waiver.[2] And even if I considered that a real issue of waiver had been shown and was properly before us, I would decide it here. I cannot agree to the Court's judgment remanding the case to the state courts for a hearing on that issue alone, thereby giving the State a chance to supplement the trial record to save its conviction from constitutional challenge in a summary hearing before a court without a jury. * * *

Nor do I believe that Mississippi's procedural rule concerning the stage of a trial at which constitutional objections should be made is the kind of rule that we should accept as an independent, adequate ground for the State Supreme Court's refusal to decide the constitutional question raised by petitioner. * * * [T]his Court held that where a State allows constitutional questions "to be raised at a late stage and be determined by its courts as a matter of discretion, we are not concluded from assuming jurisdiction and deciding whether the state court action in the particular circumstances is, in effect, an avoidance of the federal right."

2 I think that the very "evidence" cited in the Court's opinion points up the fact that there was no evidence from which it can be inferred that a conscious waiver was made. I can find no support, as the Court does, from an affidavit filed for the first time as an appendix to the State's brief in this Court, stating that the district attorney who tried the case had seen one of petitioner's counsel start to rise from his chair when the evidence from the search was introduced, but that another of petitioner's counsel gave a "jerk on the coat tail" of the lawyer, "returning him to his seat." It is hard for me to see how one could infer from this "jerk on the coat tail" even a suspicion that petitioner had consciously and knowingly waived his right to object to the evidence offered against him.

No Mississippi court opinions or state statutes have been called to our attention that I read as denying power of the State Supreme Court, should that court wish to do so, to consider and determine constitutional questions presented at the time this one was. In fact, as I understand counsel for the State, the Supreme Court of Mississippi does have power in its discretion to consider such questions regardless of when they are presented. As that court has said most persuasively: "Constitutional rights in serious criminal cases rise above mere rules of procedure. * * * Errors affecting fundamental rights are exceptions to the rule that questions not raised in the trial court cannot be raised for the first time on appeal."

After stating this to be the rule it followed, and citing a number of its past decisions which stated and applied the same rule, the highest court of Mississippi, in the opinion quoted from, because of that rule reversed a conviction obtained through the use of unconstitutionally seized evidence, even though as in the present case there had been no objection made at the time the evidence was presented. The court noted that it had applied this same rule in other cases where proper objection had not been made at the trial * * * . In all of those cases the defendant appears to have been represented by local counsel. Yet this Court now apparently holds that the state court may, if it chooses to do so, depart from its prior cases and apply a new, stricter rule against this defendant and thereby prevent this Court from reviewing the case to see that his federal constitutional rights were safeguarded. I do not believe the cherished federal constitutional right of a defendant to object to unconstitutionally seized evidence offered against him can be cut off irrevocably by state-court discretionary rulings which might be different in particular undefined circumstances in other cases. I think such a procedural device for shutting off our review of questions involving constitutional rights is too dangerous to be tolerated.

Food for Thought

Does Justice Black suggest here that he sees *Henry* as a latter-day Herndon v. Georgia?

For these reasons I dissent from the disposition of this case.

MR. JUSTICE HARLAN, with whom MR. JUSTICE CLARK and MR. JUSTICE STEWART join, dissenting.

Flying banners of federalism, the Court's opinion actually raises storm signals of a most disquieting nature. While purporting to recognize the traditional principle that an adequate procedural, as well as substantive, state ground of decision bars direct review here of any federal claim asserted in the state litigation, the Court, unless I wholly misconceive what is lurking in today's opinion, portends a severe dilution, if not complete abolition, of the concept of "adequacy" as pertaining to state procedural grounds.

In making these preliminary observations I do not believe I am seeing ghosts. For I cannot account for the remand of this case in the face of what is a demonstrably adequate state procedural ground of decision by the Mississippi Supreme Court except as an early step toward extending in one way or another the doctrine of *Fay v. Noia*, to direct review. In that case, decided only two Terms ago, the Court turned its back on history * * * and did away with the adequate state ground doctrine in federal habeas corpus proceedings.

Believing that any step toward extending *Noia* to direct review should be flushed out and challenged at its earliest appearance in an opinion of this Court, I respectfully dissent.

I

The Mississippi Supreme Court did not base its ultimate decision upon petitioner's federal claim that his wife's consent could not validate an otherwise improper police search of the family car, but on the procedural ground that petitioner (who was represented by three experienced lawyers) had not objected at the time the fruits of this search were received in evidence. This Court now strongly implies, but does not decide (in view of its remand on the "waiver" issue) that enforcement of the State's "contemporaneous-objection" rule was inadequate as a state ground of decision because the petitioner's motion for a directed verdict of acquittal afforded the trial judge a satisfactory opportunity to take "appropriate corrective action" with reference to the allegedly inadmissible evidence. Thus, it is suggested, this may be a situation where "giving effect to the contemporaneous-objection rule for its own sake 'would be to force resort to an arid ritual of meaningless form.' "

From the standpoint of the realities of the courtroom, I can only regard the Court's analysis as little short of fanciful. The petitioner's motion for a verdict could have provoked one of three courses of action by the trial judge, none of which can reasonably be considered as depriving the State's contemporaneous-objection rule of its capacity to serve as an adequate state ground.

1. The trial judge might have granted the directed verdict. But had this action been appropriate, the Supreme Court of Mississippi, in its first opinion, would have ordered the prosecution dismissed. Since it did not, and the matter is entirely one of state law, further speculation by this Court should be foreclosed.

2. The trial judge might have directed a mistrial. The State's interest in preventing mistrials through the contemporaneous-objection requirement is obvious.

3. The remaining course of action is the example given by the Court; the trial judge could have denied the motion for a directed verdict, but, ***sua sponte***, called

for elaboration of the argument, determined that the search of the automobile was unconstitutional, and given cautionary instructions to the jury to disregard the inadmissible evidence when the case was submitted to it.

The practical difficulties with this approach are manifestly sufficient to show a substantial state interest in their avoidance, and thus to show an "adequate" basis for the State's adherence to the contemporaneous-objection rule.

* * *

As every trial lawyer of any experience knows, motions for directed verdicts are generally made as a matter of course at the close of the prosecution's case, and are generally denied without close consideration unless the case is clearly borderline. It is simply unrealistic in this context to have expected the trial judge to pick out the single vague sentence from the directed verdict motion and to have acted upon it with the refined imagination the Court would require of him. Henry's three lawyers apparently regarded the search and seizure claim as make-weight. They had not mentioned it earlier in the trial and gave no explanation for their laxity in raising it. And when they did mention it, they did so in a cursory and conclusional sentence placed in a secondary position in a directed verdict motion. The theory underlying the search and seizure argument—that a wife's freely given permission to search the family car is invalid—is subtle to say the very least, and as the matter was presented to the trial judge it would have been extraordinary had he caught it, or even realized that there was a serious problem to catch. But this is not all the Court would require of him. He must, in addition, realize that despite the inappropriateness of granting the directed verdict requested of him, he could partially serve the cause of the defense by taking it upon himself to frame and give cautionary instructions to the jury to disregard the evidence obtained as fruits of the search.[2]

Contrast with this the situation presented by a contemporaneous objection. The objection must necessarily be directed to the single question of admissibility; the judge must inevitably focus on it; there would be no doubt as to the appropriate form of relief, and the effect of the trial judge's decision would be immediate rather than remote. Usually the proper timing of an objection will force an elaboration of it. Had objection been made in this case during the officer's testimony about the search, it would have called forth of its own force the specific answer that the wife had given her permission and, in turn, the assertion that the permis-

2 Furthermore, even if counsel had fully elaborated the argument and had made it in the context of a motion to strike rather than a motion for directed verdict, the trial judge could properly have exercised his discretion (as the Mississippi Supreme Court did) and denied any relief. This power is recognized in trial judges in the federal system in order to prevent the "ambushing" of a trial through the withholding of an objection that should have been made when questionable evidence was first introduced. Federalism is turned upside down if it is denied to judges in the state systems.

sion was ineffective. The issue, in short, would have been advertently faced by the trial judge and the likelihood of achieving a correct result maximized.

Thus the state interest which so powerfully supports the contemporaneous-objection rule is that of maximizing correct decisions and concomitantly minimizing errors requiring mistrials and retrials. The alternative for the State is to reverse a trial judge who, from a long motion, fails to pick out and act with remarkable imagination upon a single vague sentence relating to admissibility of evidence long since admitted. A trial judge is a decision-maker, not an advocate. To force him out of his proper role by requiring him to coax out the arguments and imaginatively reframe the requested remedies for the counsel before him is to place upon him more responsibility than a trial judge can be expected to discharge.

There was no "appropriate corrective action" that could have realistically satisfied the purposes of the contemporaneous-objection rule. Without question the State had an interest in maintaining the integrity of its procedure, and thus without doubt reliance on the rule in question is 'adequate' to bar direct review of petitioner's federal claim by this Court.[3]

II

The real reason for remanding this case emerges only in the closing pages of the Court's opinion. It is pointed out that even were the contemporaneous-objection rule considered to be an adequate state ground, this would not, under Fay v. Noia, preclude consideration of Henry's federal claim in federal habeas corpus unless it were made to appear that Henry had deliberately waived his federal claim in the state proceedings. It is then said that in the interest of "efficient administration of criminal justice" and "harmonious" relations between the federal and state judiciaries the Mississippi courts should be given the opportunity to pass, in the first instance, on the waiver issue; the prospect is entertained that such action on the part of this Court will encourage the States to grasp the "opportunity" afforded by * * * providing "state procedures, direct or collateral, for a full airing of federal claims." It is "suggested" that were this to be done "irritation" and "friction" respecting the exercise of federal habeas corpus power vis-à-vis state convictions "might be ameliorated."

3 As the first opinion by the Mississippi Supreme Court shows, there is discretion in certain circumstances to lower the procedural bar. It does not follow that this Court is completely free to exercise that discretion. Even in cases from lower federal courts we do so only if there has been an abuse. If, in order to insulate its decisions from reversal by this Court, a state court must strip itself of the discretionary power to differentiate between different sets of circumstances, the rule operates in a most perverse way.

What does all this signify? The States are being invited to voluntarily obliterate all state procedures, however conducive they may be to the orderly conduct of litigation, which might thwart state-court consideration of federal claims. But what if the States do not accept the invitation? Despite the Court's soft-spoken assertion that "settled principles" will be applied in the future, I do not think the intimation will be missed by any discerning reader of the Court's opinion that at the least a substantial dilution of the adequate state-ground doctrine may be expected. A contrary prediction is belied by the implication of the opinion that under "settled principles," the contemporaneous-objection rule relied upon in this case could be declared inadequate.

To me this would not be a move toward "harmonious" federalism; any further disrespect for state procedures, no longer cognizable at all in federal habeas corpus, would be the very antithesis of it. While some may say that, given Fay v. Noia, what the Court is attempting to do is justifiable as a means of promoting "efficiency" in the administration of criminal justice, it is the sort of efficiency which, though perhaps appropriate in some watered-down form of federalism, is not congenial to the kind of federalism I had supposed was ours. I venture to say that to all who believe the federal system as we have known it to be a priceless aspect of our Constitutionalism, the spectre implicit in today's decision will be no less disturbing than what the Court has already done in Fay v. Noia.

Believing that the judgment below rests on an adequate independent state ground, I would dismiss the writ issued in this case as improvidently granted.

Notes and Questions

1. *Henry v. Mississippi* was certainly not the ordinary case; it had great political and social significance not reflected in the record. After the Court's decision above, the Mississippi Supreme Court, perhaps contrary to the United States Supreme Court's hopes, declined to find that the directed verdict motion sufficiently satisfied the state's interest to permit litigation of the federal issue and specifically found that there had been a deliberate and knowing waiver of the Fourth Amendment claim. Henry again sought review, but the Supreme Court denied the petition for certiorari while appending an unusual note that Henry was free to seek federal habeas corpus relief, which he subsequently did.

> The intransigence of the Mississippi Supreme Court and the desire of the U.S. Supreme Court to intervene is more understandable when one notes that Aaron Henry was not an ordinary criminal defendant. Henry, in fact, was the president of the local NAACP chapter. The prosecution was in Mississippi and the year

was 1962. There is some question as to whether Henry was being singled out for prosecution.

Robert Jerome Glennon, *The Jurisdictional Legacy of the Civil Rights Movement*, 61 TENN.L.REV. 869, 899 (1994) (citation omitted).

2. Suppose federal law made the wife's consent to the inspection of the automobile effective as to the husband. Could Mississippi take a contrary position? Assuming that Mississippi did so, would that have any effect on the appealability of the case?

3. The Court notes that the adequate and independent state ground rule applies whether the state ground is substantive or procedural; however, the rule applies differently in the two contexts. What are the differences? The Court appears to say the rule is jurisdictional in one context but not in the other. In which context is it jurisdictional? When the rule is not jurisdictional, does the Court's refusal to hear the case amount to another abstention doctrine? The Court goes on to state that "the question of when and how defaults in compliance with state procedural rules can preclude our consideration of a federal question is itself a federal question." If the state procedural default constitutes an "adequate" ground, the Court will not review the federal question. What test does the Court announce for assessing whether a state ground is adequate?

4. a) Discussing the contemporaneous-objection rule, Justice Brennan notes that it "clearly does serve a legitimate state interest," but observes that Henry's motion for directed verdict "substantially serve[s]" the purpose. Who ought to make the judgment of whether an alternate procedure sufficiently protects the state's interest? Does the majority imply either that the state is obligated to adopt the least restrictive rules possible to protect its interests or that if litigants devise their own ways to protect the state's interest, the state must accept them?

b) This is a point that draws Justice Harlan's attention in dissent. On what basis, if any, should the Supreme Court decide that a state procedural rule is inappropriate? Does the majority hold that the contemporaneous-objection rule is unconstitutional as applied? If not, then what is the federal issue that supports the Court's appellate jurisdiction under 28 U.S.C. § 1257? Does the Court owe any deference to the state's perception of its own interests and selection of rules to protect them?

5. In *Michel v. Louisiana*, 350 U.S. 91 (1955), the Court considered whether to review a case where the substantive constitutional challenge involved the composition of the grand jury pool. Louisiana law required defendants to raise challenges to the composition of the grand jury "before the expiration of the third judicial day following the end of the grand jury's term or before trial, whichever is earlier." The defendants in Michel had not filed timely challenges. The Court characterized the issue before it as follows: "In these cases, we are asked to decide whether this statute as applied violates

the Fourteenth Amendment." This challenge to the adequacy of the state procedural rule is of a different nature than the challenge to adequacy of the procedural rule in *Henry*. How are the challenges different? Does *Henry* overrule Michel, or can the different kinds of challenges coexist?

6. Justice Black's dissent raises a different question. He notes that Mississippi's Supreme Court has discretion to waive compliance with the rule and has done so on occasion in the past. Does he implicitly take the position that having exercised such discretion, the Mississippi Supreme Court has made the contemporaneous-objection rule forever unavailable as a basis for resisting review in the United States Supreme Court?

7. The Court tends to follow a two-step inquiry when the respondent seeks to block Supreme Court review based on a state procedural default. First, is there an independent state procedural ground that is adequate to support the judgment? If not, then the Court may proceed to hear the petitioner's federal claims. If the answer is "Yes," the Court moves to the second inquiry: Do circumstances exist that will excuse the petitioner's noncompliance with the state procedural rule?

a) As to the first inquiry, *Henry* took a very searching look at the adequacy of the Mississippi contemporaneous objection rule, observing that raising the Fourth Amendment claim in a motion for a directed verdict would serve the legitimate state interest equally well. This portion of Justice Brennan's opinion plainly is strained. In fact, *Henry* did not usher in a new era of aggressive examination of the adequacy of state procedural rules. On occasion, the Court found state court reliance on a procedural rule to bar a constitutional claim to be an inadequate ground. For example, in *Douglas v. Alabama*, 380 U.S. 415 (1965), the Court found an Alabama rule requiring multiple objections to the admission of a confession inadequate to bar Supreme Court review. But such cases were rare. The Court was much more likely to stress the importance of state contemporaneous objection rules.

Recently, however, the Court appeared to adopt *Henry*'s approach in a different context in *Lee v. Kemna*, 534 U.S. 362 (2002). A state prisoner seeking federal habeas corpus relief had been denied an overnight continuance in his murder trial when his subpoenaed alibi witnesses disappeared from the courthouse. The trial court refused the continuance because of other schedule commitments. The state appellate courts had upheld the denial, but only on the ground that the defendant had not complied with the state rule requiring such requests to be in writing and with a certain amount of detail. Neither the trial court nor the prosecutor had raised either concern. The inferior federal courts denied relief, but a majority of the Supreme Court held that the procedural default noted for the first time at the appellate level should not bar review. The Court freely acknowledged that the state rules served a legitimate state interest, but it also noted that the manner in which the defendant had sought the continuance gave the trial court the relevant information at the relevant time. (The latter might distinguish the case from *Henry*). At the same time, the majority explicitly denied that it relied on *Henry* in reaching the result, a claim that Justice Kennedy, in dissent, could not accept.

Despite the majority's insistence that Henry did not underlie the decision, the fact remains that the Court did evaluate concededly legitimate state procedural rules on an as-applied basis, just as the *Henry* Court did. Moreover, Note 16 of the majority opinion appears to approve the as-applied approach that the Court used in *Henry* and later endorsed in *Osborne v. Ohio*, 495 U.S. 103 (1990). The Court seemed at pains only to distance itself from *Henry*'s permitting later events to substitute for actions that the defendant should have taken earlier. (In some ways, *Lee* seems more defensible than *Henry*, since Lee moved timely for the continuance whereas Henry did not lodge a contemporaneous objection to the introduction of the evidence from the search.) Although the majority did not use the term, it appeared implicitly to find the facially legitimate state rules unconstitutional as applied to Lee's case, just as the *Henry* majority seemed to reach the same sort of conclusion. The open question now may be whether *Lee* signifies that the Court will take a more searching look at procedural defaults to ensure that application of the state rules in the case in fact serves the legitimate state interest that the rules, considered in the abstract, address.

b) *Henry* appeared to suggest that the standards for assessing the second inquiry—whether to excuse a failure to obey a state rule found adequate to support the judgment—may be quite lax. Two years before *Henry*, *Fay v. Noia*, 372 U.S. 391 (1963), held that a state procedural default would not bar federal court review of a state judgment in a habeas corpus case unless the applicant "deliberately by-passed the orderly procedures of the state courts and in so doing * * * forfeited his state court remedies." To Justice Harlan's distress, Justice Brennan seemed to imply that the habeas standard would also apply in § 1257 cases.

Coleman v. Thompson, 501 U.S. 722 (1991), imposes a much stricter standard for excusing procedural default in habeas cases and it probably also applies in § 1257 cases. *Coleman* explicitly overruled *Fay v. Noia*'s deliberate-by-pass standard and replaced it with the so-called cause-and-prejudice standard. Under this new standard, a federal habeas court will excuse non-compliance with a state procedural rule only if the petitioner shows good cause for not complying with the rule and that the result of his case would have been different if the state court had considered his constitutional claim. Although the Court did not specifically address whether the cause-and-prejudice standard would apply to § 1257 cases, it is hard to see why it should not. The conclusion that it does apply is strengthened by the Court's reminder in *Coleman* that it applies the standards of *Michigan v. Long*, a § 1257 case, to habeas cases. Treating like cases alike should work both ways.

If the cause-and-prejudice standard applies to Supreme Court review of state court decisions, the petitioner in a case like Michel would have to persuade the Court that there was a good reason underlying the failure to comply with the three-day rule *and* that if the court heard the grand jury challenge, no conviction would have ensued. Similarly, in *Henry,* the Court might defer the inquiry into the "legitimate state interest" until the petitioner satisfies the cause-and-prejudice inquiry Coleman now mandates. It is not yet clear whether the Court will adopt a similar standard in civil cases, but the breadth of Coleman's language at least suggests that it will. Does such a standard mean that a state procedural default almost inevitably bars subsequent consideration of the federal constitutional claim?

There have been three broad categories of cases in which a state procedural default does not preclude Supreme Court review. The first, discussed in Michel, involves state procedural rules that are themselves unconstitutional, ordinarily because they deny due process of law. The second, hinted at in Michel, involves state procedural rules that, while constitutional on their face, are applied haphazardly or discriminatorily. In 1991, the Court reaffirmed its view of such rules, noting that a state procedural rule must be "firmly established and regularly followed" if it is to bar review. The third, exemplified by *Henry,* concerns circumstances in which the Court finds either that the state procedural rule serves no legitimate state interest or that the legitimate state interest the rule does represent may be satisfied in other ways. What effect do you think Coleman will have on each of these three categories?

8. Counsel's rigorous adherence to state timing rules may also present problems. Where a state allows a comparatively short time in which to make certain motions (*e.g.* a state rule potentially requiring objections to the composition of a grand jury panel to be filed within three days of indictment, (as in Michel v. Louisiana)), what is counsel's best course upon entering a complex case? If the state has a counterpart to FED.R.CIV.P. 11, which requires counsel to make a reasonable inquiry into the basis for a motion, does that affect the answer? Should existence of a counterpart affect the Court's analysis in procedural default cases?

3. With the Final Judgment Rule

Cox Broadcasting Corp. v. Cohn

Supreme Court of the United States, 1975.
420 U.S. 469.

MR. JUSTICE WHITE delivered the opinion of the Court.

The issue before us in this case is whether, consistently with the First and Fourteenth Amendments, a State may extend a cause of action for damages for invasion of privacy caused by the publication of the name of a deceased rape victim which was publicly revealed in connection with the prosecution of the crime.

I

In August 1971, appellee's 17-year-old daughter was the victim of a rape and did not survive the incident. Six youths were soon indicted for murder and rape. Although there was substantial press coverage of the crime and of subsequent developments, the identity of the victim was not disclosed pending trial, perhaps because of GA. CODE ANN. § 26-9901 (1972), which makes it a misdemeanor to publish or broadcast the name or identity of a rape victim. In April 1972, some eight months later, the six defendants appeared in court. Five pleaded guilty to rape or attempted rape, the charge of murder having been dropped. The guilty pleas were accepted by the court, and the trial of the defendant pleading not guilty was set for a later date.

In the course of the proceedings that day, appellant Wassell, a reporter covering the incident for his employer, learned the name of the victim from an examination of the indictments which were made available for his inspection in the courtroom. That the name of the victim appears in the indictments and that the indictments were public records available for inspection are not disputed. Later that day, Wassell broadcast over the facilities of station WSB-TV, a television station owned by appellant Cox Broadcasting Corp., a news report concerning the court proceedings. The report named the victim of the crime and was repeated the following day.

In May 1972, appellee brought an action for money damages against appellants, relying on § 26-9901 and claiming that his right to privacy had been invaded by the television broadcasts giving the name of his deceased daughter. Appellants admitted the broadcasts but claimed that they were privileged under both state law and the First and Fourteenth Amendments. The trial court, rejecting appellants' constitutional claims and holding that the Georgia statute gave a civil remedy to those injured by its violation, granted summary judgment to appellee as to liability, with the determination of damages to await trial by jury.

On appeal, the Georgia Supreme Court, in its initial opinion, held that the trial court had erred in construing § 26-9901 to extend a civil cause of action for invasion of privacy and thus found it unnecessary to consider the constitutionality of the statute. The court went on to rule, however, that the complaint stated a cause of action "for the invasion of the appellee's right of privacy, or for the tort of public disclosure"—a "common law tort exist[ing] in this jurisdiction without the help of the statute that the trial judge in this case relied on." Although the privacy invaded was not that of the deceased victim, the father was held to have stated a claim for invasion of his own privacy by reason of the publication of his daughter's name. The court explained, however, that liability did not follow as a matter of law and that summary judgment was improper; whether the public disclosure of the name actually invaded appellee's "zone of privacy," and if so, to what extent, were issues to be determined by the trier of fact. Also, "in formulating such an issue for determination by the fact-finder, it is reasonable to require the appellee to prove that the appellants invaded his privacy with wilful or negligent disregard for the fact that reasonable men would find the invasion highly offensive." The Georgia Supreme Court did agree with the trial court, however, that the First and Fourteenth Amendments did not, as a matter of law, require judgment for appellants. * * *

Upon motion for rehearing the Georgia court countered the argument that the victim's name was a matter of public interest and could be published with impunity by relying on § 26-9901 as an authoritative declaration of state policy that the name of a rape victim was not a matter of public concern. This time the court felt compelled to determine the constitutionality of the statute and sustained it as a "legitimate limitation on the right of freedom of expression contained in the First Amendment." The court could discern "no public interest or general concern about the identity of the victim of such a crime as will make the right to disclose the identity of the victim rise to the level of First Amendment protection."

Food for Thought

Is there a problem with the trial court's wording here? Can a state statute limit a constitutional right?

We postponed decision as to our jurisdiction over this appeal to the hearing on the merits. We conclude that the Court has jurisdiction, and reverse the judgment of the Georgia Supreme Court.

II

Appellants invoke the appellate jurisdiction of this Court under 28 U.S.C. § 1257(2) and, if that jurisdictional basis is found to be absent, through a petition for certiorari under 28 U.S.C. § 2103. Two questions concerning our jurisdiction must be resolved: (1) whether the constitutional validity of § 26-9901 was "drawn in question," with the Georgia Supreme Court upholding its validity, and (2) whether the decision from which this appeal has been taken is a "[f]inal judgment or decree."

* * *

A

[The Court answered the first question in the affirmative.]

B

Since 1789, Congress has granted this Court appellate jurisdiction with respect to state litigation only after the highest state court in which judgment could be had has rendered a "[f]inal judgment or decree." Title 28 U.S.C. § 1257 retains this limitation on our power to review cases coming from state courts. The Court has noted that "[considerations] of English usage as well as those of judicial policy" would justify an interpretation of the final-judgment rule to preclude review "where anything further remains to be determined by a State court, no matter how dissociated from the only federal issue that has finally been adjudicated by the highest court of the State." *Radio Station WOW, Inc. v. Johnson (1945)*. But the Court there observed that the rule had not been administered in such a mechanical fashion and that there were circumstances in which there has been "a departure from this requirement of finality for federal appellate jurisdiction."

These circumstances were said to be "very few," but as the cases have unfolded, the Court has recurringly encountered situations in which the highest court of a State has finally determined the federal issue present in a particular case, but in which there are further proceedings in the lower state courts to come. There are now at least four categories of such cases in which the Court has treated the decision on the federal issue as a final judgment for the purposes of 28 U.S.C. § 1257 and has taken jurisdiction without awaiting the completion of the additional proceedings anticipated in the lower state courts. In most, if not all, of the cases in these categories, these additional proceedings would not require the decision of other federal questions that might also require review by the Court at a later date, and immediate rather than delayed review would be the best way to avoid "the mischief of economic waste and of delayed justice," as well as precipitate interference with state litigation.[7] In the cases in the first two categories considered below, the federal issue would not be mooted or otherwise affected by the proceedings yet to be had because those proceedings have little substance, their outcome is certain, or they are wholly unrelated to the federal question. In the other two categories, however, the federal issue would be mooted if the petitioner or appellant seeking to bring the action here prevailed on the merits in the later state-court proceedings, but there is nevertheless sufficient justification for immediate review of the federal question finally determined in the state courts.

Food for Thought

With respect to the first two categories that Justice White mentions, why are they separate?

In the first category are those cases in which there are further proceedings—even entire trials—yet to occur in the state courts but where for one reason or another the federal issue is conclusive or the outcome of further proceedings preordained. In these circumstances, because the case is for all practical purposes concluded, the judgment of the state court on the federal issue is deemed final. In Mills v. Alabama (1966), for example, a demurrer to a criminal complaint was sustained on federal constitutional grounds by a state trial court. The State Supreme Court reversed, remanding for jury trial. This Court took jurisdiction on the reasoning that the appellant had no defense other than his federal claim and could not prevail at trial on the facts or any nonfederal ground. To dismiss the appeal "would not only be an inexcusable delay of the benefits Congress intended to grant by providing for appeal to this Court, but it would also result in a completely unnecessary waste of time and energy in judicial systems already troubled by delays due to congested dockets."

Second, there are cases such as *Radio Station WOW*, and *Brady v. Maryland* (1963) in which the federal issue, finally decided by the highest court in the State, will survive and require decision regardless of the outcome of future state-court proceedings. In *Radio Station WOW*, the Nebraska Supreme Court directed

---

7 Gillespie v. United States Steel Corp., 379 U.S. 148 (1964), arose in the federal courts and involved the requirement of 28 U.S.C. § 1291 that judgments of district courts be final if they are to be appealed to the courts of appeals. In the course of deciding that the judgment of the District Court in the case had been final, the Court indicated its approach to finality requirements:

> And our cases long have recognized that whether a ruling is "final" within the meaning of § 1291 is frequently so close a question that decision of that issue either way can be supported with equally forceful arguments, and that it is impossible to devise a formula to resolve all marginal cases coming within what might well be called the "twilight zone" of finality. Because of this difficulty this Court has held that the requirement of finality is to be given a "practical rather than a technical construction." [We also] pointed out that in deciding the question of finality the most important competing considerations are "the inconvenience and costs of piecemeal review on the one hand and the danger of denying justice by delay on the other."

the transfer of the properties of a federally licensed radio station and ordered an accounting, rejecting the claim that the transfer order would interfere with the federal license. The federal issue was held reviewable here despite the pending accounting on the "presupposition * * * that the federal questions that could come here have been adjudicated by the State court, and that the accounting which remains to be taken could not remotely give rise to a federal question * * * that may later come here * * * ." The judgment rejecting the federal claim and directing the transfer was deemed "dissociated from a provision for an accounting even though that is decreed in the same order." Nothing that could happen in the course of the accounting, short of settlement of the case, would foreclose or make unnecessary decision on the federal question. Older cases in the Court had reached the same result on similar facts. * * *[9]

In the third category are those situations where the federal claim has been finally decided, with further proceedings on the merits in the state courts to come, but in which later review of the federal issue cannot be had, whatever the ultimate outcome of the case. Thus, in these cases, if the party seeking interim review ultimately prevails on the merits, the federal issue will be mooted; if he were to lose on the merits, however, the governing state law would not permit him again to present his federal claims for review. The Court has taken jurisdiction in these circumstances prior to completion of the case in the state courts. California v. Stewart (1966) (decided with Miranda v. Arizona), epitomizes this category. There the state court reversed a conviction on federal constitutional grounds and remanded for a new trial. Although the State might have prevailed at trial, we granted its petition for certiorari and affirmed, explaining that the state judgment was "final" since an acquittal of the defendant at trial would preclude, under state law, an appeal by the State.

A recent decision in this category is North Dakota State Board of Pharmacy v. Snyder's Drug Stores, Inc., in which the Pharmacy Board rejected an application for a pharmacy operating permit relying on a state statute specifying ownership requirements which the applicant did not meet. The State Supreme Court held the statute unconstitutional and remanded the matter to the Board for further consideration of

Make the Connection

Note here that the Court assumes that there is a cognizable state interest in not being subject to an overbroad interpretation of federal law. Contrast this assumption with Justice Stevens's argument in Michigan v. Long, at page 939.

9 In Brady v. Maryland, the Maryland courts had ordered a new trial in a criminal case but on punishment only, and the petitioner asserted here that he was entitled to a new trial on guilt as well. We entertained the case, saying that the federal issue was separable and would not be mooted by the new trial on punishment ordered in the state courts.

the application, freed from the constraints of the ownership statute. The Board brought the case here, claiming that the statute was constitutionally acceptable under modern cases. After reviewing the various circumstances under which the finality requirement has been deemed satisfied despite the fact that litigation had not terminated in the state courts, we entertained the case over claims that we had no jurisdiction. The federal issue would not survive the remand, whatever the result of the state administrative proceedings. The Board might deny the license on state-law grounds, thus foreclosing the federal issue, and the Court also ascertained that under state law the Board could not bring the federal issue here in the event the applicant satisfied the requirements of state law except for the invalidated ownership statute. Under these circumstances, the issue was ripe for review.

Lastly, there are those situations where the federal issue has been finally decided in the state courts with further proceedings pending in which the party seeking review here might prevail on the merits on nonfederal grounds, thus rendering unnecessary review of the federal issue by this Court, and where reversal of the state court on the federal issue would be preclusive of any further litigation on the relevant cause of action rather than merely controlling the nature and character of, or determining the admissibility of evidence in, the state proceedings still to come. In these circumstances, if a refusal immediately to review the state-court decision might seriously erode federal policy, the Court has entertained and decided the federal issue, which itself has been finally determined by the state courts for purposes of the state litigation.

Food for Thought

Does the Court suggest here that the length of the ordinary litigation process may itself justify Supreme Court review before the state courts are finished with the case?

In Construction Laborers v. Curry (1963), the state courts temporarily enjoined labor union picketing over claims that the National Labor Relations Board had exclusive jurisdiction of the controversy. The Court took jurisdiction for two independent reasons. First, the power of the state court to proceed in the face of the preemption claim was deemed an issue separable from the merits and ripe for review in this Court, particularly "when postponing review would seriously erode the national labor policy requiring the subject matter of respondents' cause to be heard by the * * * Board, not by the state courts." Second, the Court was convinced that in any event the union had no defense to the entry of a permanent injunction other than the preemption claim that

Food for Thought

Does the Court's second reason mean that it is more accurate to characterize Curry as a Category 1 case?

had already been ruled on in the state courts. Hence the case was for all practical purposes concluded in the state tribunals.

In Mercantile National Bank v. Langdeau (1963), two national banks were sued, along with others, in the courts of Travis County, Tex. The claim asserted was conspiracy to defraud an insurance company. The banks as a preliminary matter asserted that a special federal venue statute immunized them from suit in Travis County and that they could properly be sued only in another county. Although trial was still to be had and the banks might well prevail on the merits, the Court, relying on Curry, entertained the issue as a "separate and independent matter, anterior to the merits and not enmeshed in the factual and legal issues comprising the plaintiff's cause of action." Moreover, it would serve the policy of the federal statute "to determine now in which state court appellants may be tried rather than to subject them * * * to long and complex litigation which may all be for naught if consideration of the preliminary question of venue is postponed until the conclusion of the proceedings."

Miami Herald Publishing Co. v. Tornillo (1974) is the latest case in this category. There a candidate for public office sued a newspaper for refusing, allegedly contrary to a state statute, to carry his reply to the paper's editorial critical of his qualifications. The trial court held the act unconstitutional, denying both injunctive relief and damages. The State Supreme Court reversed, sustaining the statute against the challenge based upon the First and Fourteenth Amendments and remanding the case for a trial and appropriate relief, including damages. The newspaper brought the case here. We sustained our jurisdiction, relying on the principles elaborated in the North Dakota case and observing:

> **Take Note**
>
> The Court's approach here is reminiscent of its handling of double-jeopardy cases. The Double Jeopardy Clause protects the defendant from being *tried* a second time, not merely from being convicted in a second trial.

> Whichever way we were to decide on the merits, it would be intolerable to leave unanswered, under these circumstances, an important question of freedom of the press under the First Amendment; an uneasy and unsettled constitutional posture of § 104.38 could only further harm the operation of a free press.

In light of the prior cases, we conclude that we have jurisdiction to review the judgment of the Georgia Supreme Court rejecting the challenge under the First and Fourteenth Amendments to the state law authorizing damage suits against the press for publishing the name of a rape victim whose identity is revealed in the course of a public prosecution. The Georgia Supreme Court's judgment is plainly final on the federal issue and is not subject to further review in the state courts. Appellants will be liable for damages if the elements of the state cause of action are proved. They may prevail at trial on nonfederal grounds, it is true, but if the Georgia court erroneously upheld the statute, there should be no trial at all. Moreover, even if appellants prevailed at trial and made unnecessary further consideration of the constitutional question, there would remain in effect the unreviewed decision of the State Supreme Court that a civil action for publishing the name of a rape victim disclosed in a public judicial proceeding may go forward despite the First and Fourteenth Amendments. Delaying final decision of the First Amendment claim until after trial will "leave unanswered * * * an important question of freedom of the press under the First Amendment," "an uneasy and unsettled constitutional posture [that] could only further harm the operation of a free press."

Food for Thought

Again the Court echoes its interpretation of the Double Jeopardy Clause. But how far does the Court's argument go? Does this mean that in any state case where the trial court denies a motion to dismiss on constitutional grounds the defendant should immediately pursue appeals on that ruling through the state courts or, if state law permits no such interlocutory appeal, to the Supreme Court directly, similar to the procedure followed in Thompson v. City of Louisville, at page 907? Perhaps equally important, if counsel fails to seek Supreme Court review in such a situation, might the prevailing party in the state courts oppose a petition for certiorari on the ground that the relevant date for measuring the ninety days during which a petitioner may seek certiorari under 28 U.S.C. § 2101(c) is the date on which the interlocutory decision of the federal issue became final? Justice Rehnquist's dissent focuses on this issue.

On the other hand, if we now hold that the First and Fourteenth Amendments bar civil liability for broadcasting the victim's name, this litigation ends. Given these factors—that the litigation could be terminated by our decision on the merits[13] and that a failure to decide the question now will leave the press

13 Mr. Justice Rehnquist is correct in saying that this factor involves consideration of the merits in determining jurisdiction. But it does so only to the extent of determining that the issue is substantial and only in the context that if the state court's final decision on the federal issue is incorrect, federal law forecloses further proceedings in the state court. That the petitioner who protests against the state court's decision on the federal question might prevail on the merits on nonfederal grounds in the course of further proceedings anticipated in the state court and hence obviate later review of the federal issue here is not preclusive of our jurisdiction. Curry, Langdeau, North Dakota State Board of Pharmacy, California v. Stewart, decided with Miranda v. Arizona, and Miami Herald Publishing Co. v. Tornillo, make this clear. In those cases, the federal issue having been decided, arguably wrongly, and being determinative of the litigation if decided the other way, the finality rule was satisfied.

The author of the dissent, a member of the majority in Tornillo, does not disavow that decision. He seeks only to distinguish it by indicating that the First Amendment issue at stake there was more important and pressing than the one here. This seems to embrace the thesis of that case and of this one as far as the approach to finality is concerned, even though the merits and the avoidance doctrine are to some extent involved.

in Georgia operating in the shadow of the civil and criminal sanctions of a rule of law and a statute the constitutionality of which is in serious doubt—we find that reaching the merits is consistent with the pragmatic approach that we have followed in the past in determining finality.

Take Note

Remember that on many other occasions, the Court has admonished that it sits to decide cases, not to answer questions.

Reversed.

MR. JUSTICE REHNQUIST, dissenting.

Because I am of the opinion that the decision which is the subject of this appeal is not a "final" judgment or decree, as that term is used in 28 U.S.C. § 1257, I would dismiss this appeal for want of jurisdiction.

Radio Station WOW, Inc. v. Johnson established that in a "very few" circumstances review of state-court decisions could be had in this Court even though something "further remain[ed] to be determined by a State court." Over the years, however, and despite vigorous protest by Mr. Justice Harlan, this Court has steadily discovered new exceptions to the finality requirement, such that they can hardly any longer be described as "very few." Whatever may be the unexpressed reasons for this process of expansion, it has frequently been the subject of no more formal an express explanation than cursory citations to preceding cases in the line. * * * Although the Court's opinion today does accord detailed consideration to this problem, I do not believe that the reasons it expresses can support its result.

I

The Court has taken what it terms a "pragmatic" approach to the finality problem presented in this case. In so doing, it has relied heavily on Gillespie v. United States Steel Corp. As the Court acknowledges, Gillespie involved 28 U.S.C. § 1291, which restricts the appellate jurisdiction of the federal courts of appeals to "final decisions of the district courts." Although acknowledging this distinction, the Court accords it no importance and adopts Gillespie's approach without any consideration of whether the finality requirement for this Court's jurisdiction over a "judgment or decree" of a state court is grounded on more serious concerns than is the limitation of court of appeals jurisdiction to final "decisions" of the district courts. I believe that the underlying concerns are different, and that the difference counsels a more restrictive approach when § 1257 finality is at issue.

According to Gillespie, the finality requirement is imposed as a matter of minimizing "the inconvenience and costs of piecemeal review." This proposition is undoubtedly sound so long as one is considering the administration of the federal court system. Were judicial efficiency the only interest at stake there would be less inclination to challenge the Court's resolution in this case, although, as discussed below, I have serious reservations that the standards the Court has formulated are effective for achieving even this single goal. The case before us, however, is an appeal from a state court, and this fact introduces additional interests which must be accommodated in fashioning any exception to the literal application of the finality requirement. I consider § 1257 finality to be but one of a number of congressional provisions reflecting concern that uncontrolled federal judicial interference with state administrative and judicial functions would have untoward consequences for our federal system.[4] This is by no means a novel view of the § 1257 finality requirement. In Radio Station WOW, Inc. v. Johnson, Mr. Justice Frankfurter's opinion for the Court explained the finality requirement as follows:

> * * * *This prerequisite to review derives added force when the jurisdiction of this Court is invoked to upset the decision of a State court.* Here we are in the realm of potential conflict between the courts of two different governments. And so, ever since 1789, Congress has granted this Court the power to intervene in State litigation only after "the highest court of a State in which a decision in the suit could be had" has rendered a "final judgment or decree." § 237 of the Judicial Code, 28 U.S.C. § 344(a). *This requirement is not one of those technicalities to be easily scorned. It is an important factor in the smooth working of our federal system.* [Emphasis added.]

* * *

That comity and federalism are significant elements of § 1257 finality has been recognized by other members of the Court as well, perhaps most notably by Mr. Justice Harlan. * * * [H]e argued that one basis of the finality rule was that it foreclosed "this Court from passing on constitutional issues that may be dissipated by the final outcome of a case, thus helping to keep to a minimum undesirable federal-state conflicts." One need cast no doubt on the Court's decision in such cases as *Langdeau* to recognize that Mr. Justice Harlan was focusing on a consideration which should be of significance in the Court's disposition of this case.

"Harmonious state-federal relations" are no less important today * * * . Indeed, we have in recent years emphasized and re-emphasized the importance of comity and federalism in dealing with a related problem, that of district court interference with ongoing state judicial proceedings. Because these concerns are

---

4 *See, e.g.*, 28 U.S.C. § 1341 (limitation on power of district courts to enjoin state taxing systems); 28 U.S.C. § 1739 (*sic*, probably intending § 1738) (requiring that state judicial proceedings be accorded full faith and credit in federal courts); 28 U.S.C. §§ 2253-2254 (prescribing various restrictions on federal habeas corpus for state prisoners); 28 U.S.C. § 2281 (three-judge district court requirement) [now repealed]; 28 U.S.C. § 2283 (restricting power of federal courts to enjoin state-court proceedings).

important, and because they provide "added force" to § 1257's finality requirement, I believe that the Court has erred by simply importing the approach of cases in which the only concern is efficient judicial administration.

II

But quite apart from the considerations of federalism which counsel against an expansive reading of our jurisdiction under § 1257, the Court's holding today enunciates a virtually formless exception to the finality requirement, one which differs in kind from those previously carved out. By contrast, *Construction Laborers v. Curry* and *Mercantile National Bank v. Langdeau* are based on the understandable principle that where the proper forum for trying the issue joined in the state courts depends on the resolution of the federal question raised on appeal, sound judicial administration requires that such a question be decided by this Court, if it is to be decided at all, sooner rather than later in the course of the litigation. *Organization for a Better Austin v. Keefe (1971)* and *Mills v. Alabama (1966)* rest on the premise that where as a practical matter the state litigation has been concluded by the decision of the State's highest court, the fact that in terms of state procedure the ruling is interlocutory should not bar a determination by this Court of the merits of the federal question.

Still other exceptions, as noted in the Court's opinion, have been made where the federal question decided by the highest court of the State is bound to survive and be presented for decision here regardless of the outcome of future state-court proceedings, and for the situation in which later review of the federal issue cannot be had, whatever the ultimate outcome of the subsequent proceedings directed by the highest court of the State. While the totality of these exceptions certainly indicates that the Court has been willing to impart to the language "final judgment or decree" a great deal of flexibility, each of them is arguably consistent with the intent of Congress in enacting § 1257, if not with the language it used, and each of them is relatively workable in practice.

To those established exceptions is now added one so formless that it cannot be paraphrased, but instead must be quoted:

> Given these factors—that the litigation could be terminated by our decision on the merits and that a failure to decide the question now will leave the press in Georgia operating in the shadow of the civil and criminal sanctions of a rule of law and a statute the constitutionality of which is in serious doubt—we find that reaching the merits is consistent with the pragmatic approach that we have followed in the past in determining finality.

There are a number of difficulties with this test. One of them is the Court's willingness to look to the merits. It is not clear from the Court's opinion, however, exactly how great a look at the merits we are to take. On the one hand, the Court emphasizes that if we reverse the Supreme Court of Georgia the litigation will end, and it refers to cases in which the federal issue has been decided "arguably wrongly." On the other hand, it claims to look to the merits "only to the extent of determining that the issue is substantial." If the latter is all the Court means, then the inquiry is no more extensive than is involved when we determine whether a case is appropriate for plenary consideration; but if no more is meant, our decision is just as likely to be a costly intermediate step in the litigation as it is to be the concluding event. If, on the other hand, the Court really intends its doctrine to reach only so far as cases in which our decision in all probability will terminate the litigation, then the Court is reversing the traditional sequence of judicial decisionmaking. Heretofore, it has generally been thought that a court first assumed jurisdiction of a case, and then went on to decide the merits of the questions it presented. But henceforth in determining our own jurisdiction we may be obliged to determine whether or not we agree with the merits of the decision of the highest court of a State.

Yet another difficulty with the Court's formulation is the problem of transposing to any other case the requirement that "failure to decide the question now will leave the press in Georgia operating in the shadow of the civil and criminal sanctions of a rule of law and a statute the constitutionality of which is in serious doubt." Assuming that we are to make this determination of "serious doubt" at the time we note probable jurisdiction of such an appeal, is it enough that the highest court of the State has ruled against any federal constitutional claim? If that is the case, then because § 1257 by other language imposes that requirement, we will have completely read out of the statute the limitation of our jurisdiction to a "final judgment or decree." Perhaps the Court's new standard for finality is limited to cases in which a First Amendment freedom is at issue. The language used by Congress, however, certainly provides no basis for preferring the First Amendment, as incorporated by the Fourteenth Amendment, to the various other Amendments which are likewise "incorporated," or indeed for preferring any of the "incorporated" Amendments over the due process and equal protection provisions which are embodied literally in the Fourteenth Amendment.

Another problem is that in applying the second prong of its test, the Court has not engaged in any independent inquiry as to the consequences of permitting the decision of the Supreme Court of Georgia to remain undisturbed pending final state-court resolution of the case. This suggests that in order to invoke the benefit of today's rule, the "shadow" in which an appellant must stand need be neither deep nor wide. In this case nothing more is at issue than the right to report the name of the victim of a rape. No hindrance of any sort has been imposed on reporting the fact of a rape or the circumstances surrounding it. Yet the Court unquestioningly places this issue on a par with the core First Amendment interest involved in Miami Herald Publishing Co. v. Tornillo and Mills v. Alabama, that of protecting the press in its role of providing uninhibited political discourse.

But the greatest difficulty with the test enunciated today is that it totally abandons the principle that constitutional issues are too important to be decided save when absolutely necessary, and are to be avoided if there are grounds for decision of lesser dimension. The long line of cases which established this rule makes clear that it is a principle primarily designed, not to benefit the lower courts, or state-federal relations, but rather to safeguard this Court's own process of constitutional adjudication.

* * *

In this case there has yet to be an adjudication of liability against appellants, and unlike the appellant in Mills v. Alabama, they do not concede that they have no nonfederal defenses. Nonetheless, the Court rules on their constitutional defense. Far from eschewing a constitutional holding in advance of the necessity for one, the Court construes § 1257 so that it may virtually rush out and meet the prospective constitutional litigant as he approaches our doors.

III

This Court is obliged to make preliminary determinations of its jurisdiction at the time it votes to note probable jurisdiction. At that stage of the proceedings, prior to briefing on the merits or oral argument, such determinations must of necessity be based on relatively cursory acquaintance with the record of the proceedings below. The need for an understandable and workable application of a jurisdictional provision such as § 1257 is therefore far greater than for a similar interpretation of statutes dealing with substantive law.[7] We, of course, retain the authority to dismiss a case for want of a final judgment after having studied briefs on the merits and having heard oral argument, but I can recall not a single instance of such a disposition during the last three Terms of the Court. While in theory this may be explained by saying that during these Terms we have never accorded plenary consideration to a § 1257 case which was not a "final judgment or decree," I would guess it just as accurate to say that after the Court has studied briefs and heard oral argument, it has an understandable tendency to proceed to a decision on the merits in preference to dismissing for want of jurisdiction. It is thus especially disturbing that the rule of this case, unlike the more workable and straightforward exceptions which the Court has previously formulated, will seriously compound the already difficult task of accurately determining, at

7 *Cf.* United States v. Sisson: "Clarity is to be desired in any statute, but in matters of jurisdiction it is especially important. Otherwise the courts and the parties must expend great energy, not on the merits of dispute settlement, but on simply deciding whether a court has the power to hear a case."

a preliminary stage, whether an appeal from a state-court judgment is a "final judgment or decree."

A further aspect of the difficulties which the Court is generating is illustrated by a petition for certiorari recently filed in this Court, *Time, Inc. v. Firestone.* The case was twice before the Florida Supreme Court. That court's first decision was rendered in December 1972; it rejected Time's First Amendment defense to a libel action, and remanded for further proceedings on state-law issues. The second decision was rendered in 1974, and dealt with the state-law issues litigated on remand. Before this Court, Time seeks review of the First Amendment defense rejected by the Florida Supreme Court in December 1972. Under the Court's decision today, one could conclude that the 1972 judgment was itself a final decision from which review might have been had. If it was, then petitioner Time is confronted by 28 U.S.C. § 2101(c), which restricts this Court's jurisdiction over state civil cases to those in which review is sought within 90 days of the entry of a reviewable judgment.

I in no way suggest either my own or the Court's views on our jurisdiction over *Time, Inc. v. Firestone.* This example is simply illustrative of the difficulties which today's decision poses not only for this Court, but also for a prudent counsel who is faced with an adverse interlocutory ruling by a State's highest court on a federal issue asserted as a dispositive bar to further litigation. I suppose that such counsel would be unwilling to presume that this Court would flout both the meaning of words and the command of Congress by employing loose standards of finality to obtain jurisdiction, but strict ones to prevent its loss. He thus would be compelled to judge his situation in light of today's formless, unworkable exception to the finality requirement. I would expect him frequently to choose to seek immediate review in this Court, solely as a matter of assuring that his federal contentions are not lost for want of timely filing. The inevitable result will be totally unnecessary additions to our docket and serious interruptions and delays of the state adjudicatory process.

Although unable to persuade my Brethren that we do not have in this case a final judgment or decree of the Supreme Court of Georgia, I nonetheless take heart from the fact that we are concerned here with an area in which "*stare decisis* has historically been accorded considerably less than its usual weight." I would dismiss for want of jurisdiction.

Notes and Questions

1. To understand fully the Court's four categories of non-final cases that will be treated as final for purposes of 28 U.S.C.A. § 1257, it is necessary not only to identify the general criteria for each category but also to review carefully the examples the Court gives of each to see exactly how the federal issue arises and what is likely to happen to it in further state court proceedings. *Cox's* analysis raises many questions about the functioning of the federal courts generally. As a preliminary matter, consider the purposes of the finality requirement. The Court most often mentions judicial efficiency—the need to conserve judicial time, but particularly federal judicial time. The Court believes there times when that goal may be better served by allowing review of a non-final judgment—times when the "custom is more honored in the breach than in the observance." WILLIAM SHAKESPEARE, HAMLET, act I, sc. iv, lines 17-18.

2. Does the Court subdivide the fourth category into three parts? It first cites *Construction Laborers v. Curry*. The Court argued intervention was justified because of the need to avoid erosion of important federal policy. Then it reviews *Mercantile National Bank v. Langdeau* as an example of deciding a preliminary matter to avoid complex, costly, and potentially futile litigation. Finally, the Court cites *Miami Herald Publishing Co. v. Tornillo* as exemplifying cases where important federal issues, though they may well survive further state court litigation, ought not to be left unsettled in the interim. Are these three cases fungible or do they represent different concerns that may call for a common solution?

3. The Court notes its long-standing "pragmatic" approach to determining what "final" means. Does "final" mean the same thing in all four categories? By definition, does the fourth category, in any of its manifestations, involve judgments that are demonstrably not final?

4. With respect to the fourth category, are there any discernible limits to the Court's asserted ability to review federal issues that it considers important, or is that category a roving commission for the court to seek out issues to which at least four Justices wish to speak? *Cox* notes that "if Georgia erroneously upheld the statute, there should be no trial at all." Accepting the characterization as an indication that summary disposition in defendant's favor would be appropriate, either by summary judgment or under FED. R. CIV. P. 12(b)(6), does *Cox* mean that any erroneous denial of a defendant's federally-based motion for summary disposition is reviewable under § 1257? If not, how is this case different from any other case where a legal issue disposes of the plaintiff's claim?

5. Applying the *Cox* categories, especially the fourth, can be difficult. In *Nike, Inc. v. Kasky*, 539 U.S. 654 (2003) (dismissing the writ of certiorari as improvidently

granted), Justices Stevens and Breyer battled over how far the *Cox* pattern extended. The underlying issue was whether certain statements that Nike had made were entitled to First Amendment protection as noncommercial speech or only as commercial speech, which might have left Nike vulnerable to an adverse judgment under California's Unfair Competition Law and its False Advertising Law. When Kasky appealed the lower state courts' ruling that Nike's speech was entitled to full First Amendment protection as "part of a public dialogue on a matter of public concern within the core area of expression protected by the First Amendment," which led them to dismiss the action, the California Supreme Court had reversed, finding that the speech was commercial, entitled to less embracing First Amendment protection, and that Nike therefore had to go to trial on whether its speech had been false and misleading within the meaning of the California statutes. Nike sought Supreme Court review, and the Court originally granted certiorari.

Ultimately, the Court dismissed the writ. The case raised a critical issue of whether the Supreme Court had statutory jurisdiction to review under 28 U.S.C. § 1257. The California Supreme Court's ruling that Nike's speech was commercial was not a final defeat for Nike; Kasky might have been unable to demonstrate that the speech satisfied the California criteria for liability, so Nike might have prevailed. Even had it lost, it might have preserved the First Amendment question that it had lost on the interlocutory appeal in California and ultimately sought to present it to the United States Supreme Court. These circumstances make Nike resemble *Cox*. Had Cox been required to go to trial, it might have won, as the Georgia Supreme Court had observed, on the issue of whether the publication had invaded the victim's father's zone of privacy. Ultimately, had Cox lost, it might have sought review in the United States Supreme Court.

That parallel did not satisfy Justices Stevens and Ginsburg, who concurred in the dismissal of the writ. Justice Stevens's opinion distinguished Nike from *Cox* on the ground that the First Amendment issue in Nike involved multiple statements made at different times and in different circumstances, and it criticized Nike's argument as assuming that all of the speech involved was classifiable uniformly as commercial or noncommercial. "[E]ven if we were to decide the First Amendment issues presented to us today, more First Amendment issues might well remain in this case, making piecemeal review of the Federal First Amendment issues likely." This caused Justice Stevens to view the state judgment as insufficiently final to support the exercise of Supreme Court jurisdiction and to conclude that it was not sufficiently likely that a decision by the Court could end the litigation on Kasky's claim, because he saw several possible decisions on the merits of the First Amendment questions.

Justices Breyer and O'Connor dissented from the dismissal. Justice Breyer identified four criteria from *Cox* and concluded that Nike satisfied each. The primary areas of dispute with Justice Stevens were the first and third criteria. Justice Breyer conceded that it was conceivable that additional First Amendment issues would arise in the course of further litigation, but he took the position that every case in the fourth category, particularly including *Cox* itself, presented that possibility.

Make the Connection

Cox required 1) a final decision of the federal issue at the state level, 2) the possibility of the party seeking review prevailing on nonfederal grounds that would prevent Supreme Court consideration of the federal issue, 3) "reversal of the state court on the federal issue [being] preclusive of any further litigation on the relevant cause of action rather than merely controlling the nature and character of, or determination the admissibility of evidence in, the state proceedings still to come," (internal quotation marks omitted) and 4) erosion of important federal policy as a result of refusal to review)

With respect to the third criterion, Justice Breyer noted that some potential decisions by the Court would leave Kasky's claim alive, thus not satisfying the criterion, but he was not willing to conclude that "outright reversal [which would have ended the litigation] is not a very realistic possibility." He argued that the line between commercial and noncommercial speech was not sharp or bright and speculated that the Court might well conclude that even if some commercial speech were mixed with some noncommercial speech, the First Amendment required a protective rule with a broad embrace. One may agree or disagree with either Justice about the proper decision on the merits of the First Amendment question(s), but perhaps that misses the point, at least for present purposes.

To what extent do you think the Justices' forecast of how the Court might decide the merits of the federal issue should be relevant to the question of whether the Court can exercise jurisdiction over cases in the *Cox* category? Should the mere theoretical possibility of a litigation-ending decision be sufficient to satisfy the third criterion that Justice Breyer described, or is it appropriate (or even mandatory) that the Justices making the decision on certiorari engage in some sort of determination of the probabilities of one or another result? If the former, does that approach underscore the separation-of-powers problems that underlie the Court's decidedly non-literal interpretation of § 1257's finality requirement? If the latter, what sorts of standards can you suggest for the Court to use?

6. Was the Court's treatment of the finality issue consistent with its oft-repeated insistence that constitutional issues be decided only when unavoidable? *See, e.g.*, *Ashwander v. TVA*, 297 U.S. 288 (1936) (Brandeis, J., concurring), which Justice Rehnquist cited in his dissent.

In *Nike*, Justices Stevens and Breyer also clashed over application of the prudential rule derived from *Ashwander v. TVA*, 297 U.S. 288 (1936) (Brandeis, J., concurring), which counsels that the Court should strain to avoid deciding constitutional questions when possible. Justice Stevens took the position that the very novelty and indeterminateness of the First Amendment questions presented argued powerfully for avoiding them unless it was absolutely necessary at some future point (presumably after Nike had lost at trial) to decide them. Justice Breyer argued that prudence was on the side of the Court deciding the issue, largely because

> waiting extracts a heavy First Amendment price. If this suit goes forward, both Nike and other potential speakers, out of reasonable caution or even an excess of caution, may censor their own expression well beyond what the law may constitutionally demand. That is what a "chilling effect" means. It is present here.

For Justice Breyer, the novelty and indeterminateness of the First Amendment questions provided a strong reason to go forward rather than to refuse review.

Should the existence of both the third and fourth categories of review of non-final state court judgments cause the Court to reexamine more generally its position on the Ashwander rule? In the third category, it is entirely certain that the federal issues will not survive for presentation to the Court; that is the criterion for allowing review. Are the third criterion and Ashwander irreconcilably in conflict? With respect to the fourth category, by definition it may be possible for the Court to avoid deciding the federal issues. Is not that enough to demonstrate that decision is not unavoidable? Perhaps the Court should undertake to articulate standards or some sort of balancing test to describe when the nature of the federal issues presented is such that the federal courts should ignore Ashwander's counsel. Can you suggest any such standards that will not have the effect of gutting the rule?

7. Justice Rehnquist's dissent in *Cox* deserves considerable attention. Note that he has a variety of objections to the Court's reviewing cases before they have been entirely terminated in the state courts.

a) Does his objection to the rationale and result of *Cox* apply to each category of non-final final review described by the majority?

b) Is it appropriate for the Court to rely on cases construing 28 U.S.C.A. § 1291, which concerns finality for purposes of appeals from federal district courts to the United States Court of Appeals? Justice Rehnquist argues powerfully that federalism concerns that have no force within the federal judicial system may counsel strongly against permitting review of non-final state court judgments.

c) Does Justice Rehnquist's argument about the impropriety of the Court's interpretation of "final judgment" in § 1257 change in light of the 1988 amendment to the Rules Enabling Act, 28 U.S.C.A. § 2072, that allows the Supreme Court to prescribe rules that "may define when a ruling of a district court is final for the purposes of appeal under section 1291 of this title"?

The Justice Rehnquist's objections notwithstanding, the *Cox* doctrine appears to be entrenched. In *Kansas v. Marsh*, 548 U.S. 163 (2006), the Court reviewed a case in the third *Cox* category, citing *Cox* with approval. Although the Court split 5-4 on the merits, none of the Justices argued that review was inappropriate because of the finality requirement of 28 U.S.C. § 1257.

8. Is there an unrealized separation-of-powers question underlying the debate in *Cox* as well? Justice Rehnquist notes with some force the federalism concerns implicated by the Court's willingness to review non-final cases. Is the Court also ignoring legislatively-imposed limits on its power when it construes "[f]inal judgments or decrees" to mean only that "the judgment of the state court on the federal issue is deemed final"? If Congress meant to allow interlocutory review from conclusive determinations of federal issues, why did it not say so? On the other hand, if Congress does not at least acquiesce in the construction of § 1257, why has it never objected, despite having amended or recodified § 1257 several times?

Chapter 10

The Rooker-Feldman Doctrine

A. Introduction

Martin v. Hunter's Lessee[1] clearly illustrates the states' resistance to the idea that the Supreme Court of the United States could review the judgments of state courts. Given the great concern in the post-colonial period about the potential evils of centralized government, manifested scarcely thirty years before Martin in the Articles of Confederation and then in the Constitutional Convention, the surprise might have been if the states had acquiesced too readily. The relationship of federal courts to state courts was thus one of the early battlegrounds of federalism.

Imagine, if you will, what the reaction of the states might have been to the idea that even the inferior federal courts could review state court judgments. In one way, Ex parte Young[2] and its immediate aftermath demonstrate that the issue was very much alive at the beginning of the twentieth century, as it remains today. Shortly after the Court's decision, there was a movement to remove cases challenging the constitutionality of state statutes from the jurisdiction of the district courts. In response, Congress passed the Three-Judge-Court Act,[3] which provided that a three-judge district court comprised of one circuit judge and two district judges should hear constitutional challenges to a state statute. The legislative history of that statute makes clear that Congress intended it to avoid the specter of a single district judge overturning a state statutory scheme (as had happened in Ex parte Young).[4] As one district court put it, Congress's goal was "protecting

---

1 14 U.S. (1 Wheat.) 304 (1816).

2 209 U.S. 123 (1908). Chapter 7 covers Young at pages 663-80.

3 Act of June 18, 1910, ch. 309, § 17, 36 Stat. 557.

4 Writing for the majority in Swift & Company v. Wickham, 382 U.S. 111 (1965), Justice Harlan noted:

> The three-judge district court is a unique feature of our jurisprudence, created to alleviate a specific discontent within the federal system. * * * [It was] passed to assuage growing popular displeasure with the frequent grants of injunctions by federal courts against the operation of state legislation regulating railroads and utilities in particular. * * * The advent of the Granger and labor movements in the late nineteenth century, and the acceleration of state social legislation

the states from the imprudent exercise of federal injunctive power."[5] The Act, provided, inter alia, that the losing party in such a case could appeal directly to the Supreme Court.[6] The Act lasted, largely unchanged, until Congress substantially narrowed it in 1976, limiting its applicability to congressional or statewide legislative apportionment cases or other cases in which legislation might direct use of such a court.[7]

The problem of inferior federal court review of state court decisions, however, came cloaked, as it were. No one would have thought of filing a notice of appeal with a state's highest court seeking appellate review in the federal district court. There are other ways, nonetheless, that one may ask one court to do something that affects the judgment of another. The question then becomes one of deciding when something not called an appeal nonetheless functions as one. The Supreme Court turned to that problem in 1923.

B. The Basic Doctrine

Rooker v. Fidelity Trust Co.

Supreme Court of the United States, 1923.
263 U.S. 413.

MR. JUSTICE VAN DEVANTER delivered the opinion of the Court.

This is a bill in equity to have a judgment of a circuit court in Indiana, which was affirmed by the Supreme Court of the state, declared null and void, and to obtain other relief dependent on that outcome. An effort to have the judgment reviewed by this court on writ of error had failed because the record did not disclose the presence of any question constituting a basis for such a review.

---

especially through the creation of regulatory bodies met with opposition in the federal judiciary. [T]his Court held that the setting of rates not permitting a fair return violated the Due Process Clause of the Fourteenth Amendment. Ex parte Young established firmly the corollary that inferior federal courts could enjoin state officials from enforcing such unconstitutional state laws. * * * The sponsor of the bill establishing the three-judge procedure for these cases, Senator Overman of North Carolina, noted:

> Whenever one judge stands up in a State and enjoins the governor and the attorney-general, the people resent it, and public sentiment is stirred, as it was in my State, when there was almost a rebellion, whereas if three judges declare that a state statute is unconstitutional the people would rest easy under it.

Id. at 116-18.

5 Webber v. White, 422 F. Supp. 416, 425 (N.D. Tex. 1976).

6 Swift & Company v. Wickham, 382 U.S. at 119.

7 *See* 28 U.S.C. § 2284 (2006).

The parties to the bill are the same as in the litigation in the state court, but with an addition of two defendants whose presence does not need special notice. All are citizens of the same state. The grounds advanced for resorting to the District Court are that the judgment was rendered and affirmed in contravention of the contract clause of the Constitution of the United States and the due process of law and equal protection clauses of the Fourteenth Amendment, in that it gave effect to a state statute alleged to be in conflict with those clauses and did not give effect to a prior decision in the same cause by the Supreme Court of the State which is alleged to have become the "law of the case." The District Court was of opinion that the suit was not within its jurisdiction as defined by Congress, and on that ground dismissed the bill. The plaintiffs have appealed directly to this court under section 238 of the Judicial Code.

Food for Thought

The writ of error was the method of taking an appeal as of right; the Supreme Court had no discretion in whether to hear the appeal. Any decision in a writ-of-error case operated as a decision on the merits, even if the Court did not give the case plenary consideration. When the record failed to show the presence of an issue qualifying the case for review under the predecessor of 28 U.S.C. § 1257, the Court would "dismiss for want of a substantial federal question." Given that, should the district court have dismissed the action on preclusion grounds?

The appellees move that the appeal be dismissed, or in the alternative that the decree be affirmed.

The appeal is within the first clause of section 238, so the motion to dismiss must be overruled. But the suit is so plainly not within the District Court's jurisdiction as defined by Congress that the motion to affirm must be sustained.

It affirmatively appears from the bill that the judgment was rendered in a cause wherein the [state] circuit court had jurisdiction of both the subject-matter and the parties, that a full hearing was had therein, that the judgment was responsive to the issues, and that it was affirmed by the Supreme Court of the state on an appeal by the plaintiffs. If the constitutional questions stated in the bill actually arose in the cause, it was the province and duty of the state courts to decide them; and their decision, whether right or wrong, was an exercise of jurisdiction. If the decision was wrong, that did not make the judgment void, but merely left it open to reversal or modification in an appropriate and timely appellate proceeding. Unless and until so reversed or modified, it would be an effective and conclusive adjudication. Under the legislation of Congress, no court of the United States other than this court could entertain a proceeding to reverse or modify the judgment for errors of that character. To do so would be an exercise of appellate jurisdiction. The jurisdiction possessed by the District Courts is strictly original.

Besides, the period within which a proceeding might be begun for the correction of errors such as are charged in the bill had expired before it was filed, and * * * after that period elapses an aggrieved litigant cannot be permitted to do indirectly what he no longer can do directly.

Some parts of the bill speak of the judgment as given without jurisdiction and absolutely void; but this is merely mistaken characterization. A reading of the entire bill shows indubitably that there was full jurisdiction in the state courts and that the bill at best is merely an attempt to get rid of the judgment for alleged errors of law committed in the exercise of that jurisdiction.

In what has been said we have proceeded on the assumption that the constitutional questions alleged to have arisen in the state courts respecting the validity of a state statute and the effect to be given to a prior decision in the same cause by the Supreme Court of the state were questions of substance, but we do not hold that they were such—the assumption being indulged merely for the purpose of testing the nature of the bill and the power of the District Court to entertain it.

* * *

Decree affirmed.

Notes and Questions

1. Why did the district court not simply refuse to act on the ground that the state court's judgment was entitled to res judicata effect, preventing a collateral attack?

When the Indiana legislature enacted the statute that the plaintiff challenged in this litigation, could the plaintiff have sued to enjoin enforcement of the statute (assuming that the plaintiff could satisfy justiciability requirements)? Would such an action have been an appeal? Is there a difference in effect between such an approach and what actually happened in the case?

2. Since its original enactment in 1793, the Anti-Injunction Act, 28 U.S.C. § 2283 (2006), has signaled Congress's intense concern that federal courts not interfere with state judicial proceedings by staying them, except in three circumstances.[8] Is it significant that for more than a century before Rooker reached the Supreme Court, Congress had forbidden stays but had not forbidden collateral attacks on state court judgments when the state litigation was no longer pending?

---

8 Chapter 8 A discusses the Anti-Injunction Act. Note that in the *Atlantic Coast Line* case presented in that chapter, *supra* at 784, the Court construed the three exceptions to the Act's prohibition quite narrowly.

3. Where does federal habeas corpus for state prisoners fit into this structure? Is a habeas challenge to state confinement, brought pursuant to 28 U.S.C. § 2254, an appeal within the meaning of *Rooker*? If not, how can one differentiate a case in that procedural posture from *Rooker* itself? If so, how can habeas proceed in the federal courts? The federal courts have been saying for a long time that federal habeas corpus is an exception to the *Rooker-Feldman* doctrine because 28 U.S.C. § 2241 is a grant of jurisdiction to the federal courts. *See, e.g., Zadvydas v. Davis*, 533 U.S. 678, 687 (2001). Take a look at § 2241. Does it sound like a jurisdiction-vesting statute in the manner of 28 U.S.C. §§ 1330-1338? Does Congress's conferring the power to issue a writ represent a jurisdictional grant or merely provision of a specific remedy? If the former, does the All Writs Act, 28 U.S.C. § 1651 (2006) become a font of jurisdiction? If not, whence the district courts' jurisdiction to entertain habeas cases? If one were to read § 2241 as not vesting jurisdiction, but rather limiting the courts' ability to issue the writ under jurisdiction conferred elsewhere (§ 1331, for example), would that make any difference for *Rooker-Feldman* purposes? Assuming § 2241 is a grant of jurisdiction, does that necessarily resolve the matter? Does Congress have the power under Article III to grant the inferior federal courts appellate jurisdiction over state court decisions?

4. *Rooker* is, despite some questions, a fairly straightforward case. It contained, however, hidden problems inherent in the idea that something not styled an appeal might nonetheless be an appeal. It forced the courts to consider, inter alia, what sorts of decisions were "judicial" in nature. The Supreme Court waited only sixty years to reach that issue.

District of Columbia Court of Appeals v. Feldman

Supreme Court of the United States, 1983.
460 U.S. 462.

JUSTICE BRENNAN delivered the opinion of the Court.

We must decide in these cases what authority the United States District Court for the District of Columbia and the United States Court of Appeals for the District of Columbia Circuit have to review decisions of the District of Columbia Court of Appeals in bar admission matters. The United States Court of Appeals for the District of Columbia Circuit, reversing the United States District Court, held that the District Court had jurisdiction to review the District of Columbia Court of Appeals' denials of the respondents' requests for waivers of a bar admission rule that requires applicants to have graduated from an approved law school.

fed. ct. of appeals

We vacate the decision of the United States Court of Appeals for the District of Columbia Circuit and remand the case for proceedings consistent with this opinion.

I

We have discussed in detail in earlier opinions the changes in the structure of the District of Columbia court system effected by the District of Columbia Court Reform and Criminal Procedure Act of 1970. For purposes of this case, three provisions of that legislation are crucial. One provision made "final judgments and decrees of the District of Columbia Court of Appeals * * * reviewable by the Supreme Court of the United States in accordance with section 1257 of title 28, United States Code." Another provision amended 28 U.S.C. § 1257 to specify that the term "highest court of a state" as used in § 1257 includes the District of Columbia Court of Appeals. These provisions make the judgments of the District of Columbia Court of Appeals, like the judgments of state courts, directly reviewable in this Court. Cases no longer have to proceed from the local courts to the United States Court of Appeals and then to this Court under 28 U.S.C. § 1254. The third provision authorized the District of Columbia Court of Appeals to "make such rules as it deems proper respecting the examination, qualification, and admission of persons to membership in its bar, and their censure, suspension, and expulsion." This provision divested the United States District Court of its former authority to supervise admission to the District of Columbia bar.

Pursuant to its new rulemaking authority, the District of Columbia Court of Appeals adopted, as part of its general rules, Rule 46 I (1973), which governs admission to the bar. Rule 46 I(b)(3) states:

> (3) Proof of Legal Education. An applicant who has graduated from a law school that at the time of graduation was approved by the American Bar Association or who shall be eligible to be graduated from an approved law school within 60 days of the date of the examination will be permitted to take the bar examination. Under no circumstances shall an applicant be admitted to the bar without having first submitted to the Secretary to the Committee [on Admissions] a certificate verifying that he has graduated from an approved law school.[1]

Neither of the respondents graduated from an approved law school. Their efforts to avoid the operation of Rule 46 I(b)(3) form the foundation of this case.

1 Under Rule 46 I(b)(4), a graduate of an unaccredited law school "may be permitted admission to an examination only after receiving credit for 24 semester hours of study in a law school that at the time of study was approved by the American Bar Association and with Committee approval."

A

Respondent Feldman did not attend law school. Instead, he pursued an alternative path to a legal career provided by the State of Virginia involving a highly structured program of study in the office of a practicing attorney. In addition to his work and study at a law firm in Charlottesville, Virginia, Feldman formally audited classes at the University of Virginia School of Law. For the final six months of his alternative course of study, Feldman served as a law clerk to a United States District Judge.

Having passed the Virginia bar examination, Feldman was admitted to that state's bar in April, 1976. In March of that year he had begun working as a staff attorney for the Baltimore, Maryland Legal Aid Bureau. He continued in that job until January, 1977. Like the District of Columbia, Maryland has a rule limiting access to the bar examination to graduates of ABA-approved law schools, but the Maryland Board of Law Examiners waived the rule for Feldman. Feldman passed the Maryland examination and later was admitted to that state's bar.

In November, 1976 Feldman applied to the Committee on Admissions of the District of Columbia Bar for admission to the District bar under a rule which, prior to its recent amendment, allowed a member of a bar in another jurisdiction to seek membership in the District bar without examination. In January, 1977 the Committee denied Feldman's application on the ground that he had not graduated from an approved law school. Initially, the Committee stated that waivers of Rule 46 I(b)(3), or exceptions to it, were not authorized. Following further contact with the Committee, however, Feldman was granted an informal hearing. After the hearing, the Committee reaffirmed its denial of Feldman's application and stated that only the District of Columbia Court of Appeals could waive the requirement of graduation from an approved law school.

In June, 1977 Feldman submitted to the District of Columbia Court of Appeals a petition for admission to the bar without examination. Alternatively, Feldman requested that he be allowed to sit for the bar examination. In his petition, Feldman described his legal training, work experience, and other qualifications. He suggested that his professional training and education were "equal to that received by those who have attended an A.B.A. approved law school." In view of his training, experience, and success in passing the bar examinations in other jurisdictions, Feldman stated that "the objectives of the District of Columbia's procedures and requirements for admission to the Bar will not be frustrated by granting this petition."

The District of Columbia Court of Appeals did not act on Feldman's petition for several months. In March, 1978, Feldman's counsel wrote to the Chief Judge of the District of Columbia Court of Appeals to urge favorable action on Feldman's petition. The letter stated that Feldman had "abundantly demonstrated his fitness to practice law" and suggested that "it would be a gross injustice to exclude him from the Bar without even considering his individual qualifications." The letter went on to state that "in the unique circumstances of his case, barring Mr. Feldman from the practice of law merely because he has not graduated from an accredited law school would raise important questions under the United States Constitution and the federal antitrust laws—questions that Mr. Feldman is prepared to pursue in the United States District Court if necessary." In support of Feldman's position, the letter again stressed the strength of his training and the breadth of his experience. While acknowledging that a strict reading of Rule 46 I(b)(3) prevented Feldman from taking the bar examination, Feldman's counsel suggested that the court was not precluded from considering "Mr. Feldman's application on its merits." The court has plenary power to regulate the licensing of attorneys, which, in the view of Feldman's counsel, includes the discretion to waive the requirements of Rule 46 in a deserving case. In view of Feldman's "unusually high qualifications for admission" his case provided "an ideal occasion for the exercise of such discretion."

Practice Pointer

Note counsel's tactics here. By suggesting (some would say threatening) that there are some thorny issues of constitutional and antitrust law in the offing, he simultaneously offers the Court of Appeals a way out: neither it nor the District Court will have to deal with these issues if a waiver is forthcoming. To the extent that courts share a disinclination to decide constitutional questions when possible, pointing out such a question—particularly if it is novel—gives the court some incentive to avoid the matter by deciding for the party on some other ground.

Feldman's counsel also pointed out that the court had granted waivers of the rule in the past and suggested that a "failure to consider Mr. Feldman's application would be highly arbitrary and would raise serious questions about the fairness and even-handedness of the Court's policies regarding bar admissions." He went on to state that "serious questions under the United States Constitution are raised by any bar admissions procedure which automatically rejects applicants who have not graduated from an A.B.A. accredited law school, without any opportunity to show that their experience and education provide equivalent evidence of their fitness to practice law." Feldman's counsel cited case authority in support of his position. Finally, Feldman's counsel stated that "the federal antitrust laws provide an alternative basis for questioning the legality of a bar admissions procedure which presumes applicants to be unqualified if they lack a law degree and denies them any opportunity to show that their individual training and experience still qualify them to practice law." Feldman's counsel also cited cases in support of this position.

In late March, 1978, the Chief Judge of the District of Columbia Court of Appeals responded to the letter from Feldman's counsel. The Chief Judge stated that while the Committee on Admissions had recognized Mr. Feldman's "exceptional opportunity for training" and his fine personal qualities, the purpose of the rule at issue was "to prevent the Committee and the Court from assuming the practicably impossible task of making separate subjective evaluations of each applicant's training and education; hence, an objective and reasonable standard as prescribed by the rule must be utilized." In this light, the court decided not to waive the rule and upheld the Committee's denial of Feldman's application.

Food for Thought

This seems a bit odd. What is the purpose of the bar examination if not to serve as an "evaluation[ ] of each applicant's training and education * * * "? If the court wanted to avoid making a *subjective* evaluation, should it have granted Feldman's request to be allowed to take the bar examination?

On March 30, 1978, the District of Columbia Court of Appeals issued a *per curiam* order denying Feldman's petition. The order stated simply that "[o]n consideration of the petition of Marc Feldman to waive the provisions of Rule 46 of the General Rules of this Court, it is ORDERED that applicant's petition is denied."

In May, 1978, Feldman filed a complaint in the United States District Court for the District of Columbia challenging the District of Columbia Court of Appeals' refusal to waive Rule 46 I(b)(3) on his behalf.[2] The complaint stated that the "defendants' refusal to consider plaintiff's individual qualifications to practice law is unlawful in view of his demonstrated fitness and competence, as well as the prior admission to the D.C. bar of several other individuals who did not attend an accredited law school." Feldman sought "a declaration that defendants' actions have violated the Fifth Amendment to the Constitution and the Sherman Act, and * * * an injunction requiring defendants either to grant plaintiff immediate admission to the District of Columbia bar or to permit him to sit for the bar examination as soon as possible."

The District Court granted the defendants' motion to dismiss on the ground that it lacked subject matter jurisdiction over the action. The court found that the District of Columbia Court of Appeals' order denying Feldman's petition was a judicial act "which fully encompassed the constitutional and statutory issues raised." The court stated that if it were "to assume jurisdiction over the subject matter of this lawsuit, it would find itself in the unsupportable position of reviewing an order of a jurisdiction's highest court."

2 The complaint named as defendants the District of Columbia Court of Appeals, the Chief Judge of the District of Columbia Court of Appeals in his official capacity, the Committee on Admissions, and the Chairman and Secretary of that Committee.

* * *

B

[Hickey, the second respondent, similarly sought permission to sit for the bar examination, and the Court detailed his qualifications and experience. The details of Hickey's background are not important for present purposes. The only significant potential difference is that Hickey was apparently not represented by counsel and advanced only policy arguments in favor of his application, not raising his Fifth Amendment and antitrust arguments until he filed his complaint in the United States District Court.]

C

Both Hickey and Feldman appealed the dismissals of their complaints to the United States Court of Appeals for the District of Columbia Circuit. The District of Columbia Circuit affirmed the dismissals of Hickey's and Feldman's antitrust claims on the ground that they were insubstantial.[11] The court, however, concluded that the waiver proceedings in the District of Columbia Court of Appeals "were not judicial in the federal sense, and thus did not foreclose litigation of the constitutional contentions in the District Court." The court therefore reversed the dismissals of the constitutional claims and remanded them for consideration on the merits.

Although the District of Columbia Circuit acknowledged that "review of a final judgment of the highest judicial tribunal of a state is vested solely in the Supreme Court of the United States," (footnote omitted), and that the United States District Court therefore is without authority to review determinations by the District of Columbia Court of Appeals in judicial proceedings, the court found that the District Court has jurisdiction over these cases because the proceedings in the District of Columbia Court of Appeals "were not judicial * * * ." The court based this conclusion on a finding that neither Feldman nor Hickey asserted in their waiver petitions "any sort of *right* to be admitted to the District of Columbia bar, or even to take the examination therefor." ([E]mphasis in original). Feldman and Hickey simply sought an exemption from the rule. In particular, Hickey did not present any legal arguments nor did "he demand admission to the examination as a matter of legal entitlement." He "merely asked the court to exercise its administrative discretion to permit him to take the test." This amounted to a request that the court "make a policy decision equating his personal qualities with accredited legal education, not an adjudication requiring resort to legal principles." ([F]ootnote omitted).

no right asserted

Hickey

11 We denied respondents' cross-petitions for certiorari from the disposition of the antitrust claims. Those claims, therefore, are not before us.

The District of Columbia Circuit found Feldman's case more difficult, but still concluded that the proceedings on his waiver petition were not judicial in nature because the "claim-of-right element" was lacking. Feldman's petition did not "claim that a refusal of his waiver request would deny him any right at all." Instead, the petition "invoked the administrative discretion of [the court], simply asking that it temper its rule in his favor, for personal and not legal reasons." The District of Columbia Circuit rejected the argument that the letter from Feldman's counsel, which raised certain legal arguments, changed the nature of the proceedings. The District of Columbia Circuit stated: "We are unable to discern in the letter any desire that the court consider Feldman's legal criticisms of the rule on their merits, or hand down a decision dealing with them. The letter made unmistakably clear that these criticisms would be litigated, if at all, in the District Court * * * ." ([F]ootnotes omitted).[12]

II

The District of Columbia Circuit properly acknowledged that the United States District Court is without authority to review final determinations of the District of Columbia Court of Appeals in judicial proceedings. Review of such determinations can be obtained only in this Court. A crucial question in this case, therefore, is whether the proceedings before the District of Columbia Court of Appeals were judicial in nature.[13]

A

This Court has considered the distinction between judicial and administrative or ministerial proceedings on several occasions. In *Prentis v. Atlantic Coast Line (1908)*, a railroad challenged in federal court the constitutionality of rail passenger rates set by the state corporation commission. The question presented by the case was whether the federal court was free to enjoin implementation of the rate order. In considering this question, we assumed that the state corporation

---

12 The District of Columbia Circuit rejected the petitioners' alternative argument that consideration of the legal issues Feldman sought to raise in District Court was barred by principles of res judicata. The court did so on the ground that the proceedings in the District of Columbia Court of Appeals were non-judicial in nature.

In an opinion concurring in part and dissenting in part, Judge Robb expressed the view that the District Court had no jurisdiction to review the orders of the District of Columbia Court of Appeals. He noted that the District of Columbia Court of Appeals has the status of a state supreme court and stated:

> The adverse decisions in the appellants' cases were reviewable in the Supreme Court of the United States. Although the appellants cast their petitions to the Court of Appeals in terms of requests for waivers, the petitions in essence were demands that the court declare the petitioners qualified to sit for the bar examination. Those demands were denied by en banc orders of the Court of Appeals. The denials were judicial acts and as such were reviewable on writ of certiorari to the Supreme Court. They were not reviewable in the District Court.

13 As the District of Columbia Circuit recognized, it is a question of federal law whether "a particular proceeding before another tribunal was truly judicial" for purposes of ascertaining the jurisdiction of a federal court.

commission was, at least for some purposes, a court. We held, however, that the federal court could enjoin implementation of the rate order because the commission had acted in a legislative as opposed to a judicial capacity in setting the rates. In reaching this conclusion, we stated:

> A judicial inquiry investigates, declares and enforces liabilities as they stand on present or past facts and under laws supposed already to exist. That is its purpose and end. Legislation on the other hand looks to the future and changes existing conditions by making a new rule to be applied thereafter to all or some part of those subject to its power. The establishment of a rate is the making of a rule for the future, and therefore is an act legislative not judicial in kind * * * .

We went on to suggest that the nature of a proceeding "depends not upon the character of the body but upon the character of the proceedings."

Food for Thought

Do you think this language gets the Court where it needs to go? The rule affecting graduates of non-ABA-accredited schools looked to the future, did it not? If the difference between that rule and the situation in *Prentis* was that individual bar candidates could petition for relief from the rules provisions, could the *Prentis* state corporation commission have insulated its rate decisions from review in the lower federal courts by publishing a presumptive rate schedule but allowing individual carriers to petition for adjustment of the schedule?

In *In re Summers (1945)*, we considered the petitioner's challenge to the constitutionality of a state Supreme Court's refusal to admit him to the practice of law. At the outset, we noted that the record was not in the "customary form" because the state court had not treated the proceeding as "judicial." In fact, the state court contested our certiorari jurisdiction on the ground that the state court proceedings had not been judicial in nature and that no case or controversy therefore existed in this Court under Article III of the Federal Constitution. In considering this contention, we conceded that the state court proceeding might not have been judicial under state law and that the denial of the petitioner's application for admission to the bar was treated "as a ministerial act which is performed by virtue of the judicial power, such as the appointment of a clerk or bailiff or the specification of the requirements of eligibility or the course of study for applicants for admission to the bar, rather than a judicial proceeding." We stated, however, that in determining the nature of the proceedings "we must for ourselves appraise the circumstances of the refusal."

In conducting this appraisal, we first stated:

> A case arises, within the meaning of the Constitution, when any question respecting the Constitution, treaties or laws of the United States has assumed

> "such a form that the judicial power is capable of acting on it." * * * A declaration on rights as they stand must be sought, not on rights which may arise in the future, and there must be an actual controversy over an issue, not a desire for an abstract declaration of the law. The form of the proceeding is not significant. It is the nature and effect which is controlling.

Applying this standard, we noted that the state court had concluded that the report of the Committee on Character and Fitness, which refused to issue a favorable certificate, should be sustained. The state court, therefore, considered the petitioner's petition "on its merits." Although "no entry was placed by the Clerk in the file, on a docket, or in a judgment roll," we found that the state court had taken "cognizance of the petition and passed an order which [was] validated by the signature of the presiding officer." ([F]ootnote omitted). We stated:

> Where relief is thus sought in a state court against the action of a committee, appointed to advise the court, and the court takes cognizance of the complaint without requiring the appearance of the committee or its members, we think the consideration of the petition by the Supreme Court, the body which has authority itself by its own act to give the relief sought, makes the proceeding adversary in the sense of a true case or controversy.
>
> A claim of a present right to admission to the bar of a state and a denial of that right is a controversy. When the claim is made in a state court and a denial of the right is made by judicial order, it is a case which may be reviewed under Article III of the Constitution when federal questions are raised and proper steps taken to that end, in this Court. ([F]ootnote omitted).

Food for Thought

Query whether the characterization of state proceedings as judicial or non-judicial should be a question of federal or state law. If the state courts interpret state law as making the proceeding non-judicial, is it open to the federal courts to take issue with that conclusion, or are they then forced to take the position that the state law, as interpreted by the state's highest court, is unconstitutional?

B

These precedents clearly establish that the proceedings in the District of Columbia Court of Appeals surrounding Feldman's and Hickey's petitions for waiver were judicial in nature. The proceedings were not legislative, ministerial, or administrative. The District of Columbia Court of Appeals did not "loo[k] to the future and chang[e] existing conditions by making a new rule to be applied thereafter to all or some part of those subject to its power." Nor did it engage in rulemaking or specify "the requirements of eligibility or the course of study for applicants for admission to the bar * * * ." Nor did the District of Columbia Court of Appeals simply engage in ministerial action. Instead, the proceedings before the District of Columbia Court of Appeals involved a "judicial inquiry" in which the court was called upon to investigate, declare, and enforce "liabilities as they [stood] on present or past facts and under laws supposed already to exist."

In his petition to the District of Columbia Court of Appeals, discussed in detail above, Feldman contended that he possessed "the requisite fitness and good moral character necessary to practice law in this jurisdiction." In support of his position, he described in detail his legal training and experience. He asserted that his professional education and training were "equal to that received by those who have attended an A.B.A. approved law school." He further argued that granting his petition would not frustrate the objectives of the District of Columbia's procedures and requirements for admission to the bar. In his later letter, Feldman pointed out that the court's former practice of granting waivers to graduates of unaccredited law schools raised questions about the fairness of denying his petition. He also made explicit legal arguments against the rule based both on the Constitution and on the federal antitrust laws. All of this was done against the background of an existing rule.

In essence, Feldman argued on policy grounds that the rule should not be applied to him because he had fulfilled the spirit, if not the letter, of Rule 46 I(b)(3). Alternatively, he argued in his letter that the rule was invalid. In short, he was seeking "a declaration on rights as they [stood] * * * not on rights which [might] arise in the future * * * ." This required the District of Columbia Court of Appeals to determine in light of existing law and in light of Feldman's qualifications and arguments whether Feldman's petition should be granted. The court also had before it legal arguments against the validity of the rule. When it issued a *per curiam* order denying Feldman's petition, it determined as a legal matter that Feldman was not entitled to be admitted to the bar without examination or to sit for the bar examination. The court had adjudicated Feldman's "claim of a present right to admission to the bar," and rejected it. This is the essence of a judicial proceeding.

The same conclusion obtains with respect to the proceedings on Hickey's petition for waiver.

* * *

Admittedly, the proceedings in both Feldman's and Hickey's case did not assume the form commonly associated with judicial proceedings. As we said in In re Summers, however, "the form of the proceeding is not significant. It is the nature and effect which is controlling."[15]

---

15 Our conclusion that the proceedings before the District of Columbia Court of Appeals were judicial in nature is consistent with our grants of certiorari to review state court decisions on bar-related matters in [eight cases from 1957 to 1982].

III

A

A determination that the proceedings on Feldman's and Hickey's petitions were judicial does not finally dispose of this case. As we have noted, a United States District Court has no authority to review final judgments of a state court in judicial proceedings. Review of such judgments may be had only in this Court. Therefore, to the extent that Hickey and Feldman sought review in District Court of the District of Columbia Court of Appeals' denial of their petitions for waiver the District Court lacked subject matter jurisdiction over their complaints. Hickey and Feldman should have sought review of the District of Columbia Court of Appeals' judgments in this Court.[16] To the extent that Hickey and Feldman mounted a general challenge to the constitutionality of Rule 46 I(b)(3), however, the District Court did have subject matter jurisdiction over their complaints.

The difference between seeking review in a federal district court of a state court's final judgment in a bar admission matter and challenging the validity of a state bar admission rule has been recognized in the lower courts and, at least implicitly, in the opinions of this Court.

* * *

B

16 It is possible that review of a state court decision by this Court could be barred by a petitioner's failure to raise his constitutional claims in the state courts. * * * The United States Court of Appeals for the Fifth Circuit has relied on this limit on our certiorari jurisdiction to hold that a federal district court has jurisdiction over constitutional claims asserted by a plaintiff who has been denied admission to a state bar in a state court judicial proceeding if he failed to raise his constitutional claims in the state court. The Circuit Court of Appeals' reasoning * * * is flawed. As we noted "lower federal courts possess no power whatever to sit in direct review of state court decisions." If the constitutional claims presented to a United States District Court are inextricably intertwined with the state court's denial in a judicial proceeding of a particular plaintiff's application for admission to the state bar, then the District Court is in essence being called upon to review the state court decision. This the District Court may not do.

Moreover, the fact that we may not have jurisdiction to review a final state court judgment because of a petitioner's failure to raise his constitutional claims in state court does not mean that a United States District Court should have jurisdiction over the claims. By failing to raise his claims in state court a plaintiff may forfeit his right to obtain review of the state court decision in any federal court. This result is eminently defensible on policy grounds. We have noted the competence of state courts to adjudicate federal constitutional claims. * * * [O]ne of the policies underlying the requirement that constitutional claims be raised in state court as a predicate to our certiorari jurisdiction is the desirability of giving the state court the first opportunity to consider a state statute or rule in light of federal constitutional arguments. A state court may give the statute a saving construction in response to those arguments.

Finally, it is important to note in the context of this case the strength of the state interest in regulating the state bar. * * * "[T]he interest of the States in regulating lawyers is especially great since lawyers are essential to the primary governmental function of administering justice, and have historically been "officers of the courts."

Applying this standard to the respondents' complaints, it is clear that their allegations that the District of Columbia Court of Appeals acted arbitrarily and capriciously in denying their petitions for waiver and that the court acted unreasonably and discriminatorily in denying their petitions in view of its former policy of granting waivers to graduates of unaccredited law schools, required the District Court to review a final judicial decision of the highest court of a jurisdiction in a particular case. These allegations are inextricably intertwined with the District of Columbia Court of Appeals' decisions, in judicial proceedings, to deny the respondents' petitions. The District Court, therefore, does not have jurisdiction over these elements of the respondents' complaints.

The remaining allegations in the complaints, however, involve a general attack on the constitutionality of Rule 46 I(b)(3). The respondents' claims that the rule is unconstitutional because it creates an irrebuttable presumption that only graduates of accredited law schools are fit to practice law, discriminates against those who have obtained equivalent legal training by other means, and impermissibly delegates the District of Columbia Court of Appeals' power to regulate the bar to the American Bar Association, do not require review of a judicial decision in a particular case. The District Court, therefore, has subject matter jurisdiction over these elements of the respondents' complaints.

In deciding that the District Court has jurisdiction over those elements of the respondents' complaints that involve a general challenge to the constitutionality of Rule 46 I(b)(3), we expressly do not reach the question of whether the doctrine of res judicata forecloses litigation on these elements of the complaints. We leave that question to the District Court on remand.

IV

The judgment of the District of Columbia Circuit is vacated and the cases are remanded to the District Court for further proceedings consistent with this opinion.

So ordered.

JUSTICE STEVENS, dissenting.

There are many crafts in which the State performs a licensing function. That function is important, not only to those seeking access to a gainful occupation but to the members of the public served by the profession as

Food for Thought

Why would preclusion embarrass the plaintiffs here? Is the Court suggesting that they should have raised their constitutional and antitrust arguments as a part of their petitions for waivers of the rule? Note that the D.C. bar rules, insofar as the opinion reflects them, make no provision for a waiver petition at all. Would the plaintiffs have been better off simply to have commenced in the district court, raising their federal claims *ab initio*?

well. State-created rules governing the grant or denial of licenses must comply with constitutional standards and must be administered in accordance with due process of law. Given these acknowledged constitutional limitations on action by the State, it should be beyond question that a federal district court has subject matter jurisdiction over an individual's lawsuit raising federal constitutional challenges either to licensing rules themselves or to their application in his own case. Curiously, however, the Court today ignores basic jurisdictional principles when it decides a jurisdictional issue affecting the licensing of members of the legal profession.

The Court holds that respondents may make a general constitutional attack on the rules governing the admission of lawyers to practice in the District of Columbia. I agree. But the Court also concludes that a United States District Court has no subject matter jurisdiction over a claim that those rules have been administered in an unconstitutional manner. According to the Court's opinion, respondents' contentions that bar admission rules have been unconstitutionally applied to them by the District of Columbia Court of Appeals somehow constitute impermissible attempts to secure appellate review of final judgments of that court. There are two basic flaws in the Court's analysis.

First, neither Feldman nor Hickey requested the District of Columbia Court of Appeals to pass on the validity of Rule 46 I(b)(3) or to grant them admission to the bar or the bar examination as a matter of right. Rather, each of them asked the court to waive the requirements of the rule for a variety of reasons. I would not characterize the court's refusal to grant a requested waiver as an adjudication. Unlike the decision of the Supreme Court of Illinois reviewed in *In re Summers*, the order of the District of Columbia Court of Appeals did not determine a claim of right, nor did it even apply standard equitable principles to a prayer for relief. Rather, that court performed no more and no less than the administrative function of a licensing board. As the United States Court of Appeals wrote, Hickey asked the court "to make a policy decision equating his personal qualities with accredited legal education, not an adjudication requiring resort to legal principles," and Feldman "invoked the administrative discretion of that body, simply asking that it temper its rule in his favor, for personal and not legal reasons." Rejection of those petitions was not "adjudicative" and was therefore not susceptible to certiorari review in this Court.

Second, even if the refusal to grant a waiver were an adjudication, the federal statute that confers jurisdiction upon the United States District Court to entertain a constitutional challenge to the rules themselves also authorizes that court to entertain a collateral attack upon the unconstitutional application of those rules. The Court's opinion fails to distinguish between two concepts: appellate review and collateral attack. If a challenge to a state court's decision is brought in United

States District Court and alleges violations of the United States Constitution, then by definition it does not seek appellate review. It is plainly within the federal-question jurisdiction of the federal court.

> **Food for Thought**
>
> Does Justice Stevens overstate his case here? Suppose a plaintiff commences an action in the state court, filing a complaint that would satisfy the Court's federal-question-jurisdiction standards (well-pleaded, outcome determinative and substantial federal issue). Suppose also that the defendant does not remove the case. As Justice Stevens formulates his argument, what will prevent whichever litigant loses in the state court from going next to the United States District Court to seek a different result?
>
> Perhaps there is a subtle conflation going on here. To assert that a case is a federal-question case does not necessarily mean that what the plaintiff asks the district court to do is not appellate in nature

There may be other reasons for denying relief to the plaintiff—such as failure to state a cause of action, claim or issue preclusion, or failure to prove a violation of constitutional rights.[2] But it does violence to jurisdictional concepts for this Court to hold, as it does, that the federal district court has no *jurisdiction* to conduct independent review of a specific claim that a licensing body's action did not comply with federal constitutional standards. The fact that the licensing function in the legal profession is controlled by the judiciary is not a sufficient reason to immunize allegedly unconstitutional conduct from review in the federal courts.

I therefore respectfully dissent.

Notes and Questions

1. What is the basis for the *Rooker-Feldman* doctrine? Does the Constitution compel it? Is it a creature of statute? Is it federal common law? Does the answer make any difference?

2. Suppose a state permits collateral attacks on judgments. In such circumstances, if the party entitled to make a collateral attack in the state courts instead mounts one in federal court, do the premises on which the *Rooker-Feldman* doctrine relies still counsel the federal court to refuse to entertain the case?

---

2 Constitutional challenges to specific licensing actions may, of course, fail on the merits. But in my view, if plaintiffs challenging a bar admissions decision by a state court prove facts comparable to the allegations made by the appellants in *Yick Wo v. Hopkins* (1886), they would clearly be entitled to relief in the United States District Court. If they were seeking admission to any other craft regulated by the state, they would unquestionably have such a right.

3. In *Federal Maritime Commission v. South Carolina State Ports Authority*, 535 U.S. 743 (2002), a case involving Eleventh Amendment immunity from federal suit, the Court characterized a proceeding before a federal executive branch agency brought by a private company as within the state's sovereign immunity protection, quoting with approval the Fourth Circuit's declaration that the proceeding " 'walks, talks, and squawks very much like a lawsuit' and that '[i]ts placement within the Executive Branch cannot blind us to the fact that the proceeding is truly an adjudication.' " Do the proceedings involving Feldman's and Hickey's applications to the District of Columbia bar qualify as judicial proceedings under the Court's new Duck Test?

a) The Court makes much of the fact that Feldman's attorney spoke the language of the law in specifying constitutional and other legal problems he thought attended refusal to allow his client to become a member of the District of Columbia bar or even to sit for the examination. Is an application for a driver's license a judicial proceeding within the meaning of the *Rooker-Feldman* rule? If so, was it unnecessary for the Court to call attention to the nature of counsel's argument on Feldman's behalf? If not, does it become one if counsel for a driver-applicant states in a letter to the commissioner of motor vehicles that denying a license to his client violates one or more constitutional or statutory provisions?

Suppose the District of Columbia had instead established a board of bar examiners to perform the admission functions now entrusted to the Court of Appeals. If the plaintiffs here had presented the same information to the board rather than to the Court, would that have made the proceeding judicial? Would it matter whether the District authorized the board to consider legal challenges to the District's admission rules? If it had done so, and if no appeal lay to any District of Columbia court, would disappointed applicant's only recourse have been to seek review in the Supreme Court?

b) The Court notes that Hickey's application "did not present any legal arguments nor did 'he demand admission to the examination as a matter of legal entitlement.' " Should that put Hickey on different footing from Feldman? Does that alter whether the proceedings of the District of Columbia Court of Appeals on applications to sit for the bar examination (or to be admitted without having taken the bar examination) are "judicial"?

What are the hallmarks of a judicial proceeding? Clearly not everything a judge does is judicial in nature; the Court has recognized that in cases denying absolute immunity to judges for actions that are administrative in nature. *See, e.g.*, *Forrester v. White*, 484 U.S. 219 (1988), *supra* page 622.

4. The Court's discussion of *Prentis* raises an interesting possibility. There the Court allowed the railroad to challenge conditions of operation (rates) set by the state corporation commission. If Feldman and Hickey had restructured their challenges, going directly to the district court and arguing that the District of Columbia require-

ment that all applicants have attended ABA-approved law schools was unconstitutional on its face, would they have been entitled to a hearing on the merits? Was their mistake in presenting too particularized a case to the federal courts? Or, if they had adopted this alternative approach, would they also have been entitled to a determination of whether the requirement was unconstitutional as applied to them?

5. *In re Summers* appeared to pit the United States Supreme Court against the Supreme Court of Illinois, the latter declaring that its bar admission proceedings were not judicial, and the former ruling that state courts could not make such a determination for purposes of federal law.

> The return of the [Illinois Supreme Court] states that the correspondence and communications of petitioner with the Justices were not spread upon the records of the Supreme Court of Illinois and that under the law of Illinois this petition for admission to the bar does not constitute a case or controversy or a judicial proceeding but is a mere application for appointment as an officer of the court. We of course accept this authoritative commentary upon the law of Illinois as establishing for that state the non-judicial character of an application for admission to the bar. We take it that the law of Illinois treats the action of the Supreme Court on this petition as a ministerial act which is performed by virtue of the judicial power, such as the appointment of a clerk or bailiff or the specification of the requirements of eligibility or the course of study for applicants for admission to the bar, rather than a judicial proceeding.
>
> For the purpose of determining whether the action of the Supreme Court of Illinois is a judgment in a judicial proceeding which involves a case or controversy reviewable in this Court under Article III, Sec. 2, Cl. 1, of the Constitution of the United States, we must for ourselves appraise the circumstances of this refusal.

In re Summers, 325 U.S. 561, 565-66 (1945) (footnotes omitted). Thus, whether the Illinois Supreme Court's proceedings were judicial for *Rooker* purposes was a question of federal, not state law. One should note that the *Summers* Court did not cite *Rooker*. More than that, the Court engaged in the quoted discussion as a way of demonstrating that it *could* reach and decide the merits (which, by the way, involved the Court's affirming Illinois's refusal to admit Summers to the practice of law because he was a conscientious objector and a pacifist). Nonetheless, does the language of that Court imply that the *Rooker-Feldman* doctrine is a matter of constitutional imperative? To the extent that the doctrine exists to protect the dignity of state courts against intrusion by the inferior federal courts, should it be relevant that the state courts themselves characterize a proceeding as non-judicial?

As *Rooker* and *Feldman* suggest, a doctrine comparatively simple to state ("The inferior federal courts cannot hear appeals of state court decisions[ ]") nonetheless presents considerable difficulties of application. The following materials elaborate some the difficulties that the lower federal courts have experienced.

C. Problems of Interpretation

1. The Source of the Injury: Independent Act or State Court Judgment?

Exxon Mobil Corporation v. Saudi Basic Industries Corporation

Supreme Court of the United States, 2005.
544 U.S. 280.

JUSTICE GINSBURG delivered the opinion of the Court.

This case concerns what has come to be known as the *Rooker-Feldman* doctrine, applied by this Court only twice, first in *Rooker v. Fidelity Trust Co.* (1923), then, 60 years later, in *District of Columbia Court of Appeals v. Feldman* (1983). Variously interpreted in the lower courts, the doctrine has sometimes been construed to extend far beyond the contours of the *Rooker* and *Feldman* cases, overriding Congress' conferral of federal-court jurisdiction concurrent with jurisdiction exercised by state courts, and superseding the ordinary application of preclusion law pursuant to 28 U.S.C. § 1738.

> **Take Note**
>
> "Concurrent" may have two meanings here. First, Justice Ginsburg may be referring to the fact that the subject matter jurisdiction of state and federal courts overlaps to a considerable extent. Second, she may be referring to the possibility of parallel (or otherwise related) actions in the two court systems proceeding at the same time.

Rooker was a suit commenced in Federal District Court to have a judgment of a state court, adverse to the federal court plaintiffs, "declared null and void." In *Feldman*, parties unsuccessful in the District of Columbia Court of Appeals (the District's highest court) commenced a federal-court action against the very court that had rejected their applications. Holding the federal suits impermissible, we emphasized that appellate jurisdiction to reverse or modify a state-court judgment is lodged, initially by § 25 of the Judiciary Act of 1789 and now by 28 U.S.C. § 1257, exclusively in this Court. Federal district courts, we noted, are empowered to exercise original, not appellate, jurisdiction. Plaintiffs in *Rooker* and *Feldman* had litigated and lost in state court. Their federal complaints, we observed, essentially invited federal courts of first instance to review and reverse unfavorable state-court judgments. We declared such suits out of bounds, *i.e.*, properly dismissed for want of subject-matter jurisdiction.

holding

The *Rooker-Feldman* doctrine, we hold today, is confined to cases of the kind from which the doctrine acquired its name: cases brought by state-court losers complaining of injuries caused by state-court judgments rendered before the district court proceedings commenced and inviting district court review and rejection of those judgments. *Rooker-Feldman* does not otherwise override or supplant preclusion doctrine or augment the circumscribed doctrines that allow federal courts to stay or dismiss proceedings in deference to state-court actions.

In the case before us, the Court of Appeals for the Third Circuit misperceived the narrow ground occupied by *Rooker-Feldman*, and consequently erred in ordering the federal action dismissed for lack of subject-matter jurisdiction. We therefore reverse the Third Circuit's judgment.

I

In *Rooker v. Fidelity Trust Co.*, the parties defeated in state court turned to a Federal District Court for relief. Alleging that the adverse state-court judgment was rendered in contravention of the Constitution, they asked the federal court to declare it "null and void." This Court noted preliminarily that the state court had acted within its jurisdiction. If the state-court decision was wrong, the Court explained, "that did not make the judgment void, but merely left it open to reversal or modification in an appropriate and timely appellate proceeding." Federal district courts, the *Rooker* Court recognized, lacked the requisite appellate authority, for their jurisdiction was "strictly original." Among federal courts, the *Rooker* Court clarified, Congress had empowered only this Court to exercise appellate authority "to reverse or modify" a state-court judgment. Accordingly, the Court affirmed a decree dismissing the suit for lack of jurisdiction.

Sixty years later, the Court decided *District of Columbia Court of Appeals v. Feldman*. The two plaintiffs in that case, Hickey and Feldman, neither of whom had graduated from an accredited law school, petitioned the District of Columbia Court of Appeals to waive a court Rule that required D.C. bar applicants to have graduated from a law school approved by the American Bar Association. After the D.C. court denied their waiver requests, Hickey and Feldman filed suits in the United States District Court for the District of Columbia. The District Court and the Court of Appeals for the District of Columbia Circuit disagreed on the question whether the federal suit could be maintained, and we granted certiorari.

Recalling *Rooker*, this Court's opinion in *Feldman* observed first that the District Court lacked authority to review a final judicial determination of the D.C. high court. "Review of such determinations," the *Feldman* opinion reiterated, "can be obtained only in this Court." The "crucial question," the Court next stated, was whether the proceedings in the D.C. court were "judicial in nature." Addressing that question, the Court concluded that the D.C. court had acted both judicially and legislatively.

In applying the accreditation Rule to the Hickey and Feldman waiver petitions, this Court determined, the D.C. court had acted judicially. As to that adjudication, *Feldman* held, this Court alone among federal courts had review authority. Hence, "to the extent that Hickey and Feldman sought review in the District Court of the District of Columbia Court of Appeals' denial of their petitions for waiver, the District Court lacked subject-matter jurisdiction over their complaints." But that determination did not dispose of the entire case, for in promulgating the bar admission rule, this Court said, the D.C. court had acted legislatively, not judicially. "Challenges to the constitutionality of state bar rules," the Court elaborated, "do not necessarily require a United States district court to review a final state-court judgment in a judicial proceeding." Thus, the Court reasoned, 28 U.S.C. § 1257 did not bar District Court proceedings addressed to the validity of the accreditation Rule itself. The Rule could be contested in federal court, this Court held, so long as plaintiffs did not seek review of the Rule's application in a particular case.

The Court endeavored to separate elements of the Hickey and Feldman complaints that failed the jurisdictional threshold from those that survived jurisdictional inspection. Plaintiffs had urged that the District of Columbia Court of Appeals acted arbitrarily in denying the waiver petitions of Hickey and Feldman, given that court's "former policy of granting waivers to graduates of unaccredited law schools." That charge, the Court held, could not be pursued, for it was "inextricably intertwined with the District of Columbia Court of Appeals' decisions, in judicial proceedings, to deny [plaintiffs'] petitions."[1]

On the other hand, the Court said, plaintiffs could maintain

> claims that the [bar admission] rule is unconstitutional because it creates an irrebuttable presumption that only graduates of accredited law schools are fit to practice law, discriminates against those who have obtained equivalent legal training by other means, and impermissibly delegates the District of Columbia Court of Appeals' power to regulate the bar to the American Bar Association,

for those claims "do not require review of a judicial decision in a particular case." The Court left open the question whether the doctrine of res judicata foreclosed

1 Earlier in the opinion the Court had used the same expression. In a footnote, the Court explained that a district court could not entertain constitutional claims attacking a state-court judgment, even if the state court had not passed directly on those claims, when the constitutional attack was "inextricably intertwined" with the state court's judgment.

litigation of the elements of the complaints spared from dismissal for want of subject-matter jurisdiction.

Since Feldman, this Court has never applied *Rooker-Feldman* to dismiss an action for want of jurisdiction. The few decisions that have mentioned Rooker and Feldman have done so only in passing or to explain why those cases did not dictate dismissal. * * * [The Court cited numerous examples.]"

II

In 1980, two subsidiaries of petitioner Exxon Mobil Corporation (then the separate companies Exxon Corp. and Mobil Corp.) formed joint ventures with respondent Saudi Basic Industries Corp. (SABIC) to produce polyethylene in Saudi Arabia. Two decades later, the parties began to dispute royalties that SABIC had charged the joint ventures for sublicenses to a polyethylene manufacturing method.

SABIC preemptively sued the two ExxonMobil subsidiaries in Delaware Superior Court in July 2000 seeking a declaratory judgment that the royalty charges were proper under the joint venture agreements. About two weeks later, ExxonMobil and its subsidiaries countersued SABIC in the United States District Court for the District of New Jersey, alleging that SABIC overcharged the joint ventures for the sublicenses. ExxonMobil invoked subject-matter jurisdiction in the New Jersey action under 28 U.S.C. § 1330, which authorizes district courts to adjudicate actions against foreign states.[4]

In January 2002, the ExxonMobil subsidiaries answered SABIC's state-court complaint, asserting as counterclaims the same claims ExxonMobil had made in the federal suit in New Jersey. The state suit went to trial in March 2003, and the jury returned a verdict of over $400 million in favor of the ExxonMobil subsidiaries. SABIC appealed the judgment entered on the verdict to the Delaware Supreme Court.

Before the state-court trial, SABIC moved to dismiss the federal suit, alleging, *inter alia,* immunity under the Foreign Sovereign Immunities Act of 1976. The Federal District Court denied SABIC's motion to dismiss. SABIC took an interlocutory appeal, and the Court of Appeals heard argument in December 2003, over eight months after the state-court jury verdict.

The Court of Appeals, on its own motion, raised the question whether "subject matter jurisdiction over this case fails under the *Rooker-Feldman* doctrine

---

4 SABIC is a Saudi Arabian corporation, 70% owned by the Saudi Government and 30% owned by private investors.

because ExxonMobil's claims have already been litigated in state court." The court did not question the District Court's possession of subject-matter jurisdiction at the outset of the suit, but held that federal jurisdiction terminated when the Delaware Superior Court entered judgment on the jury verdict. The court rejected ExxonMobil's argument that *Rooker-Feldman* could not apply because ExxonMobil filed its federal complaint well before the state-court judgment. The only relevant consideration, the court stated, "is whether the state judgment precedes a federal judgment on the same claims." If *Rooker-Feldman* did not apply to federal actions filed prior to a state-court judgment, the Court of Appeals worried, "we would be encouraging parties to maintain federal actions as 'insurance policies' while their state court claims were pending." Once ExxonMobil's claims had been litigated to a judgment in state court, the Court of Appeals held, *Rooker-Feldman* "preclude[d] [the] federal district court from proceeding." ([I]nternal quotation marks omitted).

ExxonMobil, at that point prevailing in Delaware, was not seeking to overturn the state-court judgment. Nevertheless, the Court of Appeals hypothesized that, if SABIC won on appeal in Delaware, ExxonMobil would be endeavoring in the federal action to "invalidate" the state-court judgment, "the very situation," the court concluded, "contemplated by *Rooker-Feldman's* 'inextricably intertwined' bar."

Food for Thought

Was there another way that the Third Circuit could have reached the same result—dismissal—at that point in the dispute?

We granted certiorari to resolve conflict among the Courts of Appeals over the scope of the *Rooker-Feldman* doctrine. We now reverse the judgment of the Court of Appeals for the Third Circuit.

III

Rooker and *Feldman* exhibit the limited circumstances in which this Court's appellate jurisdiction over state-court judgments, 28 U.S.C. § 1257, precludes a United States district court from exercising subject-matter jurisdiction in an action it would otherwise be empowered to adjudicate * * * . In both cases, the losing party in state court filed suit in federal court after the state proceedings ended, complaining of an injury caused by the state-court judgment and seeking review and rejection of that judgment. Plaintiffs in both cases, alleging federal-question jurisdiction, called upon the District Court to overturn an injurious state-court judgment. Because § 1257, as long interpreted, vests authority to review a state court's judgment solely in this Court, the District Courts in *Rooker* and *Feldman* lacked subject-matter jurisdiction.[8]

> **Take Note!**
>
> The position the Court takes in Footnote 8 is surprising, since it had previously characterized habeas proceedings in the district courts as reviewing the *custody* exercised by the state rather than the judgment of the state court.
>
> When a federal district court reviews a state prisoner's habeas corpus petition pursuant to 28 U.S.C. § 2254, it must decide whether the petitioner is "in custody in violation of the Constitution or laws or treaties of the United States." The court does not review a judgment, but the lawfulness of the petitioner's custody *simpliciter*.
>
> *Coleman v. Thompson*, 501 U.S. 722, 730 (1991). That is what the Court said. It probably is only a small exaggeration to say that no one believed it, since the custodian's defense to the habeas proceeding was invariably that the custody was lawful because of the state court conviction. Now, at least, the Court appears to have discarded the unsustainable fiction.

When there is parallel state and federal litigation, *Rooker-Feldman* is not triggered simply by the entry of judgment in state court. This Court has repeatedly held that "the pendency of an action in the state court is no bar to proceedings concerning the same matter in the Federal court having jurisdiction." Comity or abstention doctrines may, in various circumstances, permit or require the federal court to stay or dismiss the federal action in favor of the state-court litigation. But neither *Rooker* nor *Feldman* supports the notion that properly invoked concurrent jurisdiction vanishes if a state court reaches judgment on the same or related question while the case remains *sub judice* in a federal court.

Disposition of the federal action, once the state-court adjudication is complete, would be governed by preclusion law. The Full Faith and Credit Act * * * requires the federal court to "give the same preclusive effect to a state-court judgment as another court of that State would give." Preclusion, of course, is not a jurisdictional matter. In parallel litigation, a federal court may be bound to recognize the claim- and issue-preclusive effects of a state-court judgment, but federal jurisdiction over an action does not terminate automatically on the entry of judgment in the state court.

Nor does § 1257 stop a district court from exercising subject-matter jurisdiction simply because a party attempts to litigate in federal court a matter previously litigated in state court. If a federal plaintiff "present[s] some independent claim, albeit one that denies a legal conclusion that a state court has reached in a case to

---

8 Congress, if so minded, may explicitly empower district courts to oversee certain state-court judgments and has done so, most notably, in authorizing federal habeas review of state prisoners' petitions.

which he was a party * * * , then there is jurisdiction and state law determines whether the defendant prevails under principles of preclusion."

This case surely is not the "paradigm situation in which *Rooker-Feldman* precludes a federal district court from proceeding." ExxonMobil plainly has not repaired to federal court to undo the Delaware judgment in its favor. Rather, it appears ExxonMobil filed suit in Federal District Court (only two weeks after SABIC filed in Delaware and well before any judgment in state court) to protect itself in the event it lost in state court on grounds (such as the state statute of limitations) that might not preclude relief in the federal venue.[9] *Rooker-Feldman* did not prevent the District Court from exercising jurisdiction when ExxonMobil filed the federal action, and it did not emerge to vanquish jurisdiction after ExxonMobil prevailed in the Delaware courts.

* * *

For the reasons stated, the judgment of the Court of Appeals for the Third Circuit is reversed, and the case is remanded for further proceedings consistent with this opinion.

It is so ordered.

Notes and Questions

1. Does the Court effectively say that if the object of a federal action when filed is not to overturn an existing state court judgment, *Rooker-Feldman* has no application? In *Garry v. Geils*, 82 F.3d 1362 (7th Cir. 1996), the court noted just such a distinction:

> If the injury alleged resulted from the state court judgment itself, Rooker-Feldman directs that the lower federal courts lack jurisdiction. If the injury alleged is distinct from that judgment, i.e., the party maintains an injury apart from the loss in state court and not "inextricably intertwined" with the state judgment, res judicata may apply, but Rooker-Feldman does not.

Has *ExxonMobil* embraced the Seventh Circuit's view? If it has, does that connote at least that *Rooker-Feldman* can never apply unless there is a state court judgment that antedates commencement of the federal action?

---

9 The Court of Appeals criticized ExxonMobil for pursuing its federal suit as an "insurance policy" against an adverse result in state court. There is nothing necessarily inappropriate, however, about filing a protective action.

2. *ExxonMobil* seems to raise the question of whether *Rooker-Feldman* is simply a redundant doctrine given the Full Faith and Credit Statute, which requires federal courts to give preclusive effect to state court judgments. Is the answer a technical rather than a practical one? Recall that preclusion is not jurisdictional; that is why it appears as an affirmative defense that the party relying on it must plead pursuant to FED. R. CIV. P. 8(c). Does *Rooker-Feldman* exist because the Court has characterized it as going to the subject matter jurisdiction of the inferior federal courts, making ita threshold matter? Does that difference in treatment underscore the dividing point suggested in Note 1 above: that if there is a state court judgment when the federal action begins, *Rooker-Feldman* may apply, but otherwise preclusion principles will have to do?

3. The *Feldman* Court rejected part of the plaintiffs' challenge (based on alleged arbitrariness in granting waivers to graduates of unaccredited schools) because it was "inextricably intertwined" with the judicial decisions that aggrieved the plaintiffs. Is ExxonMobil's action here "inextricably intertwined" with the Delaware action that SABIC began and in which ExxonMobil successfully counterclaimed? Does one even need to ask the question? Note that the Court, although mentioning that part of the *Feldman* opinion more than once, never analyzes *ExxonMobil* on that basis. Why not?

4. Given *ExxonMobil's* approach, is there anything left for the "inextricably intertwined" language from *Feldman* to do or has the Court read it out of the calculus? Does *Facio v. Jones* (*infra* at 1075) predict an answer?

Some courts think that the inextricably-intertwined criterion continues to have teeth. In *Industrial Communications and Electronics, Inc. v. Monroe County*, 134 Fed. Appx. 314 (11th Cir. 2005), the court set out a four-part test for determining whether *Rooker-Feldman* bars a federal action:

> (1) the party in federal court is the same as the party in state court; (2) the prior state court ruling was a final or conclusive judgment on the merits; (3) the party seeking relief in federal court had a reasonable opportunity to raise its federal claims in the state court proceeding; and (4) the issue before the federal court was either adjudicated by the state court or was inextricably intertwined with the state court's judgment.

The court suggested that a claim is inextricably intertwined if the federal plaintiff had "a reasonable opportunity to raise it during the state court proceeding." Thus, although the Supreme Court was careful to distinguish between *Rooker-Feldman* and res judicata, it appears that the latter concept is useful for determining whether *Rooker-Feldman* prevents assertion of a claim not raised in earlier state court proceedings.

5. Suppose a state court issued a preliminary injunction in an on-going case. After *ExxonMobil*, would the *Rooker-Feldman* doctrine prevent a federal district court

from hearing a challenge to the preliminary injunction, assuming that the state case has not reached final judgment? The Court discusses *Rooker-Feldman* in terms of "state court losers." Is the party against whom a preliminary injunction operates a state court loser? On the other hand, the Court also refers to situations in which the federal action begins "after the state proceedings ended [*supra* page 1043]." Might that suggest that the *Rooker-Feldman* doctrine would not prevent review of interlocutory orders in pending state actions?

6. Since *ExxonMobil*, lower federal courts have been careful to limit *Rooker-Feldman* to the paradigmatic situation of the loser in the state court challenging that court's judgment in a federal proceeding commenced after the state court decision. Nonetheless, the Supreme Court has still had to deal with some vestiges of the lower courts' overbroad reading of *Rooker-Feldman*. In *Lance v. Dennis*, 546 U.S. 459 (2006), a per curiam Court vacated a three-judge-district-court judgment holding that *Rooker-Feldman* deprived the court of jurisdiction to hear a federal challenge that parties in privity with state court losers (for preclusion purposes) brought. The three-judge court rendered its decision four months after *ExxonMobil* but explained that it felt bound by Tenth Circuit precedent on the privity question that antedated *ExxonMobil*. The Court again tried to separate preclusion law from *Rooker-Feldman*:

> Whatever the impact of privity principles on preclusion rules, *Rooker-Feldman* is not simply preclusion by another name. * * * The *Rooker-Feldman* doctrine does not bar actins by nonparties to the earlier state-court judgment simply because, for purposes of preclusion law, they could be considered in privity with a party to the judgment.[9]

7. For a thoughtful discussion of the issues that *ExxonMobil* raises without resolving, see Thomas D. Rowe, Jr. & Edward L. Baskauskas, *"Inextricably Intertwined" Explicable at Last?*: Rooker-Feldman *Analysis After the Supreme Court's* ExxonMobil *Decision*, 2006 FED.CTS.L.REV. 1 (2006).

8. The post-*ExxonMobil* debate on *Rooker-Feldman* now seems to center on whether the doctrine protects only final state court judgments from review by the inferior federal courts or whether it protects interlocutory orders as well. To the extent that the doctrine rests on strict interpretation of 28 U.S.C. §§ 1257, 1331, cannot one argue that the lower federal courts have no jurisdiction to review any state court order? On the other hand, the Supreme Court's cases have all talked about "final" judgments. (Then, too, the Court has not yet considered the problem of interlocutory orders, so even had it said something, it would have been *obiter dictum*.) The circuit courts have split into three groups, one limiting the doctrine to final judgments, one extending the

9 In an omitted footnote, the Court reserved the question of whether the doctrine could ever apply to a non-party in the state court, offering the example of an estate commencing a federal action aimed at avoiding the effect of a state court judgment against the decedent.

doctrine to all state court orders, and the third extending the doctrine to some, but not all orders, the difference being whether the interlocutory order is appealable to the United States Supreme Court under *Cox Broadcasting Co. v. Cohn*, presented in Chapter 9 at page 999. Which is the best reading?

For More Information

See Dustin E. Buehler, *Revisiting* Rooker-Feldman*: Extending the Doctrine to State Court Interlocutory Orders*, 36 FLA. ST. L. REV. 373 (2009).

---

2. The Type of Relief Sought

Centifanti v. Nix

United States Court of Appeals for the Third Circuit, 1989.
865 F.2d 1422.

COWEN, Circuit Judge.

J. Benedict Centifanti appeals the order of the district court dismissing his complaint for lack of subject matter jurisdiction and denying his motion for leave to amend the complaint. Centifanti filed a complaint under 42 U.S.C. § 1983 (1982) against the Chief Justice and the Justices of the Supreme Court of Pennsylvania ("the Justices" or "Justice Nix"), following the Court's denial of his petition for reinstatement to the bar of the Supreme Court of Pennsylvania. The complaint alleged various constitutional defects in the procedural rules under which the Supreme Court considers petitions for the reinstatement of suspended attorneys.

We hold that the complaint, properly framed, raises a permissible general constitutional challenge to state rules, and does not improperly seek review of a state court decision. Therefore, we will reverse the district court's dismissal of the complaint for lack of subject matter jurisdiction. We will also reverse the district court's denial of Centifanti's motion for leave to amend his complaint to eliminate improper factual detail contained in the complaint. * * * Finally, we conclude that Centifanti's suit is not barred by either the statute of limitations or the doctrine of res judicata.

Food for Thought

Why does the court characterize the case this way?

I.

BACKGROUND

Before discussing the facts of this case, we briefly examine the relevant provisions of the Pennsylvania Rules of Disciplinary Enforcement ("R.D.E."), which govern the investigation and sanction of attorney misconduct. The Rules designate the Supreme Court of Pennsylvania as the ultimate decisionmaker on matters of attorney discipline. The Rules provide for a Disciplinary Board and hearing committees which make findings and submit recommendations to the Supreme Court.

The Disciplinary Board has "the power and the duty * * * [t]o consider and investigate the conduct of any person subject to these rules * * * ." More specifically, the Board has the authority to appoint three or more hearing committees within each disciplinary district, and to assign formal charges to a hearing committee. The Board is also authorized "[t]o review the conclusions of hearing committees with respect to formal charges and to prepare and forward its own findings and recommendations, together with the record of the proceeding before the hearing committee, to the Supreme Court." Hearing committees, in turn, are authorized to conduct hearings into formal charges of misconduct upon assignment by the Board, to submit their conclusions (together with the record of the hearing) to the Board, and to review and approve or modify recommendations by Disciplinary Counsel for dismissals, informal admonitions, private reprimands and institution of formal charges.

hearing comm.

With regard to decisions on initial disciplinary actions, R.D.E. 208(e)(5) provides that the Supreme Court "shall review the record, where appropriate consider oral argument, and enter an order." R.D.E. 208(e)(4) states, however, that "[e] xcept as provided in [R.D.E. 208](e)(2) and (e)(3), respondent-attorney will not be afforded the right of oral argument." R.D.E. 208(e)(2) provides that if the Board recommends disbarment, the attorney may submit to the Supreme Court a request to present oral argument. R.D.E. 208(e)(3) provides that if the Board recommends a sanction less than disbarment, the Court may issue a rule to show cause why an order of disbarment should not be entered, if the Court so decides after considering the Board's recommendation. In the latter case, the attorney "shall have the absolute right upon request for oral argument." R.D.E. 208(e)(3).

R.D.E. 218(a) provides that "[n]o attorney suspended for a period exceeding three months * * * may resume practice until reinstated by order of the Supreme Court after petition therefor pursuant to these rules." R.D.E. 218(b) provides that, with exceptions which are not germane here, "[a] person who has been disbarred may not apply for reinstatement until the expiration of at least five years from the effective date of the disbarment * * * ." With regard to reinstatement petitions of disbarred or suspended attorneys, R.D.E. 218(c)(6) states: "The Supreme Court shall review the record [of the hearing committee and Disciplinary Board] and enter an appropriate order. Unless otherwise ordered, matters arising under this rule will be considered without oral argument."

Centifanti is an attorney admitted to the bar of the Supreme Court of Pennsylvania in 1972. In 1980, by order of the Supreme Court of Pennsylvania, Centifanti was retroactively suspended from the practice of law for five years, resulting from a plea of *nolo contendere* to two charges of aggravated assault on his wife in 1976.

On August 10, 1983, having successfully completed his criminal probation, Centifanti filed a petition for reinstatement with the Disciplinary Board of the Supreme Court of Pennsylvania. Following the completion of hearings, a hearing committee of the Disciplinary Board submitted a report to the Board unanimously recommending that Centifanti's petition for reinstatement be granted.

Upon review, the Disciplinary Board remanded the petition to the hearing committee to consider certain factual questions which it believed were presented by the record and to consider independent medical testimony concerning Centifanti's mental health. The hearing committee reviewed additional evidence and again unanimously recommended reinstatement. On review of the record, the Disciplinary Board issued an opinion recommending Centifanti's reinstatement by a vote of eight to one.

Centifanti filed an application for leave to file a brief in support of his petition for reinstatement with the Supreme Court of Pennsylvania. By letter dated July 9, 1986, the Court, with one Justice dissenting, denied the petition for reinstatement to the Bar as well as the application for leave to file a brief. The decision was unaccompanied by an opinion or statement of reasons.

1983 claim

On January 2, 1987, Centifanti filed a complaint in the district court alleging a cause of action under 42 U.S.C. § 1983 against the Chief Justice and the Justices of the Supreme Court of Pennsylvania. The complaint alleges that the court-promulgated procedural rules governing attorney reinstatement violate the due process and equal protection clauses of the fourteenth amendment to the United States Constitution. Although we do not decide the merits of Centifanti's constitutional claims in this opinion, an understanding of these claims is necessary to resolve the jurisdictional issue in this case. The complaint, fairly read, essentially alleges the following due process defects in the rules:

> 1) that the rules fail to provide for a hearing before the Justices prior to action on a petition for reinstatement, following favorable action on the petition by the hearing committee and the Disciplinary Board;

2) that the rules fail to allow petitioners to submit briefs to the Justices in support of the recommendation of the Disciplinary Board that petitioners be reinstated, or to address any concerns or comments expressed by the Board;

3) that the rules fail to provide notification to petitioners, following favorable action by the Board, that the Justices may believe that reinstatement may not be in order, and fail to allow petitioners a hearing before the Justices and to submit a brief addressing any concerns the Justices may have; and

4) that the rules fail to require issuance of a statement of reasons when the Justices reject a petition for reinstatement which had been favorably acted upon by the Board.

Centifanti's complaint also alleges that the rules violate the constitutional guarantee of equal protection. The complaint notes that the rules provide that attorneys suspended for more than three months may not resume practice without first formally petitioning for reinstatement and obtaining the approval of a hearing committee, the Disciplinary Board and the Justices. Yet, although such attorneys are subject to "*de facto* disbarment," they are not afforded the same procedural safeguards as attorneys who are formally disbarred.

In a memorandum opinion and order dated June 1, 1988, the district court dismissed Centifanti's complaint for lack of subject matter jurisdiction, and also denied his application for leave to amend the complaint. The court considered Centifanti's complaint to be identical in effect to the complaint filed in Stern v. Nix, in which this Court held that the district court lacked subject matter jurisdiction over the complaint. The district court viewed Centifanti's complaint as an attempt to obtain improper review of the decision of the highest court of a state, rather than a permissible generalized constitutional challenge to a state law. The district court also determined that his "proposal to amend the complaint by deleting much of the personal detail does not alter the fundamental nature of this action which is, as it has always been, to challenge the Pennsylvania Supreme Court's judgment." ([F]ootnote omitted). Centifanti appeals to this Court.

II.

THE APPLICABLE LAW

Congress has provided that "[f]inal judgments or decrees rendered by the highest court of a State in which a decision could be had, may be reviewed by the Supreme Court * * * ." In Rooker v. Fidelity Trust Co., the Supreme Court held that section 1257 provides that *only* the Supreme Court, and not lower federal courts, may review decisions of the highest court of a state.

In District of Columbia Court of Appeals v. Feldman, the Court reaffirmed * * * Rooker, stating that a district court has "no authority to review final judgments of a state court in judicial proceedings" and "[r]eview of such judgments may be had only in this Court."[3] The Court in Feldman also added an important qualification to this rule, however, in the following discussion:

> We have recognized that state supreme courts may act in a nonjudicial capacity in promulgating rules regulating the bar. Challenges to the constitutionality of state bar rules, therefore, do not necessarily require a United States district court to review a final state-court judgment in a judicial proceeding. Instead, the district court may simply be asked to assess the validity of a rule promulgated in a nonjudicial proceeding. If this is the case, the district court is not reviewing a state court judicial decision. In this regard, 28 U.S.C. § 1257 does not act as a bar to the district court's consideration of the case and because the proceedings giving rise to the rule are nonjudicial the policies prohibiting United States district court review of final state-court judgments are not implicated. *United States district courts, therefore, have subject-matter jurisdiction over general challenges to state bar rules, promulgated by state courts in nonjudicial proceedings, which do not require review of a final state-court judgment in a particular case.*

([E]mphasis added) (citations omitted).

* * *

The Feldman Court held that the district court lacked subject matter jurisdiction over those claims which alleged that the denial by the state court of the attorneys' petitions for waiver was arbitrary and capricious, but that it *did* have subject matter jurisdiction over those claims which raised general challenges to the constitutionality of the rules.

3 After an extensive analysis, the Feldman Court found the state court proceedings to be "judicial," rather than legislative, ministerial or administrative, and thus subject to the proscription against appeal in the lower federal courts. The Court stated that

> "[a] judicial inquiry investigates, declares and enforces liabilities as they stand on present or past facts and under laws supposed already to exist * * * . Legislation on the other hand looks to the future and changes existing conditions by making a new rule to be applied thereafter to all or some part of those subject to its power."

([Q]uoting *Prentis v. Atlantic Coast Line Co.*, 211 U.S. 210, 226 (1908)).

Another court has aptly noted:

> Following the decision in *Feldman*, courts have consistently found state court decisions regarding the application of bar rules to be judicial rather than ministerial, even when the decisions are made not by the state's supreme court, but by a committee appointed by that court. The determination in these cases turns on whether the state court or its designee considers a present claim of right by applying the terms of a rule to the facts of a petitioner's case.

The parties in the instant case do not appear to dispute that when the Pennsylvania Supreme Court decided Centifanti's petition, it was applying existing rules to the facts to reach a decision and was thus acting in a judicial capacity.

The Court in Feldman recognized the occasional difficulty in distinguishing between a general challenge to court-promulgated attorney disciplinary or admission rules, and a specific challenge to a particular decision involving these rules by a state supreme court. The Court suggested that "[i]f the constitutional claims presented to a United States district court are *inextricably intertwined* with the state court's denial in a judicial proceeding of a particular plaintiff's application for admission to the state bar, then the district court is in essence being called upon to review the state-court decision * * * [which] the district court may not do." ([E]mphasis added).

> **FYI**
>
> The phrase "inextricably intertwined" may seem to be unworkably vague, and it has drawn considerable attention from commentators. *See, e.g.*, Thomas D. Rowe Jr. & Edward L. Baskauskas, *"Inextricably Intertwined" Explicable at Last?* Rooker-Feldman *Analysis After the Supreme Court's* ExxonMobil *Decision*, 2006 FED. CTS. L. REV. 1 (2006).

We recently had occasion to apply the so-called *Rooker-Feldman* doctrine in Stern v. Nix. Stern, a Pennsylvania attorney, was the subject of a disciplinary investigation by state bar authorities. A hearing committee of the Disciplinary Board recommended a private reprimand as a sanction against Stern for his misbehavior. The Disciplinary Board on review recommended the higher sanction of public censure. The Supreme Court rejected the factual findings of both the committee and the Board, which the disciplinary rules allowed it to do, and imposed the penalty of disbarment.

Stern then filed a section 1983 action in federal district court against the Justices of the Supreme Court, challenging the combined effect of two state court rules. The first rule was a court-made rule which provides that the Pennsylvania Supreme Court may review *de novo* attorney disciplinary hearings without being bound by the findings of the hearing committee or the Disciplinary Board. The second rule was a Pennsylvania Rule of Disciplinary Enforcement which provided that attorneys facing disciplinary charges had the right to oral argument before the Supreme Court, but made no provision for an evidentiary hearing before the Court. Stern challenged the Supreme Court's practice of rejecting administrative findings of fact without conducting an evidentiary hearing.

The district court denied the Justices' motion to dismiss the action on the basis of lack of subject matter jurisdiction, but also denied the injunction requested by Stern. On appeal, we held that the district court lacked subject matter jurisdiction over Stern's complaint, because the complaint sought reversal of the decision of the Supreme Court of Pennsylvania, in contravention of *Rooker-Feldman*.

We based our decision in Stern on our determination that the remedy sought would, if granted, force the district court to review the merits of the state court's decision, for two reasons. First, Stern sought a permanent injunction preventing the state court from disbarring him and others without a hearing. We noted that this remedy, if granted, would effectively reverse the state court judgment, and thus improperly review that judgment.

Second, Stern also requested a temporary restraining order and a preliminary injunction. We noted that both of these remedies "required him to demonstrate the likelihood of success on the merits and irreparable harm to *himself*, thus shifting the focus to the actions of the Supreme Court of Pennsylvania in his particular case." ([E]mphasis in original). Thus we concluded that Stern's complaint, although couched in terms of a general challenge to the constitutionality of the state rules, was in reality an attempt to obtain reversal of the state court judgment which disbarred him.[7]

III.

DISCUSSION

A. *Subject Matter Jurisdiction*

We must determine on which side of the *Rooker-Feldman* line Centifanti's complaint falls. * * *

Our first task is to characterize the precise object of Centifanti's constitutional challenge. In Feldman, the appellants challenged the decisions of a state court not to waive bar application requirements in their cases, but they also made a general challenge to the constitutionality of those requirements. The Supreme Court emphasized the fundamental difference between the two types of challenges. Here Centifanti challenges the constitutionality of the Pennsylvania rules as they exist, rather than the state court's application of them to deny his petition. As in Feldman, Centifanti's claims reflect "general challenges to state bar rules, promulgated by [a] state court[ ] in nonjudicial proceedings, which do not require review of a final state-court judgment in a particular case." Thus, Centifanti's complaint is in the nature of those Feldman-type claims (general challenges to the constitutionality of state supreme court rules) over which the district court

7 Our decision in Stern was also influenced by the excessive factual detail in Stern's complaint. We noted that "[t]he complaint and the stipulation of facts contained extensive exposition of the specific facts in Stern's case, which hardly would have been necessary if the district court were being asked only to 'assess the validity' of the rule in its general application." ([Q]uoting Feldman.)

has jurisdiction, and does not run afoul of the prohibition against appeals of state court decisions to lower federal courts.

As in Stern, examining the nature of the specific relief requested will aid us in determining what is being challenged and, thus, whether the district court has subject matter jurisdiction. In his due process claim, Centifanti requests a declaratory judgment that "the rules and procedures for considering petitions for reinstatement of suspended attorneys are unconstitutional." This would not require the district court to review the state supreme court decision. The declaratory judgment Centifanti seeks is prospective and directed toward "the rules and procedures for considering [future] petitions for reinstatement," rather than toward the decision of the state supreme court on Centifanti's prior petition. In Stern, we noted that Stern requested a declaratory judgment as well as injunctive relief, and we expressed no jurisdictional difficulty with the former.[8]

Centifanti also sought "injunctive relief directing the Defendant Justices to afford plaintiff and all similarly situated future petitioners for reinstatement Due Process prior to denial of their petitions," including the right to a hearing before the Justices, and the right to submit briefs to them and to receive a statement of reasons from them. Centifanti's request for a permanent injunction differs significantly from the injunction sought in Stern. Stern sought an injunction restraining the state supreme court from disbarring him and similarly situated attorneys unless the court, in cases where it plans to reject the findings of the hearing committee ("which of course would include Stern's case," we noted), first grants an evidentiary hearing. We considered this an improper attempt to enjoin, albeit conditionally, the enforcement of the state supreme court judgment disbarring Stern.

In contrast to the injunction sought in Stern, Centifanti seeks to enjoin the Justices to direct that they "afford *plaintiff and all similarly situated future petitioners for reinstatement* Due Process prior to the denial of their petitions." ([E]mphasis added). Centifanti argues, and we agree, that the complaint's joint reference to Centifanti "and all similarly situated future petitioners" indicates that he seeks *prospective* relief. He does not request the district court to interfere in any way with the decision of the Pennsylvania Supreme Court to deny his petition, or with

8 In fact, we strongly implied in Stern that a challenge seeking declaratory relief did *not* violate the *Rooker-Feldman* doctrine. Stern had argued that his case was similar to a case from another circuit in which the court of appeals held that the district court had jurisdiction over a challenge to a state's procedural rule governing attorney discipline. We rejected Stern's comparison, noting that [that case], the plaintiff requested *only declaratory relief* and a hearing, *not an injunction*. ([E]mphasis added).

Of course, the substance and not the form of the requested relief is ultimately controlling. For example, a federal court would not have jurisdiction over a complaint seeking a "declaration" that a state court's decision not to waive a bar application requirement was arbitrary and capricious. This certainly would raise a retrospective challenge to a state court decision.

the enforcement of that decision. Instead, he requests an injunction ordering the state court to correct alleged constitutional defects in the procedural rules applied in reaching that decision. Although such relief, if granted, could affect *future* decisions of the state supreme court, it would not require review of a past decision. Thus, we hold that the district court has subject matter jurisdiction over the due process claim.

Centifanti's requests for injunctive relief in his equal protection claim * * * are framed in terms identical to his due process claim. That is, they seek prospective relief in the form of ordering the Justices to remedy the alleged defects for the purposes of future reinstatement proceedings. Thus, the analysis we have set forth above of his due process claim applies as well to these additional constitutional challenges.

We must also determine whether Centifanti's claims are "inextricably intertwined" with the merits of the state court's denial of Centifanti's petition. In his concurring opinion in Pennzoil Co. v. Texaco, Inc., Justice Marshall addressed the problem of determining when a constitutional claim is "inextricably intertwined" with the particular decision of a state court:

> While the question whether a federal constitutional challenge is inextricably intertwined with the merits of a state-court judgment may sometimes be difficult to answer, it is apparent, as a first step, that the federal claim is inextricably intertwined with the state-court judgment if the federal claim succeeds only to the extent that the state court wrongly decided the issues before it. Where federal relief can only be predicated upon a conviction that the state court was wrong, it is difficult to conceive the federal proceeding as, in substance, anything other than a prohibited appeal of the state-court judgment.

In the instant case, the district court could hold that the state rules in question violate the Constitution, without holding that the Pennsylvania Supreme Court erred in denying Centifanti's petition for reinstatement. Thus, the federal claim is not inextricably intertwined with the state court judgment.

Food for Thought

If a favorable judgment will not change Centifanti's status as a suspended attorney, does he have standing to raise the challenge or will the court dismiss the action because it fails to meet the redressability prong of the constitutional standing inquiry? Or does the fact that Centifanti can again apply for reinstatement after a favorable federal ruling save him?

B. *Amendment of the Complaint*

In order for the district court to have subject matter jurisdiction over

Centifanti's complaint, the complaint must challenge the *rules* promulgated by the court, rather than the court's *decision* on Centifanti's petition for reinstatement. Thus, Centifanti's complaint need only contain enough factual detail to enable him to establish standing to bring an action pursuant to 42 U.S.C. § 1983 challenging the state supreme court rules.

Centifanti includes in his complaint far more detail than is necessary to mount a general constitutional challenge to the Pennsylvania rules. He describes his productivity since his suspension from the practice of law, his rehabilitation from an alcohol problem, his completion of probation, and his numerous character references. He also describes the hearing committee's and Disciplinary Board's strong recommendations for reinstatement. However, the facts alleged are simply outside the scope of and irrelevant to a federal district court's review of state court-promulgated rules. The excessive detail undermines the validity of Centifanti's general constitutional challenge, and his complaint begins to resemble an attempt to seek improper review of the state supreme court decision.

In his supplemental response to defendant's motion for summary judgment, Centifanti moved, in the alternative, for leave to amend his complaint to eliminate the improper factual detail from the complaint. The district court denied the motion, stating that "plaintiff's proposal to amend the complaint by deleting much of the personal detail does not alter the fundamental nature of this action which is, as it has always been, to challenge the Pennsylvania Supreme Court's judgment." ([F]ootnote omitted).

* * *

The district court determined that it lacked subject matter jurisdiction over Centifanti's complaint under the *Rooker-Feldman* doctrine. Based on this conclusion, it denied the motion to amend the complaint, asserting simply that an amendment would not cure the jurisdictional defect, and thus by implication, that the amendment would not survive a motion to dismiss. Because we hold that the district court has subject matter jurisdiction over the complaint, we determine that the amendment would survive a motion to dismiss for lack of subject matter jurisdiction.

Take Note

As the court observes in footnote 7, a plaintiff seeking federal judicial intervention to permit him to resume practice may plead himself out of court under *Rooker-Feldman*. Ordinarily mere surplusage in a complaint poses no problem, but here focusing on the facts of the applicant's situation rather than on the rules of decision may cause the court to conclude that the plaintiff is attacking the judgment in his case rather than the rules governing review of attorney cases generally.

The district court abused its discretion in denying the motion for leave to amend the complaint, and we will reverse the district court's order.[11]

FYI

Abuse of discretion is the most difficult review standard for an appellant to meet. The court had noted that Centifanti made a motion to amend the complaint rather than amending as of right as Rule 15 would have permitted. The Third Circuit said it would therefore consider the case as if leave to amend was necessary. Do you think the fact that Centifanti could have amended without the district court's permission nonetheless influenced the appellate judges in finding that there had been an abuse of discretion?

* * *

D. *Statute of Limitations and Res Judicata*

The district court, having decided that it lacked jurisdiction over the instant matter and having denied leave to amend the complaint, expressly did not reach the Justices' claims that the proposed amended complaint would be barred by Pennsylvania's two year statute of limitations for tort actions and by principles of issue and claim preclusion. We address these two questions now.

Food for Thought

What is going on here? Ordinarily, if a lower court has not considered one or more issues in reaching its decision, the appellate court will remand so that the lower court can address the remaining issues. Why do you think that the Third Circuit did not follow that practice here?

With regard to the statute of limitations, the Justices argue that Centifanti's cause of action accrued in 1983, when Centifanti filed his petition for reinstatement. They note that Centifanti's section 1983 action was brought in 1987, beyond the two-year statute of limitations for tort actions—and thus for section 1983 actions—in Pennsylvania. The Justices argue that because Centifanti is alleging a general infirmity in the state supreme court rules rather than a defect in the decision on his petition, Centifanti did not have to wait until his petition was denied to bring suit.

11 We recognize that in Stern the excessive factual detail in the complaint was a factor in our characterizing that complaint as an attempt at improper review of the state court decision. In that case, however, we did not have occasion to address the issue of amending the defective complaint, as Stern apparently did not file an amended complaint or move for leave to do so. Moreover, our decision in Stern was based primarily on the retrospective nature of the specific injunction sought, as discussed above. Thus, Stern does not prevent us from reversing the district court on its denial of the motion to amend.

We find the Justices' arguments unpersuasive. First, we observe that Centifanti remains suspended from the practice of law, and thus he alleges what is in essence a continuing wrong. His cause of action continues to accrue on each day of the alleged wrong. Second, even if we did not determine that the cause of action continued to accrue each day, we would nevertheless find the complaint not barred by the statute of limitations. Although we agree with the Justices that Centifanti is alleging a defect in the rules and not in the state court's decision, this does not mean that the cause of action accrued as soon as he filed his reinstatement petition. Centifanti did not have standing to challenge the rules until he had suffered or was about to suffer an actual injury. This did not occur until the Pennsylvania Supreme Court denied his petition in July of 1986, or at least until the hearing committee and the Disciplinary Board recommended his reinstatement. He filed his complaint in the federal district court in January of 1987, well within two years of both the Court's denial and the Board's recommendation.

Take Note

Observe that the defendants are characterizing Centifanti's challenge inconsistently here. With respect to the *Rooker-Feldman* doctrine, they argued that the challenge was to their *decision* on the petition for reinstatement, but with respect to the statute-of-limitations question, they argue that the challenge was to the general rules and therefore that Centifanti's claim accrued much earlier.

The Justices also argue that Centifanti could have raised his constitutional claims in the reinstatement proceeding in the state supreme court, or before the hearing committee or Disciplinary Board, and that his failure to do so bars the district court from hearing those claims under the doctrine of res judicata. In Feldman, the Supreme Court expressly declined to reach the issue of res judicata. The Justices cite several cases in their brief which hold that res judicata may apply to an attorney's constitutional challenges to procedural rules where the claims could have been but were not litigated in the state-court attorney disciplinary proceedings.

Take Note!

In one sense, this is where Pennsylvania's R.D.E. rules bite back. The court noted they provide for very limited petitioner participation. That *may* be constitutional (note that the court says nothing about the merits), but the court appears to conclude that those truncated procedures do not satisfy the general rule of claim preclusion that prevents later consideration of matters that were or could have been litigated.

Centifanti does not dispute that res judicata *may* apply in such cases, but he argues that he did not have a realistic opportunity to raise his federal constitutional claims in the state court proceeding. We agree that on the record before us and in the factual context of his particular application for reinstatement, Centifanti did not have a realistic opportunity to fully and fairly litigate these issues. Thus, we determine that he is not barred by res judicata from bringing his constitutional claims in the district court.

IV.

CONCLUSION

For the reasons discussed, we will reverse the district court's order dismissing the complaint for lack of subject matter jurisdiction. We will also reverse the court's order denying Centifanti leave to amend his complaint to delete the improper factual detail. * * * Finally, we determine that neither the statute of limitations nor res judicata preclude this action.

Costs taxed against appellees.

Notes and Questions

1. Centifanti is attempting to have the federal courts declare unconstitutional the Pennsylvania Supreme Court's rules for adjudicating applications for reinstatement to the bar. Was the injury of which Centifanti complains suffered at the hands of the Pennsylvania Supreme Court's judgment or from some independent source? Does the *Rooker-Feldman* doctrine aim to protect state *courts* or state *judgments* from federal judicial interference?

2. a) If Centifanti gets relief, clearly it will affect the efficacy of the Pennsylvania Supreme Court's previous orders denying him leave to file a brief or have an evidentiary hearing. Why does that not violate *Rooker-Feldman*?

b) Is it really possible for the federal court to say that the rules denying Centifanti reinstatement were unconstitutional without saying that the Pennsylvania Supreme Court committed constitutional error in reaching its decision under those rules? Is the difference that the court here is making no effort to give its ruling coercive effect with respect to the state courts? If the ruling can have no coercive effect at all, then does it amount to an advisory opinion?

c) Does the court's distinction between declaratory and injunctive relief hold up? See particularly Note 8 in the opinion. In the Younger abstention context, the Supreme Court has noted that a declaratory judgment may interfere with state judicial proceedings just as much as an injunction. (Note 10 on page 835 discusses *Samuels v. Mackell*, the case decided with Younger v. Harris in which the Court declined to allow a plaintiff to evade Younger's admonition against enjoining pending state criminal proceedings by seeking declaratory relief instead.) For that matter, the second section of the Declaratory Judgment Act, 28 U.S.C. § 2202, explicitly authorizes " * * * further necessary or proper relief based on a declaratory judgment * * * ." Under the Third Circuit's reasoning, could Stern have accomplished in two steps what the court forbade him to do in one? On the other hand, if one takes the position that the successful declaratory judgment plaintiff cannot avail himself of § 2202 without running afoul of *Rooker-Feldman*, then is there an insurmountable standing problem under the doctrine of *Simon v. Eastern Kentucky Welfare Rights Organization*, 426 U.S. 26 (1976), because the relief requested will not redress the plaintiff's injury?

3. a) Why is Centifanti's claim not subject to the same objections as Stern's? He is in court only because of the adverse decision. If the Pennsylvania Supreme Court had not acted on his application when he filed the federal suit, or if he had not yet sought reinstatement, would his case be justiciable under Article III?

b) Is the real difference between Centifanti and Stern the fact that Stern was trying to undo a state court judgment that had expelled him from the bar, whereas Centifanti was trying to set up a future application for reentry?

4. Is it only Centifanti's on-going entitlement to apply for reinstatement that enables him to evade the *Rooker-Feldman* bar that Stern encountered? If so, should one conclude that only "applications" cases can survive a *Rooker-Feldman* attack?

5. Would Stern have been better off for *Rooker-Feldman* purposes if he mounted his federal challenge to Pennsylvania's rules while his state proceeding was still before the state's Rule of Disciplinary Enforcement Board? Then there would have been no state court judgment. On the other hand, would Stern then have faced insurmountable problems under either the Anti-Injunction Act, 28 U.S.C. § 2283 (*see* pages 784-98 of the text) or under the Younger abstention doctrine (*see* pages 821-75 of the text)?

3. Appeal vs. Collateral Attack vs. Independent Action

Kamilewicz v. Bank of Boston Corporation

United States Court of Appeals for the Seventh Circuit, 1996.
92 F.3d 506.

TERENCE T. EVANS, Circuit Judge.

A class action in Alabama cost Dexter Kamilewicz $91.33 in attorney fees to recover $2.19 on the merits. When he learned of this news, he and the other plaintiffs (his wife and Martha Preston) sued the class action attorneys (as well as certain defendants in the Alabama action) in the District Court for the Northern District of Illinois. There, to add to their chagrin, they ran up against another obstacle—the *Rooker-Feldman* doctrine. This is their appeal from an order dismissing their federal case for lack of subject matter jurisdiction.

Kamilewicz and the other plaintiffs have had mortgages serviced by BancBoston Mortgage Corporation, one of the defendants. They were among an estimated 715,000 members of a class in a nationwide class action filed in the circuit court for Mobile County, Alabama. The suit [*Hoffman*] challenged the manner in which BancBoston calculated the amount of surplus each member of the class was required to maintain in their escrow accounts. Deposits to the escrow accounts were paid as part of the class members' monthly mortgage payments. There was no question regarding the ultimate ownership of the surplus; it belonged to the mortgagor and was to be returned when the mortgage debt was satisfied. The issue in the lawsuit was the propriety of BancBoston's holding the surplus until the time it would be returned to the mortgagor.

In October 1993, the Alabama court granted partial summary judgment in favor of the plaintiff class. The court found that BancBoston's practice was, in fact, inconsistent with the terms of the mortgages. Then in October 1995, counsel for the class prepared a notice of a proposed settlement of the suit. The notice stated that the settlement was "fair, reasonable, adequate, and in the best interests of the class" and that the attorney fees sought were "reasonable" and would "not exceed one-third of the economic benefit" to the class. Bank of Boston—one of the defendants—objected to the notice because it failed to advise the class that there were "substantial adverse effects" to the proposed settlement.

Those perceived adverse effects were that if BancBoston were ordered to refund the escrow surplus and if the

Food for Thought

Why did the class action defendants have standing to raise this argument? Were they exposed to harm if the adverse effects came to pass?

attorneys for the class were to seek attorney fees out of the refund, some class members would suffer an out-of-pocket loss as a result of the lawsuit. It should be noted here that the Bank of Boston and BancBoston had offered, prior to the grant of partial summary judgment in 1993, to settle the litigation. As part of that proposed settlement, the bank and BancBoston would have had to pay $500,000 in attorney fees out of the banks' own funds, and the entire amount of the escrow refund would have gone to the class members.

Nevertheless, the Alabama court approved the proposed notice and held a fairness hearing on January 10 and 11, 1994. On January 24, 1994, the court approved the settlement under which the class members received one-time interest payments ranging from $0.00 to $8.76. The court also found the attorney fees reasonable. The fee award was a percentage of the escrow accounts, or, the complaint in the present case asserts, in excess of $14 million. The fact may be that the award was closer to $8,500,000, but because in either event we are talking about significant amounts of money, the actual amount is not material and, of course, the allegations of the complaint are accepted as true at this point in the litigation. Under the settlement, BancBoston deducted attorney fees from the class members' escrow accounts. The deduction was recorded on the 1994 annual tax and interest statements as a "miscellaneous disbursement." In most cases, the "miscellaneous disbursement" was more—far more—than the interest refund. It was this statement that, understandably, caught Mr. Kamilewicz's eye.

Unhappy with the peculiar result of the class action suit in Alabama, Mr. and Mrs. Kamilewicz and Ms. Preston filed the present federal class action against the bank and the mortgage company, and the plaintiffs' attorneys in the Alabama action. The complaint contained allegations of violations of the Racketeer Influenced and Corrupt Organizations Act, 18 U.S.C. § 1962, and of the Civil Rights Act, 42 U.S.C. § 1983, as well as claims of common law fraud, negligent misrepresentation, attorney malpractice, breach of fiduciary duty, and conversion. In turn, the defendants in the federal case filed a motion with the Alabama court seeking an order directed to the Kamilewicz plaintiffs to show cause why they were not bound by the January 1994 order of that court. A hearing was scheduled in Alabama, to which the Kamilewicz plaintiffs sent an attorney for the purpose of stating that they would not participate in the hearing because they contested whether Alabama had personal jurisdiction over them. On January 30, 1996, the Alabama court reaffirmed the order of settlement.

Meanwhile, back in Chicago, on December 15, 1995, Judge Paul Plunkett of the Northern District of Illinois had entered his order dismissing the federal case for lack of subject matter jurisdiction. He found that even though the federal case was "dressed up" as a claim for RICO damages or for attorney malpractice, it was, nevertheless, a collateral attack on a state court judgment which would require that he consider issues "inextricably intertwined" with the state court case. This he was prohibited to do, he concluded, under the doctrine known as *Rooker-Feldman.*

* * * [W]e find ourselves in agreement with the district court.

We first note that the exact ground on which the plaintiffs and, for that matter, the *Amici*, who are attorneys general from several states, stand in this appeal is a little like shifting sand. The plaintiffs argue that the judgment of the Alabama court is null and void because the court did not have personal jurisdiction over them and that the special protections required for class actions—notice, adequate representation, etc.—were not complied with. However, they also say that they are not seeking to overturn the Alabama judgment. Then, they state that where the district court went wrong was to use a state court judgment which was "null and void" as the basis for the *Rooker-Feldman* bar. In addition, plaintiffs veer into a claim that the January 30, 1996, Alabama court order cannot be a basis for the *Rooker-Feldman* bar because there was no personal jurisdiction over them, and furthermore that fraud claims are somehow outside the *Rooker-Feldman* bar. The *Amici* say that they do not want to establish an exception to the general rule that absent class members may be bound by a nationwide class action settlement, but that on the unusual—and egregious—facts of this case, the Kamilewicz action should be allowed to proceed.

* * *

Food for Thought

If *Amici* did not want an exception to the general rule, on what legal theory could the district court have allowed the case to proceed?

It becomes necessary to our analysis * * * to determine whether what the federal court was asked to do in this case was, essentially, review a decision of a state court. Our cases offer means by which that determination is made. We ask whether the federal plaintiff seeks to set aside a state court judgment or whether he is, in fact, presenting an independent claim. Put another way, if the injury which the federal plaintiff alleges resulted from the state court judgment itself, then *Rooker-Feldman* controls, and the lower federal courts lack jurisdiction over the claim. It does not matter that the state court judgment might be erroneous or even unconstitutional. Nor does it matter that the time for appeal to the United States Supreme Court may have passed.

In addition, the state and federal cases also do not need to be directly on point. The Court found a lack of jurisdiction in Feldman itself when the federal constitutional claims were "inextricably intertwined," with the state court judgment. As we have explained, lower federal courts might be engaging in impermissible appellate review even when asked to entertain a claim that was not argued in the state court but was "inextricably intertwined" with the state court judgment.

Our cases have attempted to make the analysis of this issue easier by offering a sometimes helpful tip. That tip is that often, if a federal plaintiff was the plaintiff in the state court action, the doctrine he must contend with is res judicata, not *Rooker-Feldman.* On the other hand, if the federal plaintiff was the defendant in state court, *Rooker-Feldman* is the applicable doctrine. The tip, however, is merely that, and allows exceptions. * * * [B]oth the *Rooker* and *Feldman* plaintiffs were also plaintiffs in the state judicial proceedings. Although it may be that the federal plaintiff's position as either a plaintiff or a defendant in the state court proceeding will "usually coalesce with the source-of-the-injury standard," as we said in *Garry,* it may not always do so, and the important issue remains the source of the injury: the issue is whether the federal plaintiff is injured by the state court judgment or by a prior injury at the hands of the defendant.

How does all of this theory apply to the case before us? As a preliminary matter, we note that the Alabama court specifically found the settlement to be fair and approved the fees. In his order of January 24, 1994, the state judge found that the notice complied with all requirements of due process, that the consent decree was fair and reasonable, and that the attorney fees were reasonable.

Plaintiffs seem to be urging us to reach the conclusion that we can overturn the decision of the Alabama court insofar as it involved a determination that procedural due process was complied with. As support for this proposition, they rely on decisions which hold that a party can attack a *default* judgment against him if it is entered by a court without personal jurisdiction over him. We see significant differences between default judgments and the judgment under attack here. We reject the plaintiffs' far-reaching proposed exception to the *Rooker-Feldman* doctrine.

Another argument which seems slightly off-center is that the January 30, 1996, order, finding the allegations of fraud "baseless," is not subject to a *Rooker-Feldman* bar because it was entered in the absence of personal jurisdiction over the plaintiffs and it was entered after the federal lawsuit was filed. This argument is tied to the claim that the plaintiffs were precluded from litigating their fraud claim in the state court, and thus were required to—or had a right to—litigate it in federal court.

The January 30 order itself is not material to the issues before us. It is not necessary to rely on it to determine that the federal lawsuit was properly dismissed. The fact is that the proper court for an assertion of fraud in the procurement of a judgment is the one which rendered the judgment. * * *

Alabama has a procedure by which a litigant can assert an independent action for fraud upon the court within three years of the entry of the fraudulently induced judgment. In addition, the Alabama court retained continuing jurisdiction over the class action. It is not for the federal court to decide these issues.

* * *

The Kamilewiczes were class member/plaintiffs in the Alabama suit. The part of the judgment they are unhappy with is the approval of the settlement as to the fees to be paid to their attorneys—fees which were assessed against them. The district court concluded that the *Kamilewicz* plaintiffs were in the position of defendants in this aspect of the state court proceedings. That conclusion has some support in logic and bolsters a finding of a *Rooker-Feldman* bar. More important, however, is the fact that the plaintiffs' injuries are a result of the state court judgment. Their claim in federal court is a multi-pronged attack on the approval of the settlement regarding the attorney fees issue. Regardless of which of the specific federal claims the district court were to consider, it would run directly into the state court finding, entered after a two-day fairness hearing—that the fees were reasonable. The federal claims are "inextricably intertwined" with the state court judgment, whether that judgment is right or wrong.

We won't deny that the Alabama judgment seems questionable on the surface. How can it be right that a plaintiff should recover less than $10 and have to pay nearly $100 in fees? But how can we—or the district court—know that we would have ruled another way? To determine that, we would have to go through the steps already taken in the state court—precisely what lower federal courts are not allowed to do under *Rooker-Feldman*. And perhaps if we undertook that analysis we would find that some less tangible economic benefit to the class justified the settlement.

That the facts seem at least superficially egregious brings us to the arguments of *Amici* that on facts such as these an exception of some undefined sort should be carved out, and that if the plaintiff class was actually in the position of defendants on the attorney fees issue, then even under Phillips Petroleum Co. v. Shutts (1985), perhaps personal jurisdiction was lacking in the Alabama court. We decline to take the step urged by the *Amici*.

Take Note

The Shutts Court's rationale does not stand up well to even cursory scrutiny. The typical case exposes defendants to monetary loss. A class action exposes absent plaintiffs to loss of property—the causes of action they possess individually. *Kamilewicz* may be the perfect case to demonstrate the Court's shortsightedness.

In Shutts, the Court loosened somewhat the requirements for assertion of personal jurisdiction over members of a plaintiff class and determined that due process would be satisfied if there was notice, an opportunity to appear in person or by counsel, an opportunity to opt out of the class, and adequate representation. The rationale was, in part, that absent plaintiffs ordinarily do not face the same exposure as defendants. *Amici* argue that if on the attorney fees issue the *Kamilewicz* plaintiffs were actually in the position of defendants, then due process requires that issues of personal jurisdiction be assessed under the traditional minimum contacts analysis of International Shoe Co. v. Washington (1945).

Even were we to accept the argument, it does not change the fact that lower federal courts cannot review decisions of the state court. Here, the state court approved the settlement, including the fees. The Supreme Court of Alabama or the United States Supreme Court could reverse the decision were either so inclined. The federal district court, on the other hand, cannot review the Alabama decision. We also note the obvious—that the posture of the Alabama case is not unique. In class actions, often the fees are a percentage of the award granted to the plaintiff class. The argument of Amici, if accepted, could have ramifications far beyond this case.

Because we agree that *Rooker-Feldman* bars this action, the judgment of the district court is AFFIRMED.

Kamilewicz v. Bank of Boston Corporation

United States Court of Appeals for the Seventh Circuit, 1996.
100 F.3d 1348.

ON PETITION FOR REHEARING WITH SUGGESTION
FOR REHEARING EN BANC

ORDER

A panel decided this case on August 8, 1996. On August 22, 1996, the plaintiffs-appellants filed a petition for rehearing and suggestion for rehearing en banc. Subsequently, the judges on the panel voted to deny the petition for rehearing, and a vote was requested on the suggestion for rehearing en banc. A majority of the active members of the court have voted to deny rehearing en banc. Chief Judge Posner and Circuit Judges Easterbrook, Manion, Rovner, and Diane P. Wood voted to grant rehearing en banc.

IT IS THEREFORE ORDERED that the petition for rehearing is hereby DENIED. Because a majority of judges voted to deny rehearing en banc, the suggestion to do so is also DENIED.

Easterbrook, Circuit Judge, with whom Posner, Chief Judge, and Manion, Rovner, and Diane P. Wood, Circuit Judges, join, dissenting from the denial of rehearing en banc.

A class action contending that the Bank of Boston and its affiliates (collectively, the Bank) did not promptly post interest to real estate escrow accounts was filed in Alabama by a Chicago law firm. Settlement ensued, and the class members learned only what the notice told them. Few opted out or objected, because the maximum award to any class member was less than $9. Any recovery, however small, seemed preferable to initiating a separate suit or even bearing the costs of protesting the settlement's terms. After the state judge approved the pact, the Bank carried out its part: it disbursed more than $8 million to the class attorneys in legal fees and credited most accounts with paltry sums. Problem: the fees, equal to 5.32 percent of the balance in each account, were debited to the accounts. For many accounts the debit exceeded the credit. Dexter J. Kamilewicz, for example, received a credit of $2.19 and a debit of $91.33, for a loss of $89.14.

Outraged account holders hired new lawyers to sue their "champions" from the state case for malpractice, breach of fiduciary duty, indeed for fraud. Defendants insist that most members of the class emerged with net benefits, but they do not deny that many suffered net losses—and that these impending losses, known to those who negotiated the settlement, were not disclosed to the class members. Kamilewicz believes that even when the credit exceeded the debit the account holder lost, because the credit would have been made when the mortgage terminated and the escrowed sum was released; the real economic benefit was not the amount of the credit but the interest that could be earned from investing the payment sooner.

Kamilewicz and the other representative plaintiffs sued not only the lawyers for the plaintiff class in *Hoffman* but also the Bank and the Bank's lawyers. Everything the Bank did to affect Kamilewicz's interests was authorized by the judgment based on the settlement, so the Bank's inclusion in the case marked an effort to obtain collateral review of the state court's judgment. Kamilewicz argued that the judgment is void with respect to account holders who live outside Alabama—for what right does Alabama have to instruct financial institutions in Florida to debit the accounts of citizens of Maine and other states? (Despite its name, BancBoston's headquarters are in Florida, and the Kamilewiczes hail from Maine.) Class members are not bound when a state court exceeds its jurisdiction. The Attorneys General of Florida, Maine, and seven other states have filed a brief as amicus curiae to protest their citizens' treatment by Alabama. According to Kamilewicz, the Alabama judgment is doubly flawed, because the notice was so misleading that it denied the class members due process of law. A deficient notice means that the class members' right to opt out was defeated, which has jurisdictional consequences of its own. Lack of jurisdiction and unconstitutional procedures are recognized grounds for disregarding a judgment in a class action. But by asking for collateral review of a judgment, the Kamilewicz class invited the response: "In federal court?" Under the *Rooker-Feldman* doctrine, * * * the Supreme Court of the United States is the only federal court authorized to review a state court's judgment in civil litigation. Defendants invoked this rule and argued that the Kamilewicz class could obtain relief only from a state court. The district court agreed and dismissed the entire complaint for want of jurisdiction, and a panel of this court affirmed.

Suppose A sues B in a state that lacks any connection to B or to the dispute. B refuses to appear and the court enters a default judgment, which A attempts to collect using the processes of the federal court under the diversity jurisdiction. Would the court really direct B to pay, without inquiring into the jurisdiction of the state court? Certainly not in the fifth circuit, which has held that the *Rooker-Feldman* doctrine permits the kinds of collateral attacks that any state court of general jurisdiction could entertain. * * * When Hansberry v. Lee (1940) held that a judgment rendered without personal jurisdiction over members of the class is not entitled to full faith and credit, the Justices did not add: "except in federal court." Granted, the defendants in today's case are not trying to execute a judgment; they want to fend off a challenge to the status quo. But the difference between offensive and defensive use of a judgment is not important to the panel's conclusion, or to mine—which is that a judgment that is not entitled to full faith and credit does not acquire extra force via the *Rooker-Feldman* doctrine.

Collateral attacks based on lack of personal or subject-matter jurisdiction are proper, no less in class actions than in other cases—indeed, they are especially appropriate where class members are stunned to find that, although aligned as plaintiffs, they are net losers, just as if the original defendants had filed and prevailed on a counterclaim of which they received no notice and over which the state court had no jurisdiction. In effect, though not in name, this was a defendant class, attempting (unbeknownst to its members) to fend off predatory lawyers' claims to the balances in the escrow accounts. The substantial jurisdictional problems entailed by defendant classes, were aggravated by the class members' ignorance of their exposure.

In Matsushita Electric Industrial Co. v. Epstein (1996), members of a class in a securities case filed in state court initiated an independent action in federal court for the purpose of attacking the

Take Note!

Ordinarily, collateral attacks based on jurisdictional defects arise when the judgment creditor seeks to enforce the judgment in another forum. The judgment debtor, *if she defaulted on the original action*, then can resist enforcement on the ground that the judgment, entered in the absence of jurisdiction, is not entitled to full faith and credit, as you saw long ago in Pennoyer v. Neff (1877). Here, on the other hand, there was no ancillary enforcement action; the defendant banks simply handed over the money to the class attorneys, and the absent plaintiffs had "appeared" by counsel when they did not opt out of the class. By the time the class members found out about it, it was a *fait accompli*. This is why the banks objected to the proposed notice of settlement.

terms on which the state case had been settled. They argued that the state court lacked jurisdiction to resolve claims based on federal securities law. Ultimately they lost—but not on *Rooker-Feldman* grounds. The Supreme Court concluded that state judges may accept and enforce settlements of federal claims. This it held on the merits. It did not mention the possibility that the federal court lacked jurisdiction, which I think signifies how obvious it was to all concerned that the *Rooker-Feldman* doctrine is inapplicable. If it was inapplicable in *Matsushita*, it is inapplicable here too. I grant that *Matsushita* did not "hold" this, because it did not discuss jurisdiction. Shared assumptions are revealing nonetheless. And in today's case as in *Matsushita* the aggrieved class members may choose a new forum; they need not return to a court whose lack of jurisdiction is the basis of their position. None of this is to say that the Alabama court actually lacked jurisdiction, or that the notice was inadequate; to get anywhere against the Bank the Kamilewicz class must establish these things; but under the panel's approach the state court's judgment blocks federal litigation even if it lacked jurisdiction.

Next consider plaintiffs' claim against the *Hoffman* class counsel, which is not a collateral attack on a judgment. It takes the judgment as a given—indeed, it is only so long as the judgment stands that the litigant has a compensable loss. Neither state nor federal law requires a malpractice suit to be filed in the same court that handled the initial litigation. The *Rooker-Feldman* doctrine therefore does not apply to malpractice suits, which may be litigated in federal courts without regard to the location of the initial case. If the panel is right, no malpractice suit growing out of state litigation in which the judge awarded attorneys' fees—maybe no malpractice suit, period—may be brought in federal court, even if all requirements of the diversity jurisdiction have been satisfied. This holding is sufficiently troubling and affects so many other cases that it is worth the time of our court to consider the subject en banc.

The *Rooker-Feldman* doctrine has two rationales: first, that the decision of a state court reached after notice and opportunity for hearing is not an independent violation of the Constitution, and therefore is not actionable under 42 U.S.C. § 1983; second, that by virtue of 28 U.S.C. § 1257 only the Supreme Court may review the decision of a state court in civil litigation. The rationales of the doctrine identify important limits: the first theme is irrelevant to a malpractice suit, and the second is beside the point, because the plaintiff does not seek review of the decision. The original parties' entitlements *vis-à-vis* each other are fixed by the judgment. The contest now is between the litigant and his lawyer. We have emphasized this distinction many times—not only in malpractice cases, but also when the loser tries to get relief from judgment because of the lawyer's incompetence.

Consider a related sequence of litigation. A sells a painting to B, and before delivering the painting to B sells it again to C. Then A learns that the painting has increased in value and holds onto it. B sues A in state court for specific performance and prevails. Next C sues A for damages. Surely the *Rooker-Feldman* doctrine does not foreclose C from using federal court. C's suit does not attack the judgment (B keeps the painting); C wasn't even a party to B v. A; and the cause of C's loss wasn't the judgment, but A's double dealing. So too with malpractice litigation: it is a suit against a nonparty (the lawyer) alleging harm from incompetent or deceitful acts. That the lawyer's misconduct occurred in a judicial proceeding doesn't insulate the lawyer from liability, even when the *Rooker-Feldman* doctrine insulates the *judgment*.

The Supreme Court's most recent discussion of the *Rooker-Feldman* doctrine strongly implies that it does not bar malpractice litigation. Johnson v. De Grandy (1994), holds that the *Rooker-Feldman* doctrine does not bar voting rights litigation filed by the United States, even though the districts being challenged were approved by a state court in adversarial litigation. The Court observed that the United States was not a party to the state case and therefore could not have presented its claim by petition for certiorari under § 1257; the inability to do so meant that it could litigate independently. We, too, have held that the *Rooker-Feldman* doctrine does not affect suits by or against persons who were not parties to the initial case. It may apply when the non-parties occupy positions functionally identical to the parties (for example, when a person whose property has been condemned by a city retaliates with a suit against the mayor), but the class attorneys are not the Bank's alter egos. The attorneys representing the *Hoffman* class were not parties to the Alabama case. Neither were the class members. Absent class members are represented by the named plaintiffs and their lawyers, but they aren't parties, a point reflected in federal litigation by disregarding their citizenship. They are ignored in negotiating settlements as well. A real party's lack of assent means that there is no settlement; but the missing class members don't sign the settlement, and their objection is not dispositive. It is crammed down the throats of objectors, which cannot be done to real parties. What is more, the members of the Kamilewicz class could not have presented their malpractice arguments to the Supreme Court by petition for certiorari under § 1257: they did not discover the malpractice until later (it was not reflected in the record of the state proceeding); it was not litigated in the *Hoffman* case; class members can't seek appellate review without intervening, which further illustrates their non-party status; and of course malpractice is not a federal claim, so it is outside the scope of § 1257. For some purposes missing class members are treated *like* parties, but only if the named plaintiffs adequately represent the interests of the class, and only if the unnamed members of the class receive adequate notice and elect not to opt out—which in this case is the very thing in dispute! It gets the cart before the horse to reject, as barred by a judgment, an effort by the absent class members to show that they were not properly brought into the state case and therefore are not affected by the judgment.

From all of this it follows that a malpractice action is not affected by the *Rooker-Feldman* doctrine. Does the fairness hearing required to approve the settlement of a class action make a difference? I think not. For the reasons just explained, absent class members (*especially* those who deny the state court's jurisdiction over them) are not parties and cannot be treated as bound by the findings implicit in the approval of the settlement and the award of fees to attorneys. The panel implied approval of the district court's conclusion that the class members were effectively defendants resisting financial demands by the attorneys, which makes the jurisdictional shortcoming clear and establishes that the judgment is not entitled to full faith and credit.

Take Note

The timing of the events is significant. The Alabama court entered its judgment in January, 1994. The only apparent notice to the absent class members of the actual monetary effects on them came "the 1994 annual tax and interest statements as a 'miscellaneous disbursement.' " Those statements reached the absent class members long after expiration of their time to seek to appeal the judgment of the Alabama court, and, as Judge Easterbrook points out, the Alabama trial court would have had to allow them to intervene before they could appeal. Query, though, what would have happened if they had sought direct review on jurisdictional grounds of the Alabama court's 1996 order reaffirming the settlement.

All jurisdictional doubts to one side, a settlement followed by a fairness hearing remains more like a contract than like litigation. Accordingly there is even less reason to apply the *Rooker-Feldman* doctrine than in a normal malpractice case, where the loss ensues from a genuine contest. Representative plaintiffs and their lawyers may be imperfect agents of the other class members—may even put one over on the court, in a staged performance. The lawyers support the settlement to get fees; the defendants support it to evade liability; the court can't vindicate the class's rights because the friendly presentation means that it lacks essential information. This possibility, a staple of the literature about class actions, enjoys judicial recognition. Recall that even the active opposition of class members does not automatically block the settlement, which therefore rests on the *lawyers'* consent, not the litigants' agreement or the legal decision of a court.

The Kamilewicz class asserts that it suffered harm from the *Hoffman* class lawyers' breach of their duties of care and loyalty in negotiating the settlement, which was concealed from the Alabama judge (and the class) by a further breach of the duty of loyalty in drafting the notice about the settlement. The notice not only didn't alert the absent class members to the impending loss but also pulled the wool over the state judge's eyes. Suing faithless agents is far from the core of the *Rooker-Feldman* doctrine, which should not be extended to block suits like this. "Were [plaintiff] merely claiming that the decision of the state court was incorrect, even that it denied him some constitutional right, the doctrine would indeed bar his claim. But if he claims, as he does, that people involved in the decision violated some independent right of his * * * then he can, without being blocked by the *Rooker-Feldman* doctrine, sue to vindicate that right."

The panel's decision is important. If I am right that the state court's award of attorneys' fees does not matter, then the decision logically bars all malpractice and related fiduciary-duty suits arising out of state litigation. We have entertained many, without seeing jurisdictional problems. And even if I am wrong about the sweep of the panel's decision, the issue is recurrent. * * * If the *Rooker-Feldman* doctrine applies to suits by the absent class members because a malpractice action is a collateral attack on the order approving the settlement and awarding attorneys' fees, then the law of preclusion (res judicata) should bar malpractice actions in any court, state or federal, and without regard to which judicial system handled the first case. Yet no one thinks that. A malpractice suit is an independent action. A (potential) defense of issue preclusion is defeated by the very theory of the claim: that the first judgment is unreliable because of the attorney's bungling. The bungler cannot point to the adverse judgment produced by his own incompetence to ward off the client's demand. The Kamilewicz class may fail in its proof, or it may encounter other obstacles, but the *Rooker-Feldman* doctrine does not close the door of the federal courthouse.

Notes and Questions

1. As Judge Easterbrook points out, one can attack a state court default judgment collaterally on jurisdictional grounds in a federal court enforcement proceeding. When a defendant receives a summons and fails to appear, he may resist a subsequent enforcement action on the ground that the state court lacked jurisdiction over him, either because the court had no basis upon which to exercise jurisdiction or because the summons was defective. (There are other possible attacks as well, but they are not relevant here.) In *Kamilewicz*, the plaintiffs had received a notice that they ignored and that they now claim conferred no jurisdiction on the Alabama court because both the notice itself and the representation of the class did not comport with the constitutional standards that *Phillips Petroleum Co. v. Shutts*, 472 U.S. 797 (1985), articulated. Is their position truly distinguishable from that of a defaulting defendant? Note that the Seventh Circuit's panel concedes that for purposes of the fee awards, the nominal plaintiffs were in fact in the position of defendants.

2. The plaintiffs' position is aggravated here because under the terms of the settlement, the attorneys essentially got automatic enforcement of the judgment. If the attorneys had had to bring an enforcement action against the plaintiffs to recover the fees (and before you say that it would not be worth their while for such small individual amounts, remember that they just represented a plaintiff class in exactly such a case), would the plaintiffs have been allowed to resist on jurisdictional grounds? Does the difference between a case in which the plaintiffs can resist and one in which they cannot simply depend on which side of the "v." the plaintiffs find themselves?

3. Given the Alabama court's determination that the attorneys' fees were reasonable, is there anything that *Rooker-Feldman* accomplishes here that res judicata would not do just as well? Does *Rooker-Feldman* ever accomplish anything beyond the reach of the preclusion doctrines? See Suzanna Sherry, *Judicial Federalism in the Trenches: The* Rooker-Feldman *Doctrine in Action*, 74 NOTRE DAME L. REV. 1085 (1999).

4. Judge Evans notes that the Alabama judgment may be "questionable" but says that the federal courts are in no position to evaluate it without reopening and relitigating the Alabama case. Are the plaintiffs asking the federal courts to evaluate the fairness of the Alabama proceedings or the fee award on the merits, or are they raising jurisdictional objections relying on *Shutts*?

5. Is there a meaningful distinction between attacking a judgment and attacking the correctness of a judgment? The plaintiffs here seek to file a malpractice claim against the attorneys. Malpractice claims generally do not have to be brought in the same court in which the alleged malpractice occurred. Why should this one? If the attorneys had not applied for a fee award from the Alabama court, would the malpractice action lie for *Rooker-Feldman* purposes? Suppose at the conclusion of a trial, the state judge tells a party's counsel that she has done "an excellent job." Would *Rooker-Feldman* then say that the federal courts are without jurisdiction to entertain a malpractice action from the unappreciative client?

6. Should the panel have dealt with *Matsushita*? Is Judge Easterbrook correct that it is apposite? Granted, *Matsushita* did not discuss *Rooker-Feldman*. Nonetheless, since the courts have emphasized that the doctrine goes to subject matter jurisdiction, and since a court can raise subject matter jurisdiction questions **sua sponte** (*see, e.g.*, *Louisville & Nashville Railroad v. Mottley* and *Smith v. Kansas City Title & Trust Co.*), does the fact that the Court decided the case on the merits suggest that it found no subject matter jurisdiction problem?

7. Is Judge Easterbrook's "painting" hypothetical apposite? Are the plaintiffs here analogous to B or C (or to both)? Does the hypothetical suggest that Judge Evans is correct that the plaintiffs are attacking the Alabama court's judgment of fairness?

8. Note that the lawyers will receive the money from the escrow accounts, which is all that the Alabama court ordered. The plaintiffs are not seeking an injunction against the disbursement; they seek damages in a separate action for claims not adjudicated in the first action. Should that make a difference for *Rooker-Feldman* purposes?

9. Is it really true, as Judge Easterbrook says, that absent class members are not parties to the action even though they have received service? If that is correct, then how can a judgment bind them? Is it possible to view someone as a party for some purposes and not for others? Are the provisions of Federal Rule of Civil Procedure 23 relevant insofar as they talk about intervention for absent class members?

10. Is *DeGrandy* helpful to the plaintiffs? Are they in a position analogous to the United States in that case? In this connection, consider *Devlin v. Scardelletti*, 536 U.S. 1 (2002), in which the Court ruled that an unnamed class member who was denied intervention can state objections to a proposed settlement and then appeal from an unfavorable ruling without intervening, provided that the appeal also challenges denial of the motion to intervene.

---

4. Threading the Needle: *Rooker-Feldman* and Standing

Facio v. Jones

United States Court of Appeals for the Tenth Circuit, 1991.
929 F.2d 541.

EBEL, Circuit Judge.

This is an appeal and cross-appeal from a judgment of the federal district court under 42 U.S.C. § 1983 which declared unconstitutional the Utah state rule requiring that a default judgment debtor show a meritorious defense before the default judgment against him could be vacated. The district court also granted plaintiff costs and attorney's fees under 42 U.S.C. § 1988. In addition, plaintiff cross-appeals the district court's denial of a request for attorney's fees against the state court judge. We do not reach the merits of this appeal because we find that the district court lacked subject matter jurisdiction to hear the original case.

FACTS

Gary Facio, the plaintiff below, wrote a bad check. Mr. Facio received notice that the check had bounced and thereafter sent a money order to cover the debit and expenses. For reasons not entirely clear, one appellant, Collection Agency Management, nevertheless instituted a civil action against Mr. Facio in a Utah state court based on the bad check. Although Mr. Facio was validly served with process and thus had received notice of that litigation, he failed to answer because he apparently believed that the money order had settled the controversy. Ultimately, a default judgment was entered against him. Mr. Facio then filed a motion to set aside the default judgment pursuant to Utah Rules of Civil Procedure 55(c) and 60(b). The state court judge—the Honorable Maurice Jones—denied the motion because Mr. Facio failed to present proof of a meritorious defense as required by the Utah Supreme Court's interpretation of Rules 55(c) and 60(b). Eventually, the judgment was satisfied through garnishment of Mr. Facio's wages and bank account.

Thereafter, Mr. Facio filed suit in federal district court. He sought

> declaratory relief under 42 U.S.C. § 1983 for deprivation of property without due process of law in violation of the Fourteenth Amendment * * * . Specifically, plaintiff contend[ed] that Judge Jones' application of Utah Rules of Civil Procedure 55(c) and 60(b) [was] unconstitutional to the extent that a defendant [was] required to offer proof of a meritorious defense * * * . By pendant [*sic*] claim, plaintiff challenge[d] the validity of the default and default judgment entered against him.

The district court agreed with Mr. Facio, finding that the Utah procedural requirement that a meritorious defense be presented before a default judgment could be set aside was unconstitutional. The district court set aside the default judgment and ordered costs to be paid by both Judge Jones and the collection agency and attorney's fees to be paid by the collection agency only. Judge Jones and the collection agency appealed. Mr. Facio cross-appealed, claiming that the district court did not articulate reasons sufficient to exempt Judge Jones from paying attorney's fees.

DISCUSSION

The district court considered the possibility that it did not have jurisdiction over the case. In particular, the court referred to the Tenth Circuit case of *Razatos v. Colorado Supreme Court,* 746 F.2d 1429 (10th Cir.1984), *cert. denied,* 471 U.S. 1016 (1985) for the proposition that "[i]t is clearly established law that the Supreme Court has the exclusive power to review state court decisions. However, federal trial courts can adjudicate civil rights complaints such as that brought by plaintiff without directly reviewing state court decisions." We disagree with that conclusion as it applies to the particular facts of this case. We hold that the district court did not have jurisdiction to consider Mr. Facio's lawsuit and, therefore, we do not reach the merits on appeal.

In his federal action, Mr. Facio seeks two types of relief. First, he wants the default judgment against him set aside. Second, he asks the federal courts to declare the Utah Rules of Civil Procedure 55(c) and 60(b) unconstitutional as applied by the Utah courts.

relief sought

To the extent that Mr. Facio sought to have the federal district court set aside a state default judgment, the federal court lacked jurisdiction to grant that relief. * * * Any such federal review has to be addressed directly to the United States Supreme Court from the state's highest court pursuant to 28 U.S.C. § 1257.

Mr. Facio also seeks a second form of relief that would have the federal court declare the Utah default rules unconstitutional as applied. However, *Feldman* not only prohibited direct review of state judgments by lower federal courts, but it also prohibited those federal courts from issuing any declaratory relief that is "inextricably intertwined" with the state court judgment. We believe that Mr. Facio's request for declaratory relief is inextricably intertwined with his request to vacate and to set aside the default judgment. In this case, the two forms of relief are so intertwined, in fact, that if Mr. Facio is not able to set aside the default judgment against him, he would lack standing to assert his second claim, which is the request that the federal court declare Utah's default judgment procedures unconstitutional. Unless Mr. Facio's default judgment is upset, his only interest in Utah's default judgment procedures is prospective and hypothetical in nature. He cannot establish a sufficient interest in the future application of those procedures to him to establish a constitutional case or controversy.

Because Mr. Facio's threshold ability to establish standing with regard to his claim for declaratory relief is dependent upon his ability to upset the default judgment against him, that presents a classic case of an inextricably intertwined relationship between the two requested types of relief. * * * For instance, this court * * * refused to allow a plaintiff to hide behind the language of a general attack on state procedures while bringing what was in reality a claim to overturn a state court decision. We stated * * * in a holding that is equally applicable here, that "[w]here a constitutional issue could have been reviewed on direct appeal by the state appellate courts, a litigant may not seek to reverse or modify the state court judgment by bringing a constitutional claim under 42 U.S.C. § 1983."

If the two forms of relief Mr. Facio seeks are separated and the request for declaratory relief is looked at in isolation, Mr. Facio lacks standing to assert that claim. He has not demonstrated any real chance of being subjected in the future to Utah's procedures for reversing default judgments. Indeed, after separating out Mr. Facio's impermissible request that the federal district court overturn the state judgment against him, his situation is indistinguishable from that of any other citizen of Utah who, without any palpable chance of being subjected to those procedures in the future, might desire to challenge that state's default judgment rule.

Our analysis is consistent with, and well-grounded in, Supreme Court cases which have held that while a plaintiff who has been constitutionally injured can bring a § 1983 action to recover damages, that same plaintiff cannot maintain a declaratory or injunctive action unless he or she can demonstrate a good chance of being likewise injured in the future. * * *

In [*City of Los Angeles v.*] *Lyons* [1983], a citizen brought suit under § 1983 in federal district court, alleging that Los Angeles police officers had unconstitutionally applied a dangerous "chokehold" to his neck. Plaintiff sought damages and also requested an injunction that would have prevented the police from using chokeholds in similar situations. The Court found that although Lyons had allegedly suffered actual harm—and could presumably recover damages under § 1983—he could not "demonstrate a case or controversy with the City that would justify the equitable relief sought" because "standing to seek the injunction requested depended on whether he was likely to suffer future injury from the use of the chokeholds by police officers."

* * *

The cases of *Feldman* and *Razatos* involved plaintiffs who had been denied admission to a particular state's bar, and therefore wanted to have the allegedly unconstitutional law invalidated so that they could practice law in the state or district. But in each case, it was clear that even though the federal district court could not reverse the adverse state court judgment that had been rendered against the plaintiffs, the plaintiffs still had standing because they could reapply to the state's bar. In other words, even though the individual state court decisions stood against them, they each still had an interest in practicing law in the state or district involved and therefore had standing to assert that the restrictive bar admission rules should be declared unconstitutional. Thus, in each of those cases the federal court had before it a real case or controversy.

In contrast, if Mr. Facio's default judgment stands—and it must because it is final under state law and under 28 U.S.C. § 1257 the federal district court has no jurisdiction to review it—he cannot demonstrate any continuing interest in having Utah's default judgment rules set aside. The default against him is final, whether or not the default judgment rules may later be held unconstitutional. Any ruling now that Utah's procedures to vacate default judgments are unconstitutional could not undo the judgment against Mr. Facio anymore than it would undo the countless other default judgments that presumably have been entered in Utah pursuant to this rule and have long since become final.

Unable to attack the final default judgment rendered against him and without any evidence that he will again be subject to Utah's default provisions, Mr. Facio is left with no interest greater than that of any other citizen of Utah. Accordingly,

Mr. Facio's action must be dismissed; the federal courts have "no jurisdiction to pronounce any statute, either of a State or of the United States, void, because irreconcilable with the Constitution, except as it is called upon to adjudge the legal rights of litigants in actual controversies."

We should add that any concern about whether the *Feldman* rule effectively isolates state court decisions from federal review is unfounded. First, there is the obvious alternative open to litigants—and it was open to Mr. Facio—to appeal the state court decision through the state courts and then to seek certiorari review by the United States Supreme Court. Second, it may be possible for some litigants (as, perhaps, credit companies) to demonstrate that the repeated application of default judgment rules operate to their continuing harm even though a particular case may be final. Thus, they may be able to attack the rule *if* they are able to establish that the particular rule sufficiently impedes their future action. However, Mr. Facio cannot demonstrate that requirement because for him this was a one-shot case. Indeed, the Supreme Court has stated that "[p]ast exposure to illegal conduct does not in itself show a present case or controversy regarding injunctive relief * * * if unaccompanied by any continuing, present adverse effects."

The *Feldman* rule is soundly and clearly based in the language of 28 U.S.C. § 1257 and in the public policy of federalism. Federal district courts are specifically proscribed from the business of reviewing state court judgments. Mr. Facio's request for an order reversing his final default judgment was outside the district court's jurisdiction. Likewise, his request for declaratory relief was hopelessly intertwined with his claim for retrospective relief. If the different remedies Mr. Facio seeks *are* separated, then he is left with no case or controversy to challenge the future application of that rule.

Thus, the district court did not have jurisdiction to consider Mr. Facio's claims. The district court order is hereby vacated and the matter is remanded with instructions that the action be dismissed for lack of jurisdiction.

Notes and Questions

1. Would (should) it make any difference in the disposition of this case if Utah law allows Facio to make an additional application in a state court to have the default judgment vacated? If so, why?

2. Assume (as the court implies) that the creditor knew the money order had satisfied the debt represented by the bounced check before the creditor sued on the check. If Utah allowed a tort action for either wrongful civil proceedings (a civil

equivalent of the tort of malicious prosecution) or for abuse of process, would Facio be able to pursue such a suit against the creditor in federal court (assuming that subject matter jurisdiction was not a problem) despite *Rooker-Feldman*? If not, why not? If so, then did Facio's counsel blunder by not including such a count in Facio's complaint?

3. Note that if Facio brought an abuse-of-process action independent of any other claim (such as one to set aside the Utah default judgment), the Utah judgment would remain intact and in effect, irrespective of the outcome of the abuse claim. Does *Rooker-Feldman* compel dismissal of any federal case that might tend do undo the practical effect of a state judgment, or does it only bar actions that would act upon the state judgment itself?

The Anti-Injunction Act, 28 U.S.C. § 2283, allows a federal court to enjoin state courts from proceeding with cases if necessary "to protect or effectuate its judgments." This is known as the "relitigation exception" and allows the federal courts to prevent state courts from relitigating claims or issues already decided in federal court. ERWIN CHEMERINSKY, FEDERAL COURTS § 11.2.4, at 749-52 (5th ed. 2007). Does that shed any light on how narrowly or broadly the federal courts should interpret *Rooker-Feldman*?

If Congress thought it necessary in the Anti-Injunction Act to create res-judicata-by-injunction (and that in cases in which the state trial courts certainly lack appellate jurisdiction with respect to federal judgments), should one conclude that Congress would regard res judicata as a sufficient protection for state judgments in federal courts, given the Full Faith and Credit Act, 28 U.S.C. § 1738? If so, does that suggest whether Congress would simultaneously have contemplated regulating this particular kind of federal court behavior through the various subject matter jurisdictional statutes? To put it another way, if the federal jurisdictional statutes create res judicata protection for state judgments, should one assume that Congress enacted a superfluous res judicata protection in § 1738?

4. Is the court's use of *City of Los Angeles v. Lyons* apt? If it is not, where does the analogy break down? If it is, does that not raise again the question of what *Rooker-Feldman* adds to the effects of § 1738 and justiciability doctrine? Now, one might say that *Rooker-Feldman*, insofar as one regards it as jurisdictional, in some sense preempts the effect of § 1738 because the courts decide subject matter jurisdiction issues before other issues, but one cannot raise the same point with respect to standing, which also goes to subject matter jurisdiction under Article III, § 2.

In some sense, there may be a sequencing problem in reconciling 28 U.S.C. § 1331 (and other subject matter jurisdiction statutes) as seen through the eyes of the *Rooker-Feldman* doctrine and 28 U.S.C. § 1738. If those jurisdictional statutes necessarily include the *Rooker-Feldman* concept because they do not authorize the inferior courts to hear appeals from the state courts, why did Congress think it necessary also to enact the Full Faith and Credit Act, 28 U.S.C. § 1738, which ostensibly accomplishes the same thing. If, on the other hand, those jurisdictional statutes do not include the *Rooker-Feldman* concept, then the need for § 1738 is clear, but the foundation for the Court's articulation of *Rooker-Feldman* is gone.

5. At bottom, what is it that the *Rooker-Feldman* doctrine should protect? Should it guard only against federal actions that by their terms might prevent enforcement of all or parts of state court judgments (such an action to set aside a judgment)? On the other hand, should it forbid any federal action that might have the practical (but not legal) effect of making the relief afforded by a state judgment less satisfying to the state court victor than it might otherwise have been? In *Kamilewicz*, for example, if the plaintiffs pursued a malpractice action against the class attorneys, that would not deprive the state judgment for attorneys fees of any force; the attorneys would still get the fees from the escrow accounts. They might, of course, be less than satisfied with that multimillion dollar fee if the *Kamilewicz* class succeeded in recovering from them an even larger sum as malpractice damages. Should that rise to the level of *Rooker-Feldman*?

6. You can now see why the doctrine is creating such consternation in the inferior federal courts. There is an almost Zen-like quality to the doctrine: when is something that is not an appeal actually an appeal? This parallels a common question in the area of Supreme Court review of state court decisions under 28 U.S.C. § 1257: when is a non-final state court ruling in a case final within the meaning of § 1257? Cox Broadcasting Corp. v. Cohn, presented at page 999, discusses that issue. Then-Justice Rehnquist dissented vigorously from the majority's conclusion that four categories of cases from the state courts were final for § 1257 purposes even though there were further state court proceedings to come. He argued that "final" actually means "final," but was not able to persuade his colleagues. In the *Rooker-Feldman* context, could one argue that "appeal" means "appeal," so that the jurisdictional base for the doctrine crumbles? If *Rooker-Feldman* is not based in the jurisdictional statutes, is there any other justification for it?

For More Information

For some excellent scholarly consideration of the *Rooker-Feldman* doctrine before *Exxon-Mobil*, see the symposium issue of Notre Dame Law Review that includes papers presented to the Federal Courts section at the 1999 Annual Meeting of the Association of American Law Schools: Thomas D. Rowe, Jr., Rooker-Feldman: *Worth Only the Powder to Blow It Up?*, 74 NOTRE DAME L. REV. 1081 (1999); Suzanna Sherry, *Judicial Federalism in the Trenches: The* Rooker-Feldman *Doctrine in Action*, 74 NOTRE DAME L. REV. 1085 (1999); Barry Friedman & James E. Gaylord, Rooker-Feldman *from the Ground Up*, 74 NOTRE DAME L. REV. 1129 (1999); Susan Bandes, *The* Rooker-Feldman *Doctrine: Evaluating Its Jurisdictional Status*, 74 NOTRE DAME L. REV. 1175 (1999); Jack M. Beermann, *Comments on* Rooker-Feldman *or Let State Law Be Our Guide*, 74 NOTRE DAME L. REV. 1209 (1999).

Chapter 11

Federal Habeas Corpus

A. Introduction

"Habeas corpus" is Latin for "you have the body."[1] Although the writ of habeas corpus took different forms at common law, this chapter concerns only the writ of ***habeas corpus ad subjiciendum***, known as the Great Writ. A person claiming to be held in custody in violation of federal law may petition a federal court to issue a writ of habeas corpus to inquire into the legality of the detention. Most often, the custody is the result of a state criminal conviction, but the proceeding is not a direct appeal of the conviction.[2] Instead, it is a separate civil lawsuit called a "collateral proceeding." Habeas corpus is a remarkably appropriate finale for studying the federal courts as an institution. The enduring themes of federalism and separation of powers figure heavily in the jurisprudence of The Great Writ, and the manner in which federal habeas corpus operates connotes much about the oft-debated subject of parity. Although habeas corpus lies to challenge civil or criminal custody, the huge majority of the cases (and all that attract public attention) involve criminal cases.[3] That is one of the things that makes habeas corpus a focal point of emotional and political attention in a society so preoccupied with the problem of crime. As Professor William Hellerstein once observed, "You're selling a product nobody wants to buy: reversal of a criminal conviction." That observation, although made in the context of direct rather than collateral attack on a conviction, illustrates one of the things that has made federal habeas corpus an especially hot topic over the past two decades.

> **It's Latin to Me!**
>
> A writ directed to someone detaining another person and commanding that the detainee be brought to court.

1 Black's Law Dictionary 728 (8th ed. 2004).

2 As Chapter 10 discussed, as a formal matter inferior federal courts may not review state court decisions.

3 *See, e.g.*, Erwin Chemerinsky, Federal Jurisdiction § 15.1, at 896 (5th ed. 2007).

How one feels about federal habeas corpus will depend, in no small part, on one's view of the appropriate role of the federal courts and how those courts, particularly the inferior federal courts, should relate to the states generally and to the state judiciaries in particular. Although a habeas proceeding is not an appeal, the inferior federal courts in effect sit in review of state courts' conduct of criminal cases.

> [T]he availability of federal habeas as a sequel to state court consideration of the same claim does, in the nature of things, place a district court in position to second-guess the state court. In this practical sense, postconviction federal habeas has an undeniable appellate flavor. The great intellectual challenge has always been to reconcile the theoretical (original) nature of the federal courts' jurisdiction * * * with the practical (appellate) character of the federal courts' function when the state courts have previously adjudicated prisoners' claims.[4]

When a federal court grants habeas corpus relief, it often vacates a conviction.[5] Although technically the relief runs against the custodian, not the court that issued the order of confinement,[6] the emotional and political impact is little different from true appellate reversal. The federalism and parity implications are obvious. When a federal court orders habeas relief for a state prisoner, it imposes its own view of federal law, almost always displacing a contrary state court view, in an area of intense state concern. In an individual case, one might simply regard the doctrine as another error-correcting mechanism. The existence of federal habeas itself, however, connotes to some the underlying judgment that state courts are institutionally not quite up to the job of properly interpreting and applying federal constitutional principles.

The separation-of-powers issues raised by habeas corpus are not always as apparent as the federalism concerns. Nonetheless, there is tension between Congress and the federal courts over habeas. It appears most often in judges' statements appearing to chafe over the congressionally imposed responsibility to hear habeas cases. Consider Justice Frankfurter's comments in *Brown v. Allen*, 344 U.S. 443 (1953):

---

4 Larry W. Yackle, *A Primer on the New Habeas Corpus Statute*, 44 BUFF. L. REV. 381, 403 (1996).

5 Even vacating a conviction, moreover, does not necessarily compel release of the prisoner. Often, the state retries the defendant successfully.

There have been cases, however, in which habeas corpus relief goes to the sentence a prisoner has received (usually the death penalty), not to the validity of the conviction. To some extent, the Antiterrorism and Effective Death Penalty Act appears to restrict such relief, at least when the prisoner seeks it in a second or successive petition. *See* 28 U.S.C. § 2244(b)(2)(B).

6 It would be unthinkable, for example, for a federal court granting habeas corpus relief to attempt to return the case to the state courts with instructions, as is common when an appellate court reverses a lower court.

Congress could have left the enforcement of federal constitutional rights governing the administration of criminal justice in the States exclusively to the State courts. These tribunals are under the same duty as the federal courts to respect rights under the United States Constitution. * * * It is not for us to determine whether this power should have been vested in the federal courts. As Mr. Justice Bradley, with his usual acuteness, commented not long after the passage of [the 1867 statute authorizing the federal courts to hear habeas petitions from state prisoners], "although it may appear unseemly that a prisoner, after conviction in a state court, should be set at liberty by a single judge on habeas corpus, there seems to be no escape from the law." His feeling has been recently echoed in a proposal of the Judicial Conference of Senior Circuit Judges that these cases be heard by three-judge courts. But the wisdom of such a modification in the law is for Congress to consider, particularly in view of the effect of the expanding concept of due process upon enforcement by the States of their criminal laws. It is for this Court to give fair effect to the habeas corpus jurisdiction as enacted by Congress.

In the late 1980's, Chief Justice Rehnquist openly lobbied Congress to restrict the writ, and Congress finally responded in the Antiterrorism and Effective Death Penalty Act of 1996 (AEDPA). Judicial actions, whether expanding or contracting the writ, take place in an area of extensive legislation; modification of the rules concerning the availability of habeas corpus inevitably involves that statutory structure. The cases that follow demonstrate the Justices' frequent awareness of the separation-of-powers implications of their actions.

Habeas corpus came to the American colonies from England. The Constitution provides: "The Privilege of the Writ of Habeas Corpus shall not be suspended unless when in Cases of Rebellion or Invasion the public Safety may require it."[7] The Judiciary Act of 1789 made the writ available to federal prisoners. After some piecemeal extension of the writ to state prisoners,[8] in 1867 Congress authorized federal courts to issue writs of habeas corpus in "all cases where any person may be restrained of his or her liberty in violation of the constitution, or of any treaty or law of the United States."[9] This statute, as many others adopted during Reconstruction, aimed at reforming Southern criminal and civil justice systems that were being used systematically to re-enslave the freed African-Americans and to harass whites serving in the Union Army or the Freedmen's Bureau.[10] Given the depth of Congress' anger and frustration with the South in the aftermath of the Civil War, it is not surprising that legislators openly favored broad construction of the statute during the limited debate on the measure.

---

7 U.S. CONST. art. 1, § 9, cl. 2.

8 The Force Act of 1833, for example, made the writ available to federal officials held in state custody. Act of Mar. 2, 1833, c. 57, § 3, 4 Stat. 633.

9 Habeas Corpus Act of 1867, ch. 28, 14 Stat. 385.

10 *See generally*, Donald H. Zeigler, *A Reassessment of the* Younger *Doctrine in Light of the Legislative History of Reconstruction*, 1983 DUKE L.J. 987, 990-1020.

Scholars disagree about the actual scope of habeas corpus both before and after the Civil War. Paul M. Bator contended that habeas was limited to deciding whether the convicting court had subject matter jurisdiction and proper jurisdiction over the defendant's person,[11] while Gary Peller concluded that federal courts exercised a broader power to review constitutional errors.[12] Ann Woolhandler presented a more nuanced, middle view:

> [T]he federal habeas remedy was not uniformly available to address all constitutional wrongs arising in criminal cases in the nineteenth century. Nevertheless, the scope of habeas review reflected the Court's gradual willingness to address ad hoc or random acts of official illegality (that is, official action not specifically authorized by legislation) as constitutional violations rather than common law violations, and to provide federal remedies for such abuses.[13]

B. The Statutory Structure

The statutes governing federal habeas corpus appear at 28 U.S.C.A. §§ 2241-2266.[14] They may generate more questions than they answer, and that is particularly so today, because of the amendments contained in the Antiterrorism and Effective Death Penalty Act of 1996. The courts are struggling to interpret and clarify the Act's sometimes murky language and confusing structure. As Professor Yackle observed:

> The new law is not well drafted. It bears the influence of various bills that were fiercely debated for nearly forty years. Along the way, proponents of habeas legislation adjusted their initiatives in light of contemporaneous events and circumstances: the Powell Committee Report in 1989, for example, as well as shifting levels of political support for particular measures and new Supreme Court decisions on point. Proponents often kept abreast of the times by adding new elements to their bills without, at the same time, reexamining old formulations in order to maintain an intellectually coherent whole. The

11 Paul M. Bator, *Finality in Criminal Law and Federal Habeas Corpus for State Prisoners*, 76 HARV.L.REV. 441 (1963).

12 Gary Peller, *In Defense of Federal Habeas Corpus Relitigation*, 16 HARV.C.R.-C.L. L. REV. 579 (1982).

13 Ann Woolhandler, *Demodeling Habeas*, 45 STAN. L. REV. 575, 580 (1993).

14 A brief word about vocabulary is appropriate. The statutes, particularly 28 U.S.C. § 2243, reflect the common law heritage of habeas corpus. The writ originally required the custodian of a prisoner to present the prisoner to the court so the court could evaluate the legality of the detention. The writ itself was not a release from the custody; it was merely the instrument by which the inquiry was launched. Accordingly, § 2243 notes that the judge "shall forthwith award the writ * * * ," but follows that command by noting that the custodian shall make a return on the writ specifying the reasons that the detention is lawful. Nonetheless, today the writ is frequently equated with the relief sought: (most often) release from custody. Even the Supreme Court has lapsed into this misusage, as in Coleman v. Thompson, *infra* page 1163, in which the Court notes that the district court, after considering the petitioner's claims on the merits, "denied the petition." In more traditional parlance, the writ was granted but relief was denied.

result, I am afraid, is extraordinarily arcane verbiage that will require considerable time and resources to sort out.[15]

Section 2241 contains the basic authorization for federal judges to grant writs of habeas corpus. All three levels of the federal judiciary are authorized to grant a writ, but, for obvious reasons, Supreme Court justices and circuit judges may transfer an application to the district court having jurisdiction to entertain it. The Military Commissions Act of 2006[16] amended § 2241(e) to deny the federal courts jurisdiction to hear habeas petitions by aliens determined by the United States to have been properly detained as enemy combatants or to be awaiting such determination. Sections 2242 and 2243 contain relatively straightforward provisions for the application, return, and hearing of a habeas petition. Section 2244, entitled "Finality of determination," is the first section AEDPA substantially revised. It is lengthy and confusing; nonetheless, the language evinces a clear intent drastically to limit second or successive habeas corpus petitions by state prisoners. Prior to AEDPA, the Supreme Court announced rules greatly limiting second or successive petitions. Section D-5 explores whether amended § 2244 limits even further the circumstances when second or successive petitions can be filed. Two new procedural hurdles are apparent on the face of § 2244. First, a prisoner seeking to file a second or successive petition must get permission from a three-judge panel of the court of appeals. Second, § 2244(d) imposes a one-year limitation on state prisoners' habeas petitions, running generally from the time the state judgment became final "by the conclusion of direct review or the expiration of the time for seeking such review." More time is available in certain extraordinary circumstances. The one year period is tolled during the pendency of state post-conviction proceedings; however, the Court held in *Lawrence v. Florida*, 549 U.S. 327 (2007), that the period is not tolled during the pendency of a petition for certiorari to the Supreme Court from the state court judgment rendered on direct review.

Sections 2245-2252 are short sections containing specific procedural directions for habeas proceedings. Section 2253, as amended in 1996, sharply limits appeals in habeas cases, proscribing appeals unless a circuit judge issues a certificate of appealability and defining appealability in terms of a petitioner's "substantial showing" of constitutional violation. What is a substantial showing? Given the denial of relief, the petitioner's showing clearly did not persuade the district court. We are familiar with standards of appellate review involving abuse of discretion or "clear error." Where does "substantial showing" fit on that spectrum? Prior to AEDPA, Section 2253 allowed an appeal if either a district or circuit judge issued a "certificate of probable cause." A certificate issued if a judge felt there was "probable cause to believe that the petitioner ha[d] raised a 'substantial question'

15 Larry W. Yackle, *A Primer on the New Habeas Corpus Statute*, 44 BUFF.L.REV. 381, 281 (1996).

16 Pub.L. 109-366, 120 Stat. 2600 (2006).

that [was] at least not totally 'devoid of merit.' "[17] Although the courts never clearly articulated the distinction between frivolous and non-frivolous unsuccessful claims, it was plainly easier to appeal before AEDPA.

Section 2254 contains most of the major restrictions on habeas corpus applications by state prisoners. Section 2254(a) appears to permit broad review by authorizing a federal court to hear any application by a state prisoner claiming "that he is in custody in violation of the Constitution or laws or treaties of the United States." Subsequent subsections, however, impose substantial limitations. Section 2254(b) requires a petitioner to have exhausted any available state procedures for raising the question presented. What if a petition contains both exhausted and unexhausted claims? May a federal court hear the exhausted claims and dismiss the rest to allow the petitioner to comply with the statute as to the unexhausted claims, or, if the prisoner chooses to press the exhausted claims, does he waive his opportunity to re-present the unexhausted claims after presenting them to the state courts? Section D-3 addresses these questions. Section D-4 considers the related rule that a state procedural default by the petitioner (*e.g.*, letting the time to file a notice of appeal pass) will normally constitute an adequate and independent state ground barring federal habeas review.

Section 2254(d)(1) says a habeas petition "shall not be granted with respect to any claim that was adjudicated on the merits in State court proceedings" unless the state ruling "resulted in a decision that was contrary to, or involved an unreasonable application of, clearly established Federal law, as determined by the Supreme Court of the United States." Congress may have intended this provision to codify the Supreme Court's decision in *Teague v. Lane*, 489 U.S. 288 (1989). *Teague*, and § 2254(d)(1) raises many thorny issues. For example, how is a court to decide whether Supreme Court cases "clearly establish" a federal constitutional rule? And what does "resulted in a decision that was contrary to, or involved an unreasonable application of" mean? Does it simply mean incorrect, or does it require a higher degree of error? Section D-2 of this Chapter addresses these and related issues

Section 2254(e) addresses the weight to be given to state court factual findings and the circumstances permitting a federal evidentiary hearing. Prior to enactment of the current § 2254(e) of AEDPA, the Supreme Court substantially narrowed the standards *Townsend v. Sain* (1963) set forth and Congress incorporated in 1966 into what was then § 2254(d). Section 2254(e) appears further to limit petitioners' opportunities for federal evidentiary hearings, although by how much is still unclear. Section D-1 addresses these matters.

---

17 Donald H. Zeigler & Michele G. Hermann, *The Invisible Litigant: An Inside View of Pro Se Actions in the Federal Courts*, 47 N.Y.U.L.Rev. 157, 220-21 (1972).

One special feature of AEDPA deserves separate comment. Sections 2261-2266 provide expedited procedures applicable only to capital cases and limit the grounds for relief that the federal courts may consider. Section 2261(e) specifically excludes ineffective assistance of counsel in post-conviction proceedings (state or federal) as a ground for federal habeas corpus relief, a point on which Congress must have been especially intent given that § 2254(i) already contained an identical provision. Section 2261(e) does, however, note that the court may appoint effective counsel to *replace* ineffective counsel *during* post-conviction proceedings. Section 2263 limits a prisoner's time to seek federal habeas relief in a capital case to 180 days from the time the conviction becomes final (subject to certain tolling provisions), half that permitted in non-capital cases under § 2244(d) (subject to quite similar tolling provisions), and § 2266 directs the inferior federal courts to give priority to capital cases and to complete their consideration within specified time limits. AEDPA also sharply limits stays of execution, including prohibiting them with respect to second or successive petitions "unless the court of appeals approves the filing * * * ." The statute also limits the scope of review, directing the district courts only to consider claims upon which the state courts have ruled, excepting only claims not presented to the state courts because of some violation of federal law by the state, claims based on a new federal right that is retroactive, or claims based on previously undiscoverable facts.

These features are not automatically available, however. Section 2261(b, c, d) establishes prerequisites that the state must satisfy to reap the benefit of these sections. It must establish a formal, regular procedure to appoint competent counsel for post-conviction procedures in the state courts. The state must formally and affirmatively offer post-conviction counsel to all capital prisoners; merely giving prisoners the right to counsel does not suffice. Such counsel cannot, without the consent of both the prisoner and counsel, have previously been involved in the trial or appeal of the case. Finally, the state's rules must explicitly "provide standards of competency for the appointment of such counsel." Early experience suggests that the lower federal courts will interpret these requirements quite strictly. Thus, district courts have required an "affirmative, institutionalized, formal commitment" to a post-conviction review system, something more "than the general supervision of a state high court." One court found that merely setting aside funds for a "general category of state court expenditures" did not establish a " 'mechanism for the compensation and payment of reasonable expenses' as required by § 2261(b)." On the other hand, the Fifth Circuit upheld Texas rules providing funds for post-conviction review but limiting attorney compensation to $7,500 and expenses to $2,500. With respect to the competence of post-conviction counsel, however, the same court found that a "flexible mechanism" for ensuring competent counsel, such as evaluation of attorney questionnaires on a case-by-case basis, failed to meet the statutory requirement of "explicit standards of competency." A court found that one state's standard of five years of membership in the state bar and two years' experience in criminal law failed to guarantee competency. A district court approved Virginia's approach because Virginia has a statute that establishes seven criteria by which to judge counsel's competency.[18] On balance, although Congress sought through these provisions to make good on AEDPA's title, lower court experience to date suggests that it will not be easy for states to qualify under this particular "fast-track" legislation.

A final ironic note: In 1997, the year after the AEDPA was enacted, the number of state prisoner petitions jumped by over 5,000, reaching 19,956. By 2000, 21,345 applications were filed.[19] John Scalia, a researcher with the Department of Justice's Bureau of Justice Statistics, concluded after a mathematical analysis that "[b]etween April 1996 and September 2000 an estimated 18,000 additional habeas corpus petitions were filed in U.S. district courts by State prison inmates directly as a result of the enactment of the AEDPA."[20] Why a dramatic increase followed legislation designed to curtail habeas petitions is a mystery.

C. Habeas Corpus and the War on Terror

The continuing "War on Terror" raises many controversial military, political, and legal issues. Intense controversy has centered on detained individuals. What are their rights, if any? Are they prisoners of war, entitled to the full protections of the Geneva Conventions, or illegal "enemy combatants," with few or no rights? Should the military alone determine their status and punishments, or should some or all of their cases go to the federal criminal justice system? Should it matter whether they are aliens or American citizens, or whether the government is holding them inside or outside of United States territory? These are complex and profound issues that have engaged the attention of all three branches of government and the citizenry.

In Chapter 2, *Boumediene v. Bush* touches on some of these questions, but its role in this book is to explain how the Suspension Clause limits Congress' power to restrict the subject matter jurisdiction of the federal courts. The Guantanamo cases, and more generally the cases where habeas petitioners are complaining of executive detention rather than about their state convictions, are generally covered more fully in courses on Constitutional Law. The executive detention

---

18 VA. CODE. § 19.2-163.8(A):

> (i) license or permission to practice law in Virginia; (ii) general background in criminal litigation; (iii) demonstrated experience in felony practice at trial and appeal; (iv) experience in death penalty litigation; (v) familiarity with the requisite court system; (vi) current training in death penalty litigation; and (vii) demonstrated proficiency and commitment to quality representation.

19 JOHN SCALIA, BUREAU OF JUSTICE STATISTICS SPECIAL REPORT: PRISONER PETITIONS FILED IN U.S. DISTRICT COURTS, 2000, WITH TRENDS 1980-2000, at 2 (2002).

20 *Id.* at 7.

cases do not implicate judicial federalism and thus this book does not attempt to explore the many important issues that attend the executive detention cases.

D. Federal Court Review of State Convictions

1. State Factual Findings and Federal Evidentiary Hearings

When a federal habeas court holds an evidentiary hearing, it treads in an area of great sensitivity. Consider, after all, that the state has already held a full trial and has expended appellate time on the case as well. There is a state court record that contains "the facts." For the federal court to proceed in such circumstances clearly implies that the state court record is somehow defective and that the state court proceeding was not adequate to develop the relevant facts fully. That the states should take offense at the implication is not surprising.

As explained in Section A, *Townsend v. Sain* (1963) and the 1966 amendments to 28 U.S.C. § 2254(d) liberalized the standards for granting evidentiary hearings. Although § 2254(d) said that state factual findings "shall be presumed to be correct," the presumption was rebuttable in the circumstances the statute listed. When the state court hearing did not develop the material facts adequately (circumstance 5 in the *Townsend* list, circumstance 3 in the statute), *Townsend* held that the deliberate-bypass standard applied; that is, a hearing could be denied only if the petitioner was guilty of "inexcusable neglect."

Keeney v. Tamayo-Reyes (1992), shifted from the deliberate-bypass standard to a cause-and-prejudice standard that had developed in the context of prisoners' failure to raise legal arguments in state proceedings. The old standard placed the burden on the state to demonstrate that a petitioner had deliberately bypassed an opportunity to develop the material facts during state proceedings. Under the new standard, a prisoner was not entitled to an evidentiary hearing unless he could demonstrate good cause (some objective reason) for having failed to develop the facts in state court *and* prejudice—a substantial probability that the result in the state proceeding would have been different in a trial without the alleged constitutional violation. The shift to the cause-and-prejudice standard made it much more difficult for petitioners to obtain an evidentiary hearing.

AEDPA replaced § 2254(d) of the 1966 statute with a new provision, § 2254(e). Section 2254(e)(1) continues the presumption that state fact findings were correct. Section 2254(e)(2) contains a new provision governing cases where the material facts were not adequately developed at the state court hearing. The Supreme Court considered the new provision in the following case.

Williams (Michael) v. Taylor

Supreme Court of the United States, 2000.
529 U.S. 420.

JUSTICE KENNEDY delivered the opinion of the Court.

Petitioner Michael Wayne Williams received a capital sentence for the murders of Morris Keller, Jr., and Keller's wife, Mary Elizabeth. Petitioner later sought a writ of habeas corpus in federal court. Accompanying his petition was a request for an evidentiary hearing on constitutional claims which, he alleged, he had been unable to develop in state-court proceedings. The question in this case is whether 28 U.S.C. § 2254(e)(2) as amended by the Antiterrorism and Effective Death Penalty Act of 1996 (AEDPA), bars the evidentiary hearing petitioner seeks. If petitioner "has failed to develop the factual basis of [his] claim[s] in State court proceedings," his case is subject to § 2254(e)(2), and he may not receive a hearing because he concedes his inability to satisfy the statute's further stringent conditions for excusing the deficiency.

I

[Petitioner and Jeffrey Alan Cruse committed the murders in 1993. Cruse was the State's main witness. After the petitioner was convicted and sentenced to death, Cruse pleaded guilty in a separate proceeding. Upon the prosecutor's recommendation to spare Cruse' life because of his testimony against the petitioner, Cruse was sentenced to life imprisonment. Petitioner's conviction and sentence were upheld by the Virginia appellate courts, and the Supreme Court denied certiorari. Petitioner then filed a state collateral attack claiming the State failed to disclose a second plea agreement it had reached with Cruse. (An earlier agreement was revoked when prosecutors discovered Cruse had failed to admit some of his wrongdoing.) The state courts denied relief and the Supreme Court again denied certiorari.]

* * *

Petitioner filed a habeas petition in the United States District Court for the Eastern District of Virginia on November 20, 1996. In addition to his claim regarding the alleged undisclosed agreement between the Commonwealth and Cruse, the petition raised three claims relevant to questions now before us. First, petitioner claimed the prosecution had violated *Brady v. Maryland* (1963) in failing to disclose a report of a confidential pretrial psychiatric examination of Cruse. Second, petitioner alleged his trial was rendered unfair by the seating of a juror who at *voir dire* had not revealed possible sources of bias. Finally, petitioner alleged one of the prosecutors committed misconduct in failing to reveal his knowledge of the juror's possible bias.

The District Court granted an evidentiary hearing on the undisclosed agreement and the allegations of juror bias and prosecutorial misconduct but denied a hearing on the psychiatric report. Before the evidentiary hearing could be held, the Commonwealth filed an application for an emergency stay and a petition for a writ of mandamus and prohibition in the Court of Appeals. The Commonwealth argued that petitioner's evidentiary hearing was prohibited by 28 U.S.C. § 2254(e)(2). A divided panel of the Court of Appeals granted the emergency stay and remanded for the District Court to apply the statute to petitioner's request for an evidentiary hearing. On remand, the District Court vacated its order granting an evidentiary hearing and dismissed the petition, having determined petitioner could not satisfy § 2254(e)(2)'s requirements.

The Court of Appeals affirmed. It first considered petitioner's argument that § 2254(e)(2) did not apply to his case because he had been diligent in attempting to develop his claims in state court. Citing its decision in *Cardwell v. Greene*, the Court of Appeals agreed with petitioner that § 2254(e)(2) would not apply if he had exercised diligence in state court. The court held, however, that petitioner had not been diligent and so had "failed to develop" in state court the factual bases of his *Brady*, juror bias, and prosecutorial misconduct claims. The Court of Appeals concluded petitioner could not satisfy the statute's conditions for excusing his failure to develop the facts and held him barred from receiving an evidentiary hearing. The Court of Appeals ruled in the alternative that, even if § 2254(e)(2) did not apply, petitioner would be ineligible for an evidentiary hearing under the cause and prejudice standard of pre-AEDPA law.

Addressing petitioner's claim of an undisclosed informal agreement between the Commonwealth and Cruse, the Court of Appeals rejected it on the merits under 28 U.S.C. § 2254(d)(1) and, as a result, did not consider whether § 2254(e)(2) applied.

On October 18, 1999, petitioner filed an application for stay of execution and a petition for a writ of certiorari. On October 28, we stayed petitioner's execution and granted certiorari to decide whether § 2254(e)(2) precludes him from receiving an evidentiary hearing on his claims. We now affirm in part and reverse in part.

II

A

Petitioner filed his federal habeas petition after AEDPA's effective date, so the statute applies to his case. The Commonwealth argues AEDPA bars petitioner from receiving an evidentiary hearing on any claim whose factual basis was not developed in state court, absent narrow circumstances not applicable here. Petitioner did not develop, or raise, his claims of juror bias, prosecutorial misconduct, or the prosecution's alleged Brady violation regarding Cruse's psychiatric report until he filed his federal habeas petition. Petitioner explains he could not have developed the claims earlier because he was unaware, through no fault of his own, of the underlying facts. As a consequence, petitioner contends, AEDPA erects no barrier to an evidentiary hearing in federal court.

Section 2254(e)(2), the provision which controls whether petitioner may receive an evidentiary hearing in federal district court on the claims that were not developed in the Virginia courts, becomes the central point of our analysis. It provides as follows:

> If the applicant has failed to develop the factual basis of a claim in State court proceedings, the court shall not hold an evidentiary hearing on the claim unless the applicant shows that—
>
> (A) the claim relies on—
>
> (i) a new rule of constitutional law, made retroactive to cases on collateral review by the Supreme Court, that was previously unavailable; or
>
> (ii) a factual predicate that could not have been previously discovered through the exercise of due diligence; and
>
> (B) the facts underlying the claim would be sufficient to establish by clear and convincing evidence that but for constitutional error, no reasonable factfinder would have found the applicant guilty of the underlying offense.

By the terms of its opening clause the statute applies only to prisoners who have "failed to develop the factual basis of a claim in State court proceedings." If the prisoner has failed to develop the facts, an evidentiary hearing cannot be granted unless the prisoner's case meets the other conditions of § 2254(e)(2). Here, petitioner concedes his case does not comply with § 2254(e)(2)(B), so he may receive an evidentiary hearing only if his claims fall outside the opening clause.

* * *

B

We start, as always, with the language of the statute. Section 2254(e)(2) begins with a conditional clause, "[i]f the applicant has failed to develop the factual basis of a claim in State court proceedings," which directs attention to the prisoner's efforts in state court. We ask first whether the factual basis was indeed developed in state court, a question susceptible, in the normal course, of a simple yes or no answer. Here the answer is no.

The Commonwealth would have the analysis begin and end there. Under its no-fault reading of the statute, if there is no factual development in the state court, the federal habeas court may not inquire into the reasons for the default when determining whether the opening clause of § 2254(e)(2) applies. We do not agree with the Commonwealth's interpretation of the word "failed."

We do not deny "fail" is sometimes used in a neutral way, not importing fault or want of diligence. So the phrase "We fail to understand his argument" can mean simply "We cannot understand his argument." This is not the sense in which the word "failed" is used here, however.

We give the words of a statute their " 'ordinary, contemporary, common meaning,' " absent an indication Congress intended them to bear some different import. In its customary and preferred sense, "fail" connotes some omission, fault, or negligence on the part of the person who has failed to do something. To say a person has failed in a duty implies he did not take the necessary steps to fulfill it. He is, as a consequence, at fault and bears responsibility for the failure. In this sense, a person is not at fault when his diligent efforts to perform an act are thwarted, for example, by the conduct of another or by happenstance. Fault lies, in those circumstances, either with the person who interfered with the accomplishment of the act or with no one at all. We conclude Congress used the word "failed" in the sense just described. Had Congress intended a no-fault standard, it would have had no difficulty in making its intent plain. It would have had to do no more than use, in lieu of the phrase "has failed to," the phrase "did not."

* * *

Our interpretation of § 2254(e)(2)'s opening clause has support in *Keeney v. Tamayo-Reyes* (1992), a case decided four years before AEDPA's enactment. In *Keeney*, a prisoner with little knowledge of English sought an evidentiary hearing in federal court, alleging his *nolo contendere* plea to a manslaughter charge was not knowing and voluntary because of inaccuracies in the translation of the plea proceedings. The prisoner had not developed the facts of his claim in state collateral proceedings, an omission caused by the negligence of his state postconviction counsel. The Court characterized this as the "prisoner's failure to develop material facts in state court." We required the prisoner to demonstrate cause and prejudice excusing the default before he could receive a hearing on his claim, unless the prisoner could "show that a fundamental miscarriage of justice would result from failure to hold a federal evidentiary hearing."

Section 2254(e)(2)'s initial inquiry into whether "the applicant has failed to develop the factual basis of a claim in State court proceedings" echoes *Keeney*'s language regarding "the state prisoner's failure to develop material facts in state court." In *Keeney*, the Court borrowed the cause and prejudice standard applied to procedurally defaulted claims, *see* Wainwright v. Sykes (1977), deciding there was no reason "to distinguish between failing to properly assert a federal claim in state court and failing in state court to properly develop such a claim." As is evident from the similarity between the Court's phrasing in Keeney and the opening clause of § 2254(e)(2), Congress intended to preserve at least one aspect of Keeney's holding: prisoners who are at fault for the deficiency in the state-court record must satisfy a heightened standard to obtain an evidentiary hearing. To be sure, in requiring that prisoners who have not been diligent satisfy § 2254(e)(2)'s provisions rather than show cause and prejudice, and in eliminating a freestanding "miscarriage of justice" exception, Congress raised the bar Keeney imposed on prisoners who were not diligent in state-court proceedings. Contrary to the Commonwealth's position, however, there is no basis in the text of § 2254(e)(2) to believe Congress used "fail" in a different sense than the Court did in Keeney or otherwise intended the statute's further, more stringent requirements to control the availability of an evidentiary hearing in a broader class of cases than were covered by Keeney's cause and prejudice standard.

* * *

Interpreting § 2254(e)(2) so that "failed" requires lack of diligence or some other fault avoids putting it in needless tension with § 2254(d). A prisoner who developed his claim in state court and can prove the state court's decision was "contrary to, or involved an unreasonable application of, clearly established Federal law, as determined by the Supreme Court of the United States," is not barred from obtaining relief by § 2254(d)(1). If the opening clause of § 2254(e)(2) covers a request for an evidentiary hearing on a claim which was pursued with diligence but remained undeveloped in state court because, for instance, the prosecution concealed the facts, a prisoner lacking clear and convincing evidence of innocence could be barred from a hearing on the claim even if he could satisfy § 2254(d). *See* 28 U.S.C. § 2254(e)(2)(B). The "failed to develop" clause does not bear this harsh reading, which would attribute to Congress a purpose or design to bar evidentiary hearings for diligent prisoners with meritorious claims just because the prosecution's conduct went undetected in state court. We see no indication that Congress by this language intended to remove the distinction between a prisoner who is at fault and one who is not.

The Commonwealth argues a reading of "failed to develop" premised on fault empties § 2254(e)(2)(A)(ii) of its meaning. To treat the prisoner's lack of diligence in state court as a prerequisite for application of § 2254(e)(2), the Commonwealth contends, renders a nullity of the statute's own diligence provision requiring the prisoner to show "a factual predicate [of his claim] could not have been previously discovered through the exercise of due diligence." § 2254(e)(2)(A)(ii). We disagree.

The Commonwealth misconceives the inquiry mandated by the opening clause of § 2254(e)(2). The question is not whether the facts could have been discovered but instead whether the prisoner was diligent in his efforts. The purpose of the fault component of "failed" is to ensure the prisoner undertakes his own diligent search for evidence. Diligence for purposes of the opening clause depends upon whether the prisoner made a reasonable attempt, in light of the information available at the time, to investigate and pursue claims in state court; it does not depend, as the Commonwealth would have it, upon whether those efforts could have been successful. Though lack of diligence will not bar an evidentiary hearing if efforts to discover the facts would have been in vain, see § 2254(e)(2)(A)(ii), and there is a convincing claim of innocence, see § 2254(e)(2)(B), only a prisoner who has neglected his rights in state court need satisfy these conditions. The statute's later reference to diligence pertains to cases in which the facts could not have been discovered, whether there was diligence or not. In this important respect § 2254(e)(2)(A)(ii) bears a close resemblance to (e)(2)(A)(i), which applies to a new rule that was not available at the time of the earlier proceedings. ("[W]ords and people are known by their companions"). In these two parallel provisions Congress has given prisoners who fall within § 2254(e)(2)'s opening clause an opportunity to obtain an evidentiary hearing where the legal or factual basis of the claims did not exist at the time of state-court proceedings.

We are not persuaded by the Commonwealth's further argument that anything less than a no-fault understanding of the opening clause is contrary to AEDPA's purpose to further the principles of comity, finality, and federalism. There is no doubt Congress intended AEDPA to advance these doctrines. Federal habeas corpus principles must inform and shape the historic and still vital relation of mutual respect and common purpose existing between the States and the federal courts. In keeping this delicate balance we have been careful to limit the scope of federal intrusion into state criminal adjudications and to safeguard the States' interest in the integrity of their criminal and collateral proceedings. * * *

It is consistent with these principles to give effect to Congress' intent to avoid unneeded evidentiary hearings in federal habeas corpus, while recognizing the statute does not equate prisoners who exercise diligence in pursuing their claims with those who do not. Principles of exhaustion are premised upon recognition by Congress and the Court that state judiciaries have the duty and competence to vindicate rights secured by the Constitution in state criminal proceedings. Diligence will require in the usual case that the prisoner, at a minimum, seek an evidentiary hearing in state court in the manner prescribed by state law. "Comity * * * dictates that when a prisoner alleges that his continued confinement for a state court conviction violates federal law, the state courts should have the first opportunity to review this claim and provide any necessary relief." For state courts to have their rightful opportunity to adjudicate federal rights, the prisoner must be diligent in developing the record and presenting, if possible, all claims of constitutional error. If the prisoner fails to do so, himself or herself contributing to the absence of a full and fair adjudication in state court, § 2254(e)(2) prohibits an evidentiary hearing to develop the relevant claims in federal court, unless the statute's other stringent requirements are met. Federal courts sitting in habeas are not an alternative forum for trying facts and issues which a prisoner made insufficient effort to pursue in state proceedings. Yet comity is not served by saying a prisoner "has failed to develop the factual basis of a claim" where he was unable to develop his claim in state court despite diligent effort. In that circumstance, an evidentiary hearing is not barred by § 2254(e)(2).

III

Now we apply the statutory test. If there has been no lack of diligence at the relevant stages in the state proceedings, the prisoner has not "failed to develop" the facts under § 2254(e)(2)'s opening clause, and he will be excused from showing compliance with the balance of the subsection's requirements. We find lack of diligence as to one of the three claims but not as to the other two.

A

Petitioner did not exercise the diligence required to preserve the claim that nondisclosure of Cruse's psychiatric report was in contravention of *Brady v. Maryland* (1963). The report concluded Cruse "ha[d] little recollection of the [murders of the Kellers], other than vague memories, as he was intoxicated with alcohol and marijuana at the time." The report had been prepared in September 1993, before petitioner was tried; yet it was not mentioned by petitioner until he filed his federal habeas petition and attached a copy of the report. Petitioner explained that an investigator for his federal habeas counsel discovered the report in Cruse's court file but state habeas counsel had not seen it when he had reviewed the same file. State habeas counsel averred as follows:

> Prior to filing [petitioner's] habeas corpus petition with the Virginia Supreme Court, I reviewed the Cumberland County court files of [petitioner] and of his co-defendant, Jeffrey Cruse* * *. I have reviewed the attached psychiatric evaluation of Jeffrey Cruse * * *. I have no recollection of seeing this report in Mr. Cruse's court file when I examined the file. Given the contents of the report, I am confident that I would remember it.

The trial court was not satisfied with this explanation for the late discovery. Nor are we.

There are repeated references to a "psychiatric" or "mental health" report in a transcript of Cruse's sentencing proceeding, a copy of which petitioner's own state habeas counsel attached to the state habeas petition he filed with the Virginia state hab. atty was on notice of report

Supreme Court. The transcript reveals that Cruse's attorney described the report with details that should have alerted counsel to a possible *Brady* claim.

* * *

The transcript put petitioner's state habeas counsel on notice of the report's existence and possible materiality. The sole indication that counsel made some effort to investigate the report is an October 30, 1995, letter to the prosecutor in which counsel requested "[a]ll reports of physical and mental examinations, scientific tests, or experiments conducted in connection with the investigation of the offense, including but not limited to: * * * [a]ll psychological test or polygraph examinations performed upon any prosecution witness and all documents referring or relating to such tests * * *." After the prosecution declined the requests absent a court order, it appears counsel made no further efforts to find the specific report mentioned by Cruse's attorney. Given knowledge of the report's existence and potential importance, a diligent attorney would have done more. Counsel's failure to investigate these references in anything but a cursory manner triggers the opening clause of § 2254(e)(2).

As we hold there was a failure to develop the factual basis of this *Brady* claim in state court, we must determine if the requirements in the balance of § 2254(e)(2) are satisfied so that petitioner's failure is excused. Subparagraph (B) of § 2254(e)(2) conditions a hearing upon a showing, by clear and convincing evidence, that no reasonable factfinder would have found petitioner guilty of capital murder but for the alleged constitutional error. Petitioner concedes he cannot make this showing, and the case has been presented to us on that premise. For these reasons, we affirm the Court of Appeals' judgment barring an evidentiary hearing on this claim.

B

We conclude petitioner has met the burden of showing he was diligent in efforts to develop the facts supporting his juror bias and prosecutorial misconduct claims in collateral proceedings before the Virginia Supreme Court.

Petitioner's claims are based on two of the questions posed to the jurors by the trial judge at *voir dire*. First, the judge asked prospective jurors, "Are any of you related to the following people who may be called as witnesses?" Then he read the jurors a list of names, one of which was "Deputy Sheriff Claude Meinhard." Bonnie Stinnett, who would later become the jury foreperson, had divorced Meinhard in 1979, after a 17-year marriage with four children. Stinnett remained silent, indicating the answer was "no." Meinhard, as the officer who investigated the crime scene and interrogated Cruse, would later become the prosecution's lead-off witness at trial.

After reading the names of the attorneys involved in the case, including one of the prosecutors, Robert Woodson, Jr., the judge asked, "Have you or any member of your immediate family ever been represented by any of the aforementioned attorneys?" Stinnett again said nothing, despite the fact Woodson had represented her during her divorce from Meinhard.

In an affidavit she provided in the federal habeas proceedings, Stinnett claimed "[she] did not respond to the judge's [first] question because [she] did not consider [herself] 'related' to Claude Meinhard in 1994 [at *voir dire*] * * * . Once our marriage ended in 1979, I was no longer related to him." As for Woodson's earlier representation of her, Stinnett explained as follows: "When Claude and I divorced in 1979, the divorce was uncontested and Mr. Woodson drew up the papers so that the divorce could be completed. Since neither Claude nor I was contesting anything, I didn't think Mr. Woodson 'represented' either one of us."

Woodson provided an affidavit in which he admitted "[he] was aware that Juror Bonnie Stinnett was the ex-wife of then Deputy Sheriff Claude Meinhard and [he] was aware that they had been divorced for some time." Woodson stated, however, "[t]o [his] mind, people who are related only by marriage are no longer 'related' once the marriage ends in divorce." Woodson also "had no recollection of having been involved as a private attorney in the divorce proceedings between Claude Meinhard and Bonnie Stinnett." He explained that "[w]hatever [his] involvement was in the 1979 divorce, by the time of trial in 1994 [he] had completely forgotten about it."

wtf

Even if Stinnett had been correct in her technical or literal interpretation of the question relating to Meinhard, her silence after the first question was asked could suggest to the finder of fact an unwillingness to be forthcoming; this in turn could bear on the veracity of her explanation for not disclosing that Woodson had been her attorney. Stinnett's failure to divulge material information in response to the second question was misleading as a matter of fact because, under any interpretation, Woodson had acted as counsel to her and Meinhard in their divorce. Coupled with Woodson's own reticence, these omissions as a whole disclose the need for an evidentiary hearing. It may be that petitioner could establish that Stinnett was not impartial, or that Woodson's silence so infected the trial as to deny due process.

In ordering an evidentiary hearing on the juror bias and prosecutorial misconduct claims, the District Court concluded the factual basis of the claims was not reasonably available to petitioner's counsel during state habeas proceedings. After the Court of Appeals vacated this judgment, the District Court dismissed the petition and the Court of Appeals affirmed under the theory that state habeas counsel should have discovered Stinnett's relationship to Meinhard and Woodson.

We disagree with the Court of Appeals on this point. The trial record contains no evidence which would have put a reasonable attorney on notice that Stinnett's nonresponse was a deliberate omission of material information. State habeas counsel did attempt to investigate petitioner's jury, though prompted by concerns about a different juror. Counsel filed a motion for expert services with the Virginia Supreme Court, alleging "irregularities, improprieties and omissions exist[ed] with respect to the empaneling [*sic*] of the jury." Based on these suspicions, counsel requested funding for an investigator "to examine all circumstances relating to the empanelment of the jury and the jury's consideration of the case." The Commonwealth opposed the motion, and the Virginia Supreme Court denied it and dismissed the habeas petition, depriving petitioner of a further opportunity to investigate. The Virginia Supreme Court's denial of the motion is understandable in light of petitioner's vague allegations, but the vagueness was not the fault of petitioner. Counsel had no reason to believe Stinnett had been married to Meinhard or been represented by Woodson. The underdevelopment of these matters was attributable to Stinnett and Woodson, if anyone. We do not suggest the State has an obligation to pay for investigation of as yet undeveloped claims; but if the prisoner has made a reasonable effort to discover the claims to commence or continue state proceedings, § 2254(e)(2) will not bar him from developing them in federal court.

The Court of Appeals held state habeas counsel was not diligent because petitioner's investigator on federal habeas discovered the relationships upon interviewing two jurors who referred in passing to Stinnett as "Bonnie Meinhard." The investigator later confirmed Stinnett's prior marriage to Meinhard by checking Cumberland County's public records. We should be surprised, to say the least, if a district court familiar with the standards of trial practice were to hold that in all cases diligent counsel must check public records containing personal information pertaining to each and every juror. Because of Stinnett and Woodson's silence, there was no basis for an investigation into Stinnett's marriage history. Section 2254(e)(2) does not apply to petitioner's related claims of juror bias and prosecutorial misconduct.

We further note the Commonwealth has not argued that petitioner could have sought relief in state court once he discovered the factual bases of these claims some time between appointment of federal habeas counsel on July 2, 1996, and the filing of his federal habeas petition on November 20, 1996. * * * As state postconviction relief was no longer available at the time the facts came to light, it would have been futile for petitioner to return to the Virginia courts. In these circumstances, though the state courts did not have an opportunity to consider the new claims, petitioner cannot be said to have failed to develop them in state court by reason of having neglected to pursue remedies available under Virginia law.

Our analysis should suffice to establish cause for any procedural default petitioner may have committed in not presenting these claims to the Virginia courts in the first instance. Questions regarding the standard for determining the prejudice that petitioner must establish to obtain relief on these claims can be addressed by the Court of Appeals or the District Court in the course of further proceedings. These courts, in light of cases such as Smith ("[T]he remedy for allegations of juror partiality is a hearing in which the defendant has the opportunity to prove actual bias"), will take due account of the District Court's earlier decision to grant an evidentiary hearing based in part on its belief that "Juror Stinnett deliberately failed to tell the truth on voir dire."

IV

Petitioner alleges the Commonwealth failed to disclose an informal plea agreement with Cruse. The Court of Appeals rejected this claim on the merits under § 2254(d)(1), so it is unnecessary to reach the question whether § 2254(e)(2) would permit a hearing on the claim.

The judgment of the Court of Appeals is affirmed in part and reversed in part, and the case is remanded for further proceedings consistent with this opinion.

It is so ordered.

Notes and Questions

1. As *Williams* reflects, AEDPA supersedes *Townsend*, the 1966 amendment to § 2254(d), and *Tamayo-Reyes* for some purposes. *Tamayo-Reyes* substituted the cause-prejudice standard for *Townsend*'s deliberate-bypass standard when a petitioner sought a federal evidentiary hearing on the ground that state proceedings did not develop the material facts adequately. What is left of the cause-prejudice standard in such cases after *Williams*? When does it apply? When does § 2254(e)(2) supersede it?

2. Look at the language of § 2254(e)(2). *Williams* tells us only that by replacing the cause-prejudice standard with this provision, Congress "raised the bar *Keeney* [v. *Tamayo-Reyes*] imposed on prisoners who were not diligent in state-court proceedings." How much did Congress raise the bar? To satisfy the "prejudice" element, a petitioner needs to show a substantial probability that the result of the state proceeding would have been different in a trial without the constitutional violation. What exactly must a petitioner show under § 2254(e)(2)(B)? How does that compare to "prejudice?"

3. Remember that Townsend and the 1966 amendments to then § 2254(d) laid out many circumstances requiring an evidentiary hearing. Tamayo-Reyes, § 2254(e)(2), and *Williams* all appear to apply only to the single circumstance when the state court hearing did not develop the material facts adequately. The only other provision of current law dealing with a review of state factual findings is in § 2254(d)(2), which states that a court shall not grant a state prisoner's application for a writ of habeas corpus that the state court adjudicated on the merits unless the state adjudication "resulted in a decision that was based on an unreasonable determination of the facts in light of the evidence presented in the State court proceeding." What happened to all of the other particular circumstances for granting a federal evidentiary hearing listed in Townsend and the former § 2254(d)? Has AEDPA eliminated them by omission? Should the general language of current § 2254(d)(2) be interpreted to encompass the other circumstances or should the other *Townsend* circumstances have a continuing life of their own? If your answer to the last question is "yes," consider whether a Supreme Court decision survives when Congress codifies it and subsequently deletes the codification. If your answer is "no," what do you make of Tamayo-Reyes's statement that "it is evident that [the 1966 version of] § 2254(d) does not codify Townsend's specifications of when a hearing is required?" At least one district judge has concluded that the answer should be "yes." *See Lawrie v. Snyder*, 9 F.Supp.2d 428 (D.Del. 1998) ("The remainder of Townsend, however, appears to have been left intact, including the other five factors under which an evidentiary hearing is mandatory, as well as the court's overriding ability to hold a hearing in its discretion.").

Professor Yackle attempted to resolve this interpretive problem by a liberal reading of the current sections (d)(2) and (e)(1):

> Under [(d)(2)], a federal court can scarcely be indifferent to the process by which a state court reached a factual finding or the evidentiary support that finding enjoys.
>
> I read § 2254(e)(1) to drop the specific procedural and substantive standards contained in the former § 2254(d). But I do not read it to dispense with a federal court's rudimentary responsibility to ensure that it is deciding a constitutional claim based on factual findings that were forged in a procedurally adequate way and were anchored in a sufficient evidentiary record. In this sense, § 2254(e)(1) departs from prior law, but only to substitute general notions of procedural regularity and substantive accuracy for detailed statutory standards.

Larry W. Yackle, *Federal Evidentiary Hearings Under the New Habeas Corpus Statute*, 6 B.U.PUB.INT.L.J. 135, 141 (1996) (footnotes omitted).

4. In a series of cases, the Supreme Court has repeatedly (often *per curiam*) reversed habeas decisions coming out of the Ninth Circuit on the ground that the Court of Appeals was too quick to conclude that the state court's decision involved an "objectively unreasonable" application of the facts to clearly established federal law. These cases include, but are not limited to, *Rice v. Collins*, 546 U.S. 333 (2006); *Schriro*

v. Landrigan, 550 U.S. 465 (2007); *Waddington v. Sarausad*, 555 U.S. 179 (2009), and *Knowles v. Mirzayance*, 556 U.S. 111 (2009). The Ninth Circuit does not shows no signs of simply allowing a larger percentage of state court constitutional decisions to stand, and the Supreme Court has not further elaborated, in general terms, what "objectively reasonable" means; it simply continues to reverse case after case. Is the Ninth Circuit acting properly under these circumstances? Irrespective of the answer to that question, is the Supreme Court using its docket in the most prudent manner? If the Court is unable or unwilling to articulate a more granular standard, ought it expect a lower court to simply leave a larger number of state court decisions undisturbed without any greater guidance as to which decisions fall into that category? Or is the Court right to expect that all experienced lawyers and judges know "objectively reasonableness" when they see it? (In other areas of the law, does "reasonableness" vary from one sub-specialty to another?)

---

2. Constitutional Claims Cognizable on Habeas Corpus

Brown v. Allen (1953) greatly expanded habeas corpus by holding that federal courts generally must review federal constitutional claims raised by state prisoners if the petitioner exhausted available state court remedies. Notwithstanding *Brown*'s blanket nature, *Stone v. Powell*, 428 U.S. 465 (1976), held that federal habeas corpus does not extend to relitigation of Fourth Amendment claims when the state provides a full and fair opportunity to litigate them. The majority based its ruling on two themes: 1) the exclusionary rule being not a personal right but rather a judicially-created remedy for the benefit of society as a deterrent measure, and 2) that the interests the rule protects do not affect the integrity of the trial itself. Justice Brennan dissented vigorously, decrying the majority's "arrogation of power committed solely to Congress."

Many speculated that *Stone* presaged a general restricting of federal habeas jurisdiction because state courts generally provide opportunities to litigate federal claims. The defense community's alarm, at least on that ground, appears to have been premature. *Rose v. Mitchell*, 443 U.S. 545 (1979), declined to extend *Stone* to a challenge to an allegedly racially discriminatory grand jury system, and *Jackson v. Virginia*, 443 U.S. 307 (1979) ruled that *Stone* does not apply to a challenge based on the constitutionality of the reasonable doubt standard of criminal guilt. The latter issue goes directly to the integrity of the trial process as a manner of determining guilt, but the former is not so easily related to it. *Kimmelman v. Morrison* (1986) refused to extend *Stone* to Sixth Amendment claims of ineffective assistance of counsel where the claim of inadequate representation rested on failure to make a timely motion to suppress evidence allegedly seized in violation of the Fourth Amendment. The state argued that every Fourth Amendment claim where the defendant loses or defaults in raising it will thus be litigated in federal court in Sixth Amendment guise. The Court responded that the rigorous standard for ineffective assistance claims that *Strickland v. Washington*, 466 U.S. 668 (1984), set forth would prevent this easy circumvention of *Stone v. Powell*. Finally, *Withrow v. Williams*, 507 U.S. 680 (1993), declined to extend to claims involving confessions obtained in violation of *Miranda v. Arizona*, 384 U.S. 436 (1966). Has the Court implicitly limited *Stone* to Fourth Amendment claims?

Teague v. Lane

Supreme Court of the United States, 1989.
489 U.S. 288.

JUSTICE O'CONNOR announced the judgment of the Court and delivered the opinion of the Court with respect to Parts I, II, and III, and an opinion with respect to Parts IV and V, in which THE CHIEF JUSTICE, JUSTICE SCALIA, and JUSTICE KENNEDY join.

In *Taylor v. Louisiana* (1975), this Court held that the Sixth Amendment required that the jury **venire** be drawn from a fair cross section of the community. The Court stated, however, that "in holding that petit juries must be drawn from a source fairly representative of the community we impose no requirement that petit juries actually chosen must mirror the community and reflect the various distinctive groups in the population. Defendants are not entitled to a jury of any particular composition." The principal question presented in this case is whether the Sixth Amendment's fair cross section requirement should now be extended to the petit jury. Because we adopt Justice Harlan's approach to retroactivity for cases on collateral review, we leave the resolution of that question for another day.

I

Petitioner, a black man, was convicted by an all-white Illinois jury of three counts of attempted murder, two counts of armed robbery, and one count of aggravated battery. During jury selection for petitioner's trial, the prosecutor used all 10 of his peremptory challenges to exclude blacks. Petitioner's counsel used one of his 10 peremptory challenges to exclude a black woman who was married to a police officer. After the prosecutor had struck six blacks, petitioner's counsel moved for a mistrial. The trial court denied the motion. When the prosecutor struck four more blacks, petitioner's counsel again moved for a mistrial, arguing that petitioner was "entitled to a jury of his peers." The prosecutor defended the challenges by stating that he was trying to achieve a balance of men and women on the jury. The trial court denied the motion, reasoning that the jury "appear[ed] to be a fair [one]."

[Teague pursued his direct appeals in Illinois. The Illinois and United States Supreme Courts denied review. Teague then sought federal habeas relief, arguing that, even before Batson v. Kentucky, under Swain v. Alabama a prosecutor who offered an explanation on his use of peremptory challenges could be questioned further. The lower federal courts rejected that argument and ruled that the fair cross section rule only applied to jury venires, not to juries selected from such venires. Since Teague's conviction became final before the Court decided Batson, the courts declined to afford him relief based on that case.]

* * *

II

Petitioner's first contention is that he should receive the benefit of our decision in Batson even though his conviction became final before Batson was decided. Before addressing petitioner's argument, we think it helpful to explain how Batson modified Swain. Swain held that a "State's purposeful or deliberate denial" to blacks of an opportunity to serve as jurors solely on account of race violates the Equal Protection Clause of the Fourteenth Amendment. * * *

In Batson, the Court overruled that portion of Swain setting forth the evidentiary showing necessary to make out a *prima facie* case of racial discrimination under the Equal Protection Clause. The Court held that a defendant can establish a *prima facie* case by showing that he is a "member of a cognizable racial group," that the prosecutor exercised "peremptory challenges to remove from the venire members of the defendant's race," and that those "facts and any other relevant circumstances raise an inference that the prosecutor used that practice to exclude the veniremen from the petit jury on account of their race." Once the defendant makes out a *prima facie* case of discrimination, the burden shifts to the prosecutor "to come forward with a neutral explanation for challenging black jurors."

In Allen v. Hardy, the Court held that Batson constituted an "explicit and substantial break with prior precedent" because it overruled a portion of Swain. Employing the retroactivity standard of Linkletter v. Walker, the Court concluded that the rule announced in Batson should not be applied retroactively on collateral review of convictions that became final before Batson was announced. The Court defined final to mean a case " 'where the judgment of conviction was rendered, the availability of appeal exhausted, and the time for petition for certiorari had elapsed before our decision in' Batson * * * ."

Petitioner's conviction became final 2 years prior to Batson, thus depriving petitioner of any benefit from the rule announced in that case.

* * *

We find that *Allen v. Hardy* is dispositive, and that petitioner cannot benefit from the rule announced in *Batson*.

IV

Petitioner's third and final contention is that the Sixth Amendment's fair cross section requirement applies to the petit jury. As we noted at the outset, *Taylor* expressly stated that the fair cross section requirement does not apply to the petit jury. Petitioner nevertheless contends that the *ratio decidendi* of *Taylor* cannot be limited to the jury venire, and he urges adoption of a new rule. Because we hold that the rule urged by petitioner should not be applied retroactively to cases on collateral review, we decline to address petitioner's contention.

A

In the past, the Court has, without discussion, often applied a new constitutional rule of criminal procedure to the defendant in the case announcing the new rule, and has confronted the question of retroactivity later when a different defendant sought the benefit of that rule. In several cases, however, the Court has addressed the retroactivity question in the very case announcing the new rule. These two lines of cases do not have a unifying theme, and we think it is time to clarify how the question of retroactivity should be resolved for cases on collateral review.

> **FYI**
>
> "Collateral review" means judicial examination of a case after all direct appeals have been exhausted. It is generally prohibited in civil cases, but habeas proceedings have long been an exception to that rule.

* * *

In our view, the question "whether a decision [announcing a new rule should] be given prospective or retroactive effect should be faced at the time of [that] decision." Retroactivity is properly treated as a threshold question, for, once a new rule is applied to the defendant in the case announcing the rule, evenhanded justice requires that it be applied retroactively to all who are similarly situated. Thus, before deciding whether the fair cross section requirement should be extended to the petit jury, we should ask whether such a rule would be applied retroactively to the case at issue. This retroactivity determination would normally entail application of the *Linkletter* standard, but we believe that our approach to retroactivity for cases on collateral review requires modification.

It is admittedly often difficult to determine when a case announces a new rule, and we do not attempt to define the spectrum of what may or may not constitute a new rule for retroactivity purposes. In general, however, a case announces a new rule when it breaks new ground or imposes a new obligation on the States or the Federal Government. To put it differently, a case announces a new rule if the result was not dictated by precedent existing at the time the defendant's conviction became final. Given the strong language in *Taylor* and our statement that "[f]airness in [jury] selection has never been held to require proportional representation of races upon a jury," application of the fair cross section requirement to the petit jury would be a new rule.

Not all new rules have been uniformly treated for retroactivity purposes. Nearly a quarter of a century ago, in *Linkletter*, the Court attempted to set some standards by which to determine the retroactivity of new rules. The question in *Linkletter* was whether *Mapp v. Ohio*, which made the exclusionary rule applicable to the States, should be applied retroactively to cases on collateral review. The Court determined that the retroactivity of *Mapp* should be determined by examining the purpose of the exclusionary rule, the reliance of the States on prior law, and the effect on the administration of justice of a retroactive application of the exclusionary rule. Using that standard, the Court held that *Mapp* would only apply to trials commencing after that case was decided.

The *Linkletter* retroactivity standard has not led to consistent results. Instead, it has been used to limit application of certain new rules to cases on direct review, other new rules only to the defendants in the cases announcing such rules, and still other new rules to cases in which trials have not yet commenced. Not surprisingly, commentators have "had a veritable field day" with the *Linkletter* standard, with much of the discussion being "more than mildly negative."

Application of the *Linkletter* standard led to the disparate treatment of similarly situated defendants on direct review. * * * This inequity also generated vehement criticism.

Dissatisfied with the *Linkletter* standard, Justice Harlan advocated a different approach to retroactivity. He argued that new rules should always be applied retroactively to cases on direct review, but that generally they should not be applied retroactively to criminal cases on collateral review.

In [1987], we rejected as unprincipled and inequitable the *Linkletter* standard for cases pending on direct review at the time a new rule is announced, and adopted the first part of the retroactivity approach advocated by Justice Harlan. We agreed with Justice Harlan that "failure to apply a newly declared constitutional rule to criminal cases pending on direct review violates basic norms of constitutional adjudication." We gave two reasons for our decision. First, because we can only promulgate new rules in specific cases and cannot possibly decide all cases in which review is sought, "the integrity of judicial review" requires the application of the new rule to "all similar cases pending on direct review." * * *

Second, because "selective application of new rules violates the principle of treating similarly situated defendants the same," we refused to continue to tolerate the inequity that resulted from not applying new rules retroactively to defendants whose cases had not yet become final. Although new rules that constituted clear breaks with the past generally were not given retroactive effect under the *Linkletter* standard, we held that "a new rule for the conduct of criminal prosecutions is to be applied retroactively to all cases, state or federal, pending on direct review or not yet final, with no exception for cases in which the new rule constitutes a 'clear break' with the past."

The *Linkletter* standard also led to unfortunate disparity in the treatment of similarly situated defendants on collateral review. * * * This disparity in treatment was a product of two factors: our failure to treat retroactivity as a threshold question and the *Linkletter* standard's inability to account for the nature and function of collateral review. Having decided to rectify the first of those inadequacies, we now turn to the second.

B

Justice Harlan believed that new rules generally should not be applied retroactively to cases on collateral review. He argued that retroactivity for cases on collateral review could "be responsibly [determined] only by focusing, in the first instance, on the nature, function, and scope of the adjudicatory process in which such cases arise. The relevant frame of reference, in other words, is not the purpose of the new rule whose benefit the [defendant] seeks, but instead the purposes for which the writ of habeas corpus is made available." With regard to the nature of habeas corpus, Justice Harlan wrote:

> Habeas corpus always has been a collateral remedy, providing an avenue for upsetting judgments that have become otherwise final. It is not designed as a substitute for direct review. The interest in leaving concluded litigation in a state of repose, that is, reducing the controversy to a final judgment not subject to further judicial revision, may quite legitimately be found by those responsible for defining the scope of the writ to outweigh in some, many, or most instances the competing interest in readjudicating convictions according to all legal standards in effect when a habeas petition is filed.

Given the "broad scope of constitutional issues cognizable on habeas," Justice Harlan argued that it is "sounder, in adjudicating habeas petitions, generally to apply the law prevailing at the time a conviction became final than it is to seek to dispose of [habeas] cases on the basis of intervening changes in constitutional interpretation." As he had explained,

> the threat of habeas serves as a necessary additional incentive for trial and appellate courts throughout the land to conduct their proceedings in a manner

consistent with established constitutional standards. In order to perform this deterrence function, * * * the habeas court need only apply the constitutional standards that prevailed at the time the original proceedings took place.

Justice Harlan identified only two exceptions to his general rule of nonretroactivity for cases on collateral review. First, a new rule should be applied retroactively if it places "certain kinds of primary, private individual conduct beyond the power of the criminal law-making authority to proscribe." Second, a new rule should be applied retroactively if it requires the observance of "those procedures that * * * are 'implicit in the concept of ordered liberty.'" [Citing Palko v. Connecticut.]

exceptions

* * *

We agree with Justice Harlan's description of the function of habeas corpus. * * * Rather, we have recognized that interests of comity and finality must also be considered in determining the proper scope of habeas review. Thus, if a defendant fails to comply with state procedural rules and is barred from litigating a particular constitutional claim in state court, the claim can be considered on federal habeas only if the defendant shows cause for the default and actual prejudice resulting therefrom. We have declined to make the application of the procedural default rule dependent on the magnitude of the constitutional claim at issue, or on the State's interest in the enforcement of its procedural rule.

* * *

Application of constitutional rules not in existence at the time a conviction became final seriously undermines the principle of finality which is essential to the operation of our criminal justice system. Without finality, the criminal law is deprived of much of its deterrent effect.

* * *

The "costs imposed upon the State[s] by retroactive application of new rules of constitutional law on habeas corpus * * * generally far outweigh the benefits of this application." In many ways the application of new rules to cases on collateral review may be more intrusive than the enjoining of criminal prosecutions, for it continually forces the States to marshal resources in order to keep in prison defendants whose trials and appeals conformed to then-existing constitutional standards. Furthermore, as we recognized, "[s]tate courts are understandably frustrated when they faithfully apply existing constitutional law only to have a federal court discover, during a [habeas] proceeding, new constitutional commands."

We find these criticisms to be persuasive, and we now adopt Justice Harlan's view of retroactivity for cases on collateral review. Unless they fall within an exception to the general rule, new constitutional rules of criminal procedure will not be applicable to those cases which have become final before the new rules are announced.

V

Petitioner's conviction became final in 1983. As a result, the rule petitioner urges would not be applicable to this case, which is on collateral review, unless it would fall within an exception.

The first exception suggested by Justice Harlan—that a new rule should be applied retroactively if it places "certain kinds of primary, private individual conduct beyond the power of the criminal law-making authority to proscribe,"—is not relevant here. * * *

The second exception suggested by Justice Harlan—that a new rule should be applied retroactively if it requires the observance of "those procedures that * * * are 'implicit in the concept of ordered liberty,' "—we apply with a modification. The language used by Justice Harlan * * * leaves no doubt that he meant the second exception to be reserved for watershed rules of criminal procedure * * * .

Justice Harlan had reasoned that one of the two principal functions of habeas corpus was "to assure that no man has been incarcerated under a procedure which creates an impermissibly large risk that the innocent will be convicted," and concluded "from this that all 'new' constitutional rules which significantly improve the pre-existing fact-finding procedures are to be retroactively applied on habeas." Justice Harlan gave three reasons for [later] shifting to the less defined *Palko* approach. First, he observed that recent precedent led "ineluctably * * * to the conclusion that it is not a principal purpose of the writ to inquire whether a criminal convict did in fact commit the deed alleged." Second, he noted that cases gave him reason to doubt the marginal effectiveness of claimed improvements in factfinding. Third, he found "inherently intractable the purported distinction between those new rules that are designed to improve the factfinding process and those designed principally to further other values."

We believe it desirable to combine the accuracy element of the * * * second exception with the * * * requirement that the procedure at issue must implicate the fundamental fairness of the trial. * * * [O]ur cases have moved in the direction of reaffirming the relevance of the likely accuracy of convictions in determining the available scope of habeas review. * * * [W]e believe that Justice Harlan's concerns about the difficulty in identifying both the existence and the value of accuracy-enhancing procedural rules can be addressed by limiting the scope of the second exception to those new procedures without which the likelihood of an accurate conviction is seriously diminished.

Because we operate from the premise that such procedures would be so central to an accurate determination of innocence or guilt, we believe it unlikely that many such components of basic due process have yet to emerge. We are also of the view that such rules are "best illustrated by recalling the classic grounds for the issuance of a writ of habeas corpus—that the proceeding was dominated by mob violence; that the prosecutor knowingly made use of perjured testimony; or that the conviction was based on a confession extorted from the defendant by brutal methods."

An examination of our decision in *Taylor* applying the fair cross section requirement to the jury venire leads inexorably to the conclusion that adoption of the rule petitioner urges would be a far cry from the kind of absolute prerequisite to fundamental fairness that is "implicit in the concept of ordered liberty." * * * Because the absence of a fair cross section on the jury venire does not undermine the fundamental fairness that must underlie a conviction or seriously diminish the likelihood of obtaining an accurate conviction, we conclude that a rule requiring that petit juries be composed of a fair cross section of the community would not be a "bedrock procedural element" that would be retroactively applied under the second exception we have articulated.

Were we to recognize the new rule urged by petitioner in this case, we would have to give petitioner the benefit of that new rule even though it would not be applied retroactively to others similarly situated. In the words of Justice Brennan, such an inequitable result would be "an unavoidable consequence of the necessity that constitutional adjudications not stand as mere dictum." But the harm caused by the failure to treat similarly situated defendants alike cannot be exaggerated: such inequitable treatment "hardly comports with the ideal of 'administration of justice with an even hand.'" Our refusal to allow such disparate treatment in the direct review context led us to adopt the first part of Justice Harlan's retroactivity approach in *Griffith*. "The fact that the new rule may constitute a clear break with the past has no bearing on the 'actual inequity that results' when only one of many similarly situated defendants receives the benefit of the new rule."

If there were no other way to avoid rendering advisory opinions, we might well agree that the inequitable treatment described above is "an insignificant cost for adherence to sound principles of decision-making." But there is a more principled way of dealing with the problem. We can simply refuse to announce a new rule in a given case unless the rule would be applied retroactively to the defendant in the case and to all others similarly situated. We think this approach is a sound one. Not only does it eliminate any problems of rendering advisory opinions, it also avoids the inequity resulting from the uneven application of new rules to similarly situated defendants. We therefore hold that, implicit in the retroactivity approach we adopt today, is the principle that habeas corpus cannot be used as a vehicle to create new constitutional rules of criminal procedure unless those rules would be applied retroactively to all defendants on collateral review through one of the two exceptions we have articulated. Because a decision extending the fair cross section requirement to the petit jury would not be applied retroactively to cases on collateral review under the approach we adopt today, we do not address petitioner's claim.

For the reasons set forth above, the judgment of the Court of Appeals is affirmed.

It is so ordered.

JUSTICE STEVENS, with whom JUSTICE BLACKMUN joins as to Part I, concurring in part and concurring in the judgment.

I

* * *

I do not agree * * * with the plurality's dicta proposing a "modification" of Justice Harlan's fundamental fairness exception. "[I]t has been the law, presumably for at least as long as anyone currently in jail has been incarcerated," Justice Harlan wrote, "that procedures utilized to convict them must have been fundamentally fair, that is, in accordance with the command of the Fourteenth Amendment that '[n]o State shall * * * deprive any person of life, liberty, or property, without due process of law.' " He continued: "[T]he writ ought always to lie for claims of nonobservance of those procedures that, as so aptly described by Mr. Justice Cardozo, are 'implicit in the concept of ordered liberty.' * * * " In embracing Justice Cardozo's notion that errors "violat[ing] those 'fundamental principles of liberty and justice which lie at the base of all our civil and political institutions,' " must be rectified, Justice Harlan expressly rejected a previous statement linking the fundamental fairness exception to factual innocence.

The plurality wrongly resuscitates Justice Harlan's early view, indicating that the only procedural errors deserving correction on collateral review are those that undermine "an accurate determination of innocence or guilt * * * ." I cannot agree that it is "unnecessarily anachronistic," to issue a writ of habeas corpus to a petitioner convicted in a manner that violates fundamental principles of liberty. * * * Even when assessing errors at the guilt phase of a trial, factual innocence is too capricious a factor by which to determine if a procedural change is sufficiently "bedrock" or "watershed" to justify application of the fundamental fairness exception.

* * *

JUSTICE BRENNAN, with whom JUSTICE MARSHALL joins, dissenting.

Today a plurality of this Court, without benefit of briefing and oral argument, adopts a novel threshold test for federal review of state criminal convictions on habeas corpus. It does so without regard for—indeed, without even mentioning—our contrary decisions over the past 35 years delineating the broad scope of habeas relief. The plurality further appears oblivious to the importance we have consistently accorded the principle of *stare decisis* in nonconstitutional cases. Out of an exaggerated concern for treating similarly situated habeas petitioners the same, the plurality would for the first time preclude the federal courts from considering on collateral review a vast range of important constitutional challenges; where those challenges have merit, it would bar the vindication of personal constitutional rights and deny society a check against further violations until the same claim is presented on direct review. In my view, the plurality's "blind adherence to the principle of treating like cases alike" amounts to "letting the tail wag the dog" when it stymies the resolution of substantial and unheralded constitutional questions. Because I cannot acquiesce in this unprecedented curtailment of the reach of the Great Writ, particularly in the absence of any discussion of these momentous changes by the parties or the lower courts, I dissent.

I

The federal habeas corpus statute provides that a federal court "shall entertain an application for a writ of habeas corpus in behalf of a person in custody pursuant to the judgment of a State court only on the ground that he is in custody in violation of the Constitution or laws or treaties of the United States." For well over a century, we have read this statute and its forbears to authorize federal courts to grant writs of habeas corpus whenever a person's liberty is unconstitutionally restrained. Shortly after the Habeas Corpus Act of 1867 empowered federal courts to issue writs of habeas corpus to state authorities, we noted: "This legislation is of the most comprehensive character. It brings within the habeas corpus jurisdiction of every court and of every judge every possible case of privation of liberty contrary to the National Constitution, treaties, or laws. It is impossible to widen this jurisdiction." Nothing has happened since to persuade us to alter that judgment. * * * Our subsequent rulings have not departed from that teaching in cases where the presentation of a petitioner's claim on collateral review is not barred by a procedural default.

In particular, our decisions have made plain that the federal courts may collaterally review claims such as Teague's once state remedies have been exhausted.

* * *

II

* * *

D

These are massive changes, unsupported by precedent.[6] They also lack a reasonable foundation. By exaggerating the importance of treating like cases alike and granting relief to all identically positioned habeas petitioners or none, "the Court acts as if it has no choice but to follow a mechanical notion of fairness without pausing to consider 'sound principles of decisionmaking.'" Certainly it is desirable, in the interest of fairness, to accord the same treatment to all habeas petitioners with the same claims. Given a choice between deciding an issue on direct or collateral review that might result in a new rule of law that would not warrant retroactive application to persons on collateral review other than the petitioner who brought the claim, we should ordinarily grant certiorari and decide the question on direct review. Following our decision in *Griffith v. Kentucky*, a new rule would apply equally to all persons whose convictions had not become final before the rule was announced, whereas habeas petitioners other than the one whose case we decided might not benefit from such a rule if we adopted it on collateral review. Taking cases on direct review ahead of those on habeas is especially attractive because the retrial of habeas petitioners usually places a heavier burden on the States than the retrial of persons on direct review. Other things being equal, our concern for fairness and finality ought to therefore lead us to render our decision in a case that comes to us on direct review.

Other things are not always equal, however. Sometimes a claim which, if successful, would create a new rule not appropriate for retroactive application on collateral review is better presented by a habeas case than by one on direct review. In fact, sometimes the claim is only presented on collateral review. In that case, while we could forgo deciding the issue in the hope that it would eventually be presented squarely on direct review, that hope might be misplaced, and even if it were in time fulfilled, the opportunity to check constitutional violations and to further the evolution of our thinking in some area of the law would in the meanwhile have been lost. In addition, by preserving our right and that of the lower federal courts to hear such claims on collateral review, we would not discourage their litigation on federal habeas corpus and thus not deprive ourselves

6 The plurality's claim that "our cases have moved in the direction of reaffirming the relevance of the likely accuracy of convictions in determining the available scope of habeas review," has little force. Two of the cases it cites discuss the conditions under which a habeas petitioner may obtain review even though his claim would otherwise be procedurally barred. They do not hold that a petitioner's likely guilt or innocence bears on the cognizability of habeas claims in the absence of procedural default. And the Court has limited *Stone v. Powell* to Fourth Amendment exclusionary rule claims, passing up several opportunities to extend it.

and society of the benefit of decisions by the lower federal courts when we must resolve these issues ourselves.

The plurality appears oblivious to these advantages of our settled approach to collateral review. Instead, it would deny itself these benefits because adherence to precedent would occasionally result in one habeas petitioner's obtaining redress while another petitioner with an identical claim could not qualify for relief.[7] In my view, the uniform treatment of habeas petitioners is not worth the price the plurality is willing to pay. Permitting the federal courts to decide novel habeas claims not substantially related to guilt or innocence has profited our society immensely. Congress has not seen fit to withdraw those benefits by amending the statute that provides for them. And although a favorable decision for a petitioner might not extend to another prisoner whose identical claim has become final, it is at least arguably better that the wrong done to one person be righted than that none of the injuries inflicted on those whose convictions have become final be redressed, despite the resulting inequality in treatment.

* * *

Notes and Questions

1. a) When does existing precedent clearly dictate a decision? One could analogize to the official immunity decisions. In *Wood v. Strickland*, 420 U.S. 308 (1975), a case involving official immunity to § 1983 claims, Justice Powell argued strongly that "settled, indisputable law" and "unquestioned constitutional rights" were chimerical and unworkable as a standard of liability, but in *Harlow v. Fitzgerald*, 457 U.S. 800 (1982), he ruled that officials have immunity from § 1983 actions only "insofar as their conduct does not violate clearly established statutory or constitutional rights of which a reasonable person would have known." How many cases that recognize constitutional rights are "dictated by existing precedent"? If precedent so clearly dictates a particular result, how does the case survive for Supreme Court review? Conversely, should one conclude that whenever the Supreme Court grants plenary review, either

7 The plurality's complaint that prior retroactivity decisions have sometimes led to more than one habeas petitioner's reaping the benefit of a new rule while most habeas petitioners obtained no relief because of "our failure to treat retroactivity as a threshold question" is misguided. The disparity resulting from our deciding three years later not to apply retroactively the rule of *Edwards v. Arizona* should not be ascribed to our failure to make retroactivity a threshold question, but rather to our failure to decide the retroactivity question at the same time that we decided the merits issue. If both decisions are made contemporaneously, then only one exception need be made to the rule of equal treatment. The plurality may find even this slight inequality unacceptable, but the magnitude of the disparity is not and need not be as large as its example suggests.

the precedent was not clearly established or the lower courts ignored their constitutional responsibility?

b) The Court has made clear that a case need not be on all fours to establish precedent sufficiently clear to avoid *Teague*. *Stringer v. Black*, 503 U.S. 222 (1992), found that although no single case established the rule upon which the petitioner relied, a "long line of authority" strongly suggested it; *Teague* did not bar review. Still, it remains unclear just how much not-directly-on-point precedent is enough.

c) Neither the Supreme Court nor the inferior federal courts have had an easy time defining what a new rule is. In *Butler v. McKellar*, 494 U.S. 407 (1990), the majority held that reasonable disagreement among courts or counsel about the outcome of a case meant that the result was not dictated by existing precedent and therefore was "new." Does that mean that whenever there is a dissenting opinion or a split among the circuits on an issue that it is by definition "new" and cannot be considered on collateral review? *See also Saffle v. Parks*, 494 U.S. 484 (1990) (disagreement among lower courts establishes a rule as "new" as long as it is "logically distinct" from precedent); *Beard v. Banks*, 542 U.S. 406 (2004) (dissent by four Justices reasoning that existing Supreme Court precedent did not compel result adopted by majority precludes finding that the result was dictated by precedent because the unlawfulness of conviction was not apparent to all reasonable jurists).

CLICK FOR UPDATE
UPDATES FOUND ON PAGES 1191-1195

(d) *Whorton v. Bockting*, 549 U.S. 406 (2007), continued the Court's practice of defining "new rule" very broadly for *Teague* purposes but defining the exceptions that would allow a new rule to apply in a collateral proceeding very narrowly. *Crawford v. Washington*, 541 U.S. 36 (2004), redefined the Sixth Amendment's Confrontation Clause. Prior to *Crawford*, *Ohio v. Roberts*, 448 U.S. 56 (1980), allowed admission of a hearsay statement by a declarant unavailable to testify if the statement "bore sufficient indicia of reliability," either because the statement fell within a firmly rooted exception to the hearsay rule or bore "particularized guarantees of trustworthiness." *Crawford* overruled *Roberts*, holding that "[t]estimonial statements of witnesses absent from trial" are admissible "only where the declarant is unavailable *and* only where the defendant had a prior opportunity to cross-examine [the witness]." (Emphasis added.) Quoting *Saffle* and *Teague*, the Court said a rule is "new" if it is not "dictated by precedent existing at the time the defendant's conviction became final." Finding *Crawford* "flatly inconsistent" with *Roberts*, the Court held that *Crawford* established a new rule of criminal procedure.

The *Whorton* Court noted that a new rule of procedure applies retroactively in a collateral proceeding only if it is a " 'watershed rul[e] of criminal procedure' implicating the fundamental fairness and accuracy of the criminal proceeding" (again quoting *Saffle* and *Teague*). A new rule is a watershed only if it is necessary to prevent an impermissibly large risk of an inaccurate conviction and "alter[s] our understanding of the bedrock procedural elements essential to the fairness of a proceeding." The Court noted that while excluding uncross-examined hearsay statements might improve the accuracy of trial, absence of this safeguard nonetheless did not pose an "impermissibly large risk" of an inaccurate conviction. Nor did Crawford find a new, previously *undiscovered* part of the bedrock because live testimony and cross-examination have long been considered important procedural guarantees.

If the Crawford rule is not a watershed, it is difficult to imagine what new rule might be. The Court stated it to be "unlikely" that any such rules will emerge, and noted that in the years since *Teague*, it has rejected every claim that a new rule satisfied the requirements for watershed status. To date, the Supreme Court has not found any new rule of criminal procedure to fall within the watershed exception to *Teague*. For the Court's latest refusal to denominate a new rule "watershed," see *Chaidez v. United States*, 133 S.Ct. 1103 (2013) (holding that *Padilla v. Kentucky*, 559 U.S. 356 (2010) (Sixth Amendment requirement that defense counsel advise non-citizen clients of deportation risks of entering guilty pleas) does not apply retroactively).

(e) The *Teague* plurality believes that retroactivity is a threshold issue; that is, a court must decide whether a new rule will be applied retroactively before deciding whether to announce the rule. The plurality then adopts Justice Harlan's suggestion that new rules not be applied retroactively if announced in cases on collateral review, except in two very limited circumstances. From these premises, the plurality concludes that new rules cannot be announced at all in a collateral proceeding. The plurality reaches this conclusion because of problems the justices perceive with announcing a new rule but not applying the rule retroactively. A court might decide not to apply the rule to the petitioner or to others similarly situated. What does the plurality suggest would be wrong with that? A court might apply the new rule just to the petitioner and not to others similarly situated. What does the plurality say would be wrong with that? Having found these alternatives unacceptable, the plurality is left with the conclusion that new rules simply cannot be announced in habeas corpus cases.

(f) To make the threshold retroactivity decision, is a court forced to hypothesize a substantive rule in order to test its novelty? Where the hypothesized rule would not be retroactive, has not the court rendered an advisory opinion? Professor Arkin describes how the lower courts have apparently finessed the issue.

> When a petitioner is claiming relief under an after-decided rule, courts treat the requirement that retroactivity is to be given threshold consideration as one of priority; they simply decide the retroactivity of petitioner's claims—with whatever weighing of the merits is practically necessary—before proceeding to any other issue. Indeed, the fact that the issue of threshold consideration was passed over entirely by the Supreme Court in its affirmance of *Sawyer* [*v. Butler*] may well signal a recognition that the extreme position of *Teague* was unworkable from the

start. Certainly, no court has expended much effort sorting out novelty from the constitutional merits.

Marc M. Arkin, *The Prisoner's Dilemma: Life in the Lower Federal Courts After* Teague v. Lane, 69 N.C. L. REV. 371, 397-98 (1991).

g) It is not yet clear whether a state litigant can waive *Teague* problems, but the Supreme Court has effectively held that the state courts cannot. In *Horn v. Banks*, 536 U.S. 266 (2002), petitioner sought habeas relief after the state courts affirmed his murder conviction and denied post-conviction relief. He argued in his state and federal petitions that *Mills v. Maryland*, 486 U.S. 367 (1988), which postdated petitioner's conviction by six years, compelled the state to afford him a new sentencing proceeding because the sentencing court's charge implied that the jury had to be unanimous with respect to the existence of mitigating factors. The state courts denied relief on the ground that the procedure at Banks's sentencing did not violate Mills, but they did not consider *Teague*. The Third Circuit granted relief, foregoing a *Teague* analysis because "we do not need to focus on anything other than the reasoning and determination of the Pennsylvania Supreme Court." A per curiam Supreme Court reversed, holding that "the Court of Appeals committed a clear error by failing to perform a *Teague* analysis," and describing Teague analysis as a threshold question.

2. *Teague* divides constitutional rights into two categories: those that are retroactive and those that are not. After *Teague*, how will previously-unrecognized constitutional rights receive the federal courts' *imprimatur*?

3. The Court disapproves disparity of treatment among similarly-situated individuals, arguing that recognition of a new but non-retroactive constitutional entitlement on habeas would allow only the petitioner to benefit, not others convicted at the same time.

a) Suppose all individuals convicted on a given day whose cases present a new constitutional question were to persevere through the state appellate and federal habeas corpus processes. What becomes of the anomaly the Court perceives? To the extent that it disappears, does a petitioner in Teague's position suffer because other prisoners had less astute counsel?

b) Suppose Teague and another person involved in the same incident were convicted on the same day but in separate trials. If Teague's state appellate process ran particularly quickly and his confederate's did not, is it not possible that the confederate would receive the benefit of a newly-recognized constitutional right during his direct appeal while Teague would not because his trip through the appellate process was more expeditious?

4. Justice Brennan's dissent argued that the lower federal courts recognized many constitutional rights in habeas corpus cases. *Teague* halts that phenomenon. Although only a plurality supported the *Teague* rule, the Court has since made clear its intention to apply it rigorously. In *Penry v. Lynaugh*, 492 U.S. 302 (1989), a majority ruled that *Teague* applies to whether the Constitution permits execution of a retarded prisoner. The Court reached the merits because existing precedent dictated the claimed right, but in three subsequent decisions, the Court applied *Teague* in capital cases and refused review. Justice Brennan dissented vigorously:

> [Applying *Teague* to capital cases] means that a person may be killed although he or she has a sound constitutional claim that would have barred his or her execution had this Court only announced the constitutional rule before his or her conviction and sentence became final. It is intolerable that the difference between life and death should turn on such a fortuity of timing and beyond my comprehension that a majority of this Court will so blithely allow a State to take a human life though the method by which the sentence was determined violates our Constitution.

5. *Teague* has provoked considerable critical scholarly commentary. One commentator suggested strongly that the decision damages the Court's institutional integrity.

> The decisions in *Teague* and its progeny are subject to criticism on several fronts. The judicial crafting of the *Teague* decision was uneven at best, all too disingenuous at worst. The Court adopted an extremely restrictive view of habeas corpus jurisdiction and did so virtually as a passing aside. For anyone familiar with the climate surrounding the decision it is difficult to conclude that the Court's determination was the product of much more than unseemly impatience with a Congress that was considering related issues, but evidently too slowly for the Court. Moreover, the result in the *Teague* cases plainly was the work of a Court anxious to speed the pace of executions.
>
> * * *
>
> None of the *Teague* decisions seriously discussed [the] radical redefinition of habeas corpus. Rather, the Court disingenuously characterized *Teague* as nothing more than one further decision in a long line of cases attempting to resolve perplexing problems regarding the retroactivity of criminal constitutional rules. The entire premise of *Teague* was that existing retroactivity rules denied "even-handed justice" to "similarly situated" individuals seeking application of constitutional rules in their cases. Thus, *Teague* masqueraded as an exercise in achieving fairness. Moreover, in doing so the *Teague* Court purported to adopt a theory of retroactivity advanced by Justice Harlan twenty years ago. *Teague*, however, did neither of these things, or at least it did not do them very well.

Barry Friedman, *Habeas and Hubris*, 45 VAND.L.REV. 797, 800, 803 (1992). *See also, e.g.*, Vivian Berger, *Justice Delayed or Justice Denied—A Comment on Recent Proposals to Reform Death Penalty Habeas Corpus*, 90 COLUM. L. REV. 1665 (1990); Richard H.

Fallon, Jr. & Daniel J. Meltzer, *New Law, Non-retroactivity and Constitutional Remedies*, 104 HARV.L.REV. 1731 (1991).

Williams (Terry) v. Taylor

Supreme Court of the United States, 2000.
529 U.S. 362.

JUSTICE STEVENS announced the judgment of the Court and delivered the opinion of the Court with respect to Parts, I, III, and IV, and an opinion with respect to Parts II and V.*

The questions presented are whether Terry Williams' constitutional right to the effective assistance of counsel as defined in *Strickland v. Washington* was violated, and whether the judgment of the Virginia Supreme Court refusing to set aside his death sentence "was contrary to, or involved an unreasonable application of, clearly established Federal law, as determined by the Supreme Court of the United States," within the meaning of 28 U.S.C. § 2254(d)(1). We answer both questions affirmatively.

I

On November 3, 1985, Harris Stone was found dead in his residence on Henry Street in Danville, Virginia. Finding no indication of a struggle, local officials determined that the cause of death was blood alcohol poisoning, and the case was considered closed. Six months after Stone's death, Terry Williams, who was then incarcerated in the "I" unit of the city jail for an unrelated offense, wrote a letter to the police stating that he had killed " 'that man down on Henry Street' " and also stating that he " 'did it' " to that " 'lady down on West Green Street' " and was " 'very sorry.' " The letter was unsigned, but it closed with a reference to "I cell." The police readily identified Williams as its author, and, on April 25, 1986, they obtained several statements from him. In one Williams admitted that, after Stone refused to lend him " 'a couple of dollars,' " he had killed Stone with a mattock and took the money from his wallet. In September 1986, Williams was convicted of robbery and capital murder.

At Williams' sentencing hearing, the prosecution proved that Williams had been convicted of armed robbery in 1976 and burglary and grand larceny in 1982. The prosecution also introduced the written confessions that Williams had made

* Justice Souter, Justice Ginsburg, and Justice Breyer join this opinion in its entirety. Justice O'Connor and Justice Kennedy join Parts I, III, and IV of this opinion.

in April. The prosecution described two auto thefts and two separate violent assaults on elderly victims perpetrated after the Stone murder. On December 4, 1985, Williams had started a fire outside one victim's residence before attacking and robbing him. On March 5, 1986, Williams had brutally assaulted an elderly woman on West Green Street—an incident he had mentioned in his letter to the police. That confession was particularly damaging because other evidence established that the woman was in a "vegetative state" and not expected to recover. Williams had also been convicted of arson for setting a fire in the jail while awaiting trial in this case. Two expert witnesses employed by the State testified that there was a "high probability" that Williams would pose a serious continuing threat to society.

The evidence offered by Williams' trial counsel at the sentencing hearing consisted of the testimony of Williams' mother, two neighbors, and a taped excerpt from a statement by a psychiatrist. One of the neighbors had not been previously interviewed by defense counsel, but was noticed by counsel in the audience during the proceedings and asked to testify on the spot. The three witnesses briefly described Williams as a "nice boy" and not a violent person. The recorded psychiatrist's testimony did little more than relate Williams' statement during an examination that in the course of one of his earlier robberies, he had removed the bullets from a gun so as not to injure anyone.

In his cross-examination of the prosecution witnesses, Williams' counsel repeatedly emphasized the fact that Williams had initiated the contact with the police that enabled them to solve the murder and to identify him as the perpetrator of the recent assaults, as well as the car thefts. In closing argument, Williams' counsel characterized Williams' confessional statements as "dumb," but asked the jury to give weight to the fact that he had "turned himself in, not on one crime but on four * * * that the [police otherwise] would not have solved." The weight of defense counsel's closing, however, was devoted to explaining that it was difficult to find a reason why the jury should spare Williams' life.[2]

The jury found a probability of future dangerousness and unanimously fixed Williams' punishment at death. The trial judge concluded that such punishment was "proper" and "just" and imposed the death sentence. The Virginia Supreme Court affirmed the conviction and sentence. It rejected Williams' argument that

2 In defense counsel's words: "I will admit too that it is very difficult to ask you to show mercy to a man who maybe has not shown much mercy himself. I doubt very seriously that he thought much about mercy when he was in Mr. Stone's bedroom that night with him. I doubt very seriously that he had mercy very highly on his mind when he was walking along West Green and the incident with Alberta Stroud. I doubt very seriously that he had mercy on his mind when he took two cars that didn't belong to him. Admittedly it is very difficult to get us [*sic*, probably intending "up"] and ask that you give this man mercy when he has shown so little of it himself. But I would ask that you would."

when the trial judge imposed sentence, he failed to give mitigating weight to the fact that Williams had turned himself in.

State Habeas Corpus Proceedings

In 1988 Williams filed for state collateral relief in the Danville Circuit Court. The petition was subsequently amended, and the Circuit Court (the same judge who had presided over Williams' trial and sentencing) held an evidentiary hearing on Williams' claim that trial counsel had been ineffective.[3] Based on the evidence adduced after two days of hearings, Judge Ingram found that Williams' conviction was valid, but that his trial attorneys had been ineffective during sentencing. Among the evidence reviewed that had not been presented at trial were documents prepared in connection with Williams' commitment when he was 11 years old that dramatically described mistreatment, abuse, and neglect during his early childhood, as well as testimony that he was "borderline mentally retarded," had suffered repeated head injuries, and might have mental impairments organic in origin. The habeas hearing also revealed that the same experts who had testified on the State's behalf at trial believed that Williams, if kept in a "structured environment," would not pose a future danger to society.

Counsel's failure to discover and present this and other significant mitigating evidence was "below the range expected of reasonable, professional competent assistance of counsel." Counsel's performance thus "did not measure up to the standard required under the holding of Strickland, and [if it had,] there is a reasonable probability that the result of the sentencing phase would have been different." Judge Ingram therefore recommended that Williams be granted a rehearing on the sentencing phase of his trial.

The Virginia Supreme Court did not accept that recommendation. Although it assumed, without deciding, that trial counsel had been ineffective, it disagreed with the trial judge's conclusion that Williams had suffered sufficient prejudice to warrant relief. Treating the prejudice inquiry as a mixed question of law and fact, the Virginia Supreme Court accepted the factual determination that available evidence in mitigation had not been presented at the trial, but held that the trial judge had misapplied the law in two respects. First, relying on our decision in *Lockhart v. Fretwell*, the court held that it was wrong for the trial judge to rely " 'on mere outcome determination' " when assessing prejudice. Second, it construed the trial judge's opinion as having "adopted a *per se* approach" that would establish prejudice whenever any mitigating evidence was omitted.

3 While Williams' petition was pending before the Circuit Court, Virginia amended its state habeas statute to vest in the State Supreme Court exclusive jurisdiction to award writs of habeas corpus in capital cases. Shortly after the Circuit Court held its evidentiary hearing, the Supreme Court assumed jurisdiction over Williams' petition and instructed the Circuit Court to issue findings of fact and legal recommendation[s] regarding Williams' ineffective-assistance claims.

The court then reviewed the prosecution evidence supporting the "future dangerousness" aggravating circumstance, reciting Williams' criminal history, including the several most recent offenses to which he had confessed. In comparison, it found that the excluded mitigating evidence—which it characterized as merely indicating "that numerous people, mostly relatives, thought that defendant was nonviolent and could cope very well in a structured environment"—"barely would have altered the profile of this defendant that was presented to the jury." On this basis, the court concluded that there was no reasonable possibility that the omitted evidence would have affected the jury's sentencing recommendation, and that Williams had failed to demonstrate that his sentencing proceeding was fundamentally unfair.

no prejudice

Federal Habeas Corpus Proceedings

Having exhausted his state remedies, Williams sought a federal writ of habeas corpus. After reviewing the state habeas hearing transcript and the state courts' findings of fact and conclusions of law, the federal trial judge agreed with the Virginia trial judge: The death sentence was constitutionally infirm.

fed trial judge: state S.C. didn't address IAC

After noting that the Virginia Supreme Court had not addressed the question whether trial counsel's performance at the sentencing hearing fell below the range of competence demanded of lawyers in criminal cases, the judge began by addressing that issue in detail. He identified five categories of mitigating evidence that counsel had failed to introduce,[4] and he rejected the argument that counsel's failure to conduct an adequate investigation had been a strategic decision to rely almost entirely on the fact that Williams had voluntarily confessed.

According to Williams' trial counsel's testimony before the state habeas court, counsel did not fail to seek Williams' juvenile and social services records because he thought they would be counterproductive, but because counsel erroneously believed that " 'state law didn't permit it.' " Counsel also acknowledged in the course of the hearings that information about Williams' childhood would have been important in mitigation. And counsel's failure to contact a potentially persuasive character witness was likewise not a conscious strategic choice, but simply a failure to return that witness' phone call offering his service. Finally, even if counsel neglected to conduct such an investigation at the time as part of a tactical

4 (i) Counsel did not introduce evidence of the Petitioner's background * * * . (ii) Counsel did not introduce evidence that Petitioner was abused by his father. (iii) Counsel did not introduce testimony from correctional officers who were willing to testify that defendant would not pose a danger while incarcerated. Nor did counsel offer prison commendations awarded to Williams for his help in breaking up a prison drug ring and for returning a guard's wallet. (iv) Several character witnesses were not called to testify * * * . [T]he testimony of Elliott, a respected CPA in the community, could have been quite important to the jury * * * . (v) Finally, counsel did not introduce evidence that Petitioner was borderline mentally retarded, though he was found competent to stand trial.

decision, the District Judge found, tactics as a matter of reasonable performance could not justify the omissions.

Turning to the prejudice issue, the judge determined that there was " 'a reasonable probability that, but for counsel's unprofessional errors, the result of the proceeding would have been different.' *Strickland*." He found that the Virginia Supreme Court had erroneously assumed that *Lockhart* had modified the *Strickland* standard for determining prejudice, and that it had made an important error of fact in discussing its finding of no prejudice.[5] Having introduced his analysis of Williams' claim with the standard of review applicable on habeas appeals provided by 28 U.S.C. § 2254(d), the judge concluded that those errors established that the Virginia Supreme Court's decision "was contrary to, or involved an unreasonable application of, clearly established Federal law" within the meaning of § 2254(d)(1).

The Federal Court of Appeals reversed. It construed § 2254(d)(1) as prohibiting the grant of habeas corpus relief unless the state court "decided the question by interpreting or applying the relevant precedent in a manner that reasonable jurists would all agree is unreasonable." Applying that standard, it could not say that the Virginia Supreme Court's decision on the prejudice issue was an unreasonable application of the tests developed in either *Strickland* or *Lockhart*. It explained that the evidence that Williams presented a future danger to society was "simply overwhelming"; it endorsed the Virginia Supreme Court's interpretation of *Lockhart*, and it characterized the state court's understanding of the facts in this case as "reasonable."

We granted certiorari and now reverse.

II

In 1867, Congress enacted a statute providing that federal courts "shall have power to grant writs of habeas corpus in all cases where any person may be restrained of his or her liberty in violation of the constitution, or of any treaty or law of the United States * * * ." Over the years, the federal habeas corpus statute has been repeatedly amended, but the scope of that jurisdictional grant remains the same. It is, of course, well settled that the fact that constitutional

5 Specifically, the Virginia Supreme Court found no prejudice, reasoning: "The mitigation evidence that the prisoner says, in retrospect, his trial counsel should have discovered and offered barely would have altered the profile of this defendant that was presented to the jury. At most, this evidence would have shown that numerous people, mostly relatives, thought that defendant was nonviolent and could cope very well in a structured environment." The Virginia Supreme Court ignored or overlooked the evidence of Williams' difficult childhood and abuse and his limited mental capacity. It is also unreasonable to characterize the additional evidence as coming from "mostly relatives." As stated, Bruce Elliott, a respected professional in the community, and several correctional officers offered to testify on Williams behalf.

error occurred in the proceedings that led to a state-court conviction may not alone be sufficient reason for concluding that a prisoner is entitled to the remedy of habeas. On the other hand, errors that undermine confidence in the fundamental fairness of the state adjudication certainly justify the issuance of the federal writ. The deprivation of the right to the effective assistance of counsel recognized in Strickland is such an error.

The warden here contends that federal habeas corpus relief is prohibited by the amendment to 28 U.S.C. § 2254, enacted as a part of the Antiterrorism and Effective Death Penalty Act of 1996 (AEDPA). The relevant portion of that amendment provides:

> (d) An application for a writ of habeas corpus on behalf of a person in custody pursuant to the judgment of a State court shall not be granted with respect to any claim that was adjudicated on the merits in State court proceedings unless the adjudication of the claim—
>
> (1) resulted in a decision that was contrary to, or involved an unreasonable application of, clearly established Federal law, as determined by the Supreme Court of the United States * * * .

In this case, the Court of Appeals applied the construction of the amendment that it had adopted in its earlier opinion in *Green v. French*. It read the amendment as prohibiting federal courts from issuing the writ unless:

> (a) the state court decision is in "square conflict" with Supreme Court precedent that is controlling as to law and fact or (b) if no such controlling decision exists, the state court's resolution of a question of pure law rests upon an objectively unreasonable derivation of legal principles from the relevant [S]upreme [C]ourt precedents, or if its decision rests upon an objectively unreasonable application of established principles to new facts.

Accordingly, it held that a federal court may issue habeas relief only if "the state courts have decided the question by interpreting or applying the relevant precedent in a manner that reasonable jurists would all agree is unreasonable."

We are convinced that that interpretation of the amendment is incorrect. It would impose a test for determining when a legal rule is clearly established that simply cannot be squared with the real practice of decisional law.[9] It would apply

---

9 Although we explain our understanding of "clearly established law," we note that the Fourth Circuit's construction of the amendment's inquiry in this respect is especially problematic. It separates cases into those for which a "controlling decision" exists and those for which no such decision exists. The former category includes very few cases, since a rule is "controlling" only if it matches the case before the court both "as to law and fact," and most cases are factually distinguishable in some respect. A literal application of the Fourth Circuit test would yield a particularly perverse outcome in cases involving the Strickland rule for establishing ineffective assistance of counsel, since that case, which established the "controlling" rule of law on the issue, contained facts insufficient to show ineffectiveness.

a standard for determining the "reasonableness" of state-court decisions that is not contained in the statute itself, and that Congress surely did not intend. And it would wrongly require the federal courts, including this Court, to defer to state judges' interpretations of federal law.

As the Fourth Circuit would have it, a state-court judgment is "unreasonable" in the face of federal law only if all reasonable jurists would agree that the state court was unreasonable. Thus, in this case, for example, even if the Virginia Supreme Court misread our opinion in Lockhart, we could not grant relief unless we believed that none of the judges who agreed with the state court's interpretation of that case was a "reasonable jurist." But the statute says nothing about "reasonable judges," presumably because all, or virtually all, such judges occasionally commit error; they make decisions that in retrospect may be characterized as "unreasonable." Indeed, it is most unlikely that Congress would deliberately impose such a requirement of unanimity on federal judges. As Congress is acutely aware, reasonable lawyers and lawgivers regularly disagree with one another. Congress surely did not intend that the views of one such judge who might think that relief is not warranted in a particular case should always have greater weight than the contrary, considered judgment of several other reasonable judges.

The inquiry mandated by the amendment relates to the way in which a federal habeas court exercises its duty to decide constitutional questions; the amendment does not alter the underlying grant of jurisdiction in § 2254(a).[10] When federal judges exercise their federal-question jurisdiction under the "judicial Power" of Article III of the Constitution, it is "emphatically the province and duty" of those judges to "say what the law is." At the core of this power is the federal courts' independent responsibility—independent from its coequal branches in the Federal Government, and independent from the separate authority of the several States—to interpret federal law. A construction of AEDPA that would require the federal courts to cede this authority to the courts of the States would be inconsistent with the practice that federal judges have traditionally followed in discharging their duties under Article III of the Constitution. If Congress had intended to require such an important change in the exercise of our jurisdiction, we believe it would have spoken with much greater clarity than is found in the text of AEDPA.

10 Indeed, Congress roundly rejected an amendment to the bill eventually adopted that directly invoked the text of the jurisdictional grant, 28 U.S.C. § 2254(a) (providing that the federal courts "*shall entertain* an application for a writ of habeas corpus" (emphasis added)). The amendment read: "Notwithstanding any other provision of law, an application for a writ of habeas corpus in behalf of a person in custody pursuant to a judgment or order of a State court *shall not be entertained* by a court of the United States unless the remedies in the courts of the State are inadequate or ineffective to test the legality of the person's detention." ([A]mendment of Sen. Kyl) (emphasis added). In speaking against the Kyl amendment, Senator Specter (a key proponent of the eventual habeas reform) explained that when "dealing with the question of jurisdiction of the Federal courts to entertain questions on Federal issues, on constitutional issues, I believe it is necessary that the Federal courts retain that jurisdiction as a constitutional matter."

This basic premise informs our interpretation of both parts of § 2254(d)(1): first, the requirement that the determinations of state courts be tested only against "clearly established Federal law, as determined by the Supreme Court of the United States," and second, the prohibition on the issuance of the writ unless the state court's decision is "contrary to, or involved an unreasonable application of," that clearly established law. We address each part in turn.

The "clearly established law" requirement

In *Teague v. Lane*, we held that the petitioner was not entitled to federal habeas relief because he was relying on a rule of federal law that had not been announced until after his state conviction became final. The antiretroactivity rule recognized in Teague, which prohibits reliance on "new rules," is the functional equivalent of a statutory provision commanding exclusive reliance on "clearly established law." Because there is no reason to believe that Congress intended to require federal courts to ask both whether a rule sought on habeas is "new" under Teague—which remains the law—and also whether it is "clearly established" under AEDPA, it seems safe to assume that Congress had congruent concepts in mind. It is perfectly clear that AEDPA codifies Teague to the extent that Teague requires federal habeas courts to deny relief that is contingent upon a rule of law not clearly established at the time the state conviction became final.[12]

Teague's core principles are therefore relevant to our construction of this requirement. Justice Harlan recognized the "inevitable difficulties" that come with "attempting 'to determine whether a particular decision has really announced a "new" rule at all or whether it has simply applied a well-established constitutional principle to govern a case which is closely analogous to those which have been previously considered in the prior case law.' " But *Teague* established some guidance for making this determination, explaining that a federal habeas court operates within the bounds of comity and finality if it applies a rule "dictated by precedent existing at the time the defendant's conviction became final." ([E]mphasis

---

12 We are not persuaded by the argument that because Congress used the words "clearly established law" and not "new rule," it meant in this section to codify an aspect of the doctrine of executive qualified immunity rather than *Teague*'s antiretroactivity bar. The warden refers us specifically to § 2244(b)(2)(A) and 28 U.S.C. § 2254(e)(2), in which the statute does in so many words employ the "new rule" language familiar to *Teague* and its progeny. Congress thus knew precisely the words to use if it had wished to codify *Teague per se*. That it did not use those words in § 2254(d) is evidence, the argument goes, that it had something else in mind entirely in amending that section. We think, quite the contrary, that the verbatim adoption of the *Teague* language in these other sections bolsters our impression that Congress had *Teague*—and not any unrelated area of our jurisprudence—specifically in mind in amending the habeas statute. These provisions, seen together, make it impossible to conclude that Congress was not fully aware of, and interested in codifying into law, that aspect of this Court's habeas doctrine. We will not assume that in a single subsection of an amendment entirely devoted to the law of habeas corpus, Congress made the anomalous choice of reaching into the doctrinally distinct law of qualified immunity, for a single phrase that just so happens to be the conceptual twin of a dominant principle in habeas law of which Congress was fully aware.

deleted). A rule that "breaks new ground or imposes a new obligation on the States or the Federal Government," falls outside this universe of federal law.

To this, AEDPA has added, immediately following the "clearly established law" requirement, a clause limiting the area of relevant law to that "determined by the Supreme Court of the United States." If this Court has not broken sufficient legal ground to establish an asked-for constitutional principle, the lower federal courts cannot themselves establish such a principle with clarity sufficient to satisfy the AEDPA bar. In this respect, we agree with the Seventh Circuit that this clause "extends the principle of *Teague* by limiting the source of doctrine on which a federal court may rely in addressing the application for a writ."

* * *

A rule that fails to satisfy the foregoing criteria is barred by *Teague* from application on collateral review, and, similarly, is not available as a basis for relief in a habeas case to which AEDPA applies.

In the context of this case, we also note that, as our precedent interpreting *Teague* has demonstrated, rules of law may be sufficiently clear for habeas purposes even when they are expressed in terms of a generalized standard rather than as a bright-line rule. As Justice Kennedy has explained:

> If the rule in question is one which of necessity requires a case-by-case examination of the evidence, then we can tolerate a number of specific applications without saying that those applications themselves create a new rule * * * . Where the beginning point is a rule of this general application, a rule designed for the specific purpose of evaluating a myriad of factual contexts, it will be the infrequent case that yields a result so novel that it forges a new rule, one not dictated by precedent.

Moreover, the determination whether or not a rule is clearly established at the time a state court renders its final judgment of conviction is a question as to which the "federal courts must make an independent evaluation."

It has been urged, in contrast, that we should read *Teague* and its progeny to encompass a broader principle of deference requiring federal courts to "validat[e] 'reasonable, good-faith interpretations' of the law" by state courts. The position has been bolstered with references to our statements elucidating the "new rule" inquiry as one turning on whether "reasonable jurists" would agree the rule was not clearly established. This presumption of deference was in essence the position taken by three Members of this Court in *Wright* (opinion of Thomas, J.) ("[A] federal habeas court must defer to the state court's decision rejecting the claim unless that decision is patently unreasonable.").

Teague, however, does not extend this far. The often repeated language that *Teague* endorses "reasonable, good-faith interpretations" by state courts is an explanation of policy, not a statement of law. The *Teague* cases reflect this Court's view that habeas corpus is not to be used as a second criminal trial, and federal courts are not to run roughshod over the considered findings and judgments of the state courts that conducted the original trial and heard the initial appeals. On the contrary, we have long insisted that federal habeas courts attend closely to those considered decisions, and give them full effect when their findings and judgments are consistent with federal law. But as Justice O'Connor explained in *Wright*:

> [T]he duty of the federal court in evaluating whether a rule is "new" is not the same as deference; * * * *Teague* does not direct federal courts to spend less time or effort scrutinizing the existing federal law, on the ground that they can assume the state courts interpreted it properly.
>
> [T]he maxim that federal courts should "give great weight to the considered conclusions of a coequal state judiciary" * * * does not mean that we have held in the past that federal courts must presume the correctness of a state court's legal conclusions on habeas, or that a state court's incorrect legal determination has ever been allowed to stand because it was reasonable. We have always held that federal courts, even on habeas, have an independent obligation to say what the law is.

We are convinced that in the phrase, "clearly established law," Congress did not intend to modify that independent obligation.

The "contrary to, or an unreasonable application of," requirement

The message that Congress intended to convey by using the phrases, "contrary to" and "unreasonable application of" is not entirely clear. The prevailing view in the Circuits is that the former phrase requires *de novo* review of "pure" questions of law and the latter requires some sort of "reasonability" review of so-called mixed questions of law and fact.

We are not persuaded that the phrases define two mutually exclusive categories of questions. Most constitutional questions that arise in habeas corpus proceedings—and therefore most "decisions" to be made—require the federal judge to apply a rule of law to a set of facts, some of which may be disputed and some undisputed. For example, an erroneous conclusion that particular circumstances established the voluntariness of a confession, or that there exists a conflict of interest when one attorney represents multiple defendants, may well be described either as "contrary to" or as an "unreasonable application of" the governing rule of law. In constitutional adjudication, as in the common law, rules of law often develop incrementally as earlier decisions are applied to new factual situations.

But rules that depend upon such elaboration are hardly less lawlike than those that establish a bright-line test.

Indeed, our pre-AEDPA efforts to distinguish questions of fact, questions of law, and "mixed questions," and to create an appropriate standard of habeas review for each, generated some not insubstantial differences of opinion as to which issues of law fell into which category of question, and as to which standard of review applied to each. We thus think the Fourth Circuit was correct when it attributed the lack of clarity in the statute, in part, to the overlapping meanings of the phrases "contrary to" and "unreasonable application of."

The statutory text likewise does not obviously prescribe a specific, recognizable standard of review for dealing with either phrase. Significantly, it does not use any term, such as "de novo" or "plain error," that would easily identify a familiar standard of review. Rather, the text is fairly read simply as a command that a federal court not issue the habeas writ unless the state court was wrong as a matter of law or unreasonable in its application of law in a given case. The suggestion that a wrong state-court "decision"—a legal judgment rendered "after consideration of *facts, and* * * * *law*," BLACK'S LAW DICTIONARY 414 (7th ed.1999) (emphasis added)—may no longer be redressed through habeas (because it is unreachable under the "unreasonable application" phrase) is based on a mistaken insistence that the § 2254(d)(1) phrases have not only independent, but mutually exclusive, meanings. Whether or not a federal court can issue the writ "under [the] 'unreasonable application' clause," the statute is clear that habeas may issue under § 2254(d)(1) if a state court "decision" is "contrary to * * * clearly established Federal law." We thus anticipate that there will be a variety of cases, like this one, in which both phrases may be implicated.

Even though we cannot conclude that the phrases establish "a body of rigid rules," they do express a "mood" that the federal judiciary must respect. In this respect, it seems clear that Congress intended federal judges to attend with the utmost care to state-court decisions, including all of the reasons supporting their decisions, before concluding that those proceedings were infected by constitutional error sufficiently serious to warrant the issuance of the writ. Likewise, the statute in a separate provision provides for the habeas remedy when a state-court decision "was based on an unreasonable determination of the facts *in light of the evidence presented in the State court proceeding.*" ([E]mphasis added). While this provision is not before us in this case, it provides relevant context for our interpretation of § 2254(d)(1); in this respect, it bolsters our conviction that federal habeas courts must make as the starting point of their analysis the state courts' determinations of fact, including that aspect of a "mixed question" that rests on a finding of fact. AEDPA plainly sought to ensure a level of "deference to the determinations of state courts," provided those determinations did not conflict with federal law or apply federal law in an unreasonable way. Congress wished to curb delays, to prevent "retrials" on federal habeas, and to give effect to state convictions to the extent possible under law. When federal courts are able to fulfill these goals within the bounds of the law, AEDPA instructs them to do so.

On the other hand, it is significant that the word "deference" does not appear in the text of the statute itself. Neither the legislative history, nor the statutory text, suggests any difference in the so-called "deference" depending on which of the two phrases is implicated.[13] Whatever "deference" Congress had in mind with respect to both phrases, it surely is not a requirement that federal courts actually defer to a state-court application of the federal law that is, in the independent judgment of the federal court, in error. As Judge Easterbrook noted with respect to the phrase "contrary to": "Section 2254(d) requires us to give state courts' opinions a respectful reading, and to listen carefully to their conclusions, but when the state court addresses a legal question, it is the law 'as determined by the Supreme Court of the United States' that prevails."[14]

---

13 As Judge Easterbrook has noted, the statute surely does not require the kind of "deference" appropriate in other contexts:

> It does not tell us to "defer" to state decisions, as if the Constitution means one thing in Wisconsin and another in Indiana. Nor does it tell us to treat state courts the way we treat federal administrative agencies. Deference * * * depends on delegation. Congress did not delegate interpretive or executive power to the state courts. They exercise powers under their domestic law, constrained by the Constitution of the United States. "Deference" to the jurisdictions bound by those constraints is not sensible.

14 The Court advances three reasons for adopting its alternative construction of the phrase "unreasonable application of." First, the use of the word "unreasonable" in the statute suggests that Congress was directly influenced by the "patently unreasonable" standard advocated by Justice Thomas in his opinion in Wright v. West; second, the legislative history supports this view; and third, Congress must have intended to change the law more substantially than our reading 28 U.S.C. § 2254(d)(1) permits. None of these reasons is persuasive. First, even though, as the Court recognizes, the term "unreasonable" is "difficult to define," neither the statute itself nor the Court's explanation of it, suggests that AEDPA's "unreasonable application of" has the same meaning as Justice Thomas' " 'patently unreasonable' " standard mentioned in his dictum in Wright. To the extent the "broader debate" in Wright touched upon the Court's novel distinction today between what is "wrong" and what is "unreasonable," it was in the context of a discussion not about the *standard of review* habeas courts should use for law-application questions, but about whether a rule is "new" or "old" such that Teague's retroactivity rule would bar habeas relief; Justice Thomas contended that Teague barred habeas "whenever the state courts have interpreted old precedents *reasonably*, not [as Justice O'Connor suggested] only when they have done so 'properly.' " Teague, of course, as Justice O'Connor correctly pointed out, "did not establish a standard of review at all"; rather than instructing a court how to review a claim, it simply asks, in absolute terms, *whether* a rule was clear at the time of a state-court decision. We thus do not think Wright "confirms" anything about the meaning of § 2254(d)(1), which is, as our division reflects, anything but "clear."

As for the other bases for Justice O'Connor's view, the only two specific citations to the legislative history upon which she relies do no more than beg the question. One merely quotes the language of the statute without elaboration, and the other goes to slightly greater length in stating that state-court judgments must be upheld unless "unreasonable." Neither sheds any light on what the content of the hypothetical category of "decisions" that are wrong but nevertheless not "unreasonable." Finally, while we certainly agree with the Court that AEDPA wrought substantial changes in habeas law, there is an obvious fallacy in the assumption that because the statute changed pre-existing law in some respects, it must have rendered this specific change here.

Our disagreement with Justice O'Connor about the precise meaning of the phrase "contrary to," and the word "unreasonable," is, of course, important, but should affect only a narrow category of cases. The simplest and first definition of "contrary to" as a phrase is "in conflict with." In this sense, we think the phrase surely capacious enough to include a finding that the state-court "decision" is simply "erroneous" or wrong. (We hasten to add that even "diametrically different" from, or "opposite" to, an established federal law would seem to include "decisions" that are wrong in light of that law.) And there is nothing in the phrase "contrary to"—as Justice O'Connor appears to agree—that implies anything less than independent review by the federal courts. Moreover, state-court decisions that do not "conflict" with federal law will rarely be "unreasonable" under either her reading of the statute or ours. We all agree that state-court judgments must be upheld unless, after the closest examination of the state-court judgment, a federal court is firmly convinced that a federal constitutional right has been violated. Our difference is as to the cases in which, at first-blush, a state-court judgment seems entirely reasonable, but thorough analysis by a federal court produces a firm conviction that that judgment is infected by constitutional error. In our view, such an erroneous judgment is "unreasonable" within the meaning of the act even though that conclusion was not immediately apparent.

In sum, the statute directs federal courts to attend to every state-court judgment with utmost care, but it does not require them to defer to the opinion of every reasonable state-court judge on * * * federal law. If, after carefully weighing all the reasons for accepting a state court's judgment, a federal court is convinced that a prisoner's custody—or, as in this case, his sentence of death—violates the Constitution, that independent judgment should prevail. Otherwise the federal "law as determined by the Supreme Court of the United States" might be applied by the federal courts one way in Virginia and another way in California. In light of the well-recognized interest in ensuring that federal courts interpret federal law in a uniform way,[15] we are convinced that Congress did not intend the statute to produce such a result.

III

In this case, Williams contends that he was denied his constitutionally guaranteed right to the effective assistance of counsel when his trial lawyers failed to investigate and to present substantial mitigating evidence to the sentencing jury. The threshold question under AEDPA is whether Williams seeks to apply a rule of law that was clearly established at the time his state-court conviction became

15 Indeed, a contrary rule would be in substantial tension with the interest in uniformity served by Congress' modification in AEDPA of our previous *Teague* jurisprudence—now the law on habeas review must be "clearly established" by this Court alone. It would thus seem somewhat perverse to ascribe to Congress the entirely inconsistent policy of perpetuating disparate readings of our decisions under the guise of deference to anything within a conceivable spectrum of reasonableness.

final. That question is easily answered because the merits of his claim are squarely governed by our holding in *Strickland*.

We explained in *Strickland* that a violation of the right on which Williams relies has two components:

> First, the defendant must show that counsel's performance was deficient. This requires showing that counsel made errors so serious that counsel was not functioning as the "counsel" guaranteed the defendant by the Sixth Amendment. Second, the defendant must show that the deficient performance prejudiced the defense. This requires showing that counsel's errors were so serious as to deprive the defendant of a fair trial, a trial whose result is reliable.

To establish ineffectiveness, a "defendant must show that counsel's representation fell below an objective standard of reasonableness." To establish prejudice he "must show that there is a reasonable probability that, but for counsel's unprofessional errors, the result of the proceeding would have been different. A reasonable probability is a probability sufficient to undermine confidence in the outcome."

It is past question that the rule set forth in *Strickland* qualifies as "clearly established Federal law, as determined by the Supreme Court of the United States." That the *Strickland* test "of necessity requires a case-by-case examination of the evidence," obviates neither the clarity of the rule nor the extent to which the rule must be seen as "established" by this Court. This Court's precedent "dictated" that the Virginia Supreme Court apply the *Strickland* test at the time that court entertained Williams' ineffective-assistance claim. And it can hardly be said that recognizing the right to effective counsel "breaks new ground or imposes a new obligation on the States." Williams is therefore entitled to relief if the Virginia Supreme Court's decision rejecting his ineffective-assistance claim was either "contrary to, or involved an unreasonable application of," that established law. It was both.

IV

The Virginia Supreme Court erred in holding that our decision in *Lockhart v. Fretwell* modified or in some way supplanted the rule set down in *Strickland*. It is true that while the *Strickland* test provides sufficient guidance for resolving virtually all ineffective-assistance-of-counsel claims, there are situations in which the overriding focus on fundamental fairness may affect the analysis. Thus, on the one hand, as *Strickland* itself explained, there are a few situations in which prejudice may be presumed. And, on the other hand, there are also situations in which it would be unjust to characterize the likelihood of a different outcome as legitimate "prejudice." Even if a defendant's false testimony might have persuaded the jury to acquit him, it is not fundamentally unfair to conclude that he was not prejudiced by counsel's interference with his intended perjury.

Similarly, in Lockhart, we concluded that, given the overriding interest in fundamental fairness, the likelihood of a different outcome attributable to an incorrect interpretation of the law should be regarded as a potential "windfall" to the defendant rather than the legitimate "prejudice" contemplated by our opinion in *Strickland*. The death sentence that Arkansas had imposed on Bobby Ray Fretwell was based on an aggravating circumstance (murder committed for pecuniary gain) that duplicated an element of the underlying felony (murder in the course of a robbery). Shortly before the trial, the United States Court of Appeals for the Eighth Circuit had held that such "double counting" was impermissible, but Fretwell's lawyer (presumably because he was unaware of the * * * decision) failed to object to the use of the pecuniary gain aggravator. Before Fretwell's claim for federal habeas corpus relief reached this Court, the case was overruled. Accordingly, even though the Arkansas trial judge probably would have sustained a timely objection to the double counting, it had become clear that the State had a right to rely on the disputed aggravating circumstance. Because the ineffectiveness of Fretwell's counsel had not deprived him of any substantive or procedural right to which the law entitled him, we held that his claim did not satisfy the "prejudice" component of the *Strickland* test.

Cases such as *Nix v. Whiteside* and *Lockhart v. Fretwell* do not justify a departure from a straightforward application of *Strickland* when the ineffectiveness of counsel does deprive the defendant of a substantive or procedural right to which the law entitles him.[18] In the instant case, it is undisputed that Williams had a right—indeed, a constitutionally protected right—to provide the jury with the mitigating evidence that his trial counsel either failed to discover or failed to offer.

Nevertheless, the Virginia Supreme Court read our decision in *Lockhart* to require a separate inquiry into fundamental fairness even when Williams is able to show that his lawyer was ineffective and that his ineffectiveness probably affected the outcome of the proceeding. It wrote:

> The prisoner argues there "is a 'reasonable probability' that at least one juror would have been moved to spare Petitioner's life had he heard" the mitigation evidence developed at the habeas hearing that was not presented at the trial. Summarizing, he contends there "is a 'reasonable probability' that had at least

18 In her concurring opinion in *Lockhart*, Justice O'Connor stressed this precise point.

> I write separately only to point out that today's decision will, in the vast majority of cases, have no effect on the prejudice inquiry under *Strickland*. The determinative question—whether there is "a reasonable probability that, but for counsel's unprofessional errors, the result of the proceeding would have been different,"—remains unchanged. This case, however, concerns the unusual circumstance where the defendant attempts to demonstrate prejudice based on considerations that, as a matter of law, ought not inform the inquiry.

one juror heard any of this evidence—let alone all of this evidence—the outcome of this case would have been different."

We reject these contentions. The prisoner's discussion flies in the face of the Supreme Court's admonition in Lockhart that "an analysis focusing solely on mere outcome determination, without attention to whether the result of the proceeding was fundamentally unfair or unreliable, is defective."

Unlike the Virginia Supreme Court, the state trial judge omitted any reference to Lockhart and simply relied on our opinion in Strickland as stating the correct standard for judging ineffective-assistance claims. With respect to the prejudice component, he wrote:

> Even if a Petitioner shows that counsel's performance was deficient, however, he must also show prejudice. Petitioner must show "that there is a reasonable probability that but for counsel's unprofessional errors, the result * * * would have been different." "A reasonable probability is a probability sufficient to undermine confidence in the outcome." Indeed, it is insufficient to show only that the errors had some conceivable effect on the outcome of the proceeding, because virtually every act or omission of counsel would meet that test. The petitioner bears the "highly demanding" and "heavy burden" in establishing actual prejudice.

The trial judge analyzed the ineffective-assistance claim under the correct standard; the Virginia Supreme Court did not.

We are likewise persuaded that the Virginia trial judge correctly applied both components of that standard to Williams' ineffectiveness claim. Although he concluded that counsel competently handled the guilt phase of the trial, he found that their representation during the sentencing phase fell short of professional standards—a judgment barely disputed by the State in its brief to this Court. The record establishes that counsel did not begin to prepare for that phase of the proceeding until a week before the trial. They failed to conduct an investigation that would have uncovered extensive records graphically describing Williams' nightmarish childhood, not because of any strategic calculation but because they incorrectly thought that state law barred access to such records. Had they done so, the jury would have learned that Williams' parents had been imprisoned for the criminal neglect of Williams and his siblings, that Williams had been severely and repeatedly beaten by his father, that he had been committed to the custody of the social services bureau for two years during his parents' incarceration (including one stint in an abusive foster home), and then, after his parents were released from prison, had been returned to his parents' custody.

Counsel failed to introduce available evidence that Williams was "borderline mentally retarded" and did not advance beyond sixth grade in school. They failed to seek prison records recording Williams' commendations for helping to crack a prison drug ring and for returning a guard's missing wallet, or the testimony of prison officials who described Williams as among the inmates "least likely to act in a violent, dangerous or provocative way." Counsel failed even to return the phone call of a certified public accountant who had offered to testify that he had visited Williams frequently when Williams was incarcerated as part of a prison ministry program, that Williams "seemed to thrive in a more regimented and structured environment," and that Williams was proud of the carpentry degree he earned while in prison.

Of course, not all of the additional evidence was favorable to Williams. The juvenile records revealed that he had been thrice committed to the juvenile system—for aiding and abetting larceny when he was 11 years old, for pulling a false fire alarm when he was 12, and for breaking and entering when he was 15. But as the Federal District Court correctly observed, the failure to introduce the comparatively voluminous amount of evidence that did speak in Williams' favor was not justified by a tactical decision to focus on Williams' voluntary confession. Whether or not those omissions were sufficiently prejudicial to have affected the outcome of sentencing, they clearly demonstrate that trial counsel did not fulfill their obligation to conduct a thorough investigation of the defendant's background.

We are also persuaded, unlike the Virginia Supreme Court, that counsel's unprofessional service prejudiced Williams within the meaning of *Strickland*. After hearing the additional evidence developed in the postconviction proceedings, the very judge who presided at Williams' trial and who once determined that the death penalty was "just" and "appropriate," concluded that there existed "a reasonable probability that the result of the sentencing phase would have been different" if the jury had heard that evidence. We do not agree with the Virginia Supreme Court that Judge Ingram's conclusion should be discounted because he apparently adopted "a *per se* approach to the prejudice element" that placed undue "emphasis on mere outcome determination." Judge Ingram did stress the importance of mitigation evidence in making his "outcome determination," but it is clear that his predictive judgment rested on his assessment of the totality of the omitted evidence rather than on the notion that a single item of omitted evidence, no matter how trivial, would require a new hearing.

The Virginia Supreme Court's own analysis of prejudice reaching the contrary conclusion was thus unreasonable in at least two respects. First, as we have already explained, the State Supreme Court mischaracterized at best the appropriate rule, made clear by this Court in *Strickland*, for determining whether counsel's assistance was effective within the meaning of the Constitution. While it may also have conducted an "outcome determinative" analysis of its own, it is evident to us that the court's decision turned on its erroneous view that a "mere" difference in outcome is not sufficient to establish constitutionally ineffective assistance of counsel. Its analysis in this respect was thus not only "contrary to," but also, inasmuch as the Virginia Supreme Court relied on the inapplicable exception recognized in *Lockhart*, an "unreasonable application of" the clear law as established by this Court.

Second, the State Supreme Court's prejudice determination was unreasonable insofar as it failed to evaluate the totality of the available mitigation evidence—both that adduced at trial, and the evidence adduced in the habeas proceeding—in reweighing it against the evidence in aggravation. This error is apparent in its consideration of the additional mitigation evidence developed in the postconviction proceedings. The court correctly found that as to "the factual part of the mixed question," there was "really * * * n[o] * * * dispute" that available mitigation evidence was not presented at trial. As to the prejudice determination comprising the "legal part" of its analysis, it correctly emphasized the strength of the prosecution evidence supporting the future dangerousness aggravating circumstance.

But the state court failed even to mention the sole argument in mitigation that trial counsel did advance—Williams turned himself in, alerting police to a crime they otherwise would never have discovered, expressing remorse for his actions, and cooperating with the police after that. While this, coupled with the prison records and guard testimony, may not have overcome a finding of future dangerousness, the graphic description of Williams' childhood, filled with abuse and privation, or the reality that he was "borderline mentally retarded," might well have influenced the jury's appraisal of his moral culpability. The circumstances recited in his several confessions are consistent with the view that in each case his violent behavior was a compulsive reaction rather than the product of cold-blooded premeditation. Mitigating evidence unrelated to dangerousness may alter the jury's selection of penalty, even if it does not undermine or rebut the prosecution's death-eligibility case. The Virginia Supreme Court did not entertain that possibility. It thus failed to accord appropriate weight to the body of mitigation evidence available to trial counsel.

V

In our judgment, the state trial judge was correct both in his recognition of the established legal standard for determining counsel's effectiveness, and in his conclusion that the entire postconviction record, viewed as a whole and cumulative of mitigation evidence presented originally, raised "a reasonable probability that the result of the sentencing proceeding would have been different" if competent counsel had presented and explained the significance of all the available evidence. It follows that the Virginia Supreme Court rendered a "decision that was contrary to, or involved an unreasonable application of, clearly established

Federal law." Williams' constitutional right to the effective assistance of counsel as defined in Strickland was violated.

Accordingly, the judgment of the Court of Appeals is reversed, and the case is remanded for further proceedings consistent with this opinion.

It is so ordered.

JUSTICE O'CONNOR delivered the opinion of the Court with respect to Part II (except as to the footnote), concurred in part, and concurred in the judgment.*

* * * The relevant provision prohibits a federal court from granting an application for a writ of habeas corpus with respect to a claim adjudicated on the merits in state court unless that adjudication "resulted in a decision that was contrary to, or involved an unreasonable application of, clearly established Federal law, as determined by the Supreme Court of the United States." The Court holds today that the Virginia Supreme Court's adjudication of Terry Williams' application for state habeas corpus relief resulted in just such a decision. I agree with that determination and join Parts I, III, and IV of the Court's opinion. Because I disagree, however, with the interpretation of § 2254(d)(1) set forth in Part II of Justice Stevens' opinion, I write separately to explain my views.

I

Before 1996, this Court held that a federal court entertaining a state prisoner's application for habeas relief must exercise its independent judgment when deciding both questions of constitutional law and mixed constitutional questions (*i.e.*, application of constitutional law to fact). In other words, a federal habeas court owed no deference to a state court's resolution of such questions of law or mixed questions. In * * * Wright v. West, we revisited our prior holdings by asking the parties to address the following question in their briefs:

> In determining whether to grant a petition for writ of habeas corpus by a person in custody pursuant to the judgment of a state court, should a federal court give deference to the state court's application of law to the specific facts of the petitioner's case or should it review the state court's determination *de novo*?" Although our ultimate decision did not turn on the answer to that question, our several opinions did join issue on it.

Justice Thomas, announcing the judgment of the Court, acknowledged that our precedents had "treat[ed] as settled the rule that mixed constitutional questions are 'subject to plenary federal review' on habeas." He contended,

* Justice Kennedy joins this opinion in its entirety. The Chief Justice and Justice Thomas join this opinion with respect to Part II. Justice Scalia joins this opinion with respect to Part II, except as to the footnote.

nevertheless, that those decisions did not foreclose the Court from applying a rule of deferential review for reasonableness in future cases. According to Justice Thomas, the reliance of our precedents on Brown v. Allen was erroneous because the Court in Brown never explored in detail whether a federal habeas court, to deny a state prisoner's application, must conclude that the relevant state-court adjudication was "correct" or merely that it was "reasonable." Justice Thomas suggested that the time to revisit our decisions may have been at hand, given that our more recent habeas jurisprudence in the nonretroactivity context, *see, e.g.*, Teague v. Lane, had called into question the then-settled rule of independent review of mixed constitutional questions.

I wrote separately in Wright because I believed Justice Thomas had "understate[d] the certainty with which Brown v. Allen rejected a deferential standard of review of issues of law." I also explained that we had considered the standard of review applicable to mixed constitutional questions on numerous occasions and each time we concluded that federal habeas courts had a duty to evaluate such questions independently. * * *

* * * Under the federal habeas statute as it stood in 1992, then, our precedents dictated that a federal court should grant a state prisoner's petition for habeas relief if that court were to conclude in its independent judgment that the relevant state court had erred on a question of constitutional law or on a mixed constitutional question.

If today's case were governed by the federal habeas statute prior to Congress' enactment of AEDPA in 1996, I would agree with Justice Stevens that Williams' petition for habeas relief must be granted if we, in our independent judgment, were to conclude that his Sixth Amendment right to effective assistance of counsel was violated.

II

A

Williams' case is *not* governed by the pre-1996 version of the habeas statute. Because he filed his petition in December 1997, Williams' case is governed by the statute as amended by AEDPA. * * * Accordingly, for Williams to obtain federal habeas relief, he must first demonstrate that his case satisfies the condition set by § 2254(d)(1). That provision modifies the role of federal habeas courts in reviewing petitions filed by state prisoners.

Justice Stevens' opinion in Part II essentially contends that § 2254(d)(1) does not alter the previously settled rule of independent review. Indeed, the opinion concludes its statutory inquiry with the somewhat empty finding that

§ 2254(d)(1) does no more than express a " 'mood' that the federal judiciary must respect." For Justice Stevens, the congressionally enacted "mood" has two important qualities. First, "federal courts [must] attend to every state-court judgment with utmost care" by "carefully weighing all the reasons for accepting a state court's judgment." Second, if a federal court undertakes that careful review and yet remains convinced that a prisoner's custody violates the Constitution, "that independent judgment should prevail."

* * * Justice Stevens' interpretation of § 2254(d)(1) gives the 1996 amendment no effect whatsoever. The command that federal courts should now use the "utmost care" by "carefully weighing" the reasons supporting a state court's judgment echoes our pre-AEDPA statement * * * that federal habeas courts "should, of course, give great weight to the considered conclusions of a coequal state judiciary." Similarly, the requirement that the independent judgment of a federal court must in the end prevail essentially repeats the conclusion we reached in the very next sentence * * * with respect to the specific issue presented there: "But, as we now reaffirm, the ultimate question whether, under the totality of the circumstances, the challenged confession was obtained in a manner compatible with the requirements of the Constitution *is a matter for independent federal determination*." ([E]mphasis added).

That Justice Stevens would find the new § 2254(d)(1) to have no effect on the prior law of habeas corpus is remarkable given his apparent acknowledgment that Congress wished to bring change to the field. That acknowledgment is correct and significant to this case. It cannot be disputed that Congress viewed § 2254(d)(1) as an important means by which its goals for habeas reform would be achieved.

Justice Stevens arrives at his erroneous interpretation by means of one critical misstep. He fails to give independent meaning to both the "contrary to" and "unreasonable application" clauses of the statute. By reading § 2254(d)(1) as one general restriction on the power of the federal habeas court, Justice Stevens manages to avoid confronting the specific meaning of the statute's "unreasonable application" clause and its ramifications for the independent-review rule. It is, however, a cardinal principle of statutory construction that we must " 'give effect, if possible, to every clause and word of a statute.' " Section 2254(d)(1) defines two categories of cases in which a state prisoner may obtain federal habeas relief with respect to a claim adjudicated on the merits in state court[:] * * * if the relevant state-court decision was either (1) "*contrary to* * * * clearly established Federal law, as determined by the Supreme Court of the United States," or (2) "*involved an unreasonable application of* * * * clearly established Federal law, as determined by the Supreme Court of the United States." (Emphases added.)

The Court of Appeals for the Fourth Circuit properly accorded both the "contrary to" and "unreasonable application" clauses independent meaning. * * * With respect to the first of the two statutory clauses, the Fourth Circuit held in *Green* that a state-court decision can be "contrary to" this Court's clearly established precedent in two ways. First, a state-court decision is contrary to this Court's precedent if the state court arrives at a conclusion opposite to that reached by this Court on a question of law. Second, a state-court decision is also contrary to this Court's precedent if the state court confronts facts that are materially indistinguishable from a relevant Supreme Court precedent and arrives at a result opposite to ours.

The word "contrary" is commonly understood to mean "diametrically different," "opposite in character or nature," or "mutually opposed." The text of § 2254(d)(1) therefore suggests that the state court's decision must be substantially different from the relevant precedent of this Court. The Fourth Circuit's interpretation of the "contrary to" clause accurately reflects this textual meaning. A state-court decision will certainly be contrary to our clearly established precedent if the state court applies a rule that contradicts the governing law set forth in our cases. * * * A state-court decision will also be contrary to this Court's clearly established precedent if the state court confronts a set of facts that are materially indistinguishable from a decision of this Court and nevertheless arrives at a result different from our precedent. Accordingly, in either of these two scenarios, a federal court will be unconstrained by § 2254(d)(1) because the state-court decision falls within that provision's "contrary to" clause.

On the other hand, a run-of-the-mill state-court decision applying the correct legal rule from our cases to the facts of a prisoner's case would not fit comfortably within § 2254(d)(1)'s "contrary to" clause. Assume, for example, that a state-court decision on a prisoner's ineffective-assistance claim correctly identifies *Strickland* as the controlling legal authority and, applying that framework, rejects the prisoner's claim. Quite clearly, the state-court decision would be in accord with our decision in *Strickland* as to the legal prerequisites for establishing an ineffective-assistance claim, even assuming the federal court considering the prisoner's habeas application might reach a different result applying the *Strickland* framework itself. It is difficult, however, to describe such a run-of-the-mill state-court decision as "diametrically different" from, "opposite in character or nature" from, or "mutually opposed" to *Strickland*, our clearly established precedent. Although the state-court decision may be contrary to the federal court's conception of how *Strickland* ought to be applied in that particular case, the decision is not "mutually opposed" to *Strickland* itself.

Justice Stevens would instead construe § 2254(d)(1)'s "contrary to" clause to encompass such a routine state-court decision. That construction, however, saps the "unreasonable application" clause of any meaning. If a federal habeas court can, under the "contrary to" clause, issue the writ whenever it concludes that the state court's *application* of clearly established federal law was incorrect, the "unreasonable application" clause becomes a nullity. We must, however, if possible, give meaning to every clause of the statute. Justice Stevens not only makes no attempt to do so, but also construes the "contrary to" clause in a manner that ensures that the "unreasonable application" clause will have no independent meaning. We reject that expansive interpretation of the statute. Reading § 2254(d)(1)'s "contrary to" clause to permit a federal court to grant relief in cases where a state court's error is limited to the manner in which it *applies* Supreme Court precedent is suspect given the logical and natural fit of the neighboring "unreasonable application" clause to such cases.

The Fourth Circuit's interpretation of the "unreasonable application" clause of § 2254(d)(1) is generally correct. That court held in Green that a state-court decision can involve an "unreasonable application" of this Court's clearly established precedent in two ways. First, a state-court decision involves an unreasonable application of this Court's precedent if the state court identifies the correct governing legal rule from this Court's cases but unreasonably applies it to the facts of the particular state prisoner's case. Second, a state-court decision also involves an unreasonable application of this Court's precedent if the state court either unreasonably extends a legal principle from our precedent to a new context where it should not apply or unreasonably refuses to extend that principle to a new context where it should apply.

A state-court decision that correctly identifies the governing legal rule but applies it unreasonably to the facts of a particular prisoner's case certainly would qualify as a decision "involv[ing] an unreasonable application of * * * clearly established Federal law." Indeed, we used the almost identical phrase "application of law" to describe a state court's application of law to fact in the certiorari question we posed to the parties in Wright.*

The Fourth Circuit also held in Green that state-court decisions that unreasonably extend a legal principle from our precedent to a new context where it should not apply (or unreasonably refuse to extend a legal principle to a new context where it should apply) should be analyzed under § 2254(d)(1)'s "unreasonable application" clause. Although that holding may perhaps be correct, the classification does have some problems of precision. Just as it is sometimes difficult to distinguish a mixed question of law and fact from a question of fact, it will

* The legislative history of § 2254(d)(1) also supports this interpretation. ("[U]nder the bill deference will be owed to State courts' decisions on the application of Federal law to the facts. Unless it is unreasonable, a State court's decision applying the law to the facts will be upheld"); ("[W]e allow a Federal court to overturn a State court decision only if it is contrary to clearly established Federal law or if it involves an 'unreasonable application' of clearly established Federal law to the facts").

often be difficult to identify separately those state-court decisions that involve an unreasonable application of a legal principle (or an unreasonable failure to apply a legal principle) to a new context. Indeed, on the one hand, in some cases it will be hard to distinguish a decision involving an unreasonable extension of a legal principle from a decision involving an unreasonable application of law to facts. On the other hand, in many of the same cases it will also be difficult to distinguish a decision involving an unreasonable extension of a legal principle from a decision that "arrives at a conclusion opposite to that reached by this Court on a question of law." Today's case does not require us to decide how such "extension of legal principle" cases should be treated under § 2254(d)(1). For now it is sufficient to hold that when a state-court decision unreasonably applies the law of this Court to the facts of a prisoner's case, a federal court applying § 2254(d)(1) may conclude that the state-court decision falls within that provision's "unreasonable application" clause.

B

There remains the task of defining what exactly qualifies as an "unreasonable application" of law under § 2254(d)(1). The Fourth Circuit held in *Green* that a state-court decision involves an "unreasonable application of * * * clearly established Federal law" only if the state court has applied federal law "in a manner that reasonable jurists would all agree is unreasonable." The placement of this additional overlay on the "unreasonable application" clause was erroneous. It is difficult to fault the Fourth Circuit for using this language given the fact that we have employed nearly identical terminology to describe the related inquiry undertaken by federal courts in applying the nonretroactivity rule of *Teague*. * * *

Defining an "unreasonable application" by reference to a "reasonable jurist," however, is of little assistance to the courts that must apply § 2254(d)(1) and, in fact, may be misleading. Stated simply, a federal habeas court making the "unreasonable application" inquiry should ask whether the state court's application of clearly established federal law was objectively unreasonable. The federal habeas court should not transform the inquiry into a subjective one by resting its determination instead on the simple fact that at least one of the Nation's jurists has applied the relevant federal law in the same manner the state court did in the habeas petitioner's case. The "all reasonable jurists" standard would tend to mislead federal habeas courts by focusing their attention on a subjective inquiry rather than on an objective one. * * * As I explained in *Wright* with respect to the "reasonable jurist" standard in the *Teague* context, "[e]ven though we have characterized the new rule inquiry as whether 'reasonable jurists' could disagree as to whether a result is dictated by precedent, the standard for determining when a case establishes a new rule is 'objective,' and the mere existence of conflicting authority does not necessarily mean a rule is new."

test for unreasonableness

The term "unreasonable" is no doubt difficult to define. That said, it is a common term in the legal world and, accordingly, federal judges are familiar with its meaning. For purposes of today's opinion, the most important point is that an *unreasonable* application of federal law is different from an *incorrect* application of federal law. Our opinions in Wright, for example, make that difference clear. Justice Thomas' criticism of this Court's subsequent reliance on Brown turned on that distinction. The Court in *Brown*, Justice Thomas contended, held only that a federal habeas court must determine whether the relevant state-court adjudication resulted in a " 'satisfactory conclusion.' " In Justice Thomas' view, Brown did not answer "the question whether a 'satisfactory' conclusion was one that the habeas court considered correct, as opposed to merely *reasonable*." ([E]mphases in original). In my separate opinion in Wright, I made the same distinction, maintaining that "a state court's *incorrect* legal determination has [never] been allowed to stand because it was *reasonable*. We have always held that federal courts, even on habeas, have an independent obligation to say what the law is." ([E]mphases added). In § 2254(d)(1), Congress specifically used the word "unreasonable," and not a term like "erroneous" or "incorrect." Under § 2254(d)(1)'s "unreasonable application" clause, then, a federal habeas court may not issue the writ simply because that court concludes in its independent judgment that the relevant state-court decision applied clearly established federal law erroneously or incorrectly. Rather, that application must also be unreasonable.

Justice Stevens turns a blind eye to the debate in Wright because he finds no indication in § 2254(d)(1) itself that Congress was "directly influenced" by Justice Thomas' opinion in Wright. As Justice Stevens himself apparently recognizes, however, Congress need not mention a prior decision of this Court by name in a statute's text in order to adopt either a rule or a meaning given a certain term in that decision. In any event, whether Congress intended to codify the standard of review suggested by Justice Thomas in Wright is beside the point. Wright is important for the light it sheds on § 2254(d)(1)'s requirement that a federal habeas court inquire into the reasonableness of a state court's application of clearly established federal law. The separate opinions in Wright concerned the very issue addressed by § 2254(d)(1)'s "unreasonable application" clause—whether, in reviewing a state-court decision on a state prisoner's claims under federal law, a federal habeas court should ask whether the state-court decision was correct or simply whether it was reasonable. Justice Stevens' claim that the debate in Wright concerned only the meaning of the Teague nonretroactivity rule is simply incorrect. As even a cursory review of Justice Thomas' opinion and my own opinion reveals, both the broader debate and the specific statements to which we refer concerned precisely the issue of the standard of review to be employed by federal habeas courts. The Wright opinions confirm what § 2254(d)(1)'s language already makes clear—that an *unreasonable* application of federal law is different from an *incorrect* or *erroneous* application of federal law.

Throughout this discussion the meaning of the phrase "clearly established Federal law, as determined by the Supreme Court of the United States" has been put to the side. That statutory phrase refers to the holdings, as opposed to the *dicta*, of this Court's decisions as of the time of the relevant state-court decision. In this respect, the "clearly established Federal law" phrase bears only a slight connection to our *Teague* jurisprudence. With one caveat, whatever would qualify as an old rule under our *Teague* jurisprudence will constitute "clearly established Federal law, as determined by the Supreme Court of the United States" under § 2254(d)(1). The one caveat, as the statutory language makes clear, is that § 2254(d)(1) restricts the source of clearly established law to this Court's jurisprudence.

In sum, § 2254(d)(1) places a new constraint on the power of a federal habeas court to grant a state prisoner's application for a writ of habeas corpus with respect to claims adjudicated on the merits in state court. Under § 2254(d)(1), the writ may issue only if one of the following two conditions is satisfied—the state-court adjudication resulted in a decision that (1) "was contrary to * * * clearly established Federal law, as determined by the Supreme Court of the United States," or (2) "involved an unreasonable application of * * * clearly established Federal law, as determined by the Supreme Court of the United States." Under the "contrary to" clause, a federal habeas court may grant the writ if the state court arrives at a conclusion opposite to that reached by this Court on a question of law or if the state court decides a case differently than this Court has on a set of materially indistinguishable facts. Under the "unreasonable application" clause, a federal habeas court may grant the writ if the state court identifies the correct governing legal principle from this Court's decisions but unreasonably applies that principle to the facts of the prisoner's case.

III

Although I disagree with Justice Stevens concerning the standard we must apply under § 2254(d)(1) in evaluating Terry Williams' claims on habeas, I agree with the Court that the Virginia Supreme Court's adjudication of Williams' claim of ineffective assistance of counsel resulted in a decision that was both contrary to and involved an unreasonable application of this Court's clearly established precedent. Specifically, I believe that the Court's discussion in Parts III and IV is correct and that it demonstrates the reasons that the Virginia Supreme Court's decision in Williams' case, even under the interpretation of § 2254(d)(1) I have set forth above, was both contrary to and involved an unreasonable application of our precedent.

* * *

To be sure, as The Chief Justice notes, the Virginia Supreme Court did also inquire whether Williams had demonstrated a reasonable probability that, but for his trial counsel's unprofessional errors, the result of his sentencing would have been different. It is impossible to determine, however, the extent to which the Virginia Supreme Court's error with respect to its reading of Lockhart affected its ultimate finding that Williams suffered no prejudice. For example, at the conclusion of its discussion of whether Williams had demonstrated a reasonable probability of a different outcome at sentencing, the Virginia Supreme Court faulted the Virginia Circuit Court for its "emphasis on mere outcome determination, without proper attention to whether the result of the criminal proceeding was fundamentally unfair or unreliable." As the Court explains, however, Williams' case did not implicate the unusual circumstances present in cases like Lockhart or Nix v. Whiteside. Accordingly, for the very reasons I set forth in my Lockhart concurrence, the emphasis on outcome was entirely appropriate in Williams' case.

Third, I also agree with the Court that, to the extent the Virginia Supreme Court did apply Strickland, its application was unreasonable. * * * The Virginia Supreme Court's decision reveals an obvious failure to consider the totality of the omitted mitigation evidence. For that reason, and the remaining factors discussed in the Court's opinion, I believe that the Virginia Supreme Court's decision "involved an unreasonable application of * * * clearly established Federal law, as determined by the Supreme Court of the United States."

Accordingly, although I disagree with the interpretation of § 2254(d)(1) set forth in Part II of Justice Stevens' opinion, I join Parts I, III, and IV of the Court's opinion and concur in the judgment of reversal.

[Chief Justice Rehnquist, joined by Justices Scalia and Thomas, agreed with the Court's analytical framework as set out in Justice Stevens's and O'Connor's opinions. He diverged, however, from the Court's conclusion that the omitted evidence might have changed the result, finding as a practical matter that the omission was similar to harmless error.]

Notes and Questions

1. Both Justice Stevens and Justice O'Connor address, at least to some extent, the relationship between Teague v. Lane (1989), *supra* at 1105, and the current version of § 2254(d)(1), enacted as part of the AEDPA in 1996. The exact relationship, however, is unclear. Teague held that new constitutional rules of criminal procedure cannot be announced in habeas corpus cases unless such rules apply retroactively to all defendants on collateral review under one of the Teague two exceptions. Thus, habeas petitioners basically are limited to asserting claims based on "old rules," that is, rules that existed when their convictions became final. Section 2254(d)(1) prohibits

the grant of a state prisoner's habeas petition unless the state adjudication of the claim "resulted in a decision that was contrary to, or involved an unreasonable application of, clearly established Federal law, as determined by the Supreme Court of the United States." The use of the phrase "clearly established Federal law" raised the question whether Congress meant to codify the holding of Teague. The circuit courts disagreed.

Justice Stevens, speaking only for himself and three other Justices on this point in *Williams*, states that Teague's prohibition of reliance on new rules "is the functional equivalent of [the] statutory provision commanding exclusive reliance on 'clearly established law.' " Consequently, he concludes that "AEDPA codifies Teague to the extent that Teague requires federal habeas courts to deny relief that is contingent upon a rule of law not clearly established at the time the state conviction became final." Justice O'Connor, speaking for a majority on this point, appears to agree, although she points out (and Justice Stevens agrees) that the statute limits "clearly established law" to that "determined by the Supreme Court." The additional language of § 2254(d)(1) ("a decision that was contrary to, or involved an unreasonable application of" clearly established law) is not taken from Teague, and this muddies the waters considerably.

The Court revisited the question of the relationship between Teague and § 2254(d)(1) in *Horn v. Banks*, 536 U.S. 266 (2002). *Banks*, a *per curiam* opinion, stated that Teague has a continued authority independent of AEDPA:

> While it is of course a necessary prerequisite to federal habeas relief that a prisoner satisfy the AEDPA standard of review set forth in 28 U.S.C. § 2254(d) ("[a]n application * * * shall not be granted * * * *unless*" the AEDPA standard of review is satisfied (emphasis added)), none of our post-AEDPA cases have suggested that a writ of habeas corpus should automatically issue if a prisoner satisfies the AEDPA standard, or that AEDPA relieves courts from the responsibility of addressing properly raised Teague arguments. To the contrary, if our post-AEDPA cases suggest anything about AEDPA's relationship to Teague, it is that the AEDPA and Teague inquires are distinct. Thus, in addition to performing any analysis required by AEDPA, a federal court considering a habeas petition must conduct a threshold Teague analysis when the issue is properly raised by the state.

It would have been helpful if the Court had explained each inquiry and specified exactly *how* the AEDPA and Teague inquiries are different rather than simply asserting it. Because the Court spoke so generally, the relationship between Teague and § 2254(d)(1) remains unclear. Consider Larry Yackle's summary of the relationship: "The statute neither displaces nor codifies the Teague doctrine wholesale. It is accurate to say only that § 2254(d) absorbs the central ideas in Teague into a statutory framework for handling habeas petitions, seeking, in effect, to upset prior state court decisions on the merits of prisoners' claims." LARRY W. YACKLE, FEDERAL COURTS 567 (2d ed. 2003).

2. a) Justice Stevens says that whether a particular rule is "clearly established" is itself a federal question. If the federal courts find that a rule is not clearly established, how will it ever become so? Pursuant to § 2254(d)(1), even the Supreme Court cannot order habeas relief if the federal rule was not clearly established. Has Congress effectively put a cap on the scope of federal rights to which a state prisoner is entitled?

b) Section 2254(d)(1) now clearly limits the source of federal constitutional law binding on the states to Supreme Court decisions. Does that effectively put pressure on the Court to accept for review cases in which the Circuits are unanimous (and correct in the Court's view) about the existence of a constitutional rule? If so, is that a wise use of Supreme Court resources? Should Congress or the Court make that decision?

3. a) Justice Stevens thinks the phrases "contrary to" and "unreasonable application of" are not mutually exclusive, and that Congress did not mean to alter the settled rule that federal habeas courts may conduct essentially *de novo* review of state court decisions of issues of law and the application of law to fact. Justice O'Connor thinks the phrases impose different standards (and has the majority to prove it). Justice Stevens' attempt to merge them, she contends, "saps the 'unreasonable application' clause of any meaning." If you were on the Court, how would you vote? Why?

b) Note that Justice O'Connor endorses the Fourth Circuit's categorization of the kinds of cases that will fall under the two phrases. It is interesting to juxtapose her characterization of the cases in each category:

> First, a state-court decision is contrary to this Court's precedent if the state court arrives at a conclusion opposite to that reached by this Court on a question of law. Second, a state-court decision is also contrary to this Court's precedent if the state court confronts facts that are materially indistinguishable from a relevant Supreme Court precedent and arrives at a result opposite to ours.
>
> * * *
>
> [Third,] a state-court decision involves an unreasonable application of this Court's precedent if the state court identifies the correct governing legal rule from this Court's cases but unreasonably applies it to the facts of the particular state prisoner's case. [Fourth,] a state-court decision also involves an unreasonable application of this Court's precedent if that state court either unreasonably extends a legal principle from our precedent to a new context where it should not apply or unreasonably refuses to extend that principle to a new context where it should apply.

How different are the second and third categories? If the state court confronts materially indistinguishable facts and reaches an opposite result, is that different from a state court using the correct rule but unreasonably applying it to the facts? How can we know that the state court application is unreasonable save by comparing the state case with the facts of the Supreme Court case that announced the rule (and perhaps other Supreme Court cases that elaborated it)? If you think the second and third categories are different, can you construct cases that would satisfy one but not the other? Is it also possible that there are cases that satisfy both?

To the extent that the two categories do overlap, does that give some support, however unintended, to Justice Stevens's view that the two statutory phrases overlap? Assuming that they do, does the fourth category nonetheless give "unreasonable application of" something to do, thus supporting Justice O'Connor's criticism of Justice Stevens's approach?

4. Having concluded that the phrases "contrary to" and "unreasonable application of" have different meanings, Justice O'Connor interprets the latter in a way that imposes a substantial new restriction on federal habeas corpus review of state convictions. Admitting that the term "unreasonable" is difficult to define, Justice O'Connor defines it in the negative. According to her, what is an unreasonable application of federal law *not*? In assessing whether a state court decision involved an unreasonable application of federal law, should the federal court apply an objective or subjective standard?

5. Should federal courts defer to state interpretations of federal law? Assume that Congress indeed intended to codify a rule of deference by federal courts to opinions of state courts on federal law. Is that permissible, or does it violate separation of powers by intruding on the judicial function? Could Congress simply withdraw Supreme Court power to review such adjudications under § 1257 (*cf.* Martin v. Hunter's Lessee), making them unreviewable, thus making impossible Supreme Court review of state court decisions on federal constitutional matters?

6. Closely related to the question of what claims are cognizable on federal habeas corpus is the question of what facts the habeas court may take into account when determining whether the state court adjudication was "contrary to" or "involved an unreasonable application of" clearly established federal law. In the next case, the Supreme Court decided that a federal habeas court's inquiry is limited to those facts that were before the state courts when they adjudicated the federal claims that the prisoner seeks to relitigate in the federal forum.

Cullen v. Pinholster

Supreme Court of the United States, 2011.
131 S.Ct. 1388.

JUSTICE THOMAS delivered the opinion of the Court.

Scott Lynn Pinholster and two accomplices broke into a house in the middle of the night and brutally beat and stabbed to death two men who happened to interrupt the burglary. A jury convicted Pinholster of first-degree murder, and he was sentenced to death.

After the California Supreme Court twice unanimously denied Pinholster habeas relief, a Federal District Court held an evidentiary hearing and granted Pinholster habeas relief under 28 U.S.C. § 2254. The District Court concluded that Pinholster's trial counsel had been constitutionally ineffective at the penalty phase of trial. Sitting en banc, the Court of Appeals for the Ninth Circuit affirmed. * * * Considering the new evidence adduced in the District Court hearing, the Court of Appeals held that the California Supreme Court's decision "was contrary to, or involved an unreasonable application of, clearly established Federal law." § 2254(d)(1).

We granted certiorari and now reverse.

I

A

On the evening of January 8, 1982, Pinholster solicited Art Corona and Paul David Brown to help him rob Michael Kumar, a local drug dealer. On the way, they stopped at Lisa Tapar's house, where Pinholster put his buck knife through her front door and scratched a swastika into her car after she refused to talk to him. The three men, who were all armed with buck knives, found no one at Kumar's house, broke in, and began ransacking the home. They came across only a small amount of marijuana before Kumar's friends, Thomas Johnson and Robert Beckett, arrived and shouted that they were calling the police.

Pinholster and his accomplices tried to escape through the rear door, but Johnson blocked their path. Pinholster backed Johnson onto the patio, demanding drugs and money and repeatedly striking him in the chest. Johnson dropped his wallet on the ground and stopped resisting. Beckett then came around the corner, and Pinholster attacked him, too, stabbing him repeatedly in the chest. Pinholster forced Beckett to the ground, took both men's wallets, and began kicking Beckett in the head. Meanwhile, Brown stabbed Johnson in the chest, " 'bury[ing] his knife to the hilt.' " * * * Johnson and Beckett died of their wounds.

Corona drove the three men to Pinholster's apartment. While in the car, Pinholster and Brown exulted, " 'We got em, man, we got em good.' " At the apartment, Pinholster washed his knife, and the three split the proceeds of the robbery: $23 and one quarter-ounce of marijuana. Although Pinholster instructed Corona to "lay low," Corona turned himself in to the police two weeks later. Pinholster was arrested shortly thereafter and threatened to kill Corona if he did not keep quiet about the burglary and murders. Corona later became the State's primary witness. The prosecution brought numerous charges against Pinholster, including two counts of first-degree murder.

B

The California trial court appointed Harry Brainard and Wilbur Dettmar to defend Pinholster on charges of first-degree murder, robbery, and burglary. Before their appointment, Pinholster had rejected other attorneys and insisted on representing himself. During that time, the State had mailed Pinholster a letter in jail informing him that the prosecution planned to offer aggravating evidence during the penalty phase of trial to support a sentence of death.

The guilt phase of the trial began on February 28, 1984. Pinholster testified on his own behalf and presented an alibi defense. He claimed that he had broken into Kumar's house alone at around 8 p.m. on January 8, 1982, and had stolen marijuana but denied killing anyone. Pinholster asserted that later that night around 1 a.m., while he was elsewhere, Corona went to Kumar's house to steal more drugs and did not return for three hours. Pinholster told the jury that he was a "professional robber," not a murderer. He boasted of committing hundreds of robberies over the previous six years but insisted that he always used a gun, never a knife. The jury convicted Pinholster on both counts of first-degree murder.

Before the penalty phase, Brainard and Dettmar moved to exclude any aggravating evidence on the ground that the prosecution had failed to provide notice of the evidence to be introduced * * * . At a hearing on April 24, Dettmar argued that, in reliance on the lack of notice, he was "not presently prepared to offer anything by way of mitigation." He acknowledged, however, that the prosecutor "possibly ha[d] met the [notice] requirement." The trial court asked whether a continuance might be helpful, but Dettmar declined, explaining that he could not think of a mitigation witness other than Pinholster's mother and that additional time would not "make a great deal of difference." Three days later, after hearing testimony, the court found that Pinholster had received notice while representing himself and denied the motion to exclude.

The penalty phase was held before the same jury that had convicted Pinholster. The prosecution produced eight witnesses, who testified about Pinholster's history of threatening and violent behavior, including resisting arrest and assaulting police officers, involvement with juvenile gangs, and a substantial prison disciplinary record. Defense counsel called only Pinholster's mother, Burnice Brashear. She gave an account of Pinholster's troubled childhood and adolescent years, discussed Pinholster's siblings, and described Pinholster as "a perfect gentleman at home." Defense counsel did not call a psychiatrist, though they had consulted Dr. John Stalberg at least six weeks earlier. Dr. Stalberg noted Pinholster's "psychopathic personality traits," diagnosed him with antisocial personality disorder, and concluded that he "was not under the influence of extreme mental or emotional disturbance" at the time of the murders.

After 2½ days of deliberation, the jury unanimously voted for death on each of the two murder counts. On mandatory appeal, the California Supreme Court affirmed the judgment.

C

In August 1993, Pinholster filed his first state habeas petition. Represented by new counsel, Pinholster alleged, *inter alia*, ineffective assistance of counsel at the penalty phase of his trial. He alleged that Brainard and Dettmar had failed to adequately investigate and present mitigating evidence, including evidence of mental disorders. Pinholster supported this claim with school, medical, and legal records, as well as declarations from family members, Brainard, and Dr. George Woods, a psychiatrist who diagnosed Pinholster with bipolar mood disorder and seizure disorders. Dr. Woods criticized Dr. Stalberg's report as incompetent, unreliable, and inaccurate. The California Supreme Court unanimously and summarily denied Pinholster's penalty-phase ineffective-assistance claim "on the substantive ground that it is without merit."

Pinholster filed a federal habeas petition in April 1997. He reiterated his previous allegations about penalty-phase ineffective assistance and also added new allegations that his trial counsel had failed to furnish Dr. Stalberg with adequate background materials. In support of the new allegations, Dr. Stalberg provided a declaration stating that in 1984, Pinholster's trial counsel had provided him with only some police reports and a 1978 probation report. Dr. Stalberg explained that, had he known about the material that had since been gathered by Pinholster's habeas counsel, he would have conducted "further inquiry" before concluding that Pinholster suffered only from a personality disorder. He noted that Pinholster's school records showed evidence of "some degree of brain damage." Dr. Stalberg did not, however, retract his earlier diagnosis. The parties stipulated that this declaration had never been submitted to the California Supreme Court, and the federal petition was held in abeyance to allow Pinholster to go back to state court.

In August 1997, Pinholster filed his second state habeas petition, this time including Dr. Stalberg's declaration and requesting judicial notice of the documents previously submitted in support of his first state habeas petition. His allegations of penalty-phase ineffective assistance of counsel mirrored those in his federal habeas petition. The California Supreme Court again unanimously and summarily denied the petition "on the substantive ground that it is without merit."

Having presented Dr. Stalberg's declaration to the state court, Pinholster returned to the District Court. In November 1997, he filed an amended petition for a writ of habeas corpus. His allegations of penalty-phase ineffective assistance of counsel were identical to those in his second state habeas petition. Both parties moved for summary judgment and Pinholster also moved, in the alternative, for an evidentiary hearing.

The District Court concluded that the Antiterrorism and Effective Death Penalty Act of 1996 (AEDPA) did not apply and granted an evidentiary hearing. Before the hearing, the State deposed Dr. Stalberg, who stated that none of the new material he reviewed altered his original diagnosis. Dr. Stalberg disagreed with Dr. Woods' conclusion that Pinholster suffers from bipolar disorder. Pinholster did not call Dr. Stalberg to testify at the hearing. He presented two new medical experts: Dr. Sophia Vinogradov, a psychiatrist who diagnosed Pinholster with organic personality syndrome and ruled out antisocial personality disorder, and Dr. Donald Olson, a pediatric neurologist who suggested that Pinholster suffers from partial epilepsy and brain injury. The State called Dr. F. David Rudnick, a psychiatrist who, like Dr. Stalberg, diagnosed Pinholster with antisocial personality disorder and rejected any diagnosis of bipolar disorder.

D

The District Court granted habeas relief. Applying pre-AEDPA standards, the court granted the habeas petition "for inadequacy of counsel by failure to investigate and present mitigation evidence at the penalty hearing." After *Woodford v. Garceau*, 538 U.S. 202 (2003), clarified that AEDPA applies to cases like Pinholster's, the court amended its order but did not alter its conclusion. Over a dissent, a panel of the Court of Appeals for the Ninth Circuit reversed. On rehearing en banc, the Court of Appeals vacated the panel opinion and affirmed the District Court's grant of habeas relief. The en banc court held that the District Court's evidentiary hearing was not barred by 28 U.S.C. § 2254(e)(2). The court then determined that new evidence from the hearing could be considered in assessing whether the California Supreme Court's decision "was contrary to, or involved an unreasonable application of, clearly established Federal law" under § 2254(d)(1). See 590 F.3d, at 666 ("Congress did not intend to restrict the inquiry under

§ 2254(d)(1) only to the evidence introduced in the state habeas court"). Taking the District Court evidence into account, the en banc court determined that the California Supreme Court unreasonably applied *Strickland* v. *Washington*, 466 U.S. 668 (1984), in denying Pinholster's claim of penalty-phase ineffective assistance of counsel.

* * *

We granted certiorari to resolve two questions. First, whether review under § 2254(d)(1) permits consideration of evidence introduced in an evidentiary hearing before the federal habeas court. Second, whether the Court of Appeals properly granted Pinholster habeas relief on his claim of penalty-phase ineffective assistance of counsel.

II

We first consider the scope of the record for a § 2254(d)(1) inquiry. The State argues that review is limited to the record that was before the state court that adjudicated the claim on the merits. Pinholster contends that evidence presented to the federal habeas court may also be considered. We agree with the State.

A

As amended by AEDPA, 28 U.S.C. § 2254 sets several limits on the power of a federal court to grant an application for a writ of habeas corpus on behalf of a state prisoner. Section 2254(a) permits a federal court to entertain only those applications alleging that a person is in state custody "in violation of the Constitution or laws or treaties of the United States." Sections 2254(b) and (c) provide that a federal court may not grant such applications unless, with certain exceptions, the applicant has exhausted state remedies.

If an application includes a claim that has been "adjudicated on the merits in State court proceedings," § 2254(d), an additional restriction applies. Under § 2254(d), that application "shall not be granted with respect to [such a] claim * * * unless the adjudication of the claim":

> (1) resulted in a decision that was contrary to, or involved an unreasonable application of, clearly established Federal law, as determined by the Supreme Court of the United States; or
>
> (2) resulted in a decision that was based on an unreasonable determination of the facts in light of the evidence presented in the State court proceeding.

This is a "difficult to meet," *Harrington v. Richter*, 131 S. Ct. 770 (2011), and "highly deferential standard for evaluating state-court rulings, which demands that state-court decisions be given the benefit of the doubt," Woodford v. Visciotti (2002) *(per curiam)*. The petitioner carries the burden of proof.

We now hold that review under § 2254(d)(1) is limited to the record that was before the state court that adjudicated the claim on the merits. Section 2254(d)(1) refers, in the past tense, to a state-court adjudication that "resulted in" a decision that was contrary to, or "involved" an unreasonable application of, established law. This backward-looking language requires an examination of the state-court decision at the time it was made. It follows that the record under review is limited to the record in existence at that same time—*i.e.*, the record before the state court.

This understanding of the text is compelled by "the broader context of the statute as a whole," which demonstrates Congress' intent to channel prisoners' claims first to the state courts. "The federal habeas scheme leaves primary responsibility with the state courts * * * ." Section 2254(b) requires that prisoners must ordinarily exhaust state remedies before filing for federal habeas relief. It would be contrary to that purpose to allow a petitioner to overcome an adverse state-court decision with new evidence introduced in a federal habeas court and reviewed by that court in the first instance effectively *de novo*.

Limiting § 2254(d)(1) review to the state-court record is consistent with our precedents interpreting that statutory provision. Our cases emphasize that review under § 2254(d)(1) focuses on what a state court knew and did. State-court decisions are measured against this Court's precedents as of "the time the state court renders its decision." To determine whether a particular decision is "contrary to" then-established law, a federal court must consider whether the decision "applies a rule that contradicts [such] law" and how the decision "confronts [the] set of facts" that were before the state court. If the state-court decision "identifies the correct governing legal principle" in existence at the time, a federal court must assess whether the decision "unreasonably applies that principle to the facts of the prisoner's case." It would be strange to ask federal courts to analyze whether a state court's adjudication resulted in a decision that unreasonably applied federal law to facts not before the state court.

Our recent decision in *Schriro v. Landrigan* (2007), is consistent as well with our holding here. We explained that "[b]ecause the deferential standards prescribed by § 2254 control whether to grant habeas relief, a federal court must take into account those standards in deciding whether an evidentiary hearing is appropriate." In practical effect, we went on to note, this means that when the state-court record "precludes habeas relief" under the limitations of § 2254(d), a district court is "not required to hold an evidentiary hearing."

The Court of Appeals wrongly interpreted *Williams v. Taylor*, 529 U.S. 420 (2000) *(Michael Williams)*, as supporting the contrary view. The question there was whether the lower court had correctly determined that § 2254(e)(2) barred the petitioner's request for a federal evidentiary hearing. *Michael Williams* did not concern whether evidence introduced in such a hearing could be considered under § 2254(d)(1). In fact, only one claim at issue in that case was even subject to § 2254(d); the rest had not been adjudicated on the merits in state-court proceedings.

* * *

B

Pinholster's contention that our holding renders § 2254(e)(2) superfluous is incorrect. Section 2254(e)(2) imposes a limitation on the discretion of federal habeas courts to take new evidence in an evidentiary hearing. Like § 2254(d)(1), it carries out "AEDPA's goal of promoting comity, finality, and federalism by giving state courts the first opportunity to review [a] claim, and to correct any constitutional violation in the first instance."

Section 2254(e)(2) continues to have force where § 2254(d)(1) does not bar federal habeas relief. For example, not all federal habeas claims by state prisoners fall within the scope of § 2254(d), which applies only to claims "adjudicated on the merits in State court proceedings." At a minimum, therefore, § 2254(e)(2) still restricts the discretion of federal habeas courts to consider new evidence when deciding claims that were not adjudicated on the merits in state court. *See, e.g.*, Michael Williams v. Taylor.

Although state prisoners may sometimes submit new evidence in federal court, AEDPA's statutory scheme is designed to strongly discourage them from doing so. Provisions like §§ 2254(d)(1) and (e)(2) ensure that "[f]ederal courts sitting in habeas are not an alternative forum for trying facts and issues which a prisoner made insufficient effort to pursue in state proceedings." *Michael Williams v. Taylor*, 529 U.S. 420, 437 (2000). [*See*] *Richter*, 131 S. Ct. 770, 787 ("Section 2254(d) is part of the basic structure of federal habeas jurisdiction, designed to confirm that state courts are the principal forum for asserting constitutional challenges to state convictions"); *Wainwright v. Sykes*, 433 U.S. 72, 90 (1977) ("[T]he state trial on the merits [should be] the 'main event,' so to speak, rather than a 'tryout on the road' for what will later be the determinative federal habeas hearing").

C

Accordingly, we conclude that the Court of Appeals erred in considering the District Court evidence in its review under § 2254(d)(1). Although we might ordinarily remand for a properly limited review, the Court of Appeals also ruled, in the alternative, that Pinholster merited habeas relief even on the state-court record alone. Remand is therefore inappropriate, and we turn next to a review of the state-court record.

[The Court then found that Pinholster had failed to demonstrate that the California Supreme Court had unreasonably applied *Strickland v. Washington* to his penalty-hase ineffective assistance claim, based exclusively on the state court record.]

The judgment of the United States Court of Appeals for the Ninth Circuit is reversed.

It is so ordered.

JUSTICE SOTOMAYOR, with whom JUSTICE GINSBURG and JUSTICE KAGAN join as to Part II, dissenting.

Some habeas petitioners are unable to develop the factual basis of their claims in state court through no fault of their own. Congress recognized as much when it enacted the Antiterrorism and Effective Death Penalty Act of 1996 (AEDPA) and permitted therein the introduction of new evidence in federal habeas proceedings in certain limited circumstances. See 28 U.S.C. § 2254(e)(2). Under the Court's novel interpretation of § 2254(d)(1), however, federal courts must turn a blind eye to new evidence in deciding whether a petitioner has satisfied § 2254(d)(1)'s threshold obstacle to federal habeas relief—even when it is clear that the petitioner would be entitled to relief in light of that evidence. In reading the statute to "compe[l]" this harsh result, the Court ignores a key textual difference between §§ 2254(d)(1) and 2254(d)(2) and discards the previous understanding in our precedents that new evidence can, in fact, inform the § 2254(d)(1) inquiry. I therefore dissent from the Court's first holding.

Notes and Questions

1. With respect to Pinholster's claim, the Court observed that he could satisfy the "unreasonable application" prong of § 2254(d)(1) only by showing that

> "there was no reasonable basis" for the California Supreme Court's decision. "[A] habeas court must determine what arguments or theories * * * could have supporte[d] the state court's decision; and then it must ask whether it is possible fairminded jurists could disagree that those arguments or theories are inconsistent with the holding in a prior decision of this Court." After a thorough review of the state-court record, we conclude that Pinholster has failed to meet that high threshold.

In the quotation within the quotation above, does the Court articulate a defensible approach? Do you think it is appropriate for the reviewing court to consider what arguments "could have supporte[d]" the state court's decision, or should it consider only the arguments on which the state court actually relied?

The Court has expressed concern about affirming decisions where there were multiple possible bases for a decision, at least one of the bases was illegitimate, and the adjudicator did not reveal upon which basis it relied. For example, *Stromberg v. California* (1931) overturned a conviction on a general jury verdict where the trial court had charged the jury that there were three possible grounds under the statute to support conviction. One of the three clauses in the statute was unconstitutional. The Court applied the same principle to administrative proceedings in *Clay v. United States*, (1971), explaining that it was not appropriate for the reviewing court to hypothesize a basis upon which the reviewed decision *might have* rested when the record contained both legitimate and illegitimate bases. *Clay* involved boxer Muhammad Ali, convicted of violating the Selective Service Act despite his claim of exemption as a conscientious objector. Even before *Clay*, some of the circuit court had begun requiring statements of reasons for denials of deferments or exemptions, at least for claims *prima facie* valid. Should state and federal courts have to state their reasons for deciding? If so, what justifies the Court's imposition of such a burden on them? If not, how can a reviewing court be sure it is reviewing the decision that the body being reviewed actually made, rather than one that it might have made?

2. In 2011, the Supreme Court handed down another decision bearing on the scope of deference to state court adjudications of federal claims required by Section 2254(d)(1). In *Harrington v. Richter*, 131 S.Ct. 770 (2011), the Court confronted the issue of how a federal habeas court analyzes the reasonableness of a state court adjudication unaccompanied by any explanation. In non-capital cases, at least, state courts very frequently affirm convictions on direct appeal or refuse state post-conviction relief by way of "postcard denials" — orders that simply state the result. In *Harrington*, the Court held that a federal habeas court may not grant relief unless the result was objectively unreasonable, as per *(Terry) Williams v. Taylor.* In other words, a federal habeas court must let stand any state court ruling on a federal claim if it can conceive of any reasonable explanation for the ruling. For a contrary argument, *see* Evan Tsen Lee, *Section 2254(d) of the Federal Habeas Statute: Is It Beyond Reason?*, 56 HASTINGS L.J. 283 (2004) (long history of habeas reform efforts by conservatives centered on reasoning of decisions, not results).

CLICK FOR UPDATE
UPDATES FOUND ON PAGES 1191-1195

3. Exhaustion of Remedies

The federal courts have long required state prisoners to exhaust available state remedies before filing a habeas petition in federal court. Congress codified this requirement in 1948, but the statute did not address how the courts should deal with so-called "mixed" petitions—petitions containing both exhausted and unexhausted claims. In *Rose v. Lundy*, 455 U.S. 509 (1982), the Court held a district court must dismiss mixed petitions, thus leaving the petitioner with the choice of returning to state court to adjudicate unexhausted claims or amending the petition to present only exhausted claims.

Congress addressed exhaustion requirements in AEDPA (1996):

§ 2254

* * *

(b)(1) An application for a writ of habeas corpus on behalf of a person in custody pursuant to the judgment of a State court shall not be granted unless it appears that

(A) the applicant has exhausted the remedies available in the courts of the State; or

(B) (i) there is an absence of available state corrective process; or

(ii) circumstances exist that render such process ineffective to protect the rights of the applicant.

(2) An application for a writ of habeas corpus may be denied on the merits, notwithstanding the failure of the applicant to exhaust the remedies available in the courts of the State.

(3) A State shall not be deemed to have waived the exhaustion requirement or be estopped from reliance upon the requirement unless the State, through counsel, expressly waives the requirement.

(c) An applicant shall not be deemed to have exhausted the remedies available in the courts of the State, within the meaning of this section, it he has the right under the law of the State to raise, by any available procedure, the question presented.

AEDPA left the basic exhaustion requirements of § 2254 unchanged. Note that the statute does specifically permit the habeas court to rule on an unexhausted claim provided that the court rules *against* the prisoner. The statute also prohibits the federal courts from inferring state waiver of the requirement or from finding that the state is estopped to raise the issue, requiring instead an explicit waiver through counsel. What do these two provisions tell us about the nature of even Congress's exhaustion rule?

The amended exhaustion provisions do not say what should happened to mixed petitions of the type presented in Lundy. Should the courts continue to dismiss such petitions in their entirety, or should they hear the exhausted claims and dismiss only the unexhausted ones? If the former, then has Congress implicitly taken the position that a prisoner who has some claims that are ripe for federal adjudication and some that are not should remain imprisoned until all are ripe, despite the fact that the earlier-ripened claims may be sufficient to secure his release? Is the prisoner thus faced with the dilemma of abandoning some (perhaps winning) claims or suffering longer-than-necessary imprisonment?

What does AEDPA mean when it refers in § 2254(c) to "any available procedure" for raising a claim in the state courts? Does that include having sought certiorari from the state's highest court even in the face of indications that the court only wishes to receive petitions for review if the case presents unsettled issues of law with broad application rather than fact-specific claims relating to the application of established law? *O'Sullivan v. Boerckel*, 526 U.S. 838 (1999), answered affirmatively. Boerckel sought federal habeas relief on six grounds, only three of which he had sought (unsuccessfully) to present to the Illinois Supreme Court through certiorari. Illinois had a rule discussing the scope of its Supreme Court's discretion; it referred *inter alia* to "the general importance of the question presented; the existence of a conflict between the decision sought to be reviewed and a decision of the Supreme Court, or of another division of the Appellate Court; [and] the need for the exercise of the Supreme Court's supervisory authority * * * ." Boerckel argued that the three excluded claims related to "routine allegations of error" and were highly fact-specific, involving only particularized application of well established legal principles. A six-to-three Court ruled that he should have given Illinois's Supreme Court the opportunity to exercise its discretion and that his failure to do so constituted a procedural default barring federal consideration of the omitted claims. The majority did appear to leave room for states to pass rules of discretionary review that make it clear that such review is "unavailable" to certain types of cases.

Justice Stevens's dissent accused the majority of confusing the exhaustion and procedural default doctrines. He argued that the Court actually showed less, not more, respect for the states, by threatening to flood their discretionary review processes with futile petitions, wasting state judicial time and delaying inevitable federal habeas review. Assuming that Justice Stevens is correct about the Illinois Supreme Court's not wanting to be troubled with appeals on fact-intensive claims with no systemic importance, how would you craft a certiorari policy the embodies that goal without excluding cases that the court might want to hear?

Generally, a petitioner who uses one of several available means to present a claim to the state court satisfies the exhaustion requirement. Once the state's highest court has either rejected the claim or denied discretionary review, exhaustion is complete. Is this a reasonable interpretation of § 2254(c) (unchanged by AEDPA), which apparently precludes review if there is "any" available procedure? Why should one not understand that word to include, in addition to applications to the state's highest court for discretionary review, requests for rehearing, resort to the extraordinary writs, and invocation of state habeas corpus procedures? Is it of any significance that AEDPA reenacted this section without change?

Does the majority's view place state prisoners in an impossible position with respect to characterizing their claims? Professor Carlos Vasquez has suggested that this creates an irreconcilable conflict for state prisoners. Given the ordinary workings of a discretionary review procedure, persons seeking discretionary review will have no realistic possibility of obtaining it unless they can demonstrate that the issues they raise are novel and, as Justice Stevens says, "of broad significance." Yet to make such a showing in the state's certiorari proceeding may undermine the chance to secure federal habeas corpus relief, since the doctrine of *Teague v. Lane*, supplemented now by 28 U.S.C. § 2254(d), requires a decision to have been "contrary to * * * clearly established Federal law, as determined by the Supreme Court of the United States" to be reviewable by federal habeas corpus. How likely is it that an issue will satisfy both of those criteria?

What policies does the Court serve by dismissing exhausted claims joined with unexhausted ones? How does deferring federal adjudication serve those policies? In this connection, consider one of the perhaps unanticipated effects that AEDPA may have. The statute establishes a one-year filing deadline, typically running from the end of the direct review process. Lundy directs the federal courts to dismiss petitions containing exhausted and unexhausted claims, and threatens prisoners with the loss of the unexhausted claims if the prisoners press on with only the exhausted claims. "The idea in *Lundy* is to encourage prisoners to slow down litigation of some claims until all are ready for federal adjudication." Larry W. Yackle, *A Primer on the New Habeas Corpus Statute*, 44 BUFF.L.REV. 381, 387 (1996). Suppose a prisoner faces the one-year filing deadline with respect to some (exhausted) claims but has not completed state proceedings with respect to other (obviously unexhausted) claims. What is he to do?

AEDPA directs that "[a] claim presented in a second or successive habeas corpus application under section 2254 that was presented in a prior application shall be dismissed." If a district court follows *Lundy* and dismisses a mixed petition at the outset without any consideration of the merits, were the claims in such a petition "presented"? *Stewart v. Martinez-Villareal*, 523 U.S. 637 (1998), says no.

4. The Effect of State Procedural Defaults

Coleman v. Thompson

Supreme Court of the United States, 1991.
501 U.S. 722.

JUSTICE O'CONNOR delivered the opinion of the Court.

This is a case about federalism. It concerns the respect that federal courts owe the States and the States' procedural rules when reviewing the claims of state prisoners in federal habeas corpus.

> **Food for Thought**
>
> The underlying criminal proceeding involves the murder of a human being, and the proposed execution of another one. It is curious that Justice O'Connor, not known as a particularly abstract thinker, would begin the majority opinion with this characterization.

I

A Buchanan County, Virginia, jury convicted Roger Keith Coleman of rape and capital murder and fixed the sentence at death for the murder. The trial court imposed the death sentence, and the Virginia Supreme Court affirmed both the convictions and the sentence. This Court denied certiorari.

Coleman then filed a petition for a writ of habeas corpus in the Circuit Court for Buchanan County, raising numerous federal constitutional claims that he had not raised on direct appeal. After a two-day evidentiary hearing, the Circuit Court ruled against Coleman on all claims.

Coleman filed his notice of appeal with the Circuit Court * * * 33 days after the entry of final judgment. Coleman subsequently filed a petition for appeal in the Virginia Supreme Court. The Commonwealth of Virginia, as appellant, filed a motion to dismiss the appeal. The sole ground for dismissal urged in the motion was that Coleman's notice of appeal had been filed late. Virginia Supreme Court Rule 5:9(a) provides that no appeal shall be allowed unless a notice of appeal is filed with the trial court within 30 days of final judgment.

The Virginia Supreme Court did not act immediately on the Commonwealth's motion, and both parties filed several briefs on the subject of the motion to dismiss and on the merits of the claims in Coleman's petition. On May 19, 1987, the Virginia Supreme Court issued the following order, dismissing Coleman's appeal:

> On December 4, 1986 came the appellant, by counsel, and filed a petition for appeal in the above-styled case.
>
> Thereupon came the appellee, by the Attorney General of Virginia, and filed a motion to dismiss the petition for appeal; on December 19, 1986 the appellant filed a memorandum in opposition to the motion to dismiss; on December 19, 1986 the appellee filed a reply to the appellant's memorandum; on December 23, 1986 the appellee filed a brief in opposition to the petition for appeal; on December 23, 1986 the appellant filed a surreply in opposition to the appellee's motion to dismiss; and on January 6, 1987 the appellant filed a reply brief.
>
> Upon consideration whereof, the motion to dismiss is granted and the petition for appeal is dismissed.
>
> This Court again denied certiorari.

Coleman next filed a petition for writ of habeas corpus in the United States District Court for the Western District of Virginia. In his petition, Coleman presented four federal constitutional claims he had raised on direct appeal in the Virginia Supreme Court and seven claims he had raised for the first time in state habeas. The District Court concluded that, by virtue of the dismissal of his appeal by the Virginia Supreme Court in state habeas, Coleman had procedurally defaulted the seven claims. The District Court nonetheless went on to address the merits of all 11 of Coleman's claims. The court ruled against Coleman on all of the claims and denied the petition.

The United States Court of Appeals for the Fourth Circuit * * * held that Coleman had defaulted all of the claims that he had presented for the first time in state habeas. Coleman argued that the Virginia Supreme Court had not "clearly and expressly" stated that its decision in state habeas was based on a procedural default, and therefore the federal courts could not treat it as such under the rule of *Harris v. Reed* (1989). The Fourth Circuit disagreed. It concluded that the Virginia Supreme Court had met the "plain statement" requirement of *Harris* by granting a motion to dismiss that was based solely on procedural grounds. The Fourth Circuit held that the Virginia Supreme Court's decision rested on independent and adequate state grounds and that Coleman had not shown cause to excuse the default. As a consequence, federal review of the claims Coleman presented only in the state habeas proceeding was barred. We granted certiorari to resolve several issues concerning the relationship between state procedural defaults and federal habeas review, and now affirm.

II

A

This Court will not review a question of federal law decided by a state court if the decision of that court rests on a state law ground that is independent of the federal question and adequate to support the judgment. This rule applies whether the state law ground is substantive or procedural. In the context of direct review of a state court judgment, the independent and adequate state ground doctrine is jurisdictional. Because this Court has no power to review a state law determination that is sufficient to support the judgment, resolution of any independent federal ground for the decision could not affect the judgment and would therefore be advisory.

We have applied the independent and adequate state ground doctrine not only in our own review of state court judgments, but in deciding whether federal district courts should address the claims of state prisoners in habeas corpus actions. The doctrine applies also to bar federal habeas when a state court declined to address a prisoner's federal claims because the prisoner had failed to meet a state procedural requirement. * * *

The basis for application of the independent and adequate state ground doctrine in federal habeas is somewhat different than on direct review by this Court. When this Court reviews a state court decision on direct review pursuant to 28 U.S.C. § 1257 it is reviewing the *judgment*; if resolution of a federal question cannot affect the judgment, there is nothing for the Court to do. This is not the case in habeas. When a federal district court reviews a state prisoner's habeas corpus petition pursuant to 28 U.S.C. § 2254 it must decide whether the petitioner is "in custody in violation of the Constitution or laws or treaties of the United States." The court does not review a judgment, but the lawfulness of the petitioner's custody *simpliciter*.

Nonetheless, a state prisoner is in custody *pursuant* to a judgment. When a federal habeas court releases a prisoner held pursuant to a state court judgment that rests on an independent and adequate state ground, it renders ineffective the state rule just as completely as if this Court had reversed the state judgment on direct review. In such a case, the habeas court ignores the State's legitimate reasons for holding the prisoner.

In the habeas context, the application of the independent and adequate state ground doctrine is grounded in concerns of comity and federalism. Without the rule, a federal district court would be able to do in habeas what this Court could not do on direct review; habeas would offer state prisoners whose custody was supported by independent and adequate state grounds an end run around the limits of this Court's jurisdiction and a means to undermine the State's interest in enforcing its laws.

When the independent and adequate state ground supporting a habeas petitioner's custody is a state procedural default, an additional concern comes into play. This Court has long held that a state prisoner's federal habeas petition should be dismissed if the prisoner has not exhausted available state remedies as to any of his federal claims. This exhaustion requirement is also grounded in principles of comity; in a federal system, the States should have the first opportunity to address and correct alleged violations of state prisoner's federal rights. * * *

These same concerns apply to federal claims that have been procedurally defaulted in state court. Just as in those cases in which a state prisoner fails to exhaust state remedies, a habeas petitioner who has failed to meet the State's procedural requirements for presenting his federal claims has deprived the state courts of an opportunity to address those claims in the first instance. A habeas petitioner who has defaulted his federal claims in state court meets the technical requirements for exhaustion; there are no state remedies any longer "available" to him. In the absence of the independent and adequate state ground doctrine in federal habeas, habeas petitioners would be able to avoid the exhaustion requirement by defaulting their federal claims in state court. The independent and adequate state ground doctrine ensures that the State's interest in correcting their own mistakes is respected in all federal habeas cases.

B

* * *

In Michigan v. Long (1983), * * * in order to minimize the costs associated with resolving ambiguities in state court decisions while still fulfilling our obligation to determine if there was an independent and adequate state ground for the decision, we established a conclusive presumption of jurisdiction in these cases:

> [W]hen, as in this case, a state court decision fairly appears to rest primarily on federal law, or to be interwoven with the federal law, and when the adequacy and independence of any possible state law ground is not clear from the face of the opinion, we will accept as the most reasonable explanation that the state court decided the case the way it did because it believed that federal law required it to do so.

After Long, a state court that wishes to look to federal law for guidance or as an alternative holding while still relying on an independent and adequate state ground can avoid the presumption by stating "clearly and expressly that [its decision] is * * * based on bona fide separate, adequate, and independent grounds."

In Caldwell v. Mississippi (1985) we applied the Long presumption in the context of an alleged independent and adequate state procedural ground.

Long and Caldwell were direct review cases. We first considered the problem of ambiguous state court decisions in the application of the independent and adequate state ground doctrine in a federal habeas case in Harris v. Reed. * * *

The situation presented to this Court was nearly identical to that in Long and Caldwell: a state court decision that fairly appeared to rest primarily on federal law in a context in which a federal court has an obligation to determine if the state court decision rested on an independent and adequate state ground. "Faced with a common problem, we adopt[ed] a common solution." Harris applied in federal habeas the presumption this Court adopted in Long for direct review cases. Because the Illinois Appellate Court did not "clearly and expressly" rely on waiver as a ground for rejecting Harris' ineffective assistance of counsel claims, the Long presumption applied and Harris was not barred from federal habeas.

After Harris, federal courts on habeas corpus review of state prisoner claims, like this Court on direct review of state court judgments, will presume that there is no independent and adequate state ground for a state court decision when the decision "fairly appears to rest primarily on federal law, or to be interwoven with the federal law, and when the adequacy and independence of any possible state law ground is not clear from the face of the opinion." In habeas, if the decision of the last state court to which the petitioner presented his federal claims fairly appeared to rest primarily on resolution of those claims, or to be interwoven with those claims, and did not clearly and expressly rely on an independent and adequate state ground, a federal court may address the petition.[1]

III

A

Coleman contends that the presumption of Long and Harris applies in this case, and precludes a bar to habeas, because the Virginia Supreme Court's order dismissing Coleman's appeal did not "clearly and expressly" state that it was based on state procedural grounds. Coleman reads Harris too broadly. A predicate to the application of the Harris presumption is that the decision of the last state court to which the petitioner presented his federal claims must fairly appear to rest primarily on federal law or to be interwoven with federal law.

---

1 This rule does not apply if the petitioner failed to exhaust state remedies and the court to which petitioner would be required to present his claims in order to meet the exhaustion requirement would now find the claims procedurally barred. In such a case there is a procedural default for purposes of federal habeas regardless of the decision of the last state court to which the petitioner actually presented his claims.

* * *

Coleman urges a broader rule: that the presumption applies in all cases in which a habeas petitioner presented his federal claims to the state court. This rule makes little sense. * * * The presumption, like all conclusive presumptions, is designed to avoid the costs of excessive inquiry where a *per se* rule will achieve the correct result in almost all cases. * * *

Per se rules should not be applied, however, in situations where the generalization is incorrect as an empirical matter; the justification for a conclusive presumption disappears when application of the presumption will not reach the correct result most of the time. The Long and Harris presumption works because in the majority of cases in which a state court decision fairly appears to rest primarily on federal law or to be interwoven with such law, and the state court does not plainly state that it is relying on an independent and adequate state ground, the state court decision did not in fact rest on an independent and adequate state ground. We accept errors in those small number of cases where there was nonetheless an independent and adequate state ground in exchange for a significant reduction in the costs of inquiry.

The tradeoff is very different when the factual predicate does not exist. In those cases in which it does not fairly appear that the state court rested its decision primarily on federal grounds, it is simply not true that the "most reasonable explanation" is that the state judgment rested on federal grounds. * * * Any efficiency gained by applying a conclusive presumption, and thereby avoiding inquiry into state law, is simply not worth the cost in the loss of respect for the State that such a rule would entail.

* * *

In any event, we decline to establish such a rule here, for it would place burdens on the States and state courts in exchange for very little benefit to the federal courts. We are, as an initial matter, far from confident that the empirical assumption of the argument for such a rule is correct. It is not necessarily the case that state courts will take pains to provide a clear and express statement of procedural default in all cases, even after announcement of the rule. State courts presumably have a dignitary interest in seeing that their state law decisions are not ignored by a federal habeas court, but most of the price paid for federal review of state prisoner claims is paid by the State. When a federal habeas court considers the federal claims of a prisoner in state custody for independent and adequate state law reasons, it is the State that must respond. It is the State that pays the price in terms of the uncertainty and delay added to the enforcement of its criminal laws. It is the State that must retry the petitioner if the federal courts reverse his conviction. If a state court, in the course of disposing of cases on its overcrowded docket, neglects to provide a clear and express statement of procedural default, or is insufficiently motivated to do so, there is little the State can do about it. Yet it is primarily respect for the State's interests that underlies the application of the independent and adequate state ground doctrine in federal habeas.

A broad presumption would also put too great a burden on the state courts. It remains the duty of the federal courts, whether this Court on direct review, or lower federal courts in habeas, to determine the scope of the relevant state court judgment. We can establish a *per se* rule that eases the burden of inquiry on the federal courts in those cases where there are few costs to doing so, but we have no power to tell state courts how they must write their opinions. We encourage state courts to express plainly, in every decision potentially subject to federal review, the grounds upon which its judgment rests, but we will not impose on state courts the responsibility for using particular language in every case in which a state prisoner presents a federal claim—every state appeal, every denial of state collateral review—in order that federal courts might not be bothered with reviewing state law and the record in the case.

Nor do we believe that the federal courts will save much work by applying the Harris presumption in all cases. * * * In the absence of a clear indication that a state court rested its decision on federal law, a federal court's task will not be difficult.

* * *

B

The Harris presumption does not apply here. Coleman does not argue, nor could he, that it "fairly appears" that the Virginia Supreme Court's decision rested primarily on federal law or was interwoven with such law. The Virginia Supreme Court stated plainly that it was granting the Commonwealth's motion to dismiss the petition for appeal. That motion was based solely on Coleman's failure to meet the Supreme Court's time requirements. There is no mention of federal law in the Virginia Supreme Court's three-sentence dismissal order. It "fairly appears" to rest primarily on state law.

* * *

IV

In Daniels v. Allen (1953), the companion case to Brown v. Allen, we confronted a situation nearly identical to that here. Petitioners were convicted in a North Carolina trial court, and then were one day late in filing their appeal as of right in the North Carolina Supreme Court. That court rejected the appeals as procedurally barred. We held that federal habeas was also barred unless petitioners could prove that they were "detained without opportunity to appeal because of lack of counsel, incapacity, or some interference by officials."

Fay v. Noia (1963) overruled this holding. Noia failed to appeal at all in state court his state conviction, and then sought federal habeas review of his claim that his confession had been coerced. This Court held that such a procedural default in state court does not bar federal habeas review unless the petitioner has deliberately bypassed state procedures by intentionally forgoing an opportunity for state review. Fay thus created a presumption in favor of federal habeas review of claims procedurally defaulted in state court. The Court based this holding on its conclusion that a State's interest in orderly procedure are sufficiently vindicated by the prisoner's forfeiture of his state remedies. "Whatever residuum of state interest there may be under such circumstances is manifestly insufficient in the face of the federal policy * * * of affording an effective remedy for restraints contrary to the Constitution."

Our cases after Fay that have considered the effect of state procedural default on federal habeas review have taken a markedly different view of the important interests served by state procedural rules.

* * *

We concluded in Francis [v. Henderson (1976), a case challenging grand jury composition where defendant failed to raise the issue as required by state law] that a proper respect for the States required that federal courts give to the state procedural rule the same effect they give to the federal rule * * * . We held that Francis' claim was barred in federal habeas unless he could establish cause and prejudice.

Wainwright v. Sykes (1977) applied the cause and prejudice standard more broadly. Sykes did not object at trial to the introduction of certain inculpatory statements he had earlier made to the police. Under Florida law, this failure barred state courts from hearing the claim on either direct appeal or state collateral review. We recognized that this contemporaneous objection rule served strong state interests in the finality of its criminal litigation. To protect these interests, we adopted the same presumption against federal habeas review of claims defaulted in state court for failure to object at trial that Francis had adopted in the grand jury context: the cause and prejudice standard. "We believe the adoption of the Francis rule in this situation will have the salutary effect of making the state trial on the merits the 'main event,' so to speak, rather than a 'tryout on the road' for what will later be the determinative federal habeas hearing."

In so holding, Wainwright limited Fay to its facts. The cause and prejudice standard in federal habeas evinces far greater respect for state procedural rules than does the deliberate bypass standard of Fay. These incompatible rules are based on very different conceptions of comity and of the importance of finality in state criminal litigation. In Wainwright, we left open the question whether the deliberate bypass standard still applied to a situation like that in Fay, where a petitioner has surrendered entirely his right to appeal his state conviction. We rejected explicitly, however, "the sweeping language of Fay v. Noia, going far beyond the facts of the case eliciting it."

Our cases since Sykes have been unanimous in applying the cause and prejudice standard. Engle v. Isaac (1982) held that the standard applies even in cases in which the alleged constitutional error impaired the truthfinding function of the trial. Respondents had failed to object at trial to jury instructions that placed on them the burden of proving self defense. Ohio's contemporaneous objection rule barred respondents' claim on appeal that the burden should have been on the State. We held that this independent and adequate state ground barred federal habeas as well, absent a showing of cause and prejudice.

Recognizing that the writ of habeas corpus "is a bulwark against convictions that violate fundamental fairness," we also acknowledged that "the Great Writ entails significant costs." The most significant of these is the cost to finality in criminal litigation that federal collateral review of state convictions entails * * * . Moreover, "[f]ederal intrusions into state criminal trials frustrate both the States' sovereign power to punish offenders and their good-faith attempts to honor constitutional rights." These costs are particularly high, we explained, when a state prisoner, through a procedural default, prevents adjudication of his constitutional claims in state court. Because these costs do not depend on the type of claim the prisoner raised, we reaffirmed that a state procedural default of any federal claim will bar federal habeas unless the petitioner demonstrates cause and actual prejudice. We also explained in Engle that the cause and prejudice standard will be met in those cases where review of a state prisoner's claim is necessary to correct "a fundamental miscarriage of justice." ("[W]here a constitutional violation has probably resulted in the conviction of one who is actually innocent, a federal habeas court may grant the writ even in the absence of a showing of cause for the procedural default").

* * *

We now make it explicit: In all cases in which a state prisoner has defaulted his federal claims in state court pursuant to an independent and adequate state procedural rule, federal habeas review of the claims is barred unless the prisoner can demonstrate cause for the default and actual prejudice as a result of the alleged violation of federal law, or demonstrate that failure to consider the claims will result in a fundamental miscarriage of justice. Fay was based on a conception of federal/state relations that undervalued the importance of state procedural rules. The several cases after Fay that applied the cause and prejudice standard to a variety of state procedural defaults represent a different view. We now recognize the important interest in finality served by state procedural rules, and the significant harm to the States that results from the failure of federal courts to respect them.

* * *

V

A

Coleman maintains that there was cause for his default. The late filing was, he contends, the result of attorney error of sufficient magnitude to excuse the default in federal habeas.

Murray v. Carrier (1986) considered the circumstances under which attorney error constitutes cause. Carrier argued that his attorney's inadvertence in failing to raise certain claims in his state appeal constituted cause for the default sufficient to allow federal habeas review. We rejected this claim, explaining that the costs associated with an ignorant or inadvertent procedural default are no less than where the failure to raise a claim is a deliberate strategy: it deprives the state courts of the opportunity to review trial errors. When a federal habeas court hears such a claim, it undercuts the State's ability to enforce its procedural rules just as surely as when the default was deliberate. We concluded: "So long as a defendant is represented by counsel whose performance is not constitutionally ineffective under the standard established in Strickland v. Washington, we discern no inequity in requiring him to bear the risk of attorney error that results in a procedural default."

Applying the Carrier rule as stated, this case is at an end. There is no constitutional right to an attorney in state post-conviction proceedings. * * *

Coleman attempts to avoid this reasoning by arguing that Carrier does not stand for such a broad proposition. He contends that Carrier applies by its terms only in those situations where it is possible to state a claim for ineffective assistance of counsel. Where there is no constitutional right to counsel, Coleman argues, it is enough that a petitioner demonstrate that his attorney's conduct would meet the Strickland standard, even though no independent Sixth Amendment claim is possible.

* * *

Attorney ignorance or inadvertence is not "cause" because the attorney is the petitioner's agent when acting, or failing to act, in furtherance of the litigation, and the petitioner must "bear the risk of attorney error." Attorney error that constitutes ineffective assistance of counsel is cause, however. This is not because, as Coleman contends, the error is so bad that "the lawyer ceases to be an agent of the petitioner." In a case such as this, where the alleged attorney error is inadvertence in failing to file a timely notice, such a rule would be contrary to well-settled principles of agency law. Rather, as Carrier explains, "if the procedural default is the result of ineffective assistance of counsel, the Sixth Amendment itself requires that responsibility for the default be imputed to the State." In other words, it is not the gravity of the attorney's error that matters, but that it constitutes a violation of petitioner's right to counsel, so that the error must be seen as an external factor, *i.e.*, "imputed to the State."

Where a petitioner defaults a claim as a result of the denial of the right to effective assistance of counsel, the State, which is responsible for the denial as a constitutional matter, must bear the cost of any resulting default and the harm to state interests that federal habeas review entails. A different allocation of costs is appropriate in those circumstances where the State has no responsibility to ensure that the petitioner was represented by competent counsel. As between the State and the petitioner, it is the petitioner who must bear the burden of a failure to follow state procedural rules. In the absence of a constitutional violation, the petitioner bears the risk in federal habeas for all attorney errors made in the course of the representation, as Carrier says explicitly.

B

Among the claims Coleman brought in state habeas, and then again in federal habeas, is ineffective assistance of counsel during trial, sentencing, and appeal. Coleman contends that, at least as to these claims, attorney error in state habeas must constitute cause. This is because, under Virginia law at the time of Coleman's trial and direct appeal, ineffective assistance of counsel claims related to counsel's conduct during trial or appeal could be brought only in state habeas. Coleman argues that attorney error in failing to file timely in the first forum in which a federal claim can be raised is cause.

We reiterate that counsel's ineffectiveness will constitute cause only if it is an independent constitutional violation. * * * [T]here is no right to counsel in state collateral proceedings. For Coleman to prevail, therefore, there must be an exception to the rule * * * in those cases where state collateral review is the first place a prisoner can present a challenge to his conviction. We need not answer this question broadly, however, for one state court has addressed Coleman's claims: the state habeas trial court. The effectiveness of Coleman's counsel before that court is not at issue here. Coleman contends that it was the ineffectiveness of his counsel during the appeal from that determination that constitutes cause to excuse his default. We thus need to decide only whether Coleman had a constitutional right to counsel on appeal from the state habeas trial court judgment. We conclude that he did not.

* * *

Coleman has had his "one and only appeal," if that is what a state collateral proceeding may be considered; the Buchanan County Circuit Court, after a two-day evidentiary hearing, addressed Coleman's claims of trial error, including his ineffective assistance of counsel claims. What Coleman requires here is a right to counsel on appeal from that determination. Our case law will not support it.

* * *

Because Coleman had no right to counsel to pursue his appeal in state habeas, any attorney error that led to the default of Coleman's claims in state court cannot constitute cause to excuse the default in federal habeas. As Coleman does not argue in this Court that federal review of his claims is necessary to prevent a fundamental miscarriage of justice, he is barred from bringing these claims in federal habeas. Accordingly, the judgment of the Court of Appeals is

Affirmed.

JUSTICE BLACKMUN, with whom JUSTICE MARSHALL and JUSTICE STEVENS join, dissenting.

Federalism; comity; state sovereignty; preservation of state resources; certainty: the majority methodically inventories these multifarious state interests before concluding that the plain-statement rule of Michigan v. Long does not apply to a summary order. One searches the majority's opinion in vain, however, for any mention of petitioner Coleman's right to a criminal proceeding free from constitutional defect or his interest in finding a forum for his constitutional challenge to his conviction and sentence of death. Nor does the majority even allude to the "important need for uniformity in federal law," which justified this Court's adoption of the plain-statement rule in the first place. Rather, displaying obvious exasperation with the breadth of substantive federal habeas doctrine and the expansive protection afforded by the Fourteenth Amendment's guarantee of fundamental fairness in state criminal proceedings, the Court today continues its crusade to erect petty procedural barriers in the path of any state prisoner seeking review of his federal constitutional claims. Because I believe that the Court is creating a Byzantine morass of arbitrary, unnecessary, and unjustifiable impediments to the vindication of federal rights, I dissent.

I

The Court cavalierly claims that "[t]his is a case about federalism," and proceeds without explanation to assume that the purposes of federalism are advanced whenever a federal court refrains from reviewing an ambiguous state court judgment. Federalism, however, has no inherent normative value: it does not, as the majority appears to assume, blindly protect the interests of States from any incursion by the federal courts. Rather, federalism secures to citizens the liberties that derive from the diffusion of sovereign power. * * * In this context, it cannot lightly be assumed that the interests of federalism are fostered by a rule that impedes federal review of federal constitutional claims.

Moreover, the form of federalism embraced by today's majority bears little resemblance to that adopted by the Framers of the Constitution and ratified by the original States. The majority proceeds as if the sovereign interests of the States and the Federal Government were co-equal. Ours, however, is a federal republic, conceived on the principle of a supreme federal power and constituted first and foremost of citizens, not of sovereign States. The citizens expressly declared: "This Constitution, and the Laws of the United States which shall be made in Pursuance thereof * * * shall be the supreme Law of the Land." * * * The ratification of the Fourteenth Amendment by the citizens of the several States expanded federal powers even further, with a corresponding diminution of state sovereignty. Thus, "the sovereignty of the States is limited by the Constitution itself."

Federal habeas review of state court judgments, respectfully employed to safeguard federal rights, is no invasion of State sovereignty. Since 1867, Congress has acted within its constitutional authority to " 'interpose the federal courts between the States and the people, as guardians of the people's federal rights—to protect the people from unconstitutional action.' " Justice Frankfurter, in his separate opinion in Brown v. Allen, recognized this: "Insofar as [federal habeas] jurisdiction enables federal district courts to entertain claims that State Supreme Courts have denied rights guaranteed by the United States Constitution, it is not a case of a lower court sitting in judgment on a higher court. It is merely one aspect of respecting the Supremacy Clause of the Constitution whereby federal law is higher than State law." Thus, the considered exercise by federal courts—in vindication of fundamental constitutional rights—of the habeas jurisdiction conferred on them by Congress exemplifies the full expression of this Nation's federalism.

* * *

II

* * *

B

* * * In its attempt to justify a blind abdication of responsibility by the federal courts, the majority's opinion marks the nadir of the Court's recent habeas jurisprudence, where the discourse of rights is routinely replaced with the functional dialect of interests. The Court's habeas jurisprudence now routinely, and without evident reflection, subordinates fundamental constitutional rights to mere utilitarian interests. Such unreflective cost-benefit analysis is inconsistent with the very idea of rights. The Bill of Rights is not, after all, a collection of technical interests, and "surely it is an abuse to deal too casually and too lightly with rights guaranteed" therein. Brown v. Allen (opinion of Frankfurter, J.).

It is well settled that the existence of a state procedural default does not divest a federal court of jurisdiction on collateral review. Rather, the important office of the federal courts in vindicating federal rights gives way to the States' enforcement of their procedural rules to protect the States' interest in being an equal partner in safeguarding federal rights. This accommodation furthers the values underlying federalism in two ways. First, encouraging a defendant to assert his federal rights in the appropriate state forum makes it possible for transgressions to be arrested sooner and before they influence an erroneous deprivation of liberty. Second, thorough examination of a prisoner's federal claims in state court permits more effective review of those claims in federal court, honing the accuracy of the writ as an implement to eradicate unlawful detention. The majority ignores these purposes in concluding that a State need not bear the burden of making clear its intent to rely on such a rule. When it is uncertain whether a state court judgment denying relief from federal claims rests on a procedural bar, it is inconsistent with federalism principles for a federal court to exercise discretion to decline to review those federal claims.

* * *

The majority's attempt to distinguish between the interests of state courts and the interests of the States in this context is inexplicable. States do not exist independent of their officers, agents, and citizens. Rather, "[t]hrough the structure of its government, and the character of those who exercise government authority, a State defines itself as a sovereign." *See also* Ex parte Virginia ("A State acts by its legislative, its executive, or its judicial authorities. It can act in no other way"). The majority's novel conception of dichotomous interests is entirely unprecedented.

* * *

III

* * * Whether unprofessional attorney conduct in a state postconviction proceeding should bar federal habeas review of a state prisoner's conviction and sentence of death is not a question of costs to be allocated most efficiently. It is, rather, another circumstance where this Court must determine whether federal rights should yield to state interests. * * *

The majority first contends that this Court's decision in Murray v. Carrier expressly resolves this issue. Of course, that cannot be so, as the procedural default at issue in Murray occurred on direct review, not collateral attack, and this Court has no authority to resolve issues not before it. Moreover, notwithstanding the majority's protestations to the contrary, the language of Murray strongly suggests that the Court's resolution of the issue would have been the same regardless of when the procedural default occurred. The Court in Murray explained: "A State's procedural rules serve vital purposes at trial, on appeal, and *on state collateral attack* " (emphasis added). Rejecting Carrier's argument that, with respect to the standard for cause, procedural defaults on appeal should be treated differently from those that occur during the trial, the Court stated that "the standard for cause should not vary depending on the timing of a procedural default or on the strength of an uncertain and difficult assessment of the relative magnitude of the benefits attributable to the state procedural rules that attach at *each successive stage of the judicial process*" (emphasis added).

The rule foreshadowed by this language, which the majority today evades, most faithfully adheres to a principled view of the role of federal habeas jurisdiction. As noted above, federal courts forgo the exercise of their habeas jurisprudence over claims that are procedurally barred out of respect for the state interests served by those rules. Recognition of state procedural forfeitures discourages petitioners from attempting to avoid state proceedings, and accommodates the State's interest in finality. No rule, however, can deter gross incompetence. To permit a procedural default caused by attorney error egregious enough to constitute ineffective assistance of counsel to preclude federal habeas review of a state prisoner's federal claims in no way serves the State's interest in preserving the integrity of its rules and proceedings. The interest in finality, standing alone, cannot provide a sufficient reason for a federal habeas court to compromise its protection of constitutional rights.

The majority's conclusion that Coleman's allegations of ineffective assistance of counsel, if true, would not excuse a procedural default that occurred in the state post-conviction proceeding is particularly disturbing because, at the time of Coleman's appeal, state law precluded defendants from raising certain claims on direct appeal. As the majority acknowledges, under state law as it existed at the time of Coleman's trial and appeal, Coleman could raise his ineffective assistance of counsel claim with respect to counsel's conduct during trial and appeal only in state habeas.

* * *

* * * "[F]undamental fairness is the central concern of the writ of habeas corpus." It is the quintessence of inequity that the Court today abandons that safeguard while continuing to embrace the cause and prejudice standard.

I dissent.

Notes and Questions

1. a) The majority notes that the adequate-and-independent-state-ground rule is a jurisdictional limitation of direct review and links that assertion to the inhibition against advisory opinions. Although the Court's disinclination to render advisory opinions is two centuries old, why is it a jurisdictional bar? From what constitutional provision does it derive?

b) The Court clearly feels that the rule is not jurisdictional in cases of collateral review. Why not? Why should the presence of a state ground for decision either always or never preclude review? If there is a distinction, does it shed any light on whether the rule is *always* jurisdictional in the context of direct review?

c) The Court reaffirmed the non-jurisdictional nature of the state-procedural-default rule in the habeas context in *Trest v. Cain*, 522 U.S. 87 (1997), holding that "a procedural default, that is, a critical failure to comply with state procedural law, is not a jurisdictional matter." Justice Breyer's opinion for a unanimous Court viewed state procedural default as a defense that the state must preserve. The Court also recognized that there is uncertainty about whether a habeas court may raise the issue ***sua sponte***, but declined to reach that question because the Fifth Circuit had thought itself compelled to raise the issue, the petition for certiorari had not embraced that question, and the factual record was inadequate to permit the court to adjudicate that issue.

(d) In *Beard v. Kindler*, 558 U.S. 53 (2009), the Justices ruled that a state court's refusal to entertain a habeas claim because the prisoner had escaped served as an adequate and independent ground barring federal habeas review despite the discretionary nature of the determination.

2. a) *Coleman* reaffirms the decision in Harris v. Reed to apply the standards for interpreting ambiguous state court decisions developed in the context of direct Supreme Court review in Michigan v. Long and Caldwell v. Mississippi to habeas corpus cases. Thus, both the Supreme Court and district courts faced with an ambiguous state court decision will presume there is no independent and adequate state ground barring federal review if the state court decision "fairly appears to rest primarily on federal law, or to be interwoven with the federal law" unless the adequacy and independence of any possible state law ground is clear from the face of the state court opinion. While there clearly is logic in the Court's determination when "[f]aced with a common problem [to] adopt a common solution," there also is irony. The Michigan v. Long standard expanded the Supreme Court's jurisdiction. Presuming the state court decision did not rest upon an adequate and independent state ground enabled the Court in Long to review and reverse a state court ruling that granted the defendant relief on the grounds his Fourth Amendment rights were violated. The Michigan v. Long standard, however, also expands the scope of habeas corpus, making it easier for district courts to review state court decisions denying petitioners' federal constitutional claims. This expansion runs counter to the Court's apparent desire to limit the scope of habeas corpus.

b) The Court of Appeals and the Supreme Court both concluded the Virginia Supreme Court decision rested on an adequate and independent state ground, so Coleman could not rely on Long. Do you agree?

c) Justice Blackmun, dissenting, accuses the majority of embracing a federalism that "blindly protect[s] the interests of the States from any incursion by the federal courts." He contends federal habeas review, "respectfully employed to safeguard federal rights, is no invasion of State sovereignty." Who is right?

3. *Wainwright v. Sykes*, 433 U.S. 72 (1977), upon which *Coleman* so heavily relies, deserves extended consideration. Sykes challenged a conviction based in part upon his own statement. Counsel had not objected to the introduction of the statement, violating the state's contemporaneous objection rule. Sykes argued in the federal proceeding that he had not understood his Miranda rights and persuaded the district court to order a hearing on the question of the voluntariness of his statement. The Supreme Court denied habeas relief, adopting the cause-and-prejudice standard echoed in *Coleman*.

a) In rejecting the "deliberate bypass" standard in favor of the "cause and prejudice" standard, Sykes noted (and *Coleman* echoes) that "proper respect" for the states and their adjudicative processes compels the latter standard. From whence do either the cause-and-prejudice standard or the deliberate-bypass standard derive? Are they constitutionally compelled or are they prudential limitations on federal judicial power?

b) The Sykes Court adopted the cause-and-prejudice standard because it worried that a more lenient rule encouraged "sandbagging."

> We think that the [deliberate bypass] rule of Fay v. Noia, broadly stated, may encourage "sandbagging" on the part of defense lawyers, who may take their chances on a verdict of not guilty in a state trial court with the intent to raise their constitutional claims in a federal habeas court if their initial gamble does not pay off. The refusal of federal habeas courts to honor contemporaneous-objection rules may also make state courts themselves less stringent in their enforcement. Under the rule of Fay v. Noia, state appellate courts know that a federal constitutional issue raised for the first time in the proceeding before them may well be decided in any event by a federal habeas tribunal. Thus, their choice is between addressing the issue notwithstanding the petitioner's failure to timely object, or else face the prospect that the federal habeas court will decide the question without the benefit of their views.

Justice Brennan's dissent insisted that sandbagging was unlikely because it would violate even the deliberate-bypass standard. He argued that the majority's new rule was inconsistent with proper respect for constitutional rights and established law regarding their abandonment. Apart from questions of the proper standard for surrender of important constitutional rights, discussed below, consider whether sandbagging is practical. Assuming defense counsel could conceal deliberate failure to raise an issue, what does it profit the defense in a criminal case to hold it back?

c) Sykes and *Coleman* also raise questions about the ease or difficulty of losing constitutional rights. In Sykes, the petitioner sought to assert a Fifth Amendment right. In *Coleman*, petitioner urged several constitutional defects in the state proceedings[21] that the Court barred because Coleman's counsel had filed a state notice of appeal three days late. In both cases, the Court found that the asserted constitutional rights had been waived. In Sykes, Justice Brennan took sharp issue with the majority, arguing that *Johnson v. Zerbst*, 304 U.S. 458 (1938), which required a knowing and deliberate waiver by the defendant, should continue to govern waiver of constitutional rights. The majority, shifting away from that standard, noted:

> We leave open for resolution in future decisions the precise definition of the "cause"-and-"prejudice" standard, and note here only that it is narrower than the standard set forth in dicta in Fay v. Noia, which would make federal habeas review generally available to state convicts absent a knowing and deliberate waiver of the federal constitutional contention.

Thus, the majority clearly repudiated Johnson v. Zerbst in this context.

---

21 Coleman argued, *inter alia*, the following: pre-judgment of his case one juror, ineffective assistance of counsel, exclusion, in violation of Witherspoon v. Illinois, 391 U.S. 510 (1968), of jurors opposed to the death penalty, and the prosecution's failure to disclose exculpatory evidence.

In Sykes, the defendant's failure to object contemporaneously to introduction of his statement waived his right to do so. In *Edelman v. Jordan*, 415 U.S. 651 (1974), the Court ruled on whether Illinois's participation in a federal program waived the state's Eleventh Amendment immunity. Refusing to find waiver, the majority said:

> Constructive consent is not a doctrine commonly associated with the surrender of constitutional rights, and we see no place for it here. In deciding whether a State has waived its constitutional protection under the Eleventh Amendment, we will find waiver only where stated "by the most express language or by such overwhelming implications from the text as [will] leave no room for any other reasonable construction."[a]

Plainly, Sykes/*Coleman* and Edelman are flatly inconsistent as to the conduct necessary to waive a constitutional right. Are the different standards for state and individual waiver justifiable?

4. What exactly constitutes "cause" and "prejudice"? *Maples v. Thomas*, 132 S.Ct. 912 (2012), defines "cause" for overcoming a procedural default as "something *external* to the petitioner, something that cannot fairly be attributed to him [and has] impeded his efforts to comply with the State's procedural rule" (Court's brackets deleted). In most cases where the petitioner tries to overcome a procedural default, the claimed "cause" is ineffective assistance of counsel, and governed generally by *Strickland v. Washington* (1984). Normally, the deficiencies of state post-conviction counsel cannot constitute "ineffective assistance," and therefore cannot constitute cause to excuse a procedural default, but in *Maples*, the big firm lawyers who abandoned their death-row client without telling him or the firm's management actually brought about the default, so their conduct did constitute "cause." (As a general rule, there is no right to counsel in post-conviction proceedings, so there normally cannot be ineffective assistance rendered in such proceedings.)

Following *Strickland*, the Court has recently reaffirmed the definition of "prejudice" as meaning that there is a "reasonable probability" that there would have been a different result if not for the constitutional violation. *See Lafler v. Cooper*, 132 S.Ct. 1376 (2012). Note that the "result" at issue depends on the case—it could be a jury verdict of guilty; it could be a death sentence rather than life, or, as in *Lafler*, it could be that the petitioner would have taken a more favorable plea offer than the one he ultimately took if not for his lawyer's failure to communicate it to him.

5. The Court notes that a petitioner must exhaust available state remedies as a prerequisite to federal habeas review. How does this relate to the rule that a state procedural default constitutes an adequate and independent state ground barring

---

a [AUTHORS' NOTE] The Court did note that the Eleventh Amendment concerns an area in which sovereignties collide, paying homage to the special position of the Eleventh Amendment. Nonetheless, the Court's thoughts on waiver were expressed in terms far broader than necessary merely to defer to the Eleventh Amendment.

habeas review? Note that *all* procedurally defaulted claims are by definition exhausted, because there is no state court currently available to hear the merits of them. On the other hand, not all unexhausted claims are necesarily defaulted—for example, newly-discovered evidence claims. State post-conviction courts are always available to hear claims of new exculpatory evidence, but they are not exhausted until brought to state court.

6. *Coleman* raises questions on many levels, some concerning the "federalism" on which Justice O'Connor focuses. Lurking in the background, however, is a more general issue about federal habeas corpus. Perhaps only by considering what the institution of federal habeas is supposed to do can one sensibly approach federalism and other problems. Justice Blackmun's dissent suggests as much. Is he correct? Is there a "chicken and egg" problem with respect to which issue drives the inquiry?

CLICK FOR UPDATE
UPDATES FOUND ON PAGES 1191-1195

7. The Problem of Successive Petitions

Sanders v. United States (1963) set permissive standards for second or successive habeas petitions. The court could dismiss such petitions without reaching the merits only if an earlier petition presenting the same claim had been denied on the merits *and* the ends of justice would not be served by reaching the merits of the subsequent petition. The court could deny subsequent applications based on new grounds or on grounds not previously determined on the merits only if the petitioner was guilty of abuse of the writ. If the court found that the failure to raise the present claim in a previous application was a deliberate by-pass within the meaning of *Fay v. Noia* (1963), that was an abuse. Thus, res judicata, which precludes not only claims that were litigated but also claims that might have been litigated in an earlier lawsuit, had only limited application in habeas cases. In 1966, Congress essentially codified this standard in an amendment to § 2244(b).

Coleman v. Thompson (1991), presented at page 1163, formally interred *Fay v. Noia*. *McCleskey v. Zant*, 499 U.S. 467 (1991) did the same to *Sanders* by applying the cause-and-prejudice standard to successive petitions:

> We conclude from the unity of structure and purpose in the jurisprudence of state procedural defaults and abuse of the writ that the standard for excusing a failure to raise a claim at the appropriate time should be the same in both contexts. We have held that a procedural default will be excused upon a showing of cause and prejudice. We now hold that the same standard applies to determine if there has been an abuse of the writ through inexcusable neglect.
>
> In procedural default cases, the cause standard requires the petitioner to show that "some objective factor external to the defense impeded counsel's efforts" to raise the claim in state court. Objective factors that constitute cause include " 'interference by officials' " that makes compliance with the state's procedural rule impracticable, and "a showing that the factual or legal basis for a claim was not reasonably available to counsel." In addition, constitutionally "ineffective as-

sistance of counsel * * * is cause." Attorney error short of ineffective assistance of counsel, however, does not constitute cause and will not excuse a procedural default. Once the petitioner has established cause, he must show " 'actual prejudice' resulting from the errors of which he complains."

Federal courts retain the authority to issue the writ of habeas corpus in a further, narrow class of cases despite a petitioner's failure to show cause for a procedural default. These are extraordinary instances when a constitutional violation probably has caused the conviction of one innocent of the crime. We have described this class of cases as implicating a fundamental miscarriage of justice.

The cause and prejudice analysis we have adopted for cases of procedural default applies to an abuse of the writ inquiry in the following manner. When a prisoner files a second or subsequent application, the government bears the burden of pleading abuse of the writ. The government satisfies this burden if, with clarity and particularity, it notes petitioner's prior writ history, identifies the claims that appear for the first time, and alleges that petitioner has abused the writ. The burden to disprove abuse then becomes petitioner's. To excuse his failure to raise the claim earlier, he must show cause for failing to raise it and prejudice therefrom as those concepts have been defined in our procedural default decisions. The petitioner's opportunity to meet the burden of cause and prejudice will not include an evidentiary hearing if the district court determines as a matter of law that petitioner cannot satisfy the standard. If petitioner cannot show cause, the failure to raise the claim in an earlier petition may nonetheless be excused if he or she can show that a fundamental miscarriage of justice would result from a failure to entertain the claim. Application of the cause and prejudice standard in the abuse of the writ context does not mitigate the force of Teague v. Lane, which prohibits, with certain exceptions, the retroactive application of new law to claims raised in federal habeas. Nor does it imply that there is a constitutional right to counsel in federal habeas corpus.

In 1996, AEDPA amended the language of § 2244 that governed successive petitions and abuse of the writ. Whether one considers McClesky still to be good law depends on whether one reads the new language to codify McClesky or to impose even greater restrictions on successive petitions. The applicable provisions of § 2244 read as follows:

(b) (1) A claim presented in a second or successive habeas corpus application under section 2254 that was presented in a prior application shall be dismissed.

(2) A claim presented in a second or successive habeas corpus application under section 2254 that was not presented in a prior application shall be dismissed unless—

(A) the applicant shows that the claim relies on a new rule of constitutional law, made retroactive to cases on collateral review by the Supreme Court, that was previously unavailable; or

(B) (i) the factual predicate for the claim could not have been discovered previously through the exercise of due diligence; and

> (ii) the facts underlying the claim, if proven and viewed in light of the evidence as a whole, would be sufficient to establish by clear and convincing evidence that, but for constitutional error, no reasonable factfinder would have found the applicant guilt of the underlying offense.

Notice that the statute does not use the language "cause and prejudice." Review the guidelines for cause and prejudice described in note 4 following *Coleman*. What similarities do you see between the guidelines and the language of the statute? What differences? Do you think the statute imposes any new restrictions on successive petitions? In an extended discussion, *Daniels v. United States*, 254 F.3d 1180, 1195-98 (10th Cir. 2001), concluded that AEDPA replaces the old cause-and-prejudice and *Teague* standards but then interprets the new language to mean almost the same thing as the old standards. Section 2244(b)(3) contains one requirement that is indisputably new. Before filing a second or successive petition permitted under (b)(2), the applicant must receive permission from the appropriate court of appeals.

As difficult as the questions in the preceding paragraph are to answer, § 2244(b) poses even more difficult questions when petitioners claim they are actually innocent. In a series of cases decided before AEDPA where petitioners claimed they could make compelling showings of innocence, the Court relied upon its general equitable powers to establish standards for entertaining a first, second or successive habeas petition despite a state procedural default or other defect that would normally preclude federal review. Moreover, if the petitioner was able to present strong evidence of innocence in a second or successive federal petition, the Court did not pay much attention to whether the petition repeated a claim raised in an earlier federal petition or presented a claim that might have been but was not raised in the earlier petition. The cases were not consistent, however, in specifying the burden of proof a petitioner must satisfy to obtain relief.

The Court addressed this inconsistency in *Schlup v. Delo*, 513 U.S. 298 (1995). *Schlup* held that a person whose petition would otherwise be barred as a successive petition or for some procedural default could have the petition heard because of "actual innocence" by showing that "a constitutional violation has probably resulted in the conviction of one who is actually innocent." The Court made clear it was adopting a "more likely than not" or preponderance standard rather than the "clear and convincing evidence" standard the dissenters proposed.

Consider again the language of § 2244 (b). Note that (b)(1) and (b)(2) distinguish between claims presented in a second or successive petition that were presented in a prior application and claims that were not. Under (b)(1), claims that were previously presented "shall be dismissed," period. Under (b)(2), claims that were not presented can be heard if the conditions of (b)(2)(A) or (B) can be satisfied.

In *Magwood v. Patterson*, 130 S.Ct. 2788 (2010), an oddly split Court announced one way around § 2244(b)'s apparent prohibition on second or successive petitions. Following his state conviction and death sentence for murder, Magwood obtained federal habeas relief from the sentence because the state court had not considered mitigating circumstances. The federal habeas court upheld the conviction but granted the writ conditionally because of the sentencing error. The state court held a new sentencing hearing, finding Magwood's age, mental state and lack of criminal history to be mitigating factors. It nonetheless reimposed the death penalty. Magwood appealed within the state system, arguing that the statute failed to give him fair warning that his offense was punishable by death[22] and that his attorney at the resentencing was constitutionally ineffective. The state argued that Magwood could have raised the fair-warning claim in the federal challenge to his first sentence and that his failure to do so made that part of his challenge to the new sentence a "second or successive" petition. Justice Thomas, writing for the Court (with Justices Stevens, Scalia, Breyer and Sotomayor), held that the new sentencing gave rise to an entirely new judgment within the meaning of § 2244(a). The majority thus restricted the "second or successive" language of § 2244(b) to petitions directed at the same judgment.

The majority rejected the state's (and the dissent's) argument that § 2244(b) contemplates only a single opportunity to raise a *claim*, finding instead that the phrase "second or successive" modified "application," not "claim." The dissent argued that § 2244(b)(2)'s reference to claims rather than applications mandated rejection of Magwood's application. Thus, what separated the Justices was whether the limiting language referred to claims, applications or judgments. Perhaps the majority had the better of the argument here, on a strictly (and, the dissent argued, unrealistically) textual approach, given the statute's wording: "a claim presented in a second or successive habeas corpus application under section 2254 that was not presented in a prior application shall be dismissed." Magwood could not have raised the fair-warning challenge to the second judgment in his habeas application in opposition to the first. The dissent argued that the Court's exception was actually atextual and that the Court should have treated the case under its abuse-of-the-writ jurisprudence that antedated AEDPA.

State prisoners sometimes seek to avoid the severe restrictions on successive habeas petitions by raising their claims in a plenary civil action under 42 U.S.C. § 1983. Although the federal courts generally disallow this gambit, it has been successful in a few instances. *Hill v. McDonough*, 547 U.S. 573 (2006), allowed a Florida death row inmate to bring a § 1983 action challenging the lethal injection procedure the state was likely to use on him. Hill claimed the procedure would cause him severe pain, thus violating the Eighth Amendment's prohibition of cruel and unusual punishments. Because Hill did not challenge the lethal injection sentence as a general matter

22 Magwood argued that the state penal statute then in effect gave insufficient warning that the death sentence was possible even in the absence of any aggravating circumstance.

and appeared to leave the state free to use an alternative lethal injection procedure, the lawsuit would not actually bar implementation of the sentence and thus could proceed.

The proper line of demarcation between habeas corpus and § 1983 claims has concerned the Court for some time. Many of the procedural restrictions on habeas corpus do not exist in § 1983 cases, thus giving state prisoners an incentive to raise their claims under that statute. The Supreme Court first considered the issue in *Preiser v. Rodriguez*, 411 U.S. 475 (1973). In 1973, the main impediment to access to a federal forum in habeas cases was the requirement that a prisoner exhaust available state remedies before proceeding to federal court. Because there is no exhaustion requirement in § 1983 actions,[23] they provided an attractive alternative to habeas corpus. *Preiser* set the dividing line as follows: "[W]hen a state prisoner is challenging the very fact or duration of his physical imprisonment, and the relief he seeks is a determination that he is entitled to immediate release or a speedier release * * * his sole federal remedy is a writ of habeas corpus." Challenges to the *conditions* of confinement, by contrast, were appropriate for § 1983 actions.

The *Preiser* standard worked reasonably well in the main, but applying it was sometimes uncertain. The lethal injection cases provide a dramatic example. *Nelson v. Campbell*, 541 U.S. 637 (1994), presaged *Hill v. McDonough*. Three days before he was to die by lethal injection, Nelson filed a § 1983 action in federal court. Nelson had severely compromised peripheral veins from drug abuse, and he challenged the so-called "cut-down" procedure the warden planned to use to gain access to a vein as cruel and unusual punishment and deliberate indifference to his serious medical needs in violation of the Eighth Amendment. The district court and court of appeals held Nelson's action the "functional equivalent" of a habeas corpus proceeding and denied relief because Nelson had filed a previous federal habeas petition and could not surmount the restrictions on successive petitions.

In her opinion for a unanimous Court, Justice O'Connor explained the difficulty in applying the *Preiser* standard to Nelson's claims. She noted that the labels "conditions of confinement" and "fact or duration" of confinement were not "particularly apt." Nor did a suit seeking to enjoin a particular means of execution directly call into question the "fact" or "validity" of the sentence. On the other hand, when a state has directed that executions be by lethal injection, the Court may rule that a suit seeking to enjoin lethal injections permanently is a challenge to the fact of the sentence itself. In addition, while it "makes little sense" to talk about the "duration" of a death sentence, allowing a § 1983 action clearly delays imposition of the sentence. Ultimately, the Court held Nelson's lawsuit could proceed, reasoning that Nelson was not actually

23 *See* Patsy v. Board of Regents, 457 U.S. 496 (1982) (*supra* at 799; Monroe v. Pape, 365 U.S. 167 (1961), *supra* at 564.

challenging the sentence itself. Because the "cut-down" procedure was not necessary to the lethal injection, the sentence could be implemented by other means.

The analysis in *Hill v. McDonough* proceeded along similar lines. Although Hill challenged the chemical injection sequence rather than a surgical procedure prior to the injections, he did not actually ask to stop his execution or to change the sentence. Hill, like Nelson, sought only to enjoin state officials from executing him in the manner they presently intended.

CLICK FOR UPDATE
UPDATES FOUND ON PAGES 1191-1195

8. Statute of Limitations

AEDPA imposes a one-year limitation period for filing a federal habeas petition, measured generally (with certain limited exceptions) from the time direct state review is final. The statute tolls the limitation for the time during which a properly filed application for state collateral review is pending. The statutory provisions read as follows:

§ 2244. Finality of Determination

* * * *

(d)(1) A 1-year period of limitation shall apply to an application for a writ of habeas corpus by a person in custody pursuant to the judgment of a State court. The limitation period shall run from the latest of—

(A) the date on which the judgment became final by the conclusion of direct review or the expiration of the time for seeking such review;

(B) the date on which the impediment to filing an application created by State action in violation of the Constitution or laws of the United States if removed, if the applicant was prevented from filing by such State action;

(C) the date on which the constitutional right asserted was initially recognized by the Supreme Court, if the right has been newly recognized by the Supreme Court and made retroactively applicable to cases on collateral review; or

(D) the date on which the factual predicate of the claim or claims presented could have been discovered through the exercise of due diligence.

(2) The time during which a properly filed application for State post-conviction or other collateral review with respect to the pertinent judgment or claim is pending shall not be counted toward any period of limitation under this subsection.

Several issues as to the proper interpretation of these provisions reached the Supreme Court in recent terms. *Day v. McDonough*, 547 U.S. 198 (2006), held that district courts are permitted, but not obliged, to consider the timeliness of a state prisoner's habeas petition **sua sponte**. In answering Day's petition, the state failed to raise § 2244(d)'s one-year limitation as a defense. The state mistakenly overlooked controlling Eleventh Circuit precedent, which, if applied, would require dismissal of the petition as untimely. A federal Magistrate Judge noticed the state's computation error and recommended the petition be dismissed. The district court adopted the recommendation, and the Eleventh Circuit affirmed.

Day argued that under the applicable habeas corpus rules, the Federal Rules of Civil Procedure should govern. Under Federal Rules 8(c) and 12(b), a defendant waives a statute of limitations defense that is not raised in its answer. The Court declined to apply these rules in this situation, applying a more flexible, discretionary approach. Where the state had not affirmatively decided to waive the defense and failure to raise it resulted from a mathematical error, the Court thought dismissal was appropriate. The Court noted that instead of acting on its own motion, the Magistrate Judge might have invited the state to amend it's answer when the Judge noticed the computation error. Because this procedure would have resulted in dismissal of the petition, it seemed unreasonable to require a different result simply because the Magistrate Judge acted *sua sponte*.

Jimenez v. Quarterman, 555 U.S. 113 (2009), held that a state court's decision during collateral review to grant the defendant the right to file a out-of-time direct appeal postponed the date on which a defendant's state conviction becomes final under § 2241(d)(1)(A). A Texas court convicted Jimenez of burglary. His appellate attorney filed a motion to be relieved of the representation, pursuant to *Anders v. California*, 386 U.S. 738 (1967), stating that he was unable to find any non-frivolous issues on which to base an appeal. He left a copy of the motion papers and a letter to Jimenez at the county jail, advising him that he was entitled to file a *pro se* brief. Jimenez, however, had been transferred to a state facility and did not receive the papers. He also did not receive the later appellate court order dismissing his appeal. Subsequently, Jimenez filed a state collateral proceeding claiming he was denied a meaningful appeal because he did not have a chance to file a *pro se* appellate brief. The state court agreed and allowed Jimenez to file an out-of-time direct appeal. Many years passed by the time Jimenez finished the appeal and another state collateral proceeding. When he filed a federal habeas petition, the district court held that § 2244(d)(1)'s one-year limitation period ran from one month following dismissal of Jimenez's original direct appeal because his right to seek discretionary review expired at that time. The Court of Appeals affirmed. The Supreme Court reversed, holding that Jimenez's state conviction became final for purposes of § 2241(d)(1)(A) when his actual appeal concluded.

28 U.S.C. 2244(d)(2) tolls the one-year limitation period during the time when state collateral challenges are pending. In *Carey v. Saffold*, 536 U.S. 214 (2002), the Court held that the proceeding is "pending" for § 2244(d)(2) purposes during the period from a lower state court's final judgment in a collateral proceeding to the filing of a notice of appeal to a higher court. Most states require an appellant to file a notice of appeal within a few days of final judgment, so tolling the limitation period does not undermine with the reasons for having one. California follows a different procedure. It permits the petitioner to file new original petitions in successively higher

state courts as long as they come within a "reasonable time." In Carey, petitioner promptly filed after an adverse decision in the California Superior Court, but when the California Court of Appeal ruled against him, he allowed 4½ months to elapse before seeking relief from the California Supreme Court, which denied Saffold's petition "on the merits and for lack of diligence." One week after that decision, Saffold sought federal habeas relief.

When the case reached Washington, the Court vacated the judgment for the petitioner and directed the Ninth Circuit to determine whether the California Supreme Court thought the appeal was timely and denied it on the merits or thought the appeal was untimely and denied it for that reason. The United States Supreme Court stated that the words "lack of diligence" did not necessarily mean Saffold was untimely seeking relief from the California Supreme Court, because the lack of diligence might have referred to some earlier delay not relevant to whether Saffold timely sought relief from the California Supreme Court. The five-member majority also observed that the words "on the merits" might not have necessarily meant the application was timely, because courts sometimes deny a case on the merits even though it is untimely. Unfortunately, the Court left it unclear how the Ninth Circuit should proceed if it could not rely on any of the words the California Supreme Court used, although they certifying the question of timeliness to the California Supreme Court for clarification. This rather bizarre approach caused Justice Kennedy's dissent to heap some perhaps well deserved scorn on the majority's method of analysis.

Rhines v. Weber, 544 U.S. 269 (2005), addressed the interplay between the rules governing mixed petitions and the one-year statute of limitations in 28 U.S.C. § 2244(d). If a state prisoner files a petition within the limitation period, and the district court determines it to be a mixed petition after the one-year period has run, may the petitioner exercise the *Rose v. Lundy* option of returning to state court to present the unexhausted claims, later to present all of his claims to the federal court, or does § 2244(d) bar a return to federal court? In *Rhines*, the district court granted the petitioner's motion to hold his habeas petition in abeyance (rather than dismiss it) while he returned to state court to present his unexhausted claims, but the Court of Appeals held the district had no authority to do this except in "truly exceptional" cases.

The Supreme Court held that a stay in these circumstances may be appropriate, although it imposed several conditions. The Court thought a stay may be appropriate because a contrary rule would put petitioners in an unfair position. If a petitioner files a timely mixed petition, and the court dismisses it under Rose, the petitioner is likely to forfeit federal review of any of his claims because of the one-year limitation period. Thus, the petitioner's only course would be to drop his unexhausted claims, forfeiting any chance for federal court review of those claims. The Court cautioned against too frequent use of stay and abeyance, which it thought would undermine AEDPA's twin goals of reducing delays in the execution of sentences and streamlining habeas proceedings. Thus, a stay should be granted only if 1) there was "good cause" for the failure to exhaust all claims; 2) the unexhausted claims are not plainly meritless; 3) the petitioner complies with any time limits set by the district court for pursuing state review; and 4) the petitioner does not engage in "abusive litigation tactics or intentional delay."

When a properly-filed petition for state post-conviction relief tolls the statute of limitations, it is referred to as "statutory tolling." In recent years, the Court has begun to explore tolling on the basis of fairness— referred to as "equitable tolling." In *Holland v. Florida*, 130 S.Ct. 2549 (2010), the Court explicitly held that equitable tolling of § 2244(d)(1)'s one-year limitation period is possible, agreeing with the eleven circuits (including the Eleventh) that had previously considered the question. Following his conviction and unsuccessful attempt to get state post-conviction relief, Holland had repeatedly directed counsel to seek federal habeas relief. Apparently, counsel did not do the research necessary to inform himself of the filing deadline, although Holland's directions to counsel even identified the applicable legal rules. Counsel also failed to respond to Holland's requests for information so Holland could monitor the case. Finally, counsel failed to communicate with Holland for several years. On several occasions, Holland had attempted to get the state courts and the state bar to remove the attorney from the case. The Eleventh Circuit ruled that the facts could not constitute "extraordinary circumstances" justifying an equitable toll unless Holland could show counsel's dishonesty, bad faith, divided loyalty, mental impairment or some similar circumstance.

The Supreme Court reversed. The majority noted the Court's prior ruling that the limitation period was not jurisdictional, and Justice Breyer's opinion stated a rebuttable presumption (not satisfied here) in favor of equitable tolling. The Court found the Eleventh Circuit's restrictions unreasonably rigid and incongruent with the spirit of equity, refusing to read *Coleman v. Thompson* (*supra* at 1163) as demanding a *per se* approach. Said the Court,

> In short, no pre-existing rule of law or precedent demands a rule like the one set forth by the Eleventh Circuit in this case. That rule is difficult to reconcile with more general equitable principles in that it fails to recognize that, at least sometimes, professional misconduct that fails to meet the Eleventh Circuit's standard could nonetheless amount to egregious behavior and create an extraordinary circumstance that warrants equitable tolling. And, given the long history of judicial application of equitable tolling, courts can easily find precedents that can guide their judgments. Several lower courts have specifically held that unprofessional attorney conduct may, in certain circumstances, prove "egregious" and can be "extraordinary" even though the conduct in question may not satisfy the Eleventh Circuit's rule.

Because neither lower court had considered equitable tolling under the proper standard, the Court remanded for further proceedings.

CLICK FOR UPDATE
UPDATES FOUND ON PAGES 1191-1195

Supplementary Material

Chapter 3

p. 313, Note 8

Update

It is still true that the plaintiff is the master of the complaint, but only of his own. In *Standard Fire Ins. Co. v. Knowles*, 133 S.Ct. 1345 (2013), the plaintiff tried to bring a class action and to evade the Class Action Fairness Act of 2005 (CAFA) (*see* 28 U.S.C. § 1332(d)). He filed in state court and submitted a stipulation that the class would not seek damages in excess of $5,000,000, CAFA's floor amount. Standard Fire Insurance removed the case, but the district court, accepting Knowles's stipulation, granted his motion to remand. When the case arrived in the Supreme Court, a unanimous Court overturned the district court's decision (the court of appeals had declined review) and remanded to the district court.

The district court had found that in the absence of the stipulation, the amount in controversy "would have fallen just above the $5 million threshold." The Supreme Court declined to recognize the stipulation as a limiting factor. Justice Breyer's opinion pointed out that stipulations must be binding to be effective and that, prior to class certification, Knowles could bind only himself. In addition, the Court noted that the district court might find that Knowles was an inadequate class representative because of "the artificial cap he purports to impose on the class' recovery." In part, the Court seemed concerned that future enterprising plaintiffs (or their lawyers) would simply subdivide large class actions into separate actions not meeting CAFA's jurisdictional-amount requirement, thus evading Congress's evident purpose in enacting CAFA.

Chapter 7

p. 719, New Note 7.1

Update

The Court continues to hew closely to the congruent-and-proportional standard. In Coleman v. Court of Appeals of Maryland, 132 S.Ct. 1323 (2012), the Justices considered the self-care leave provisions of FMLA and rejected on Eleventh Amendment grounds the plaintiff's attempt to sue the state. Having found in *Hibbs* that the family-care provision of FMLA that allowed actions against states was congruent and proportional, the Court declined to extend that ruling to the self-care provisions, reasoning that, as in *Garrett*, Congress had not assembled a sufficient factual record with respect to that portion of FMLA.

In that respect, *Coleman* adds nothing doctrinal to *Garrett*. The case is noteworthy because there was no majority opinion. Justice Thomas joined the result, but argued in a one-paragraph dissent that the Court had blundered in deciding *Hibbs*. Justice Scalia wrote a two-paragraph dissent, arguing first that the Court's outcomes using "the 'congruence and proportionality' test make no sense." Second, he argued that the Court should read Section 5 of the Fourteenth Amendment to apply only to "conduct that *itself* violates the Fourteenth Amendment"—that is, declining to recognize prophylactic legislation as appropriate under Section 5 "outside of the context of racial discrimination (which is different for *stare decisis* reasons) * * * ."

Justice Ginsburg, joined for the most part by Justices Breyer, Sotomayor and Kagan, thought the statute proper and called for revisiting the assertion in Geduldig v. Aiello, 417 U.S. 484, 496 n.20 (1974), that discrimination on the basis of pregnancy is not sex discrimination.

Chapter 11

p. 1117, Note 1(c)

Update

There is no bright-line test for whether a decision announces a new rule within the meaning of *Teague*. Instead, the novelty of a decision can be plotted along a continuum, with incremental expansions of precedent at one end and categorical expansions at the other.

In Chaidez v. United States, 133 S.Ct. 1103 (2013), the Supreme Court considered whether Padilla v. Kentucky, 559 U.S. 356 (2010), announced a new rule. *Padilla* held that a defense lawyer renders ineffective assistance of counsel when he fails to advise a defendant of the risk of deportation arising from a guilty plea. Justice Kagan's opinion for the Court stated that a decision creates no new rule when it merely applies a pre-existing rule to a new fact situation. She contrasted *Padilla* with several other Supreme Court decisions applying *Strickland v. Washington,* 466 U.S. 668 (1984) to disparate fact patterns. Unlike those cases, *Padilla* required the Court to answer a logically prior question: "Was advice about deportation 'categorically removed' from the scope of the Sixth Amendment right to counsel because it involved only a 'collateral consequence' of a conviction, rather than a component of the criminal sentence?" By answering this question in the negative, *Padilla* opened a whole new category to which *Strickland* applied.

p. 1159, Note 2

Update

Suppose the last state court opinion addressed some, but not all, of petitioner's federal claims. Does Harrington v. Richter apply? In Johnson v. Williams, 133 S.Ct. 1088 (2013), the Supreme Court unanimously said yes. The Court stated that the reasoning of *Richter* dictated the result in *Johnson.* "Although *Richter* itself concerned a state-court order that did not address *any* of the defendant's claims, we see no reason why the *Richter* presumption should not also apply when a state-court opinion addresses some but not all of a defendant's claims," stated Justice Alito's opinion for the Court. "[I]t is not the uniform practice of busy state courts to discuss separately every single claim to which a defendant makes even a passing reference," the Court noted.

p. 1182, Note 6

Update

The most commonly invoked form of "cause" is ineffective assistance of counsel—at trial, or, as in *Coleman*, on direct appeal. Some states require that claims of ineffective assistance of trial counsel be raised during direct appeal or be forfeited. Normally, a federal court will respect such a rule. However, in Martinez v. Ryan, 132 S.Ct. 1309 (2012), the Court held that a procedural default will not defeat federal habeas review when a state's procedural rules require that any ineffective-assistance-of-trial-counsel claim be brought in an initial-review collateral proceeding, *and* where the prisoner had no or ineffective counsel in that initial-review collateral proceeding. In *Trevino v. Thaler*, 133 S.Ct. 1911 (2013), the Supreme Court extended *Martinez v. Ryan* to states whose systems practically, if not formally, require petitioners to raise ineffective assistance claims for the first time on collateral review. *Trevino* arose in Texas, which formally permits a petitioner to raise ineffective assistance on direct review. By a 5-4 vote, however, the Court held that *Martinez* applies to Texas because, as a practical matter, it is "nearly impossible" to raise a claim of ineffective assistance by trial counsel on direct review. The ultimate question, stated the majority, is whether the state system provides a "fair, meaningful opportunity" to assert an ineffective assistance claim on direct review.

The majority cited several factors that made it highly impractical to raise ineffective assistance claims on direct review in Texas. If trial counsel was ineffective, the trial record is unlikely to be adequate to demonstrate such ineffectiveness. Time limits and the unavailability of trial transcripts exacerbate the likely deficiencies in the record.

p. 1187, Note 7

Update

Several issues as to the proper interpretation of these provisions reached the Supreme Court in recent terms. *McQuiggin v. Perkins*, 133 S.Ct. 1924 (2013), presented the issue of whether a showing of actual innocence affects the statute of limitations. By a 5-4 vote, the Supreme Court held that the "fundamental miscarriage of justice" exception (*i.e.*, actual innocence) applies not only to the judge-made doctrine of procedural default, but to § 2244(d)(1) as well.

Writing for the majority, Justice Ginsburg said it would be ironic not to recognize an actual innocence exception to AEDPA's statute of limitations. When a federal court recognizes an exception to the procedural default doctrine, it effectively excuses a failure to fulfill state procedure. The AEDPA limitation is a federal procedural requirement. "It would be passing strange to interpret a statute seeking to promote federalism and comity as requiring stricter enforcement of federal procedural rules than procedural rules established and enforced by the *States*," she wrote.

McQuiggin had filed for federal habeas relief after three exculpatory post-trial affidavits had been sworn out, but he waited until almost six years after the last of the three was executed. He clearly was not entitled to "equitable tolling" of the one-year statute of limitations, for he had not acted diligently. But the Supreme Court distinguished equitable tolling from an application of the fundamental miscarriage of justice exception to the statute of limitations. The latter constitutes an "equitable *exception*" to the statute, and therefore diligence was not required.

The Court made it clear that the actual innocence exception to the statute of limitations was only a "gateway" exception, as with the actual innocence exception to the procedural default doctrine. In other words, when a petitioner brings forward evidence in the face of which a reasonable jury probably would not have convicted, he is entitled to proceed with his showing that one of his constitutional rights was violated in a prejudicial manner, procedural violation notwithstanding. The *McQuiggin* Court stressed that it was not reaching the question of whether a petitioner is ever entitled to a "freestanding" claim of innocence, which would be an entitlement to habeas relief based on the proof of innocence alone without any accompanying violation of federal law. Recall that § 2254(d) limits the grant of federal habeas relief to violations of clearly established federal law.

p. 1190

Update

A petitioner is not, however, entitled to a stay of federal habeas based on his mental incompetence. In *Ryan v. Valencia-Gonzalez*, 133 S.Ct. 696 (2013), the Supreme Court unanimously held that neither 18 U.S.C. § 3599 nor § 4241 creates a right to such a stay.

The Ninth Circuit had held that § 3599, which guarantees federal habeas petitioners on death row the right to federally funded counsel, by implication created a right to effective counsel during federal habeas proceedings. That right could not be ensured unless the petitioner were able to assist counsel in the representation, according to the Ninth Circuit. The Supreme Court disagreed. Effective representation at trial requires that the petitioner be competent to assist in his defense, but habeas proceedings are limited to the record. "Given the backward-looking, record-based nature of most federal habeas proceedings, counsel can generally provide effective representation to a habeas petitioner regardless of the petition's competence," wrote Justice Thomas.

The Sixth Circuit had held that § 4241 creates a right to inmate competence during federal habeas. Justice Thomas made short work of that holding, pointing out that § 4241 by its own terms applies only to trial proceedings *prior to sentencing* and at any time *after the commencement of probation or supervised release.* A habeas petitioner has already been sentenced, and, Justice Thomas said, by definition, is incarcerated, not on probation.

Recall that there is no constitutional right to counsel in federal habeas proceedings, which means there can be no Sixth Amendment right to competence in such litigation.

Appendix A

The Constitution of the United States of America

We The People of the United States, in Order to form a more perfect Union, establish Justice, insure domestic Tranquility, provide for the common defence, promote the general Welfare, and secure the Blessings of Liberty to ourselves and our Posterity, do ordain and establish this Constitution for the United States of America.

Article I

Section 1. All legislative Powers herein granted shall be vested in a Congress of the United States, which shall consist of a Senate and House of Representatives.

Section 2. [1] The House of Representatives shall be composed of Members chosen every second Year by the People of the several States, and the Electors in each State shall have the Qualifications requisite for Electors of the most numerous Branch of the State Legislature.

[2] No Person shall be a Representative who shall not have attained to the Age of twenty five Years, and been seven Years a Citizen of the United States, and who shall not, when elected, be an Inhabitant of that State in which he shall be chosen.

[3] Representatives and direct Taxes shall be apportioned among the several States which may be included within this Union, according to their respective Numbers, which shall be determined by adding to the whole Number of free Persons, including those bound to Service for a Term of Years, and excluding Indians not taxed, three fifths of all other Persons. The actual Enumeration shall be made within three Years after the first Meeting of the Congress of the United States, and within every subsequent Term of ten Years, in such Manner as they shall by Law direct. The Number of Representatives shall not exceed one for every thirty Thousand, but each State shall have at Least one Representative; and until such enumeration shall be made, the State of New Hampshire shall be entitled to chuse three, Massachusetts eight, Rhode–Island and Providence Plantations one, Connecticut five, New–York six, New Jersey four,

Pennsylvania eight, Delaware one, Maryland six, Virginia ten, North Carolina five, South Carolina five, and Georgia three.

[4] When vacancies happen in the Representation from any State, the Executive Authority thereof shall issue Writs of Election to fill such Vacancies.

[5] The House of Representatives shall chuse their Speaker and other Officers; and shall have the sole Power of Impeachment.

SECTION 3. [1] The Senate of the United States shall be composed of two Senators from each State, chosen by the Legislature thereof, for six Years; and each Senator shall have one Vote.

[2] Immediately after they shall be assembled in Consequence of the first Election, they shall be divided as equally as may be into three Classes. The Seats of the Senators of the first Class shall be vacated at the Expiration of the second Year, of the second Class at the Expiration of the fourth Year, and of the third Class at the Expiration of the sixth Year, so that one third may be chosen every second Year; [and if Vacancies happen by Resignation, or otherwise, during the Recess of the Legislature of any State, the Executive thereof may make temporary Appointments until the next Meeting of the Legislature, which shall then fill such Vacancies].

[3] No Person shall be a Senator who shall not have attained to the Age of thirty Years, and been nine Years a Citizen of the United States, and who shall not, when elected, be an Inhabitant of that State for which he shall be chosen.

[4] The Vice President of the United States shall be President of the Senate, but shall have no Vote, unless they be equally divided.

[5] The Senate shall chuse their other Officers, and also a President pro tempore, in the Absence of the Vice President, or when he shall exercise the Office of President of the United States.

[6] The Senate shall have the sole Power to try all Impeachments. When sitting for that Purpose, they shall be on Oath or Affirmation. When the President of the United States is tried, the Chief Justice shall preside: And no Person shall be convicted without the Concurrence of two thirds of the Members present.

[7] Judgment in Cases of Impeachment shall not extend further than to removal from Office, and disqualification to hold and enjoy any Office of honor, Trust or Profit under the United States: but the Party convicted shall nevertheless be liable and subject to Indictment, Trial Judgment and Punishment, according to Law.

SECTION 4. [1] The Times, Places and Manner of holding Elections for Senators and Representatives, shall be prescribed in each State by the Legislature thereof; but the Congress may at any time by Law make or alter such Regulations, except as to the Places of chusing Senators.

[2] The Congress shall assemble at least once in every Year, and such Meeting shall be on the first Monday in December, unless they shall by Law appoint a different Day.

Section 5. [1] Each House shall be the Judge of the Elections, Returns and Qualifications of its own Members, and a Majority of each shall constitute a Quorum to do Business; but a smaller Number may adjourn from day to day, and may be authorized to compel the Attendance of absent Members, in such Manner, and under such Penalties as each House may provide.

[2] Each House may determine the Rules of its Proceedings, punish its Members for disorderly Behaviour, and, with the Concurrence of two thirds, expel a Member.

[3] Each House shall keep a Journal of its Proceedings, and from time to time publish the same, excepting such Parts as may in their Judgment require Secrecy; and the Yeas and Nays of the Members of either House on any question shall, at the Desire of one fifth of those Present, be entered on the Journal.

[4] Neither House, during the Session of Congress, shall, without the Consent of the other, adjourn for more than three days, nor to any other Place than that in which the two Houses shall be sitting.

Section 6. [1] The Senators and Representatives shall receive a Compensation for their Services, to be ascertained by Law, and paid out of the Treasury of the United States. They shall in all Cases, except Treason, Felony and Breach of the Peace, be privileged from Arrest during their Attendance at the Session of their respective Houses, and in going to and returning from the same; and for any Speech or Debate in either House, they shall not be questioned in any other Place.

[2] No Senator or Representative shall, during the Time for which he was elected, be appointed to any civil Office under the Authority of the United States, which shall have been created, or the Emoluments whereof shall have been encreased during such time; and no Person holding any Office under the United States, shall be a Member of either House during his Continuance in Office.

Section 7. [1] All Bills for raising Revenue shall originate in the House of Representatives; but the Senate may propose or concur with Amendments as on other Bills.

[2] Every Bill which shall have passed the House of Representatives and the Senate, shall, before it become a Law, be presented to the President of the United States; If he approve he shall sign it, but if not he shall return it, with his Objections to that House in which it shall have originated, who shall enter the Objections at large on their Journal, and proceed to reconsider it. If after such Reconsideration two thirds of that House shall agree to pass the Bill, it shall be sent, together with the Objections, to the other House, by which it shall likewise be reconsidered, and if approved by two thirds of that House, it shall become a Law. But in all such Cases the Votes of both

Houses shall be determined by yeas and Nays, and the Names of the Persons voting for and against the Bill shall be entered on the Journal of each House respectively. If any Bill shall not be returned by the President within ten Days (Sundays excepted) after it shall have been presented to him, the Same shall be a Law, in like Manner as if he had signed it, unless the Congress by their Adjournment prevent its Return, in which Case it shall not be a Law.

[3] Every Order, Resolution, or Vote to which the Concurrence of the Senate and House of Representatives may be necessary (except on a question of Adjournment) shall be presented to the President of the United States; and before the Same shall take Effect, shall be approved by him, or being disapproved by him, shall be repassed by two thirds of the Senate and House of Representatives, according to the Rules and Limitations prescribed in the Case of a Bill.

SECTION 8. [1] The Congress shall have Power To lay and collect Taxes, Duties, Imposts and Excises, to pay the Debts and provide for the common Defence and general Welfare of the United States; but all Duties, Imposts and Excises shall be uniform throughout the United States;

[2] To borrow Money on the credit of the United States;

[3] To regulate Commerce with foreign Nations, and among the several States, and with the Indian Tribes;

[4] To establish an uniform Rule of Naturalization, and uniform Laws on the subject of Bankruptcies throughout the United States;

[5] To coin Money, regulate the Value thereof, and of foreign Coin, and fix the Standard of Weights and Measures;

[6] To provide for the Punishment of counterfeiting the Securities and current Coin of the United States;

[7] To establish Post Offices and post Roads;

[8] To promote the Progress of Science and useful Arts, by securing for limited Times to Authors and Inventors the exclusive Right to their respective Writings and Discoveries;

[9] To constitute Tribunals inferior to the supreme Court;

[10] To define and punish Piracies and Felonies committed on the high Seas, and Offences against the Law of Nations;

[11] To declare War, grant Letters of Marque and Reprisal, and make Rules concerning Captures on Land and Water;

[12] To raise and support Armies, but no Appropriation of Money to that Use shall be for a longer Term than two Years;

[13] To provide and maintain a Navy;

[14] To make Rules for the Government and Regulation of the land and naval Forces;

[15] To provide for calling forth the Militia to execute the Laws of the Union, suppress Insurrections and repel Invasions;

[16] To provide for organizing, arming, and disciplining, the Militia, and for governing such Part of them as may be employed in the Service of the United States, reserving to the States respectively, the Appointment of the Officers, and the Authority of training the Militia according to the discipline prescribed by Congress

[17] To exercise exclusive Legislation in all Cases whatsoever, over such District (not exceeding ten Miles square) as may, by Cession of particular States, and the Acceptance of Congress, become the Seat of the Government of the United States, and to exercise like Authority over all Places purchased by the Consent of the Legislature of the State in which the Same shall be, for the Erection of Forts, Magazines, Arsenals, dock-Yards, and other needful Buildings;—And

[18] To make all Laws which shall be necessary and proper for carrying into Execution the foregoing Powers, and all other Powers vested by this Constitution in the Government of the United States, or in any Department or Officer thereof.

Section 9. [1] The Migration or Importation of such Persons as any of the States now existing shall think proper to admit, shall not be prohibited by the Congress prior to the Year one thousand eight hundred and eight, but a Tax or duty may be imposed on such Importation, not exceeding ten dollars for each Person.

[2] The Privilege of the Writ of Habeas Corpus shall not be suspended, unless when in Cases of Rebellion or Invasion the public Safety may require it.

[3] No Bill of Attainder or ex post facto Law shall be passed.

[4] No Capitation, or other direct, Tax shall be laid, unless in Proportion to the Census or Enumeration herein before directed to be taken.

[5] No Tax or Duty shall be laid on Articles exported from any State.

[6] No Preference shall be given by any Regulation of Commerce or Revenue to the Ports of one State over those of another: nor shall Vessels bound to, or from, one State, be obliged to enter, clear, or pay Duties in another.

[7] No Money shall be drawn from the Treasury, but in Consequence of Appropriations made by Law; and a regular Statement and Account of the Receipts and Expenditures of all public Money shall be published from time to time.

[8] No Title of Nobility shall be granted by the United States: And no Person holding any Office of Profit or Trust under them, shall, without the Consent of the Congress, accept of any present, Emolument, Office, or Title, of any kind whatever, from any King, Prince, or foreign State.

SECTION 10. [1] No State shall enter into any Treaty, Alliance, or Confederation; grant Letters of Marque and Reprisal; coin Money; emit Bills of Credit; make any Thing but gold and silver Coin a Tender in Payment of Debts; pass any Bill of Attainder, ex post facto Law, or Law impairing the Obligation of Contracts, or grant any Title of Nobility.

[2] No State shall, without the Consent of the Congress, lay any Imposts or Duties on Imports or Exports, except what may be absolutely necessary for executing its inspection Laws: and the net Produce of all Duties and Imposts, laid by any State on Imports or Exports, shall be for the Use of the Treasury of the United States; and all such Laws shall be subject to the Revision and Controul of the Congress.

[3] No State shall, without the Consent of Congress, lay any Duty of Tonnage, keep Troops, or Ships of War in time of Peace, enter into any Agreement or Compact with another State, or with a foreign Power, or engage in War, unless actually invaded, or in such imminent Danger as will not admit of delay.

ARTICLE II

SECTION 1. [1] The executive Power shall be vested in a President of the United States of America. He shall hold his Office during the Term of four Years, and, together with the Vice President, chosen for the same Term, be elected, as follows

[2] Each State shall appoint, in such Manner as the Legislature thereof may direct, a Number of Electors, equal to the whole Number of Senators and Representatives to which the State may be entitled in the Congress: but no Senator or Representative, or Person holding an Office of Trust or Profit under the United States, shall be appointed an Elector.

[3] The Congress may determine the Time of chusing the Electors, and the Day on which they shall give their Votes; which Day shall be the same throughout the United States.

[4] No Person except a natural born Citizen, or a Citizen of the United States, at the time of the Adoption of this Constitution, shall be eligible to the Office of President; neither shall any Person be eligible to that Office who shall not have attained to the Age of thirty five Years, and been fourteen Years a Resident within the United States.

[5] In Case of the Removal of the President from Office, or of his Death, Resignation, or Inability to discharge the Powers and Duties of the said Office, the Same shall devolve on the Vice President, and the Congress may by Law provide for the Case of Removal, Death, Resignation or Inability, both of the President and Vice President, declaring what Officer shall then act as President, and such Officer shall act accordingly, until the Disability be removed, or a President shall be elected.

[6] The President shall, at stated Times, receive for his Services, a Compensation, which shall neither be encreased nor diminished during the Period for which he shall have been elected, and he shall not receive within that Period any other Emolument from the United States, or any of them.

[7] Before he enter on the Execution of his Office, he shall take the following Oath or Affirmation:—"I do solemnly swear (or affirm) that I will faithfully execute the Office of President of the United States, and will to the best of my Ability, preserve, protect and defend the Constitution of the United States."

Section 2. [1] The President shall be Commander in Chief of the Army and Navy of the United States, and of the Militia of the several States, when called into the actual Service of the United States; he may require the Opinion, in writing, of the principal Officer in each of the executive Departments, upon any Subject relating to the Duties of their respective Offices, and he shall have Power to grant Reprieves and Pardons for Offenses against the United States, except in Cases of Impeachment.

[2] He shall have Power, by and with the Advice and Consent of the Senate, to make Treaties, provided two thirds of the Senators present concur; and he shall nominate, and by and with the Advice and Consent of the Senate, shall appoint Ambassadors, other public Ministers and Consuls, Judges of the supreme Court, and all other Officers of the United States, whose Appointments are not herein otherwise provided for, and which shall be established by Law: but the Congress may by Law vest the Appointment of such inferior Officers, as they think proper, in the President alone, in the Courts of Law, or in the Heads of Departments.

[3] The President shall have Power to fill up all Vacancies that may happen during the Recess of the Senate, by granting Commissions which shall expire at the End of their next Session.

Section 3. He shall from time to time give to the Congress Information of the State of the Union, and recommend to their Consideration such Measures as he shall judge necessary and expedient; he may, on extraordinary Occasions, convene both Houses, or either of them, and in Case of Disagreement between them, with Respect to the Time of Adjournment, he may adjourn them to such Time as he shall think proper; he shall receive Ambassadors and other public Ministers; he shall take Care that the Laws be faithfully executed, and shall Commission all the Officers of the United States.

SECTION 4. The President, Vice President and all civil Officers of the United States, shall be removed from Office on Impeachment for, and Conviction of, Treason, Bribery, or other high Crimes and Misdemeanors.

ARTICLE III

SECTION 1. The judicial Power of the United States, shall be vested in one supreme Court, and in such inferior Courts as the Congress may from time to time ordain and establish. The Judges, both of the supreme and inferior Courts, shall hold their Offices during good Behaviour, and shall, at stated Times, receive for their Services, a Compensation, which shall not be diminished during their Continuance in Office.

SECTION 2. [1] The judicial Power shall extend to all Cases, in Law and Equity, arising under this Constitution, the Laws of the United States, and Treaties made, or which shall be made, under their Authority;—to all Cases affecting Ambassadors, other public Ministers and Consuls;—to all Cases of admiralty and maritime Jurisdiction;—to Controversies to which the United States shall be a Party;—to Controversies between two or more States;—between a State and Citizens of another State;—between Citizens of different States;—between Citizens of the same State claiming Lands under Grants of different States, and between a State, or the Citizens thereof, and foreign States, Citizens or Subjects.

[2] In all Cases affecting Ambassadors, other public Ministers and Consuls, and those in which a State shall be Party, the supreme Court shall have original Jurisdiction. In all the other Cases before mentioned, the supreme Court shall have appellate Jurisdiction, both as to Law and Fact, with such Exceptions, and under such Regulations as the Congress shall make.

[3] The Trial of all Crimes, except in Cases of Impeachment, shall be by Jury; and such Trial shall be held in the State where the said Crimes shall have been committed; but when not committed within any State, the Trial shall be at such Place or Places as the Congress may by Law have directed.

SECTION 3. [1] Treason against the United States, shall consist only in levying War against them, or in adhering to their Enemies, giving them Aid and Comfort. No Person shall be convicted of Treason unless on the Testimony of two Witnesses to the same overt Act, or on Confession in open Court.

[2] The Congress shall have power to declare the Punishment of Treason, but no Attainder of Treason shall work Corruption of Blood, or Forfeiture except during the Life of the Person attainted.

ARTICLE IV

SECTION 1. Full Faith and Credit shall be given in each State to the public Acts, Records, and judicial Proceedings of every other State. And the Congress may by general Laws prescribe the Manner in which such Acts, Records and Proceedings shall be proved, and the Effect thereof.

SECTION 2. [1] The Citizens of each State shall be entitled to all Privileges and Immunities of Citizens in the several States.

[2] A person charged in any State with Treason, Felony, or other Crime, who shall flee from Justice, and be found in another State, shall on Demand of the executive Authority of the State from which he fled, be delivered up, to be removed to the State having Jurisdiction of the Crime.

[3] No Person held to Service or Labour in one State, under the Laws thereof, escaping into another, shall, in Consequence of any Law or Regulation therein, be discharged from such Service or Labour, but shall be delivered up on Claim of the Party to whom such Service or Labour may be due.

SECTION 3. [1] New States may be admitted by the Congress into this Union; but no new State shall be formed or erected within the Jurisdiction of any other State; nor any State be formed by the Junction of two or more States, or Parts of States, without the Consent of the Legislatures of the States concerned as well as of the Congress.

[2] The Congress shall have Power to dispose of and make all needful Rules and Regulations respecting the Territory or other Property belonging to the United States; and nothing in this Constitution shall be so construed as to Prejudice any Claims of the United States, or of any particular State.

SECTION 4. The United States shall guarantee to every State in this Union a Republican Form of Government, and shall protect each of them against Invasion; and on Application of the Legislature, or of the Executive (when the Legislature cannot be convened) against domestic Violence.

ARTICLE V

The Congress, whenever two thirds of both Houses shall deem it necessary, shall propose Amendments to this Constitution, or on the Application of the Legislatures of two thirds of the several States, shall call a Convention for proposing Amendments, which, in either Case, shall be valid to all Intents and Purposes, as Part of this Constitution, when ratified by the Legislatures of three fourths of the several States, or by Conventions in three fourths thereof, as the one or the other Mode of Ratification may be proposed by the Congress; Provided that no Amendment which may be made prior to the Year One thousand eight hundred and eight shall in any Manner affect the first and fourth Clauses in the Ninth Section of the first Article; and that no State, without its Consent, shall be deprived of its equal Suffrage in the Senate.

ARTICLE VI

[1] All Debts contracted and Engagements entered into, before the Adoption of this Constitution, shall be as valid against the United States under this Constitution, as under the Confederation.

[2] This Constitution, and the Laws of the United States which shall be made in Pursuance thereof; and all Treaties made, or which shall be made, under the Authority of the United States, shall be the supreme Law of the Land; and the Judges in every State shall be bound thereby, any Thing in the Constitution or Laws of any State to the Contrary notwithstanding.

[3] The Senators and Representatives before mentioned, and the Members of the several State Legislatures, and all executive and judicial Officers, both of the United States and of the several States, shall be bound by Oath or Affirmation, to support this Constitution; but no religious Test shall ever be required as a Qualification to any Office or public Trust under the United States.

ARTICLE VII

The Ratification of the Conventions of nine States, shall be sufficient for the Establishment of this Constitution between the States so ratifying the Same.

AMENDMENT I [1791]

Congress shall make no law respecting an establishment of religion, or prohibiting the free exercise thereof; or abridging the freedom of speech, or of the press; or the right of the people peaceably to assemble, and to petition the Government for a redress of grievances.

AMENDMENT II [1791]

A well regulated Militia, being necessary to the security of a free State, the right of the people to keep and bear Arms, shall not be infringed.

AMENDMENT III [1791]

No Soldier shall, in time of peace be quartered in any house, without the consent of the Owner, nor in time of war, but in a manner to be prescribed by law.

AMENDMENT IV [1791]

The right of the people to be secure in their persons, houses, papers, and effects, against unreasonable searches and seizures, shall not be violated, and no Warrants shall issue, but upon probable cause, supported by Oath or affirmation, and particularly describing the place to be searched, and the persons or things to be seized.

Amendment V [1791]

No person shall be held to answer for a capital, or otherwise infamous crime, unless on a presentment or indictment of a Grand Jury, except in cases arising in the land or naval forces, or in the Militia, when in actual service in time of War or public danger; nor shall any person be subject for the same offence to be twice put in jeopardy of life or limb; nor shall be compelled in any criminal case to be a witness against himself, nor be deprived of life, liberty, or property, without due process of law; nor shall private property be taken for public use, without just compensation.

Amendment VI [1791]

In all criminal prosecutions, the accused shall enjoy the right to a speedy and public trial, by an impartial jury of the State and district wherein the crime shall have been committed, which district shall have been previously ascertained by law, and to be informed of the nature and cause of the accusation; to be confronted with the witnesses against him; to have compulsory process for obtaining witnesses in his favor, and to have the Assistance of Counsel for his defence.

Amendment VII [1791]

In Suits at common law, where the value in controversy shall exceed twenty dollars, the right of trial by jury shall be preserved, and no fact tried by a jury, shall be otherwise reexamined in any Court of the United States, than according to the rules of the common law.

Amendment VIII [1791]

Excessive bail shall not be required, nor excessive fines imposed, nor cruel and unusual punishments inflicted.

Amendment IX [1791]

The enumeration in the Constitution, of certain rights, shall not be construed to deny or disparage others retained by the people.

Amendment X [1791]

The powers not delegated to the United States by the Constitution, nor prohibited by it to the States, are reserved to the States respectively, or to the people.

Amendment XI [1798]

The Judicial power of the United States shall not be construed to extend to any suit in law or equity, commenced or prosecuted against one of the United States by Citizens of another State, or by Citizens or Subjects of any Foreign State.

AMENDMENT XII [1804]

The Electors shall meet in their respective states and vote by ballot for President and Vice–President, one of whom, at least, shall not be an inhabitant of the same state with themselves; they shall name in their ballots the person voted for as President, and in distinct ballots the person voted for as Vice–President, and they shall make distinct lists of all persons voted for as President, and of all persons voted for as Vice–President, and of the number of votes for each, which lists they shall sign and certify, and transmit sealed to the seat of the government of the United States, directed to the President of the Senate;—The President of the Senate shall, in the presence of the Senate and House of Representatives, open all the certificates and the votes shall then be counted;—The person having the greatest number of votes for President, shall be the President, if such number be a majority of the whole number of Electors appointed; and if no person have such majority, then from the persons having the highest numbers not exceeding three on the list of those voted for as President, the House of Representatives shall choose immediately, by ballot, the President. But in choosing the President, the votes shall be taken by states, the representation from each state having one vote; a quorum for this purpose shall consist of a member or members from two-thirds of the states, and a majority of all the states shall be necessary to a choice. And if the House of Representatives shall not choose a President whenever the right of choice shall devolve upon them, before the fourth day of March next following, then the Vice–President shall act as President, as in the case of the death or other constitutional disability of the President.—The person having the greatest number of votes as Vice–President, shall be the Vice–President, if such number be a majority of the whole number of Electors appointed, and if no person have a majority, then from the two highest numbers on the list, the Senate shall choose the Vice–President; a quorum for the purpose shall consist of two-thirds of the whole number of Senators, and a majority of the whole number shall be necessary to a choice. But no person constitutionally ineligible to the office of President shall be eligible to that of Vice–President of the United States.

AMENDMENT XIII [1865]

SECTION 1. Neither slavery nor involuntary servitude, except as a punishment for crime whereof the party shall have been duly convicted, shall exist within the United States, or any place subject to their jurisdiction.

SECTION 2. Congress shall have power to enforce this article by appropriate legislation.

AMENDMENT XIV [1868]

SECTION 1. All persons born or naturalized in the United States, and subject to the jurisdiction thereof, are citizens of the United States and of the State wherein they reside. No State shall make or enforce any law which shall abridge the privileges or immunities of citizens of the United States; nor shall any State deprive any person of life, liberty, or property, without due process of law; nor deny to any person within its jurisdiction the equal protection of the laws.

SECTION 2. Representatives shall be apportioned among the several States according to their respective numbers, counting the whole number of persons in each State, excluding Indians not taxed. But when the right to vote at any election for the choice of electors for President and Vice President of the United States, Representatives in Congress, the Executive and Judicial officers of a State, or the members of the Legislature thereof, is denied to any of the male inhabitants of such State, being twenty-one years of age, and citizens of the United States, or in any way abridged, except for participation in rebellion, or other crime, the basis of representation therein shall be reduced in the proportion which the number of such male citizens shall bear to the whole number of male citizens twenty-one years of age in such State.

SECTION 3. No person shall be a Senator or Representative in Congress, or elector of President and Vice President, or hold any office, civil or military, under the United States, or under any State, who, having previously taken an oath, as a member of Congress, or as an officer of the United States, or as a member of any State legislature, or as an executive or judicial officer of any State, to support the Constitution of the United States, shall have engaged in insurrection or rebellion against the same, or given aid or comfort to the enemies thereof. But Congress may by a vote of two-thirds of each House, remove such disability.

SECTION 4. The validity of the public debt of the United States, authorized by law, including debts incurred for payment of pensions and bounties for services in suppressing insurrection or rebellion, shall not be questioned. But neither the United States nor any State shall assume or pay any debt or obligation incurred in aid of insurrection or rebellion against the United States, or any claim for the loss or emancipation of any slave; but all such debts, obligations and claims shall be held illegal and void.

SECTION 5. The Congress shall have power to enforce, by appropriate legislation, the provisions of this article.

AMENDMENT XV [1870]

SECTION 1. The right of citizens of the United States to vote shall not be denied or abridged by the United States or by any State on account of race, color, or previous condition of servitude.

SECTION 2. The Congress shall have power to enforce this article by appropriate legislation.

AMENDMENT XVI [1913]

The Congress shall have power to lay and collect taxes on incomes, from whatever source derived, without apportionment among the several States, and without regard to any census or enumeration.

AMENDMENT XVII [1913]

The Senate of the United States shall be composed of two Senators from each State, elected by the people thereof, for six years; and each Senator shall have one vote. The electors in each State shall have the qualifications requisite for electors of the most numerous branch of the State legislatures.

When vacancies happen in the representation of any State in the Senate, the executive authority of such State shall issue writs of election to fill such vacancies: Provided, That the legislature of any State may empower the executive thereof to make temporary appointments until the people fill the vacancies by election as the legislature may direct.

This amendment shall not be so construed as to affect the election or term of any Senator chosen before it becomes valid as part of the Constitution.

AMENDMENT XVIII [1919]

SECTION 1. After one year from the ratification of this article the manufacture, sale, or transportation of intoxicating liquors within, the importation thereof into, or the exportation thereof from the United States and all territory subject to the jurisdiction thereof for beverage purposes is hereby prohibited.

SECTION 2. The Congress and the several States shall have concurrent power to enforce this article by appropriate legislation.

SECTION 3. This article shall be inoperative unless it shall have been ratified as an amendment to the Constitution by the legislatures of the several States, as provided in the Constitution, within seven years from the date of the submission hereof to the States by the Congress.

AMENDMENT XIX [1920]

The right of citizens of the United States to vote shall not be denied or abridged by the United States or by any State on account of sex.

Congress shall have power to enforce this article by appropriate legislation.

AMENDMENT XX [1933]

SECTION 1. The terms of the President and Vice President shall end at noon on the 20th day of January, and the terms of Senators and Representatives at noon on the 3d day of January, of the years in which such terms would have ended if this article had not been ratified; and the terms of their successors shall then begin.

SECTION 2. The Congress shall assemble at least once in every year, and such meeting shall begin at noon on the 3d day of January, unless they shall by law appoint a different day.

SECTION 3. If, at the time fixed for the beginning of the term of the President, the President elect shall have died, the Vice President elect shall become President. If a President shall not have been chosen before the time fixed for the beginning of his term, or if the President elect shall have failed to qualify, then the Vice President elect shall act as President until a President shall have qualified; and the Congress may by law provide for the case wherein neither a President elect nor a Vice President elect shall have qualified, declaring who shall then act as President, or the manner in which one who is to act shall be selected, and such person shall act accordingly until a President or Vice President shall have qualified.

SECTION 4. The Congress may by law provide for the case of the death of any of the persons from whom the House of Representatives may choose a President whenever the right of choice shall have devolved upon them, and for the case of the death of any of the persons from whom the Senate may choose a Vice President whenever the right of choice shall have devolved upon them.

SECTION 5. Sections 1 and 2 shall take effect on the 15th day of October following the ratification of this article.

SECTION 6. This article shall be inoperative unless it shall have been ratified as an amendment to the Constitution by the legislatures of three-fourths of the several States within seven years from the date of its submission.

AMENDMENT XXI [1933]

SECTION 1. The eighteenth article of amendment to the Constitution of the United States is hereby repealed.

SECTION 2. The transportation or importation into any State, Territory, or possession of the United States or delivery or use therein of intoxicating liquors in violation of the laws thereof, is hereby prohibited.

SECTION 3. This article shall be inoperative unless it shall have been ratified as an amendment to the Constitution by conventions in the several States, as provided in the Constitution, within seven years from the date of the submission hereof to the States by the Congress.

AMENDMENT XXII [1951]

SECTION 1. No person shall be elected to the office of the President more than twice, and no person who has held the office of President, or acted as President, for more than two years of a term to which some other person was elected President shall be elected to the office of the President more than once. But this Article shall not apply to any person holding the office of President when this Article was proposed by the Congress, and shall not prevent any person who may be holding the office of President, or acting as President, during the term within which this Article becomes operative from holding the office of President or acting as President during the remainder of such term.

SECTION 2. This article shall be inoperative unless it shall have been ratified as an amendment to the Constitution by the legislatures of three-fourths of the several States within seven years from the date of its submission to the States by the Congress.

AMENDMENT XXIII [1961]

SECTION 1. The District constituting the seat of Government of the United States shall appoint in such manner as the Congress may direct:

A number of electors of President and Vice President equal to the whole number of Senators and Representatives in Congress to which the District would be entitled if it were a State, but in no event more than the least populous State; they shall be in addition to those appointed by the States, but they shall be considered, for the purposes of the election of President and Vice President, to be electors appointed by a State; and they shall meet in the District and perform such duties as provided by the twelfth article of amendment.

SECTION 2. The Congress shall have power to enforce this article by appropriate legislation.

AMENDMENT XXIV [1964]

SECTION 1. The right of citizens of the United States to vote in any primary or other election for President or Vice President, for electors for President or Vice President, or for Senator or Representative in Congress, shall not be denied or abridged by the United States or any State by reason of failure to pay any poll tax or other tax.

SECTION 2. The Congress shall have power to enforce this article by appropriate legislation.

AMENDMENT XXV [1967]

SECTION 1. In case of the removal of the President from office or of his death or resignation, the Vice President shall become President.

SECTION 2. Whenever there is a vacancy in the office of the Vice President, the President shall nominate a Vice President who shall take office upon confirmation by a majority vote of both Houses of Congress.

SECTION 3. Whenever the President transmits to the President pro tempore of the Senate and the Speaker of the House of Representatives his written declaration that he is unable to discharge the powers and duties of his office, and until he transmits to them a written declaration to the contrary, such powers and duties shall be discharged by the Vice President as Acting President.

Section 4. Whenever the Vice President and a majority of either the principal officers of the executive departments or of such other body as Congress may by law provide, transmit to the President pro tempore of the Senate and the Speaker of the House of Representatives their written declaration that the President is unable to discharge the powers and duties of his office, the Vice President shall immediately assume the powers and duties of the office as Acting President.

Thereafter, when the President transmits to the President pro tempore of the Senate and the Speaker of the House of Representatives his written declaration that no inability exists, he shall resume the powers and duties of his office unless the Vice President and a majority of either the principal officers of the executive department or of such other body as Congress may by law provide, transmit within four days to the President pro tempore of the Senate and the Speaker of the House of Representatives their written declaration that the President is unable to discharge the powers and duties of his office. Thereupon Congress shall decide the issue, assembling within forty-eight hours for that purpose if not in session. If the Congress, within twenty-one days after receipt of the latter written declaration, or, if Congress is not in session, within twenty-one days after Congress is required to assemble, determines by two-thirds vote of both Houses that the President is unable to discharge the powers and duties of his office, the Vice President shall continue to discharge the same as Acting President; otherwise, the President shall resume the powers and duties of his office.

Amendment XXVI [1971]

Section 1. The right of citizens of the United States, who are eighteen years of age or older, to vote shall not be denied or abridged by the United States or by any State on account of age.

Section 2. The Congress shall have power to enforce this article by appropriate legislation.

Amendment XXVII [1992]

No law, varying the compensation for the services of the Senators and Representatives, shall take effect, until an election of Representatives shall have intervened.

Appendix B

Excerpts from Title 18, United States Code Annotated

§ 3626. Appropriate remedies with respect to prison conditions

(a) Requirements for relief.—

(1) Prospective relief.—

(A) Prospective relief in any civil action with respect to prison conditions shall extend no further than necessary to correct the violation of the Federal right of a particular plaintiff or plaintiffs. The court shall not grant or approve any prospective relief unless the court finds that such relief is narrowly drawn, extends no further than necessary to correct the violation of the Federal right, and is the least intrusive means necessary to correct the violation of the Federal right. The court shall give substantial weight to any adverse impact on public safety or the operation of a criminal justice system caused by the relief.

(B) The court shall not order any prospective relief that requires or permits a government official to exceed his or her authority under State or local law or otherwise violates State or local law, unless—

(i) Federal law requires such relief to be ordered in violation of State or local law;

(ii) the relief is necessary to correct the violation of a Federal right; and

(iii) no other relief will correct the violation of the Federal right.

(C) Nothing in this section shall be construed to authorize the courts, in exercising their remedial powers, to order the construction of prisons or the raising of taxes, or to repeal or detract from otherwise applicable limitations on the remedial powers of the courts.

(2) Preliminary injunctive relief.—In any civil action with respect to prison conditions, to the extent otherwise authorized by law, the court may enter a temporary restraining order or an order for preliminary injunctive relief. Preliminary injunctive relief must be narrowly drawn, extend no further than necessary to correct the harm the court finds requires preliminary relief, and be the least intrusive means necessary to correct that harm. The court shall give substantial weight to any adverse impact on public safety or the operation of a criminal justice system caused by the preliminary relief and shall respect the principles of comity set out in paragraph (1)(B) in tailoring any preliminary relief. Preliminary injunctive relief shall automatically expire on the date that is 90 days after its entry, unless the court makes the findings required under subsection (a)(1) for the entry of prospective relief and makes the order final before the expiration of the 90- day period.

(3) Prisoner release order.—

(A) In any civil action with respect to prison conditions, no court shall enter a prisoner release order unless—

(i) a court has previously entered an order for less intrusive relief that has failed to remedy the deprivation of the Federal right sought to be remedied through the prisoner release order; and

(ii) the defendant has had a reasonable amount of time to comply with the previous court orders.

(B) In any civil action in Federal court with respect to prison conditions, a prisoner release order shall be entered only by a three-judge court in accordance with section 2284 of title 28, if the requirements of subparagraph (E) have been met.

(C) A party seeking a prisoner release order in Federal court shall file with any request for such relief, a request for a three-judge court and materials sufficient to demonstrate that the requirements of subparagraph (A) have been met.

(D) If the requirements under subparagraph (A) have been met, a Federal judge before whom a civil action with respect to prison conditions is pending who believes that a prison release order should be considered may sua sponte request the convening of a three-judge court to determine whether a prisoner release order should be entered.

(E) The three-judge court shall enter a prisoner release order only if the court finds by clear and convincing evidence that—

(i) crowding is the primary cause of the violation of a Federal right; and

(ii) no other relief will remedy the violation of the Federal right.

(F) Any State or local official including a legislator or unit of government whose jurisdiction or function includes the appropriation of funds for the construction, operation, or maintenance of prison facilities, or the prosecution or custody of persons who may be released from, or not admitted to, a prison as a result of a prisoner release order shall have standing to oppose the imposition or continuation in effect of such relief and to seek termination of such relief, and shall have the right to intervene in any proceeding relating to such relief.

(b) Termination of relief.—

(1) Termination of prospective relief.—

(A) In any civil action with respect to prison conditions in which prospective relief is ordered, such relief shall be terminable upon the motion of any party or intervener—

(i) 2 years after the date the court granted or approved the prospective relief;

(ii) 1 year after the date the court has entered an order denying termination of prospective relief under this paragraph; or

(iii) in the case of an order issued on or before the date of enactment of the Prison Litigation Reform Act, 2 years after such date of enactment.

(B) Nothing in this section shall prevent the parties from agreeing to terminate or modify relief before the relief is terminated under subparagraph (A).

(2) Immediate termination of prospective relief.—In any civil action with respect to prison conditions, a defendant or intervener shall be entitled to the immediate termination of any prospective relief if the relief was approved or granted in the absence of a finding by the court that the relief is narrowly drawn, extends no further than necessary to correct the violation of the Federal right, and is the least intrusive means necessary to correct the violation of the Federal right.

(3) Limitation.—Prospective relief shall not terminate if the court makes written findings based on the record that prospective relief remains necessary to correct a current and ongoing violation of the Federal right, extends no further than necessary to correct the violation of the Federal right, and that the prospective relief is narrowly drawn and the least intrusive means to correct the violation.

(4) Termination or modification of relief.—Nothing in this section shall prevent any party or intervener from seeking modification or termination before the relief is terminable under paragraph (1) or (2), to the extent that modification or termination would otherwise be legally permissible.

(c) Settlements.—

(1) Consent decrees.—In any civil action with respect to prison conditions, the court shall not enter or approve a consent decree unless it complies with the limitations on relief set forth in subsection (a).

(2) Private settlement agreements.—

(A) Nothing in this section shall preclude parties from entering into a private settlement agreement that does not comply with the limitations on relief set forth in subsection (a), if the terms of that agreement are not subject to court enforcement other than the reinstatement of the civil proceeding that the agreement settled.

(B) Nothing in this section shall preclude any party claiming that a private settlement agreement has been breached from seeking in State court any remedy available under State law.

(d) State law remedies.—The limitations on remedies in this section shall not apply to relief entered by a State court based solely upon claims arising under State law.

(e) Procedure for motions affecting prospective relief.—

(1) Generally.—The court shall promptly rule on any motion to modify or terminate prospective relief in a civil action with respect to prison conditions. Mandamus shall lie to remedy any failure to issue a prompt ruling on such a motion.

(2) Automatic stay.—Any motion to modify or terminate prospective relief made under subsection (b) shall operate as a stay during the period—

(A) (i) beginning on the 30th day after such motion is filed, in the case of a motion made under paragraph (1) or (2) of subsection (b); or

(ii) beginning on the 180th day after such motion is filed, in the case of a motion made under any other law; and

(B) ending on the date the court enters a final order ruling on the motion.

(3) Postponement of automatic stay.—The court may postpone the effective date of an automatic stay specified in subsection (e)(2)(A) for not more than 60 days for good cause. No postponement shall be permissible because of general congestion of the court's calendar.

(4) Order blocking the automatic stay.—Any order staying, suspending, delaying, or barring the operation of the automatic stay described in paragraph (2) (other than an order to postpone the effective date of the automatic stay under paragraph (3)) shall be treated as an order refusing to dissolve or modify an injunction and shall be appealable pursuant to section 1292(a)(1) of title 28, United States Code, regardless of how the order is styled or whether the order is termed a preliminary or a final ruling.

* * *

(g) Definitions.—As used in this section—

(1) the term "consent decree" means any relief entered by the court that is based in whole or in part upon the consent or acquiescence of the parties but does not include private settlements;

(2) the term "civil action with respect to prison conditions" means any civil proceeding arising under Federal law with respect to the conditions of confinement or the effects of actions by government officials on the lives of

persons confined in prison, but does not include habeas corpus proceedings challenging the fact or duration of confinement in prison;

(3) the term "prisoner" means any person subject to incarceration, detention, or admission to any facility who is accused of, convicted of, sentenced for, or adjudicated delinquent for, violations of criminal law or the terms and conditions of parole, probation, pretrial release, or diversionary program;

(4) the term "prisoner release order" includes any order, including a temporary restraining order or preliminary injunctive relief, that has the purpose or effect of reducing or limiting the prison population, or that directs the release from or nonadmission of prisoners to a prison;

(5) the term "prison" means any Federal, State, or local facility that incarcerates or detains juveniles or adults accused of, convicted of, sentenced for, or adjudicated delinquent for, violations of criminal law;

(6) the term "private settlement agreement" means an agreement entered into among the parties that is not subject to judicial enforcement other than the reinstatement of the civil proceeding that the agreement settled;

(7) the term "prospective relief" means all relief other than compensatory monetary damages;

* * *

(9) the term "relief" means all relief in any form that may be granted or approved by the court, and includes consent decrees but does not include private settlement agreements.

Appendix C

Excerpts from Title 28, United States Code Annotated

§ 1257. State courts; certiorari

(a) Final judgments or decrees rendered by the highest court of a State in which a decision could be had, may be reviewed by the Supreme Court by writ of certiorari where the validity of a treaty or statute of the United States is drawn in question or where the validity of a statute of any State is drawn in question on the ground of its being repugnant to the Constitution, treaties, or laws of the United States, or where any title, right, privilege, or immunity is specially set up or claimed under the Constitution or the treaties or statutes of, or any commission held or authority exercised under, the United States.

(b) For the purposes of this section, the term "highest court of a State" includes the District of Columbia Court of Appeals.

§ 1292. Interlocutory decisions

(a) Except as provided in subsections (c) and (d) of this section, the courts of appeals shall have jurisdiction of appeals from:

(1) Interlocutory orders of the district courts of the United States, the United States District Court for the District of the Canal Zone, the District Court of Guam, and the District Court of the Virgin Islands, or of the judges thereof, granting, continuing, modifying, refusing or dissolving injunctions, or refusing to dissolve or modify injunctions, except where a direct review may be had in the Supreme Court;

(2) Interlocutory orders appointing receivers, or refusing orders to wind up receiverships or to take steps to accomplish the purposes thereof, such as directing sales or other disposals of property;

(3) Interlocutory decrees of such district courts or the judges thereof determining the rights and liabilities of the parties to admiralty cases in which appeals from final decrees are allowed.

(b) When a district judge, in making in a civil action an order not otherwise appealable under this section, shall be of the opinion that such order involves a controlling question of law as to which there is substantial ground for difference of opinion and that an immediate appeal from the order may materially advance the ultimate termination of the litigation, he shall so state in writing in such order. The Court of Appeals which would have jurisdiction of an appeal of such action may thereupon, in its discretion, permit an appeal to be taken from such order, if application is made to it within ten days after the entry of the order: *Provided, however,* That application for an appeal hereunder shall not stay proceedings in the district court unless the district judge or the Court of Appeals or a judge thereof shall so order.

(c) The United States Court of Appeals for the Federal Circuit shall have exclusive jurisdiction—

(1) of an appeal from an interlocutory order or decree described in subsection (a) or (b) of this section in any case over which the court would have jurisdiction of an appeal under section 1295 of this title; and

(2) of an appeal from a judgment in a civil action for patent infringement which would otherwise be appealable to the United States Court of Appeals for the Federal Circuit and is final except for an accounting.

(d) (1) When the chief judge of the Court of International Trade issues an order under the provisions of section 256(b) of this title, or when any judge of the Court of International Trade, in issuing any other interlocutory order, includes in the order a statement that a controlling question of law is involved with respect to which there is a substantial ground for difference of opinion and that an immediate appeal from that order may materially advance the ultimate termination of the litigation, the United States Court of Appeals for the Federal Circuit may, in its discretion, permit an appeal to be taken from such order, if application is made to that Court within ten days after the entry of such order.

(2) When the chief judge of the United States Court of Federal Claims issues an order under section 798(b) of this title, or when any judge of the United States Court of Federal Claims, in issuing an interlocutory order, includes in the order a statement that a controlling question of law is involved with respect to which there is a substantial ground for difference of opinion and that an immediate appeal from that order may materially advance the ultimate termination of the litigation, the United States Court of Appeals for the Federal Circuit may, in its discretion, permit an appeal to be taken from such order, if application is made to that Court within ten days after the entry of such order.

(3) Neither the application for nor the granting of an appeal under this subsection shall stay proceedings in the Court of International Trade or in the Court of Federal Claims, as the case may be, unless a stay is ordered by

a judge of the Court of International Trade or of the Court of Federal Claims or by the United States Court of Appeals for the Federal Circuit or a judge of that court.

(4)(A) The United States Court of Appeals for the Federal Circuit shall have exclusive jurisdiction of an appeal from an interlocutory order of a district court of the United States, the District Court of Guam, the District Court of the Virgin Islands, or the District Court for the Northern Mariana Islands, granting or denying, in whole or in part, a motion to transfer an action to the United States Court of Federal Claims under section 1631 of this title.

(B) When a motion to transfer an action to the Court of Federal Claims is filed in a district court, no further proceedings shall be taken in the district court until 60 days after the court has ruled upon the motion. If an appeal is taken from the district court's grant or denial of the motion, proceedings shall be further stayed until the appeal has been decided by the Court of Appeals for the Federal Circuit. The stay of proceedings in the district court shall not bar the granting of preliminary or injunctive relief, where appropriate and where expedition is reasonably necessary. However, during the period in which proceedings are stayed as provided in this subparagraph, no transfer to the Court of Federal Claims pursuant to the motion shall be carried out.

(e) The Supreme Court may prescribe rules, in accordance with section 2072 of this title, to provide for an appeal of an interlocutory decision to the courts of appeals that is not otherwise provided for under subsection (a), (b), (c), or (d).

§ 1331. Federal question

The district courts shall have original jurisdiction of all civil actions arising under the Constitution, laws, or treaties of the United States.

§ 1332. Diversity of citizenship; amount in controversy; costs

(a) The district courts shall have original jurisdiction of all civil actions where the matter in controversy exceeds the sum or value of $75,000, exclusive of interest and costs, and is between—

(1) citizens of different States;

(2) citizens of a State and citizens or subjects of a foreign state, except that the district courts shall not have original jurisdiction under this subsection of an action between citizens of a State and citizens or subjects of a foreign state who are lawfully admitted for permanent residence in the United States and are domiciled in the same State;

(3) citizens of different States and in which citizens or subjects of a foreign state are additional parties; and

(4) a foreign state, defined in section 1603(a) of this title, as plaintiff and citizens of a State or of different States.

(b) Except when express provision therefor is otherwise made in a statute of the

United States, where the plaintiff who files the case originally in the Federal courts is finally adjudged to be entitled to recover less than the sum or value of $75,000, computed without regard to any setoff or counterclaim to which the defendant may be adjudged to be entitled, and exclusive of interest and costs, the district court may deny costs to the plaintiff and, in addition, may impose costs on the plaintiff.

(c) For the purposes of this section and section 1441 of this title—

(1) a corporation shall be deemed to be a citizen of every State and foreign state by which it has been incorporated and of the State or foreign state where it has its principal place of business, except that in any direct action against the insurer of a policy or contract of liability insurance, whether incorporated or unincorporated, to which action the insured is not joined as a party-defendant, such insurer shall be deemed a citizen of —

(A) every State and foreign state of which the insured is a citizen;

(B) every State and foreign state by which the insurer has been incorporated; and

(C) the State or foreign state where the insurer has its principal place of business; and

(2) the legal representative of the estate of a decedent shall be deemed to be a citizen only of the same State as the decedent, and the legal representative of an infant or incompetent shall be deemed to be a citizen only of the same State as the infant or incompetent.

(d) (1) In this subsection—

(A) the term "class" means all of the class members in a class action;

(B) the term "class action" means any civil action filed under rule 23 of the Federal Rules of Civil Procedure or similar State statute or rule of judicial procedure authorizing an action to be brought by 1 or more representative persons as a class action;

(C) the term "class certification order" means an order issued by a court approving the treatment of some or all aspects of a civil action as a class action; and

(D) the term "class members" means the persons (named or unnamed) who fall within the definition of the proposed or certified class in a class action.

(2) The district courts shall have original jurisdiction of any civil action in which the matter in controversy exceeds the sum or value of $5,000,000, exclusive of interest and costs, and is a class action in which—

(A) any member of a class of plaintiffs is a citizen of a State different from any defendant;

(B) any member of a class of plaintiffs is a foreign state or a citizen or subject of a foreign state and any defendant is a citizen of a State; or

(C) any member of a class of plaintiffs is a citizen of a State and any defendant is a foreign state or a citizen or subject of a foreign state.

(3) A district court may, in the interests of justice and looking at the totality of the circumstances, decline to exercise jurisdiction under paragraph (2) over a class action in which greater than one-third but less than two-thirds of the members of all proposed plaintiff classes in the aggregate and the primary defendants are citizens of the State in which the action was originally filed based on consideration of—

(A) whether the claims asserted involve matters of national or interstate interest;

(B) whether the claims asserted will be governed by laws of the State in which the action was originally filed or by the laws of other States;

(C) whether the class action has been pleaded in a manner that seeks to avoid Federal jurisdiction;

(D) whether the action was brought in a forum with a distinct nexus with the class members, the alleged harm, or the defendants;

(E) whether the number of citizens of the State in which the action was originally filed in all proposed plaintiff classes in the aggregate is substantially larger than the number of citizens from any other State, and the citizenship of the other members of the proposed class is dispersed among a substantial number of States; and

(F) whether, during the 3-year period preceding the filing of that class action, 1 or more other class actions asserting the same or similar claims on behalf of the same or other persons have been filed.

(4) A district court shall decline to exercise jurisdiction under paragraph (2)—

(A) (i) over a class action in which—

(I) greater than two-thirds of the members of all proposed plaintiff classes in the aggregate are citizens of the State in which the action was originally filed;

(II) at least 1 defendant is a defendant—

(aa) from whom significant relief is sought by members of the plaintiff class;

(bb) whose alleged conduct forms a significant basis for the claims asserted by the proposed plaintiff class; and

(cc) who is a citizen of the State in which the action was originally filed; and

(III) principal injuries resulting from the alleged conduct or any related conduct of each defendant were incurred in the

State in which the action was originally filed; and

(ii) during the 3-year period preceding the filing of that class action, no other class action has been filed asserting the same or similar factual allegations against any of the defendants on behalf of the same or other persons; or

(B) two-thirds or more of the members of all proposed plaintiff classes in the aggregate, and the primary defendants, are citizens of the State in which the action was originally filed.

(5) Paragraphs (2) through (4) shall not apply to any class action in which—

(A) the primary defendants are States, State officials, or other governmental entities against whom the district court may be foreclosed from ordering relief; or

(B) the number of members of all proposed plaintiff classes in the aggregate is less than 100.

(6) In any class action, the claims of the individual class members shall be aggregated to determine whether the matter in controversy exceeds the sum or value of $5,000,000, exclusive of interest and costs.

(7) Citizenship of the members of the proposed plaintiff classes shall be determined for purposes of paragraphs (2) through (6) as of the date of filing of the complaint or amended complaint, or, if the case stated by the initial pleading is not subject to Federal jurisdiction, as of the date of service by plaintiffs of an amended pleading, motion, or other paper, indicating the existence of Federal jurisdiction.

(8) This subsection shall apply to any class action before or after the entry of a class certification order by the court with respect to that action.

(9) Paragraph (2) shall not apply to any class action that solely involves a claim—

(A) concerning a covered security as defined under 16(f)(3) of the Securities Act of 1933 (15 U.S.C. 78p(f)(3)[*]) and section 28(f)(5)(E) of the Securities Exchange Act of 1934 (15 U.S.C. 78bb(f)(5)(E));

(B) that relates to the internal affairs or governance of a corporation or other form of business enterprise and that arises under or by virtue of the laws of the State in which such corporation or business enterprise is incorporated or organized; or

(C) that relates to the rights, duties (including fiduciary duties), and obligations relating to or created by or pursuant to any security (as defined under section 2(a)(1) of the Securities Act of 1933 (15 U.S.C. 77b(a)(1)) and the regulations issued thereunder).

(10) For purposes of this subsection and section 1453, an unincorporated association shall be deemed to be a citizen of the State where it has its principal place of business and the State under whose laws it is organized.

(11) (A) For purposes of this subsection and section 1453, a mass action shall be deemed to be a class action removable under paragraphs (2) through (10) if it otherwise meets the provisions of those paragraphs.

---

* *Sic*, probably intending "77p(f)(3)."

(B) (i) As used in subparagraph (A), the term "mass action" means any civil action (except a civil action within the scope of section 1711(2)) in which monetary relief claims of 100 or more persons are proposed to be tried jointly on the ground that the plaintiffs' claims involve common questions of law or fact, except that jurisdiction shall exist only over those plaintiffs whose claims in a mass action satisfy the jurisdictional amount requirements under subsection (a).

(ii) As used in subparagraph (A), the term "mass action" shall not include any civil action in which—

(I) all of the claims in the action arise from an event or occurrence in the State in which the action was filed, and that allegedly resulted in injuries in that State or in States contiguous to that State;

(II) the claims are joined upon motion of a defendant;

(III) all of the claims in the action are asserted on behalf of the general public (and not on behalf of individual claimants or members of a purported class) pursuant to a State statute specifically authorizing such action; or

(IV) the claims have been consolidated or coordinated solely for pretrial proceedings.

(C) (i) Any action(s) removed to Federal court pursuant to this subsection shall not thereafter be transferred to any other court pursuant to section 1407, or the rules promulgated thereunder, unless a majority of the plaintiffs in the action request transfer pursuant to section 1407.

(ii) This subparagraph will not apply—

(I) to cases certified pursuant to rule 23 of the Federal Rules of Civil Procedure; or

(II) if plaintiffs propose that the action proceed as a class action pursuant to rule 23 of the Federal Rules of Civil Procedure.

(D) The limitations periods on any claims asserted in a mass action that is removed to Federal court pursuant to this subsection shall be deemed tolled during the period that the action is pending in Federal court.

(e) The word "States", as used in this section, includes the Territories, the District of Columbia, and the Commonwealth of Puerto Rico.

§ 1333. Admiralty, maritime and prize cases

The district courts shall have original jurisdiction, exclusive of the courts of the States, of:

(1) Any civil case of admiralty or maritime jurisdiction, saving to suitors in all cases all other remedies to which they are otherwise entitled.

(2) Any prize brought into the United States and all proceedings for the condemnation of property taken as prize.

§ 1334. Bankruptcy cases and proceedings

(a) Except as provided in subsection (b) of this section, the district courts shall have original and exclusive jurisdiction of all cases under title 11.

(b) Except as provided in subsection (e)(2), and notwithstanding any Act of Congress that confers exclusive jurisdiction on a court or courts other than the district courts, the district courts shall have original but not exclusive jurisdiction of all civil proceedings arising under title 11, or arising in or related to cases under title 11.

(c) (1) Except with respect to a case under chapter 15 of title 11, nothing in this section prevents a district court in the interest of justice, or in the interest of comity with State courts or respect for State law, from abstaining from hearing a particular proceeding arising under title 11 or arising in or related to a case under title 11.

(2) Upon timely motion of a party in a proceeding based upon a State law claim or State law cause of action, related to a case under title 11 but not arising under title 11 or arising in a case under title 11, with respect to which an action could not have been commenced in a court of the United States absent jurisdiction under this section, the district court shall abstain from hearing such proceeding if an action is commenced, and can be timely adjudicated, in a State forum of appropriate jurisdiction.

(d) Any decision to abstain or not to abstain made under subsection (c) (other than a decision not to abstain in a proceeding described in subsection (c)(2)) is not reviewable by appeal or otherwise by the court of appeals under section 158(d), 1291, or 1292 of this title or by the Supreme Court of the United States under section 1254 of this title. Subsection (c) and this subsection shall not be construed to limit the applicability of the stay provided for by section 362 of title 11, United States Code, as such section applies to an action affecting the property of the estate in bankruptcy.

(e) The district court in which a case under title 11 is commenced or is pending shall have exclusive jurisdiction—

(1) of all the property, wherever located, of the debtor as of the commencement of such case, and of property of the estate; and

(2) over all claims or causes of action that involve construction of section 327 of title 11, United States Code, or rules relating to disclosure requirements under section 327.

§ 1337. Commerce and antitrust regulations; amount in controversy, costs

(a) The district courts shall have original jurisdiction of any civil action or proceeding arising under any Act of Congress regulating commerce or protecting trade and commerce against restraints and monopolies: *Provided, however,* That the district courts shall have original jurisdiction of an action brought under section 11706 or 14706 of title 49, only if the matter in controversy for each receipt or bill of lading exceeds $10,000, exclusive of interest and costs.

(b) Except when express provision therefor is otherwise made in a statute of the United States, where a plaintiff who files the case under section 11706 or 14706 of title 49, originally in the Federal courts is finally adjudged to be entitled to recover less than the sum or value of $ 10,000, computed without regard to any setoff or counterclaim to which the defendant may be adjudged to be entitled, and exclusive of any interest and costs, the district court may deny costs to the plaintiff and, in addition, may impose costs on the plaintiff.

(c) The district courts shall not have jurisdiction under this section of any matter within the exclusive jurisdiction of the Court of International Trade under chapter 95 of this title.

§ 1338. Patents, plant variety protection, copyrights, mask works, designs, trademarks, and unfair competition

(a) The district courts shall have original jurisdiction of any civil action arising under any Act of Congress relating to patents, plant variety protection, copyrights and trademarks. No State court shall have jurisdiction over any claim for relief arising under any Act of Congress relating to patents, plant variety protection, copyrights and trademarks. For purposes of this subsection, the term "State" includes any State of the United States, the District of Columbia, the Commonwealth of Puerto Rico, the United States Virgin Islands, American Samoa, Guam, and the Northern Mariana Islands.

(b) The district courts shall have original jurisdiction of any civil action asserting a claim of unfair competition when joined with a substantial and related claim under the copyright, patent, plant variety protection or trademark laws.

(c) Subsections (a) and (b) apply to exclusive rights in mask works under chapter 9 of title 17, and to exclusive rights in designs under chapter 13 of title 17, to the same extent as such subsections apply to copyrights.

§ 1343. Civil rights and elective franchise

(a) The district courts shall have original jurisdiction of any civil action authorized by law to be commenced by any person:

> (1) To recover damages for injury to his person or property, or because of the deprivation of any right or privilege of a citizen of the United States, by any act done in furtherance of any conspiracy mentioned in section 1985 of Title 42;
>
> (2) To recover damages from any person who fails to prevent or to aid in preventing any wrongs mentioned in section 1985 of Title 42 which he had knowledge were about to occur and power to prevent;
>
> (3) To redress the deprivation, under color of any State law, statute, ordinance, regulation, custom or usage, of any right, privilege or immunity secured by the Constitution of the United States or by any Act of Congress providing for equal rights of citizens or of all persons within the jurisdiction of the United States;
>
> (4) To recover damages or to secure equitable or other relief under any Act of Congress providing for the protection of civil rights, including the right to vote.

(b) For purposes of this section—

(1) the District of Columbia shall be considered to be a State; and

(2) any Act of Congress applicable exclusively to the District of Columbia shall be considered to be a statute of the District of Columbia.

§ 1345. United States as plaintiff

Except as otherwise provided by Act of Congress, the district courts shall have original jurisdiction of all civil actions, suits or proceedings commenced by the United States, or by any agency or officer thereof expressly authorized to sue by Act of Congress.

§ 1346. United States as defendant

(a) The district courts shall have original jurisdiction, concurrent with the United States Court of Federal Claims, of:

(1) Any civil action against the United States for the recovery of any internal-revenue tax alleged to have been erroneously or illegally assessed or collected, or any penalty claimed to have been collected without authority or any sum alleged to have been excessive or in any manner wrongfully collected under the internal-revenue laws;

(2) Any other civil action or claim against the United States, not exceeding $10,000 in amount, founded either upon the Constitution, or any Act of Congress, or any regulation of an executive department, or upon any express or implied contract with the United States, or for liquidated or unliquidated damages in cases not sounding in tort, except that the district courts shall not have jurisdiction of any civil action or claim against the United States founded upon any express or implied contract with the United States or for liquidated or unliquidated damages in cases not sounding in tort which are subject to sections 7104(b)(1) and 7107(a)(1) of title 41. For the purpose of this paragraph, an express or implied contract with the Army and Air Force Exchange Service, Navy Exchanges, Marine Corps Exchanges, Coast Guard Exchanges, or Exchange Councils of the National Aeronautics and Space Administration shall be considered an express or implied contract with the United States.

(b) (1) Subject to the provisions of chapter 171 of this title, the district courts, together with the United States District Court for the District of the Canal Zone and the District Court of the Virgin Islands, shall have exclusive jurisdiction of civil actions on claims against the United States, for money damages, accruing on and after January 1, 1945, for injury or loss of property, or personal injury or death caused by the negligent or wrongful act or omission of any employee of the Government while acting within the scope of his office or employment, under circumstances where the United States, if a private person, would be liable to the claimant in accordance with the law of the place where the act or omission occurred.

(2) No person convicted of a felony who is incarcerated while awaiting sentencing or while serving a sentence may bring a civil action against the

United States or an agency, officer, or employee of the Government, for mental or emotional injury suffered while in custody without a prior showing of physical injury.

(c) The jurisdiction conferred by this section includes jurisdiction of any set-off, counterclaim, or other claim or demand whatever on the part of the United States against any plaintiff commencing an action under this section.

(d) The district courts shall not have jurisdiction under this section of any civil action or claim for a pension.

(e) The district courts shall have original jurisdiction of any civil action against the United States provided in section 6226, 6228(a), 7426, or 7428 (in the case of the United States district court for the District of Columbia) or section 7429 of the Internal Revenue Code of 1986.

(f) The district courts shall have exclusive original jurisdiction of civil actions under section 2409a to quiet title to an estate or interest in real property in which an interest is claimed by the United States.

(g) Subject to the provisions of chapter 179, the district courts of the United States shall have exclusive jurisdiction over any civil action commenced under section 453(2) of title 3, by a covered employee under chapter 5 of such title.

§ 1367. Supplemental jurisdiction

(a) Except as provided in subsections (b) and (c) or as expressly provided otherwise by Federal statute, in any civil action of which the district courts have original jurisdiction, the district courts shall have supplemental jurisdiction over all other claims that are so related to claims in the action within such original jurisdiction that they form part of the same case or controversy under Article III of the United States Constitution. Such supplemental jurisdiction shall include claims that involve the joinder or intervention of additional parties.

(b) In any civil action of which the district courts have original jurisdiction founded solely on section 1332 of this title, the district courts shall not have supplemental jurisdiction under subsection (a) over claims by plaintiffs against persons made parties under Rule 14, 19, 20, or 24 of the Federal Rules of Civil Procedure, or over claims by persons proposed to be joined as plaintiffs under Rule 19 of such rules, or seeking to intervene as plaintiffs under Rule 24 of such rules, when exercising supplemental jurisdiction over such claims would be inconsistent with the jurisdictional requirements of section 1332.

(c) The district courts may decline to exercise supplemental jurisdiction over a claim under subsection (a) if—

(1) the claim raises a novel or complex issue of State law,

(2) the claim substantially predominates over the claim or claims over which the district court has original jurisdiction,

(3) the district court has dismissed all claims over which it has original jurisdiction, or

(4) in exceptional circumstances, there are other compelling reasons for declining jurisdiction.

(d) The period of limitations for any claim asserted under subsection (a), and for any other claim in the same action that is voluntarily dismissed at the same time as or after the dismissal of the claim under subsection (a), shall be tolled while the claim is pending and for a period of 30 days after it is dismissed unless State law provides for a longer tolling period.

(e) As used in this section, the term "State" includes the District of Columbia, the Commonwealth of Puerto Rico, and any territory or possession of the United States.

§ 1441. Removal of civil actions

(a) Generally. —Except as otherwise expressly provided by Act of Congress, any civil action brought in a State court of which the district courts of the United States have original jurisdiction, may be removed by the defendant or the defendants, to the district court of the United States for the district and division embracing the place where such action is pending.

(b) Removal based on diversity of citizenship.—

(1) In determining whether a civil action is removable on the basis of the jurisdiction under section 1332(a) of this title, the citizenship of defendants sued under fictitious names shall be disregarded.

(2) A civil action otherwise removable solely on the basis of the jurisdiction under section 1332(a) of this title may not be removed if any of the parties in interest properly joined and served as defendants is a citizen of the State in which such action is brought.

(c) Joinder of Federal law claims and State law claims.—

(1) If a civil action includes—

(A) a claim arising under the Constitution, laws, or treaties of the United States (within the meaning of section 1331 of this title), and

(B) a claim not within the original or supplemental jurisdiction of the district court or a claim that has been made nonremovable by statute, the entire action may be removed if the action would be removable without the inclusion of the claim described in subparagraph (B).

(2) Upon removal of an action described in paragraph (1), the district court shall sever from the action all claims described in paragraph (1)(B) and shall remand the severed claims to the State court from which the action was removed. Only defendants against whom a claim described in paragraph (1)(A) has been asserted are required to join in or consent to the removal under paragraph (1).

(d) Actions against foreign States.—Any civil action brought in a State court against a foreign state as defined in section 1603(a) of this title may be removed by the foreign state to the district court of the United States for the district and division embracing the place where such action is pending. Upon removal the action shall be tried by the court without jury. Where removal is based upon this subsection, the time limitations of section 1446(b) of this chapter may be enlarged at any time for cause shown.

(e) Multiparty, multiforum jurisdiction.—

(1) Notwithstanding the provisions of subsection (b) of this section, a defendant in a civil action in a State court may remove the action to the district court of the United States for the district and division embracing the place where the action is pending if—

(A) the action could have been brought in a United States district court under section 1369 of this title; or

(B) the defendant is a party to an action which is or could have been brought, in whole or in part, under section 1369 in a United States district court and arises from the same accident as the action in State court, even if the action to be removed could not have been brought in a district court as an original matter.

The removal of an action under this subsection shall be made in accordance with section 1446 of this title, except that a notice of removal may also be filed before trial of the action in State court within 30 days after the date on which the defendant first becomes a party to an action under section 1369 in a United States district court that arises from the same accident as the action in State court, or at a later time with leave of the district court.

(2) Whenever an action is removed under this subsection and the district court to which it is removed or transferred under section 1407(j) has made a liability determination requiring further proceedings as to damages, the district court shall remand the action to the State court from which it had been removed for the determination of damages, unless the court finds that, for the convenience of parties and witnesses and in the interest of justice, the action should be retained for the determination of damages.

(3) Any remand under paragraph (2) shall not be effective until 60 days after the district court has issued an order determining liability and has certified its intention to remand the removed action for the determination of damages. An appeal with respect to the liability determination of the district court may be taken during that 60-day period to the court of appeals with appellate jurisdiction over the district court. In the event a party files such an appeal, the remand shall not be effective until the appeal has been finally disposed of. Once the remand has become effective, the liability determination shall not be subject to further review by appeal or otherwise.

(4) Any decision under this subsection concerning remand for the determination of damages shall not be reviewable by appeal or otherwise.

(5) An action removed under this subsection shall be deemed to be an action under section 1369 and an action in which jurisdiction is based on section 1369 of this title for purposes of this section and sections 1407, 1697, and 1785 of this title.

(6) Nothing in this subsection shall restrict the authority of the district court to transfer or dismiss an action on the ground of inconvenient forum.

(f) Derivative removal jurisdiction.—The court to which a civil action is removed under this section is not precluded from hearing and determining any claim in such civil action because the State court from which such civil action is removed did not have jurisdiction over that claim.

§ 1442. Federal officers or agencies sued or prosecuted

(a) A civil action or criminal prosecution that is commenced in a State court and that is against or directed to any of the following may be removed by them to the district court of the United States for the district and division embracing the place wherein it is pending:

(1) The United States or any agency thereof or any officer (or any person acting under that officer) of the United States or of any agency thereof, sued in an official or individual capacity for any act under color of such office or on account of any right, title or authority claimed under any Act of Congress for the apprehension or punishment of criminals or the collection of the revenue.

(2) A property holder whose title is derived from any such officer, where such action or prosecution affects the validity of any law of the United States.

(3) Any officer of the courts of the United States, for any Act under color of office or in the performance of his duties;

(4) Any officer of either House of Congress, for any act in the discharge of his official duty under an order of such House.

(b) A personal action commenced in any State court by an alien against any citizen of a State who is, or at the time the alleged action accrued was, a civil officer of the United States and is a nonresident of such State, wherein jurisdiction is obtained by the State court by personal service of process, may be removed by the defendant to the district court of the United States for the district and division in which the defendant was served with process.

(c) Solely for purposes of determining the propriety of removal under subsection (a), a law enforcement officer, who is the defendant in a criminal prosecution, shall be deemed to have been acting under the color of his office if the officer—

(1) protected an individual in the presence of the officer from a crime of violence;

(2) provided immediate assistance to an individual who suffered, or who was threatened with, bodily harm; or

(3) prevented the escape of any individual who the officer reasonably believed to have committed, or was about to commit, in the presence of the officer, a crime of violence that resulted in, or was likely to result in, death or serious bodily injury.

(d) In this section, the following definitions apply:

(1) The terms "civil action" and "criminal prosecution" include any proceeding (whether or not ancillary to another proceeding) to the extent that in such proceeding a judicial order, including a subpoena for testimony or documents, is sought or issued. If removal is sought for a proceeding described in the previous sentence, and there is no other basis for removal, only that proceeding may be removed to the district court.

(2) The term "crime of violence" has the meaning given that term in section 16 of title 18.

(3) The term "law enforcement officer" means any employee described in subparagraph (A), (B), or (C) of section 8401(17) of title 5 and any special agent in the Diplomatic Security Service of the Department of State.

(4) The term "serious bodily injury" has the meaning given that term in section 1365 of title 18.

(5) The term "State" includes the District of Columbia, United States territories and insular possessions, and Indian country (as defined in section 1151 of title 18).

(6) The term "State court" includes the Superior Court of the District of Columbia, a court of a United States territory or insular possession, and a tribal court..

§ 1443. Civil rights cases

Any of the following civil actions or criminal prosecutions, commenced in a State court may be removed by the defendant to the district court of the United States for the district and division embracing the place wherein it is pending:

(1) Against any person who is denied or cannot enforce in the courts of such State a right under any law providing for the equal civil rights of citizens of the United States, or of all persons within the jurisdiction thereof;

(2) For any act under color of authority derived from any law providing for equal rights, or for refusing to do any act on the ground that it would be inconsistent with such law.

§ 1445. Nonremovable actions

(a) A civil action in any State court against a railroad or its receivers or trustees, arising under sections 1-4 and 5-10 of the Act of April 22, 1908 (45 U.S.C. 51-54, 55-60), may not be removed to any district court of the United States.

(b) A civil action in any State court against a carrier or its receivers or trustees to recover damages for delay, loss, or injury of shipments, arising under section 11706 or 14706 of title 49, may not be removed to any district court of the United States unless the matter in controversy exceeds $10,000, exclusive of interest and costs.

(c) A civil action in any State court arising under the workmen's compensation laws of such State may not be removed to any district court of the United States.

(d) A civil action in any State court arising under section 40302 of the Violence Against Women Act of 1994 may not be removed to any district court of the United States.

§ 1446. Procedure for removal of civil actions

(a) Generally.—A defendant or defendants desiring to remove any civil action from a State court shall file in the district court of the United States for the district and division within which such action is pending a notice of removal signed pursuant to Rule 11 of the Federal Rules of Civil Procedure and containing a short and plain statement of the grounds for removal, together with a copy of all process, pleadings, and orders served upon such defendant or defendants in such action.

(b) Requirements; generally.—

(1) The notice of removal of a civil action or proceeding shall be filed within 30 days after the receipt by the defendant, through service or otherwise, of a copy of the initial pleading setting forth the claim for relief upon which such action or proceeding is based, or within 30 days after the service of summons upon the defendant if such initial pleading has then been filed in court and is not required to be served on the defendant, whichever period is shorter.

(2) (A) When a civil action is removed solely under section 1441(a), all defendants who have been properly joined and served must join in or consent to the removal of the action.

(B) Each defendant shall have 30 days after receipt by or service on that defendant of the initial pleading or summons described in paragraph (1) to file the notice of removal.

(C) If defendants are served at different times, and a later-served defendant files a notice of removal, any earlier-served defendant may consent to the removal even though that earlier-served defendant did not previously initiate or consent to removal.

(3) Except as provided in subsection (c), if the case stated by the initial pleading is not removable, a notice of removal may be filed within 30 days after receipt by the defendant, through service or otherwise, of a copy of an amended pleading, motion, order or other paper from which it may first be ascertained that the case is one which is or has become removable.

(c) Requirements; removal based on diversity of citizenship.—(1) A case may not be removed under subsection (b)(3) on the basis of jurisdiction conferred by section 1332 more than 1 year after commencement of the action, unless the district court finds that the plaintiff has acted in bad faith in order to prevent a defendant from removing the action.

(2) If removal of a civil action is sought on the basis of the jurisdiction conferred by section 1332(a), the sum demanded in good faith in the initial pleading shall be deemed to be the amount in controversy, except that--

(A) the notice of removal may assert the amount in controversy if the initial pleading seeks--

(i) nonmonetary relief; or

(ii) a money judgment, but the State practice either does not permit demand for a specific sum or permits recovery of damages in excess of the amount demanded; and

(B) removal of the action is proper on the basis of an amount in controversy asserted under subparagraph (A) if the district court finds, by the preponderance of the evidence, that the amount in controversy exceeds the amount specified in section 1332(a).

(3) (A) If the case stated by the initial pleading is not removable solely because the amount in controversy does not exceed the amount specified in section 1332(a), information relating to the amount in controversy in the record of the State proceeding, or in responses to discovery, shall be treated as an 'other paper' under subsection (b)(3).

(B) If the notice of removal is filed more than 1 year after commencement of the action and the district court finds that the plaintiff deliberately failed to disclose the actual amount in controversy to prevent removal, that finding shall be deemed bad faith under paragraph (1).

(d) Notice to adverse parties and state court.—Promptly after the filing of such notice of removal of a civil action the defendant or defendants shall give written notice thereof to all adverse parties and shall file a copy of the notice with the clerk of such State court, which shall effect the removal and the State court shall proceed no further unless and until the case is remanded.

(e) Counterclaim in 337 proceeding.—With respect to any counterclaim removed to a district court pursuant to section 337(c) of the Tariff Act of 1930, the district court shall resolve such counterclaim in the same manner as an original complaint under the Federal Rules of Civil Procedure, except that the payment of a filing fee shall not be required in such cases and the counterclaim shall relate back to the date of the original complaint in the proceeding before the International Trade Commission under section 337 of that Act.

[(f) redesignated (e)]

(g) Where the civil action or criminal prosecution that is removable under section 1442(a) is a proceeding in which a judicial order for testimony or documents is sought or issued or sought to be enforced, the 30-day requirement of subsection (b) of this section and paragraph (1) of section 1455(b) is satisfied if the person or entity desiring to remove the proceeding files the notice of removal not later than 30 days after receiving, through service, notice of any such proceeding.

§ 1447. Procedure after removal generally

(a) In any case removed from a State court, the district court may issue all necessary orders and process to bring before it all proper parties whether served by process issued by the State court or otherwise.

(b) It may require the removing party to file with its clerk copies of all records and proceedings in such State court or may cause the same to be brought before it by writ of certiorari issued to such State court.

(c) A motion to remand the case on the basis of any defect other than lack of subject matter jurisdiction must be made within 30 days after the filing of the notice of removal under section 1446(a). If at any time before final judgment it appears that the district court lacks subject matter jurisdiction, the case shall be remanded. An order remanding the case may require payment of just costs and any actual expenses, including attorney fees, incurred as a result of the removal. A certified copy of the order of remand shall be mailed by the clerk to the clerk of the State court. The State court may thereupon proceed with such case.

(d) An order remanding a case to the State court from which it was removed is not reviewable on appeal or otherwise, except that an order remanding a case to the State court from which it was removed pursuant to section 1442 or 1443 of this title shall be reviewable by appeal or otherwise.

(e) If after removal the plaintiff seeks to join additional defendants whose joinder would destroy subject matter jurisdiction, the court may deny joinder, or permit joinder and remand the action to the State court.

§ 1455. Procedure for removal of criminal prosecutions

(a) Notice of removal.—A defendant or defendants desiring to remove any criminal prosecution from a State court shall file in the district court of the United States for the district and division within which such prosecution is pending a notice of removal signed pursuant to Rule 11 of the Federal Rules of Civil Procedure and containing a short and plain statement of the grounds for removal, together with a copy of all process, pleadings, and orders served upon such defendant or defendants in such action.

(b) Requirements.—

(1) A notice of removal of a criminal prosecution shall be filed not later than 30 days after the arraignment in the State court, or at any time before trial, whichever is earlier, except that for good cause shown the United States district court may enter an order granting the defendant or defendants leave to file the notice at a later time.

(2) A notice of removal of a criminal prosecution shall include all grounds for such removal. A failure to state grounds that exist at the time of the filing of the notice shall constitute a waiver of such grounds, and a second notice may be filed only on grounds not existing at the time of the original notice. For good cause shown, the United States district court may grant relief from the limitations of this paragraph.

(3) The filing of a notice of removal of a criminal prosecution shall not prevent the State court in which such prosecution is pending from proceeding further, except that a judgment of conviction shall not be entered unless the prosecution is first remanded.

(4) The United States district court in which such notice is filed shall examine the notice promptly. If it clearly appears on the face of the notice and any exhibits annexed thereto that removal should not be permitted, the court shall make an order for summary remand.

(5) If the United States district court does not order the summary remand of such prosecution, it shall order an evidentiary hearing to be held promptly and, after such hearing, shall make such disposition of the prosecution as justice shall require. If the United States district court determines that removal shall be permitted, it shall so notify the State court in which prosecution is pending, which shall proceed no further.

(c) Writ of habeas corpus.—If the defendant or defendants are in actual custody on process issued by the State court, the district court shall issue its writ of habeas corpus, and the marshal shall thereupon take such defendant or defendants into the marshal's custody and deliver a copy of the writ to the clerk of such State court.

§ 1500. Pendency of claims in other courts

The United States Court of Federal Claims shall not have jurisdiction of any claim for or in respect to which the plaintiff or his assignee has pending in any other court any suit or process against the United States or any person who, at the time when the cause of action alleged in such suit or process arose, was, in respect thereto, acting or professing to act, directly or indirectly under the authority of the United States.

§ 1602. Findings and declaration of purpose

The Congress finds that the determination by United States courts of the claims of foreign states to immunity from the jurisdiction of such courts would serve the interests of justice and would protect the rights of both foreign states and litigants in United States courts. Under international law, states are not immune from the jurisdiction of foreign courts insofar as their commercial activities are concerned, and their commercial property may be levied upon for the satisfaction of judgments rendered against them in connection with their commercial activities. Claims of foreign states to immunity should henceforth be decided by courts of the United States and of the States in conformity with the principles set forth in this chapter.

§ 1603. Definitions

For purposes of this chapter—

(a) A "foreign state", except as used in section 1608 of this title, includes a political subdivision of a foreign state or an agency or instrumentality of a foreign state as defined in subsection (b).

(b) An "agency or instrumentality of a foreign state" means any entity—

(1) which is a separate legal person, corporate or otherwise, and

(2) which is an organ of a foreign state or political subdivision thereof, or a majority of whose shares or other ownership interest is owned by a foreign state or political subdivision thereof, and

(3) which is neither a citizen of a State of the United States as defined in section 1332(c) and (e) of this title, nor created under the laws of any third country.

(c) The "United States" includes all territory and waters, continental or insular, subject to the jurisdiction of the United States.

(d) A "commercial activity" means either a regular course of commercial conduct or a particular commercial transaction or act. The commercial character of an activity shall be determined by reference to the nature of the course of conduct or particular transaction or act, rather than by reference to its purpose.

(e) A "commercial activity carried on in the United States by a foreign state" means commercial activity carried on by such state and having substantial contact with the United States.

§ 1604. Immunity of a foreign state from jurisdiction

Subject to existing international agreements to which the United States is a party at the time of enactment of this Act a foreign state shall be immune from the jurisdiction of the courts of the United States and of the States except as provided in sections 1605 to 1607 of this chapter.

§ 1605. General exceptions to the jurisdictional immunity of a foreign state

(a) A foreign state shall not be immune from the jurisdiction of courts of the United States or of the States in any case—

> (1) in which the foreign state has waived its immunity either explicitly or by implication, notwithstanding any withdrawal of the waiver which the foreign state may purport to effect except in accordance with the terms of the waiver;
>
> (2) in which the action is based upon a commercial activity carried on in the United States by the foreign state; or upon an act performed in the United States in connection with a commercial activity of the foreign state elsewhere; or upon an act outside the territory of the United States in connection with a commercial activity of the foreign state elsewhere and that act causes a direct effect in the United States;
>
> (3) in which rights in property taken in violation of international law are in issue and that property or any property exchanged for such property is present in the United States in connection with a commercial activity carried on in the United States by the foreign state; or that property or any property exchanged for such property is owned or operated by an agency or instrumentality of the foreign state and that agency or instrumentality is engaged in a commercial activity in the United States;
>
> (4) in which rights in property in the United States acquired by succession or gift or rights in immovable property situated in the United States are in issue;
>
> (5) not otherwise encompassed in paragraph (2) above, in which money damages are sought against a foreign state for personal injury or death, or damage to or loss of property, occurring in the United States and caused by the tortious act or omission of that foreign state or of any official or employee of that foreign state while acting within the scope of his office or employment; except this paragraph shall not apply to—

(A) any claim based upon the exercise or performance or the failure to exercise or perform a discretionary function regardless of whether the discretion be abused, or

(B) any claim arising out of malicious prosecution, abuse of process, libel, slander, misrepresentation, deceit, or interference with contract rights; or

(6) in which the action is brought, either to enforce an agreement made by the foreign state with or for the benefit of a private party to submit to arbitration all or any differences which have arisen or which may arise between the parties with respect to a defined legal relationship, whether contractual or not, concerning a subject matter capable of settlement by arbitration under the laws of the United States, or to confirm an award made pursuant to such an agreement to arbitrate, if (A) the arbitration takes place or is intended to take place in the United States, (B) the agreement or award is or may be governed by a treaty or other international agreement in force for the United States calling for the recognition and enforcement of arbitral awards, (C) the underlying claim, save for the agreement to arbitrate, could have been brought in a United States court under this section or section 1607, or (D) paragraph (1) of this subsection is otherwise applicable.

(7) Repealed.

(b) A foreign state shall not be immune from the jurisdiction of the courts of the United States in any case in which a suit in admiralty is brought to enforce a maritime lien against a vessel or cargo of the foreign state, which maritime lien is based upon a commercial activity of the foreign state: *Provided,* That—

(1) notice of the suit is given by delivery of a copy of the summons and of the complaint to the person, or his agent, having possession of the vessel or cargo against which the maritime lien is asserted; and if the vessel or cargo is arrested pursuant to process obtained on behalf of the party bringing the suit, the service of process of arrest shall be deemed to constitute valid delivery of such notice, but the party bringing the suit shall be liable for any damages sustained by the foreign state as a result of the arrest if the party bringing the suit had actual or constructive knowledge that the vessel or cargo of a foreign state was involved; and

(2) notice to the foreign state of the commencement of suit as provided in section 1608 of this title is initiated within ten days either of the delivery of notice as provided in paragraph (1) of this subsection or, in the case of a party who was unaware that the vessel or cargo of a foreign state was involved, of the date such party determined the existence of the foreign state's interest.

(c) Whenever notice is delivered under subsection (b)(1), the suit to enforce a maritime lien shall thereafter proceed and shall be heard and determined according to the principles of law and rules of practice of suits in rem whenever it appears that, had the vessel been privately owned and possessed, a suit in rem might have been maintained. A decree against the foreign state may include costs of the suit and, if the decree is for a money judgment, interest as ordered by the court, except that the court may not award judgment against the foreign state in an amount greater than the value of the vessel or cargo upon which the maritime lien arose. Such value shall be determined as of the time notice is served under subsection (b)(1). Decrees shall be subject to appeal and revision as provided in other cases of admiralty and maritime jurisdiction. Nothing shall preclude the plaintiff in any proper case from seeking relief in personam in the same action brought to enforce a maritime lien as provided in this section.

(d) A foreign state shall not be immune from the jurisdiction of the courts of the United States in any action brought to foreclose a preferred mortgage, as defined in section 31301 of title 46. Such action shall be brought, heard, and determined in accordance with the provisions of chapter 313 of title 46 and in accordance with the principles of law and rules of practice of suits in rem, whenever it appears that had the vessel been privately owned and possessed a suit in rem might have been maintained.

(e), (f) Repealed.

(g) Limitation on discovery.—

(1) In general.—

(A) Subject to paragraph (2), if an action is filed that would otherwise be barred by section 1604, but for section 1605A, the court, upon request of the Attorney General, shall stay any request, demand, or order for discovery on the United States that the Attorney General certifies would significantly interfere with a criminal investigation or prosecution, or a national security operation, related to the incident that gave rise to the cause of action, until such time as the Attorney General advises the court that such request, demand, or order will no longer so interfere.

(B) A stay under this paragraph shall be in effect during the 12-month period beginning on the date on which the court issues the order to stay discovery. The court shall renew the order to stay discovery for additional 12-month periods upon motion by the United States if the Attorney General certifies that discovery would significantly interfere with a criminal investigation or prosecution, or a national security operation, related to the incident that gave rise to the cause of action.

(2) Sunset.—

(A) Subject to subparagraph (B), no stay shall be granted or continued in effect under paragraph (1) after the date that is 10 years after the date on which the incident that gave rise to the cause of action occurred.

(B) After the period referred to in subparagraph (A), the court, upon request of the Attorney General, may stay any request, demand, or order for discovery on the United States that the court finds a substantial likelihood would—

(i) create a serious threat of death or serious bodily injury to any person;

(ii) adversely affect the ability of the United States to work in cooperation with foreign and international law enforcement agencies in investigating violations of United States law; or

(iii) obstruct the criminal case related to the incident that gave rise to the cause of action or undermine the potential for a conviction in such case.

(3) Evaluation of evidence.—The court's evaluation of any request for a stay under this subsection filed by the Attorney General shall be conducted ex parte and in camera.

(4) Bar on motions to dismiss.—A stay of discovery under this subsection shall constitute a bar to the granting of a motion to dismiss under rules 12(b)(6) and 56 of the Federal Rules of Civil Procedure.

(5) Construction.—Nothing in this subsection shall prevent the United States from seeking protective orders or asserting privileges ordinarily available to the United States.

§ 1606. Extent of liability

As to any claim for relief with respect to which a foreign state is not entitled to immunity under section 1605 or 1607 of this chapter, the foreign state shall be liable in the same manner and to the same extent as a private individual under like circumstances; but a foreign state except for an agency or instrumentality thereof shall not be liable for punitive damages; if, however, in any case wherein death was caused, the law of the place where the action or omission occurred provides, or has been construed to provide, for damages only punitive in nature, the foreign state shall be liable for actual or compensatory damages measured by the pecuniary injuries resulting from such death which were incurred by the persons for whose benefit the action was brought.

§ 1651. Writs

(a) The Supreme Court and all courts established by Act of Congress may issue all writs necessary or appropriate in aid of their respective jurisdictions and agreeable to the usages and principles of law.

(b) An alternative writ or rule nisi may be issued by a justice or judge of a court which has jurisdiction.

§ 1652. State laws as rules of decision

The laws of the several states, except where the Constitution or treaties of the United States or Acts of Congress otherwise require or provide, shall be regarded as rules of decision in civil actions in the courts of the United States, in cases where they apply.

§ 1738. State and Territorial statutes and judicial proceedings; full faith and credit

The Acts of the legislature of any State, Territory, or Possession of the United States, or copies thereof, shall be authenticated by affixing the seal of such State, Territory or Possession thereto.

The records and judicial proceedings of any court of any such State, Territory or Possession, or copies thereof, shall be proved or admitted in other courts within the United States and its Territories and Possessions by the attestation of the clerk and seal of the court annexed, if a seal exists, together with a certificate of a judge of the court that the said attestation is in proper form.

Such Acts, records and judicial proceedings or copies thereof, so authenticated, shall have the same full faith and credit in every court within the United States and its Territories and Possessions as they have by law or usage in the courts of such State, Territory or Possession from which they are taken.

§ 1932. Revocation of earned release credit1[2]

In any civil action brought by an adult convicted of a crime and confined in a Federal correctional facility, the court may order the revocation of such earned good time credit under section 3624(b) of title 18, United States Code, that has not yet vested, if, on its own motion or the motion of any party, the court finds that—

(1) the claim was filed for a malicious purpose;

(2) the claim was filed solely to harass the party against which it was filed; or

(3) the claimant testifies falsely or otherwise knowingly presents false evidence or information to the court.

§ 2071. Rule-making power generally

(a) The Supreme Court and all courts established by Act of Congress may from time to time prescribe rules for the conduct of their business. Such rules shall be consistent with Acts of Congress and rules of practice and procedure prescribed under section 2072 of this title.

(b) Any rule prescribed by a court, other than the Supreme Court, under subsection (a) shall be prescribed only after giving appropriate public notice and an opportunity for comment. Such rule shall take effect upon the date specified by the prescribing court and shall have such effect on pending proceedings as the prescribing court may order.

---

1 Congress, in its wisdom, has enacted two § 1932s (your tax dollars at work). The other one concerns the Judicial Panel on Multidistrict Litigation and authorizes the Judicial Conference of the United States to set the fees and costs that the Panel may collect.

(c) (1) A rule of a district court prescribed under subsection (a) shall remain in effect unless modified or abrogated by the judicial council of the relevant circuit.

(2) Any other rule prescribed by a court other than the Supreme Court under subsection (a) shall remain in effect unless modified or abrogated by the Judicial Conference.

(d) Copies of rules prescribed under subsection (a) by a district court shall be furnished to the judicial council, and copies of all rules prescribed by a court other than the Supreme Court under subsection (a) shall be furnished to the director of the Administrative Office of the United States Courts and made available to the public.

(e) If the prescribing court determines that there is an immediate need for a rule, such court may proceed under this section without public notice and opportunity for comment, but such court shall promptly thereafter afford such notice and opportunity for comment.

(f) No rule may be prescribed by a district court other than under this section.

§ 2072. Rules of procedure and evidence; power to prescribe

(a) The Supreme Court shall have the power to prescribe general rules of practice and procedure and rules of evidence for cases in the United States district courts (including proceedings before magistrates thereof) and courts of appeals.

(b) Such rules shall not abridge, enlarge or modify any substantive right. All laws in conflict with such rules shall be of no further force or effect after such rules have taken effect.

(c) Such rules may define when a ruling of a district court is final for the purposes of appeal under section 1291 of this title.

§ 2201. Creation of remedy

(a) In a case of actual controversy within its jurisdiction, except with respect to Federal taxes other than actions brought under section 7428 of the Internal Revenue Code of 1986, a proceeding under section 505 or 1146 of title 11, or in any civil action involving an antidumping or countervailing duty proceeding regarding a class or kind of merchandise of a free trade area country (as defined in section 516A(f)(10) of the Tariff Act of 1930), as determined by the administering authority, any court of the United States, upon the filing of an appropriate pleading, may declare the rights and other legal relations of any interested party seeking such declaration, whether or not further relief is or could be sought. Any such declaration shall have the force and effect of a final judgment or decree and shall be reviewable as such.

(b) For limitations on actions brought with respect to drug patents see section 505 or 512 of the Federal Food, Drug, and Cosmetic Act, or section 351 of the Public Health Service Act.

§ 2202. Further relief

Further necessary or proper relief based on a declaratory judgment or decree may be granted, after reasonable notice and hearing, against any adverse party whose rights have been determined by such judgment.

§ 2241. Power to grant writ

(a) Writs of habeas corpus may be granted by the Supreme Court, any justice thereof, the district courts and any circuit judge within their respective jurisdictions. The order of a circuit judge shall be entered in the records of the district court of the district wherein the restraint complained of is had.

(b) The Supreme Court, any justice thereof, and any circuit judge may decline to entertain an application for a writ of habeas corpus and may transfer the application for hearing and determination to the district court having jurisdiction to entertain it.

(c) The writ of habeas corpus shall not extend to a prisoner unless—

(1) He is in custody under or by color of the authority of the United States or is committed for trial before some court thereof; or

(2) He is in custody for an act done or omitted in pursuance of an Act of Congress, or an order, process, judgment or decree of a court or judge of the United States; or

(3) He is in custody in violation of the Constitution or laws or treaties of the United States; or

(4) He, being a citizen of a foreign state and domiciled therein is in custody for an act done or omitted under any alleged right, title, authority, privilege, protection, or exemption claimed under the commission, order or sanction of any foreign state, or under color thereof, the validity and effect of which depend upon the law of nations; or

(5) It is necessary to bring him into court to testify or for trial.

(d) Where an application for a writ of habeas corpus is made by a person in custody under the judgment and sentence of a State court of a State which contains two or more Federal judicial districts, the application may be filed in the district court for the district wherein such person is in custody or in the district court for the district within which the State court was held which convicted and sentenced him and each of such district courts shall have concurrent jurisdiction to entertain the application. The district court for the district wherein such an application is filed in the exercise of its discretion and in furtherance of justice may transfer the application to the other district court for hearing and determination.

(e) (1) No court, justice, or judge shall have jurisdiction to hear or consider an application for a writ of habeas corpus filed by or on behalf of an alien detained by the United States who has been determined by the United States to have been properly detained as an enemy combatant or is awaiting such determination.

(2) Except as provided in paragraphs (2) and (3) of section 1005(e) of the Detainee Treatment Act of 2005 (10 U.S.C. 801 note), no court, justice, or judge shall have jurisdiction to hear or consider any other action against the United States or its agents relating to any aspect of the detention, transfer, treatment, trial, or conditions of confinement of an alien who is or was detained by the United States and has been determined by the United States to have been properly detained as an enemy combatant or is awaiting such determination.

§ 2242. Application

Application for a writ of habeas corpus shall be in writing signed and verified by the person for whose relief it is intended or by someone acting in his behalf.

It shall allege the facts concerning the applicant's commitment or detention, the name of the person who has custody over him and by virtue of what claim or authority, if known.

It may be amended or supplemented as provided in the rules of procedure applicable to civil actions.

If addressed to the Supreme Court, a Justice thereof or a circuit judge it shall state the reasons for not making application to the district court of the district in which the applicant is held.

§ 2243. Issuance of writ; return; hearing; decision

A court, justice or judge entertaining an application for a writ of habeas corpus shall forthwith award the writ or issue an order directing the respondent to show cause why the writ should not be granted, unless it appears from the application that the applicant or person detained is not entitled thereto.

The writ, or order to show cause shall be directed to the person having custody of the person detained. It shall be returned within three days unless for good cause additional time, not exceeding twenty days, is allowed.

The person to whom the writ or order is directed shall make a return certifying the true cause of the detention.

When the writ or order is returned a day shall be set for hearing, not more than five days after the return unless for good cause additional time is allowed.

Unless the application for the writ and the return present only issues of law the person to whom the writ is directed shall be required to produce at the hearing the body of the person detained.

The applicant or the person detained may, under oath, deny any of the facts set forth in the return or allege any other material facts.

The return and all suggestions made against it may be amended, by leave of court, before or after being filed.

The court shall summarily hear and determine the facts, and dispose of the matter as law and justice require.

§ 2244. Finality of determination

(a) No circuit or district judge shall be required to entertain an application for a writ of habeas corpus to inquire into the detention of a person pursuant to a judgment of a court of the United States if it appears that the legality of such detention has been determined by a judge or court of the United States on a prior application for a writ of habeas corpus, except as provided in section 2255.

(b) (1) A claim presented in a second or successive habeas corpus application under section 2254 that was presented in a prior application shall be dismissed.

(2) A claim presented in a second or successive habeas corpus application under section 2254 that was not presented in a prior application shall be dismissed unless—

(A) the applicant shows that the claim relies on a new rule of constitutional law, made retroactive to cases on collateral review by the Supreme Court, that was previously unavailable; or

(B) (i) the factual predicate for the claim could not have been discovered previously through the exercise of due diligence; and

(ii) the facts underlying the claim, if proven and viewed in light of the evidence as a whole, would be sufficient to establish by clear and convincing evidence that, but for constitutional error, no reasonable factfinder would have found the applicant guilty of the underlying offense.

(3) (A) Before a second or successive application permitted by this section is filed in the district court, the applicant shall move in the appropriate court of appeals for an order authorizing the district court to consider the application.

(B) A motion in the court of appeals for an order authorizing the district court to consider a second or successive application shall be determined by a three-judge panel of the court of appeals.

(C) The court of appeals may authorize the filing of a second or successive application only if it determines that the application makes a prima facie showing that the application satisfies the requirements of this subsection.

(D) The court of appeals shall grant or deny the authorization to file a second or successive application not later than 30 days after the filing of the motion.

(E) The grant or denial of an authorization by a court of appeals to file a second or successive application shall not be appealable and shall not be the subject of a petition for rehearing or for a writ of certiorari.

(4) A district court shall dismiss any claim presented in a second or successive application that the court of appeals has authorized to be filed unless the applicant shows that the claim satisfies the requirements of this section.

(c) In a habeas corpus proceeding brought in behalf of a person in custody pursuant to the judgment of a State court, a prior judgment of the Supreme Court of the United States on an appeal or review by a writ of certiorari at the instance of the prisoner of the decision of such State court, shall be conclusive as to all issues of fact or law with respect to an asserted denial of a Federal right which constitutes ground for discharge in a habeas corpus proceeding, actually adjudicated by the Supreme Court therein, unless the applicant for the writ of habeas corpus shall plead and the court shall find the existence of a material and controlling fact which did not appear in the record of the proceeding in the Supreme Court and the court shall further find that the applicant for the writ of habeas corpus could not have caused such fact to appear in such record by the exercise of reasonable diligence.

(d) (1) A 1-year period of limitation shall apply to an application for a writ of habeas corpus by a person in custody pursuant to the judgment of a State court. The limitation period shall run from the latest of—

(A) the date on which the judgment became final by the conclusion of direct review or the expiration of the time for seeking such review;

(B) the date on which the impediment to filing an application created by State action in violation of the Constitution or laws of the United States is removed, if the applicant was prevented from filing by such State action;

(C) the date on which the constitutional right asserted was initially recognized by the Supreme Court, if the right has been newly recognized by the Supreme Court and made retroactively applicable to cases on collateral review; or

(D) the date on which the factual predicate of the claim or claims presented could have been discovered through the exercise of due diligence.

(2) The time during which a properly filed application for State post-conviction or other collateral review with respect to the pertinent judgment or claim is pending shall not be counted toward any period of limitation under this subsection.

§ 2245. Certificate of trial judge admissible in evidence

On the hearing of an application for a writ of habeas corpus to inquire into the legality of the detention of a person pursuant to a judgment the certificate of the judge who presided at the trial resulting in the judgment, setting forth the facts occurring at the trial, shall be admissible in evidence. Copies of the certificate shall be filed with the court in which the application is pending and in the court in which the trial took place.

§ 2246. Evidence; depositions; affidavits

On application for a writ of habeas corpus, evidence may be taken orally or by deposition, or, in the discretion of the judge, by affidavit. If affidavits are admitted any party shall have the right to propound written interrogatories to the affiants, or to file answering affidavits.

§ 2247. Documentary evidence

On application for a writ of habeas corpus documentary evidence, transcripts of proceedings upon arraignment, plea and sentence and a transcript of the oral testimony introduced on any previous similar application by or in behalf of the same petitioner, shall be admissible in evidence.

§ 2248. Return or answer; conclusiveness

The allegations of a return to the writ of habeas corpus or of an answer to an order to show cause in a habeas corpus proceeding, if not traversed, shall be accepted as true except to the extent that the judge finds from the evidence that they are not true.

§ 2249. Certified copies of indictment, plea and judgment; duty of respondent

On application for a writ of habeas corpus to inquire into the detention of any person pursuant to a judgment of a court of the United States, the respondent shall promptly file with the court certified copies of the indictment, plea of petitioner and the judgment, or such of them as may be material to the questions raised, if the petitioner fails to attach them to his petition, and same shall be attached to the return to the writ, or to the answer to the order to show cause.

§ 2250. Indigent petitioner entitled to documents without cost

If on any application for a writ of habeas corpus an order has been made permitting the petitioner to prosecute the application in forma pauperis, the clerk of any court of the United States shall furnish to the petitioner without cost certified copies of such documents or parts of the record on file in his office as may be required by order of the judge before whom the application is pending.

§ 2251. Stay of State court proceedings

(a) In general.—

(1) Pending matters.—A justice or judge of the United States before whom a habeas corpus proceeding is pending, may, before final judgment or after final judgment of discharge, or pending appeal, stay any proceeding against the person detained in any State court or by or under the authority of any State for any matter involved in the habeas corpus proceeding.

(2) Matter not pending.—For purposes of this section, a habeas corpus proceeding is not pending until the application is filed.

(3) Application for appointment of counsel.—If a State prisoner sentenced to death applies for appointment of counsel pursuant to section 3599(a)(2) of title 18 in a court that would have jurisdiction to entertain a habeas corpus application regarding that sentence, that court may stay execution of the sentence of death, but such stay shall terminate not later than 90 days after counsel is appointed or the application for appointment of counsel is withdrawn or denied.

(b) No further proceedings.—After the granting of such a stay, any such proceeding in any State court or by or under the authority of any State shall be void. If no stay is granted, any such proceeding shall be as valid as if no habeas corpus proceedings or appeal were pending.

§ 2252. Notice

Prior to the hearing of a habeas corpus proceeding in behalf of a person in custody of State officers or by virtue of State laws notice shall be served on the attorney general or other appropriate officer of such State as the justice or judge at the time of issuing the writ shall direct.

§ 2253. Appeal

(a) In a habeas corpus proceeding or a proceeding under section 2255 before a district judge, the final order shall be subject to review, on appeal, by the court of appeals for the circuit in which the proceeding is held.

(b) There shall be no right of appeal from a final order in a proceeding to test the validity of a warrant to remove to another district or place for commitment or trial a person charged with a criminal offense against the United States, or to test the validity of such person's detention pending removal proceedings.

(c) (1) Unless a circuit justice or judge issues a certificate of appealability, an appeal may not be taken to the court of appeals from—

(A) the final order in a habeas corpus proceeding in which the detention complained of arises out of process issued by a State court; or

(B) the final order in a proceeding under section 2255.

(2) A certificate of appealability may issue under paragraph (1) only if the applicant has made a substantial showing of the denial of a constitutional right.

(3) The certificate of appealability under paragraph (1) shall indicate which specific issue or issues satisfy the showing required by paragraph (2).

§ 2254. State custody; remedies in Federal courts

(a) The Supreme Court, a Justice thereof, a circuit judge, or a district court shall entertain an application for a writ of habeas corpus in behalf of a person in custody pursuant to the judgment of a State court only on the ground that he is in custody in violation of the Constitution or laws or treaties of the United States.

(b) (1) An application for a writ of habeas corpus on behalf of a person in custody pursuant to the judgment of a State court shall not be granted unless it appears that—

(A) the applicant has exhausted the remedies available in the courts of the State; or

(B) (i) there is an absence of available State corrective process; or

(ii) circumstances exist that render such process ineffective to protect the rights of the applicant.

(2) An application for a writ of habeas corpus may be denied on the merits, notwithstanding the failure of the applicant to exhaust the remedies available in the courts of the State.

(3) A State shall not be deemed to have waived the exhaustion requirement or be estopped from reliance upon the requirement unless the State, through counsel, expressly waives the requirement.

(c) An applicant shall not be deemed to have exhausted the remedies available in the courts of the State, within the meaning of this section, if he has the right under the law of the State to raise, by any available procedure, the question presented.

(d) An application for a writ of habeas corpus on behalf of a person in custody pursuant to the judgment of a State court shall not be granted with respect to any claim that was adjudicated on the merits in State court proceedings unless the adjudication of the claim—

(1) resulted in a decision that was contrary to, or involved an unreasonable application of, clearly established Federal law, as determined by the Supreme Court of the United States; or

(2) resulted in a decision that was based on an unreasonable determination of the facts in light of the evidence presented in the State court proceeding.

(e) (1) In a proceeding instituted by an application for a writ of habeas corpus by a person in custody pursuant to the judgment of a State court, a determination of a factual issue made by a State court shall be presumed to be correct. The applicant shall have the burden of rebutting the presumption of correctness by clear and convincing evidence.

(2) If the applicant has failed to develop the factual basis of a claim in State court proceedings, the court shall not hold an evidentiary hearing on the claim unless the applicant shows that—

(A) the claim relies on —

(i) a new rule of constitutional law, made retroactive to cases on collateral review by the Supreme Court, that was previously unavailable; or

(ii) a factual predicate that could not have been previously discovered through the exercise of due diligence; and

(B) the facts underlying the claim would be sufficient to establish by clear and convincing evidence that but for constitutional error, no reasonable factfinder would have found the applicant guilty of the underlying offense.

(f) If the applicant challenges the sufficiency of the evidence adduced in such State court proceeding to support the State court's determination of a factual issue made therein, the applicant, if able, shall produce that part of the record pertinent to a determination of the sufficiency of the evidence to support such determination. If the applicant, because of indigency or other reason is unable to produce such part of the record, then the State shall produce such part of the record and the Federal court shall direct the State to do so by order directed to an appropriate State official. If the State cannot provide such pertinent part of the record, then the court shall determine under the existing facts and circumstances what weight shall be given to the State court's factual determination.

(g) A copy of the official records of the State court, duly certified by the clerk of such court to be a true and correct copy of a finding, judicial opinion, or other reliable written indicia showing such a factual determination by the State court shall be admissible in the Federal court proceeding.

(h) Except as provided in section 408 of the Controlled Substances Act, in all proceedings brought under this section, and any subsequent proceedings on review, the court may appoint counsel for an applicant who is or becomes financially unable to afford counsel, except as provided by a rule promulgated by the Supreme Court pursuant to statutory authority. Appointment of counsel under this section shall be governed by section 3006A of title 18.

(i) The ineffectiveness or incompetence of counsel during Federal or State collateral post-conviction proceedings shall not be a ground for relief in a proceeding arising under section 2254.

§ 2255. Federal custody; remedies on motion attacking sentence

(a) A prisoner in custody under sentence of a court established by Act of Congress claiming the right to be released upon the ground that the sentence was imposed in violation of the Constitution or laws of the United States, or that the court was without jurisdiction to impose such sentence, or that the sentence was in excess of the maximum authorized by law, or is otherwise subject to collateral attack, may move the court which imposed the sentence to vacate, set aside or correct the sentence.

(b) Unless the motion and the files and records of the case conclusively show that the prisoner is entitled to no relief, the court shall cause notice thereof to be served upon the United States attorney, grant a prompt hearing thereon, determine the issues and make findings of fact and conclusions of law with respect thereto. If the court finds that the judgment was rendered without jurisdiction, or that the sentence imposed was not authorized by law or otherwise open to collateral attack, or that there has been such a denial or infringement of the constitutional rights of the prisoner as to render the judgment vulnerable to collateral attack, the court shall vacate and set the judgment aside and shall discharge the prisoner or resentence him or grant a new trial or correct the sentence as may appear appropriate.

(c) A court may entertain and determine such motion without requiring the production of the prisoner at the hearing.

(d) An appeal may be taken to the court of appeals from the order entered on the motion as from a final judgment on application for a writ of habeas corpus.

(e) An application for a writ of habeas corpus in behalf of a prisoner who is authorized to apply for relief by motion pursuant to this section, shall not be entertained if it appears that the applicant has failed to apply for relief, by motion, to the court which sentenced him, or that such court has denied him relief, unless it also appears that the remedy by motion is inadequate or ineffective to test the legality of his detention.

(f) A 1-year period of limitation shall apply to a motion under this section. The limitation period shall run from the latest of—

(1) the date on which the judgment of conviction becomes final;

(2) the date on which the impediment to making a motion created by governmental action in violation of the Constitution or laws of the United States is removed, if the movant was prevented from making a motion by such governmental action;

(3) the date on which the right asserted was initially recognized by the Supreme Court, if that right has been newly recognized by the Supreme Court and made retroactively applicable to cases on collateral review; or

(4) the date on which the facts supporting the claim or claims presented could have been discovered through the exercise of due diligence.

(g) Except as provided in section 408 of the Controlled Substances Act, in all proceedings brought under this section, and any subsequent proceedings on review, the court may appoint counsel, except as provided by a rule promulgated by the Supreme Court pursuant to statutory authority. Appointment of counsel under this section shall be governed by section 3006A of title 18.

(h) A second or successive motion must be certified as provided in section 2244 by a panel of the appropriate court of appeals to contain—

(1) newly discovered evidence that, if proven and viewed in light of the evidence as a whole, would be sufficient to establish by clear and convincing evidence that no reasonable factfinder would have found the movant guilty of the offense; or

(2) a new rule of constitutional law, made retroactive to cases on collateral review by the Supreme Court, that was previously unavailable.

§ 2261. Prisoners in State custody subject to capital sentence; appointment of counsel; requirement of rule of court or statute; procedures for appointment

(a) This chapter shall apply to cases arising under section 2254 brought by prisoners in State custody who are subject to a capital sentence. It shall apply only if the provisions of subsections (b) and (c) are satisfied.

(b) Counsel.—This chapter is applicable if—

(1) the Attorney General of the United States certifies that a State has established a mechanism for providing counsel in postconviction proceedings as provided in section 2265; and

(2) counsel was appointed pursuant to that mechanism, petitioner validly waived counsel, petitioner retained counsel, or petitioner was found not to be indigent.

(c) Any mechanism for the appointment, compensation, and reimbursement of counsel as provided in subsection (b) must offer counsel to all State prisoners under capital sentence and must provide for the entry of an order by a court of record—

(1) appointing one or more counsels to represent the prisoner upon a finding that the prisoner is indigent and accepted the offer or is unable competently to decide whether to accept or reject the offer;

(2) finding, after a hearing if necessary, that the prisoner rejected the offer of counsel and made the decision with an understanding of its legal consequences; or

(3) denying the appointment of counsel upon a finding that the prisoner is not indigent.

(d) No counsel appointed pursuant to subsections (b) and (c) to represent a State prisoner under capital sentence shall have previously represented the prisoner at trial in the case for which the appointment is made unless the prisoner and counsel expressly request continued representation.

(e) The ineffectiveness or incompetence of counsel during State or Federal post-conviction proceedings in a capital case shall not be a ground for relief in a proceeding arising under section 2254. This limitation shall not preclude the appointment of different counsel, on the court's own motion or at the request of the prisoner, at any phase of State or Federal post-conviction proceedings on the basis of the ineffectiveness or incompetence of counsel in such proceedings.

§ 2262. Mandatory stay of execution; duration; limits on stays of execution; successive petitions

(a) Upon the entry in the appropriate State court of record of an order under section 2261(c), a warrant or order setting an execution date for a State prisoner shall be stayed upon application to any court that would have jurisdiction over any proceedings filed under section 2254. The application shall recite that the State has invoked the post-conviction review procedures of this chapter and that the scheduled execution is subject to stay.

(b) A stay of execution granted pursuant to subsection (a) shall expire if—

(1) a State prisoner fails to file a habeas corpus application under section 2254 within the time required in section 2263;

(2) before a court of competent jurisdiction, in the presence of counsel, unless the prisoner has competently and knowingly waived such counsel, and after having been advised of the consequences, a State prisoner under capital sentence waives the right to pursue habeas corpus review under section 2254; or

(3) a State prisoner files a habeas corpus petition under section 2254 within the time required by section 2263 and fails to make a substantial showing of the denial of a Federal right or is denied relief in the district court or at any subsequent stage of review.

(c) If one of the conditions in subsection (b) has occurred, no Federal court thereafter shall have the authority to enter a stay of execution in the case, unless the court of appeals approves the filing of a second or successive application under section 2244(b).

§ 2263. Filing of habeas corpus application; time requirements; tolling rules

(a) Any application under this chapter for habeas corpus relief under section 2254 must be filed in the appropriate district court not later than 180 days after final State court affirmance of the conviction and sentence on direct review or the expiration of the time for seeking such review.

(b) The time requirements established by subsection (a) shall be tolled—

(1) from the date that a petition for certiorari is filed in the Supreme Court until the date of final disposition of the petition if a State prisoner files the petition to secure review by the Supreme Court of the affirmance of a capital sentence on direct review by the court of last resort of the State or other final State court decision on direct review;

(2) from the date on which the first petition for post-conviction review or other collateral relief is filed until the final State court disposition of such petition; and

(3) during an additional period not to exceed 30 days, if—

(A) a motion for an extension of time is filed in the Federal district court that would have jurisdiction over the case upon the filing of a habeas corpus application under section 2254; and

(B) a showing of good cause is made for the failure to file the habeas corpus application within the time period established by this section.

§ 2264. Scope of Federal review; district court adjudications

(a) Whenever a State prisoner under capital sentence files a petition for habeas corpus relief to which this chapter applies, the district court shall only consider a claim or claims that have been raised and decided on the merits in the State courts, unless the failure to raise the claim properly is—

(1) the result of State action in violation of the Constitution or laws of the United States;

(2) the result of the Supreme Court's recognition of a new Federal right that is made retroactively applicable; or

(3) based on a factual predicate that could not have been discovered through the exercise of due diligence in time to present the claim for State or Federal post-conviction review.

(b) Following review subject to subsections (a), (d), and (e) of section 2254, the court shall rule on the claims properly before it.

§ 2265. Certification and judicial review

(a) Certification.—

(1) In general.—If requested by an appropriate State official, the Attorney General of the United States shall determine—

(A) whether the State has established a mechanism for the appointment, compensation, and payment of reasonable litigation expenses of competent counsel in State postconviction proceedings brought by indigent prisoners who have been sentenced to death;

(B) the date on which the mechanism described in subparagraph (A) was established; and

(C) whether the State provides standards of competency for the appointment of counsel in proceedings described in subparagraph (A).

(2) Effective date.—The date the mechanism described in paragraph (1)(A) was established shall be the effective date of the certification under this subsection.

(3) Only express requirements.—There are no requirements for certification or for application of this chapter other than those expressly stated in this chapter.

(b) Regulations.—The Attorney General shall promulgate regulations to implement the certification procedure under subsection (a).

(c) Review of certification.—

(1) In general.—The determination by the Attorney General regarding whether to certify a State under this section is subject to review exclusively as provided under chapter 158 of this title.

(2) Venue.—The Court of Appeals for the District of Columbia Circuit shall have exclusive jurisdiction over matters under paragraph (1), subject to review by the Supreme Court under section 2350 of this title.

(3) Standard of review.—The determination by the Attorney General regarding whether to certify a State under this section shall be subject to de novo review.

§ 2266. Limitation periods for determining applications and motions

(a) The adjudication of any application under section 2254 that is subject to this chapter, and the adjudication of any motion under section 2255 by a person under sentence of death, shall be given priority by the district court and by the court of appeals over all noncapital matters.

(b)(1)(A) A district court shall render a final determination and enter a final judgment on any application for a writ of habeas corpus brought under this chapter in a capital case not later than 450 days after the date on which the application is filed, or 60 days after the date on which the case is submitted for decision, whichever is earlier.

(B) A district court shall afford the parties at least 120 days in which to complete all actions, including the preparation of all pleadings and briefs, and if necessary, a hearing, prior to the submission of the case for decision.

(C)(i) A district court may delay for not more than one additional 30-day period beyond the period specified in subparagraph (A), the rendering of a determination of an application for a writ of habeas corpus if the court issues a written order making a finding, and stating the reasons for the finding, that the ends of justice that would be served by allowing the delay outweigh the best interests of the public and the applicant in a speedy disposition of the application.

(ii) The factors, among others, that a court shall consider in determining whether a delay in the disposition of an application is warranted are as follows:

(I) Whether the failure to allow the delay would be likely to result in a miscarriage of justice.

(II) Whether the case is so unusual or so complex, due to the number of defendants, the nature of the prosecution, or the existence of novel questions of fact or law, that it is unreasonable to expect adequate briefing within the time limitations established by subparagraph (A).

(III) Whether the failure to allow a delay in a case that, taken as a whole, is not so unusual or so complex as described in subclause (II), but would otherwise deny the applicant reasonable time to obtain counsel, would unreasonably deny the applicant or the government continuity of counsel, or would deny counsel for the applicant or the government the reasonable time necessary for effective preparation, taking into account the exercise of due diligence.

(iii) No delay in disposition shall be permissible because of general congestion of the court's calendar.

(iv) The court shall transmit a copy of any order issued under clause (i) to the Director of the Administrative Office of the United States Courts for inclusion in the report under paragraph (5).

(2) The time limitations under paragraph (1) shall apply to—

(A) an initial application for a writ of habeas corpus;

(B) any second or successive application for a writ of habeas corpus; and

(C) any redetermination of an application for a writ of habeas corpus following a remand by the court of appeals or the Supreme Court for further proceedings, in which case the limitation period shall run from the date the remand is ordered.

(3) (A) The time limitations under this section shall not be construed to entitle an applicant to a stay of execution, to which the applicant would otherwise not be entitled, for the purpose of litigating any application or appeal.

(B) No amendment to an application for a writ of habeas corpus under this chapter shall be permitted after the filing of the answer to the application, except on the grounds specified in section 2244(b).

(4) (A) The failure of a court to meet or comply with a time limitation under this section shall not be a ground for granting relief from a judgment of conviction or sentence.

(B) The State may enforce a time limitation under this section by petitioning for a writ of mandamus to the court of appeals. The court of appeals shall act on the petition for a writ of mandamus not later than 30 days after the filing of the petition.

(5) (A) The Administrative Office of the United States Courts shall submit to Congress an annual report on the compliance by the district courts with the time limitations under this section.

(B) The report described in subparagraph (A) shall include copies of the orders submitted by the district courts under paragraph (1)(B)(iv).

(c) (1) (A) A court of appeals shall hear and render a final determination of any appeal of an order granting or denying, in whole or in part, an application brought under this chapter in a capital case not later than 120 days after the date on which the reply brief is filed, or if no reply brief is filed, not later than 120 days after the date on which the answering brief is filed.

(B) (i) A court of appeals shall decide whether to grant a petition for rehearing or other request for rehearing en banc not later than 30 days after the date on which the petition for rehearing is filed unless a responsive pleading is required, in which case the court shall decide whether to grant the petition not later than 30 days after the date on which the responsive pleading is filed.

(ii) If a petition for rehearing or rehearing en banc is granted, the court of appeals shall hear and render a final determination of the appeal not later than 120 days after the date on which the order granting rehearing or rehearing en banc is entered.

(2) The time limitations under paragraph (1) shall apply to—

(A) an initial application for a writ of habeas corpus;

(B) any second or successive application for a writ of habeas corpus; and

(C) any redetermination of an application for a writ of habeas corpus or related appeal following a remand by the court of appeals en banc or the Supreme Court for further proceedings, in which case the limitation period shall run from the date the remand is ordered.

(3) The time limitations under this section shall not be construed to entitle an applicant to a stay of execution, to which the applicant would otherwise not be entitled, for the purpose of litigating any application or appeal.

(4) (A) The failure of a court to meet or comply with a time limitation under this section shall not be a ground for granting relief from a judgment of conviction or sentence.

(B) The State may enforce a time limitation under this section by applying for a writ of mandamus to the Supreme Court.

(5) The Administrative Office of the United States Courts shall submit to Congress an annual report on the compliance by the courts of appeals with the time limitations under this section.

§ 2283. Stay of State court proceedings

A court of the United States may not grant an injunction to stay proceedings in a State court except as expressly authorized by Act of Congress, or where necessary in aid of its jurisdiction, or to protect or effectuate its judgments.

Appendix D

Excerpts from Title 42, United States Code Annotated

§ 1981. Equal rights under the law[3]

(a) Statement of equal rights

All persons within the jurisdiction of the United States shall have the same right in every State and Territory to make and enforce contracts, to sue, be parties, give evidence, and to the full and equal benefit of all laws and proceedings for the security of persons and property as is enjoyed by white citizens, and shall be subject to like punishment, pains, penalties, taxes, licenses, and exactions of every kind, and to no other.

(b) "Make and enforce contracts" defined

For purposes of this section, the term "make and enforce contracts" includes the making, performance, modification, and termination of contracts, and the enjoyment of all benefits, privileges, terms, and conditions of the contractual relationship.

(c) Protection against impairment

The rights protected by this section are protected against impairment by nongovernmental discrimination and impairment under color of State law.

§ 1982. Property rights of citizens

All citizens of the United States shall have the same right, in every State and Territory, as is enjoyed by white citizens thereof to inherit, purchase, lease, sell, hold, and convey real and personal property.

3 Keller v. City of Fremont, 853 F.Supp.2d 959 (D. Neb. 2012), ruled that the Immigration Control and Reform Act of 1986 implicitly repealed § 1981 to the extent that that section would otherwise have protected the entitlement of undocumented aliens to enter into contracts.

§ 1983. Civil action for deprivation of rights

Every person who, under color of any statute, ordinance, regulation, custom, or usage, of any State or Territory or the District of Columbia, subjects, or causes to be subjected, any citizen of the United States or other person within the jurisdiction thereof to the deprivation of any rights, privileges, or immunities secured by the Constitution and laws, shall be liable to the party injured in an action at law, suit in equity, or other proper proceeding for redress, except that in any action brought against a judicial officer for an act or omission taken in such officer's judicial capacity, injunctive relief shall not be granted unless a declaratory decree was violated or declaratory relief was unavailable. For the purposes of this section, any Act of Congress applicable exclusively to the District of Columbia shall be considered to be a statute of the District of Columbia.

§ 1985. Conspiracy to interfere with civil rights

(1) Preventing officer from performing duties

If two or more persons in any State or Territory conspire to prevent, by force, intimidation, or threat, any person from accepting or holding any office, trust, or place of confidence under the United States, or from discharging any duties thereof; or to induce by like means any officer of the United States to leave any State, district, or place, where his duties as an officer are required to be performed, or to injure him in his person or property on account of his lawful discharge of the duties of his office, or while engaged in the lawful discharge thereof, or to injure his property so as to molest, interrupt, hinder, or impede him in the discharge of his official duties;

(2) Obstructing justice; intimidating party, witness, or juror

If two or more persons in any State or Territory conspire to deter, by force, intimidation, or threat, any party or witness in any court of the United States from attending such court, or from testifying to any matter pending therein, freely, fully, and truthfully, or to injure such party or witness in his person or property on account of his having so attended or testified, or to influence the verdict, presentment, or indictment of any grand or petit juror in any such court, or to injure such juror in his person or property on account of any verdict, presentment, or indictment lawfully assented to by him, or of his being or having been such juror; or if two or more persons conspire for the purpose of impeding, hindering, obstructing, or defeating, in any manner, the due course of justice in any State or Territory, with intent to deny to any citizen the equal protection of the laws, or to injure him or his property for lawfully enforcing, or attempting to enforce, the right of any person, or class of persons, to the equal protection of the laws;

(3) Depriving persons of rights or privileges

If two or more persons in any State or Territory conspire or go in disguise on the highway or on the premises of another, for the purpose of depriving, either directly or indirectly, any person or class of persons of the equal protection of the laws, or of equal privileges and immunities under the laws; or for the purpose of preventing or hindering the constituted authorities of any State or Territory from giving or securing to all persons within such State or Territory the equal protection of the laws; or if two or more persons conspire to prevent by force, intimidation, or threat, any citizen who is lawfully entitled to vote, from giving his support or advocacy in a legal manner, toward or in favor of the election of any lawfully qualified person as an elector for President or Vice President, or as a Member of Congress of the United States; or to injure any citizen in person or property on account of such support or advocacy; in any case of conspiracy set forth in this section, if one or more persons engaged therein do, or cause to be done, any act in furtherance of the object of such conspiracy, whereby another is injured in his person or property, or deprived of having and exercising any right or privilege of a citizen of the United States, the party so injured or deprived may have an action for the recovery of damages occasioned by such injury or deprivation, against any one or more of the conspirators.

§ 1988. Proceedings in vindication of civil rights; attorney's fees; expert fees

(a) Applicability of statutory and common law

The jurisdiction in civil and criminal matters conferred on the district courts by the provisions of titles 13, 24, and 70 of the Revised Statutes for the protection of all persons in the United States in their civil rights, and for their vindication, shall be exercised and enforced in conformity with the laws of the United States, so far as such laws are suitable to carry the same into effect; but in all cases where they are not adapted to the object, or are deficient in the provisions necessary to furnish suitable remedies and punish offenses against law, the common law, as modified and changed by the constitution and statutes of the State wherein the court having jurisdiction of such civil or criminal cause is held, so far as the same is not inconsistent with the Constitution and laws of the United States, shall be extended to and govern the said courts in the trial and disposition of the cause, and, if it is of a criminal nature, in the infliction of punishment on the party found guilty.

(b) Attorney's fees

In any action or proceeding to enforce a provision of sections 1981, 1981a, 1982, 1983, 1985, and 1986 of this title, title IX of Public Law 92-318 [20

U.S.C.A. § 1681 et seq.], the Religious Freedom Restoration Act of 1993 [42 U.S.C.A. § 2000bb et seq.], the Religious Land Use and Institutionalized Persons Act of 2000 [42 U.S.C.A. § 2000cc et seq.], title VI of the Civil Rights Act of 1964 [42 U.S.C.A. § 2000d et seq.], or section 13981 of this title, the court, in its discretion, may allow the prevailing party, other than the United States, a reasonable attorney's fee as part of the costs, except that in any action brought against a judicial officer for an act or omission taken in such officer's judicial capacity such officer shall not be held liable for any costs, including attorney's fees, unless such action was clearly in excess of such officer's jurisdiction.

(c) Expert fees

In awarding an attorney's fee under subsection (b) of this section in any action or proceeding to enforce a provision of section 1981 or 1981a of this title, the court, in its discretion, may include expert fees as part of the attorney's fee.

Index

References are to pages